THE PHILOSOPHICAL QUEST
A Cross-Cultural Reader

THE PHILOSOPHICAL QUEST

A Cross-Cultural Reader

Gail M. Presbey

Marist College

Karsten J. Struhl

Adelphi University

Richard E. Olsen

Adelphi University

McGraw-Hill, Inc.

New York   St. Louis   San Francisco   Auckland   Bogotá   Caracas
Lisbon   London   Madrid   Mexico City   Milan   Montreal   New Delhi
San Juan   Singapore   Sydney   Tokyo   Toronto

This book was set in Times Roman by Ruttle, Shaw & Wetherill, Inc.
The editors were Judith R. Cornwell, Cynthia Ward, and Tom Holton;
the production supervisor was Denise L. Puryear.
The cover was designed by Karen K. Quigley;
the cover illustration was done by Cathy Hull.
R. R. Donnelley & Sons Company was printer and binder.

THE PHILOSOPHICAL QUEST

A Cross-Cultural Reader

Permissions Acknowledgments appear on pages 564–570, and on this page by reference.

This book is printed on acid-free paper.

234567890 DOC/DOC 998765

ISBN 0-07-062547-6

Library of Congress Cataloging-in-Publication Data

The philosophical quest: a cross-cultural reader / [edited by] Gail
   M. Presbey, Karsten J. Struhl, Richard E. Olsen.
        p.   cm.
     Includes bibliographical references and index.
     ISBN 0-07-062547-6
     1. Philosophy—Introductions.   I. Presbey, Gail M.   II. Struhl,
   Karsten J.   III. Olsen, Richard E., (date).
   BD21.P466   1995
   100—dc20   94-33149

ABOUT THE AUTHORS

GAIL M. PRESBEY is Assistant Professor of Philosophy at Marist College in Poughkeepsie, New York. She earned her doctorate at Fordham University, concentrating in the field of social and political philosophy. She has pursued postgraduate studies and independent research at Gandhigram Rural University in Tamil Nadu, India, and at University of Nairobi, Kenya. She has authored several articles in publications such as *Acorn: Journal of the Gandhi-King Society,* and the book *Nonviolence: Social and Psychological Issues.* She is active in Concerned Philosophers for Peace and the Radical Philosophy Association. She is a participant in the yearly Institute for Global Cultural Studies conferences.

KARSTEN J. STRUHL teaches philosophy and political theory in adult education programs (B.A. programs) at Adelphi University, the New School for Social Research, Iona College, and the College of New Rochelle. He has also taught at Long Island University, La Guardia Community College, the Queens House of Detention, Harlem Hospital, and several senior citizen centers. His articles have appeared in philosophical, psychological, educational, and political journals and anthologies. He is the coeditor of *Philosophy Now: An Introductory Reader* (Random House) and *Ethics in Perspective* (McGraw-Hill). He has recently coauthored the entry on human nature for the forthcoming edition of *The Encyclopedia of Bioethics* (Macmillan). He is a member of the American Philosophical Association, the Radical Philosophy Association, and Educators for Social Responsibility.

RICHARD E. OLSEN is Professor of Philosophy at Adelphi University and chair of that university's philosophy department. He received his Ph.D. in Philosophy from Brown University. He is the author of several journal articles and a book, *Karl Marx* (1979). He has also participated in National Endowment for the Humanities and Mellon Foundation grant projects. Professor Olsen has been a scholar of both Western and Asian philosophy for over twenty years and lived for a time as an ordained Buddhist monk in Thailand while pursuing his studies of Buddhism in that country. He is a member of the American Philosophical Association, the Phi Beta Kappa Society and the Sigma Xi Honorary Science Fraternity.

CONTENTS

PREFACE

Education in the United States is presently confronting the challenge of multiculturalism. This term covers a variety of concerns: the inclusion in the curriculum of the history and points of view of different ethnic and racial groups; a greater emphasis on African-American, feminist, and gay and lesbian studies; and a greater sensitivity to the literature and history of non-western cultures. All of the above senses of "multicultural" are included in our text, although the last may be properly termed "cross-cultural," and is emphasized in our text.

A number of disciplines have begun to respond to this challenge, most notably literature, history, sociology, and anthropology. For the most part, however, philosophy has been taught and continues to be taught as an essentially Western enterprise.

College students who studied philosophy in the 1950s and early 1960s were taught a historical canon that began with the Greeks, emphasizing Plato and Aristotle, passed quickly over the Middle Ages, and entered "modern philosophy" with Descartes in France, Locke and Berkeley in England, Hume in Scotland, and Kant, sometimes Hegel, and very occasionally Nietzsche in Germany. What was called contemporary philosophy might take a passing glance at phenomenology, existentialism, and American pragmatism but was for the most part positivism and the analytic school of Russell, Moore, Wittgenstein, Strawson, Austin, and so on. One could, in fact, go through a complete undergraduate and graduate curriculum in philosophy without ever encountering a non-Western philosopher. The introductory textbook anthologies of this era, reflecting this orientation, usually offered an almost exclusively Western "dialogue" within the traditional branches of philosophy—metaphysics, epistemology, ethics, social and political philosophy, and aesthetics.

In the late 1960s and early 1970s a new wave of introductory philosophy anthologies appeared, often labeled "relevance" textbooks (One of the editors of this anthology was a coeditor of such a textbook.) These attempted both to expand the philosophical categories in a manner which made them more timely—human nature, philosophy of sexuality, the nature of consciousness, medical ethics, etc.—and to include more specific ethical and political issues. The philosophical canon was broadened to include more continental (nonanalytic European) philosophy and theoretical readings by authors in other disciplines. The late 1970s and the 1980s represented a return to a more traditional approach that yet retained some of the concerns of the 1960s, an integration of the old canon with what was rapidly becoming a new canon.

However, left out of these changing perspectives concerning the philosophical dialogue was any serious attempt to reflect upon non-Western philosophical traditions. At most a few Indian and Chinese authors might be thrown in as spice for an essentially Western philosophical brew.

This situation has now reached an almost embarrassing conjuncture. There are now significantly more students from China, Japan, and other Asian countries, from the Middle East, from Latin America, and from Africa. These students do not see themselves represented in either the traditional or the new canon, and they have begun to say so.

We know that many philosophers have wanted to respond to this deficiency but are uncertain about how to begin. While there have been several recent conferences and workshops focusing on philosophy in a cross-cultural perspective, the standard complaint is that there is a general lack of adequate resources. This is especially true when it comes to introductory texts. It was our own frustration with the overall unavailability of a suitable cross-cultural introductory text as well as a recognition that others felt this same frustration that led us to collaborate on this anthology.

Our text is designed to be used in an introductory philosophy course, but it might also be used as part of a core humanities program and in a comparative philosophy course. Each of its nine chapters introduces the student to a fundamental question of philosophy through a wide variety of Western and non-Western philosophical readings. In fact, almost half of the selections in our text are by non-Western authors. The non-Western readings include classical and contemporary representatives of Asian, African, Middle Eastern, and Native American thought. Among the Western selections are classical and contemporary readings from diverse philosophical schools (analytic, positivist, pragmatist, phenomenological, and existential). We have also tried to include selections from Russian, Iberian, and Latin American philosophy, which are on the periphery of the Western philosophical tradition and generally not included very much in standard introductory philosophical anthologies. These voices are also interesting because, while grounded in the Western tradition, they tend to speak in their own unique idioms. Finally, our text also includes African-American and both Western and non-Western feminist thinkers.

Each chapter positions selections from Western and non-Western philosophical traditions in such a way as to highlight the parallels and differences between them and to present the writers from these different traditions in dialogue with each other. In addition, the Western readings in themselves often raise issues that reveal an awareness of non-Western philosophical traditions. An obvious example is an article by Derek Parfit, a contemporary analytic philosopher, who defends a Humean and Buddhist view of the self.

The juxtaposition of non-Western philosophical readings beside Western ones within established philosophical categories has several other important functions. First, it serves to demonstrate the philosophical contributions of non-Western cultures. Second, it specifically emphasizes the way in which similar philosophical debates and concepts have occurred within these different philosophical traditions. Third, it shows the different ways in which these other traditions have interpreted and responded to these perennial questions. Finally, by presenting philosophical thinkers from different cultures in dialogue with one another, it expands the meaning of the traditional categories themselves.

Each chapter in our text has two or more sections. There is a general introduction to each chapter and a separate introduction to each of the sections within the chapter. There are questions for discussion at the end of each section within the chapter and some explanatory footnotes within the readings themselves. Each chapter introduction also refers the student to related readings that appear in other chapters. This cross referencing will, we hope, enable the student to appreciate more clearly the interrelation of fundamental philosophical questions in a cross-cultural perspective.

The editors would like to thank Wayne Somers for his bibliographical expertise; Susan Weisser and Bernard Witlieb for reading and commenting on portions of the text; Liza Greenwald for help in selecting illustrations; Richard Schiffman for his suggestions concerning Asian sources; James Fenneley for consultation on Islamic sources; Lucius Outlaw, Henry Odera Oruka, and Emmanuel Eze for leads on African sources; Alison Jaggar for suggestions concerning feminist sources; Barbara Krieger for leads on Jewish sources; and Ofelia Schutte for suggestions about Latin American readings.

Acknowledgment is also due to the publisher's reviewers whose comments and suggestions helped refine the manuscript: Mary Ann Gardell Cutter, University of Colorado at Colorado Springs; Burton Hurdle, Virginia State University; Laura Lyn Inglis, Buena Vista College; Eric Kraemer, University of Wisconsin–La Crosse; and Katherine Shamey, Santa Monica College.

The creation of a book requires considerable labor by those who often go unrecognized, those who do the editing, production, design, etc. Our special thanks, therefore, goes to those at McGraw-Hill: Cynthia Ward, Patricia Rodney, Judy Cornwell, Tom Holton, and Diane Schadoff; and to Jo-Anne Naples for her persistent efforts to secure permissions for the readings that appear in our book.

Gail Presbey would like to thank the following friends for encouragement and practical help: Josef Velazquez, Anna Brown, and Nancy Benignus. She would like thank Dikirr Patrick Maison for help with questions and ideas concerning chapters 7 and 8. She would also like to thank the following faculty at Marist College for support and encouragement: Vincent Toscano, Mar Peter-Raoul, Susan Gronewold, and Irma Casey-Blanco.

Karsten Struhl would especially like to thank Carole Lapidus for her support and encouragement throughout the entire process.

Gail M. Presbey
Karsten J. Struhl
Richard E. Olsen

INTRODUCTION

For this is essentially the pathos of a philosopher, to be astonished; there is no other determining point of departure for philosophy than this.
—Plato

WONDER AND THE EXPERIENCE OF PHILOSOPHIZING

Wonder is probably as old as humanity; it is also the starting point of philosophy.

Perhaps we are most familiar with wonder as we ponder the remarkable accomplishments of humans throughout history and the astounding events of our times: the Egyptian pyramids, the Taj Mahal, the medieval cathedral in Chartres, the first astronaut's steps on the moon, and so on. Human history is filled with great accomplishments as well as great cruelties, both of which can stun the inquirer and send thought spinning. Likewise, nature's grandeur and terrors—oceans and mountain ranges, hurricanes and volcanoes—seize our attention and either mesmerize with their beauty or stupefy with their power. Witnessing a birth or a death can also bring to mind questions of human meaning with an urgency we do not often experience. At times like these our everyday consciousness is arrested, and we wonder why, just marvel at the fact of existence, or ponder the pain or joy such sights evoke in us.

Karl Jasper describes those moments that so often give rise to philosophical reflection. He speaks of them as times of either joy or despair that jar a person into a state of wonderment, where all former answers and beliefs are called into question. We all have probably had such experiences. We are all philosophers on at least some occasions.

Humans can certainly function practically in an immediate "survival" mode without wondering about the above matters. But a lifetime of such shortsightedness may begin to feel unfulfilling. Of course, one could take a shortcut and bypass philosophical inquiry by embracing a prepackaged ideology which provides ready-made answers to our fundamental questions. The philosopher, however, strikes out on his or her own, searching for wisdom in a reflective fashion. It is this that we call the philosophical quest.

Here it might be helpful to contrast the informal sense of "having" a philosophy with the formal sense of "doing" philosophy, or philosophizing, where we scrutinize our experiences and beliefs in a search for insight and understanding. In the first sense, each of us already has a philosophy; indeed, we are creating our philosophy of life—more or less unconsciously— all the time. "Don't trust people," "pain can be a growing experience," "try new things," "don't be afraid," "there *is* life after death": such viewpoints, held unreflectively, influence our daily lives and guide our decisions. In contrast, when we engage directly in *doing* philosophy, it is a time to take inventory of our preconceptions and challenge them. With this more formal sense of philosophizing comes an emphasis on reason, analysis, and argumentation.

In fact, philosophy could be understood as the discipline that criticizes received opinions, in all subjects, from daily life to aesthetic and religious experience. In this sense we can say that philosophy is *radical* in the most literal meaning of the word; for whereas practitioners of a religion or citizens of a state may take for granted the validity of the assumptions of their belief systems, philosophers question those assumptions. Philosophers go to the "roots" of ideas by clarifying, questioning, and evaluating our most basic assumptions. Often this challenge to accepted norms and ideas can lead to views that are at odds with one's culture. Buddha challenged the Hindu views on caste and social position; Socrates challenged the Athenians on their notions of piety, justice, and wisdom; both the French existentialists and the logical positivists, in our own century, have questioned received religious opinion. In this way, philosophy never rests, never reaches the final answer; all past answers are subject to continuing scrutiny and revision by those who come after. Philosophy is, in short, a radical critical inquiry into the fundamental assumptions of any field of inquiry, including itself.

As we have seen, one doesn't have to be a professional "philosopher" to philosophize; wherever assumptions are being questioned, and opinions are challenged, philosophizing is going on. Anyone willing to observe the overlooked, to reflect, to analyze, and to put forth an argument can be a philosopher. However, those who make philosophical reflection a lifetime habit perhaps deserve the label "philosopher" most. For, with practice, comes skill. The more one philosophizes and studies the philosophies of the past, the more likely one is to gain real philosophic insight.

PHILOSOPHY IN WORLD PERSPECTIVE:
THE EUROCENTRIC PROBLEM

People around the globe have been engaging in philosophical reflection for centuries. And yet the most often promulgated view of philosophy in so many Western introductory textbooks is that the Greeks began philosophy, the Romans continued it, and then the Germans, French, and British have carried it to its present state. Some texts follow philosophy to the New World but only to observe its practice in the essentially Anglo-German cultures of English-speaking Canada and the United States. One gets the impression that other peoples in the world do not philosophize. What were then the Asian and African peoples, the Persians, Iberians, and Slavs doing and thinking over the centuries? What of the aboriginal societies in North, Central, and South America? The popular Western view is that others were content to wallow in superstition, unthinkingly perpetuating a system of belief that could never stand the scrutiny of Western reason. Whole continents have been seen as prereflective, never asking philosophical questions, never criticizing received opinions. It is the view of the editors, and of many now engaged in a careful study of the intellectual history of the world, that such a vision of philosophy goes against the facts and results from "Eurocentrism."

Often the contributions of other cultures to the foundations of Western philosophy are recognized at the time of the influence but then are downplayed in later historical accounts. Greece, considered the cradle of Western philosophy, was a seafaring nation that regularly interacted with many other cultures. But most modern Western readers will not realize that at the birth and heyday of Greek civilization, Greece was surrounded by advanced and powerful civilizations which had a detailed knowledge of medicine, science, astronomy, and a practice of philosophical speculation and debate. That the Greeks built upon this background knowledge and came up with their own unique contributions to thought and method that radically clarified and furthered philosophy is not to be disputed; it is with real merit that the Greeks deserve an important place in the history of philosophy. But it is crucial to realize that the Greeks did not appear in a vacuum but rather in a context of an interactive dialogue with other civilizations.

Some contemporary thinkers, such as Enrique Dussel and W. E. B. DuBois, have developed theories to explain the seeming tunnel vision of many Western accounts of the history of philosophy. Since we are in the "West," we receive a view of our cultural heritage that emphasizes the accomplishments of those who are considered to be a part of this heritage; those who are historical enemies or rivals are always seen in the worst light. To take one example, the fledgling European nations were awed by the power of the Indian and Chinese empires and envied their riches. In the years of colonialism and imperialism, Britain conquered India militarily and came to dominate China during the Opium Wars. With the theory of the "white man's burden," Britain attempted to see itself as a civilizing influence bringing order where there had formerly been chaos, and instituting progress, where there had formerly been backwardness. In such a context, it was difficult to admit the good points of cultures that were being forced to submit to British models of right and progress.

This same theory of military-political rivalry and/or domination affecting perceptions of cultural history can account, at least partially, for the meager attention paid to Islam, Africa, and Native America in Western philosophy texts. The Greco-Roman world and Western Europe have, throughout much of history, been involved in military battles to check the spread of Islam westward. It is probably no accident, then, that the flourishing of Islamic philosophy between the tenth and fourteenth centuries is rarely mentioned in the more superficial Western accounts of philosophy, even though this Islamic philosophical renaissance directly influenced the West.

In a similar vein, it has been argued that the European and American engagement in the African slave trade encouraged thinkers to justify such an atrocity by interpreting African culture as primitive, asserting that Africans are not "rational animals." It is no wonder that G. W. F. Hegel, one of the greatest German philosophers of the nineteenth century, said in his *Philosophy of History* that Africans were not even a part of the unfolding human story of progress toward ultimate rationality. For, if Africans were humans with complex thought patterns and an insightful and sensitive relationship to the world and themselves, then how could their enslavement be justified? Earlier justifications of slavery based on the slave's "inferior nature" were first argued by Aristotle. Aristotle's arguments were resurrected by the Spanish conquistadores to defend their enslavement of Native Americans in Mexico and Central and South America.

Europe itself—and then later the United States—has had its own "peripheries," which have given rise to their own style of philosophy. Iberian, Latin American, and Russian philosophers often find themselves marginalized in most textbooks, if they find themselves included at all. Once again, coincidentally, the political marginalizations of these areas may account for their philosophical marginalization. Yet great thinkers such as Dostoevsky and Unamuno have pondered questions of life with marvelous insight and have earned themselves the spotlight of world renown. It has even been suggested that being on the periphery of a culture affords one a better perspective for asking the most basic questions, so necessary for philosophy.

The twentieth-century French philosopher Michel Foucault has observed that often so-called objective and impartial knowledge serves the powers-that-be. Fortunately for us, philosophy always entails the questioning of assumptions, so that later philosophical inquiry can expose the mistakes of former positions. In fact, all knowledge seems to be perspectival; no human being can have a God's-eye view of our world; each of us has been influenced by our culture to interpret our experience according to certain conceptual categories. Does this mean that objectivity is a goal never to be reached? This question is the focus of a centuries-long debate; all we editors wish to suggest is that objectivity can be encouraged by seeking out a multiplicity of perspectives on any given topic. Immanuel Kant referred to an "enlarged mentality" as the ability to represent the views of others in one's own mind, and he saw it as a crucial step in making a sound judgment. This text is structured with the idea that looking at multiple perspectives on any given issue will help the reader make a more informed judgment.

Our goal in this collection is not to pit civilizations against one another and rate their relative merits or demerits. Rather, our hope is to present each culture in its best light, with selections taken from its most interesting contributions to the philosophical dialogue. We also hope to dispel some misconceptions. For example, it is often suggested that all Hindu thought is alike, all Chinese thought is alike, and so on, and it is only in the Western tradition that we have truly interesting debate. The reality is, however, quite different. The Chinese philosophers debated a number of issues within the Taoist, Confucian, and Buddhist schools. Ancient China saw a lively debate concerning the question of whether human nature was good or evil. Debates concerning science can be found within the Islamic tradition. Hinduism also saw debates between dualists, monists, and materialists. These and other such controversies are represented in this anthology. Also within this text the reader will find a number of parallel debates carried on within two or more cultures. Plato's world of the forms finds echoes in a Native American Lakota vision. Western skepticism concerning the problem of induction was preceded by Indian skepticism by several thousand years. Hume's critique of the self was preceded by the Buddha's and is revived by a contemporary British philosopher in the analytic tradition, Derek Parfit. Arguments for dualism, idealism, and materialism appear within the African, Indian, and Western traditions. Parallel debates concerning human nature occur within both China and the Western world.

The project of this book is embedded in a sociopolitical context; the contemporary educational setting demands such works. In our own American society, a web of interrelating immigrant cultures, we need to let all voices be heard. We have our own "peripheries," and those at the edge of power in our society, women, African-Americans, and other minorities, have felt their voices stifled. Thus we have included some of these voices as well.

160°W 140°W 120°W 100°W 80°W 60°W 40°W 20°W

80°N

60°N

KALAALLIT NUNAAT
(DEN.)

ALASKA
(U.S.)

ICELAND

UNITED
KINGDOM

CANADA

IRELAND

40°N

PORTUGAL

UNITED STATES

ATLANTIC

AZORES
(PORT.)

MADEIRA IS.
(PORT.)

Tropic of Cancer

MEXICO

BAHAMAS

CANARY IS.
(SP.)

20°N

CUBA

DOMINICAN
REPUBLIC
27

WESTERN SAHARA
(MOR.)

HAWAII (U.S.)

BELIZE
HONDURAS

HAITI

JAMAICA

29
30
31
32
33
34

MAURITANI

CAPE
VERDE

SENEGAL
GAMBIA

GUATEMALA
EL SALVADOR

NICARAGUA

28
GRENADA

GUINEA BISSAU

GUINEA

COSTA RICA

GUYANA

SIERRA
LEONE

PANAMA

VENEZUELA

SURINAME

LIBERIA

PACIFIC

COLOMBIA

FRENCH GUIANA (FR.)

CÔ
D'IVOIR

EQUATOR

GALÁPAGOS IS.
(EC.)

ECUADOR

KIRIBATI

OCEAN

OCEAN

WESTERN
SAMOA

AMERICAN
SAMOA (U.S.)

FRENCH POLYNESIA
(FR.)

BRAZIL

PERU

TONGA

BOLIVIA

20°S

Tropic of Capricorn

PARAGUAY

CHILE

40°S

ARGENTINA

URUGUAY

FALKLAND IS. (U.K.)

60°S

80°S

```
0        1000      2000 Miles

0      1000    2000 Kilometers
```

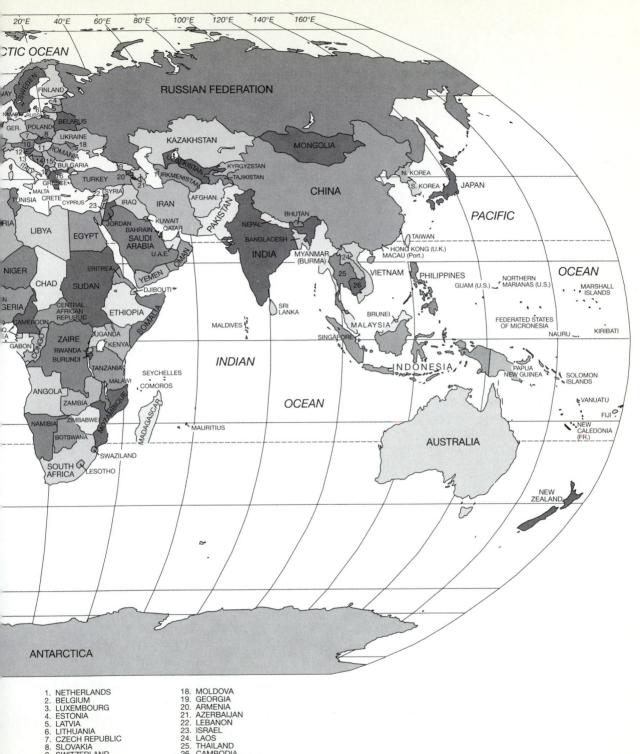

20°E 40°E 60°E 80°E 100°E 120°E 140°E 160°E

CTIC OCEAN

RUSSIAN FEDERATION

NAY
SWEDEN
FINLAND
4
NMARK
RUSS.
GER. POLAND
7 8
BELARUS
UKRAINE
10 11
12
14 15
1
KAZAKHSTAN
MONGOLIA
18
ROMANIA
BULGARIA
19
TURKEY
GREECE
MALTA
TUNISIA
CRETE
CYPRUS
16
20
21
TURKMENISTAN
TAJIKISTAN
KYRGYZSTAN
PAKISTAN
AFGHAN.
CHINA
N. KOREA
S. KOREA
JAPAN

(SYRIA)
IRAQ
IRAN
23

RIA
LIBYA
EGYPT
JORDAN
BAHRAIN
SAUDI
ARABIA
KUWAIT
QATAR
U.A.E.
BHUTAN
NEPAL
BANGLADESH

TAIWAN
HONG KONG (U.K.)
MACAU (Port.)

PACIFIC

NIGER
CHAD
SUDAN
ERITREA
YEMEN
DJIBOUTI
INDIA
MYANMAR
(BURMA)
24
VIETNAM
PHILIPPINES
GUAM (U.S.)
NORTHERN
MARIANAS (U.S.)
OCEAN
MARSHALL
ISLANDS

GERIA
CENTRAL
AFRICAN
REPUBLIC
ETHIOPIA
SOMALIA
25
26

CAMEROON
ZAIRE
UGANDA
KENYA
SRI
LANKA
MALDIVES
BRUNEI
MALAYSIA
FEDERATED STATES
OF MICRONESIA
NAURU
KIRIBATI

EA
CONGO
GABON
RWANDA
BURUNDI
TANZANIA
SINGAPORE
INDONESIA
PAPUA
NEW GUINEA
SOLOMON
ISLANDS

INDIAN
SEYCHELLES
COMOROS

ANGOLA
ZAMBIA
MALAWI
MOZAMBIQUE
VANUATU
FIJI

NAMIBIA
ZIMBABWE
BOTSWANA
MADAGASCAR
OCEAN
MAURITIUS
AUSTRALIA
NEW
CALEDONIA
(FR.)

SWAZILAND
SOUTH
AFRICA
LESOTHO

NEW
ZEALAND

ANTARCTICA

1. NETHERLANDS	18. MOLDOVA
2. BELGIUM	19. GEORGIA
3. LUXEMBOURG	20. ARMENIA
4. ESTONIA	21. AZERBAIJAN
5. LATVIA	22. LEBANON
6. LITHUANIA	23. ISRAEL
7. CZECH REPUBLIC	24. LAOS
8. SLOVAKIA	25. THAILAND
9. SWITZERLAND	26. CAMBODIA
10. AUSTRIA	27. PUERTO RICO (U.S.)
11. HUNGARY	28. ST. KITTS AND NEVIS
12. SLOVENIA	29. ANTIGUA AND BARBUDA
13. CROATIA	30. DOMINICA
14. BOSNIA AND HERCEGOVINA	31. ST. LUCIA
15. YUGOSLAVIA	32. ST. VINCENT AND THE GRENADINES
16. MACEDONIA	33. BARBADOS
17. ALBANIA	34. TRINIDAD AND TOBAGO

THE PHILOSOPHICAL QUEST
A Cross-Cultural Reader

The World of the Forms
Plato, *The Parable of the Cave*
Plato, *The Symposium*
Black Elk, *A Lakota Vision*

Idealism: Western and Indian
The Upanishads, *Thou Art That*
Shankara, *A Commentary on the Upanishads*
George Berkeley, *Subjective Idealism*
Arthur Schopenhauer, *The World as Will and Idea*

Zen Buddhism
Hui Neng, *The Sutra of Hui Neng*
Thich Nhat Hanh, *Zen Keys*

The Tao
Lao Tzu, *The Way and Its Power*

Materialism
Wang Fu-Chih, *Neo-Confucian Materialism*
Friedrich Engels, *Materialism and the Scientific World View*

M. C. Escher, *Day and Night,* 1938, M. C. Escher Heirs, c/o Cordon Art, Baarn, Holland.

CHAPTER 1

APPEARANCE AND REALITY

The philosophical question concerning the distinction between appearance and reality—that is, the question which concerns itself with the relationship between what things appear to be to the senses and what they really are—has been especially prominent in Western philosophy since the time of the scientific revolution. It has also, in the West since that time, been closely tied to questions which concern the nature of knowledge. However, the puzzles of the appearance/reality distinction are neither specifically Western nor specifically modern. They seem to be both universal and universally deemed important, though the forms the questions take may vary from culture to culture and age to age.

The selections in Section One begin with Plato's famous parable of the cave, in which he likens the world of appearances to a world of shadows, a comparison which is echoed in the teachings of the Native American sage Black Elk. The Plato and Black Elk selections are followed by a variety of views which argue that reality is created by the mind, the position which philosophers call "idealism," using this term in a technical sense which has little in common with its everyday meaning. Zen Buddhism, following the teachings of the ancient Indian Mahayana Buddhist philosophers, puts a special twist on this "idealist" theme, arguing that a true understanding of the nature of mind and its world pushes us beyond concepts and language. This view is commonly called "mysticism." The ancient Chinese philosopher Lao Tzu also expresses this mystical view of the world in the classic *Tao te Ching*.

Finally, there are the views of the world which see its appearances as grounded in—not mind—but matter. "Materialists," those who hold that the world is entirely physical in its nature, have existed in most cultures that practice philosophical reflection, though their denial of an independent spiritual realm has often made them unpopular with their contemporaries. The selections presented here are taken from the seventeenth-century Chinese materialist Wang Fu-Chih and the famous German socialist Friedrich Engels, who is better known for his political than his philosophical efforts (he coauthored, with Karl Marx, the *Communist Manifesto* and several other revolutionary socialist works). A selection from the *Communist Manifesto* can be found in Chapter 9 of this book.

Readers interested in Section One, "The World of the Forms," may also want to refer to a further selection of Black Elk's teachings in Chapter 3 and the Plato selection found in Chapter 5. Idealism is also dealt with in Chapter 5 in the selections taken from Edmund Husserl, the *Upanishads,* and Toshiko Izutsu's work. Reflections on mysticism are found in the Daisetz Suzuki and Milton Munitz selections of Chapter 2 and the section on "The Religious Experience" in Chapter 3. In Chapter 5, T. R. V. Murti explains the Indian philosophical doctrine on which the Zen view of "emptiness" or "void" is based. A further discussion of Taoism is found in Chapter 8.

THE WORLD OF THE FORMS

The ancient Greek philosopher Plato's (427?–347? B.C.) famous dialogue *Republic,* from which "The Parable of the Cave" is taken, begins with a discussion between Plato's teacher, Socrates, and some fellow Athenians concerning an ethical question: What is justice? Although it does, in its own way, continue always to hark back to that question, the dialogue takes us on several fascinating journeys in its attempt to discover the true meaning of what it is to be just. On one of these, Socrates speaks extensively on the most basic aspects of his philosophical world view—the metaphysics or first philosophy on which his ethical and other views are based. There is, he argues, a higher world, the "world of mind," compared to which our tangible and visible world is an insubstantial copy, a world of "shadows," to use the metaphor he employs in the long analogy he draws between our own condition and that of prisoners confined in a dimly lit cave.

It is important to stress here that the "world of mind," as he speaks about it, is not something subjective and therefore *in* the mind, but an objective realm which is more deeply real, on his view, than is the realm of the senses. The ideas or "Forms" which the world of mind contains are not lodged in our consciousness any more than the things which our eyes see are lodged in our eyeballs. The mind, for Plato, is more like a sixth sense than a container. We apprehend the higher world through mind in much the same way that we apprehend this world with our eyes and ears and fingers.

Socrates returns to this theme in the dialogue *Symposium.* The occasion this time is a drinking party to celebrate the successful production of a friend's play. In order not to become too drunk, since some of the party are still suffering from hangovers from the night before's festivities, the participants have decided to water their wine and test their poetic skills in making speeches in honor of the god of Love, the god which the Greeks called "Eros." The selection begins with the speech of Socrates' playwright friend, Agathon, who waxes eloquent in his praises of the god, presenting a perfect foil for Socrates' speech which is to follow. For Socrates maintains that Love is not a god at all but merely a messenger to the divine. Love is, however, he adds, not to be dismissed lightly on account of this, since—if he is used correctly—Love can lead you to the higher world of the perfect Forms and the supreme God which governs that world. In making his case for this account of Love, Plato contrasts Socrates with Agathon and the speakers who came before him, not merely in the content of what Socrates says but also in his method. Where Agathon and the others rely mainly upon references to mythology in presenting their accounts of Love, Socrates employs reasoned argument. We see his own teacher, the wise woman Diotima, lead him through the series of questions and answers which were to become his staple and a staple in Greek philosophy, the Socratic dialogue or dialectic.

Though separated from Plato's Athens by an ocean and over two thousand years, the metaphysics espoused by Socrates is also voiced by the Native American Sioux or Lakota shaman Black Elk in his account of the journey of his cousin, the famous holy man and war chief Crazy Horse, to a higher spirit world which seems indistinguishable from that which Socrates and Diotima sought. Being a horseback Indian of the Western American plains, Crazy Horse took his horse along on the journey, but, aside from that, the nature of the quest appears to be nearly identical. It is also interesting to note the striking parallels between the account of Crazy Horse's character, which Black Elk presents, and those usually given of Socrates; they are both strange men, never wholly present, seemingly not subject to the needs of ordinary people, but loved by many for their unselfishness, despite their strangeness, though feared by others because of it.

Black Elk presented this account of Crazy Horse

in unfolding the story of his life to the poet and journalist John Niehardt in the early 1930s, when Black Elk was an old man in his seventies. In his lifetime, he had seen perhaps the most painful period in his people's history, beginning with a childhood of fear during the Sioux Indian wars, when the Lakota were convinced that the whites meant to exterminate them. There were moments of glory, of course;

he—like Crazy Horse—had visions, and he fought in the victory over the U.S. cavalry at Little Big Horn. But this was followed by defeat and demoralization and the vanishing of a way of life that the Sioux loved enough to defend fiercely. It was only to preserve a little piece of this, a fragment of its wisdom, that he agreed to tell John Niehardt things he had never told a white before.

THE PARABLE OF THE CAVE

Plato

"Next, then," I said, "take the following parable of education and ignorance as a picture of the condition of our nature. Imagine mankind as dwelling in an underground cave with a long entrance open to the light across the whole width of the cave; in this they have been from childhood, with necks and legs fettered, so they have to stay where they are. They cannot move their heads round because of the fetters, and they can only look forward, but light comes to them from fire burning behind them higher up at a distance. Between the fire and the prisoners is a road above their level, and along it imagine a low wall has been built, as puppet showmen have screens in front of their people over which they work their puppets."

"I see," he said.

"See, then, bearers carrying along this wall all sorts of articles which they hold projecting above the wall, statues of men and other living things,[1] made of stone or wood and all kinds of stuff, some of the bearers speaking and some silent, as you might expect."

"What a remarkable image," he said, "and what remarkable prisoners!"

"Just like ourselves," I said. "For, first of all, tell

me this: What do you think such people would have seen of themselves and each other except their shadows, which the fire cast on the opposite wall of the cave?"

"I don't see how they could see anything else," said he, "if they were compelled to keep their heads unmoving all their lives!"

"Very well, what of the things being carried along? Would not this be the same?"

"Of course it would."

"Suppose the prisoners were able to talk together, don't you think that when they named the shadows which they saw passing they would believe they were naming things?"[2]

"Necessarily."

"Then if their prison had an echo from the opposite wall, whenever one of the passing bearers uttered a sound, would they not suppose that the passing shadow must be making the sound? Don't you think so?"

"Indeed I do," he said.

"If so," said I, "such persons would certainly believe that there were no realities except those shadows of handmade things."[3]

"So it must be," said he.

"Now consider," said I, "what their release would be like, and their cure from these fetters and their folly; let us imagine whether it might naturally

---

[1]Including models of trees, etc.

[2]Which they have never seen. They would say "tree" when it was only a shadow of the model of a tree.

[3]Shadows of artificial things, not even the shadow of a growing tree: another stage from reality.

be something like this. One might be released, and compelled suddenly to stand up and turn his neck round, and to walk and look towards the firelight; all this would hurt him, and he would be too much dazzled to see distinctly those things whose shadows he had seen before. What do you think he would say, if someone told him that what he saw before was foolery, but now he saw more rightly, being a bit nearer reality and turned towards what was a little more real? What if he were shown each of the passing things, and compelled by questions to answer what each one was? Don't you think he would be puzzled, and believe what he saw before was more true than what was shown to him now?"

"Far more," he said.

"Then suppose he were compelled to look towards the real light, it would hurt his eyes, and he would escape by turning them away to the things which he was able to look at, and these he would believe to be clearer than what was being shown to him."

"Just so," said he.

"Suppose, now," said I, "that someone should drag him thence by force, up the rough ascent, the steep way up, and never stop until he could drag him out into the light of the sun, would he not be distressed and furious at being dragged; and when he came into the light, the brilliance would fill his eyes and he would not be able to see even one of the things now called real?"[4]

"That he would not," said he, "all of a sudden."

"He would have to get used to it, surely, I think, if he is to see the things above. First he would most easily look at shadows, after that images of mankind and the rest in water, lastly the things themselves. After this he would find it easier to survey by night the heavens themselves and all that is in them, gazing at the light of the stars and moon, rather than by day the sun and the sun's light."

"Of course."

"Last of all, I suppose, the sun; he could look on the sun itself by itself in its own place, and see what it is like, not reflections of it in water or as it appears in some alien setting."

"Necessarily," said he.

"And only after all this he might reason about it, how this is he who provides seasons and years, and is set over all there is in the visible region, and he is in a manner the cause of all things which they saw."

"Yes, it is clear," said he, "that after all that, he would come to this last."

"Very good. Let him be reminded of his first habitation, and what was wisdom in that place, and of his fellow-prisoners there; don't you think he would bless himself for the change, and pity them?"

"Yes, indeed."

"And if there were honours and praises among them and prizes for the one who saw the passing things most sharply and remembered best which of them used to come before and which after and which together, and from these was best able to prophesy accordingly what was going to come—do you beleive he would set his desire on that, and envy those who were honoured men or potentates among them? Would he not feel as Homer says,[5] and heartily desire rather to be serf or some landless man on earth and to endure anything in the world, rather than to opine as they did and to live in that way?"

"Yes indeed," said he, "he would rather accept anything than live like that."

"Then again," I said, "just consider; if such a one should go down again and sit on his old seat, would he not get his eyes full of darkness coming in suddenly out of the sun?"

"Very much so," said he.

"And if he should have to compete with those who had been always prisoners, by laying down the law about those shadows while he was blinking before his eyes were settled down—and it would take a good long time to get used to things—wouldn't they all laugh at him and say he had spoiled his eyesight by going up there, and it was not worth-while

---

[4]To the next stage of knowledge: the real thing, not the artificial puppet.

[5]*Odyssey* xi. 489.

so much as to try to go up? And would they not kill anyone who tried to release them and take them up, if they could somehow lay hands on him and kill him?"[6]

"That they would!" said he.

"Then we must apply this image, my dear Glaucon," said I, "to all we have been saying. The world of our sight is like the habitation in prison, the firelight there to the sunlight here, the ascent and the view of the upper world is the rising of the soul into the world of mind; put it so and you will not be far from my own surmise, since that is what you want to hear; but God knows if it is really true. At least, what appears to me is, that in the world of the known, last of all,[7] is the idea of the good, and with what toil to be seen! And seen, this must be inferred to be the cause of all right and beautiful things for all, which gives birth to light and the king of light in the world of sight, and, in the world of mind, herself the queen produces truth and reason; and she must be seen by one who is to act with reason publicly or privately."

"I believe as you do," he said, "in so far as I am able."

"Then believe also, as I do," said I, "and do not be surprised, that those who come thither are not willing to have part in the affairs of men, but their souls ever strive to remain above; for that surely may be expected if our parable fits the case."

"Quite so," he said.

"Well then," said I, "do you think it surprising if one leaving divine contemplations and passing to the evils of men is awkward and appears to be a great fool, while he is still blinking—not yet accustomed to the darkness around him, but compelled to struggle in law courts or elsewhere about shadows of justice, or the images which make the shadows, and to quarrel about notions of justice in those who have never seen justice itself?"

"Not surprising at all," said he.

"But any man of sense," I said, "would remember that the eyes are doubly confused from two dif-ferent causes, both in passing from light to darkness and from darkness to light; and believing that the same things happen with regard to the soul also, whenever he sees a soul confused and unable to discern anything he would not just laugh carelessly; he would examine whether it had come out of a more brilliant life, and if it were darkened by the strangeness; or whether it had come out of greater ignorance into a more brilliant light, and if it were dazzled with the brighter illumination. Then only would he congratulate the one soul upon its happy experience and way of life, and pity the other; but if he must laugh, his laugh would be a less downright laugh than his laughter at the soul which came out of the light above."

"That is fairly put," said he.

"Then if this is true," I said, "our belief about these matters must be this, that the nature of education is not really such as some of its professors say it is; as you know, they say that there is not understanding in the soul, but they put it in, as if they were putting sight into blind eyes."

"They do say so," said he.

"But our reasoning indicates," I said, "that this power is already in the soul of each, and is the instrument by which each learns; thus if the eye could not see without being turned with the whole body from the dark towards the light, so this instrument must be turned round with the whole soul away from the world of becoming until it is able to endure the sight of being and the most brilliant light of being: and this we say is the good, don't we?"

"Yes."

THE SYMPOSIUM

Plato

"Quite right, Phaidros," said Agathon, "I am ready to speak; Socrates will be there another time, and often, to talk to.

"First, then, I wish to describe how I ought to

---

[6]Plato probably alludes to the death of Socrates.
[7]The end of our search.

speak; then to speak. It seems to me that all who have spoken so far have not praised the god, but have congratulated mankind on the good things which the god has caused for them: what that god was himself who gave these gifts, no one has described. But the one right way for any laudation of anyone is to describe what he is, and then what he causes, whoever may be our subject. Thus, you see, with Love: we also should first praise him for what he is, and then praise his gifts.

"I say then that all gods are happy, but if it is lawful to say this without offence, I say that Love is happiest of them all, being most beautiful and best. And how he is most beautiful, I am about to describe. First of all, Phaidros, he is youngest of the gods. He himself supplies one great proof of what I say, for he flies in full flight away from Old Age, who is a quick one clearly, since he comes too soon to us all. Love hates him naturally and will not come anywhere near him. But he is always associated with the young, and with them he consorts, for the old saying is right, 'Like ever comes to like.' I am ready to admit many other things to Phaidros, but one I do not admit, that Love is older than Cronos and Iapetos[1]; no, I say he is youngest of the gods, and ever young; but that old business of the gods, which Hesiod and Parmenides tell about, was done through Necessity and not though Love, if they told the truth; for if Love had been in them, there would have been no gelding or enchaining of each other and all those violent things, but friendship and peace, as there is now, and has been ever since Love has reigned over the gods. So then he is young, and besides being young he is tender; but we need a poet like Homer to show the god's tenderness. For Homer says of Ate[2] that she was a god and tender—at least her feet were tender—when he says that

Tender are her feet; she comes not near
The ground, but walks upon the heads of men.

I think he gives good proof of her tenderness, that she walks not on the hard but on the soft. Then let us use the same proof for Love, that he is tender. For he walks not on the earth nor on top of heads, which are not so very soft, but both walks and abides in the softest things there are; for his abode is settled in the tempers and souls of gods and men, and again, not in all souls without exception; no, whenever he meets a soul with a hard temper, he departs, but where it is soft, he abides. So since he always touches with feet and all else the softest of the soft, he must needs be tender. You see, then, he is youngest and tenderest, but besides this his figure is supple, for if he were stiff, he could not fold himself in everywhere, or throughout every soul, and come in and go out unnoticed from the first. A great proof of his good proportion and supple shape in his gracefulness, which, as we know, Love has in high degree; for there is always war between gracelessness and Love. Colours and beauty are testified by the god's nestling in flowers; for where there is no flower, or flower is past, in body and soul and everything else, Love sits not, but where the place is flowery and fragrant there he both sits and stays.

"Of the god's beauty much more might be said, but this is enough; the virtue of Love comes next. Chief is that Love wrongs not and is not wronged, wrongs no god and is wronged by none, wrongs no man and is wronged by none. Nothing that happens to him comes by violence, for violence touches not Love; nothing he does is violent, for everyone willingly serves Love in everything, and what a willing person grants to a willing, is just—so say 'the city's king, the laws.'[3] And besides justice, he is full of temperance. It is agreed that temperance is the mastery and control of pleasures and desires, and that no pleasure is stronger than Love. But if they are weaker, then Love would master and control them; and being master of pleasure and desires, Love would be especially temperate. Furthermore, in courage 'not even Ares[4] stands up against Love,' for

---

[1]In Greek mythology these were two of the Titans who were children of Ouranos (Heaven) and Gaia (Earth). They existed even before Zeus.
[2]Atē, presumptuous Madness, something like Sin. *Iliad* xix, 92.

[3]Quoted from Alcidamas, a stylist.
[4]Ares, god of war. The quotation is from Sophocles' lost play *Thyestes,* fragment 235 N.

it is not Ares that holds Love, but Love Ares—love of Aphrodite, as they say; stronger is he that holds than he that is held, and the master of the bravest of all would be himself bravest. Now the justice and temperance and courage of the god have been spoken of, and wisdom is left; so one must try to do the best one is able to do. And first, that I may honour our art as Eryximachos honoured his, Love is so wise a poet that he can make another the same; at least, everyone becomes a poet whom Love touches, even one who before that, had 'no music in his soul.'[5] This we may fittingly use as a proof that Love is a good poet[6] or active maker in practically all the creations of the fine arts; for what one has not or knows not, one can neither give to another nor teach another. Now take the making of all living things; who will dispute that they are the clever work of Love, by which all living things are made and begotten? And craftsmanship in the arts; don't we know that where this god is teacher, art turns out notable and illustrious, but where there is no touch of Love, it is all in the dark? Archery, again, and medicine and divination were invented by Apollo, led by desire and love, so that even he would be a pupil of Love; so also the Muses in music and Hephaistos in smithcraft and Athena in weaving and Zeus in 'pilotage of gods and men.' Hence you see also, all that business of the gods was arranged when Love came among them—love of beauty, that is plain, for there is no Love in ugliness. Before that, as I said at the beginning, many terrible things happened to the gods because of the reign of Necessity—so the story goes; but when this god Love was born, all became good both for gods and men from loving beautiful things.

"Thus it seems to me, Phaidros, that Love comes first, himself most beautiful and best, and thereafter he is cause of other such things in others. And I am moved to speak something of him in verse myself, that it is he who makes

Peace among men, calm weather on the deep,
Respite from winds, in trouble rest and sleep.[7]

He empties us of estrangement, and fills us with friendliness, ordaining all such meetings as this one, of people one with another, in feasts, in dances, in sacrifices becoming men's guide; he provides gentleness and banishes savagery; he loves to give good will, hates to give ill will; gracious, mild, illustrious to the wise, admirable to the gods; enviable to those who have none of him, treasured by those who have some of him; father of luxury, daintiness, delicacy, grace, longing, desire; careful of good things, careless of bad things; in hardship, in fear, in drinking,[8] in talk a pilot, a comrade, a stand-by[9] and the best of saviours; of all gods and men an ornament, a guide most beautiful and best, whom every man must follow, hymning him well, sharing in the song he sings as he charms the mind of gods and men.

"This, Phaidros, is my speech," he said, "may the god accept my dedication, partly play, partly modest seriousness, and the best that I am able to do."

When Agathon had spoken (Aristodemos told me), all applauded; the young man was thought to have spoken becomingly for himself and for the god. Then Socrates looked at Eryximachos, and said, "Now then, son of Acumenos, do you think there was no reason to fear in the fears I feared?[10] Was I not a prophet when I said, as I did just now, that Agathon would make a wonderful speech, and leave me with nothing to say?"

"Yes, to the first," said Eryximachos, "you were a prophet there, certainly, about the wonderful speech; but nothing to say? I don't think so!"

"Bless you," said Socrates, "and how have I anything to say, I or anyone else, when I have to speak after that beautiful speech, with everything in it?

---

[5]Euripides, *Stheneboea*, fragment 663 N.
[6]The Greek word ποιητης, poet, means a maker, and he uses this here to indicate creative arts and crafts and even the "creation" of living things.

[7]Compare *Odyssey* v. 391.
[8]This word "drinking" is doubtful in the Greek text.
[9]The three words used by Plato mean a ship's pilot, a fighter (not the driver) in a chariot or a marine on a ship, and a man who stands by another in battle.
[10]He puts in his own little drop of parody.

The first part was wonderful enough, but the end! The beauty of those words and phrases! It was quite overwhelming for any listener. The fact is, when I considered that I shall not be able to get anywhere near it, and I have nothing fine to say at all—I was so ashamed that I all but took to my heels and ran, but I had nowhere to go. The speech reminded me of Gorgias,[11] and I really felt quite as in Homer's story[12]; I was afraid that Agathon at the end of his speech might be going to produce the Gorgon's head of Gorgias—the terror in speech-making—directed against *my* speech, and turn me into stone with dumbness. And I understood then that I was a fool when I told you I would take my turn in singing the honours of Love, and admitted I was terribly clever in love affairs, whereas it seems I really had no idea how a eulogy ought to be made. For I was stupid enough to think that we ought to speak the truth about each person eulogised, and to make this the foundation, and from these truths to choose the most beautiful things and arrange them in the most elegant way; and I was quite proud to think how well I should speak, because I believed that I knew the truth. However, apparently this was not the right way to praise anything, but we should dedicate all that is greatest and most beautiful to the work, whether things are so or not; if they were false it did not matter. For it seems the task laid down was not for each of us to praise Love, but to seem to praise him. For this reason then, I think, you rake up every story, and dedicate it to Love, and say he is so-and-so and the cause of such-and-such, that he may seem to be most beautiful and best, of course to those who don't know—not to those who do, I suppose—and the laudation is excellent and imposing. But indeed I did not know how an encomium was made, and it was without this knowledge that I agreed to take my part in praising. Therefore the

tongue promised, but not the mind,[13] so good-bye to that. For I take it back now; I make no eulogy in this fashion: I could not do it. However, the truth, if you like: I have no objection to telling the truth, in my own fashion, not in rivalry with your speeches, or I should deserve to be laughed at. Then see whether you want a speech of that sort, Phaidros. Will you listen to the truth being told about Love, in any words and arrangement of phrases such as we may hit on as we go?"

Phaidros and the others (continued Aristodemos) told him to go on just as he thought best. "Then, Phaidros," he said, "let us ask Agathon a few little things, that I may get his agreement before I speak."

"Oh, I don't mind," said Phaidros, "ask away." After that Socrates began something like this:

"Indeed, my dear Agathon, I thought you were quite right in the beginning of your speech, when you said that you must first show what Love was like, and afterwards come to his works. That beginning I admire very much. Now then, about Love: you described what he is magnificently well, and so on; but tell me this too—is Love such as to be a love of something, or of nothing? I don't mean to ask if he is a love of mother or father; for that would be a ridiculous question, whether Love is love for mother or father; I mean it in the sense that one might apply to 'father' for instance; is the father a father of something or not? You would say, I suppose, if you wanted to answer right, that the father is father of son or daughter. Is that correct?"

"Certainly," said Agathon.

"And the same with the mother?"

This was agreed.

"Another, please," said Socrates, "answer me one or two more, that you may better understand what I want. What if I were to ask: 'A brother now, in himself, is he brother of something?'"

He said yes.

"Of a brother or sister?"

He agreed.

---

[11]Gorgias, the celebrated Sophist, adopted an artificial, affected style.

[12]*Odyssey* xi, 634. Odysseus, at the end of his visit to the Kingdom of the Dead, grew pale with fear that Persephone might out of Hades send upon him a Gorgonhead, and turn him to stone.

---

[13]A modification of Euripides' *Hippolytos* 612.

"Then tell me," he said, "about Love. Is Love love of nothing or of something?"

"Certainly he is love of something."

"Now then," said Socrates, "keep this in your memory, what the object of Love is[14]; and say whether Love desires the object of his love?"

"Certainly," said Agathon.

"Is it when he *has* what he desires and loves that he desires and loves it, or when he has not?"

"Most likely, when he has not," said he.

"Just consider," said Socrates, "put 'necessary' for 'likely'; isn't it necessary that the desiring desires what it lacks, or else does not desire if it does not lack? I think positively myself, Agathon, that it is absolutely necessary; what do you think?"

"I think the same," said he.

"Good. Then would one being big want to be big, or being strong want to be strong?"

"Impossible, according to what we have agreed."

"For I suppose he would not be lacking in whichever of these he is?"

"True."

"For if being strong he wanted to be strong," said Socrates, "and being swift he wanted to be swift, and being healthy he wanted to be healthy—you might go on forever like this, and you might think that those who were so-and-so and had such-and-such did also desire what they had; but to avoid our being deceived I say this—if you understand me, Agathon, it is obvious that these *must* have at this present time all they have, whether they wish to or not—and can anyone desire that? And when one says, 'I am healthy and want to be healthy,' 'I am rich and want to be rich,' 'I desire what I have,' we should answer, 'You, my good man, being possessed of riches and health and strength, wish to go on being possessed of them in the future, since at present you have them whether you want it or not; and when you say, "I desire what I have," consider—you mean only that you want to have in the future what you have now.' Wouldn't he agree?"

Agathon said yes.

Then Socrates went on, "Therefore this love for these blessings to be preserved for him into the future and to be always present for him—this is really loving that which is not yet available for him or possessed by him?"

"Certainly," he said.

"Then he, and every other who desires, desires what is not in his possession and not there, what he has not, and what he is not himself and what he lacks? Those are the sorts of things of which there is desire and love?"

"Certainly," he said.

"Come now," said Socrates, "let us run over again what has been agreed. Love is, first of all, of something; next, of those things which one lacks?"

"Yes," he said.

"This being granted, then, remember what things you said in your speech were the objects of Love. I will remind you, if you wish. I think you said something like this; the gods arranged their business through love of beautiful things, for there could not be a love for ugly things. Didn't you say something like that?"

"Yes, I did," said Agathon.

"And quite reasonably too, my friend," said Socrates; "and if this is so, would not Love be love of beauty, not of ugliness?"

He agreed.

"Well now, it has been agreed that he loves what he lacks and has not?"

"Yes," he said.

"Then Love lacks and has not beauty."

"That must be," said he.

"Very well: do you say that what lacks beauty and in no wise has beauty is beautiful?"

"Certainly not."

"Then if that is so, do you still agree that Love is beautiful?"

Agathon answered, "I fear, Socrates, I knew nothing of what I said!"

"Oh no," said he, "it was a fine speech, Agathon! But one little thing more: don't you think good things are also beautiful?"

"I do."

---

[14]Agathon had just said it was beauty.

"Then if Love lacks beautiful things, and good things are beautiful, he should lack the good things too."

"Socrates," he said, "I really could not contradict you; let it be as you say."

"Contradict the truth, you should say, beloved Agathon," he replied; "you can't do that, but to contradict Socrates is easy enough.

"And now you shall have peace from me; but there is a speech about Love which I heard once from Diotima of Mantineia,[15] who was wise in this matter and in many others; by making the Athenians perform sacrifices before the plague she even managed to put off the disease for ten years. And she it was who taught me about love affairs. This speech, then, which she made I will try to narrate to you now, beginning with what is agreed between me and Agathon; I will tell it by myself, as well as I can. You will see that I must describe first, as you did, Agathon, who Love is and what like, and then his works. I think it easiest to do it as the lady did in examining me. I said to her very much what Agathon just now did to me, that Love was a great god, and was a love of beautiful things; and she convinced me by saying the same as I did to Agathon, that he is neither beautiful, according to my argument, nor good. Then I said, 'What do you mean, Diotima? Is Love then ugly and bad?' And she said, 'Hush, for shame! Do you think that what is not beautiful must necessarily be ugly?' 'Yes, I do.' 'And what is not wise, ignorant? Do you not perceive that there is something between wisdom and ignorance?' 'What is that?' 'To have right opinion without being able to give a reason,' she said, 'is neither to understand (for how could an unreasoned thing be understanding?) nor is it ignorance (for how can ignorance hit the truth?). Right opinion is no doubt something between knowledge and ignorance.' 'Quite true,' I said. 'Then do not try to compel what is not beautiful to be ugly, or what is not good to be bad. So also with Love. He is not good and not beautiful, as you admit yourself, but do not imagine for that reason any the more that he must be ugly and bad, but something between these two,' said she. 'Well, anyway,' I said, 'he is admitted by all to be a great god.' 'All who don't know,' she said, 'or all who know too?' 'All without exception.' At this she said, with a laugh, 'And how could he be admitted to be a great god, Socrates, by those who say he is not a god at all?' 'Who are these?' said I. 'You for one,' said she, 'and I for another.' And I asked, 'How can that be?' She said, 'Easily. Tell me, don't you say that all the gods are happy and beautiful? Or would you dare to say that any one of them is not happy and beautiful?' 'Indeed I would not," said I. 'Then don't you call happy those possessed of good and beautiful things?' 'Certainly.' 'Yet you admitted that Love, because of a lack of good and beautiful things, actually desired those things which he lacked.' 'Yes, I admitted that.' 'Then how could he be a god who has no share in beautiful and good things?' 'He could not be a god, as it seems.' 'Don't you see then,' said she, 'that you yourself deny Love to be a god?'

" 'Then what could Love be?' I asked. 'A mortal?' 'Not at all.' 'What then?' I asked. 'Just as before, between mortal and immortal.' 'What is he then, Diotima?' 'A great spirit, Socrates; for all the spiritual is between divine and mortal.' 'What power has it?' said I. 'To interpret and to ferry across to the gods things given by men, and to men things from the gods, from men petitions and sacrifices, from the gods commands and requitals in return; and being in the middle it completes them and binds all together into a whole. Through this intermediary moves all the art of divination, and the art of priests, and all concerned with sacrifice and mysteries and incantations, and all sorcery and witchcraft. For God mingles not with man, but through this comes all the communion and conversation of gods with men and men with gods, both awake and asleep; and he who is expert in this is a spiritual man, but the expert in something other than this, such as common arts or crafts, is a vulgar man. These spirits are many and of all sorts and kinds, and one of them is Love.'

---

[15]A well-known Greek city in the Peloponnesus. The names perhaps suggest "the prophetess Fearthelord of Prophetville."

"'Who was his father,' said I, 'and who was his mother?' She answered, 'That is rather a long story, but still I will tell you. When Aphrodite was born, the gods held a feast, among them Plenty,[16] the son of Neverataloss. When they had dined, Poverty came in begging, as might be expected with all that good cheer, and hung about the doors. Plenty then got drunk on the nectar—for there was no wine yet—and went into Zeus's park all heavy and fell asleep. So Poverty because of her penury made a plan to have a child from Plenty, and lay by his side and conceived Love. This is why Love has become follower and servant of Aphrodite, having been begotten at her birthday party, and at the same time he is by nature a lover busy with beauty because Aphrodite is beautiful. Then since Love is the son of Plenty and Poverty he gets his fortunes from them. First, he is always poor; and far from being tender and beautiful, as most people think, he is hard and rough and unshod and homeless, lying always on the ground without bedding, sleeping by the doors and in the streets in the open air, having his mother's nature, always dwelling with want. But from his father again he has designs upon beautiful and good things, being brave and go-ahead and high-strung, a mighty hunter, always weaving devices, and a successful coveter of wisdom, a philosopher all his days, a great wizard and sorcerer and sophist. He was born neither mortal nor immortal; but on the same day, sometimes he is blooming and alive, when he has plenty, sometimes he is dying; then again he gets new life through his father's nature; but what he procures in plenty always trickles away, so that Love is not in want nor in wealth, and again he is between wisdom and ignorance. The truth is this: no god seeks after wisdom or desires to become wise—for wise he is already; nor does anyone else seek after wisdom, if he is wise already. And again, the ignorant do not seek after wisdom nor desire to become wise; for this is

the worst of ignorance, that one who is neither beautiful and good[17] nor intelligent should think himself good enough, so he does not desire it, because he does not think he is lacking in what he does not think he needs.'

"'Then who are the philosophers, Diotima,' said I, 'if those who seek after wisdom are neither the wise nor the ignorant?' 'That's clear enough even to a child,' she answered; 'they are those between these two, as Love is. You see, wisdom is one of the most beautiful things, and Love is a love for the beautiful, so Love must necessarily be a philosopher, and, being a philosopher, he must be between wise and ignorant. His birth is the cause of this, for he comes of a wise and resourceful father, but of a mother resourceless and not wise. Well then, dear Socrates, this is the nature of the spirit; but it was no wonder you thought Love what you did think. You thought, if I may infer it from what you say, that Love was the beloved, not the lover. That was why, I think, Love seemed to you wholly beautiful; for the thing loved is in fact beautiful and dainty and perfect and blessed, but the loving thing has a different shape, such as I have described.'

"Then I said, 'Very well, madam, what you say is right; but Love being such as you describe, of what use is he to mankind?' 'I will try to teach you that next, Socrates,' she said. 'Love then is like that, and born like that, and he is love of beautiful things, as you said he is. But suppose someone should ask us: "Socrates and Diotima, what is meant by love of beautiful things?"—I will put it more clearly: "He that loves beautiful things loves what?"' Then I answered, 'To get them.' 'Still,' she said, 'that answer needs another question, like this: "What will he get who gets the beautiful things?"' I said I could not manage at all to answer that question offhand. 'Well,' said she, 'suppose one should change "beautiful" to "good" and ask that? See here, Socrates, I will say: "What does he love who loves good things?"' 'To get them,' said I. 'And what will he

---

[16]So Spenser calls him in the "Hymn to Love"; Lamb has "Resource, the son of Cunning," in his translation in the Loeb Classical Library.

[17]The Greeks meant by this what we might call a cultured gentleman.

get who gets the good things?' 'That's easier,' said I; 'I can answer that he will be happy.' 'Then,' said she, 'by getting good things the happy are happy, and there is no need to ask further, why he who wishes to be happy does wish that, but the answer seems to be finished.' 'Quite true,' said I. 'But do you think this wish and this love is common to all mankind,' Diotima said, 'and do you think that all men always wish to have the good things, or what do you say?' 'That's it,' said I, 'it's common to all.' 'Why then, Socrates,' said she, 'do we not say that all men are lovers, if they do in fact all love the same things and always, instead of saying that some are lovers and some are not?' 'That surprises me too,' I said. 'Don't let it surprise you,' she said. 'For we have taken one kind of love, and given it the name of the whole, love; and there are other cases in which we misapply other names.' 'For example?' said I. 'Here is one,' she said. 'You know that poetry is many kinds of making, for when anything passes from not-being to being, the cause is always making, or poetry, so that in all the arts the process is making, and all the craftsmen in these are makers, or poets.' 'Quite true,' I said. 'But yet,' said she, 'they are not all called poets; they have other names, and one bit of this making has been taken, that concerning music and verse, and this is called by the name of the whole. For this only is called poetry, and those who have this bit of making are called poets.' 'That is true,' I said. 'So with love, then; in its general sense it is all the desire for good things and for happiness—Love most mighty and all-ensnaring; but those who turn to him by any other road, whether by way of moneymaking, or of a taste for sports or philosophy, are not said to be in love and are not called lovers, but only those who go after one kind and are earnest about that have the name of the whole, love, and are said to love and to be lovers.' 'I think you are right there,' said I. 'And there is a story,' said she, 'that people in love are those who are seeking for their other half, but my story tells that love is not for a half, nor indeed the whole, unless that happens to be something good, my friend; since men are willing to cut off their own hands and feet, if their own seem to them to be nasty. For really, I think, no one is pleased with his own thing, except one who calls the good thing his own and his property, and the bad thing another's; since there is nothing else men love but the good. Don't you think so?' 'Yes,' I said. 'Then,' said she, 'we may say simply that men love the good?' 'Yes,' I said. 'Shall we add,' she asked, 'that they love to have the good?' 'Yes, add that,' I said. 'Not only to have it, but always to have it?' 'Add that too.' 'Then to sum up,' she said, 'it is the love of having the good for oneself always.' 'Most true, indeed,' I said.

"She went on, 'Now if love is the love of having this always, what is the way men pursue it, and in what actions would their intense earnestness be expressed so as to be called love? What is this process? Can you tell me?' 'No,' said I, 'or else, Diotima, why should I, in admiration of your wisdom, have come to you as your pupil to find out these very matters?' 'Well then, I will tell you,' she said. 'It is a breeding in the beautiful, both of body and soul.' 'It needs divination,' I said, 'to tell what on earth you mean, and I don't understand.' 'Well,' she said, 'I will tell you clearer. All men are pregnant, Socrates, both in body and in soul, and when they are of the right age, our nature desires to beget. But it cannot beget in an ugly thing, only in a beautiful thing. And this business is divine, and this is something immortal in a mortal creature, breeding and birth. These cannot be in what is discordant. But the ugly is discordant with everything divine, and the beautiful is concordant. Beauty therefore is Portioner and Lady of Labour at birth. Therefore when the pregnant comes near to a beautiful thing it becomes gracious, and being delighted it is poured out and begets and procreates; when it comes near to an ugly thing, it becomes gloomy and grieved and rolls itself up and is repelled and shrinks back and does not procreate, but holds back the conception and is in a bad way. Hence in the pregnant thing swelling full already, there is great agitation about the beautiful thing because he that has it gains relief from great agony. Finally, Socrates, love is not for the beautiful, as you think.' 'Why not?' 'It is for begetting and birth in the beautiful.' 'Oh, indeed?' said I. 'Yes indeed,' said she. 'Then why for begetting?'

'Because begetting is, for the mortal, something everlasting and immortal. But one must desire immortality along with the good, according to what has been agreed, if love is love of having the good for oneself always. It is necessary then from this argument that love is for immortality also.'

"All this she taught me at different times whenever she came to speak about love affairs; and once she asked, 'What do you think, Socrates, to be the cause of this love and desire? You perceive that all animals get into a dreadful state when they desire to procreate, indeed birds and beasts alike; all are sick and in a condition of love, about mating first, and then how to find food for their young, and they are ready to fight hard for them, the weakest against the strongest, and to die for them, and to suffer the agonies of starvation themselves in order to feed them, ready to do anything. One might perhaps think that man,' she said, 'would do all this from reasoning; but what about beasts? What is the cause of their enamoured state? Can you tell me?' And I said again that I did not know; and she said, 'Then how do you ever expect to become expert in love affairs, if you do not understand that?' 'Why, Diotima, this is just why I have come to you, as I said; I knew I needed a teacher. Pray tell me the cause of this, and all the other love lore.'

"'Well then,' she said, 'if you believe love is by nature love of that which we often agreed on, don't be surprised. For on the same principle as before, here mortal nature seeks always as far as it can be to be immortal; and this is the only way it can, by birth, because it leaves something young in place of the old. Consider that for a while each single living creature is said to live and to be the same; for example, a man is said to be the same from boyhood to old age; he has, however, by no means the same things in himself, yet he is called the same: he continually becomes new, though he loses parts of himself, hair and flesh and bones and blood and all the body. Indeed, not only body, even in soul, manners, opinions, desires, pleasures, pains, fears, none of these remains the same, but some perish and others are born. And far stranger still, this happens to knowledge too; not only do some kinds of knowl-

edge perish in us, not only are other kinds born, and not even in our knowledge are we ever the same, but the same happens even in each single kind of knowledge. For what is called study and practice means that knowledge is passing out; forgetting is knowledge leaving us, and study puts in new knowledge instead of that which is passing away, and preserves our knowledge so that it seems to be the same. In this way all the mortal is preserved, not by being wholly the same always, like the divine, but because what grows old and goes leaves behind something new like its past self. By this device, Socrates,' said she, 'mortality partakes of immortality, both in body and in all other respects; but it cannot otherwise. Then do not be surprised that everything naturally honours its own offspring; immortality is what all this earnestness and love pursues.'

"I heard this with admiration; and I said, 'Really, Diotima most wise! Is that really and truly so?' She answered as the complete Sophists do,[18] and said, 'You may be sure of that, Socrates. Just think, if you please, of men's ambition. You would be surprised at its unreasonableness if you didn't bear in mind what I have told you; observe what a terrible state they are in with love of becoming renowned, "and to lay up their fame for evermore"[19] and for this how ready they are to run all risks even more than for their children, and to spend money and endure hardship to any extent, and to die for it. Do you think Alcestis would have died for Admetos, or Achilles would have died over Patroclos, or your Codros[20] would have died for the royalty of his sons, if they had not thought that "immortal memory of Virtue" would be theirs, which we still keep! Far from it,' she said; 'for eternal virtue and glorious fame like that all men do everything, I think, and the better they are, the more they do so; for the immortal is what they love. So those who are pregnant in body,' she said, 'turn rather to women and

---

[18]That is, she made a speech rather than answered questions.
[19]A line of poetry.
[20]A legendary King of Athens, who gave his life for this in the Dorian invasion.

are enamoured in this way, and thus, by begetting children, secure for themselves, so they think, immortality and memory and happiness, "Providing all things for the time to come";[21] but those who are pregnant in soul—for there are some,' she said, 'who conceive in soul still more than in body, what is proper for the soul to conceive and bear; and what is proper? wisdom and virtue in general—to this class belong all creative poets, and those artists and craftsmen who are said to be inventive. But much the greatest wisdom,' she said, 'and the most beautiful, is that which is concerned with the ordering of cities and homes, which we call temperance and justice. So again a man with divinity in him, whose soul from his youth is pregnant with these things, desires when he grows up to beget and procreate; and thereupon, I think, he seeks and goes about to find the beautiful thing in which he can beget; for in the ugly he never will. Being pregnant, then, he welcomes bodies which are beautiful rather than ugly, and if he finds a soul beautiful and generous and well-bred, he gladly welcomes the two body and soul together, and for a human being like that he has plenty of talks about virtue, and what the good man ought to be and to practise, and he tries to educate him. For by attaching himself to a person of beauty, I think, and keeping company with him, he begets and procreates what he has long been pregnant with; present and absent he remembers him, and with him fosters what is begotten, so that as a result these people maintain a much closer communion together and a firmer relationship than parents of children, because they have shared between them children more beautiful and more immortal. And everyone would be content to have such children born to him rather than human children; he would look to Homer and Hesiod and the other good poets, and wish to rival them, who leave such offspring behind them, which give their parents the same immortal fame and memory as they have themselves; or if you like,' she said, 'think what children Lycurgos[22] left in Lacedaimon, the saviours of Lacedai-

mon and, one may say, of all Hellas. Honour came to Solon also, in your country, by the begetting of his laws; and to many others in many countries and times, both Hellenes and barbarians, who performed many beautiful works and begat all kinds of virtue; in their names many sanctuaries have been made because they had such children, but never a one has been so honoured because of human children.

"'These are some of the mysteries of Love, Socrates, in which perhaps even you may become an initiate; but as for the higher revelations, which initiation leads to if one approaches in the right way, I do not know if you could ever become an adept. At least I will instruct you,' she said, 'and no pains will be lacking; you try to follow if you can. It is necessary,' she said, 'that one who approaches in the right way should begin this business young, and approach beautiful bodies. First, if his leader leads aright, he should love one body and there beget beautiful speech; then he should take notice that the beauty in one body is akin to the beauty in another body, and if we must pursue beauty in essence, it is great folly not to believe that the beauty in all such bodies is one and the same. When he has learnt this, he must become the lover of all beautiful bodies, and relax the intense passion for one, thinking lightly of it and believing it to be a small thing. Next he must believe beauty in souls to be more precious than beauty in the body; so that if anyone is decent in soul, even if it has little bloom, it should be enough for him to love and care for, and to beget and seek such talks as will make young people better; that he may moreover be compelled to contemplate the beauty in our pursuits and customs, and to see that all beauty is of one and the same kin, and that so he may believe that bodily beauty is a small thing. Next, he must be led from practice to knowledge, that he may see again the beauty in different kinds of knowledge, and, directing his gaze from now on towards beauty as a whole, he may no longer dwell upon one, like a servant, content with the beauty of one boy or one human being or one pursuit, and so be slavish and petty; but he should turn to the great ocean of beauty, and in contempla-

---

[21] A line of poetry.
[22] The Spartan lawgiver.

tion of it give birth to many beautiful and magnificent speeches and thoughts in the abundance of philosophy, until being strengthened and grown therein he may catch sight of some one knowledge, the one science of this beauty now to be described. Try to attend,' she said, 'as carefully as you can.

"'Whoever shall be guided so far towards the mysteries of love, by contemplating beautiful things rightly in due order, is approaching the last grade. Suddenly he will behold a beauty marvellous in its nature, that very Beauty, Socrates, for the sake of which all the earlier hardships had been borne: in the first place, everlasting, and never being born nor perishing, neither increasing nor diminishing; secondly, not beautiful here and ugly there, not beautiful now and ugly then, not beautiful in one direction and ugly in another direction, not beautiful in one place and ugly in another place. Again, this beauty will not show itself to him like a face or hands or any bodily thing at all, nor as a discourse or a science, nor indeed as residing in anything, as in a living creature or in earth or heaven or anything else, but being by itself with itself always in simplicity; while all the beautiful things elsewhere partake of this beauty in such manner, that when *they* are born and perish *it* becomes neither less nor more and nothing at all happens to it; so that when anyone by right boy-loving goes up from these beautiful things to that beauty, and begins to catch sight of it, he would almost touch the perfect secret. For let me tell you, the right way to approach the things of love, or to be led there by another, is this: beginning from these beautiful things, to mount for that beauty's sake ever upwards, as by a flight of steps, from one to two, and from two to all beautiful bodies, and from beautiful bodies to beautiful pursuits and practices, and from practices to beautiful learnings, so that from learnings he may come at last to that perfect learning which is the learning solely of that beauty itself, and may know at last that which is the perfection of beauty. There in life and there alone, my dear Socrates,' said the inspired woman, 'is life worth living for man, while he contemplates Beauty itself. If ever you see this, it will seem to you to be far above gold and raiment and beautiful boys and men, whose beauty you are now entranced to

see and you and many others are ready, so long as they see their darlings and remain ever with them, if it could be possible, not to eat nor drink but only to gaze at them and to be with them. What indeed,' she said, 'should we think, if it were given to one of us to see beauty undefiled, pure, unmixed, not adulterated with human flesh and colours and much other mortal rubbish, and if he could behold beauty in perfect simplicity? Do you think it a mean life for a man,' she said, 'to be looking thither and contemplating that and abiding with it? Do you not reflect,' said she, 'that there only it will be possible for him, when he sees the beautiful with the mind, which alone can see it, to give birth not to likenesses of virtue, since he touches no likeness, but to realities, since he touches reality; and when he has given birth to real virtue and brought it up, will it not be granted him to be the friend of God, and immortal if any man ever is?'

"This then, Phaidros and gentlemen, is what Diotima said, and I am quite convinced, and, being convinced, I try to persuade other people also to believe that to attain this possession one could not easily find a better helper for human nature than Love. And so I say that every man ought to honour Love, and I honour love matters myself, and I practise them particularly and encourage others; and now and always I sing the praises of Love's power and courage, as much as I am able. Then let this be my speech of eulogy to Love, if you please, Phaidros, or call it anything else you like."

A LAKOTA VISION

Black Elk

Crazy Horse's father was my father's cousin, and there were no chiefs in our family before Crazy Horse; but there were holy men; and he became a chief because of the power he got in a vision when he was a boy. When I was a man, my father told me something about that vision. Of course he did not know all of it; but he said that Crazy Horse dreamed and went into the world where there is nothing but the spirits of all things. That is the real world that is behind this one, and everything we see here is something like a shadow from that world. He was on his horse in that world, and the horse and himself on it and the trees and the grass and the stones and everything were made of spirit, and nothing was hard, and everything seemed to float. His horse was standing still there, and yet it danced around like a horse made only of shadow, and that is how he got his name, which does not mean that his horse was crazy or wild, but that in his vision it danced around in that queer way.

It was this vision that gave him his great power, for when he went into a fight, he had only to think of that world to be in it again, so that he could go through anything and not be hurt. Until he was murdered by the Wasichus* at the Soldiers' Town on White River, he was wounded only twice, once by accident and both times by some one of his own people when he was not expecting trouble and was not thinking; never by an enemy. He was fifteen years old when he was wounded by accident; and the other time was when he was a young man and another man was jealous of him because the man's wife liked Crazy Horse.

They used to say too that he carried a sacred stone with him, like one he had seen in some vision, and that when he was in danger, the stone always got very heavy and protected him somehow. That, they used to say, was the reason no horse he ever rode lasted very long. I do not know about this; maybe people only thought it; but it is a fact that he never kept one horse long. They wore out. I think it was only the power of his great vision that made him great.

Now and then he would notice me and speak to me before this; and sometimes he would have the crier call me into his tepee to eat with him. Then he would say things to tease me, but I would not say anything back, because I think I was a little afraid of him. I was not afraid that he would hurt me; I was

just afraid. Everybody felt that way about him, for he was a queer man and would go about the village without noticing people or saying anything. In his own tepee he would joke, and when he was on the warpath with a small party, he would joke to make his warriors feel good. But around the village he hardly ever noticed anybody, except little children. All the Lakotas* like to dance and sing; but he never joined a dance, and they say nobody ever heard him sing. But everyone liked him, and they would do anything he wanted or go anywhere he said. He was a small man among the Lakotas and he was slender and had a thin face and his eyes looked through things and he always seemed to be thinking hard about something. He never wanted to have many things for himself, and did not have many ponies like a chief. They say that when game was scarce and the people were hungry, he would not eat at all. He was a queer man. Maybe he was always part way into that world of his vision. He was a very great man, and I think if the Wasichus had not murdered him down there, maybe we should still have the Black Hills and be happy. They could not have killed him in battle. They had to lie to him and murder him. And he was only about thirty years old when he died.

___

QUESTIONS FOR DISCUSSION

1. Why does Socrates believe that Love is not a god, even though Love was traditionally accepted as a god by the Greek people? Do you think that Socrates' argument concerning Love's true nature is a sound one? Why or why not?
2. If a time machine could carry Black Elk to Socrates' Athens or Socrates to the American plains, they surely would have had much in common to talk about, despite their great differences in culture. What might they say to each other? What might seem familiar? What would seem strange?

Wasichus is the name Black Elk uses for the whites (Eds.).

*Lakota or Dakota is the name the Sioux call themselves (Eds.).

IDEALISM: WESTERN AND INDIAN

Beginning about 800 B.C.—or perhaps even earlier—in the great river valleys of North India, small groups of men turned their backs on established society in order to undertake a journey deep within themselves to find their own true nature and the true nature of God. Out of these spiritual journeys came the philosophical reflections known to the world as Vedanta or the *Upanishads,* a word which, roughly translated, means teachings received sitting at a sage's feet. Over time, these teachings were accepted as scriptural by the priests of the emerging Hindu religion. These scriptures in turn were interpreted in a variety of ways by the philosophers and theologians of Hinduism.

Our first selection is perhaps the most famous *Upanishad* of all. In the second, the most famous of its interpreters, the ninth-century philosopher Shankara, presents a philosophical interpretation of it and related passages which is known as *Advaita Vedanta. Advaita* in the Sanskrit language means "nondual" or "Absolute," to use a technical term for nonduality taken from the Western tradition. The *Upanishad,* on Shankara's view, teaches that God or *Brahman* (the True) is in reality identical to the true self or *Atman,* a nondual unity without an other. The world and the false self that we usually mistakenly take ourselves to be are, on the other hand, a mere appearance of God and not the underlying reality. The material world is thus, from God's point of view, a purely mind-created entity, a product of God's consciousness with no substance of its own. This view of reality is called in philosophy "idealism," not in the sense that its proponents are necessarily high-minded idealists but in the more basic sense that they view the world as mental or a mere idea.

In the West, 900 years after the time of Shankara, the Anglo-Irish philosopher-bishop George Berkeley (1685–1753) argued for a form of idealism which rests on premises somewhat different than those which Shankara employed. The world is not appearance as opposed to a unitary reality; the world of appearance *is* reality; the things around us are ideas in our minds, though ultimately they do have their origin in ideas which are contained in the mind of God. This form of idealism is often termed "subjective idealism" to contrast it with the nondual "objective" or "absolute idealism" of the form one finds in Shankara's work.

Absolute idealism is not, however, a purely Indian invention. In Germany in the nineteenth century, following suggestions in the work of the great philosopher Immanuel Kant, several philosophers began exploring this avenue of understanding. When translations of classical Indian philosophy began to appear simultaneously in Germany, they were greeted with amazed enthusiasm. This, in turn, was reinforced by the discovery of the common ancestry of most European and North Indian languages. It was as if, in India, a long lost, if distant, cousin had been found. Of all the German idealists, the most knowledgeable on the subject of Indian idealism and the one working most closely in spirit to the Indians was Schopenhauer. Indeed he often referred to himself as a Buddhist. In the selection presented here, he relates his own work to the famous "Thou art that" passage from the *Chandogya Upanishad* with which the section begins.

✗ THOU ART THAT

The Upanishads

"As the bees, my son, make honey by collecting the juices of distant trees, and reduce the juice into one form,

"And as these juices have no discrimination, so that they might say, I am the juice of this tree or that, in the same manner, my son, all these creatures when they have become merged in the True (either in deep sleep or in death), know not that they are merged in the True.

"Whatever these creatures are here, whether a lion, or a wolf, or a boar, or a worm, or a midge, or a gnat, or a musquito, that they become again and again.

"Now that which is that subtile essence, in it all that exists has its self. It is the True. It is the Self, and thou, O *Svetaketu*, art it."

"Please, Sir, inform me still more," said the son.

"Be it so, my child," the father replied.

"These rivers, my son, run, the eastern (like the Gangâ) toward the east, the western (like the Sindhu) toward the west. They go from sea to sea (i.e. the clouds lift up the water from the sea to the sky, and send it back as rain to the sea). They become indeed sea. And as those rivers, when they are in the sea, do not know, I am this or that river,

"In the same manner, my son, all these creatures, when they have come back from the True, know not that they have come back from the True. Whatever these creatures are here, whether a lion, or a wolf, or a boar, or a worm, or a midge, or a gnat, or a musquito, that they become again and again.

"That which is that subtile essence, in it all that exists has its self. It is the True. It is the Self, and thou, O *Svetaketu*, art it." (Sveta Kay tu)

"Please, Sir, inform me still more," said the son.

"Be it so, my child," the father replied.

"If some one were to strike at the root of this large tree here, it would bleed, but live. If he were to strike at its stem, it would bleed, but live. If he were to strike at its top, it would bleed, but live. Per-vaded by the living Self that tree stands firm, drinking in its nourishment and rejoicing;

"But if the life (the living Self) leaves one of its branches, that branch withers; if it leaves a second, that branch withers; if it leaves a third, that branch withers. If it leaves the whole tree, the whole tree withers. In exactly the same manner, my son, know this." Thus he spoke:

"This (body) indeed withers and dies when the living Self has left it; the living Self dies not.

"That which is that subtile essence, in it all that exists has its self. It is the True. It is the Self, and thou, *Svetaketu*, art it."

"Please, Sir, inform me still more," said the son.

"Be it so, my child," the father replied.

"Fetch me from thence a fruit of the Nyagrodha tree."

"Here is one, Sir."

"Break it."

"It is broken, Sir."

"What do you see there?"

"These seeds, almost infinitesimal."

"Break one of them."

"It is broken, Sir."

"What do you see there?"

"Not anything, Sir."

The father said: "My son, that subtile essence which you do not perceive there, of that very essence this great Nyagrodha tree exists.

"Believe it, my son. That which is the subtile essence, in it all that exists has its self. It is the True. It is the Self, and thou, O *Svetaketu*, art it."

"Please, Sir, inform me still more," said the son.

"Be it so, my child," the father replied.

"Place this salt in water, and then wait on me in the morning."

The son did as he was commanded.

The father said to him: "Bring me the salt, which you placed in the water last night."

The son having looked for it, found it not, for, of course, it was melted.

The father said: "Taste it from the surface of the water. How is it?"

The son replied: "It is salt."

"Taste it from the middle. How is it?"

The son replied: "It is salt."

"Taste it from the bottom. How is it?"

The son replied: "It is salt."

The father said: "Throw it away and then wait on me."

He did so; but salt exists for ever.

Then the father said: "Here also, in this body, forsooth, you do not perceive the True (Sat), my son; but there indeed it is.

"That which is the subtle essence, in it all that exists has its self. It is the True. It is the Self, and thou, O *Svetaketu*, art it."

A COMMENTARY ON THE UPANISHADS

Shankara

That same highest Brahman* constitutes—as we know from passages such as "that art thou"—the real nature of the individual soul, while its second nature, i.e. that aspect of it which depends on fictitious limiting conditions, is not its real nature. For as long as the individual soul does not free itself from Nescience in the form of duality—which Nescience may be compared to the mistake of him who in the twilight mistakes a post for a man—and does not rise to the knowledge of the Self, whose nature is unchangeable, eternal Cognition—which expresses itself in the form "I am Brahman"—so long it remains the individual soul. But when, discarding the aggregate of body, sense-organs and mind, it arrives, by means of Scripture, at the knowledge that it is not itself that aggregate, that it does not form part of transmigratory existence, but is the True, the Real, the Self, whose nature is pure intelligence; then knowing itself to be of the nature

---

*Brahman is the term that the *Upanishads* use to designate God in the deep sense that Western mystics sometimes call "the God-head" or "the Ground of Being" (Eds.).

of unchangeable, eternal Cognition, it lifts itself above the vain conceit of being one with this body, and itself becomes the Self, whose nature is unchanging, eternal Cognition. As is declared in such scriptural passages as "He who knows the highest Brahman becomes even Brahman." And this is the real nature of the individual soul by means of which it arises from the body and appears in its own form.

Here an objection may be raised. How, it is asked, can we speak of the true nature (svarûpa) of that which is unchanging and eternal, and then say that "it appears in its own form (true nature)"? Of gold and similar substances, whose true nature becomes hidden, and whose specific qualities are rendered non-apparent by their contact with some other substance, it may be said that their true nature is rendered manifest when they are cleaned by the application of some acid substance; so it may be said, likewise, that the stars, whose light is during daytime overpowered (by the superior brilliancy of the sun), become manifest in their true nature at night when the overpowering (sun) has departed. But it is impossible to speak of an analogous overpowering of the eternal light of intelligence by whatever agency, since, like ether, it is free from all contact, and since, moreover, such an assumption would be contradicted by what we actually observe. For the (energies of) seeing, hearing, noticing, cognising constitute the character of the individual soul, and that character is observed to exist in full perfection, even in the case of that individual soul which has not yet risen beyond the body. Every individual soul carries on the course of its practical existence by means of the activities of seeing, hearing, cognising; otherwise no practical existence at all would be possible. If, on the other hand, that character would realise itself in the case of that soul only which has risen above the body, the entire aggregate of practical existence, as it actually presents itself prior to the soul's rising, would thereby be contradicted. We therefore ask: Wherein consists that (alleged) rising from the body? Wherein consists that appearing (of the soul) in its own form?

To this we make the following reply.—Before the rise of discriminative knowledge the nature of the individual soul, which is (in reality) pure light, is non-discriminated as it were from its limiting adjuncts consisting of body, senses, mind, sense-objects and feelings, and appears as consisting of the energies of seeing and so on. Similarly—to quote an analogous case from ordinary experience—the true nature of a pure crystal, i.e. its transparency and whiteness, is, before the rise of discriminative knowledge (on the part of the observer), non-discriminated as it were from any limiting adjuncts of red or blue colour; while, as soon as through some means of true cognition discriminative knowledge has arisen, it is said to have now accomplished its true nature, i.e. transparency and whiteness, although in reality it had already done so before. Thus the discriminative knowledge, effected by *Sruti*, on the part of the individual soul which previously is non-discriminated as it were from its limiting adjuncts, is (according to the scriptural passage under discussion) the soul's rising from the body, and the fruit of that discriminative knowledge is its accomplishment in its true nature, i.e. the comprehension that its nature is the pure Self. Thus the embodiedness and the non-embodiedness of the Self are due merely to discrimination and non-discrimination, in agreement with the mantra, "Bodiless within the bodies," &c., and the statement of *Smriti* as to the non-difference between embodiedness and non-embodiedness "Through dwelling in the body, O Kaunteya, it does not act and is not tainted."* The individual soul is therefore called "That whose true nature is non-manifest" merely on account of the absence of discriminative knowledge, and it is called "That whose nature has become manifest" on account of the presence of such knowledge. Manifestation and non-manifestation of its nature of a different kind are not possible, since its nature is nothing but its nature (i.e. in reality is always the same). Thus the difference between the individual soul and the highest Lord is owing to wrong knowledge only, not to any reality, since, like ether, the highest Self is not in real contact with anything.

---

*From the *Bhagavad Gita,* Chapter 13; see Chapter 5 (Eds.).

• • •

As the magician is not at any time affected by the magical illusion produced by himself, because it is unreal, so the highest Self is not affected by the world-illusion. And as one dreaming person is not affected by the illusory visions of his dream because they do not accompany the waking state and the state of dreamless sleep; so the one permanent witness of the three states (viz. the highest Self which is the one unchanging witness of the creation, subsistence, and reabsorption of the world) is not touched by the mutually exclusive three states. For that the highest Self appears in those three states is a mere illusion, not more substantial than the snake for which the rope is mistaken in the twilight. With reference to this point teachers knowing the true tradition of the Vedânta have made the following declaration, "When the individual soul which is held in the bonds of slumber by the beginningless Mâyâ awakes, then it knows the eternal, sleepless, dreamless non-duality."

• • •

In the same way as those parts of ethereal space which are limited by jars and waterpots are not really different from the universal ethereal space, and as the water of a mirage is not really different from the surface of the salty steppe—for the nature of that water is that it is seen in one moment and has vanished in the next, and moreover, it is not to be perceived by its own nature (i.e. apart from the surface of the desert)—; so this manifold world with its objects of enjoyment, enjoyers and so on has no existence apart from Brahman.—But—it might be objected—Brahman has in itself elements of manifoldness. As the tree has many branches, so Brahman possesses many powers and energies dependent on those powers. Unity and manifoldness are therefore both true. Thus, a tree considered in itself is one, but it is manifold if viewed as having branches; so the sea in itself is one, but manifold as having waves and foam; so the clay in itself is one, but manifold if viewed with regard to the jars and dishes made of it. On this assumption the process of final release resulting from right knowledge may be established in connexion with the element of unity (in Brahman), while the two processes of common worldly activity and of activity according to the Veda—which depend on the karmakânda—may be established in connexion with the element of manifoldness. And with this view the parallel instances of clay &c. agree very well.

This theory, we reply, is untenable because in the instance (quoted in the Upanishad) the phrase "as clay they are true" asserts the cause only to be true while the phrase "having its origin in speech" declares the unreality of all effects. And with reference to the matter illustrated by the instance given (viz. the highest cause, Brahman) we read, "In that all this has its Self"; and, again, "That is true"; whereby it is asserted that only the one highest cause is true. The following passage again, "That is the Self; thou art that, O *S*vetaketu!" teaches that the embodied soul (the individual soul) also is Brahman. (And we must note that) the passage distinctly teaches that the fact of the embodied soul having its Self in Brahman is self-established, not to be accomplished by endeavour. This doctrine of the individual soul having its Self in Brahman, if once accepted as the doctrine of the Veda, does away with the independent existence of the individual soul, just as the idea of the rope does away with the idea of the snake (for which the rope had been mistaken). And if the doctrine of the independent existence of the individual soul has to be set aside, then the opinion of the entire phenomenal world—which is based on the individual soul—having an independent existence is likewise to be set aside. But only for the establishment of the latter an element of manifoldness would have to be assumed in Brahman, in addition to the element of unity.— Scriptural passages also (such as, "When the Self only is all this, how should he see another?") declare that for him who sees that everything has its Self in Brahman the whole phenomenal world with its actions, agents, and results of actions is non-existent. Nor can it be said that this non-existence of the phenomenal world is declared (by Scripture) to be limited to certain states; for the passage "Thou art that" shows that the general fact of Brahman

being the Self of all is not limited by any particular state.

 # SUBJECTIVE IDEALISM

George Berkeley

THE FIRST DIALOGUE

Philonous: Good morrow, Hylas: I did not expect to find you abroad so early.

Hylas: It is indeed something unusual: but my thoughts were so taken up with a subject I was discoursing of last night, that finding I could not sleep, I resolved to rise and take a turn in the garden.

Phil.: It happened well, to let you see what innocent and agreeable pleasures you lose every morning. Can there be a pleasanter time of the day, or a more delightful season of the year? . . .

But I am afraid I interrupt your thoughts; for you seemed very intent on something.

Hyl.: It is true, I was, and shall be obliged to you if you will permit me to go on in the same vein; not that I would by any means deprive myself of your company, for my thoughts always flow more easily in conversation with a friend, than when I am alone: but my request is, that you would suffer me to impart my reflections to you.

Phil.: With all my heart, it is what I should have requested myself, if you had not prevented me.

Hyl.: I was considering the odd fate of those men who have in all ages, through an affectation of being distinguished from the vulgar, or some unaccountable turn of thought, pretended either to believe nothing at all, or to believe the most extravagant things in the world. This however might be borne, if their paradoxes and scepticism did not draw after them some consequences of general disadvantage to mankind. But the mischief lieth here; that when men of less leisure see them who are supposed to have spent their whole time in the pursuits of knowledge, professing an entire ignorance of all things, or advancing such notions as are repugnant to plain and commonly received principles, they will be tempted to entertain suspicions concerning the most important truths, which they had hitherto held sacred and unquestionable.

Phil.: I entirely agree with you, as to the ill tendency of the affected doubts of some philosophers, and fantastical conceits of others. I am even so far gone of late in this way of thinking, that I have quitted several of the sublime notions I had got in their schools for vulgar opinions. And I give it you on my word, since this revolt from metaphysical notions to the plain dictates of nature and common sense, I find my understanding strangely enlightened, so that I can now easily comprehend a great many things which before were all mystery and riddle.

Hyl.: I am glad to find there was nothing in the accounts I heard of you.

Phil.: Pray, what were those?

Hyl.: You were represented in last night's conversation, as one who maintained the most extravagant opinion that ever entered into the mind of man, to wit, that there is no such thing as *material substance* in the world.

Phil.: That there is no such thing as what philosophers call *material substance,* I am seriously persuaded: but if I were made to see any thing absurd or sceptical in this, I should then have the same reason to renounce this, that I imagine I have now to reject the contrary opinion.

Hyl.: What! can any thing be more fantastical, more repugnant to common sense, or a more manifest piece of scepticism, than to believe there is no such thing as *matter?*

Phil.: Softly, good Hylas. What if it should prove, that you who hold there is, are by virtue of that opinion a greater sceptic, and maintain more paradoxes and repugnances to common sense, than I who believe no such thing?

Hyl.: You may as soon persuade me, the part is greater than the whole, as that, in order to avoid absurdity and scepticism, I should ever be obliged to give up my opinion in this point.

Phil.: Well then, are you content to admit that opinion for true, which upon examination shall appear most agreeable to common sense, and remote from scepticism?

Hyl.: With all my heart. Since you are for raising disputes about the plainest things in nature, I am content for once to hear what you have to say.

Phil.: Pray, Hylas, what do you mean by a *sceptic?*

Hyl.: I mean what all men mean, one that doubts of every thing.

Phil.: He then who entertains no doubt concerning some particular point, with regard to that point cannot be thought a *sceptic.*

Hyl.: I agree with you.

Phil.: Whether doth doubting consist in embracing the affirmative or negative side of a question?

Hyl.: In neither; for whoever understands English, cannot but know that *doubting* signifies a suspense between both.

Phil.: He then that denieth any point, can no more be said to doubt of it than he who affirmeth it with the same degree of assurance.

Hyl.: True.

Phil.: And consequently, for such his denial is no more to be esteemed a *sceptic* than the other.

Hyl.: I acknowledge it.

Phil.: How cometh it to pass then, Hylas, that you pronounce me a *sceptic,* because I deny what you affirm, to wit, the existence of matter? Since, for ought you can tell, I am as peremptory in my denial, as you in your affirmation.

Hyl.: Hold, Philonous, I have been a little out in my definition; but every false step a man makes in discourse is not to be insisted on. I said, indeed, that a *sceptic* was one who doubted of every thing; but I should have added, or who denies the reality and truth of things.

Phil.: What things? Do you mean the principles and theorems of sciences? but these you know are universal intellectual notions, and consequently independent of matter; the denial therefore of this doth not imply the denying them.

Hyl.: I grant it. But are there no other things? What think you of distrusting the senses, of denying the real existence of sensible things, or pretending to know nothing of them? Is not this sufficient to denominate a man a *sceptic?*

Phil.: Shall we therefore examine which of us it is that denies the reality of sensible things, or professes the greatest ignorance of them; since, if I take you rightly, he is to be esteemed the greatest *sceptic?*

Hyl.: That is what I desire.

Phil.: What mean you by sensible things?

Hyl.: Those things which are perceived by the senses. Can you imagine that I mean any thing else?

Phil.: Pardon me, Hylas, if I am desirous clearly to apprehend your notions, since this may much shorten our inquiry. Suffer me then to ask you this further question. Are those things only perceived by the senses which are perceived immediately? or may those things properly be said to be *sensible,* which are perceived mediately, or not without the intervention of others?

Hyl.: I do not sufficiently understand you.

Phil.: In reading a book, what I immediately perceive are the letters, but mediately, or by means of these, are suggested to my mind the notions of God, virtue, truth, &c. Now that the letters are truly sensible things, or perceived by sense, there is no doubt: but I would know whether you take the things suggested by them to be so too.

Hyl.: No, certainly, it were absurd to think *God* or *virtue* sensible things, though they may be signified and suggested to the mind by sensible marks, with which they have an arbitrary connexion.

Phil.: It seems then, that by *sensible things* you mean those only which can be perceived immediately by sense.

Hyl.: Right.

Phil.: Doth it not follow from this, that though I see one part of the sky red, and another blue, and that my reason doth thence evidently conclude there must be some cause of that diversity of colours, yet that cause cannot be said to be a sensible thing, or perceived by the sense of seeing?

Hyl.: It doth.

Phil.: In like manner, though I hear variety of sounds, yet I cannot be said to hear the causes of these sounds.

Hyl.: You cannot.

Phil.: And when by my touch I perceive a thing to be hot and heavy, I cannot say with any truth or propriety, that I feel the cause of its heat or weight.

Hyl.: To prevent any more questions of this kind, I tell you once for all, that by *sensible things* I mean those only which are perceived by sense, and that in truth the senses perceive nothing which they do not perceive immediately: for they make no inferences. The deducing therefore of causes or occasions from effects and appearances, which alone are perceived by sense, entirely relates to reason.

Phil.: This point then is agreed between us, that *sensible things are those only which are immediately perceived by sense.* You will further inform me, whether we immediately perceive by sight any thing beside light, and colours, and figures: or by hearing any thing but sounds: by the palate, any thing besides tastes: by the smell, besides odours: or by the touch, more than tangible qualities.

Hyl.: We do not.

Phil.: It seems therefore, that if you take away all sensible qualities, there remains nothing sensible.

Hyl.: I grant it.

Phil.: Sensible things therefore are nothing else but so many sensible qualities, or combinations of sensible qualities.

Hyl.: Nothing else.

Phil.: Heat then is a sensible thing.

Hyl.: Certainly.

Phil.: Doth the reality of sensible things consist in being perceived? or, is it something distinct from their being perceived, and that bears no relation to the mind?

Hyl.: To *exist* is one thing, and to be *perceived* is another.

Phil.: I speak with regard to sensible things only; and of these I ask, whether by their real existence you mean a subsistence exterior to the mind, and distinct from their being perceived?

Hyl.: I mean a real absolute being, distinct from, and without any relation to their being perceived.

Phil.: Heat, therefore, if it be allowed a real being, must exist without the mind.

Hyl.: It must.

Phil.: Tell me, Hylas, is this real existence equally compatible to all degrees of heat, which we perceive: or is there any reason why we should attribute it to some, and deny it others? and if there be, pray let me know that reason.

Hyl.: Whatever degree of heat we perceive by sense, we may be sure the same exists in the object that occasions it.

Phil.: What, the greatest as well as the least?

Hyl.: I tell you, the reason is plainly the same in respect of both: they are both perceived by sense; nay, the greater degree of heat is more sensibly perceived; and consequently, if there is any difference, we are more certain of its real existence than we can be of the reality of a lesser degree.

Phil.: But is not the most vehement and intense degree of heat a very great pain?

Hyl.: No one can deny it.

Phil.: And is any unperceiving thing capable of pain or pleasure?

Hyl.: No, certainly.

Phil.: Is your material substance a senseless being, or a being endowed with sense and perception?

Hyl.: It is senseless without doubt.

Phil.: It cannot therefore be the subject of pain.

Hyl.: By no means.

Phil.: Nor consequently of the greatest heat perceived by sense, since you acknowledge this to be no small pain.

Hyl.: I grant it.

Phil.: What shall we say then of your external object; is it a material substance, or no?

Hyl.: It is a material substance with the sensible qualities inhering in it.

Phil.: How then can a great heat exist in it, since you own it cannot in a material substance? I desire you would clear this point.

Hyl.: Hold, Philonous; I fear I was out in yielding intense heat to be a pain. It should seem rather, that pain is something distinct from heat, and the consequence or effect of it.

Phil.: Upon putting your hand near the fire, do you perceive one simple uniform sensation, or two distinct sensations?

Hyl.: But one simple sensation.

Phil.: Is not the heat immediately perceived?

Hyl.: It is.

Phil.: And the pain?

Hyl.: True.

Phil.: Seeing therefore they are both immediately perceived at the same time, and the fire affects you only with one simple, or uncompounded idea, it follows that this same simple idea is both the intense heat immediately perceived, and the pain; and consequently, that the intense heat immediately perceived, is nothing distinct from a particular sort of pain.

Hyl.: It seems so.

Phil.: Again, try in your thoughts, Hylas, if you can conceive a vehement sensation to be without pain, or pleasure.

Hyl.: I cannot.

Phil.: Or can you frame to yourself an idea of sensible pain or pleasure in general, abstracted from every particular idea of heat, cold, tastes, smells, &c.?

Hyl.: I do not find that I can.

Phil.: Doth it not therefore follow, that sensible pain is nothing distinct from those sensations or ideas, in an intense degree?

Hyl.: It is undeniable; and to speak the truth, I begin to suspect a very great heat cannot exist but in a mind perceiving it.

Phil.: What! are you then in that *sceptical* state of suspense, between affirming and denying?

Hyl.: I think I may be positive in the point. A very violent and painful heat cannot exist without the mind.

Phil.: It hath not therefore, according to you, any real being.

Hyl.: I own it.

Phil.: Is it therefore certain, that there is no body in nature really hot?

Hyl.: I have not denied there is any real heat in bodies. I only say, there is no such thing as an intense real heat.

Phil.: But did you not say before, that all degrees of heat were equally real: or if there was any difference, that the greater were more undoubtedly real than the lesser?

Hyl.: True: but it was, because I did not then consider the ground there is for distinguishing between them, which I now plainly see. And it is this: because intense heat is nothing else but a particular kind of painful sensation; and pain cannot exist but in a perceiving being; it follows that no intense heat can really exist in an unperceiving corporeal substance. But this is no reason why we should deny heat in an inferior degree to exist in such a substance.

Phil.: But how shall we be able to discern those degrees of heat which exist only in the mind, from those which exist without it?

Hyl.: That is no difficult matter. You know, the least pain cannot exist unperceived; whatever therefore degree of heat is a pain, exists only in the mind. But as for all other degrees of heat, nothing obliges us to think the same of them.

Phil.: I think you granted before, that no unperceiving being was capable of pleasure, any more than of pain.

Hyl.: I did.

Phil.: And is not warmth, or a more gentle degree of heat than what causes uneasiness, a pleasure?

Hyl.: What then?

Phil.: Consequently it cannot exist without the mind in any unperceiving substance, or body.

Hyl.: So it seems.

Phil.: Since therefore, as well those degrees of heat that are not painful, as those that are, can exist only in a thinking substance; may we not conclude that external bodies are absolutely incapable of any degree of heat whatsoever?

Hyl.: On second thoughts, I do not think it so evident that warmth is a pleasure, as that a great degree of heat is a pain.

Phil.: I do not pretend that warmth is as great a pleasure as heat is a pain. But if you grant it to be even a small pleasure, it serves to make good my conclusion.

Hyl.: I could rather call it an *indolence*. It seems to be nothing more than a privation of both pain and pleasure. And that such a quality or state as this may agree to an unthinking substance, I hope you will not deny.

Phil.: If you are resolved to maintain that warmth, or a gentle degree of heat, is no pleasure, I know not how to convince you otherwise, than by appealing to your own sense. But what think you of cold?

Hyl.: The same that I do of heat. An intense degree of cold is a pain; for to feel a very great cold, is to perceive a great uneasiness: it cannot therefore exist without the mind; but a lesser degree of cold may, as well as a lesser degree of heat.

Phil.: Those bodies therefore, upon whose application to our own we perceive a moderate degree of heat, must be concluded to have a moderate degree of heat or warmth in them; and those, upon whose application we feel a like degree of cold, must be thought to have cold in them.

Hyl.: They must.

Phil.: Can any doctrine be true that necessarily leads a man into an absurdity?

Hyl.: Without doubt it cannot.

Phil.: Is it not an absurdity to think that the same thing should be at the same time both cold and warm?

Hyl.: It is.

Phil.: Suppose now one of your hands hot, and the other cold, and that they are both at once put into the same vessel of water, in an intermediate state; will not the water seem cold to one hand, and warm to the other?

Hyl.: It will.

Phil.: Ought we not therefore by your principles to conclude, it is really both cold and warm at the same time, that is, according to your own concession, to believe an absurdity?

Hyl.: I confess it seems so.

Phil.: Consequently, the principles themselves are false, since you have granted that no true principle leads to an absurdity.

Hyl.: But after all, can any thing be more absurd than to say, *there is no heat in the fire?*

Phil.: To make the point still clearer; tell me, whether in two cases exactly alike, we ought not to make the same judgment?

Hyl.: We ought.

Phil.: When a pin pricks your finger, doth it not rend and divide the fibres of your flesh?

Hyl.: It doth.

Phil.: And when a coal burns your finger, doth it any more?

Hyl.: It doth not.

Phil.: Since therefore you neither judge the sensation itself occasioned by the pin, nor any thing like it to be in the pin; you should not, conformably to what you have now granted, judge the sensation occasioned by the fire, or any thing like it, to be in the fire.

Hyl.: Well, since it must be so, I am content to yield this point, and acknowledge, that heat and cold are only sensations existing in our minds: but there still remain qualities enough to secure the reality of external things.

Phil.: But what will you say, Hylas, if it shall appear that the case is the same with regard to all otrher sensible qualities, and that they can no more be supposed to exist without the mind, than heat and cold?

Hyl.: Then indeed you will have done something to the purpose; but that is what I despair of seeing proved.

Phil.: Let us examine them in order. What think you of tastes, do they exist without the mind, or no?

Hyl.: Can any man in his senses doubt whether sugar is sweet, or wormwood bitter?

Phil.: Inform me, Hylas. Is a sweet taste a particular kind of pleasure or pleasant sensation, or is it not?

Hyl.: It is.

Phil.: And is not bitterness some kind of uneasiness or pain?

Hyl.: I grant it.

Phil.: If therefore sugar and wormwood are unthinking corporeal substances existing without the mind, how can sweetness and bitterness, that is, pleasure and pain, agree to them?

Hyl.: Hold, Philonous; I now see what it was deluded me all this time. You asked whether heat and cold, sweetness and bitterness, were not particular sorts of pleasure and pain; to which I answered simply, that they were. Whereas I should have thus distinguished: those qualities, as perceived by us, are pleasures or pains, but not as existing in the external objects. We must not therefore conclude absolutely, that there is no heat in the fire, or sweetness in the sugar, but only that heat or sweetness, as perceived by us, are not in the fire or sugar. What say you to this?

Phil.: I say it is nothing to the purpose. Our discourse proceeded altogether concerning sensible things, which you defined to be the things we *immediately perceive by our senses.* Whatever other qualities therefore you speak of, as distinct from these, I know nothing of them, neither do they at all belong to the point in dispute. You may indeed pretend to have discovered certain qualities which you do not perceive, and assert those insensible qualities exist in fire and sugar. But what use can be made of this to your present purpose, I am at a loss to conceive. Tell me then once more, do you acknowledge that heat and cold, sweetness and bitterness (meaning those qualities which are perceived by the senses), do not exist without the mind?

Hyl.: I see it is to no purpose to hold out, so I give up the cause as to those mentioned qualities. Though I profess it sounds oddly, to say that sugar is not sweet.

Phil.: But for your further satisfaction, take this along with you: that which at other times seems sweet, shall to a distempered palate appear bitter. And nothing can be plainer, than that divers persons perceive different tastes in the same food, since that which one man delights in, another abhors. And how could this be, if the taste was something really inherent in the food?

Hyl.: I acknowledge I know not how.

Phil.: In the next place, odours are to be considered. And with regard to these, I would fain know, whether what hath been said of tastes doth not exactly agree to them? Are they not so many pleasing or displeasing sensations?

Hyl.: They are.

Phil.: Can you then conceive it possible that they should exist in an unperceiving thing?

Hyl.: I cannot.

Phil.: Or can you imagine, that filth and ordure affect those brute animals that feed on them out of choice, with the same smells which we perceive in them?

Hyl.: By no means.

Phil.: May we not therefore conclude of smells,

as of the other forementioned qualities, that they cannot exist in any but a perceiving substance or mind?

Hyl.: I think so.

Phil.: Then as to sounds, what must we think of them: are they accidents really inherent in external bodies, or not?

Hyl.: That they inhere not in the sonorous bodies, is plain from hence; because a bell struck in the exhausted receiver of an air-pump, sends forth no sound. The air therefore must be thought the subject of sound.

Phil.: What reason is there for that, Hylas?

Hyl.: Because when any motion is raised in the air, we perceive a sound greater or lesser, in proportion to the air's motion; but without some motion in the air, we never hear any sound at all.

Phil.: And granting that we never hear a sound but when some motion is produced in the air, yet I do not see how you can infer from thence, that the sound itself is in the air.

Hyl.: It is this very motion in the external air, that produces in the mind the sensation of *sound.* For striking on the drum of the ear, it causeth a vibration, which by the auditory nerves being communicated to the brain, the soul is thereupon affected with the sensation called *sound.*

Phil.: What! is sound then a sensation?

Hyl.: I tell you, as perceived by us, it is a particular sensation in the mind.

Phil.: And can any sensation exist without the mind?

Hyl.: No, certainly.

Phil.: How then can sound, being a sensation, exist in the air, if by the *air* you mean a senseless substance existing without the mind.

Hyl.: You must distinguish, Philonous, between sound, as it is perceived by us, and as it is in itself; or, (which is the same thing) between the sound we immediately perceive, and that which exists without us. The former indeed is a particular kind of sensation, but the latter is merely a vibrative or undulatory motion in the air.

Phil.: I thought I had already obviated that distinction by the answer I gave when you were applying it in a like case before. But to say no more of

that: are you sure then that sound is really nothing but motion?

Hyl.: I am.

Phil.: Whatever therefore agrees to real sound, may with truth be attributed to motion.

Hyl.: It may.

Phil.: It is then good sense to speak of *motion,* as of a thing that is *loud, sweet, acute,* or *grave.*

Hyl.: I see you are resolved not to understand me. Is it not evident, those accidents or modes belong only to sensible sound, or *sound* in the common acceptation of the word, but not to *sound* in the real and philosophic sense, which, as I just now told you, is nothing but a certain motion of the air?

Phil.: It seems then there are two sorts of sound, the one vulgar, or that which is heard, the other philosophical and real.

Hyl.: Even so.

Phil.: And the latter consists in motion.

Hyl.: I told you so before.

Phil.: Tell me, Hylas, to which of the senses, think you, the idea of motion belongs: to the hearing?

Hyl.: No, certainly, but to the sight and touch.

Phil.: It should follow then, that according to you, real sounds may possibly be *seen* or *felt,* but never *heard.*

Hyl.: Look you, Philonous, you may if you please make a jest of my opinion, but that will not alter the truth of things. I own, indeed, the inferences you draw me into sound something oddly: but common language, you know, is framed by, and for the use of the vulgar: we must not therefore wonder, if expressions adapted to exact philosophic notions, seem uncouth and out of the way.

Phil.: Is it come to that? I assure you, I imagine myself to have gained no small point, since you make so light of departing from common phrases and opinions; it being a main part of our inquiry, to examine whose notions are widest of the common road, and most repugnant to the general sense of the world. But can you think it no more than a philosophical paradox, to say that *real sounds are never heard,* and that the idea of them is obtained by some other sense. And is there nothing in this contrary to nature and the truth of things?

Hyl.: To deal ingenuously, I do not like it. And after the concessions already made, I had as well grant that sounds too have no real being without the mind.

Phil.: And I hope you will make no difficulty to acknowledge the same of colours.

Hyl.: Pardon me; the case of colours is very different. Can any thing be plainer, than that we see them on the objects?

Phil.: The objects you speak of are, I suppose, corporeal substances existing without the mind.

Hyl.: They are.

Phil.: And have true and real colours inhering in them?

Hyl.: Each visible object hath that colour which we see in it.

Phil.: How! is there any thing visible but what we perceive by sight.

Hyl.: There is not.

Phil.: And do we perceive any thing by sense, which we do not perceive immediately?

Hyl.: How often must I be obliged to repeat the same thing? I tell you, we do not.

Phil.: Have patience, good Hylas; and tell me once more whether there is any thing immediately perceived by the senses, except sensible qualities. I know you asserted there was not: but I would now be informed, whether you still persist in the same opinion.

Hyl.: I do.

Phil.: Pray, is your corporeal substance either a sensible quality or made up of sensible qualities?

Hyl.: What a question that is! who ever thought it was?

Phil.: My reason for asking was, because in saying, *each visible object hath that colour which we see in it,* you make visible objects to be corporeal substances; which implies either that corporeal substances are sensible qualities, or else that there is something beside sensible qualities perceived by sight: but as this point was formerly agreed between us, and is still maintained by you, it is a clear consequence, that your corporeal substance is nothing distinct from sensible qualities.

Hyl.: You may draw as many absurd consequences as you please, and endeavour to perplex the plainest things; but you shall never persuade me out of my senses. I clearly understand my own meaning.

Phil.: I wish you would make me understand it too. But since you are unwilling to have your notion of corporeal substance examined, I shall urge that point no further. Only be pleased to let me know, whether the same colours which we see, exist in external bodies, or some other.

Hyl.: The very same.

Phil.: What! are then the beautiful red and purple we see on yonder clouds, really in them? Or do you imagine they have in themselves any other form than that of a dark mist or vapour?

Hyl.: I must own, Philonous, those colours are not really in the clouds as they seem to be at this distance. They are only apparent colours.

Phil.: Apparent call you them? how shall we distinguish these apparent colours from real?

Hyl.: Very easily. Those are to be thought apparent, which, appearing only at a distance, vanish upon a nearer approach.

Phil.: And those I suppose are to be thought real, which are discovered by the most near and exact survey.

Hyl.: Right.

Phil.: Is the nearest and exactest survey made by the help of a microscope, or by the naked eye?

Hyl.: By a microscope, doubtless.

Phil.: But a microscope often discovers colours in an object different from those perceived by the unassisted sight. And in case we had microscopes magnifying to any assigned degree; it is certain, that no object whatsoever viewed through them, would appear in the same colour which it exhibits to the naked eye.

Hyl.: And what will you conclude from all this? You cannot argue that there are really and naturally no colours on objects; because by artificial managements they may be altered, or made to vanish.

Phil.: I think it may evidently be concluded from your own concessions, that all the colors we see with our naked eyes, are only apparent as those on the clouds, since they vanish upon a more close and accurate inspection, which is afforded us by a microscope. Then as to what you say by way of prevention; I ask you, whether the real and natural state of an object is better discovered by a very sharp and piercing sight, or by one which is less sharp.

Hyl.: By the former without doubt.

Phil.: Is it not plain from *dioptrics,* that microscopes make the sight more penetrating, and represent objects as they would appear to the eye, in case it were naturally endowed with a most exquisite sharpness?

Hyl.: It is.

Phil.: Consequently the microscopical representation is to be thought that which best sets forth the real nature of the thing, or what it is in itself. The colours therefore by it perceived, are more genuine and real, than those perceived otherwise.

Hyl.: I confess there is something in what you say.

Phil.: Besides, it is not only possible but manifest, that there actually are animals, whose eyes are by nature framed to perceive those things, which by reason of their minuteness escape our sight. What think you of those inconceivably small animals perceived by glasses? must we suppose they are all stark blind? Or, in case they see, can it be imagined their sight hath not the same use in preserving their bodies from injuries, which appears in that of all other animals? And if it hath, is it not evident, they must see particles less than their own bodies, which will present them with a far different view in each object, from that which strikes our senses? Even our own eyes do not always represent objects to us after the same manner. In the *jaundice,* every one knows that all things seem yellow. Is it not therefore highly probable, those animals in whose eyes we discern a very different texture from that of ours, and whose bodies abound with different humours, do not see the same colours in every object that we do? From all of which, should it not seem to follow that all colours are equally apparent, and that none of those which we perceive are really inherent in any outward object?

Hyl.: It should.

Phil.: The point will be past all doubt, if you consider, that in case colours were real properties or affections inherent in external bodies, they could admit of no alteration, without some change

wrought in the very bodies themselves; but is it not evident from what hath been said, that upon the use of microscopes, upon a change happening in the humours of the eye, or a variation of distance, without any manner of real alteration in the thing itself, the colours of any object are either changed, or totally disappear? Nay, all other circumstances remaining the same, change but the situation of some objects, and they shall present different colours to the eye. The same thing happens upon viewing an object in various degrees of light. And what is more known, than that the same bodies appear differently coloured by candle-light from what they do in the open day? Add to these the experiment of a prism, which, separating the heterogeneous rays of light, alters the colour of any object; and will cause the whitest to appear of a deep blue or red to the naked eye. And now tell me, whether you are still of opinion, that every body hath its true, real colour inhering in it; and if you think it hath, I would fain know further from you, what certain distance and position of the object, what peculiar texture and formation of the eye, what degree or kind of light is necessary for ascertaining that true colour, and distinguishing it from apparent ones.

Hyl.: I own myself entirely satisfied, that they are all equally apparent; and that there is no such thing as colour really inhering in external bodies, but that it is altogether in the light. And what confirms me in this opinion, is, that in proportion to the light, colours are still more or less vivid; and if there be no light, then are there no colours perceived. Besides, allowing there are colours on external objects, yet how is it possible for us to perceive them? For no external body affects the mind, unless it act first on our organs of sense. But the only action of bodies is motion; and motion cannot be communicated otherwise than by impulse. A distant object therefore cannot act on the eye, nor consequently make itself or its properties perceivable to the soul. Whence it plainly follows, that it is immediately some contiguous substance, which operating on the eye occasions a perception of colours: and such is light.

Phil.: How! is light then a substance?

Hyl.: I tell you, Philonous, external light is noth-

ing but a thin fluid substance, whose minute particles being agitated with a brisk motion, and in various manners reflected from the different surfaces
of outward objects to the eyes, communicate different motions to the optic nerves; which being propa-
gated to the brain, cause therein various impressions: and these are attended with the sensations of
red, blue, yellow, &c.

Phil.: It seems, then, the light doth no more than
shake the optic nerves.

Hyl.: Nothing else.

Phil.: And consequent to each particular motion
of the nerves the mind is affected with a sensation,
which is some particular colour.

Hyl.: Right.

Phil.: And these sensations have no existence
without the mind.

Hyl.: They have not.

Phil.: How then do you affirm that colours are in
the light, since by *light* you understand a corporeal
substance external to the mind?

Hyl.: Light and colours, as immediately perceived by us, I grant cannot exist without the mind.
But in themselves they are only the motions and
configurations of certain insensible particles of
matter.

Phil.: Colours then, in the vulgar sense, or taken
for the immediate objects of sight, cannot agree to
any but a perceiving substance.

Hyl.: That is what I say.

Phil.: Well then, since you give up the point as to
those sensible qualities, which are alone thought
colours by all mankind beside, you may hold what
you please with regard to those invisible ones of the
philosophers. It is not my business to dispute about
them; only I would advise you to bethink yourself,
whether, considering the inquiry we are upon, it be
prudent for you to affirm *the red and blue which we
see are not real colours, but certain unknown motions and figures which no man ever did or can see,
are truly so.* Are not these shocking notions, and are
not they subject to as many ridiculous inferences, as
those you were obliged to renounce before in the
case of sounds?

Hyl.: I frankly own, Philonous, that it is in vain
to stand out any longer. Colours, sounds, tastes, in a
word, all those termed *secondary qualities,* have
certainly no existence without the mind. But by this
acknowledgment I must not be supposed to dero-
gate any thing from the reality of matter or external
objects, seeing it is no more than several philosophers maintain, who nevertheless are the furthest
imaginable from denying matter. For the clearer understanding of this, you must know sensible qualities are by philosophers divided into *primary* and
secondary. The former are extension, figure, solidity, gravity, motion, and rest. And these they hold
exist really in bodies. The latter are those above
enumerated; or briefly, all sensible qualities beside
the primary, which they assert are only so many
sensations or ideas existing no where but in the
mind. But all this, I doubt not, you are already ap-
prised of. For my part, I have been a long time sensible there was such an opinion current among
philosophers, but was never thoroughly convinced
of its truth till now.

Phil.: You are still then of opinion, that extension and figures are inherent in external unthinking
substances.

Hyl.: I am.

Phil.: But what if the same arguments which are
brought against secondary qualities, will hold proof
against these also?

Hyl.: Why then I shall be obliged to think, they
too exist only in the mind.

Phil.: Is it your opinion, the very figure and extension which you perceive by sense, exist in the
outward object or material substance?

Hyl.: It is.

Phil.: Have all other animals as good grounds to
think the same of the figure and extension which
they see and feel?

Hyl.: Without doubt, if they have any thought at
all.

Phil.: Answer me, Hylas. Think you the senses
were bestowed upon all animals for their preservation and well-being in life? or were they given to
men alone for this end?

Hyl.: I make no question but they have the same
use in all other animals.

Phil.: If so, is it not necessary they should be
enabled by them to perceive their own limbs,

and those bodies which are capable of harming them?

Hyl.: Certainly.

Phil.: A mite therefore must be supposed to see his own foot, and things equal or even less than it, as bodies of some considerable dimension; though at the same time they appear to you scarce discernible, or at best as so many visible points.

Hyl.: I cannot deny it.

Phil.: And to creatures less than the mite they will seem yet larger.

Hyl.: They will.

Phil.: Insomuch that what you can hardly discern, will to another extremely minute animal appear as some huge mountain.

Hyl.: All this I grant.

Phil.: Can one and the same thing be at the same time in itself of different dimensions?

Hyl.: That were absurd to imagine.

Phil.: But from what you have laid down it follows, that both the extension by you perceived, and that perceived by the mite itself, as likewise all those perceived by lesser animals, are each of them the true extension of the mite's foot, that is to say, by your own principles you are led into an absurdity.

Hyl.: There seems to be some difficulty in the point.

Phil.: Again, have you not acknowledged that no real inherent property of any object can be changed, without some change in the thing itself?

Hyl.: I have.

Phil.: But as we approach to or recede from an object, the visible extension varies, being at one distance ten or a hundred times greater than at another. Doth it not therefore follow from hence likewise, that it is not really inherent in the object?

Hyl.: I own I am at a loss what to think.

Phil.: Your judgment will soon be determined, if you will venture to think as freely concerning this quality, as you have done concerning the rest. Was it not admitted as a good argument, that neither heat nor cold was in the water, because it seemed warm to one hand, and cold to the other?

Hyl.: It was.

Phil.: Is it not the very same reasoning to conclude, there is no extension or figure in an object, because to one eye it shall seem little, smooth, and round, when at the same time it appears to the other, great, uneven, and angular?

Hyl.: The very same. But doth this latter fact ever happen?

Phil.: You may at any time make the experiment, by looking with one eye bare, and with the other through a microscope.

Hyl.: I know not how to maintain it, and yet I am loath to give up *extension,* I see so many odd consequences following upon such a concession.

Phil.: Odd, say you? After the concessions already made, I hope you will stick at nothing for its oddness. But on the other hand should it not seem very odd, if the general reasoning which includes all other sensible qualities did not also include extension? If it be allowed that no idea nor any thing like an idea can exist in an unperceiving substance, then surely it follows, that no figure or mode of extension, which we can either perceive or imagine, or have any idea of, can be really inherent in matter; not to mention the peculiar difficulty there must be, in conceiving a material substance, prior to and distinct from extension, to be the *substratum* of extension. Be the sensible quality what it will, figure, or sound, or colour; it seems alike impossible it should subsist in that which doth not perceive it.

Hyl.: I give up the point for the present, reserving still a right to retract my opinion, in case I shall hereafter discover any false step in my progress to it.

Phil.: That is a right you cannot be denied. Figures and extension being despatched, we proceed next to *motion.* Can a real motion in any external body be at the same time both very swift and very slow?

Hyl.: It cannot.

Phil.: Is not the motion of a body swift in a reciprocal proportion to the time it takes up in describing any given space? Thus a body that describes a mile in an hour, moves three times faster than it would in case it described only a mile in three hours.

Hyl.: I agree with you.

Phil.: And is not time measured by the succession of ideas in our minds?

Hyl.: It is.

Phil.: And is it not possible ideas should succeed one another twice as fast in your mind, as they do in mine, or in that of some spirit of another kind?

Hyl.: I own it.

Phil.: Consequently the same body may to another seem to perform its motion over any space in half the time that it doth to you. And the same reasoning will hold as to any other proportion: that is to say, according to your principles (since the motions perceived are both really in the object) it is possible one and the same body shall be really moved the same way at once, both very swift and very slow. How is this consistent either with common sense, or with what you just now granted?

Hyl.: I have nothing to say to it.

Phil.: Then as for *solidity;* either you do not mean any sensible quality by that word, and so it is beside our inquiry: or if you do, it must be either hardness or resistance. But both the one and the other are plainly relative to our senses: it being evident, that what seems hard to one animal, may appear soft to another, who hath greater force and firmness of limbs. Nor is it less plain, that the resistance I feel is not in the body.

Hyl.: I own the very sensation of resistance, which is all you immediately perceive, is not in the *body,* but the cause of that sensation is.

Phil.: But the causes of our sensations are not things immediately perceived, and therefore not sensible. This point I thought had been already determined.

Hyl.: I own it was; but you will pardon me if I seem a little embarrassed: I know not how to quit my old notions.

Phil.: To help you out, do but consider, that if extension be once acknowledged to have no existence without the mind, the same must necessarily be granted of motion, solidity, and gravity, since they all evidently suppose extension. It is therefore su-

perfluous to inquire particularly concerning each of them. In denying extension, you have denied them all to have any real existence.

• • •

THE SECOND DIALOGUE

Hylas: I beg your pardon, Philonous, for not meeting you sooner. All this morning my head was so filled with our late conversation that I had not leisure to think of the time of the day, or indeed of any thing else.

Philonous: I am glad you were so intent upon it, in hopes if there were any mistakes in your concessions, or fallacies in my reasonings from them, you will now discover them to me.

Hyl.: I assure you, I have done nothing ever since I saw you, but search after mistakes and fallacies, and with that view have minutely examined the whole series of yesterday's discourse: but all in vain, for the notions it led me into, upon review appear still more clear and evident; and the more I consider them, the more irresistibly do they force my assent.

Phil.: And is not this, think you, a sign that they are genuine, that they proceed from nature, and are conformable to right reason? Truth and beauty are in this alike, that the strictest survey sets them both off to advantage. While the false lustre of error and disguise cannot endure being reviewed, or too nearly inspected.

Hyl.: I own there is a great deal in what you say. Nor can any one be more entirely satisfied of the truth of those odd consequences, so long as I have in view the reasonings that lead to them. But when these are out of my thoughts, there seems on the other hand something so satisfactory, so natural and intelligible in the modern way of explaining things, that I profess I know not how to reject it.

Phil.: I know not what way you mean.

Hyl.: I mean the way of accounting for our sensations or ideas.

Phil.: How is that?

Hyl.: It is supposed the soul makes her residence

in some part of the brain, from which the nerves take their rise, and are thence extended to all parts of the body: and that outward objects, by the different impressions they make on the organs of sense, communicate certain vibrative motions to the nerves; and these being filled with spirits, propagate them to the brain or seat of the soul, which according to the various impressions or traces thereby made in the brain, is variously affected with ideas.

Phil.: And call you this an explication of the manner whereby we are affected with ideas.

Hyl.: Why not, Philonous? have you any thing to object against it?

Phil.: I would first know whether I rightly understand your hypothesis. You make certain traces in the brain to be the causes or occasions of our ideas. Pray tell me, whether by the *brain* you mean any sensible thing?

Hyl.: What else think you I could mean?

Phil.: Sensible things are all immediately perceivable; and those things which are immediately perceivable, are ideas; and these exist only in the mind. Thus much you have, if I mistake not, long since agreed to.

Hyl.: I do not deny it.

Phil.: The brain therefore you speak of, being a sensible thing, exists only in the mind. Now, I would fain know whether you think it reasonable to suppose, that one idea or thing existing in the mind, occasions all other ideas. And if you think so, pray how do you account for the origin of that primary idea or brain itself?

Hyl.: I do not explain the origin of our ideas by that brain which is perceivable to sense, this being itself only a combination of sensible ideas, but by another which I imagine.

Phil.: But are not things imagined as truly in the mind as things perceived?

Hyl.: I must confess they are.

Phil.: It comes therefore to the same thing; and you have been all this while accounting for ideas, by certain motions or impressions in the brain, that is, by some alterations in an idea, whether sensible or imaginable, it matters not.

Hyl.: I begin to suspect my hypothesis.

Phil.: Besides spirits, all that we know or conceive are our own ideas. When therefore you say, all ideas are occasioned by impressions in the brain, do you conceive this brain or no? If you do, then you talk of ideas imprinted in an idea, causing that same idea, which is absurd. If you do not conceive it, you talk unintelligibly, instead of forming a reasonable hypothesis.

Hyl.: I now clearly see it was a mere dream. There is nothing in it.

Phil.: You need not be much concerned at it; for after all, this way of explaining things, as you called it, could never have satisfied any reasonable man. What connexion is there between a motion in the nerves, and the sensations of sound or colour in the mind? Or how is it possible these should be the effect of that?

Hyl.: But I could never think it had so little in it, as now it seems to have.

Phil.: Well then, are you at length satisfied that no sensible things have a real existence; and that you are in truth an arrant *sceptic?*

Hyl.: It is too plain to be denied.

Phil.: Look! are not the fields covered with a delightful verdure? . . .

The motion and situation of the planets, are they not admirable for use and order. Were those globes ever known to stray, in their repeated journeys through the pathless void? Do they not measure areas round the sun ever proportioned to the times? So fixed, so immutable are the laws by which the unseen Author of nature actuates the universe. . . .

Is not the whole system immense, beautiful, glorious beyond expression and beyond thought? What treatment then do those philosophers deserve, who would deprive these noble and delightful scenes of all reality? How should these principles be entertained, that lead us to think all the visible beauty of the creation a false imaginary glare? To be plain, can you expect this scepticism of yours will not be thought extravagantly absurd by all men of sense?

Hyl.: Other men may think as they please: but for your part you have nothing to reproach me with. My confort is, you are as much a *sceptic* as I am.

Phil.: There, Hylas, I must beg leave to differ with you.

Hyl.: What! have you all along agreed to the

premises, and do you now deny the conclusion, and leave me to maintain those paradoxes by myself which you led me into? This surely is not fair.

Phil.: I deny that I agreed with you in those notions that led to scepticism. You indeed said, the reality of sensible things consisted in an *absolute existence* out of the minds of spirits, or distinct from their being perceived. And pursuant to this notion of reality, you are obliged to deny sensible things any real existence: that is, according to your own definition, you profess yourself a *sceptic.* But I neither said nor thought the reality of sensible things was to be defined after that manner. To me it is evident, for the reasons you allow of, that sensible things cannot exist otherwise than in a mind or spirit. Whence I conclude, not that they have no real existence, but that seeing they depend not on my thought, and have an existence distinct from being perceived by me, *there must be some other mind wherein they exist.* As sure therefore as the sensible world really exists, so sure is there an infinite, omnipresent Spirit who contains and supports it.

Hyl.: What! this is no more than I and all Christians hold; nay, and all others too who believe there is a God, and that he knows and comprehends all things.

Phil.: Ay, but here lies the difference. Men commonly believe that all things are known or perceived by God, because they believe the being of a God, whereas I, on the other side, immediately and necessarily conclude the being of a God, because all sensible things must be perceived by him.

THE WORLD AS WILL AND IDEA

Arthur Schopenhauer

We have recognised *temporal justice,* which has its seat in the state, as requiting and punishing, and have seen that this only becomes justice through a reference to the *future.* For without this reference all

punishing and requiting would be an outrage without justification, and indeed merely the addition of another evil to that which has already occurred, without meaning or significance. But it is quite otherwise with *eternal justice,* which was referred to before, and which rules not the state but the world, is not dependent upon human institutions, is not subject to chance and deception, is not uncertain, wavering, and erring, but infallible, fixed, and sure. The conception of requital implies that of time; therefore *eternal justice* cannot be requital. Thus it cannot, like temporal justice, admit of respite and delay, and require time in order to triumph, equalising the evil deed by the evil consequences only by means of time. The punishment must here be so bound up with the offence that both are one.

• • •

Now that such an eternal justice really lies in the nature of the world will soon become completely evident to whoever has grasped the whole of the thought which we have hitherto been developing.

The world, in all the multiplicity of its parts and forms, is the manifestation, the objectivity, of the one will to live. Existence itself, and the kind of existence, both as a collective whole and in every part, proceeds from the will alone. The will is free, the will is almighty. The will appears in everything, just as it determines itself in itself and outside time. The world is only the mirror of this willing; and all finitude, all suffering, all miseries, which it contains, belong to the expression of that which the will wills, are as they are because the will so wills. Accordingly with perfect right every being supports existence in general, and also the existence of its species and its peculiar individuality, entirely as it is and in circumstances as they are, in a world such as it is, swayed by chance and error, transient, ephemeral, and constantly suffering; and in all that it experiences, or indeed can experience, it always gets its due. For the will belongs to it; and as the will is, so is the world. Only this world itself can bear the responsibility of its own existence and nature—no other; for by what means could another have assumed it? Do we desire to know what men, morally considered, are worth as a whole and in general, we have only to consider their fate as a whole and in general. This is want, wretchedness, affliction, misery, and death. Eternal justice reigns; if they were not, as a whole, worthless, their fate, as a whole, would not be so sad. In this sense we may say, the world itself is the judgment of the world. If we could lay all the misery of the world in one scale of the balance, and all the guilt of the world in the other, the needle would certainly point to the centre.

Certainly, however, the world does not exhibit itself to the knowledge of the individual as such, developed for the service of the will, as it finally reveals itself to the inquirer as the objectivity of the one and only will to live, which he himself is. But the sight of the uncultured individual is clouded, as the Hindus say, by the veil of Mâyâ.* He sees not the thing-in-itself but the phenomenon in time and space, the *principium individuationis,* and in the other forms of the principle of sufficient reason. And in this form of his limited knowledge he sees not the inner nature of things, which is one, but its phenomena as separated, disunited, innumerable, very different, and indeed opposed. For to him pleasure appears as one thing and pain as quite another thing: one man as a tormentor and a murderer, another as a martyr and a victim; wickedness as one thing and evil as another. He sees one man live in joy, abundance, and pleasure, and even at his door another die miserably of want and cold. Then he asks, Where is the retribution? And he himself, in the vehement pressure of will which is his origin and his nature, seizes upon the pleasures and enjoyments of life, firmly embraces them, and knows not that by this very act of his will he seizes and hugs all those pains and sorrows at the sight of which he shudders. He sees the ills and he sees the wickedness in the world, but far from knowing that both of these are but different sides of the manifestation of the one will to live, he regards them as very different, and indeed quite opposed, and often seeks to

escape by wickedness, *i.e.,* by causing the suffering of another, from ills, from the suffering of his own individuality, for he is involved in the *principium individuationis,* deluded by the veil of Mâyâ. Just as a sailor sits in a boat trusting to his frail barque in a stormy sea, unbounded in every direction, rising and falling with the howling mountainous waves; so in the midst of a world of sorrows the individual man sits quietly, supported by and trusting to the *principium individuationis,* or the way in which the individual knows things as phenomena. The boundless world, everywhere full of suffering in the infinite past, in the infinite future, is strange to him, indeed is to him but a fable; his ephemeral person, his extensionless present, his momentary satisfaction, this alone has reality for him; and he does all to maintain this, so long as his eyes are not opened by a better knowledge. Till then, there lives only in the inmost depths of his consciousness a very obscure presentiment that all that is after all not really so strange to him, but has a connection with him, from which the *principium individuationis* cannot protect him. From this presentiment arises that ineradicable *awe* common to all men (and indeed perhaps even to the most sensible of the brutes) which suddenly seizes them if by any chance they become puzzled about the *principium individuationis,* because the principle of sufficient reason in some one of its forms seems to admit of an exception. For example, if it seems as if some change took place without a cause, or some one who is dead appears again, or if in any other way the past or the future becomes present or the distant becomes near. The fearful terror at anything of the kind is founded on the fact that they suddenly become puzzled about the forms of knowledge of the phenomenon, which alone separate their own individuality from the rest of the world. But even this separation lies only in the phenomenon, and not in the thing-in-itself; and on this rests eternal justice. In fact, all temporal happiness stands, and all prudence proceeds, upon ground that is undermined. They defend the person from accidents and supply its pleasures; but the person is merely phenomenon, and its difference from other individuals, and exemption from the sufferings which they endure, rests merely in the form of the

---

*Maya literally is a veil, but Western writers still persist in using the phrase "the veil of Maya" as if "Maya" had a veil. The metaphor of a veil which hides reality and produces illusion is a common one in Indian thought, especially in the *Upanishads* (Eds.).

phenomenon, the *principium individuationis.* According to the true nature of things, every one has all the suffering of the world as his own, and indeed has to regard all merely possible suffering as for him actual, so long as he is the fixed will to live, *i.e.,* asserts life with all his power. For the knowledge that sees through the *principium individuationis,* a happy life in time, the gift of chance or won by prudence, amid the sorrows of innumerable others, is only the dream of a beggar in which he is a king, but from which he must awake and learn from experience that only a fleeting illusion had separated him from the suffering of his life.

Eternal justice withdraws itself from the vision that is involved in the knowledge which follows the principle of sufficient reason in the *principium individuationis;* such vision misses it altogether unless it vindicates it in some way by fictions. It sees the bad, after misdeeds and cruelties of every kind, live in happiness and leave the world unpunished. It sees the oppressed drag out a life full of suffering to the end without an avenger, a requiter appearing. But that man only will grasp and comprehend eternal justice who raises himself above the knowledge that proceeds under the guidance of the principle of sufficient reason, bound to the particular thing, and recognises the Ideas, sees through the *principium individuationis,* and becomes conscious that the forms of the phenomenon do not apply to the thing-in-itself. Moreover, he alone, by virtue of the same knowledge, can understand the true nature of virtue, as it will soon disclose itself to us in connection with the present inquiry, although for the practice of virtue this knowledge in the abstract is by no means demanded. Thus it becomes clear to whoever has attained to the knowledge referred to, that because the will is the in-itself of all phenomena, the misery which is awarded to others and that which he experiences himself, the bad and the evil, always concerns only that one inner being which is everywhere the same, although the phenomena in which the one and the other exhibits itself exist as quite different individuals, and are widely separated by time and space. He sees that the difference between him who inflicts the suffering and him who must bear it is only the phenomenon, and does not concern the

thing-in-itself, for this is the will living in both, which here, deceived by the knowledge which is bound to its service, does not recognise itself, and seeking an increased happiness in *one* of its phenomena, produces great suffering in *another,* and thus, in the pressure of excitement, buries its teeth in its own flesh, not knowing that it always injures only itself, revealing in this form, through the medium of individuality, the conflict with itself which it bears in its inner nature. The inflicter of suffering and the sufferer are one. The former errs in that he believes he is not a partaker in the suffering; the latter, in that he believes he is not a partaker in the guilt. If the eyes of both were opened, the inflicter of suffering would see that he lives in all that suffers pain in the wide world, and which, if endowed with reason, in vain asks why it was called into existence for such great suffering, its desert of which it does not understand. And the sufferer would see that all the wickedness which is or ever was committed in the world proceeds from that will which constitutes *his* own nature also, appears also in *him,* and that through this phenomenon and its assertion he has taken upon himself all the sufferings which proceed from such a will and bears them as his due, so long as he is this will. From this knowledge speaks the profound poet Calderon in "Life a Dream"—

> For the greatest crime of man
> Is that he ever was born.

Why should it not be a crime, since, according to an eternal law, death follows upon it? Calderon has merely expressed in these lines the Christian dogma of original sin.

The living knowledge of eternal justice, of the balance that inseparably binds together the *malum culpæ* with the *malum pœnæ,* demands the complete transcending of individuality and the principle of its possibility. Therefore it will always remain unattainable to the majority of men, as will also be the case with the pure and distinct knowledge of the nature of all virtue, which is akin to it, and which we are about to explain. Accordingly the wise ancestors of the Hindu people have directly expressed it in the Vedas, which are only allowed to the three regenerate castes, or in their esoteric teaching, so far at any rate as conception and language comprehend it, and their method of exposition, which always remains pictorial and even rhapsodical, admits; but in the religion of the people, or exoteric teaching, they only communicate it by means of myths. The direct exposition we find in the Vedas, the fruit of the highest human knowledge and wisdom, the kernel of which has at last reached us in the Upanishads as the greatest gift of this century. It is expressed in various ways, but especially by making all the beings in the world, living and lifeless, pass successively before the view of the student, and pronouncing over every one of them that word which has become a formula, and as such has been called the Mahavakya: Tatoumes,—more correctly, Tat twam asi,—which means, "This thou art." But for the people, that great truth, so far as in their limited condition they could comprehend it, was translated into the form of knowledge which follows the principle of sufficient reason. This form of knowledge is indeed, from its nature, quite incapable of apprehending that truth pure and in itself, and even stands in contradiction to it, yet in the form of a myth it received a substitute for it which was sufficient as a guide for conduct. For the myth enables the method of knowlege, in accordance with the principle of sufficient reason, to comprehend by figurative representation the ethnical significance of conduct, which itself is ever foreign to it. This is the aim of all systems of religion, for as a whole they are the mythical clothing of the truth which is unattainable to the uncultured human intellect. In this sense this myth might, in Kant's language, be called a postulate of the practical reason; but regarded as such, it has the great advantage that it contains absolutely no elements but such as lie before our eyes in the course of actual experience, and can therefore support all its conceptions with perceptions. What is here referred to is the myth of the transmigration of souls. It teaches that all sufferings which in life one inflicts upon other beings must be expiated in a subsequent life in this world, through precisely the same sufferings; and this extends so far, that he who only kills a brute must, some time in endless time,

be born as the same kind of brute and suffer the same death. It teaches that wicked conduct involves a future life in this world in suffering and despised creatures, and, accordingly, that one will then be born again in lower castes, or as a woman, or as a brute, as Pariah or Tschandala, as a leper, or as a crocodile, and so forth. All the pains which the myth threatens it supports with perceptions from actual life, through suffering creatures which do not know how they have merited their misery, and it does not require to call in the assistance of any other hell. As a reward, on the other hand, it promises rebirth in better, nobler forms, as Brahmans, wise men, or saints. The highest reward, which awaits the noblest deeds and the completest resignation, which is also given to the woman who in seven successive lives has voluntarily died on the funeral pile of her husband, and not less to the man whose pure mouth has never uttered a single lie,—this reward the myth can only express negatively in the language of this world by the promise, which is so often repeated, that they shall never be born again, *Non adsumes iterum existentiam apparentem;* or, as the Buddhists, who recognise neither Vedas nor castes, express it, "Thou shalt attain to Nirvâna," *i.e.,* to a state in which four things no longer exist— birth, age, sickness, and death.

Never has a myth entered, and never will one enter, more closely into the philosophical truth which is attainable to so few than this primitive doctrine of the noblest and most ancient nation. Broken up as this nation now is into many parts, this myth yet reigns as the universal belief of the people, and has the most decided influence upon life to-day, as four thousand years ago. Therefore Pythagoras and Plato have seized with admiration on that *ne plus ultra* of mythical representation, received it from India or Egypt, honoured it, made use of it, and, we know not how far, even believed it. We, on the contrary, now send the Brahmans English clergymen and evangelical linen-weavers to set them right out of sympathy, and to show them that they are created out of nothing, and ought thankfully to rejoice in the fact. But it is just the same as if we fired a bullet against a cliff. In India our religions will never take root. The ancient wisdom of the human race will not be displaced by what happened in Galilee. On the contrary, Indian philosophy streams back to Europe, and will produce a fundamental change in our knowledge and thought.

QUESTIONS FOR DISCUSSION

1. Shankara, at one point, speaks of reality using the now famous metaphor of "the rope and the snake." What is he trying to express about the true nature of reality in using this metaphor? Do you agree with this way of looking at the world? Why or why not?

2. Berkeley claims that his philosophy is compatible with the views of the ordinary person (the "vulgar" to use his own term, although that word has since taken on negative connotations it didn't have in his day). Why does he claim that he speaks for the ordinary human? Do you think he is correct in making this claim? Why or why not?

3. Evaluate Schopenhauer's claim that, if the misery of the world were weighed against its guilt, the needle would balance at the center.

ZEN BUDDHISM

Legend says that Buddha each day would retire with his monks at the day's end and lecture them on his teachings. On one occasion, however, instead of speaking, he merely held up before them a bouquet of flowers, which a lay follower had given him earlier in the day. All the monks but one were puzzled. Only Kasyapa smiled and understood. Buddha therefore handed him the flowers, saying, "There is a teaching which is beyond words. I have given this teaching to Maha Kasyapa." This, says the legend, was the birth of Zen Buddhism.

Many centuries later, says another legend, the Indian monk Bodhidharma carried the teachings over the mountains to China. At this time they were called "Dhyana," though the Zen school seems to put no special emphasis on the dhyana or trance states induced by intense meditative concentration. Like Buddha with Kasyapa, Bodhidharma—if we are to believe the legend—brought the Chinese not trance but a teaching beyond words, a teaching which was "a direct pointing into the heart that we might see our true nature." The Chinese took up Bodhidharma's teachings, calling them "Ch'an" because they couldn't pronounce "Dhyana"; they mixed the teachings also with styles derived from their indigenous Taoist mysticism. When Ch'an was brought to Japan in its Chinese form by Chinese monks, the Japanese in turn mispronounced Ch'an as Zen. It was in their Japanese form that the teachings first became popular in the West. They are, however, a very pure version of mysticism, the doctrine that reality cannot be expressed in language; their ultimate origin is actually Indian, as the legends suggest, and a version of the school can be found in several Buddhist countries.

The first selection is Chinese. In it, the sixth patriarch of the Ch'an school, Hui Neng (638–713), relates the story of his life and spiritual development. He describes his enlightenment through the use of the philosophical concept of *sunya* or emptiness, a notion developed to point to the unsayable many centuries earlier by the Indian thinker Nagarjuna and his *Madhyamika* (Mod-ya-mik̇-a) or "Middle Way" school of Buddhism. In the second selection presented, the contemporary Vietnamese Zen master Thich Nhat Hanh explicates the notion of emptiness and further explains its use in Zen.

THE SUTRA OF HUI NENG*

Hui Neng

Once, when the Patriarch had arrived in Pao Lin Monastery, Prefect Wei of Shao Chou and other officials went there to ask him to deliver public lectures on Buddhism in the hall of Ta Fan Temple in the City (of Canton).

In due course, there were assembled (in the lecture hall) Prefect Wei, government officials and Confucian scholars, about thirty each, and bhikkhus, bhikkhunis,* Taoists and laymen to the number of about one thousand. After the Patriarch had taken his seat, the congregation in a body paid him homage and asked him to preach on the fundamental laws of Buddhism. Whereupon, His Holiness delivered the following address:

Learned Audience, our Essence of Mind (literally, self-nature) which is the seed or kernel of en-

---

*A "sutra" is a short discourse usually delivered by the Buddha himself or a Bodhisattva or Buddhist saint. This sutra is, in fact, the sole exception to this general rule (Eds.).

---

*"Bhikkhus and bhikkhunis" are Buddhist monks and nuns (Eds.).

lightenment (Bodhi) is pure by nature, and by making use of this mind alone we can reach Buddhahood directly. Now let me tell you something about my own life and how I came into possession of the esoteric teaching of the Dhyana (or the Zen) School.

My father, a native of Fan Yang, was dismissed from his official post and banished to be a commoner in Hsin Chou in Kwangtung. I was unlucky in that my father died when I was very young, leaving my mother poor and miserable. We moved to Kwang Chou (Canton) and were then in very bad circumstances.

I was selling firewood in the market one day, when one of my customers ordered some to be brought to his shop. Upon delivery being made and payment received, I left the shop, outside of which I found a man reciting a sutra. As soon as I heard the text of this sutra my mind at once became enlightened. Thereupon I asked the man the name of the book he was reciting and was told that it was the Diamond Sutra (Vajracchedika or Diamond Cutter). I further enquired whence he came and why he recited this particular sutra. He replied that he came from Tung Ch'an Monastery in the Huang Mei District of Ch'i Chou; that the Abbot in charge of this temple was Hung Yen, the Fifth Patriarch; that there were about one thousand disciples under him; and that when he went there to pay homage to the Patriarch, he attended lectures on this sutra. He further told me that His Holiness used to encourage the laity as well as the monks to recite this scripture, as by doing so they might realise their own Essence of Mind, and thereby reach Buddhahood directly.

It must be due to my good karma in past lives that I heard about this, and that I was given ten taels for the maintenance of my mother by a man who advised me to go to Huang Mei to interview the Fifth Patriarch. After arrangements had been made for her, I left for Huang Mei, which took me less than thirty days to reach.

I then went to pay homage to the Patriarch, and was asked where I came from and what I expected to get from him. I replied, "I am a commoner from Hsin Chou of Kwangtung. I have travelled far to pay you respect and I ask for nothing but Buddhahood." "You are a native of Kwangtung, a barbarian? How can you expect to be a Buddha?" asked the Patriarch. I replied, "Although there are northern men and southern men, north and south make no difference to their Buddha-nature. A barbarian is different from Your Holiness physically, but there is no difference in our Buddha-nature." He was going to speak further to me, but the presence of other disciples made him stop short. He then ordered me to join the crowd to work.

"May I tell Your Holiness," said I, "that Prajna (transcendental Wisdom) often rises in my mind. When one does not go astray from one's own Essence of Mind, one may be called the 'field of merits.'[1] I do not know what work Your Holiness would ask me to do."

"This barbarian is too bright," he remarked. "Go to the stable and speak no more." I then withdrew myself to the backyard and was told by a lay brother to split firewood and to pound rice.

More than eight months after, the Patriarch saw me one day and said, "I know your knowledge of Buddhism is very sound, but I have to refrain from speaking to you lest evil doers should do you harm. Do you understand?" "Yes, Sir, I do," I replied. "To avoid people taking notice of me, I dare not go near your hall."

The Patriarch one day assembled all his disciples and said to them, "The question of incessant rebirth is a momentous one. Day after day, instead of trying to free yourselves from this bitter sea of life and death, you seem to go after tainted merits only (*i.e.,* merits which will cause rebirth). Yet merits will be of no help, if your Essence of Mind is obscured. Go and seek for Prajna (wisdom) in your own mind and then write me a stanza (*gatha*) about it. He who understands what the Essence of Mind is will be given the robe (the insignia of the Patriarchate) and the Dharma (*i.e.,* the esoteric teaching of the Dhyana School), and I shall make him the Sixth

---

[1]A title of honour given to monks, as they afford the best opportunities to others to sow the "seed" of merits.

Patriarch. Go away quickly. Delay not in writing the stanza, as deliberation is quite unnecessary and of no use. The man who has realised the Essence of Mind can speak of it at once, as soon as he is spoken to about it; and he cannot lose sight of it, even when engaged in battle."

Having received this instruction, the disciples withdrew and said to one another, "It is of no use for us to concentrate our mind to write the stanza and submit it to His Holiness, since the Patriarchate is bound to be won by Shen Hsiu, our instructor. And if we write perfunctorily, it will only be a waste of energy." Upon hearing this, all of them made up their minds not to write and said, "Why should we take the trouble? Hereafter, we will simply follow our instructor, Shen Hsiu, wherever he goes, and look to him for guidance."

Meanwhile, Shen Hsiu reasoned thus with himself. "Considering that I am their teacher, none of them will take part in the competition. I wonder whether I should write a stanza and submit it to His Holiness. If I do not, how can the Patriarch know how deep or superficial my knowledge is? If my object is to get the Dharma, my motive is a pure one. If I were after the Patriarchate, then it would be bad. In that case, my mind would be that of a worldling and my action would amount to robbing the Patriarch's holy seat. But if I do not submit the stanza, I shall never have a chance of getting the Dharma. A very difficult point to decide, indeed!"

In front of the Patriarch's hall there were three corridors, the walls of which were to be painted by a court artist, named Lu Chen, with pictures from the Lankavatara (Sutra) depicting the transfiguration of the assembly, and with scenes showing the genealogy of the five Patriarchs for the information and veneration of the public.

When Shen Hsiu had composed his stanza he made several attempts to submit it to the Patriarch, but as soon as he went near the hall his mind was so perturbed that he sweated all over. He could not screw up courage to submit it, although in the course of four days he made altogether thirteen attempts to do so.

Then he suggested to himself, "It would be better for me to write it on the wall of the corridor and let the Patriarch see it for himself. If he approves it, I shall come out to pay homage, and tell him that it is done by me; but if he disapproves it, then I shall have wasted several years in this mountain in receiving homage from others which I by no means deserve! In that case, what progress have I made in learning Buddhism?"

At 12 o'clock that night he went secretly with a lamp to write the stanza on the wall of the south corridor, so that the Patriarch might know what spiritual insight he had attained. The stanza read:

> Our body is the Bodhi-tree,
> And our mind a mirror bright.
> Carefully we wipe them hour by hour,
> And let no dust alight.

As soon as he had written it he left at once for his room; so nobody knew what he had done. In his room he again pondered: "When the Patriarch sees my stanza tomorrow and is pleased with it, I shall be ready for the Dharma; but if he says that it is badly done, it will mean that I am unfit for the Dharma, owing to the misdeeds in previous lives which thickly becloud my mind. It is difficult to know what the Patriarch will say about it!" In this vein he kept on thinking until dawn, as he could neither sleep nor sit at ease.

But the Patriarch knew already that Shen Hsiu had not entered the door of enlightenment, and that he had not known the Essence of Mind.

In the morning, he sent for Mr. Lu, the court artist, and went with him to the south corridor to have the walls there painted with pictures. By chance, he saw the stanza. "I am sorry to have troubled you to come so far," he said to the artist. "The walls need not be painted now, as the Sutra says, 'All forms or phenomena are transient and illusive.' It will be better to leave the stanza here, so that people may study it and recite it. If they put its teaching into actual practice, they will be saved from the misery of being born in these evil realms of existence (*gatis*). The merit gained by one who practises it will be great indeed!"

He then ordered incense to be burnt, and all his disciples to pay homage to it and to recite it, so that they might realise the Essence of Mind. After they had recited it, all of them exclaimed, "Well done!"

At midnight, the Patriarch sent for Shen Hsiu to come to the hall, and asked him whether the stanza was written by him or not. "It was, Sir," replied Shen Hsiu. "I dare not be so vain as to expect to get the Patriarchate, but I wish Your Holiness would kindly tell me whether my stanza shows the least grain of wisdom."

"Your stanza," replied the Patriarch, "shows that you have not yet realised the Essence of Mind. So far you have reached the 'door of enlightenment,' but you have not yet entered it. To seek for supreme enlightenment with such an understanding as yours can hardly be successful.

"To attain supreme enlightenment, one must be able to know spontaneously one's own nature or Essence of Mind, which is neither created nor can it be annihilated. From ksana to ksana (thought-moment to thought-moment), one should be able to realise the Essence of Mind all the time. All things will then be free from restraint (i.e., emancipated). Once the Tathata (Suchness, another name for the Essence of Mind) is known, one will be free from delusion for ever; and in all circumstances one's mind will be in a state of 'Thusness.' Such a state of mind is absolute Truth. If you can see things in such a frame of mind you will have known the Essence of Mind, which is supreme enlightenment.

"You had better go back to think it over again for a couple of days, and then submit me another stanza. If your stanza shows that you have entered the 'door of enlightenment,' I will transmit you the robe and the Dharma."

Shen Hsiu made obeisance to the Patriarch and left. For several days, he tried in vain to write another stanza. This upset his mind so much that he was as ill at ease as if he were in a nightmare, and he could find comfort neither in sitting nor in walking.

Two days after, it happened that a young boy who was passing by the room where I was pounding rice recited loudly the stanza written by Shen Hsiu. As soon as I heard it, I knew at once that the composer of it had not yet realised the Essence of Mind. For although I had not been taught about it at that time, I already had a general idea of it.

"What stanza is this?" I asked the boy. "You barbarian," he replied, "don't you know about it? The Patriarch told his disciples that the question of incessant rebirth was a momentous one, that those who wished to inherit his robe and Dharma should write him a stanza, and that the one who had an understanding of the Essence of Mind would get them and be made the Sixth Patriarch. Elder Shen Hsiu wrote this 'Formless' Stanza on the wall of the south corridor and the Patriarch told us to recite it. He also said that those who put its teaching into actual practice would attain great merit, and be saved from the misery of being born in the evil realms of existence."

I told the boy that I wished to recite the stanza too, so that I might have an affinity with its teaching in future life. I also told him that although I had been pounding rice there for eight months I had never been to the hall, and that he would have to show me where the stanza was to enable me to make obeisance to it.

The boy took me there and I asked him to read it to me, as I am illiterate. A petty officer of the Chiang Chou District named Chang Tih-Yung, who happened to be there, read it out to me. When he had finished reading I told him that I also had composed a stanza, and asked him to write it for me. "Extraordinary indeed," he exclaimed, "that you also can compose a stanza!"

"Don't despise a beginner," said I, "if you are a seeker of supreme enlightenment. You should know that the lowest class may have the sharpest wit, while the highest may be in want of intelligence. If you slight others, you commit a very great sin."

"Dictate your stanza," said he. "I will take it down for you. But do not forget to deliver me, should you succeed in getting the Dharma!"

My stanza read:

> There is no Bodhi-tree,
> Nor stand of a mirror bright.
> Since all is void,
> Where can the dust alight?

When he had written this, all disciples and others who were present were greatly surprised. Filled with admiration, they said to one another, "How wonderful! No doubt we should not judge people by appearance. How can it be that for so long we have made a Bodhisattva incarnate work for us?"

Seeing that the crowd was overwhelmed with amazement, the Patriarch rubbed off the stanza with his shoe, lest jealous ones should do me injury. He expressed the opinion, which they took for granted, that the author of this stanza had also not yet realised the Essence of Mind.

Next day the Patriarch came secretly to the room where the rice was pounded. Seeing that I was working there with a stone pestle, he said to me, "A seeker of the Path risks his life for the Dharma. Should he not do so?" Then he asked, "Is the rice ready?" "Ready long ago," I replied, "only waiting for the sieve." He knocked the mortar thrice with his stick and left.

Knowing what his message meant, in the third watch of the night I went to his room. Using the robe as a screen so that none could see us, he expounded the Diamond Sutra to me. When he came to the sentence, "One should use one's mind in such a way that it will be free from any attachment,"[2] I at once became thoroughly enlightened, and realised that all things in the universe are the Essence of Mind itself.

"Who would have thought," I said to the Patriarch, "that the Essence of Mind is intrinsically pure! Who would have thought that the Essence of Mind is intrinsically free from becoming or annihilation! Who would have thought that the Essence of Mind is intrinsically self-sufficient! Who would have

thought that the Essence of Mind is intrinsically free from change! Who would have thought that all things are the manifestation of the Essence of Mind!"

Knowing that I had realised the Essence of Mind, the Patriarch said, "For him who does not know his own mind there is no use learning Buddhism. On the other hand, if he knows his own mind and sees intuitively his own nature, he is a Hero, a 'Teacher of gods and men,' 'Buddha'."

Thus, to the knowledge of no one, the Dharma was transmitted to me at midnight, and consequently I became the inheritor of the teaching of the 'Sudden' School as well as of the robe and the begging bowl.

"You are now the Sixth Patriarch," said he. "Take good care of yourself, and deliver as many sentient beings as possible. Spread and preserve the teaching, and don't let it come to an end. Take note of my stanza:

Sentient beings who sow the seeds of enlightenment
In the field of causation will reap the fruit of Buddha-
    hood.
Inanimate objects void of Buddha-nature
Sow not and reap not.

He further said, "When the Patriarch Bodhidharma first came to China, most Chinese had no confidence in him, and so this robe was handed down as a testimony from one Patriarch to another. As to the Dharma, this is transmitted from heart to heart, and the recipient must realise it by his own efforts. From time immemorial it has been the practice for one Buddha to pass to his successor the quintessence of the Dharma, and for one Patriarch to transmit to another the esoteric teaching from heart to heart. As the robe may give cause for dispute, you are the last one to inherit it. Should you hand it down to your successor, your life would be in imminent danger. Now leave this place as quickly as you can, lest some one should do you harm."

"Whither should I go?" I asked. "At Huai you stop and at Hui you seclude yourself," he replied.

Upon receiving the robe and the begging bowl in

---

[2]Note by Dhyana Master Hui An: "'To be free from any attachment' means not to abide in form or matter, not to abide in sound, not to abide in delusion, not to abide in enlightenment, not to abide in the quintessence, not to abide in the attribute. 'To use the mind' means to let the 'One Mind' (i.e., the Universal mind) manifest itself everywhere. When we let our mind dwell on piety or on evil, piety or evil manifests itself, but our Essence of Mind (or Primordial mind) is thereby obscured. But when our mind dwells on nothing, we realise that all the worlds of the ten quarters are nothing but the manifestation of 'One Mind.'"

the middle of the night, I told the Patriarch that, being a Southerner, I did not know the mountain tracks, and that it was impossible for me to get to the mouth of the river (to catch a boat). "You need not worry," said he. "I will go with you."

He then accompanied me to Kiukiang, and there ordered me into a boat. As he did the rowing himself, I asked him to sit down and let me handle the oar. "It is only right for me to carry you across," he said (an allusion to the sea of birth and death which one has to go across before the shore of Nirvana can be reached). To this I replied, "While I am under illusion, it is for you to get me across; but after enlightenment, I should cross it by myself. (Although the term 'to go across' is the same, it is used differently in each case.) As I happen to be born on the frontier, even my speaking is incorrect in pronunciation, (but in spite of this) I have had the honour to inherit the Dharma from you. Since I am now enlightened, it is only right for me to cross the sea of birth and death myself by realising my own Essence of Mind."

"Quite so, quite so," he agreed. "Beginning from you the Dhyana School will become very popular. Three years after your departure from me I shall leave this world. You may start on your journey now. Go as fast as you can towards the South. Do not preach too soon, as Buddhism is not so easily spread."

After saying good-bye, I left him and walked towards the South. In about two months' time, I reached the Ta Yü Mountain. There I noticed that several hundred men were in pursuit of me with the intention of robbing me of my robe and begging bowl.

Among them there was a monk named Hui Ming, whose lay surname was Ch'en. He was a general of the fourth rank in lay life. His manner was rough and his temper hot. Of all the pursuers, he was the most vigilant in search of me. When he was about to overtake me, I threw the robe and the begging bowl on a rock, saying, "This robe is nothing but a symbol. What is the use of taking it away by force?" (I then hid myself). When he got to the rock, he tried to pick them up, but found he could

not. Then he shouted out, "Lay Brother, Lay Brother, (for the Patriarch had not yet formally joined the Order) I come for the Dharma, not for the robe."

Whereupon I came out from my hiding place and squatted on the rock. He made obeisance and said, "Lay Brother, preach to me, please."

"Since the object of your coming is the Dharma," said I, "refrain from thinking of anything and keep your mind blank. I will then teach you." When he had done this for a considerable time, I said, "When you are thinking of neither good nor evil, what is at that particular moment, Venerable Sir, your real nature (literally, original face)?"

As soon as he heard this he at once became enlightened. But he further asked, "Apart from those esoteric sayings and esoteric ideas handed down by the Patriarch from generation to generation, are there any other esoteric teachings?" "What I can tell you is not esoteric," I replied. "If you turn your light inwardly,[3] you will find what is esoteric within you."

"In spite of my staying in Huang Mei," said he, "I did not realise my self-nature. Now thanks to your guidance, I know it as a water-drinker knows how hot or how cold the water is. Lay Brother, you are now my teacher."

I replied, "If that is so, then you and I are fellow disciples of the Fifth Patriarch. Take good care of yourself."

---

[3]The most important point in the teaching of the Dhyana School lies in "Introspection," which means the turning of one's own "light" to reflect inwardly. To illustrate, let us take the analogy of a lamp. We know that the light of a lamp, when surrounded by a shade, will reflect inwardly with its radiance centering on itself, whereas the rays of a naked flame will diffuse and shine outwardly. Now when we are engrossed with criticising others, as is our wont, we hardly turn our thoughts on ourselves, and hence scarcely know anything about ourselves. Contrary to this, the followers of the Dhyana School turn their attention completely within and reflect exclusively on their own "real nature," known in Chinese as one's "original face."

Lest our readers should overlook this important passage, let it be noted that in China alone thousands of Buddhists have attained enlightenment by acting on this wise saying of the Sixth Patriarch.—DIH PING TSZE.

In answering his question whither he should go thereafter, I told him to stop at Yuan and to take up his abode in Meng. He paid homage and departed.

Sometime after I reached Ts'ao Ch'i. There the evildoers again persecuted me and I had to take refuge in Szu Hui, where I stayed with a party of hunters for a period as long as fifteen years.

Occasionally I preached to them in a way that befitted their understanding. They used to put me to watch their nets, but whenever I found living creatures therein I set them free. At meal times I put vegetables in the pan in which they cooked their meat. Some of them questioned me, and I explained to them that I would eat the vegetables only, after they had been cooked with the meat.

One day I bethought myself that I ought not to pass a secluded life all the time, and that it was high time for me to propagate the Law. Accordingly I left there and went to the Fa Hsin Temple in Canton.

At that time Bhikkhu Yin Tsung, Master of the Dharma, was lecturing on the Maha Parinirvana Sutra in the Temple. It happened that one day, when a pennant was blown about by the wind, two Bhikkhus entered into a dispute as to what it was that was in motion, the wind or the pennant. As they could not settle their difference I submitted to them that it was neither, and that what actually moved was their own mind. The whole assembly was startled by what I said, and Bhikkhu Yin Tsung invited me to take a seat of honour and questioned me about various knotty points in the Sutras.

Seeing that my answers were precise and accurate, and that they showed something more than book-knowledge, he said to me, "Lay Brother, you must be an extraordinary man. I was told long ago that the inheritor of the Fifth Patriarch's robe and Dharma had come to the South. Very likely you are the man."

To this I politely assented. He immediately made obeisance and asked me to show the assembly the robe and the begging bowl which I had inherited.

He further asked what instructions I had when the Fifth Patriarch transmitted me the Dharma. "Apart from a discussion on the realisation of the Essence of Mind," I replied, "he gave me no other instruction, nor did he refer to Dhyana and Emancipation." "Why not?" he asked. "Because that would mean two ways," I replied. "And there cannot be two ways in Buddhism. There is one way only."

He asked what was the only way. I replied, "The Maha Parinirvana Sutra which you expound explains that Buddha-nature is the only way. For example, in that Sutra King Kao Kuei-Teh, a Bodhisattva, asked Buddha whether or not those who commit the four acts of gross misconduct,[4] or the five deadly sins,[5] and those who are *icchantika* (heretics) etc., would eradicate their 'element of goodness' and their Buddha-nature. Buddha replied, 'There are two kinds of 'element of goodness,' the eternal and the non-eternal. Since Buddha-nature is neither eternal nor non-eternal, therefore their 'element of goodness' is not eradicated. Now Buddhism is known as having no two ways. There are good ways and evil ways, but since Buddha-nature is neither, therefore Buddhism is known as having no two ways. From the point of view of ordinary folks, the component parts of a personality (*skandhas*) and factors of consciousness (*dhatus*) are two separate things: but enlightened men understand that they are not dual in nature. Buddha-nature is non-duality."

Bhikkhu Yin Tsung was highly pleased with my answer. Putting his two palms together as a sign of respect, he said, "My interpretation of the Sutra is as worthless as a heap of debris, while your discourse is as valuable as genuine gold." Subsequently he conducted the ceremony of hair-cutting for me (*i.e.*, the ceremony of Initiation into the Order) and asked me to accept him as my pupil.

Thenceforth, under the Bodhi-tree I preached the teaching of the Tung Shan School (the School of the Fourth and the Fifth Patriarchs, who lived in Tung Shan).

Since the time when the Dharma was transmitted

---

[4]Killing, stealing, carnality and lying.
[5]Patricide, matricide, setting the Buddhist Order in discord, killing an Arhat, and causing blood to flow from the body of a Buddha.

to me in Tung Shan, I have gone through many hardships and my life often seemed to be hanging by a thread. Today, I have had the honour of meeting you in this assembly, and I must ascribe this to our good connection in previous *kalpas* (cyclic periods), as well as to our common accumulated merits in making offerings to various Buddhas in our past reincarnations; otherwise, we should have had no chance of hearing the above teaching of the 'Sudden' School, and thereby laying the foundation of our future success in understanding the Dharma.

This teaching was handed down from the past Patriarchs, and it is not a system of my own invention. Those who wish to hear the teaching should first purify their own mind, and after hearing it they should each clear up their own doubts in the same way as the Sages did in the past."

At the end of the address, the assembly felt rejoiced, made obeisance and departed.

ZEN KEYS

Thich Nhat Hanh

The second century B.C. saw the appearance of the first *Prajnaparamita* Sutra* text and the rise of the doctrine of *emptiness,* in an effort aimed at regaining the original spirit of Buddhism. The *Prajnaparamita* texts, as well as other Mahayanistic texts, such as the *Sadharmapundarika,* the *Lankavatara,* the *Mahaparinirvana,* and the *Avatamsaka,* continued to appear in the following century.

• • •

The texts mentioned are used in the Zen tradition. It can be said that Zen Buddhism reflects the essence of all these Mahayanist scriptures in a harmonious way.

RETURN TO THE SOURCE

The point of departure of the *Prajnaparamita* thought is the notion of *emptiness.* In the beginning . . . the word *emptiness* signified the absence of permanent identity. When the Sarvastivada school declared that from the phenomenal point of view things do not exist as permanent identities, but that the true nature of things exists from the ontological standpoint, it can be seen that this permanent identity of things is now disguised as an ontological entity. The *Prajnaparamita* explains: "Things do not have their own nature; the ontological entity of things does not exist." The *Prajnaparamita,* through this declaration, tends to bring us back to the source of Buddhism.

The notions of impermanence, of non-identity, of interdependent relation, and emptiness are means aimed at revealing the errors of knowledge rather than at giving a description of the objects of knowledge. These notions must be considered as *methods* and not as *knowledge.* We must correct the habit we have of seeing things while having principles of conduct as our basis. According to the *Vajracchedika-prajnaparamita,* this problem is *the most important problem of all.* Buddha said to Subhuti, who asked him what was the method to correct understanding:

> Subhuti, the great bodhisattvas must correct their understanding in the following way. It is necessary for them to think: while living beings exist, whether they are oviparous, viviparous, exudative, or metamorphosics, whether they possess a form or not, whether they are gifted with perception or not, I must bring them all to Nirvana. But, although these innumerable living beings must be brought to Nirvana, in reality no living being has to be so brought. Why is this? It is very simple. If a bodhisattva maintains in his mind the concepts of self, others, of living beings, of person, then he is not a true bodhisattva.

Why are concepts the source of errors that must

---

*"Prajnaparamita" (pronounced Pra-na-para-meet'-a) means "knowledge that has gone beyond"; it refers to the mystical knowledge of Mahayana Buddhism which is said to go beyond ordinary thought and language (Eds.).

be corrected? Because the concept is not reality. "To bring all living beings to Nirvana" is reality itself; but "to bring," "living beings," "Nirvana," "the bringer," and the "brought'" are only concepts. And why is there this great distance between reality and the concept? There is no discrimination in reality in itself. But "reality" in the world of concepts is full of discriminations: subject/object, I/Not-I, etc. This is not truly reality but an erroneous image of reality. The origin of this erroneous image is called *discrimination* or *imagination* (*vikalpa*) in the Vijanavada school.

This flower, for example, which is near the window, is a true flower in its non-discriminated reality. Because we discriminate it is no longer revealed. In its place stands an erroneous image of it. The word "empty" which at first signified the ab-

sence of permanent identity, now acquires another meaning: the image created by the concept does not represent any reality, it is imaginary.

QUESTIONS FOR DISCUSSION

1. Why does Hui Neng challenge Shen Hsiu's interpretation of the Zen teachings? Using Thich Nhat Hanh's account of "emptiness," explain Hui Neng's alternative view.

2. Thich Nhat Hanh claims that concepts are a source of error that needs correcting if we are to know the truth. Why does he hold this view? Do you agree or disagree with him? Why or why not?

THE TAO

Like Zen, which it influenced, Taoism and its central scripture, the *Tao Te Ching,* represent a very pure form of mysticism. The very first sentences of the work set this out in a direct manner, telling us that the eternal Tao or "way" and the eternal Name are beyond telling and naming. Like Zen also, and the Indian mystical schools from which it was derived, the *Tao* uses the images of "emptiness" and "nonbeing" as central in its attempt to express the mystical inexpressibility of truth.

The author of the work is traditionally said to be Lao Tzu, who, legend tells us, was a contemporary of Confucius, which would date the book from the fifth or sixth century B.C. However, "Lao Tzu" is probably not a name but a phrase meaning "the old sage," so the author is, in a sense, anonymous. And the "history" of his life and of his meeting with Confucius is, as likely as not, a fiction, the latter story merely serving to dramatize the tension between the aloof mysticism of the Tao and Confucian moralism in classical Chinese thought.

THE WAY AND ITS POWER

Lao Tzu

1

Tao can be talked about, but not the Eternal Tao.
Names can be named, but not the Eternal Name.

As the origin of heaven-and-earth, it is nameless:
As "the Mother" of all things, it is nameable.

So, as ever hidden, we should look at its inner
    essence:
As always manifest, we should look at its outer aspects.

These two flow from the same source, though differently named;
And both are called mysteries.

The Mystery of mysteries is the Door of all
    essence.

. . .

4

The Tao is like an empty bowl,
Which in being used can never be filled up.
Fathomless, it seems to be the origin of all things.
It blunts all sharp edges,
It unties all tangles,
It harmonizes all lights,
It unites the world into one whole.
Hidden in the deeps,
Yet it seems to exist for ever.
I do not know whose child it is;
It seems to be the common ancestor of all, the father of things.

5

Heaven-and-Earth is not sentimental;
It treats all things as straw-dogs.
The Sage is not sentimental;
He treats all his people as straw-dogs.

Between Heaven and Earth,
There seems to be a Bellows:
It is empty, and yet it is inexhaustible;
The more it works, the more comes out of it.

No amount of words can fathom it:
Better look for it within you.

• • •

11

Thirty spokes converge upon a single hub;
It is on the hole in the center that the use of the
    cart hinges.

We make a vessel from a lump of clay;
It is the empty space within the vessel that makes
    it useful.

We make doors and windows for a room;
But it is these empty spaces that make the room
    livable.

Thus, while the tangible has advantages,
It is the intangible that makes it useful.

• • •

25

There was Something undefined and yet complete
    in itself,
Born Before Heaven-and-Earth.

Silent and boundless,
Standing alone without change,
Yet pervading all without fail,
It may be regarded as the Mother of the world.
I do not know its name;
I style it "Tao";
And, in the absence of a better word, call it "The
    Great."

To be great is to go on,
To go on is to be far,
To be far is to return.

Hence, "Tao is great,
Heaven is great,
Earth is great,
King is great."
Thus, the king is one of the great four in the Uni-
    verse.

Man follows the ways of the Earth.
The Earth follows the ways of Heaven,
Heaven follows the ways of Tao,
Tao follows its own ways.

• • •

32

Tao is always nameless.
Small as it is in its Primal Simplicity,
It is inferior to nothing in the world.
If only a ruler could cling to it,
Everything will render homage to him.
Heaven and Earth will be harmonized
And send down sweet dew.
Peace and order will reign among the people
Without any command from above.

When once the Primal Simplicity diversified,
Different names appeared.
Are there not enough names now?

Is this not the time to stop?
To know when to stop is to preserve ourselves
    from danger.
The Tao is to the world what a great river or an
    ocean is to the streams and brooks.

• • •

34

The Great Tao is universal like a flood.
How can it be turned to the right or to the left?

All creatures depend on it,
And it denies nothing to anyone.

It does its work,
But it makes no claims for itself.

It clothes and feeds all,
But it does not lord it over them:
Thus, it may be called "the Little."

All things return to it as to their home,
But it does not lord it over them:
Thus, it may be called "the Great."

It is just because it does not wish to be great
That its greatness is fully realized.

35

He who holds the Great Symbol will attract all
    things to him.
They flock to him and receive no harm, for in him
    they find peace, security and happiness.

Music and dainty dishes can only make a passing
    guest pause.
But the words of Tao possess lasting effects,
Though they are mild and flavourless,
Though they appeal neither to the eye nor to the
    ear.

. . .

37

Tao never makes any ado,
And yet it does everything.
If a ruler can cling to it,
All things will grow of themselves.
When they have grown and tend to make a stir,
It is time to keep them in their place by the aid of
    the nameless Primal Simplicity,
Which alone can curb the desires of men.
When the desires of men are curbed, there will be
    peace,
And the world will settle down of its own accord.

. . .

51

Tao gives them life,
Virtue nurses them,
Matter shapes them,
Environment perfects them.
Therefore all things without exception worship
    Tao and do homage to Virtue.
They have not been commanded to worship Tao
    and do homage to Virtue,
But they always do so spontaneously.

It is Tao that gives them life:
It is Virtue that nurses them, grows them, fosters
    them, shelters them, comforts them, nourishes
    them, and covers them under her wings.
To give life but to claim nothing,
To do your work but to set no store by it,
To be a leader, not a butcher,
This is called hidden Virtue.

. . .

77

Perhaps the Way of Heaven may be likened to the
    stretching of a composite bow! The upper part is
    depressed, while the lower is raised. If the bow-
    string is too long, it is cut short: if too short, it is
    added to.

The Way of Heaven diminishes the more-than-
    enough to supply the less-than-enough. The way
    of man is different: it takes from the less-than-
    enough to swell the more-than-enough. Who ex-
    cept a man of the Tao can put his superabundant
    riches to the service of the world?

Therefore, the Sage does his work without setting
    any store by it, accomplishes his task without
    dwelling upon it. He does not want his merits to
    be seen.

QUESTION FOR DISCUSSION

1. The Tao seems to encompass everything, making the following of it appear inevitable, and yet
   the world's rulers are urged to remain centered in
   it, implying that it is possible to defy it. Does this
   paradox, on your view, leave Lao Tzu in an impossible contradiction, or is there a deeper meaning in his words which will resolve that contradiction?

MATERIALISM

Just as philosophical idealism in no way implies an idealistic attitude in the popular sense of this term, so also philosophical materialism implies no preoccupation with the acquisition of material goods. Rather, as *idealism* in philosophy refers to a doctrine that teaches that the world is the product of mind, *materialism* refers to the opposite position; the world consists only of independent physical things, the mind being not the creator of the material world but its product. Where idealists such as Bishop Berkeley claim that the brain is paradoxically lodged in the mind, the materialist sees the brain as the source of the mind, as something which is either actually identical with the mind or a necessary prerequisite for mind to exist in the world. This, of course, challenges most religious beliefs and puts materialism in direct conflict with spiritual interpretations of the world.

The first selection presented comes from the work of the seventeenth-century neo-Confucian philosopher Wang Fu-Chi, who argues that both Tao, the "Way," and Li, or "Principle," are not prior to Chi or "material force" but inseparable from it. In this he challenges all other neo-Confucians who generally hold the view that Li is prior to Chi, that is to say, that a conscious intelligence is necessary for the operation of the laws of physical nature, that a Supreme Principle or a Supreme Being governs the world. As a materialist, Wang has come in for much praise in recent years in China, where the officially materialist communist regime views him as a traditional ally and forerunner of its official world view.

The cofounder of Marxism—Karl Marx's lifelong collaborator—Friedrich Engels (1820–1895) provides the second selection. The selection begins with his account of the origin and development of the world in exclusively scientific terms—a world of matter and energy governed wholly by natural law. Very quickly, however, he moves on to the question of humanity's place in this world of unthinking matter, ending with a faith that, though intelligent life is eventually likely to perish here on this planet, it will emerge elsewhere in the universe in matter's "eternal cycle."

NEO-CONFUCIAN MATERIALISM

Wang Fu-Chih

THE WORLD OF CONCRETE THINGS

The world consists only of concrete things. The Way (*Tao*) is the Way of concrete things, but concrete things may not be called concrete things of the Way. People generally are capable of saying that without its Way there cannot be the concrete thing. However, if there is the concrete thing, there need be no worry about there not being its Way. A sage knows what a superior man does not know, but an ordinary man or woman can do what a sage cannot do. A person may be ignorant of the Way of a thing, and the concrete thing therefore cannot be completed. But not being completed does not mean that there is no concrete thing. Few people are capable of saying that without a concrete thing there cannot be its Way, but it is certainly true.

In the period of wilderness and chaos, there was no Way to bow and yield a throne. At the time of Yao and Shun,[1] there was no Way to pity the suffer-

---

[1]Legendary emperors (3rd millennium B.C.).

ing people and punish the sinful rulers. During the Han (206 B.C.–A.D. 220) and T'ang (618–907) dynasties there were no Ways as we have today, and there will be many in future years which we do not have now. Before bows and arrows existed, there was no Way of archery. Before chariots and horses existed, there was no Way to drive them. Before sacrificing oxen and wine, presents of jade and silk, or bells, chimes, flutes, and strings existed, there were no Ways of ceremonies and music. Thus there is no Way of the father before there is a son, there is no Way of the elder brother before there is a younger brother, and there are many potential Ways which are not existent. Therefore without a concrete thing, there cannot be its Way. This is indeed a true statement. Only people have not understood it.

Sages of antiquity could manage concrete things but could not manage the Way. What is meant by the Way is the management of concrete things. When the Way is fulfilled, we call it virtue. When the concrete thing is completed, we call it operation. When concrete things function extensively, we call it transformation and penetration. When its effect becomes prominent, we call it achievement. . . .

By "what exists before physical form" [and is therefore without it][2] does not mean there is no physical form. There is already physical form. As there is physical form, there is that which exists before it. Even if we span past and present, go through all the myriad transformations, and investigate Heaven, Earth, man, and things to the utmost, we will not find any thing existing before physical form [and is without it]. Therefore it is said, "It is only the sage who can put his physical form into full use."[3] He puts into full use what is within a physical form, not what is above it. Quickness of apprehension and intelligence are matters of the ear and the eye, insight and wisdom those of the mind and thought, humanity that of men, righteousness that of events, equilibrium and harmony those of ceremonies and music, great impartiality and perfect correctness those of reward and punishment, advantage and utility those of water, fire, metal, and wood, welfare that of grains, fruits, silk, and hemp, and correct virtue that of the relationship between ruler and minister and between father and son. If one discarded these and sought for that which existed before concrete things, even if he spanned past and present, went through all the myriad transformations, and investigated Heaven, Earth, man, and things to the utmost, he would not be able to give it a name. How much less could he find its reality! Lao Tzu was blind to this and said that the Way existed in vacuity. But vacuity is the vacuity of concrete things. The Buddha was blind to this and said that the Way existed in silence. But silence is the silence of concrete things. One may keep on uttering such extravagant words to no end, but one can never escape from concrete things. Thus if one plays up some name that is separated from concrete things as though he were a divine being, whom could he deceive?

SUBSTANCE AND FUNCTION

All functions in the world are those of existing things. From their functions I know they possess substance. Why should we entertain any doubt? Function exists to become effect, and substance exists to become nature and feelings. Both substance and function exist, and each depends on the other to be concrete. Therefore all that fills the universe demonstrates the principle of mutual dependence. Therefore it is said, "Sincerity (realness) is the beginning and end of things. Without sincerity there will be nothing."[4]

What is the test for this? We believe in what exists but doubt what does not exist. I live from the time I was born to the time I die. As there were ancestors before, so there will be descendants later. From observing the transformations throughout heaven and earth, we see the productive process. Is any of these facts doubtful?. . . Hold on to the con-

---

[2]*Changes,* "Appended Remarks," pt. 1, ch. 12. Cf. Legge, trans., *Yi King,* 377.
[3]*Mencius,* 7A:38.

[4]*The Mean,* ch. 25.

crete things and its Way will be preserved. Cast aside the concrete things and its Way will be destroyed. . . . Therefore those who are expert in speaking of the Way arrive at substance from function but those who are not expert in speaking of the Way erroneously set up substance and dismiss function in order to conform to it.

· · ·

PRINCIPLE AND MATERIAL FORCE

Principle depends on material force. When material force is strong, principle prevails. When Heaven accumulates strong and powerful material force, there will be order, and transformations will be refined and totally renewed. This is why on the day of religious fasting an emperor presents an ox [to Heaven] so that the material force will fill the universe and sincerity will penetrate everything. All products in the world are results of refined and beautiful material force. Man takes the best of it to nourish his life, but it is all from Heaven. Material force naturally becomes strong. Sincerity naturally becomes solidified. And principle naturally becomes self-sufficient. If we investigate into the source of these phenomena, we shall find that it is the refined and beautiful transformation of Heaven and Earth.

At bottom principle is not a finished product that can be grasped. It is invisible. The details and order of material force is principle that is visible. Therefore the first time there is any principle is when it is seen in material force.

MATERIALISM AND THE SCIENTIFIC WORLD VIEW

Friedrich Engels

The new conception of nature was complete in its main features; all rigidity was dissolved, all fixity dissipated, all particularity that had been regarded

as eternal became transient, the whole of nature shown as moving in eternal flux and cyclical course.

Thus we have once again returned to the point of view of the great founders of Greek philosophy, the view that the whole of nature, from the smallest element to the greatest, from grains of sand to suns, from protista[1] to men, has its existence in eternal coming into being and passing away, in ceaseless flux, in unresting motion and change, only with the essential difference that what for the Greeks was a brilliant intuition, is in our case the result of strictly scientific research in accordance with experience, and hence also it emerges in a much more definite and clear form. It is true that the empirical proof of this motion is not wholly free from gaps, but these are insignificant in comparison with what has already been firmly established, and with each year they become more and more filled up. And how could the proof in detail be otherwise than defective when one bears in mind that the most essential branches of science—trans-planetary astronomy, chemistry, geology—have a scientific existence of barely a hundred years, and the comparative method in physiology one of barely fifty years, and that the basic form of almost all organic development, the cell, is a discovery not yet forty years old?

The innumerable suns and solar systems of our island universe,[2] bounded by the outermost stellar rings of the Milky Way, developed from swirling, glowing masses of vapour, the laws of motion of which will perhaps be disclosed after the observations of some centuries have given us an insight into the proper motion of the stars. Obviously, this development did not proceed everywhere at the same rate. Recognition of the existence of dark bodies, not merely planetary in nature, hence extinct suns in our stellar system, more and more forces itself on

---

[1]*Protista.* Single-celled animals and plants such as Paramœcium, Amœba, Bacillus.
[2]This refers to the system of stars of which the sun is one, and the Milky Way represents the densest portions. Mädler was right in maintaining that many of the other bodies then described as nebulæ were similar masses of stars. His view that there are extinct suns is more doubtful. Nor is it clear that the gaseous nebulæ are likely to condense into suns.

astronomy (Mädler); on the other hand (according to Secchi) a part of the vaporous nebular patches belong to our stellar system as suns not yet fully formed, whereby it is not excluded that other nebulæ, as Mädler maintains, are distant independent island universes, the relative stage of development of which must be determined by the spectroscope.

How a solar system develops from an individual nebular mass has been shown in detail by Laplace in a manner still unsurpassed; subsequent science has more and more confirmed him.[3]

On the separate bodies so formed—suns as well as planets and satellites—the form of motion of matter at first prevailing is that which we call heat. There can be no question of chemical compounds of the elements even at a temperature like that still possessed by the sun; the extent to which heat is transformed into electricity or magnetism[4] under such conditions, continued solar observations will show; it is already as good as proved that the mechanical motion taking place in the sun arises solely from the conflict of heat with gravity.

The smaller the individual bodies, the quicker they cool down, the satellites, asteroids, and meteors first of all, just as our moon has long been extinct. The planets cool more slowly, the central body slowest of all.

With progressive cooling the interplay of the physical forms of motion which become transformed into one another comes more and more to the forefront until finally a point is reached from when on chemical affinity begins to make itself felt, the previously chemically indifferent elements become differentiated chemically one after another, obtain chemical properties, and enter into combination with one another. These compounds change continually with the decreasing temperature, which affects differently not only each element but also each separate compound of the elements, changing also with the consequent passage of part of the

gaseous matter first to the liquid and then the solid state, and with the new conditions thus created.

The period when the planet has a firm shell and accumulations of water on its surface coincides with that when its intrinsic heat diminishes more and more in comparison to the heat emitted to it from the central body. Its atmosphere becomes the arena of meteorological phenomena in the sense in which we now understand the word; its surface becomes the arena of geological changes in which the deposits resulting from atmospheric precipitation become of ever greater importance in comparison to the slowly decreasing external effects of the hot fluid interior.

If, finally, the temperature becomes so far equalised that over a considerable portion of the surface at least it does not exceed the limits within which protein[5] is capable of life, then, if other chemical conditions are favourable, living protoplasm is formed. What these conditions are, we do not yet know, which is not to be wondered at since so far not even the chemical formula of protein has been established—we do not even know how many chemically different protein bodies there are—and since it is only about ten years ago that the fact became known that completely structureless protein[6] exercises all the essential functions of life, digestion, excretion, movement, contraction, reaction to stimuli, and reproduction.

Thousands of years may have passed before the

_____

[3]Laplace's theory is fairly certainly incorrect.
[4]Huge magnetic fields have been discovered in the sunspots, and it is also known that the matter shot out in solar prominences is electrically charged. Both these facts were unsuspected by most, if not all, astronomers when Engels wrote.

[5]Throughout this book Engels's word "*Eiweiss*" is translated as "*protein.*" The word "*albumen,*" which has been used in the translation of some of Engels' other works, is now applied to one group of the proteins only. The chemical formulæ of a few proteins were first discovered with fair accuracy by Bergmann, a German-Jewish refugee in New York, in 1936. However, the order in which their constituents are arranged is still incompletely known. There are probably many millions of different proteins.
[6]*Structureless protein: Bathybius Haeckeli,* which was supposed to be an organism composed of a mere mass of structureless protein, proved to be an artefact, that is to say not a natural object, but one produced by the chemicals intended to preserve it. However Engels was fundamentally right. Some of the "viruses," that is to say the smallest agents of disease, are simply large protein molecules, as first shown by Stanley in 1936. They do not appear to exercise all the functions of life, but only some of them.

conditions arose in which the next advance could take place and this formless protein produce the first cell by formation of nucleus and cell membrane. But this first cell also provided the foundation for the morphological development of the whole organic world; the first to develop, as it is permissible to assume from the whole analogy of the palæontological record, were innumerable species of non-cellular and cellular protista, of which *Eozoon canadense*[7] alone has come down to us, and of which some were gradually differentiated into the first plants and others into the first animals. And from the first animals were developed, essentially by further differentiation, the numerous classes, orders, families, genera, and species of animals; and finally mammals, the form in which the nervous system attains its fullest development; and among these again finally that mammal in which nature attains consciousness of itself—man.

Man too arises by differentiation. Not only individually, by differentiation from a single egg cell to the most complicated organism that nature produces—no, also historically. When after thousands of years[8] of struggle the differentiation of hand from foot, and erect gait, were finally established, man became distinct from the monkey and the basis was laid for the development of articulate speech and the mighty development of the brain that has since made the gulf between man and monkey an unbridgeable one. The specialisation of the hand— this implies the *tool,* and the tool implies specific human activity, the transforming reaction of man on nature, production. Animals in the narrower sense also have tools, but only as limbs of their bodies: the ant, the bee, the beaver; animals also produce, but their productive effect on surrounding nature in relation to the latter amounts to nothing at all. Man alone has succeeded in impressing his stamp on nature, not only by shifting the plant and animal world from one place to another, but also by so altering the

aspect and climate of his dwelling place, and even the plants and animals themselves, that the consequences of his activity can disappear only with the general extinction of the terrestrial globe. And he has accomplished this primarily and essentially by means of *the hand*. Even the steam engine, so far his most powerful tool for the transformation of nature, depends, because it is a tool, in the last resort on the hand. But step by step with the development of the hand went that of the brain; first of all consciousness of the conditions for separate practically useful actions, and later, among the more favoured peoples and arising from the preceding, insight into the natural laws governing them. And with the rapidly growing knowledge of the laws of nature the means for reacting on nature also grew; the hand alone would never have achieved the steam engine if the brain of man had not attained a correlative development with it, and parallel to it, and partly owing to it.

With men we enter *history.* Animals also have a history, that of their derivation and gradual evolution to their present position. This history, however, is made for them, and in so far as they themselves take part in it, this occurs without their knowledge or desire. On the other hand, the more that human beings become removed from animals in the narrower sense of the word, the more they make their own history consciously, the less becomes the influence of unforeseen effects and uncontrolled forces on this history, and the more accurately does the historical result correspond to the aim laid down in advance. If, however, we apply this measure to human history, to that of even the most developed peoples of the present day, we find that there still exists here a colossal disproportion between the proposed aims and the results arrived at, that unforeseen effects predominate, and that the uncontrolled forces are far more powerful than those set into motion according to plan. And this cannot be otherwise as long as the most essential historical activity of men, the one which has raised them from bestiality to humanity and which forms the material foundation of all their other activities, namely the production of their requirements of life, that is to-day social production, is above all subject to the in-

---

[7]*Eozoon canadense* is almost certainly not an organic product. Nevertheless there is every reason to believe in the essential truth of this paragraph.

[8]The geological time-scale is longer than was believed fifty years ago. "Millions of years" would be more correct.

terplay of unintended effects from uncontrolled forces and achieves its desired end only by way of exception and, much more frequently, the exact opposite. In the most advanced industrial countries we have subdued the forces of nature and pressed them into the service of mankind; we have thereby infinitely multiplied production, so that a child now produces more than a hundred adults previously did. And what is the result? Increasing overwork and increasing misery of the masses, and every ten years a great collapse. Darwin did not know what a bitter satire he wrote on mankind, and especially on his countrymen, when he showed that free competition, the struggle for existence, which the economists celebrate as the highest historical achievement, is the normal state of the *animal kingdom*. Only conscious organisation of social production, in which production and distribution are carried on in a planned way, can lift mankind above the rest of the animal world as regards the social aspect, in the same way that production in general has done this for men in their aspect as species. Historical evolution makes such an organisation daily more indispensable, but also with every day more possible. From it will date a new epoch of history, in which mankind itself, and with mankind all branches of its activity, and especially natural science, will experience an advance that will put everything preceding it in the deepest shade.

Nevertheless, "all that comes into being deserves to perish." Millions of years may elapse, hundreds of thousands of generations be born and die, but inexorably the time will come when the declining warmth of the sun[9] will no longer suffice to melt the ice thrusting itself forward from the poles; when the human race, crowding more and more

about the equator, will finally no longer find even there enough heat for life; when gradually even the last trace of organic life will vanish; and the earth, an extinct frozen globe like the moon, will circle in deepest darkness and in an ever narrower orbit about the equally extinct sun, and at last fall into it. Other planets will have preceded it, others will follow it; instead of the bright, warm solar system with its harmonious arrangement of members, only a cold, dead sphere will still pursue its lonely path through universal space. And what will happen to our solar system will happen sooner or later to all the other systems of our island universe; it will happen to all the other innumerable island universes, even to those the light of which will never reach the earth while there is a living human eye to receive it.

And when such a solar system has completed its life history and succumbs to the fate of all that is finite, death, what then? Will the sun's corpse roll on for all eternity through infinite space, and all the once infinitely diverse, differentiated natural forces pass for ever into one single form of motion, attraction? "Or"—as Secchi asks—"do forces exist in nature which can re-convert the dead system into its original state of an incandescent nebular and reawake it to new life? We do not know."

At all events we do not know in the sense that we know that $2 \times 2 = 4$, or that the attraction of matter increases and decreases according to the square of the distance. In theoretical natural science, however, which as far as possible builds up its view of nature into a harmonious whole, and without which nowadays even the most thoughtless empiricist cannot get anywhere, we have very often to reckon with incompletely known magnitudes; and logical consistency of thought must at all times help to get over defective knowledge. Modern natural science has had to take over from philosophy the principle of the indestructibility of motion; it cannot any longer exist without this principle. But the motion of matter is not merely crude mechanical motion, mere change of place, it is heat and light, electric and magnetic stress, chemical combination and dissociation, life and, finally, consciousness. To say that matter during the whole unlimited time of its existence has only once, and for what is an infini-

---

[9]Until quite recently these rather gloomy conclusions appeared inevitable, even if the time-scale proved to be vastly longer than was supposed. But in 1936–1938 Milne and Dirac independently arrived at the conclusion that the laws of nature themselves evolve, and in particular (according to Milne) that chemical changes are speeded up (at the rate of about one two-thousand-millionth part per year) in relation to physical changes. If so it is at least conceivable that this process may be rapid enough to compensate for the cooling of the stars, and that life may never become impossible.

tesimally short period in comparison to its eternity, found itself able to differentiate its motion and thereby to unfold the whole wealth of this motion, and that before and after this remains restricted for eternity to mere change of place—this is equivalent to maintaining that matter is mortal and motion transitory. The indestructibility of motion cannot be merely quantitative, it must also be conceived qualitatively; matter whose purely mechanical change of place includes indeed the possibility under favourable conditions of being transformed into heat, electricity, chemical action, or life, but which is not capable of producing these conditions from out of itself, such matter has *forfeited motion;* motion which has lost the capacity of being transformed into the various forms appropriate to it may indeed still have *dynamis* but no longer *energeia,*[10] and so has become partially destroyed. Both, however, are unthinkable.

This much is certain: there was a time when the matter of our island universe had *transformed* a quantity of motion—of what kind we do not yet know—into heat, such that there could be developed from it the solar systems appertaining to (according to Mädler) at least twenty million stars, the gradual extinction of which is likewise certain. How did this transformation take place? We know just as little as Father Secchi knows whether the future *caput mortuum* of our solar system will once again be converted into the raw material of a new solar system. But here either we must have recourse to a creator, or we are forced to the conclusion that the incandescent raw material for the solar system of our universe was produced in a natural way by transformations of motion which are *by nature inherent* in moving matter, and the conditions of which therefore also must be reproduced by matter, even if only after millions and millions of years and more or less by chance but with the necessity that is also inherent in chance.

The possibility of such a transformation is more

and more being conceded. The view is being arrived at that the heavenly bodies are ultimately destined to fall into one another, and one even calculates the amount of heat which must be developed on such collisions. The sudden flaring up of new stars, and the equally sudden increase in brightness of familiar ones, of which we are informed by astronomy, is most easily explained[11] by such collisions. Not only does our group of planets move about the sun, and our sun within our island universe, but our whole island universe also moves in space in temporary, relative equilibrium with the other island universes, for even the relative equilibrium of freely moving bodies can only exist where the motion is reciprocally determined; and it is assumed by many that the temperature in space is not everywhere the same. Finally, we know that, with the exception of an infinitesimal portion, the heat of the innumerable suns of our island universe vanishes into space and fails to raise the temperature of space even by a millionth of a degree centigrade.[12] What becomes of all this enormous quantity of heat? Is it for ever dissipated in the attempt to heat universal space, has it ceased to exist practically, and does it only continue to exist theoretically, in the fact that universal space has become warmer by a decimal fraction of a degree beginning with ten or more noughts? The indestructibility of motion forbids such an assumption, but it allows the possibility that by the successive falling into one another of the bodies of the universe all existing mechanical motion will be converted into heat and the latter radiated into space, so that in spite of all "indestructibility of force" all motion in general would have ceased. (Incidentally it is seen here how inaccurate is the term "indestructibility of force"[13] instead of "indestructibility of motion.") Hence we arrive at the conclu-

---

[10]"Dynamis" and "energeia" are Greek words used by Aristotle. They can roughly be translated as "power" and "activity."

[11]The flaring up of new stars is now generally explained not by collision, but by an internal crisis in the star, in fact in a more dialectical manner.

[12]Actually the temperature of dust particles in the space between the galaxies is probably several degrees above absolute zero.

[13]Engels rightly protests against the use of the same word "Kraft" for "force" and "energy."

sion that in some way, which it will later be the task of scientific research to demonstrate, the heat radiated into space must be able to become transformed into another form of motion, in which it can once more be stored up and rendered active. Thereby the chief difficulty in the way of the reconversion of extinct suns into incandescent vapour disappears.

For the rest, the eternally repeated succession of worlds in infinite time is only the logical complement to the co-existence of innumerable worlds in infinite space—a principle the necessity of which has forced itself even on the anti-theoretical Yankee brain of Draper.[14]

It is an eternal cycle[15] in which matter moves, a cycle that certainly only completes its orbit in periods of time for which our terrestrial year is no adequate measure, a cycle in which the time of highest development, the time of organic life and still more that of the life of beings conscious of nature and of themselves, is just as narrowly restricted as the space in which life and self-consciousness come into operation; a cycle in which every finite mode of existence of matter, whether it be sun or nebular

vapour, single animal or genus of animals, chemical combination or dissociation, is equally transient, and wherein nothing is eternal but eternally changing, eternally moving matter and the laws according to which it moves and changes. But however often, and however relentlessly, this cycle is completed in time and space, however many millions of suns and earths may arise and pass away, however long it may last before the conditions for organic life develop, however innumerable the organic beings that have to arise and to pass away before animals with a brain capable of thought are developed from their midst, and for a short span of time find conditions suitable for life, only to be exterminated later without mercy, we have the certainty that matter remains eternally the same in all its transformations, that none of its attributes can ever be lost, and therefore, also, that with the same iron necessity that it will exterminate on the earth its highest creation, the thinking mind, it must somewhere else and at another time again produce it.

---

[14]"The multiplicity of worlds in infinite space leads to the conception of a succession of worlds in infinite time." J. W. Draper, *History of the Intellectual Development of Europe,* 1864. Vol. 2, p. 825. [*Note by F. Engels.*]

[15]At present physicists are divided on this question. A few take Engels' view that the universe goes through cyclical changes, entropy being somehow diminished by processes at present unknown (*e.g.* formation of matter from radiation in interstellar space). Others think as Clausius did, that it will run down. But there is a third possibility. As pointed out above, the work of Milne suggests that the universe as a whole has a history, though probably an infinite one both in the past and the future. It is almost certain that Engels would have welcomed this idea, although he here admits the eternity of the laws according to which matter moves and changes.

QUESTIONS FOR DISCUSSION

1. Where Engels speaks of scientifically derived natural laws, Wang Fu-Chi speaks of "Principle." Do you think these two notions can be equated? That is, is Wang Fu-Chi's materialism at bottom the same as that of Engels or significantly different?

2. Engels presents a picture of the universe without a god or any other sort of supreme being. Do you agree with this materialist picture of the world? Why or why not?

Jacob Lawrence, *The Library,* 1960, National Museum of American Art, Washington, D.C./Art Resource, NY

CHAPTER 2

KNOWLEDGE AND SCIENCE

The theory of knowledge, which is also known as *epistemology,* has been seen as central to philosophy by most Western philosophers in the period since the scientific revolution. As the prestige of science has grown, the philosophy of science has in turn increasingly been seen as central to most epistemological investigations. In this chapter, knowledge is examined both generally and in its specifically "scientific" form. The chapter begins with a traditional epistemological problem which has proved to have important ramifications for the methods of the sciences—the problem of induction.

Few of us have any real worries that the sun will not rise tomorrow. The philosopher David Hume, however, has demonstrated that absolute certainty is impossible to obtain for even so firmly held a belief as this. The problem which he presents for our knowledge of the world is known as the problem of induction. Its appearance in two cultures—Indian and European—is chronicled in the chapter's opening section. The discussion found there leads naturally to the question of method in knowledge gathering: What is the scientific method? Does such a method really, in practice, exist? Is it sufficient for a full understanding of the world? Is there, in addition to scientific knowledge, spiritual or religious knowledge of the world? What of the knowledge that we seem to obtain through the arts? Are there cultural limitations on the acquisition of knowledge? Can all understanding be contained within the bounds of reason? These questions are debated by thinkers from a variety of times and cultures. We have given special emphasis to contemporary thought, for the problems of knowledge have become more acute than ever before in the world's history, as Marshall McLuhan's "global village" and the post–Cold War global market begin to take shape.

Readers of Section One might also want to look at the further selections from the Carvaka philosophers which are found in Chapter 5 of the book. Those interested in Mao Tse-tung's thought will find other examples of Marxist philosophy in Friedrich Engels's essay in Chapter 1, in his and Karl Marx's critique of religion in Chapter 3, and their *Communist Manifesto* in the book's final chapter. Further examples of both traditional and contemporary Islamic philosophy are found in the second section of Chapter 4 and the first section of Chapter 8. Chuang Tzu's Taoism is also explored further in Chapter 8. The subject of mysticism, and Zen mysticism in particular, is addressed in the third section of the first chapter, the second section of Chapter 3, Section One of Chapter 4, and Section Three of Chapter 5.

INDUCTION

Induction has proved to be the central problem of the philosophy of science. From the time of the ancient Greek geometers, many thinkers had held out the possibility that a complete system of knowledge could be obtained from self-evident principles, using reason alone. In the West, these hopes were finally dashed forever when the Scottish philosopher David Hume (1711–1776) demonstrated that it was impossible to reach absolute logical certainty with respect to any generalization of the sort that is called "empirical"—i.e., one based on sense experience. This includes all those found routinely in the natural sciences.

Bertrand Russell (1872–1971), in the first of our selections, explains Hume's argument, using the example of chickens with an expectation that the farmer who daily feeds them will continue to do so indefinitely, only to find out too late that such general expectations are unfounded when they meet an untimely end at the farmer's hands.

The same difficulty which Hume uncovered in the eighteenth-century Western world had emerged in India over 2500 years earlier. The argument against the process of induction is, in all essentials, set out by the Carvaka philosophers (the *C* is pronounced like *Ch,* that is, "Char-va-ka") in their critique of inference. The Carvaka were a group at least as old as the Buddhists who taught an antispiritual philosophy which recommended that one trust nothing but immediate sense experience. Like David Hume they were skeptics at odds with the priests and spiritual aspirants of their day.

It should be noted in reading the Carvaka selection that Indian logic does not distinguish between logical inference and inductive inference, a distinction which has become almost second nature to students of Western philosophy. Thus, the critique of induction is, for the Carvaka, carried out in the context of an attack on inference generally considered.

Readers interested in this section will probably also want to consult the closely related next section of the chapter.

THE PROBLEM OF INDUCTION

Bertrand Russell

. . . Let us take as an illustration a matter about which none of us, in fact, feel the slightest doubt. We are all convinced that the sun will rise to-morrow. Why? Is this belief a mere blind outcome of past experience, or can it be justified as a reasonable belief? It is not easy to find a test by which to judge whether a belief of this kind is reasonable or not, but we can at least ascertain what sort of general beliefs would suffice, if true, to justify the judgement that the sun will rise to-morrow, and the many other similar judgements upon which our actions are based.

It is obvious that if we are asked why we believe that the sun will rise to-morrow, we shall naturally answer, "Because it always has risen every day." We have a firm belief that it will rise in the future, because it has risen in the past. If we are challenged as to why we believe that it will continue to rise as heretofore, we may appeal to the laws of motion: the earth, we shall say, is a freely rotating body, and such bodies do not cease to rotate unless something interferes from outside, and there is nothing outside to interfere with the earth between now and to-morrow. Of course it might be doubted whether we are quite certain that there is nothing outside to interfere, but this is not the interesting doubt. The interesting doubt is as to whether the laws of motion will remain in operation until to-morrow. If this doubt is raised, we find ourselves in the same position as when the doubt about the sunrise was first raised.

The *only* reason for believing that the laws of motion will remain in operation is that they have operated hitherto, so far as our knowledge of the past enables us to judge. It is true that we have a greater body of evidence from the past in favour of the laws of motion than we have in favour of the sunrise, because the sunrise is merely a particular case of fulfillment of the laws of motion, and there are countless other particular cases. But the real question is: Do *any* number of cases of a law being fulfilled in the past afford evidence that it will be fulfilled in the future? If not, it becomes plain that we have no ground whatever for expecting the sun to rise to-morrow, or for expecting the bread we shall eat at our next meal not to poison us, or for any of the other scarcely conscious expectations that control our daily lives. It is to be observed that all such expectations are only *probable;* thus we have not to seek for a proof that they *must* be fulfilled, but only for some reason in favour of the view that they are *likely* to be fulfilled.

Now in dealing with this question we must, to begin with, make an important distinction, without which we should soon become involved in hopeless confusions. Experience has shown us that, hitherto, the frequent repetition of some uniform succession or coexistence has been a *cause* of our expecting the same succession or coexistence on the next occasion. Food that has a certain appearance generally has a certain taste, and it is a severe shock to our expectations when the familiar appearance is found to be associated with an unusual taste. Things which we see become associated, by habit, with certain tactile sensations which we expect if we touch them; one of the horrors of a ghost (in many ghost-stories) is that it fails to give us any sensations of touch. Uneducated people who go abroad for the first time are so surprised as to be incredulous when they find their native language not understood.

And this kind of association is not confined to men; in animals also it is very strong. A horse which has been often driven along a certain road resists the attempt to drive him in a different direction. Do-mestic animals expect food when they see the person who usually feeds them. We know that all these rather crude expectations of uniformity are liable to be misleading. The man who has fed the chicken every day throughout its life at last wrings its neck instead, showing that more refined views as to the uniformity of nature would have been useful to the chicken.

But in spite of the misleadingness of such expectations, they nevertheless exist. The mere fact that something has happened a certain number of times causes animals and men to expect that it will happen again. Thus our instincts certainly cause us to believe that the sun will rise to-morrow, but we may be in no better a position than the chicken which unexpectedly has its neck wrung. We have therefore to distinguish the fact that past uniformities *cause* expectations as to the future, from the question whether there is any reasonable ground for giving weight to such expectations after the question of their validity has been raised.

The problem we have to discuss is whether there is any reason for believing in what is called "the uniformity of nature." The belief in the uniformity of nature is the belief that everything that has happened or will happen is an instance of some general law to which there are *no* exceptions. The crude expectations which we have been considering are all subject to exceptions, and therefore liable to disappoint those who entertain them. But science habitually assumes, at least as a working hypothesis, that general rules which have exceptions can be replaced by general rules which have no exceptions. "Unsupported bodies in air fall" is a general rule to which balloons and aeroplanes are exceptions. But the laws of motion and the law of gravitation, which account for the fact that most bodies fall, also account for the fact that balloons and aeroplanes can rise; thus the laws of motion and the law of gravitation are not subject to these exceptions.

The belief that the sun will rise to-morrow might be falsified if the earth came suddenly into contact with a large body that destroyed its rotation; but the laws of motion and the law of gravitation would not be infringed by such an event. The business of science is to find uniformities, such as the laws of motion and the law of gravitation, to which, so far as our experience extends, there are no exceptions. In this search science has been remarkably successful, and it may be conceded that such uniformities have held hitherto. This brings us back to the question: Have we any reason, assuming that they have always held in the past, to suppose that they will hold in the future?

It has been argued that we have reason to know that the future will resemble the past, because what was the future has constantly become the past, and has always been found to resemble the past, so that we really have experience of the future, namely of times which were formerly future, which we may call past futures. But such an argument really begs the very question at issue. We have experience of past futures, but not of future futures, and the question is: Will future futures resemble past futures? This question is not to be answered by an argument which starts from past futures alone. We have therefore still to seek for some principle which shall enable us to know that the future will follow the same laws as the past.

The reference to the future in this question is not essential. The same question arises when we apply the laws that work in our experience to past things of which we have no experience—as, for example, in geology, or in theories as to the origin of the Solar System. The question we really have to ask is: "When two things have been found to be often associated, and no instance is known of the one occurring without the other, does the occurrence of one of the two, in a fresh instance, give any good ground for expecting the other?" On our answer to this question must depend the validity of the whole of our expectations as to the future, the whole of the results obtained by induction, and in fact practically all the beliefs upon which our daily life is based.

It must be conceded, to begin with, that the fact that two things have been found often together and never apart does not, by itself, suffice to *prove* demonstratively that they will be found together in the next case we examine. The most we can hope is that the oftener things are found together, the more probable it becomes that they will be found together another time, and that, if they have been found together often enough, the probability will amount *almost* to certainty. It can never quite reach certainty, because we know that in spite of frequent repetitions there sometimes is a failure at the last, as in the case of the chicken whose neck is wrung. Thus probability is all we ought to seek.

It might be urged, as against the view we are advocating, that we know all natural phenomena to be subject to the reign of law, and that sometimes, on the basis of observation, we can see that only one law can possibly fit the facts of the case. Now to this view there are two answers. The first is that, even if *some* law which has no exceptions applies to our case, we can never, in practice, be sure that we have discovered that law and not one to which there are exceptions. The second is that the reign of law would seem to be itself only probable, and that our belief that it will hold in the future, or in unexamined cases in the past, is itself based upon the very principle we are examining.

The principle we are examining may be called the *principle of induction,* and its two parts may be stated as follows:

a. When a thing of a certain sort A has been found to be associated with a thing of a certain other sort B, and has never been found dissociated from a thing of the sort B, the greater the number of cases in which A and B have been associated, the greater is the probability that they will be associated in a fresh case in which one of them is known to be present;

b. Under the same circumstances, a sufficient number of cases of association will make the probability of a fresh association nearly a certainty, and will make it approach certainty without limit.

As just stated, the principle applies only to the verification of our expectation in a single fresh instance. But we want also to know that there is a probability in favour of the general law that things of the sort A are *always* associated with things of the sort B, provided a sufficient number of cases of association are known, and no cases of failure of association are known. The probability of the general law is obviously less than the probability of the particular case, since if the general law is true, the particular case must also be true, whereas the particular case may be true without the general law being true. Nevertheless the probability of the general law is increased by repetitions, just as the probability of the particular case is. We may therefore repeat the two parts of our principle as regards the general law, thus:

a. The greater the number of cases in which a thing of the sort A has been found associated with a thing of the sort B, the more probable it is (if no cases of failure of association are known) that A is always associated with B;

b. Under the same circumstances, a sufficient number of cases of the association of A with B will make it nearly certain that A is always associated with B, and will make this general law approach certainty without limit.

It should be noted that probability is always relative to certain data. In our case, the data are merely the known cases of coexistence of A and B. There may be other data, which *might* be taken into account, which would gravely alter the probability. For example, a man who had seen a great many white swans might argue, by our principle, that on the data it was *probable* that all swans were white, and this might be a perfectly sound argument. The argument is not disproved by the fact that some swans are black, because a thing may very well happen in spite of the fact that some data render it improbable. In the case of the swans, a man might know that colour is a very variable characteristic in many species of animals, and that, therefore, an induction as to colour is peculiarly liable to error. But this knowledge would be a fresh datum, by no means proving that the probability relatively to our previous data had been wrongly estimated. The fact, therefore, that things often fail to fulfil our expectations is no evidence that our expectations will not *probably* be fulfilled in a given case or a given class of cases. Thus our inductive principle is at any

rate not capable of being *disproved* by an appeal to experience.

The inductive principle, however, is equally incapable of being *proved* by an appeal to experience. Experience might conceivably confirm the inductive principle as regards the cases that have been already examined; but as regards unexamined cases, it is the inductive principle alone that can justify any inference from what has been examined to what has not been examined. All arguments which, on the basis of experience, argue as to the future or the unexperienced parts of the past or present, assume the inductive principle; hence we can never use experience to prove the inductive principle without begging the question. Thus we must either accept the inductive principle on the ground of its intrinsic evidence, or forgo all justification of our expectations about the future. If the principle is unsound, we have no reason to expect the sun to rise tomorrow, to expect bread to be more nourishing than a stone, or to expect that if we throw ourselves off the roof we shall fall. When we see what looks like our best friend approaching us, we shall have no reason to suppose that his body is not inhabited by the mind of our worst enemy or of some total stranger. All our conduct is based upon the associations which have worked in the past, and which we therefore regard as likely to work in the future; and this likelihood is dependent for its validity upon the inductive principle.

The general principles of science, such as the belief in the reign of law, and the belief that every event must have a cause, are as completely dependent upon the inductive principle as are the beliefs of daily life. All such general principles are believed because mankind have found innumerable instances of their truth and no instances of their falsehood. But this affords no evidence for their truth in the future, unless the inductive principle is assumed.

Thus all knowledge which, on a basis of experience tells us something about what is not experienced, is based upon a belief which experience can neither confirm nor confute, yet which, at least in its more concrete applications, appears to be as firmly rooted in us as many of the facts of experience. The existence and justification of such beliefs . . . raises some of the most difficult and most debated problems of philosophy.

SCEPTICISM

The Carvaka School

Inference, then, is now being examined—Well, what is inference? "Inference is preceded by it [perception]" (*Nyāya Sūtra* I.i.5).* Why is this so? It is explained thus: In a kitchen, one apprehends the relation between fire and smoke through the function of the eyes, etc. By this a connection between them is formed in the mind; thereafter, the sign [smoke] is perceived in something for a second time. Then one remembers the universal relation [between the smoke and fire]. After this, there is a consideration of the thing [the hill] as related to smoke which is pervaded by [universally related to] fire, and this leads to the inference [of fire in the thing] from the sign [the smoke].†

In the absence of one, there is an absence of the other, for the one precedes the other. In this world, no effect is seen to have taken place without its cause; perception is declared to be the cause, and in its absence how can there be any possibility of inference? If there were [such a] possibility, it would be a case of an event being produced without a cause. In the absence of perception, it is said, "It is impossible to apprehend an invariable relation [between events]."

There is another reason why the knowledge of an invariable relation cannot be established. Is it the cognition of a relation between two universals, or between two particulars, or between a universal and a particular? If it be the cognition of a relation between two universals, then that is incorrect for the universal itself is not demonstrated (*anupapatti*). That it is not demonstrated has already been shown. Nor is it possible to conceive of such a relation subsisting between a universal and a particular object because of the indemonstrability [or impossibility, *asaṁbhavāt*] of universals.

Nor is it [possible to think of] such a relation between two particulars for there are innumerable cases of particular fires and particular smokes, and also because [as proved by us] no common element exists among the many particulars. Even if that were possible, the numberlessness [of individual objects] would still persist. Or, if that [the numberlessness], too, were to disappear, then there would be no existence of particulars and, in their absence, tell me, by reference to what would the relation be apprehended?

Moreover, perception is not competent to establish any relation among particulars on account of the remoteness of time, place, and the essence [of things]. Nor is it possible to have any knowledge of a relation without the perception of the related terms, because that is the basis of the relation and of the knowledge of it. Nor is it the case that all the related terms are perceived at the time when the relation is being perceived, for they do not appear to be perceived at all [at the time]. It is not logical to regard something as perceived unless it appears to be perceived, as that would be an undue assumption; otherwise, when, as the result of a palatal perception, the taste of an object is being experienced, the perception of its color (*rūpa*) would also occur.

Well, then, if [it be argued that] the existence of such a relation could be apprehended in the case of a few particular objects that are present at the time of apprehending the relation of invariability, though not with regard to all of them, then only those particular objects [that are present at the time of perception] can be taken as signs (or marks, *gamaka*) [for inference], and not the others. A relation sub-

---

* The *Nyāya Sūtra* is a work of the Nyaya school of logicians, an orthodox Hindu group of thinkers who oppose the views of the Carvaka school (Eds.).
† That is, the connection observed in the kitchen leads to an inference that smoke on a hill indicates fire there (Eds.).

sisting between one pair of terms cannot serve as the ground of inference for another [pair], for that would be an undue extension. Indeed, a visual contact being established between the eye of Devadatta and a jar, no knowledge of water, etc., can be had, for it is an essential characteristic of a contact that it gives rise to the knowledge of an object with reference only to a particular time and place.

. . . Individual objects differ; hence, upon the contact of one, another cannot be perceived, due to the difference in their form. Should the difference in form not be recognized, all varieties of smoke on a mountain would fall into the category of smoke, which having taken place, the perception of smoke could not give rise to the inference of fire, because the relation [of invariability] subsisting between them is as unknown [to the perceiver] as it is to a resident of a Coconut Island. Without the knowledge of such a relation, the inferred fire is only like the god of the goblins.

If from the cognition of that which is related to fire [smoke] you argue to a cognition of the relation [between the two], then there is the fallacy of undue assumption [*atiprasaṅga*]. Therefore, the smokes are like the cognitions of the signs . . . [and this] cannot, on the right view, be explained in any way. Thus, in fact, why is it not acceptable that the knowledge of the one [smoke] does not depend upon the [knowledge of the] other [fire]? . . . [Well,

if it be argued that even without the cognition of the relation of interdependence, smoke by itself is competent to give rise to the knowledge of fire on a mountain], then, it is to be asked whether the smokeness in smoke has just arisen, or had arisen long before, or has arisen due to some other cause, or without any cause. . . . [In the absence of any conclusive factor to prove any one of the first three alternatives, the only alternative left is to believe] in the accidental rise of the phenomenon, for complex, indeed, is the nature of the universe. In the case of its being accidental, it is not valid to object that it will have no relation to a fixed time and place, for even in the case of the accidental rise of a phenomenon, its non-reference to time and place has not been observed. Thus, also, a phenomenon which has arisen without a cause can have its existence with reference to a particular time and place. Under such circumstances, even after the perception of smoke, there could be no inferential knowledge of fire, for it is simply not admissible.

QUESTION FOR DISCUSSION

1. Both Russell and the Carvaka philosophers seem to feel that the problem of induction is an insoluble problem. Are they correct? Why or why not?

THE PROBLEM OF METHOD

The question of method—that is to say, what method or methods prove best in assuring reliable knowledge—has both great practical and great theoretical importance. It therefore is one of the most central questions in epistemology. In the West and other industrialized parts of the world today, the methods of science are held in high esteem. In the first selection presented in this section, the turn-of-the-century American philosopher Charles Sanders Peirce (pronounced "Purse") attempts in a cheerfully open-minded manner to demonstrate why science is, for many purposes at least, superior to other methods of knowledge gathering or—to put the matter in his terms—for the "fixing of belief." In doing this, he very briefly sketches out some main features of the "method of scientific investigation." The question of whether the view of scientific investigation presented here really *is* the method employed by working scientists is left, however, unexamined by him.

If we are to believe the next two authors, this is not a clear-cut issue. After warning us to trust the deeds of scientists rather than what they say about their methods, the famous theoretical physicist Albert Einstein suggests that much of science involves the free play of the imagination. He nonetheless concludes that the mathematical description of the world, which has had so much success in physics, provides a master key to obtaining future knowledge—at least in that field. He also points out that, for science, experience remains the ultimate criterion of adequacy.

Contemporary philosopher Paul Feyerabend, however, finds himself unconvinced of this. In a selection taken from his critique of science, "Against Method," he claims that the scientists' decisions concerning the role that experience will play in their work are far more arbitrary than they are usually taken to be. There is no scientific method, argues Feyerabend; the claim that there is a single foolproof method in science is merely a piece of propaganda which scientists use to undercut their opponents.

So far the question of method has centered around science. But what of the knowledge imparted through art? Is it really knowledge? And how does it illuminate us? In a brilliant reflection on his craft, the contemporary Nigerian novelist Chinua Achebe tries to uncover the mystery of how a fictional account of the world might lead us to truth.

THE FIXATION OF BELIEF

Charles Sanders Peirce

GUIDING PRINCIPLES

The object of reasoning is to find out, from the consideration of what we already know, something else which we do not know. Consequently, reasoning is good if it be such as to give a true conclusion from true premises, and not otherwise. Thus, the question of validity is purely one of fact and not of thinking. A being the facts stated in the premisses and B being that concluded, the question is, whether these facts are really so related that if A were B would generally be. If so, the inference is valid; if not, not. It is not in the least the question whether, when the premisses are accepted by the mind, we feel an impulse to accept the conclusion also. It is true that we do generally reason correctly by nature. But that is an accident; the true conclusion would remain true if we had no impulse to accept it; and the false one would remain false, though we could not resist the tendency to believe in it.

We are, doubtless, in the main logical animals,

but we are not perfectly so. Most of us, for example, are naturally more sanguine and hopeful than logic would justify. We seem to be so constituted that in the absence of any facts to go upon we are happy and self-satisfied; so that the effect of experience is continually to contract our hopes and aspirations. Yet a lifetime of the application of this corrective does not usually eradicate our sanguine disposition. Where hope is unchecked by any experience, it is likely that our optimism is extravagant. Logicality in regard to practical matters (if this be understood, not in the old sense, but as consisting in a wise union of security with fruitfulness of reasoning) is the most useful quality an animal can possess, and might, therefore, result from the action of natural selection; but outside of these it is probably of more advantage to the animal to have his mind filled with pleasing and encouraging visions, independently of their truth; and thus, upon unpractical subjects, natural selection might occasion a fallacious tendency of thought.[1]

That which determines us, from given premisses, to draw one inference rather than another, is some habit of mind, whether it be constitutional or acquired. The habit is good or otherwise, according as it produces true conclusions from true premises or not; and an inference is regarded as valid or not, without reference to the truth or falsity of its conclusion specially, but according as the habit which determines it is such as to produce true conclusions in general or not. The particular habit of mind which governs this or that inference may be formulated in a proposition whose truth depends on the validity of the inferences which the habit determines; and such a formula is called a *guiding principle* of inference. Suppose, for example, that we observe that a rotating disk of copper quickly comes to rest when placed between the poles of a magnet, and we infer that this will happen with every disk of copper. The guiding principle is, that what is true of

one piece of copper is true of another. Such a guiding principle with regard to copper would be much safer than with regard to many other substances—brass, for example.

A book might be written to signalize all the most important of these guiding principles of reasoning. It would probably be, we must confess, of no service to a person whose thought is directed wholly to practical subjects, and whose activity moves along thoroughly-beaten paths. The problems that present themselves to such a mind are matters of routine which he has learned once for all to handle in learning his business. But let a man venture into an unfamiliar field, or where his results are not continually checked by experience, and all history shows that the most masculine intellect will oft times lose his orientation and waste his efforts in directions which bring him no nearer to his goal, or even carry him entirely astray. He is like a ship in the open sea, with no one on board who understands the rules of navigation. And in such a case some general study of the guiding principles of reasoning would be sure to be found useful.

The subject could hardly be treated, however, without being first limited; since almost any fact may serve as a guiding principle. But it so happens that there exists a division among facts, such that in one class are all those which are absolutely essential as guiding principles, while in the others are all which have any other interest as objects of research. This division is between those which are necessarily taken for granted in asking why a certain conclusion is thought to follow from certain premisses, and those which are not implied in such a question. A moment's thought will show that a variety of facts are already assumed when the logical question is first asked. It is implied, for instance, that there are such states of mind as doubt and belief—that a passage from one to the other is possible, the object of thought remaining the same, and that this transition is subject to some rules by which all minds are alike bound. As these are facts which we must already know before we can have any clear conception of reasoning at all, it cannot be supposed to be any longer of much interest to inquire into their

---

[1] Let us not, however, be cocksure that natural selection is the only factor of evolution; and until this momentous proposition has been much better proved than as yet it has been, let it not blind us to the force [of] very sound reasoning.—1903.

truth or falsity. On the other hand, it is easy to believe that those rules of reasoning which are deduced from the very idea of the process are the ones which are the most essential; and, indeed, that so long as it conforms to these it will, at least, not lead to false conclusions from true premises. In point of fact, the importance of what may be deduced from the assumptions involved in the logical question turns out to be greater than might be supposed, and this for reasons which it is difficult to exhibit at the outset. The only one which I shall here mention is, that conceptions which are really products of logical reflection, without being readily seen to be so, mingle with our ordinary thoughts, and are frequently the causes of great confusion. This is the case, for example, with the conception of quality. A quality, as such, is never an object of observation. We can see that a thing is blue or green, but the quality of being blue and the quality of being green are not things which we see; they are products of logical reflections. The truth is, that common-sense, or thought as it first emerges above the level of the narrowly practical, is deeply imbued with that bad logical quality to which the epithet *metaphysical* is commonly applied; and nothing can clear it up but a severe course of logic.

DOUBT AND BELIEF

We generally know when we wish to ask a question and when we wish to pronounce a judgment, for there is a dissimilarity between the sensation of doubting and that of believing.

But this is not all which distinguishes doubt from belief. There is a practical difference. Our beliefs guide our desires and shape our actions. The Assassins, or followers of the Old Man of the Mountain, used to rush into death at his least command, because they believed that obedience to him would insure everlasting felicity. Had they doubted this, they would not have acted as they did. So it is with every belief, according to its degree. The feeling of believing is a more or less sure indication of there being established in our nature some habit which

will determine our actions.[2] Doubt never has such an effect.

Nor must we overlook a third point of difference. Doubt is an uneasy and dissatisfied state from which we struggle to free ourselves and pass into the stage of belief; while the latter is a calm and satisfactory state which we do not wish to avoid, or to change to a belief in anything else. On the contrary, we cling tenaciously, not merely to believing, but to believing just what we do believe.

Thus, both doubt and belief have positive effects upon us, though very different ones. Belief does not make us act at once, but puts us into such a condition that we shall behave in some certain way, when the occasion arises. Doubt has not the least such active effect, but stimulates us to inquiry until it is destroyed. This reminds us of the irritation of a nerve and the reflex action produced thereby; while for the analogue of belief, in the nervous system, we must look to what are called nervous associations—for example, to that habit of the nerves in consequence of which the smell of a peach will make the mouth water.

THE END OF INQUIRY

The irritation of doubt causes a struggle to attain a state of belief. I shall term this struggle *Inquiry,* though it must be admitted that this is sometimes not a very apt designation.

The irritation of doubt is the only immediate motive for the struggle to attain belief. It is certainly best for us that our beliefs should be such as may truly guide our actions so as to satisfy our desires; and this reflection will make us reject every belief which does not seem to have been so formed as to

---

[2]Doubt, however, is not usually hesitancy about what is to be done then and there. It is anticipated hesitancy about what I shall do hereafter, or a feigned hesitancy about a fictitious state of things. It is the power of making believe we hesitate, together with the pregnant fact that the decision upon the merely make-believe dilemma goes toward forming a bona fide habit that will be operative in a real emergency. It is these two things in conjunction that constitute us intellectual beings.

insure this result. But it will only do so by creating a doubt in the place of that belief. With the doubt, therefore, the struggle begins, and with the cessation of doubt it ends. Hence, the sole object of inquiry is the settlement of opinion. We may fancy that this is not enough for us, and that we seek, not merely an opinion, but a true opinion. But put this fancy to the test, and it proves groundless; for as soon as a firm belief is reached we are entirely satisfied, whether the belief be true or false. And it is clear that nothing out of the sphere of our knowledge can be our object, for nothing which does not affect the mind can be the motive for mental effort. The most that can be maintained is, that we seek for a belief that we shall *think* to be true. But we think each one of our beliefs to be true, and, indeed, it is mere tautology to say so.[3]

That the settlement of opinion is the sole end of inquiry is a very important proposition. It sweeps away, at once, various vague and erroneous conceptions of proof. A few of these may be noticed here.

1. Some philosophers have imagined that to start an inquiry it was only necessary to utter a question whether orally or by setting it down upon paper, and have even recommended us to begin our studies with questioning everything! But the mere putting of a proposition into the interrogative form does not stimulate the mind to any struggle after belief. There must be a real and living doubt, and without this all discussion is idle.

2. It is a very common idea that a demonstration must rest on some ultimate and absolutely indubitable propositions. These, according to one school, are first principles of a general nature; according to another, are first sensations. But, in point of fact, an inquiry, to have that completely

satisfactory result called demonstration, has only to start with propositions perfectly free from all actual doubt. If the premises are not in fact doubted at all, they cannot be more satisfactory than they are.[4]

3. Some people seem to love to argue a point after all the world is fully convinced of it. But no further advance can be made. When doubt ceases, mental action on the subject comes to an end; and, if it did go on, it would be without a purpose.

METHODS OF FIXING BELIEF

If the settlement of opinion is the sole object of inquiry, and if belief is of the nature of a habit, why should we not attain the desired end, by taking as answer to a question any we may fancy, and constantly reiterating it to ourselves, dwelling on all which may conduce to that belief, and learning to turn with contempt and hatred from anything that might disturb it? This simple and direct method is really pursued by many men. I remember once being entreated not to read a certain newspaper lest it might change my opinion upon free-trade. "Lest I might be entrapped by its fallacies and misstatements," was the form of expression. "You are not," my friend said "a special student of political economy. You might, therefore, easily be deceived by fallacious arguments upon the subject. You might, then, if you read this paper, be led to believe in protection. But you admit that free-trade is the true doctrine; and you do not wish to believe what is not true." I have often known this system to be deliberately adopted. Still oftener, the instinctive dislike of an undecided state of mind, exaggerated into a vague dread of doubt, makes men cling spasmodi-

---

[3]For truth is neither more nor less than that character of a proposition which consists in this, that belief in the proposition would, with sufficient experience and reflection, lead us to such conduct as would tend to satisfy the desires we should then have. To say that truth means more than this is to say that it has no meaning at all.—1903.

[4]We have to acknowledge that doubts about them may spring up later; but we can find no propositions which are not subject to this contingency. We ought to construct our theories so as to provide for such discoveries; first, by making them rest on as great a variety of different considerations as possible, and second, by leaving room for the modifications which cannot be foreseen but which are pretty sure to prove needful.

cally to the views they already take. The man feels that, if he only holds to his belief without wavering, it will be entirely satisfactory. Nor can it be denied that a steady and immovable faith yields great peace of mind. It may, indeed, give rise to inconveniences, as if a man should resolutely continue to believe that fire would not burn him, or that he would be eternally damned if he received his *ingesta* otherwise than through a stomach-pump. But then the man who adopts this method will not allow that its inconveniences are greater than its advantages. He will say, "I hold steadfastly to the truth, and the truth is always wholesome." And in many cases it may very well be that the pleasure he derives from his calm faith overbalances any inconveniences resulting from its deceptive character. Thus, if it be true that death is annihilation, then the man who believes that he will certainly go straight to heaven when he dies, provided he have fulfilled certain simple observances in this life, has a cheap pleasure which will not be followed by the least disappointment. A similar consideration seems to have weight with many persons in religious topics, for we frequently hear it said, "Oh, I could not believe so-and-so, because I should be wretched if I did." When an ostrich buries its head in the sand as danger approaches, it very likely takes the happiest course. It hides the danger, and then calmly says there is no danger; and, if it feels perfectly sure there is none, why should it raise its head to see? A man may go through life, systematically keeping out of view all that might cause a change in his opinions, and if he only succeeds—basing his method, as he does, on two fundamental psychological laws—I do not see what can be said against his doing so. It would be an egotistical impertinence to object that his procedure is irrational, for that only amounts to saying that his method of settling belief is not ours. He does not propose to himself to be rational, and, indeed, will often talk with scorn of man's weak and illusive reason. So let him think as he pleases.

But this method of fixing belief, which may be called the method of tenacity, will be unable to hold its ground in practice. The social impulse is against it. The man who adopts it will find that other men think differently from him, and it will be apt to occur to him, in some saner moment, that their opinions are quite as good as his own, and this will shake his confidence in his belief. This conception, that another man's thought or sentiment may be equivalent to one's own, is a distinctly new step, and a highly important one. It arises from an impulse too strong in man to be suppressed, without danger of destroying the human species. Unless we make ourselves hermits, we shall necessarily influence each other's opinions; so that the problem becomes how to fix belief, not in the individual merely, but in the community.

Let the will of the state act, then, instead of that of the individual. Let an institution be created which shall have for its object to keep correct doctrines before the attention of the people, to reiterate them perpetually, and to teach them to the young; having at the same time power to prevent contrary doctrines from being taught, advocated, or expressed. Let all possible causes of a change of mind be removed from men's apprehensions. Let them be kept ignorant, lest they should learn of some reason to think otherwise than they do. Let their passions be enlisted, so that they may regard private and unusual opinions with hatred and horror. Then, let all men who reject the established belief be terrified into silence. Let the people turn out and tar-and-feather such men, or let inquisitions be made into the manner of thinking of suspected persons, and when they are found guilty of forbidden beliefs, let them be subjected to some signal punishment. When complete agreement could not otherwise be reached, a general massacre of all who have not thought in a certain way has proved a very effective means of settling opinion in a country. If the power to do this be wanting, let a list of opinions be drawn up, to which no man of the least independence of thought can assent, and let the faithful be required to accept all these propositions, in order to segregate them as radically as possible from the influence of the rest of the world.

This method has, from the earliest times, been one of the chief means of upholding correct theological and political doctrines, and of preserving their universal or catholic character. In Rome, especially, it has been practised from the days of Numa Pompilius to those of Pius Nonus. This is the most perfect example in history; but wherever there is a priesthood—and no religion has been without one—this method has been more or less made use of. Wherever there is an aristocracy, or a guild, or any association of a class of men whose interests depend, or are supposed to depend, on certain propositions, there will be inevitably found some traces of this natural product of social feeling. Cruelties always accompany this system; and when it is consistently carried out, they become atrocities of the most horrible kind in the eyes of any rational man. Nor should this occasion surprise, for the officer of a society does not feel justified in surrendering the interests of that society for the sake of mercy, as he might his own private interests. It is natural, therefore, that sympathy and fellowship should thus produce a most ruthless power.

In judging this method of fixing belief, which may be called the method of authority, we must, in the first place, allow its immeasurable mental and moral superiority to the method of tenacity. Its success is proportionately greater; and, in fact, it has over and over again worked the most majestic results. The mere structures of stone which it has caused to be put together—in Siam, for example, in Egypt, and in Europe—have many of them a sublimity hardly more than rivaled by the greatest works of Nature. And, except the geological epochs, there are no periods of time so vast as those which are measured by some of these organized faiths. If we scrutinize the matter closely, we shall find that there has not been one of their creeds which has remained always the same; yet the change is so slow as to be imperceptible during one person's life, so that individual belief remains sensibly fixed. For the mass of mankind, then, there is perhaps no better method than this. If it is their highest impulse to be intellectual slaves, then slaves they ought to remain.

But no institution can undertake to regulate opinions upon every subject. Only the most important ones can be attended to, and on the rest men's minds must be left to the action of natural causes. This imperfection will be no source of weakness so long as men are in such a state of culture that one opinion does not influence another—that is, so long as they cannot put two and two together. But in the most priest-ridden states some individuals will be found who are raised above that condition. These men possess a wider sort of social feeling; they see that men in other countries and in other ages have held to very different doctrines from those which they themselves have been brought up to believe; and they cannot help seeing that it is the mere accident of their having been taught as they have, and of their having been surrounded with the manners and associations they have, that has caused them to believe as they do and not far differently. Nor can their candour resist the reflection that there is no reason to rate their own views at a higher value than those of other nations and other centuries; thus giving rise to doubts in their minds.

They will further perceive that such doubts as these must exist in their minds with reference to every belief which seems to be determined by the caprice either of themselves or of those who originated the popular opinions. The willful adherence to a belief, and the arbitrary forcing of it upon others, must, therefore, both be given up. A different new method of settling opinions must be adopted, that shall not only produce an impulse to believe, but shall also decide what proposition it is which is to be believed. Let the action of natural preferences be unimpeded, then, and under their influence let men, conversing together and regarding matters in different lights, gradually develop beliefs in harmony with natural causes. This method resembles that by which conceptions of art have been brought to maturity. The most perfect example of it is to be found in the history of metaphysical philosophy. Systems of this sort have not usually rested upon any observed facts, at least not in any great degree. They have been chiefly adopted because their fundamental propositions seemed "agreeable to reason." This is an apt expression; it does not mean that which agrees with experience, but that which we find ourselves inclined to believe. Plato, for example, finds it agreeable to reason that the distances of the celestial spheres from one another should be proportional to the different lengths of strings which produce harmonious chords. Many philosophers have been led to their main conclusions by considerations like this[5]; but this is the lowest and least developed form which the method takes, for it is clear that another man might find Kepler's theory, that the celestial spheres are proportional to the inscribed and circumscribed spheres of the different regular solids, more agreeable to *his* reason. But the shock of opinions will soon lead men to rest on preferences of a far more universal nature. Take, for example, the doctrine that man only acts selfishly— that is, from the consideration that acting in one way will afford him more pleasure than acting in another. This rests on no fact in the world, but it has had a wide acceptance as being the only reasonable theory.

This method is far more intellectual and respectable from the point of view of reason than either of the others which we have noticed. Indeed, as long as no better method can be applied, it ought to be followed, since it is then the expression of instinct which must be the ultimate cause of belief in all cases. But its failure has been the most manifest. It makes of inquiry something similar to the development of taste; but taste, unfortunately, is always more or less a matter of fashion, and accordingly metaphysicians have never come to any fixed agreement, but the pendulum has swung backward and forward between a more material and a more spiritual philosophy, from the earliest times to the latest. And so from this, which has been called the *a*

priori method, we are driven, in Lord Bacon's phrase, to a true induction. We have examined this *a priori* method as something which promised to deliver our opinions from their accidental and capricious element. But development, while it is a process which eliminates the effect of some casual circumstances, only magnifies that of others. This method, therefore, does not differ in a very essential way from that of authority. The government may not have lifted its finger to influence my convictions; I may have been left outwardly quite free to choose, we will say, between monogamy and polygamy, and, appealing to my conscience only, I may have concluded that the latter practice is in itself licentious. But when I come to see that the chief obstacle to the spread of Christianity among a people of as high culture as the Hindoos has been a conviction of the immorality of our way of treating women, I cannot help seeing that, though governments do not interfere, sentiments in their development will be very greatly determined by accidental causes. Now, there are some people, among whom I must suppose that my reader is to be found, who, when they see that any belief of theirs is determined by any circumstance extraneous to the facts, will from that moment not merely admit in words that that belief is doubtful, but will experience a real doubt of it, so that it ceases in some degree at least to be a belief.

To satisfy our doubts, therefore, it is necessary that a method should be found by which our beliefs may be determined by nothing human, but by some external permanency—by something upon which our thinking has no effect. Some mystics imagine that they have such a method in a private inspiration from on high. But that is only a form of the method of tenacity, in which the conception of truth as something public is not yet developed. Our external permanency would not be external, in our sense, if it was restricted in its influence to one individual. It must be something which affects, or might affect, every man. And, though these affections are necessarily as various as are individual conditions, yet the method must be such that the ultimate conclusion of every man shall be the same. Such is the

---

[5]Let us see in what manner a few of the greatest philosophers have undertaken to settle opinion, and what their success has been. Descartes, who would have a man begin by doubting everything, remarks that there is one thing he will find himself unable to doubt, and that is, that he does doubt; and when he reflects that he doubts, he can no longer doubt that he exists. Then, because he is all the while doubting whether there are any such things as shape and motion, Descartes thinks he must be persuaded that shape and motion do not belong to his nature, or anything else but consciousness. This is taking it for granted that nothing in his nature lies hidden beneath the surface.

method of science. Its fundamental hypothesis, re-stated in more familiar language, is this: There are Real things, whose characters are entirely independent of our opinions about them; those Reals affect our senses according to regular laws, and, though our sensations are as different as are our relations to the objects, yet, by taking advantage of the laws of perception, we can ascertain by reasoning how things really and truly are; and any man, if he have sufficient experience and he reason enough about it, will be led to the one True conclusion. The new conception here involved is that of Reality. It may be asked how I know that there are any Reals. If this hypothesis is the sole support of my method of inquiry, my method of inquiry must not be used to support my hypothesis. The reply is this: (1) If investigation cannot be regarded as proving that there are Real things, it at least does not lead to a contrary conclusion; but the method and the conception on which it is based remain ever in harmony. No doubts of the method, therefore, necessarily arise from its practice, as is the case with all the others. (2) The feeling which gives rise to any method of fixing belief is a dissatisfaction at two repugnant propositions. But here already is a vague concession that there is some *one* thing which a proposition should represent. Nobody, therefore, can really doubt there are Reals, for, if he did, doubt would not be a source of dissatisfaction. The hypothesis, therefore, is one which every mind admits. So that the social impulse does not cause men to doubt it. (3) Everybody uses the scientific method about a great many things, and only ceases to use it when he does not know how to apply it. (4) Experience of the method has not led us to doubt it, but, on the contrary, scientific investigation has had the most wonderful triumphs in the way of settling opinion. These afford the explanation of my not doubting the method or the hypothesis which it supposes; and not having any doubt, nor believing that anybody else whom I could influence has, it would be the merest babble for me to say more about it. If there be anybody with a living doubt upon the subject, let him consider it.

To describe the method of scientific investiga-tion is the object of this series of papers. At present I have only room to notice some points of contrast between it and other methods of fixing belief.

This is the only one of the four methods which presents any distinction of a right and a wrong way. If I adopt the method of tenacity, and shut myself out from all influences, whatever I think necessary to doing this, is necessary according to that method. So with the method of authority: the state may try to put down heresy by means which, from a scientific point of view, seem very ill-calculated to accomplish its purposes; but the only test *on that method* is what the state thinks; so that it cannot pursue the method wrongly. So with the *a priori* method. The very essence of it is to think as one is inclined to think. All metaphysicians will be sure to do that, however they may be inclined to judge each other to be perversely wrong. The Hegelian system recognizes every natural tendency of thought as logical, although it be certain to be abolished by counter-tendencies. Hegel thinks there is a regular system in the succession of these tendencies, in consequence of which, after drifting one way and the other for a long time, opinion will at last go right. And it is true that metaphysicians do get the right ideas at last; Hegel's system of Nature represents tolerably the science of his day; and one may be sure that whatever scientific investigation shall have put out of doubt will presently receive *a priori* demonstration on the part of the metaphysicians. But with the scientific method the case is different. I may start with known and observed facts to proceed to the unknown; and yet the rules which I follow in doing so may not be such as investigation would approve. The test of whether I am truly following the method is not an immediate appeal to my feelings and purposes, but, on the contrary, itself involves the application of the method. Hence it is that bad reasoning as well as good reasoning is possible; and this fact is the foundation of the practical side of logic.

It is not to be supposed that the first three methods of settling opinion present no advantage whatever over the scientific method. On the contrary, each has some peculiar convenience of its own. The *a priori* method is distinguished for its comfortable conclusions. It is the nature of the process to adopt whatever belief we are inclined to, and there are certain flatteries to the vanity of man which we all believe by nature, until we are awakened from our pleasing dream by rough facts. The method of authority will always govern the mass of mankind; and those who wield the various forms of organized force in the state will never be convinced that dangerous reasoning ought not to be suppressed in some way. If liberty of speech is to be untrammeled from the grosser forms of constraint, then uniformity of opinion will be secured by a moral terrorism to which the respectability of society will give its thorough approval. Following the method of authority is the path of peace. Certain non-conformities are permitted; certain others (considered unsafe) are forbidden. These are different in different countries and in different ages; but, wherever you are, let it be known that you seriously hold a tabooed belief, and you may be perfectly sure of being treated with a cruelty less brutal but more refined than hunting you like a wolf. Thus, the greatest intellectual benefactors of mankind have never dared, and dare not now, to utter the whole of their thought; and thus a shade of *prima facie* doubt is cast upon every proposition which is considered essential to the security of society. Singularly enough, the persecution does not all come from without; but a man torments himself and is oftentimes most distressed at finding himself believing propositions which he has been brought up to regard with aversion. The peaceful and sympathetic man will, therefore, find it hard to resist the temptation to submit his opinions to authority. But most of all I admire the method of tenacity for its strength, simplicity, and directness. Men who pursue it are distinguished for their decision of character, which becomes very easy with such a mental rule. They do not waste time in trying to make up their minds what they want, but, fastening like lightning upon whatever alternative comes first, they hold to it to the end, whatever happens, without an instant's irresolution. This is one of the splendid qualities which generally accompany brilliant, unlasting success. It is impos-

sible not to envy the man who can dismiss reason, although we know how it must turn out at last.

• • •

Yes, the other methods do have their merits: a clear logical conscience does cost something—just as any virtue, just as all that we cherish, costs us dear. But we should not desire it to be otherwise. The genius of a man's logical method should be loved and reverenced as his bride, whom he has chosen from all the world. He need not contemn the others; on the contrary, he may honor them deeply, and in doing so he only honors her the more. But she is the one that he has chosen, and he knows that he was right in making that choice. And having made it, he will work and fight for her, and will not complain that there are blows to take, hoping that there may be as many and as hard to give, and will strive to be the worthy knight and champion of her from the blaze of those splendors he draws his inspiration and his courage.

CREATIVITY AND SCIENCE

Albert Einstein

ON THE METHOD OF THEORETICAL PHYSICS

The Herbert Spencer lecture, delivered at Oxford, June 10, 1933. Published in Mein Weltbild, *Amsterdam: Querido Verlag, 1934.*

If you want to find out anything from the theoretical physicists about the methods they use, I advise you to stick closely to one principle: don't listen to their words, fix your attention on their deeds. To him who is a discoverer in this field, the products of his imagination appear so necessary and natural that he regards them, and would like to have them regarded by others, not as creations of thought but as given realities.

These words sound like an invitation to you to walk out of this lecture. You will say to yourselves, the fellow's a working physicist himself and ought therefore to leave all questions of the structure of theoretical science to the epistemologists.

Against such criticism I can defend myself from the personal point of view by assuring you that it is not at my own instance but at the kind invitation of others that I have mounted this rostrum, which serves to commemorate a man who fought hard all his life for the unity of knowledge. Objectively, however, my enterprise can be justified on the ground that it may, after all, be of interest to know how one who has spent a lifetime in striving with all his might to clear up and rectify its fundamentals looks upon his own branch of science. The way in which he regards its past and present may depend too much on what he hopes for the future and aims at in the present; but that is the inevitable fate of anybody who has occupied himself intensively with a world of ideas. The same thing happens to him as to the historian, who in the same way, even though perhaps unconsciously, groups actual events round ideals which he has formed for himself on the subject of human society.

Let us now cast an eye over the development of the theoretical system, paying special attention to the relations between the content of the theory and the totality of empirical fact. We are concerned with the eternal antithesis between the two inseparable components of our knowledge, the empirical and the rational, in our department.

We reverence ancient Greece as the cradle of western science. Here for the first time the world witnessed the miracle of a logical system which proceeded from step to step with such precision that every single one of its propositions was absolutely indubitable—I refer to Euclid's geometry. This admirable triumph of reasoning gave the human intellect the necessary confidence in itself for its subsequent achievements. If Euclid failed to kindle your youthful enthusiasm, then you were not born to be a scientific thinker.

But before mankind could be ripe for a science which takes in the whole of reality, a second fundamental truth was needed, which only became common property among philosophers with the advent of Kepler and Galileo. Pure logical thinking cannot yield us any knowledge of the empirical world; all knowledge of reality starts from experience and ends in it. Propositions arrived at by purely logical means are completely empty as regards reality. Because Galileo saw this, and particularly because he drummed it into the scientific world, he is the father of modern physics—indeed, of modern science altogether.

If, then, experience is the alpha and the omega of all our knowledge of reality, what is the function of pure reason in science?

A complete system of theoretical physics is made up of concepts, fundamental laws which are supposed to be valid for those concepts and conclusions to be reached by logical deduction. It is these conclusions which must correspond with our separate experiences; in any theoretical treatise their logical deduction occupies almost the whole book.

This is exactly what happens in Euclid's geometry, except that there the fundamental laws are called axioms and there is no question of the conclusions having to correspond to any sort of experience. If, however, one regards Euclidean geometry as the science of the possible mutual relations of practically rigid bodies in space, that is to say, treats it as a physical science, without abstracting from its original empirical content, the logical homogeneity of geometry and theoretical physics becomes complete.

We have thus assigned to pure reason and experience their places in a theoretical system of physics. The structure of the system is the work of reason; the empirical contents and their mutual relations must find their representation in the conclusions of the theory. In the possibility of such a representation lie the sole value and justification of the whole system, and especially of the concepts and fundamental principles which underlie it. Apart from that, these latter are free inventions of the human intellect, which cannot be justified either by the nature of that intellect or in any other fashion *a priori*.

These fundamental concepts and postulates, which cannot be further reduced logically, form the essential part of a theory, which reason cannot touch. It is the grand object of all theory to make these irreducible elements as simple and as few in number as possible, without having to renounce the adequate representation of any empirical content whatever.

The view I have just outlined of the purely fictitious character of the fundamentals of scientific theory was by no means the prevailing one in the eighteenth and nineteenth centuries. But it is steadily gaining ground from the fact that the distance in thought between the fundamental concepts and laws on one side and, on the other, the conclusions which have to be brought into relation with our experience grows larger and larger, the simpler the logical structure becomes—that is to say, the smaller the number of logically independent conceptual elements which are found necessary to support the structure.

Newton, the first creator of a comprehensive, workable system of theoretical physics, still believed that the basic concepts and laws of his system could be derived from experience. This is no doubt the meaning of his saying, *hypotheses non fingo*.

Actually the concepts of time and space appeared at that time to present no difficulties. The concepts of mass, inertia, and force, and the laws connecting them, seemed to be drawn directly from experience. Once this basis is accepted, the expression for the force of gravitation appears derivable from experience, and it was reasonable to expect the same in regard to other forces.

We can indeed see from Newton's formulation of it that the concept of absolute space, which comprised that of absolute rest, made him feel uncomfortable; he realized that there seemed to be nothing in experience corresponding to this last concept. He was also not quite comfortable about the introduction of forces operating at a distance. But the tremendous practical success of his doctrines may

well have prevented him and the physicists of the eighteenth and nineteenth centuries from recognizing the fictitious character of the foundations of his system.

The natural philosophers of those days were, on the contrary, most of them possessed with the idea that the fundamental concepts and postulates of physics were not in the logical sense free inventions of the human mind but could be deduced from experience by "abstraction"—that is to say, by logical means. A clear recognition of the erroneousness of this notion really only came with the general theory of relativity, which showed that one could take account of a wider range of empirical facts, and that, too, in a more satisfactory and complete manner, on a foundation quite different from the Newtonian. But quite apart from the question of the superiority of one or the other, the fictitious character of fundamental principles is perfectly evident from the fact that we can point to two essentially different principles, both of which correspond with experience to a large extent; this proves at the same time that every attempt at a logical deduction of the basic concepts and postulates of mechanics from elementary experiences is doomed to failure.

If, then, it is true that the axiomatic basis of theoretical physics cannot be extracted from experience but must be freely invented, can we ever hope to find the right way? Nay, more, has this right way any existence outside our illusions? Can we hope to be guided safely by experience at all when there exist theories (such as classical mechanics) which to a large extent do justice to experience, without getting to the root of the matter? I answer without hesitation that there is, in my opinion, a right way, and that we are capable of finding it. Our experience hitherto justifies us in believing that nature is the realization of the simplest conceivable mathematical ideas. I am convinced that we can discover by means of purely mathematical constructions the concepts and the laws connecting them with each other, which furnish the key to the understanding of natural phenomena. Experience may suggest the appropriate mathematical concepts, but they most certainly cannot be deduced from it. Experience remains, of course, the sole criterion of the physical utility of a mathematical construction. But the creative principle resides in mathematics.

AGAINST METHOD

Paul Feyerabend

The following essay has been written in the conviction that *anarchism,* while perhaps not the most attractive *political* philosophy, is certainly an excellent foundation for *epistemology,* and for the *philosophy of science.*

The reason is not difficult to find.

"History generally, and the history of revolutions in particular, is always richer in content, more varied, more manysided, more lively and 'subtle' than even" the best historian and the best methodologist can imagine.[1] "Accidents and conjunctures, and curious juxtapositions of events"[2] are the very substance of history, and the "complexity of human change and the unpredictable character of the ultimate consequences of any given act or decision of men"[3] its most conspicuous feature. Are we really to believe that a bunch of rather naive and simple-minded rules will be capable of explaining such a "maze of interactions"?[4] And is it not clear that a person who *participates* in a complex process of this kind will succeed only if he is a ruthless *opportunist,* and capable of quickly changing from one method to another?

This is indeed the lesson that has been drawn by intelligent and thoughtful observers. "From this [character of the historical process]," writes Lenin, continuing the passage just quoted, "follow two very important practical conclusions: first, that in order to fulfill its task, the revolutionary class [i.e., the class of those who want to change either a part of society, such as science, or society as a whole] must be able to master *all* forms and sides of social activity [it must be able to understand, and to apply not only one particular methodology, but any methodology, and any variation thereof it can imagine], without exception; second, [it] must be ready to pass from one to another in the quickest and most unexpected manner."[5] "The external conditions," writes Einstein, "which are set for [the scientist] by the facts of experience do not permit him to let himself be too much restricted in the construction of his conceptual world by the adherence to an epistemological system. He therefore must appear to the systematic epistemologist as a type of unscrupulous opportunist . . ."[6]

The difference between epistemological (political, theological) *theory* and scientific (political, religious) *practice* that emerges from these quotations is usually formulated as a difference between "certain and infallible" (or, at any rate, clear, systematic, and objective) *rules,* or *standards,* and "our fallible and uncertain faculties [which] depart from them and fall into error."[7] Science as it should be, third-world science,[8] agrees with the proscribed rules. Science as we actually find it in history is a combination of such rules and of *error.* It follows that the scientist who works in a particular historical situation must learn how to recognize error and how to live with it, always keeping in mind that he himself

---

[1]V. I. Lenin, *'Left Wing' Communism, an Infantile Disorder* (Peking: Foreign Language Press, 1965), p. 100. Lenin speaks of parties and the revolutionary vanguard rather than of scientists and methodologists. The lesson is, however, the same.
[2]H. Butterfield, *The Whig Interpretation of History* (New York: Norton, 1965), p. 66.
[3]*Ibid.,* p. 21.
[4]*Ibid.,* p. 25.

[5]Lenin, *'Left Wing' Communism,* p. 100. It is interesting to see how a few substitutions can turn a political lesson into a lesson for methodology which, after all, is part of the process by means of which we move from one historical stage to another.
[6]P. A. Schilpp, ed., *Albert Einstein, Philosopher-Scientist* (Evanston, Ill.: Tudor, 1948), p. 683.
[7]D. Hume, *A Treatise of Human Nature* (Oxford: Oxford University Press, 1888), p. 180.
[8]Popper and his followers distinguish between the socio-psychological process of science where errors abound and rules are constantly broken and a "third world" where knowledge is changed in a rational manner, and without interference from "mob psychology."

is liable to add fresh error at any stage of the investigation. He needs a *theory of error* in addition to the "certain and infallible" rules which define the "approach to the truth."

Now error, being an expression of the idiosyncrasies of an individual thinker, observer, even of an individual measuring instrument, *depends on* circumstances, on the particular phenomena or theories one wants to analyze, and it *develops* in highly unexpected ways. *Error is itself a historical phenomenon.* A theory of error will therefore contain rules of thumb, useful hints, heuristic suggestions rather than general laws, and it will relate these hints and these suggestions to historical episodes so that one sees in detail how some of them have led some people to success in some situations. It will develop the imagination of the student without ever providing him with cut-and-dried prescriptions and procedures. It will be more a collection of stories than a theory in the proper sense and it will contain a sizable amount of aimless gossip from which everyone may choose what fits in with his intentions. Good books on the art of recognizing and avoiding error will have much in common with good books on the art of singing, or boxing, or making love. Such books consider the great variety of character, of vocal (muscular, glandular, emotional) equipment, of personal idiosyncrasies, and they pay attention to the fact that each element of this variety may develop in most unexpected directions (a woman's voice may bloom forth after her first abortion). They contain numerous rules of thumb, useful hints, and they leave it to the reader to choose what fits his case. Clearly the reader will not be able to make the correct choice unless he has already *some* knowledge of vocal (muscular, emotional) matters and this knowledge he can acquire only by throwing himself into the process of learning and hoping for the best. In the case of singing he must start using his organs, his throat, his brain, his diaphragm, his buttocks before he really knows how to use them, and he must learn from their reactions the way of learning most appropriate to him. And this is true of all learning: choosing a certain way the student, or the "mature scientist," creates a situation as yet unknown to him from which he must

learn how best to approach situations of this kind. This is not as paradoxical as it sounds as long as we keep our options open and as long as we refuse to settle for a particular method, including a particular set of rules, without having examined alternatives. "Let people emancipate themselves," says Bakunin, "and they will instruct themselves of their own accord."[9] In the case of *science* the necessary tact can be developed only by *direct participation* (where "participation" means something different for different individuals) or, if such direct participation cannot be had, or seems undesirable, from a study of past episodes in the *history* of the subject. *Considering their great and difficult complexity these episodes must be approached with a novelist's love for character and for detail,* or with a gossip columnist's love for scandal and for surprising turns; they must be approached with insight into the positive function of strength as well as of weakness, of intelligence as well as of stupidity, of love for truth as well as of the will to deceive, of modesty as well as of conceit, rather than with the crude and laughably inadequate instruments of the logician. For nobody can say in abstract terms, without paying attention to idiosyncrasies of person and circumstance, what precisely it was that led to progress in the past, and nobody can say what moves will succeed in the future.

Now it is of course possible to simplify the historical medium in which a scientist works by simplifying its main actors. The history of science, after all, consists not only of facts and conclusions drawn therefrom. It consists also of ideas, interpretations of facts, problems created by a clash of interpretations, actions of scientists, and so on. On closer analysis we even find that there are no "bare facts" at all but that the facts that enter our knowledge are already viewed in a certain way and are therefore essentially ideational. This being the case the history of science will be as complex, as chaotic, as full of error, and as entertaining as the ideas it contains and these ideas in turn will be as complex, as

---

9E. H. Carr, *Michael Bakunin* (London: Macmillan, 1937), pp. 8–9.

chaotic, as full of error, and as entertaining as are the minds of those who invented them. Conversely, a little brainwashing will go a long way in making the history of science more simple, more uniform, more dull, more "objective," and more accessible to treatment by "certain and infallible" rules: a theory of errors is superfluous when we are dealing with well-trained scientists who are kept in place by an internal slave master called "professional conscience" and who have been convinced that it is good and rewarding to attain, and then to forever keep, one's "professional integrity."[10]

Scientific education as we know it today has precisely this purpose. It has the purpose of carrying out a rationalistic simplification of the process "science" by simplifying its participants. One proceeds as follows. First, a domain of research is defined. Next, the domain is separated from the remainder of history (physics, for example, is separated from metaphysics and from theology) and receives a "logic" of its own.[11] A thorough training in such a logic then conditions those working in the domain so that they may not unwittingly disturb the purity (read: the sterility) that has already been achieved. An essential part of the training is the inhibition of intuitions that might lead to a blurring of boundaries. A person's religion, for example, or his metaphysics, or his sense of humor must not have the slightest connection with his scientific activity. His imagination is restrained[12] and even his language will cease to be his own.[13]

It is obvious that such an education, such a cutting up of domains and of consciousness, cannot be easily reconciled with a humanitarian attitude. It is in conflict "with the cultivation of individuality which [alone] produces, or can produce well developed human beings";[14] it "maim[s] by compression, like a Chinese lady's foot, every part of human nature which stands out prominently, and tends to make a person markedly dissimilar in outline"[15] from the ideal of rationality that happens to be fashionable with the methodologists.

Now it is precisely such an ideal that finds expression either in "certain and infallible rules" or else in *standards* which separate what is correct, or rational, or reasonable, or "objective" from what is incorrect, or irrational, or unreasonable, or "subjective." Abandoning the ideal as being unworthy of a free man means abandoning standards and relying on theories of error entirely. Only these theories, these hints, these rules of thumb must now be renamed. Without universally enforced standards of truth and rationality we can no longer speak of universal error. We can only speak of what does, or does not, seem appropriate when viewed from a particular and restricted point of view, different views, temperaments, attitudes giving rise to different judgments and different methods of approach. Such an *anarchistic epistemology*—for this is what our theories of error now turn out to be—is not only a better means for improving knowledge, or of understanding history. It is also more appropriate for a free man to use than are its rigorous and "scientific" alternatives.

We need not fear that the diminished concern for law and order in science and society that is entailed by the use of anarchistic philosophies will lead to chaos. The human nervous system is too well organized for that.[16] Of course, there may arrive an

---

[10] Thus external pressure is replaced by bad conscience, and freedom remains restricted as before.

[11] "This unique prevalence of the *inner* logic of a subject over and above the *outer* influences is not . . . to be found at the beginning of modern science." H. Blumenberg, *Die Kopernikanische Wende* (Frankfurt: Suhrkamp, 1965), p. 8.

[12] "Nothing is more dangerous to reason than the flights of the imagination . . ." Hume, *A Treatise of Human Nature,* p. 267.

[13] An *expert* is a man or a woman who has decided to achieve excellence in a narrow field at the expense of a balanced development. He has decided to subject himself to standards which restrict him in many ways, his style of writing and the patterns of his speech included, and he is prepared to conduct most of his waking life in accordance with these standards (this being the case, it is likely that his dreams will be governed by these standards, too).

[14] John Stuart Mill, *On Liberty,* quoted from *The Philosophy of John Stuart Mill,* ed. Marshall Cohen (New York: Modern Library, 1961), p. 258.

[15] *Ibid.,* p. 265.

[16] Even in undetermined and ambiguous situations uniformity of action is soon achieved, and adhered to tenaciously. Cf. M. Sherif, *The Psychology of Social Norms* (New York: Harper Torchbooks, 1964).

epoch when it becomes necessary to give reason a temporary advantage and when it is wise to defend *its* rules to the exclusion of everything else. I do not think we are living in such an epoch today.

> When we see that we have arrived at the utmost extent of human [understanding] we sit down contented.   HUME[17]

> The more solid, well defined, and splendid the edifice erected by the understanding, the more restless the urge of life . . . to escape from it into freedom. [Appearing as] reason it is negative and dialectical, for it dissolves into nothing the detailed determinations of the understanding.   HEGEL[18]

> Although science taken as whole is a nuisance, one can still learn from it.   BENN[19]

• • •

The idea of a method that contains firm, unchanging, and absolutely binding principles for conducting the business of science gets into considerable difficulty when confronted with the results of historical research. We find, then, that there is not a single rule, however plausible, and however firmly grounded in epistemology, that is not violated at some time or other. It becomes evident that such violations are not accidental events, they are not the results of insufficient knowledge or of inattention which might have been avoided. On the contrary, we see that they are necessary for progress. Indeed, one of the most striking features of recent discussions in the history and philosophy of science is the realization that developments such as the Copernican Revolutions, or the rise of atomism in antiquity and recently (kinetic theory; dispersion theory; stereochemistry; quantum theory), or the gradual

emergence of the wave theory of light occurred either because some thinkers *decided* not to be bound by certain "obvious" methodological rules or because they *unwittingly broke* them.[20]

This liberal practice, I repeat, is not just a *fact* of the history of science. It is not merely a manifestation of human inconstancy and ignorance. It is reasonable *and absolutely necessary* for the growth of knowledge. More specifically, the following can be shown: considering any rule, however "fundamental," there are always circumstances when it is advisable not only to ignore the rule, but to adopt its opposite. For example, there are circumstances when it is advisable to introduce, elaborate, and defend ad hoc hypotheses, or hypotheses which contradict well-established and generally accepted experimental results, or hypotheses whose content is smaller than the content of the existing and empirically adequate alternatives, or self-inconsistent hypotheses, and so on.[21]

There are even circumstances—and they occur rather frequently—when *argument* loses its forward-looking aspect and becomes a hindrance to progress. Nobody wants to assert that the teaching of *small children* is exclusively a matter of argument (though argument may enter into it and should enter into it to a larger extent than is customary), and almost everyone now agrees that what looks like a result of reason—the mastery of a language, the existence of a richly articulated perceptual world, logical ability—is due partly to indoctrina-

---

[17] *A Treatise of Human Nature,* p. xxii. The word "reason" has been replaced by "understanding" in order to establish coherence with the terminology of the German idealists.

[18] The first part of the quotation, up to "appearing as," is taken from *Differenz des Fichte'schen und Schelling'schen Systems der Philosophie,* ed. G. Lasson (Hamburg: Felix Meiner, 1962), p. 13. The second part is from the *Wissenschaft der Logik,* vol. I (Hamburg: Felix Meiner, 1965), p. 6.

[19] Letter to Gert Micha Simon of October 11, 1949. Quoted from *Gottfried Benn, Lyrik und Prosa, Briefe und Dokuments* (Wiesbaden: Limes Verlag, 1962), p. 235.

[20] For details and further literature see "Problems of Empiricism, Part II," in *The Nature and Function of Scientific Theory,* ed. R. G. Colodny (Pittsburgh: University of Pittsburgh Press, 1970).

[21] One of the few physicists to see and to understand this feature of the development of scientific knowledge was Niels Bohr: ". . . he would never try to outline any finished picture, but would patiently go through all the phases of the development of a problem, starting from some apparent paradox, and gradually leading to its elucidation. In fact, he never regarded achieved results in any other light than as starting points for further exploration. In speculating about the prospects of some line of investigation, he would dismiss the usual considerations of simplicity, elegance or even consistency with the remark that such qualities can only be properly judged *after* [my italics] the event . . ." L. Rosenfeld in S. Rozental, ed., *Niels Bohr, His Life and Work as Seen by His Friends and Colleagues* (New York: Interscience, 1967), p. 117.

tion, partly to a process of *growth* that proceeds with the force of natural law. And where arguments do seem to have an effect this must often be ascribed to their *physical repetition* rather than to their *semantic content.*[22] This much having been admitted, we must also concede the possibility of non-argumentative growth in the *adult* as well as in (the theoretical parts of) *institutions* such as science, religion, and prostitution. We certainly cannot take it for granted that what is possible for a small child—to acquire new modes of behavior on the slightest provocation, to slide into them without any noticeable effort—is beyond the reach of his elders. One should expect that catastrophic changes of the physical environment, wars, the breakdown of encompassing systems of morality, political revolutions, will transform adult reaction patterns, too, including important patterns of argumentation. This may again be an entirely natural process and rational argument may but increase the mental tension that precedes and causes the behavioral outburst.

Now, if there are events, not necessarily arguments, which cause us to adopt new standards, including new and more complex forms of argumentation, will it then not be up to the defenders of the status quo to provide, not just arguments, but also contrary causes? (Virtue without terror is ineffective, says Robespierre.) And if the old forms of argumentation turn out to be too weak a cause, must not these defenders either give up or resort to stronger and more "irrational" means? (It is very difficult, and perhaps entirely impossible, to combat the effect of brainwashing by argument.) Even the most puritanical rationalist will then be forced

to stop reasoning and to use, say, *propaganda* and *coercion,* not because some of his *reasons* have ceased to be valid, but because the *psychological conditions* which make them effective, and capable of influencing others, have disappeared. And what is the use of an argument that leaves people unmoved?

Of course, the problem never arises quite in this form. The teaching of standards never consists in merely putting them before the mind of the student and making them as *clear* as possible. The standards are supposed to have maximal *causal efficacy* as well. This makes it very difficult to distinguish between the *logical force* and the *material effect* of an argument. Just as a well-trained pet will obey his master no matter how great the confusion he finds himself in and no matter how urgent the need to adopt new patterns of behavior, in the very same way a well-trained rationalist will obey the mental image of *his* master, he will conform to the standards of argumentation he has learned, he will adhere to these standards no matter how great the difficulty he finds himself in, and he will be quite unable to discover that what he regards as the "voice of reason" is but *a causal aftereffect* of the training he has received. We see here very clearly how the appeal to "reason" works. At first sight this appeal seems to be to some *ideas* which *convince* a man instead of *pushing* him. But conviction cannot remain an ethereal state; it is supposed to lead to *action*. It is supposed to lead to the *appropriate* action, and it is supposed to *sustain* this action as long as necessary. What is the force that upholds such a development? It is the causal efficacy of the standards to which appeal was made and this causal efficacy in turn is but an effect of training, as we have seen. It follows that appeal to argument either has no content at all, and can be made to agree with any procedure, or else will often have a conservative function: it will set limits to what is about to become a natural way of behavior. In the latter case, however, the appeal is nothing but a concealed *political maneuver.* This becomes very clear when a rationalist wants to restore an earlier point of view. Basing his argument on natural habits of reasoning which ei-

---

[22] Commenting on his early education by his father, and especially on the explanations he received on matters of logic, J. S. Mill made the following observations: "The explanations did not make the matter at all clear to me at the time; but they were not therefore useless; they remained as a nucleus for my observations and reflections to crystallize upon; the import of his general remarks being interpreted to me, by the particular instances which came under my notice afterwards." *Autobiography* (London: Oxford University Press, 1963), p. 16. In "Problems of Empiricism, Part II" I have argued that the development of science exhibits phase differences of precisely this kind.

ther have become extinct or have no point of attack in the new situation, such a champion of "rationality" must first restore the earlier material and psychological conditions. This, however, involves him in "a struggle of interests and forces, not of argument."[23]

That interests, forces, propaganda, brainwashing techniques play a much greater role in the growth of our knowledge and, a fortiori, of science than is commonly believed can also be seen from an analysis of the *relation between idea and action.* One often takes it for granted that a clear and distinct understanding of new ideas precedes and should precede any formulation and any institutional expression of them. (An investigation starts with a problem, says Popper.) *First,* we have an idea, or a problem; *then* we act, i.e., either speak, or build, or destroy. This is certainly not the way in which small children develop. They use words, they combine them, they play with them until they grasp a meaning that so far has been beyond their reach. And the initial playful activity is an essential presupposition of the final act of understanding. There is no reason why this mechanism should cease to function in the adult. On the contrary, we must expect, for example, that the *idea* of liberty could be made clear only by means of the very same actions which were supposed to *create* liberty. Creation of a *thing,* and creation plus full understanding of a *correct idea* of the thing, *very often are parts of one and the same indivisible process* and they cannot be separated without bringing the process to a standstill. The process itself is not guided by a well-defined program; it cannot be guided by such a program for it contains the conditions of the realization of programs. It is rather guided by a vague urge, by a "passion" (Kierkegaard). The passion gives rise to specific behavior which in turn creates the circumstances and the ideas necessary for analyzing and explaining the whole development, for making it "rational."

The development of the Copernican point of view from Galileo up to the twentieth century is a perfect example of the situation we want to describe. We start with a strong belief that runs counter to contemporary reason. The belief spreads and finds support from other beliefs which are equally unreasonable, if not more so (law of inertia; telescope). Research now gets deflected in new directions, new kinds of instruments are built, "evidence" is related to theories in new ways until there arises a new ideology that is rich enough to provide independent arguments for any particular part of it and mobile enough to find such arguments whenever they seem to be required. *Today* we can say that Galileo was on the right track, for his persistent pursuit of what once seemed to be a silly cosmology created the material needed for the defense of this cosmology against those of us who accept a view only if it is told in a certain way and who trust it only if it contains certain magical phrases, called "observational reports."[24] And this is not an exception—it is the normal case: theories become clear and "reasonable" only *after* incoherent parts of them have been used for a long time. Such unreasonable, nonsensical, unmethodical foreplay thus turns out to be an unavoidable precondition of clarity and of empirical success.[25]

Trying to describe developments of this kind in a general way, we are of course obliged to appeal to the existing forms of speech which do not take them into account and which must be distorted, misused, and beaten into new patterns in order to fit unfore-

---

[23] Leon Trotsky, *The Revolution Betrayed,* trans. M. Eastman (Garden City, N.Y.: Doubleday, 1937), pp. 86–87.

[24] The phrase "magical" is quite appropriate, for the inclusion of well-formed observational reports was demanded in books on magic, down to Agrippa's *De occulta philosophia.*

[25] Our understanding of ideas and concepts, says Hegel (*Gymnasialreden;* quoted from K. Loewith and J. Riedel, eds., *Hegel, Studienausgabe,* vol. I, Frankfurt: Fischer Bücherei, 1968, p. 54), starts with "an uncomprehended knowledge of them. . ."

It is also interesting to note to what extent Kierkegaard's ideas about the role of faith, passion, subjectivity apply to our scientific life (provided, of course, we are interested in fundamental discoveries, and not just in the preservation of the status quo, in methodology, and elsewhere). Cf. *Concluding Unscientific Postscript,* trans. David F. Swensen and Walter Lowrie (Princeton, N.J.: Princeton University Press, 1941), especially chapter II: "Truth as Subjectivity. . ."

seen situations (without a constant misuse of language there cannot be any discovery and any progress). "Moreover, since the traditional categories are the gospel of everyday thinking (including ordinary scientific thinking) and of everyday practice, [such an attempt at understanding] in effect presents rules and forms of false thinking and action—false, that is, from the standpoint of [scientific] commonsense."[26] This is how *dialectical thinking* arises as a form of thought that "dissolves into nothing the detailed determinations of the understanding."[27]

It is clear, then, that the idea of a fixed method, or of a fixed (theory of) rationality, arises from too naive a view of man and of his social surroundings. To those who look at the rich material provided by history, and who are not intent on impoverishing it in order to please their lower instincts, their craving for intellectual security as it is provided, for example, by clarity and precision, to such people it will seem that there is only *one* principle that can be defended under all circumstances, and in *all* stages of human development. It is the principle: *anything goes.*[28]

THE TRUTH OF FICTION

Chinua Achebe

Picasso once pronounced that all art was false. Since the West gave him credit for something like

90 percent of its twentieth-century artistic achievement, Picasso no doubt felt free to say whatever he liked on the matter! Even so, I believe he was merely drawing attention in the exaggerated manner of seers and prophets to the important but simple fact that art cannot be a carbon copy of life; and thus, in that specific sense, cannot be "true." And if not true, it must therefore be false!

But if art may dispense with the constraining exactitude of literal truth, it does acquire in return incalculable powers of persuasion in the imagination. Which was why a single canvas, *Guernica,* by Picasso himself could so frighten the state machinery of Spanish fascism. For how could a mere painting on canvas exercise such awe unless in some way it accorded with, or had a disquieting relationship to, recognizable reality? Unless, in other words, it spoke a kind of truth?

• • •

Actually, art is man's constant effort to create for himself a different order of reality from that which is given to him; an aspiration to provide himself with a second handle on existence *through his imagination.* For practical considerations, I shall limit myself to just one of the forms he has fashioned out of his experience with language—the art of fiction.

In his brilliant essay *The Sense of an Ending,* Frank Kermode defines fiction simply as "something we know does not exist but which helps us to make sense of, and move in, the world."[1] Defining it in this practical way does prepare us not for one but for many varieties of fiction. Kermode himself draws attention to some of them, for example the mathematical fiction of "infinity plus one" which does not exist and yet facilitates the solution of certain problems in pure mathematics; or the legal fiction in certain legal systems which holds that when a man and his wife die at the same time the law, in pursuit of equity, will pretend that the woman dies

---

[26] H. Marcuse, *Reason and Revolution* (London: Oxford University Press, 1941), p. 130. The quotation is about Hegel's logic.
[27] Cf. note 18.
[28] "It would be absurd to formulate a recipe or general rule . . . to serve all cases. One must use one's own brains and be able to find one's bearings in each separate case." Lenin, *'Left Wing' Communism,* p. 64.

The reader should remember that despite all my praise for Marxism and its various proponents I am defending its *anarchistic* elements only and that I am defending those elements only insofar as they can be used for a criticism of epistemological and moral rules.

[1] Frank Kermode, *The Sense of an Ending,* New York, Oxford University Press, 1967.

before her husband, so that excessive hardship may not be brought upon their estate.

In other words, we invent different fictions to help us out of particular problems we encounter in living. But of course these problems are not always as specific and clear-cut, or indeed as consciously perceived, as the lawyer's or the mathematician's formulations. When two very young children say to each other, "Let us pretend . . ." and begin to act such roles as father and mother they are obviously creating a fiction for a less definite, more spontaneous and, I dare say, more profound purpose.

• • •

Given the great gulf between being and knowing, between his essence and existence, man has no choice really but to make and believe in some fiction or other. Perhaps the ultimate judgement on a man is not whether he acquiesces to a fiction but rather what *kind* of fiction will persuade him into that acquiescence, that willing suspension of disbelief which Coleridge spoke about or that "experimental submission," to quote I. A. Richards.

However, we must not overlook the carefulness displayed by both Coleridge and Richards in their choice of words; and for a very good reason. Coleridge's disbelief is only *suspended,* not abolished, and will presumably return at the appropriate moment; and Richards's submission is experimental, not definitive or permanent.

It is important to stress this point because man makes not only fictions to which he gives guarded or temporary acquiescence like the pretending games of healthy children; he has the capacity also to create fictions that demand and indeed impose upon him absolute and unconditional obedience. I will shortly return to this, but first of all let me extend what I have said about man's desire for fictions to include the question of his capacity. Man's desire for fictions goes with his ability for making them, just as his need for language is inseparable from his capacity for speech. If man only had the need to speak but lacked his peculiar speech organs, he could not have invented language. For all we know, other animals in the jungle might be in just as much need to talk to one another as man ever was and

might have become just as eloquent had they been endowed with the elaborate apparatus for giving expression to that need. And certainly no one would suggest that the mute is silent because he has no need to speak or nothing to say. If we apply the same reasoning to man's propensity for fictions we can see that his need to create them would not adequately explain their existence; there must also be an effective apparatus.

This equipment, I suggest, is man's imagination. For just as man is a tool-making animal and has recreated his natural world with his tools, so is he a fiction-making animal and refashions his imaginative landscape with his fictions.

• • •

In the 1950s a Nigerian microbiologist, Dr. Sanya Onabamiro, published a book which he entitled, with great perspicacity, *Why Our Children Die,* echoing what must have been one of the most poignant and heartrending questions asked by our ancestors down the millennia. Why do our children die? Being a modern scientist, Dr. Onabamiro gave appropriate twentieth-century answers: disease, undernourishment and ignorance. Every reasonable person will accept that this "scientific" answer is more satisfactory than answers we might be given from other quarters. For example, a witch doctor might tell us that our children die because they are bewitched; because someone else in the family has offended a god or, in some other secret way, erred. Some years ago I watched the pitiful spectacle of an emaciated little child brought out and sat on a mat in the midst of the desperate *habitués* of a prayer-house while the prophetess with maniacal authority pronounced it possessed by the devil and ordered its parents to fast for seven days.

The point of these examples is to suggest two things: first, the richness, the sheer prodigality, of man's inventiveness in creating aetiological fictions; second, that not all his fictions are equally useful or desirable.

But first of all I must explain my temerity in thus appearing to lump together under the general rubric of fictions the cool, methodical and altogether marvellous procedures of modern medicine with the erratic "visions" of a religious psychopath. In all truth, the two ought never to be mentioned in the same breath. And yet they share, however remotely it may seem, the same need of man to explain and alleviate his intolerable condition. And they both make use of theories of disease—the germ theory, on the one hand, and the theory of diabolical possession, on the other. And theories are no more than fictions which help us to make sense of experience and which are subject to disconfirmation when their explanations are no longer adequate. There is no doubt, for instance, that scientists in the twenty-first and later centuries will look at some of the most cherished scientific notions of our day with the same amused indulgence that we show towards the fumblings of past generations.

And yet we can say, indeed we must say, that the insights given by Dr. Onabamiro into the problem of high infant mortality, however incomplete future generations may find them, are infinitely more helpful to us than the diagnosis of a half-mad religious fanatic. In conclusion, there are fictions that help and fictions that hinder. For simplicity, let us call them beneficent and malignant fictions.

• • •

Given our questioning nature the end of which is discovery, and given our existential limitations especially the vastness of our ignorance, one can begin to appreciate the immeasurable blessing that our imagination could confer on us. It is a truism and a cliché that experience is the best teacher; it is even arguable whether we can truly *know* anything which we have not personally experienced. But our imagination can narrow the existential gap by giving us in a wide range of human situations the closest approximation to experience that we are ever likely to get, and sometimes the safest too, as anyone who has travelled on Nigerian roads can tell you! For it is hardly desirable to be run over by a car in order to *know* that automobiles are dangerous.

• • •

The life of the imagination is a vital element of our total nature. If we starve it or pollute it the quality of our life is depressed or soiled.

We must not, however, celebrate the beauties of imagination and the beneficent fictions that are spun in its golden looms without mentioning the terrible danger to which it can be exposed.

Belief in superior and inferior races; belief that some people who live across our frontiers or speak a different language from ourselves are the cause of all the trouble in the world, or that our own particular group or class or caste has a right to certain things which are denied to others; the belief that men are superior to women, and so on—all are fictions generated by the imagination. What then makes them different from the beneficent fiction for which I am making rather large claims? One might reply: By their fruits, ye shall know them. Logically that may be a good answer, but strategically it is inadequate. For it might imply that Hitler should first commit genocide before we can conclude that racism is a horrendous evil, or that South Africa should go up in flames to confirm it. So we must find a criterion with an alarm system that screams red whenever we begin to spin virulent fictions.

Such an early-warning system is ready to hand and really quite simple. You remember the example of the children at play, how they preface their little drama by saying, "Let us pretend." What distinguishes beneficent fiction from such malignant cousins as racism is that the first never forgets that it is fiction and the other never knows that it is.

• • •

Malignant fictions like racial superiority, on the other hand, never say, "Let us pretend." They assert their fictions as a proven fact and a way of life. Holders of such fictions are really like lunatics, for while a sane person might act a play now and again a madman lives it permanently. Some people would describe malignant fictions as myths, but I find no justification for soiling the reputation of myths in that way. I would prefer to call malignant fictions by their proper name, which is superstitions. But whatever we call them, it is essential to draw a clear distinction between beneficent fiction and any arbitrary nonsense emanating from a sick imagination. Watching a magician and marvelling at his sleight of hand and management of optical tricks is something quite different from seeing him and *believing* that his powers derive from midnight visits to cemeteries or from reading the Sixth and Seventh Books of Moses.

• • •

The fiction which imaginative literature offers us does not enslave; it liberates the mind of man. Its truth is not like the canons of an orthodoxy or the irrationality of prejudice and superstition. It begins as an adventure in self-discovery and ends in wisdom and humane conscience.

QUESTIONS FOR DISCUSSION

1. Compare Peirce's account of science with that of Einstein. Are they, on your view, compatible? Why or why not?

2. Compare Feyerabend's views on method with those of Peirce. Compare his view with those expressed by Einstein.

3. Evaluate Feyerabend's claim that the only epistemological principle that can be adequately defended for all times and places is "Anything goes."

4. Discuss Achebe's distinction between "beneficent fictions" and "malignant fictions." Is the distinction, in your opinion, always easily drawn in the world?

MAO TSE-TUNG ON KNOWLEDGE AND PRACTICE

Marxism and the scientific attitude often entered modern Chinese thought together. The view that a scientific approach was adequate for the understanding of the world, coupled with a political activism that applied Marx's scientific socialism to the problems which beset China, was popular with Chinese intellectuals in the period between the two world wars. Among Chinese Marxists, the Stalin-oriented "Marxist-Leninists," who enjoyed the Soviet Union's support, became the dominant group. The most important figure among them was undoubtedly Mao Tse-tung, the leader of the Communist guerrilla army that eventually seized power in China. Mao was essentially a military and political leader but he dabbled in Marxist philosophy, more often than not—it should be noted—for political purposes; but, as his essay "On Practice," the first selection, demonstrates, this is a consistent position for him. Knowledge comes from social practice and

this in turn takes three forms—economic production, science, and the political practice involved in Marxist class struggle. One may question whether Mao's politics were always in the service of the oppressed classes, but he is at pains always to present them as such.

Although the two essays presented are similar in content, it is interesting to note the difference in tone between them. The first, "On Practice," written in 1937, when Mao was leading his peasant army, seems thoughtful and reasoned. The second, the famous "Where Do Correct Ideas Come From?" appears almost flippant. It dates from the time when Mao was in the process of purging his enemies within the Chinese Communist Party and preparing to rule China like a traditional emperor rather than the leader of a large, faction-ridden political movement.

ON PRACTICE

Mao Tse-tung

The Marxist holds that man's social practice alone is the criterion of the truth of his knowledge of the external world. In reality, man's knowledge becomes verified only when, in the process of social practice (in the process of material production, of class struggle, and of scientific experiment), he achieves the anticipated results. If man wants to achieve success in his work, that is, to achieve the anticipated results, he must make his thoughts correspond to the laws of the objective world surrounding him; if they do not correspond, he will fail in practice. If he fails he will derive lessons from his failure, alter his ideas, so as to make them correspond to the laws of the objective world, and thus

turn failure into success; that is what is meant by "failure is the mother of success," and "a fall into the pit, a gain in your wit."

• • •

If a man wants to know certain things or certain kinds of things directly, it is only through personal participation in the practical struggle to change reality, to change those things or those kinds of things, that he can come into contact with the phenomena of those things or those kinds of things; and it is only during the practical struggle to change reality, in which he personally participates, that he can disclose the essence of those things or those kinds of things and understand them. This is the path to knowledge along which everyone actually travels, only some people, distorting things deliberately, argue to the contrary. The most ridiculous person in the world is the "wiseacre" who, having gained some half-baked knowledge by hearsay, proclaims himself "the world's number one"; this merely shows that he has not taken a proper measure of himself. The question of knowledge is one of science, and there must not be the least bit of insincerity or conceit; what is required is decidedly the reverse—a sincere and modest attitude. If you want to gain knowledge you must participate in the practice of changing reality. If you want to know the taste of a pear you must change the pear by eating it yourself. If you want to know the composition and properties of atoms you must make experiments in physics and chemistry to change the state of atoms. If you want to know the theory and methods of revolution, you must participate in revolution. All genuine knowledge originates in direct experience. But man cannot have direct experience in everything; as a matter of fact, most of our knowledge comes from indirect experience, *e.g.* all knowledge of ancient times and foreign lands. To the ancients and foreigners, such knowledge comes from direct experience; if, as the direct experience of the ancients and foreigners, such knowledge fulfils the condition of "scientific abstraction" mentioned by Lenin, and scientifically reflects objective things, then it is reliable, otherwise it is not. Hence a man's knowledge consists of two parts and nothing else, of direct experience and indirect experience. And what is indirect experience to me is nevertheless direct experience to other people. Consequently, taking knowledge in its totality, any kind of knowledge is inseparable from direct experience.

• • •

Let us also look at war. If those who direct a war lack war experience, then in the initial stage they will not understand the profound laws for directing a particular war (*e.g.* our Agrarian Revolutionary War of the past ten years). In the initial stage they merely undergo the experience of a good deal of fighting, and what is more, suffer many defeats. But from such experience (of battles won and especially of battles lost), they are able to understand the inner thread of the whole war, namely, the laws governing that particular war, to understand strategy and

tactics, and consequently they are able to direct the war with confidence. At such a time, if an inexperienced person takes over the command, he, too, cannot understand the true laws of war until after he has suffered a number of defeats (after he has gained experience).

• • •

Thus the first step in the process of knowledge is contact with the things of the external world; this belongs to the stage of perception. The second step is a synthesis of the data of perception by making a rearrangement or a reconstruction; this belongs to the stage of conception, judgment and inference. It is only when the preceptual data are extremely rich (not fragmentary or incomplete) and are in correspondence to reality (not illusory) that we can, on the basis of such data, form valid concepts and carry out correct reasoning.

Here two important points must be emphasised. The first, a point which has been mentioned before, but should be repeated here, is the question of the dependence of rational knowledge upon perceptual knowledge. The person is an idealist who thinks that rational knowledge need not be derived from perceptual knowledge. In the history of philosophy there is the so-called "rationalist" school which admits only the validity of reason, but not the validity of experience, regarding reason alone as reliable and perceptual experience as unreliable; the mistake of this school consists in turning things upside down. The rational is reliable precisely because it has its source in the perceptual, otherwise it would be like water without a source or a tree without roots, something subjective, spontaneous and unreliable. As to the sequence in the process of knowledge, perceptual experience comes first; we emphasise the significance of social practice in the process of knowledge precisely because social practice alone can give rise to man's knowledge and start him on the acquisition of perceptual experience from the objective world surrounding him. For a person who shuts his eyes, stops his ears and totally cuts himself off from the objective world, there can be no knowledge to speak of. Knowledge starts with experience—this is the materialism of the theory of knowledge.

The second point is that knowledge has yet to be deepened, the perceptual stage of knowledge has yet to be developed to the rational stage—this is the dialectics of the theory of knowledge. It would be a repetition of the mistake of "empiricism" in history to hold that knowledge can stop at the lower stage of perception and that perceptual knowledge alone is reliable while rational knowledge is not. This theory errs in failing to recognise that, although the data of perception reflect certain real things of the objective world (I am not speaking here of idealist empiricism which limits experience to so-called introspection), yet they are merely fragmentary and superficial, reflecting things incompletely instead of representing their essence. To reflect a thing fully in its totality, to reflect its essence and its inherent laws, it is necessary, through thinking, to build up a system of concepts and theories by subjecting the abundant perceptual data to a process of remodelling and reconstructing—discarding the crude and selecting the refined, eliminating the false and retaining the true, proceeding from one point to another, and going through the outside into the inside; it is necessary to leap from perceptual knowledge to rational knowledge. Knowledge which is such a reconstruction does not become emptier or less reliable; on the contrary, whatever has been scientifically reconstructed on the basis of practice in the process of knowledge is something which, as Lenin said, reflects objective things more deeply, more truly, more fully. As against this, the vulgar plodders, respecting experience yet despising theory, cannot take a comprehensive view of the entire objective process, lack clear direction and long-range perspective, and are self-complacent with occasional successes and peep-hole views. Were those persons to direct a revolution, they would lead it up a blind alley.

• • •

But the process of knowledge does not end here. The statement that the dialectical-materialist process of knowledge stops at rational knowledge, covers only half the problem. And so far as Marxist philosophy is concerned, it covers only the half that is not particularly important. What Marxist philosophy regards as the most important problem does not lie in understanding the laws of the objective world and thereby becoming capable of explaining it, but in actively changing the world by applying the knowledge of its objective laws. From the Marxist viewpoint, theory is important, and its importance is fully shown in Lenin's statement: "Without a revolutionary theory there can be no revolutionary movement." But Marxism emphasises the importance of theory precisely and only because it can guide action. If we have a correct theory, but merely prate about it, pigeonhole it, and do not put it into practice, then that theory, however good, has no significance.

Knowledge starts with practice, reaches the theoretical plane via practice, and then has to return to practice. The active function of knowledge not only manifests itself in the active leap from perceptual knowledge to rational knowledge, but also—and this is the more important—in the leap from rational knowledge to revolutionary practice. The knowledge which enables us to grasp the laws of the world must be redirected to the practice of changing the world, that is, it must again be applied in the practice of production, in the practice of the revolutionary class struggle and revolutionary national struggle, as well as in the practice of scientific experimentation. This is the process of testing and developing theory, the continuation of the whole process of knowledge.

• • •

When we get to this point, is the process of knowledge completed? Our answer is: it is and yet it is not. When man in society devotes himself to the practice of changing a certain objective process at a certain stage of its development (whether changing a natural or social process), he can, by the reflection of the objective process in his thought and by the functioning of his own subjective activity, advance his knowledge from the perceptual to the rational and bring forth ideas, theories, plans or programmes which on the whole correspond to the laws of that objective process; he then puts these ideas, theories, plans or programmes into practice in the same objective process; and the process of knowledge as regards this concrete process can be considered as completed if, through the practice in that objective process, he can realise his preconceived aim, viz. if he can turn or on the whole turn these preconceived ideas, theories, plans or programmes into facts. For example, in the process of changing nature, such as in the realisation of an engineering plan, the verification of a scientific hypothesis, the production of a utensil or instrument, the reaping of a crop; or in the process of changing society, such as in the victory of a strike, the victory of a war, the fulfilment of an educational plan—all these can be considered as the realisation of preconceived aims. But generally speaking, whether in the practice of changing nature or of changing society, people's original ideas, theories, plans or programmes are seldom realised without any change whatever. This is because people engaged in changing reality often suffer from many limitations: they are limited not only by the scientific and technological conditions, but also by the degree of development and revelation of the objective process itself (by the fact that the aspects and essence of the objective process have not yet been fully disclosed). In such a situation, ideas, theories, plans or programmes are often altered partially and sometimes even wholly along with the discovery of unforeseen circumstances during practice. That is to say, it does happen that the original ideas, theories, plans or programmes fail partially or wholly to correspond to reality and are partially or entirely incorrect. In many instances, failures have to be repeated several times before erroneous knowledge can be rectified and made to correspond to the laws of the objective process, so that subjective things can be transformed into objective things, viz. the anticipated results can be achieved in practice. But in any case, at such a point, the process of man's knowledge of a certain objective process at a certain stage of its development is regarded as completed.

As regards man's process of knowledge, however, there can be no end to it. As any process, whether in the natural or social world, advances and develops through its internal contradictions and struggles, man's process of knowledge must also advance and develop accordingly. In terms of social movement, not only must a true revolutionary leader be adept at correcting his ideas, theories, plans or programmes when they are found to be erroneous, as we have seen, but he must also, when a certain objective process has already advanced and changed from one stage of development to another, be adept at making himself and all his fellow revolutionaries advance and revise their subjective ideas accordingly, that is to say, he must propose new revolutionary tasks and new working programmes corresponding to the changes in the new situation. Situations change very rapidly in a revolutionary period; if the knowledge of revolutionaries does not change rapidly in accordance with the changed situation, they cannot lead the revolution towards victory.

• • •

The development of the objective process is one full of contradictions and struggles. The development of the process of man's knowledge is also one full of contradictions and struggles. All the dialectical movements of the objective world can sooner or later be reflected in man's knowledge. As the process of emergence, development and disappearance in social practice is infinite, the process of emergence, development and disappearance in human knowledge is also infinite. As the practice directed towards changing objective reality on the basis of definite ideas, theories, plans or programmes develops farther ahead each time, man's knowledge of objective reality likewise becomes deeper each time. The process of change in the objective world will never end, nor will man's knowledge of truth through practice.

• • •

To discover truth through practice, and through practice to verify and develop truth. To start from perceptual knowledge and actively develop it into rational knowledge, and then, starting from rational knowledge, actively direct revolutionary practice so as to remould the subjective and the objective world. Practice, knowledge, more practice, more knowledge; the cyclical repetition of this pattern to infinity, and with each cycle, the elevation of the content of practice and knowledge to a higher level. Such is the whole of the dialectical materialist theory of knowledge, and such is the dialectical materialist theory of the unity of knowing and doing.

WHERE DO CORRECT IDEAS COME FROM?

Mao Tse-tung

Where do correct ideas come from? Do they drop from the skies? No. Are they innate in the mind? No. They come from social practice, and from it alone; they come from three kinds of social practice, the struggle for production, the class struggle and scientific experiment. It is man's social being that determines his thinking. Once the correct ideas characteristic of the advanced class are grasped by the masses, these ideas turn into a material force which changes society and changes the world. In their social practice, men engage in various kinds of struggle and gain rich experience, both from their successes and from their failures. Countless phenomena of the objective external world are reflected in a man's brain through his five sense organs—the organs of sight, hearing, smell, taste and touch. At first, knowledge is perceptual. The leap to conceptual knowledge, i.e., to ideas, occurs when sufficient perceptual knowledge is accumulated. This is one process in cognition. It is the first stage in the whole process of cognition, the stage leading from objective matter to subjective consciousness, from existence to ideas. Whether or not one's consciousness or ideas (including theories, policies, plans or measures) do correctly reflect the laws of the objective external world is not yet proved at this stage, in which it is not yet possible to ascertain whether they are correct or not. Then comes the second stage in the process of cognition, the stage leading from consciousness back to matter, from ideas back to existence, in which the knowledge gained in the first stage is applied in social practice to ascertain whether the theories, policies, plans or measures meet with the anticipated success. Generally speaking, those that succeed are correct and those that fail are incorrect, and this is especially true of man's struggle with nature. In social struggle, the forces representing the advanced class sometimes suffer defeat not because their ideas are incorrect but because, in the balance of forces engaged in struggle, they are not as powerful for the time being as the forces of reaction; they are therefore temporarily defeated, but they are bound to triumph sooner or later. Man's knowledge makes another leap through the test of practice. This leap is more important than the previous one. For it is this leap alone that can prove the correctness or incorrectness of the first leap in cognition, i.e., of the ideas, theories, policies, plans or measures formulated in the course of reflecting the objective external world. There is no other way of testing truth.

QUESTION FOR DISCUSSION

1. Evaluate Mao's claim that, speaking generally, the ideas we have that succeed are correct and those which fail are incorrect. Does the inclusion of the "speaking generally" rider in this formula present any problems for Mao's analysis of knowledge?

A CONTEMPORARY ISLAMIC CRITIQUE OF SCIENCE

Islamic civilization was at one time the most powerful in the world, not merely politically and militarily but also in terms of its widespread intellectual influence. It was through Islam that Europe recovered the lost portions of its classical heritage, as Aristotle and other ancient Greek thinkers were reintroduced to the West by Islamic philosophers in the later Middle Ages. It was also through Islam that Indian mathematics—algebra and an efficient arithmetic notation (our "Arabic numerals")—were transmitted to Europe, laying the groundwork for the European scientific revolution of the seventeenth century. The great medieval civilizations of Western Africa also benefited from Islamic thought. The Islamic thinkers not only acted as a conduit for classical philosophy and science in both Europe and Africa, they also added to it, making significant contributions to astronomy, philosophy, architecture, medicine, and mathematics. Today Islam finds itself frustrated, treated as if it were a barbarous backwater, valued more for its oil reserves than its knowledge and wisdom.

In this situation, a movement has arisen that is usually referred to as "Islamic fundamentalism." This movement has made great inroads both politically and intellectually in most major Islamic countries. In Iran, the movement has actually seized the reins of power. The Ayatollah Murtaza Mutahhari was an important figure in the Iranian revolution. Popular with traditionalists and author of several works on Islamic theology, he was a student of the Ayatollah Khomeini and held political office under him. Muttahhrari's political and religious career was, however, cut short, when he was assassinated by a car bomb relatively early in the history of the Khomeini regime.

In the selection presented here, Mutahhari argues for the supremacy of a religious world view and comments upon the limitations of science.

THE LIMITS OF SCIENCE

Ayatollah Murtaza Mutahhari

THREE WORLD VIEWS

World views or schemes of world knowledge (the ways man defines or explains the world) generally fall into three classes: scientific, philosophic, and religious.

Scientific World View

Science is based on two things: hypothesis and experiment. In the scientist's mind, to discover and explain a phenomenon, one first forms a hypothesis, and then one subjects it to concrete experiment, in the laboratory. If the experiment supports the hypothesis, it becomes an accepted scientific principle. As long as no more comprehensive hypothesis, better supported by experimentation, appears, that scientific principle retains its standing. The more comprehensive hypothesis with its advent clears the field for itself. Science thus engages in discovering causes and effects: Through concrete experiments, it discovers a thing's cause or effect; then it pursues the cause of that cause or the effect of that effect. It continues this course of discovery as far as possible.

The work of science, in being based on concrete experiments, has advantages and shortcomings. The greatest advantage of scientific research is that it is exact, precise, and discriminating. Science is able to give man thousands of data about some slight being; it can fill a book with knowledge about a leaf. Because it acquaints man with the special laws of every being, it enables man to control and dominate that being. Thus, it brings about industry and technology.

But precisely because of these qualities, the compass of science is also limited to experiment. It advances as far as can be subjected to experiment. But can one bring all of being in all its aspects within the confines of experiment? Science in practice pursues causes and effects to a certain limit and then reaches a point where it must say "I don't know." Science is like a powerful searchlight in the long winter night, illuminating a certain area without disclosing anything beyond its border. Can one determine by experiment whether the universe has a beginning and an end or is limitless in time? Or does the scientist, on reaching this point, consciously or unconsciously mount the pinions of philosophy in order to express an opinion?

From the standpoint of science, the universe is like an old book the first and last pages of which have been lost. Neither the beginning nor the end is known. Thus, the world view of science is a knowledge of the part, not of the whole. Our science acquaints us with the situation of some parts of the universe, not with the shape, mien, and character of the whole universe. The scientist's world view is like the knowledge about the elephant gained by those who touched it in the dark. The one who felt the elephant's ear supposed the animal to be shaped like a fan; the one who felt its leg supposed it to be shaped like a column; and the one who felt its back supposed it to be shaped like a throne.

Another shortcoming of the scientific world view as a basis for an ideology is that science is unstable and unenduring from a theoretical standpoint, that is, from the standpoint of presenting reality as it is or of attracting faith to the nature of the reality of being. From the viewpoint of science, the face of the world changes from day to day because science is based on hypothesis and experiment, not on rational and self-evident first principles. Hypothesis and experiment have a provisional value; so the scientific world view is shaky and inconsistent and cannot serve as a foundation for faith. Faith

demands a firmer, an unshakable foundation, a foundation characterized by eternity.

The scientific world view, in accordance with the limitations that the tools of science (hypothesis and experiment) have inevitably brought about for science, falls short of answering a series of basic cosmological questions that an ideology is obliged to answer decisively, such as: Where did the universe come from? Where is it going? How are we situated within the totality of being? Does the universe have a beginning and an end in time or in space? Is being in its totality right or a mistake, true or vain, beautiful or ugly? Do inevitable and immutable norms preside over the universe, or does no immutable norm exist? Is being in its totality a single living, conscious entity, or is it dead and unconscious, man's existence being an aberration, an accident? Can that which exists cease to exist? Can that which does not exist come into existence? Is the return of that which has lapsed from existence possible or impossible? Are the universe and history exactly repeatable, even after billions of years (the cyclical theory)? Does unity truly preside, or does multiplicity? Is the universe divisible into the material and the nonmaterial, and is the material universe a small part of the universe as a whole? Is the universe under guidance and seeing, or is it blind? Is the universe transacting with man? Does the universe respond in kind to man's good and evil? Does an enduring life exist after this transient one?

Science arrives at "I don't know" in trying to answer all these questions because it cannot subject them to experiment. Science answers limited, partial questions but is incapable of representing the totality of the universe. An analogy will clarify this point. It is possible for an individual to be well acquainted with a neighborhood or a quarter of Tehran. For instance, he may know South Tehran or some part of it in detail, such that he can sketch the streets, alleys, and even the houses of that area from memory. Someone else may know another neighborhood, a third person, a third area, and so on. If we bring together everything they know, we shall know enough of Tehran, part by part. But if we learn about Tehran in this way, shall we have learned about Tehran from every standpoint? Can we gain a complete picture of Tehran? Is it circular? Is it square? Is it shaped like the leaf of a tree? Of what tree? What relationships do the neighborhoods have with one another? Which bus lines connect how many neighborhoods? Is Tehran as a whole beautiful or ugly? If we want to inform ourselves on subjects such as these, if, for instance, we want to learn what the shape of Tehran is, or whether it is beautiful or ugly, we must board a plane and take in the whole city from above. In this sense, science is incapable of answering the most basic questions, as a whole view must; that is, it can form no general conceptions of the universe as a whole and of its form.

The importance of the scientific world view lies in its practical, technical value, not in its theoretical value. What can serve as the support for an ideology is a theoretical value, not a practical one. The theoretical value of science lies in the reality of the universe being just as it is represented in the mirror of science. The practical and technical value of science lies in science's empowering man in his work and being fruitful, whether or not it represents reality. Today's industry and technology display the practical and technical value of science.

One of the remarkable things about science in today's world is that, to the extent that its practical and technical value increases, its theoretical value diminishes. Those on the sidelines suppose that the progress of science as an illumination of the human conscience and as a source of faith and certitude relative to reality (which is how science represents itself) is in direct proportion to the extent of irrefutable concrete progress, whereas the truth is just the opposite.

An ideology requires a world view that, first, answers the basic cosmological questions of relevance to the universe as a whole, not just to some certain part; second, provides a well-grounded, reliable, and eternally valid comprehension, not a provisional, transient one; and third, provides something of theoretical, not purely practical and technical value, something revealing reality. The scientific

world view, for all its advantages from other standpoints, fails to fulfill these three conditions.

Philosophical World View

Although the philosophical world view lacks the exactitude and definition of the scientific world view, it enjoys an assurance and has none of the instability of the scientific world view. The reason for this is that it rests on a series of principles that are in the first place self-evident and undeniable to the mind, carried forward by demonstration and deduction, and in the second place general and comprehensive (in the language of philosophy, they relate to that by virtue of which the being is being). The world view of philosophy answers those same questions on which ideologies rest. Philosophical thought discerns the mien of the universe as a whole.

The scientific world view and the philosophical world view both conduce to action, but in two different ways. The scientific world view conduces to action by giving man the power and capacity to "change" and to "control" nature; it allows him to render nature subservient to his own desires. But the philosophical world view conduces to action and influences action by distinguishing the reasons for action and the criteria for human choice in life. The philosophical world view is influential in the way man encounters and responds to the universe. It fixes the attitude of man to the universe and shapes his outlook toward being and the universe. It gives man ideas or takes them away. It imparts meaning to his life or draws him into futility and emptiness. Thus, science is incapable but philosophy is capable of giving man a world view as the foundation of an ideology.

Religious World View

If we regard every general viewpoint expressed toward being and the universe as philosophical, regardless of the source of that world view (that is, syllogism, demonstration, and deduction or revelation received from the unseen world), we must regard the religious world view as philosophical. The religious world view and the philosophic world view cover the same domain, by contrast with the scientific world view. But if we take into account the source of knowledge, we must certainly admit that the religious and the philosophical cosmologies are different in kind. In some religions, such as Islam, the religious cosmology within the religion has taken on a philosophical quality, that is, a rational quality. It relies on reason and deduction and adduces demonstrations in answering the questions that are raised. From this standpoint, the Islamic world view is likewise a rational and philosophical world view.

Among the advantages of the religious world view (in addition to the two advantages it shares with the philosophical world view—stability and eternality, and generality and comprehensiveness) is its sanctification of the bases of the world view.

An ideology demands faith. For a school of thought to attract faith calls not only for a belief in that eternity and immutability of its principles, which the scientific world view in particular lacks, but for a respect approaching reverence. Thus, a world view becomes the basis of ideology and the foundation of belief when it takes on a religious character. A world view can become the basis of an ideology when it has attained the firmness and breadth of philosophical thought as well as the holiness and sanctity of religious principles.

CRITERIA FOR A WORLD VIEW

The good, sublime world view has the following characteristics:

1. It can be deduced and proven (is supported by reason and logic).
2. It gives meaning to life; it banishes from minds the idea that life is vain and futile, that all roads lead to vanity and nothingness.
3. It gives rise to ideals, enthusiasm, and aspiration.

4. It has the power to sanctify human aims and social goals.
5. It promotes commitment and responsibility.

That a world view is logical paves the way to rational acceptance of it and renders it admissible to thought. It eliminates the ambiguities and obscurities that are great barriers to action.

That the world view of a school of thought gives rise to ideals lends it a magnetism as well as a fervor and force.

That a world view sanctifies the aims of a school of thought leads to individuals' easily making sacrifices and taking risks for the sake of these aims. So long as a school is unable to sanctify its aims, to induce feelings in individuals of worshipfulness, sacrifice, and idealism in relation to the aims of the school, that school of thought has no assurance that its aims will be carried out.

That a world view promotes commitment and responsibility commits the individual, to the depths of his heart and conscience, and makes him responsible for himself and society.

THE ALL-ENCOMPASSING WORLD VIEW OF TAUHID

All the features and properties that are organic to a good world view are summed up in the world view of *tauhid,* which is the only world view that can have all these features. The world view of *tauhid* means perceiving that the universe has appeared through a sagacious will and that the order of being is founded on goodness, generosity, and mercy, to convey existents to attainments worthy of them. The world view of *tauhid* means the universe is unipolar and uniaxial. The world view of *tauhid* means the universe has for its essence "from Himness" (*inna lillah*) and "to Him-ness" (*inna ilayhi raji'un*) [Qur'an, 2:156].

The beings of the universe evolve in a harmonious system in one direction, toward one center. No being is created in vain, aimlessly. The universe is regulated through a series of definitive rules named the divine norms (*sunan ilahiya*). Man enjoys a special nobility and greatness among beings and has a special role and mission. He is responsible for his own evolution and upbringing and for the improvement of his society. The universe is the school for man, and God rewards every human being according to his right intention and right effort.

The world view of *tauhid* is backed by the force of logic, science, and reason. In every particle of the universe, there are indications of the existence of a wise, omniscient God; every tree leaf is a compendium of knowledge of the solicitous Lord.

The world view of *tauhid* gives meaning, spirit, and aim to life because it sets man on the course of perfection that stops at no determinate limit but leads ever onward.

The world view of *tauhid* has a magnetic attraction; it imparts joy and confidence to man; it presents sublime and sacred aims; and it leads individuals to be self-sacrificing.

The world view of *tauhid* is the only world view in which individuals' mutual commitment and responsibility find meaning, just as it is the only world view that saves man from falling into the terrible valley of belief in futility and worship of nothingness.

The Islamic world view is the world view of *tauhid*. *Tauhid* is presented in Islam in the purest form and manner. According to Islam, God has no peer—"There is nothing like Him" (42:11). God resembles nothing and no thing can be compared to God. God is the Absolute without needs; all need Him; He needs none—"You are the ones needing God, and God is the One Free of Need, the Praiseworthy" (35:15). "He is aware of all things" (42:12) and "He is capable of all things" (22:6). He is everywhere, and nowhere is devoid of Him; the highest heaven and the depths of the earth bear the same relationship to Him. Wherever we turn we face Him—"Wherever you turn, there is the presence of God" (2:115). He is aware of all the secrets of the heart, all the thoughts passing through the mind, all the intentions and designs, of everyone—"We created man, and We know what his soul whispers to him, and We are nearer to him than his jugular vein" (50:16). He is the summation of all perfections and is above and devoid of all defect—"The most beautiful names belong to God" (7:180). He is not a body; He is not to be seen with the eye—"No visions can grasp Him, but He comprehends all vision" (6:103).

According to the Islamic world view, the world view of *tauhid*, the universe is a created thing preserved through the divine providence and will. If for an instant this divine providence were withdrawn from the world, it would cease to be.

The universe has not been created in vain, in jest. Wise aims are at work in the creation of the universe and of man. Nothing inappropriate, devoid of wisdom and value, has been created. The existing order is the best and most perfect of possible orders. The universe rests on justice and truth. The order of the universe is based on causes and effects, and one must seek for every result in its unique cause and antecedents. One must expect a unique cause for every result and a unique result for every cause. Divine decree and foreordination bring about the existence of every being only through its own unique cause. A thing's divinely decreed fate is identical with the fate decreed for it by the sequence of causes leading to it.

The intent of the divine will operates in the world in the form of a norm (*sunna*), that is, in the form of a universal law and principle. The divine norms do not change.

QUESTION FOR DISCUSSION

1. Ayatollah Mutahhari criticizes science, in large part, on the basis of the problem of induction. Evaluate his critique of science. Evaluate his more positive attitude toward religion as a source of knowledge.

THE LIMITS OF REASON AND THE LIMITS OF KNOWLEDGE

This cross-cultural reader is predicated on the assumption that significant communication between cultures is possible. Yet, in true philosophical spirit, it must nevertheless be asked what the limits of such communication might be. Chuang Tzu, the well-known Taoist mystic of fourth-century B.C. China, asks this question at an even deeper level, testing the limits of understanding between species. In a famous paradox, he observes that he once dreamt that he was a butterfly, a dream so vivid that, when he awoke, he did not know whether the dream was his or the butterfly's. Another paradoxalist, the modern Argentine writer Jorge Luis Borges, poignantly dramatizes our limitations in an imagined account of the very real Islamic philosopher, Averroës, and his futile search to understand Aristotle's theory of drama while living in a culture that has no theatre! In a final irony, Borges notes the absurdity of his own position, a twentieth-century Argentine trying to understand a medieval Arab intellectual.

The question of the limits of our knowledge is coupled in this section with the question of the limits of reason in knowledge. The selections are here taken from two twentieth-century "mystics"—one Asian, the Japanese scholar of Zen D. T. Suzuki, the other Western, the American philosopher Milton Munitz.

KNOWLEDGE AND RELATIVITY

Chuang Tzu

How can Tao be so obscured that there should be a distinction of true and false? How can speech be so obscured that there should be a distinction of right and wrong? Where can you go and find Tao not to exist? Where can you go and find speech impossible? Tao is obscured by petty biases and speech is obscured by flowery expressions. Therefore there have arisen the controversies between the Confucianists and the Moists, each school regarding as right what the other considers as wrong, and regarding as wrong what the other considers as right. But to show that what each regards as right is wrong or to show that what each regards as wrong is right, there is no better way than to use the light (of Nature).

There is nothing that is not the "that" and there is nothing that is not the "this." Things do not know that they are the "that" of other things; they only know what they themselves know. Therefore I say that the "that" is produced by the "this" and the "this" is also caused by the "that." This is the theory of mutual production.[1] Nevertheless, when there is life there is death,[2] and when there is death there is life. When there is possibility, there is impossibility, and when there is impossibility, there is possibility. Because of the right, there is the wrong, and because of the wrong, there is the right. Therefore the sage does not proceed along these lines (of right and wrong, and so forth) but illuminates the matter with Nature. This is the reason.

The "this" is also the "that." The "that" is also the "this." The "this" has one standard of right and

---

[1]According to Ch'ien Mu, *Chuang Tzu tsuan-chien* (Collected Commentaries on the *Chuang Tzu*), 1951, *fang-sheng* means simultaneously coming into being. It means simultaneous production or causation. The idea is that one implies or involves the other, or coexistence. The emphasis here, however, is the causal relation rather than coexistence.

[2]The same saying appears in Hui Shih's (380–305 B.C.) paradoxes.

wrong, and the "that" also has a standard of right and wrong. Is there really a distinction between "that" and "this"? Or is there really no distinction between "that" and "this"? When "this" and "that" have no opposites,[3] there is the very axis of Tao. Only when the axis occupies the center of a circle can things in their infinite complexities be responded to. The right is an infinity. The wrong is also an infinity. Therefore I say that there is nothing better than to use the light (of Nature).

To take a mark (*chih*) to show that a mark is not a mark is not as good as to take a non-mark to show that a mark is not a mark. To take a horse to show that a [white] horse is not a horse (as such) is not as good as to take a non-horse to show that a horse is not a horse.[4] The universe is but one mark, and all things are but a horse. When [people say], "All right," then [things are] all right. When people say, "Not all right," then [things are] not all right. A road becomes so when people walk on it,[5] and things become so-and-so [to people] because people call them so-and-so. How have they become so? They have become so because [people say they are] so. How have they become not so? They have become not so because [people say they are] not so. In their own way things are so-and-so. In their own way things are all right. There is nothing that is not so-and-so. There is nothing that is not all right. Let us take, for instance, a large beam and a small beam, or an ugly woman and Hsi-shih (famous beauty of ancient China), or generosity, strangeness, deceit, and abnormality. The Tao identifies them all as one. What is division [to some] is production [to others], and what is production [to others] is destruction [to some]. Whether things are produced or destroyed, [Tao] again identifies them all as one.

Only the intelligent knows how to identify all things as one. Therefore he does not use [his own judgment] but abides in the common [principle]. The common means the useful and the useful means identification. Identification means being at ease with oneself. When one is at ease with himself, one is near Tao. This is to let it (Nature) take its own course.[6] He has arrived at this situation,[7] and does not know it. This is Tao.

Those who wear out their intelligence to try to make things one without knowing that they are really the same may be called "three in the morning." What is meant by "three in the morning"? A monkey keeper once was giving out nuts and said, "Three in the morning and four in the evening." All the monkeys became angry. He said, "If that is the case, there will be four in the morning and three in the evening." All the monkeys were glad. Neither the name nor the actuality has been reduced but the monkeys reacted in joy and anger [differently]. The keeper also let things take their own course. Therefore the sage harmonizes the right and wrong and rests in natural equalization. This is called following two courses at the same time.

The knowledge of the ancients was perfect. In what way was it perfect? There were those who believed that nothing existed. Such knowledge is indeed perfect and infinite and cannot be improved. The next were those who believed there were things but there was no distinction between them. Still the next were those who believed there was distinction but there was neither right nor wrong. When the distinction between right and wrong became prominent, Tao was thereby reduced. Because Tao was reduced, individual bias was formed. But are there really production and reduction? Is there really no production or reduction? That there are production and reduction is like Chao Wen[8] playing the lute [with petty opinions produced in his mind]. That there is no production or reduction is like Chao Wen

---

[3]Interpretation following Kuo Hsiang, whose commentary on *Chuang Tzu* is the most important of all. However, Kuo's commentary is more a system of his own philosophy than explanation of the text.
[4]This is clearly a criticism of Kung-sun Lung (b. 380 B.C.?).
[5]According to Wang Hsien-ch'ien, *tao* here does not mean Tao but a road.

[6]Other interpretations: (1) This is because he relies on this (that is, Tao); (2) he stops with this.
[7]Another interpretation: He has stopped.
[8]Identity unknown.

not playing the lute,[9] [thus leaving things alone].
Chao Wen played the lute. Master K'uang[10] wielded
the stick to keep time. And Hui Tzu[11] leaned against
a drayanda tree [to argue]. The knowledge of these
three gentlemen was almost perfect, and therefore
they practiced their art to the end of their lives. Because they liked it, they became different from others, and they wished to enlighten others with what
they liked. They were not to be enlightened and yet
they insisted on enlightening them. Therefore Hui
Tzu lived throughout his life discussing the obscure
doctrines of hardness and whiteness.[12] And Chao
Wen's son devoted his whole life to his heritage but
ended with no success. Can these be called success?
If so, even I am a success. Can these not be called
success? If so, then neither I nor anything else can
be called a success. Therefore the sage aims are removing the confusions and doubts that dazzle people. Because of this he does not use [his own judg-
ment] but abides in the common principle. This is
what is meant by using the light (of Nature).

Suppose we make a statement. We don't know
whether it belongs to one category or another.
Whether one or the other, if we put them in one,
then one is not different from the other. However,
let me explain. There was a beginning. There was a
time before that beginning. And there was a time
before the time which was before that beginning.
There was being. There was non-being. There was
a time before that non-being. And there was a time
before the time that was before that non-being. Suddenly there is being and there is non-being, but I
don't know which of being and non-being is really
being or really non-being. I have just said something, but I don't know if what I have said really
says something or says nothing.

There is nothing in the world greater than the tip
of a hair that grows in the autumn, while Mount T'ai

is small. No one lives a longer life than a child who
dies in infancy, but P'eng-tsu (who lived many hundred years) died prematurely. The universe and I
exist together, and all things and I are one. Since all
things are one, what room is there for speech? But
since I have already said that all things are one, how
can speech not exist? Speech and the one then make
two. These two (separately) and the one (the two together) make three. Going from this, even the best
mathematician cannot reach [the final number].
How much less can ordinary people! If we proceed
from nothing to something and arrive at three, how
much more shall we reach if we proceed from
something to something! Let us not proceed. Let us
let things take their course.[13]

In reality Tao has no limitation, and speech has
no finality. Because of this there are clear demarcations. Let me talk about clear demarcations. There
are the left and the right. There are discussions and
theories. There are analyses and arguments. And
there are competitions and quarrels. These are
called the eight characteristics. What is beyond the
world, the sage leaves it as it exists and does not discuss it. What is within the world, the sage discusses
but does not pass judgment. About the chronicles of
historical events and the records of ancient kings,
the sage passes judgments but does not argue.
Therefore there are things which analysis cannot
analyze, and there are things which argument cannot argue. Why? The sage keeps it in his mind while
men in general argue in order to brag before each
other. Therefore it is said that argument arises from
failure to see [the greatness of Tao].

Great Tao has no appellation. Great speech does
not say anything. Great humanity (*jen*) is not humane (through any special effort).[14] Great modesty
is not yielding. Great courage does not injure. Tao
that is displayed is not Tao. Speech that argues is fu-

---

[9]Kuo Hsiang said in his commentary, "Not all sounds can be produced."
[10] Ancient musician famous for his sharpness in listening.
[11] Hui Shih.
[12] In ch. 5 of the *Chuang Tzu,* NHCC, 2:44a, Giles, pp. 69-70,
Chuang Tzu refers to Hui Tzu's discussion and doctrines.

[13] Another interpretation is: Let us stop.
[14] It means that a man of humanity is not humane in a deliberate
or artificial way, and that he is not partial. The word *jen* is often
rendered as love, kindness, human-heartedness, true mankind,
etc. In its broad sense, it denotes the general virtue.

tile. Humanity that is specially permanent or specially attached to someone or something will not be comprehensive.[15] Modesty that is too apparent is not real. Courage that injures the nature of things will not succeed. These five are all-comprehensive and all-embracing but tend to develop sharp edges. Therefore he who knows to stop at what he does not know is perfect. Who knows the argument that requires no speech or the Tao that cannot be named? If anyone can know, he is called the store of Nature (which embraces all). This story is not full when more things are added and not empty when things are taken out. We don't know where it comes from. This is called dimmed light.[16]

Of old Emperor Yao said to Shun,[17] "I want to attack the states of Tsung, Kuei, and Hsü-ao. Since I have been on the throne, my mind has not been free from them. Why?"

"The rulers of these states are as lowly as weeds," replied Shun. "Why is your mind not free from them? Once there were ten suns shining simultaneously and all things were illuminated. How much more can virtue illuminate than the suns?"

Nieh Ch'üeh asked Wang I,[18] "Do you know in what respect all things are right?"

"How can I know?" replied Wang I.

"Do you know that you do not know?"

Wang I said, "How can I know?"

"Then have all things no knowledge?"

"How can I know?" answered Wang I. "Nevertheless, I will try to tell you. How can it be known that what I call knowing is not really not knowing and that what I call not knowing is not really knowing? Now let me ask you this: If a man sleeps in a damp place, he will have a pain in his loins and will dry up and die. Is that true of eels? If a man lives up in a tree, he will be frightened and tremble. Is that true of monkeys? Which of the three knows the right place to live? Men eat vegetables and flesh,

and deer eat tender grass. Centipedes enjoy snakes, and owls and crows like mice. Which of the four knows the right taste? Monkey mates with the dog-headed female ape and the buck mates with the doe, and eels mate with fishes. Mao Ch'iang[19] and Li Chi[20] were considered by men to be beauties, but at the sight of them fish plunged deep down in the water, birds soared high up in the air, and deer dashed away. Which of the four knows the right kind of beauty? From my point of view, the principle of humanity and righteousness and the doctrines of right and wrong are mixed and confused. How do I know the difference among them?"

"If you do not know what is beneficial and what is harmful," said Nieh Ch'üeh, "does it mean that the perfect man does not know them also?"

"The perfect man is a spiritual being," said Wang I. "Even if great oceans burned up, he would not feel hot. Even if the great rivers are frozen, he would not feel cold. And even if terrific thunder were to break up mountains and the wind were to upset the sea, he would not be afraid. Being such, he mounts upon the clouds and forces of heaven, rides on the sun and the moon, and roams beyond the four seas. Neither life nor death affects him. How much less can such matters as benefit and harm?"

Ch'ü-ch'iao Tzu asked Ch'ang-wu Tzu,[21] "I have heard from my grand master (Confucius) that the sage does not devote himself to worldly affairs. He does not go after gain nor avoid injury. He does not like to seek anything and does not purposely adhere to Tao. He speaks without speaking, and he does not speak when he speaks. Thus he roams beyond this dusty world. My grand master regarded

---

[15] This is Kuo Hsiang's interpretation.

[16] This phrase is obscure. Each commentator has his own interpretation, which is mostly subjective.

[17] Legendary sage-emperors (3rd millennium B.C.).

[18] A virtuous man at the time of Yao, and teacher of Nieh Ch'üeh.

[19] Concubine of a king of Yüeh, which state ended in 334 B.C.

[20] Favorite of Duke Hsien (r. 676–651 B.C.) of Chin.

[21] The identities of these men have not been established. Most probably they are fictitious, products of Chuang Tzu's creative imagination. Yü Yüeh (1821–1906), in his *Chu-tzu p'ing-i* (Textual Critiques of the Various Philosophers), ch. 17, 1899 ed., 17:6b, argues that since the term "grand master" which is the honorific for Confucius, is used, the questioner must have been a pupil of Confucius. This is not necessarily the case, for Chuang Tzu freely put words into the mouths of people, historic or imaginary.

this as a rough description of the sage, but I regard this to be the way the wonderful Tao operates. What do you think, sir?"

"What you have said would have perplexed even the Yellow Emperor," replied Ch'ang-wu Tzu. "How could Confucius be competent enough to know? Moreover, you have drawn a conclusion too early. You see an egg and you immediately want a cock to crow, and you see a sling and you immediately want to roast a dove. Suppose I say a few words to you for what they are worth and you listen to them for what they are worth. How about it?

"The sage has the sun and moon by his side. He grasps the universe under the arm. He blends everything into a harmonious whole, casts aside whatever is confused or obscured, and regards the humble as honorable. While the multitude toil, he seems to be stupid and nondiscriminative. He blends the disparities of ten thousand years into one complete purity. All things are blended like this and mutually involve each other.

"How do I know that the love of life is not a delusion? And how do I know that the hate of death is not like a man who lost his home when young and does not know where his home is to return to? Li Chi was the daughter of the border warden of Ai. When the Duke of Chin first got her, she wept until the bosom of her dress was drenched with tears. But when she came to the royal residence, shared with the duke his luxurious couch and ate delicate food, she regretted that she had wept. How do I know that the dead will not repent having previously craved for life?

"Those who dream of the banquet may weep the next morning, and those who dream of weeping may go out to hunt after dawn. When we dream we do not know that we are dreaming. In our dreams we may even interpret our dreams. Only after we are awake do we know we have dreamed. Finally there comes a great awakening, and then we know life is a great dream. But the stupid think they are awake all the time, and believe they know it distinctly. Are we (honorable) rulers? Are we (humble) shepherds? How vulgar! Both Confucius and you were dreaming. When I say you were dreaming, I

am also dreaming. This way of talking may be called perfectly strange. If after ten thousand generations we could meet one great sage who can explain this, it would be like meeting him in as short a time as in a single morning or evening.

"Suppose you and I argue. If you beat me instead of my beating you, are you really right and am I really wrong? If I beat you instead of your beating me, am I really right and are you really wrong? Or are we both partly right and partly wrong? Or are we both wholly right and wholly wrong? Since between us neither you nor I know which is right, others are naturally in the dark. Whom shall we ask to arbitrate? If we ask someone who agrees with you, since he has already agreed with you, how can he arbitrate? If we ask someone who agrees with me, since he has already agreed with me, how can he arbitrate? If we ask someone who disagrees with both you and me to arbitrate, since he has already disagreed with you and me, how can he arbitrate? If we ask someone who agrees with both you and me to arbitrate, since he has already agreed with you and me, how can he arbitrate? Thus among you, me, and others, none knows which is right. Shall we wait for still others? The great variety of sounds are relative to each other just as much as they are not relative to each other. To harmonize them in the functioning of Nature[22] and leave them in the process of infinite evolution is the way to complete our lifetime."[23]

"What is meant by harmonizing them with the functioning of Nature?"

"We say this is right or wrong, and is so or is not so. If the right is really right, then the fact that it is different from the wrong leaves no room for argument. If what is so is really so, then the fact that it is different from what is not so leaves no room for argument. Forget the passage of time (life and death)

---

[22] This interpretation follows Kuo Hsiang. Ma Hsü-lun in his *Chuang Tzu i-cheng* (Textual Studies of the Meaning of the *Chuang Tzu*), 1930, 2:23b, says that it means the revolving process of Nature.

[23] In the text these two sentences follow the next four. Following some editions, I have shifted them here. It seems a most logical thing to do.

and forget the distinction of right and wrong. Relax in the realm of the infinite and thus abide in the realm of the infinite."

The Shade asks the Shadow, "A little while ago you moved, and now you stop. A little while ago you sat down and now you stand up. Why this instability of purpose?"

"Do I depend on something else to be this way?" answered the Shadow. "Does that something on which I depend also depend on something else? Do I depend on anything any more than a snake depends on its discarded scale or a cicada on its new wings? How can I tell why I am so or why I am not so?"

Once I, Chuang Chou,* dreamed that I was a butterfly and was happy as a butterfly. I was conscious that I was quite pleased with myself, but I did not know that I was Chou. Suddenly I awoke, and there I was, visibly Chou. I do not know whether it was Chou dreaming that he was a butterfly or the butterfly dreaming that it was Chou. Between Chou and the butterfly there must be some distinction. [But one may be the other.] This is called the transformation of things.

• • •

THE JOY OF FISHES

Chuang Tzu and Hui Tzu
Were crossing Hao river
By the dam.

Chuang said:
"See how free
The fishes leap and dart:
That is their happiness."

Hui replied:
"Since you are not a fish
How do you know
What makes fishes happy?"

Chuang said:
"Since you are not I
How can you possibly know

That I do not know
What makes fishes happy?"

Hui argued:
"If I, not being you,
Cannot know what you know
It follows that you
Not being a fish
Cannot know what they know."

Chuang said:
"Wait a minute!
Let us get back
To the original question.
What you asked me was
'*How do you know
What makes fishes happy?*'
From the terms of your question
You evidently know I know
What makes fishes happy.

"I know the joy of fishes
In the river
Through my own joy, as I go walking
Along the same river."

AVERROËS' SEARCH

Jorge Luis Borges

*S'imaginant que la tragédie
n'est autre que l'art de louer . . .*
—ERNEST RENAN, *AVERROËS,* 48 (1861).

Abu-al-Walīd Muhammad ibn-Ahmad ibn-Rushd (a century would be needed for this lengthy name to become simply Averroës, after first becoming Benraist and then Avenryz and even Aben-Rassad and Filius Rosadis) was busy redacting the eleventh chapter of the *Tahāfut al Tahāfut* ("The Incoherence of Incoherence"), in which he maintains, against the

---

* Chuang Tzu here refers to himself as Chuang Chou (Eds.).

opinion of the Persian ascetic al-Ghazzāli,* author of the *Tahāfut al Falasifa* ("The Incoherence of Philosophers"), that the Divinity knows only the general laws of the universe, those concerning the species, not those relating to the individual. He wrote with slow assurance, from right to left; the task of composing syllogisms and of linking up vast paragraphs did not prevent him from feeling, as if it were a sense of well-being, the cool deep house around him. In the depths of the siesta hour, amorous doves cooed huskily; from some invisible patio arose the murmur of a fountain; something in the blood of Averroës, whose ancestors came from Arabian deserts, was grateful for the constancy of water. Down below lay the gardens, the orchard; down below, the bustling Guadalquivir, and beyond, the beloved city of Córdoba, no less illustrious than Baghdad or Cairo, like a complex and delicate instrument; and all around (Averroës heard and felt it, too), the land of Spain stretched out to the border, the land of Spain, where there are few things, but where each one seems to exist in a substantive and eternal way.

His pen raced across the page, his proofs, irrefutable, interwove themselves; but a slight preoccupation dimmed Averroës' felicity. It was not the fault of the *Tahāfut,* a fortuitous piece of work, but was caused by a problem of a philological nature, relating to the monumental work which would justify him in the eyes of mankind: his commentary on Aristotle. Fountainhead of all wisdom, the Greek had been given to the world to teach men all they might know. Averroës' lofty purpose was to interpret his books in the way that the ulema interpret the Koran. History records few acts more beautiful and more pathetic than this Arabic physician's consecration to the thoughts of a man from whom he was separated by fourteen centuries. To the intrinsic difficulties we should add the fact that Averroës, who had no knowledge of Syriac or Greek, was working on the translation of a translation. On the previous evening he had been nonplussed by two equivocal

words at the beginning of the *Poetics:* the words *tragedy* and *comedy.* He had encountered them years before in the third book of the *Rhetoric.* No one within the compass of Islam intuited what they meant. Averroës had exhausted the pages of Alexander of Aphrodisia in vain; vainly he had collated the versions of the Nestorian philosopher Hunain ibn-Ishaq and of abu-Bashar Mata. The two arcane words pullulated in the text of the *Poetics;* it was impossible to elude them.

Averroës put down his pen. He told himself (without too much conviction) that whatever we seek is never very far away. He put aside the manuscript of the *Tahāfut* and went over to the book shelf where the many volumes of the *Mohkam,* composed by blind Abensida and copied by Persian calligraphers, stood in a row. It was ludicrous to think that he might not have consulted them already, but he was tempted anew by the idle pleasure of turning their pages again: From this deliberate distraction he was in turn distracted by a kind of melody. He looked down over the railed balcony; below, in the narrow earthen patio, some half-clad boys were playing. One of them, standing on the shoulders of another, was obviously acting the part of the muezzin; with his eyes closed tight he chanted *There is no god but God.* The boy who sustained him, unmoving, was the minaret. A third, abjectly on his knees in the dust, was the congregation of the Faithful. The game did not last long: each one wanted to be the muezzin, no one cared to be the congregation or the tower. Averroës heard them arguing in *gross* dialect: that is, in the incipient Spanish of the Peninsula's Moslem plebs. He opened the *Quitah Ul Ain* of Jalal and thought proudly of how in all Córdoba (perhaps even in all Al-Andalus) there was not another copy of that perfect work, only this one which the emir Yacub Almansur had sent him from Tangier. The name of this seaport reminded him that the traveler Abulcasim Al-Ashari, who had just come back from Morocco, would be dining with him that evening at the home of the Koranic scholar Farach. Abulcasim claimed to have voyaged as far as the dominions of the Empire of Shin (China). His detractors, equipped with the pe-

* A selection from the work of al-Ghazali is found in Chapter 4 of this volume (Eds.).

culiar logic supplied by hatred, swore that he had never set foot in China and that he had blasphemed against Allah in that country's temples. The gathering would, inevitably, last several hours. Hurriedly, Averroës resumed writing his *Tahāfut.* He worked until nightfall.

At Farach's house, the conversation went from a discussion of the incomparable virtues of the Governor to those of his brother the emir; later, in the garden, they spoke of roses. Abulcasim, who had not looked at them, swore that there were no roses like those which decorate the country houses of Andalusia. Farach did not let himself be flattered; he observed that the learned ibn-Qutaiba describes an excellent variety of perpetual rose which grows in the gardens of Hindustan and whose petals—blood red—have characters written on them saying: *There is no other god like God. Mohammed is the Apostle of God.* He added that Abulcasim surely knew of these roses. Abulcasim looked at him with alarm. If he answered that he did, everyone would judge him, justifiably, the readiest and most gratuitous of imposters; if he replied that he did not, they would consider him an infidel. He chose to mumble that the keys to occult matters are kept by the Lord, and that in all the earth there is nothing, either green or faded, that is not noted in His Book. These words are part of one of the first sutras of the Koran, and they were received with a murmur of reverence. Stimulated by this dialectical victory, Abulcasim was about to announce that the Lord is perfect in His works, and inscrutable. Whereupon Averroës, prefiguring the remote arguments of an as yet problematical Hume, declared:

"It is easier for me to admit of an error in the learned ibn-Qutaiba, or in the copyists, than admit that the earth yields roses embodying a profession of Faith."

"Just so. Great words and true," said Abulcasim.

"One traveler speaks of a tree whose fruit are green birds," recalled the poet Abdalmalik. "It would take a less painful effort for me to believe in that tree than in roses which bore words."

"The color of the birds," said Averroës, "would seem to favor the first mentioned prodigy. Besides, fruits and birds belong to the natural world, but writing is an art. To go from leaves to birds is easier than to go from roses to letters."

Another guest indignantly denied that writing was an art, inasmuch as the original of the Koran— *the mother of the Book*—is older than the Creation and is kept in Heaven. Another man cited Chahiz of Basra, who had said that the Koran is an essence which can take the form of a man or of an animal, an opinion apparently in concord with the theory that it has two faces. Farach then lengthily expounded the orthodox doctrine. The Koran, he said, is one of the attributes of God, like His mercy; it is copied in a book, it is pronounced with the tongue, it is remembered in one's heart, and the language and the signs and the writing are all works of man, while the Koran is eternal and irrevocable. Averroës, who had written a commentary on the *Republic,* could have mentioned that the mother of the Book is something on the order of its Platonic model, but he had already noticed that theology was a subject altogether inaccessible to Abulcasim.

Others, who had also noticed the same thing, urged Abulcasim to tell them the tale of some marvel. Then as now the world was an atrocious place; the audacious could move about in it, and so could the poor in spirit, the wretches who adjusted to anything. Abulcasim's memory was a mirror of intimate acts of cowardice. What tale could he tell? Besides, they demanded marvels of him, and marvels are probably not communicable; the moon in Bengal is not the same as the moon in the Yemen, though it be described by the same words. Abulcasim hesitated; then he spoke:

"Whoever travels through climes and cities," he unctuously announced, "will see many things worthy of credit. For instance, the following, which I have related only once before, to the King of the Turks. It took place at Sin Kalan (Canton), where the river of the Water of Life spills into the sea."

Farach asked if the city was to be found many leagues away from the Wall which had been built by Iskandar Zul Qarnain (Alexander Bicornis of Macedonia) to halt Gog and Magog.

"Deserts separate them," said Abulcasim, with involuntary arrogance. "It would take a *kafila* (a caravan) forty days to get within sight of its towers, and another forty days, they say, to reach it. I don't know of a single man in Sin Kalan who has ever seen the Wall, or who has ever seen anyone who did."

Terror of the crassly infinite, of mere space, of mere matter, laid a hand on Averroës for an instant. He gazed on the symmetrical garden; he knew himself grown old, useless, unreal. Abulcasim was saying:

"One afternoon, the Moslem merchants in Sin Kalan led me to a painted wood house inhabited by a large number of people. It is impossible to describe that house, which was more like a single room, with rows of chambers or of balconies, one on top of the other. People were eating and drinking in these cavities; the same activity was taking place on the floor and on a terrace. The people on the terrace played on drums and lutes, except for some score or so (who wore crimson masks) who were praying, singing, and conversing. They suffered imprisonment, but no one could see the prison: they rode on horseback, but no one saw the horse; they fought in combat, but their swords were reeds; they died and then stood up again."

"The activity of madmen," said Farach, "goes beyond the previsions of the sane."

"They were not mad," Abulcasim was forced to explain. "They were representing a story, a merchant told me."

No one understood, no one seemed to want to understand. In confusion, Abulcasim turned from the narrative which they had heard to cumbersome explanations. With the help of his hands, he said:

"Let us imagine that someone shows a story instead of telling it. Suppose this story is the one about the Seven Sleepers of Ephesus. We see them retire to the cave, we see them pray and sleep, sleep with their eyes open, we see them growing while they sleep, we see them awake at the end of three hundred and nine years, we see them awake in Paradise, we seem them awake with the dog. Something of the sort was shown us that afternoon by the persons on the terrace."

"Did these people speak?" asked Farach.

"Of course they spoke," said Abulcasim, now become the apologist for a performance he scarcely remembered and which had only vexed him at the time. "They spoke and sang and perorated!"

"In that case," said Farach, "there was no need for *twenty* people. A single speaker can relate anything, however complex it may be."

Everyone approved this dictum. The virtues of Arabic were next extolled, for it is the language used by God to direct the angels; and Arabic poetry was praised. Abdalmalik, after properly considering the subject, held that the poets of Damascus or Córdoba who insisted on pastoral images and a Bedouin vocabulary were old-fashioned. He said it was absurd that a man before whose eyes the Guadalquivir ran wide should celebrate the still waters of a well. He urged the convenience of renovating the ancient metaphors; he stated that at the time Zuhair compared Destiny with a blind camel, this figure of speech could move people to astonishment, but that five centuries of wonder had exhausted the surprise. This dictum, too, was approved by all: they had heard it often, from many men. Averroës was silent. But at last he spoke, less for the sake of the others than for himself.

"With less eloquence," said Averroës, "but with arguments of the same order, I have defended the proposition now sustained by Abdalmalik. In Alexandria, they say that the only man incapable of a crime is the man who has already committed it and already repented; to be free of error, let us add, it is well to have professed it. In his *mohalaca,* Zuhair stated that in the course of eighty years of pain and glory he has often seen Destiny suddenly trample men, like a blind camel. Abdalmalik finds that this figure of speech can no longer cause wonder. Many rejoinders could be made to this objection. The first, that if the end purpose of the poem was surprise, its life would be measured not by centuries but by days and hours and even perhaps by minutes. The second, that a renowned poet is less an inventor than he is a discoverer. In praise of ibn-Sharaf of Berja it has been said and repeated that only he could imagine that the stars at dawn fall slowly, like leaves falling from a tree; if such an attribution were true, it would be evidence that the image is worthless. An image one man alone can compose is an image that touches no man. There are an infinite number of things on earth; any one of them can be equated to any other. To equate stars to leaves is no less arbitrary than to equate them with fishes or birds. On the other hand, there is no one who has not felt at some time that Destiny is hard and awkward, that it is innocent and also inhuman. It was with this conviction in mind, a conviction which may be ephemeral or may be continuous but which no one may elude, that Zuhair's verse was written. What was said in that verse will not ever be said better. Besides (and perhaps here lies the essence of my reflections), time, which despoils fortresses, enriches verses. When Zuhair composed his verse in Araby, it served to bring two images face to face: the image of the old camel and the image of Destiny. Repeated now, it serves to evoke the memory of Zuhair and to fuse our regrets with those of the dead Arabian. The figure had two terms then, and now it has four. Time dilates the compass of verse, and I know of some which, like music, are all things to all men. Thus, when years ago in Marrakesh I was tormented by memories of Córdoba, I took pleasure in repeating the apostrophe Abdurrahman addressed to an African palm in the gardens of Ruzafa:

You, too, O palm!
are a stranger to this shore . . .

And this is the singular merit of poetry: that words written by a King who longed for the East served me, an exile in Africa, in my nostalgia for Spain."

Averroës then spoke of the first poets, of those who in the Time of Ignorance, before Islam, already said everything there was to say and said it in the infinite language of the desert. Alarmed—not without reason—by ibn-Sharaf's ostentation, he pointed out that all poetry was summarized in the ancients and in the Koran, and he condemned the ambition to innovate as both illiterate and vainglorious. The other guests heard him with pleasure, for he vindicated tradition.

The muezzins were calling the Faithful to early morning prayer when Averroës entered his library

again. (In the harem, the raven-haired slave girls had been torturing a red-haired slave girl, but Averroës wouldn't know about this until that afternoon.) The sense of the two equivocal words had somehow been revealed to him. With a firm and careful calligraphy he added the following lines to the manuscript.

> *Aristu* (Aristotle) *calls panegyrics by the name of tragedy, and satires and anathemas he calls comedies. The Koran abounds in remarkable tragedies and comedies, and so do the* mohalacas *of the sanctuary.*

He felt sleepy, he felt a bit cold. He unwound his turban and looked at himself in a metal mirror. I do not know what his eyes saw, for no historian has ever described the forms of his face. I do know that he suddenly disappeared, as if fulminated by a bolt of flameless fire, and that with him disappeared the house and the invisible fountain and the books and the manuscripts and the doves and the many raven-haired slave girls and the quivering red-haired slave girl and Farach and Abulcasim and the rose trees and perhaps even the Guadalquivir.

In the foregoing story I have striven to narrate the process involved in a defeat. I thought, first, of the Bishop of Canterbury who proposed to demonstrate the existence of God; then, of the alchemists who sought the philosopher's stone; next, of the vain trisectors of the angle and squarers of the circle. Later I reflected that even more poetic is the case of the man who sets himself a goal not inaccessible to other men, but inaccessible to him. I remembered Averroës, who, circumscribed by the compass of Islam, could never know the significance of the words *tragedy* and *comedy*. I told the tale; as I progressed, I felt what the god mentioned by Buffon must have felt, the god who set out to create a bull and instead created a buffalo. I sensed that the work was making mock of me. I sensed that Averroës, striving to imagine a drama without ever having suspected what a theater was, was no more absurd than I, who strove to imagine Averroës with no material other than some fragments from Renan, Lane, and Asín Palacios. I sensed, on the last page, that my narrative was a symbol of the man I was while I wrote it, and that to write that story I had to be that man, and that to be that man I had to write that story, and so to infinity. (The instant I stop believing in him, "Averroës" disappears.)

ZEN KNOWLEDGE

Daisetz T. Suzuki

Satori is a Japanese term, *wu* in Chinese. The Sanskrit *bodhi* and *buddha* come from the same root, *bud,* "to be aware of," "to wake." *Buddha* is thus "the awakened one," "the enlightened one," while *bodhi* is "enlightenment." "Buddhism" means the teaching of the enlightened one, that is to say, Buddhism is the doctrine of enlightenment. What Buddha teaches, therefore, is the realisation of bodhi, which is satori. Satori is the centre of all Buddhist teachings. Some may think satori is characteristic of Mahayana Buddhism, but it is not so. Earlier Buddhists also talk about this, the realization of *bodhi;* and as long as they talk about *bodhi* at all they must be said to base their doctrine on the experience of satori.

We have to distinguish between *prajna* and *vijnana.* We can divide knowledge into two categories: intuitive knowledge which is *prajna* whereas discursive knowledge is *vijnana.* To distinguish further: *prajna* grasps reality in its oneness, in its totality; *vijnana* analyses it into subject and object. Here is a flower; we can take this flower as representing the universe itself. We talk about the petals, pollen, stamen and stalk; that is physical analysis. Or we can analyse it chemically into so much hydrogen, oxygen, etc. Chemists analyse a flower, enumerate all its elements and say that the aggregate of all those elements makes up the flower. But they have not exhausted the flower; they have simply analysed it. That is the *vijnana* way of understanding a flower. The *prajna* way is to understand it just as it is without analysis or chopping it into pieces. It is to grasp it in its oneness, in its totality, in its suchness (*sono mame*) in Japanese.

We are generally attracted to analytical knowledge or discriminative understanding, and we divide reality into several pieces. We dissect it and by dissecting it we kill reality. When we have finished our analysis we have murdered reality, and this dead reality we think is our understanding of it. When we see reality dead, after analysing it, we say that we understand it, but what we understand is not reality itself but its corpse after it has been mutilated by our intellect and senses. We fail to see that this result of dissection is not reality itself, and when we take this analysis as a basis of our understanding it is inevitable that we go astray, far away from the truth. Because in this way we shall never reach the final solution of the problem of reality.

Prajna grasps this reality in its oneness, in its totality, in its suchness. *Praja* does not divide reality into any form of dichotomy; it does not dissect it either metaphysically or physically or chemically. The dividing of reality is the function of *vijnana* which is very useful in a practical way, but *prajna* is different.

Vijnana can never reach infinity. When we write the numbers 1, 2, 3, etc., we never come to an end, for the series goes on to infinity. By adding together all those individual numbers we try to reach the total of the numbers, but as numbers are endless this totality can never be reached. *Prajna,* on the other hand, intuits the whole totality instead of moving through 1, 2, 3 to infinity; it grasps things as a whole. It does not appeal to discrimination; it grasps reality from inside, as it were. Discursive *vijnana* tries to grasp reality objectively, that is, by addition objectively one after another. But this objective method can never reach its end because things are infinite, and we can never exhaust them objectively. Subjectively, however, we turn that position upside down and get to the inside. By looking at this flower objectively we can never reach its essence or life, but when we turn that position inside out, enter into the flower, and become the flower itself, we live through the process of growth: I am the shoot, I am the stem, I am the bud, and finally I am the flower and the flower is me. That is the *prajna* way of comprehending the flower.

In Japan there is a seventeen syllable poem called *haiku,* and one composed by a modern woman-poet reads in literal translation:

Oh, Morning Glory!
Bucket taken captive,
I beg for water.

The following was the incident that led her to compose it. One early morning the poet came outdoors to draw water from the well, and saw the morning glory winding round the bamboo pole attached to the bucket. The morning glory in full bloom looks its best in the early morning after a dewy night. It is bright, refreshing, vivifying; it reflects heavenly glory not yet tarnished by things earthly. She was so struck with its untainted beauty that she remained silent for a little while; she was so absorbed in the flower that she lost the power of speech. It took a few seconds at least before she could exclaim: "Oh, Morning Glory!" Physically, the interval was a space of a second or two or perhaps more; but metaphysically, it was eternity as beauty itself is. Psychologically, the poet was the unconscious itself in which there was no dichotomization of any kind.

The poet was the morning glory and the morning glory was the poet. There was self-identity of flower and poet. It was only when she became conscious of herself seeing the flower that she cried: "Oh, Morning Glory!" When she said that, consciousness revived in her. But she did not like to disturb the flower, because although it is not difficult to unwind the flower from the bamboo pole she feared that to touch the flower with human hands would be the desecration of the beauty. So she went to a neighbour and asked for water.

When you analyse that poem you can picture to yourself how she stood before the flower, losing herself. There was then no flower, no human poet; just a "something" which was neither flower nor poet. But when she recovered her consciousness, there was the flower, there was herself. There was an object which was designated as morning glory

and there was one who spoke—a bifurcation of subject-object. Before the bifurcation there was nothing to which she could give expression, she herself was non-existent. When she uttered, "Oh, Morning Glory!" the flower was created and along with it herself, but before that bifurcation, that dualisation of subject and object, there was nothing. And yet there was a "something" which could divide itself into subject-object, and this "something" which had not yet divided itself, not become subject to bifurcation, to discriminative understanding (i.e. before *vijnana* asserted itself)—this is *prajna*. For *Prajna* is subject and at the same time object; it divides itself into subject-object and also stands by itself, but that standing by itself is not to be understood on the level of duality. Standing by itself, being absolute in its complete totality or oneness—that is the moment which the poet realised, and that is satori. Satori consists in not staying in that oneness, not remaining with itself, but in awakening from it and being just about to divide itself into subject and object. Satori is the staying in oneness and yet rising from it and dividing itself into subject-object. First, there is "something" which has not divided itself into subject-object, this is oneness as it is. Then this "something," becoming conscious of itself, divides itself into flower and poet. The becoming conscious is the dividing. Poet now sees flower and flower sees poet, there is mutual seeing. When this seeing each other, not just from one side alone but from the other side as well when this kind of seeing actually takes place, there is a state of satori.

When I talk like this it takes time. There is something which has not divided itself but which then becomes conscious of itself, and this leads to an utterance, and so on. But in actual satori there is no time interval, hence no consciousness of the bifurcation. The oneness dividing itself into subject-object and yet retaining its oneness at the very moment that there is the awakening of a consciousness—this is satori.

From the human point of view we talk of *prajna* and *vijnana* as the integral understanding and the discriminative understanding of reality respectively. We speak of these things in order to satisfy our human understanding. Animals and plants do not divide themselves; they just live and act, but humans have awakened this consciousness. By the awakening of consciousness we become conscious of this and that, and this universe of infinite diversity arises. Because of this awakening we discriminate, and because of discrimination we talk of *prajna* and *vijnana* and make these distinctions, which is characteristic of human beings. To satisfy this demand we talk about having satori, or the awakening of this self-identity consciousness.

When the poet saw the flower, that very moment before she spoke even a word there was an intuitive apprehension of something which eludes our ordinary intuition. This *sui generis* intuition is what I would call *prajna*-intuition. The moment grasped by *prajna*-intuition is satori. That is what made Buddha the Enlightened one. Thus, to attain satori, *prajna*-intuition is to be awakened.

That is more or less a metaphysical explanation of satori, but psychologically satori may be said to take place this way. Our consciousness contains all things; but there must be at least two things whereby consciousness is possible. Consciousness takes place when two things stand opposing one another. In our ordinary life, consciousness is kept too busy with all things going on in it and has not time to reflect within itself. Consciousness has thus no opportunity to become conscious of itself. It is so deeply involved in action, it is in fact action itself. Satori never takes place as long as consciousness is kept turning outwardly, as it were. Satori is born of self-consciousness. Consciousness must be made to look within itself before it is awakened to satori.

To get satori, all things which crowd into our daily-life consciousness must be wiped off clean. This is the function of *samadhi,* which Indian philosophers emphasize so much. "Entering into *samadhi*" is to attain uniformity of consciousness, i.e. to wipe consciousness clean, though practically speaking, this wiping clean is something almost impossible. But we must try to do it in order to attain this state of uniformity, which, according to early Buddhist thinkers, is a perfect state of mental equilibrium, for here there are no passions, no intellectual functions, but only a perfectly balanced state of indifference. When this takes place it is known as *samadhi,* or entering into the fourth stage of *dhyana* or *jhana,* as described in most early Buddhist sutras. This is not, however, a state of satori. *Samadhi* is not enough, which is no more than the unification of consciousness. There must be an awakening from this state of unification or uniformity. The awakening is becoming aware of consciousness in its own activities. When consciousness starts to move, begins to divide itself into subject-object and says: I am sorry, or glad, or I hear, and so on—this very moment as it moves on is caught up in satori. But as soon as you say "I have caught it" it is no more there. Therefore, satori is not something you can take hold of and show to others, saying, "See, it is here!"

Consciousness is something which never ceases to be active though we may be quite unconscious of it, and what we call perfect uniformity is not a state of sheer quietness, that is, of death. As consciousness thus goes on unceasingly, no one can stop it for inspection. Satori must take place while consciousness is going through states or instant points of becoming. Satori is realized along with the becoming, which knows no stoppage. Satori is no particular experience like other experiences of our daily life. Particular experiences are experiences of particular events while the satori experience is the one that runs through all experiences. It is for this reason that satori cannot be singled out of other experiences and pronounced, "See, here is my satori!" It is always elusive and alluring. It can never be separated from our everyday life, it is forever there, inevitably there. Becoming, not only in its each particularisable moment but through its never-terminating totality is the body of satori.

The nature of human understanding and reasoning is to divide reality into the dichotomy of this and that, of "A" and "not-A" and then to take reality so divided as really reality. We do not seem to understand reality in any other way. This being so, as long as we are depending on "the understanding," there will be no grasping of reality, no intuitive taking hold of reality, and satori is no other than this intuitive taking hold of reality. There is no reality beside becoming, becoming is reality and reality is becoming. Therefore, the satori intuition of reality consists in identifying oneself with becoming, to take becoming as it goes on becoming. We are not to cut becoming into pieces, and, picking up each separate piece which drops from "becoming," to say to people, "Here is reality." While making this announcement we will find that becoming is no more there; reality is flown away into the realm of the irrevocable past.

This is illustrated by a Zen story. A woodman went to the mountains and saw a strange animal on the other side of the tree which he was cutting. He thought: "I might kill that animal." The animal then spoke to the woodman and said: "Are you going to kill me?" Having his mind read, the woodman got angry and wondered what to do. The animal said: "Now you are thinking what to do with me." Whatever thought the woodman had, the animal intuited, and told him so. Finally, the woodman said: "I will stop thinking about the animal and go on cutting wood." While he was so engaged the top of the axe flew off and killed the animal.

This illustrates that when you are thinking of it there is satori. When you try to realise satori, the more you struggle the farther it is away. You cannot help pursuing satori, but so long as you make that special effort satori will never be gained. But you cannot forget about it altogether. If you expect satori to come to you of its own accord, you will not get it.

To realise satori is very difficult, as the Buddha found. When he wished to be liberated from the bondage of birth and death he began to study philosophy, but this did not avail him, so he turned to asceticism. This made him so weak that he could not move, so he took milk and decided to go on with his search for liberation. Reasoning did not do any good and pursuing moral perfection did not help him either. Yet the urge to solve this problem was still there. He could go no farther, yet he could not retreat, so he had to stay where he was, but even that would not do. This state of spiritual crisis means that you cannot go on, nor retreat, nor stay where you are. When this dilemma is genuine, there prevails a state of consciousness ready for satori. When we really come to this stage (but we frequently think that what is not real is real), when we find ourselves at this critical moment, something is sure to rise from the depths of reality, from the depths of our own being. When this comes up there is satori. Then you understand all things and are at peace with the world as well as with yourself.

BOUNDLESS EXISTENCE

Milton Munitz

Does the existence of the observable universe, and what can be established as its contents and structure, exhaust all that belongs to Reality in its most fundamental nature? If not, what more needs to be said? The answer I wish to propose is that there is something more.

I will use the expression "Boundless Existence" to designate this "something more." I will use it to refer to a crucial aspect of Reality beyond or transcendent to that of the observable universe insofar as the latter is understood. This transcendent aspect of Reality, however, should not be equated with the fact that the observable universe, for scientific cosmology, is unendingly open to further enlargement both on the levels of increasing information (through enrichment of the fund of observational data) and through bringing to bear novel forms of conceptual understanding. Boundless Existence always outstrips and transcends any actual or possible scientific knowledge of the known universe. Boundless Existence always looms as the "unintelligible more," no matter how far scientific understanding has progressed. As the transcendent aspect of Reality, Boundless Existence is not accessible either to observation or to scientific understanding by human beings, hence not open to investigation by either means. A scientific enlargement of knowledge of the observable universe leaves untouched and undiminished the transcendent unintelligibility of Boundless Existence.

But this does not mean that we could obtain reliable knowledge of Boundless Existence by metaphysical means. For there are no properties or structural features belonging to Boundless Existence that are open to discovery and conceptual articulation by metaphysics, any more than it is the case they could be investigated by science. The term "Boundless Existence," accordingly, will hereinafter be used to refer to an aspect of Reality that totally frustrates any search for intelligibility, whether this search is carried out by science *or* metaphysics.

What the term "Boundless Existence" stands for is best approached by pursuing a number of different routes, all of which, if successfully followed, converge on the same result. That result is always "there"—open to a type of intensified *awareness,* though not to any form of *understanding or knowledge.* The awareness, consequently, is an experience wholly different from that in which it is possible to discriminate various properties or a structural pattern in some subject matter and which, when found, can be described in language.

• • •

On the view here proposed, the drive by reason, as traditionally pursued, to discover order and intelligibility *in* the world is blocked—not because of human limitations and incompetence, but because there is a fundamental, inherent aspect of *unintelligibility* both in the very existence of the world and in what it is "in itself" apart from the use of humanly devised conceptual schemes. It is the radical presence on a metaphysical level of this aspect of unintelligibility—defeating all actual or possible efforts by human reason to *discover* intelligible order everywhere—that is brought to the fore in recognizing Boundless Existence as a crucial aspect of Reality.

• • •

In order to indicate the types of consideration that lead to recognizing Boundless Existence as a fundamental aspect of Reality and to making clear in what sense the observable universe is unintelligible, we need, first of all, to distinguish two principal ways in which the term "exist" can be used in connection with the observable universe. Having done this, we should also recall the distinction we made earlier between the two principal ways (the Platonic and Kantian) in which the term "intelligible" can be used—a distinction that will clarify in what sense we can say Boundless Existence is unintelligible.

I turn, first, to distinguish two principal uses of the term "exist." One is the sense in which we say that various items found in the known observable universe exist, the other is employed in the nominalized and capitalized expression, "Boundless Existence."

The first of these two senses of "existence" comes to the fore wherever, for example, from the perspective of a cosmologist's interest, one asks for the criteria for establishing whether something exists, and—given these criteria and applying them—what confirming evidence there is for accepting a particular account as a true description or explanation of some feature of the observable universe. Where confirming evidence is available that supports the description or explanation being considered, one says of some object, occurrence, process, or regularity that it exists. The use of the term "galaxy" (specified in one or another of its special types) is an accepted description for certain visually or otherwise perceived and measured data. Evidence can be offered in particular cases to support the classification and description as true—as establishing the existence of galaxies. The microwave background radiation is another existent feature of the observable universe. So is the law or regularity reporting the fact that the redshifts of galaxies is linearly correlated with their distance. So is the fact that the value of the cosmological constant (the difference between the critical density of mass and the actual density) is close to zero. And so on. In each case there are normally available conceptual tools for describing these specific features of the observable universe and for accepting these descriptions as true—as reporting existing features or components of the observable universe. In addition, of course, there are further questions that arise concerning how to *explain* these features. Where such explanations are forthcoming, additional considerations come to the fore concerning the criteria to be employed in accepting them as true when applied, and therefore for determining in what sense, or to what extent, the explanation also points to something existent in the observable universe. In this process of rendering some existent feature of the observable universe intelligible, we must recognize, of course, that any achieved successes may involve giving explanations that depend at some point on taking some other matters as unexplained, but not necessarily as unexplainable, by science. We must expect, therefore, that no cognitive enlargement of the observable universe by the use of scientific resources will ever eventuate in the finding of an account in which there are no further questions to be asked or possibly answered. This amounts to accepting the view that there will never be an absolute terminus to the search for scientific intelligibility with respect to existent features or contents of the observable universe, whatever the extent of the cumulative successes of science at any particular stage of inquiry.

Thus far, let us assume, there are no intractable objections to using the ordinary term "exists" in application to the observable universe and its contents. There is, however, another, special use of the term "exists" (or its nominative form "existence") that comes to the fore and that leads to the use of the qualifying term "boundless" in connection with it. Here the term "boundless" will be used, not in any quantitative or metric sense, but rather to signify the total absence, inapplicability, and radical unavailability of *any* form of description or explanation: of the use of any scheme of *conceptual bounds*. The ordinary or scientific use of the term "exists" ("existent," or "existence"), previously alluded to, does not provide any occasion or incentive for using the qualifying adjective "boundless" in this way. We should not come upon Boundless Existence in considering this or that feature of the known observable universe as described, questioned, explained, or understood at any stage of scientific cosmological inquiry.

I shall distinguish two major routes to this latter, special sense of "exists," viz., "Exists" or its nominalization, "Existence." One route to this special sense is best recaptured by stressing the kinds of metaphysical questions raised by traditional theology about the existence of the world. The other route to the special use of "exists" is of a more directly epistemological character.

Let us consider, to begin with, the special use of the term "exists" that arises from taking a primarily metaphysical orientation of the sort to which the theist directs our attention. In a theistic metaphysics, one starts with the fact *that* the observed world exists and that it has a determinable structure and contents. For the sake of brevity, I shall refer to the latter (its structure and contents) as its *what*. By asking "*Why* does the world exist at all?" and "*Why* does it have *what* properties (the structure and contents) it does?" and by answering these questions by relying on the creation model, the resulting main feature of theistic metaphysics (whatever its manifold variations in detail) is based on a fundamental division into two main entities: the created world and its Creator. Each "entity" (the created world, and God as Creator) has its own *that* (its own mode or level of existence) and its own *what* (its own set of properties and attributes). As it concerns both the existence of the world and its properties, the *why* question is given an answer: God created it.

Part of the intellectual price paid in accepting this answer is to admit that while we are assured, whether by argument, analogy, faith, or revelation, *that* God exists, we do not have any detailed knowledge of the *what* of God. Furthermore, it is commonly claimed, it makes no sense to ask the question "Why?" concerning God's existence. Accordingly, while this metaphysical view achieves its own type of consistency and simplification by answering the "why" question concerning the existence and properties of the observed world, an acceptance of this answer also carries with it an *increase* in the number of mysteries and unanswerable questions. These include God's own "that," "why," "what," and "how," as well as those surrounding the lack of full human understanding of God's purposes in establishing various features of the world. The latter type of unanswerability holds for the kinds of questions raised in the *Book of Job.*

It will not serve our present interest to rehearse the familiar history of attempts to prove the existence of God or to examine the equally familiar criticisms and "rebuttals" of these arguments. If we accept Wittgenstein's analysis of how we should regard the beliefs that make up a world picture of whatever sort as distinguished from "fluid" or nonfoundational beliefs, then one cannot refute the position of the theist. All that can be done is to rely on the possible effectiveness of "persuasion" to bring about a change in the groundless commitments that define his world picture.

I shall confine myself, therefore, to examining the point from which the theist's metaphysics takes its departure: the conviction that there *must* be a reason for the very existence of the world, whatever the success of science in explaining the existence of one or another detail or aspect of the observable universe. It is this conviction of "mustness" that fuels and supports all efforts at meeting the metaphysical hunger for an explanation of the existence of the world.

Let us use the capitalized term "Existence" in connection with the observable universe to refer to what is disclosed in the awareness *that* the observable universe exists—whatever the particular features of the observable universe and their actual or possible scientific explanation. In this sense, Existence lies beyond the range of any conceptual tools of the sort that science employs in its dealings with the observable universe. *It is the having of this awareness of the fact that the universe Exists, that our own world picture shares with the viewpoint of the theist.* It serves as the matrix from which our respective, though ultimately divergent metaphysical journeys take their common point of departure.

Given *that* the known observable universe Exists, whatever its observed or scientifically understood features may be at any stage of the enlargement of the known observable universe, those who adopt the viewpoint of the traditional theist ask: Should we not be able to ask various questions about the "that" (about the Existence) of the known

observable universe? Should we not be able to ask, for example, "*How* did it come into Existence?" and "*Why* does it Exist?" If we were able to answer these questions, the fact of the Existence of the observable universe would not be a total mystery; it would be conceptually bound, it would be amenable to encompassment by some conceptual scheme, whether literal, metaphorical or analogical.

It is precisely here where the world picture I am proposing deviates from those who subscribe to the foregoing type of outlook. It takes the "that" of the world's Existence, of which we have an awareness, as *not* amenable to any form of conceptual understanding. It leaves the Existence of the observable universe a not further analyzable, describable, or explainable metaphysical fact: a groundless aspect of Reality. It finds no justification for the belief in being able successfully to find reasons for the Existence of the observable universe in any of the various standard uses of the expression "reason."[1]

As approached in the present account, Boundless Existence is not an entity of a special type, as, for example, God is thought to be: one having a mind, creative abilities, solicitude for human beings, causal efficacy, and so on. Boundless Existence is not an entity at all. Instead, in the search for intelligibility and the fulfillment of that search through the use of humanly produced conceptual schemes, we restrict ourselves to distinguishing the "that" and the "what" of the various contents of the observable universe, as well as asking, with the scientist, various types of "why" questions about the details of the observable universe. However, the Existence of the known observable universe remains altogether outside the scope and powers of conferring intelligibility upon it by means of a standard conceptual sort. An acknowledgment of this unintelligibility is one aspect of what is signified by the use of the term "Boundless Existence." Boundless Existence is a way of referring to the total un-

---

[1] For a discussion, in some detail, see my book, *The Mystery of Existence,* chaps. 10 and 11.

intelligibility of the Existence of the universe, regardless of how much intelligibility science achieves with respect to the existent parts (objects, occurrences, processes, spatial and temporal scope) of the observable universe.

Thus, in the face of the acknowledged fact of the persistent human search for rationality and intelligibility on a metaphysical level, we should pose our own form of "why" question: Why need the very Existence of the world (apart from the existence of its internal details and observable features) be explainable? Mystery for mystery, why should we not allow that the Existence of the world is beyond all possible explanation? Why should we not regard the very Existence of the observable universe as a metaphysical datum in the same way as God's existence is accepted by the theist as that which must remain forever unintelligible? And why should we not ascribe the unintelligibility of the Existence of the observable universe, not to the fact of our human "finitude" and incapacity to find such a reason, but simply to the fact that the world's Existence is that for which the search for a reason is unsatisfiable? An awareness of Boundless Existence would then consist in the realization that the Existence of the observable universe is unintelligible: an irreducible and ineliminable feature of Reality. "Boundless Existence" could then serve as a way of emphasizing the metaphysical fact that inevitable failure faces any search to find an answer to the question "Why is there a universe at all?" In this respect, and to the extent we equate the "question of reality" with a search for an answer to the question "Why does the universe Exist at all?" there is *no answer.*

So much for a brief review of the basically different ways of responding to the awareness of the Existence of the universe—that of the theist and of our own account—and why, according to the latter, this awareness is accompanied by the realization that Existence is unintelligible: that it is conceptually Boundless.

In addition to the foregoing way of approaching the notion of Boundless Existence as signifying the unintelligibility (the unavailability of an explanation) of the Existence of the observable universe— and thus in opposition to the Platonic view that there is such an explanation and that the "question of reality" *can be answered*—there is another route that leads to the same conclusion. This is the route of epistemology. It does not fasten, as does the first route we have just briefly explored, on attempts to solve the mystery of Existence—to answering the question "*Why* does the universe Exist at all?" Instead, it focuses primarily on the question of the *what* of the observable universe: its having a certain structure and contents. And it seeks to answer the following kinds of questions: In what does the intelligibility of the contents and structure of the universe consist? In what sense, or to what extent, can we as human beings hope to understand and know the nature of that intelligible order? What is the source of this intelligibility? On what grounds do claims to have been able to establish intelligibility rest? And if sustained, what makes any such claims true? These questions are of a fundamentally epistemological sort.

The variety of ways in which these questions have been answered again points to a fundamental divergence in philosophical viewpoints. The divergence centers on the different ways of interpreting the meaning of "intelligibility": the Platonic and Kantian ways. As we have seen, the Kantian way, which we have followed here, offers its own way of analyzing what is involved in saying that the observable universe *can* be made intelligible. If by the "question of reality" one means "How can we describe and explain (render intelligible) the various observable features (the 'what') of the observable universe?" then, for the Kantian, this question can be answered. It consists in the application of humanly created sets of "grammatical rules," as in science, to the materials of observational experience, and by making the choice from among available proposals of those that prove most successful in practice. This process of creating conceptual schemes for purposes of description and explanation, and of choosing at a particular stage of inquiry the most successful ones, is an unending one when considered historically. The evaluation of "success" is not determined by looking among competing accounts for that one which matches perfectly (or even with increasing approximation and probability) the supposedly unique, objective, independently existing structure of the world "in itself." The "question of reality," if interpreted as asking for the criteria to be used in describing and explaining the materials of observational experience, is *not to be answered in a Platonic way,* that is, by finding which is the inherent, unique, intelligible order already implanted in the world by a Divine Intelligence. It involves, rather, a comparison of any proposed conceptual scheme with rival accounts that are also products of human creative intelligence. The goal is to see which, among available schemes, is *better* than any of the others available at a given stage of inquiry. There need be no presumption that there is a *best* one, and that it will be found when human beings will be able to match the unique pattern of intelligibility already supposedly embedded in the world in itself. If we surrender all reliance on and appeal to the analogy of craftsmanship on a cosmic and metaphysical level, as in the Platonic model, then the idea that the world contains "in itself" some discoverable, unique intelligible structure goes with it. This conception of the "in itself" is the echo and relic of the craftsman model and should be abandoned.

If, despite the foregoing objections using the Platonic sense of an intelligible order in the world "in itself," we wish nevertheless to retain, from a Kantian perspective, the use of the expression "in itself," this can be done only by saying that what is "in itself" is the Existence of the observable universe. Man does not create the Existence of the observable universe. Human beings, at most, are *aware that* the observable universe Exists. But *what* the Existence of the observable universe is "in itself" is unintelligible. The Existence of the observable universe "in itself" gives no foothold for the application of descriptive expressions or explanatory theories, no basis for exemplifying the use of general terms in predicative position.

In this respect, the "that" of the Existence of the observable universe is to be contrasted with the "that" of a recognized existent part or phase of development *within* the observable universe. *That* this person, or this building, this blade of grass, this thunderstorm, this supernova explosion, this planet, exists is open to description and explanation, to the application of some conceptual scheme. Where successful and accepted, the "that" of an existent within the observable universe is thereby made intelligible by links of one sort or another (causal, purposive, historical, etc.) to other existents that are also within the observable universe. But this way of rendering intelligible the "that" of an existent within the observable universe is not available for describing or explaining the "that" of the Existence of the observable universe. The "that" of the Existence of the observable universe has no properties, qualities, or structure of its own. It cannot be described or explained by linkage, via an acceptable scheme, to one or more existents. The Existence of the observable universe is devoid of anything that could sanction this way of thinking. *That* the observable universe Exists is Boundless; it is not "in itself" intelligible. The term "Boundless Existence" is used to mark this unintelligibility.

To sum up our main conclusions: The "positive" answer to the question of reality depends on making and applying appropriate distinctions in the uses of the expressions "existence" and "intelligibility."

In connection with "existence," the basic distinction is between (1) existents within the observable universe, or the observable universe insofar as it is a limited collection of existent objects, events, and processes, and is identified and understood at a particular stage of scientific inquiry; and (2) the Boundless Existence of the observable universe.

In connection with "intelligibility," the basic distinction is between a Platonic and Kantian sense of this term. The observable universe, as known at a given stage of scientific inquiry, *is* intelligible—but only in a Kantian way, not in a Platonic one. However, Boundless Existence, as manifested by the Existence of the observable universe, is unintelligible; it *cannot be rendered intelligible* either in a Platonic way (whether it be through a theistic metaphysics or a philosophy of epistemological realism) or in a

Kantian way. It cannot be described or explained by any acceptable conceptual scheme; it is conceptually Boundless. Insofar as the question of reality seeks an answer to *what* the intelligible structure of the Existence of the observable universe is *in itself,* there is *no answer.* Because Reality includes Boundless Existence, and the latter is the locus of a radical unintelligibility "in" Reality, we must also accept the negative conclusion that there is no answer to the question of reality. From this perspective, one must abandon the pursuit of metaphysics as a knowledge-yielding discipline.

The observable universe and Boundless Existence are the two basic aspects or dimensions of Reality—but they are not differentiated from one another by being two distinct types of entities. Boundless Existence is not transcendent to and distinct from the observable universe in the same way in which, according to traditional theology, God is distinct from and transcendent to the world. The presence in Reality of both the observable universe and Boundless Existence is altogether unique. No model or analogy drawn from ordinary experience of what is found in the observable universe will adequately serve to describe the presence in Reality of the observable universe and Boundless Existence.

QUESTIONS FOR DISCUSSION

1. Chuang Tzu says he knows the joy of fishes through his own joy, while walking by the river in which they swim. Do you think this empathy is a reliable indicator? Or are we being too literal in thus trying to understand Chuang Tzu?

2. Compare Borges's views on knowledge with those of Chuang Tzu.

3. Suzuki says that, so long as we depend on "the understanding," there will be no grasping of reality. Do you agree with this mystical conclusion? Why or why not?

Theistic Arguments and Atheistic Challenges
  A. C. Ewing, *Proofs of God's Existence*
  Antony Flew, *Theology and Falsification*
  Sigmund Freud, *A Philosophy of Life*

The Religious Experience
  Sarvepalli Radhakrishnan, *Personal Experience of God*
  Black Elk, *The Sacred Pipe*

Kitaro Nishida, *The Essence of Religion*
Buddhadasa, *No Religion*

Religion, Society, and Politics
  Karl Marx and Friedrich Engels, *Critique of Religion*
  Leonardo Boff and Clodovis Boff, *Liberation Theology*
  Carol P. Christ, *Why Women Need the Goddess*

William H. Johnson, *I Baptize Thee,* c. 1940, National Museum of American Art, Washington, D.C./Art Resource, NY.

122

CHAPTER 3

PHILOSOPHY OF RELIGION

The contemporary German-born psychoanalyst and social thinker Erich Fromm claims that all cultures and, indeed, all human beings are religious in that they develop a general frame of orientation to understand the fundamental problems of human existence. Such a framework attempts to locate one's own life within a larger scheme of things. Whether or not we want to conceptualize religion so broadly, it is clear that from the dawn of human civilization every culture has been concerned with what it identified as a religious dimension of life and embodied this concern in a specific set of religious institutions and ritual practices. In this more specific sense, religion points to an ultimate spiritual foundation of physical reality and human existence, a spiritual dimension that can provide us with an answer to questions of life and death, which attempts to explain the relation of the individual to the universe and which can offer a guide to human self-development and ethical conduct. Such a spiritual source has been most often, although not always, identified with the idea of God. It is for this reason that in the first section of this chapter we consider the philosophical question: Does God exist?

Philosophy of religion in the Western tradition has been to a large extent the attempt to answer this question by providing, analyzing, and criticizing rational demonstrations or proofs of God's existence. In the first section the contemporary British philosopher A. C. Ewing presents three of these proofs and gives qualified support to two of them. The second two selections in this section—by the contemporary British philosopher Antony Flew and the renowned founder of psychoanalysis Sigmund Freud—answer the question in the negative.

Philosophical proofs of the existence of God have been a much more important philosophical enterprise within the West than it has been for other religious traditions. In part this is because these other traditions tend to be more concerned with religious experience as such, or what is sometimes called "the mystical experience." While those who have had such experiences often talk about them as experiences of God, they do not always do so. In fact, while religious or mystical experiences as such seem to be cross-cultural, they tend to be interpreted through the cultural and philosophical categories of each religious tradition. This leads to the proposition expressed by the contemporary Thai Buddhist, Buddhadasa, that the essence of religion transcends all religions.

In the final section of this chapter we examine

the relationship of religion to social and political change. Although the nineteenth-century revolutionary German philosopher Karl Marx characterized religion as the "opium of the people," religion has also been used to challenge the ruling powers. In Latin America, for example, a powerful revolutionary current has emerged in the last several decades known as "liberation theology." The selection by two Brazilian theologians and priests who are also brothers, Leonardo and Clodovis Boff, attempts to explain the political, theological, and philosophical significance of this movement. Finally, the last selection by the feminist writer Carol Christ challenges the patriarchal categories of traditional religious thought and suggests that women might do well to disavow God the Father and embrace the Goddess.

Readers of Section One might also want to look at Chapter 2, especially Section Two, for a discussion of the nature of scientific method and the value of the scientific world view. Those who are particular interested in Antony Flew's logical positivist approach might want to see an application of this same approach to another philosophical problem by Moritz Schlick in the fourth section of Chapter 6.

Readers of Section Two who want to know more about the Hindu point of view should see another reading by Radhakrishnan in Section One of Chapter 6 and the reading by Bitheka Mukerji in Section One of Chapter 4. Those who want to know more about the Buddhist approach should consult the selection by Chogyam Trungpa in the third section of Chapter 8 and, more specifically, for the Zen Buddhist approach should read the third section of Chapter 1, the article by Shin'Ichi Hisamatsu in Section One of Chapter 4, but especially the articles by Daisetz Suzuki in Section Five of Chapter 2 and by Toshiko Izutsu in Section Three of Chapter 5. Those particularly interested in learning more about Kitaro Nishida's philosophy should read the other selection by him in Section Four of Chapter 6. Although the Taoist point of view is not represented in this section, Taoist metaphysics is represented by Lao Tzu in Section Four of Chapter 1, its epistemology by Chuang Tzu in Section Five of Chapter 2, and its general position concerning how to live in Section Two of Chapter 8.

Readers of Section Three might be interested in Chapter 9 in its entirety but especially selections by Karl Marx and Friedrich Engels and by Paulo Freire, who has been an important influence on liberation theology, both of which appear in Section Two of that chapter. Finally, for those interested in Carol Christ's article on feminist spirituality, we recommend Section Two of Chapter 4 and especially the readings by Simone de Beauvoir and Ann Ferguson.

THEISTIC ARGUMENTS AND ATHEIST CHALLENGES

The Bible does not attempt to prove the existence of God but rather assumes it. For those who lived in the community for whom the Bible was originally meaningful, God's existence was beyond question. Only when a system of beliefs begins to break down do people feel the need to question that system. This happens when one culture meets another or when the development of a new mode of thinking emerges. Modern science is such a new mode of thinking.

The scientific ethos puts belief in God in question in two ways. First, the ethos insists that ideas about the world must be, in some way, verified in experience. Second, specific theories of science pose challenges to, at least, some traditional Western religious beliefs. Before Galileo looked through his telescope and found evidence that Copernicus was right, it was generally assumed that God created the earth at the center of the universe so that his human creation would also be so situated. Darwin's theory of evolution challenged the idea of Adam and Eve as a separate creation. And Sigmund Freud's psychoanalytic theories imply that belief in God might have less than spiritual motives.

Although the main arguments for the existence of God were originally formulated in the Middle Ages or earlier, they take on a special urgency in the modern scientific era. A. C. Ewing, a twentieth-century British philosopher, in the first selection of this section, presents a version of three classical arguments. The first, the ontological argument which attempts to deduce the existence of God from the very concept of God, Ewing finds unsatisfying. But he gives qualified support to the cosmological argument, which assumes that we need an ultimate reason or First Cause to account for the existence of the world, and the argument from design (sometimes called the "teleological argument") which argues from the appearance of orderliness and design in the universe to the existence of a Grand Designer. These arguments, Ewing asserts, do not provide a definitive proof of God's existence but give the world view of the *theist* (one who believes in the existence of God) a higher probability value than the world view of the *atheist* (one who denies God's existence). In the last analysis, Ewing claims that "it does remain incredible that the physical universe should just have happened."

Antony Flew, the contemporary British philosopher and proponent of logical positivism, is the second author in this section. Logical positivism is a philosophical method which assumes that a statement about the world is meaningful only if we can say what kinds of conditions and observations would lead us to accept it as true or false. Emphasizing the latter consideration, Flew insists that for a statement to be meaningful it must in principle be capable of falsification. This is known as the "falsifiability criteria." Using a parable of an invisible gardener, Flew attempts to show that the falsifiability criteria cannot be satisfied with regard to statements about God, and, therefore, such assertions as "God exists" or "God loves us" are neither true nor false but simply meaningless.

It is important to note that when Flew claims that statements about God are not meaningful, he is denying their cognitive status, not talking about whether they have emotional significance for our lives. It is hardly to be doubted that for many people in the world belief in the existence of God is of great psychological importance. Indeed, some might argue that this fact alone establishes the existence of God. How is it possible for so many people to believe in God, if the belief itself is false or meaningless? Sigmund Freud, in the last article in this section, speaks directly to this question. Freud uses his psychoanalytic method to trace the origin of belief in God to the child's helplessness in relation to his or her parents. For Freud, "God the Father" functions precisely as the infant once viewed his real father—as a creator of his or her existence, as an omnipotent protector, and as one who imposes prohibitions and threatens punishment. Religion, then, is a fantasy which attempts to relive this aspect of our childhood experiences. In this sense, religion speaks to some real human desires and fears but remains an illusion which cannot provide an adequate account of the real world. For that we need the scientific world view. In another of his works, *The Future of an Illusion,* Freud describes religion as a universal cultural neurosis which must be transcended if civilization as a whole is to move from its childhood to maturity.

PROOFS OF GOD'S EXISTENCE

A. C. Ewing

By "God" I shall understand . . . a supreme mind regarded as either omnipotent or at least more powerful than anything else and supremely good and wise. It is not within the scope of a purely philosophical work to discuss the claims of revelation on which belief in God and his attributes has so often been based, but philosophers have also formulated a great number of *arguments* for the existence of God.

THE ONTOLOGICAL ARGUMENT

To start with the most dubious and least valuable of these, the *ontological* argument claims to prove the existence of God by a mere consideration of our idea of him. God is defined as the most perfect being or as a being containing all positive attributes.[1] It is then argued that existence is a "perfection" or a positive attribute, and that therefore, if we are to avoid contradicting ourselves, we must grant the existence of God. The most important of the objections to the argument is to the effect that existence is not a "perfection" or an attribute. To say that something exists is to assert a proposition of a very different kind from what we assert when we ascribe any ordinary attribute to a thing. It is not to increase the concept of the thing by adding a new characteristic, but merely to affirm that the concept is realized in fact. This is one of the cases where we are apt to be misled by language. Because "cats exist" and "cats sleep," or "cats are existent" and "cats are carnivorous," are sentences of the same grammatical form, people are liable to suppose that they also express the same form of proposition, but this is not the case. To say that cats are carnivorous is to ascribe an additional quality to beings already presupposed as existing; to say that cats are existent is to say that propositions ascribing to something the properties which constitute the definition of a cat are sometimes true. The distinction is still more obvious in the negative case. If "dragons are not existent animals" were a proposition of the same form as "lions are not herbivorous animals," to say that dragons are not existent would already be to presuppose their existence. A lion has to exist in order to have the negative property of not being herbivorous, but in order to be non-existent a dragon need not first exist.[2] "Dragons are non-existent" means that nothing has the properties commonly implied by the word "dragon."

It has sometimes been said that "the ontological proof" is just an imperfect formulation of a principle which no one can help admitting and which is a necessary presupposition of all knowledge. This is the principle that what we really must think must be

---

[1] "Positive" (1) enables us to exclude evil attributes on the ground that they are negative, (2) implies the infinity of God, for there would be an element of negativity in him if he possessed any attribute in any limited degree, i.e. superior degrees would be denied of him.

[2] We can of course say that dragons are not herbivorous if we are merely making a statement about the content of fictitious stories of dragons.

true of reality. ("Must" here is the logical, not the psychological must.) If we did not assume this principle, we should never be entitled to accept something as a fact because it satisfies our best intellectual criteria, and therefore we should have no ground for asserting anything at all. Even experience would not help us, since any proposition contradicting experience might well be true if the law of contradiction were not assumed to be objectively valid. This, however, is so different from what the ontological proof as formulated by its older exponents says that it should not be called by the same name. And in any case the principle that what we must think must be true of reality could only be used to establish the existence of God if we already had reached the conclusion that we must think this, i.e. had already justified the view that God exists (or seen it to be self-evident).

THE FIRST CAUSE ARGUMENT

The *cosmological* or first cause argument is of greater importance. The greatest thinker of the Middle Ages, St. Thomas Aquinas (*circ.* 1225-74), while rejecting the ontological argument, made the cosmological the main intellectual basis of his own theism, and in this respect he has been followed by Roman Catholic orthodoxy. To this day it is often regarded in such circles as proving with mathematical certainty the existence of God. It has, however, also played a very large part in Protestant thought; and an argument accepted in different forms by such varied philosophers of the highest eminence as Aristotle, St. Thomas, Descartes, Locke, Leibniz, and many modern thinkers certainly ought not to be despised. The argument is briefly to the effect that we require a reason to account for the world and this ultimate reason must be of such a kind as itself not to require a further reason to account for it. It is then argued that God is the only kind of being who could be conceived as self-sufficient and so as not requiring a cause beyond himself but being his own reason. The argument has an appeal because we are inclined to demand a reason for things, and the notion of a first cause is the only alternative to the notion

of an infinite regress, which is very difficult and seems even self-contradictory. Further, if any being is to be conceived as necessarily existing and so not needing a cause outside itself, it is most plausible to conceive God as occupying this position. But the argument certainly makes assumptions which may be questioned. It assumes the principle of causation in a form in which the cause is held to give a reason for the effect, a doctrine with which I have sympathy but which would probably be rejected by the majority of modern philosophers outside the Roman Catholic Church. Further, it may be doubted whether we can apply to the world as a whole the causal principle which is valid within the world; and if we say that the causal principle thus applied is only analogous to the latter the argument is weakened. Finally, and this I think the most serious point, it is exceedingly difficult to see how anything could be its own reason. To be this it would seem that it must exist necessarily *a priori.** Now we can well see how it can be necessary *a priori* that something, p, should be true if something else, q, is, or again how it can be necessary *a priori* that something self-contradictory should not exist, but it is quite another matter to see how it could be *a priori* necessary in the logical sense that something should positively exist. What contradiction could there be in its not existing?[3] In the mere blank of non-existence there can be nothing to contradict. I do not say that it can be seen to be absolutely impossible that a being could be its own logical reason, but I at least have not the faintest notion how this could be. The advocates of the cosmological proof might, however, contend that God was necessary in some non-logical sense, which is somewhat less unplausible though still quite incomprehensible to us.

Can the cosmological argument, clearly invalid as a complete proof, be stated in a form which retains some probability value? It may still be argued

---

* *A priori:* A Latin phrase meaning, literally, "from what comes before." In philosophy, this phrase refers to something which precedes or is independent of sensory experience. Thus, what is *a priori* is true, valid, or exists by necessity (Eds.).

[3] It is one of the objections to the ontological proof that it claims to find a contradiction in God not existing.

that the world will at least be more rational if it is as the theist pictures it than if it is not, and that it is more reasonable to suppose that the world is rational than to suppose that it is irrational. Even the latter point would be contradicted by many modern thinkers, but though we cannot prove the view they reject to be true, we should at least note that it is the view which is presupposed by science, often unconsciously, in its own sphere. For, as we have seen, practically no scientific propositions can be established by strict demonstration and/or observation alone. Science could not advance at all if it did not assume some criterion beyond experience and the laws of logic and mathematics. What is this criterion? It seems to be coherence in a rational system. We have rejected the view that this is the only criterion, but it is certainly one criterion of truth. For of two hypotheses equally in accord with the empirical facts, scientists will always prefer the one which makes the universe more of a rational system to the one which does not. Science does this even though neither hypothesis is capable of rationalizing the universe completely or even of giving a complete ultimate explanation of the phenomena in question. It is sufficient that the hypothesis adopted brings us a step nearer to the ideal of a fully coherent, rationally explicable world. Now theism cannot indeed completely rationalize the universe till it can show how God can be his own cause, or how it is that he does not need a cause, and till it can also overcome the problem of evil completely, but it does come nearer to rationalizing it than does any other view. The usual modern philosophical views opposed to theism do not try to give any rational explanation of the world at all, but just take it as a brute fact not to be explained, and it must certainly be admitted that we come at least nearer to a rational explanation if we regard the course of the world as determined by purpose and value than if we do not. So it may be argued that according to the scientific principle that we should accept the hypothesis which brings the universe nearest to a coherent rational system theism should be accepted by us. The strong point of the cosmological argument is that after all it does

remain incredible that the physical universe should just have happened, even if it be reduced to the juxtaposition of some trillions of electrons. It calls out for some further explanation of some kind.

THE ARGUMENT FROM DESIGN

The *teleological argument* or the *argument from design* is the argument from the adaptation of the living bodies of organisms to their ends and the ends of their species. This is certainly very wonderful: there are thousands of millions of cells in our brain knit together in a system which works; twenty or thirty different muscles are involved even in such a simple act as a sneeze; directly a wound is inflicted or germs enter an animal's body all sorts of protective mechanisms are set up, different cells are so cunningly arranged that, if we cut off the tail of one of the lower animals, a new one is grown, and the very same cells can develop according to what is needed into a tail or into a leg. Such intricate arrangements seem to require an intelligent purposing mind to explain them. It may be objected that, even if such an argument shows wisdom in God, it does not show goodness and is therefore of little value. The reply may be made that it is incredible that a mind who is so much superior to us in intelligence as to have designed the whole universe should not be at least as good as the best men and should not, to put it at its lowest, care for his offspring at least as well as a decent human father and much more wisely because of his superior knowledge and intellect. Still it must be admitted that the argument could not at its best establish all that the theist would ordinarily wish to establish. It might show that the designer was very powerful, but it could not show him to be omnipotent or even to have created the world as opposed to manufacturing it out of given material; it might make it probable that he was good, but it could not possibly prove him perfect. And of course the more unpleasant features of the struggle for existence in nature are far from supporting the hypothesis of a good God.

But does the argument justify any conclusion at

all? It has been objected that it does not on the following ground. It is an argument from analogy, it is said, to this effect: animal bodies are like machines, a machine has a designer, therefore animal bodies have a designer. But the strength of an argument from analogy depends on the likeness between what is compared. Now animal bodies are really not very like machines, and God is certainly not very like a man. Therefore the argument from analogy based on our experience of men designing machines has not enough strength to give much probability to its conclusion. This criticism, I think, would be valid if the argument from design were really in the main an argument from analogy,[4] but I do not think it is. The force of the argument lies not in the analogy, but in the extraordinary intricacy with which the details of a living body are adapted to serve its own interests, an intricacy far too great to be regarded as merely a coincidence. Suppose we saw pebbles on the shore arranged in such a way as to make an elaborate machine. It is theoretically possible that they might have come to occupy such positions by mere chance, but it is fantastically unlikely, and we should feel no hesitation in jumping to the conclusion that they had been thus deposited not by the tide but by some intelligent agent. Yet the body of the simplest living creature is a more complex machine than the most complex ever devised by a human engineer.

Before the theory of evolution was accepted the only reply to this argument was to say that in an infinite time there is room for an infinite number of possible combinations, and therefore it is not, even apart from a designing mind, improbable that there should be worlds or stages in the development of worlds which display great apparent purposiveness. If a monkey played with a typewriter at random, it is most unlikely that it would produce an intelligible book; but granted a sufficient number of billions of years to live and keep playing, the creature would probably eventually produce quite by accident a great number. For the number of possible combinations of twenty-six letters in successions of words is finite, though enormously large, and therefore given a sufficiently long time it is actually probable that any particular one would be reached. This may easily be applied to the occurrence of adaptations in nature. Out of all the possible combinations of things very few would display marked adaptation; but if the number of ingredients of the universe is finite the number of their combinations is also finite, and therefore it is only probable that, given an infinite time, some worlds or some stages in a world process should appear highly purposeful, though they are only the result of a chance combination of atoms. The plausibility of this reply is diminished when we reflect what our attitude would be to somebody who, when playing bridge, had thirteen spades in his hand several times running—according to the laws of probability an enormously less improbable coincidence than would be an unpurposed universe with so much design unaccounted for—and then used such an argument to meet the charge of cheating. Our attitude to his reply would surely hardly be changed even if we believed that people had been playing bridge for an infinite time. If only we were satisfied that matter had existed and gone on changing for ever, would we conclude that the existence of leaves or pebbles on the ground in such positions as to make an intelligible book no longer provided evidence making it probable that somebody had deliberately arranged them? Surely not. And, if not, why should the supposition that matter had gone on changing for ever really upset the argument from design? Of course the appearance of design *may be* fortuitous; the argument from design never claims to give certainty but only probability. But, granted the universe as we have it, is it not a much less improbable hypothesis that it should really have been designed than that it should constitute one of the fantastically rare stages which showed design in an infinite series of chance universes? Further, that matter has been changing for

---

[4] Hume's criticisms of it in the famous *Dialogues concerning Natural Religion* depend mainly on the assumption that it is such an argument.

an infinite time is a gratuitous assumption and one not favoured by modern science.[5]

But now the theory of evolution* claims to give an alternative explanation of the adaptation of organisms that removes the improbability of which we have complained. Once granted the existence of some organisms their offspring would not all be exactly similar. Some would necessarily be somewhat better equipped than others for surviving and producing offspring in their turn, and their characteristics would therefore tend to be more widely transmitted. When we take vast numbers into account, this will mean that a larger and larger proportion of the species will have had relatively favourable variations transmitted to them by their parents, while unfavourable variations will tend to die out. Thus from small beginnings accumulated all the extraordinarily elaborate mechanism which now serves the purpose of living creatures.

There can be no question for a properly informed person of denying the evolution theory, but only of considering whether it is adequate by itself to explain the striking appearance of design. If it is not, it may perfectly well be combined with the metaphysical hypothesis that a mind has designed and controls the universe. Evolution will then be just the way in which God's design works out. Now in reply to the purely evolutionary explanation it has been said that for evolution to get started at all some or-

ganisms must have already appeared. Otherwise the production of offspring and their survival or death in the struggle for existence would not have come into question at all. But even the simplest living organism is a machine very much more complex than a motor car. Therefore, if it would be absurd to suppose inorganic matter coming together fortuitously of itself to form a motor car, it would be even more absurd to suppose it thus coming together to form an organism, so without design the evolutionary process would never get started at all. Nor, even granting that this miracle had occurred, could the evolutionists claim that they had been altogether successful in removing the antecedent improbability of such an extensive adaptation as is in fact shown by experience. It has been urged that, since we may go wrong in a vast number of ways for one in which we may go right, the probability of favourable variations is very much less than that of unfavourable; that in order to produce the effect on survival required a variation would have to be large, but if it were large it would usually lessen rather than increase the chance of survival, unless balanced by other variations the occurrence of which simultaneously with the first would be much more improbable still; and that the odds are very great against either a large number of animals in a species having the variations together by chance or their spreading from a single animal through the species by natural selection. The arguments suggest that, so to speak, to weight the chances we require a purpose, which we should not need, however, to think of as intervening at odd moments but as controlling the whole process. The establishment of the evolution theory no doubt lessens the great improbability of the adaptations having occurred without this, but the original improbability is so vast as to be able to survive a great deal of lessening, and it does not remove it.

Some thinkers would regard it as adequate to postulate an unconscious purpose to explain design, but it is extraordinarily difficult to see what such a thing as an unconscious purpose could be. In one sense indeed I can understand such a phrase. "Unconscious" might mean "unintrospected" or "unin-

---

[5] Strictly speaking, what is required by those who put forward the objection in question to the argument from design is not necessarily that matter should have been changing for an infinite time but only for a sufficiently long, though finite, time. But the length of time allowed by modern science for the development of the earth and indeed for that of the whole universe does not in the faintest degree approach what would be needed to make the appearance of organized beings as a result of mere random combinations of atoms anything less than monstrously improbable.

* *Theory of evolution:* The theory developed by Charles Darwin (1809–1882) which proposes a scientific explanation of the development of different species. In brief, the theory argues that all known living organisms have evolved from the simplest living organism through a process known as "natural selection," through the capacities of certain accidental new characteristics to adapt to the environment. Evolutionary theory is generally accepted by the scientific community and is the foundation for much of modern biology (Eds.).

trospectible," and then the purpose would be one which occurred in a mind that did think on the matter but did not self-consciously notice its thinking. But this sense will not do here, for it already presupposes a mind. To talk of a purpose which is not present in any mind at all seems to me as unintelligible as it would be to talk of rectangles which had no extension. The argument from design has therefore to my mind considerable, though not, by itself at least, conclusive force. It is also strange that there should be so much beauty in the world, that there should have resulted from an unconscious unintelligent world beings who could form the theory that the world was due to chance or frame moral ideals in the light of which they could condemn it. It might be suggested that a mind designed the organic without designing the inorganic, but the connection between organic and inorganic and the unity of the world in general are too close to make this a plausible view.

The counter argument from evil is of course formidable, but I shall defer discussion of it to a later stage in the chapter, as it is rather an argument against theism in general than a specific objection to the argument from design. I must, however, make two remarks here. First, it is almost a commonplace that the very large amount of apparent waste in nature is a strong prima facie argument against the world having been designed by a good and wise being. But is there really much "wasted"? A herring may produce hundreds of thousands or millions of eggs for one fish that arrives at maturity, but most of the eggs which come to grief serve as food for other animals. We do not look on the eggs we eat at breakfast, when we can get them, as "wasted," though the hen might well do so. It is certainly very strange that a good God should have designed a world in which the living beings can only maintain their life by devouring each other, but this is part of the general problem of evil and not a specific problem of waste in nature. Secondly, the occurrence of elaborate adaptations to ends is a very much stronger argument for the presence of an intelligence than its apparent absence in a good many instances is against it. A dog would see no purpose whatever in

my present activity, but he would not therefore have adequate grounds for concluding that I had no intelligence. If there is a God, it is only to be expected *a priori* that in regard to a great deal of his work we should be in the same position as the dog is in regard to ours, and therefore the fact that we are in this position is no argument that there is no God. The occurrence of events requiring intelligence to explain them is positive evidence for the presence of intelligence, but the absence of results we think worth while in particular cases is very slight evidence indeed on the other side where we are debating the existence of a being whose intelligence, if he exists, we must in any case assume to be as much above ours as that of the maker of the whole world would have to be. The existence of positive evil of course presents a greater difficulty to the theist.

THEOLOGY AND FALSIFICATION

Antony Flew

Let us begin with a parable. It is a parable developed from a tale told by John Wisdom in his haunting and revelatory article "Gods."[1] Once upon a time two explorers came upon a clearing in the jungle. In the clearing were growing many flowers and many weeds. One explorer says, "Some gardener must tend this plot." The other disagrees, "There is no gardener." So they pitch their tents and set a watch. No gardener is ever seen. "But perhaps he is an invisible gardener." So they set up a barbed-wire fence. They electrify it. They patrol with bloodhounds. (For they remember how H. G. Wells's *The Invisible Man* could be both smelt and touched

---

[1] *P.A.S.,* 1944–5, reprinted as Ch. X of *Logic and Language,* Vol I (Blackwell, 1951), and in his *Philosophy and Psychoanalysis* (Blackwell, 1953).

though he could not be seen.) But no shrieks ever suggest that some intruder has received a shock. No movements of the wire ever betray an invisible climber. The bloodhounds never give cry. Yet still the Believer is not convinced. "But there is a gardener, invisible, intangible, insensible to electric shocks, a gardener who has no scent and makes no sound, a gardener who comes secretly to look after the garden which he loves." At last the Sceptic despairs, "But what remains of your original assertion? Just how does what you call an invisible, intangible, eternally elusive gardener differ from an imaginary gardener or even from no gardener at all?"

In this parable we can see how what starts as an assertion, that something exists or that there is some analogy between certain complexes of phenomena, may be reduced step by step to an altogether different status, to an expression perhaps of a "picture preference."[2] The Sceptic says there is no gardener. The Believer says there is a gardener (but invisible, etc.). One man talks about sexual behaviour. Another man prefers to talk of Aphrodite* (but knows that there is not really a superhuman person additional to, and somehow responsible for, all sexual phenomena). The process of qualification may be checked at any point before the original assertion is completely withdrawn and something of that first assertion will remain (Tautology). Mr. Wells's invisible man could not, admittedly, be seen, but in all others respects he was a man like the rest of us. But though the process of qualification may be, and of course usually is, checked in time, it is not always judiciously so halted. Someone may dissipate his assertion completely without noticing that he has done so. A fine brash hypothesis may thus be killed by inches, the death by a thousand qualifications.

And in this, it seems to me, lies the peculiar danger, the endemic evil, of theological utterance. Take

such utterances as "God has a plan," "God created the world," "God loves us as a father loves his children." They look at first sight very much like assertions, vast cosmological assertions. Of course, this is no sure sign that they either are, or are intended to be, assertions. But let us confine ourselves to the cases where those who utter such sentences intend them to express assertions. (Merely remarking parenthetically that those who intend or interpret such utterances as crypto-commands, expressions of wishes, disguised ejaculations, concealed ethics, or as anything else but assertions, are unlikely to succeed in making them either properly orthodox or practically effective.)

Now to assert that such and such is the case is necessarily equivalent to denying that such and such is not the case.[3] Suppose then that we are in doubt as to what someone who gives vent to an utterance is asserting, or suppose that, more radically, we are sceptical as to whether he is really asserting anything at all, one way of trying to understand (or perhaps it will be to expose) his utterance is to attempt to find what he would regard as counting against, or as being incompatible with, its truth. For if the utterance is indeed an assertion, it will necessarily be equivalent to a denial of the negation of that assertion. And anything which would count against the assertion, or which would induce the speaker to withdraw it and to admit that it had been mistaken, must be part of (or the whole of) the meaning of the negation of that assertion. And to know the meaning of the negation of an assertion is, as near as makes no matter, to know the meaning of that assertion.[4] And if there is nothing which a putative assertion denies then there is nothing which it asserts either: and so it is not really an assertion. When the Sceptic in the parable asked the Believer, "Just how does what you call an invisible, intangible, eternally elusive gardener differ from an imaginary gardener or even from no gardener at all?" he was suggesting that the Believer's earlier statement

---

[2] Cf. J. Wisdom, "Other Minds," *Mind,* 1940; reprinted in his *Other Minds* (Blackwell, 1952).

* *Aphrodite:* In ancient Greek mythology, the goddess of love, sex, and beauty. In Roman mythology, she was called "Venus" (Eds.).

[3] For those who prefer symbolism: $p \equiv \sim \sim p$.

[4] For by simply negating $\sim p$ we get $p: \sim \sim p \equiv p$.

had been so eroded by qualification that it was no longer an assertion at all.

Now it often seems to people who are not religious as if there was no conceivable event or series of events the occurrence of which would be admitted by sophisticated religious people to be a sufficient reason for conceding "There wasn't a God after all" or "God does not really love us then." Someone tells us that God loves us as a father loves his children. We are reassured. But then we see a child dying of inoperable cancer of the throat. His earthly father is driven frantic in his efforts to help, but his Heavenly Father reveals no obvious sign of concern. Some qualification is made—God's love is "not a merely human love" or it is "an inscrutable love," perhaps—and we realize that such sufferings are quite compatible with the truth of the assertion that "God loves us as a father (but, of course, . . .)." We are reassured again. But then perhaps we ask: what is this assurance of God's (appropriately qualified) love worth, what is this apparent guarantee really a guarantee against? Just what would have to happen not merely (morally and wrongly) to tempt but also (logically and rightly) to entitle us to say "God does not love us" or even "God does not exist"? I therefore put to the succeeding symposiasts the simple central questions, "What would have to occur or to have occurred to constitute for you a disproof of the love of, or of the existence of, God?"

A PHILOSOPHY OF LIFE

Sigmund Freud

If we are to give an account of the grandiose nature of religion, we must bear in mind what it undertakes to do for human beings. It gives them information about the origin and coming into existence of the universe, it assures them of its protection and of ultimate happiness in the ups and downs of life and it directs their thoughts and actions by precepts which it lays down with its whole authority. Thus it fulfils three functions. With the first of them it satisfies the human thirst for knowledge; it does the same thing that science attempts to do with *its* means, and at that point enters into rivalry with it. It is to its second function that it no doubt owes the greatest part of its influence. Science can be no match for it when it soothes the fear that men feel of the dangers and vicissitudes of life, when it assures them of a happy ending and offers them comfort in unhappiness. It is true that science can teach us how to avoid certain dangers and that there are some sufferings which it can successfully combat; it would be most unjust to deny that it is a powerful helper to men; but there are many situations in which it must leave a man to his suffering and can only advise him to submit to it. In its third function, in which it issues precepts and lays down prohibitions and restrictions, religion is furthest away from science. For science is content to investigate and to establish facts, though it is true that from its applications rules and advice are derived on the conduct of life. In some circumstances these are the same as those offered by religion, but, when this is so, the reasons for them are different.

The convergence between these three aspects of religion is not entirely clear. What has an explanation of the origin of the universe to do with the inculcation of certain particular ethical precepts? The assurances of protection and happiness are more intimately linked with the ethical requirements. They are the reward for fulfilling these commands; only those who obey them may count upon these benefits, punishment awaits the disobedient. Incidentally, something similar is true of science. Those who disregard its lessons, so it tells us, expose themselves to injury.

The remarkable combination in religion of instruction, consolation and requirements can only be understood if it is subjected to a genetic analysis. This may be approached from the most striking point of the aggregate, from its instruction on the origin of the universe; for why, we may ask, should a cosmogony be a regular component of religious systems? The doctrine is, then, that the universe was created by a being resembling a man, but magnified in every respect, in power, wisdom, and the strength of his passions—an idealized super-man. Animals as creators of the universe point to the influence of totemism, upon which we shall have a few words at least to say presently. It is an interesting fact that this creator is always only a single being, even when there are believed to be many gods. It is interesting, too, that the creator is usually a man, though there is far from being a lack of indications of female deities; and some mythologies actually make the creation begin with a male god getting rid of a female deity, who is degraded into being a monster. Here the most interesting problems of detail open out; but we must hurry on. Our further path is made easy to recognize, for this god-creator is undisguisedly called "father." Psychoanalysis infers that he really is the father, with all the magnificence in which he once appeared to the small child. A religious man pictures the creation of the universe just as he pictures his own origin.

This being so, it is easy to explain how it is that consoling assurances and strict ethical demands are combined with a cosmogony. For the same person to whom the child owed his existence, the father (or more correctly, no doubt, the parental agency compounded of the father and mother), also protected and watched over him in his feeble and helpless state, exposed as he was to all the dangers lying in wait in the external world; under his father's protection he felt safe. When a human being has himself grown up, he knows, to be sure, that he is in possession of greater strength, but his insight into the perils of life has also grown greater, and he rightly concludes that fundamentally he still remains just as helpless and unprotected as he was in his childhood, that faced by the world he is still a child. Even now, therefore, he cannot do without the protection which he enjoyed as a child. But he has long since recognized, too, that his father is a being of narrowly restricted power, and not equipped with every excellence. He therefore harks back to the mnemic image of the father whom in his childhood he so greatly overvalued. He exalts the image into a deity and makes it into something con-

temporary and real. The effective strength of this mnemic image and the persistence of his need for protection jointly sustain his belief in God.

The third main item in the religious programme, the ethical demand, also fits into this childhood situation with ease. I may remind you of Kant's famous pronouncement in which he names, in a single breath, the starry heavens and the moral law within us. However strange this juxtaposition may sound—for what have the heavenly bodies to do with the question of whether one human creature loves another or kills him?—it nevertheless touches on a great psychological truth. The same father (or parental agency) which gave the child life and guarded him against its perils taught him as well what he might do and what he must leave undone, instructed him that he must adapt himself to certain restrictions on his instinctual wishes, and made him understand what regard he was expected to have for his parents and brothers and sisters, if he wanted to become a tolerated and welcome member of the family circle and later on of larger associations. The child is brought up to a knowledge of his social duties by a system of loving rewards and punishments, he is taught that his security in life depends on his parents (and afterwards other people) loving him and on their being able to believe that he loves them. All these relations are afterwards introduced by men unaltered into their religion. Their parents' prohibitions and demands persist within them as a moral conscience. With the help of this same system of rewards and punishments, God rules the world of men. The amount of protection and happy satisfaction assigned to an individual depends on his fulfilment of the ethical demands; his love of God and his consciousness of being loved by God are the foundations of the security with which he is armed against the dangers of the external world and of his human environment. Finally, in prayer he has assured himself a direct influence on the divine will and with it a share in the divine omnipotence.

• • •

The scientific spirit, strengthened by the observation of natural processes, has begun, in the course of time, to treat religion as a human affair and to submit it to a critical examination. Religion was not able to stand up to this. What first gave rise to suspicion and scepticism were its tales of miracles, for they contradicted everything that had been taught by sober observation and betrayed too clearly the influence of the activity of the human imagination. After this its doctrines explaining the origin of the universe met with rejection, for they gave evidence of an ignorance which bore the stamp of ancient times and to which, thanks to their increased familiarity with the laws of nature, people knew they were superior. The idea that the universe came into existence through acts of copulation or creation analogous to the origin of individual people had ceased to be the most obvious and self-evident hypothesis since the distinction between animate creatures with a mind and an inanimate Nature had impressed itself on human thought—a distinction which made it impossible to retain belief in the original animism. Nor must we overlook the influence of the comparative study of different religious systems and the impression of their mutual exclusiveness and intolerance.

Strengthened by these preliminary exercises, the scientific spirit gained enough courage at last to venture on an examination of the most important and emotionally valuable elements of the religious *Weltanschauung*.* People may always have seen, though it was long before they dared to say so openly, that the pronouncements of religion promising men protection and happiness if they would only fulfil certain ethical requirements had also shown themselves unworthy of belief. It seems not to be the case that there is a Power in the universe which watches over the well-being of individuals with parental care and brings all their affairs to a happy ending. On the contrary, the destinies of mankind can be brought into harmony neither with

the hypothesis of a Universal Benevolence nor with the partly contradictory one of a Universal Justice. Earthquakes, tidal waves, conflagrations, make no distinction between the virtuous and pious and the scoundrel or unbeliever. Even where what is in question is not inanimate Nature but where an individual's fate depends on his relations to other people, it is by no means the rule that virtue is rewarded and that evil finds its punishment. Often enough the violent, cunning or ruthless man seizes the envied good things of the world and the pious man goes away empty. Obscure, unfeeling and unloving powers determine men's fate; the system of rewards and punishments which religion ascribes to the government of the universe seems not to exist.

• • •

The last contribution to the criticism of the religious *Weltanschauung* was effected by psychoanalysis, by showing how religion originated from the helplessness of children and by tracing its contents to the survival into maturity of the wishes and needs of childhood. This did not precisely mean a contradiction of religion, but it was nevertheless a necessary rounding-off of our knowledge about it, and in one respect at least it was a contradiction, for religion itself lays claim to a divine origin. And, to be sure, it is not wrong in this, provided that our interpretation of God is accepted.

In summary, therefore, the judgement of science on the religious *Weltanschauung* is this. While the different religions wrangle with one another as to which of them is in possession of the truth, our view is that the question of the truth of religious beliefs may be left altogether on one side. Religion is an attempt to master the sensory world in which we are situated by means of the wishful world which we have developed within us as a result of biological and psychological necessities. But religion cannot achieve this. Its doctrines bear the imprint of the times in which they arose, the ignorant times of the childhood of humanity. Its consolations deserve no trust. Experience teaches us that the world is no nursery. The ethical demands on which religion seeks to lay stress need, rather, to be given another

---

* *Weltanschauung:* From the German, literally, "world view." The term refers to one's general framework or system of beliefs about the universe and life. In this essay, Freud is contrasting the religious world view with the general assumptions of science (Eds.).

basis; for they are indispensable to human society and it is dangerous to link obedience to them with religious faith. If we attempt to assign the place of religion in the evolution of mankind, it appears not as a permanent acquisition but as a counterpart to the neurosis which individual civilized men have to go through in their passage from childhood to maturity.

• • •

The struggle of the scientific spirit against the religious *Weltanschauung* is, as you know, not at an end: it is still going on to-day under our eyes. Though as a rule psycho-analysis makes little use of the weapon of controversy, I will not hold back from looking into this dispute. In doing so I may perhaps throw some further light on our attitude to *Weltanschauungen.* You will see how easily some of the arguments brought forward by the supporters of religion can be answered, though it is true that others may evade refutation.

The first objection we meet with is to the effect that it is an impertinence on the part of science to make religion a subject for its investigations, for religion is something sublime, superior to any operation of the human intellect, something which may not be approached with hair-splitting criticisms. In other words, science is not qualified to judge religion: it is quite serviceable and estimable otherwise, so long as it keeps to its own sphere. But religion is not its sphere, and it has no business there. If we do not let ourselves be put off by this brusque repulse and enquire further what is the basis of this claim to a position exceptional among all human concerns, the reply we receive (if we are thought worthy of any reply) is that religion cannot be measured by human measurements, for it is of divine origin and was given us as a revelation by a Spirit which the human spirit cannot comprehend. One would have thought that there was nothing easier than the refutation of this argument: it is a clear case of *petitio principii,* of "begging the question"—I know of no good German equivalent expression. The actual question raised is whether there *is* a divine spirit and a revelation by it; and the matter is certainly not decided by saying that

this question cannot be asked, since the diety may not be put in question. The position here is what it occasionally is during the work of analysis. If a usually sensible patient rejects some particular suggestion on specially foolish grounds, this logical weakness is evidence of the existence of a specially strong motive for the denial—a motive which can only be of an affective nature, an emotional tie.

We may also be given another answer, in which a motive of this kind is openly admitted: religion may not be critically examined because it is the highest, most precious, and most sublime thing that the human spirit has produced, because it gives expression to the deepest feelings and alone makes the world tolerable and life worthy of men. We need not reply by disputing this estimate of religion but by drawing attention to another matter. What we do is to emphasize the fact that what is in question is not in the least an invasion of the field of religion by the scientific spirit, but on the contrary an invasion by religion of the sphere of scientific thought. Whatever may be the value and importance of religion, it has no right in any way to restrict thought—no right, therefore, to exclude itself from having thought applied to it.

Scientific thinking does not differ in its nature from the normal activity of thought, which all of us, believers and unbelievers, employ in looking after our affairs in ordinary life. It has only developed certain features: it takes an interest in things even if they have no immediate, tangible use; it is concerned carefully to avoid individual factors and affective influences; it examines more strictly the trustworthiness of the sense-perceptions on which it bases its conclusions; it provides itself with new perceptions which cannot be obtained by everyday means and it isolates the determinants of these new experiences in experiments which are deliberately varied. Its endeavour is to arrive at correspondence with reality—that is to say, with what exists outside us and independently of us and, as experience has taught us, is decisive for the fulfilment or disappointment of our wishes. This correspondence with the real external world we call "truth." It remains the aim of scientific work even if we leave the practical value of that work out of account. When, therefore, religion asserts that it can take the place of science, that, because it is beneficent and elevating, it must also be true, that is in fact an invasion which must be repulsed in the most general interest. It is asking a great deal of a person who has learnt to conduct his ordinary affairs in accordance with the rules of experience and with a regard to reality, to suggest that he shall hand over the care of what are precisely his most intimate interests to an agency which claims as its privilege freedom from the precepts of rational thinking. And as regards the protection which religion promises its believers, I think none of us would be so much as prepared to enter a motor-car if its driver announced that he drove, unperturbed by traffic regulations, in accordance with the impulses of his soaring imagination.

The prohibition against thought issued by religion to assist in its self-preservation is also far from being free from danger either for the individual or for human society. Analytic experience has taught us that a prohibition like this, even if it is originally limited to a particular field, tends to widen out and thereafter to become the cause of severe inhibitions in the subject's conduct of life. This result may be observed, too, in the female sex, following from their being forbidden to have anything to do with their sexuality even in thought. Biography is able to point to the damage done by the religious inhibition of thought in the life stories of nearly all eminent individuals in the past. On the other hand intellect—or let us call it by the name that is familiar to us, reason—is among the powers which we may most expect to exercise a unifying influence on men—on men who are held together with such difficulty and whom it is therefore scarcely possible to rule. It may be imagined how impossible human society would be, merely if everyone had his own multiplication table and his own private units of length and weight. Our best hope for the future is that intellect—the scientific spirit, reason—may in process of time establish a dictatorship in the mental life of man. The nature of reason is a guarantee that afterwards it will not fail to give man's emotional impulses and what is determined by them the position they deserve. But the common compulsion exercised by such a dominance of reason will prove to be the strongest uniting bond among men and lead the way to further unions. Whatever, like religion's prohibition against thought, opposes such a development, is a danger for the future of mankind.

• • •

And what, finally, is the aim of these passionate disparagements of science? In spite of its present incompleteness and of the difficulties attaching to it, it remains indispensable to us and nothing can take its place. It is capable of undreamt-of improvements, whereas the religious *Weltanschauung* is not. This is complete in all essential respects; if it was a mistake, it must remain one for ever. No belittlement of science can in any way alter the fact that it is attempting to take account of our dependence on the real external world, while religion is an illusion and it derives its strength from its readiness to fit in with our instinctual wishful impulses.

QUESTIONS FOR DISCUSSION

1. In what respects, if at all, do you think the statement "God exists" is meaningful? In what respects, if any, is it a meaningless assertion? In your answer refer to Flew's article and to at least one other reading in this section.

2. Ewing claims that the religious world view is a more adequate explanation for the universe than that of the atheist. Freud argues for atheism on the basis of the scientific world view. Who is right? Or do you believe that science and religion are ultimately compatible?

3. Freud claims that religion is an illusion, a fantasy derived from early childhood memories and wishes. Explain his interpretation of religion. Is he correct? Why or why not?

THE RELIGIOUS EXPERIENCE

The readings in the previous section focused primarily on the Western theistic tradition in which God is understood as a transcendent being whose proof requires rational demonstration through philosophical argument. As we have seen, such arguments are problematic and lend themselves easily to the atheist's challenge which, in the scientific spirit, insists upon the experiential verification. However, there is also an undercurrent within the Western tradition which talks about an immediate experiential encounter with God—Moses and the burning bush, the Jewish mystics of the Kaballah, and such Christian mystics as Meister Eckhart and Saint Teresa of Avila. But what is only an undercurrent in Western religions is given emphasis in the Asian traditions—Hinduism, Buddhism, and Taoism. "Experience," writes Sarvepalli Radhakrishnan, "is the soul of religion." The readings in this section explore the nature of the religious experience.

Sarvepalli Radhakrishnan (1888–1975) was an Indian philosopher well known for his ability to make Hindu philosophy accessible to Western philosophers. After a long academic career he entered politics and become vice-president of India in 1952 and president of India ten years later. In the first selection of this section, he analyzes the essential characteristics of religious, or mystical, experiences. These experiences are described as being beyond our ordinary sensory and intellectual consciousness. The boundaries dividing the individual from the universe have been broken, and the self merges with an undifferentiated unity that is experienced as a higher realm. How do we know that this is not simply an hallucination? The mystic's answer is that the experience presents itself with a sense of its own validity. Beyond that not much more can be said, and, in fact, the experience is often described as ineffable.

How should we evaluate this experience? Here, according to Radhakrishnan, we must distinguish between the experience, which he believes has value in itself, and the interpretation of that experi-ence. The tendency has been to identify the mystical experience as an experience of God and, within each religious tradition, to interpret it through the categories of that religion. He concludes that such interpretations are cultural constructions and must be distinguished from the experience itself.

The next selection is by the twentieth-century Lakota holy man, Black Elk, as recorded by the anthropologist Joseph Epes Brown. Black Elk recounts the ancient tale of how the Sioux got the sacred pipe from the wakan buffalo cow woman, who was an emissary of *Wakan-Tanka,* the Great Spirit. The pipe itself represents the earth, all that grows from it, and the animals which live upon it. Those who smoke the pipe are said to be joined to everything in the universe, including their ancestors. The tale may be read as both an account of a mystic vision and an ecological parable.

The last two selections in this section are by the twentieth-century Japanese philosopher Kitaro Nishida and by the Thai Buddhist monk and meditation master Buddhadasa, who consider further implications of the religious experience. Nishida, although a Zen Buddhist, attempts to present the Eastern way of thinking in the philosophical idiom of Western theology and philosophy. The religious experience, he claims, is an experience of God—not of a transcendent God who rules the universe from outside, but rather of a God who is both the foundation and unifier of nature and yet who is identical with nature; in other words, a pantheistic God. The point of the religious experience is the unity of the self with God, which is to say the self's unity with nature and the spiritual principle which animates it.

The last selection in this section by Buddhadasa comes to a surprising conclusion about religious experiences: that while in the ordinary mode of language religions are different and tend to divide people, on a deeper level they are all the same. And at still a deeper level mystical experiences reveal that there is no religion. In other words, the deepest essence of religion goes beyond religion itself.

PERSONAL EXPERIENCE OF GOD

Sarvepalli Radhakrishnan

PERSONAL EXPERIENCE OF GOD

All the religions owe their inspiration to the personal insights of their prophet founders. The Hindu religion, for example, is characterized by its adherence to fact. In its pure form, at any rate, it never leaned as heavily as other religions do on authority. It is not a "founded" religion; nor does it centre round any historical events. Its distinctive characteristic has been its insistence on the inward life of spirit. To know, possess and be the spirit in this physical frame, to convert an obscure plodding mentality into clear spiritual illumination, to build peace and self-existent freedom in the stress of emotional satisfactions and sufferings, to discover and realize the life divine in a body subject to sickness and death has been the constant aim of the Hindu religious endeavour. The Hindus look back to the Vedic period* as the epoch of their founders. The Veda, the wisdom, is the accepted name for the highest spiritual truth of which the human mind is capable. It is the work of the *rsis* or the seers. The truths of the *rsis* are not evolved as the result of logical reasoning or systematic philosophy but they are the products of spiritual intuition, *drsti* or vision. The *rsis* are not so much the authors of the truths recorded in the Vedas† as the seers who were able to discern the eternal truths by raising their life-spirit to the plane of the universal spirit. They are the pioneer researchers in the realm of spirit who saw more in the world than their fellows. Their utterances are based not on transitory vision but on a continuous experience of resident life and power. When the Vedas are regarded as the highest authority, all that is meant is that the most exacting of all authorities is the authority of facts.

If experience is the soul of religion, expression is the body through which it fulfils its destiny. We have the spiritual facts and their interpretations by which they are communicated to others, *śruti* or what is heard, and *smrti* or what is remembered. Śamkara equates them with *pratyaksa* or intuition and *anumāna* or inference. It is the distinction between immediacy and thought. Intuitions abide, while interpretations change. *Śruti* and *smrti* differ as the authority of fact and the authority of interpretation. Theory, speculation, dogma, change from time to time as the facts become better understood. Their value is acquired from their adequacy to experience. When forms dissolve and the interpretations are doubted, it is a call to get back to the experience itself and reformulate its content in more suitable terms. While the experiential character of religion is emphasized in the Hindu faith, every religion at its best falls back on it.

The whole scheme of Buddhism centres on Buddha's enlightenment. Moses saw God in the burning bush, and Elijah heard the still small voice. In *Jeremiah* we read: "This is the covenant which I will make with the house of Israel after those days, saith the Lord. I will put my hand in their inward parts, and in their heart will I write it."[1] Jesus's experience of God is the basic fact for Christianity: "As he came up out of the river he saw the heavens parted above him and the spirit descending like a dove towards him: and he heard a voice sounding out of the heavens and saying 'Thou art my beloved son. I have chosen thee.'" According to St. Mark, the baptism in the Jordan by John was to Jesus the occasion of a vivid and intense religious experience, so much so that he felt that he had to go for a time into absolute solitude to think it over.[2] He obviously spoke of the ineffable happening, the sudden revelation,

---

* The *Vedic period* is approximately between 2500 and 600 B.C. The philosophical literature of this period is known as the Vedas (Eds.).

† The *Vedas:* There are four *Vedas,* each of which consists of hymns, guidelines for rituals and conduct, and philosophical reflection. The *Vedas* were initially transmitted through recitation and memorization. They provide us with the earliest known philosophical and religious expressions of Hinduism (Eds.).

---

[1] xxxi. 37.
[2] Mark 1. 10.

the new peace and joy in words that have come down to us. He emphasized the newness of the re-born soul as something which marks him off from all those who are religious only at second hand. "Verily I say unto you, among men born of women there hath not arisen a greater than John the Baptist; but the least in the Kingdom of God is greater than he."[3] The vision that came to Saul on the Damascus road and turned the persecutor into an apostle[4] is another illustration. Faith means in St James accep-tance of dogma; in St Paul it is the surrender of heart and mind to Christ; but in the Epistle to the He-brews, faith is defined as that outreaching of the mind by which we become aware of the invisible world.[5] The life of Mohammad is full of mystic ex-periences. Witnesses to the personal sense of the di-vine are not confined to the East. Socrates and Plato, Plotinus and Porphyry, Augustine and Dante, Bunyan and Wesley, and numberless others, testify to the felt reality of God. It is as old as humanity and is not confined to any one people. The evidence is too massive to run away from.

CHARACTER OF RELIGIOUS EXPERIENCE

To study the nature of this experience is rather a dif-ficult matter. All that one can hope to do is to set down a few general impressions. It is a type of ex-perience which is not clearly differentiated into a subject-object state, an integral, undivided con-sciousness in which not merely this or that side of man's nature but this whole being seems to find it-self. It is a condition of consciousness in which feel-ings are fused, ideas melt into one another, bound-aries broken and ordinary distinctions transcended. Past and present fade away in a sense of timeless being. Consciousness and being are not there dif-ferent from each other. All being is consciousness and all consciousness being. Thought and reality coalesce and a creative merging of subject and ob-

ject results. Life grows conscious of its incredible depths. In this fulness of felt life and freedom, the distinction of the knower and the known disappears. The privacy of the individual self is broken into and invaded by a universal self which the individual feels as his own.

The experience itself is felt to be sufficient and complete. It does not come in a fragmentary or trun-cated form demanding completion by something else. It does not look beyond itself for meaning or validity. It does not appeal to external standards of logic or metaphysics. It is its own cause and expla-nation. It is sovereign in its own rights and carries its own credentials. It is self-established (*svatassid-dha*) self-evidencing (*svasaṁvedya*) self-luminous (*svayam-prakāśa*). It does not argue or explain but it knows and is. It is beyond the bounds of proof and so touches completeness. It comes with a constraint that brooks no denial. It is pure comprehension, en-tire significance, complete validity. Patañjali, the author of the *Yoga Sūtra,* tells us that the insight is truth-filled, or truth-bearing.[6]

The tension of normal life disappears, giving rise to inward peace, power and joy. The Greeks called it ataraxy, but the word sounds more negative than the Hindu term "*Śānti*" or peace, which is a positive feeling of calm and confidence, joy and strength in the midst of outward pain and defeat, loss and frustration. The experience is felt as profoundly satisfying, where darkness is turned into light, sad-ness into joy, despair into assurance. The continu-ance of such an experience constitutes dwelling in heaven, which is not a place where God lives but a mode of being which is fully and completely real.

However much we may quarrel about the impli-cations of this kind of experience, we cannot ques-tion the actuality of the experience itself. While the profound intuitions do not normally occur, milder forms are in the experience of all who feel an an-swering presence in deep devotion or share the spell which great works of art cast on us. When we expe-rience the illumination of new knowledge, the

---

[3] See also Matt. xi. ii.
[4] Acts ix. 1–9.
[5] See also i Cor. xiii. 12; Romans viii. 18–25; Rev. xxi. 22.

[6] Rtambharā tatra prajñā (*Yoga Sūtra,* I. 48).

ecstasy of poetry or the subordination of self to something greater, family or nation, the self-abandonment of falling in love, we have faint glimpses of mystic moods. Human love perhaps takes us nearest to them. It can become an experience deep and profound, a portal through which we enter the realm of the sublime. "My life, My all, My more," said Sappho to Philaenis. To have one's heart and mind absorbed in love seems to unveil the mystery of the universe. We forget the sense of the outward world in our communion with the grandeur beyond. Religious mysticism often falls into the language of passionate love. It has been so from the Upaniṣads and the Song of Songs.

Since the intuitive experiences are not always given but occur only at rare intervals, they possess the character of revelation. We cannot command or continue them at our will. We do not know how or why they occur. They sometimes occur even against our will. Their mode of comprehension is beyond the understanding of the normal, and the supernormal is traced to the supernatural. Those who are gifted with the insight tend to regard themselves as the chosen ones, the privileged few. Conscious of a light which other men had not, they feel inclined to believe that the light has been directed on them and that they are not only the seekers but the sought. "Only he who is chosen by the Supreme is able to realize it."

If all our experience were possessed of intrinsic validity (*svataḥpramāṇya*) there would be no question of truth and falsehood. There would be nothing with which our experience will have to cohere or to correspond. There would not arise any need or desire to test its value. All our experience will be self-valid, i.e. all reality will be present in its own immediate validity. But even the noblest human minds have only glimpses of self-valid experiences. The moments of vision are transitory and intermittent. We therefore do not attain an insight, permanent and uninterrupted, where reality is present in its own immediate witness. But we are convinced that such an ideal is not an impossible one.

So long as the experience lasts, the individual remains rapt in contemplation, but no man can rest in that state for all time. Life is a restless surge.

Scarcely is the seer assured of the unique character of the experience than he is caught in the whirl of desire and temptation, discord and struggle. During the vision, its influence was so potent and overwhelming that he had neither the power nor the desire to analyse it. Now that the vision is no more, he strives to recapture it and retain in memory what cannot be realized in fact. The process of reflection starts. He cannot forget the blessed moments which have a weight for the rest of his life and give to his beliefs a power and a vividness that nothing can shake. The individual adopts an attitude of faith which is urged by its own needs to posit the transcendental reality. He affirms that the soul has dealings, direct, intimate and luminous, with a plane of being different from that with which the senses deal, a world more resplendent but not less real than the conventional one. The experience is felt as of the nature of a discovery or a revelation, not a mere conjecture or a creation. The real was there actually confronting us, it was not conjured out of the resources of our mind.[7] He claims for his knowledge of reality an immediate and intuitive certainy, transcending any which mere reason can reach. No further experience or rational criticism can disturb his sense of certainty. Doubt and disbelief are no more possible. He speaks without hesitation and with the calm accents of finality. Such strange simplicity and authoritativeness do we find in the utterances of the seers of the Upaniṣads, of Buddha, of Plato, of Christ, of Dante, of Eckhart, of Spinoza, of Blake. They speak of the real, not as the scribes, but as those who were in the immediate presence of "that which was, is and ever shall be." St Theresa says: "If you ask how it is possible that the soul can see and understand that she has been in God, since during the union she has neither sight nor understanding, I reply that she does not see it then, but that she sees it clearly later, after she has returned to herself, not by any vision, but by a certitude which abides with her and which God alone can give her."[8]

In addition to the feeling of certitude is found the

---

[7] Śaṁkara on *Brahma Sūtra*, i. 1. 1.
[8] James: *Varieties of Religious Experience* (1906), p. 409.

sense of the ineffability of the experience. It transcends expression even while it provokes it. It is just what it is and not like anything else. There is no experience by which we can limit it, no conception by which we can define it. The *Kena Upaniṣad* says that "it is other than the known and above the unknown."[9] As Lao Tze expresses it at the beginning of his *Tao Teh King**: "The Tao which can be expressed is not the unchanging Tao; the Name which can be named is not the unchanging Name."

The unquestionable content of the experience is that about which nothing more can be said.[10] Indian scriptures give cases of teachers who dispelled the doubts of their pupils by assuming an attitude of silence on this question.[11] When we hear enthusiastic descriptions about the ultimate reality, let us remember the dictum of Lao Tze that he who knows the Tao may be recognized by the fact that he is reluctant to speak of it.

Conceptual substitutes for ineffable experiences are not adequate. They are products of rational thinking. All forms, according to Śaṁkara, contain an element of untruth and the real is beyond all forms. Any attempt to describe the experience falsifies it to an extent. In the experience itself the self is wholly integrated and is therefore both the knower and the known, but it is not so in any intellectual description of the experience. The profoundest being of man cannot be brought out by mental pictures or logical counters. God is too great for words to explain. He is like light, making things luminous but himself invisible.

And yet we cannot afford to be absolutely silent.

---

[9] i. 3.
* *Lao Tze and Tao Teh King:* This is an alternative English spelling of Lao Tzu and the *Tao Te Ching*. Selections from Lao Tzu appear in this book in Section Four of Chapter 1 and Section Two of Chapter 8 (Eds.).
[10] There is an endless world, O my brother, and there is the Nameless Being, of whom nought can be said.
  Only he knows it who has reached that region: it is other than all that is heard and said.
  No form, no body, no length, no breadth is seen there: how can I tell you that which it is?
              (*Kabir:* Rabindranath Tagore's E.T., 76.)
[11] Cp. Lao Tze: "To teach without words and to be useful without action, few among men are capable of this."

Though the tools of sense and understanding cannot describe adequately, creative imagination with its symbols and suggestions may be of assistance. The profoundest wisdom of the past is transmitted to us in the form of myths and metaphors which do not have any fixed meaning and therefore can be interpreted as life requires. The seers who were at least as wise and as subtle as ourselves, by letting their imagination work on experience, devised symbolic conceptions such as crossing the ocean of *saṁsāra,* ascending into heaven, meeting God face to face. Plato expressed his deepest convictions, which were incapable of proof, in the language of poetry, saying, "Not this perhaps, but something like this must be true." If we insist on interpreting these symbols literally, difficulties arise. But if we go behind the words to the moods they symbolize, agreement is possible.

The symbols and suggestions employed are derived from the local and historical traditions. An Orphic describes to us Charon and the spring on either side of the road and the tall cypress tree. The Vaiṣṇava speaks to us of the cowherd, the Brindāvan and the river Yamunā. The myths require to be changed as they lose their meaning with the lapse of time, but they are in no case to be accepted as literal truths: They require to be interpreted "according to their meaning and not their lisping expression," as Aristotle suggests in speaking of Empedocles. Much of the rationalistic criticism of the sacred scriptures is due to a confusion between symbolic statements and literal truths. It is easy to prove that the world was not made in seven days or that Eve was not made out of Adam's rib. What they say is not scientifically true; what they mean is a different matter.

EXPERIENCE AND THE VARIETY OF EXPRESSIONS

If all our experiences were adequately intuited at once, such immediate intuitions could not be doubted under any circumstances; but, as it is, we are compelled to relate our intuitive experiences with others and here we are obliged to employ formulas. The pedestrian function of consolidation and revaluation seems to be indispensable. The only way to impart our experiences to others and elucidate their implications for the rest of our life and defend their validity against hostile criticism is by means of logic. When we test the claim of the experience to truth, we are really discussing the claims of the forms or propositions in which the nature of the experience is unfolded. In the utterances of the seers, we have to distinguish the given and the interpreted elements. What is regarded as immediately given may be the product of inference. Immediacy does not mean absence of psychological mediation, but only non-mediation by conscious thought. Ideas which seem to come to us with compelling force, without any mediate intellectual process of which we are aware, are generally the results of previous training in traditions imparted to us in our early years. Our past experience supplies the materials to which the new insight adds fresh meanings. When we are told that the souls have felt in their lives the redeeming power of Kṛṣṇa or Buddha, Jesus or Mohammad, we must distinguish the immediate experience or intuition which might conceivably be infallible and the interpretation which is mixed up with it. St Theresa tells us that after her experience she learned to understand the Trinity. Surely she would not have recognized the revelation as that of the Trinity if she had not already known something of the Trinity.[12] Similarly, if Paul had not learned something about Jesus, he would not have identified the voice that came to him on the Damascus road as Jesus's. We must distinguish the simple facts of religion from the accounts which reach us through the depth of theological preconceptions. That the soul is in contact with a mighty spiritual power other than its normal self and yet within and that its contact means the beginning of the creation of a new self is the fact, while the identification of this power with the historic figures of Buddha or Christ, the confusion of the simple realization of the universal self in us with a catastrophic revelation from without, is an interpretation, a personal confession and not necessarily an objective truth. Something is directly experienced but it is unconsciously interpreted in the terms of the tradition in which the individual is trained. The frame of reference which each individual adopts is determined by heredity and culture.

Again, there is no such thing as pure experience, raw and undigested. It is always mixed up with layers of interpretation. The alleged immediate datum is psychologically mediated. The scriptural statements give us knowledge, or interpreted experience, a that-what. The "that" is merely the affirmation of a fact, of a self-existent spiritual experience in which all distinctions are blurred and the individual seems to overflow into the whole and belong to it. The experience is real though inarticulate.

Among the religious teachers of the world, Buddha is marked out as the one who admitted the reality of the spiritual experience and yet refused to interpret it as a revelation of anything beyond itself. For him the view that the experience gives us direct contact with God is an interpretation and not an immediate datum. Buddha gives us a report of the experience rather than an interpretation of it, though strictly speaking there are no experiences which we do not interpret. It is only a question of degree. But Buddha keeps closest to the given and is content with affirming that a deeper world of spirit penetrates the visible and the tangible world. Such a world certified as valid by the witness of perfect intuition exists beyond or rather within the world of multiplicity and change which the senses and understanding present to us. The primary reality is an unconditional existence beyond all potentiality of adequate expression by thought or description by symbol, in which the word "existence" itself loses its meaning and the symbol of *nirvāṇa* alone seems to be justified. The only liberty in which Buddha indulges when obliged to give a positive content to it is to identify it with Eternal righteousness (*dharma*), which is the principle of the universe[13] and the foundation of all conduct. It is on account of it that we have the implicit belief in the worth of life.

---

[12] Evelyn Underhill: *Mysticism,* p. 132, 5th Ed.

[13] See Appendix to the writer's work on *Indian Philosophy,* vol. 1, 2nd Edn. (1929).

The Hindu thinkers admit the ineffability of the experience but permit themselves a graduated scale of interpretations from the most "impersonal" to the most "personal." The freedom of interpretation is responsible for what may be called the hospitality of the Hindu mind. The Hindu tradition by its very breadth seems to be capable of accommodating varied religious conceptions.

Hinduism admits that the unquestionable content of the experience is a *that* about which nothing more can be said. The deeper and more intimate a spiritual experience, the more readily does it dispense with signs and symbols. Deep intuition is utterly silent. Through silence we "confess without confession" that the glory of spiritual life is inexplicable and beyond the reach of speech and mind. It is the great unfathomable mystery and words are treacherous.

The empirical understanding is quite competent within its own region, but it cannot be allowed to criticize its foundation, that which it, along with other powers of man, takes for granted. The Supreme is not an object presented to knowledge but is the condition of knowledge. While for Buddha, who was ethically disposed, the eternal spirit is righteousness or *dharma,* in the strength of which we live and struggle, for many Hindu thinkers it is the very condition of knowledge. It is the eternal light which is not one of the things seen but the condition of seeing. The ultimate condition of being where all dualities disappear, where life and death do not matter since they spring from it, where spirit seems to enjoy spirit and reason does not stir, can be expressed only in negative terms. The Upanisads and Śaṁkara* try to express the nature of the ultimate being in negative terms. "The eye goes not thither nor speech nor mind."[14]

There is a danger in these negative descriptions. By denying all attributes and relations we expose ourselves to the charge of reducing the ultimate being to bare existence which is absolute vacuity. The negative account is intended to express the soul's sense of the transcendence of God, the "wholly other," of whom naught may be predicted save in negations, and not to deprive God of his positive being. It is the inexhaustible positivity of God that bursts through all conceptual forms. When we call it nothing we mean that it is nothing which created beings can conceive or name and not that it is nothing absolutely. The scriptures do not demonstrate or describe him but only bear witness to him. The three noteworthy features of spiritual experience are reality, awareness and freedom. If some parts of our experience come to us with these characteristics, it implies the possibility that all experience is capable of being received in the same manner. The consciousness to which all experience is present in its own immediacy, revealedness and freedom from anything which is not itself is the divine consciousness, that which is our ideal. We picture it as a glowing fire, a lucid flame of consciousness ever shining and revealing itself. In the divine status reality is its own immediate witness, its own self-awareness, its own freedom of complete being. There is nothing which is not gathered up in its being, nothing which is not revealed in it, and there is utter absence of all discord. It is perfect being, perfect consciousness and perfect freedom, *sat, cit* and *ānanda.* Being, truth and freedom are distinguished in the divine but not divided. The true and ultimate condition of the human being is the divine status. The essence of life is the movement of the universal being; the essence of emotion is the play

---

* The *Upanishads* and *Samkara:* The *Upanishads,* a Sanskrit word which means teachings received sitting at the feet of the sage, are the last and most philosophical part of the *Vedas* (see our explanatory footnote above). There are 108 authenticated *Upanishads,* 13 of which are taken to be major texts. They are perhaps the best known of Hindu scriptural literature and are taken as the basis of Hindu philosophy. *Samkara* is an alternative English spelling of *Shankara,* a ninth-century Indian philosopher who is the most famous interpreter of the *Upanishads.* A selection of his work can be found in this text in Section Two of Chapter 1. Selections from the *Upanishads* themselves appear in Section Two of Chapter 1 and Section Three of Chapter 5 (Eds.).

---

[14] *Bṛhadāraṇyaka Upaniṣad,* iii. 8. 8. For Śamkara it is *nirguna* (without qualities), *nirākāra* (without form), *nirviśeṣa* (without particularity), *nirupādhika* (without limitations). It is what it is. Isaiah's words are true, "Verily, thou art a God that hidest thyself." For Dionysius the Areopagite, God is the nameless supra-essential one elevated above goodness itself. St Augustine speaks of the Absolute, selfsame. One, that which is.

of the self-existent delight in being; the essence of thought is the inspiration of the all-pervading truth; the essence of activity is the progressive realization of a universal and self-effecting good. Thought and its formations, will and its achievements, love and its harmonies are all based on the Divine Spirit. Only the human counterparts involve duality, tension, strain, and so are inadequate to the fulness of the divine. The supreme is real, not true, perfect, not good. Its freedom is its life, its essential spontaneity.

THE SACRED PIPE

Black Elk

In the great vision which came to me in my youth, when I had known only nine winters, there was something which has seemed to me to be of greater and greater importance as the moons have passed by. It is about our sacred pipe and its importance to our people.

We have been told by the white men, or at least by those who are Christian, that God sent to men His son, who would restore order and peace upon the earth; and we have been told that Jesus the Christ was crucified, but that he shall come again at the Last Judgment, the end of this world or cycle. This I understand and know that it is true, but the white men should know that for the red people too, it was the will of *Wakan-Tanka,* the Great Spirit, that an animal turn itself into a two-legged person in order to bring the most holy pipe to His people; and we too were taught that this White Buffalo Cow Woman who brought our sacred pipe will appear again at the end of this "world," a coming which we Indians know is now not very far off.

Most people call it a "peace pipe," yet now there is no peace on earth or even between neighbors, and I have been told that it has been a long time since there has been peace in the world. There is much talk of peace among the Christians, yet this is just talk. Perhaps it may be, and this is my prayer that, through our sacred pipe, and through this book in which I shall explain what our pipe really is, peace may come to those peoples who can understand, an understanding which must be of the heart and not of the head alone. Then they will realize that we Indians know the One true God, and that we pray to Him continually.

I have wished to make this book through no other desire than to help my people in understanding the greatness and truth of our own tradition, and also to help in bringing peace upon the earth, not only among men, but within men and between the whole of creation.

We should understand well that all things are the works of the Great Spirit. We should know that He is within all things; the trees, the grasses, the rivers, the mountains, and all the four-legged animals, and the winged peoples; and even more important, we should understand that He is also above all these things and peoples. When we do understand all this deeply in our hearts, then we will fear, and love, and know the Great Spirit, and then we will be and act and live as He intends.

Early one morning, very many winters ago, two Lakota were out hunting with their bows and arrows, and as they were standing on a hill looking for game, they saw in the distance something coming towards them in a very strange and wonderful manner. When this mysterious thing came nearer to them, they saw that it was a very beautiful woman, dressed in white buckskin, and bearing a bundle on her back. Now this woman was so good to look at that one of the Lakota had bad intentions, and told his friend of his desire, but this good man said that he must not have such thoughts, for surely this is a *wakan* woman.[1] The mysterious person was now

---

[1] Throughout this work I shall translate the Lakota word *wakan* as "holy" or "sacred," rather than as "power" or "powerful" as used by some ethnologists. This latter term may be a true translation, yet is not really complete, for with the Sioux, and with all traditional peoples in general, the "power" (really the sacredness) of a being or a thing is in proportion to its nearness to its prototype; or better, it is in proportion to the ability of the object or act to reflect most directly the principle or principles which are in *Wakan-Tanka,* the Great Spirit, who is One.

very close to the men, and then putting down her bundle, she asked the one with bad intentions to come over to her. As the young man approached the mysterious woman, they were both covered by a great cloud, and soon when it lifted the sacred woman was standing there, and at her feet was the man with the bad thoughts who was now nothing but bones, and terrible snakes were eating him.[2]

"Behold what you see!" the strange woman said to the good man. "I am coming to your people and wish to talk with your chief *Hehlokecha Najin* [Standing Hollow Horn]. Return to him, and tell him to prepare a large tipi in which he should gather all his people, and make ready for my coming. I wish to tell you something of great importance!"

The young man then returned to the tipi of his chief, and told him all that had happened: that this *wakan* woman was coming to visit them and that they must all prepare. The chief, Standing Hollow Horn, then had several tipis taken down, and from them a great lodge was made as the sacred woman had instructed.[3] He sent out a crier to tell the people to put on their best buckskin clothes and to gather immediately in the lodge. The people were, of course, all very excited as they waited in the great lodge for the coming of the holy woman, and everybody was wondering where this mysterious woman came from and what it was that she wished to say.

Soon the young men who were watching for the coming of the *wakan* person announced that they saw something in the distance approaching them in a beautiful manner, and then suddenly she entered

the lodge, walked around sun-wise,[4] and stood in front of Standing Hollow Horn.[5] She took from her back the bundle, and holding it with both hands in front of the chief, said: "Behold this and always love it! It is *lela wakan* [very sacred], and you must treat it as such. No impure man should ever be allowed to see it, for within this bundle there is a sacred pipe. With this you will, during the winters to come, send your voices to *Wakan-Tanka,* your Father and Grandfather."[6]

After the mysterious woman said this, she took from the bundle a pipe, and also a small round stone which she placed upon the ground. Holding the pipe up with its stem to the heavens, she said: "With this sacred pipe you will walk upon the Earth; for the Earth is your Grandmother and Mother,[7] and She is

---

[2] Black Elk emphasized that this should not only be taken as an event in time, but also as an eternal truth. "Any man," he said, "who is attached to the senses and to the things of this world, is one who lives in ignorance and is being consumed by the snakes which represent his own passions."

[3] The Sioux ceremonial lodge is constructed with twenty-eight poles. One of these poles is the "key," holding up all the others, and this pole the holy men say represents *Wakan-Tanka,* who sustains the universe, which is represented by the lodge as a whole.

[4] The sun-wise or clockwise circumambulation is almost always used by the Sioux; occasionally, however, the counter-clockwise movement is used in a dance or some occasion prior to or after a great catastrophe, for this movement is in imitation of the Thunder-beings who always act in an antinatural way and who come in a terrifying manner, often bringing destruction.

　　The reason for the sun-wise circumambulation was once explained by Black Elk in this manner: "Is not the south the source of life, and does not the flowering stick truly come from there? And does not man advance from there toward the setting sun of his life? Then does he not approach the colder north where the white hairs are? And does he not then arrive, if he lives, at the source of light and understanding, which is the east? Then does he not return to where he began, to his second childhood, there to give back his life to all life, and his flesh to the earth whence it came? The more you think about this, the more meaning you will see in it." (*Black Elk Speaks,* recorded by John G. Neihardt).

[5] Standing Hollow Horn, as leader of his people, should be seated at the west, the place of honor; for in sitting at the west of a tipi, one faces the door, or east, from which comes the light, representing wisdom, and this illumination a leader must always possess if he is to guide his people in a sacred manner.

[6] *Wakan-Tanka* as Grandfather is the Great Spirit independent of manifestation, unqualified, unlimited, identical to the Christian Godhead, or to the Hindu *Brahma-Nirguna. Wakan-Tanka* as Father is the Great Spirit considered in relation to His manifestation, either as Creator, Preserver, or Destroyer, identical to the Christian God, or to the Hindu *Brahma-Saguna.*

[7] As in the distinction made within *Wakan-Tanka* between Grandfather and Father, so the Earth is considered under two aspects, that of Mother and Grandmother. The former is the earth considered as the producer of all growing forms, in act; whereas Grandmother refers to the ground or substance of all growing things—potentiality. This distinction is the same as that made by the Christian Scholastics between *natura naturans* and *natura naturata.*

sacred. Every step that is taken upon Her should be as a prayer. The bowl of this pipe is of red stone; it is the Earth. Carved in the stone and facing the center is this buffalo calf who represents all the four-leggeds[8] who live upon your Mother. The stem of the pipe is of wood, and this represents all that grows upon the Earth. And these twelve feathers which hang here where the stem fits into the bowl are from *Wanbli Galeshka,* the Spotted Eagle,[9] and they represent the eagle and all the wingeds of the air. All these peoples, and all the things of the universe, are joined to you who smoke the pipe—all send their voices to *Wakan-Tanka,* the Great Spirit. When you pray with this pipe, you pray for and with everything."

The *wakan* woman then touched the foot of the pipe to the round stone which lay upon the ground, and said: "With this pipe you will be bound to all your relatives: your Grandfather and Father, your Grandmother and Mother. This round rock, which is made of the same red stone as the bowl of the pipe, your Father *Wakan-Tanka* has also given to you. It is the Earth, your Grandmother and Mother, and it is where you will live and increase. This Earth which He has given to you is red, and the two-leggeds who live upon the Earth are red; and the Great Spirit has also given to you a red day, and a red road.[10] All of this is sacred and so do not forget! Every dawn as it comes is a holy event, and every day is holy, for the light comes from your Father *Wakan-Tanka;* and also you must always remember that the two-leggeds and all the other peoples who stand upon this earth are sacred and should be treated as such.

"From this time on, the holy pipe will stand upon this red Earth, and the two-leggeds will take the pipe and send their voices to *Wakan-Tanka.* These seven circles[11] which you see on the stone have much meaning, for they represent the seven rites in which the pipe will be used. The first large circle represents the first rite which I shall give to you, and the other six circles represent the rites which will in time be revealed to you directly.[12] Standing Hollow Horn, be good to these gifts and to your people, for they are *wakan!* With this pipe the two-leggeds will increase, and there will come to them all that is good. From above *Wakan-Tanka* has given to you

---

[8] The buffalo was to the Sioux the most important of all four-legged animals, for it supplied their food, their clothing, and even their houses, which were made from the tanned hides. Because the buffalo contained all these things within himself, and for many other reasons, he was a natural symbol of the universe, the totality of all manifested forms. Everything is symbolically contained within this animal: the earth and all that grows from her, all animals, and even the two-legged peoples; and each specific part of the beast represents the Indian, one of these "parts" of creation. Also the buffalo has four legs, and these represent the four ages which are an integral condition of creation.

[9] Since *Wanbli Galeshka* (the Spotted Eagle) flies the highest of all created creatures and sees everything, he is regarded as *Wakan-Tanka* under certain aspects. He is a solar bird, His feathers being regarded as rays of the sun, and when one is carried or worn by the Indian it represents, or rather *is,* the "Real Presence." In wearing the eagle-feathered "war-bonnet," the wearer actually becomes the eagle, which is to say that he identifies himself, his real Self, with *Wakan-Tanka.*

The Spotted Eagle corresponds exactly, in the Hindu tradition, to the *Buddhi,* which is the Intellect, or the formless and transcendant principle of all manifestation; further, the *Buddhi* is often expressed as being a ray directly emanating from the *Atma,* the spiritual sun.

From this it should be clear what is really being expressed in the often misunderstood Ghost Dance song: *"Wanbli galeshka wana ni he o who e,"* "The Spotted Eagle is coming to carry me away."

---

[10] The "red road" is that which runs north and south and is the good or straight way, for to the Sioux the north is purity and the south is the source of life. This "red road" is thus similar to the Christian "straight and narrow way"; it is the vertical of the cross, or the *ec-cirata el-mustaqim* of the Islamic tradition.

On the other hand, there is the "blue" or "black road" of the Sioux, which runs east and west and which is the path of error and destruction. He who travels on this path is, Black Elk has said, "one who is distracted, who is ruled by his senses, and who lives for himself rather than for his people."

[11] The seven circles are arranged in this manner:

[12] According to Black Elk, two of these rites were known to the Sioux prior to the coming of the sacred Woman; these were the purification rites of the sweat lodge, and the *Hanblecheyapi* (crying for a vision); the ritual of the pipe was, however, now added to both of these.

this sacred pipe, so that through it you may have knowledge. For this great gift you should always be grateful! But now before I leave I wish to give to you instructions for the first rite in which your people will use this pipe.

"It should be for you a sacred day when one of your people dies. You must then keep his soul[13] as I shall teach you, and through this you will gain much power; for if this soul is kept, it will increase in you your concern and love for your neighbor. So long as the person, in his soul, is kept with your people, through him you will be able to send your voice to *Wakan-Tanka.*[14]

"It should also be a sacred day when a soul is released and returns to its home, *Wakan-Tanka,* for on this day four women will be made holy, and they will in time bear children who will walk the path of life in a sacred manner, setting an example to your people. Behold Me, for it is I that they will take in their mouths, and it is through this that they will become *wakan.*

"He who keeps the soul of a person must be a good and pure man, and he should use the pipe so that all the people, with the soul, will together send their voices to *Wakan-Tanka.* The fruit of your

Mother the Earth and the fruit of all that bears will be blessed in this manner, and your people will then walk the path of life in a sacred way. Do not forget that *Wakan-Tanka* has given you seven days in which to send your voices to Him. So long as you remember this you will live; the rest you will know from *Wakan-Tanka* directly."

The sacred woman then started to leave the lodge, but turning again to Standing Hollow Horn, she said: "Behold this pipe! Always remember how sacred it is, and treat it as such, for it will take you to the end. Remember, in me there are four ages.[15] I am leaving now, but I shall look back upon your people in every age, and at the end I shall return."

Moving around the lodge in a sun-wise manner, the mysterious woman left, but after walking a short distance she looked back towards the people and sat down. When she rose the people were amazed to see that she had become a young red and brown buffalo calf. Then this calf walked farther, lay down, and rolled, looking back at the people, and when she got up she was a white buffalo. Again the white buffalo walked farther and rolled on the ground, becoming now a black buffalo. This buffalo then walked farther away from the people, stopped, and after bowing to each of the four quarters of the universe, disappeared over the hill.

---

[13] In translating the Lakota word *wanagi,* I have used the term "soul" in preference to "spirit," which has been used by many ethnologists; I believe this term, understood in its scholastic Christian sense, to be more accurate, for what is kept and purified in this rite is really the totality of the psychic entities of the being, which, although localized within a particular gross form (usually the lock of hair), are really of a subtle nature, intermediate between the gross body and the pure spirit. At the same time it should always be remembered that it is the pure spirit, which is the presence of *Wakan-Tanka,* which is at the "center" of both the subtle and gross entities. The soul is thus kept in the manner to be described so that there may be a prolongation of the individual state and, thus, that the subtle or psychic part of the being may be purified, so that a virtual liberation will be achieved. This corresponds very closely to the Christian state of Purgatory. For further explanation of this important question, see René Guénon, *Man and His Becoming* (London, 1945).

[14] "It is good," Black Elk has said, "to have a reminder of death before us, for it helps us to understand the impermanence of life on this earth, and this understanding may aid us in preparing for our own death. He who is well prepared is he who knows that he is nothing compared with *Wakan-Tanka,* who is everything; then he knows that world which is real."

---

[15] According to Siouan mythology, it is believed that at the beginning of the cycle a buffalo was placed at the west in order to hold back the waters. Every year this buffalo loses one hair, and every age he loses one leg. When all his hair and all four legs are gone, then the waters rush in once again, and the cycle comes to an end.

A striking parallel to this myth is found in the Hindu tradition, where it is the Bull *Dharma* (the divine law) who has four legs, each of which represents an age of the total cycle. During the course of these four ages (*yugas*) true spirituality becomes increasingly obscured, until the cycle (*manvantara*) closes with a catastrophe, after which the primordial spirituality is restored, and the cycle begins once again.

It is believed by both the American Indian and the Hindu that at the present time the buffalo or bull is on his last leg, and he is very nearly bald. Corresponding beliefs could be cited from many other traditions. See René Guénon, *The Crisis of the Modern World* (London, 1942).

THE ESSENCE OF RELIGION

Kitaro Nishida

Religion is the relationship between God and human beings. We can think about God in various ways, but it is perhaps most appropriate to view God as the foundation of the universe; and by "human beings" I am referring to our individual consciousness. Various religions come into being in accordance with different ways of thinking about the relationship between God and humans. But what sort of relationship is the true religious relationship?

If we assume that the essences of God and humans differ fundamentally and that God is merely some sort of great power above and beyond us, then there is no true religious motive in our response to God. We might fear God and therefore follow God's commands, or we might curry favor with God and thereby seek happiness and benefit. These approaches are rooted in selfishness, and a mutual relationship between those with different natures cannot be established without an element of selfishness. William Robertson Smith stated that religion does not emerge from fear of an unknowable power but from loving reverence for a God who has a blood relationship with oneself. Religion is not an individual's optional relation with a supernatural power, but a communal relationship between members of a society and the power that maintains the peace and order of the society. At the base of all religions must be a relationship between God and humans in which they share the same nature—that is, a relationship like that between father and child. But for God and the human to share the same losses and gains and for God to save and protect us is not yet true religion. God must be the foundation of the universe and our own foundation as well. To take refuge in God is to take refuge in that foundation. God must also be the goal of the myriad things in the universe and therefore the goal of humans as well. Each person finds in God his or her own true goal. Just as the hands and feet are parts of the

human, the human is a part of God. Our taking refuge in God seems in a certain respect to be a loss of the self, but in another respect it is the way we find the self. Christ said, "He who finds his life shall lose it, and he who loses his life for my sake will find it,"[1] and this is the purest form of religion.

The relationship between God and the human in true religion must be of this sort. We pray and offer thanks to God not for the sake of the self's existence, but for our return to God as the source of the self—and we are grateful for our return to God. Moreover, God loves people not to give worldly happiness but to return them to God. God is the source of life, and we live only in God. In this respect alone is religion filled with life and does the feeling of true piety arise. If we merely resign and entrust ourselves to God, then we have yet to rid ourselves of the scent of the self and to realize the heart of true piety. That one finds the true self in God might be seen as emphasizing the self, but this is actually the reason for abandoning the self and praising God.

I think it is a fundamental idea of all religions that God and humans have the same nature, that in God humans return to their origin, and that only what is based on these two points can be called true religion. Beginning with this idea, however, we can conceptualize various kinds of relationships between God and humans. We can conceive of God as a transcendent entity apart from the universe who controls the world—including people—from the outside. Or we can think of God as immanent and functioning within people, who are all parts of God. The former is theism, the latter is pantheism. It might be rational to think along the lines of pantheism, but many religious figures oppose that view, for to see God and nature as identical is to eliminate God's personal character. When the myriad things in the universe are regarded as variant forms of God, not only is the transcendence of God lost and God's majesty marred, but the objectionable problem of having to attribute the origin of evil to God

---

[1] Matthew 10:39.

also arises. Thinking about this carefully, however, we see that pantheistic thought does not necessarily have such flaws and that theistic thought is not necessarily without them. If we view God and the essential nature of reality as identical while also viewing the foundation of reality as spiritual, then we will not necessarily lose God's personal character. Additionally, no form of pantheism holds that individual things are God just as they are. In Spinoza's philosophy, for example, the myriad things in this world are modes of God.* Moreover, even in theism God's omniscience and omnipotence are not easily reconcilable with the existence of evil in the world; in fact, this problem plagued many medieval philosophers.

The idea of a transcendent God who controls the world from without not only conflicts with our reason but also falls short of the most profound religiosity. The only thing we can know to be the will of God is the laws of nature, and apart from these laws there is no divine revelation; of course, because God is unfathomable, what we know is perhaps only one part of God. Though we might assume a revelation apart from the laws of nature, we cannot know it; and if we assume that revelation opposes the laws of nature, then God involves a contradiction. People believe in the divinity of Jesus Christ because his life exhibits the deepest truth of human life. Our God must be the internal unifying power of the universe, which orders heaven and earth and nurtures the myriad things in them; apart from this power there is no God. If we say that God is personal, then at the base of reality we ascertain significance that involves personality. Otherwise, what we speak of as supernatural is either based on a historical legend or our own subjective fancy. It is moreover by directly seeing God at the base of nature and at the base of the self that we can feel God's infinite warmth and attain to the essence of religion, which is to live in God. The sense of true reverence

and love for God can emerge only from living in God. Love means that two personalities have merged and become one, and reverence arises when a partial personality faces a perfect one. Reverence and love must be based on a unity of personality.

The feelings of love and reverence arise not only between people but also in one's own consciousness. Because our mutually divergent consciousness of today and yesterday possess the same center of consciousness, they are filled with feelings of self-reverence and self-love; likewise, the reason we revere and love God must be that we possess the same foundation as God and that our spirit is a part of God's consciousness. Even though God and humans have the same foundation of spirit, they can of course be regarded as independent in the same way that the minds of two people with the same thought are independent. This approach, however, makes temporal and spatial distinctions in spirit just as we do between physical bodies. In the case of spirit, whatever has the same foundation is the same spirit. We can view our consciousness, which changes from day to day, as always being the same spirit because it always possesses the same unity; in the same way, our spirit must be identical to God. The statement that we live in God is, then, not simply a metaphor but a fact. (In a commentary on John 17:21, even Bishop Wescott stated that the unity of believers is not merely a moral unity in terms of such factors as goal-emotion but a vital unity in the sense of life unity.)

The most profound religion is thus established upon the unity of God and humans, and the true meaning of religion is found in grasping the significance of this unity, in breaking beyond one's own consciousness and experiencing the lofty universal spirit that functions at the base of consciousness. Faith should not be bestowed from without by a legend or theory—it should be cultivated from within. As Jakob Boehme said, we arrive at God through the deepest internal birth (*die innerste Geburt*).* In

---

* *Baruch Spinoza* (1632–1677) was a Dutch philosopher who used the mathematical method of axioms and theorems to develop a metaphysical and ethical system. Through this method he attempted to demonstrate the unity of thought and matter, mind and body, God and Nature (Eds.).

* *Jakob Boehme* (1575–1624) was a German cobbler who wrote a systematic treatise expressing a mystical view of the universe (Eds.).

this internal rebirth we see God directly and believe in God, and at the same time we find our true life and feel infinite power. Faith is not mere knowledge, but an intuition and a vital force in the above sense. One unifying power functions at the base of all our mental activity, and we call it our self or personality. Subjective things such as desires as well as highly objective things such as knowledge take on the color of this unifying force, the personality of each person. Both knowledge and desire are established by this power.

Faith is thus a unifying power that transcends knowledge. It is not that faith is supported by knowledge and the will, but that knowledge and the will are supported by faith. In this sense, faith is mystical. But to say that faith is mystical does not mean that it is contrary to knowledge, for faith that conflicts with knowledge cannot become the basis of life. If we exhaust our intellect and will, then we will acquire from within a faith we cannot lose.

I have argued that nature and spirit are not two completely different kinds of reality. The distinction between them results from differing ways of looking at one and the same reality. Anyone who deeply comprehends nature discerns a spiritual unity at its base. Moreover, complete, true spirit is united with nature; only one reality exists in the universe. And, as I said before, this sole reality is both infinite opposition and conflict and infinite unity. It is an independent, self-fulfilled, infinite activity. We call the base of this infinite activity God. God is not something that transcends reality, God is the base of reality. God is that which dissolves the distinction between subjectivity and objectivity and unites spirit and nature.

Regardless of the historical age or the cultural group, everyone has a word for "God." Due to differences in the level of knowledge and the diversity of demands, the word is interpreted in a variety of ways. Most people of religion conceive of God as something like a great human who stands outside the universe and controls it. This notion of God is extremely infantile, and it not only conflicts with present-day learning and knowledge but in the religious sphere falls short of being something with which we humans can achieve intimate unity in our hearts. At the same time, however, I cannot follow the lead of hard-core scientists these days and argue that matter is the only reality and that material force is the basis of the universe. As previously stated, there is a fundamental spiritual principle at the base of reality, and this principle is God. This idea accords with the fundamental truth of Indian religion: Ātman and Brahman are identical.* God is the great spirit of the universe.

Since long ago, there have been many attempts to prove the existence of God. Some people argue that because this world could not have begun from nothing it must have been created by something, namely, God. Thus relying on the law of causality, such people consider God to be the cause of the world. Others hold that this world does not exist by accident, that it is in all respects something with meaning, organized with a certain fixed goal; they then infer that something gave this organization to the world and conclude by claiming that the organizing guide is God. They view the relation between the world and God like that between an artistic work and the artist. Both of these arguments attempt to prove the existence of God from the standpoint of knowledge and to determine God's qualities. There are others who try to prove God's existence by referring to moral demands totally divorced from knowledge. They argue that humans have moral demands, that is, consciences, and that if there were no great supervisor in the world to encourage good and admonish evil, then our morality would be meaningless. It is for this reaon, they say, that we must acknowledge the existence of God as the upholder of morality. Kant is one who advanced this proof.

But can these arguments really prove the existence of God? Although some contend that because there has to be a cause of the world we must acknowledge the existence of God, if we base our ar-

---

* *Atman and Brahman: Atman* is a Sanskrit term signifying the True Self. *Brahman* is a term used in the *Upanishads* to designate God in the deeper sense of the Godhead. It has also been variously translated as the Ground of Being, the Ultimate Reality, and the World-Soul. If the Atman and Brahman are identical, then the True Self is one with God, or the Ultimate Reality (Eds.).

gument on the law of causality can we not proceed another step and ask about the cause of God? And if we were to say that God is beginningless and endless and hence exists without a cause, is there any reason why we cannot say the same thing about the world? Also, to infer an omniscient controller from the fact that the world is organized favorably according to a certain goal, one must prove that the myriad things in the universe are in fact created purposefully, but this is extremely difficult to do. If the proof of God's existence hinges on this, then the existence of God becomes quite uncertain. Some might believe it, while others might not. Even supposing that this fact is proven, we can still think of the world as coming into being by chance and yet having a goal.

The attempt to prove the existence of God from moral demands is even weaker. If there is an omniscient, omnipotent God who upholds our morality, we do gain great strength in the moral realm; but though the belief that God exists has a valuable impact on our behavior, it does not prove that God does indeed exist. We can even view this belief as simply an expediency.

The aforementioned theories attempt to prove the existence of God indirectly from without and thus have not proven God immediately in the direct experience of the self. How can we verify the existence of God in facts of our direct experience? An infinite power is hidden even in our small chests that are restricted by time and space; the infinite unifying power of reality is latent in us. Possessing this power, we can search for the truth of the universe in learning, we can express the true meaning of reality in art, and we can know the foundation of reality that forms the universe in the depths of our hearts—we can grasp the true face of God. The infinitely free activity of the human heart proves God directly. As Jakob Boehme said, we see God with a "reversed eye" (*umgewandtes Auge*).

If we seek God in the facts of the external world, God must inescapably be a hypothetical God. Further, a God set up outside the universe as a creator or overseer of the universe cannot be deemed a true, absolutely infinite God. The religion of India of the distant past and the mysticism that flourished in Europe in the fifteenth and sixteenth centuries sought God in intuition realized in the inner soul, and this I consider to be the deepest knowledge of God.

In what form does God exist? From one perspective, taken by such thinkers as Nicholas of Cusa,* God is all negation, whereas that which can be affirmed or grasped is not God; if there is some entity that can be grasped, it is already finite and cannot perform the infinite activity of unifying the universe. From this standpoint, God is absolute nothingness. God is not, however, mere nothingness. An immovable unifying activity clearly functions at the base of the establishment of reality, and it is by means of this activity that reality is established. For example, where is the law that the sum of the three angles in a triangle is equal to the sum of two right angles? We can neither see nor hear this law, yet does there not exist an indisputable law? Further, in response to a great painting, we see that something in its entirety strikes sensitive people as enlivened by a superb spirit; but if we try to determine how each object or scene in the painting is enlivened by this spirit, we inevitably fail. God is in these senses the unifier of the universe, the base of reality; and because God is no-thing, there is no place where God is not, and no place where God does not function.

In the same way that profound mathematics gives no knowledge to those who cannot understand mathematical principles and that a sublime painting does not move those who have no feel for beauty, the existence of God is considered a fancy or felt to be meaningless and therefore ignored by mediocre and shallow humans. Those who desire to know the true God must discipline themselves and provide themselves with eyes that can know God. To such people, the power of God is active in the universe just as a painter's spirit is active in a great

---

* *Nicholas of Cusa* (1401–1464) was a bishop and a cardinal in the Catholic Church who developed a philosophy which utilized elements of medieval, early Renaissance, and German mystical thought (Eds.).

painting; God's power is felt as a fact of direct experience. This is the fact of seeing God.

Given what I have said so far, God might be felt to be a cold philosophical existence—the base of the unity of the universe—totally unrelated to the activity of our warm feelings, but this is hardly the case. As stated, since our desires arise in the search for a greater unity, we experience joy when we attain to this unity. The so-called self-love of an individual is ultimately nothing more than this demand for unity. Because our infinite spirit is never fundamentally satisfied by the unity constituted by an individual self, it inevitably seeks a larger unity, a great self that envelops both oneself and others. We come to express sympathy toward others and seek congruence and unity between oneself and others. Our love for others is the demand for such a supra-individual unity with them. Accordingly, we feel greater peace and joy in love for others than in love for ourselves. God, the unity of the universe, is the base of this unifying activity, the foundation of our love, the source of our joy. God is infinite love, infinite joy, and peace.

NO RELIGION

Buddhadāsa Bhikkhu

I didn't come here today to give any formal sermon or lecture, but to have an informal chat among friends. I hope that you all agree to this, so that we can speak and listen to each other without formality and rituals, even if our talk here becomes somewhat different or unusual. Further, I intend to speak only about the most essential matters, important topics which people consider to be profound. Therefore, if you don't listen carefully you may find it difficult to follow and might misunderstand, especially those of you who haven't heard the previous talks in this series. (As a matter of fact, it's also difficult for me,

for with each new talk I must maintain a connection with the previous ones.)

The last talk was called "What To Do To Be Void." This time I intend to talk about "No Religion." If you find the subject strange or incomprehensible, or if don't agree, please take the time to think it over. But remember, it isn't necessary to believe or subscribe to what I say right away.

When we meet together like this, I feel there is something which prevents us from understanding each other and this thing is simply the problem of language itself. You see, there are two kinds of language. One is conventional language that ordinary people speak, what I call "people language."

People language is used by the ordinary people who don't understand Dhamma very well and by those worldly people who are so dense that they are blind to everything but material things. Then, there is the language which is spoken by those who understand reality (Dhamma), especially those who know and understand reality in the ultimate sense. This is another kind of language. Sometimes, when only a few words or even just a few syllables are uttered, the ordinary listener finds Dhamma language paradoxical, completely opposite to the language he speaks. We can call it "Dhamma language." You always must take care to recognize which language is being spoken.

People who are blind to the true reality (Dhamma) can speak only people language, the conventional language of ordinary people. On the other hand, people who have genuinely realized the ultimate truth (Dhamma) can speak either language. They can handle people language quite well and are also comfortable using Dhamma language, especially when speaking among those who know reality, who have already realized the truth (Dhamma). Amongst those with profound understanding, Dhamma language is used almost exclusively; unfortunately, ordinary people can't understand a word. Dhamma language is understood only by those who are in the know. What is more, in Dhamma language it isn't even necessary to make a sound. For example, a finger is pointed or an eyebrow raised and the ultimate meaning of reality is understood. So, please take interest in these two kinds of language—people language and Dhamma language.

To illustrate the importance of language, let's consider the following example. Ordinary, ignorant worldly people are under the impression that there is this religion and that religion, and that these religions are different, so different that they're opposed to each other. Such people speak of "Christianity," "Islam," "Buddhism," "Hinduism," "Sikhism," and so on, and consider these religions to be different, separate, and incompatible. These people think and speak according to their personal feelings and thus turn the religions into enemies. Because of this mentality, there come to exist different religions which are hostilely opposed to each other.

Those who have penetrated to the essential nature of religion will regard all religions as being the same. Although they may say there is Buddhism, Judaism, Taoism, Islam, or whatever, they will also say that all religions are inwardly the same. However, those who have penetrated to the highest understanding of Dhamma will feel that the thing called "religion" doesn't exist after all. There is no Buddhism; there is no Christianity; there is no Islam. How can they be the same or in conflict when they don't exist? It just isn't possible. Thus, the phrase "No religion!" is actually Dhamma language of the highest level. Whether it will be understood or not is something else, depending upon the listener, and has nothing to do with the truth or with religion.

I'd like to give a simple example of people language, the language of materialism. "Water" will suffice. People who don't know much about even the simplest things think that there are many different kinds of water. They view these various kinds of water as if they have nothing in common. They distinguish rain-water, well-water, underground-water, canal-water, swamp-water, ditch-water, gutter-water, sewer-water, toilet-water, urine, diarrhea, and many other kinds of water from each other. Average people will insist that these waters are com-

pletely different, because such people take external appearances as their criteria.

A person with some knowledge, however, knows that pure water can be found in every kind of water. If we take rain-water and distill it, we will get pure water. If we take river-water and distill it, we will get pure water. If we take canal-water, sewer-water, or toilet-water, and distill it, we will still get pure water. A person with this understanding knows that all those different kinds of water are the same as far as the water component is concerned. As for those elements which make it impure and look different, they aren't the water itself. They may combine with water, and alter water, but they are never water itself. If we look through the polluting elements, we can see the water that is always the same, for in every case the essential nature of water is the same. However many kinds of water there may seem to be, they are all the same as far as the essential nature of water is concerned. When we look at things from this viewpoint, we can see that all religions are the same. If they appear different it's because we are making judgments on the basis of external forms.

On an even more intelligent level, we can take that pure water and examine it further. Then, we must conclude that there is no water, only two parts hydrogen and one part oxygen. There's no water left. That substance which we have been calling "water" has disappeared, it's void. The same is true everywhere, no matter where we find the two parts of hydrogen and one part oxygen. In the sky, in the ground, or wherever these parts happen to be found, the state of water has disappeared and the term "water" is no longer used. For one who has penetrated to this level of truth, there is no such thing as "water."

In the same way, one who has attained to the ultimate truth sees that there's no such thing as "religion." There is only a certain nature which can be called whatever we like. We can call it "Dhamma," we can call it "Truth," we can call it "God," "Tao," or whatever, but we shouldn't particularize that Dhamma or that Truth as Buddhism, Christianity,

Taoism, Judaism, Sikhism, Zoroastranism, or Islam, for we can neither capture nor confine it with labels and concepts. Still, such divisions occur because people haven't yet realized this nameless truth for themselves. They have only reached the external levels, just as with canal-water, muddy-water, and the rest. . . .

QUESTIONS FOR DISCUSSION

1. For Radhakrishnan mystical or religious experiences have certain universal characteristics. Discuss several of these characteristics. In your discussions consider at least two of the following: (a) whether there is any value to these experiences; (b) the epistemological status of the experience; and (c) whether they are experiences of God.
2. Would you like to smoke the sacred pipe of the Oglala Sioux? Why or why not?
3. Explain Nishida's pantheism. Is a pantheist God preferable to the traditional theistic conception of a transcendent God? Is there a difference between a God who is identical with nature and no God at all?
4. Evaluate Buddhadasa's claim that, even though from the perspective of ordinary language religions are different, on a deeper level they are all the same. Then, evaluate his further claim that on a still deeper level there are no religions. In your answer to the last questions consider his comparison of religion at the deepest level and water as ultimately two parts hydrogen and one part oxygen.
5. We generally feel justified in calling something real if it is capable of being publically verified. But mystical experiences are, by their very nature, private. How then, if at all, can we distinguish between a mystical experience and a hallucination?

RELIGION, SOCIETY, AND POLITICS

Religion has always had an ambivalent relationship with those in power. "Render unto Caesar," said Jesus Christ, "what is due to Caesar," but he left unclear what fits into this category. Although often supporting the status quo, religion has been used also by revolutionaries against the status quo. How, then, should we evaluate its social and political significance?

The first reading in this section is composed of excerpts from the works of the nineteenth-century social theorists and revolutionaries Karl Marx and Friedrich Engels. For these thinkers, religion is an expression of an oppressive and alienated society. Since human beings experience intense suffering in such a world, they create an illusory happiness in a world beyond (the reader might want to compare this analysis of religion as an illusion with Freud's psychological analysis in Section One of this chapter). It is in this sense that religion is "the opium of the people." Just as the use of actual opiate derivatives or other similar drugs tends to reinforce the status quo by pacifying people and diverting their attention from the problems which make them need drugs in the first place, so religion pacifies and diverts people's attention from the social roots of their suffering. In addition, both Marx and Engels believe that the class which wields economic and political power, the ruling class, uses religion directly as an instrument to legitimate its interest and its rule. Marx notes that Christianity in particular has historically justified slavery, serfdom, and capitalist exploitation and that it has attempted to justify these forms of oppression as "either the just punishment of original sin and other sins or trials that the Lord in his infinite wisdom imposes on those redeemed." Religion, Marx claims, will not vanish through the force of rational argument but only when the oppressive social conditions which generate the need for it have been overthrown. "The demand to give up the illusions about its condition is the demand to give up a condition which needs illusions. The crit-

icism of religion is therefore in embryo the criticism of the vale of woe, the halo of which is religion."

Nevertheless, even Marx knows that there is another side to religion. In the same text that he discusses religion as "the opium of the people" he also calls religion "the protest against real distress" and the "heart of a heartless world." And Engels writes that Christianity "was originally a movement of oppressed people" and that it, like socialism, preaches a liberation from oppression. The problem, however, is that "Christianity places this salvation in a life beyond, after death, in heaven," whereas "socialism places it in this world in a transformatrion of society."

In 1968, in Medellin, Colombia, 130 Catholic bishops met and called for a radical social transformation with an emphasis on the "option for the poor." This call spoke to a movement that was already emerging known as "liberation theology," and this movement was to become a dynamic movement for and by the poor in every country in Latin America. It was often led by priests who helped their parishioners establish "Christian base communities" which were often engaged in revolutionary struggle.

In this section, two Brazilian theologians and priests, Leonardo Boff and Clodovis Boff (they are brothers), discuss some of the key theological and philosophical foundations of liberation theology. Liberation from oppression, according to liberation theology, does not await a life beyond, after death, as Engels would have it, because God's kingdom exists not only in eternity but also within history.

Although liberation theology is revolutionary, it is also still theology. The poor are not merely Marx's proletariat but all the oppressed who are represented by the "disfigured Son of God." The revolutionary stance of liberation theology is rooted in what Boff and Boff call a "hermeneutics of liberation," a rereading of the Bible from the standpoint of the poor. This also entails reinterpreting the fundamental stories and symbols of Christianity as revolutionary indicators. The Exodus is the story of a God who stands with the oppressed against their oppressors. The Prophets present a revolutionary challenge to all forms of social injustice. Christ is the symbol of liberation itself. The Holy Spirit struggles with the people against their oppressors. Mary is the liberating woman of the people.

Symbols in general and religious symbols in particular have profound psychological and political significance. As Carol Christ, a feminist writer—she is the author of *Laughter of Aphrodite*—involved in the movement of women's spirituality, observes, symbols shape our cultural ethos and resonate at a deep unconscious level. But, with perhaps the exception of Mary, the symbols of Western religion—and, we might add, of all the major religions—are overwhelmingly male. Of special significance is the symbol of God the Father which Carol Christ claims devalues and delegitimatizes the power of women. Thus, in the last selection in this section and in this chapter, Christ argues in favor of asserting the symbol of the Goddess as an affirmation of female power.

CRITIQUE OF RELIGION[*]

Karl Marx and Friedrich Engels

The basis of irreligious criticism is: *Man makes religion, religion does not make man.* In other words, religion is the self-consciousness and self-feeling of man who has either not yet found himself or has already lost himself again. But *man* is no abstract being squatting outside the world. Man is *the world of man,* the state, society. This state, this society, produce religion, *a reversed world-consciousness,* because they are *a reversed world.* Religion is the general theory of that world, its encyclopaedic compendium, its logic in a popular form, its spiritualistic *point d'honneur,* its enthusiasm, its moral sanction, its solemn completion, its universal ground for consolation and justification. It is *the fantastic realization* of the human essence because the *human essence* has no true reality. The struggle against religion is therefore mediately the fight against *the other world,* of which religion is the spiritual *aroma.*

Religious distress is at the same time the *expression* of real distress and the *protest* against real distress. Religion is the sigh of the oppressed creature, the heart of a heartless world, just as it is the spirit of a spiritless situation. It is the *opium* of the people.

The abolition of religion as the *illusory* happiness of the people is required for their *real* happiness. The demand to give up the illusions about its condition is the *demand to give up a condition which needs illusions.* The criticism of religion is therefore *in embryo the criticism of the vale of woe,* the *halo* of which is religion.

Criticism has plucked the imaginary flowers from the chain not so that man will wear the chain without any fantasy or consolation but so that he will shake off the chain and cull the living flower. The criticism of religion disillusions man to make him think and act and shape his reality like a man who has been disillusioned and has come to reason, so that he will revolve round himself and therefore round his true sun. Religion is only the illusory sun which revolves round man as long as he does not revolve round himself.

The task of history, therefore, once the *world beyond the truth* has disappeared, is to establish the *truth of this world.* The immediate *task of philosophy,* which is at the service of history, once the *saintly form* of human self-alienation has been un-

---

[*]The following are short selections from the writings of Marx and Engels. The first selection is from Marx's "Contribution to the Critique of Hegel's Philosophy of Right." The second is excerpted from Marx's *Capital,* Volume One. The third and fourth selections are from Engel's *Anti-Dühring* and *On the History of Early Christianity,* respectively. The final selection is from Marx's "The Communism of the Paper *Rheinischer Beobachter.*"

masked, is to unmask self-alienation in its *unholy forms.* Thus the criticism of heaven turns into the criticism of the earth, the *criticism of religion* into the *criticism of right* and the *criticism of theology* into the *criticism of politics.* *

• • •

. . . The religious world is but the reflex of the real world. And for a society based upon the production of commodities,† in which the producers in general enter into social relations with one another by treating their products as commodities and values, whereby they reduce their individual private labour to the standard of homogeneous human labour—for such a society, Christianity with its *cultus* of abstract man, more especially in its bourgeois developments, Protestantism, Deism, &c., is the most fitting form of religion. In the ancient Asiatic and other ancient modes of production,‡ we find that the conversion of products into commodities, and therefore the conversion of men into producers of commodities, holds a subordinate place, which, however, increases in importance as the primitive communities approach nearer and nearer to their dissolution. Trading nations, properly so called, exist in the ancient world only in its interstices, like the gods of Epicurus in the Intermundia,§ or like

Jews in the pores of Polish society. Those ancient social organisms of production are, as compared with bourgeois society, extremely simple and transparent. But they are founded either on the immature development of man individually, who has not yet severed the umbilical cord that unites him with his fellowmen in a primitive tribal community, or upon direct relations of subjection. They can arise and exist only when the development of the productive power of labour has not risen beyond a low stage, and when, therefore, the social relations within the sphere of material life, between man and man, and between man and nature, are correspondingly narrow. This narrowness is reflected in the ancient worship of nature, and in the other elements of the popular religions. The religious reflex of the real world can, in any case, only then finally vanish, when the practical relations of every-day life offer to man none but perfectly intelligible and reasonable relations with regard to his fellowmen and to nature.

The life-process of society, which is based on the process of material production, does not strip off its mystical veil until it is treated as production by freely associated men, and is consciously regulated by them in accordance with a settled plan.** This, however, demands for society a certain material groundwork or set of conditions of existence which in their turn are the spontaneous product of a long and painful process of development.

• • •

All religion, however, is nothing but the fantastic reflection in men's minds of those external forces which control their daily life, a reflection in which the terrestrial forces assume the form of supernatural forces. In the beginnings of history it was the forces of nature which were first so reflected and which in the course of further evolution under-

---

* Marx is referring here to the German philosopher Ludwig Feuerbach's (1804–1872) critique of religion as an alienated projection of human nature. Marx is arguing that it is not enough to expose religion as self-alienation but that we must further expose the alienating social and political conditions which provide the ground for religious self-alienation (Eds.).

† Commodities are not just objects for use but objects to be bought and sold. A society based upon the production of commodities is a capitalist society (Eds.).

‡ A mode of production is the economic structure of a society in both its physical and social dimensions. According to Marx there have been several different modes of production throughout history: ancient (Asiatic and slave), feudal, and capitalist (Eds.).

§ Epicurus (341–270 B.C.E.) was an ancient Greek philosopher who speculated that the gods are material, pleasure seeking beings who exist in a realm separate from the human world—Intermundia—and who pursue their own affairs without concern for human beings (Eds.).

** ". . . production by freely associated men . . . consciously regulated by them in accordance with a settled plan" was Marx's concept of a communist society (Eds.).

went the most manifold and varied personifications among the various peoples. This early process has been traced back by comparative mythology, at least in the case of the Indo-European peoples, to its origin in the Indian Vedas, and in its further evolution it has been demonstrated in detail among the Indians, Persians, Greeks, Romans, Germans and, so far as material is available, also among the Celts, Lithuanians and Slavs. But it is not long before, side by side with the forces of nature, social forces begin to be active—forces which confront man as equally alien and at first equally inexplicable, dominating him with the same apparent natural necessity as the forces of nature themselves. The fantastic figures, which at first only reflected the mysterious forces of nature, at this point acquire social attributes, become representatives of the forces of history. At a still further stage of evolution, all the natural and social attributes of the numerous gods are transferred to *one* almighty god, who is but a reflection of the abstract man. Such was the origin of monotheism, which was historically the last product of the vulgarized philosophy of the later Greeks and found its incarnation in the exclusively national god of the Jews, Jehovah. In this convenient, handy and universally adaptable form, religion can continue to exist as the immediate, that is, the sentimental form of men's relation to the alien natural and social forces which dominate them, so long as men remain under the control of these forces. However, we have seen repeatedly that in existing bourgeois society men are dominated by the economic conditions created by themselves, by the means of production which they themselves have produced, as if by an alien force. The actual basis of the reflective activity that gives rise to religion therefore continues to exist, and with it the religious reflection itself. And although bourgeois political economy has given a certain insight into the causal connection of this alien domination, this makes no essential difference. Bourgeois economics can neither prevent crises in general, nor protect the individual capitalists from losses, bad debts and bankruptcy, nor secure the individual workers against unemployment and destitution. It is still true that

man proposes and God (that is, the alien domination of the capitalist mode of production) disposes. Mere knowledge, even if it went much further and deeper than that of bourgeois economic science, is not enough to bring social forces under the domination of society. What is above all necessary for this, is a social *act*. And when this act has been accomplished, when society, by taking possession of all means of production and using them on a planned basis, has freed itself and all its members from the bondage in which they are now held by these means of production which they themselves have produced but which confront them as an irresistible alien force; when therefore man no longer merely proposes, but also disposes—only then will the last alien force which is still reflected in religion vanish; and with it will also vanish the religious reflection itself, for the simple reason that then there will be nothing left to reflect.

• • •

The history of early Christianity has notable points of resemblance with the modern working-class movement. Like the latter, Christianity was originally a movement of oppressed people: it first appeared as the religion of slaves and emancipated slaves, of poor people deprived of all rights, of peoples subjugated or dispersed by Rome. Both Christianity and the workers' socialism preach forthcoming salvation from bondage and misery; Christianity place this salvation in a life beyond, after death, in heaven; socialism places it in this world, in a transformation of society. Both are persecuted and baited, their adherents are despised and made the objects of exclusive laws, the former as enemies of the human race, the latter as enemies of the state, enemies of religion, the family, social order. And in spite of all persecution, nay, even spurred on by it, they forge victoriously, irresistibly ahead. Three hundred years after its appearance Christianity was the recognized state religion in the Roman World Empire, and in barely sixty years socialism has won itself a position which makes its victory absolutely certain.

If, therefore, Prof. Anton Menger wonders in his *Right to the Full Product of Labour* why, with the enormous concentration of landownership under the Roman emperors and the boundless sufferings of the working class of the time, which was composed almost exclusively of slaves, "socialism did not follow the overthrow of the Roman Empire in the West," it is because he cannot see that this "socialism" did in fact, as far as it was possible at the time, exist and even became dominant—in Christianity. Only this Christianity, as was bound to be the case in the historic conditions, did not want to accomplish the social transformation in this world, but beyond it, in heaven, in eternal life after death, in the impending "millennium."

• • •

. . . Besides income tax, the Consistorial Councillor has another means of introducing communism as he conceives it:

"What is the alpha and omega of Christian faith? The dogma of original sin and the redemption. And therein lies the solidary link between men at its highest potential; one for all and all for one."

Happy people! The *cardinal question* is solved for ever. Under the double wings of the Prussian eagle and the Holy Ghost the proletariat will find two inexhaustible sources of life: first the surplus of income tax over and above the ordinary and extra-ordinary needs of the state, a surplus which is equal to nought; second, the revenues from the heavenly domains of original sin and the redemption which are also equal to nought. These two noughts provide a splendid ground for one-third of the nation who have no ground for their subsistence and a wonderful support for another third which is on the decline. In any case, the imaginary surpluses, original sin and the redemption, will appease the hunger of the people in quite a different way than the long speeches of the liberal deputies!

Further we read:

"In the 'Our Father' we say: lead us not into temptation. And we must practise towards our neighbour what we ask for ourselves. But our social conditions tempt man and excessive need incites to crime."

And we, the honourable bureaucrats, judges and consistorial councillors of the Prussian state, take this into consideration by having people racked on the wheel, beheaded, imprisoned, and flogged and thereby "lead" the proletarians "into temptation" to have us later similarly racked on the wheel, beheaded, imprisoned and flogged. And that will not fail to happen.

"Such conditions," the Consistorial Councillor declares, "a Christian state *cannot* tolerate, it must find a remedy for them."

Yes, with absurd prattle on society's duties of solidarity, with imaginary surpluses and unprovided bills drawn on God the Father, Son and Co.

"We can also be spared the already boring talk about communism," our observant Consistorial Councillor asserts. "If only those whose calling it is to develop the social principles of Christianity do so, the Communists will soon be put to silence."

The social principles of Christianity have now had eighteen hundred years to develop and need no further development by Prussian consistorial councillors.

The social principles of Christianity justified the slavery of Antiquity, glorified the serfdom of the Middle Ages and equally know, when necessary, how to defend the oppression of the proletariat, although they make a pitiful face over it.

The social principles of Christianity preach the necessity of a ruling and an oppressed class, and all they have for the latter is the pious wish the former will be charitable.

The social principles of Christianity transfer the consistorial councillors' adjustment of all infamies to heaven and thus justify the further existence of those infamies on earth.

The social principles of Christianity declare all vile acts of the oppressors against the oppressed to be either the just punishment of original sin and other sins or trials that the Lord in his infinite wisdom imposes on those redeemed.

The social principles of Christianity preach cowardice, self-contempt, abasement, submission, dejection, in a word all the qualities of the *canaille;* and the proletariat, not wishing to be treated as *canaille,* needs its courage, its self-feeling, its pride and its sense of independence more than its bread.

The social principles of Christianity are sneakish and the proletariat is revolutionary.

So much for the social principles of Christianity.

LIBERATION THEOLOGY

Leonardo Boff and Clodovis Boff

What lies behind liberation theology? Its starting point is the perception of scandals such as those described above, which exist not only in Latin America but throughout the Third World. According to "conservative" estimates, there are in those countries held in underdevelopment:

- five-hundred million persons starving;
- one billion, six-hundred million persons, whose life expectancy is less than sixty years (when a person in one of the developed countries reaches the age of forty-five, he or she is reaching middle age; in most of Africa or Latin America, a person has little hope of living to that age);
- one billion persons living in absolute poverty;
- one billion, five-hundred million persons with no access to the most basic medical care;
- five-hundred million with no work or only occasional work and a per capita income of less than $150 a year;
- eight-hundred-fourteen million who are illiterate;
- two billion with no regular, dependable water supply.

Who cannot be filled with righteous anger at such a human and social hell? Liberation theology presupposes an energetic protest at such a situation, for that situation means:

- on the social level: collective oppression, exclusion, and marginalization;
- on the individual level: injustice and denial of human rights;
- on the religious level: social sinfulness, "contrary to the plan of the Creator and to the honor that is due to him" (Puebla, §28).[1]

Without a minimum of "suffering with" this suffering that affects the great majority of the human race, liberation theology can neither exist nor be understood. Underlying liberation theology is a prophetic and comradely commitment to the life, cause, and struggle of these millions of debased and marginalized human beings, a commitment to ending this historical-social iniquity. The Vatican Instruction "Some Aspects of Liberation Theology" (August 6, 1984), put it well: "It is not possible for a single instant to forget the situations of dramatic poverty from which the challenge set to theologians springs—the challenge to work out a genuine theology of liberation."

MEETING THE POOR CHRIST IN THE POOR

Every true theology springs from a spirituality—that is, from a true meeting with God in history. Liberation theology was born when faith confronted

---

[1] The Latin American bishops' conference, CELAM, has held three General Conferences since the Second Vatican Council. The second, held at Medellín, Columbia, in 1968, can be considered the "official launching" of the theme of liberation. The third, held at Puebla, Mexico, in 1979, with Pope John Paul II in attendance, developed in some ways, but also watered down, the conclusions reached at Medellín. Puebla produced its own "Final Document," published in England as *Puebla: Evangelization at Present in the Future: Conclusions of the Third General Conference of the Latin American Bishops.* Catholic Institute for International Relations (Slough, Berkshire: St. Paul Publications, 1979) and in the U.S.A. as *Puebla and Beyond: Documentation and Commentary.* Ed. John Eagleson and Philip Scharper (Maryknoll, N.Y.: Orbis, 1979).—Trans.

the injustice done to the poor. By "poor" we do not really mean the poor individual who knocks on the door asking for alms. We mean a collective poor, the "popular classes," which is a much wider category than the "proletariat" singled out by Karl Marx (it is a mistake to identify the poor of liberation theology with the proletariat, though many of its critics do): the poor are also the workers exploited by the capitalist system; the underemployed, those pushed aside by the production process—a reserve army always at hand to take the place of the employed; they are the laborers of the countryside, and migrant workers with only seasonal work.

All this mass of the socially and historically oppressed makes up the poor as a social phenomenon. In the light of faith, Christians see in them the challenging face of the Suffering Servant, Jesus Christ. At first there is silence, silent and sorrowful contemplation, as if in the presence of a mystery that calls for introspection and prayer. Then this presence speaks. The Crucified in these crucified persons weeps and cries out: "I was hungry . . . in prison . . . naked" (Matt. 25:31–46).

Here what is needed is not so much contemplation as effective action for liberation. The Crucified needs to be raised to life. We are on the side of the poor only when we struggle alongside them against the poverty that has been unjustly created and forced on them. Service in solidarity with the oppressed also implies an act of love for the suffering Christ, a liturgy pleasing to God.

THE FIRST STEP: LIBERATING ACTION, LIBER-A(C)TION[2]

What is the action that will effectively enable the oppressed to move out of their inhuman situation? Many years of reflection and practice suggest that it

---

[2] The Portuguese word for "liberation" is *liberação,* which is composed of the root *liber,* "free," and, by chance, the Portuguese word for "action," *ação.* This coupling cannot be reproduced in English.—TRANS.

has to go beyond two approaches that have already been tried: aid and reformism.

"Aid" is help offered by individuals moved by the spectacle of widespread destitution. They form agencies and organize projects: the "Band-Aid" or "corn-plaster" approach to social ills. But however perceptive they become and however well-intentioned—and successful—aid remains a strategy for helping the poor, but treating them as (collective) objects of charity, not as subjects of their own liberation. The poor are seen simply as those who have nothing. There is a failure to see that the poor are oppressed and made poor *by others;* and what they do possess—strength to resist, capacity to understand their rights, to organize themselves and transform a subhuman situation—tends to be left out of account. Aid increases the dependence of the poor, tying them to help from others, to decisions made by others: again, not enabling them to become their own liberators.

"Reformism" seeks to improve the situation of the poor, but always wihin existing social relationships and the basic structuring of society, which rules out greater participation by all and diminution in the privileges enjoyed by the ruling classes. Reformism can lead to great feats of development in the poorer nations, but this development is nearly always at the expense of the oppressed poor and very rarely in their favor. For example, in 1964 the Brazilian economy ranked 46th in the world; in 1984 it ranked 8th. The last twenty years have seen undeniable technological and industrial progress, but at the same time there has been a considerable worsening of social conditions for the poor, with exploitation, destitution, and hunger on a scale previously unknown in Brazilian history. This has been the price paid by the poor for this type of elitist, exploitative, and exclusivist development in which, in the words of Pope John Paul II, the rich become ever richer at the expense of the poor who become ever poorer.

The poor can break out of their situation of oppression only by working out a strategy better able to change social conditions: the strategy of liberation. In liberation, the oppressed come together, come to understand their situation through the process of conscientization,[3] discover the causes of their oppression, organize themselves into movements, and act in a coordinated fashion. First, they claim everything that the existing system can give: better wages, working conditions, health care, education, housing, and so forth; then they work toward the transformation of present society in the direction of a new society characterized by widespread participation, a better and more just balance among social classes and more worthy ways of life.

In Latin America, where liberation theology originated, there have always been movements of liberation since the early days of the Spanish and Portuguese conquest. Amerindians, slaves, and the oppressed in general fought against the violence of the colonizers, created redoubts of freedom, such as the *quilombos* and *reducciones,*[4] led movements of revolt and independence. And among the colonizers were bishops such as Bartolomé de Las Casas, Antonio Valdivieso, and Toribio de Mogrovejo, and other missionaries and priests who defended the rights of the colonized peoples and made evangelization a process that included advancement of their rights.

Despite the massive and gospel-denying domination of the colonial centuries, dreams of freedom were never entirely extinguished. But it is only in the past few decades that a new consciousness of liberation has become widespread over the whole of Latin America. The poor, organized and conscientized, are beating at their masters' doors, demanding life, bread, liberty, and dignity. Courses of action are being taken with a view to release the

liberty that is now held captive. Liberation is emerging as the strategy of the poor themselves, confident in themselves and in their instruments of struggle: free trade unions, peasant organizations, local associations, action groups and study groups, popular political parties, base Christian communities.[5] They are being joined by groups and individuals from other social classes who have opted to change society and join the poor in their struggle to bring about change.

The growth of regimes of "national security" (for which read "capital security"), of military dictatorships, with their repression of popular movements in many countries of Latin America, is a reaction against the transforming and liberating power of the organized poor.

THE SECOND STEP: FAITH REFLECTS ON LIBERATING PRACTICE

Christians have always been and still are at the heart of these wider movements for liberation. The great majority of Latin Americans are not only poor but also Christian. So the great question at the beginning and still valid today was—and is—what role Christianity has to play. How are we to be Christians in a world of destitution and injustice? There can be only one answer: we can be followers of Jesus and true Christians only by making common cause with the poor and working out the gospel of liberation. Trade union struggles, battles for land and for the territories belonging to Amerindians, the fight for human rights and all other forms of commitment always pose the same question: What part is Christianity playing in motivating and carrying on the process of liberating the oppressed?

---

[3] "Conscientization" was a term brought into general use by the Brazilian educator Paulo Freire. In his work with illiterate Brazilians, the basic learning unit was always linked with the social and political context of the learner, as distinguished from purely objective learning or indoctrination.—TRANS.

[4] *Quilombos* were villages formed and inhabited by runaway slaves. *Reducciones* were enclaves of relative freedom from colonial powers for baptized Latin Americans, especially Amerindians, supervised by religious orders, especially the Jesuits, in Paraguay and elsewhere in the seventeenth and eighteenth centuries.—TRANS.

[5] The Portuguese term *comunidade* (in Spanish, *comunidad*) *eclesial de base* is variously translated "base church community," "basic Christian community," "grass-roots community," etc. They are small groups that come together for Bible study, liturgy, and social action, usually without a priest but with trained leaders. Smaller than parishes, they represent the "base" of society. They are the operational base of liberation theology in practice.—TRANS.

Inspired by their faith—which must include commitment to one's neighbor, particularly to the poor, if it is to be true (Matt. 25:31–46)—and motivated by the proclamation of the kingdom of God—which begins in this world and culminates only in eternity—and by the life, deeds, and death of Christ, who made a historic option for the poor, and by the supremely liberating significance of his resurrection, many Christians—bishops, priests, religious, nuns, lay men and women—are throwing themselves into action alongside the poor, or joining the struggles already taking place. The Christian base communities, Bible societies, groups for popular evangelization, movements for the promotion and defense of human rights, particularly those of the poor, agencies involved in questions of land tenure, indigenous peoples, slums, marginalized groups, and the like, have all shown themselves to have more than a purely religious and ecclesial significance, and to be powerful factors for mobilization and dynamos of liberating action, particularly when they have joined forces with other popular movements.

Christianity can no longer be dismissed as the opium of the people, nor can it be seen as merely fostering an attitude of critique: it has now become an active commitment to liberation. Faith challenges human reason and the historical progress of the powerful, but in the Third World it tackles the problem of poverty, now seen as the result of oppression. Only from this starting point can the flag of liberation be raised.

The gospel is not aimed chiefly at "modern" men and women with their critical spirit, but first and foremost at "nonpersons," those whose basic dignity and rights are denied them. This leads to reflection in a spirit of prophecy and solidarity aimed at making nonpersons full human beings, and then new men and women, according to the design of the "new Adam," Jesus Christ.

Reflecting on the basis of practice, within the ambit of the vast efforts made by the poor and their allies, seeking inspiration in faith and the gospel for the commitment to fight against poverty and for the integral liberation of all persons and the whole person—that is what liberation theology means.

Christians who have been inspired by its principles and who live out its practices have chosen the harder way, exposing themselves to defamation, persecution, and even martyrdom. Many have been led by its insights and the practice of solidarity at its origins to a process of true conversion. Archbishop Oscar Romero of San Salvador, who had been conservative in his views, became a great advocate and defender of the poor when he stood over the dead body of Fr. Rutilio Grande, assassinated for his liberating commitment to the poor. The spilt blood of the martyr acted like a salve on his eyes, opening them to the urgency of the task of liberation. And he himself was to follow to a martyr's death in the same cause.

Commitment to the liberation of the millions of the oppressed of our world restores to the gospel the credibility it had at the beginning and at the great periods of holiness and prophetic witness in history. The God who pitied the downtrodden and the Christ who came to set prisoners free proclaim themselves with a new face and in a new image today. The eternal salvation they offer is mediated by the historical liberations that dignify the children of God and render credible the coming utopia of the kingdom of freedom, justice, love, and peace, the kingdom of God in the midst of humankind.

From all this, it follows that if we are to understand the theology of liberation, we must first understand and take an active part in the real and historical process of liberating the oppressed. In this field, more than in others, it is vital to move beyond a merely intellectual approach that is content with comprehending a theology through its purely theoretical aspects, by reading articles, attending conferences, and skimming through books. We have to work our way into a more biblical framework of reference, where "knowing" implies loving, letting oneself become involved body and soul, communing wholly—being committed, in a word—as the prophet Jeremiah says: "He used to examine the cases of poor and needy, then all went well. Is not that what it means to know me?—it is Yahweh who speaks" (Jer. 22:16). So the criticisms made of liberation theology by those who judge it on a purely conceptual level, devoid of any real commitment to the oppressed, must be seen as radically irrelevant. Liberation theology responds to such criticism with just one question: What part have *you* played in the effective and integral liberaton of the oppressed?

. . .

ENLARGING ON THE CONCEPT OF "THE POOR"

The Poor as Blacks, Indigenous Peoples, Women

Liberation theology is about liberation of the oppressed—in their totality as persons, body and soul,—and in their totality as a class: the poor, the subjected, the discriminated against. We cannot confine ourselves to the purely socioeconomic aspect of oppression, the "poverty" aspect, however basic and "determinant" this may be. We have to look also to other levels of social oppression, such as:

* racist oppression: discrimination against blacks;
* ethnic oppression: discrimination against indigenous peoples or other minority groups;
* sexual oppression: discrimination against women.

Each of these various oppressions—or discriminations—and more (oppression of children, juveniles, the elderly) has its specific nature and therefore needs to be treated (in both theory and practice) specifically. So we have to go beyond an exclusively "classist" concept of the oppressed, which would restrict the oppressed to the socio-economically poor. The ranks of the oppressed are filled with others besides the poor.

Nevertheless, we have to observe here that the socio-economically oppressed (the poor) do not simply exist *alongside* other oppressed groups,

such as blacks, indigenous peoples, women—to take the three major categories in the Third World. No, the "class-oppressed"—the socio-economically poor—are the infrastructural expression of the process of oppression. The other groups represent "superstructural" expressions of oppression and because of this are deeply conditioned by the infrastructural. It is one thing to be a black taxi-driver, quite another to be a black football idol; it is one thing to be a woman working as a domestic servant, quite another to be the first lady of the land; it is one thing to be an Amerindian thrown off your land, quite another to be an Amerindian owning your own farm.

This shows why, in a class-divided society, class struggles—which are a fact and an ethical demonstration of the presence of the injustice condemned by God and the church—are the main sort of struggle. They bring antagonistic groups, whose basic interests are irreconcilable, face to face. On the other hand, the struggles of blacks, indigenes, and women bring groups that are not naturally antagonistic into play, whose basic interests can in principle be reconciled. Although exploiting bosses and exploited workers can never finally be reconciled (so long as the former remain exploiters and the latter exploited), blacks can be reconciled with whites, indigenes with nonindigenes, and women with men. We are dealing here with nonantagonistic contradictions mixed in with the basic, antagonist class conflict in our societies. But it must also be noted that noneconomic types of oppression aggravate preexisting socio-economic oppression. The poor are additionally oppressed when, beside being poor, they are also black, indigenous, women, or old.

The Poor as "Degraded and Deprived"

The socio-analytical approach is undoubtedly important for a critical understanding of the situation of the poor and all classes of oppressed. Nevertheless, its insight into oppression is limited to what an academic sort of approach can achieve. Such an approach has its limitations, which are those of analytical scholarship. It can only (but this is already a great deal) grasp the basic and overall structure of oppression; it leaves out of account all the shadings that only direct experience and day-by-day living can appreciate. Attending just to the rational, scientific understanding of oppression falls into rationalism and leaves more than half the reality of the oppressed poor out of account.

The oppressed are more than what social analysts—economists, sociologists, anthropologists—can tell us about them. We need to listen to the oppressed themselves. The poor, in their popular wisdom, in fact "know" much more about poverty than does any economist. Or rather, they know in another way, in much greater depth.

For example, what is "work" for popular wisdom and what is it for an economist? For the latter it is usually a simple category or a satirical calculation, whereas for the people, "work" means drama, anguish, dignity, security, exploitation, exhaustion, life—a whole series of complex and even contradictory perceptions. Again, what does "land" mean to an agricultural worker and what does it mean to a sociologist? For the former, it is much more than an economic and social entity; it is human greatness, with a deeply affective and even mystical significance. And if it is your ancestral land, then it means even more.

Finally, "poor" for the people means dependence, debt, exposure, anonymity, contempt, and humiliation. The poor do not usually refer to themselves as "poor," which would offend their sense of honor and dignity. It is the non-poor who call them poor. So a poor woman from Tacaimbó in the interior of Pernambuco, hearing someone call her poor, retorted: "Poor, no! Poor is the end. We are the dispossessed, but fighting!"

From which we conclude that liberation theologians in contact with the people cannot be content with social analyses but also have to grasp the whole rich interpretation made by the poor of their world, linking the socio-analytical approach with the indispensable understanding provided by folk wisdom.

The Poor as the Disfigured Son of God

Finally, the Christian view of the poor is that they are all this and more. Faith shows us the poor and all the oppressed in the light that liberation theology seeks to project (and here we anticipate the hermeneutical mediation):

- the disfigured image of God;
- the Son of God made the suffering servant and rejected;
- the memorial of the poor and persecuted Nazarene;
- the sacrament of the Lord and Judge of history.

Without losing any of its specific substance, the conception of the poor is thus infinitely enlarged through being opened up to the Infinite. In this way, seen from the standpoint of faith and the mission of the church, the poor are not merely human beings with needs; they are not just persons who are socially oppressed and at the same time agents of history. They are all these and more: they are also bearers of an "evangelizing potential" (Puebla, §1147) and beings called to eternal life.

HERMENEUTICAL MEDIATION*

Once they have understood the real situation of the oppressed, theologians have to ask: What has the word of God to say about this? This is the second stage in the theological construct—a specific stage, in which discourse is *formally* theological.

It is therefore a question, at this point, of seeing the "oppression/liberation" process "in the light of faith." What does this mean? The expression does not denote something vague or general; it is something that has a positive meaning in scripture, where we find that "in the light of faith" and "in the light of the word of God" have the same meaning.

---

* Hermeneutics is the process of interpreting the deeper meaning of a text. In this context it is the attempt to interpret scriptures through the categories of liberation and oppression. The scriptures are, thus, mediated by those categories (Eds.).

The liberation theologian goes to the scriptures bearing the whole weight of the problems, sorrows, and hopes of the poor, seeking light and inspiration from the divine word. This is a new way of reading the Bible: the hermeneutics of liberation.

• • •

The Marks of a Theological-liberative Hermeneutics

The rereading of the Bible done from the basis of the poor and their liberation project has certain characteristic marks.

It is a hermeneutics that favors *application* rather than explanation. In this the theology of liberation takes up the kind of probing that has been the perennial pursuit of all true biblical reading, as can be seen, for example, in the church fathers—a pursuit that was neglected for a long time in favor of a rationalistic exegesis concerned with dragging out the meaning-in-itself.

Liberative hermeneutics reads the Bible as a book of life, not as a book of strange stories. The textual meaning is indeed sought, but only as a function of the *practical* meaning: the important thing is not so much interpreting the text of the scriptures as interpreting life "according to the scriptures." Ultimately, this old/new reading aims to find contemporary actualization (practicality) for the textual meaning.

Liberative hermeneutics seeks to discover and activate the *transforming energy* of biblical texts. In the end, this is a question of finding an interpretation that will lead to individual change (conversion) and change in history (revolution). This is not a reading from ideological preconceptions: biblical religion is an open and dynamic religion thanks to its messianic and eschatological character. Ernst Bloch once declared: "It would be difficult to make a revolution without the Bible."

Finally, without being reductionist, this theological-political rereading of the Bible stresses the *social context* of the message. It places each text in its historical context in order to construct an appropriate—not literal—translation into our own historical context. For example, liberative hermeneutics will stress (but not to the exclusion of other aspects) the social context of oppression in which Jesus lived and the markedly political context of his death on the cross. Obviously, when it is approached in this way, the biblical text takes on particular relevance in the context of the oppression now being experienced in the Third World, where liberating evangelization has immediate and serious political implications—as the growing list of martyrs in Latin America proves.

Biblical Books Favored by Liberation Theology

Theology must, of course, take all the books of the Bible into account. Nevertheless, hermeneutical preferences are inevitable and even necessary, as the liturgy and the practice of homiletics demonstrate. The books most appreciated by liberation theology, on its three levels—professional, pastoral, and especially popular—are:

- Exodus, because it recounts the epic of the politico-religious liberation of a mass of slaves who, through the power of the covenant with God, became the people of God;
- the *Prophets,* for their uncompromising defense of the liberator God, their vigorous denunciation of injustices, their revindication of the rights of the poor, and their proclamation of the messianic world;
- the *Gospels,* obviously, for the centrality of the divine person of Jesus, with his announcement of the kingdom, his liberating actions, and his death and resurrection—the final meaning of history;
- the *Acts of the Apostles,* because they portray the ideal of a free and liberating Christian community;
- *Revelation,* because in collective and symbolic terms it describes the immense struggles of the

people of God against all the monsters of history.

SOME KEY THEMES OF LIBERATION THEOLOGY

1. Living and True Faith Includes the Practice of Liberation   Faith is the original standpoint of all theology, including liberation theology. Through the act of faith we place our life, our pilgrimage through this world, and our death in God's hands. By the light of faith we see that divine reality penetrates every level of history and the world. As a way of life, faith enables us to discern the presence or negation of God in various human endeavors. It is living faith that provides a contemplative view of the world.

But faith also has to be true, the faith necessary for salvation. In the biblical tradition it is not enough for faith to be true in the terms in which it is expressed (orthodoxy); it is verified, made true, when it is informed by love, solidarity, hunger and thirst for justice. St. James teaches that "faith without good deeds is useless" and that believing in the one God is not enough, for "the demons have the same belief" (2:21, 20). Therefore, ortho-doxy has to be accompanied by ortho-praxis.* Living and true faith enables us to hear the voice of the eschatological Judge in the cry of the oppressed: "I was hungry . . ." (Matt. 25:35). This same faith bids us give heed to that voice, resounding through an act of liberation: "and you gave me to eat." Without this liberating practice that appeases hunger, faith barely plants a seed, let alone produces fruit: not only would we be failing to love our sisters and brothers but we would be failing to love God too: "If a man who was rich enough in this world's goods saw that one of his brothers was in need, but closed his heart to him, how could the love of God be living in him?" (1 John 3:17). Only the faith that leads on to love of God and love of others is the faith that saves, and therefore promotes integral liberation: "Our love is not to be just words and mere talk, but something real and active" (1 John 3:18).

It is the task of liberation theology to recover the practical dimension inherent in biblical faith: in the world of the oppressed this practice can only be liberating.

2. The Living God Sides with the Oppressed against the Pharaohs of This World   In a world in which death from hunger and repression have become commonplace, it is important to bring out those characteristics of the Christian God that directly address the practice of liberation. God will always be God and as such will constitute the basic mystery of our faith. We cannot struggle with God; we can only cover our faces and, like Moses, adore God (Exod. 3:6). God, who "dwells in inaccessible light" (1 Tim. 6:16), is beyond the scope of our understanding, however enlightened. But beyond the divine transcendence, God is not a terrifying mystery, but full of tenderness. God is especially close to those who are oppressed; God hears their cry and resolves to set them free (Exod. 3:7–8). God is father of all, but most particularly father and defender of those who are oppressed and treated unjustly. Out of love for them, God takes sides, takes *their* side against the repressive measures of all the pharaohs.

This partiality on God's part shows that life and justice should be a universal guarantee to all, starting with those who are at present denied them; no one has the right to offend another human being, the image and likeness of God. God is glorified in the life-sustaining activities of men and women; God is worshiped in the doing of justice. God does not stand by impassively watching the drama of human history, in which, generally speaking, the strong impose their laws and their will on the weak. The biblical authors often present Yahweh as *Go'el,* which means: he who does justice to the weak, father of

---

* *Praxis* literally means "practice" in German but refers philosophically to the unity of thought and action, theory and practice. *Ortho-praxis* is, then, the unity of faith and social activism. According to liberation theology, that "ortho-doxy has to be accompanied by ortho-praxis" means that true faith must be accompanied by political struggle for liberation (Eds.).

orphans and comforter of widows (see Ps. 146:9; Isa. 1:17; Jer. 7:6, 22:3; Job 29:13, 31:16).

In the experience of slavery in Egypt, which bound the Israelites together as a people, they realized their longing for liberation and witnessed to the intervention of Yahweh as liberator. The liberation from slavery in Egypt was a political event, but one that became the basis for the religious experience of full liberation—that is, liberation also from sin and death. As the bishops of Latin America said at Medellín in 1968:

> Just as formerly the first people, Israel, experienced the saving presence of God when he set them free from slavery in Egypt, so we too, the new people of God, cannot fail to feel his saving deliverance when there is real development—that is, deliverance for each and every one from less human to more human conditions of life [Introduction to Conclusions, no. 6].

Finally, the Christian God is a trinity of persons, Father, Son, and Holy Spirit. Each distinct from the other, they coexist eternally in a relationship of absolute equality and reciprocity. In the beginning there was not merely the oneness of a divine nature, but the full and perfect communion of three divine persons. This mystery provides the prototype for what society should be according to the plan of the triune God: by affirming and respecting personal individuality, it should enable persons to live in such communion and collaboration with each other as to constitute a unified society of equals and fellow citizens. The society we commonly find today, full of divisions, antagonisms, and discriminations, does not offer an environment in which we can experience the mystery of the Holy Trinity. It has to be transformed if it is to become the image and likeness of the communion of the divine persons.

3. The Kingdom Is God's Project in History and Eternity Jesus Christ, second person of the Blessed Trinity, incarnated in our misery, revealed the divine plan that is to be realized through the course of history and to constitute the definitive future in eternity; the kingdom of God. The kingdom is not just in the future, for it is "in our midst" (Luke 17:21); it is not a kingdom "of this world" (John 18:36), but it nevertheless begins to come about in this world. The kingdom or reign of God means the full and total liberation of all creation, in the end, purified of all that oppresses it, transfigured by the full presence of God.

No other theological or biblical concept is as close to the ideal of integral liberation as this concept of the kingdom of God. This was well expressed by the bishops at Puebla, in the hearing of John Paul II:

> There are two complementary and inseparable elements. The first is liberation from all the forms of bondage, from personal and social sin, and from everything that tears apart the human individual and society; all this finds its source in egotism, in the mystery of iniquity. The second element is liberation for progressive growth in being through communion with God and other human beings; this reaches its culmination in the perfect communion of heaven, where God is all in all and weeping forever ceases [§482; cf. *Evangelii nuntiandi,* no. 9].

Because the kingdom is the absolute, it embraces all things: sacred and profane history, the church and the world, human beings and the cosmos. Under different sacred and profane signs, the kingdom is always present where persons bring about justice, seek comradeship, forgive each other, and promote life. However, the kingdom finds a particular expression in the church, which is its perceptible sign, its privileged instrument, its "initial budding forth" and principle (see Puebla, §§227–28) insofar as it lives the gospel and builds itself up from day to day as the Body of Christ.

Seeing the kingdom as God's universal project helps us to understand the link joining creation and redemption, time and eternity. The kingdom of God is something more than historical liberations, which are always limited and open to further perfectioning, but it is anticipated and incarnated in them in time, in preparation for its full realization with the coming of the new heaven and the new earth.

4. Jesus, the Son of God, Took on Oppression in Order to Set Us Free   Jesus is God in our human misery, the Son of God become an individual Jew, at a certain time in history and in a particular social setting. The incarnation of the Word of God implies the assumption of human life as marked by the contradictions left by sin, not in order to consecrate them, but in order to redeem them. In these conditions, Jesus became a "servant" and made himself "obedient even to death on a cross" (Phil. 2:6–11; Mark 10:45). His first public word was to proclaim that the kingdom of God was "at hand" and already present as "good news" (Mark 1:14). When he publicly set out his program in the synagogue in Nazareth (Luke 4:16–21), he took on the hopes of the oppressed and announced that they were not— "this day"—being fulfilled. So the Messiah is the one who brings about the liberation of all classes of unfortunates. The kingdom is also liberation from sin (Luke 24:27; Acts 2:38; 5:31; 13:38), but this must not be interpreted in a reductionist sense to the point where the infrastructural dimension in Jesus' preaching stressed by the evangelists is lost sight of.

The kingdom is not presented simply as something to be hoped for in the future; it is already being made concrete in Jesus' actions. His miracles and healings, besides demonstrating his divinity, are designed to show that his liberating proclamation is already being made history among the oppressed, the special recipients of his teaching and first beneficiaries of his actions. The kingdom is a gift of God offered gratuitously to all. But the way into it is through the process of conversion. The conversion demanded by Jesus does not mean just a change of convictions (theory) but above all a change of attitude (practice) toward all one's previous personal, social, and religious relationships.

The liberation wrought by Jesus outside the law and customs of the time, and his radical requirements for a change of behavior along the lines of the Beatitudes, led him into serious conflict with all the authorities of his age. He knew defamation and demoralization, persecution and the threat of death. His capture, torture, judicial condemnation, and crucifixion can be understood only as a consequence of his activity and his life. In a world that refused to listen to his message and to take up the way of conversion, the only alternative open to Jesus as a way of staying faithful to the Father and to his own preaching was to accept martyrdom. The cross is the expression of the human rejection of Jesus, on the one hand, and of his sacrificial acceptance by the Father, on the other.

The resurrection uncovers the absolute meaning of the message of the kingdom, and of Jesus' life and death. It is the definitive triumph of life and of hope for a reconciled kingdom in which universal peace is the fruit of divine justice and the integration of all things in God. The resurrection has to be seen as full liberation from all the obstacles standing in the way of the lordship of God and the full realization of all the dynamic forces for life and glory placed by God within human beings and the whole of creation.

The resurrection also, and especially, reveals the meaning of the death of the innocent, of those who are rejected for having proclaimed a greater justice—God's justice—and of all those who, like Jesus, support a good cause and are anonymously liquidated. It was not a Caesar at the height of his power who was raised from the dead, but someone destroyed by crucifixion on Calvary. Those who have been unjustly put to death in a good cause share in his resurrection.

Following Jesus means taking up his cause, being ready to bear the persecution it brings and brave enough to share his fate in the hope of inheriting the full liberation that the resurrection offers us.

5. The Holy Spirit, "Father of the Poor," Is Present in the Struggles of the Oppressed   Like the Son, the Holy Spirit was sent into the world to further and complete the work of integral redemption and liberation. The special field of action for the Spirit is history. Like the wind (the biblical meaning of "spirit"), the Spirit is present in everything that implies movement, transformation, growth. No one and nothing is beyond the reach of the Spirit, inside and outside the Christian sphere. The Spirit takes hold of persons, fills them with enthusiasm, endows them with special charisms and abilities to change religion and society, break open rigid institutions and make things new. The Spirit presides over the religious experience of peoples, not allowing them to forget the dimension of eternity or succumb to the appeals of the flesh.

The Holy Spirit becomes a participant in the struggles and resistance of the poor in a quite special way. Not without reason is the Spirit called "Father of the poor" in the liturgy: giving them strength, day after day, to face up to the arduous struggle for their own survival and that of their families, finding the strength to put up with a socio-economic system that oppresses them, one that they have no hope of changing from one day to the next; helping keep alive their hope that some things will get better and that, united, they will eventually set themselves free. Their piety, their sense of God; their solidarity, hospitality, and fortitude; their native wisdom, fed on suffering and experience; their love for their own children and those of others; their capacity for celebration and joy in the midst of the most painful conflicts; the serenity with which they face the harshness of their struggle for life; their perception of what is possible and viable; their moderation in the use of force and their virtually limitless powers of resistance to the persistent, daily aggression of the socio-economic system with its consequent social marginalization—all these qualities are gifts of the Holy Spirit, forms of the ineffable presence and activity of the Spirit among the oppressed.

But this activity is seen even more clearly when they rise up, decide to take history into their own hands, and organize themselves to bring about the transformation of society in the direction of the dream in which there will be a place for all with dignity and peace. The history of the struggles of the oppressed for their liberation is the history of the call of the Holy Spirit to the heart of a divided world. It is because of the Spirit that the ideals of equality and fellowship, the utopia of a world in which it will be easier to love and recognize in the face of the other the maternal and paternal features

of God, will never be allowed to die or be forgotten under the pressure of resignation.

It is also in the light of the action of the Spirit that the emergence of base Christian communities should be understood. More a happening than an institution, they bring into the present the movement Jesus started and commit themselves to the justice of the kingdom of God. This is where the church can be seen to be the sacrament of the Holy Spirit, endowed with many charisms, ministries and services for the good of all and the building of the kingdom in history.

6. Mary Is the Prophetic and Liberating Woman of the People The people's devotion to Mary has deep dogmatic roots: she is the Mother of God, the Immaculate Conception, the Virgin of Nazareth, and the one human being taken up into heavenly glory in all her human reality. From the standpoint of liberation, certain characteristics of hers stand out as dear to Christians of the base communities committed in the light of their faith to the transformation of society.

In the first place, all the theological greatness of Mary is based on the lowliness of her historical condition. She is Mary from Nazareth, a woman of the people, who observed the popular religious customs of the time (the presentation of Jesus in the temple and the pilgrimage to Jerusalem [Luke 2:21ff. and 41ff.]), who visited her relatives (Luke 1:39ff.), who would not miss a wedding (John 2), who worried about her son (Luke 2:48–51; Mark 3:31–32), and who followed him to the foot of the cross, as any devoted mother would have done (John 19:25). Because of this ordinariness, and not in spite of it, Mary was everything that faith proclaims her to be, for God did "great things" for her (Luke 1:49).

In the second place, Mary is the perfect example of faith and availability for God's purpose (Luke 1:45, 38). She certainly did not understand the full extent of the mystery being brought about through her—the coming of the Holy Spirit upon her and the virginal conception of the eternal Son of the Father in her womb (Luke 1:35; Matt. 1:18), but even so she trusted in God's purpose. She thinks not of herself but of others, of her cousin Elizabeth (Luke 1:39ff.), of her son lost on the pilgrimage (Luke 2:43), of those who have no wine at the marriage feast at Cana (John 2:3). Persons can be liberators only if they free themselves from their own preoccupations and place their lives at the service of others, as did Mary, Jesus, and Joseph.

In the third place, Mary is the prophetess of the Magnificat. Anticipating the liberating proclamation of her son, she shows herself attentive and sensitive to the fate of the humiliated and debased; in a context of praising God, she raises her voice in denunciation and invokes divine revolution in the relationship between oppressors and oppressed. Paul VI gave excellent expression to this whole liberating dimension of Mary in his apostolic exhortation *Marialis Cultus* of 1974:

> Mary of Nazareth, despite her total submission to the will of God, was far from being a passively submissive woman or one given to an alienating religiosity; she was a woman who had no hesitation in affirming that God is the avenger of the humble and oppressed, who pulls down the mighty of this world from their thrones (Luke 1:51–53). We can recognize in Mary, "who stands out among the poor and humble of the Lord" (LG 55), a strong woman, who knew poverty, suffering, flight, and exile (Matt. 2:13–23)—situations that cannot escape the attention of those who with an evangelical spirit seek to channel the liberating energies of man and society [no. 37].

Finally, Mary is as she appears in the popular religion of Latin America. There is no part of Latin America in which the name of Mary is not given to persons, cities, mountains, and innumerable shrines. Mary loves the poor of Latin America. She took on the dark face of the slaves and the persecuted Amerindians. She is the *Morenita* ("little dark girl") in Guadalupe, Mexico; she is Nossa Senhora da Aparecida, bound like the slaves in Brazil; she is the dark-complexioned Virgin of Charity in Cuba; the list is endless.

The masses of the poor bring their troubles to the centers of Marian pilgrimage; they dry their tears there and are filled with renewed strength and hope

to carry on struggling and surviving. In these places Mary becomes "the sacramental presence of the maternal features of God" (Puebla, §291), the "ever-renewed star of evangelization" (*Evangelii nuntiandi,* no. 81), and together with Christ her son, in union with the oppressed, the "protagonist of history" (Puebla, §293).

WHY WOMEN NEED THE GODDESS

Carol P. Christ*

At the close of Ntozake Shange's stupendously successful Broadway play "For Colored Girls Who Have Considered Suicide When the Rainbow Is Enuf," a tall beautiful black woman rises from despair to cry out, "I found God in myself and I loved her fiercely."[1] Her discovery is echoed by women around the country who meet spontaneously in small groups of full moons, solstices, and equinoxes to celebrate the Goddess as symbol of life and death powers and waxing and waning energies in the universe and in themselves.[2]

> It is the night of the full moon. Nine women stand in a circle, on a rocky hill above the city. The western sky is rosy with the setting sun; in the east the moon's face begins to peer above the horizon. . . . The woman pours out a cup of wine onto the earth, refills it and raises it high. "Hail, Tana, Mother of

---

* The author has requested the following: "This essay is published in a slightly shortened form. Ellipsis dots indicate places where Christ's discussion of feminist art and ritual illustrating her points was cut. Carol P. Christ is an internationally known feminist theologian. Her book *Laughter of Aphrodite: Reflections on a Journey to the Goddess* (Harper and Row) discusses issues raised in this essay in greater detail."

[1] From the original cast album, Buddah Records, 1976.

[2] See Susan Rennie and Kristen Grimstad, "Spiritual Explorations Cross-Country," *Quest,* 1975, *I* (4), 1975, 49–51; and *WomanSpirit* magazine.

mothers!" she cries. "Awaken from your long sleep, and return to your children again!"[3]

What are the political and psychological effects of this fierce new love of the divine in themselves for women whose spiritual experience has been focused by the male God of Judaism and Christianity? Is the spiritual dimension of feminism a passing diversion, an escape from difficult but necessary political work? Or does the emergence of the symbol of Goddess among women have significant political and psychological ramifications for the feminist movement?

To answer this question, we must first understand the importance of religious symbols and rituals in human life and consider the effect of male symbolism of God on women. According to anthropologist Clifford Geertz, religious symbols shape a cultural ethos, defining the deepest values of a society and the persons in it. "Religion," Geertz writes "is a system of symbols which act to produce powerful, pervasive, and long-lasting moods and motivations"[4] in the people of a given culture. A "mood" for Geertz is a psychological attitude such as awe, trust, and respect, while a "motivation" is the *social* and *political* trajectory created by a mood that transforms mythos into ethos, symbol system into social and political reality. Symbols have both psychological and political effects, because they create the inner conditions (deep-seated attitudes and feelings) that lead people to feel comfortable with or to accept social and political arrangements that correspond to the symbol system.

Because religion has such a compelling hold on the deep psyches of so many people, feminists cannot afford to leave it in the hands of the fathers. Even people who no longer "believe in God" or participate in the institutional structure of patriarchal religion still may not be free of the power of the symbolism of God the Father. A symbol's effect does not depend on rational assent, for a symbol also functions on levels of the psyche other than the rational. Religion fulfills deep psychic needs by providing symbols and rituals that enable people to cope with limit situations[5] in human life (death, evil, suffering) and to pass through life's important transitions (birth, sexuality, death). Even people who consider themselves completely secularized will often find themselves sitting in a church or synagogue when a friend or relative gets married, or when a parent or friend has died. The symbols associated with these important rituals cannot fail to affect the deep or unconscious structures of the mind of even a person who has rejected these symbolisms on a conscious level—especially if the person is under stress. The reason for the continuing effect of religious symbols is that the mind abhors a vacuum. Symbol systems cannot simply be rejected, they must be replaced. Where there is not any replacement, the mind will revert to familiar structures at times of crisis, bafflement, or defeat.

Religions centered on the worship of a male God create "moods" and "motivations" that keep women in a state of psychological dependence on men and male authority, while at the same legitimating the *political* and *social* authority of fathers and sons in the institutions of society.

Religious symbol systems focused around exclusively male images of divinity create the impression that female power can never be fully legitimate or wholly beneficent. This message need never be explicitly stated (as, for example, it is in the story of Eve) for its effect to be felt. A woman completely ignorant of the myths of female evil in biblical religion nonetheless acknowledges the anomaly of female power when she prays exclusively to a male God. She may see herself as like God (created in the image of God) only by denying her own sexual identify and affirming God's transcendence of sexual identity. But she can never have the experience that is freely available to every man and boy in her

---

[3] See Starhawk, "Witchcraft and Women's Culture," in *Womanspirit Rising,* ed. Carol P. Christ and Judith Plaskow (New York: Harper and Row, 1979), p. 260.

[4] "Religion as a Cultural System," in William L. Lessa and Evon V. Vogt, eds., *Reader in Comparative Religion,* 2nd ed. (New York: Harper & Row, 1972), p. 206.

[5] Geertz, p. 210.

culture, of having her full sexual identity affirmed as being in the image and likeness of God. In Geertz' terms, her "mood" is one of trust in male power as salvific and distrust of female power in herself and other women as inferior or dangerous. Such a powerful, pervasive, and longlasting "mood" cannot fail to become a "motivation" that translates into social and political reality.

In *Beyond God the Father,* feminist theologian Mary Daly detailed the psychological and political ramifications of father religion for women. "If God in 'his' heaven is a father ruling his people," she wrote, "then it is the 'nature' of things and according to divine plan and the order of the universe that society be male dominated. Within this context, a *mystification of roles* takes place: The husband dominating his wife represents God 'himself.' The images and values of a given society have been projected into the realm of dogmas and 'Articles of Faith,' and these in turn justify the social structures which have given rise to them and which sustain their plausibility."[6]

Philosopher Simone de Beauvoir was well aware of the function of patriarchal religion as legitimater of male power. As she wrote, "Man enjoys the great advantage of having a god endorse the code he writes; and since man exercises a sovereign authority over women it is especially fortunate that this authority has been vested in him by the Supreme Being. For the Jew, Mohammedans, and Christians, among others, man is Master by divine right; the fear of God will therefore repress any impulse to revolt in the downtrodden female."[7]

This brief discussion of the psychological and political effects of God religion puts us in an excellent position to begin to understand the significance of the symbol of Goddess for women. In discussing the meaning of the Goddess, my method will first be phenomenological. I will isolate a meaning of the symbol of the Goddess as it has emerged in the lives of contemporary women. I will then discuss its

psychological and political significance by contrasting the "moods" and "motivations" engendered by Goddess symbols with those engendered by Christian symbolism. I will also correlate Goddess symbolism with themes that have emerged in the women's movement, in order to show how Goddess symbolism undergirds and legitimates the concerns of the women's movement, much as God symbolism in Christianity undergirded the interests of men in patriarchy. I will discuss four aspects of Goddess symbolism here: the Goddess as affirmation of female power, the female body, the female will, and women's bonds and heritage. There are, of course, many other meanings of the Goddess that I will not discuss here.

The sources for the symbol of the Goddess in contemporary spirituality are traditions of Goddess worship and modern women's experience. The ancient Mediterranean, pre-Christian European, native American, Mesoamerican, Hindu, African, and other traditions are rich sources for Goddess symbolism. But these traditions are filtered through modern women's experiences. Traditions of Goddesses, subordination to Gods, for example, are ignored. Ancient traditions are tapped selectively and eclectically, but they are not considered authoritative for modern consciousness. The Goddess symbol has emerged spontaneously in the dreams, fantasies, and thoughts of many women around the country in the past several years. Kirsten Grimstad and Susan Rennie reported that they were surprised to discover widespread interest in spirituality, including the Goddess, among feminists around the country in the summer of 1974.[8] *WomanSpirit* magazine, which published its first issue in 1974 and has contributors from across the United States, has expressed the grass roots nature of the women's spirituality movement. In 1976, a journal, *Lady Unique,* devoted to the Goddess emerged. In 1975, the first women's spirituality conference was held in Boston and attended by 1,800 women. In 1978, a University of Santa Cruz course on the Goddess drew over

---

[6] Boston: Beacon Press, 1974, p. 13, italics added.
[7] *The Second Sex,* trans. H. M. Parshleys (New York: Alfred A. Knopf, 1953).

[8] See Grimstad and Rennie.

500 people. Sources for this essay are these manifestations of the Goddess in modern women's experiences as reported in *WomanSpirit, Lady Unique,* and elsewhere, and as expressed in conversations I have had with women who have been thinking about the Goddess and women's spirituality.

The simplest and most basic meaning of the symbol of Goddess is the acknowledgement of the legitimacy of female power as a beneficient and independent power. A woman who echoes Ntosake Shange's dramatic statement, "I found God in myself and I loved her fiercely," is saying "Female power is strong and creative." She is saying that the divine principle, the saving and sustaining power, is in herself, that she will no longer look to men or male figures as saviors. The strength and independence of female power can be intuited by contemplating ancient and modern images of the Goddess.

• • •

The affirmation of female power contained in the Goddess symbol has both psychological and political consequences. Psychologically, it means the defeat of the view engendered by patriarchy that women's power is inferior and dangerous. This new "mood" of affirmation of female power also leads to new "motivations"; it supports and undergirds women's trust in their own power and the power of other women in family and society.

If the simplest meaning of the Goddess symbol is an affirmation of the legitimacy and beneficience of female power, then a question immediately arises, "Is the Goddess simply female power writ large, and if so, why bother with the symbol of Goddess at all? Or does the symbol refer to a Goddess 'out there' who is not reducible to a human potential?" The many women who have rediscovered the power of Goddess would give three answers to this question: (1) The Goddess is divine female, a personification who can be invoked in prayer and ritual; (2) the Goddess is symbol of the life, death, and rebirth energy in nature and culture, in personal and communal life and (3) the Goddes is symbol of the affirmation of the legitimacy and beauty of female power (made possible by the new becoming of

women in the women's liberation movement). If one were to ask these women which answer is the "correct" one, different responses would be given. Some would assert that the Goddess definitely is *not* "out there," that the symbol of a divinity "out there" is part of the legacy of patriarchal oppression, which brings with it the authoritarianism, hierarchicalism, and dogmatic rigidity associated with biblical monotheistic religions. They might assert that the Goddess symbol reflects the sacred power within women and nature, suggesting the connectedness between women's cycles of menstruation, birth, and menopause, and the life and death cycles of the universe. Others seem quite comfortable with the notion of Goddess as a divine female protector and creator and would find their experience of Goddess limited by the assertion that she is not *also* out there as well as within themselves and in all natural processes. When asked what the symbol of Goddess means, feminist priestess Starhawk replied, "It all depends on how I feel. When I feel weak, she is someone who can help and protect me. When I feel strong, she is the symbol of my own power. At other times I feel her as the natural energy in my body and the world."[9] How are we to evaluate such a statement? Theologians might call these the words of a sloppy thinker. But my deepest intuition tells me they contain a wisdom that Western theological thought has lost.

To theologians, these differing views of the "meaning" of the symbol of Goddess might seem to threaten a replay of the trinitarian controversies. Is there, perhaps, a way of doing theology, which would not lead immediately into dogmatic controversy, which would not require theologians to say definitively that one understanding is true and the others are false? Could people's relation to a common symbol be made primary and varying interpretations be acknowledged? The diversity of explications of the meaning of the Goddess symbol suggests that symbols have a richer significance than any explications of their meaning can express,

---

[9] Personal communication.

a point literary critics have long insisted on. This phenomenological fact suggests that theologians may need to give more than lip service to a theory of symbol in which the symbol is viewed as the primary fact and the meanings are viewed as secondary. It also suggests that a *thea*logy[10] of the Goddess would be very different from the *theo*logy we have known in the West. But to spell out this notion of the primacy of *symbol* in thealogy in contrast to the primacy of the *explanation* in theology would be the topic of another paper. Let me simply state that women, who have been deprived of a female religious symbol system for centuries, are therefore in an excellent position to recognize the power and primacy of symbols. I believe women must develop a theory of symbol and thealogy congruent with their experience at the same time as they "remember and invent" new symbol systems.

A second important implication of the Goddess symbol for women is the affirmation of the female body and the life cycle expressed in it. Because of women's unique position as menstruants, birthgivers, and those who have traditionally cared for the young and the dying, women's connection to the body, nature, and this world has been obvious. Women were denigrated because they seemed more carnal, fleshy, and earthy than the culture-creating males.[11] The misogynist anti*body* tradition in Western thought is symbolized in the myth of Eve who is traditionally viewed as a sexual temptress, the epitome of women's carnal nature. This tradition reaches its nadir in the *Malleus Maleficarum (The Hammer of Evil-Doing Women),* which states, "All witchcraft stems from carnal lust, which in women is insatiable."[12] The Virgin Mary, the positive female image in Christianity does not contradict Christian denigration of the female body and its powers. The Virgin Mary is revered because she, in her perpetual virginity, transcends the carnal sexuality attributed to most women.

The denigration of the female body is expressed in cultural and religious taboos surrounding menstruation, childbirth, and menopause in women. While menstruation taboos may have originated in a perception of the awesome powers of the female body,[13] they degenerated into a simple perception that there is something "wrong" with female bodily functions. Menstruating women were forbidden to enter the sanctuary in ancient Hebrew and premodern Christian communities. Although only Orthodox Jews still enforce religious taboos against menstruant women, few women in our culture grow up affirming their menstruation as a connection to sacred power. Most women learn that menstruation is a curse and grow up believing that the bloody facts of menstruation are best hidden away. Feminists challenge this attitude to the female body. Judy Chicago's art piece "Menstruation Bathroom" broke these menstrual taboos. In a sterile white bathroom, she exhibited boxes of Tampax and Kotex on an open shelf, and the wastepaper basket was overflowing with bloody tampons and sanitary napkins.[14] Many women who viewed the piece felt relieved to have their "dirty secret" out in the open.

The denigration of the female body and its powers is further expressed in Western culture's attitudes toward childbirth.[15] Religious iconography does not celebrate the birthgiver, and there is no theology or ritual that enables a woman to celebrate the process of birth as a spiritual experience. Indeed, Jewish and Christian traditions also had blood taboos concerning the woman who had recently given birth. While these religious taboos are rarely

---

[10] A term coined by Naomi Goldenberg to refer to reflection on the meaning of the symbol of Goddess.

[11] This theory of the origins of the Western dualism is stated by Rosemary Ruether in *New Woman: New Earth* (New York: Seabury Press, 1975), and elsewhere.

[12] Heinrich Kramer and Jacob Sprenger (New York: Dover, 1971), p. 47.

[13] See Rita M. Gross, "Menstruation and Childbirth as Ritual and Religious Experience in the Religion of the Australian Aborigines," in *The Journal of the American Academy of Religion,* 1977, *45* (4), Supplement 1147–1181.

[14] *Through the Flower* (New York: Doubleday & Company, 1975), plate 4, pp. 106–107.

[15] See Adrienne Rich, *Of Woman Born* (New York: Bantam Books, 1977), chaps. 6 and 7.

enforced today (again, only by Orthodox Jews), they have secular equivalents. Giving birth is treated as a disease requiring hospitalization, and the woman is viewed as a passive object, anesthetized to ensure her acquiescence to the will of the doctor. The women's liberation movement has challenged these cultural attitudes, and many feminists have joined with advocates of natural childbirth and home birth in emphasizing the need for women to control and take pride in their bodies, including the birth process.

Western culture also gives little dignity to the postmenopausal or aging woman. It is no secret that our culture is based on a denial of aging and death, and that women suffer more severely from this denial than men. Women are placed on a pedestal and considered powerful when they are young and beautiful, but they are said to lose this power as they age. As feminists have pointed out, the "power" of the young woman is illusory, since beauty standards are defined by men, and since few women are considered (or consider themselves) beautiful for more than a few years of their lives. Some men are viewed as wise and authoritative in age, but old women are pitied and shunned. Religious iconography supports this cultural attitude towards aging women. The purity and virginity of Mary and the female saints is often expressed in the iconographic convention of perpetual youth. Moreover, religious mythology associates aging women with evil in the symbol of the wicked old witch. Feminists have challenged cultural myths of aging women and have urged women to reject patriarchal beauty standards and to celebrate the distinctive beauty of women of all ages.

The symbol of Goddess aids the process of naming and reclaiming the female body and its cycles and processes. In the ancient world and among modern women, the Goddess symbol represents the birth, death, and rebirth processes of the natural and human worlds. The female body is viewed as the direct incarnation of waxing and waning, life and death, cycles in the universe. This is sometimes expressed through the symbolic connection between the twenty-eight-day cycles of menstruation and the twenty-eight-day cycles of the moon. Moreover, the Goddess is celebrated in the triple aspect of youth, maturity, and age, or maiden, mother, and crone. The potentiality of the young girl is celebrated in the nymph or maiden aspect of the Goddess. The Goddess as mother is sometimes depicted giving birth, and giving birth is viewed as a symbol for all the creative, life-giving powers of the universe.[16] The life-giving powers of the Goddess in her creative aspect are not limited to physical birth, for the Goddess is also seen as the creator of all the arts of civilization, including healing, writing, and the giving of just law. Women in the middle of life who are not physical mothers may give birth to poems, songs, and books, or nurture other women, men, and children. They too are incarnations of the Goddess in her creative, life-giving aspect. At the end of life, women incarnate the crone aspect of the Goddess. The wise old woman, the woman who knows from experience what life is about, the woman whose closeness to her own death gives her a distance and perspective on the problems of life, is celebrated as the third aspect of the Goddess. Thus, women learn to value youth, creativity, and wisdom in themselves and other women.

• • •

A third important implication of the Goddess symbol for women is the positive valuation of will in a Goddess-centered ritual, especially in Goddess-centered ritual magic and spellcasting in womanspirit and feminist witchcraft circles. The basic notion behind ritual magic and spellcasting is energy as power. Here the Goddess is a center or focus of power and energy; she is the personification of the energy that flows between beings in the natural and human worlds. In Goddess circles, energy is raised by chanting or dancing. According to Starhawk, "Witches conceive of psychic energy, as having form and substance that can be perceived and directed by those with a trained awareness. The power

---

[16] See James Mellaart, *Earliest Civilizations of the Near East* (New York: McGraw-Hill, 1965), p. 92.

generated within the circle is built into a cone form, and at its peak is released—to the Goddess, to reenergize the members of the coven, or to do a specific work such as healing."[17] In ritual magic, the energy raised is directed by willpower. Women who celebrate in Goddess circles believe they can achieve their wills in the world.

The emphasis on the will is important for women, because women traditionally have been taught to devalue their wills, to believe that they cannot achieve their will through their own power, and even to suspect that the assertion of will is evil.

• • •

Patriarchal religion has enforced the view that female initiative and will are evil through the juxtaposition of Eve and Mary. Eve caused the fall by asserting her will against the command of God, while Mary began the new age with her response to God's initiative, "Let it be done to me according to thy word" (Luke 1:38). Even for men, patriarchal religion values the passive will subordinate to divine initiative. The classical doctrines of sin and grace view sin as the prideful assertion of will and grace as the obedient subordination of the human will to the divine initiative or order. While this view of will might be questioned from a human perspective, Valerie Saiving has argued that it has particularly deleterious consequences for women in Western culture. According to Saiving, Western culture encourages males in the assertion of will, and thus it may make some sense to view the male form of sin as an excess of will. But since culture discourages females in the assertion of will, the traditional doctrines of sin and grace encourage women to remain in their form of sin, which is self-negation or insufficient assertion of will.[18] One possible reason the will is denigrated in a patriarchal religious framework is that both human and divine will are often pictured as arbitrary, self-initiated, and exercised without regard for other wills.

In a Goddess-centered context, in contrast, the will is valued. *A woman is encouraged to know her will, to believe that her will is valid, and to believe that her will can be achieved in the world,* three powers traditionally denied to her in patriarchy. In a Goddess-centered framework, a woman's will is not subordinated to the Lord God as king and ruler, nor to men as his representatives. Thus a woman is not reduced to waiting and acquiescing in the wills of others as she is in patriarchy. But neither does she adopt the egocentric form of will that pursues self-interest without regard for the interests of others.

The Goddess-centered context provides a different understanding of the will than that available in the traditional patriarchal religious framework. In the Goddess framework, will can be achieved only when it is exercised in harmony with the energies and wills of other beings. Wise women, for example, raise a cone of healing energy at the full moon or solstice when the lunar or solar energies are at their high points with respect to the earth. This discipline encourages them to recognize that not all times are propitious for the achieving of every will. Similarly, they know that spring is a time for new beginnings in work and love, summer a time for producing external manifestations of inner potentialities, and fall or winter times for stripping down to the inner core and extending roots. Such awareness of waxing and waning processes in the universe discourages arbitrary ego-centered assertion of will, while at the same time encouraging the assertion of individual will in cooperation with natural energies and the energies created by the wills of others. Wise women also have a tradition that whatever is sent out will be returned and this reminds them to assert their wills in cooperative and healing rather than egocentric and destructive ways. This view of will allows women to begin to recognize, claim, and assert their wills without adopting the worst characteristics of the patriarchal understanding and use of will. In the Goddess-centered framework, the "mood" is one of positive affirmation of personal will in the context of the energies of other wills or beings. The "motivation" is for women to know and assert their wills in cooperation with

---

[17] Starhawk, *op. cit.,* p. 266.
[18] "The Human Situation: A Feminine View," in *Journal of Religion,* 1960, *40,* 100–112.

other wills and energies. This of course does not mean that women always assert their wills in positive and life-affirming ways. Women's capacity for evil is, of course, as great as men's. My purpose is simply to contrast the differing attitudes toward the exercise of will *per se,* and the female will in particular, in Goddess-centered religion and in the Christian God-centered religion.

The fourth and final aspect of Goddess symbolism that I will discuss here is the significance of the Goddess for a revaluation of woman's bonds and heritage. As Virginia Woolf has said, "Chloe liked Olivia," a statement about a woman's relation to another woman, is a sentence that rarely occurs in fiction. Men have written the stories, and they have written about women almost exclusively in their relations to men.[19] The celebrations of women's bonds to each other, as mothers and daughters, as colleagues and coworkers, as sisters, friends, and lovers, is beginning to occur in the new literature and culture created by women in the women's movement. While I believe that the revaluating of each of these bonds is important, I will focus on the mother-daughter bond, in part because I believe it may be the key to the others.

Adrienne Rich has pointed out that the mother-daughter bond, perhaps the most important of woman's bonds, "resonant with charges . . . the flow of energy between two biologically alike bodies, one of which has lain in amniotic bliss inside the other, one of which has labored to give birth to the other,"[20] is rarely celebrated in patriarchal religion and culture. Christianity celebrates the father's relation to the son and the mother's relation to the son, but the story of mother and daughter is missing. So, too, in patriarchal literature and psychology the mothers and the daughters rarely exist. Volumes have been written about the oedipal complex, but little has been written about the girl's relation to her mother. Moreover, as de Beauvoir has noted, the mother-daughter relation is distorted in partriarchy because the mother must give her daughter over to men in a male-defined culture in which women are viewed as inferior. The mother must socialize her daughter to become subordinate to men, and if her daughter challenges patriarchal norms, the mother is likely to defend the patriarchal structures against her own daughter.[21]

These patterns are changing in the new culture created by women in which the bonds of women to women are beginning to be celebrated. Holly Near has written several songs that celebrate women's bonds and women's heritage. In one of her finest songs she writes of an "old-time woman" who is "waiting to die." A young woman feels for the life that has passed the old woman by and begins to cry, but the old woman looks her in the eyes and says, "If I had not suffered, you wouldn't be wearing those jeans / Being an old-time woman ain't as bad as it seems."[22] This song, which Near has said was inspired by her grandmother, expresses and celebrates a bond and a heritage passed down from one woman to another. In another of Near's songs, she sings of "a hiking-boot mother who's seeing the world / For the first time with her own little girl." In this song, the mother tells the drifter who has been traveling with her to pack up and travel alone if he things "traveling three is a drag" because "I've got a little one who loves me as much as you need me / And darling, that's loving enough."[23] This song is significant because the mother places her relationship to her daughter above her relationship to a man, something women rarely do in patriarchy.[24]

Almost the only story of mothers and daughters that has been transmitted in Western culture is the myth of Demeter and Persephone that was the basis of religious rites celebrated by women only, the

---

[19] *A Room of One's Own* (New York: Harcourt Brace Jovanovich, 1928), p. 86.
[20] Rich, p. 226.

[21] De Beauvior, pp. 448–449.
[22] "Old Time Woman," lyrics by Jeffrey Langley and Holly Near, from *Holly Near: A Live Album,* Redwood Records, 1974.
[23] "Started Out Fine," by Holly Near from *Holly Near: A Live Album.*
[24] Rich, p. 223.

Thesmophoria, and later formed the basis of the Eleusian mysteries, which were open to all who spoke Greek. In this story, the daughter, Persephone, is raped away from her mother, Demeter, by the God of the underworld. Unwilling to accept this state of affairs, Demeter rages and withholds fertility from the earth until her daughter is returned to her. What is important for women in this story is that a mother fights for her daughter and for her relation to her daughter. This is completely different from the mother's relation to her daughter in patriarchy. The "mood" created by the story of Demeter and Persephone is one of celebration of the mother-daughter bond, and the "motivation" is for mothers and daughters to affirm the heritage passed on from mother to daughter and to reject the patriarchal pattern where the primary loyalties of mother and daughter must be to men.

The symbol of Goddess has much to offer women who are struggling to be rid of the "powerful, pervasive, and long-lasting moods and motivations" of devaluation of female power, denigration of the female body, distrust of female will, and denial of the women's bonds and heritage that have been engendered by patriarchal religion. As women struggle to create a new culture in which women's power, bodies, will, and bonds are celebrated, it seems natural that the Goddess would reemerge as symbol of the newfound beauty, strength, and power of women.

QUESTIONS FOR DISCUSSION

1. Discuss Marx's claim that religion is "the opium of the people." What does he mean by this? Is he right?

2. Is liberation theology simply Marxism with a Christian face, or is it a genuine theology in its own right? Be specific.

3. Both Marx and Freud (Section One) believe that religion is an illusion, but their respective analyses of the origin and function of this illusion are quite different. Compare their respective positions. Who is right, or are their analyses compatible and perhaps even complementary?

4. Is worshiping the Goddess more or less problematic than worshiping God? Are both equally problematic? For those who worship the Goddess, is the Goddess real or simply a useful fiction?

Universal Human Nature

Is Human Nature Good or Evil? A Chinese Debate
Mencius, *Human Nature Is Good*
Hsün Tzu, *Human Nature Is Evil*
Ch'eng Hao, *Human Nature Is Good But Can Become Evil*
Han Yü, *Three Grades of Human Nature*

Bitheka Mukerji, *A Hindu View*
Thomas Hobbes, *Human Nature as Competitive*
Petr Kropotkin, *Mutual Aid*
John Dewey, *Changing Human Nature*

Jean-Paul Sartre, *There Is No Human Nature*
Shin'Ichi Hisamatsu, *A Zen View*

Gender Nature

Women's Nature: Two Islamic Views
Abu Hamid Muhammad al-Ghazali, *The Proper Role for Women*
Fatima Mernissi, *Beyond the Veil*

Simone de Beauvoir, *The Second Sex*
Ann Ferguson, *Androgyny as an Ideal for Human Development*
Richard D. Mohr, *Is Homosexuality Unnatural?*

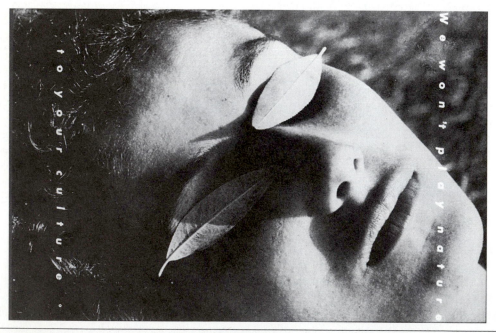

Barbara Kruger, *Untitled (We Won't Play Nature to Your Culture)*, 1983, Collection Ydessa Hendeles, Toronto. Courtesy Ydessa Hendeles Art Foundation. Photo: Robert Keziere.

CHAPTER 4

HUMAN NATURE

What does it mean to be human? Behind this seemingly straightforward question is a set of interrelated issues. What distinguishes human beings from nonhuman animals? That human beings are featherless bipeds is true but not very enlightening. Some other definitions are more interesting. Human beings are rational animals (Aristotle), symbolic animals (language users), tool makers; the human being is the only animal who can laugh, who can be bored, who can fear its own death. But these answers still do not go far enough. We do not merely want a taxonomy. We want to know whether there are certain modes of feeling, thinking, and behaving which are *natural* and which, because they are natural, have profound implications for our individual and collective lives. In other words, are there certain innate psychological characteristics which are socially significant and which can be ascribed to all human beings throughout history? Such characteristics would determine the limits of personal or social change or would suggest possibilities for a more human existence. This may be called the "universal and transhistorical" concept of human nature.

The readings in Section One of this chapter examine the idea of a universal human nature and its implications for personal and social change. The section begins with a Chinese debate in the Confucian tradition concerning whether human nature is good or evil. This question recurs in more modern forms: The seventeenth-century British philosopher Thomas Hobbes argues that human nature is aggressive, competitive, selfish, and, if left to its own devices, destructive. The nineteenth-century Russian naturalist and political anarchist Petr Kropotkin argues that human beings are naturally cooperative and altruistic. The Indian philosopher Bitheka Mukerji and the Japanese philosopher Shin'Ichi Hisamatsu offer, respectively, a Hindu and a Zen view of human nature; both suggest the possibility of profound personal transformation. The pragmatic philosopher John Dewey argues that human nature can be changed. And the French existentialist philosopher Jean-Paul Sartre claims that there is no human nature.

Not all theories of human nature are universal. Some theories make a point of noting the social differences between human beings and claim that these differences derive from certain innate characteristics. Such theories tend to justify the dominance of one group over the other; specifically, they tend to legitimate racial, class, or sexual domination. The readings in the second section of this chapter focus on the problem of gender nature. Is there a woman's nature distinct from a man's nature? If so, do their differences justify each sex occupying different social positions with different advantages and responsibilities? Or is gender itself a social construction, a set of social meanings ascribed to sexual embodiment? Would it be possible to eliminate gender and create an androgynous society? What would happen to sex itself in such a society? Would heterosexuality still be the norm? Is there anything unnatural about homosexuality? The readings in the second section give a variety of answers to these and related questions.

Readers of Section One who want to know more about Chinese views of human nature might be interested in the reading by the neo-Confucian Wang Fu Chih in Section Five of Chapter 1 and in some of the Taoist selections in this anthology. These appear in the fourth section of Chapter 1 (Lao Tzu), the fifth section of Chapter 2 (Chuang Tzu), and we especially recommend the whole of Section Two in Chapter 8. For those especially interested in the Hindu point of view we recommend the selection from the Upanishads in the second section of Chapter 1, the excerpt from the Bhagavad-Gita in the first section of Chapter 7, and the selections by Sarvepalli Radhakrishnan in Section Two of Chap-

ter Three and Section One of Chapter 6. Those interested in reading more about the Zen Buddhist point of view should look at Section Three of Chapter 1, Daisetz's Suzuki's account of knowledge in Section Five of Chapter 2, Toshiko Izutsu's phenomenological discussion of egoless consciousness in Section Three of Chapter 5, and the selections by Kitaro Nishida in the second section of Chapter 3 and the fourth section of Chapter 6. Those who want to better understand Jean-Paul Sartre's existentialism should read the selection from his *Being and Nothingness* reprinted in Section Two of Chapter 6 and Edmund Husserl's discussion of phenomenology and transcendental subjectivity in Section Two of Chapter 5. Also recommended for the further consideration of the problem of human nature are the selections by René Descartes and Risieri Frondizi in Chapter 5, by Okot p'Bitek in Chapter 6, by Ayn Rand in Chapter 7, and by Aristotle, Chogyam Trungpa, and Carl Rogers in Chapter 8. Those reading Section Two of this chapter might also want to read the selections by Carol Christ in the third section of Chapter 3, by Nancy Holmstrom in the fourth section of Chapter 6, by Virginia Held in the first section of Chapter 7, and by Sandra Lee Bartky in the second section of Chapter 9.

UNIVERSAL HUMAN NATURE

"**M**an's Nature is naturally good," writes Mencius, "just as water naturally flows downward." Mencius (372–289 B.C.E.) was one of the most illustrious followers of Confucius and was himself a pupil of Confucius's grandson. In making the above claim, he thought he was only making explicit what he took to be already implicit in Confucian thought. However, as the Chinese debate in this section demonstrates, not all followers of Confucius agreed. To appreciate the nuances of this Chinese debate, which spans a period from ancient to medieval times, it is important to reflect upon the Confucian tradition within which it took place. For Confucius, the individual was immediately a social being. Individual and society were inseparable. The goal of social organization and government was to bring about the happiness of the individual within it, and it was the task of these individuals to take their place within the social order by following *Li,* often translated "ritual," "rules of propriety," "etiquette," and "principles." In effect, *Li* was a set of social conventions which held society together and through which, according to Confucius, an individual became a social and ethical being. It is important to add that Confucius did not believe in following all social conventions but only those which were morally correct. *Li* originally meant "sacrifice," and indeed following *Li* required the sacrifice of self-discipline, as it imposed upon each individual a set of obligations which must be willingly assumed. This self-discipline, Confucius believed, required extensive education which was at once moral and intellectual. From this followed the special esteem which Confucius accorded the role of the teacher.

To return to Mencius, human nature is good because human beings have within them a sense of right and wrong, a natural sympathy for those who suffer, and a sense of propriety; in effect the desire to conform to *Li* is already within our original nature. Therefore, Mencius argues that "if you let people follow their feelings (original nature), they will

be able to do good." If this is so, how do we account for the differences in human moral behavior? Mencius's answer is to compare these differences to the way in which the same kind of seed fares differently in different soils. In other words, our original goodness needs cultivation and nourishment, or it will be corrupted and decay. For Mencius, like Confucius, education was extremely important to cultivate our innate moral sense.

Hsün Tzu (298–238 B.C.E.), a contemporary of Mencius and a significant figure within the Confucian tradition, also extolled education but saw its function as extremely different. For Hsün Tzu, human nature was fundamentally evil. What was innate within us was greed, envy, and hatred. Realizing this, the sage kings—the wise rulers of even more ancient times—created certain "ritual principles," *Li,* to control our natural (evil) emotions. It is only by being educated to follow these principles that the unruly impulses of human beings could be controlled. Morality, then, did not derive from our original nature but was opposed to it and had to be painfully inculcated in each individual. If we did away with these principles and, Hsün adds, the authority of the ruler, "chaos and destruction" would surely follow. In Hsün Tzu's words, we are originally a "warped piece of wood" which must be "laid against the straightening board."

The contrasts between Mencius and Hsün Tzu do not exhaust the alternatives. Ch'eng Hao (1032–1085), a neo-Confucian of the eleventh century, argues that although human beings are originally good, they can become evil. To make his point he uses Mencius's metaphor of the water flowing downhill but notes that it may become dirty as it flows. The task of education, then, is purification, to eliminate the external filth and to restore our original nature.

Han Yü (768–824), who is generally considered a forerunner of the neo-Confucian school, argued that there were three "grades" of human nature—the superior, the medium, and the inferior, each of which contained within them a different proportion of moral elements. Each side of the argument between Mencius and Hsün Tzu applied correctly to one "grade" of human nature. Those who were of a superior nature were naturally good; for them education is an aid to further cultivating their innate goodness. In contrast those of an inferior nature were innately evil. For them the solution is not so much education as such but control. As for the middle range, whose original nature is a mixture of the good and the bad, they must be led by those of a superior nature.

The idea that human nature may be a mixture of positive and negative elements is also contained in the Hindu view of human nature. Bitheka Mukerji, a contemporary Indian scholar who has taught at Hindu Benares University and is revered as a spiritual mother, explains that for Hinduism human nature is a different combination of *tamas* (negativity, apathy), *sattva* (joy), and *raja* (the energizing quality). The proportion and strength of these elements differ from one individual to another. These elements are also subject to change; specifically, by asking the question "Who am I?" we can find the God who dwells within the innermost Self, thus bringing about the predominance of *sattva*. In doing so, we transcend our present existence and fulfill our deeper essence. Mukerji compares this process to "falling in love" (with the God within). Thus, our ultimate possibility is to transcend our present nature and become that most ethical of human beings, the saint, who is in accord with the cosmic whole.

The debate concerning whether human nature is good or evil can be found in a variety of cultures from ancient times to the modern era. Echoing Hsün Tzu, the seventeenth-century British philosopher Thomas Hobbes argues that human beings are naturally competitive, greedy, antisocial, and bellicose and that left to themselves they would be in continuous war with one another—a war of each against each. The result would be that life would be "nasty, brutish, and short" (remember that Hsün Tzu had declared that without moral education there would be chaos and destruction). Hobbes's *Leviathan,* from which this reading was excerpted,

appeared in 1654, shortly after the British Revolution of 1648. This revolution had convinced Hobbes, who sympathized with the monarchy against the parliament, that it was folly for there to be a division of authority and that peace and order required a Leviathanlike state—the Leviathan was a crocodile in the Old Testment who ruled the animal kingdom and who, because of his tough scales, could not be overthrown—which had absolute authority over its subjects. Thus, just as Hsün Tzu emphasizes the need for moral principles to control our evil impulses, Hobbes argues for the necessity of an absolute sovereign to accomplish the same purpose.

Although Hobbes was long dead by the time Charles Darwin wrote his *Origins of the Species,* Hobbes's analysis of human nature is often taken to be a precursor of Darwin's "survival of the fittest." Darwin had used this phrase to indicate the mechanism through which evolutionary development, or "natural selection," occurred. Certain new traits, or mutations, that appeared accidentally would survive if they were adaptive to the environmental conditions within which the organism lived. If so, a new species developed which was "fit" to survive. Those who did not survive were "unfit."

In the hands of the British philosopher and sociologist Herbert Spencer* (1820–1903) the idea of the survival of the fittest came to imply that social progress was like biological evolution in that it was the result of a competition between individuals—and, he asserted, also races—in which the superior, who he identified with the economically prosperous, overcome their inferiors, who he identified with the poor. The latter then tended to die off, leaving the human species with a greater stock of superior characteristics. This, he argued, gave scientific credence to laissez-faire economics, as it implied that social welfare measures would retard social progress.

---

*Spencer was, in fact, the first to use the phrase "survival of the fittest" to describe Darwin's idea. Darwin himself subsequently borrowed the term from Spencer in the fifth edition of his *Origin of the Species.*

Spencer's theory, which became known as Social Darwinism, was popularized in the United States by William Graham Sumner, a major economist and sociologist, who specifically equated the "fittest" with the rich and wrote an entire work justifying the concentration of wealth. Sumner's ideas were adopted by the Episcopalian minister Henry Ward Beecher who had such luminaries in his congregation as J. P. Morgan and John D. Rockefeller. They, needless to say, found Social Darwinism a very agreeable doctrine. Rockefeller is quoted as having said: "The growth of a large business is merely the survival of the fittest. . . . It is merely the working-out of a law of nature and a law of God."

What Social Darwinists failed to note was that Darwin himself was at least ambivalent about the ethical implications of his ideas. He had argued that the "social instinct," which he considered the biological basis for morality, was an adaptive trait, specifically, that human tribal groups whose members were altruistic and who engaged in mutual support had an evolutionary advantage over those tribes whose members lacked these traits. From this it is not very difficult to draw the conclusion that cooperation and mutual support rather than rapacious competition are what helped the human species to survive.

It was precisely this interpretation of Darwinism which was advanced by Prince Petr Kropotkin (1842–1921), a Russian aristocrat who eventually renounced his social standing. Kropotkin was a renowned naturalist and political anarchist known for his work in geography and zoology—he studied animal life in Siberia for several years—as well as his work in sociology, politics, and history. His goal in writing *Mutual Aid,* from which the reading in this chapter is taken, was to put his anarcho-communist ideas on a scientific foundation. In this work he argues that Darwin's "fittest" should not be equated with the strong who dominate the weak but rather with the species whose members learn to cooperate and support one another for their mutual advantage. Competition within a species, then, is ultimately disadvantageous. With numerous examples of animal life and early human societies he attempts

to demonstrate that mutual aid is a general rule and that it, rather than mutual struggle, is the major force of evolution. In the reading reprinted in this chapter he specifically attacks Hobbes's notion of the state of nature, pointing out that rather than being characterized by a war of each against each, early human societies, and most higher mammals, lived in tribes or bands based on mutual aid.

· · ·

Who is right? Is human nature essentially good or is it evil? Is it essentially competitive and selfish or cooperative and altruistic? The assumption behind these questions is that human nature is transhistorically the same. However, there is another concept of human nature, one that has been advanced by the twentieth-century U.S. philosopher and pragmatist John Dewey among others. This we may call the *social and historical* concept of human nature insofar as it understands human nature as necessarily social and sees human beings as changing themselves collectively in response to the changes in historical and social conditions.

What human beings share universally, according to Dewey, is a variety of impulses and a reflective intelligence. These impulses are quite flexible; they do not generally act singly but tend to interact with each other and become meaningful only within a social context as habits. Habits are predispositions to ways of thinking and acting embodied in social institutions. These social habits constitute our historically specific social nature. Although habits have a tendency to remain relatively stable over time, when new social problems arise which are incompatible with the social institutions of the time, human beings can use their reflective intelligence to redirect their impulses into new habits forming new social institutions. For example, as war and competitive capitalism become increasingly obsolete solutions to international problems and new economic developments, human impulses, under the direction of our reflective intelligence, may be rechanneled into alternative activities and political and economic institutions. In sum, according to

Dewey, human nature, because of its reflective capacity, continually changes its specific historical form.

It follows from Dewey's analysis that in some societies human beings may be primarily competitive and aggressive, but in other societies, whose institutional structures emphasize mutual aid, the cooperative and altruistic side of human nature will manifest itself. Although Dewey himself, like Kropotkin, would prefer the latter, the realization of such a possibility would, according to Dewey, in contrast with Kropotkin, not be the fulfillment of an innate tendency but would rather be the result of our collective intelligence reflecting upon the social problems generated by our concrete historical circumstances and collectively (democratically) choosing to construct such institutions.

The importance of choice receives special emphasis in the work of the contemporary French philosopher Jean-Paul Sartre. Sartre is perhaps the best-known proponent of existentialism, whose main theses he characterizes as "existence precedes essence." This means that there is no objective human essence, that humanity does not have within itself any necessary function or goal. From this it follows that there is nothing that a person necessarily is or has to be. What we are individually is the result of our past choices and actions, and all of us will be what we choose to be. Thus, each person must accept total responsibility for what he or she has become and will become. We cannot blame human nature, because there is no universal, unchangeable nature shared by everyone. In the course of our lives we create our specific natures and, in so doing, we give this choice the import of universal values; in other words, by choosing we simultaneously define what it is to be human and create our own values. Of course, others may choose differently, giving their choice equally universal import. There is, then, a plurality of human "natures," each based upon individual human choice. But what can guide this choice? Sartre's answer is that there are no external standards, no God, and no human nature which can make us choose or tell us how to choose. And yet, we must choose, for deciding not to choose, is still a choice. We are, therefore, "condemned to freedom."

The last article in this section is written from a Zen Buddhist perspective. Shin'Ichi Hisamatsu, a contemporary Japanese philosopher, develops a Zen view of human nature within the context of the overwhelming complexity of modern society. Human nature, he argues, is at once a unity and a multiplicity, a oneness and a manyness. As modern society becomes more complex, the sense of multiplicity begins to outstrip our sense of unity. The result is the sense of fragmentation so well documented by contemporary psychologists and sociologists. The solution, however, is not to attempt to retreat into a primitive oneness apart from the complexity of modern life but to establish a dynamic creative unity within the multiplicity. "The greater the multiplicity, the stronger in direct proportion must be the oneness or unity." This, claims Hisamatsu, requires that we return to the "Original-Subject," which he also identifies with an "Active Nothingness" and a "Formless Self." This Subject is our true Nature, which is not itself a thing but which is able to produce all things; this Subject is in time and place but never bound by it. Thus, like Sartre's existence which precedes essence, Zen too posits an existential subject which is not bound by instincts or social conditions, which is ultimately free to choose.

HUMAN NATURE IS GOOD

Mencius

Kao Tzu said, "Human nature is like the willow tree, and righteousness is like a cup or a bowl. To turn human nature into humanity and righteousness is like turning the willow into cups and bowls." Mencius said, "Sir, can you follow the nature of the willow tree and make the cups and bowls, or must you violate the nature of the willow tree before you can make the cups and bowls? If you are going to violate the nature of the willow tree in order to make cups and bowls, then must you also violate human nature in order to make it into humanity and righteousness? Your words, alas! would lead all people in the world to consider humanity and righteousness as calamity [because they required the violation of human nature]!"

Kao Tzu said, "Man's nature is like whirling water. If a breach in the pool is made to the east it will flow to the east. If a breach is made to the west it will flow to the west. Man's nature is indifferent to good and evil, just as water is indifferent to east and west." Mencius said, "Water, indeed, is indifferent to the east and west, but is it indifferent to high and low? Man's nature is naturally good just as water naturally flows downward. There is no man without this good nature; neither is there water that does not flow downward. Now you can strike water and cause it to splash upward over your forehead, and by damming and leading it, you can force it uphill. Is this the nature of water? It is the forced circumstance that makes it do so. Man can be made to do evil, for his nature can be treated in the same way."

Kao Tzu said, "What is inborn is called nature." Mencius said, "When you say that what is inborn is called nature, is that like saying that white is white?" "Yes." "Then is the whiteness of the white feather the same as the whiteness of snow? Or, again, is the whiteness of snow the same as the whiteness of white jade?" "Yes." "Then is the nature of a dog the same as the nature of an ox, and is the nature of an ox the same as the nature of a man?"

Kao Tzu said, "By nature we desire food and sex. Humanity is internal and not external, whereas righteousness is external and not internal." Mencius said, "Why do you say that humanity is internal and righteousness external?" "When I see an old man and respect him for his age, it is not that the oldness is within me, just as, when something is white and I call it white, I am merely observing its external appearance. I therefore say that righteousness is external." Mencius said, "There is no difference between our considering a white horse to be white and a white man to be white. But is there no difference between acknowledging the age of an old horse and the age of an old man? And what is it that we call righteousness, the fact that a man is old or the fact that we honor his old age?" Kao Tzu said, "I love my own younger brother but do not love the younger brother of, say, a man from the state of Ch'in. This is because I am the one to determine that pleasant feeling. I therefore say that humanity comes from within. On the other hand, I respect the old men of the state of Ch'u as well as my own elders. What determines my pleasant feeling is age itself. Therefore I say that righteousness is external." Mencius said, "We love the roast meat of Ch'in as much as we love our own. This is even so with respect to material things. Then are you going to say that our love of roast meat is also external?"

Meng Chi Tzu asked Kung-tu Tzu, "What does it mean to say that righteousness is internal?" Kung-tu Tzu said, "We practice reverence, and therefore it is called internal." "Suppose a fellow villager is one year older than your older brother. Whom are you going to serve with reverence?" "I shall serve my brother with reverence." "In offering wine at a feast, to whom will you offer first?" "I shall offer wine to the villager first." Meng Chi Tzu said, "Now you show reverence to one but honor for age to the other. What determines your actions certainly lies without and not within." Kung-tu Tzu could not reply and told Mencius about it. Mencius said, "If you ask him whether he will serve with reverence his uncle or his younger brother, he will say that he will serve with reverence his uncle. Then you ask him, in case his younger brother is acting at a sacrifice as the representative of the deceased, then to whom is he going to serve with reverence? He will say he will serve the younger brother with reverence. Then you ask him 'Where is your reverence for your uncle?' He will then say, '[I show reverence to my younger brother] because he represents the ancestral spirit in an official capacity.' You can then likewise say, '[I show reverence to the villager] because of his position.' Ordinarily, the reverence is due the elder brother, but on special occasions it is due the villager." When Chi Tzu heard this, he said, "We show reverence to uncle when reverence is due him, and we show reverence to the younger brother when reverence is due him. Certainly what determines it lies without and does not come from within." Kung-tu Tzu said, "In the winter we drink things hot. In the summer we drink things cold. Does it mean that what determines eating and drinking also lies outside?"

Kung-tu Tzu said, "Kao Tzu said that man's nature is neither good nor evil. Some say that man's nature may be made good or evil, therefore when King Wen and King Wu[1] were in power the people loved virtue, and when Kings Yu and Li[2] were in power people loved violence. Some say that some men's nature is good and some men's nature is evil. Therefore even under (sage-emperor) Yao there was Hsiang [who daily plotted to kill his brother], and even with a bad father Ku-sou, there was [a most filial] Shun (Hsiang's brother who succeeded Yao), and even with (wicked king) Chou as uncle and ruler, there were Viscount Ch'i of Wei and Prince Pi-kan. Now you say that human nature is good. Then are those people wrong?"

Mencius said, "If you let people follow their feelings (original nature), they will be able to do good. This is what is meant by saying that human nature is good. If man does evil, it is not the fault of his natural endowment. The feeling of commiseration is found in all men; the feeling of shame and dislike is found in all men; the feeling of respect and reverence is found in all men; and the feeling of right and wrong is found in all men. The feeling of commiseration is what we call humanity; the feeling of shame and dislike is what we called righteousness; the feeling of respect and reverence is what we called propriety (li); and the feeling of right and wrong is what we called wisdom. Humanity, righteousness, propriety, and wisdom are not drilled into us from outside. We originally have them with us. Only we do not think [to find them]. Therefore it is said, 'Seek and you will find it, neglect and you will lose it.' [Men differ in the development of their endowments], some twice as much as others, some five times, and some to an incalculable degree, because no one can develop his original endowment to the fullest extent. The *Book of Odes* says, 'Heaven produces the teeming multitude. As there are things there are their specific principles. When the people keep their normal nature they will love excellent virtue.' Confucius said, 'The writer of this poem indeed knew the Way (Tao). Therefore as there are things, there must be their specific principles, and since people keep to their normal nature, therefore they love excellent virtue.' "

• • •

Mencius said, "In good years most of the young people behave well. In bad years most of them abandon themselves to evil. This is not due to any difference in the natural capacity endowed by Heaven. The abandonment is due to the fact that the mind is allowed to fall into evil. Take for instance the growing of wheat. You sow the seeds and cover them with soil. The land is the same and the time of sowing is also the same. In time they all grow up luxuriantly. When the time of harvest comes, they are all ripe. Although there may be a difference between the different stalks of wheat, it is due to differences in the soil, as rich or poor, to the unequal

---

[1] Sage-kings who founded the Chou dynsty (r. 1171–1122 B.C. and 1121–1116 B.C., respectively).
[2] Wicked kings (r. 781–771 B.C. and 878–842 B.C., respectively).

nourishment obtained from the rain and the dew, and to differences in human effort. Therefore all things of the same kind are similar to one another. Why should there be any doubt about men? The sage and I are the same in kind. Therefore Lung Tzu said, 'If a man makes shoes without knowing the size of people's feet, I know that he will at least not make them to be like baskets.' Shoes are alike because people's feet are alike. There is a common taste for flavor in our mouths. I-ya was the first to know our common taste for food. Suppose one man's taste for flavor is different from that of others, as dogs and horses differ from us in belonging to different species, then why should the world follow I-ya in regard to flavor? Since in the matter of flavor the whole world regards I-ya as the standard, it shows that our tastes for flavor are alike. The same is true of our ears. Since in the matter of sounds the whole world regards Shih-k'uang as the standard, it shows that our ears are alike. The same is true of our eyes. With regard to Tzu-tu, none in the world did not know that he was handsome. Any one who did not recognize his handsomeness must have no eyes. Therefore I say there is a common taste for flavor in our mouths, a common sense for sound in our ears, and a common sense for beauty in our eyes. Can it be that in our minds alone we are not alike? What is it that we have in common in our minds? It is the sense of principle and righteousness (i-li, moral principles). The sage is the first to possess what is common in our minds. Therefore moral principles please our minds as beef and mutton and pork please our mouths."

· · ·

Mencius said, "The trees of the Niu Mountain were once beautiful. But can the mountain be regarded any longer as beautiful since, being in the borders of a big state, the trees have been hewed down with axes and hatchets? Still with the rest given them by the days and nights and the nourishment provided them by the rains and the dew, they were not without buds and sprouts springing forth. But then the cattle and the sheep pastured upon them once and again. That is why the mountain looks so bald.

When people see that it is so bald, they think that there was never any timber on the mountain. Is this the true nature of the mountain? Is there not [also] a heart of humanity and righteousness originally existing in man? The way in which he loses his originally good mind is like the way in which the trees are hewn down with axes and hatchets. As trees are cut down day after day, can a mountain retain its beauty? To be sure, the days and nights do the healing, and there is the nourishing air of the calm morning which keeps him normal in his likes and dislikes. But the effect is slight, and is disturbed and destroyed by what he does during the day. When there is repeated disturbance, the restorative influence of the night will not be sufficient to preserve (the proper goodness of the mind). When the influence of the night is not sufficient to preserve it, man becomes not much different from the beast. People see that he acts like an animal, and think that he never had the original endowment (for goodness).

· · ·

But is that his true character? Therefore with proper nourishment and care, everything grows, whereas without proper nourishment and care, everything decays. Confucius said, "Hold it fast and you preserve it. Let it go and you lose it. It comes in and goes out at no definite time and without anyone's knowing its direction.' He was talking about the human mind."

· · ·

Kung-tu Tzu asked, "We are all human beings. Why is it that some men become great and others become small?" Mencius said, "Those who follow the greater qualities in their nature become great men and those who follow the smaller qualities in their nature become small men." "But we are all human beings. Why is it that some follow their greater qualities and others follow their smaller qualities?" Mencius replied, "When our senses of sight and hearing are used without thought and are thereby obscured by material things, the material things act on the material senses and lead them astray. That is all. The function of the mind is to think. If we think, we will get them (the principles of things). If we do not think, we will not get them. This is what Heaven has given to us. If we first build up the nobler part of our nature, then the inferior part cannot overcome it. It is simply this that makes a man great."

• • •

Mencius said, "All men have the mind which cannot bear [to see the suffering of][3] others. The ancient kings had this mind and therefore they had a government that could not bear to see the suffering of the people. When a government that cannot bear to see the suffering of the people is conducted from a mind that cannot bear to see the suffering of others, the government of the empire will be as easy as making something go round in the palm."

"When I say that all men have the mind which cannot bear to see the suffering of others, my meaning may be illustrated thus: Now, when men suddenly see a child about to fall into a well, they all have a feeling of alarm and distress, not to gain friendship with the child's parents, nor to seek the praise of their neighbors and friends, nor because they dislike the reputation [of lack of humanity if they did not rescue the child]. From such a case, we see that a man without the feeling of commiseration is not a man; a man without the feeling of shame and dislike is not a man; a man without the feeling of deference and compliance is not a man; and a man without the feeling of right and wrong is not a man. The feeling of commiseration is the beginning of humanity; the feeling of shame and dislike is the beginning of righteousness; the feeling of deference and compliance is the beginning of propriety; and the feeling of right and wrong is the beginning of wisdom. Men have these Four Beginnings just as they have their four limbs. Having these Four Beginnings, but saying that they cannot develop them is to destroy themselves. When they say that their ruler cannot develop them, they are destroying their ruler. If anyone with these Four Beginnings in him knows how to give them the fullest extension and development, the result will be like fire beginning to burn or a spring beginning to shoot forth. When they are fully developed, they will be sufficient to protect all people within the four seas (the world). If they are not developed, they will not be sufficient even to serve one's parents."

HUMAN NATURE IS EVIL

Hsün Tzu

Man's nature is evil; goodness is the result of conscious activity. The nature of man is such that he is born with a fondness for profit. If he indulges this fondness, it will lead him into wrangling and strife, and all sense of courtesy and humility will disappear. He is born with feelings of envy and hate, and if he indulges these, they will lead him into violence and crime, and all sense of loyalty and good faith will disappear. Man is born with the desires of the eyes and ears, with a fondness for beautiful sights and sounds. If he indulges these, they will lead him into license and wantonness, and all ritual principles and correct forms will be lost. Hence, any man who follows his nature and indulges his emotions will inevitably become involved in wrangling and strife, will violate the forms and rules of society, and will end as a criminal. Therefore, man must first be transformed by the instructions of a teacher and guided by ritual principles, and only then will he be able to observe the dictates of courtesy and humility, obey the forms and rules of society, and achieve order. It is obvious from this, then, that man's nature is evil, and that his goodness is the result of conscious activity.

A warped piece of wood must wait until it has been laid against the straightening board, steamed, and forced into shape before it can become straight; a piece of blunt metal must wait until it has been whetted on a grindstone before it can become sharp.

---

[3] According to Chao Ch'i, "cannot bear to do evil to others."

Similarly, since man's nature is evil, it must wait for the instructions of a teacher before it can become upright, and for the guidance of ritual principles before it can become orderly. If men have no teachers to instruct them, they will be inclined towards evil and not upright; and if they have no ritual principles to guide them, they will be perverse and violent and lack order. In ancient times the sage kings realized that man's nature is evil, and that therefore he inclines toward evil and violence and is not upright or orderly. Accordingly they created ritual principles and laid down certain regulations in order to reform man's emotional nature and make it upright, in order to train and transform it and guide it in the proper channels. In this way they caused all men to become orderly and to conform to the Way. Hence, today any man who takes to heart the instructions of his teacher, applies himself to his studies, and abides by ritual principles may become a gentleman, but anyone who gives free rein to his emotional nature, is content to indulge his passions, and disregards ritual principles becomes a petty man. It is obvious from this, therefore, that man's nature is evil, and that his goodness is the result of conscious activity.

Mencius states that man is capable of learning because his nature is good, but I say that this is wrong. It indicates that he has not really understood man's nature nor distinguished properly between the basic nature and conscious activity. The nature is that which is given by Heaven; you cannot learn it, you cannot acquire it by effort. Ritual principles, on the other hand, are created by sages; you can learn to apply them, you can work to bring them to completion. That part of man which cannot be learned or acquired by effort is called the nature; that part of him which can be acquired by learning and brought to completion by effort is called conscious activity. This is the difference between nature and conscious activity.

It is a part of man's nature that his eyes can see and his ears can hear. But the faculty of clear sight can never exist separately from the eye, nor can the faculty of keen hearing exist separately from the ear. It is obvious, then, that you cannot acquire clear

sight and keen hearing by study. Mencius states that man's nature is good, and that all evil arises because he loses his original nature. Such a view, I believe, is erroneous. It is the way with man's nature that as soon as he is born he begins to depart from his original naïveté and simplicity, and therefore he must inevitably lose what Mencius regards as his original nature. It is obvious from this, then, that the nature of man is evil.

Those who maintain that the nature is good praise and approve whatever has not departed from the original simplicity and naïveté of the child. That is, they consider that beauty belongs to the original simplicity and naïveté and goodness to the original mind in the same way that clear sight is inseparable from the eye and keen hearing from the ear. Hence, they maintain that [the nature possesses goodness] in the same way that the eye possesses clear vision or the ear keenness of hearing. Now it is the nature of man that when he is hungry he will desire satisfaction, when he is cold he will desire warmth, and when he is weary he will desire rest. This is his emotional nature. And yet a man, although he is hungry, will not dare to be the first to eat if he is in the presence of his elders, because he knows that he should yield to them, and although he is weary, he will not dare to demand rest because he knows that he should relieve others of the burden of labor. For a son to yield to his father or a younger brother to yield to his elder brother, for a son to relieve his father of work or a younger brother to relieve his elder brother—acts such as these are all contrary to man's nature and run counter to his emotions. And yet they represent the way of filial piety and the proper forms enjoined by ritual principles. Hence, if men follow their emotional nature, there will be no courtesy or humility; courtesy and humility in fact run counter to man's emotional nature. From this it is obvious, then, that man's nature is evil, and that his goodness is the result of conscious activity.

Someone may ask: if man's nature is evil, then where do ritual principles come from? I would reply: all ritual principles are produced by the conscious activity of the sages; essentially they are not products of man's nature. A potter molds clay and makes a vessel, but the vessel is the product of the conscious activity of the potter, not essentially a product of his human nature. A carpenter carves a piece of wood and makes a utensil, but the utensil is the product of the conscious activity of the carpenter, not essentially a product of his human nature. The sage gathers together his thoughts and ideas, experiments with various forms of conscious activity, and so produces ritual principles and sets forth laws and regulations. Hence, these ritual principles and laws are the products of the conscious activity of the sage, not essentially products of his human nature.

Phenomena such as the eye's fondness for beautiful forms, the ear's fondness for beautiful sounds, the mouth's fondness for delicious flavors, the mind's fondness for profit, or the body's fondness for pleasure and ease—these are all products of the emotional nature of man. They are instinctive and spontaneous; man does not have to do anything to produce them. But that which does not come into being instinctively but must wait for some activity to bring it into being is called the product of conscious activity. These are the products of the nature and of conscious activity respectively, and the proof that they are not the same. Therefore, the sage transforms his nature and initiates conscious activity; from this conscious activity he produces ritual principles, and when they have been produced he sets up rules and regulations. Hence, ritual principles and rules are produced by the sage. In respect to human nature the sage is the same as all other men and does not surpass them; it is only in his conscious activity that he differs from and surpasses other men.

It is man's emotional nature to love profit and desire gain. Suppose now that a man has some wealth to be divided. If he indulges his emotional nature, loving profit and desiring gain, then he will quarrel and wrangle even with his own brothers over the division. But if he has been transformed by the proper forms of ritual principle, then he will be capable of yielding even to a complete stranger. Hence, to indulge the emotional nature leads to the quarreling of brothers, but to be transformed by rit-

ual principles makes a man capable of yielding to strangers.

Every man who desires to do good does so precisely because his nature is evil. A man whose accomplishments are meager longs for greatness; an ugly man longs for beauty; a man in cramped quarters longs for spaciousness; a poor man longs for wealth; a humble man longs for eminence. Whatever a man lacks in himself he will seek outside. But if a man is already rich, he will not long for wealth, and if he is already eminent, he will not long for greater power. What a man already possesses in himself he will not bother to look for outside. From this we can see that men desire to do good precisely because their nature is evil. Ritual principles are certainly not a part of man's original nature. Therefore, he forces himself to study and to seek to possess them. An understanding of ritual principles is not a part of man's original nature, and therefore he ponders and plans and thereby seeks to understand them. Hence, man in the state in which he is born neither possesses nor understands ritual principles. If he does not possess ritual principles, his behavior will be chaotic, and if he does not understand them, he will be wild and irresponsible. In fact, therefore, man in the state in which he is born possesses this tendency towards chaos and irresponsibility. From this it is obvious, then, that man's nature is evil, and that his goodness is the result of conscious activity.

Mencius states that man's nature is good, but I say that this view is wrong. All men in the world, past and present, agree in defining goodness as that which is upright, reasonable, and orderly, and evil as that which is prejudiced, irresponsible, and chaotic. This is the distinction between good and evil. Now suppose that man's nature was in fact intrinsically upright, reasonable, and orderly—then what need would there be for sage kings and ritual principles? The existence of sage kings and ritual principles could certainly add nothing to the situation. But because man's nature is in fact evil, this is not so. Therefore, in ancient times the sages, realizing that man's nature is evil, that it is prejudiced and not upright, irresponsible and lacking in order, for this reason established the authority of the ruler to control it, elucidated ritual principles to transform it, set up laws and standards to correct it, and meted out strict punishments to restrain it. As a result, all the world achieved order and conformed to goodness. Such is the orderly government of the sage kings and the transforming power of ritual principles. Now let someone try doing away with the authority of the ruler, ignoring the transforming power of ritual principles, rejecting the order that comes from laws and standards, and dispensing with the restrictive power of punishments, and then watch and see how the people of the world treat each other. He will find that the powerful impose upon the weak and rob them, the many terrorize the few and extort from them, and in no time the whole world will be given up to chaos and mutual destruction. It is obvious from this, then, that man's nature is evil, and that his goodness is the result of conscious activity.

Those who are good at discussing antiquity must demonstrate the validity of what they say in terms of modern times; those who are good at discussing Heaven must show proofs from the human world. In discussions of all kinds, men value what is in accord with the facts and what can be proved to be valid. Hence if a man sits on his mat propounding some theory, he should be able to stand right up and put it into practice, and show that it can be extended over a wide area with equal validity. Now Mencius states that man's nature is good, but this is neither in accord with the facts, nor can it be proved to be valid. One may sit down and propound such a theory, but he cannot stand up and put it into practice, nor can he extend it over a wide area with any success at all. How, then, could it be anything but erroneous?

If the nature of man were good, we could dispense with sage kings and forget about ritual principles. But if it is evil, then we must go along with the sage kings and honor ritual principles. The straightening board is made because of the warped wood; the plumb line is employed because things are crooked; rulers are set up and ritual principles elucidated because the nature of man is evil. From this it is obvious, then, that man's nature is evil, and

that his goodness is the result of conscious activity. A straight piece of wood does not have to wait for the straightening board to become straight; it is straight by nature. But a warped piece of wood must wait until it has been laid against the straightening board, steamed, and forced into shape before it can become straight, because by nature it is warped. Similarly, since man's nature is evil, he must wait for the ordering power of the sage kings and the transforming power of ritual principles; only then can he achieve order and conform to goodness. From this it is obvious, then, that man's nature is evil, and that his goodness is the result of conscious activity.

Someone may ask whether ritual principles and concerted conscious activity are not themselves a part of man's nature, so that for that reason the sage is capable of producing them. But I would answer that this is not so. A potter may mold clay and produce an earthen pot, but surely molding pots out of clay is not a part of the potter's human nature. A carpenter may carve wood and produce a utensil, but surely carving utensils out of wood is not a part of the carpenter's human nature. The sage stands in the same relation to ritual principles as the potter to the things he molds and produces. How, then, could ritual principles and concerted conscious activity be a part of man's basic human nature?

As far as human nature goes, the sages Yao and Shun possessed the same nature as the tyrant Chieh or Robber Chih, and the gentleman possesses the same nature as the petty man. Would you still maintain, then, that ritual principles and concerted conscious activity are a part of man's nature? If you do so, then what reason is there to pay any particular honor to Yao, Shun, or the gentleman? The reason people honor Yao, Shun, and the gentleman is that they are able to transform their nature, apply themselves to conscious activity, and produce ritual principles. The sage, then, must stand in the same relation to ritual principles as the potter to the things he molds and produces. Looking at it this way, how could ritual principles and concerted conscious activity be a part of man's nature? The reason people despise Chieh, Robber Chih, or the petty man is that they give free rein to their nature, follow their emotions, and are content to indulge their passions, so that their conduct is marked by greed and contentiousness. Therefore, it is clear that man's nature is evil, and that his goodness is the result of conscious activity.

HUMAN NATURE IS GOOD BUT CAN BECOME EVIL

Ch'eng Hao

"What is inborn is called nature." Nature is the same as material force and material force is the same as nature. They are both inborn. According to principle, there are both good and evil in the material force with which man is endowed at birth. However, man is not born with these two opposing elements in his nature to start with. Due to the material force with which men are endowed some become good from childhood and others become evil. Man's nature is of course good, but it cannot be said that evil is not his nature. For what is inborn is called nature. "By nature man is tranquil at birth." The state preceding this cannot be discussed. As soon as we talk about human nature, we already go beyond it. Actually, in our discussion of nature, we only talk about (the idea expressed in the *Book of Changes* as) "What issues from the Way is good." This is the case when Mencius speaks of the original goodness of human nature. The fact that whatever issues from the Way is good may be compared to the fact that water always flows downward. Water as such is the same in all cases. Some water flows onward to the sea without becoming dirty. What human effort is needed here? Some flows only a short distance before growing turbid. Some travels a long distance before growing turbid. Some becomes extremely turbid, some only slightly so. Although water differs in being clean or turbid, we cannot say that the turbid water (evil) ceases to be

water (nature). This being the case, man must make an increasing effort at purification. With diligent and vigorous effort, water will become clear quickly. With slow and lazy effort, water will become clear slowly. When it is clear, it is then the original water. Not that clear water has been substituted for turbid water, nor that turbid water has been taken out and left in a corner. The original goodness of human nature is like the original clearness of water. Therefore it is not true that two distinct and opposing elements of good and evil exist in human nature and that each of them issues from it.

THREE GRADES OF HUMAN NATURE

Han Yü

The nature of man comes into existence with birth, whereas the feelings are produced when there is contact with external things. There are three grades of human nature, and what constitute that nature are five. There are three grades of feelings, and what constitute feelings are seven. What are these? I say: The three grades of nature are: superior, the medium, and the inferior. The superior is good, and good only. The medium may be led to be either superior or inferior. The inferior is evil, and evil only. Human nature consists in five virtues, namely, humanity, (*jen*), propriety (*li*), faithfulness, righteousness (*i*), and wisdom. In the superior grade, one of these five is the ruling factor while the other four also are practiced. In the medium grade, there is more or less of one of the five while the other four are not pure. In the inferior grade, one rebels against one of these and is out of accord with the other four. The relation of nature to feelings depends on its grade.

Similarly, there are three grades of feelings: the superior, the medium, and the inferior, and what constitute the feelings are seven: pleasure, anger, sorrow, fear, love, hate, and desire. In the superior grade, when any of these seven becomes active, it abides by the Mean. In the medium grade, some of the seven are excessive and some are deficient but there is an effort to be in accord with the Mean. In the inferior grade, whether they are excessive or deficient, action is directed by whichever feeling happens to be predominant. The relation between feelings and nature depends on their grade.

In discussing human nature, Mencius said, "Man's nature is good." Hsün Tzu said, "Man's nature is evil." And Yang Hsiung said, "Man's nature is a mixture of good and evil." Now to say that nature is good at first but subsequently becomes evil, or bad at first and subsequently becomes good, or mixed at first and is now either good or evil, is to mention only the medium grade and leave the superior and inferior grades out of account and to take care of one case but to lose sight of the other two.

When Shu-yü was born, his mother knew, as soon as she looked at him, that he would die of love of bribes. When Yang I-wo was born, Shu-hsiang's mother new, as soon as she heard him cry, that he would cause the destruction of all his kindred. When Yüeh-chiao was born, Tzu-wen considered it a great calamity, knowing that because of him the ghosts of Jo-ao family would be famished. [With all these evidences] can we say that human nature is good?

When Hou-chi was born, his mother did not suffer. As soon as he began to creep, he displayed understanding and intelligence. When King Wen was in his mother's womb, she had no trouble. After he was born, those who assisted him did not have to work hard, and those who taught him did not have to labor. [With all these evidences] can we say that human nature is evil?

Emperor Yao's son Chu, Emperor Shun's son Chün, and King Wen's sons Kuan and Ts'ai were not without good in their practice, but they eventually became wicked. Ku-sou's son Shun and Kun's son Yü were not without evil in their practice but they eventually became sages. [With all these evidences,] can we say that human nature is a mixture of good and evil?

I therefore say that the three philosophers, in their theories on human nature, mentioned the medium grade and left the superior and inferior grades out of account. They took care of one case but lost sight of the other two.

It may be asked: In that case, does it mean that the nature of the superior and inferior grades can never be changed?

I reply: The nature of the superior grade becomes more intelligent through education. The nature of the inferior grade comes to have few faults through an awe of power. Therefore the superior nature can be taught and the inferior nature can be controlled. But their grades have been pronounced by Confucius to be unchangeable.

A HINDU VIEW

Bitheka Mukerji

How shall we understand man's way of life in the world whence the quest for salvation is to begin? The first things that strikes us is that a definition of man in terms of the usual *pergenus at differentia* does not suffice. In view of the complex nature of the *definiendum,* the definition of man as a rational animal, even if logically cogent, will always remain a too narrow definition. The best that could be done, perhaps, is to list a descriptive series of paradoxes. For example, although man obviously and by nature is a social being, as often as not he seeks solitude (not to escape society, but to be alone with himself); although he must have a lot of pleasurable experiences, too soon he has a revulsion of feeling, again not after satiation, but in the midst of enjoyment; he talks of equality but he would like to preserve at almost any cost his singularity and individuality; we hear of scientists who are devout and also of lay people who find the question of God meaningless because of the discoveries of science; we are not unfamiliar with rationalists who are passionately committed to reason and mystics who are able to describe their experience in sober, rational language.

This list of paradoxes could easily be extended. What emerges is the picture of a being never satisfied with what is, but always concerned with the question of what might be or even what ought to be. Most human lives are spun out in constant oscillation from one to the other. This is not to say that the "is" is not accepted sometimes as a value in itself. It is not the polarity that needs to be stressed, but the fact that evaluation of our situation is endemic to human nature. The systems and structures may change, but the questioning of all that obtains at a given point in time remains an ongoing process.

The Self or "I" for whom this question is meaningful is located somewhere in the psychophysical complex which is the total personality of man. According to some, the Self has its being only in its agency; that is, it is known only in action. Others believe that the essence is in thinking, and yet others emphasize emotional or ecstatic awareness as the clue to the true identity of the Self. However this may be, it is hardly realistic to separate will, awareness, and thought; action, passion, and contemplation; creativity, vision, and insight. Thought is not static. In contemplation we change imperceptibly and become a little like the object we contemplate; in willing or creativity are incorporated vast realms of thought processes; on the other hand, there is no thinking or willing in a vacuum, so to speak. An awareness which is satisfying becomes the incentive for regulating thought or action. In this constantly shifting, dynamic, psychical process, where should we locate the Self?

To come to this question from another angle: Each man is situated in his own particular existential milieu. What is given is the environment in which we participate by acting and reacting to it. We erect for ourselves a world of values that is meaningful for us. Each person lives inside a thought-castle, as it were. Experience and evaluation, action and thought intermingle, succeed, and determine each other constantly—this is our own world of personal relationships. Nobody escapes it.

Even if one were to retire to a monastery, one's thoughts would continue to determine one's behavior. A man is what he is by virtue of what he believes in and the way he acts upon his belief.

Now it so happens that sometimes this castle of meaning or significance crumbles partially or totally. Anything may act as a catalyst that dissolves the carefully built protection around us—a sudden "transvaluation of values" which throws up the question "Who am I?" in all its stark urgency. It cannot be said that this moment of lucidity is always assessed as such by all human beings. It may come and then be overcome again by the forces of the world around us, leaving a mood of nostalgia for a strange world glimpsed as if in a dream.

Since this questioning lies in the vicinity of the region of grace, why are we not able to abide in it for any appreciable length of time? Especially as the scriptures keep on reiterating the supreme worthwhileness of this quest? The texts proclaim with great certainty the exalted status of man, albeit not as he is but as he might be. A *de facto* difference is stated between his essence and his existence. It is his destiny to supercede his human condition. Yet, as we live our lives, the gap between the human and the divine does seem to be absolute.

The crucial point, then, it would seem, is how man should transform himself so that he can hope to stay with the quest for spiritual fulfillment. In other words, let us examine the question of the separation of man's essence and existence. It is perhaps well known that Indian thought in general subscribes to the view of the Samkhya system with regard to the creation of the world and all that there is in it. The primal source is called *Prakriti,* the repository of the basic three elements of creation—*sattva, rajas,* and *tamas.* These are known as qualities or *gunas. Sattva* is the source of lightness, illumination, buoyancy of spirit, joy, serenity, etc. *Tamas* is the opposite quality of heaviness, darkness, sloth, obstruction, apathy, etc. *Rajas* signifies the energizing quality that activates both—it supplies movement, excitement, exhilaration, etc. The three strands are held in a perfect state of equilibrium before creation. The world order is an unfoldment into complexities of the original three qualities and their infinite ways of combinations and permutations. The quiescent stage of *prakriti* is dynamic. Many points of view are advanced as to why this original state of equilibrium is disturbed. For our purposes here we need not take into account the theologies regarding first cause (especially as they are variations on the same idea)—only that once equilibrium is upset—*Sattva* becomes prominent as the first evolute because that is light and buoyant. This is the dimension of the intellect, the most pure in the scale of evolution. Thereupon other stages are reached, such as the I-consciousness, the sensations, and the subtle elements which transform into the material objects of these sensations.

All things are a co-mingling of these three qualities. The nature of a thing is determined by the predominant *guna* in its composition. A stone is predominantly of the quality of *tamas* and *sattva*. Human beings differ according to the elements of *sattva* and *tamas* in their natures. An apathetic, negative attitude denotes *tamas,* a light, cheerful, happy disposition denotes the presence of *sattva* in an abundant degree. The quality of *rajas* is to be seen in very active people who are capable of experiencing great excitement and who can be very joyous as well as greatly anguished.

Human beings behave in accordance with their nature and behavior in turn formulates further the dispositions that result in activity. The crux of the notion is this: This nature is of the stuff of matter; it is malleable; it can be improved upon; it is the nonessential that fills our horizon and keeps us away from the essential question of the Self that resides well hidden within the "cave of the heart." If and when *sattva* in our nature predominates, then we can stay permanently and not fleetingly with the question "Who am I?" We may then look for the guidance of the scriptures. In fact, the asking of the question already presages the coming of the compassionate teacher because in the ultimate analysis the Self knows itself.

It is not of the essence of the Self to dwell forever in the world as if experiencing joys and sorrows. At times, therefore, human beings are seized with longings for an abiding state of happiness. This "longing" must be carefully distinguished from the wishes and wants a man may have and also see fulfilled in his life.

The variations in temperament are not fortuitous but strictly in accordance with how the material is handled by the person concerned. This is known as the law of karma, which accounts for the difference in aptitude, that is, *adhikari bheda* (difference in eligibility). Karma and eligibility go together. The law of karma is to be understood as an instrument of freedom in the hands of man. What greater power can one enjoy than the freedom to effect changes in the very texture of our nature and density. But this power is not unlimited—it operates within the realm of influence of *Prakriti* only. Its greatest achievement is to bring about a predominance of *sattva* in one's nature so that the spiritual yearning is felt. Human nature is already transcended with the asking of the question, "Who am I." So the moment of alienation from the alien world is nothing but the grace of God. Self-realization, therefore, is God's grace rather than fulfillment of human ambition for transcendence.

The human condition, according to the Hindu tradition, therefore, is preeminently a happy condition. It is happiness indeed to be born a human being because one may attain God's grace in this life. God dwells in man as his innermost Self. He catches glimpses of this presence now and then in moments of turning around from the world. The Self is the footprint of the supreme reality (Brihaderanyakopanisad I.4–7).

What stands out clearly here is the fact that pursuit of what is considered the highest value in life must come as free choice. Salvation is for he who seeks God's grace in life. To pray to God in sorrow or to take refuge at his feet in distress is of spiritual value, but the highest ideal is to seek God for himself only and not for anything else. In the language of the mystics, it is called "falling in love." The lover says to the beloved, "You are my one and only concern." Certainly not less than this is required of the man in search of God. This state of mind is not a condition of rejection of the world. Just as a human lover has his interest centered on one person, similarly the pilgrim is preoccupied with finding a way for himself. It is quite conceivable that he may even be leading a full and active life in the world, but from the perspective of his ultimate commitment, the world is now insubstantial and shadowy where he goes through the motions of participation without self-involvement. This can be called the mood of detachment *vairagya,* which is indispensable as an item of the wherewithal of a spiritual journey.

The figure of a lover in the secular world is that of an admired hero of countless books and dramas in numberless languages of the world. The figure of the ascetic in total self-surrender to God and in search of his high destiny is equally pleasing to the Indian mind. The ascetic is the idea; man—a man who by his calling is confirming what the books have to say about the ultimately worthwhile quest (*sreyas*) of human life. He is the exemplar because he is trying to bring about a radical change in the quality of human stuff, in the very texture of our being.

By an ascetic, we do not mean a man in saffron clothes. An ascetic is he who is living the question about his Self. The questioning is being emphasized because the answer is inevitably related to it. To seek is to find such a man, who then becomes an asset to the world. People may recognize him as a man of wisdom and call him a saint.

THE ROLE OF THE SAINT

A saint may be recognized by his humility and his tranquility. He is at peace with himself and with the world. He is simply an onlooker and makes no proclamations or exhortations. He knows that the world is as God has made it and he does not abrogate to himself any special powers to improve upon it. He is in tune with the cosmic scheme of things; if he is called upon to expound, he may do so, but he may also be content to abide in solitude. He does not seek to change the world, but only to render help to those who are in need of it. The saint's tranquility and affirmation is not the inertness of matter but rather the dynamic point of stillness, which bal-

ances to a nicety the boundless compassion for suffering humanity and a joyous acceptance of the divine order of things. These ascetics are, therefore, the compassionate ones who as living examples concretize for us the message of the scriptures:

I know the Supreme Person of Sunlike Color [luster] beyond the darkness. Only by knowing Him does one pass over death. There is no other path for going there.

—*Sveta Svatara* III.8

HUMAN NATURE AS COMPETITIVE

Thomas Hobbes

Nature hath made men so equal, in the faculties of the body, and mind; as that though there be found one man sometimes manifestly stronger in body, or of quicker mind than another; yet when all is reckoned together, the difference between man, and man, is not so considerable, as that one man can thereupon claim to himself any benefit, to which another may not pretend, as well as he. For as to the strength of body, the weakest has strength enough to kill the strongest, either by secret machination, or by confederacy with others, that are in the same danger with himself.

And as to the faculties of the mind, setting aside the arts grounded upon words, and especially that skill of proceeding upon general, and infallible rules, called science; which very few have, and but in few things; as being not a native faculty, born with us; nor attained, as prudence, while we look after somewhat else, I find yet a greater equality amongst men, than that of strength. For prudence, is but experience; which equal time, equally bestows on all men, in those things they equally apply themselves unto. That which may perhaps make such equality incredible, is but a vain conceit of one's own wisdom, which almost all men think they have in a greater degree, than the vulgar; that is, than all men but themselves, and a few others, whom by fame, or for concurring with themselves, they approve. For such is the nature of men, that howsoever they may acknowledge many others to be more witty, or more eloquent, or more learned; yet they will hardly believe there be many so wise as themselves; for they see their own wit at hand, and other men's at a distance. But this proveth rather that men are in that point equal, than unequal. For there is not ordinarily a greater sign of the equal distribution of any thing, than that every man is contented with his share.

• • •

From this equality of ability, ariseth equality of hope in the attaining of our ends. And therefore if any two men desire the same thing, which nevertheless they cannot both enjoy, they become enemies; and in the way to their end, which is principally their own conservation, and sometimes their delectation only, endeavour to destroy, or subdue one another. And from hence it comes to pass, that where an invader hath no more to fear, than another man's single power; if one plant, sow, build, or possess a convenient seat, others may probably be expected to come prepared with forces united, to dispossess, and deprive him, not only of the fruit of his labour, but also of his life, or liberty. And the invader again is in the like danger of another.

From Diffidence War And from this diffidence of one another, there is no way for any man to secure himself, so reasonable, as anticipation; that is, by force, or wiles, to master the persons of all men he can, so long, till he see no other power great enough to endanger him: and this is no more than his own conservation requireth, and is generally allowed. Also because there be some, that taking pleasure in contemplating their own power in the acts of conquest, which they pursue farther than their security requires; if others, that otherwise would be glad to be at ease within modest bounds, should not by invasion increase their power, they would not be able, long time, by standing only on their defence, to subsist. And by consequence, such augmentation of dominion over men being neces-

sary to a man's conservation, it ought to be allowed him.

Again, men have no pleasure, but on the contrary a great deal of grief, in keeping company, where there is no power able to over-awe them all. For every man looketh that his companion should value him, at the same rate he sets upon himself: and upon all signs of contempt, or undervaluing, naturally endeavours, as far as he dares, (which amongst them that have no common power to keep them in quiet, is far enough to make them destroy each other), to extort a greater value from his contemners, by damage; and from others, by the example.

So that in the nature of man, we find three principal causes of quarrel. First, competition; secondly, diffidence; thirdly, glory.

The first, maketh men invade for gain; the second, for safety; and the third, for reputation. The first use violence, to make themselves masters of other men's persons, wives, children, and cattle; the second, to defend them; the third, for trifles, as a word, a smile, a different opinion, and any other sign of undervalue, either direct in their persons, or by reflection in their kindred, their friends, their nation, their profession, or their name.

• • •

Hereby it is manifest, that during the time men live without a common power to keep them all in awe, they are in that condition which is called war; and such a war, as is of every man, against every man. For *war,* consisteth not in battle only, or the act of fighting; but in a tract of time, wherein the will to contend by battle is sufficiently known: and therefore the notion of *time,* is to be considered in the nature of war; as it is in the nature of weather. For as the nature of foul weather, lieth not in a shower or two of rain; but in an inclination thereto of many days together: so the nature of war, consisteth not in actual fighting; but in the known disposition thereto, during all the time there is no assurance to the contrary. All other time is *peace.*

• • •

Whatsoever therefore is consequent to a time of war, where every man is enemy to every man; the same is consequent to the time, wherein men live without other security, than what their own strength, and their own invention shall furnish them withal. In such condition, there is no place for industry; because the fruit thereof is uncertain: and consequently no culture of the earth; no navigation, nor use of the commodities that may be imported by sea; no commodious building; no instruments of moving, and removing, such things as require much force; no knowledge of the face of the earth; no account of time; no arts; no letters; no society; and which is worst of all, continual fear, and danger of violent death; and the life of man, solitary, poor, nasty, brutish, and short.

It may seem strange to some man, that has not well weighed these things; that nature should thus dissociate, and render men apt to invade, and destroy one another: and he may therefore, not trusting to this inference, made from the passions, desire perhaps to have the same confirmed by experience. Let him therefore consider with himself, when taking a journey, he arms himself, and seeks to go well accompanied; when going to sleep, he locks his doors; when even in his house he locks his chests; and this when he knows there be laws, and public officers, armed, to revenge all injuries shall be done him; what opinion he has of his fellow-subjects, when he rides armed; of his fellow citizens, when he locks his doors; and of his children, and servants, when he locks his chests. Does he not there as much accuse mankind by his actions, as I do by my words? But neither of us accuse man's nature in it. The desires, and other passions of man, are in themselves no sin. No more are the actions, that proceed from those passions, till they know a law that forbids them: which till laws be made they cannot know: nor can any law be made, till they have agreed upon the person that shall make it.

It may peradventure be thought, there was never such a time, nor condition of war as this; and I believe it was never generally so, over all the world: but there are many places, where they live so now. For the savage people in many places of America, except the government of small families, the concord whereof dependeth on natural lust, have no government at all; and live at this day in that brutish

manner, as I said before. Howsoever, it may be perceived what manner of life there would be, where there were no common power to fear, by the manner of life, which men that have formerly lived under a peaceful government, use to degenerate into, in a civil war.

But though there had never been any time, wherein particular men were in a condition of war one against another; yet in all times, kings, and persons of sovereign authority, because of their independency, are in continual jealousies, and in the state and posture of gladiators; having their weapons pointing, and their eyes fixed on one another; that is, their forts, garrisons, and guns upon the frontiers of their kingdoms; and continual spies upon their neighbours; which is a posture of war. But because they uphold thereby, the industry of their subjects; there does not follow from it, that misery, which accompanies the liberty of particular men.

. . . To this war of every man, against every man, this also is consequent; that nothing can be unjust. The notions of right and wrong, justice and injustice have there no place. Where there is no common power, there is no law: where no law, no injustice. Force, and fraud, are in war the two cardinal virtues. Justice, and injustice are none of the faculties neither of the body, nor mind. If they were, they might be in a man that were alone in the world, as well as his senses, and passions. They are qualities, that relate to men in society, not in solitude. It is consequent also to the same condition, that there be no propriety, no dominion, no *mine* and *thine* distinct; but only that to be every man's, that he can get: and for so long, as he can keep it. And thus much for the ill condition, which man by mere nature is actually placed in; though with a possibility to come out of it, consisting partly in the passions, partly in his reason.

• • •

The passions that incline men to peace, are fear of death; desire of such things as are necessary to commodious living; and a hope by their industry to obtain them. And reason suggesteth convenient articles of peace, upon which men may be drawn to agreement. These articles, are they, which otherwise are called the Laws of Nature: whereof I shall speak more particularly, in the two following chapters.

MUTUAL AID

Petr Kropotkin

The conception of struggle for existence as a factor of evolution, introduced into science by Darwin and Wallace, has permitted us to embrace an immensely-wide range of phenomena in one single generalization, which soon became the very basis of our philosophical, biological, and sociological speculations. An immense variety of facts:—adaptations of function and structure of organic beings to their surroundings; physiological and anatomical evolution; intellectual progress, and moral development itself, which we formerly used to explain by so many different causes, were embodied by Darwin in one general conception. We understood them as continued endeavours—as a struggle against adverse circumstances—for such a development of individuals, races, species and societies, as would result in the greatest possible fulness, variety, and intensity of life. It may be that at the outset Darwin himself was not fully aware of the generality of the factor which he first invoked for explaining one series only of facts relative to the accumulation of individual variations in incipient species. But he foresaw that the term which he was introducing into science would lose its philosophical and its only true meaning if it were to be used in its narrow sense only—that of a struggle between separate individuals for the sheer means of existence. And at the very beginning of his memorable work he insisted upon the term being taken in its "large and metaphorical sense including dependence of one being on another, and including (which is more important) not only the life of the individual, but success in leaving progeny."[1]

While he himself was chiefly using the term in its narrow sense for his own special purpose, he warned his followers against committing the error (which he seems once to have committed himself) of overrating its narrow meaning. In *The Descent of Man* he gave some powerful pages to illustrate its proper, wide sense. He pointed out how, in numberless animal societies, the struggle between separate individuals for the means of existence disappears, how *struggle* is replaced by *co-operation,* and how that substitution results in the development of intellectual and moral faculties which secure to the species the best conditions of survival. He intimated that in such cases the fittest are not the physically strongest, nor the cunningest, but those who learn to combine so as mutually to support each other, strong and weak alike, for the welfare of the community. "Those communities," he wrote, "which included the greatest number of the most sympathetic members would flourish best, and rear the greatest number of offspring" (2nd edit., p. 163). The term, which originated from the narrow Malthusian conception of competition between each and all, thus lost its narrowness in the mind of one who knew Nature.

⋯

As soon as we study animals—not in laboratories and museums only, but in the forest and the prairie, in the steppe and the mountains—we at once perceive that though there is an immense amount of warfare and extermination going on amidst various species, and especially amidst various classes of animals, there is, at the same time, as much, or perhaps even more, of mutual support, mutual aid, and mutual defence amidst animals belonging to the same species or, at least, to the same society. Sociability is as much a law of nature as mutual struggle. Of course it would be extremely difficult to estimate, however roughly, the relative numerical importance of both these series of facts. But if we resort to an indirect test, and ask Nature: "Who are the fittest: those who are continually at war with each other, or those who support one another?" we at once see that those animals which acquire habits of mutual aid are undoubtedly the

---

[1] *Origin of Species,* chap. iii.

fittest. They have more chances to survive, and they attain, in their respective classes, the highest development of intelligence and bodily organization. If the numberless facts which can be brought forward to support this view are taken into account, we may safely say that mutual aid is as much a law of animal life as mutual struggle, but that, as a factor of evolution, it most probably has a far greater importance, inasmuch as it favours the development of such habits and characters as insure the maintenance and further development of the species, together with the greatest amount of welfare and enjoyment of life for the individual, with the least waste of energy.

Of the scientific followers of Darwin, the first, as far as I know, who understood the full purport of Mutual Aid *as a law of Nature and the chief factor of evolution,* was a well-known Russian zoologist, the late Dean of the St. Petersburg University, Professor Kessler. He developed his ideas in an address which he delivered in January 1880, a few months before his death, at a Congress of Russian naturalists; but, like so many good things published in the Russian tongue only, that remarkable address remains almost entirely unknown.[2]

"As a zoologist of old standing," he felt bound to protest against the abuse of a term—the struggle for existence—borrowed from zoology, or, at least, against overrating its importance. Zoology, he said, and those sciences which deal with man, continually insist upon what they call the pitiless law of struggle for existence. But they forget the existence of another law which may be described as the law of mutual aid, which law, at least for the animals, is far more essential than the former. He pointed out how the need of leaving progeny necessarily brings animals together, and, "the more the individuals keep together, the more they mutually support each other, and the more are the chances of the species for surviving, as well as for making further progress in its intellectual development." "All classes of animals," he continued, "and especially the higher ones, practise mutual aid," and he illustrated the idea by examples borrowed from the life of the burying beetles and the social life of birds and some mammalia. The examples were few, as might have been expected in a short opening address, but the chief points were clearly stated; and, after mentioning that in the evolution of mankind mutual aid played a still more prominent part, Professor Kessler concluded as follows:—

I obviously do not deny the struggle for existence, but I maintain that the progressive development of the animal kingdom, and especially of mankind, is favoured much more by mutual support than by mutual struggle. . . . All organic beings have two essential needs: that of nutrition, and that of propagating the species. The former brings them to a struggle and to mutual extermination, while the needs of maintaining the species bring them to approach one another and to support one another. But I am inclined to think that in the evolution of the organic world—in the progressive modification of organic beings—mutual support among individuals plays a much more important part than their mutual struggle.[3]

• • •

---

[2] Leaving aside the pre-Darwinian writers, like Toussenel, Fée, and many others, several works containing many striking instances of mutual aid—chiefly, however, illustrating animal intelligence—were issued previously to that date. I may mention those of Houzeau, *Les facultés mentales des animaux,* 2 vols., Brussels, 1872; L. Büchner's *Aus dem Geistesleben der Thiere,* 2nd ed. in 1877; and Maximilian Perty's *Ueber das Seelenleben der Thiere,* Leipzig, 1876. Espinas published his most remarkable work, *Les Sociétés animales,* in 1877, and in that work he pointed out the importance of animal societies, and their bearing upon the preservation of species, and entered upon a most valuable discussion of the origin of societies. In fact, Espinas's book contains all that has been written since upon mutual aid, and many good things besides. If I nevertheless make a special mention of Kessler's address, it is because he raised mutual aid to the height of a law much more important in evolution than the law of mutual struggle. The same ideas were developed next year (in April 1881) by J. Lanessan in a lecture published in 1882 under this title: *La lutte pour l'existence et l'association pour la lutte.* G. Romanes's capital work, *Animal Intelligence,* was issued in 1882, and followed next year by the *Mental Evolution in Animals.* About the same time (1883), Büchner published another work, *Liebe und Liebes-Leben in der Thierwelt,* a second edition of which was issued in 1885. The idea, as seen, was in the air.

[3] *Memoirs (Trudy) of the St. Petersburg Society of Naturalists,* vol. xi. 1880.

Happily enough, competition is not the rule either in the animal world or in mankind. It is limited among animals to exceptional periods, and natural selection finds better fields for its activity. Better conditions are created by the *elimination of competition* by means of mutual aid and mutual support.[4] In the great struggle for life—for the greatest possible fulness and intensity of life with the least waste of energy—natural selection continually seeks out the ways precisely for avoiding competition as much as possible. The ants combine in nests and nations; they pile up their stores, they rear their cattle—and thus avoid competition; and natural selection picks out of the ants' family the species which know best how to avoid competition, with its unavoidably deleterious consequences. Most of our birds slowly move southwards as the winter comes, or gather in numberless societies and undertake long journeys—and thus avoid competition. Many rodents fall asleep when the time comes that competition should set in; while other rodents store food for the winter, and gather in large villages for obtaining the necessary protection when at work. The reindeer, when the lichens are dry in the interior of the continent, migrate towards the sea. Buffaloes cross an immense continent in order to find plenty of food. And the beavers, when they grow numerous on a river, divide into two parties, and go, the old ones down the river, and the young ones up the river—and avoid competition. And when animals can neither fall asleep, nor migrate, nor lay in stores, nor themselves grow their food like the ants, they do what the titmouse does, and what Wallace (*Darwinism,* ch. v.) has so charmingly described: they resort to new kinds of food—and thus, again, avoid competition.

"Don't compete!—competition is always injurious to the species, and you have plenty of resources to avoid it!" That is the *tendency* of nature, not always realized in full, but always present. That is the watchword which comes to us from the bush, the forest, the river, the ocean. "Therefore combine—practise mutual aid! That is the surest means for giving to each and to all the greatest safety, the best guarantee of existence and progress, bodily, intellectual, and moral." That is what Nature teaches us; and that is what all those animals which have attained the highest position in their respective classes have done. That is also what man—the most primitive man—has been doing; and that is why man has reached the position upon which we stand now, as we shall see in the subsequent chapters devoted to mutual aid in human societies.

The immense part played by mutual aid and mutual support in the evolution of the animal world has been briefly analyzed in the preceding chapters. We have now to cast a glance upon the part played by the same agencies in the evolution of mankind. We saw how few are the animal species which live an isolated life, and how numberless are those which live in societies, either for mutual defence, or for hunting and storing up food, or for rearing their offspring, or simply for enjoying life in common. We also saw that, though a good deal of warfare goes on between different classes of animals, or different species, or even different tribes of the same species, peace and mutual support are the rule within the tribe or the species; and that those species which best know how to combine, and to avoid competition, have the best chances of survival and of a further progressive development. They prosper, while the unsociable species decay.

It is evident that it would be quite contrary to all that we know of nature if men were an exception to so general a rule: if a creature so defenceless as man was at his beginnings should have found his protection and his way to progress, not in mutual support, like other animals, but in a reckless competition for personal advantages, with no regard to the interests of the species. To a mind accustomed to the idea of unity in nature, such a proposition appears utterly indefensible. And, yet, improbable and unphilosophical as it is, it has never found a lack of supporters. There always were writers who took a pes-

---

[4] "One of the most frequent modes in which Natural Selectino acts is, by adapting some individuals of a species to a somewhat different mode of life, whereby they are able to seize unappropriated places in Nature" (*Origin of Species,* p. 145)—in other words, to avoid competition.

simistic view of mankind. They knew it, more or less superficially, through their own limited experience; they knew of history what the annalists, always watchful of wars, cruelty, and oppression, told of it, and little more besides; and they concluded that mankind is nothing but a loose aggregation of beings, always ready to fight with each other, and only prevented from so doing by the intervention of some authority.

Hobbes took that position; and while some of his eighteenth-century followers endeavoured to prove that at no epoch of its existence—not even in its most primitive condition—mankind lived in a state of perpetual warfare; that men have been sociable even in "the state of nature," and that want of knowledge, rather than the natural bad inclinations of man, brought humanity to all the horrors of its early historical life,—his idea was, on the contrary, that the so-called "state of nature" was nothing but a permanent fight between individuals, accidentally huddled together by the mere caprice of their bestial existence. True, that science has made some progress since Hobbes's time, and that we have safer ground to stand upon than the speculations of Hobbes or Rousseau. But the Hobbesian philosophy has plenty of admirers still; and we have had of late quite a school of writers who, taking possession of Darwin's terminology rather than of his leading ideas, made of it an argument in favour of Hobbes's views upon primitive man, and even succeeded in giving them a scientific appearance. Huxley, as is known, took the lead of that school, and in a paper written in 1888 he represented primitive men as a sort of tigers or lions, deprived of all ethical conceptions, fighting out the struggle for existence to its bitter end, and living a life of "continual free fight"; to quote his own words—"beyond the limited and temporary relations of the family, the Hobbesian war of each against all was the normal state of existence."[5]

It has been remarked more than once that the chief error of Hobbes, and the eighteenth-century

philosophers as well, was to imagine that mankind began its life in the shape of small straggling families, something like the "limited and temporary" families of the bigger carnivores, while in reality it is now positively known that such as *not* the case. Of course, we have no direct evidence as to the modes of life of the first man-like beings. We are not yet settled even as to the time of their first appearance, geologists being inclined at present to see their traces in the pliocene, or even the miocene, deposits of the Tertiary period. But we have the indirect method which permits us to throw some light even upon that remote antiquity. A most careful investigation into the social institutions of the lowest races has been carried on during the last forty years, and it has revealed among the present institutions of primitive folk some traces of still older institutions which have long disappeared, but nevertheless left unmistakable traces of their previous existence. A whole science devoted to the embryology of human institutions has thus developed in the hands of Bachofen, MacLennan, Morgan, Edwin Tylor, Maine, Post, Kovalevsky, Lubbock, and many others. And that science has established beyond any doubt that mankind did *not* begin its life in the shape of small isolated families.

Far from being a primitive form of organization, the family is a very late product of human evolution. As far as we can go back in the palæo-ethnology of mankind, we find men living in societies—in tribes similar to those of the highest mammals; and an extremely slow and long evolution was required to bring these societies to the gentile, or clan organization, which, in its turn, had to undergo another, also very long evolution, before the first germs of family, polygamous or monogamous, could appear. Societies, bands, or tribes—not families—were thus the primitive form of organization of mankind and its earliest ancestors. That is what ethnology has come to after its painstaking researches. And in so doing it simply came to what might have been foreseen by the zoologist. None of the higher mammals, save a few carnivores and a few undoubtedly-decaying species of apes (orang-outans and gorillas), live in small families, isolat-

---

[5] *Nineteenth Century,* February 1888, p. 165.

edly straggling in the woods. All others live in societies. And Darwin so well understood that isolately-living apes never could have developed into man-like beings, that he was inclined to consider man as descended from some comparatively weak *but social species,* like the chimpanzee, rather than from some stronger but unsociable species, like the gorilla.[6] Zoology and palæo-ethnology are thus agreed in considering that the band, not the family, was the earliest form of social life. The first human societies simply were a further development of those societies which constitute the very essence of life of the higher animals.

---

[6] *The Descent of Man,* end of ch. ii. pp. 63 and 64 of the 2nd edition.

CHANGING HUMAN NATURE

John Dewey

Incidentally we have touched upon a most far-reaching problem: The alterability of human nature. Early reformers, following John Locke,* were inclined to minimize the significance of native activities, and to emphasize the possibilities inherent in practice and habit-acquisition. There was a political slant to this denial of the native and a priori, this magnifying of the accomplishments of acquired experience. It held out a prospect of continuous development, of improvement without end. Thus writers like Helvetius† made the idea of the complete malleability of a human nature which originally is wholly empty and passive, the basis for asserting

---

* John Locke (1632–1704) was a British philosopher who claimed that the human mind in its initial state was a *tabula rasa,* a blank tablet, and that our ideas are derived from experience (Eds.).
† Claude Adrien Helvétius (1715–1771) was a French Enlightenment philosopher who believed that human beings can be fundamentally changed through education and legislation (Eds.).

the omnipotence of education to shape human society, and the ground of proclaiming the infinite perfectibility of mankind.

Wary, experienced men of the world have always been sceptical of schemes of unlimited improvement. They tend to regard plans for social change with an eye of suspicion. They find in them evidences of the proneness of youth to illusion, or of incapacity on the part of those who have grown old to learn anything from experience. This type of conservative has thought to find in the doctrine of native instincts a scientific support for asserting the practical unalterability of human nature. Circumstances may change, but human nature remains from age to age the same. Heredity is more potent than environment, and human heredity is untouched by human intent. Effort for a serious alteration of human institutions is utopian. As things have been so they will be. The more they change the more they remain the same.

Curiously enough both parties rest their case upon just the factor which when it is analyzed weakens their respective conclusions. That is to say, the radical reformer rests his contention in behalf of easy and rapid change upon the psychology of habits, of institutions in shaping raw nature, and the conservative grounds his counter-assertion upon the psychology of instincts. As matter of fact, it is precisely custom which has greatest inertia, which is least susceptible of alteration; while instincts are more readily modifiable through use, most subject to educative direction. The conservative who begs scientific support from the psychology of instincts is the victim of an outgrown psychology which derived its notion of instinct from an exaggeration of the fixity and certainty of the operation of instincts among the lower animals. He is a victim of a popular zoology of the bird, bee and beaver, which was largely framed to the greater glory of God. He is ignorant that instincts in the animals are less infallible and definite than is supposed, and also that the human being differs from the lower animals in precisely the fact that his native activities lack the complex ready-made organization of the animals' original abilities.

But the short-cut revolutionist fails to realize the full force of the things about which he talks most, namely institutions as embodied habits. Any one with knowledge of the stability and force of habit will hesitate to propose or prophesy rapid and sweeping social changes. A social revolution may effect abrupt and deep alterations in external customs, in legal and political institutions. But the habits that are behind these institutions and that have, willy-nilly, been shaped by objective conditions, the habits of thought and feeling, are not so easily modified. They persist and insensibly assimilate to themselves the outer innovations—much as American judges nullify the intended changes of statute law by interpreting legislation in the light of common law. The force of lag in human life is enormous.

Actual social change is never so great as is apparent change. Ways of belief, of expectation, of judgment and attendant emotional dispositions of like and dislike, are not easily modified after they have once taken shape. Political and legal institutions may be altered, even abolished; but the bulk of popular thought which has been shaped to their pattern persists. This is why glowing predictions of the immediate coming of a social millennium terminate so uniformly in disappointment, which gives point to the standing suspicion of the cynical conservative about radical changes. Habits of thought outlive modifications in habits of overt action. The former are vital, the latter, without the sustaining life of the former, are muscular tricks. Consequently as a rule the moral effects of even great political revolutions, after a few years of outwardly conspicuous alterations, do not show themselves till after the lapse of years. A new generation must come upon the scene whose habits of mind have been formed under the new conditions. There is pith in the saying that important reforms cannot take real effect until after a number of influential persons have died. Where general and enduring moral changes do accompany an external revolution it is because appropriate habits of thought have previously been insensibly matured. The external change merely registers the removal of an external superficial barrier to the operation of existing intellectual tendencies.

Those who argue that social and moral reform is impossible on the ground that the Old Adam of human nature remains forever the same, attribute however to native activities the permanence and inertia that in truth belong only to acquired customs. To Aristotle slavery was rooted in aboriginal human nature. Native distinctions of quality exist such that some persons are by nature gifted with power to plan, command and supervise, and others possess merely capacity to obey and execute. Hence slavery is natural and inevitable. There is error in supposing that because domestic and chattel slavery has been legally abolished, therefore slavery as conceived by Aristotle has disappeared. But matters have at least progressed to a point where it is clear that slavery is a social state not a psychological necessity. Nevertheless the worldlywise Aristotles of today assert that the institutions of war and the present wage-system are so grounded in immutable human nature that effort to change them is foolish.

Like Greek slavery or feudal serfdom, war and the existing economic regime are social patterns woven out of the stuff of instinctive activities. Native human nature supplies the raw materials, but custom furnishes the machinery and the designs. War would not be possible without anger, pugnacity, rivalry, self-display, and such like native tendencies. Activity inheres in them and will persist under every condition of life. To imagine they can be eradicated is like supposing that society can go on without eating and without union of the sexes. But to fancy that they must eventuate in war is as if a savage were to believe that because he uses fibers having fixed natural properties in order to weave baskets, therefore his immemorial tribal patterns are also natural necessities and immutable forms.

From a humane standpoint our study of history is still all too primitive. It is possible to study a multitude of histories, and yet permit history, the record of the transitions and transformations of human activities, to escape us. Taking history in separate doses of this country and that, we take it as a succession of isolated finalities, each one in due season giving way to another, as supernumeraries succeed one another in a march across the stage. We thus miss the fact of history and also its lesson; the diversity of institutional forms and customs which the same human nature may produce and employ. An infantile logic, now happily expelled from physical science, taught that opium put men to sleep because of its dormitive potency. We follow the same logic in social matters when we believe that war exists because of bellicose instincts; or that a particular economic regime is necessary because of acquisitive and competitive impulses which must find expression.

Pugnacity and fear are no more native than are pity and sympathy. The important thing morally is the way these native tendencies interact, for their interaction may give a chemical transformation not a mechanical combination. Similarly, no social institution stands alone as a product of one dominant force. It is a phenomenon or function of a multitude of social factors in their mutual inhibitions and reinforcements. If we follow an infantile logic we shall reduplicate the unity of result in an assumption of unity of force behind it—as men once did with natural events, employing teleology as an exhibition of causal efficiency. We thus take the same social custom twice over: once as an existing fact and then as an original force which produced the fact, and utter sage platitudes about the unalterable workings of human nature or of race. As we account for war by pugnacity, for the capitalistic system by the necessity of an incentive of gain to stir ambition and effort, so we account for Greece by power of esthetic observation, Rome by administrative ability, the middle ages by interest in religion and so on. We have constructed an elaborate political zoology as mythological and not nearly as poetic as the other zoology of phœnixes, griffins and unicorns. Native racial spirit, the spirit of the people or of the time, national destiny are familiar figures in this social zoo. As names for effects, for existing customs, they are sometimes useful. As names for explanatory forces they work havoc with intelligence.

An immense debt is due William James* for the

* William James (1842–1910), the brother of the U.S. novelist Henry James, was a major U.S. philosopher and psychological theorist. He was one of the initiators of the movement in philosophy known as "pragmatism," a movement which John Dewey further developed (Eds.).

mere title of his essay: The Moral Equivalents of War. It reveals with a flash of light the true psychology. Clans, tribes, races, cities, empires, nations, states have made war. The argument that this fact proves an ineradicable belligerent instinct which makes war forever inevitable is much more respectable than many arguments about the immutability of this and that social tradition. For it has the weight of a certain empirical generality back of it. Yet the suggestion of an *equivalent* for war calls attention to the medley of impulses which are casually bunched together under the caption of belligerent impulse; and it calls attention to the fact that the elements of this medley may be woven together into many differing types of activity, some of which may function the native impulses in much better ways than war has ever done.

Pugnacity, rivalry, vainglory, love of booty, fear, suspicion, anger, desire for freedom from the conventions and restrictions of peace, love of power and hatred of oppression, opportunity for novel displays, love of home and soil, attachment to one's people and to the altar and the hearth, courage, loyalty, opportunity to make a name, money or a career, affection, piety to ancestors and ancestral gods—all of these things and many more make up the war-like force. To suppose there is some one unchanging native force which generates war is as naïve as the usual assumption that our enemy is actuated solely by the meaner of the tendencies named and we only by the nobler. In earlier days there was something more than a verbal connection between pugnacity and fighting; anger and fear moved promptly through the fists. But between a loosely organized pugilism and the highly organized warfare of today there intervenes a long economic, scientific and political history. Social conditions rather than an old and unchangeable Adam have generated wars; the ineradicable impulses that are utilized in them are capable of being drafted into many other channels. The century that has witnessed the triumph of the scientific doctrine of the convertibility of natural energies ought not to balk at the lesser miracle of social equivalences and substitutes.

It is likely that if Mr. James had witnessed the world war, he would have modified his mode of treatment. So many new transformations entered into the war, that the war seems to prove that though an equivalent has not been found for war, the psychological forces traditionally associated with it have already undergone profound changes. We may take the Iliad as a classic expression of war's traditional psychology as well as the source of the literary tradition regarding its motives and glories. But where are Helen, Hector and Achilles in modern warfare? The activities that evoke and incorporate a war are no longer personal love, love of glory, or the soldier's love of his own privately amassed booty, but are of a collective, prosaic political and economic nature.

Universal conscription, the general mobilization of all agricultural and industrial forces of the folk not engaged in the trenches, the application of every conceivable scientific and mechanical device, the mass movements of soldiery regulated from a common center by a depersonalized general staff: these factors relegate the traditional psychological apparatus of war to a now remote antiquity. The motives once appealed to are out of date; they do not now induce war. They simply are played upon after war has been brought into existence in order to keep the common soldiers keyed up to their task. The more horrible a depersonalized scientific mass war becomes, the more necessary it is to find universal ideal motives to justify it. Love of Helen of Troy has become a burning love for all humanity, and hatred of the foe symbolizes a hatred of all the unrighteousness and injustice and oppression which he embodies. The more prosaic the actual causes, the more necessary is it to find glowingly sublime motives.

Such considerations hardly prove that war is to be abolished at some future date. But they destroy that argument for its necessary continuance which is based on the immutability of specified forces in original human nature. Already the forces that once caused wars have found other outlets for themselves; while new provocations, based on new economic and political conditions, have come into being. War is thus seen to be a function of social institutions, not of what is natively fixed in human constitution. The last great war has not, it must be confessed, made the problem of finding social equivalents simpler and easier. It is now naïve to attribute war to specific isolable human impulses for which separate channels of expression may be found, while the rest of life is left to go on about the same. A general social reorganization is needed which will redistribute forces, immunize, divert and nullify. Hinton was doubtless right when he wrote that the only way to abolish war was to make peace heroic. It now appears that the heroic emotions are not anything which may be specialized in a sideline, so that the war-impulses may find a sublimation in special practices and occupations. They have to get an outlet in all the tasks of peace.

The argument for the abiding necessity of war turns out, accordingly, to have this much value. It makes us wisely suspicious of all cheap and easy equivalencies. It convinces us of the folly of striving to eliminate war by agencies which leave other institutions of society pretty much unchanged. History does not prove the inevitability of war, but it does prove that customs and institutions which organize native powers into certain patterns in politics and economics will also generate the war-pattern. The problem of war is difficult because it is serious. It is none other than the wider problem of the effective moralizing or humanizing of native impulses in times of peace.

The case of economic institutions is as suggestive as that of war. The present system is indeed much more recent and more local than is the institution of war. But no system has ever as yet existed which did not in some form involve the exploitation of some human beings for the advantage of others. And it is argued that this trait is unassailable because it flows from the inherent, immutable qualities of human nature. It is argued, for example, that economic inferiorities and disabilities are incidents of an institution of private property which flows from an original proprietary instinct; it is contended they spring from a competitive struggle for wealth which in turn flows from the absolute need of profit as an inducement to industry. The pleas are worth examination for the light they throw upon the place of impulses in organized conduct.

No unprejudiced observer will lightly deny the

existence of an original tendency to assimilate objects and events to the self, to make them part of the "me." We may even admit that the "me" cannot exist without the "mine." The self gets solidity and form through an appropriation of things which identifies them with whatever we call myself. Even a workman in a modern factory where depersonalization is extreme gets to have "his" machine and is perturbed at a change. Possession shapes and consolidates the "I" of philosophers. "I own, therefore I am" expresses a truer psychology than the Cartesian "I think, therefore I am." A man's deeds are imputed to him as their owner, not merely as their creator. That he cannot disown them when the moment of their occurrence passes is the root of responsibility, moral as well as legal.

But these same considerations evince the versatility of possessive activity. My worldly goods, my good name, my friends, my honor and shame all depend upon a possessive tendency. The need for appropriation has had to be satisfied; but only a calloused imagination fancies that the institution of private property as it exists A.D. 1921 is the sole or the indispensable means of its realization. Every gallant life is an experiment in different ways of fulfilling it. It expends itself in predatory aggression, in forming friendships, in seeking fame, in literary creation, in scientific production. In the face of this elasticity, it requires an arrogant ignorance to take the existing complex system of stocks and bonds, of wills and inheritance, a system supported at every point by manifold legal and political arrangements, and treat it as the sole legitimate and baptized child of an instinct of appropriation. Sometimes, even now, a man most accentuates the fact of ownership when he gives something away; use, consumption, is the normal end of possession. We can conceive a state of things in which the proprietary impulse would get full satisfaction by holding goods as mine in just the degree in which they were visibly administered for a benefit in which a corporate community shared.

Does the case stand otherwise with the other psychological principle appealed to, namely, the need of an incentive of personal profit to keep men engaged in useful work? We need not content ourselves with pointing out the elasticity of the idea of gain, and possible equivalences for pecuniary gain, and the possibility of a state of affairs in which only those things would be counted personal gains which profit a group. It will advance the discussion if we instead subject to analysis the whole conception of incentive and motive.

There is doubtless some sense in saying that every conscious act has an incentive or motive. But this sense is as truistic as that of the not dissimilar saying that every event has a cause. Neither statement throws any light on any particular occurrence. It is at most a maxim which advises us to search for some other fact with which the one in question may be correlated. Those who attempt to defend the necessity of existing economic institutions as manifestations of human nature convert this suggestion of a concrete inquiry into a generalized truth and hence into a definitive falsity. They take the saying to mean that nobody would do anything, or at least anything of use to others, without a prospect of some tangible reward. And beneath this false proposition there is another assumption still more monstrous, namely, that man exists naturally in a state of rest so that he requires some external force to get him into action.

The idea of a thing intrinsically wholly inert in the sense of absolutely passive is expelled from physics and has taken refuge in the psychology of current economics. In truth man acts anyway, he can't help acting. In every fundamental sense it is false that a man requires a motive to make him do something. To a healthy man inaction is the greatest of woes. Any one who observes children knows that while periods of rest are natural, laziness is an acquired vice—or virtue. While a man is awake he will do something, if only to build castles in the air. If we like the norm of words we may say that a man eats only because he is "moved" by hunger. The statement is nevertheless mere tautology. For what does hunger mean except that one of the things which man does naturally, instinctively, is to search for food—that his activity naturally turns that way? Hunger primarily names an act or active process not a motive to an act. It is an act if we take it grossly, like a babe's blind hunt for the mother's breast; it is an activity if we take it minutely as a chemico-phys-iological occurrence.

The whole concept of motives is in truth ex-trapsychological. It is an outcome of the attempt of men to influence human action, first that of others, then of a man to influence his own behavior. No sensible person thinks of attributing the acts of an animal or an idiot to a motive. We call a biting dog ugly, but we don't look for his motive in biting. If however we were able to direct the dog's action by inducing him to reflect upon his acts, we should at once become interested in the dog's motives for act-ing as he does, and should endeavor to get him in-terested in the same subject. It is absurd to ask what induces a man to activity generally speaking. He is an active being and that is all there is to be said on that score. But when we want to get him to act in this specific way rather than in that, when we want to direct his activity that is to say in a specified channel, then the question of motive is pertinent. A motive is then that element in the total complex of a man's activity which, if it can be sufficiently stim-ulated, will result in an act having specified conse-quences. And part of the process of intensifying (or reducing) certain elements in the total activity and thus regulating actual consequence is to impute these elements to a person as his actuating motives.

A child naturally grabs food. But he does it in our presence. His manner is socially displeasing and we attribute to his act, up to this time wholly innocent, the motive of greed or selfishness. Greediness sim-ply means the quality of his act as socially observed and disapproved. But by attributing it to him as his motive for acting in the disapproved way, we in-duce him to refrain. We analyze his total act and call his attention to an obnoxious element in its out-come. A child with equal spontaneity, or thought-lessness, gives way to others. We point out to him with approval that he acted considerately, gener-ously. And this quality of action when noted and en-couraged becomes a reinforcing stimulus of that factor which will induce similar acts in the future. An element in an act viewed as a tendency to pro-duce such and such consequences is a motive. A motive does not exist prior to an act and produce it. It is an act *plus* a judgment upon some element of it,

the judgment being made in the light of the conse-quences of the act.

At first, as was said, others characterize an act with favorable or condign qualities which they im-pute to an agent's character. They react in this fash-ion in order to encourage him in future acts of the same sort, or in order to dissuade him—in short to build or destroy a habit. This characterization is part of the technique of influencing the development of character and conduct. It is a refinement of the or-dinary reactions of praise and blame. After a time and to some extent, a person teaches himself to think of the results of acting in this way or that be-fore he acts. He recalls that if he acts this way or that some observer, real or imaginary, will attribute to him noble or mean disposition, virtuous or vicious motive. Thus he learns to influence his own con-duct. An inchoate activity taken in this forward-looking reference to results, especially results of approbation and condemnation, constitutes a mo-tive. Instead then of saying that a man requires a motive in order to induce him to act, we should say that when a man is going to act he needs to know *what* he is going to do—what the quality of his act is in terms of consequences to follow. In order to act properly he needs to view his act as others view it; namely, as a manifestation of a character or will which is good or bad according as it is bent upon specific things which are desirable or obnoxious. There is no call to furnish a man with incentives to activity in general. But there is every need to induce him to guide his own action by an intelligent per-ception of its results. For in the long run this is the most effective way of influencing activity to take this desirable direction rather than that objection-able one.

A motive in short is simply an impulse viewed as a constituent in a habit, a factor in a disposition. In general its meaning is simple. But in fact motives are as numerous as are original impulsive activities multiplied by the diversified consequences they produce as they operate under diverse conditions. How then does it come about that current economic psychology has so tremendously oversimplified the situation? Why does it recognize but one type of motive, that which concerns personal gain. Of course part of the answer is to be found in the natural tendency in all sciences toward a substitution of artificial conceptual simplifications for the tangles of concrete empirical facts. But the significant part of the answer has to do with the social conditions under which work is done, conditions which are such as to put an unnatural emphasis upon the prospect of reward. It exemplifies again our leading proposition that social customs are not direct and necessary consequences of specific impulses, but that social institutions and expectations shape and crystallize impulses into dominant habits.

The social peculiarity which explains the emphasis put upon profit as an inducement to productive serviceable work stands out in high relief in the identification of work with labor. For labor means in economic theory something painful, something so onerously disagreeable or "costly" that every individual avoids it if he can, and engages in it only because of the promise of an overbalancing gain. Thus the question we are invited to consider is what the social condition is which makes productive work uninteresting and toilsome. Why is the psychology of the industrialist so different from that of inventor, explorer, artist, sportsman, scientific investigator, physician, teacher? For the latter we do not assert that activity is such a burdensome sacrifice that it is engaged in only because men are bribed to act by hope of reward or are coerced by fear of loss.

The social conditions under which "labor" is undertaken have become so uncongenial to human nature that it is not undertaken because of intrinsic meaning. It is carried on under conditions which render it immediately irksome. The alleged need of an incentive to stir men out of quiescent inertness is the need of an incentive powerful enough to overcome contrary stimuli which proceed from the social conditions. Circumstances of productive service now shear away direct satisfaction from those engaging in it. A real and important fact is thus contained in current economic psychology, but it is a fact about existing industrial conditions and not a fact about native, original activity.

It is "natural" for activity to be agreeable. It tends to find fulfillment, and finding an outlet is itself satisfactory, for it marks partial accomplishment. If productive activity has become so inherently unsatisfactory that men have to be artifically induced to engage in it, this fact is ample proof that the conditions under which work is carried on balk the complex of activities instead of promoting them, irritate and frustrate natural tendencies instead of carrying them forward to fruition. Work then becomes labor, the consequence of some aboriginal curse which forces man to do what he would not do if he could help it, the outcome of some original sin which excluded man from a paradise in which desire was satisfied without industry, compelling him to pay for the means of livelihood with the sweat of his brow. From which it follows naturally that Paradise Regained means the accumulation of investments such that a man can live upon their return without labor. There is, we repeat, too much truth in this picture. But it is not a truth concerning original human nature and activity. It concerns the form human impulses have taken under the influence of a specific social environment. If there are difficulties in the way of social alteration—as there certainly are—they do not lie in an original aversion of human nature to serviceable action, but in the historic conditions which have differentiated the work of the laborer for wage from that of the artist, adventurer, sportsman, soldier, administrator and speculator.

THERE IS NO HUMAN NATURE

Jean-Paul Sartre

I should like on this occasion to defend existentialism against some charges which have been brought against it.

First, it has been charged with inviting people to remain in a kind of desperate quietism because, since no solutions are possible, we should have to consider action in this world as quite impossible. We should then end up in a philosophy of contemplation; and since contemplation is a luxury, we come in the end to a bourgeois philosophy. The communists in particular have made these charges.

On the other hand, we have been charged with dwelling on human degradation, with pointing up everywhere the sordid, shady, and slimy, and neglecting the gracious and beautiful, the bright side of human nature; for example, according to Mlle. Mercier, a Catholic critic, with forgetting the smile of the child. Both sides charge us with having ignored human solidarity, with considering man as an isolated being. The communists say that the main reason for this is that we take pure subjectivity, the *Cartesian I think,* as our starting point; in other words, the moment in which man becomes fully aware of what it means to him to be an isolated being; as a result, we are unable to return to a state of solidarity with the men who are not ourselves, a state which we can never reach in the *cogito.**

From the Christian standpoint, we are charged with denying the reality and seriousness of human undertakings, since, if we reject God's commandments and the eternal verities, there no longer remains anything but pure caprice, with everyone permitted to do as he pleases and incapable, from his own point of view, of condemning the points of view and acts of others.

I shall try today to answer these different charges. Many people are going to be surprised at what is said here about humanism, We shall try to see in what sense it is to be understood. In any case, what can be said from the very beginning is that by existentialism we mean a doctrine which makes human life possible and, in addition, declares that every truth and every action implies a human setting and a human subjectivity.

As is generally known, the basic charge against us is that we put the emphasis on the dark side of human life. Someone recently told me of a lady who, when she let slip a vulgar word in a moment of irritation, excused herself by saying, "I guess I'm becoming an existentialist." Consequently, existentialism is regarded as something ugly; that is why we are said to be naturalists; and if we are, it is rather surprising that in this day and age we cause so much more alarm and scandal than does naturalism, properly so called. The kind of person who can take in his stride such a novel as Zola's* *The Earth* is disgusted as soon as he starts reading an existentialist novel; the kind of person who is resigned to the wisdom of the ages—which is pretty sad—finds us even sadder. Yet, what can be more disillusioning than saying "true charity begins at home" or "a scoundrel will always return evil for good"?

We know the commonplace remarks made when this subject comes up, remarks which always add up to the same thing: we shouldn't struggle against the powers-that-be; we shouldn't resist authority; we shouldn't try to rise above our station; any action which doesn't conform to authority is romantic; any effort not based on past experience is doomed to failure; experience shows that man's bent is always toward trouble, that there must be a strong hand to hold him in check, if not, there will be anarchy. There are still people who go on mumbling these melancholy old saws, the people who say, "It's only human!" whenever a more or less repugnant act is pointed out to them, the people who glut themselves on *chansons réalistes;* these are the people who accuse existentialism of being too gloomy, and to such an extent that I wonder whether they are complaining about it, not for its pessimism, but much rather its optimism. Can it be that what really scares them in the doctrine I shall try to present here is that it leaves to man a possibility of choice? To answer this question, we must re-examine it on a strictly philosophical plane. What is meant by the term *existentialism?*

Most people who use the word would be rather embarrassed if they had to explain it, since, now

---

Cogito, literally, is "I think" in Latin. The reference is to the Cartesian "I think," mentioned earlier in the paragraph, which is René Descartes's epistemological starting point. See the selection by Descartes in Section Two of Chapter 5 (Eds.).

---

* Émile Zola (1840–1902) was a major French novelist who originated the naturalist movement in literature (Eds.).

that the word is all the rage, even the work of a musician or painter is being called existentialist. A gossip columnist in *Clartés* signs himself *The Existentialist,* so that by this time the word has been so stretched and has taken on so broad a meaning, that it no longer means anything at all. It seems that for want of an advance-guard doctrine analogous to surrealism, the kind of people who are eager for scandal and flurry turn to this philosophy which in other respects does not at all serve their purposes in this sphere.

Actually, it is the least scandalous, the most austere of doctrines. It is intended strictly for specialists and philosophers. Yet it can be defined easily. What complicates matters is that there are two kinds of existentialist; first, those who are Christian, among whom I would include Jaspers and Gabriel Marcel, both Catholic; and on the other hand the atheistic existentialists, among whom I class Heidegger, and then the French existentialists and myself. What they have in common is that they think that existence precedes essence, or, if you prefer, that subjectivity must be the starting point.

Just what does that mean? Let us consider some object that is manufactured, for example, a book or a paper-cutter: here is an object which has been made by an artisan whose inspiration came from a concept. He referred to the concept of what a paper-cutter is and likewise to a known method of production, which is part of the concept, something which is, by and large, a routine. Thus, the paper-cutter is at once an object produced in a certain way and, on the other hand, one having a specific use; and one can not postulate a man who produces a paper-cutter but does not know what it is used for. Therefore, let us say that, for the paper-cutter, essence—that is, the ensemble of both the production routines and the properties which enable it to be both produced and defined—precedes existence. Thus, the presence of the paper-cutter or book in front of me is determined. Therefore, we have here a technical view of the world whereby it can be said that production precedes existence.

When we conceive God as the Creator, He is generally thought of as a superior sort of artisan.

Whatever doctrine we may be considering, whether one like that of Descartes or that of Leibnitz, we always grant that will more or less follows understanding or, at the very least, accompanies it, and that when God creates He knows exactly what He is creating. Thus, the concept of man in the mind of God is comparable to the concept of paper-cutter in the mind of the manufacturer, and, following certain techniques and a conception, God produces man, just as the artisan, following a definition and a technique, makes a paper-cutter. Thus, the individual man is the realization of a certain concept in the divine intelligence.

In the eighteenth century, the atheism of the *philosophes** discarded the idea of God, but not so much for the notion that essence precedes existence. To a certain extent, this idea is found everywhere; we find it in Diderot, in Voltaire, and even in Kant. Man has a human nature; this human nature, which is the concept of the human, is found in all men, which means that each man is a particular example of a universal concept, man. In Kant, the result of this universality is that the wild-man, the natural man, as well as the bourgeois, are circumscribed by the same definition and have the same basic qualities. Thus, here too the essence of man precedes the historical existence that we find in nature.

Atheistic existentialism, which I represent, is more coherent. It states that if God does not exist, there is at least one being in whom existence precedes essence, a being who exists before he can be defined by any concept, and that this being is man, or, as Heidegger[†] says, human reality. What is meant here by saying that existence precedes essence? It means that, first of all, man exists, turns

---

* The term refers to the French Enlightenment philosophers of the eighteenth century, including Voltaire (1694–1778), Jean Jacques Rousseau (1712–1778), and Denis Diderot (1713–1784). These philosophers extolled reason against religion and superstition and generally advocated social and political reform (Eds.).

[†] Martin Heidegger (1889–1976) was a German existentialist philosopher whose major work *Being and Time* greatly influenced Sartre's philosophical development (Eds.).

up, appears on the scene, and, only afterwards, defines himself. If man, as the existentialist conceives him, is indefinable, it is because at first he is nothing. Only afterward will he be something, and he himself will have made what he will be. Thus, there is no human nature, since there is no God to conceive it. Not only is man what he conceives himself to be, but he is also only what he wills himself to be after this thrust toward existence.

Man is nothing else but what he makes of himself. Such is the first principle of existentialism. It is also what is called subjectivity, the name we are labeled with when charges are brought against us. But what do we mean by this, if not that man has a greater dignity than a stone or table? For we mean that man first exists, that is, that man first of all is the being who hurls himself toward a future and who is conscious of imagining himself as being in the future. Man is at the start a plan which is aware of itself, rather than a patch of moss, a piece of garbage, or a cauliflower; nothing exists prior to this plan; there is nothing in heaven; man will be what he will have planned to be. Not what he will want to be. Because by the word "will" we generally mean a conscious decision, which is subsequent to what we have already made of ourselves. I may want to belong to a political party, write a book, get married; but all that is only a manifestation of an earlier, more spontaneous choice that is called "will." But if existence really does precede essence, man is responsible for what he is. Thus, existentialism's first move is to make every man aware of what he is and to make the full responsibility of his existence rest on him. And when we say that a man is responsible for himself, we do not only mean that he is responsible for his own individuality, but that he is responsible for all men.

The word subjectivism has two meanings, and our opponents play on the two. Subjectivism means, on the one hand, that an individual chooses and makes himself; and, on the other, that it is impossible for man to transcend human subjectivity. The second of these is the essential meaning of existentialism. When we say that man chooses his own self, we mean that every one of us does likewise; but we also mean by that that in making this

choice he also chooses all men. In fact, in creating the man that we want to be, there is not a single one of our acts which does not at the same time create an image of man as we think he ought to be. To choose to be this or that is to affirm at the same time the value of what we choose, because we can never choose evil. We always choose the good, and nothing can be good for us without being good for all.

If, on the other hand, existence precedes essence, and if we grant that we exist and fashion our image at one and the same time, the image is valid for everybody and for our whole age. Thus, our responsibility is much greater than we might have supposed, because it involves all mankind. If I am a workingman and choose to join a Christian trade-union rather than be a communist, and if by being a member I want to show that the best thing for man is resignation, that the kingdom of man is not of this world, I am not only involving my own case—I want to be resigned for everyone. As a result, my action has involved all humanity. To take a more individual matter, if I want to marry, to have children; even if this marriage depends solely on my own circumstances or passion or wish, I am involving all humanity in monogamy and not merely myself. Therefore, I am responsible for myself and for everyone else. I am creating a certain image of man of my own choosing. In choosing myself, I choose man.

This helps us understand what the actual content is of such rather grandiloquent words as anguish, forlornness, despair. As you will see, it's all quite simple.

First, what is meant by anguish? The existentialists say at once that man is anguish. What that means is this: the man who involves himself and who realizes that he is not only the person he chooses to be, but also a lawmaker who is, at the same time, choosing all mankind as well as himself, can not help escape the feeling of his total and deep responsibility. Of course, there are many people who are not anxious; but we claim that they are hiding their anxiety, that they are fleeing from it. Certainly, many people believe that when they do something, they themselves are the only ones involved, and when someone says to them, "What if everyone acted that way?" they shrug their shoulders and answer, "Everyone doesn't act that way." But really, one should always ask himself, "What would happen if everybody looked at things that way?" There is no escaping this disturbing thought except by a kind of double-dealing. A man who lies and makes excuses for himself by saying "not everybody does that," is someone with an uneasy conscience, because the act of lying implies that a universal value is conferred upon the lie.

Anguish is evident even when it conceals itself. This is the anguish that Kierkegaard* called the anguish of Abraham. You know the story: an angel has ordered Abraham to sacrifice his son; if it really were an angel who has come and said, "You are Abraham, you shall sacrifice your son," everything would be all right. But everyone might first wonder, "Is it really an angel, and am I really Abraham? What proof do I have?"

There was a madwoman who had hallucinations; someone used to speak to her on the telephone and give her orders. Her doctor asked her, "Who is it who talks to you?" She answered, "He says it's God." What proof did she really have that it was God? If an angel comes to me, what proof is there that it's an angel? And if I hear voices, what proof is there that they come from heaven and not from hell, or from the subconscious, or a pathological condition? What proves that they are addressed to me? What proof is there that I have been appointed to impose my choice and my conception of man on humanity? I'll never find any proof or sign to convince me of that. If a voice addresses me, it is always for me to decide that this is the angel's voice; if I consider that such an act is a good one, it is I who will choose to say that it is good rather than bad.

Now, I'm not being singled out as an Abraham, and yet at every moment I'm obliged to perform exemplary acts. For every man, everything happens as if all mankind had its eyes fixed on him and were guiding itself by what he does. And every man

ought to say to himself, "Am I really the kind of man who has the right to act in such a way that humanity might guide itself by my actions?" And if he does not say that to himself, he is masking his anguish.

There is no question here of the kind of anguish which would lead to quietism, to inaction. It is a matter of a simple sort of anguish that anybody who has had responsibilities is familiar with. For example, when a military officer takes the responsibility for an attack and sends a certain number of men to death, he chooses to do so, and in the main he alone makes the choice. Doubtless, orders come from above, but they are too broad; he interprets them, and on this interpretation depend the lives of ten or fourteen or twenty men. In making a decision he can not help having a certain anguish. All leaders know this anguish. That doesn't keep them from acting; on the contrary, it is the very condition of their action. For it implies that they envisage a number of possibilities, and when they choose one, they realize that it has value only because it is chosen. We shall see that this kind of anguish, which is the kind that existentialism describes, is explained, in addition, by a direct responsibility to the other men whom it involves. It is not a curtain separating us from action, but is part of action itself.

When we speak of forlornness, a term Heidegger was fond of, we mean only that God did not exist and that we have to face all the consequences of this. The existentialist is strongly opposed to a certain kind of secular ethics which would like to abolish God with the least possible expense. About 1880, some French teachers tried to set up a secular ethics which went something like this: God is a useless and costly hypothesis; we are discarding it; but, meanwhile, in order for there to be an ethics, a society, a civilization, it is essential that certain values be taken seriously and that they be considered as having an *a priori** existence. It must be obligatory, *a priori,* to be honest, not to lie, not to beat your

---

* Soren Kierkegaard (1813–1855) was a Danish existentialist philosopher and religious thinker (Eds.).

* *a priori* is a Latin phrase meaning, literally, "from what comes before." In philosophy, it refers to something which precedes or is independent of sensory experience. Thus, what is *a priori* is true, valid, or exists by necessity (Eds.).

wife, to have children, etc., etc. So we're going to try a little device which will make it possible to show that values exist all the same, inscribed in a heaven of ideas, though otherwise God does not exist. In other words—and this, I believe, is the tendency of everything called reformism in France—nothing will be changed if God does not exist. We shall find ourselves with the same norms of honesty, progress, and humanism, and we shall have made of God an outdated hypothesis which will peacefully die off by itself.

The existentialist, on the contrary, thinks it very distressing that God does not exist, because all possibility of finding values in a heaven of ideas disappears along with Him; there can no longer be an *a priori* Good, since there is no infinite and perfect consciousness to think it. Nowhere is it written that the Good exists, that we must be honest, that we must not lie; because the fact is we are on a plane where there are only men. Dostoievsky said, "If God didn't exist, everything would be possible." That is the very starting point of existentialism. Indeed, everything is permissible if God does not exist, and as a result man is forlorn, because neither within him nor without does he find anything to cling to. He can't start making excuses for himself.

If existence really does precede essence, there is no explaining things away by reference to a fixed and given human nature. In other words, there is no determinism, man is free, man is freedom. On the other hand, if God does not exist, we find no values or commands to turn to which legitimize our conduct. So, in the bright realm of values, we have no excuse behind us, nor justification before us. We are alone, with no excuses.

That is the idea I shall try to convey when I say that man is condemned to be free. Condemned, because he did not create himself, yet, in other respects is free; because, once thrown into the world, he is responsible for everything he does. The existentialist does not believe in the power of passion. He will never agree that a sweeping passion is a ravaging torrent which fatally leads a man to certain acts and is therefore an excuse. He thinks that man is responsible for his passion.

The existentialist does not think that man is going to help himself by finding in the world some omen by which to orient himself. Because he thinks that man will interpret the omen to suit himself. Therefore, he thinks that man, with no support and no aid, is condemned every moment to invent man. Ponge, in a very fine article, has said, "Man is the future of man." That's exactly it. But if it is taken to mean that this future is recorded in heaven, that God sees it, then it is false, because it would really no longer be a future. If it is taken to mean that, whatever a man may be, there is a future to be forged, a virgin future before him, then this remark is sound. But then we are forlorn.

To give you an example which will enable you to understand forlornness better, I shall cite the case of one of my students who came to see me under the following circumstances: his father was on bad terms with his mother, and, moreover, was inclined to be a collaborationist; his older brother had been killed in the German offensive of 1940, and the young man, with somewhat immature but generous feelings, wanted to avenge him. His mother lived alone with him, very much upset by the half-treason of her husband and the death of her older son; the boy was her only consolation.

The boy was faced with the choice of leaving for England and joining the Free French Forces—that is, leaving his mother behind—or remaining with his mother and helping her to carry on. He was fully aware that the woman lived only for him and that his going-off—and perhaps his death—would plunge her into despair. He was also aware that every act that he did for his mother's sake was a sure thing, in the sense that it was helping her to carry on, whereas every effort he made toward going off and fighting was an uncertain move which might run aground and prove completely useless; for example, on his way to England he might, while passing through Spain, be detained indefinitely in a Spanish camp; he might reach England or Algiers and be stuck in an office at a desk job. As a result, he was faced with two very different kinds of action: one, concrete, immediate, but concerning only one individual; the other concerned an incomparably vaster group, a national collectivity, but for that very reason was dubious, and might be interrupted en route. And, at the same time, he was wavering between two kinds of ethics. On the one hand, an ethics of sympathy, of personal devotion; on the other, a broader ethics, but one whose efficacy was more dubious. He had to choose between the two.

Who could help him choose? Christian doctrine? No. Christian doctrine says, "Be charitable, love your neighbor, take the more rugged path, etc., etc." But which is the more rugged path? Whom should he love as a brother? The fighting man or his mother? Which does the greater good, the vague act of fighting in a group, or the concrete one of helping a particular human being to go on living? Who can decide *a priori?* Nobody. No book of ethics can tell him. The Kantian ethics says, "Never treat any person as a means, but as an end." Very well, if I stay with my mother, I'll treat her as an end and not as a means; but by virtue of this very fact, I'm running the risk of treating the people around me who are fighting, as means; and, conversely, if I go to join those who are fighting, I'll be treating them as an end, and, by doing that, I run the risk of treating my mother as a means.

If values are vague, and if they are always too broad for the concrete and specific case that we are considering, the only thing left for us is to trust our instincts. That's what this young man tried to do; and when I saw him, he said, "In the end, feeling is what counts. I ought to choose whichever pushes me in one direction. If I feel that I love my mother enough to sacrifice everything else for her—my desire for vengeance, for action, for adventure—then I'll stay with her. If, on the contrary, I feel that my love for my mother isn't enough, I'll leave."

But how is the value of a feeling determined? What gives his feeling for his mother value? Precisely the fact that he remained with her. I may say that I like so-and-so well enough to sacrifice a certain amount of money for him, but I may say so only if I've done it. I may say "I love my mother well enough to remain with her" if I have remained with her. The only way to determine the value of this affection is, precisely, to perform an act which con-

firms and defines. But, since I require this affection to justify my act, I find myself caught in a vicious circle.

On the other hand, Gide has well said that a mock feeling and a true feeling are almost indistinguishable; to decide that I love my mother and will remain with her, or to remain with her by putting on an act, amount somewhat to the same thing. In other words, the feeling is formed by the acts one performs; so, I can not refer to it in order to act upon it. Which means that I can neither seek within myself the true condition that will impel me to act, nor apply to a system of ethics for concepts which will permit me to act. You will say, "At least, he did go to a teacher for advice." But if you seek advice from a priest, for example, you have chosen this priest; you already knew, more or less, just about what advice he was going to give you. In other words, choosing your adviser is involving yourself. The proof of this is that if you are a Christian, you will say, "Consult a priest." But some priests are collaborating, some are just marking time, some are resisting. Which to choose? If the young man chooses a priest who is resisting or collaborating, he has already decided on the kind of advice he's going to get. Therefore, in coming to see me he knew the answer I was going to give him, and I had only one answer to give: "You're free, choose, that is, invent." No general ethics can show you what is to be done; there are no omens in the world. The Catholics will reply, "But there are." Granted—but, in any case, I myself choose the meaning they have.

When I was a prisoner, I knew a rather remarkable young man who was a Jesuit. He had entered the Jesuit order in the following way: he had had a number of very bad breaks; in childhood, his father died, leaving him in poverty, and he was a scholarship student at a religious institution where he was constantly made to feel that he was being kept out of charity; then, he failed to get any of the honors and distinctions that children like; later on, at about eighteen, he bungled a love affair; finally, at twenty-two, he failed in military training, a childish enough matter, but it was the last straw.

This young fellow might well have felt that he

had botched everything. It was a sign of something, but of what? He might have taken refuge in bitterness or despair. But he very wisely looked upon all this as a sign that he was not made for secular triumphs, and that only the triumphs of religion, holiness, and faith were open to him. He saw the hand of God in all this, and so he entered the order. Who can help seeing that he alone decided what the sign meant?

Some other interpretation might have been drawn from this series of setbacks; for example, that he might have done better to turn carpenter or revolutionist. Therefore, he is fully responsible for the interpretation. Forlornness implies that we ourselves choose our being. Forlornness and anguish go together.

As for despair, the term has a very simple meaning. It means that we shall confine ourselves to reckoning only with what depends upon our will, or on the ensemble of probabilities which make our action possible. When we want something, we always have to reckon with probabilities. I may be counting on the arrival of a friend. The friend is coming by rail or street-car; this supposes that the train will arrive on schedule, or that the street-car will not jump the track. I am left in the realm of possibility; but possibilities are to be reckoned with only to the point where my action comports with the ensemble of these possibilities, and no further. The moment the possibilities I am considering are not rigorously involved by my action, I ought to disengage myself from them, because no God, no scheme, can adapt the world and its possibilities to my will. When Descartes said, "Conquer your self rather than the world," he meant essentially the same thing.

The Marxists to whom I have spoken reply, "You can rely on the support of others in your action, which obviously has certain limits because you're not going to live forever. That means: rely on both what others are doing elsewhere to help you, in China, in Russia, and what they will do later on, after your death, to carry on the action and lead it to its fulfillment, which will be the revolution. You even *have* to rely upon that, otherwise you're im-

moral." I reply at once that I will always rely on fellow-fighters insofar as these comrades are involved with me in a common struggle, in the unity of a party or a group in which I can more or less make my weight felt; that is, one whose ranks I am in as a fighter and whose movements I am aware of at every moment. In such a situation, relying on the unity and will of the party is exactly like counting on the fact that the train will arrive on time or that the car won't jump the track. But, given that man is free and that there is no human nature for me to depend on, I can not count on men whom I do not know by relying on human goodness or man's concern for the good of society. I don't know what will become of the Russian revolution; I may make an example of it to the extent that at the present time it is apparent that the proletariat plays a part in Russia that it plays in no other nation. But I can't swear that this will inevitably lead to a triumph of the proletariat. I've got to limit myself to what I see.

Given that men are free and that tomorrow they will freely decide what man will be, I can not be sure that, after my death, fellow-fighters will carry on my work to bring it to its maximum perfection. Tomorrow, after my death, some men may decide to set up Fascism, and the others may be cowardly and muddled enough to let them do it. Fascism will then be the human reality, so much the worse for us.

Actually, things will be as man will have decided they are to be. Does that mean that I should abandon myself to quietism? No. First, I should involve myself; then, act on the old saw, "Nothing ventured, nothing gained." Nor does it mean that I shouldn't belong to a party, but rather that I shall have no illusions and shall do what I can. For example, suppose I ask myself, "Will socialization, as such, ever come about?" I know nothing about it. All I know is that I'm going to do everything in my power to bring it about. Beyond that, I can't count on anything. Quietism is the attitude of people who say, "Let others do what I can't do." The doctrine I am presenting is the very opposite of quietism, since it declares, "There is no reality except in action." Moreover, it goes further, since it adds, "Man is nothing else than his plan; he exists only to the extent that he fulfills himself; he is therefore nothing else than the ensemble of his acts, nothing else than his life."

According to this, we can understand why our doctrine horrifies certain people. Because often the only way they can bear their wretchedness is to think, "Circumstances have been against me. What I've been and done doesn't show my true worth. To be sure, I've had no great love, no great friendship, but that's because I haven't met a man or woman who was worthy. The books I've written haven't been very good beause I haven't had the proper leisure. I haven't had children to devote myself to because I didn't find a man with whom I could have spent my life. So there remains within me, unused and quite viable, a host of propensities, inclinations, possibilities, that one wouldn't guess from the mere series of things I've done."

Now, for the existentialist there is really no love other than one which manifests itself in a person's being in love. There is no genius other than one which is expressed in works of art; the genius of Proust* is the sum of Proust's works; the genius of Racine is his series of tragedies. Outside of that, there is nothing. Why say that Racine could have written another tragedy, when he didn't write it? A man is involved in life, leaves his impress on it, and outside of that there is nothing. To be sure, this may seem a harsh thought to someone whose life hasn't been a success. But, on the other hand, it prompts people to understand that reality alone is what counts, that dreams, expectations, and hopes warrant no more than to define a man as a disappointed dream, as miscarried hopes, as vain expectations. In other words, to define him negatively and not positively. However, when we say, "You are nothing else than your life," that does not imply that the artist will be judged solely on the basis of his works of art; a thousand other things will contribute toward summing him up. What we mean is that a man is nothing else than a series of undertakings, that he is the sum, the organization, the ensemble of the relationships which make up these undertakings.

• • •

From these few reflections it is evident that nothing is more unjust than the objections that have been raised against us. Existentialism is nothing else than an attempt to draw all the consequences of a coherent atheistic position. It isn't trying to plunge man into despair at all. But if one calls every attitude of unbelief despair, like the Christians, then the word is not being used in its original sense. Existentialism isn't so atheistic that it wears itself out showing that God doesn't exist. Rather, it declares that even if God did exist, that would change nothing. There you've got our point of view. Not that we believe that God exists, but we think that the problem of His existence is not the issue. In this sense existentialism is optimistic, a doctrine of action, and it is plain dishonesty for Christians to make no distinction between their own despair and ours and then to call us despairing.

A ZEN VIEW

Shin'Ichi Hisamatsu

It is a characteristic of man that the more he becomes involved in complexity, the more he longs for simplicity; the simpler his life becomes, the more he longs for complexity; the busier he becomes, the stronger is his desire for leisure; the more leisure he has, the more boredom he feels; the more his concerns, the more he feels the allure of unconcern, the more his unconcern, the more he suffers from vacuousness; the more tumultuous his life, the more he seeks quietude; the more placid his life, the lonelier he becomes and the more he quests for liveliness.

It is a characteristic feature of modern civilization that everything is becoming more and more

---

* Marcel Proust (1871–1922) was a French novelist most famous for his *Remembrance of Things Past* (Eds.).

complicated, that the degree of busyness increases day by day, and that the mind becomes too overburdened with concerns. Consequently, there is an increasingly strong desire on the part of people to seek simplicity, leisure, freedom from concern, and quietude in order to offset the common trend of modern life.

Recently, in the United States, which has assumed the lead in modern civilization, not only ordinary buildings but even churches have changed their architectural style from a heavy, complex, and intricate style to a straight-lined, simple, smart, modern style. That this tendency toward modernization in architecture is sweeping over not only America but also the older cities of Western Europe and, indeed, even Japan, is not simply because of practical utility, but also undoubtedly because it responds to a natural desire of modern man, who finds himself further and further enmeshed in the extreme complexities of modern life. More specifically, the fact that houses in America are gradually becoming one-storied, simple, and clean-cut, influenced by Japanese architecture, is probably because of the desire to escape complexity and to find serenity. Further, that intricate and involved painting and sculpture have given way to forms which are unconventionally informal, de-formed, or abstract may also be considered to signify a liberation from troublesome complexity, elaborateness, and formality. So, too, the change from overly heavy colors to monotone colors in the manner of monochrome *sumi-e* paintings, thus making for a beauty of simplicity, one of the special characteristics of modern art, may also be considered another aspect of this same liberation.

In the same vein, it is inevitable that modern man, thrown more and more into a whirl of pressing concerns, should seek and, in fact, greedily demand leisure time, a phenomenon which has found its expression in the current term, "leisure boom." Indeed, all of the following recent phenomena—the deep interest in the extremely primitive art of uncivilized people, the popularity of folk songs and of children's songs, the appeal generated by the rustic colloquialisms of the local dialects in contradistinc-

tion to the standard language of the cities, the attraction of the free and open world of nature (the mountains, the fields, the oceans) as opposed to the uncomfortably close and crowded urban centers, the marked tendency in recent art toward naïve artlessness, simplicity, and rustic beauty—can probably be similarly attributed to a longing for artlessness by modern men, who are suffering from the excessive contrivances and artificiality of modern civilization.

Oneness and manyness—or unity and diversity—are mutually indispensable moments within the basic structure of man. They must necessarily be one with each other and not two. Oneness without manyness is mere vacuity without content; manyness without oneness is mere segmentation without unity. Here lies the great blind spot in the mode of modern civilization. The so-called diseases of civilization—uprootedness, confusion, prostration, instability, bewilderment, skepticism, neurosis, weariness of life, etc.—are largely due to this blind spot. The greater the multiplicity, the stronger in direct proportion must be the oneness or unity. When, on the contrary, the actual situation is a relation of an inverse proportion, then man has no other alternative than to seek to escape into a oneness or simplicity alienated from manyness, whether by turning to the primitive or by simply negatively withdrawing from manyness. This, however, is no more than a superficial solution of the problem of segmented dissociation. Herein may also be found one reason that today, although anachronistic to our time, premodern, noncivilized cults and superstitions still command a following. A drowning man will grasp even at a straw, although objectively considered it is clearly untrustworthy. The attempts by contemporary man to escape from civilization or to return to the primitive, to the noncivilized and the nonmodern, may be viewed as natural but superficial countermeasures to try to compensate for the lack of unity in modern civilization. To turn from such superficial countermeasures to a genuine solution, there is no other way than by establishing within the multiplicity that oneness or unity which is appropriate to the multiplicity.

If the direction of the development of civilization is toward more and more multiplicity, more and more specialization, then no fixed, static oneness or unity will ever do. The oneness or unity must be sufficiently alive and flexible to respond freely and appropriately to the growing multiplicity. It is not enough that the oneness, while not being alienated from multiplicity, merely serve as the static basis within multiplicity. It must be a dynamic and creative oneness or unity which, as the root-origin of multiplicity, produces multiplicity from itself without limit; a oneness that can eternally produce multiplicity out of itself freely and yet remain unbound by what is produced; a unity which while producing multiplicity yet remains within multiplicity and can accord with that multiplicity appropriate to the particular time and place. Only then can the multiplicity, while unlimitedly taking its rise from such a oneness, never lose that oneness, and does the oneness, while producing the multiplicity, ever remain within and unalienated from the multiplicity it produces.

Multiplicity, in such a case, continuing to contain within itself, even as multiplicity, a oneness or unity, will thus not become disjointedly fragmented. Accordingly, there will be no need to escape from multiplicity to a hollow unity which is alienated from multiplicity. On the other hand, since the oneness even as oneness is the inexhaustible source of, and is never separated from, multiplicity, there will be no need, because of any feeling of ennui or because of having fallen into a mood of emptiness or loneliness, to seek for a liveliness within a manyness alienated from oneness. The true oneness is a oneness in manyness; the true manyness is a manyness in oneness. There is a Zen expression, "Within Nothingness [there is contained] an inexhaustible storehouse." Only when such a relation obtains between oneness and manyness, the two elements of the basic structure of man, will man, however much he may diversify toward multiplicity, be free from disjointed fragmentation and, at the same time, in his oneness never suffer from emptiness or loneliness. Then can he be at once a unity and a multiplicity without hindrance,

free from all pressure and self-contented, the true Subject eternally giving rise to civilization. Man as such a Subject is Man in his True mode of being. Precisely this Man is the human image which is the inner demand, whether or not he is conscious of it, of modern man, standing as he does right in the midst of a civilization which continues to diversify more and more as it develops. Such a human image is the Original-Subject which, even as it freely and unlimitedly creates civilization and is ever present appropriate to the time and place within the civilization which has been created, is always completely emancipated and never bound by the civilization.

This Original-Subject, which must awaken to itself and form itself right in the midst of modern civilization, is no other than the Zen image of man. It is this Man that the author in his previous writings has called "Oriental Nothingness," "Active Nothingness," and "Formless-Self." It is this Man which Hui-neng,* the Sixth Patriarch, already very early in the history of Chinese Zen, spoke of as "The Self-Nature which, unmoved in its base, is able to produce all things," and, again, as "Not a single thing to be obtained and, precisely thereby, able to give rise to all things." It is the same image of Man which is referred to when Yung-chia, a contemporary of Hui-neng, says that: "Walking is also Zen, sitting is also Zen. Whether talking or silent, whether in motion or rest, the Subject is composed." The same Man is meant by Huang-po when, in his *The Pivotal Point of Mind-to-Mind Transmission,* he declared: "Just the one who the whole day, though not apart from things, does not suffer from the world of things, is called the Free Man."

In that it infinitely creates civilization and forms history, this human image may be said to be humanistic. In that—even while it is immanent in, and the root-origin of, what is created or formed—it is not attached to or bound by, but is always free from,

---

* Hui Neng's (638–713) sutra can be found in Section Three of Chapter 1 (Eds.).

the created, it may be said to have the religiousness of Lin-chi's "Self-awakened and Self-sustaining [Man]," that is, the religiousness of being the truly Emancipated-Subject. Only when they come to be this Emancipated-Subject can the subjects—spoken of in the *Avatam-saka* teaching as the subject which "returns to and takes rise from Itself," and in the Pure Land teaching as the subject which in its "going aspect" actualizes nirvana and in its "returning aspect" "plays freely amid the thick woods of what formerly constituted self-agonizing illusions"—lend themselves to a modern application. Of course, by modern I do not mean anything temporal, that is, of any particular generation or period of history. Rather, I mean a modern Self-formation-actualization of the Eternal-Subject which is the root-origin of, and beyond all, historical periods. In the *Vimalakirtinirdesa,* this is expressed as "taking form in response to the thing confronted." Here there can be established a newer and higher humanistic religion which, on the one hand, does not degenerate into the modern type of anthropocentric, autonomous humanism which has forgotten self-criticism and, on the other, does not retrogress back toward a premodern, theocentric theonomy completely unawakened to human autonomy.

The realization of such a new, yet basic and ultimate, human image will enable us to do two things. First, it will enable us to turn away from the superficial attempt to cure the disease of modern civilization through an anachronistic, simple-minded, world-renouncing mode of escape to a naïve, premodern oneness, which is in estrangement from civilization. Secondly, it will enable us to make a more proper attempt at a radical cure of the modern predicament through the Self-awakening of that oneness which, contrary to being in estrangement from civilization, accords with, and is the source and base of, civilization. Such an image of man entertained by Zen will also sweep away every internal and external criticism or misunderstanding of Buddhism which takes it to be world-weary, world-renouncing, and removed from reality, longing for some ideal world in a sphere other than the historical world of time and space. It will, at the same time, be worthy of being presented to the Occident as a new Oriental prescription for the disease of modern civilization. For the recent surging of Zen interest in the West in such areas as psychology, the arts, the handicrafts, invention, philosophy, and religion is not accidental, but derives from an inner necessity of modern civilization.

QUESTIONS FOR DISCUSSION

1. Is there an innate human nature? If there is, what is it? If you believe that there is no human nature, then how do you explain why people act the way they do? Defend your position with respect to these questions and refer to at least two of the writers in this section.

2. Imagine Mencius, Hsün Tzu, Thomas Hobbes, and Petr Kropotkin sitting in a room together. They are discussing the question: Is human nature good or evil? What would they say to each other?

3. Can human nature be changed? If so, in what directions would you like to see it changed? What are the social and political implications of your position? In your answer refer to John Dewey and at least one of the other authors reprinted in this section.

4. Compare Sartre's claim that "existence precedes essence" with Hisamatsu's idea of an "original-subject" which is also an "active nothingness."

GENDER NATURE

That the human species is divided into male and female is hardly problematic. The problem arises when we ask what it means to be male or female. The most immediate response is that males and females have different anatomies. But this does not in itself explain the wide range of social phenomena encompassed by these terms. As Simone de Beauvoir observes: "to go for a walk with one's eyes open is enough to demonstrate that humanity is divided into two classes of individuals whose clothes, faces, bodies, smiles, gaits, interests, and occupations are manifestly different." The question, then, cannot be simply answered by referring to sex. Or rather the question needs to be reformulated more precisely: Why are there two social classes built upon the foundation of physical sexual difference? We might then distinguish between sex (in the physical sense) and gender, which is a social and psychological category; in other words, we can distinguish between male and female as physical beings and the social-psychological characteristics of *masculinity* and *femininity.*

Gender differences refer to a difference in social roles and social identity. There are at least two fundamental kinds of explanations that can be given to account for gender difference. The first is that these differences are somehow *natural,* which is why the question of gender is placed in this chapter on human nature. The second is that these differences are socially constructed, which is to say that those with different sexual anatomies are, for reasons extraneous to sex as such, given positions within the social order and are socialized to identify themselves with those positions. The implication of the first position is that gender difference is innate and, therefore, unchangeable in its general forms. The implication of the second position is that such differences can be significantly altered or perhaps eliminated altogether.

We begin this section with two Islamic views concerning women's nature. The first is that of the eleventh-century Islamic philosopher Abu Hamid Muhammad al-Ghazali (1058–1111). Al-Ghazali was born in what is now northeastern Iran, was for a time a university professor in Baghdad, but eventually left the academic life to become a Sufi mystic. Many of his philosophical works are concerned with the possibility of metaphysical knowledge. In this selection he attempts to characterize the role of women within the Islamic social order. He develops several major claims through a set of anecdotes and aphorisms: that a woman should be pious, a good helpmate, and obedient to her husband, that men must be merciful to their wives, since they "are prisoners in the hands of men," and that many of the evils in the world are caused by women.

This last characterization is examined by Fatima Mernissi, who teaches sociology at the University of Mohammed V in Rabat, Morocco. She argues that there are, in fact, two theories concerning women within Islam—an explicit theory which sees man as aggressive and woman as passive, and an implicit and unconscious theory which she derives from the writings of al-Ghazali. In the implicit theory women are not inherently inferior but must be controlled precisely because of their potential equality and power. Their power, according to this implicit theory, lies in their sexual ability to attract men and weaken their will, thus distracting men from their higher spiritual and intellectual pursuits. Women are, therefore, always a destructive force, and so their sexuality must be veiled and regulated. Thus, argues Mernissi, "the entire Muslim social structure can be seen as an attack on, and a defense against, the disruptive power of female sexuality." One of the implications she draws from this analysis is that, for Islam, humanity is constituted only by males, women being perceived as an external threat.

The next selection in this section is by Simone de Beauvoir, a well-known feminist and French existentialist philosopher, novelist, and playwright. *The*

Second Sex, from which the selection is taken, was first published in France in 1949. As one of the first major works to document women's biological, social, political, and sexual oppression, it anticipated today's feminist movement and is generally considered one of its most important theoretical works. De Beauvoir's main claim in the selection is that whereas man is defined in his own terms, woman is defined by her role in relation to man. The problem here is not only one of semantic asymmetry, but it also reflects a fundamental inequality between men and women. Hence, a women is always the "other," always "the second sex."

Since de Beauvoir's *The Second Sex,* many contemporary feminists have explored how the two genders, masculine and feminine, are socially constructed to the advantage of the male. The "masculine" is constructed from early childhood as active, independent, and self-disciplined, whereas the "feminine" is constructed as passive, dependent, and impulsive. The male is socialized to become the primary breadwinner, the female, to think of herself as wife and mother. The justification of this state of affairs is what the socialist feminist philosopher Ann Ferguson calls the "Natural Complement theory." The theory tends to permeate our entire culture and claims that each sex has certain inherent traits and capacities which are in themselves incomplete and which complement one another. Ferguson offers a thoroughgoing critique of the Natural Complement theory, citing wide cross-cultural variation in what is considered masculine and feminine and providing a historical materialist explanation for the construction of gender roles. It follows from her analysis—and in fact from all social constructionist views—that gender could as a social category be abolished, that an androgynous society in which males and females are no longer specifically "masculine" or "feminine" is possible. Ferguson further argues that androgyny is not only possible but desirable, that it is, in fact, an ideal for human development. It would lay the basis for a freer, better integrated human being who is more capable of genuine love relationships.

In an interesting footnote Ferguson suggests that, although there are no necessary sexual implications of androgyny, an androgynous society would tend to have bisexuality rather than heterosexuality as the norm. Is there any reason to give either homosexuality or heterosexuality a higher moral status? Specifically, is there any reason to claim, as is often done in this culture, that homosexuality is immoral? This claim is usually tied to another: that homosexuality goes against the laws of nature, that it is immoral. It is precisely these two claims which are challenged by Richard Mohr, who has written extensively about gay issues and who is a philosopher at the University of Illinois. Mohr notes that those who claim that homosexuality is immoral often claim that it violates the natural function of the genitals. But does that or any other organ need have only one function? Is there anything unnatural, for example, in using the mouth to lick stamps or, for that matter, to have sex? Mohr also suggests that homosexuality is more a discovery than it is a choice, in which case it would make no sense to hold the homosexual morally responsible for his or her homosexuality.

WOMEN'S NATURE:
TWO ISLAMIC VIEWS

THE PROPER ROLE FOR WOMEN

Abu Hamid Muhammad al-Ghazali

The Apostle, God bless him, stated that the best and most blessed of women are those who are most prolific in child-bearing, fairest in countenance, and least costly in dowry. He also stated, "In so far as you are able, seek a free woman in marriage; they are the purest."

The Prince of the Believers 'Umar (ibn al-Khaṭṭāb) said, "Take refuge in God from the evils caused by women, and beware (even) of the most pious of them." This means, let not (even) your own wife receive praise.

The author of this book declares that any man who desires to be sound in his religion and sound as master of his house ought not to care about nobility of birth and beauty of countenance; for a pious (wife) is the best and most beautiful.

• • •

ANECDOTE

Abū Saʿīd related that in the time of the Children of Israel there was a good man who had a pious, judicious and tactful wife. An inspiration came down to the Prophet of the Age saying, "Inform that good man that We have predestined him to spend one half of his life in poverty and one half in wealth. Let him choose now whether the poverty shall be during his youth or during his old age." The young man on hearing this went to his wife and said, "O wife, this is the command which has come down from God on High. How do you suggest that I choose?" "What is your choice?" she asked. "Come," he replied, "let us choose the poverty during our youth, so that when hardship comes we may have strength to endure it. (Moreover), when we grow old we shall need something to eat if we are to be free from cares and capable of properly obeying (God's commands)." Thereupon his wife said, "O husband, if we are poor during our youth, we shall be unable to obey God's (commands) properly then; and thereafter, when we shall have thrown to the winds the prime of our life and grown weak, how shall we perform the duties involved in obeying (God)? Let us therefore choose the wealth now, so that we may during our youth have strength both to obey God's commands and to practise charity." "Your opinion is the right one," said the husband; "let us act accordingly." Then (another) inspiration came down to the Prophet of the Age, (and the message for that man and his wife was this): "Now that you are striving to obey Us and that your intention is good, I who am the Sustainer of all life will cause you to pass (straight) to wealth. Continue striving to obey My commands, and of whatever I give you part for alms so that both this world and the next may be yours."

The author of this book declares that he has related his story to help you understand that a good helpmate will do (you) good in this world's and the next world's affairs alike.

TRADITION

Ibn 'Abbās, God be pleased with him, has related that the Prophet went into the House of Umm Salamah, God be pleased with her, and saw that she had performed the morning prayer and was reciting God's epithets. "O Umm Salamah," he asked her, "why do not you join in the congregational prayer and go to the Friday service? Why do not you make the pilgrimage and go to fight for God against the infidels? Why do not you finish memorizing the Qur'ān?" "O Apostle of God," she replied, "all these are men's activities." Then the Prophet, peace be upon him, stated: "For women too there are activities of equal worth." "Which are they, God's Apostle?" she respectfully inquired. He answered: "Whenever a woman who fulfils God's requirements and is obedient to her husband takes hold of a spinning-wheel and turns it, this is as if she were reciting God's epithets, joining in congregational prayer, and fighting against infidels."

As long as (a woman) spins at the wheel, sins vanish from her. Spinning at the wheel is women's bridge and stronghold. Three things' sounds reach to the throne of God on High: (i) the sound of bows being drawn by warriors fighting infidels; (ii) the sound of the pens of scholars; (iii) the sound of spinning by virtuous women.

APHORISM

Aḥnaf ibn Qays has said: "If you want women to like you, satisfy them sexually and treat them tenderly."

'Umar (ibn al-Khaṭṭāb), peace be upon him, has said: "Do not speak to women of love, because their hearts will be corrupted. For women are like meat left in a desert; God's (help) is needed to preserve them."

•   •   •

TRADITION

Salmān al-Fārsī, God be pleased with him, has related that the Prophet, God bless him, was (once) asked, "Which women are best?" He answered, "Those who obey you, whatever be your commands." Then he was asked, "Which are the worst?" He answered, "Those who avoid pleasing their husbands."

APHORISM

A teacher was teaching girls how to write. A sage passed by and said, "This teacher is teaching wickedness to the wicked."

APHORISM

An intelligent woman was asked, "What are the virtues of women?" ("And what," she rejoined, "are the faults of men?") "Niggardliness and cowardice," (they answered). ("These," she said,) "are among the virtues of women."

APHORISM

A sage wished (that) his short wife (might have been) tall. People asked him, "Why did not you marry a wife of full stature?" "A woman is an evil thing," he answered, "and the less (there is) of an evil thing the better."

APHORISM

A sage has said, "Men who marry women get four sorts of wife: (i) the wife who belongs wholly to her husband; (ii) the wife who belongs half to her husband; (iii) the wife who belongs one-third to her husband; (iv) the wife who is her husband's enemy. The wife who belongs wholly to her husband will be a woman who is a virgin. The wife who belongs half to her husband will be [a woman whose former husband has died but has no children]. The wife who belongs one-third to her husband will be a woman whose former husband has died but who has children by the first husband. The wife who is her husband's enemy will be a (divorced) woman whose former husband is still living. Therefore the best wives are virgins.

•   •   •

EXCURSUS DESCRIBING THE TYPES OF WOMEN

The race of women consists of ten species, and the character of each (of these) corresponds and is related to the distinctive quality of one of the animals. One (species) resembles the pig, another the ape, another the dog, another the snake, another the mule, another the scorpion, another the mouse, another the pigeon, another the fox, and another the sheep. The woman who resembles the pig in character knows full well how to eat, break (crockery), and cram her stomach, and she does not mind where she comes and goes. She does not trouble herself with religion, prayer, and fasting, and she never thinks about death, resurrection, reward and punishment, about (God's) promises, threats, commands and prohibitions, or about (His) pleasure and displeasure. She is heedless of her husband's rights and careless about nurturing and disciplining her children and teaching them knowledge of the Qur'ān. She always wears filthy clothes, and an unpleasant smell issues from her. The woman who has the character and peculiarities of the ape concerns herself with clothes of many colours—green, red, and yellow, with trinkets and jewels—pearls or rubies, and with gold and silver. She boasts of these to her relatives, but maybe her secret (self) is not the same as her (outward) appearance. The woman who has the character of the dog is one who, whenever her husband speaks, jumps at his face and shouts at him and snarls at him. If her husband's purse is full of silver and gold and the household is blessed with prosperity, she says to him, "You are the whole world to me. May God on High never let me see evil befall you, and may my own death come before yours!" But if her husband becomes insolvent, she insults and chides him, saying "You are a poor wretch," and everything is the opposite of what it was before. The woman who has the character of the mule is like a restive mule which will not stay in one place. She is stubborn and goes her own way, and is conceited. The woman who has the peculiarities of the scorpion is always visiting the houses of the neighbours, gossiping and collecting gossip; she does her utmost to cause enmity and hatred among them and to stir up strife. Like the scorpion she stings wherever she goes. She is not afraid to be one of those concerning whom the Prophet, blessings upon him, stated: "No instigator of strife will enter Paradise," meaning (in Persian) "No tale-teller will go to heaven." The woman who has the character of the mouse is a thief who steals from her husband's purse (and hides what she has stolen) in the houses of the neighbours. She steals barley, wheat, rice, and miscellaneous supplies and gives away yarn for spinning. The woman who has the peculiarities of the pigeon flits about all day long and is never still. She says to her husband, "Where are you going and whence have you come?" and she does not speak affectionately. The woman who has the peculiarities of the fox lets her husband out of the house and eats

everything there is (in it), then does not stir and pretends to be sick, and when her husband comes in, starts a quarrel and says, "You left me (alone in the house) sick." The woman who has the peculiarities of the sheep is blessed like the sheep, in which everything is useful. The good woman is the same. She is useful to her husband and to (his) family and the neighbours, compassionate with her own kinsfolk, affectionate towards the (members of the) household and towards her children, and obedient to Almighty God. The pious, veiled woman is a blessing from God on High, and few men (are able to find) a pious, veiled woman (for a wife).

• • •

(ANECDOTE)

It is related that there once lived at Bukhārā a water-carrier, who for thirty years had been carrying water to the house of a certain goldsmith. Now the goldsmith had an exceedingly beautiful and virtuous wife. One day when the water-carrier had brought the water, he saw her standing in the courtyard. Suddenly he walked up, took her hand, and squeezed it. Then he departed. When the goldsmith returned home, his wife said to hm, "Tell me truly. Did you do something (in the bazaar) today which has displeased God on High? What was it?" He replied, "I did nothing, except that at lunch-time I made a bracelet for a certain woman, and she put it on her arm. The woman was intensely beautiful, and I took her hand and squeezed it." "God is most great!" exclaimed his wife; "that is what you did, and this is the reason why the water-carrier who has been coming to this house for thirty years and has never played false with us today at lunch-time squeezed my hand (too)." "I have repented," her husband said. On the following day the water-carrier came. He grovelled on the ground before her and said, "Absolve me. It was the devil who led me astray yesterday." "It was not your fault," she replied, "because my husband the master of the house (who was at the shop) had committed the same offence; (God repaid him in kind, here in this lower world)."

A wife must be contented with her husband, whether he be capable of much or of little. She must follow the examples of the blessed Fāṭimah and of 'Ā'ishah, in order that she may become one of the Ladies of Paradise; as the following story shows.

ANECDOTE

It is related that Fāṭimah, God be pleased with her, (had been doing a lot of grinding on the hand-mill). She showed her hands to 'Alī, God ennoble his face, and they were blistered. "Tell your father," said 'Alī, "and perhaps he will buy a maidservant for you." Fāṭimah laid the matter before the Apostle, peace be upon him, and said, "O Apostle of God, buy me a maidservant. I am becoming desperate with all the work (I have to do)." The Prophet, God bless him, answered, "I will teach you something which is dearer than servants and higher than the seven heavens and earths." "What is it, God's Apostle?" she asked. He answered, "When you are about to go to sleep, say three times: "Praise be to God," "Thanks be to God," "There is no God but God" and "God is Most Great." This will be better for you than any maidservant."

In the Traditions it is reported that the Prophet, blessings be upon him, owned a rug and that when the members of his household pulled it over their heads, their legs were left bare. On the night when Fāṭimah went to 'Alī as a bride, ('Alī) had a sheepskin on which they slept. Fāṭimah owned (none of the goods) of this world (except) a rug and a palm-fibre pillow. It will therefore assuredly be proclaimed on the Resurrection Day, "Lower your eyes that the Lady of Paradise may pass!"

A wife will beome dear to her husband and gain his affection, firstly by honouring him; secondly by obeying him when they are alone together; and (further) by bearing in mind his advantage and disadvantage, adorning herself (for him), keeping herself concealed from (other) men and secluding herself in the house; by coming to him tidy and pleasantly perfumed, having meals ready (for him) at the proper) times and cheerfully preparing whatever he desires, by not making impossible demands, not nagging, keeping her nakedness covered at bedtime, and keeping her husband's secrets during his absence and in his presence.

The author of this book declares that it is the duty of gentlemen to respect the rights of their wives and veiled ones and to show mercy, kindness and forbearance to them. A man who wishes to become merciful and affectionate towards his wife must [remember] ten things (which will help him) to act fairly: (i) she cannot divorce you, while you can (divorce her whenever you wish); (ii) she can take nothing from you, while you can take everything from her; (iii) as long as she is in your net she can have no other husband, while you can have another wife; (iv) (without your permission she cannot go out of the house, while you can;) (vi) she is afraid of you, while you are not afraid of her; (vii) she is content with a cheerful look and a kind word from you, while you are not content with any action of hers; (viii) she is taken away from her mother, father and kinsfolk (for your sake), while you are not separated from any person unless you so wish; (ix) you may buy concubines and prefer them to her, while she has to endure this; (x) she kills herself (with worry) when you are sick, while you do not worry when she dies. For (all) these reasons, intelligent men will be merciful towards their wives and will not treat them unjustly; because women are prisoners in the hands of men. The intelligent man will (also) have forbearance for women; because they are deficient in intelligence. Referring to their scant intelligence, the Prophet, peace be upon him, stated: "They are deficient in (their) intellects and (their) religion." Moreover, no man ought to act upon (women's) plans; if he does, he will lose, as the following story shows.

ANECDOTE

King Parvīz was extremely fond of fish. One day when he was sitting on the terrace with Shīrīn, a fisherman brought a large fish and laid it before them. Parvīz ordered that he be given four thousand *dirhams*. Shīrīn said, "You were not right to give this fisherman four thousand *dirhams*." "Why (not)?" he asked. Shīrīn answered, "Because henceforward whenever you give four thousand *dirhams* to one of your servants and retainers, he will say "(The king) gave me the same as he gave to a fisherman"; and whenever you give less, he will say, "(The king) gave me less than he gave to a fisherman." "You are right," said Parvīz; "but it is over now, and kings cannot decently go back on their word." "(I have) a plan for dealing with the matter," said Shīrīn; "call back the fisherman, and ask him whether the fish is male or female. If he says that it is male, tell him that you wanted a female one; and if he says that it is female, tell him that you wanted a male one." So Parvīz called back the fisherman. He was a clever and very knowing man, and when Parvīz asked him "Is this fish male or female?" he kissed the ground and said: "This fish is neither male nor female. It is hermaphrodite." Parvīz laughed and ordered that he be given a further four thousand *dirhams*. The man then went to the treasurer, drew eight thousand *dirhams,* and put them into a knapsack which he slung over his shoulder. When he came out into the courtyard, one *dirham* dropped from the knapsack. He put down the knapsack and picked the *dirham* up; and Parvīz and Shīrīn saw him do this. Shīrīn turned to Parvīz and said, "What a poor mean fellow this fisherman is! One *dirham* out of the eight thousand dropped and he objected to parting with it." Parvīz was annoyed and replied, "What you say is true." Then he ordered that the fisherman be called back, and said to him, "What a poor fellow you must be! When one *dirham* out of the eight thousand dropped from your knapsack, you put down the knapsack from your shoulder and picked the *dirham* up." The fisherman kissed the ground and said, "May the king's life be long! I picked up that one *dirham* because of its importance. It has the king's face stamped on one side and the king's name inscribed on the other. I feared that some person might unknowingly trample upon it and dishonour the king's name and face, and that I should be (responsible for) the offence." Parvīz was pleased (with this answer) and ordered that he be given a further four thousand *dirhams*. So the fisherman returned (home) with twelve thousand

dirhams. Then Parvīz said, "A man who acts upon a woman's suggestion will lose two *dirhams* for every one."

The author of this book declares that the prosperity and peopling of the world depend on women. True prosperity, however, will not be achieved without (sound) planning. It is men's duty, especially after coming of age, to take precautions in matters of choosing wives and giving daughters in marriage, and so avoid falling into disgrace and embarrassment. It is a fact that all the trials, misfortunes and woes which befall men come from women, and that few men get in the end what they long and hope for from them; as the poet has said.

When slaves rebel against the Merciful,
when men in fear and dread of Sultāns stand,
it's due to women.
When robbers put their lives into the balance,
when men incur disgrace, invariably
it's due to women.
The disobedience and sad fate of Adam,
Joseph's incarceration in the dungeon,
were due to women.
Hārūt's long stay in Babylon, where he writhes
suspended by a hair, making loud groans,
was due to women.
Majnūn's flight to the nomads, sick with love,
the tale of Sindibād which makes you smile,
were due to women.
Ruin in the two worlds, and last of all
unfaithfulness, you'll learn, are what men get
from women.

BEYOND THE VEIL

Fatima Mernissi

Islam transformed a group of individuals into a community of believers. This community is defined by characteristics that determine the relations of the individuals within the *umma* both with each other and with non-believers.

"In its internal aspect the *umma* consists of the totality of individuals bound to one another by ties, not of kinship or race, but of religion, in that all its members profess their belief in the one God, Allah, and in the mission of his prophet, Muhammad. Before God and in relation to Him, all are equal without distinction of race. . . . In its external aspect, the *umma* is sharply differentiated from all other social organizations. Its duty is to bear witness to Allah in the relations of its members to one another and with all mankind. They form a single indivisible organization, charged to uphold the true faith, to instruct men in the ways of God, to persuade them to the good and to dissuade them from evil by *word and deed.*"[1]

One of the devices the Prophet used to implement the *umma* was the creation of the institutions of the Muslim family, which was quite unlike any existing sexual unions.[2] Its distinguishing feature was its strictly defined monolithic structure.

Because of the novelty of the family structure in Muhammad's revolutionary social order, he had to codify its regulations in detail. Sex is one of the instincts whose satisfaction was regulated at length by religious law during the first years of Islam. The link in the Muslim mind between sexuality and the *shari'a* has shaped the legal and ideological history of the Muslim family structure[3] and consequently of relations between the sexes. One of the most enduring characteristics of this history is that the family structure is assumed to be unchangeable, for it is considered divine.

Controversy has raged throughout this century between traditionalists who claim that Islam prohibits any change in sex roles, and modernists who claim that Islam allows for the liberation of women, the desegregation of society, and equality between the sexes. But both factions agree on one thing: Islam should remain the sacred basis of society. In this book I want to demonstrate that there is a fundamental contradiction between Islam as interpreted in official policy and equality between the sexes. Sexual equality violates Islam's premise, actualized in its laws, that heterosexual love is dangerous to Allah's order. Muslim marriage is based on male dominance. The desegregation of the sexes violates Islam's ideology on women's position in the social order: that women should be under the authority of fathers, brothers, or husbands. Since women are considered by Allah to be a destructive element, they are to be spatially confined and excluded from matters other than those of the family. Female access to non-domestic space is put under the control of males.

Paradoxically, and contrary to what is commonly assumed, Islam does not advance the thesis of women's inherent inferiority. Quite the contrary, it affirms the potential equality between the sexes. The existing inequality does not rest on an ideological or biological theory of women's inferiority, but is the outcome of specific social institutions designed to restrain her power: namely, segregation and legal subordination in the family structure. Nor have these institutions generated a systematic and convincing ideology of women's inferiority. Indeed, it was not difficult for the male initiated and male-led feminist movement to affirm the need for women's emancipation, since traditional Islam recognizes equality of potential. The democratic glorification of the human individual, regardless of sex, race, or status, is the kernel of the Muslim message.

In Western culture, sexual inequality is based on belief in women's biological inferiority. This explains some aspects of Western women's liberation movements, such as that they are almost always led by women, that their effect is often very superficial, and that they have not yet succeeded in significantly changing the male-female dynamics in that culture. In Islam there is no such belief in female inferiority. On the contrary, the whole system is based on the assumption that women are powerful and dangerous beings. All sexual institutions (polygamy, repu-

[1] H. A. R. Gigg, "Constitutional Organization" in *Origin and Development of Islamic Law,* ed. M. Khaduri and H. J. Liebesny, Vol. I (Washington, D.C.: Middle East Institute, 1955), p. 3.
[2] Gertrude Stern, *Marriage in Early Islam* (London: The Royal Asiatic Society, 1931), p. 71.
[3] Joseph Schacht, *An Introduction to Islamic Law* (London: Oxford University Press, 1964), p. 161.

diation, sexual segregation, etc.) can be perceived as a strategy for containing their power.

This belief in women's potence is likely to give the evolution of the relationship between men and women in Muslim settings a pattern entirely different from the Western one. For example, if there are any changes in the sex status and relations, they will tend to be more radical than in the West and will necessarily generate more tension, more conflict, more anxiety, and more aggression. While the women's liberation movement in the West focuses on women and their claim for equality with men, in Muslim countries it would tend to focus on the mode of relatedness between the sexes and thus would probably be led by men and women alike. Because men can see how the oppression of women works against men, women's liberation would assume the character of a generational rather than sexual conflict. This could already be seen in the opposition between young nationalists and old traditionalists at the beginning of the century, and currently it can be seen in the conflict between parents and children over the dying institution of arranged marriage.

At stake in Muslim society is not the emancipation of women (if that means only equality with men), but the fate of the heterosexual unit. Men and women were and still are socialized to perceive each other as enemies. The desegregation of social life makes them realize that besides sex, they can also give each other friendship and love. Muslim ideology, which views men and women as enemies, tries to separate the two, and empowers men with institutionalized means to oppress women. But whereas fifty years ago there was coherence between Muslim ideology and Muslim reality as embodied in the family system, now there is a wide discrepancy between that ideology and the reality that it pretends to explain. This book explores many aspects of that discrepancy and describes the *sui generis* character of male-female dynamics in Morocco, one of the most striking mixtures of modernity and Muslim tradition.

• • •

THE FUNCTION OF INSTINCTS

The Christian concept of the individual as tragically torn between two poles—good and evil, flesh and spirit, instinct and reason—is very different from the Muslim concept. Islam has a more sophisticated theory of the instincts, more akin to the Freudian concept of the libido. It views the raw instincts as energy. The energy of instincts is pure in the sense that it has no connotation of good or bad. The question of good and bad arises only when the social destiny of men is considered. The individual cannot survive except within a social order. Any social order has a set of laws. The set of laws decides which uses of the instincts are good or bad. It is the use made of the instincts, not the instincts themselves, that is beneficial or harmful to the social order. Therefore, in the Muslim order it is not necessary for the individual to eradicate his instincts or to control them for the sake of control itself, but he must use them according to the demands of religious law.

> When Muhammad forbids or censures certain human activities, or urges their omission, he does not want them to be neglected altogether, nor does he want them to be completely eradicated, or the powers from which they result to remain altogether unused. He wants those powers to be employed as much as possible for the right aims. Every inention should thus eventually become the right one and the direction of all human activities one and the same.[4]

Aggression and sexual desire, for example, if harnessed in the right direction, serve the purposes of the Muslim order; if suppressed or used wrongly, they can destroy that very order:

> Muhammad did not censure wrathfulness with the intention of eradicating it as a human quality. If the power of wrathfulness were no longer to exist in man, he would lose the ability to help the truth to

---

[4] Ibn Khaldūn, *The Muqaddimah, An Introduction to History,* translated by Franz Rosenthal (Princeton, N.J.: Princeton University Press, Bollingen Series, 1969) pp. 160–161.

become victorious. There would no longer be holy war or glorification of the word of God. Muhammad censured the wrathfulness that is in the service of Satan and reprehensible purposes, but the wrathfulness that is one in God and in the service of God deserves praise.[5]

. . . Likewise when he censures the desires, he does not want them to be abolished altogether, for a complete abolition of concupiscence in a person would make him defective and inferior. He wants the desire to be used for permissible purposes to serve the public interests, so that man becomes an active servant of God who willingly obeys the divine commands.[6]

Imam Ghazali (1050–1111) in his book *The Revivification of Religious Sciences*[7] gives a detailed description of how Islam integrated the sexual instinct in the social order and placed it at the service of God. He starts by stressing the antagonism between sexual desire and the social order: "If the desire of the flesh dominates the individual and is not controlled by the fear of God, it leads men to commit destructive acts."[8] But used according to God's will, the desire of the flesh serves God's and the individual's interests in both worlds, enhances life on earth and in heaven. Part of God's design on earth is to ensure the perpetuity of the human race, and sexual desires serve this purpose:

Sexual desire was created solely as a means to entice men to deliver the seed and to put the woman in a situation where she can cultivate it, bringing the two together softly in order to obtain progeny, as the hunter obtains his game, and this through copulation.[9]

He created two sexes, each equipped with a specific anatomic configuration which allows them to complement each other in the realization of God's design.

God the Almighty created the spouses, he created the man with his penis, his testicles and his seed in his kidneys [kidneys were believed to be the semen-producing gland]. He created for it veins and channels in the testicles. He gave the woman a uterus, the receptacle and depository of the seed. He burdened men and women with the weight of sexual desire. All these facts and organs manifest in an eloquent language the will of their creator, and address to every individual endowed with intelligence an unequivocal message about the intention of His design. Moreover, Almighty God did clearly manifest His will through his messenger (benediction and salvation upon him) who made the divine intention known when he said "Marry and multiply." How then can man not understand that God showed explicitly His intention and revealed the secret of His creation? Therefore, the man who refuses to marry fails to plant the seed, destroys it and reduces to waste the instrument created by God for this purpose.[10]

Serving God's design on earth, sexual desire also serves his design in heaven.

Sexual desire as a manifestation of God's wisdom has, independently of its manifest function, another function: when the individual yields to it and satisfies it, he experiences a delight which would be without match if it were lasting. It is a foretaste of the delights secured for men in Paradise, because to make a promise to men of delights they have not tasted before would be ineffective. . . . This earthly delight, imperfect because limited in time, is a powerful motivation to incite men to try and attain the perfect delight, the eternal delight and therefore urges men to adore God so as to reach heaven. Therefore the desire to reach the heavenly delight is so powerful that it helps men to persevere in pious activities in order to be admitted to heaven.[11]

Because of the dual nature of sexual desire (earthly and heavenly) and because of its tactical importance in God's strategy, its regulation had to

---

[5] *Ibid.*, p. 161.
[6] *Ibid.*
[7] Abu-Hamid al-Ghazali, *Ihya Ulum ad-Din*, ("The Revivification of Religious Sciences") (Cairo: al-Maktaba at Tijariya al-Kubra, n.d.).
[8] *Ibid.*, p. 28.
[9] *Ibid.*, p. 25.

[10] *Ibid.*, p. 25.
[11] *Ibid.*, p. 27.

be divine as well. In accordance with God's interests, the regulation of the sexual instinct was one of the key devices in Muhammad's implementation on earth of a new social order in then-pagan Arabia.

FEMALE SEXUALITY: ACTIVE OR PASSIVE?

According to George Murdock, societies fall into two groups with respect to the manner in which they regulate the sexual instinct. One group enforces respect of sexual rules by a "strong internalization of sexual prohibitions during the socialization process," the other enforces that respect by "external precautionary safeguards such as avoidance rules," because these societies fail to internalize sexual prohibitions in their members.[12] According to Murdock, Western society belongs to the first group while societies where veiling exists belong to the second.

> Our own society clearly belongs to the former category, so thoroughly do we instil our sex mores in the consciences of individuals that we feel quite safe in trusting our internalized sanctions. . . . We accord women a maximum of personal freedom, knowing that the internalized ethics of premarital chastity and post-marital fidelity will ordinarily suffice to prevent abuse of their liberty through fornication or adultery whenever a favourable opportunity presents itself. Societies of the other type . . . attempt to preserve premarital chastity by secluding their unmarried girls or providing them with duennas or other such external devices as veiling, seclusion in harems or constant surveillance.[13]

However, I think that the difference between these two kinds of societies resides not so much in their mechanisms of internalization as in their concept of female sexuality. In societies in which seclusion and surveillance of women prevail, the implicit concept of female sexuality is active; in societies in which there are no such methods of surveillance and coercion of women's behaviour, the concept of female sexuality is passive.

In his attempt to grasp the logic of the seclusion and veiling of women and the basis of sexual segregation, the Muslim feminist Qasim Amin came to the conclusion that women are better able to control their sexual impulses than men and that consequently sexual segregation is a device to protect men, not women.[14]

He started by asking who fears what in such societies. Observing that women do not appreciate seclusion very much and conform to it only because they are compelled to, he concluded that what is feared is *fitna*: disorder or chaos. (*Fitna* also means a beautiful woman—the connotation of a *femme fatale* who makes men lose their self-control. In the way Qasim Amin used it *fitna* could be translated as chaos provoked by sexual disorder and initiated by women.) He then asked who is protected by seclusion.

> If what men fear is that women might succumb to their masculine attraction, why did they not institute veils for themselves? Did men think that their ability to fight temptation was weaker than women's? Are men considered less able than women to control themselves and resist their sexual impulse? . . . Preventing women from showing themselves unveiled expresses men's fear of losing control over their minds, falling prey to *fitna* whenever they are confronted with a non-veiled woman. The implications of such an institution lead us to think that women are believed to be better equipped in this respect than men.[15]

Amin stopped his inquiry here and, probably thinking that his findings were absurd, concluded jokingly that if men are the weaker sex, they are the ones who need protection and therefore the ones who should veil themselves.

---

[12] George Peter Murdock, *Social Structure* (New York: MacMillan & Co. Free Press), 1965, p. 273.
[13] *Ibid.*

[14] Kacem Amin, *The Liberation of the Woman,* (Cairo: 'Umum al-Makatib Bimisr Wa-Iharij, 1928) p. 64.
[15] *Ibid.,* p. 65.

Why does Islam fear *fitna*? Why does Islam fear the power of female sexual attraction over men? Does Islam assume that the male cannot cope sexually with an uncontrolled female? Does Islam assume that women's sexual capacity is greater than men's?

Muslim society is characterized by a contradiction between what can be called "an explicit theory" and "an implicit theory" of female sexuality, and therefore a double theory of sexual dynamics. The explicit theory is the prevailing contemporary belief that men are aggressive in their interaction with women, and women are passive. The implicit theory, driven far further into the Muslim unconscious, is epitomized in Imam Ghazali's classical work.[16] He sees civilization as struggling to contain women's destructive, all-absorbing power. Women must be controlled to prevent men from being distracted from their social and religious duties. Society can survive only by creating institutions that foster male dominance through sexual segregation and polygamy for believers.

The explicit theory, with its antagonistic, machismo vision of relations between the sexes is epitomized by Abbas Mahmud al-Aqqad.[17] In *Women in the Koran* Aqqad attempted to describe male-female dynamics as they appear through the Holy Book. Aqqad opened his book with the quotation from the Koran establishing the fact of male supremacy ("the men are superior to them by a degree") and hastily concludes that "the message of the Koran, which makes men superior to women is the manifest message of human history, the history of Adam's descendants before and after civilization."[18]

What Aqqad finds in the Koran and in human civilization is a complementarity between the sexes based on their antagonistic natures. The characteristic of the male is the will to power, the will to conquer. The characteristic of the female is a negative will to power. All her energies are vested in seeking to be conquered, in wanting to be overpowered and subjugated. Therefore, "She can only expose herself and wait while the man wants and seeks."[19]

Although Aqqad has neither the depth nor the brilliant systematic deductive approach of Freud, his ideas on the male-female dynamic are very similar to Freud's emphasis on the "law of the jungle" aspect of sexuality. The complementarity of the sexes, according to Aqqad, resides in their antagonistic wills and desires and aspirations.

> Males in all kinds of animals are given the power—embodied in their biological structure—to compel females to yield to the demands of the instinct (that is, sex). . . . There is no situation where that power to compel is given to women over men.[20]

Like Freud, Aqqad endows women with a hearty appetite for suffering. Women enjoy surrender.[21] More than that, for Aqqad women experience pleasure and happiness only in their subjugation, their defeat by males. The ability to experience pleasure in suffering and subjugation is the kernel of femininity, which is masochistic by its very nature. "The woman's submission to the man's conquest is one of the strongest sources of women's pleasure.[22] The machismo theory casts the man as the hunter and the woman as his prey. This vision is widely shared and deeply ingrained in both men's and women's vision of themselves.

The implicit theory of female sexuality, as seen in Imam Ghazali's interpretation of the Koran, casts the woman as the hunter and the man as the passive victim. The two theories have one component in common, the woman's *qaid* power ("the power to

---

[16] al-Ghazali, *The Revivification of Religious Sciences,* Vol. II, chapter on marriage; and Mizan al-'Amal ("Criteria for Action") (Cairo: Dar al-Ma'arif, 1964).

[17] 'Abbas Mahmud al-Aqquad, *The Women in the Koran* (Cairo: Dar al-Hilal, n.d.).

[18] *Ibid.,* p. 7; the verse he refers to is verse 228 of Surah II which is striking by its inconsistency.

[19] *Ibid.,* p. 24.

[20] *Ibid.,* p. 25. The biological assumptions behind Aqquad's sweeping generalizations are obviously fallacious.

[21] *Ibid.,* p. 18.

[22] *Ibid.,* p. 26.

deceive and defeat men, not by force, but by cunning and intrigue"). But while Aqqad tries to link the female's *qaid* power to her weak constitution, the symbol of her divinely decreed inferiority, Imam Ghazali sees her power as the most destructive element in the Muslim social order, in which the feminine is regarded as synonymous with the satanic.

The whole Muslim organization of social interaction and spacial configuration can be understood in terms of women's *qaid* power. The social order then appears as an attempt to subjugate her power and neutralize its disruptive effects.

• • •

In the actively sexual Muslim female aggressiveness is seen as turned outward. The nature of her aggression is precisely sexual. The Muslim woman is endowed with a fatal attraction which erodes the male's will to resist her and reduces him to a passive acquiescent role. He has no choice; he can only give in to her attraction, whence her identification with *fitna,* chaos, and with the anti-divine and anti-social forces of the universe.

> The Prophet saw a woman. He hurried to his house and had intercourse with his wife Zaynab, then left the house and said, "When the woman comes towards you, it is Satan who is approaching you. When one of you sees a woman and he feels attracted to her, he should hurry to his wife. With her, it would be the same as with the other one.[23]

Commenting on this quotation, Imam Muslim, an established voice of Muslim tradition, reports that the Prophet was referring to the

> . . . fascination, to the irresistible attraction to women God instilled in man's soul, and he was referring to the pleasure man experiences when he looks at the woman, and the pleasure he experiences with anything related to her. She resembles

Satan in his irresistible power over the individual.[24]

This attraction is a natural link between the sexes. Whenever a man is faced with a woman, *fitna* might occur: "When a man and a woman are isolated in the presence of each other, Satan is bound to be their third companion."[25]

The most potentially dangerous woman is one who has experienced sexual intercourse. It is the married woman who will have more difficulties in bearing sexual frustration. The married woman whose husband is absent is a particular threat to men: "Do not go to the women whose husbands are absent. Because Satan will get in your bodies as blood rushes through your flesh."[26]

In Moroccan folk culture this threat is epitomized by the belief in Aisha Kandisha, a repugnant female demon. She is repugnant precisely because she is libidinous. She has pendulous breasts and lips and her favourite pastime is to assault men in the streets and in dark places, to induce them to have sexual intercourse with her, and ultimately to penetrate their bodies and stay with them for ever.[27] They are then said to be inhabited. The fear of Aisha Kandisha is more than ever present in Morocco's daily life. Fear of the castrating female is a legacy of tradition and is seen in many forms in popular beliefs and practices and in both religious and mundane literature, particularly novels.

Moroccan folk culture is permeated with a negative attitude towards femininity. Loving a woman is popularly described as a form of mental illness, a self-destructive state of mind. A Moroccan proverb says

---

[23] Abbi 'Issa at-Tarmidi, *Sunan at-Tarmidi* (Medina: al-Maktaba as Salafiya, n.d.) Vol. II, p. 413. Bab: 9, Hadith: 1167. (Hereinafter Bab will be indicated by the letter B, and Hadith by the letter H.)

[24] Abu al-Hassan Muslim, *al-Jami' as-Sahih* (Beirut: al-Maktaba at-Tijariya, n.d.) Vol. III, Book of Marriage, p. 130.

[25] at-Tarmidi, *Sunan at-Tarmidi,* p. 419, B:16, H:1181. See also al-Bukhari, *Kitab al-Jami' as-Sahih* (Leyden, Holland: Ludolph Krehl, 1868) Vol. III, Kitab 67, B:11. (Hereinafter Kitab will be indicated by the letter K.)

[26] at-Tarmidi, *Sunan at-Tarmidi,* p. 419, B:17, H:1172.

[27] Edward Westermarck, *The Belief in Spirits in Morocco,* (Abo, Finland: Abo-Akademi, 1920).

Love is a complicated matter
If it does not drive you crazy, it kills you.[28]

• • •

The Muslim order faces two threats: the infidel without and the woman within.

The Prophet said, 'After my disappearance there will be no greater source of chaos and disorder for my nation than women.'[29]

• • •

Different social orders have integrated the tensions between religion and sexuality in different ways. In the Western Christian experience sexuality itself was attacked, degraded as animality and condemned as anti-civilization. The individual was split into two antithetical selves: the spirit and the flesh, the ego and the id. The triumph of civilization implied the triumph of soul over flesh, of ego over id, of the controlled over the uncontrolled, of spirit over sex.

Islam took a substantially different path. What is attacked and debased is not sexuality but women, as the embodiment of destruction, the symbol is disorder. The woman is *fitna,* the epitome of the uncontrollable, a living representative of the dangers of sexuality and its rampant disruptive potential. We have seen that Muslim theory considers raw instinct as energy which is likely to be used constructively for the benefit of Allah and His society if people live according to His laws. Sexuality *per se* is not a danger. On the contrary, it has three positive, vital functions. It allows the believers to perpetuate themselves on earth, an indispensable condition if the social order is to exist at all. It serves as a "foretaste of the delights secured for men in Paradise,"[30] thus encouraging men to strive for paradise and to

obey Allah's rule on earth. Finally, sexual satisfaction is necessary to intellectual effort.

The Muslim theory of sublimation is entirely different from the Western Christian tradition as represented by Freudian psychoanalytic theory. Freud viewed civilization as a war against sexuality.[31] Civilization is sexual energy "turned aside from its sexual goal and diverted towards other ends, no longer sexual and socially more valuable.[32] The Muslim theory views civilization as the outcome of satisfied sexual energy. Work is the result not of sexual frustration but of a contented and harmoniously lived sexuality.

The soul is usually reluctant to carry out its duty because duty [work] is against its nature. If one puts pressures on the soul in order to make it do what it loathes, the soul rebels. But if the soul is allowed to relax for some moments by the means of some pleasures, it fortifies itself and becomes after that alert and ready for work again. And in the woman's company, this relaxation drives out sadness and pacifies the heart. It is advisable for pious souls to divert themselves by means which are religiously lawful.[33]

According to Ghazali, the most precious gift God gave humans is reason. Its best use is the search for knowledge. To know the human environment, to know the earth and galaxies, is to know God. Knowledge (science) is the best form of prayer for a Muslim believer. But to be able to devote his energies to knowledge, man has to reduce the tensions within and without his body, avoid being distracted by external elements, and avoid indulging in earthly pleasures. Women are a dangerous distraction that must be used for the specific purpose of providing the Muslim nation with offspring and quenching the tensions of the sexual instinct. But in no way should women be an object of

[28] Edward Westermarck, *Wit and Wisdom in Morocco: A Study of Native Proverbs* (London: MacMillan and Co., 1926) p. 330.
[29] Abu Abd Allah Muhammad Ibn Ismail al-Bukhari, *Kitab al-Jami' as-Sahih* (Leyden, Holland: Ludolph Krehl, 1868) p. 419, K:67, B:18.
[30] al-Ghazali, *Revivification,* p. 28.

[31] Sigmund Freud, *Civilization and Its Discontents* (New York: Norton and Co., Inc., 1962).
[32] Sigmund Freud, *A General Introduction to Psychoanalysis* (New York: Pocket Books, 1952) p. 27.
[33] al-Ghazali, *Revivification,* p. 32.

emotional investment or the focus of attention, which should be devoted to Allah alone in the form of knowledge-seeking, meditation, and prayer.

Ghazali's conception of the individual's task on earth is illuminating in that it reveals that the Muslim message, in spite of its beauty, considers humanity to be constituted by males only. Women are considered not only outside of humanity but a threat to it as well. Muslim wariness of heterosexual involvement is embodied in sexual segregation and its corollaries: arranged marriage, the important role of the mother in the son's life, and the fragility of the marital bond (as revealed by the institutions of repudiation and polygamy). The entire Muslim social structure can be seen as an attack on, and a defence against, the disruptive power of female sexuality.

THE SECOND SEX

Simone de Beauvoir

For a long time I have hesitated to write a book on woman. The subject is irritating, especially to women; and it is not new. Enough ink has been spilled in the quarreling over feminism, now practically over, and perhaps we should say no more about it. It is still talked about, however, for the voluminous nonsense uttered during the last century seems to have done little to illuminate the problem. After all, is there a problem? And if so, what is it? Are there women, really? Most assuredly the theory of the eternal feminine still has its adherents who will whisper in your ear: "Even in Russia women still are *women*"; and other erudite persons—sometimes the very same—say with a sigh: "Woman is losing her way, woman is lost." One wonders if women still exist, if they will always exist, whether or not it is desirable that they should, what place they occupy in this world, what their place should be. "What has become of women?" was asked recently in an ephemeral magazine.

But first we must ask: what is a woman? *"Tota mulier in utero,"* says one, "woman is a womb." But in speaking of certain women, connoisseurs declare that they are not women, although they are equipped with a uterus like the rest. All agree in recognizing the fact that females exist in the human species; today as always they make up about one half of humanity. And yet we are told that femininity is in danger; we are exhorted to be women, remain women, become women. It would appear, then, that every female human being is not necessarily a woman; to be so considered she must share in that mysterious and threatened reality known as femininity. Is this attribute something secreted by the ovaries? Or is it a Platonic essence, a product of the philosophic imagination? Is a rustling petticoat enough to bring it down to earth? Although some women try zealously to incarnate this essence, it is hardly patentable. It is frequently described in vague and dazzling terms that seem to have been borrowed from the vocabulary of the seers, and indeed in the times of St. Thomas it was considered an essence as certainly defined as the somniferous virtue of the poppy.

But conceptualism* has lost ground. The biological and social sciences no longer admit the existence of unchangeably fixed entities that determine given characteristics, such as those ascribed to woman, the Jew, or the Negro. Science regards any characteristic as a reaction dependent in part upon a *situation.* If today femininity no longer exists, then it never existed. But does the word *woman,* then, have no specific content? This is stoutly affirmed by those who hold to the philosophy of the enlightenment, of rationalism, of nominalism;† women, to

---

* *Conceptualism* is a philosophical position which holds that universal concepts exist in the mind and that, therefore, general terms—such as "man" and "woman"—refer to some universal essence (Eds.).

† *Nominalism* is a philosophical position which holds that general terms are simply words designating a collection of individuals and that there is no abstract universal essence to which they refer (Eds.).

them, are merely the human beings arbitrarily designated by the word *woman*. Many American women particularly are prepared to think that there is no longer any place for woman as such; if a backward individual still takes herself for a woman, her friends advise her to be psychoanalyzed and thus get rid of this obsession. In regard to a work, *Modern Woman: The Lost Sex,* which in other respects has its irritating features, Dorothy Parker has written: "I cannot be just to books which treat of woman as woman. . . . My idea is that all of us, men as well as women, should be regarded as human beings." But nominalism is a rather inadequate doctrine, and the antifeminists have had no trouble in showing that women simply *are not* men. Surely woman is, like man, a human being; but such a declaration is abstract. The fact is that every concrete human being is always a singular, separate individual. To decline to accept such notions as the eternal feminine, the black soul, the Jewish character, is not to deny that Jews, Negroes, women exist today—this denial does not represent a liberation for those concerned, but rather a flight from reality. Some years ago a well-known woman writer refused to permit her portrait to appear in a series of photographs especially devoted to women writers; she wished to be counted among the men. But in order to gain this privilege she made use of her husband's influence! Women who assert that they are men lay claim none the less to masculine consideration and respect. I recall also a young Trotskyite standing on a platform at a boisterous meeting and getting ready to use her fists, in spite of her evident fragility. She was denying her feminine weakness; but it was for love of a militant male whose equal she wished to be. The attitude of defiance of many American women proves that they are haunted by a sense of their femininity. In truth, to go for a walk with one's eyes open is enough to demonstrate that humanity is divided into two classes of individuals whose clothes, faces, bodies, smiles, gaits, interests, and occupations are manifestly different. Perhaps these differences are superficial, perhaps they are destined to disappear. What is certain is that right now they do most obviously exist.

If her functioning as a female is not enough to define woman, if we decline also to explain her through "the eternal feminine," and if nevertheless we admit, provisionally, that women do exist, then we must face the question: what is a woman?

To state the question is, to me, to suggest, at once, a preliminary answer. The fact that I ask it is in itself significant. A man would never get the notion of writing a book on the peculiar situation of the human male.[1] But if I wish to define myself, I must first of all say: "I am a woman"; on this truth must be based all further discussion. A man never begins by presenting himself as an individual of a certain sex; it goes without saying that he is a man. The terms *masculine* and *feminine* are used symmetrically only as a matter of form, as on legal papers. In actuality the relation of the two sexes is not quite like that of two electrical poles, for man represents both the positive and the neutral, as is indicated by the common use of *man* to designate human beings in general; whereas woman represents only the negative, defined by limiting criteria, without reciprocity. In the midst of an abstract discussion it is vexing to hear a man say: "You think thus and so because you are a woman"; but I know that my only defense is to reply: "I think thus and so because it is true," thereby removing my subjective self from the argument. It would be out of the question to reply: "And you think the contrary because you are a man," for it is understood that the fact of being a man is no peculiarity. A man is in the right in being a man; it is the woman who is in the wrong. It amounts to this: just as for the ancients there was an absolute vertical with reference to which the oblique was defined, so there is an absolute human type, the masculine. Woman has ovaries, a uterus; these peculiarities imprison her in her subjectivity, circumscribe her within the limits of her own nature. It is often said that she thinks with her glands.

---

[1] The Kinsey Report [Alfred C. Kinsey and others: *Sexual Behavior in the Human Male* (W. B. Saunders Co., 1948)] is no exception, for it is limited to describing the sexual characteristics of American men, which is quite a different matter.

Man superbly ignores the fact that his anatomy also includes glands, such as the testicles, and that they secrete hormones. He thinks of his body as a direct and normal connection with the world, which he believes he apprehends objectively, whereas he regards the body of woman as a hindrance, a prison, weighed down by everything peculiar to it. "The female is a female by virtue of a certain *lack* of qualities," said Aristotle; "we should regard the female nature as afflicted with a natural defectiveness." And St. Thomas for his part pronounced woman to be an "imperfect man," an "incidental" being. This is symbolized in Genesis where Eve is depicted as made from what Bossuet called "a supernumerary bone" of Adam.

Thus humanity is male and man defines woman not in herself but as relative to him; she is not regarded as an autonomous being. Michelet writes: "Woman, the relative being. . . ." And Benda is most positive in his *Rapport d' Uriel:* "The body of man makes sense in itself quite apart from that of woman, whereas the latter seems wanting in significance by itself. . . . Man can think of himself without woman. She cannot think of herself without man." And she is simply what man decrees; thus she is called "the sex," by which is meant that she appears essentially to the male as a sexual being. For him she is sex—absolute sex, no less. She is defined and differentiated with reference to man and not he with reference to her; she is the incidental, the inessential as opposed to the essential. He is the Subject, he is the Absolute—she is the Other.

• • •

A free individual blames only himself for his failures, he assumes responsibility for them; but everything happens to women through the agency of others, and therefore these others are responsible for her woes. Her mad despair spurns all remedies; it does not help matters to propose solutions to a woman bent on complaining: she finds none acceptable. She insists on living in her situation precisely as she does—that is, in a state of impotent rage. If some change is proposed she throws up her hands: "That's the last straw!" She knows that her

trouble goes deeper than is indicated by the pretexts she advances for it, and she is aware that it will take more than some expedient to deliver her from it. She holds the entire world responsible because it has been made without her, and against her; she has been protesting against her condition since her adolescence, ever since her childhood. She has been promised compensations, she has been assured that if she would place her fortune in man's hands, it would be returned a hundredfold—and she feels she has been swindled. She puts the whole masculine universe under indictment. Resentment is the reverse side of dependence: when one gives all, one never receives enough in return.

• • •

There are many aspects of feminine behavior that should be interpreted as forms of protest. We have seen that a woman often deceives her husband through defiance and not for pleasure; and she may be purposely careless and extravagant because he is methodical and economical. Misogynists who accuse woman of always being late think she lacks a sense of punctuality; but as we have seen, the fact is that she can adjust herself very well to the demands of time. When she is late, she has deliberately planned to be. Some coquettish women think they stimulate the man's desire in this way and make their presence the more highly appreciated; but in making the man wait a few minutes, the woman is above all protesting against that long wait: her life.

In a sense her whole existence is waiting, since she is confined in the limbo of immanence and contingence, and since her justification is always in the hands of others. She awaits the homage, the approval of men, she awaits love, she awaits the gratitude and praise of her husband or her lover. She awaits her support, which comes from man; whether she keeps the checkbook or merely gets a weekly or monthly allowance from her husband, it is necessary for him to have drawn his pay or obtained that raise if she is to be able to pay the grocer or buy a new dress. She waits for man to put in an appearance, since her economic dependence places her at his disposal; she is only one element in masculine life while man is her whole existence. The husband has his occupations outside the home, and the wife has to put up with his absence all day long; the lover—passionate as he may be—is the one who decides on their meetings and separations in accordance with his obligations. In bed, she awaits the male's desire, she awaits—sometimes anxiously—her own pleasure.

All she can do is arrive later at the rendezvous her lover has set, not be ready at the time designated by her husband; in that way she asserts the importance of her own occupations, she insists on her independence; and for the moment she becomes the essential subject to whose will the other passively submits. But these are timid attempts at revenge; however persistent she may be in keeping men waiting, she will never compensate for the interminable hours she has spent in watching and hoping, in awaiting the good pleasure of the male.

Woman is bound in a general way to contest foot by foot the rule of man, though recognizing his over-all supremacy and worshipping his idols. Hence that famous "contrariness" for which she has often been reproached. Having no independent domain, she cannot oppose positive truths and values of her own to those asserted and upheld by males; she can only deny them. Her negation is more or less thoroughgoing, according to the way respect and resentment are proportioned in her nature. But in fact she knows all the faults in the masculine system, and she has no hesitation in exposing them.

Women have no grasp on the world of men because their experience does not teach them to use logic and technique; inversely, masculine apparatus loses its power at the frontiers of the feminine realm. There is a whole region of human experience which the male deliberately chooses to ignore because he fails to *think* it: this experience woman *lives*. The engineer, so precise when he is laying out his diagrams, behaves at home like a minor god: a word, and behold, his meal is served, his shirts starched, his children quieted; procreation is an act as swift as the wave of Moses' wand; he sees nothing astounding in these miracles. The concept of the miracle is different from the idea of magic: it pre-

sents, in the midst of a world of rational causation, the radical discontinuity of an event without cause, against which the weapons of thought are shattered; whereas magical phenomena are unified by hidden forces the continuity of which can be accepted—without being understood—by a docile mind. The newborn child is miraculous to the paternal minor god, magical for the mother who has experienced its coming to term within her womb. The experience of the man is intelligible but interrupted by blanks; that of the woman is, within its own limits, mysterious and obscure but complete. This obscurity makes her weighty; in his relations with her, the male seems light: he has the lightness of dictators, generals, judges, bureaucrats, codes of law, and abstract principles. This is doubtless what a housekeeper meant when she said, shrugging her shoulders: "Men, they don't think!" Women say, also: "Men, they don't know, they don't know life." To the myth of the praying mantis, women contrast the symbol of the frivolous and obtrusive drone bee.

It is understandable, in this perspective, that woman takes exception to masculine logic. Not only is it inapplicable to her experience, but in his hands, as she knows, masculine reasoning becomes an underhand form of force; men's undebatable pronouncements are intended to confuse her. The intention is to put her in a dilemma: either you agree or you do not. Out of respect for the whole system of accepted principles she should agree; if she refuses, she rejects the entire system. But she cannot venture to go so far; she lacks the means to reconstruct society in different form. Still, she does not accept it as it is. Halfway between revolt and slavery, she resigns herself reluctantly to masculine authority. On each occasion he has to force her to accept the consequences of her halfhearted yielding. Man pursues that chimera, a companion half slave, half free: in yielding to him, he would have her yield to the convincingness of an argument, but she knows that he has himself chosen the premises on which his rigorous deductions depend. As long as she avoids questioning them, he will easily reduce her to silence; nevertheless he will not convince her, for she senses his arbitrariness. And so, annoyed, he will accuse her of being obstinate and illogical; but she refuses to play the game because she knows the dice are loaded.

ANDROGYNY AS AN IDEAL FOR HUMAN DEVELOPMENT

Ann Ferguson

In this paper I shall defend androgyny as an ideal for human development. To do this I shall argue that male/female sex roles are neither inevitable results of "natural" biological differences between the sexes, nor socially desirable ways of socializing children in contemporary societies. In fact, the elimination of sex roles and the development of androgynous human beings is the most rational way to allow for the possibility of, on the one hand, love relations among equals, and on the other, development of the widest possible range of intense and satisfying social relationships between men and women.

I. ANDROGYNY: THE IDEAL DEFINED

The term "androgyny" has Greek roots: *andros* means man and *gynē,* woman. An androgynous person would combine some of each of the characteristic traits, skills, and interests that we now associate with the stereotypes of masculinity and femininity. It is not accurate to say that the ideal androgynous person would be both masculine and feminine, for there are negative and distorted personality characteristics associated in our minds with these ideas.[1] Furthermore, as we presently understand these stereotypes, they exclude each other. A masculine person is active, independent, aggressive (demanding), more self-interested than altruistic, competent and interested in physical activities, rational, emotionally controlled, and self-disciplined. A feminine person, on the other hand, is passive, dependent, nonassertive, more altruistic than self-interested (supportive of others), neither physically competent nor interested in becoming so, intuitive but not rational, emotionally open, and impulsive rather than self-disciplined. Since our present conceptions of masculinity and femininity thus defined exclude each other, we must think of an ideal androgynous person as one to whom these categories do not apply—one who is neither masculine nor feminine, but human: who transcends those old categories in such a way as to be able to develop positive human potentialities denied or only realized in an alienated fashion in the current stereotypes.

The ideal androgynous being, because of his or her combination of general traits, skills, and interests, would have no internal blocks to attaining self-esteem. He or she would have the desire and ability to do socially meaningful productive activity (work), as well as the desire and ability to be autonomous and to relate lovingly to other human beings. Of course, whether or not such an individual would be able to *achieve* a sense of autonomy, self-worth, and group contribution will depend importantly on the way the society in which he/she lives is structured. For example, in a classist society characterized by commodity production, none of these goals is attainable by anyone, no matter how androgynous, who comes from a class lacking the material resources to acquire (relatively) nonalienating work. In a racist and sexist society there are social roles and expectations placed upon the individual which present him/her with a conflict situation: either express this trait (skill, interest) and be considered a social deviant or outcast, or repress the trait and be socially accepted. The point, however, is that the androgynous person has the requisite skills and interests to be able to achieve these goals if only the society is organized appropriately.

---

[1] I owe these thoughts to Jean Elshtain and members of the Valley Women's Union in Northampton, Massachusetts, from discussions on androgyny.

II. LIMITS TO HUMAN DEVELOPMENT: THE NATURAL COMPLEMENT THEORY

There are two lines of objection that can be raised against the view that androgyny is an ideal for human development: first, that it is not possible, given the facts we know about human nature; and second, that even if it is possible, there is no reason to think it particularly desirable that people be socialized to develop the potential for androgyny. In this section I shall present and discuss Natural Complement theories of male/female human nature and the normative conclusions about sex roles.

There are two general facts about men and women and their roles in human societies that must be taken into account by any theory of what is possible in social organizations of sex roles: first, the biological differences between men and women—in the biological reproduction of children, in relative physical strength, and in biological potential for aggressive (dominant, demanding) behavior; and second, the fact that all known human societies have had a sexual division of labor.

According to the Natural Complement theory, there are traits, capacities, and interests which inhere in men and women simply because of their biological differences, and which thus define what is normal "masculine" and normal "feminine" behavior. Since men are stronger than women, have bodies better adapted for running and throwing, and have higher amounts of the male hormone androgen, which is linked to aggressive behavior,[2] men have a greater capacity for heavy physical labor and for aggressive behavior (such as war). Thus it is natural that men are the breadwinners and play the active role in the production of commodities in society and in defending what the society sees as its interests in war. Since women bear children, it is natural that they have a maternal, nurturing instinct which enables them to be supportive of the needs of children, perceptive and sensitive to their needs, and intuitive in general in their understanding of the needs of people.

The Natural Complement theory about what men and women should do (their moral and spiritual duties, ideal love relations, etc.) is based on this conception of what are the fundamental biologically based differences between men and women. The universal human sexual division of labor is not only natural, but also desirable: men should work, provide for their families, and when necessary, make war; women should stay home, raise their children, and, with their greater emotionality and sensitivity, administer to the emotional needs of their men and children.

The ideal love relationship in the Natural Complement view is a heterosexual relationship in which man and woman complement each other. On this theory, woman needs man, and man, woman; they need each other essentially because together they form a whole being. Each of them is incomplete without the other; neither could meet all their survival and emotional needs alone. The woman needs the man as the active agent, rationally and bravely confronting nature and competitive social life; while the man needs the woman as his emotional guide, ministering to the needs he doesn't know he has himself, performing the same function for the children, and being the emotional nucleus of the family to harmonize all relationship. Love between man and woman is the attraction of complements, each being equally powerful and competent in his or her own sphere—man in the world, woman in the home—but each incompetent in the sphere of the other and therefore incomplete without the other.

The validity of the Natural Complement theory rests on the claim that there are some natural instincts (drives and abilities) inherent in men and women that are so powerful that they will determine the norm of masculine and feminine behavior for men and women under any conceivable cultural and economic conditions. That is, these natural instincts will determine not only what men and women can do well, but also what will be the most desirable (individually satisfying and socially productive) for them.

Even strong proponents of the Natural Complement theory have been uneasy with the evidence

---

[2] See Roger Brown, *Social Psychology* (New York: Free Press, 1965).

that in spite of "natural" differences between men and women, male and female sex roles are not inevitable. Not only are there always individual men and women whose abilities and inclinations make them exceptions to the sexual stereotypes in any particular society, but there is also a wide cross-cultural variation in just what work is considered masculine or feminine. Thus, although all known societies indeed do have a sexual division of labor, the evidence is that what behavior is considered masculine and what feminine is *learned* through socialization rather than mandated through biological instincts. So, for example, child care is said by the proponents of the Natural Complement theory to be women's work, supposedly on the grounds that women have a natural maternal instinct that men lack, due to women's biological role in reproduction. And it is true that in the vast majority of societies in the sexual division of labor women do bear a prime responsibility for child care. However, there are some societies where that is not so. The Arapesh have both mother and father play an equally strong nurturant role.[3] A case of sex-role reversal in child care would be the fabled Amazons, in whose society those few men allowed to survive past infancy reared the children. In the case of the Amazons, whose historical existence may never be conclusively proved, what is important for the purposes of our argument is not the question of whether such a culture actually existed. Rather, insofar as it indicated that an alternative sexual division of labor was possible, the existence of the myth of the Amazon culture in early Western civilizations was an ongoing challenge to the Natural Complement theory.

It is not only the sexual division of labor in child care that varies from society to society, but also other social tasks. Natural Complement theorists are fond of arguing that because men are physically stronger than women and more aggressive, it is a natural division of labor for men to do the heavy physical work of society as well as that of defense and war. However, in practice, societies have varied immensely in the ways in which heavy physical work is parceled out. In some African societies, women do all the heavy work of carrying wood and water, and in most South American countries Indian men and women share these physical chores. In Russia, women do the heavy manual labor involved in construction jobs, while men do the comparatively light (but higher-status) jobs of running the machinery.[4] In predominantly agricultural societies, women's work overlaps men's. From early American colonial times, farm women had to be prepared to fight native American Indians and work the land in cooperation with men. Israeli women make as aggressive and dedicated soldiers as Israeli men. Furthermore, if we pick any *one* of the traits supposed to be primarily masculine (e.g., competitiveness, aggressiveness, egotism), we will find not only whole societies of both men *and* women who seem to lack these traits, but also whole societies that exhibit them.[5]

Further evidence that general sex-linked personality traits are learned social roles rather than inevitable biological developments is found in studies done on hermaphrodites.[6] When children who are biological girls, but because of vestigial penises are mistaken for boys, are trained into male sex roles, they develop the cultural traits associated with males in their society and seem to be well adjusted to their roles.

Faced with the variability of the sexual division of labor and the evidence that human beings as social animals develop their self-concept and their sense of values from imitating models in their community rather than from innate biological urges, the Natural Complement theorists fall back on the thesis that complementary roles for men and women,

---

[3] For information on the Arapesh and variations in male/female roles in primitive societies, see Margaret Mead, *Sex and Temperament* (New York: William Morrow, 1963).

[4] See "The Political Economy of Women," *Review of Radical Political Economics,* Summer 1973.

[5] Contrast the Stone Age tribe recently discovered in the Philippines, where competition is unknown, with the competitive male and female Dobus from Melanesia. See Ruth Benedict, *Patterns of Culture* (Boston: Houghton Mifflin, 1934).

[6] See Eleanor E. Maccoby, ed., *The Development of Sex Differences* (Stanford, Calif.: Stanford University Press, 1966).

while not inevitable, are desirable. Two examples of this approach are found in the writings of Jean-Jacques Rousseau (in *Émile*) and in the contemporary writer George Gilder (in *Sexual Suicide*).[7] Both of these men are clearly male supremacists in that they feel women ought to be taught to serve, nurture, and support men.[8] What is ironic about their arguments is their belief in the biological inferiority of men, stated explicitly in Gilder and implicitly in Rousseau. Rousseau's train of reasoning suggests that men can't be nurturant and emotionally sensitive the way women can, so if we train women to be capable of abstract reasoning, to be self-interested and assertive, women will be able to do both male and female roles, and what will be left, then, for men to excel at? Gilder feels that men need to be socialized to be the breadwinners for children and a nurturant wife, because otherwise men's aggressive and competitive tendencies would make it impossible for them to cooperate in productive social work.

The desirability of complementary sex roles is maintained from a somewhat different set of premises in Lionel Tiger's book *Men in Groups*.[9] Tiger argues that the earliest sexual division of labor in hunting and gathering societies required men to develop a cooperative division of tasks in order to achieve success in hunting. Therefore, men evolved a biological predisposition toward "male bonding" (banding together into all-male cohort groups) that women lack (presumably because activities like gathering and child care didn't require a cooperative division of tasks that would develop female bonding). Because of this lack of bonding, women are doomed to subjection by men, for this biological asset of men is a trait necessary for achieving political and social power.

It is hard to take these arguments seriously. Obviously, they are biased toward what would promote male interests, and give little consideration to female interests. Also, they reject an androgynous ideal for human development, male and female, merely on the presumption that biological lacks in either men or women make it an unattainable ideal. It simply flies in the face of counter-evidence (for example, single fathers in our society) to argue as Gilder does that men will not be providers and relate to family duties of socializing children unless women center their life around the nurturing of men. And to argue as Tiger does that women cannot bond ignores not only the present example of the autonomous women's movement, but also ethnographic examples of women acting as a solidarity group in opposing men. The women of the Ba-Ila in southern Africa may collectively refuse to work if one has a grievance against a man.[10] A more likely theory of bonding seems to be that it is not biologically based, but learned through the organization of productive and reproductive work.

---

[7] George Gilder, *Sexual Suicide* (New York: Bantam Books, 1973).

[8] Rousseau says, in a typical passage from *Émile*, "When once it is proved that men and women are and ought to be unlike in constitution and in temperament, it follows that their education should be different." And on a succeeding page he concludes, "A woman's education must therefore be planned in relation to man. To be pleasing in his sight, to win his respect and love, to train him in childhood, to tend him in manhood, to counsel and console, to make his life pleasant and happy, these are the duties of woman for all time, and this is what she should be taught while she is young. The further we depart from this principle, the further we shall be from our own good, and all our precepts will fail to secure her happiness or our own" (trans. Barbara Foxley [New York: E. P. Dutton, 1911] pp. 326, 328).

Gilder's conclusion is as follows: "But at a profounder level the women are tragically wrong. For they fail to understand their own sexual power; and they fail to perceive the sexual constitution of our society, or if they see it, they underestimate its importance to our civilization and to their own interest in order and stability. In general across the whole range of the society, marriage and careers—and thus social order—will be best served if most men have a position of economic superiority over the relevant women in his [sic] community and if in most jobs in which colleagues must work together, the sexes tend to be segregated either by level or function." *Sexual Suicide,* p. 108.

---

[9] Lionel Tiger, *Men in Groups* (New York: Random House, 1969).

[10] Edwin W. Smith and Andrew M. Dale, *The Ila-Speaking Peoples of Northern Rhodesia* (London: Macmillan, 1920).

III. HISTORICAL MATERIALIST EXPLANATIONS OF SEX ROLES

Even if we reject the Natural Complement theory's claims that sex roles are either inevitable or desirable, we still have to explain the persistence, through most known societies, of a sexual division of labor and related sexual stereotypes of masculine and feminine behavior. This is due, I shall maintain, to patriarchal power relations between men and women based initially on men's biological advantages in two areas: that women are the biological reproducers of children, and that men as a biological caste are, by and large, physically stronger than women.[11] As Shulamith Firestone argues in *The Dialectic of Sex* and Simone de Beauvoir suggests in *The Second Sex,* the fact that women bear children from their bodies subjects them to the physical weaknesses and constraints that pregnancy and childbirth involve. Being incapacitated for periods of time makes them dependent on men (or at least the community) for physical survival in a way not reciprocated by men. Breast-feeding children, which in early societies continued until the children were five or six years old, meant that women could not hunt or engage in war. Men have both physical and social advantages over women because of their biological reproductive role and the fact that allocating child-rearing to women is the most socially efficient division of reproductive labor in societies with scarce material resources. Thus, in social situations in which men come to perceive their interests to lie in making women subservient to them, men have the edge in a power struggle based on sexual caste.

It is important to note at this point, however, that these biological differences between men and women are only *conditions* which may be *used* against women by men in certain economic and political organizations of society and in social roles. They are like *tools* rather than mandates. A tool is only justified if you agree with both the tool's efficiency and the worth of the task that it is being used for, given other available options in achieving the task. In a society with few material resources and no available means of birth control, the most efficient way of ensuring the reproduction of the next generation may be the sexual division of labor in which women, constantly subject to pregnancies, do the reproductive work of breast-feeding and raising the children, while the men engage in hunting, trading, and defense. In a society like ours, on the other hand, where we have the technology and means to control births, feed babies on formula food, and combat physical strength with weapons, the continuation of the sexual division of labor can no longer be justified as the most efficient mode for organizing reproductive work.

It seems that we should look for a social explanation for the continued underdevelopment and unavailability of the material resources for easing women's reproductive burden. This lack is due, I maintain, to a social organization of the forces of reproduction that perpetuates the sexual division of labor at home and in the job market, and thus benefits the perceived interests of men, not women.

The two biological disadvantages of women, relative male strength and the female role in biological reproduction, explain the persistence of the sexual division of labor and the sexual stereotypes based on this. Variations in the stereotypes seem to relate fairly directly to the power women have relative to men in the particular society. This, in turn, depends on the mode of production of the society and whether or not women's reproductive work of rais-

---

[11] It is not simply the fact that men are physically stronger than women which gives them the edge in sexual power relations. It is also women's lesser psychological capacity for violence and aggressiveness. However, this has as much to do with socialization into passive roles from early childhood as it does with any inequality in the amount of the male hormone androgen, which is correlated to aggressive behavior in higher primates. As Simone de Beauvoir points out in *The Second Sex* (New York: Knopf, 1953), male children develop training in aggressive behavior from an early age, while female children are kept from the psychological hardening process involved in physical fights. Feeling that one is by nature submissive will cause one to be submissive; so even women who are equal in strength to men will appear to themselves and to men not to be so.

ing children is in conflict with their gaining any power in the social relations of production.

• • •

Whatever the origin of the power struggle between men and women to control reproduction, the fact seems to be that the degree of a woman's oppression in a society is related to the amount of power she has at any particular historical period in the relations of reproduction in the family as well as the relations of production in society. Her oppression is thus relative to her class position as well as to her power in relation to men in her family.

There is no easy formula by which to determine the amount of power women have by simply looking at how much productive work and child care they do relative to men in a certain historical period. What is important is not the *amount* of work done, but the control a woman has over her work and the kind of independence this control offers her in the case of actual or potential conflicts with men over how the work should be done. Thus, although American slave women did as much productive work as slave men, and were almost totally responsible for the child care not only for their own children but for those of the plantation owner as well, slave women had no control over this work. Their children could be sold away from them, and they could be brutally punished if they refused to do the work assigned them by their masters. The lady of the plantation, on the other hand, did little productive work. She was more in a managerial position, usually responsible for managing the health care, clothing, and food of the slaves. She usually had little say in economic decisions about the plantation, since she was not considered a joint owner. On the other hand, the Victorian sexual division of labor and the Cult of True Womanhood gave the wealthy white woman almost total control over her children in decisions about child-rearing. Relative to her husband, all in all, she had less power; relative to her female slave she had more; and her female slave in turn had more power than the male slave because of her central role in child-rearing and the greater likelihood that fathers rather than mothers would be sold away from children.

• • •

V. CONCLUSIONS ABOUT THE NATURAL COMPLEMENT THEORY

We have discussed several different views of the "natural" sex differences between men and women prevalent in different historical periods. When we observe the shift in ideology as to what constitutes "true" female and male nature, we note that the shift has nothing to do with the further scientific discovery of biological differences between men and women. It seems rather to correlate to changes in the relation between men's and women's roles in production and reproduction, and to what serves the interests of the dominant male economic class. Given this fact of its ideological role, the Natural Complement theory, and any other static universal theory of what the "natural relationship" of man to woman should be, loses credibility.

Instead, it seems more plausible to assume that human nature is plastic and moldable, and that women and men develop their sexual identities, their sense of self, and their motivations through responding to the social expectations placed upon them. They develop the skills and personality traits necessary to carry out the productive and reproductive roles available to them in their sociohistorical context, given their sex, race, ethnic identity, and class background.

If we wish to develop a realistic ideal for human development, then, we cannot take the existing traits that differentiate men from women in this society as norms for behavior. Neither can we expect to find an ideal in some biological male and female substratum, after we strip away all the socialization processes we go through to develop our egos. Rather, with the present-day women's movement, we should ask: what traits are desirable and possible to teach people in order for them to reach their full individual human potential? And how would our society have to restructure its productive and reproductive relations in order to allow people to develop in this way?

VI. AN IDEAL LOVE RELATIONSHIP

One argument for the development of androgynous personalities (and the accompanying destruction of the sexual division of labor in production and re-production) is that without such a radical change in male and female roles an ideal love relationship be-tween the sexes is not possible. The argument goes like this. An ideal love between two mature people would be love between equals. I assume that such an ideal is the only concept of love that is histori-cally compatible with our other developed ideals of political and social equality. But, as Shulamith Fire-stone argues,[12] an equal love relationship requires the vulnerability of each partner to the other. There is today, however, an unequal balance of power in male-female relationships. Contrary to the claims of the Natural Complement theory, it is not possible for men and women to be equal while playing the complementary sex roles taught in our society. The feminine role makes a woman less equal, less pow-erful, and less free than the masculine role makes men. In fact, it is the emotional understanding of this lack of equality in love relations between men and women which increasingly influences feminists to choose lesbian love relationships.

Let us consider the vulnerabilities of women in a heterosexual love relationship under the four classi-fications Juliet Mitchell gives for women's roles[13]: production, reproduction, socialization of children, and sexuality.

1. Women's Role in Production   In the United States today, 42 percent of women work, and about 33 percent of married women work in the wage-labor force. This is much higher than the 6 percent of women in the wage-labor force around the turn of the century, and higher than in other industrial-ized countries. Nonetheless, sex-role socialization affects women's power in two important ways. First, because of job segregation by sex into part-time and low-paying jobs, women, whether single or married, are at an economic disadvantage in comparison with men when it comes to supporting

themselves. If they leave their husbands or lovers, they drop to a lower economic class, and many have to go on welfare. Second, women who have chil-dren and who also work in the wage-labor force have two jobs, not one: the responsibility for the major part of child-raising and housework, as well as the outside job. This keeps many housewives from seeking outside jobs, and makes them eco-nomically dependent on their husbands. Those who do work outside the home expend twice as much energy as the man and are less secure. Many women who try to combine career and motherhood find that the demands of both undermine their egos because they don't feel that they can do both jobs ade-quately.[14]

2. Women's Role in Reproduction   Although women currently monopolize the means of biologi-cal reproduction, they are at a disadvantage because of the absence of free contraceptives, adequate health care, and free legal abortions. A man can enjoy sex without having to worry about the conse-quences the way a woman does if a mistake occurs and she becomes pregnant. Women have some compensation in the fact that in the United States today they are favored legally over the father in their right to control of the children in case of sepa-ration or divorce. But this legal advantage (a victory won by women in the early 20th century in the on-going power struggle between the sexes for control of children, i.e. control over social reproduction) does not adequately compensate for the disadvan-tages to which motherhood subjects one in this so-ciety.

3. Women's Role in Socialization: As Wife and Mother   The social status of women, and hence their self-esteem, is measured primarily in terms of how successful they are in their relationships as

---

[12] Shulamith Firestone, *The Dialectic of Sex* (New York: William Morrow, 1970), chap. 6.

[13] Juliet Mitchell, *Woman's Estate* (New York: Random House, 1971).

[14] Socialization into complementary sex roles is responsible not only for job segregation practices' keeping women in low-paid service jobs which are extensions of the supportive work women do in the home as mothers, but also for making it difficult for women to feel confident in their ability to excel at competitive "male-defined" jobs.

lovers, wives, and mothers. Unlike men, who learn that their major social definition is success in work, women are taught from childhood that their ultimate goal is love and marriage. Women thus have more invested in a love relationship than men, and more to lose if it fails. The "old maid" or the "divorcee" is still an inferior status to be pitied, while the "swinging bachelor" is rather envied.

The fact that men achieve self- and social definition from their work means that they can feel a lesser commitment to working out problems in a relationship. Furthermore, men have more options for new relationships than do women. The double standard in sexuality allows a man to have affairs more readily than his wife. Ageism is a further limitation on women: an older man is considered a possible lover by both younger and older women, but an older woman, because she is no longer the "ideal" sex object, is not usually considered a desirable lover by either male peers or by younger men.

A woman's role as mother places her in a more vulnerable position than the man. Taking care of children and being attentive to their emotional needs is very demanding work. Many times it involves conflicts between the woman's own needs and the needs of the child. Often it involves conflict and jealousy between husband and children for her attention and emotional energy. It is the woman's role to harmonize this conflict, which she often does at the expense of herself, sacrificing her private time and interests in order to provide support for the projects of her husband and children.

No matter how devoted a parent a father is, he tends to see his time with the children as play time, not as work time. His job interests and hobbies take precedence over directing his energy to children. Thus he is more independent than the woman, who sees her job as making husband and children happy. This is the sort of job that is never completed, for there are always more ways to make people happy. Because a woman sees her job to be supporting her husband and mothering her children, the woman sees the family as her main "product." This makes her dependent on their activities, lives, and successes for her own success, and she lives vicariously through their activities. But as her "product" is human beings, when the children leave, as they must, to live independent lives, middle age brings an end to her main social function. The woman who has a career has other problems, for she has had to support her husband's career over hers wherever there was a conflict, because she knows male egos are tied up with success and "making it" in this competitive society. Women's egos, on the other hand, are primed for failure. Successful women, especially successful women with unsuccessful husbands, are considered not "true" women, but rather as deviants, "castrating bitches," "ball-busters," and "masculine women." For all these reasons, a woman in a love relationship with a man is geared by the Natural Complement view of herself as a woman to put her interests last, to define herself in terms of husband and children, and therefore to be more dependent on them than they are on her.

A woman is also vulnerable in her role as mother because there are limited alternatives if, for example, she wishes to break off her relationship with the father of her children. As a mother, her social role in bringing up children is defined as more important, more essential for the well-being of the children than the man's. Therefore, she is expected to take the children to live with her, or else she is considered a failure as a mother. But the life of a divorced or single mother with children in a nuclear-family-oriented society is lonely and hard: she must now either do two jobs without the companionship of another adult, in a society where jobs for women are inadequate, or she must survive on welfare or alimony with a reduced standard of living. When this is the alternative, is it any wonder that mothers are more dependent on maintaining a relationship—even when it is not satisfying—than the man is?

4. Women's Role in Sexuality A woman's sexual role is one in which she is both elevated by erotic romanticism and deflated to being a mere "cunt"—good for release of male sexual passions but interchangeable with other women. Because women play a subordinate role in society and are not seen as equal agents or as equally productive, men must justify a relationship with a particular woman by making her something special, mystifying her, making her better than other women. In fact, this idealization doesn't deal with her as a real *individual*; it treats her as either a beautiful object or as a mothering, supportive figure.

This idealization of women which occurs in the first stages of infatuation wears off as the couple settles into a relationship of some duration. What is left is the idea of woman as passive sex object whom one possesses and whose job as wife is to give the husband pleasure in bed. Since the woman is not seen as (and doesn't usually see herself as) active in sex, she tends to see sex as a duty rather than as a pleasure. She is not socially expected to take the active kind of initiative (even to the extent of asking for a certain kind of sex play) that would give her a sense of control over her sex life. The idea of herself as a body to be dressed and clothed in the latest media-advertised fashions "to please men" keeps her a slave to fashion and forces her to change her ego-ideal with every change in fashion. She can't see herself as an individual.

VII. ANDROGYNY AS A PROGRESSIVE IDEAL

It is the sexual division of labor in the home and at work that perpetuates complementary sex roles for men and women. In underdeveloped societies with scarce material resources such an arrangement may indeed be the most rational way to allow for the most efficient raising of children and production of goods. But this is no longer true for developed societies. In this age of advanced technology, men's relative strength compared to women's is no longer important, either in war or in the production of goods. The gun and the spinning jenny have equalized the potential role of men and women in both repression and production. And the diaphragm, the pill, and other advances in the technology of reproduction have equalized the potential power of women and men to control their bodies and to reproduce themselves.[15] (The development of cloning would mean that men and women could reproduce without the participation of the opposite sex.)

We have seen complementary sex roles and their extension to job segregation in wage labor make an ideal love relationship between equals impossible for men and women in our society. The questions that remain are: would the development of androgynous human beings through androgynous sex-role training be possible? If possible, would it allow for the development of equal love relationships? What other human potentials would androgyny allow to develop? And how would society have to be restructured in order to allow for androgynous human beings and equal love relationships?

There is good evidence that human babies are bisexual, and only *learn* a specific male or female identity by imitating and identifying with adult models. This evidence comes from the discovery that all human beings possess both male and female hormones (androgen and estrogen respectively), and also from concepts first developed at length by Freud. Freud argued that heterosexual identity is not achieved until the third stage of the child's sexual development. Sex identity is developed through the resolution of the Oedipus complex, in which the child has to give up a primary attachment to the mother and learn either to identify with, or love, the father. But Shulamith Firestone suggests that this process is not an inevitable one, as Freud presents it to be. Rather, it is due to the power dynamics of the patriarchal nuclear family.[16] Note that, on this

---

[15] Thanks to Sam Bowles for this point.

[16] Firestone, op. cit. The boy and girl both realize that the father has power in the relationship between him and the mother, and that his role, and not the mother's, represents the possibility of achieving eonomic and social power in the world and over one's life. The mother, in contrast, represents nurturing and emotionality. Both boy and girl, then, in order to get power for themselves, have to reject the mother as a love object—the boy, because he is afraid of the father as rival and potential castrator; and the girl, because the only way as a girl she can attain power is through manipulating the father. So she becomes a rival to her mother for her father's love. The girl comes to identify with her mother and to choose her father and, later, other men for love objects; while the boy identifies with his father, sublimates his sexual attraction to his mother into superego (will power), and chooses mother substitutes, other women, for his love objects.

analysis, if the sexual division of labor were destroyed, the mechanism that trains boys and girls to develop heterosexual sexual identities would also be destroyed. If fathers and mothers played equal nurturant roles in child-rearing and had equal social, economic, and political power outside the home, there would be no reason for the boy to have to reject his emotional side in order to gain the power associated with the male role. Neither would the girl have to assume a female role in rejecting her assertive, independent side in order to attain power indirectly through manipulation of males. As a sexual identity, bisexuality would then be the norm rather than the exception.

If bisexuality were the norm rather than the exception for the sexual identities that children develop,[17] androgynous sex roles would certainly be a consequence. For, as discussed above, the primary mechanism whereby complementary rather than androgynous sex roles are maintained is through heterosexual training, and through the socialization of needs for love and sexual gratification to the

search for a love partner of the opposite sex. Such a partner is sought to complement one in the traits that one has repressed or not developed because in one's own sex such traits were not socially accepted.

VIII. THE ANDROGYNOUS MODEL

I believe that only androgynous people can attain the full human potential possible given our present level of material and social resources (and this only if society is radically restructured). Only such people can have ideal love relationships; and without such relationships, I maintain that none can develop to the fullest potential. Since human beings are social animals and develop through interaction and productive activity with others, such relationships are necessary.

Furthermore, recent studies have shown that the human brain has two distinct functions: one associated with analytic, logical, sequential thinking (the left brain), and the other associated with holistic, metaphorical, intuitive thought (the right brain). Only a person capable of tapping both these sides of him/herself will have developed to full potential. We might call this characteristic of the human brain "psychic bisexuality,"[18] since it has been shown that women in fact have developed skills which allow them to tap the abilities of the right side of the brain more than men, who on the contrary excel in the analytic, logical thought characteristic of the left side. The point is that men and women have the potential for using both these functions, and yet our socialization at present tends to cut off from one or the other of these parts of ourselves.[19]

_____

[17] It should be understood here that no claim is being made that bisexuality is more desirable than homo- or heterosexuality. The point is that with the removal of the social mechanisms in the family that channel children into heterosexuality, there is no reason to suppose that most of them will develop in that direction. It would be more likely that humans with androgynous personalities would be bisexual, the assumption here being that there are no innate biological preferences in people for sexual objects of the same or opposite sex. Rather, this comes to be developed because of emotional connections of certain sorts of personality characteristics with the male and female body, characteristics which develop because of complementary sex-role training, and which would not be present without it.

The other mechanism which influences people to develop a heterosexual identity is the desire to reproduce. As long as the social institution for raising children is the heterosexual nuclear family, and as long as society continues to place social value on biological parenthood, most children will develop a heterosexual identity. Not, perhaps, in early childhood, but certainly after puberty, when the question of reproduction becomes viable. Radical socialization and collectivization of child-rearing would thus have to characterize a society before bisexuality would be the norm not only in early childhood, but in adulthood as well. For the purposes of developing androgynous individuals, however, full social bisexuality of this sort is not necessary. All that is needed is the restructuring of the sex roles of father and mother in the nuclear family so as to eliminate the sexual division of labor there.

_____

[18] Charlotte Painter, Afterword to C. Painter and M. J. Moffet, eds., _Revelations: Diaries of Women_ (New York: Random House, 1975).

[19] It is notable that writers, painters, and other intellectuals, who presumably would need skills of both sorts, have often been misfits in the prevalent complementary sex stereotyping. In fact, thinkers as diverse as Plato (in the _Symposium_) and Virginia Woolf (in _A Room of One's Own_) have suggested that writers and thinkers need to be androgynous to tap all the skills necessary for successful insight.

What would an androgynous personality be like? My model for the ideal androgynous person comes from the concept of human potential developed by Marx in *Economic and Philosophical Manuscripts*. Marx's idea is that human beings have a need (or a potential) for free, creative, productive activity which allows them to control their lives in a situation of cooperation with others. Both men and women need to be equally active and independent; with an equal sense of control over their lives; equal opportunity for creative, productive activity; and a sense of meaningful involvement in the community.

Androgynous women would be just as assertive as men about their own needs in a love relationship: productive activity outside the home, the right to private time, and the freedom to form other intimate personal and sexual relationships. I maintain that being active and assertive—traits now associated with being "masculine"—are positive traits that all people need to develop. Many feminists are suspicious of the idea of self-assertion because it is associated with the traits of aggression and competitiveness. However, there is no inevitability to this connection: it results from the structural features of competitive, hierarchical economic systems, of which our own (monopoly capitalism) is one example. In principle, given the appropriate social structure, there is no reason why a self-assertive person cannot also be nurturant and cooperative.

Androgynous men would be more sensitive and aware of emotions than sex-role stereotyped "masculine" men are today. They would be more concerned with the feelings of all people, including women and children, and aware of conflicts of interests. Being sensitive to human emotions is necessary to an effective care and concern for others. Such sensitivity is now thought of as a "motherly," "feminine," or "maternal" instinct, but in fact is a role and skill learned by women, and it can equally well be learned by men. Men need to get in touch with their own feelings in order to empathize with others, and, indeed, to understand themselves better so as to be more in control of their actions.

We have already discussed the fact that women are more vulnerable in a love relationship than men because many men consider a concern with feelings and emotions to be part of the woman's role. Women, then, are required to be more aware of everyone's feelings (if children and third parties are involved) than men, and they are under more pressure to harmonize the conflicts by sacrificing their own interests.

Another important problem with a non-androgynous love relationship is that it limits the development of mutual understanding. In general, it seems true that the more levels people can relate on, the deeper and more intimate their relationship is. The more experiences and activities they share, the greater their companionship and meaning to each other. And this is true for emotional experiences. Without mutual understanding of the complex of emotions involved in an ongoing love relationship, communication and growth on that level are blocked for both people. This means that, for both people, self-development of the sort that could come from the shared activity of understanding and struggling to deal with conflicts will not be possible.

In our society as presently structured, there are few possibilities for men and women to develop themselves through shared activities. Men and women share more activities with members of their own sex than with each other. Most women can't get jobs in our sexist, job-segregated society which allow them to share productive work with men. Most men just don't have the skills (or the time, given the demands of their wage-labor jobs) to understand the emotional needs of children and to share the activity of child-rearing equally with their wives.

How must our society be restructured to allow for the development of androgynous personalities? How can it be made to provide for self-development through the shared activities of productive and reproductive work? I maintain that this will not be possible (except for a small privileged elite) without the development of a democratic socialist society. In such a society no one would benefit from cheap labor (presently provided to the capitalist class by a part-time reserve army of women). Nor would anyone benefit from hierarchical power relationships (which encourage competition among the working class and reinforce male sex-role stereotypes as necessary to "making it" in society).

As society is presently constituted, the patriarchal nuclear family and women's reproductive work therein serve several crucial roles in maintaining the capitalist system. In the family, women do the unpaid work of social reproduction of the labor force (child-rearing). They also pacify and support the male breadwinner in an alienating society where men who are not in the capitalist class have little control of their product or work conditions. Men even come to envy their wives' relatively non-alienated labor in child-rearing rather than dealing with those with the real privilege, the capitalist class. Since those in power relations never give them up without a struggle, it is utopian to think that the capitalist class will allow for the elimination of the sexual division of labor without a socialist revolution with feminist priorities. Furthermore, men in the professional and working classes must be challenged by women with both a class and feminist consciousness to begin the process of change.

In order to eliminate the subordination of women in the patriarchal nuclear family and the perpetuation of sex-role stereotypes therein, there will need to be a radical reorganization of child-rearing. Father and mother must have an equal commitment to raising children. More of the reproductive work must be socialized—for example, by community child care, perhaps with parent cooperatives. Communal living is one obvious alternative which would de-emphasize biological parenthood and allow homosexuals and bisexuals the opportunity to have an equal part in relating to children. The increased socialization of child care would allow parents who are incompatible the freedom to dissolve their relationships without denying their children the secure, permanent loving relationships they need with both men and women. A community responsibility for child-rearing would provide children with male and female models other than their biological parent—models that they would be able to see and relate to emotionally.

Not only would men and women feel an equal

responsibility to do reproductive work, they would also expect to do rewarding, productive work in a situation where they had equal opportunity. Such a situation would of course require reduced work-weeks for parents, maternity and paternity leaves, and the development of a technology of reproduction which would allow women complete control over their bodies.

As for love relationships, with the elimination of sex roles and the disappearance, in an overpopulated world, of any biological need for sex to be associated with procreation, there would be no reason why such a society could not transcend sexual gender. It would no longer matter what biological sex individuals had. Love relationships, and the sexual relationships developing out of them, would be based on the individual meshing-together of androgynous human beings.

IS HOMOSEXUALITY UNNATURAL?

Richard D. Mohr

WHO ARE GAYS ANYWAY?

A recent Gallup poll found that only one in five Americans reports having a gay or lesbian acquaintance.[1] This finding is extraordinary given the number of practicing homosexuals in America. Alfred Kinsey's 1948 study of the sex lives of 12,000 white males shocked the nation: 37 percent had at least one homosexual experience to orgasm in their adult lives; an additional 13 percent had homosexual fantasies to orgasm; 4 percent were exclusively homosexual in their practices; another 5 percent had virtually no heterosexual experience; and nearly 20

---

[1] "Public Fears—And Sympathies," *Newsweek,* August 12, 1985, p. 23.

percent had at least as many homosexual as heterosexual experiences.[2]

Two out of five men one passes on the street have had orgasmic sex with men. Every second family in the country has a member who is essentially homosexual and many more people regularly have homosexual experiences. Who are homosexuals? They are your friends, your minister, your teacher, your bank teller, your doctor, your mail carrier, your officemate, your roommate, your congressional representative, your sibling, parent, and spouse. They are everywhere, virtually all ordinary, virtually all unknown.

Several important consequences follow. First, the country is profoundly ignorant of the actual experience of gay people. Second, social attitudes and practices that are harmful to gays have a much greater overall harmful impact on society than is usually realized. Third, most gay people live in hiding—in the closet—making the "coming out" experience the central fixture of gay consciousness and invisibility the chief characteristic of the gay community.

• • •

BUT AREN'T THEY UNNATURAL?

The most noteworthy feature of the accusation of something being unnatural (where a moral rather than an advertising point is being made) is that the plaint is so infrequently made. One used to hear the charge leveled against abortion, but that has pretty much faded as anti-abortionists have come to lay all their chips on the hope that people will come to view abortion as murder. Incest used to be considered unnatural but discourse now usually assimilates it to the moral machinery of rape and violated trust. The charge comes up now in ordinary discourse only against homosexuality. This suggests that the charge is highly idiosyncratic and has little, if any, explanatory force. It fails to put homosexuality in a class with anything else so that one can learn by comparison with clear cases of the class just exactly what it is that is allegedly wrong with it.

Though the accusation of unnaturalness looks whimsical, in actual ordinary discourse when applied to homosexuality, it is usually delivered with venom aforethought. It carries a high emotional charge, usually expressing disgust and evincing queasiness. Probably it is nothing but an emotional charge. For people get equally disgusted and queasy at all sorts of things that are perfectly natural—to be expected in nature apart from artifice—and that could hardly be fit subjects for moral condemnation. Two typical examples in current American culture are some people's responses to mothers' suckling in public and to women who do not shave body hair. When people have strong emotional reactions, as they do in these cases, without being able to give good reasons for them, we think of them not as operating morally, but rather as being obsessed and manic. So the feelings of disgust that some people have to gays will hardly ground a charge of immorality. People fling the term "unnatural" against gays in the same breath and with the same force as when they call gays "sick" and "gross." When they do this, they give every appearance of being neurotically fearful and incapable of reasoned discourse.

When "nature" is taken in *technical* rather than ordinary usages, it looks like the notion also will not ground a charge of homosexual immorality. When unnatural means "by artifice" or "made by humans," it need only be pointed out that virtually everything that is good about life is unnatural in this sense, that the chief feature that distinguishes people from other animals is their very ability to make over the world to meet their needs and desires, and that their well-being depends upon these departures from nature. On this understanding of human nature and the natural, homosexuality is perfectly unobjectionable.

Another technical sense of natural is that some-

[2] Alfred C. Kinsey, *Sexual Behavior in the Human Male* (Philadelphia: Saunders, 1948), pp. 650–651. On the somewhat lower incidences of lesbianism, see Alfred C. Kinsey, *Sexual Behavior in the Human Female* (Philadelphia: Saunders, 1953), pp. 472–475.

thing is natural and so, good, if it fulfills some function in nature. Homosexuality on this view is unnatural because it allegedly violates the function of genitals, which is to produce babies. One problem with this view is that lots of bodily parts have lots of functions and just because some one activity can be fulfilled by only one organ (say, the mouth for eating) this activity does not condemn other functions of the organ to immorality (say, the mouth for talking, licking stamps, blowing bubbles, or having sex). So the possible use of the genitals to produce children does not, without more, condemn the use of the genitals for other purposes, say, achieving ecstasy and intimacy.

The functional view of nature will only provide a morally condemnatory sense to the unnatural if a thing which might have many uses has but one proper function to the exclusion of other possible functions. But whether this is so cannot be established simply by looking at the thing. For what is seen is all its possible functions. The notion of function seemed like it might ground moral authority, but instead it turns out that moral authority is needed to define proper function. Some people try to fill in this moral authority by appeal to the "design" or "order" of an organ, saying, for instance, that the genitals are designed for the purpose of procreation. But these people cheat intellectually if they do not make explicit *who* the designer and orderer is. If it is God, we are back to square one—holding others accountable for religious beliefs.

Further, ordinary moral attitudes about childbearing will not provide the needed supplement which in conjunction with the natural function view of bodily parts would produce a positive obligation to use the genitals for procreation. Society's attitude toward a childless couple is that of pity not censure—even if the couple could have children. The pity may be an unsympathetic one, that is, not registering a course one would choose *for oneself,* but this does not make it a course one would *require* of others. The couple who discovers they cannot have children are viewed not as having thereby had a debt canceled, but rather as having to forgo some of the richness of life, just as a quadriplegic is viewed

not as absolved from some moral obligation to hop, skip, and jump, but as missing some of the richness of life. Consistency requires then that, at most, gays who do not or cannot have children are to be pitied rather than condemned. What *is* immoral is the willful preventing of people from achieving the richness of life. Immorality in this regard lies with those social customs, regulations, and statutes that prevent lesbians and gay men from establishing blood or adoptive families, not with gays themselves.

Sometimes people attempt to establish authority for a moral obligation to use bodily parts in a certain fashion simply by claiming that moral laws are natural laws and vice versa. On this account, inanimate objects and plants are good in that they follow natural laws by necessity, animals by instinct, and persons by a rational will. People are special in that they must first discover the laws that govern them. Now, even if one believes the view—dubious in the post-Newtonian, post-Darwinian world—that natural laws in the usual sense ($E = mc^2$, for instance) have some moral content, it is not at all clear how one is to discover the laws in nature that apply to people.

On the one hand, if one looks to people themselves for a model—and looks hard enough—one finds amazing variety, including homosexuality as a social ideal (upper-class fifth-century Athens) and even as socially mandatory (Melanesia today). When one looks to people, one is simply unable to strip away the layers of social custom, history, and taboo in order to see what's really there to any degree more specific than that people are the creatures that make over their world and are capable of abstract thought. That this is so should raise doubts that neutral principles are to be found in human nature that will condemn homosexuality.

On the other hand, if one looks to nature apart from people for models, the possibilities are staggering. There are fish that change gender over their lifetimes: should we "follow nature" and be operative transsexuals? Orangutans, genetically our next of kin, live completely solitary lives without social organization of any kind: ought we to "follow nature" and be hermits? There are many species where only two members per generation reproduce: should we be bees? The search in nature for people's purpose, far from finding sure models for action, is likely to leave one morally rudderless.

BUT AREN'T GAYS WILLFULLY THE WAY THEY ARE?

It is generally conceded that if sexual orientation is something over which an individual—for whatever reason—has virtually no control, then discrimination against gays is especially deplorable, as it is against racial and ethnic classes, because it holds people accountable without regard for anything they themselves have done. And to hold a person accountable for that over which the person has no control is a central form of prejudice.

Attempts to answer the question whether or not sexual orientation is something that is reasonably thought to be within one's own control usually appeal simply to various claims of the biological or "mental" sciences. But in the ensuing debate over genes, hormones, twins, early childhood development, and the like, is as unnecessary as it is currently inconclusive.[3] All that is needed to answer the question is to look at the actual experience of gays in current society and it becomes fairly clear that sexual orientation is not likely a matter of choice. For coming to have a homosexual identity simply does not have the same sort of structure that decision making has.

On the one hand, the "choice" of the gender of a sexual partner does not seem to express a trivial desire that might be as easily well fulfilled by a simple substitution of the desired object. Picking the gender of a sex partner is decidedly dissimilar, that is, to such activities as picking a flavor of ice cream.

---

[3] The preponderance of the scientific evidence supports the view that homosexuality is either genetically determined or a permanent result of early childhood development. See the Kinsey Institute's study by Alan Bell, Martin Weinberg, and Sue Hammersmith, *Sexual Preference: Its Development in Men and Women* (Bloomington: Indiana University Press, 1981); Frederick Whitam and Robin Mathy, *Male Homosexuality in Four Societies* (New York: Praeger, 1986), ch. 7.

If an ice-cream parlor is out of one's flavor, one simply picks another. And if people were persecuted, threatened with jail terms, shattered careers, loss of family and housing, and the like, for eating, say, rocky road ice cream, no one would ever eat it; everyone would pick another easily available flavor. That gay people abide in being gay even in the face of persecution shows that being gay is not a matter of easy choice.

On the other hand, even if establishing a sexual orientation is not like making a relatively trivial choice, perhaps it is nevertheless relevantly like making the central and serious life choices by which individuals try to establish themselves as being of some type. Again, if one examines gay experience, this seems not to be the case. For one never sees anyone setting out to become a homosexual, in the way one does see people setting out to become doctors, lawyers, and bricklayers. One does not find "gays-to-be" picking some end—"At some point in the future, I want to become a homosexual"—and then setting about planning and acquiring the ways and means to that end, in the way one does see people deciding that they want to become lawyers, and then sees them plan what courses to take and what sort of temperaments, habits, and skills to develop in order to become lawyers. Typically gays-to-be simply find themselves having homosexual encounters and yet at least initially resisting quite strongly the identification of being homosexual. Such a person even very likely resists having such encounters, but ends up having them anyway. Only with time, luck, and great personal effort, but sometimes never, does the person gradually come to accept her or his orientation, to view it as a given material condition of life, coming as materials do with certain capacities and limitations. The person begins to act in accordance with his or her orientation and its capacities, seeing its actualization as a requisite for an integrated personality and as a central component of personal well-being. As a result, the experience of coming out to oneself has for gays the basic structure of a discovery, not the structure of a choice. And far from signaling immorality, coming out to others affords one of the

few remaining opportunities in ever more bureaucratic, mechanistic, and socialistic societies to manifest courage.

QUESTIONS FOR DISCUSSION

1. Do "male" and "female" signify two different
   natures? How do you account for the observable
   behavior and characterological differences between men and women? Would you want there
   to be a society in which there were no specific
   sex-identified social roles? Is an androgynous
   human being a possible and/or desirable ideal?
2. Discuss the significance of the role of women
   within Islam with reference to Fatima Mernissi's
   analysis and Simone de Beauvoir's claim that
   women are the second sex.
3. Is homosexuality unnatural? Is it immoral? Defend your position with reference to Richard
   Mohr's analysis and to at least one other reading
   in this section.
4. Simone de Beauvoir writes: "A free individual
   blames only himself for his failures, he assumes
   responsibility for them; but everything happens
   to women through the agency of others, and
   therefore these others are responsible for her
   woes." Evaluate this position in the light of
   Sartre's claim that we are absolutely free and responsible for our actions.

René Magritte, *The False Mirror,* 1928, oil on canvas, 21 1/4″ x 31 7/8″. Collection, The Museum of Modern Art, New York. Purchase.

CHAPTER 5

SELF, MIND, AND BODY

The early Christian philosopher St. Augustine in his *Confessions* says, "What then is time? If no one asks me I know; if I try to explain it to someone who asks me, I know not." He might have said the same of *self.* For most of us, the concept of self when used unexamined is—like Augustine's concept of time—among the most basic and obvious that we use. But once we enter into a philosophical reflection on this concept, asking "Who am I?" or "What am I?" "Am I identical with my mind? My body? A soul that is different than either?", when questions such as these are asked, the clarity of our notion is quickly seen to vanish.

Thinkers in nearly every culture have asked such questions and come up with a variety of answers—answers that affect not only our psychological view of ourselves but also our approach to matters of the spirit. For the answer we give to the question of what and who we are will determine to a great extent the way we view our relation to this life and this body we call "my body." It will affect our views on the question of whether we will survive death and—if we do—what form an afterlife or -lives will take. Finally, it will affect our relations with others—with other "selves"—and, through this, our ethics

and our view of the community of selves we term "society."

The selections in the first section begin with the divergent answers given to the question by the two philosophers who, more than any other thinkers, have provided the foundations for both Western and Islamic philosophy—the ancient Greek philosophers Plato and Aristotle. These are followed by a section in which the discussion is continued in the current age of modern Western science. This, in turn, leads us to a similar philosophical dialogue which has been conducted down through the ages in India and the societies that it has influenced. For it is in India that the question "Who and what am I?" has been asked, perhaps most ruthlessly and most persistently, beginning with the sages of the *Upanishads* who saw it as the basis of much or all of spiritual life nearly 3000 years ago. In the section which follows this one, the two traditions are finally brought together in a contemporary article by the American philosopher Derek Parfit, in which he attempts to relate the insights of Buddhism and its "Abhidhamma" or metaphysical psychology to those of modern Western scientific psychology.

The next section deals with a view of self taken

from yet another culture, the Akan of Ghana in West Africa. Despite all cultural differences, the questions asked appear to be similar to those we have already encountered; and the answer given to them by the culture's dominant philosophy is a familiar one to those who have already read Descartes's *Meditations* or the *Bhagavad-Gita,* thus confirming the contention of author Kwame Gyekye that philosophy is not "a special relish of the people of the West and the East" alone.

Most of the philosophy described above is spiritual in its orientation. The next readings present the materialist alternative, the view that mind and spirit ultimately depend on the body and thus do not survive its death. Selections are taken from both ancient India and twentieth-century Europe, revealing a surprising similarity of viewpoint separated by over 5000 miles and 2500 years.

Finally, there is the notion of self as an organized activity or set of behaviors, as exemplified in the views of the modern Argentine philosopher Risieri Frondizi.

Readers of the Plato selection might also want to look at the Plato selections in Chapter 1. Those interested in Section Three should consult Sections Two and Three of Chapter 1 as well as the selections from Hindu and Buddhist sources in Chapters 3, 4, 7, and 8. Further selections on materialism are to be found in Section Five of Chapter 1, in the Freud reading from Chapter 3 and the Mao Tse-tung readings in Chapter 2.

TWO VIEWS FROM ANCIENT GREECE

Alfred North Whitehead once said that everyone is born either a Platonist or an Aristotelian. Although this may be an exaggeration, it seems safe to say that Plato and Aristotle in most matters reflect widely divergent viewpoints at a very basic level. It is also true that their influence has been strikingly widespread. Not only were they the major philosophers of their own native Greece, they also were central for the Romans when they took up Greek philosophy; still later, Plato and Aristotle dominated the thinking of the medieval Islamic and Jewish worlds as well as that of the medieval Christian West. Even today, Plato and Aristotle form a starting point for most Western philosophers. Nowhere is the basic dividing line set down by these thinkers more apparent than in their views of the nature of the self or "soul."

For Plato (427?–347? B.C.), in the selection presented from his dialogue *Phaedo,* the soul can exist in separation from the body, surviving the body's death and decay. He even argues for its reincarna-

tion, moving from body to body in lifetime after lifetime until it manages finally to free itself completely from the flesh. This is, of course, a viewpoint more frequently associated with India than the West, where we seldom encounter it outside the work of Plato and his disciples. It is not known if there is any connection between Plato's formulation of the doctrine and the Indian belief, though it is certainly possible that India provided his inspiration, since contact through trade did exist between India and Greece in the period when Plato and his teacher, Socrates, who sets forth the doctrine in *Phaedo,* lived.

For Aristotle (384–322 B.C.), on the other hand, essentially, "the soul is inseparable from its body." For the soul is the "form" of the body in the manner of wax and a stamp impressed on it; body and soul are matter and that which defines or molds it, neither one nor many but a unity which involves both. The notion of a full, personal survival of death thus seems a near impossibility on Aristotle's view.

THE PHAEDO

Plato

"Then from all this," said Socrates, "genuine philosophers must come to some such opinion as follows, so as to make to one another statements such as these: 'A sort of direct path, so to speak, seems to take us to the conclusion that so long as we have the body with us in our enquiry, and our soul is mixed up with so great an evil, we shall never attain sufficiently what we desire, and that, we say, is the truth. For the body provides thousands of busy distractions because of its necessary food; besides, if diseases fall upon us, they hinder us from the pursuit of the real. With loves and desires and fears and

all kinds of fancies and much rubbish, it infects us, and really and truly makes us, as they say, unable to think one little bit about anything at any time. Indeed, wars and factions and battles all come from the body and its desires, and from nothing else. For the desire of getting wealth causes all wars, and we are compelled to desire wealth by the body, being slaves to its culture; therefore we have no leisure for philosophy, from all these reasons. Chief of all is that if we do have some leisure, and turn away from the body to speculate on something, in our searches it is everywhere interfering, it causes confusion and disturbance, and dazzles us so that it will not let us see the truth; so in fact we see that if we are ever to know anything purely we must get rid of it, and examine the real things by the soul alone; and then, it seems, after we are dead, as the reasoning shows,

263

not while we live, we shall possess that which we desire, lovers of which we say we are, namely wisdom. For if it is impossible in company with the body to know anything purely, one thing of two follows: either knowledge is possible nowhere, or only after death; for then alone the soul will be quite by itself apart from the body, but not before. And while we are alive, we shall be nearest to knowing, as it seems, if as far as possible we have no commerce or communion with the body which is not absolutely necessary, and if we are not infected with its nature, but keep ourselves pure from it, until God himself shall set us free. And so, pure and rid of the body's foolishness, we shall probably be in the company of those like ourselves, and shall know through our own selves complete incontamination, and that is perhaps the truth. But for the impure to grasp the pure is not, it seems, allowed.' So we must think, Simmias, and so we must say to one another, all who are rightly lovers of learning; don't you agree?"

"Assuredly, Socrates."

"Then," said Socrates, "if this is true, my comrade, there is great hope that when I arrive where I am travelling, there if anywhere I shall sufficiently possess that for which all our study has been pursued in this past life. So the journey which has been commanded for me is made with good hope, and the same for any other man who believes he has got his mind purified, as I may call it."

"Certainly," replied Simmias.

"And is not purification really that which has been mentioned so often in our discussion, to separate as far as possible the soul from the body, and to accustom it to collect itself together out of the body in every part, and to dwell alone by itself as far as it can, both at this present and in the future, being freed from the body as if from a prison?"

"By all means," said he.

"Then is not this called death—a freeing and separation of soul from body?"

"Not a doubt of that," said he.

"But to set it free, as we say, is the chief endeavour of those who rightly love wisdom, nay of those alone, and the very care and practice of the philosophers is nothing but the freeing and separation of soul from body, don't you think so?"

"It appears to be so."

"Then, as I said at first, it would be absurd for a man preparing himself in his life to be as near as possible to death, so to live, and then when death came, to object?"

"Of course."

"Then in fact, Simmias," he said, "those who rightly love wisdom are practising dying, and death to them is the least terrible thing in the world. Look at it in this way: If they are everywhere at enmity with the body, and desire the soul to be alone by itself, and if, when this very thing happens, they shall fear and object—would not that be wholly unreasonable? Should they not willingly go to a place where there is good hope of finding what they were in love with all through life (and they loved wisdom), and of ridding themselves of the companion which they hated? When human favourites and wives and sons have died, many have been willing to go down to the grave, drawn by the hope of seeing there those they used to desire, and of being with them; but one who is really in love with wisdom and holds firm to this same hope, that he will find it in the grave, and nowhere else worth speaking of—will he then fret at dying and not go thither rejoicing? We must surely think, my comrade, that he will go rejoicing, if he is really a philosopher; he will surely believe that he will find wisdom in its purity there and there alone. If this is true, would it not be most unreasonable, as I said just now, if such a one feared death?"

• • •

When Socrates had thus finished, Cebes took up the word: "Socrates," he said, "on the whole I think you speak well; but that about the soul is a thing which people find very hard to believe. They fear that when it parts from the body it is nowhere any more; but on the day when a man dies, as it parts from the body, and goes out like a breath or a whiff of smoke, it is dispersed and flies away and is gone and is nowhere any more. If it existed anywhere, gathered together by itself, and rid of these evils which you have just described, there would be great and good hope, Socrates, that what you say is true; but this very thing needs no small reassurance and faith, that the soul exists when the man dies, and that it has some power and sense."

"Quite true," said Socrates, "quite true, Cebes; well, what are we to do? Shall we discuss this very question, whether such a thing is likely or not?"

"For my part," said Cebes, "I should very much like to know what your opinion is about it."

Then Socrates answered, "I think no one who heard us now could say, not even a composer of comedies,[1] that I am babbling nonsense and talking about things I have nothing to do with! So if you like, we must make a full enquiry.

"Let us enquire whether the souls of dead men really exist in the house of Hades or not. Well, there is the very ancient legend which we remember, that they are continually arriving there from this world, and further that they come back here and are born again from the dead. If that is true, and the living are born again from the dead, must not our souls exist there? For they could not be born again if they did not exist; and this would be sufficient proof that it is true, if it should be really shown that the living are born from the dead and from nowhere else. But if this be not true, we must take some other line."

"Certainly," said Cebes.

"Then don't consider it as regards men only," he said; "if you wish to understand more easily, think of all animals and vegetables, and, in a word, everything that was birth, let us see if everything comes into being like that, always opposite from opposite and from nowhere else; whenever there happens to be a pair of opposites, such as beautiful and ugly, just and unjust, and thousands of others like these. So let us enquire whether everything that has an opposite must come from its opposite and from nowhere else. For example, when anything becomes bigger, it must, I suppose, become bigger from being smaller before."

"Yes."

"And if it becomes smaller, it was bigger before and became smaller after that?"

"True," he said.

"And again, weaker from stronger, and slower from quicker?"

"Certainly."

"Very well, if a thing becomes worse, is it from being better, and more just from more unjust?"

"Of course."

"Have we established that sufficiently, then, that everything comes into being in this way, opposite from opposite?"

"Certainly."

"Again, is there not the same sort of thing in them all, between the two opposites two becomings, from the first to the second, and back from the second to the first; between greater and lesser increase and diminution, and we call one increasing and the other diminishing?"

"Yes," he said.

"And being separated and being mingled, growing cold and growing hot, and so with all; even if we have sometimes no names for them, yet in fact at least it must be the same everywhere, that they come into being from each other, and that there is a becoming from one to the other?"

"Certainly," said he.

"Well then," he said, "is there something opposite to being alive, as sleeping is opposite to being awake?"

"There is," he said.

"What?"

"Being dead," he said.

"Well, all these things come into being from each other, if they are opposites, and there are two becomings between each two?"

"Of course."

"Then," said Socrates, "I will speak of one of the two pairs that I mentioned just now, and its becomings; you tell me about the other. My pair is sleeping and being awake, and I say that being awake comes into being from sleeping and sleeping from being awake, and that their becomings are falling asleep and waking up. Is that satisfactory?"

"Quite so."

---

[1] As Aristophanes had done in his play *The Clouds*.

"Then you tell me in the same way about life and death. Do you not say that to be alive is the opposite of to be dead?"

"I do."

"And that they come into being from each other?"

"Yes."

"From the living, then, what comes into being?"

"The dead," he said.

"And what from the dead?"

"The living, I must admit."

"Then from the dead, Cebes, come living things and living men?"

"So it appears," he said.

"Then," said he, "our souls exist in the house of Hades."

"It seems so."

"Well, of the two becomings between them, one is quite clear. For dying is clear, I suppose, don't you think so?"

"Oh yes," said he.

"Then what shall we do?" he said. "Shall we refuse to grant in return the opposite becoming; and shall nature be lame in this point? Is it not a necessity to grant some becoming opposite to dying?"

"Surely it is," he said.

"What is that?"

"Coming to life again."

"Then," said he, "if there is coming to life again, this coming to life would be a being born from the dead into the living."

"Certainly."

"It is agreed between us, then, in this way also that the living are born from the dead, no less than the dead from the living; and since this is true, there would seem to be sufficient proof that the souls of the dead must of necessity exist somewhere, whence we assume they are born again."

• • •

"Another thing," said Cebes, putting in, "you know that favourite argument of yours, Socrates, which we so often heard from you, that our learning is simply recollection; that also makes it necessary, I suppose, if it is true, that we learnt at some former time what we now remember; but this is impossible unless our soul existed somewhere before it was born in this human shape. In this way also the soul seems to be something immortal."

Then Simmias put in, "But, Cebes, what are the proofs of this? Remind me, for I don't quite remember now."

"There is one very beautiful proof," said Cebes, "that people, when asked questions, if they are properly asked, say of themselves everything correctly; yet if there were not knowledge in them, and right reason, they would not be able to do this. You see, if you show someone a diagram or anything like that, he proves most clearly that this is true."

Socrates said, "If you don't believe this, Simmias, look at it in another way and see whether you agree. You disbelieve, I take it, how what is called learning can be recollection?"

"Disbelieve you," said Simmias, "not I! I just want to have an experience of what we are now discussing—recollection. I almost remember and believe already from what Cebes tried to say; yet none the less I should like to hear how *you* were going to put it."

"This is how," he answered. "We agree, I suppose, that if anyone remembers something he must have known it before at some time."

"Certainly," he said.

"Then do we agree on this also, that when knowledge comes to him in such a way, it is recollection? What I mean is something like this: If a man has seen or heard something or perceived it by some other sense, and he not only knows that, but thinks of something else of which the knowledge is not the same but different, is it not right for us to say he remembered that which he thought of?"

"How do you mean?"

"Here is an example: Knowledge of a man and knowledge of a lyre are different."

"Of course."

"Well, you know about lovers, that when they see a lyre or a dress or anything else which their beloved uses, this is what happens to them: they know the lyre, and they conceive in the mind the figure of the boy whose lyre it is? Now this is recollection; just as when one sees Simmias, one often remembers Cebes, and there would be thousands of things like that."

"Thousands, indeed!" said Simmias.

"Then is that sort of thing," said he, "a kind of recollection? Especially when one feels this about things which one had forgotten because of time and neglect?"

"Certainly," he said.

"Very well then," said Socrates. "When you see a horse in a picture, or a lyre in a picture, is it possible to remember a man? And when you see Simmias in a picture, to remember Cebes?"

"Yes indeed."

"Or when you see Simmias in a picture, to remember Simmias himself?"

"Oh yes," said he.

["These being either like or unlike?"

"Yes."

"It makes no difference," he said. "Whenever, seeing one thing, from sight of this you think of another thing whether like or unlike, it is necessary," he said, "that that was recollection."

"Certainly."]²

"Does it not follow from all this that recollection is both from like and from unlike things?"

"It does."

"But when a man remembers something from like things, must this not necessarily occur to him also—to reflect whether anything is lacking or not from the likeness of what he remembers?"

"He must."

"Consider then," he said, "if this is true. We say, I suppose, there is such a thing as the equal, not a stick equal to a stick, or a stone to a stone, or anything like that, but something independent which is alongside all of them, the equal itself, equality; yes or no?"

"Yes indeed," said Simmias, "upon my word, no doubt about it."

"And do we understand what that is?"

---

² The bracketed passage has been transposed from 74 C-D of the Greek text, p. 478, where it would appear to be meaningless.

"Certainly," he said. "Where did we get the knowledge of it? Was it not from such examples as we gave just now, by seeing equal sticks or stones and so forth, from these we conceived that which was something distinct from them? Don't you think it is distinct? Look at it this way also: Do not the same stones or sticks appear equal to one person and unequal to another?"

"Certainly."

"Well, did the really-equals ever seem unequal to you, I mean did equality ever seem to be inequality?"

"Never, Socrates."

"Then those equal things," said he, "are not the same as the equal itself."

"Not at all, I think, Socrates."

"Yet from these equals," he said, "being distinct from that equal, you nevertheless conceived and received knowledge of that equal?"

"Very true," he said.

"Well," said he, "how do we feel about the sticks as compared with the real equals we spoke of just now; do the equal sticks seem to us to be as equal as equality itself, or do they fall somewhat short of the essential nature of equality; or nothing short?"

"They fall short," he said, "a great deal."

"Then we agree on this: When one sees a thing, and thinks, 'This which I now see wants to be like something else—like one of the things that are, but falls short and is unable to be such as that is, it is inferior,' it is necessary, I suppose, that he who thinks thus has previous knowledge of that which he thinks it resembles but falls short of?"

"That is necessary."

"Very well, do we feel like that or not about equal things and the equal?"

"Assuredly we do."

"It is necessary then that we knew the equal before that time when, first seeing the equal things, we thought that all these aim at being such as the equal, but fall short."

"That is true."

"Well, we go on to agree here also: we did not and we could not get a notion of the equal by any other means than by seeing or grasping, or perceiving by some other sense. I say the same of equal and all the rest."

"And they are the same, Socrates, for what the argument wants to prove."

"Look here, then; it is from the senses we must get the notion that all these things of sense aim at that which is the equal, and fall short of it; or how do we say?"

"Yes."

"Then before we began to see and hear and use our other senses, we must have got somewhere knowledge of what the equal is, if we were going to compare with it the things judged equal by the senses and see that all things are eager to be such as that equal is, but are inferior to it."

"This is necessary from what we agreed, Socrates."

"Well, as soon as we were born we saw and heard and had our other senses?"

"Certainly."

"Then, we say, we must have got knowledge of the equal before that?"

"Yes."

"Before we were born, then, it is necessary that we must have got it."

"So it seems."

"Then if we got it before we were born and we were born having it, we knew before we were born and as soon as we were born, not only the equal and the greater and the less but all the rest of such things? For our argument now is no more about the equal than about the beautiful itself, and the good itself, and the just and the pious, and I mean everything which we seal with the name of 'that which is,' the essence, when we ask our questions and respond with our answers in discussion. So we must have got the proper knowledge of each of these before we were born."

• • •

"When did our souls get the knowledge of these things? For surely it is not since we became human beings."

"Certainly not."

"Then before."

"Yes."

"So, Simmias, our souls existed long ago, before they were in human shape, apart from bodies, and then had wisdom."

• • •

It appears to me that bigness itself never consents to be big and small at the same time, and not only that, even the bigness in us never accepts smallness and will not be surpassed; but one of two things, it must either depart and retreat whenever its opposite, smallness, comes near, or else must perish at its approach; it does not consent to submit and receive the smallness, and so to become other than what it was. Just so I, receiving and submitting to small, am still the man I am, I'm still this same small person; but the bigness in me, being big, has not dared to become small! In the same way, the smallness in us does not want to become or be big, nor does any other of the opposites, being still what it was, want to become and be the opposite; but either it goes away or it is destroyed in this change."

"Certainly," said Cebes, "that is what I think."

One of those present, hearing this, said—I do not clearly remember who it was—"Good heavens, didn't we admit in our former discussion the very opposite of what we are saying now—that the greater came from the less and the less from the greater, and in fact this is how opposites are generated, from opposites? Now it seems to be said that this could never be."

Socrates bent down his head to listen, and said, "Spoken like a man! I thank you for reminding me, but you don't understand the difference between what we are saying now and what we said then. For then we said that the practical opposite thing is generated from its practical opposite, but now we are saying that the opposite quality itself could never become the quality opposite to itself, either in us or in nature. Then, my friend, we were speaking of things which have opposites, these being named by the name of their (opposite) qualities, but now we are speaking of the opposite qualities themselves, from which being in the things, the things are named: those qualities themselves, we say, could never accept generation from each other." Then, with a glance at Cebes, he added, "Is it possible that you too, Cebes, were disturbed by what our friend spoke of?"

"No, not by this," replied Cebes, "but I don't deny that I get disturbed a good deal."

"Well, then, are we agreed," said Socrates, "simply on this, that nothing will ever be opposite to itself?"

"Quite agreed," he said.

"Here is something else," he said, "see if you will agree to this. You speak of hot and cold?"

"Yes."

"Is it the same as fire and snow?"

"Not at all."

"But the hot is something other than fire, and the cold other than snow?"

"Yes."

"Well, I suppose you agree that snow receiving fire (to use our former way of putting it) will never be what it was, snow, and also be hot, but when the hot approaches it will either retreat from it or be destroyed."

"Certainly."

"Fire, also, when the cold approaches, will either go away from it or be destroyed, but it will never endure to receive the coldness and still be what it was, fire, and cold too."

"True," said he.

"Then it is possible," he said, "with some such things, that not only the essence is thought worthy of the same name forever, but something else also is worthy, which is not that essence but which, when it exists, always has the form of that essence. Perhaps it will be a little clearer as follows. Odd numbers must always be called odd, I suppose, mustn't they?"

"Yes."

"Of all things do we use this name only for oddness, for that is what I ask, or is there something else, not oddness, but what must be called always by that name because its nature is never to be deserted by oddness? For example, triplet and so forth. Now consider the triplet: Don't you think it should be called always both by its own name and also by the name of odd, although oddness is not the same as triplet? Still it is the nature of triplet and quintet and half of all the numbers, that each of

them is odd although it is not the same thing as oddness; so also two and four and all the other row of numbers are each of them always even, although none is the same thing as evenness; do you agree?"

"Of course," he said.

"Now attend, this is what I want to make clear. It seems that not only those real opposites do not receive each other, but also things which not being opposites of each other yet always have those real opposites in them, these also do not look like things which receive that reality which is opposite to the reality in them, but when it approaches they either are destroyed or retire. We shall say, for example, that a triplet will be destroyed before any such thing happens to it, before it remains and becomes even, while it is still three?"

"Certainly," said Cebes.

"Nor, again," he said, "is twin the opposite of triplet."

"Not at all."

"Then not only the opposite essences do not remain at the approach of each other, but some other things do not await the approach of the opposites."

"Very true," he said.

"Then shall we distinguish what sorts of things these are," he said, "if we can?"

"Certainly."

"Then, Cebes, would they be those which compel whatever they occupy not only to get their own essence but also the essence of some opposite?"

"How so?"

"As we said just now. You know, I suppose, that whatever the essence of three occupies must necessarily be not only three but odd."

"Certainly."

"And the essence opposite to that which does this we say could never come near such a thing."

"It could not.'"

"And what has done this? Was not it oddness?"

"Yes."

"And opposite to this is the essence of even?"

"Yes."

"Then the essence of even will never approach three."

"No."

"So three has no part in the even."

"None."

"Then the triplet is uneven."

"Yes."

"Now for my distinction. What things, not being opposite to something, yet do not receive the opposite itself which is in that something? For instance now, the triplet is not the opposite to the even, yet still does not receive it because it always brings the opposite against it; and a pair brings the opposite against the odd, and fire against cold, and so with very many others. Just look then, if you distinguish thus, not only the opposite does not receive the opposite, but that also which brings anything opposite to whatever it approaches never receives the opposite to that which it brings. Recollect once more; there's no harm to hear the same thing often. Five will not receive the essence of even, or its double ten the essence of odd; yet this same double will not receive the essence of odd, although it is not opposite to anything. Again, one and a half and other such things with a half in them will not receive the essence of whole, nor will one-third and all such fractions, if you follow and agree with me in this."

"I do agree certainly, and I follow."

"Once more, then," he said, "go back to the beginning. And don't answer the questions I ask, till I show you how. I want something more than the first answer I mentioned, the safe one; I see a new safety from what we have been saying now. If you ask me what must be in any body if that body is to be hot, I will not give you that safe answer, the stupid answer, 'Heat,' but a more subtle answer from our present reasoning, 'Fire'; or if you ask what must be in a body if it is to be diseased, I will not answer 'Disease,' but 'Fever'; or if you ask what must be in a number if it is to be odd, I will not say 'Oddness,' but 'Onehood,' and so forth. Now then, do you know clearly enough what I want?"

"Oh yes," he said.

"Answer then," said he, "what must be in a body if it is to be living?"

"Soul," said he.

"Is this always true?"

"Of course," he said.

"Well now, whatever the soul occupies, she always comes to it bringing life?"

"She does, indeed," he said.

"Is there an opposite to life, or not?"

"There is."

"What?"

"Death."

"Then soul will never receive the opposite to that which she brings, as we have agreed already."

"Most assuredly," said Cebes.

"Well, what name did we give just now to that which did not receive the essence of the even?"

"Uneven," he said.

"And what name to that which does not receive what is just, or to that which does not receive music?"

"Unmusical," he said, "and unjust the other."

"Very well. What do we call that which does not receive death?"

"Immortal," he said.

"And the soul does not receive death?"

"No."

"Then the soul is a thing immortal?'"

"It is," he said.

ON THE SOUL

Aristotle

Now let us start afresh, as it were, and try to determine what the soul is, and what definition of it will be most comprehensive. We describe one class of existing things as substance; and this we subdivide into three: (1) matter, which in itself is not an individual thing; (2) shape or form, in virtue of which individuality is directly attributed, and (3) the compound of the two. Matter is potentiality, while form is realization or actuality, and the word actuality is used in two senses, illustrated by the possession of knowledge and the exercise of it. Bodies seem to be pre-eminently substances, and most particularly those which are of natural origin; for these are the sources from which the rest are derived. But of natural bodies some have life and some have not; by life we mean the capacity for self-sustenance, growth, and decay. Every natural body, then, which possesses life must be substance, and substance of the compound type. But since it is a body of a definite kind, *viz.,* having life, the body cannot be soul, for the body is not something predicated of a subject, but rather is itself to be regarded as a subject, *i.e.,* as matter. So the soul must be substance in the sense of being the form of a natural body, which potentially has life. And substance in this sense is actuality. The soul, then, is the actuality of the kind of body we have described. But actuality has two senses, analogous to the possession of knowledge and the exercise of it. Clearly actuality in our present sense is analogous to the possession of knowledge; for both sleep and waking depend upon the presence of soul, and waking is analogous to the exercise of knowledge, sleep to its possession but not its exercise. Now in one and the same person the possession of knowledge comes first. The soul may therefore be defined as the first actuality of a natural body potentially possessing life; and such will be any body which possesses organs. (The parts of plants are organs too, though very simple ones: *e.g.,* the leaf protects the pericarp, and the pericarp protects the seed; the roots are analogous to the mouth, for both these absorb food.) If then one is to find a definition which will apply to every soul, it will be "the first actuality of a natural body possessed of organs." So one need no more ask whether body and soul are one than whether the wax and the impression it receives are one, or in general whether the matter of each thing is the same as that of which it is the matter; for admitting that the terms unity and being are used in many senses, the paramount sense is that of actuality.

We have, then, given a general definition of what the soul is: it is substance in the sense of formula; *i.e.,* the essence of such-and-such a body. Suppose that an implement, *e.g.* an axe, were a natural body; the substance of the axe would be that which makes it an axe, and this would be its soul; suppose this removed, and it would no longer be an axe, except equivocally. As it is, it remains an axe, because it is not of this kind of body that the soul is the essence or formula, but only of a certain kind of natural body which has in itself a principle of movement and rest. We must, however, investigate our definition in relation to the parts of the body. If the eye were a living creature, its soul would be its vision; for this is the substance in the sense of formula of the eye. But the eye is the matter of vision, and if vision fails there is no eye, except in an equivocal sense, as for instance a stone or painted eye. Now we must apply what we have found true of the part to the whole living body. For the same relation must hold good of the whole of sensation to the whole sentient body *qua* sentient as obtains between their respective parts. That which has the capacity to live is not the body which has lost its soul, but that which possesses its soul; so seed and fruit are potentially bodies of this kind. The waking state is actuality in the same sense as the cutting of the axe or the seeing of the eye, while the soul is actuality in the same sense as the faculty of the eye for seeing, or of the implement for doing its work. The body is that which exists potentially; but just as the pupil and the faculty of seeing make an eye, so in the other case the soul and body make a living creature. It is quite clear, then, that neither the soul nor certain parts of it, if it has parts, can be separated from the body; for in some cases the actuality belongs to the parts themselves. Not but what there is nothing to prevent some parts being separated, because they are not actualities of any body. It is also uncertain whether the soul as an actuality bears the same relation to the body as the sailor to the ship. This must suffice as an attempt to determine in rough outline the nature of the soul.

QUESTIONS FOR DISCUSSION

1. Socrates feels that he has rational grounds for believing in immortality. Do you think his arguments are sound—that is, that they really demonstrate that it is highly probable that the soul lives forever? Why or why not?

2. Compare Aristotle's view of soul with that of Plato. With which do you most agree? Why?

A CONTROVERSY IN THE MODERN WESTERN TRADITION

The term *modern,* as it is used in philosophy, refers to the development in thought that has taken place since the time of the very beginnings of modern science. Modern philosophy thus extends from the seventeenth century to the present. Its founder is usually declared to be René Descartes (1596–1650) from whose *Meditations on First Philosophy* our first selection is taken.

The seventeenth century in Descartes's Europe was a time of dramatic change. Not only was Christendom immersed in a brutal civil war in which Catholicism was pitted against the new Protestant churches, it also was experiencing the challenge of a new kind of science. This new science was growing out of Copernicus's revolution in astronomy in the previous century; it appeared to be in conflict with the traditional, religious world view that had earlier grown out of the medieval synthesis of Aristotle and the Bible. The new view held that the earth was not the center of the universe and stationary; it moved. Furthermore, the earth's motion—in fact, all motion—could be explained by the principles of mechanics. The human body, like any other object, was also subject to these principles. God and "soul" seemed no longer needed for an explanation of nature.

It was at this point in history that philosophy became truly crucial. Throughout the Middle Ages, philosophy had been dominated by religious assumptions. Now those assumptions seemed to be competing with a new way of understanding the world. It was a time of great questioning and great doubt. "Better not to take anything for granted," said many, "neither the assumptions of religion nor the assumptions of science. For how is anyone to know which view of reality is correct?" Each of the world views claimed its own unique path to knowledge; the foundations of knowledge were themselves at issue.

René Descartes took up this skeptical challenge. As someone who was both a devout Catholic Christian and one of the new scientists who was questioning the traditional view, the matter was of vital importance to him. In our selection, Descartes begins by declaring that he will not accept anything as true unless it is demonstrated to be beyond doubt. He thus starts his reflections with a method that has come to be called "the method of doubt"—a method which begins with a philosophical doubt of everything that can be doubted, regardless of whether these things are really doubted in ordinary daily life. Thus, even our basic commonsense beliefs are called into question. Even the most basic "truths" of arithmetic and geometry are initially dismissed by Descartes.

However, he continues, there is one thing that is absolutely certain. I cannot doubt that there is a doubter. I cannot doubt the existence of the self that has these doubts. There is an "I" that thinks, a thinking thing, a mind as distinct from and independent of the body. One cannot, under any circumstances, deny this.

A century later, however, the Scottish philosopher David Hume (1711–1776) does just that. Not only does he question the *certainty* of Descartes's assertion; he also argues that it is in fact false. There is no single entity of which we are conscious that we can call a self. In effect, Hume is arguing that Descartes's doubting was not radical enough; what Descartes took to be certain is entirely unfounded.

It is important to understand that Hume's analysis begins from the premise that every true idea must be derived from experience—from some concrete sense impression. This view is known as "empiricism" in philosophy. From the empiricist standpoint, an accurate idea of the self would have to be derived from some sense impression. However, as Hume declares, we cannot upon reflection find any distinct impression that corresponds to a "self." What we call a "self" is merely "a bundle or collection of different perceptions, which succeed each other with an inconceivable rapidity, and are in a perpetual flux and movement."

Edmund Husserl, a philosopher of the twentieth

century and founder of the philosophical method known as phenomenology, disagrees with both Hume and Descartes. There is, for Husserl, indeed a self to be discovered in Descartes's claim that "I think therefore I am," but it is not the psychological self which Descartes took it to be; it is a "transcendental ego," a pure ego which does not enter into the natural world as an object in that world but stands, so to speak, at its borders. To use a metaphor taken from another philosopher of this century, the Austrian Ludwig Wittgenstein, the transcendental ego is to the world as the eye is to the field of vision; when you look at something, "you do not see the eye which does the looking. And from nothing in the field of vision can it be concluded that it is seen from an eye." So also with the transcendental "I." It stands beyond the "field" of the world of nature.

MEDITATIONS

René Descartes

MEDITATION I

Concerning the Things of Which We May Doubt

It is now several years since I first became aware how many false opinions I had from my childhood been admitting as true, and how doubtful was everything I have subsequently based on them. Accordingly I have ever since been convinced that if I am to establish anything firm and lasting in the sciences, I must once for all, and by a deliberate effort, rid myself of all these opinions to which I have hitherto given credence, starting entirely anew, and building from the foundations up. But as this enterprise was evidently one of great magnitude, I waited until I had attained an age so mature that I could no longer expect that I should at any later date be better able to execute my design. This is what has made me delay so long; and I should now be failing in my duty, were I to continue consuming in deliberation such time for action as still remains to me.

Today, then, as I have suitably freed my mind from all cares, and have secured for myself an assured leisure in peaceful solitude, I shall at last apply myself earnestly and freely to the general overthrow of all my former opinions. In doing so, it will not be necessary for me to show that they are one and all false; that is perhaps more than can be done. But since reason has already persuaded me that I ought to withhold belief no less carefully from things not entirely certain and indubitable than from those which appear to me manifestly false, I shall be justified in setting all of them aside, if in each case I can find any ground whatsoever for regarding them as dubitable. Nor in so doing shall I be investigating each belief separately—that, like inquiry into their falsity, would be an endless labor. The withdrawal of foundations involves the downfall of whatever rests on these foundations, and what I shall therefore begin by examining are the principles on which my former beliefs rested.

Whatever, up to the present, I have accepted as possessed of the highest truth and certainty I have learned either from the senses or through the senses. Now these senses I have sometimes found to be deceptive; and it is only prudent never to place complete confidence in that by which we have even once been deceived.

But, it may be said, although the senses sometimes deceive us regarding minute objects, or such as are at a great distance from us, there are yet many other things which, though known by way of sense, are too evident to be doubted; as, for instance, that I am in this place, seated by the fire, attired in a dressing-gown, having this paper in my hands, and other similar seeming certainties. Can I deny that these hands and this body are mine, save perhaps by comparing myself to those who are insane, and whose brains are so disturbed and clouded by dark bilious vapors that they persist in assuring us that they are kings, when in fact they are in extreme poverty; or that they are clothed in gold and purple when they are in fact destitute of any covering; or that their head is made of clay and their body of glass, or that they are pumpkins. They are mad; and I should be no less insane were I to follow examples so extravagant.

None the less I must bear in mind that I am a man, and am therefore in the habit of sleeping, and that what the insane represent to themselves in their waking moments I represent to myself, with other things even less probable, in my dreams. How often, indeed, have I dreamt of myself being in this place, dressed and seated by the fire, whilst all the time I was lying undressed in bed! At the present moment it certainly seems that in looking at this paper I do so with open eyes, that the head which I move is not asleep, that it is deliberately and of set purpose that I extend this hand, and that I am sensing the hand. The things which happen to the sleeper are not so clear nor so distinct as all of these are. I cannot, however, but remind myself that on many occasions I have in sleep been deceived by similar illusions; and on more careful study of them I see that there are no certain marks distinguishing waking from sleep; and I see this so manifestly that, lost in amazement, I am almost persuaded that I am now dreaming.

Let us, then, suppose ourselves to be asleep, and that all these particulars—namely, that we open our eyes, move the head, extend the hands—are false and illusory; and let us reflect that our hands perhaps, and the whole body, are not what we see them as being. Nevertheless we must at least agree that the things seen by us in sleep are as it were like painted images, and cannot have been formed save in the likeness of what is real and true. The types of things depicted, eyes, head, hands, etc.—these at least are not imaginary, but true and existent. For in truth when painters endeavor with all possible artifice to represent sirens and satyrs by forms the most fantastic and unusual, they cannot assign them natures which are entirely new, but only make a certain selection of limbs from different animals. Even

should they excogitate something so novel that nothing similar has ever before been seen, and that their work represents to us a thing entirely fictitious and false, the colors used in depicting them cannot be similarly fictitious; they at least must truly exist. And by this same reasoning, even should those general things, viz., a body, eyes, a head, hands and such like, be imaginary, we are yet bound to admit that there are things simpler and more universal which are real existents and by the intermixture of which, as in the case of the colors, all the images of things of which we have any awareness be they true and real or false and fantastic, are formed. To this class of things belong corporeal nature in general and its extension, the shape of extended things, their quantity or magnitude, and their number, as also the location in which they are, the time through which they endure, and other similar things.

This, perhaps, is why we not unreasonably conclude that physics, astronomy, medicine, and all other disciplines treating of composite things are of doubtful character, and that arithmetic, geometry, etc., treating only of the simplest and most general things and but little concerned as to whether or not they are actual existents, have a content that is certain and indubitable. For whether I am awake or dreaming, 2 and 3 are 5, a square has no more than four sides; and it does not seem possible that truths so evident can ever be suspected of falsity.

Yet even these truths can be questioned. That God exists, that He is all-powerful and has created me such as I am, has long been my settled opinion. How, then, do I know that He has not arranged that there be no Earth, no heavens, no extended thing, no shape, no magnitude, no location, while at the same time securing that all these things appear to me to exist precisely as they now do? Others, as I sometimes think, deceive themselves in the things which they believe they know best. How do I know that I am not myself deceived every time I add 2 and 3, or count the sides of a square, or judge of things yet simpler, if anything simpler can be suggested? But perhaps God has not been willing that I should be thus deceived, for He is said to be supremely good. If, however, it be repugnant to the goodness of God to have created me such that I am constantly subject to deception, it would also appear to be contrary to His goodness to permit me to be sometimes deceived, and that He does permit this is not in doubt.

There may be those who might prefer to deny the existence of a God so powerful, rather than to believe that all other things are uncertain. Let us, for the present, not oppose them; let us allow, in the manner of their view, that all which has been said regarding God is a fable. Even so we shall not have met and answered the doubts suggested above regarding the reliability of our mental faculties; instead we shall have given added force to them. For in whatever way it be supposed that I have come to be what I am, whether by fate or by chance, or by a continual succession and connection of things, or by some other means, since to be deceived and to err is an imperfection, the likelihood of my being so imperfect as to be the constant victim of deception will be increased in proportion as the power to which they assign my origin is lessened. To such argument I have assuredly nothing to reply; and thus at last I am constrained to confess that there is no one of all my former opinions which is not open to doubt, and this not merely owing to want of thought on my part, or through levity, but from cogent and maturely considered reasons. Henceforth, therefore, should I desire to discover something certain, I ought to refrain from assenting to these opinions no less scrupulously than in respect of what is manifestly false.

But it is not sufficient to have taken note of these conclusions; we must also be careful to keep them in mind. For long-established customary opinions perpetually recur in thought, long and familiar usage having given them the right to occupy my mind, even almost against my will, and to be masters of my belief. Nor shall I ever lose this habit of assenting to and of confiding in them, not at least so long as I consider them as in truth they are, namely, as opinions which, though in some fashion doubtful (as I have just shown), are still, none the less, highly probable and such as it is much more reasonable to believe than to deny. This is why I shall, as I think, be acting prudently if, taking a directly contrary line, I of set purpose employ every available device for the deceiving of myself, feigning that all these opinions are entirely false and imaginary. Then, in due course, having so balanced my old-time prejudices by this new prejudice that I cease to incline to one side more than to another, my judgment, no longer dominated by misleading usages, will not be hindered by them in the apprehension of things. In this course there can, I am convinced, be neither danger nor error. What I have under consideration is a question solely of knowledge, not of action, so that I cannot for the present be at fault as being over-ready to adopt a questioning attitude.

Accordingly I shall now suppose, not that a true God, who as such must be supremely good and the fountain of truth, but that some malignant genius exceedingly powerful and cunning has devoted all his powers in the deceiving of me; I shall suppose that the sky, the earth, colors, shapes, sounds and all external things are illusions and impostures of which this evil genius has availed himself for the abuse of my credulity; I shall consider myself as having no hands, no eyes, no flesh, no blood, nor any senses, but as falsely opining myself to possess all these things. Further, I shall obstinately persist in this way of thinking; and even if, while so doing, it may not be within my power to arrive at the knowledge of any truth, there is one thing I have it in me to do, viz., to suspend judgment, refusing assent to what is false. Thereby, thanks to this resolved firmness of mind, I shall be effectively guarding myself against being imposed upon by this deceiver, no matter how powerful or how craftily deceptive he may be.

This undertaking is, however, irksome and laborious, and a certain indolence drags me back into the course of my customary life. Just as a captive who has been enjoying in sleep an imaginary liberty, should he begin to suspect that his liberty is a dream, dreads awakening, and conspires with the agreeable illusions for the prolonging of the deception, so in similar fashion I gladly lapse back into my accustomed opinions. I dread to be wakened, in fear lest the wakefulness may have to be laboriously spent, not in the tranquilizing light of truth, but in the extreme darkness of the above-suggested questionings.

MEDITATION II

Concerning the Nature of the Human Mind, and How It Is More Easily Known Than the Body

So disquieting are the doubts in which yesterday's meditation has involved me that it is no longer in my power to forget them. Nor do I yet see how they are to be resolved. It is as if I had all of a sudden fallen into very deep water, and am so disconcerted that I can neither plant my feet securely on the bottom nor maintain myself by swimming on the surface. I shall, however, brace myself for a great effort, entering anew on the path which I was yesterday exploring; that is, I shall proceed by setting aside all that admits even of the very slightest doubt, just as if I had convicted it of being absolutely false; and I shall persist in following this path, until I have come upon something certain, or, failing in that, until at least I know, and know with certainty, that in the world there is nothing certain.

Archimedes, that he might displace the whole earth, required only that there might be some one point, fixed and immovable, to serve in leverage; so likewise I shall be entitled to entertain high hopes if I am fortunate enough to find some one thing that is certain and indubitable.

I am supposing, then, that all the things I see are false; that of all the happenings my memory has ever suggested to me, none has ever so existed; that I have no senses; that body, shape, extension, movement and location are but mental fictions. What is there, then, which can be esteemed true? Perhaps this only, that nothing whatsoever is certain.

But how do I know that there is not something different from all the things I have thus far enumerated and in regard to which there is not the least occasion for doubt? Is there not some God, or other being by whatever name we call Him, who puts these thoughts into my mind? Yet why suppose such a being? May it not be that I am myself capable of being their author? Am I not myself at least a something? But already I have denied that I have a body and senses. This indeed raises awkward questions. But what is it that thereupon follows? Am I so de-pendent on the body and senses that without them I cannot exist? Having persuaded myself that outside me there is nothing, that there is no heaven, no Earth, that there are no minds, no bodies, am I thereby committed to the view that I also do not exist? By no means. If I am persuading myself of something, in so doing I assuredly do exist. But what if, unknown to me, there be some deceiver, very powerful and very cunning, who is constantly employing his ingenuity in deceiving me? Again, as before, without doubt, if he is deceiving me, I exist. Let him deceive me as much as he will, he can never cause me to be nothing so long as I shall be thinking that I am something. And thus, having reflected well, and carefully examined all things, we have finally to conclude that this declaration, *Ego sum, ego existo,* is necessarily true every time I propound it or mentally apprehend it.

But I do not yet know in any adequate manner what I am, I who am certain that I am; and I must be careful not to substitute some other thing in place of myself, and so go astray in this knowledge which I am holding to be the most certain and evident of all that is knowable by me. This is why I shall now meditate anew on what, prior to my venturing on these questionings, I believed myself to be. I shall withdraw those beliefs which can, even in the least degree, be invalidated by the reasons cited, in order that at length, of all my previous beliefs, there may remain only what is certain and indubitable.

What then did I formerly believe myself to be? Undoubtedly I thought myself to be a man. But what is a man? Shall I say a rational animal? No, for then I should have to inquire what is "animal," what "rational"; and thus from the one question I should be drawn on into several others yet more difficult. I have not, at present, the leisure for any such subtle inquiries. Instead, I prefer to meditate on the thoughts which of themselves sprang up in my mind on my applying myself to the consideration of what I am, considerations suggested by my own proper nature. I thought that I possessed a face, hands, arms, and that whole structure to which I was giving the title "body," composed as it is of the limbs discernible in a corpse. In addition, I took notice that I was nourished, that I walked, that I sensed, that I thought, all of which actions I ascribed to the soul. But what the soul might be I did not stop to consider; or if I did, I imaged it as being something extremely rare and subtle, like a wind, a flame or an ether, and as diffused throughout my grosser parts. As to the nature of "body," no doubts whatsoever disturbed me. I had, as I thought, quite distinct knowledge of it; and had I been called upon to explain the manner in which I then conceived it, I should have explained myself somewhat thus: by body I understand whatever can be determined by a certain shape, and comprised in a certain location, whatever so fills a certain space as to exclude from it every other body, whatever can be apprehended by touch, sight, hearing, taste or smell, and whatever can be moved in various ways, not indeed of itself but something foreign to it by which it is touched and impressed. For I nowise conceived the power of self-movement, of sensing or knowing, as pertaining to the nature of body: on the contrary I was somewhat astonished on finding in certain bodies faculties such as these.

But what am I now to say that I am, now that I am supposing that there exists a very powerful, and if I may so speak, malignant being, who employs all his powers and skill in deceiving me? Can I affirm that I possess any one of those things which I have been speaking of as pertaining to the nature of body? On stopping to consider them with closer attention, and on reviewing all of them, I find none of which I can say that it belongs to me; to enumerate them again would be idle and tedious. What then, of those things which I have been attributing not to body, but to the soul? What of nutrition or of walking? If it be that I have no body, it cannot be that I take nourishment or that I walk. Sensing? There can be no sensing in the absence of body; and besides I have seemed during sleep to apprehend things which, as I afterwards noted, had not been sensed. Thinking? Here I find what does belong to me: it alone cannot be separated from me. *I am, I exist.* This is certain. How often? As often as I think. For it might indeed be that if I entirely ceased to think, I should thereupon altogether cease to exist. I am

not at present admitting anything which is not necessarily true; and, accurately speaking, I am therefore [taking myself to be] only a thinking thing, that is to say, a mind, an understanding or reason— terms the significance of which has hitherto been unknown to me. I am, then, a real thing, and really existent. What thing? I have said it, a thinking thing.

And what more am I? I look for aid to the imagination. [But how mistakenly!] I am not that assemblage of limbs we call the human body; I am not a subtle penetrating air distributed throughout all these members; I am not a wind, a fire, a vapor, a breath or anything at all that I can image. I am supposing all these things to be nothing. Yet I find, while so doing, that I am still assured that I am a something.

But may it not be that those very things which, not being known to me, I have been supposing nonexistent, are not really different from the self that I know? As to that I cannot say, and am not now discussing it. I can judge only of things that are known to me. Having come to know that I exist, I am inquiring as to what I am, this I that I thus know to exist. Now quite certainly this knowledge, taken in the precise manner as above, is not dependent on things the existence of which is not yet known to me; consequently and still more evidently it does not depend on any of the things which are feigned by the imagination. Indeed this word *feigning* warns me of my error; for I should in truth be feigning were I to *image* myself to be a something; since imaging is in no respect distinguishable from the contemplating of the shape or image of a *corporeal*[1] thing. Already I know with certainty that I exist, and that all these imaged things, and in general whatever relates to the nature of body, may possibly be dreams merely or deceptions. Accordingly, I see clearly that it is no more reasonable to say, "I will resort to my imagination in order to learn more distinctly what I am," than if I were to say, "I am awake and apprehend something that is real, true; but as I do not yet apprehend it sufficiently well, I

---

[1] Italics not in text.

will of express purpose go to sleep, that my dreams may represent it to me with greater truth and evidence." I know therefore that nothing of all I can comprehend by way of the imagination pertains to this knowledge I [already] have of myself, and that if the mind is to determine the nature of the self with perfect distinctness, I must be careful to restrain it, diverting it from all such imaginative modes of apprehension.

What then is it that I am? A thinking thing.[2] What is a thinking thing? It is a thing that doubts, understands, affirms, denies, wills, abstains from willing, that also can be aware of images and sensations.

Assuredly if all these things pertain to me, I am indeed a something. And how could it be they should not pertain to me? Am I not that very being who doubts of almost everything, who none the less also apprehends certain things, who affirms that one thing only is true, while denying all the rest, who yet desires to know more, who is averse to being deceived, who images many things, sometimes even despite his will, and who likewise apprehends many things which seem to come by way of the senses? Even though I should be always dreaming, and though he who has created me employs all his ingenuity in deceiving me, is there any one of the above assertions which is not as true as that I am and that I exist? Any one of them which can be distinguished from my thinking? Any one of them which can be said to be separate from the self? So manifest is it that it is I who doubt, I who apprehend, I who desire, that there is here no need to add anything by way of rendering it more evident. It is no less certain that I can apprehend images. For although it may happen (as I have been supposing) that none of the things imaged are true, the imaging, *quâ* active power, is none the less really in me, as forming part of my thinking. Again, I am the being who senses, that is to say, who apprehends corporeal things, as if by the organs of sense, since I do in truth see light, hear noise, feel heat. These things, it will be said, are false, and I am only dreaming. Even so, it is

none the less certain that it seems to me that I see, that I hear, and that I am warmed. This is what in me is rightly called sensing, and as used in this precise manner is nowise other than thinking.

PERSONAL IDENTITY

David Hume

There are some philosophers who imagine we are every moment intimately conscious of what we call our *self;* that we feel its existence and its continuance in existence; and are certain, beyond the evidence of a demonstration, both of its perfect identity and simplicity. The strongest sensation, the most violent passion, say they, instead of distracting us from this view, only fix it the more intensely and make us consider their influence on *self* either by their pain or pleasure. To attempt a further proof of this were to weaken its evidence; since no proof can be derived from any fact of which we are so intimately conscious; nor is there anything of which we can be certain if we doubt of this.

Unluckily all these positive assertions are contrary to that very experience which is pleaded for them; nor have we any idea of *self,* after the manner it is here explained. For from what impression* could this idea be derived? This question it is impossible to answer without a manifest contradiction and absurdity; and yet it is a question which must necessarily be answered, if we would have the idea of self pass for clear and intelligible. It must be some one impression that gives rise to every real idea. But self or person is not any one impression, but that to which our several impressions and ideas are supposed to have a reference. If any impression

---

[2] *Res cogitans;* Fr. *une chose qui pense.*

---

* Hume uses the term *impression* to refer to those sense experiences which are neither memories nor the result of acts of imagination; as such, impressions are, for him, sensations, passions, or emotions (Eds.).

gives rise to the idea of self, that impression must continue invariably the same, through the whole course of our lives; since self is supposed to exist after that manner. But there is no impression constant and invariable. Pain and pleasure, grief and joy, passions and sensations succeed each other, and never all exist at the same time. It cannot therefore be from any of these impressions, or from any other, that the idea of self is derived; and consequently there is no such idea.

But further, what must become of all our particular perceptions upon this hypothesis? All these are different, and distinguishable, and separable from each other, and may be separately considered, and may exist separately, and have no need of anything to support their existence. After what manner therefore do they belong to self, and how are they connected with it? For my part, when I enter most intimately into what I call *myself,* I always stumble on some particular perception or other, of heat or cold, light or shade, love or hatred, pain or pleasure. I never can catch *myself* at any time without a perception, and never can observe anything but the perception. When my perceptions are removed for any time, as by sound sleep, so long am I insensible of *myself,* and may truly be said not to exist. And were all my perceptions removed by death, and could I neither think, nor feel, nor see, nor love, nor hate, after the dissolution of my body, I should be entirely annihilated, nor do I conceive what is further requisite to make me a perfect nonentity. If any one, upon serious and unprejudiced reflection, thinks he has a different notion of *himself,* I must confess I can reason no longer with him. All I can allow him is, that he may be in the right as well as I, and that we are essentially different in this particular. He may, perhaps, perceive something simple and continued, which he calls *himself;* though I am certain there is no such principle in me.

But setting aside some metaphysicians of this kind, I may venture to affirm of the rest of mankind, that they are nothing but a bundle or collection of different perceptions, which succeed each other with an inconceivable rapidity, and are in a perpetual flux and movement. Our eyes cannot turn in their sockets without varying our perceptions. Our thought is still more variable than our sight; and all our other senses and faculties contribute to this change; nor is there any single power of the soul, which remains unalterably the same, perhaps for one moment. The mind is a kind of theatre, where several perceptions successively make their appearance; pass, repass, glide away, and mingle in an infinite variety of postures and situations. There is properly no *simplicity* in it at one time, nor *identity* in different, whatever natural propension we may have to imagine that simplicity and identity. The comparison of the theatre must not mislead us. They are the successive perceptions only, that constitute the mind; nor have we the most distant notion of the place where these scenes are represented, or of the materials of which it is composed.

What then gives us so great a propension to ascribe an identity to these successive perceptions, and to suppose ourselves possessed of an invariable and uninterrupted existence through the whole course of our lives? In order to answer this question we must distinguish betwixt personal identity, as it regards our thought or imagination, and as it regards our passions or the concern we take in ourselves. The first is our present subject; and to explain it perfectly we must take the matter pretty deep, and account for that identity, which we attribute to plants and animals; there being a great analogy betwixt it and the identity of a self or person.

We have a distinct idea of an object that remains invariable and uninterrupted through a supposed variation of time; and this idea we call that of *identity* or *sameness.* We have also a distinct idea of several different objects existing in succession, and connected together by a close relation; and this to an accurate view affords as perfect a notion of *diversity* as if there was no manner of relation among the objects. But though these two ideas of identity, and a succession of related objects, be in themselves perfectly distinct, and even contrary, yet it is certain that, in our common way of thinking, they are generally confounded with each other. That action of the imagination, by which we consider the uninterrupted and invariable object, and that by which we reflect on the succession of related objects, are almost the same to the feeling; nor is there much more effort of thought required in the latter case than in the former. The relation facilitates the transition of the mind from one object to another, and renders its passage as smooth as if it contemplated one continued object. This resemblance is the cause of the confusion and mistake, and makes us substitute the notion of identity, instead of that of related objects. However at one instant we may consider the related succession as variable or interrupted, we are sure the next to ascribe to it a perfect identity, and regard it as invariable and uninterrupted. Our propensity to this mistake is so great from the resemblance above mentioned, that we fall into it before we are aware; and though we incessantly correct ourselves by reflection, and return to a more accurate method of thinking, yet we cannot long sustain our philosophy, or take off this bias from the imagination. Our last resource is to yield to it, and boldly assert that these different related objects are in effect the same, however interrupted and variable. In order to justify to ourselves this absurdity, we often feign some new and unintelligible principle, that connects the objects together, and prevents their interruption or variation. Thus we feign the continued existence of the perceptions of our senses, to remove the interruption; and run into the notion of a *soul,* and *self,* and *substance,* to disguise the variation. But, we may further observe, that where we do not give rise to such a fiction, our propension to confound identity with relation is so great, that we are apt to imagine something unknown and mysterious, connecting the parts, beside their relation; and this I take to be the case with regard to the identity we ascribe to plants and vegetables. And even when this does not take place, we still feel a propensity to confound these ideas, though we are not able fully to satisfy ourselves in that particular, nor find anything invariable and uninterrupted to justify our notion of identity.

Thus the controversy concerning identity is not merely a dispute of words. For when we attribute identity, in an improper sense, to variable or interrupted objects, our mistake is not confined to the expression, but is commonly attended with a fiction, either of something invariable and uninterrupted, or of something mysterious and inexplicable, or at least with a propensity to such fictions. What will suffice to prove this hypothesis to the satisfaction of every fair inquirer, is to show, from daily experience and observation, that the objects which are variable or interrupted, and yet are supposed to continue the same, are such only as consist of a succession of parts, connected together by resemblance, contiguity, or causation. For as such a succession answers evidently to our notion of diversity, it can only be by mistake we ascribe to it an identity; and as the relation of parts, which leads us into this mistake, is really nothing but a quality, which produces an association of ideas, and an easy transition of the imagination from one to another, it can only be from the resemblance, which this act of the mind bears to that by which we contemplate one continued object, that the error arises.

TRANSCENDENTAL SUBJECTIVITY

Edmund Husserl

I am filled with joy at the opportunity to talk about the new phenomenology* at this most venerable place of French learning, and for very special reasons. No philosopher of the past has affected the sense of phenomenology as decisively as René Descartes, France's greatest thinker. Phenomenol-

---

* *Phenomenology* is a method of philosophizing which was invented by Husserl. It consists of an attempt to uncover solutions to philosophical problems by describing the "essences" or most general properties of phenomena. The method is nicely illustrated in the selection. In the hands of Husserl's student, Heidegger, phenomenology became the methodology of existentialism (Eds.).

ogy must honor him as its genuine patriarch. It must be said explicitly that the study of Descartes' *Meditations* has influenced directly the formation of the developing phenomenology and given it its present form, to such an extent that phenomenology might almost be called a new, a twentieth century, Cartesianism.*

Under these circumstances I may have advance assurance of your interest, especially if I start with those themes in the *Meditationes de prima philosophia* which are timeless, and if through them I point out the transformations and new concepts which give birth to what is characteristic of the phenomenological method and its problems.

Every beginner in philosophy is familiar with the remarkable train of thought in the *Meditations.* Their goal, as we remember, is a complete reform of philosophy, including all the sciences, since the latter are merely dependent members of the one universal body of knowledge which is philosophy. Only through systematic unity can the sciences achieve genuine rationality, which, as they have developed so far, is missing. What is needed is a radical reconstruction which will *satisfy* the ideal of philosophy as being the *universal unity of knowledge* by means of a unitary and *absolutely rational foundation.* Descartes carries out the demand for reconstruction in terms of a subjectively oriented philosophy. This subjective turn is carried out in two steps.

First, anyone who seriously considers becoming a philosopher must once in his life withdraw into himself and then, from within attempt to destroy and rebuild all previous learning. Philosophy is the supremely personal affair of the one who philosophizes. It is the question of *his sapientia universalis,* the aspiration of *his* knowledge for the universal. In particular, the philosopher's quest is for truly scientific knowledge, knowledge for which he can assume—from the very beginning and in every subsequent step—complete responsibility by using

his own absolutely self-evident justifications. I can become a genuine philosopher only by freely choosing to focus my life on this goal. Once I am thus committed and have accordingly chosen to begin with total poverty and destruction, my first problem is to discover an absolutely secure starting point and rules of procedure, when, in actual fact, I lack any support from the existing disciplines. Consequently, the Cartesian meditations must not be viewed as the private affair of the philosopher Descartes, but as the necessary prototype for the meditations of any beginning philosopher whatsoever.

When we now turn our attention to the content of the *Meditations,* a content which appears rather strange to us today, we notice immediately a *return to the philosophizing ego* in a second and deeper sense. It is the familiar and epoch-making return to the ego as subject of his pure *cogitationes.* It is the ego which, while it suspends all beliefs about the reality of the world on the grounds that these are not indubitable, discovers itself as the only apodictically certain being.

The ego is engaged, first of all, in philosophizing that is seriously solipsistic. He looks for apodictically certain and yet purely subjective procedures through which an objective external world can be deduced. Descartes does this in a well-known manner. He first infers both the existence and *veracitas* of God. Then, through their mediation, he deduces objective reality as a dualism of substances. In this way he reaches the objective ground of knowledge and the particular sciences themselves as well. All his inferences are based on immanent principles, *i.e.,* principles which are innate to the ego.

So much for Descartes. We now ask, is it really worthwhile to hunt critically for the eternal significance of these thoughts? Can these infuse life into our age?

Doubt is raised, in any event, by the fact that the positive sciences, for which the meditations were to have served as absolutely rational foundation, have paid so very little attention to them. Nonetheless, and despite the brilliant development experienced by the sciences over the last three centuries, they

---

* *Cartesian* refers to the views of Descartes or those of any of his followers (Eds.).

feel themselves today seriously limited by the obscurity of their foundations. But it scarcely occurs to them to refer to the Cartesian meditations for the reformulation of their foundations.

On the other hand, serious consideration must be given to the fact that the meditations constitute an altogether unique and epochal event in the history of philosophy, specifically because of their return to the *ego cogito.** As a matter of fact, Descartes inaugurates a completely new type of philosophy. Philosophy, with its style now changed altogether, experiences a radical conversion from naive objectivism to *transcendental subjectivism.* This subjectivism strives toward a pure end-form through efforts that are constantly renewed yet always remain unsatisfactory. Might it not be that this continuing tendency has eternal significance? Perhaps it is a vast task assigned to us by history itself, invoking our collective cooperation.

The splintering of contemporary philosophy and its aimless activity make us pause. Must this situation not be traced back to the fact that the motivations from which Descartes' meditations emanate have lost their original vitality? Is it not true that the only fruitful renaissance is one which reawakens these meditations, not in order to accept them, but to reveal the profound truth in the radicalism of a return to the *ego cogito* with the eternal values that reside therein?

In any case, this is the path that led to transcendental phenomenology.

Let us now pursue this path together. In true Cartesian fashion, we will become philosophers meditating in a radical sense, with, of course, frequent and critical modifications of the older Cartesian meditations. What was merely germinal in them must be freely developed here.

We thus begin, everyone for himself and in himself, with the decision to disregard all our present knowledge. We do not give up Descartes' guiding goal of an absolute foundation for knowledge. At the beginning, however, to presuppose even the possibility of that goal would be prejudice. We are satisfied to discover the goal and nature of science by submerging ourselves in scientific activity. It is the spirit of science to count nothing as really scientific which cannot be fully justified by the evidence. In other words, science demands proof *by reference to the things and facts themselves, as these are given in actual experience and intuition.* Thus guided, we, the beginning philosophers, make it a rule to judge only by the evidence. Also, the evidence itself must be subjected to critical verification, and that on the basis, of course, of further available evidence. Since from the beginning we have disregarded the sciences, we operate within our prescientific life, which is likewise filled with immediate and mediate evidences. This, and nothing else, is first given to us.

Herein arises our first question. Can we find evidence that is both immediate and apodictic?* Can we find evidence that is primitive, in the sense that it must by necessity precede all other evidence?

As we meditate on this question one thing does, in fact, emerge as both prior to all evidence and as apodictic. It is the existence of the world. All science refers to the world, and, before that, our ordinary life already makes reference to it. *That the being of the world precedes everything is* so *obvious* that no one thinks to articulate it in a sentence. Our experience of the world is continuous, incessant, and unquestionable. But is it true that this experiential evidence, even though taken for granted, is really apodictic and primary to all other evidence? We will have to deny both. Is it not the case that occasionally something manifests itself as a sensory illusion? Has not the coherent and unified totality of our experience been at times debased as a mere dream? We will ignore Descartes' attempt to prove that, notwithstanding the fact of its being constantly experienced, the world's nonbeing can be conceived. His proof is carried out by a much too superficial criticism of sensory experience. We will keep this much: experiential evidence that is to

---

* *Ego cogito* is Latin for "I think" (Eds.).

* *Apodictic* in this context means necessary or beyond doubt.

serve as radical foundation for knowledge needs, above all, a critique of its validity and range. It cannot be accepted as apodictic without question and qualification. Therefore, merely to disregard all knowledge and to treat the sciences as prejudices is not enough. Even the experience of the world as the true universal ground of knowledge becomes an unacceptably naive belief. We can no longer accept the reality of the world as a fact to be taken for granted. *It is a hypothesis that needs verification.*

Does there remain a ground of being? Do we still have a basis for all judgments and evidences, a basis on which a universal philosophy can rest apodictically? Is not "world" the name for the totality of all that is? Might it not turn out that the world is not the truly ultimate basis for judgment, but instead that its existence presupposes a prior ground of being?

Here, specifically following Descartes, we make the great shift which, when properly carried out, leads to *transcendental subjectivity.* This is the shift to the *ego cogito,* as the apodictically certain and *last basis for judgment* upon which all radical philosophy must be grounded.

Let us consider: as radically meditating philosophers we now have neither knowledge that is valid for us nor a world that exists for us. We can no longer say that the world is real—a belief that is natural enough in our ordinary experience—; instead, it merely makes a claim to reality. This skepticism also applies to other selves, so that we rightly should not speak communicatively, that is, in the plural. Other people and animals are, of course, given to me only through sensory experience. Since I have questioned the validity of the latter I cannot avail myself of it here. With the loss of other minds I lose, of course, all forms of sociability and culture. In short, the entire concrete world ceases to have reality for me and becomes instead mere appearance. However, whatever may be the veracity of the claim to being made by phenomena, whether they represent reality or appearance, phenomena in themselves cannot be disregarded as mere "nothing." On the contrary, it is precisely the phenomena themselves which, without exception, render possible for me the very existence of both reality and ap-

pearance. Again, I may freely abstain from entertaining any belief about experience—which I did. This simply means that I refuse to assert the reality of the world. Nonetheless, we must be careful to realize that this epistemological abstention is still what it is: it includes the whole stream of experienced life and all its particulars, the appearances of objects, other people, cultural situations, etc. Nothing changes, except that I no longer accept the world simply as real; I no longer judge regarding the distinction between reality and appearance. I must similarly abstain from any other of my opinions, judgments, and valuations about the world, since these likewise assume the reality of the world. But for these, as for other phenomena, epistemological abstention does not mean their disappearance, at least not as pure phenomena.

This ubiquitous detachment from any point of view regarding the objective world we term the *phenomenological epoché.* It is the methodology through which I come to understand myself as that ego and life of consciousness in which and through which the entire objective world exists for me, and is for me precisely as it is. Everything in the world, all spatio-temporal being, exists for me because I experience it, because I perceive it, remember it, think of it in any way, judge it, value it, desire it, etc. It is well known that Descartes designates all this by the term *cogito.* For me the world is nothing other than what I am aware of and what appears valid in such *cogitationes. The whole meaning and reality of the world rests exclusively on such cogitationes.* My entire worldly life takes its course within these. I cannot live, experience, think, value, and act in any world which is not in some sense in me, and derives its meaning and truth from me. If I place myself above that entire life and if I abstain from any commitment about reality, specifically one which accepts the world as existing, and if I view that life exclusively as consciousness *of* the world, then I reveal myself as the pure ego with its pure stream of *cogitationes.*

I certainly do not discover myself as one item among others in the world, since I have altogether suspended judgment about the world. I am not the ego of an individual man. I am the ego in whose stream of consciousness the world itself—including myself as an object in it, a man who exists in the world—first acquires meaning and reality.

We have reached a dangerous point. It seems simple indeed to understand the pure ego with its *cogitationes* by following Descartes. And yet it is as if we were on the brink of a precipice, where the ability to step calmly and surely decides between philosophic life and philosophic death. Descartes was thoroughly sincere in his desire to be radical and presuppositionless. However, we know through recent researches—particularly the fine and penetrating work of Messrs. Gilson and Koyré—that a great deal of Scholasticism is hidden in Descartes' meditations as unarticulated prejudice. But this is not all. We must above all avoid the prejudices, hardly noticed by us, which derive from our emphasis on the mathematically oriented natural sciences. These prejudices make it appear as if the phrase *ego cogito* refers to an apodictic and primitive axiom, one which, in conjunction with others to be derived from it, provides the foundation for a deductive and universal science, a science *ordine geometrico.* In relation to this we must under no circumstances take for granted that, with our apodictic and pure ego, we have salvaged a small corner of the world as the single indubitable fact about the world which can be utilized by the philosophizing ego. It is not true that all that now remains to be done is to infer the rest of the world through correct deductive procedures according to principles that are innate to the ego.

Unfortunately, Descartes commits this error, in the apparently insignificant yet fateful transformation of the ego to a *substantia cogitans,* to an independent human *animus,* which then becomes the point of departure for conclusions by means of the principle of causality. In short, this is the transformation which made Descartes the father of the rather absurd transcendental realism. We will keep aloof from all this if we remain true to radicalism in our self-examination and with it to the principle of pure intuition. We must regard nothing as veridical except the pure immediacy and givenness in the field of the *ego cogito* which the *epoché* has opened up to us. In other words, we must not make assertions about that which we do not ourselves *see.* In these matters Descartes was deficient. It so happens that he stands before the greatest of all discoveries—in a sense he has already made it—yet fails to see its true significance, that of transcendental subjectivity. He does not pass through the gateway that leads into genuine transcendental philosophy.

The independent *epoché* with regard to the nature of the world as it appears and is real to me—that is, "real" to the previous and natural point of view—discloses the greatest and most magnificent of all facts: I and my life remain—in my sense of reality—untouched by whichever way we decide the issue of whether the world is or is not. To say, in my natural existence, "I am, I think, I live," means that I am one human being among others in the world, that I am related to nature through my physical body, and that in this body my *cogitationes,* perceptions, memories, judgments, etc. are incorporated as psycho-physical facts. Conceived in this way, I, we, humans, and animals are subject-matter for the objective sciences, that is, for biology, anthropology, and zoology, and also for psychology. The life of the psyche, which is the subject-matter of all psychology, is understood only as the psychic life in the world. The methodology of a purified Cartesianism demands of me, the one who philosophizes, the phenomenological *epoché.* This *epoché* eliminates as worldly facts from my field of judgment both the reality of the objective world in general and the sciences of the world. *Consequently, for me there exists no "I" and there are no psychic actions,*[1] *that is, psychic phenomena in the psychological sense.* To myself I do not exist as a human being, <nor> do my *cogitationes* exist as components of a psycho-physical world. But through all this I have discovered my true self. I have discovered that I alone am the pure ego, with pure existence and pure capacities (for example, the obvious

---

[1] As a rule, "*Leistungen*" is here translated as "acts," and "*Akte*" as "actions." (Tr.).

capacity to abstain from judging). Through this ego alone does *the being of the world,* and, for that matter, any being whatsoever, make sense *to me* and has possible validity. The world—whose conceivable non-being does not extinguish my pure being but rather presupposes it—is termed *transcendent,* whereas my pure being or my pure ego is termed *transcendental.* Through the phenomenological *epoché* the natural human ego, specifically my own, is reduced to the transcendental ego. This is the meaning of the phenomenological reduction.

Further steps are needed so that what has been developed up to this point can be adequately applied. What is the philosophic use of the transcendental ego? To be sure, for me, the one who philosophizes, it obviously precedes, in an epistemological sense, all objective reality. In a way, it is the basis for all objective knowledge, be it good or bad. But does the fact that the transcendental ego precedes and presupposes all objective knowledge mean also that it is an epistemological ground in the ordinary sense? The thought is tempting. All realistic theories are guilty of it. But the temptation to look in the transcendental subjectivity for premises guaranteeing the existence of the subjective world evanesces once we realize that all arguments, considered in themselves, exist already in transcendental subjectivity itself. Furthermore, all proofs for the world have their criteria set in the world just as it is given and justified in experience. However, these considerations must not be construed as a rejection of the great Cartesian idea that the ultimate basis for objective science and the reality of the objective world is to be sought in transcendental subjectivity. Otherwise—our criticisms aside—we would not be true to Descartes' method of meditation. However, the Cartesian discovery of the ego may perhaps open up a *new concept of foundation, namely, a transcendental foundation.*

In point of fact, instead of using the *ego cogito* merely as an apodictic proposition and as an absolutely primitive premise, we notice that the phenomenological *epoché* has uncovered for us (or for me, the one who philosophizes), through the apodictic *I am,* a new kind and an endless sphere of being. This is the sphere of a new kind of experience: transcendental experience. And herewith also arises the possibility of both transcendental epistemology and transcendental science.

A most extraordinary epistemological situation is disclosed here. The phenomenological *epoché* reduces me to my transcendental and pure ego. I am, thus, at least *prima facie,* in a certain sense *solus ipse,* but not in the ordinary sense, in which one might say that a man survived a universal holocaust in a world which itself remained unaffected. Once I have banished from my sphere of judgments the world, as one which receives its being from me and within me, then I, as the transcendental ego which is prior to the world, am *the sole source and object capable of judgment* [das einzig urteilsmäßig Setzbare und Gesetzte]. And now I am supposed to develop an unheard-of and unique science, since it is one that is created exclusively by and inside my transcendental subjectivity! Furthermore, this science is meant to apply, at least at the outset, to my transcendental subjectivity alone. It thus becomes a transcendental-solipsistic science. It is therefore not the *ego cogito,* but a science about the ego—a pure *egology*—which becomes the ultimate foundation of philosophy in the Cartesian sense of a universal science, and which must provide at least the cornerstone for its absolute foundation. In actual fact this science exists already as the lowest transcendental phenomenology. And I mean the lowest, not the fully developed phenomenology, because to the latter, of course, belongs the further development from transcendental solipsism to transcendental intersubjectivity.

To make all this intelligible it is first necessary to do what was neglected by Descartes, namely, to describe the endless field of the ego's transcendental experience itself. His own experience, as is well known, and especially when he judged it to be apodictic, plays a role in the philosophy of Descartes. But he neglected to describe the ego in the full concretion of its transcendental being and life, nor did he regard it as an unlimited work-project to be pursued systematically. It is an insight central to a philosopher that, by introducing the transcendental reduction, he can reflect truthfully on his *cogitationes* and on their pure phenomenological content. In this way he can uncover all aspects of his transcendental being with respect to both his transcendental-temporal life and also his capabilities. We are clearly dealing with a train of thought parallel to what the world-centered psychologist calls inner experience or experience of the self.

One thing of the greatest, even decisive, importance remains. One cannot lightly dismiss the fact—even Descartes has so remarked on occasion—that the *epoché* changes nothing in the world. All experience is still his experience, all consciousness, still his consciousness. The expression *ego cogito* must be expanded by one term. Every *cogito* contains a meaning: its *cogitatum*. The experience of a house, as I experience it, and ignoring theories of perception, is precisely an experience of this and only this house, a house which appears in such-and-such a way, and has certain specific determinations when seen from the side, from near-by, and from afar. Similarly, a clear or a vague recollection is the recollection of a vaguely or clearly apprehended house. Even the most erroneous judgment means a judgment about such-and-such factual content, and so on. *The essence of consciousness, in which I live as my own self, is the so-called intentionality.* Consciousness is always consciousness of something. The nature of consciousness includes, as modes of being, presentations, probabilities, and non-being, and also the modes of appearance, goodness, and value, etc. Phenomenological experience as reflection must avoid any interpretative constructions. Its descriptions must reflect accurately the concrete contents of experience, precisely as these are experienced.

To interpret consciousness as a complex of sense data and then to bring forth gestalt-like qualities [*Gestaltqualitäten*] out of these—which are subsequently equated with the totality—is a sensualist invention. This interpretation is a basic error even from the worldly and psychological perspective, and much more so from the transcendental point of view. It is true that in the process of phenomenological analyses sense data do occur, and something is, in fact, disclosed about them. But what phenomenological analysis fails to find as primary is the "perception of an external world." The honest description of the unadulterated data of experience must disclose what appears first of all, *i.e.,* the *cogito.* For example, we must describe closely the perception of a house in terms of what it means as object and its modes of appearing. The same applies to all forms of consciousness.

When I focus on the object of consciousness I discover it as something which is experienced or meant as having such-and-such determinations. When I judge, the object is the repository of judgment-predicates; when I value, it is the repository of value-predicates. Looking the other way I discover the changing aspects of consciousness, *i.e.* that which is capable of perception and memory. This category comprises everything which is neither a physical object nor any determination of such an object. That is to say, it comprises the subjective mode of givenness or subjective mode of appearance, exemplified by perspective, or the distinction between vagueness and clarity, attention and inattention, etc.

To be a meditating philosopher who, through these meditations, has himself become a transcendental ego, and who constantly reflects about himself, means to enter upon often endless transcendental experience. It means to refuse to be satisfied with a vague *ego cogito* and instead pursue the steady flux of the *cogito* towards being and life. It means to see all that which is to be seen, to explain it and penetrate it, to encompass it descriptively by concepts and judgments. But these latter must only be terms which have been derived without alteration from their perceptual source.

As said before, the guiding schema for our exposition and description is a three-sided concept: *ego cogito cogitatum.* If we disregard for the time being the identical "I," notwithstanding that in a certain sense it resides in every *cogito,* then reflection will more readily disclose the various features of the *cogito* itself. Immediately there branch off descriptive types, only vaguely suggested by language, <such as> perceiving, remembering, still-being-conscious-of-the-recently-perceived, anticipating, desiring, willing, predicating, etc. Focusing on the concrete results of transcendental reflection brings out the fundamental distinction, already alluded to, between objective meaning and mode of consciousness, possible mode of appearance. That is, seen in essence, the reference here is to the two-sidedness which makes intentionality into consciousness as consciousness of such-and-such. This always yields two orientations for description.

In relation to the preceding we must thus call attention to the fact that the transcendental *epoché* performed with respect to the existing world, containing all those objects which we actually experience, perceive, remember, think, judge, and believe, does not change the fact that the world—*i.e.,* the objects as pure phenomena of experience, as pure *cogitata* of the momentary *cogitationes*—must become a central concern of phenomenological description. In that case, what is the nature of the abysmal difference between phenomenological judgments about the world of experience and natural-objective judgments? The answer can be given in these terms: as a phenomenological ego I have become a pure observer of myself. I treat as veridical only that which I encounter as inseparable from me, as pertaining purely to my life and being inseparable from it, exactly in the manner that genuine and intuitive reflection discloses my own self to me. Before the *epoché,* I was a man with the natural attitude and I lived immersed naively in the world. I accepted the experienced as such, and on the basis of it developed my subsequent positions. All this, however, took place in me without my being aware of it. I was indeed interested in my experiences, that is, in objects, values, goals, but I did not focus on the experiencing of my life, on the act of being interested, on the act of taking a position, on my subjectivity. I was a transcendental ego even while in the living natural attitude, but I knew nothing about it. In order to become aware of my true being I needed to execute the phenomenological *epoché.* Through it I do not achieve—as Descartes attempted—a critique of validity, or, in other words, the resolution of the problem of the apodictic trustworthiness of my experience and consequently of the reality of the world. Quite to the contrary, I will learn that the world and how the world is for me the

cogitatum of my *cogitationes.* I will not only discover that the *ego cogito* precedes apodictically the fact that the world exists for me, but also familiarize myself thoroughly with the concrete being of my ego and thereby *see* it. The being that I am when, immersed, I live and experience the world from the natural attitude consists of a particular transcendental life, namely, one in which I naively trust my experiences, one in which I continue to occupy myself with a naively acquired world view, etc. Therefore, the phenomenological attitude, with its *epoché,* consists in that *I reach the ultimate experiential and cognitive perspective thinkable. In it I become the disinterested spectator of my natural and worldly ego and its life.* In this manner, my natural life becomes merely one part or one particular level of what now has been disclosed as my transcendental life. I am detached inasmuch as I "suspend" all worldly interests (which I nonetheless possess), and to the degree that I—the philosophizing one—place myself above them and observe them, and take these as themes for description, as being my transcendental ego.

The phenomenological reduction thus tends to split the ego. The transcendental spectator places himself above himself, watches himself, and sees himself also as the previously world-immersed ego. In other words, he discovers that he, as a human being, exists within himself as a *cogitatum,* and, through the corresponding *cogitationes,* he discovers the transcendental life and being which make up <the> totality of the world.

QUESTIONS FOR DISCUSSION

1. Compare Descartes's view of the self with Hume's view. With which of the two philosophers do you most agree? Why?

2. Husserl tries to forge a middle ground between Descartes and Hume with his notion of transcendental subjectivity. What does Husserl mean by "transcendental ego"? Do you think his account of self works as a resolution of the Hume/Descartes conflict? Why or why not?

HINDUISM AND BUDDHISM: A SIMILAR CONTROVERSY

In the West, Hindu philosophy is often thought to be a monolithic structure—a view of the world as a mere appearance of God or the Brahman-Atman, the Ultimate Transcendent Self, which unites in itself both subject and object, a nondual "Absolute Spirit" which is, in the last analysis, open only to mystical vision. In reality, this is just one of many philosophical interpretations of Hinduism, though it *is* strongly supported by those *Upanishads* which form our second selection; as the *Upanishads* is a sacred text—being a record of the teachings of the earliest philosopher-gurus of Hinduism—the passages we have included are given a special place in the Hindu religion; still, their interpretations have been many, and they form only a portion of the large body of literature included in the *Upanishads*. In reality, all that the many philosophies of Hinduism share is a belief in some form of unified subject or soul. The view that this soul is the nondual Absolute Spirit is one of many and not, in fact, the most popular. It is probably also not the oldest. That honor goes to the Samkhya philosophy described in another sacred Indian text, the *Bhagavad-Gita* or Song of God. Samkhya is a dualism, though not precisely the mind-body dualism described in Descartes. The Samkhya philosophy is rather a dualism of a variety similar to what we have seen in Husserl. Reality consists of the natural world or *Prakriti* on the one hand and the Spirit or pure transcendental ego, *Purusha,* on the other—the "field," as the *Gita* puts it, and the "knower of the field." The psychological self, which we know by ordinary means, is a part of *Prakriti,* not the pure ego *Purusha.* The search for this pure ego, if carried to completion, would result in enlightenment, as would also, however, the realization of Self interpreted as Absolute Spirit or its realization under any of the other varieties of philosophical description known to Hinduism. Just as in Western philosophy, where St. Thomas and Descartes share the same basic Christian outlook, though their views of soul differ greatly, so also in Hinduism, a basic religious agreement can override philosophical disputes.

The passion for this quest for the pure ego or "true self" reached a zenith in the sixth century B.C., when countless young men began to flock to the forest to find enlightenment and an end to suffering by discovering what and who they truly were. Among them was a young prince from the Himalayan foothills, Gotama Siddhartha. Having exhausted the Hindu teachings and still finding himself unsatisfied and seemingly far from the knowledge of his true nature, he began to develop his own path to wisdom. The path is the eight-fold path of Buddhism, and its creator is known to history as the Buddha, the one who has awakened from the sleep of everyday awareness. At the end of the path, the Buddha discovered, not a true self, but the nonexistence of self or *anatman* in much the same manner that 2300 years later David Hume in distant Scotland was to reach the same conclusion but, apparently, not the attendant bliss. In the selection included below, the doctrine is defended by the philosopher-monk Nagasena, in a dialogue with the Greek-born Indian King Milinda, which has become a classic of Buddhist philosophy and a bridge to Western thought.

At a still later time in Indian history, Buddhism itself underwent a transformation, the development of the Mahayana or Great Vehicle school of Buddhism, which came to dominate Buddhist thought in China and Japan. Out of this school developed two new philosophies, both of which attempted a synthesis between the early Buddhist and the Hindu view of self. The first, the Madhyamika or Middle Way between self and no-self, is represented in a selection from the contemporary scholar T. R. V. Murti's work, *The Central Philosophy of Buddhism.* The second and later Yogacara philosophy, used extensively by the famous zen meditational school of Buddhism, is expounded in *Toward a Philosophy of Zen Buddhism,* an essay by another twentieth-century thinker, the Japanese Buddhist teacher, Toshiko Izutsu.

SAMKHYA DUALISM

Bhagavad-Gita

The Body called the Field, the Soul called the Knower of the Field, and Discrimination between them

THE FIELD AND THE KNOWER OF THE FIELD

Arjuna said*:

Prakṛti and *puruṣa,* the field and the knower of the field,[1] knowledge and the object of knowledge—these I should like to know, O Keśava (Kṛṣṇa).[2]

The Blessed Lord said:

1. This body, O Son of Kuntī (Arjuna), is called the field, and him who knows this those who know thereof call the knower of the field.

• • •

3. Hear briefly from Me what the field is, of what nature, what its modifications are, whence it is, what he [the knower of the field] is, and what his powers are.
4. This has been sung by sages in many ways and distinctly, in various hymns and also in well-reasoned and conclusive expressions of the aphorisms of the Absolute [*Brahma Sūtra*].[3]
5. The great [five gross] elements, self-sense, understanding, as also the unmanifested, the ten senses and mind, and the five objects of the senses.
6. Desire and hatred, pleasure and pain, the aggregate [the organism], intelligence, and steadfastness described—this in brief is the field along with its modifications.

KNOWLEDGE

7. Humility [absence of pride], integrity [absence of deceit], nonviolence, patience, uprightness, service of the teacher, purity of body and mind, steadfastness, and self-control,
8. Indifference to the objects of sense, self-effacement, and the perception of the evil of birth, death, old age, sickness, and pain,
9. Non-attachment, absence of clinging to son, wife, home, and the like, and a constant equal-mindedness to all desirable and undesirable happenings,
10. Unswerving devotion to Me with wholehearted discipline, resort to solitary places, dislike for a crowd of people,
11. Constancy in the knowledge of the Spirit, insight into the end of the knowledge of Truth—this is declared to be true knowledge, and all that is different from it is non-knowledge.
12. I will describe that which is to be known and by knowing which life eternal is gained. It is the Supreme *Brahman* who is beginningless and who is said to be neither existent nor non-existent.

THE KNOWER OF THE FIELD

13. With his hands and feet everywhere, with eyes, heads, and faces on all sides, with ears on all sides, He dwells in the world, enveloping all.
14. He appears to have the qualities of all the senses and yet is without any of the senses, unattached and yet supporting all, free from the *guṇas* [dispositions of *prakṛti*] and yet enjoying them.
15. He is without and within all beings. He is unmoving as also moving. He is too subtle to be known. He is far away and yet is He near.
16. He is undivided [indivisible] and yet He seems

---

* The "Gita" consists of a conversation which takes place on a battlefield between the famous warrior, Arjuna, and his chariot driver, the God-man Krsna (Krishna). The beginning of that conversation can be found in Chapter 7 of this volume (Eds.).

[1] *Prakṛti* (Nature) is unconscious activity, and *puruṣa* (the self) is inactive consciousness. The body is called the field in which events happen; all growth, decline, and death take place in it. The conscious principle, inactive and detached, which lies behind all active states as witness, is the knower of the field.

[2] This verse is not found in some editions. If it is included, the total number of verses in the *Bhagavad-gītā* will be 701 and not 700, which is the number traditionally accepted. So we do not include it in the numbering of the verses.

[3] The *Gītā* suggests that it is expounding the truths already contained in the Vedas, the Upaniṣads, and the *Brahma Sūtra* or the aphorisms of *Brahman* later systematized by Bādarāyaṇa.

to be divided among beings. He is to be known as supporting creatures, destroying them and creating them afresh.

17. He is the Light of lights, said to be beyond darkness. Knowledge, the object of knowledge, and the goal of knowledge—He is seated in the hearts of all.

THE FRUIT OF KNOWLEDGE

18. Thus the field, also knowledge and the object of knowledge have been briefly described. My devotee who understands thus becomes worthy of My state.

NATURE AND SPIRIT

19. Know thou that *prakṛti* [Nature] and *puruṣa* [soul] are both beginningless; and know also that the forms and modes are born of *prakṛti*.

20. Nature is said to be the cause of effect, instrument, and agent(ness) and the soul is said to be the cause, in regard to the experience of pleasure and pain.

21. The soul in nature enjoys the modes born of nature. Attachment to the modes is the cause of its births in good and evil wombs.

22. The Supreme Spirit in the body is said to be the Witness, the Permitter, the Supporter, the Experiencer, the Great Lord and the Supreme Self.

23. He who thus knows soul (*puruṣa*) and Nature (*prakṛti*) together with the modes (*guṇas*)— though he act in every way, he is not born again.

THE TRUE SELF

The Upanishads

Hari*h*, Om.* There is this city of Brahman (the body), and in it the palace, the small lotus (of the heart), and in it that small ether. Now what exists

within that small ether, that is to be sought for, that is to be understood.

And if they should say to him: "Now with regard to that city of Brahman,† and the palace in it, i.e. the small lotus of the heart, and the small ether within the heart, what is there within it that deserves to be sought for, or that is to be understood?"

Then he should say: "As large as this ether (all space) is, so large is that ether within the heart. Both heaven and earth are contained within it, both fire and air, both sun and moon, both lightning and stars; and whatever there is of him (the Self) here in the world, and whatever is not (i.e. whatever has been or will be), all that is contained within it."

And if they should say to him: "If everything that exists is contained in that city of Brahman, all beings and all desires (whatever can be imagined or desired), then what is left of it, when old age reaches it and scatters it, or when it falls to pieces?"

Then he should say: "By the old age of the body, that (the ether, or Brahman within it) does not age; by the death of the body, that (the ether, or Brahman within it) is not killed. That (the Brahman) is the true Brahma-city (not the body). In it all desires are contained. It is the Self, free from sin, free from old age, from death and grief, from hunger and thirst, which desires nothing but what it ought to desire, and imagines nothing but what it ought to imagine. Now as here on earth people follow as they are commanded, and depend on the object which they are attached to, be it a country or a piece of land.

"And as here on earth, whatever has been acquired by exertion, perishes, so perishes whatever is acquired for the next world by sacrifices and other good actions performed on earth. Those who depart from hence without having discovered the Self and those true desires, for them there is no freedom in all the worlds. But those who depart from hence, after having discovered the Self and those true desires, for them there is freedom in all the worlds."

• • •

---

* An invocation to God (Eds.).

† "Brahman" refers to God in God's deepest Being, as one finds God within oneself. Thus, Brahman in the *Upanishads* is also identified with the true "Self" (Eds.).

All this is Brahman. Let a man meditate on that (visible world) as beginning, ending, and breathing in it (the Brahman).

Now man is a creature of will. According to what his will is in this world, so will he be when he has departed this life. Let him therefore have this will and belief:

The intelligent, whose body is spirit, whose form is light, whose thoughts are true, whose nature is like ether (omnipresent and invisible), from whom all works, all desires, all sweet odours and tastes proceed; he who embraces all this, who never speaks, and is never surprised,

He is my self within the heart, smaller than a corn of rice, smaller than a corn of barley, smaller than a mustard seed, smaller than a canary seed or the kernel of a canary seed. He also is my self within the heart, greater than the earth, greater than the sky, greater than heaven, greater than all these worlds.

He from whom all works, all desires, all sweet odours and tastes proceed, who embraces all this, who never speaks and who is never surprised, he, my self within the heart, is that Brahman. When I shall have departed from hence, I shall obtain him (that Self). He who has this faith has no doubt; thus said *Sând*ilya, yea, thus he said.

NO SELF

Questions of King Milinda

Now Milinda the king went up to where the venerable Nâgasena was, and addressed him with the greetings and compliments of friendship and courtesy, and took his seat respectfully apart. And Nâgasena reciprocated his courtesy, so that the heart of the king was propitiated.

And Milinda began by asking, "How is your Reverence known, and what, Sir, is your name?"

"I am known as Nâgasena, O king, and it is by that name that my brethren in the faith address me.

But although parents, O king, give such a name as Nâgasena, or Sûrasena, or Vîrasena, or Sihasena, yet this, Sire,—Nâgasena and so on—is only a generally understood term, a designation in common use. For there is no permanent individuality (no soul) involved in the matter.

Then Milinda called upon the Yonakas and the brethren to witness: "This Nâgasena says there is no permanent individuality (no soul) implied in his name. Is it now even possible to approve him in that?" And turning to Nâgasena, he said: "If, most reverend Nâgasena, there be no permanent individuality (no soul) involved in the matter, who is it, pray, who gives to you members of the Order your robes and food and lodging and necessaries for the sick? Who is it who enjoys such things when given? Who is it who lives a life of righteousness? Who is it who devotes himself to meditation? Who is it who attains to the goal of the Excellent Way, to the Nirvâna of Arahatship? And who is it who destroys living creatures? who is it who takes what is not his own? who is it who lives an evil life of worldly lusts, who speaks lies, who drinks strong drink, who (in a word) commits any one of the five sins which work out their bitter fruit even in this life? If that be so there is neither merit nor demerit; there is neither doer nor causer of good or evil deeds; there is neither fruit nor result of good or evil Karma.—If, most reverend Nâgasena, we are to think that were a man to kill you there would be no murder, then it follows that there are no real masters or teachers in your Order, and that your ordinations are void.—You tell me that your brethren in the Order are in the habit of addressing you as Nâgasena. Now what is that Nâgasena? Do you mean to say that the hair is Nâgasena?"

"I don't say that, great king."

"Or the hairs on the body, perhaps?"

"Certainly not."

"Or is it the nails, the teeth, the skin, the flesh, the nerves, the bones, the marrow, the kidneys, the heart, the liver, the abdomen, the spleen, the lungs, the larger intestines, the lower intestines, the stomach, the fæces, the bile, the phlegm, the pus, the blood, the sweat, the fat, the tears, the serum, the saliva, the mucus, the oil that lubricates the joints, the urine, or the brain, or any or all of these, that is Nâgasena[1]?"

And to each of these he answered no.

"Is it the outward form then (Rûpa) that is Nâgasena, or the sensations (Vedanâ), or the ideas (Saññâ), or the confections (the constitutent elements of character, Samkhârâ), or the consciousness (Viññâna), that is Nâgasena[2]?"

And to each of these also he answered no.

"Then is it all these Skandhas combined that are Nâgasena?"

"No! great king."

"But is there anything outside the five Skandhas that is Nâgasena?"

And still he answered no.

"Then thus, ask as I may, I can discover no Nâgasena. Nâgasena is a mere empty sound. Who then is the Nâgasena that we see before us? It is a falsehood that your reverence has spoken, an untruth!"

And the venerable Nâgasena said to Milinda the king: "You, Sire, have been brought up in great luxury, as beseems your noble birth. If you were to walk this dry weather on the hot and sandy ground, trampling under foot the gritty, gravelly grains of the hard sand, your feet would hurt you. And as your body would be in pain, your mind would be disturbed, and you would experience a sense of bodily suffering. How then did you come, on foot, or in a chariot?"

"I did not come, Sir, on foot. I came in a carriage."

"Then if you came, Sire, in a carriage, explain to me what that is. Is it the pole that is the chariot?"

"I did not say that."

"Is it the axle that is the chariot?"

"Certainly not."

"Is it the wheels, or the framework, or the ropes, or the yoke, or the spokes of the wheels, or the goad, that are the chariot?"

And to all these he still answered no.

"Then is it all these parts of it that are the chariot?"

"No, Sir."

"But is there anything outside them that is the chariot?"

And still he answered no.

"Then thus, ask as I may, I can discover no chariot. Chariot is a mere empty sound. What then is the chariot you say you came in? It is a falsehood that your Majesty has spoken, an untruth! There is no such thing as a chariot! You are king over all India, a mighty monarch. Of whom then are you afraid that you speak untruth?" And he called upon the Yonakas and the brethren to witness, saying: "Milinda the king here has said that he came by carriage. But when asked in that case to explain what the carriage was, he is unable to establish what he averred. Is it, forsooth, possible to approve him in that?"

When he had thus spoken the five hundred Yonakas shouted their applause, and said to the king: "Now let your Majesty get out of that if you can?"

And Milinda the king replied to Nâgasena, and said: "I have spoken no untruth, reverend Sir. It is on account of its having all these things—the pole, and the axle, the wheels, and the framework, the ropes, the yoke, the spokes, and the goad—that it comes under the generally understood term, the designation in common use, of 'chariot.' "

"Very good! Your Majesty has rightly grasped the meaning of 'chariot.' And just even so it is on account of all those things you questioned me about—[28] the thirty-two kinds of organic matter in a human body, and the five constituent elements of being—that I come under the generally understood term, the designation in common use, of 'Nâgasena.' For it was said, Sire, by our Sister Vagîrâ in the presence of the Blessed One:

"Just as it is by the condition precedent of the co-existence of its various parts that the word 'chariot' is used, just so is it that when the Skandhas are there we talk of a 'being.' "

"Most wonderful, Nâgasena, and most strange.

---

[1] This list of the thirty-two forms (âkâras) of organic matter in the human body occurs already in the Khuddaka Pâtha, §3. It is the standard list always used in similar connections; and is no doubt, supposed to be exhaustive. There are sixteen (half as many) âkâras of the mind according to Dîpavamsa I, 42.

[2] These are the five Skandhas, which include in them the whole bodily and mental constituents of any being.

Well has the puzzle put to you, most difficult though it was, been solved. Were the Buddha himself here he would approve your answer. Well done, well done, Nâgasena!"

• • •

"How many years seniority have you, Nâgasena?"

"Seven, your Majesty."

"But how can you say it is your 'seven'? Is it you who are 'seven,' or the number that is 'seven'?"

Now that moment the figure of the king, decked in all the finery of his royal ornaments, cast its shadow on the ground, and was reflected in a vessel of water. And Nâgasena asked him: "Your figure, O king, is now shadowed upon the ground, and reflected in the water, how now, are you the king, or is the reflection the king?"

"I am the king, Nâgasena, but the shadow comes into existence because of me."

"Just even so, O king, the number of the years is seven, I am not seven. But it is because of me, O king, that the number seven has come into existence; and it is mine in the same sense as the shadow is yours."

• • •

The king said: "Is there, Nâgasena, such a thing as the soul?"

"What is this, O king, the soul (Vedagu)?"

"The living principle within which sees forms through the eye, hears sounds through the ear, experiences tastes through the tongue, smells odours through the nose, feels touch through the body, and discerns things (conditions, 'dhammâ') through the mind—just as we, sitting here in the palace, can look out of any window out of which we wish to look, the east window or the west, or the north or the south."

The Elder replied: "I will tell you about the five doors,[3] great king. Listen, and give heed attentively. If the living principle within sees forms through the

eye in the manner that you mention, choosing its window as it likes, can it not then see forms not only through the eye, but also through each of the other five organs of sense? And in like manner can it not then as well hear sounds, and experience taste, and smell odours, and feel touch, and discern conditions through each of the other five organs of sense, besides the one you have in each case specified?"

"No, Sir."

"Then these powers are not united one to another indiscriminately, the latter sense to the former organ, and so on. Now we, as we are seated here in the palace, with these windows all thrown open, and in full daylight, if we only stretch forth our heads, see all kinds of objects plainly. Can the living principle do the same when the doors of the eyes are thrown open? When the doors of the ear are thrown open, can it do so? Can it then not only hear sounds, but see sights, experience tastes, smell odours, feel touch, and discern conditions? And so with each of its windows?"

"No, Sir."

"Then these powers are not united one to another indiscriminately. Now again, great king, if Dinna here were to go outside and stand in the gateway, would you be aware that he had done so?"

"Yes, I should know it."

"And if the same Dinna were to come back again, and stand before you, would you be aware of his having done so?"

"Yes, I should know it."

"Well, great king, would the living principle within discern, in like manner, if anything possessing flavour were laid upon the tongue, its sourness, or its saltness, or its acidity, or its pungency, or its astringency, or its sweetness?"

"Yes, it would know it."

"But when the flavour had passed into the stomach would it still discern these things?"

"Certainly not."

"Then these powers are not united one to the other indiscriminately. Now suppose, O king, a man were to have a hundred vessels of honey brought and poured into one trough, and then, having had another man's mouth closed over and tied up, were

_____

[3] It is odd he does not say six.

to have him cast into the trough full of honey. Would he know whether that into which he had been thrown was sweet or whether it was not?"

"No, Sir."

"But why not?"

"Because the honey could not get into his mouth."

"Then, great king, these powers are not united one to another indiscriminately."[4]

"I am not capable of discussing with such a reasoner. Be pleased, Sir, to explain to me how the matter stands."

Then the Elder convinced Milinda the king with discourse drawn from the Abhidhamma, saying: "It is by reason, O king, of the eye and of forms that sight arises, and those other conditions—contact, sensation, idea, thought, abstraction, sense of vitality, and attention—arise each simultaneously with its predecessor. And a similar succession of cause and effect arises when each of the other five organs of sense is brought into play. And so herein there is no such thing as soul (Vedagu)."

---

[4] That is: "Your 'living principle within' cannot make use of whichever of its windows it pleases. And the simile of a man inside a house does not hold good of the soul."

THE MIDDLE WAY

T. R. V. Murti

There are two main currents of Indian philosophy—one having its source in the ātma-doctrine of the Upaniṣads and the other in the anātma-doctrine of Buddha. They conceive reality on two distinct and exclusive patterns. The Upaniṣads and the systems following the Brāhmanical tradition conceive reality on the pattern of an inner core or soul (ātman), immutable and identical amidst an outer region of impermanence and change, to which it is unrelated or but loosely related. This may be termed the Sub-stance-view of reality (ātma-vāda). In its radical form, as in the Advaita Vedānta, it denied the reality of the apparent, the impermanent and the many; and equated that with the false. The Sāṁkhya did not go so far; still it inclined more towards the substantial, the permanent and the universal. The Nyāya-Vaiśeṣika, with its empirical and pluralist basis, accords equal status to both substance and modes. Not only did these systems accept the ātman, but what is more, they conceived all other things also on the substance-pattern. The ātman is the very pivot of their metaphysics, epistemology and ethics. In epistemology, substance makes for unity and integration of experience; it explains perception, memory and personal identity better than other theories. Bondage is ignorance of the self or the wrong identification of the non-self with the self (ātmany anātmādhyāsa). Freedom is the discrimination between the two.

The other tradition is represented by the Buddhist denial of substance (ātman) and all that it implies. There is no inner and immutable core in things; everything is in flux. Existence for the Buddhist is momentary (kṣaṇika), unique (svalakṣaṇa) and unitary (dharmamātra). It is discontinuous, discrete and devoid of complexity. The substance (the universal and the identical) was rejected as illusory; it was but a thought-construction made under the influence of wrong belief (avidyā). This may be taken as the *Modal view of reality*. The Buddhists brought their epistemology and ethics in full accord with their metaphysics. Their peculiar conception of perception and inference and the complementary doctrine of mental construction (vikalpa) are necessary consequences of their denial of substance. Heroic attempts were made to fit this theory with the doctrine of Karma and rebirth. Avidyā (ignorance), which is the root-cause of suffering, is the wrong belief in the ātman; and prajñā (wisdom) consists in the eradication of this belief and its attendant evils.

• • •

Ātman is the chief category of the permanent. In

a restricted but more prevalent usage, it means the soul or spirit, the subject of experience; in a wider and more logical sense it is substance in general. There are two principal views of the Self (ātman): one is the conception, in vogue with the Brāhmanical systems, of a permanent and immutable entity identical amidst changing states and therefore different from them; the other is the Buddhistic conception of ātman as a conventional name (prajñaptisat) for a series of discrete momentary states (skandharūpa), sensation and feeling, intellection and conation. There is nothing unitary or identical amidst the changing states, and nothing hidden beneath them as the ātman. Like all existence, the mental states too are in a state of continual flux. The Buddhists coined a very unattractive word— 'pudgala'—for the ātman. Besides these two principal views, there is the intermediary standpoint not only of the Jainas, but of the Vātsīputrīyas (Sāmmitīyas) within the Buddhist fold itself. They held that the ātman or pudgala was a sort of quasi-permanent entity neither different from nor identical with the states like fire and fuel. The Pudgalātmavāda has been universally condemned as a heresy by the Buddhist schools, including the Mādhyamika.

If the ātman were identical with the states (skandhalaksana), it would be subject to birth, decay and death. There would be as many selves (ātman) as there are states. Of each self it could be urged that it was non-existent before it was born and would cease to exist later. Further, it would have been produced without causes, each self being a discrete independent entity, having no relation with the previous. The full weight of this criticism is realised when we consider moral responsibility. As the former self has ceased to exist and a new one has emerged into existence, the deeds done by the previous also cease to exist; for, there is no longer that entity which performed them. If the later self were to experience the result of the acts of the previous self, it would be a clear case of gratuitous burdening of responsibility. All this is repugnant to the implications of the moral act and its consequences, as done and enjoyed by the *same* agent.

This view of the states being the self really identifies the act with the agent, the feeling with the person who experiences the feeling. Such identification is unwarranted and cannot account for experience. The feeling itself is not the feeler, a content is not the *knowing* of the content. The subject of experience has to be accepted as indispensable for the occurrence of any mental state. The Buddhists, as rigorous exponents of the modal view, eschew the ātman and replace it completely by the states of feeling, sensation, conception and volition. Memory, recognition, moral responsibility and transmigration are all attempted to be explained on this hypothesis of substanceless momentary states— (upādāna-skandhas). It speaks not a little for the dialectical insight of Nāgārjuna* and his followers that they are acutely alive to the halting nature of the modal view (upādānam evātmā).

"The self is not the states that originate and cease; how can the experiencing subject (upādātā) be identical with the experienced states (upādāna)?" His main criticism of the modal view is that it wrongly identifies the agent with the act, the subject and the object (ekatvam kartrkarmanoh). A multitude of qualities is not substance; a bundle of states is not the self. Bereft of unity, they fall asunder and make for disorder. The substance or self is the unifying factor which integrates several acts, making mental life continuous and coherent.

The rejection of the Buddhist modal view of the ātman by the Mādhyamika does not of itself mean that he is committed to the opposite view of an identical and changeless self (substance) different from the states. As a keen dialectician, the Mādhyamika is equally aware of the pitfalls of the substance-view of the ātman. He rejects that too as a false view of the real.

The conception of the ātman is variously formulated by the different non-Buddhistic systems; but they all agree in considering it as eternal, and as existing apart from the states and as identical amidst

---

* The founder of the Madhyamika philosophy in the second century A.D. (Eds.).

change. The main criticism of the Mādhyamika is that if the ātman were totally different from the states, it would be apprehended apart from them, as the table is perceived apart from the chair. It is not so perceived, and hence it is merely thought to exist owing to transcendental thought-construction. The ātman is the egoity (ahaṃkāra) reflected in the states, enjoying a semblance of independence, identity and permanence. It is thus a construct (vikalpe) read into the manifold of states.

If the ātman were a real entity, there should be agreement about it. On the contrary one's (self) ātman is anātma (non-self) for another, and vice versa; and this should not be the case if it were an objective reality.

The relation of the ātman with the states cannot be formulated in any conceivable manner: whether the states are the self or different from them; whether the states are in it, or it is in them; whether the states belong to it, or vice versa, etc. There are obvious difficulties in every formulation, and most of them have been considered already.

It might be asked: if the ātman were not a real spiritual entity, then who is the mover and controller of the bodily movements? But how can an immaterial principle actuate a material thing like the body or the sense-organs and mind etc. Changeless and all-pervasive (sarvagata), ātman is not active (niṣkriya); and without action, the ātman cannot be an agent (kartā). He cannot even co-ordinate and synthesize the different states into a unity.

As in the modal view, here too moral and spiritual life becomes impossible, though for an opposite reason; an unchanging ātman cannot be benefited by any spiritual discipline, nor can it deteriorate if that effort were not made. In spiritual progress the ātman cannot be identical at any two stages of development. To say that the ātman is not really bound or free, but owing to avidyā he wrongly identifies himself with the body, sense-organs and mind, is to say that phenomenal life is the work of false belief and imagination (kalpanā). The saving knowledge then is not that the real is ātman or anātma, but that none of our conceptual patterns applies to it.

On the modal view, there are the different momentary states only; there is no principle of unity. Mental life is inexplicable without the unity of the self. On the substance-view, there is the unitary and identical self rigid and standing aloof from the states which the ātman is presumed to shape into order. The self of the Brāhmanical systems is a bare colourless unity bereft of difference and change, which alone impart significance to it. The self has no meaning apart from the states and mental activity. The two are mutually dependent, and hence unreal.

• • •

After an examination of the several views (dṛṣtis) with regard to the ātman, Nāgārjuna concludes: "The self is not different from the states, nor identical with them; (there) is no self without the states; nor is it to be considered non-existent."

The Mādhyamika position may appear to be at variance with the teaching of the Buddha; on several occasions he seems to have asserted the existence of the self. But there are texts which declare quite unequivocally that he denied the self. The contradiction, however, is but apparent. "The self does exist, the Buddhas have declared; they have taught the 'no-self' doctrine too; they have (finally) taught that there is neither self nor non-self." Buddha's teaching is adjusted to the need of the taught as the medicine of the skilled physician is to the malady of the patient. He does not blindly, mechanically, prescribe one remedy to all and sundry, He corrects those with a nihilistic tendency by affirming the self, as there is continuity of karma and its result; to those addicted to the dogmatic belief in a changeless substantial ātman and who cling to it, he teaches the 'no-self doctrine' as an antidote; his ultimate teaching is that there is neither self nor notself as these are subjective devices. The Real as the Indeterminate (śūnya) is free from conceptual construction. The indeterminacy of the Absolute allows freedom of approach; numberless are the ways by which it could be reached. The sole condition is that the method chosen should suit the disciple's disposition; this is the doctrine of upāya-kauśalya (excellence in the choice of means), and it applies to every doctrine.

EGO-LESS CONSCIOUSNESS: A ZEN VIEW

Toshiko Izutsu

THE FIRST PERSON PRONOUN "I"

In dealing with the topic of the two dimensions of ego-consciousness in Zen, it might be thought more in line with Jungian psychology to use the word "Self" instead of the word "Ego" to designate what I am going to explain as ego-consciousness in the second or deeper dimension. But there is a reason why I prefer in this particular case to use one and the same word, "ego," in reference to the two dimensions of consciousness which I shall deal with in this Essay. For it is precisely one of the most important points which Zen makes that the empirical I which is the very center of human existence in our ordinary, daily life and the other I which is supposed to be actualized through the experience of enlightenment are ultimately identical with one another. The two "egos" are radically different from each other and look almost mutually exclusive in the eyes of those who are in the pre-enlightenment stage of Zen discipline. From the viewpoint of the post-enlightenment stage, however, they are just one and the same, In the eyes of the truly enlightened Zen master, there is nothing special, nothing extraordinary about what is often called by such grandiose names as Cosmic Ego, Cosmic Unconscious, Transcendental Consciousness and the like. It is no other than the existential ground of the ordinary, commonplace man who eats when he is hungry, drinks when he is thirsty, and falls asleep when he is sleepy, that is, in short, the ordinary self which we are accustomed to regard as the subject of the day-to-day existence of the plain man.

But let us start from the beginning. The starting-point is provided by our ego-consciousness as we find it in the pre-enlightenment stage. Historically as well as structurally, Zen has always been seriously concerned with our consciousness of ourselves. Indeed, it is not going too far to say that the problem of how to deal with ego-consciousness is *the* sole and exclusive problem for Zen Buddhism. Says Dōgen,[1] one of the greatest Zen masters of Japan in the thirteenth century A.D.: "To get disciplined in the way of the Buddha means nothing other than getting disciplined in properly dealing with your own I." That is to say, an intense, unremitting self-inquiry exhausts the whole of Buddhism. It constitutes the first step into the Way of the Buddha and it constitutes the ultimate end of the same Way. There is no other problem in Zen.

Another Japanese Zen master of the 15th century, Ikkyū,[2] admonishes his disciples in a similar way saying: "Who or what am I? Search for your I from the top of your head down to your bottom." And he adds: "No matter how hard you may search for it, you will never be able to grasp it. *That* precisely is your I." In this last sentence there is a clear suggestion made as to how the problem of ego-consciousness is to be posed and settled in Zen Buddhism.

Our ordinary view of the world may be symbolically represented as a circle with the ego as its autonomous center. With individual differences that are clearly to be recognized, each circle delimits a certain spatial and temporal expanse within the boundaries of which alone everything knowable is knowable. Its circumference sets up a horizon beyond which things disappear in an unfathomable darkness. The center of the circle is occupied by what Karl Jaspers called *Ich als Dasein,* i.e. the empirical ego, the I as we ordinarily understand it.

The circle thus constituted is of a centrifugal nature in the sense that everything, every action,

---

[1] On Dōgen (1200–1253).
[2] Master Ikkyū (1394–1481). The quotation is from his *Mizukagami.*

whether mental or bodily, is considered to originate from its center and move toward its periphery. It is also centripetal in the sense that whatever happens within the circle is referred back and reduced to the center as its ultimate ground.

The center of the circle comes in this way to be vaguely represented as a permanent and enduring entity carrying and synthesizing all the disparate and divergent elements to be attributed to the various aspects and functions of the mind-body complex. Thus is born an image of the personal identity underlying all mental operations and bodily movements, remaining always the same through all the intra-organic and extra-organic processes that are observable in the mind-body complex. Linguistic usage expresses this inner vision of personal identity by the first person pronoun "I."

In our actual life we constantly use the first person pronoun as the grammatical subject for an infinite number of predicates. Long before the rise of Zen, Buddhism in India had subjected this usage of the first person pronoun to a thoroughgoing scrutiny in connection with the problem of the unreality of the ego, which, as is well known, was from the beginning the fundamental tenet of Buddhist philosophy and which, insofar as it was an idea distinguishing Buddhism from all other schools of Indian philosophy, was for the Buddhists of decisive importance.

We often say for instance "I am fat" or "I am lean" in reference to our bodily constitution. We say "I am healthy" or "I am ill" in accordance with whether our bodily organs are functioning normally or not. "I walk," "I run," etc., in reference to our bodily movements. "I am hungry," "I am thirsty," etc., in reference to the intra-organic physiological processes. "I see," "I hear," "I smell," etc., in reference to the activity of our sense organs. The first person pronoun behaves in fact as the grammatical subject of many other types of sentences, descriptive or otherwise.

Under all those propositions with the first person pronoun as the subject there is clearly observable the most primitive, primal certainty of "I am." This primal certainty we have of our "I am," that is, the

consciousness of ego, derives its supreme importance from the fact that it constitutes the very center of the existential circle of each one of us. As the center sets itself into motion, a whole world of things and events spreads itself out around it in all directions, and as it quiets down the same variegated world is reduced to the original single point. The spreading-out of the empirical world in all its possible forms around the center is linguistically reflected in the sentences whose grammatical subject is "I."

The most serious question here for Zen is: Does the grammatical subject of all these sentences represent the real personal subject in its absolute suchness? Otherwise expressed: Does the first person pronoun appearing in each of the sentences of this sort indicate pure subjectivity, the true Subject as understood by Zen Buddhism? The answer will definitely be in the negative.

The nature of the problem before us may be clarified in the following way. Suppose someone asks me, "Who are you?" or "What are you?" To this question I can give an almost infinite number of answers. I can say, for example, "I am a Japanese," "I am a student," etc. Or I can say "I am so-and-so," giving my name. None of these answers, however, presents the *whole* of myself in its absolute "suchness." And no matter how many times I may repeat the formula "I am X," changing each time the semantic referent of the X, I shall never be able to present directly and immediately the "whole man" that I am. All that is presented by this formula is nothing but a partial and relative aspect of my existence, an objectified qualification of the "whole man." Instead of presenting the pure subjectivity that I am as the "whole man," the formula presents myself only as a relative object. But what Zen is exclusively concerned with is precisely the "whole man." And herewith begins the real Zen problem concerning the ego consciousness. Zen may be said to take its start by putting a huge question mark to the word "I" as it appears as the subject-term of all sentences of the type: "I am X" or "I do X." One enters into the world of Zen only when one realizes that his own I has itself turned into an existential question mark.

In the authentic tradition of Zen Buddhism in China it was customary for a master to ask a newcomer to his monastery questions in order to probe the spiritual depth of the man. The standard question, the most commonly used for this purpose, was: "Who are you?" This simple, innocent-looking question was in reality one which the Zen disciples were most afraid of. We shall have later occasion to see how vitally important this question is in Zen. But it will already be clear enough that the question is of such grave importance because it demands of us that we reveal immediately and on the spot the reality of the I underlying the common usage of the first person pronoun, that is, the "whole man" in its absolute subjectivity. Without going into theoretical details. I shall give here a classical example.[3] Nan Yüeh Huai Jang (J.: Nangaku Ejō, 677–744) who was later to become the successor to the Sixth Patriarch of Zen Buddhism in China, the famous Hui Nêng (J.: Enō, 637–713), came to visit the latter. Quite abruptly Hui Nêng asked him: "What is *this thing* that has come to me in this way?" This put the young Nan Yüeh completely at a loss for a reply. He left the master. And it took him eight years to solve the problem. In other words, the question "What are you?" functioned for the young Nan Yüeh as a *kōan*. And, let me add, it can be or is in fact a *kōan* for anyone who wants to have an insight into the spirit of Zen. The answer, by the way, which Nan Yüeh presented to the master after eight years' struggle was a very simple one: "Whatever I say in the form of *I am X* will miss the point. That exactly is the real I."

Making reference to this famous anecdote, Master Musō, an outstanding Zen master of fourteenth century Japan,[4] makes the following remark. "To me, too," he says "many men of inferior capacity come and ask various questions about the spirit of Buddhism. To these people I usually put the question: 'Who is the one who is actually asking me such a question about the spirit of Buddhism?' To this there are some who answer: 'I am so-and-so,' or 'I am such-and-such.' There are some who answer: 'Why is it necessary at all to ask such a question? It is too obvious.' There are some who answer not by words but by gestures meant to symbolize the famous dictum: 'My own Mind, that is the Buddha.' There are still others who answer (by repeating or imitating like a parrot the sayings of ancient masters, like) 'Looking above, there is nothing to be sought after. Looking below, there is nothing to be thrown away.' All these people will never be able to attain enlightenment."

This naturally reminds us of what is known in the history of Zen as the "concluding words of Master Pai Chang." Pai Chang Huai Hai (J.: Hyakujō Ekai, 720–814) was one of the greatest Zen masters of the T'ang dynasty. It is recorded that whenever he gave a public sermon to the monks of his temple, he brought it to an end by directly addressing the audience: "You people!" And as all turned towards the master in a state of unusual spiritual tension, at that very moment he flung down upon them like a thunderbolt the shout: "WHAT IS THAT?" Those among the audience who were mature enough to get enlightened were supposed to attain enlightenment on the spot.

"What is that?" "Who are you?" "What are you?" "Where do you come from?" These and other similar questions addressed by an enlightened master to a newcomer all directly point to the real I of the latter which originally lies hidden behind the veil of his empirical I. These questions are extremely difficult to answer in a Zen context. Let us recall that Nan Yüeh had to grapple with his *kōan* for eight years before he found his own solution for it—not, of course, a verbal solution, but an existential one. The difficulty consists in that a question of this sort in the Zen context of a dialogue between master and disciple demands of the latter an immediate realization of the I as pure and unconditioned subjectivity. This is difficult almost to the extent of being utterly impossible because at the very moment that the disciple turns his attention to his own

---

[3] *Wu Têng Hui Yüan*, III.
[4] The National Teacher, Musö (1275–1351), particularly famous for initiating the tradition of landscape gardening in Japanese culture. The following passage is found in his work *Muchü Mondö Shü*, II.

self which under ordinary conditions he is wont to express quite naïvely and unreflectingly by the first person pronoun, the self becomes objectified, or we should say, petrified, and the sought-for pure subjectivity is lost. The pure Ego can be realized only through a total transformation of the empirical ego into something entirely different, functioning in an entirely different dimension of human existence.

ZEN THEORY OF CONSCIOUSNESS

In order to elucidate the nature of the problem, let me go back once again to the image of the circle with which I proposed to represent symbolically the world as experienced by man at the pre-enlightenment stage. The world in the view of the plain man, I said, may conveniently be represented as a vaguely illumined circle with the empirical ego at its center as the source of illumination. Around the empirical ego there spreads out a more or less narrowly limited circle of existence within which things are perceived and events take place. Such is the world-view of the plain man.

The circle of existence seen in this way would seem to have a peculiar structure. The center of the circle, the empirical ego, establishes itself as the "subject" and, as such, cognitively opposes itself to the "object" which is constituted by the world extending from and around it. Each of the things existing in the world and the world itself, indeed everything other than the "subject," is regarded as an "object." Zen does not necessarily criticize this structure as something entirely false or baseless. Zen takes a definitely negative attitude toward such a view as a falsification of the reality only when the "subject" becomes conscious of itself as the "subject," that is to say, when the "subjective" position of the center of the circle comes to produce the consciousness of the ego as an enduring individual entity. For in such a context, the "subject" turns into an "object." The "subject" may even then conceptually still remain "subjective," but insofar as it is conscious of itself as a self-subsistent entity, it belongs to the sphere of the "objective." It is but another "object" among myriads of other "objects."

Viewed in such a light, the entire circle of the world of Being together with its center, the ego, proves to be an "objective" order of things. That is to say, what is seemingly the center of the circle is not the real center; the "subject" is not the real Subject.

In fact, it is characteristic of the psychological mechanism of man that no matter how far he may go in search of his real self in its pure and absolute subjectivity, it goes on escaping his grip. For the very act of turning attention to the "subject" immediately turns it into an "object."

What Zen primarily aims at may be said to be the reinstatement of the "subject" in its proper, original position, at the very center of the circle, not as an "object" but in its absolute subjectivity, as the real Subject or pure Ego. But the essential nature of the "subject" being such as has just been indicated, the task of reinstating it in this sense cannot possibly be accomplished unless the illuminated circle of existence surrounding the "subject" be also completely transformed. We may perhaps describe the situaiton by saying that the primary aim of Zen consists in trying to broaden the "circle" to infinity to the extent that we might actualize an infinitely large circle with its circumference nowhere to be found, so that its center be found everywhere, always mobile and ubiquitous, fixed at no definite point. Only as the center of such a circle could the "subject" be the pure Ego.

In ancient Indian Buddhism, the pure Ego thus actualized used to be designated by the word *prajñā* or Transcendental Wisdom. Zen, using the traditional, common terminology of Buddhism that has developed in China, often calls it the "Buddha Nature," or simply "Mind," but Zen possesses also its specific vocabulary which is more colorful and more characteristically Chinese, for designating the same thing, like "No-Mind," the "Master," the "True-Man-without-any-rank," "your-original-Face-which-you-possessed-prior-to-the-birth-of-your-own-father-and-mother," or more simply, "This Thing," "That" or still more simply "It." All these and other names are designed to point to the transfigured ego functioning as the center of the transfigured "circle."

For a better understanding of the transfiguration of the ego here spoken of, we would do well to consider the Zen idea of the structure of consciousness. Buddhism, in conformity with the general trend of Indian philosophy and spirituality, was concerned from the earliest periods of its historical development in India, and later on in China, with a meticulous analysis of the psychological processes ranging from sensation, perception and imagination to logical thinking, translogical thinking and transcendental intuition. As a result, many different psychological and epistemological theories have been proposed. And this has been done in terms of the structure of consciousness. Characteristic of these theories of consciousness is that consciousness is represented as something of a multilayer structure. Consciousness, in this view, consists of a number of layers or different dimensions organically related to each other but each functioning in its own way.

The most typical of all theories of consciousness that have developed in Mahayana Buddhism is that of the Yogācāra School (otherwise called the Vijñaptimātratā School, i.e., Consciousness-Only School). The philosophers of this school recognize in human consciousness three distinctively different levels. The first or "surface" level is the ordinary psychological dimension in which the sense-organs play the preponderant role producing sensory and perceptual images of the external things. Under this uppermost layer comes the *mano-vijñāna* or Manas-Consciousness. This is the dimension of the ego-consciousness.

According to the Yogācāra School, the consciousness of ego which we ordinarily have is but an infinitesimal part of the Manas-Consciousness. It is only the tip of a huge iceberg that shows above the surface. The greater part of the iceberg is submerged beneath the water. The submerged part of the iceberg consists of the so-called "egotistic attachments" which have been accumulated there since time immemorial and which are intensely alive and active in the invisible depths of the psyche, sustaining, as it were, from below what we are ordinarily conscious of as our "I."

The Manas-Consciousness itself is sustained from below by the *ālaya-vijñāna*, the Storehouse-Consciousness which constitutes the deepest layer of human consciousness. Unlike the Manas-Consciousness of which at least the smallest part is illumined in the form of the empirical ego-consciousness, the Storehouse-Consciousness lies entirely in darkness. It is a "storehouse" or repository of all the karmic effects of our past actions, mental and bodily. They are "stored" there under the form of primordial Images which constantly come up to the above-mentioned surface level of consciousness arousing there the sensory and perceptual images of the phenomenal things and producing at the second level of consciousness i.e., the level of *mano-vijñāna,* the consciousness of the ego. What is remarkable about the nature of the Storehouse-Consciousness is that, in the view of the Yogācāra School, it is not confined to the individual person. It exceeds the boundaries of an individual mind extending even beyond the personal unconscious that belongs to the individual, for it is the "storehouse" of all the karmic vestiges that have been left by the experiences of mankind since the beginning of time. As such the concept of the Storehouse-Consciousness may be said to be the closest equivalent in Buddhism to the Collective Unconscious.

However, the philosophers of the Yogācāra School speak of transcending the Storehouse-Consciousness by the force of a spiritual illumination that issues forth from the World of Purest Reality as they call it, which they say could be opened up by man's going through the arduous process of the spiritual discipline of meditation.

As a branch of Mahayana Buddhism closely connected with the Yogācāra School, Zen bases itself philosophically on a similar conception of the structure of consciousness. However, being by nature averse to all theorizing, let alone philosophizing, Zen has elaborated no special doctrine concerning this problem, at least in an explicit form. But under the innumerable anecdotes, *kōans,* poems, and popular sermons which constitute the main body of Zen literature, a group of major ideas about the structure of consciousness is clearly discernible. And it is not so hard for us to bring them out in a theoretical form and develop them into a Zen doctrine of consciousness.

It immediately becomes clear that Zen also holds a multilayer theory of consciousness. Here, however, as in all other cases, Zen greatly simplifies the matter. It regards consciousness as consisting of two entirely different, though intimately related, layers which we may distinguish as (1) the intentional and (2) the non-intentional dimension of consciousness, the word "intentional" being used in the original sense as exemplified by the use of the Latin word *intentio* in Medieval philosophy.

In the intentional dimension, the I as the "subject" is empirically given as a correlate of the "object." There is an essential correlation between the "subject" and "object." All noetic experience in this dimension is necessarily of dualistic structure. I regard myself as "I" only insofar as I am aware of external things and events as "objects" of cognition. There would be no ego-consciousness if there were absolutely no "object" to be cognized. More generally, it is characteristic of this dimension that our consciousness is always and necessarily a "consciousness-of." It is an awareness *intending* something i.e., directed toward something; it is an awareness with an objective reference.

It is, in other words, of the very nature of consciousness in this dimension that it cannot but objectify whatever appears before it. And paradoxically or ironically enough, this holds true even of the "subject." The very moment I become aware of myself, my I turns into an objectified I, an "object" among all other "objects." This is the main reason, as I said earlier, why it is so difficult to realize the "subject" in its pure subjectivity. One can never hope to actualize the pure Ego as long as one remains in the intentional dimension of consciousness.

Zen, however, recognizes—and knows through experience—another dimension of consciousness which is what I have called above the "non-intentional" dimension, and in which consciousness functions without being divided into the subjective and objective. It is a noetic dimension which is to be cultivated through the yogic, introspective tech-

niques of *zazen,* a special dimension in which consciousness is activated not as "consciousness-of" but as Consciousness pure and simple. This would exactly correspond to what Vasubandhu, a representative philosopher of the Yogācāra School, once said:[5] "As the mind perceives no object, it remains as pure Awareness."

The non-intentional awareness is found to be at work, albeit usually in vague and indistinct form, even in our day-to-day experience. Already the Sautrāntika School of Hinayana Buddhism[6] noticed the existence of the non-intentional aspect in the mind of the plain man. The proposition, for example, "I feel happy" in contradistinction to a proposition like "I see a mountain," expresses a kind of non-intentional awareness. For being-happy is an awareness of a pleasurable mode of being, an elation which is vaguely diffused in the whole of my mind-body complex, with no definite, particular "object" of which I can say I am conscious, unless I become by *intentio secunda* conscious of my being-happy. The proposition "I see a mountain," on the contrary, is clearly a description of a perceptual event taking place between the "subject" and the "object."

What Zen is interested in, however, is not a non-intentional awareness such as is expressed by propositions of the type: "I am happy." Rather Zen is interested in opening up a special dimension of consciousness which is, we might say, systematically non-intentional. It is a dimension in which even a proposition like "I see the mountain" for example will be found to signify a peculiar state of awareness of such a nature that exactly the same propositional content may be expressed interchangeably by four linguistically different sentences: (1) "I see the mountain," (2) "The mountain sees me," (3) "The mountain sees the mountain," (4) "I see myself." The non-intentional dimension of consciousness in which Zen is interested is such

---

[5] In his *Triṃshika-Vijñaptimātratā-Siddhi.*
[6] See an excellent exposition of the matter by H. Guenther: *Buddhist Philosophy,* Harmondsworth-Baltimore, 1972, pp. 68–70.

that these four sentences are exactly synonymous with each other. Until these four sentences are realized to be exactly synonymous with each other, you are still in the intentional dimension of consciousness. Furthermore, in the non-intentional dimension of consciousness these four synonymous sentences can very well be reduced to a one word sentence: "Mountain!" and this word again can freely be reduced to one single word "I."

Here we observe how the original sentence: "I see the mountain" from which we started has ultimately been condensed into one single point of "I." The "I" thus actualized conceals within itself all the sentential variants that have been passed through, so that it can at any moment reveal itself as the "Mountain!" or expand into any of the four full sentences. In whichever form it may appear, it is a pure non-intentional awareness, a pure consciousness instead of "consciousness-of." Nothing is here objectified. What Zen considers to be the true Self or absolute Ego is precisely the I actualized in such a dimension of consciousness as an immediate self-expression of this very dimension.

QUESTIONS FOR DISCUSSION

1. The Samkhya dualism of the *Bhagavad-Gita* is somewhat different from Descartes's dualism. Compare and contrast Samkhya and Cartesian dualism. (*Note: Cartesianism* is the term usually used by philosophers to describe the work of Descartes and his followers.)
2. Compare the early Buddhist view of self with that of the Hindu *Upanishads*.
3. Compare the early Buddhist view of self with those of the Western philosophers presented in the previous section of this chapter.
4. Both the Madhyamika philosophy explained by Murti and the later Yogacara philosophy expounded by Izutsu claim to be philosophies of Mahayana Buddhism. On the basis of what you have read, do they appear to you to be different or essentially similar interpretations of this viewpoint?
5. Compare Izutsu with Husserl. How are their viewpoints similar? How do they differ?

A DEFENSE OF HUME AND BUDDHA BASED ON WESTERN PSYCHOLOGY

During the 1960s, scientists discovered that surgical separation of the two hemispheres of the brain was beneficial in cases of severe epilepsy. Unfortunately, the procedure had unanticipated side effects of a disturbing and unusual nature. When separated, the two hemispheres and the body parts they separately controlled assumed an independence of amazing proportions. In one frightening and dramatic instance, the patient reported an argument with his wife that resulted in his one hand attempting to strike her while his other hand tried to protect her from the blow. In the following article, the contemporary analytic philosopher Derek Parfit draws upon this incredible psychological discovery in an attempt to defend the "bundle" theory of the self developed by both David Hume and the Buddha against the "ego theory" of philosophers such as Descartes and the orthodox Hindu sages.

DIVIDED MINDS AND THE "BUNDLE" THEORY OF SELF

Derek Parfit

It was the split-brain cases which drew me into philosophy. Our knowledge of these cases depends on the results of various psychological tests, as described by Donald MacKay. These tests made use of two facts. We control each of our arms, and see what is in each half of our visual fields, with only one of our hemispheres. When someone's hemispheres have been disconnected, psychologists can thus present to this person two different written questions in the two halves of his visual field, and can receive two different answers written by this person's two hands.

Here is a simplified imaginary version of the kind of evidence that such tests provide. One of these people looks fixedly at the centre of a wide screen, whose left half is red and right half is blue. On each half in a darker shade are the words, "How many colours can you see?" With both hands the person writes, "Only one." The words are now changed to read, "Which is the only colour that you can see?" With one of his hands the person writes "Red," with the other he writes "Blue."

If this is how such a person responds, I would conclude that he is having two visual sensations—that he does, as he claims, see both red and blue. But in seeing each colour he is not aware of seeing the other. He has two streams of consciousness, in each of which he can see only one colour. In one stream he sees red, and at the same time, in his other stream, he sees blue. More generally, he could be having at the same time two series of thoughts and sensations, in having each of which he is unaware of having the other.

This conclusion has been questioned. It has been claimed by some that there are not *two* streams of consciousness, on the ground that the sub-dominant hemisphere is a part of the brain whose functioning involves no consciousness. If this were true, these cases would lose most of their interest. I believe that it is not true, chiefly because, if a person's dominant hemisphere is destroyed, this person is able to react in the way in which, in the split-brain cases, the sub-dominant hemisphere reacts, and we do not believe that such a person is just an automaton, without consciousness. The sub-dominant hemisphere is, of course, much less developed in certain ways, typically having the linguistic abilities of a three-year-old. But three-year-olds are conscious. This supports the view that, in split-brain cases, there *are* two streams of consciousness.

Another view is that, in these cases, there are two persons involved, sharing the same body. Like Professor MacKay, I believe that we should reject this view. My reason for believing this is, however, different. Professor MacKay denies that there are two persons involved because he believes that there is only one person involved. I believe that, in a sense, the number of persons involved is none.

THE EGO THEORY AND THE BUNDLE THEORY

To explain this sense I must, for a while, turn away from the split-brain cases. There are two theories about what persons are, and what is involved in a person's continued existence over time. On the *Ego Theory,* a person's continued existence cannot be explained except as the continued existence of a particular *Ego,* or *subject of experiences.* An Ego Theorist claims that, if we ask what unifies someone's consciousness at any time—what makes it true, for example, that I can now both see what I am typing and hear the wind outside my window—the answer is that these are both experiences which are being had by me, this person, at this time. Similarly, what explains the unity of a person's whole life is the fact that all of the experiences in this life are had by the same person, or subject of experiences. In its best-known form, the *Cartesian view,* each person is a persisting purely mental thing—a soul, or spiritual substance.

The rival view is the *Bundle Theory.* Like most styles in art—Gothic, baroque, rococo, etc.—this theory owes its name to its critics. But the name is good enough. According to the Bundle Theory, we can't explain either the unity of consciousness at any time, or the unity of a whole life, by referring to a person. Instead we must claim that there are long series of different mental states and events—thoughts, sensations, and the like—each series being what we call one life. Each series is unified by various kinds of causal relation, such as the relations that hold between experiences and later memories of them. Each series is thus like a bundle tied up with string.

In a sense, a Bundle Theorist denies the existence of persons. An outright denial is of course absurd. As Reid protested in the eighteenth century, "I am not thought, I am not action, I am not feeling; I am something which thinks and acts and feels." I am not a series of events, but a person. A Bundle Theorist admits this fact, but claims it to be only a fact about our grammar, or our language. There are persons or subjects in this language-dependent way. If, however, persons are believed to be more than this—to be separately existing things, distinct from our brains and bodies, and the various kinds of mental states and events—the Bundle Theorist denies that there are such things.

The first Bundle Theorist was Buddha, who taught "anatta," or the *No Self view.* Buddhists concede that selves or persons have "nominal existence," by which they mean that persons are merely combinations of other elements. Only what exists by itself, as a separate element, has instead what Buddhists call "actual existence." Here are some quotations from Buddhist texts:

> At the beginning of their conversation the king politely asks the monk his name, and receives the following reply: "Sir, I am known as 'Nagasena'; my fellows in the religious life address me as 'Nagasena.' Although my parents gave me the name . . . it is just an appellation, a form of speech, a description, a conventional usage. 'Nagasena' is only a name, for no person is found here."

> A sentient being does exist, you think, O Mara? You are misled by a false conception. This bundle of elements is void of Self, In it there is no sentient being. Just as a set of wooden parts Receives the name of carriage, So do we give to elements The name of fancied being.

> Buddha has spoken thus: "O Brethren, actions do exist, and also their consequences, but the person that acts does not. There is no one to cast away this set of elements, and no one to assume a new set of them. There exists no Individual, it is only a conventional name given to a set of elements."[1]

---

[1] For the sources of these and similar quotations, see my *Reasons and Persons* (1984) pp. 502–3, 532. Oxford: Oxford Univ. Press.

Buddha's claims are strikingly similar to the claims advanced by several Western writers. Since these writers knew nothing of Buddha, the similarity of these claims suggests that they are not merely part of one cultural tradition, in one period. They may be, as I believe they are, true.

WHAT WE BELIEVE OURSELVES TO BE

Given the advances in psychology and neurophysiology, the Bundle Theory may now seem to be obviously true. It may seem uninteresting to deny that there are separately existing Egos, which are distinct from brains and bodies and the various kinds of mental states and events. But this is not the only issue. We may be convinced that the Ego Theory is false, or even senseless. Most of us, however, even if we are not aware of this, also have certain beliefs about what is involved in our continued existence over time. And these beliefs would only be justified if something like the Ego Theory was true. Most of us therefore have false beliefs about what persons are, and about ourselves.

These beliefs are best revealed when we consider certain imaginary cases, often drawn from science fiction. One such case is *teletransportation.* Suppose that you enter a cubicle in which, when you press a button, a scanner records the states of all of the cells in your brain and body, destroying both while doing so. This information is then transmitted at the speed of light to some other planet, where a replicator produces a perfect organic copy of you. Since the brain of your Replica is exactly like yours, it will seem to remember living your life up to the moment when you pressed the button, its character will be just like yours, and it will be in every other way psychologically continuous with you. This psychological continuity will not have its normal cause, the continued existence of your brain, since the causal chain will run through the transmission by radio of your "blueprint."

Several writers claim that, if you chose to be teletransported, believing this to be the fastest way of travelling, you would be making a terrible mistake. This would not be a way of travelling, but a way of dying. It may not, they concede, be quite as bad as ordinary death. It might be some consolation to you that, after your death, you will have this Replica, which can finish the book that you are writing, act as parent to your children, and so on. But they insist, this Replica won't be you. It will merely be someone else, who is exactly like you. This is why this prospect is nearly as bad as ordinary death.

Imagine next a whole range of cases, in each of which, in a single operation, a different proportion of the cells in your brain and body would be replaced with exact duplicates. At the near end of this range, only 1 or 2 per cent would be replaced; in the middle, 40 or 60 per cent; near the far end, 98 or 99 per cent. At the far end of this range is pure teletransportation, the case in which all of your cells would be "replaced."

When you imagine that some proportion of your cells will be replaced with exact duplicates, it is natural to have the following beliefs. First, if you ask, "Will I survive? Will the resulting person be me?" there must be an answer to this question. Either you will survive, or you are about to die. Second, the answer to this question must be either a simple "Yes" or a simple "No." The person who wakes up either will or will not be you. There cannot be a third answer, such as that the person waking up will be half you. You can imagine yourself later being half-conscious. But if the resulting person will be fully conscious, he cannot be half you. To state these beliefs together: to the question, "Will the resulting person be me?" there must always *be* an answer, which must be all-or-nothing.

There seem good grounds for believing that, in the case of teletransportation, your Replica would not be you. In a slight variant of this case, your Replica might be created while you were still alive, so that you could talk to one another. This seems to show that, if 100 per cent of your cells were replaced, the result would merely be a Replica of you. At the other end of my range of cases, where only 1 per cent would be replaced, the resulting person clearly *would* be you. It therefore seems that, in the cases in between, the resulting person must be either you, or merely a Replica. It seems that one of these must be true, and that it makes a great difference which is true.

HOW WE ARE NOT WHAT WE BELIEVE

If these beliefs were correct, there must be some critical percentage, somewhere in this range of cases, up to which the resulting person would be you, and beyond which he would merely be your Replica. Perhaps, for example, it would be you who would wake up if the proportion of cells replaced were 49 per cent, but if just a few more cells were also replaced, this would make all the difference, causing it to be someone else who would wake up.

That there must be some critical percentage follows from our natural beliefs. But this conclusion is most implausible. How could a few cells make such a difference? Moreover, if there is such a critical percentage, no one could ever discover where it came. Since in all these cases the resulting person would believe that he was you, there could never be any evidence about where, in this range of cases, he would suddenly cease to be you.

On the Bundle Theory, we should reject these natural beliefs. Since you, the person, are not a separately existing entity, we can know exactly what would happen without answering the question of what will happen to you. Moreover, in the cases in the middle of my range, it is an empty question whether the resulting person would be you, or would merely be someone else who is exactly like you. There are not here two different possibilities, one of which must be true. These are merely two different descriptions of the very same course of events. If 50 per cent of your cells were replaced with exact duplicates, we could call the resulting person you, or we could call him merely your Replica. But since these are not here different possibilities, this is a mere choice of words.

As Buddha claimed, the Bundle Theory is hard to believe. It is hard to accept that it could be an empty question whether one is about to die, or will instead live for many years.

What we are being asked to accept may be made clearer with this analogy. Suppose that a certain club exists for some time, holding regular meetings. The meetings then cease. Some years later, several people form a club with the same name, and the same rules. We can ask, "Did these people revive the very same club? Or did they merely start up another club which is exactly similar?" Given certain further details, this would be another empty question. We could know just what happened without answering this question. Suppose that someone said: "But there must be an answer. The club meeting later must either be, or not be, the very same club." This would show that this person didn't understand the nature of clubs.

In the same way, if we have any worries about my imagined cases, we don't understand the nature of persons. In each of my cases, you would know that the resulting person would be both psychologically and physically exactly like you, and that he would have some particular proportion of the cells in your brain and body—90 per cent, or 10 per cent, or, in the case of teletransportation, 0 per cent. Knowing this, you know everything. How could it be a real question what would happen to you, unless you are a separately existing Ego, distinct from a brain and body, and the various kinds of mental state and event? If there are no such Egos, there is nothing else to ask a real question about.

Accepting the Bundle Theory is not only hard; it may also affect our emotions. As Buddha claimed, it may undermine our concern about our own futures. This effect can be suggested by redescribing this change of view. Suppose that you are about to be destroyed, but will later have a Replica on Mars. You would naturally believe that this prospect is about as bad as ordinary death, since your Replica won't be you. On the Bundle Theory, the fact that your Replica won't be you just consists in the fact that, though it will be fully psychologically continuous with you, this continuity won't have its normal cause. But when you object to teletransportation you are not objecting merely to the abnormality of this cause. You are objecting that this cause won't get *you* to Mars. You fear that the abnormal cause will fail to produce a further and all-important fact, which is different from the fact that your Replica will be psychologically continuous with you. You do not merely want there to be psychological continuity between you and some future person. You want to *be* this future person. On the Bundle Theory, there is no such special further fact. What you fear will not happen, in this imagined case, *never* happens. You want the person on Mars to be you in a specially intimate way in which no future person will ever be you. This means that, judged from the standpoint of your natural beliefs, even ordinary survival is about as bad as teletransportation. *Ordinary survival is about as bad as being destroyed and having a Replica.*

HOW THE SPLIT-BRAIN CASES SUPPORT THE BUNDLE THEORY

The truth of the Bundle Theory seems to me, in the widest sense, as much a scientific as a philosophical conclusion. I can imagine kinds of evidence which would have justified believing in the existence of separately existing Egos, and believing that the continued existence of these Egos is what explains the continuity of each mental life. But there is in fact very little evidence in favour of this Ego Theory, and much for the alternative Bundle Theory.

Some of this evidence is provided by the split-brain cases. On the Ego Theory, to explain what unifies our experiences at any one time, we should simply claim that these are all experiences which are being had by the same person. Bundle Theorists reject this explanation. This disagreement is hard to resolve in ordinary cases. But consider the simplified split-brain case that I described. We show to my imagined patient a placard whose left half is blue and right half is red. In one of this person's two streams of consciousness, he is aware of seeing only blue, while at the same time, in his other stream, he is aware of seeing only red. Each of these two visual experiences is combined with other experiences, like that of being aware of moving one of his hands. What unifies the experiences, at any time, in each of this person's two streams of consciousness? What unifies his awareness of seeing

only red with his awareness of moving one hand? The answer cannot be that these experiences are being had by the same person. This answer cannot explain the unity of each of this person's two streams of consciousness, since it ignores the disunity between these streams. This person is now having all of the experiences in both of his two streams. If this fact was what unified these experiences, this would make the two streams one.

These cases do not, I have claimed, involve two people sharing a single body. Since there is only one person involved, who has two streams of consciousness, the Ego Theorist's explanation would have to take the following form. He would have to distinguish between persons and subjects of experiences, and claim that, in split-brain cases, there are *two* of the latter. What unifies the experiences in one of the person's two streams would have to be the fact that these experiences are all being had by the same subject of experiences. What unifies the experiences in this person's other stream would have to be the fact that they are being had by another subject of experiences. When this explanation takes this form, it becomes much less plausible. While we could assume that "subject of experiences," or "Ego," simple meant "person," it was easy to believe that there are subjects of experiences. But if there can be subjects of experiences that are not persons, and if in the life of a split-brain patient there are at any time two different subjects of experiences—two different Egos—why should we believe that there really are such things? This does not amount to a refutation. But it seems to me a strong argument against the Ego Theory.

As a Bundle Theorist, I believe that these two Egos are idle cogs. There is another explanation of the unity of consciousness, both in ordinary cases and in split-brain cases. It is simply a fact that ordinary people are, at any time, aware of having several different experiences. This awareness of several different experiences can be helpfully compared with one's awareness, in short-term memory, of several different experiences. Just as there can be a single memory of just having had several experiences, such as hearing a bell strike three times, there can be a single state of awareness both of hearing the fourth striking of this bell, and of seeing, at the same time, ravens flying past the bell-tower.

Unlike the Ego Theorist's explanation, this explanation can easily be extended to cover split-brain cases. In such cases there is, at any time, not one state of awareness of several different experiences, but two such states. In the case I described, there is one state of awareness of both seeing only red and of moving one hand, and there is another state of awareness of both seeing only blue and moving the other hand. In claiming that there are two such states of awareness, we are not postulating the existence of unfamiliar entities, two separately existing Egos which are not the same as the single person whom the case involves. This explanation appeals to a pair of mental states which would have to be described anyway in a full description of this case.

I have suggested how the split-brain cases provide one argument for one view about the nature of persons. I should mention another such argument, provided by an imagined extension of these cases, first discussed at length by David Wiggins.[2]

In this imagined case a person's brain is divided, and the two halves are transplanted into a pair of different bodies. The two resulting people live quite separate lives. This imagined case shows that personal identity is not what matters. If I was about to divide, I should conclude that neither of the resulting people will be me. I will have ceased to exist. But this way of ceasing to exist is about as good— or as bad—as ordinary survival.

Some of the features of Wiggins's imagined case are likely to remain technically impossible. But the case cannot be dismissed, since its most striking feature, the division of one stream of consciousness into separate streams, has already happened. This is a second way in which the actual split-brain cases have great theoretical importance. They challenge some of our deepest assumptions about ourselves.[3]

QUESTION FOR DISCUSSION

1. Does the evidence he presents really warrant, in your opinion, the conclusion about the nature of the self that Derek Parfit draws from it? Are there other possible interpretations of the data? If so, what are they?

---

[2] At the end of his *Identity and Spatio-temporal Continuity* (1967) Oxford: Blackwell.

[3] I discuss these assumptions further in part 3 of my *Reasons and Persons*.

AN AFRICAN DUALISM

The Akan people form the majority of the population of the modern West African nation of Ghana. They encompass the Fanti and the more famous Ashanti peoples, whose empire fiercely, but ultimately unsuccessfully, resisted British colonial domination at the end of the last century. In the selection below, Kwame Gyekye (pronounced Jay-Shay), a professor of philosophy at the University of Ghana and a member of the Akan culture, explores the traditional views of his people on the question of self and presents a philosophical description and defense of these views. For Gyekye, the Akan hold an "interactionist psychophysical dualism," though one more subtle than that of Descartes and his disciples. He defends this view for the latitude it gives to religious belief, allowing for a clear theory of an afterlife, as well as for its efficacy in explaining the documented psychical healing practiced in Akan lands.

INTERACTIONIST DUALISM

Kwame Gyekye

What is a person? Is a person just the bag of flesh and bones that we see with our eyes, or is there something additional to the body that we do not see? A conception[1] of the nature of a human being in Akan philosophy is the subject of this chapter.*

ŌKRA (SOUL)

We are given to understand from a number of often quoted, though mistaken, anthropological accounts that the Akan people consider a human being to be constituted of three elements: *ōkra, sunsum,* and *honam* (or *nipadua*: body).

The *ōkra* is said to be that which constitutes the innermost self, the essence, of the individual person. *Ōkra* is the individual's life, for which reason it is usually referred to as *ōkrateasefo,* that is, the living soul, a seeming tautology that yet is significant. The expression is intended to emphasize that *ōkra* is identical with life. The *ōkra* is the embodiment and transmitter of the individual's destiny (fate: *nkrabea*). It is explained as a spark of the Supreme Being (Onyame) in man. It is thus described as divine and as having an antemundane existence with the Supreme Being. The presence of this divine essence in a human being may have been the basis of the Akan proverb, "All men are the children of God; no one is a child of the earth" (*nnipa nyinaa yē Onyame mma, obiara nnyē asase ba*). So conceived, the *ōkra* can be considered as the equivalent of the concept of the soul in other metaphysical systems. Hence, it is correct to translate *ōkra* into English as soul.

• • •

The conception of the *ōkra* as constituting the individual's life, the life force, is linked very closely with another concept, *honhom. Honhom* means "breath"; it is the noun form of *home,* to breathe. When a person is dead, it is said "His breath is gone" (*ne honhom kō*) or "His soul has withdrawn from his body" (*ne 'kra afi ne ho*). These two sentences, one with *honhom* as subject and the other with *ōkra,* do, in fact, say the same

---

[1] I say "a conception" because I believe there are other conceptions of the person held or discernible in that philosophy.

* The selection is taken from a chapter of Gyekye's book length study of Akan metaphysics, *An Essay on African Social Thought: The Akan Conceptual Scheme* (Eds.).

thing; they express the same thought, the death-of-the-person. The departure of the soul from the body means the death of the person, and so does the cessation of breath. Yet this does not mean that the *honhom* (breath) is identical with the *ōkra* (soul). It is the *ōkra* that "causes" the breathing. Thus, the *honhom* is the tangible manifestation or evidence of the presence of the *ōkra*. [In some dialects of the Akan language, however, *honhom* has come to be used interchangeably with *sunsum* ("spirit"), so that the phrase *honhom bōne* has come to mean the same thing as *sunsum bōne,* that is, evil spirit. The identification of the *honhom* with the *sunsum* seems to me to be a recent idea, and may have resulted from the translation of the Bible into the various Akan dialects; *honhom* must have been used to translate the Greek *pneuma* (breath, spirit).] The clarification of the concepts of *ōkra, honhom, sunsum* and others bearing on the Akan conception of the nature of a person is the concern of this chapter.

SUNSUM (SPIRIT)

Sunsum is another of the constituent elements of the person. It has usually been rendered in English as "spirit." It has already been observed that *sunsum* is used both generically to refer to all unperceivable, mystical beings and forces in Akan ontology, and specifically to refer to the activating principle in the person. It appears from the anthropological accounts that even when it is used specifically, "spirit" (*sunsum*) is not identical with soul (*ōkra*), as they do not refer to the same thing. However, the anthropological accounts of the *sunsum* involve some conceptual blunders, as I shall show. As for the *mind*—when it is not identified with the soul—it may be rendered also by *sunsum,* judging from the functions that are attributed by the Akan thinkers to the latter.

On the surface it might appear that "spirit" is not an appropriate rendition for *sunsum,* but after clearing away misconceptions engendered by some anthropological writings, I shall show that it is appropriate but that it requires clarification. Anthropologists and sociologists have held (1) that the

sunsum derives from the father,[2] (2) that it is not divine,[3] and (3) that it perishes with the disintegration of the *honam,*[4] that is, the material component of a person. It seems to me, however, that all these characterizations of the *sunsum* are incorrect.[5]

Let us first take up the third characterization, namely, as something that perishes with the body. Now, if the *sunsum* perishes along with the body, a physical object, then it follows that the *sunsum* also is something physical or material. Danquah's philosophical analysis concludes that "*sunsum* is, in fact, the matter or the physical basis of the ultimate ideal of which *ōkra* (soul) is the form and the spiritual or mental basis."[6] Elsewhere he speaks of an "interaction of the material mechanism (*sunsum*) with the soul," and assimilates the *sunsum* to the "sensible form" of Aristotle's metaphysics of substance and the *ōkra* to the "intelligible form."[7] One might conclude from these statements that Danquah also conceived the *sunsum* as material, although some of his other statements would seem to contradict this conclusion. The relation between the *honam* (body) and the *sunsum* (supposedly bodily), however, is left unexplained. Thus, philosophical, sociological, and anthropological accounts of the nature of the person give the impression of a tripartite conception of a human being in Akan philosophy:

---

[2] K. A. Busia, "The Ashanti of the Gold Coast," in Daryll Forde (ed.), *African Worlds,* p. 197; M. Fortes, *Kinship and the Social Order* (University of Chicago Press, Chicago, 1969), p. 199, n. 14; Robert A. Lystad, *The Ashanti, A Proud People* (Rutgers University Press, New Brunswick, N.J., 1958), p. 155; Peter K. Sarpong, *Ghana in Retrospect: Some Aspects of the Ghanaian Culture* (Ghana Publishing Corp., Accra, 1974), p. 37.
[3] Busia, p. 197; Lystad, p. 155; E. L. R. Meyerowitz, *The Sacred State of the Akan* (Faber and Faber, London, 1951), p. 86; and "Concepts of the Soul among the Akan," *Africa,* p. 26.
[4] Busia, p. 197; Lystad, p. 155; P. A. Twumasi, *Medical Systems in Ghana* (Ghana Publishing Corp., Accra, 1975), p. 22.
[5] Here the views of W. E. Abraham are excepted, for he maintains, like I do, that the *sunsum* is not "inheritable" and that it "appears to have been a spiritual substance." W. E. Abraham, *The Mind of Africa* (University of Chicago Press, Chicago, 1962), p. 60.
[6] J. B. Danquah, *The Akan Doctrine of God* (Lutterworth Press, London, 1944), p. 115.
[7] Ibid., p. 116.

Ōkra (soul)	immaterial
Sunsum ("spirit")	material (?)
Honam (body)	material

As we shall see, however, this account or analysis of a person, particularly the characterization of the *sunsum* ("spirit") as something material, is not satisfactory. I must admit, however, that the real nature of the *sunsum* presents perhaps the greatest difficulty in the Akan metaphysics of a person and has been a source of confusion for many. The difficulty, however, is not insoluble.

• • •

The explanation given by most Akans of the phenomenon of dreaming . . . indicates, it seems to me, that *sunsum* must be immaterial. In Akan thought, as in Freud's, dreams are not somatic but psychical phenomena. It is held that in a dream it is the person's *sunsum* that is the "actor." As an informant told Rattray decades ago, "When you sleep your *'Kra* (soul) does not leave you, as your *sunsum* may."[8] In sleep the *sunsum* is said to be released from the fetters of the body. As it were, it fashions for itself a new world of forms with the materials of its waking experience. Thus, although one is deeply asleep, yet one may "see" oneself standing atop a mountain or driving a car or fighting with someone or pursuing a desire like sexual intercourse; also, during sleep (that is, in dreams) a person's *sunsum* may talk with other *sunsum*. The actor in any of these "actions" is thought to be the *sunsum,* which thus can leave the body and return to it. The idea of the psychical part of a person leaving the body in sleep appears to be widespread in Africa. The Azande, for instance, maintain "that in sleep the soul is released from the body and can roam about at will and meet other spirits and have other adventures, though they admit something mysterious about its experiences. . . . During sleep a man's soul wanders everywhere."[9]

The idea that some part of the soul leaves the

body in sleep is not completely absent from the history of Western thought, even though, as Parrinder says, "the notion of a wandering soul is [are] foreign to the modern European mind."[10] The idea occurs, for instance, in Plato. In the *Republic* Plato refers to "the wild beast in us" that in pursuit of desires and pleasures bestirs itself "in *dreams* when the *gentler part of the soul* slumbers and the control of reason is withdrawn; then the wild beast in us, full-fed with meat and drink, becomes rampant and shakes off sleep to go in quest of what will gratify its own instincts."[11] The context is a discussion of tyranny. But Plato prefaces his discussion with remarks on the *psychological* foundation of the tyrannical man, and says that desire (Greek: *epithumia*) is the basis of his behavior.

It is not surprising that both scholars of Plato and modern psychologists have noted the relevance of the above passage to the analysis of the nature of the human psyche. On this passage the classical scholar James Adam wrote: "The theory is that in dreams the part of the soul concerned is not asleep, but awake and goes out to seek the object of its desire."[12] The classicist Paul Shorey observed that "The Freudians have at least discovered Plato's anticipation of their main thesis."[13] The relevance of the Platonic passage to Freud has been noted also by other scholars of Plato such as Renford Bambrough[14] and Thomas Gould,[15] and by psychologists. Valentine, a psychologist, observed: "The germ of several aspects of the Freudian view of dreams, including the characteristic doctrine of the censor, was to be found in Plato."[16]

---

[8] R. S. Rattray, *Religion and Art in Ashanti,* p. 154.
[9] E. E. Evans-Pritchard, *Witchcraft, Oracles and Magic among the Azande,* p. 136; also E. G. Parrinder, *West African Religion,* p. 197.

[10] Parrinder, *West African Religion,* p. 197.
[11] Plato, *The Republic,* 571ᶜ, beginning of Book IX.
[12] James Adam (ed.), *The Republic of Plato,* 2d ed. (Cambridge University Press, Cambridge, 1975), Vol. 2, p. 320.
[13] Plato, *The Republic,* ed. and trans. by Paul Shorey (Loeb Classical Library, Harvard University Press, Cambridge, Mass., 1935), p. 335.
[14] Plato, *The Republic,* trans. by A. D. Lindsay (J. M. Dent, London, 1976), p. 346.
[15] Thomas Gould, *Platonic Love* (Routledge and Kegan Paul, London, 1963), p. 108ff and p. 174ff.
[16] Charles W. Valentine, *Dreams and the Unconscious* (Methuen, London, 1921), p. 93; also his *The New Psychology of the Unconscious* (Macmillan, New York, 1929), p. 95.

It is clear that the passage in Plato indicates a link between dreams and (the gratification of) desires.[17] In Akan psychology the *sunsum* appears not only as unconscious but also as that which pursues and experiences desires. (In Akan dreams are also considered predictive.) But the really interesting part of Plato's thesis for our purposes relates to *the idea of some part of the human soul leaving the body in dreams.* "The wild beast in us" in Plato's passage is not necessarily equivalent to the Akan *sunsum,* but one may say that just as Plato's "wild beast" (which, like the *sunsum,* experiences dreams) is a *part* of the soul and thus not a physical object, so is *sunsum.*

It might be supposed that if the *sunsum* can engage in activity, such as traveling through space or occupying a physical location—like standing on the top of a mountain—then it can hardly be said not to be a physical object. The problem here is obviously complex. Let us assume, for the moment, that the *sunsum* is a physical object. One question that would immediately arise is: How can a purely physical object leave the person when he or she is asleep? Dreaming is of course different from imagining or thinking. The latter occurs during waking life, whereas the former occurs only during sleep: *wŏnda a wŏnso dae,* that is, "Unless you are asleep you do not dream" is a well-known Akan saying. The fact that dreaming occurs only in sleep makes it a unique sort of mental activity and its subject, namely *sunsum,* a different sort of subject. A purely physical object cannot be in two places at the same time: A body lying in bed cannot at the same time be on the top of a mountain. Whatever is on the top of the mountain, then, must be something nonphysical, nonbodily, and yet somehow connected to a physical thing—in this case, the body. This argument constitutes a *reductio ad absurdum* of the view that *sunsum* can be a physical object.

But, then, how can the *sunsum,* qua nonphysical, extrasensory object, travel in physical space and have a physical location? This question must be answered within the broad context of the African be-lief in the activities of the supernatural (spiritual) beings in the physical world. The spiritual beings are said to be insensible and intangible, but they are also said to make themselves felt in the physical world. They can thus interact with the physical world. But from this it cannot be inferred that they are physical or quasiphysical or have permanent physical properties. It means that a spiritual being can, when it so desires, take on physical properties. That is, even though a spiritual being is nonspatial in essence, it can, by the sheer operation of its power, assume spatial properties. Debrunner speaks of "temporary 'materializations,' i.e., as spirits having taken on the body of a person which afterwards suddenly vanish."[18] Mbiti observed that "Spirits are invisible, but may make themselves visible to human beings."[19] We should view the "physical" activities of the *sunsum* in dreaming from the standpoint of the activities of the spiritual beings in the physical world. As a microcosm of the world spirit, the *sunsum* can also interact with the external world. So much then for the defense of the psychical, nonphysical nature of *sunsum,* the subject of experiences in dreaming.

As the basis of personality, as the coperformer of some of the functions of the *ōkra* (soul)—undoubtedly held as a spiritual entity—and as the subject of the psychical activity of dreaming, the *sunsum* must be something spiritual (immaterial). This is the reason for my earlier assertion that "spirit" might not be an inappropriate translation for *sunsum.* On my analysis, then, we have the following picture:

$$\left.\begin{array}{l} \bar{O}kra \text{ (soul)} \\ Sunsum \text{ ("spirit")} \\ Honam \text{ (body)} \end{array}\right\} \begin{array}{l} \text{immaterial (spiritual)} \\ \\ \text{material (physical)} \end{array}$$

• • •

RELATION OF *ŌKRA* AND *SUNSUM*

Having shown that the *sunsum* is in fact something spiritual (and for this reason I shall henceforth

---

[17] Wilfred Trotter, *Instincts of the Herd in Peace and War* (T. F. Unwin, London, 1916), p. 74.

[18] H. Debrunner, *Witchcraft in Ghana* (Waterville Publishing House, Accra, 1959), p. 17.
[19] Mbiti, *African Religions and Philosophy,* p. 102.

late *sunsum* as "spirit"), we must examine whether the expressions *sunsum* and *ōkra* are identical in terms of their referent. In the course of my field research some discussants stated that the *sunsum, ōkra,* and *honhom* (breath) are identical; they denote the same object; it is one and the same object that goes under three names. I have already shown that although there is a close link between *ōkra* and *honhom,* the two cannot be identified; likewise the identification of *honhom* and *sunsum* is incorrect. What about the *sunsum* and *ōkra*? Are they identical?

The relation between the *sunsum* and *ōkra* is a difficult knot to untie. The anthropologist Rattray, perhaps the most perceptive and analytical researcher into the Ashanti culture, wrote: "It is very difficult sometimes to distinguish between the *'kra* and the next kind of soul, the *sunsum,* and sometimes the words seem synonymous, but I cannot help thinking this is a loose use of the terms."[20] Rattray was, I think, more inclined to believe that the two terms are not identical. Such a supposition, in my view, would be correct, for to say that the two are identical would logically mean that whatever can be asserted of one can or must be asserted of the other. Yet there are some things the Akans say of the *sunsum* which are not said of the *ōkra,* and vice versa; the attributes or predicates of the two are different. The Akans say:

A(1) "His *'kra* is sad" (*ne 'kra di awerēhow*); never, "His *sunsum* is sad."

(2) "His *'kra* is worried or disturbed" (*ne 'kra teetee*).

(3) "His *'kra* has run away" (*ne 'kra adwane*), to denote someone who is scared to death.

(4) "His *'kra* is good" (*ne 'kra ye*), referring to a person who is lucky or fortunate. [The negative of this statement is "His *'kra* is not good." If you used *sunsum* in lieu of *'kra,* and made the statement "His *sunsum* is not good" (*ne sunsum nnyē*), the meaning would

be quite different; it would mean that his *sunsum* is evil, that is to say, he is an evil spirit, a witch.]

(5) "His *'kra* has withdrawn from his body" (*ne 'kra afi ne ho*).

(6) "But for his *'kra* that followed him, he would have died" (*ne 'kra dii n'akyi, anka owui*).

(7) "His *'kra* is happy" (*ne 'kra aniagye*).

In all such statements the attributions are made to the *ōkra* (soul), never to the *sunsum.* On the other hand, the Akans say:

B(1) "He has *sunsum*" (*ōwō sunsum*), an expression they use when they want to refer to someone as dignified and as having a commanding presence. Here they never say, "He has *ōkra*," soul, for it is believed that it is the nature of the *sunsum* (not the *ōkra*) that differs from person to person; hence they speak of "gentle *sunsum*," "forceful *sunsum*," "weak or strong *sunsum*," etc.

(2) "His *sunsum* is heavy or weighty" (*ne sunsum yē duru*), that is, he has a strong personality.

(3) "His *sunsum* overshadows mine" (*ne sunsum hyē me so*).

(4) "Someone's *sunsum* is bigger or greater than another's" (*obi sunsum so kyēn obi deē*). To say "someone's *'kra* is greater than another's" would be meaningless.

(5) "He has a good *sunsum*" (*ōwō sunsum pa*), that is, he is a generous person.

In all such statements the attributions are made to the *sunsum* (spirit), never to the *ōkra* (soul). Rattray also pointed out correctly that "an Ashanti would never talk of washing his *sunsum.*"[21] It is the *ōkra* that is washed (*okraguare*). In the terminology of the modern linguist, sentences containing *ōkra* and *sunsum* differ, according to my analysis, not only in

---

[20] Rattray, *Religion and Art,* p. 154.

[21] Ibid., p. 318, Soul-washing is a symbolic religious rite meant to cleanse and purify the soul from defilement. "This cult," wrote Mrs. Meyerowitz, "adjures the person to lead a good and decent life." *Sacred State,* p. 117; also p. 88.

their surface structures but also in their deep structures.

It is pretty clear from this semantic analysis that *ōkra* and *sunsum* are not intersubstitutable in predications. Intersubstitution of the terms, as we saw above, leads either to nonsense as in B(4) or to change of meaning as in A(4) and B(1). Semantic analysis suggests a nonidentity relation between *sunsum* and *ōkra*. One might reject this conclusion by treating these distinctions as merely idiomatic and not, therefore, as evidence for considering *ōkra* and *sunsum* as distinct. Let us call this the "idiomatic thesis." In the English language, for instance, it is idiomatic to say "He's a sad soul" rather than "He's a sad spirit," without implying that soul and spirit are distinct. But in English the substitution of one for the other of the two terms—even if unidiomatic—will not lead to nonsense and would not change the *meaning*; in Akan it would.

• • •

It may be the easiest way out of an interpretative labyrinth to identify *ōkra* and *sunsum*,[22] but I do not think it is the most satisfactory way out. There are, I believe, other considerations for rejecting the "identity theory."

First, most Akans agree that in dreaming it is the *sunsum*, not the *ōkra*, that leaves the body. The departure of the *ōkra* (soul) from the body means the death of the person, whereas the *sunsum* can leave the body, as in dreaming, without causing the death of the person. Second, moral predicates are generally applied to the *sunsum*. Rattray wrote: "Perhaps the *sunsum* is the more volatile part of the whole *'kra*," and ". . . but the *'kra* is not volatile in life, as the *sunsum* undoubtedly is."[23] Moreover, the *ōkra* and *sunsum* appear to be different in terms of their functions or activities. The *ōkra*, as mentioned before, is the principle of life of a person and the em-

bodiment and transmitter of his or her destiny (*nkrabea*). Personality and character dispositions of a person are the function of the *sunsum*. The *sunsum* appears to be the source of dynamism of a person, the *active* part or force of the human psychological system; its energy is the ground for its interaction with the external world. It is said to have extrasensory powers; it is that which thinks, desires, feels, etc. It is in no way identical with the brain, which is a physical organ. Rather it acts upon the brain (*amene, hon*). In short, people believe that it is upon the *sunsum* that one's health, worldly power, position, influence, success, etc. would depend. The attributes and activities of the *sunsum* are therefore not ascribable to the *ōkra*. Lystad was wrong when he stated: "In many respects the *sunsum* or spirit is so identical with the *ōkra* or soul in its functions that it is difficult to distinguish between them."[25]

Now, given x and y, if whatever is asserted of x can be asserted of y, then x can be said to be identical with y. If there is at least one characteristic that x has but y does not, then x and y are not identical. On this showing, insofar as things asserted of the *ōkra* are not assertable of the *sunsum*, the two cannot logically be identified. However, although they are logically distinct, they are not *ontologically* distinct. That is to say, they are not independent existents held together in an accidental way by an external bond. They are a unity in duality, a duality in unity. The distinction is not a relation between two separate entities. The *sunsum* may, more accurately, be characterized as a *part*—the active part—of the *ōkra* (soul).

I once thought that the *sunsum* might be characterized as a state,[26] an epiphenomenon, of the *ōkra*.

---

[22] Incidentally, the "identity theory" immediately subverts any physical conception of the *sunsum*, since the *ōkra* (soul), with which it is being identified, is generally agreed to be a spiritual, not a physical, entity.

[23] Rattray, *Religion and Art*, p. 154.

[24] The dynamic and active character of the *sunsum* has given rise to metaphorical use as in the sentences, "there is 'spirit' in the game" (*agoro yi sunsum wō mu*), "the arrival of the chief brought 'spirit' into the festival celebration." Not long ago the dynamism, action and energy of a late Ghanaian army general earned him the by-name of "Sunsum!" among his soldiers.

[25] Lystad, p. 158.

[26] See Kwame Gyekye, "The Akan Concept of a Person," *International Philosophical Quarterly*, Vol. XVIII, No. 3, September 1978, p. 284.

I now think that characterization is wrong, for it would subvert the entitative nature of *sunsum*. The fact that we can speak of the inherence of the *sunsum* in natural objects as their activating principle means that in some contexts reference can be made to the *sunsum* independently of the *ōkra*. This, however, is not so in the context of the human psyche: In man *sunsum* is part of the *ōkra* (soul). Plato held a tripartite conception of the human soul, deriving that conception from his view of the functions said to be performed by the various parts of the soul. So did Freud. There is nothing inappropriate or illogical or irrational for some Akan thinkers to hold and argue for a bipartite conception of the human soul. Neither a tripartite nor a bipartite conception of the soul subverts its *ontic unity*. As already stated, the *ōkra* and *sunsum* are constitutive of a spiritual unity, which survives after death. Therefore the soul (that is, *ōkra* plus *sunsum*) does not lose its individuality after death. It survives individually. Beliefs in reincarnation (which I do not intend to explore now) and in the existence of the ancestors in the world of spirits (*asamando*) undoubtedly presuppose—and would be logically impossible without—the survival of each individual soul.

RELATION OF *ŌKRA* (SOUL) AND *HONAM* (BODY)

Understanding the *sunsum* and *ōkra* to constitute a spiritual unity, one may say that Akan philosophy maintains a dualistic, not a tripartite, conception of the person: A person is made up of two principal entities or substances, one spiritual (immaterial: *ōkra*) and the other material (*honam*: body).

But Akans sometimes speak as if the relation between the soul (that is, *ōkra* plus *sunsum*) and the body is so close that they comprise an indissoluble or indivisible unity, and that, consequently, a person is a homogeneous entity. The basis for this observation is the assertion by some discussants that "*ōkra* is blood" (*mogya*),[27] or "*ōkra* is in the blood." They

mean by this, I think, that there is some connection between the soul and the blood, and that ordinarily the former is integrated or fused with the latter. I think the supposition here is that the blood is the physical or rather physiological "medium" for the soul. However difficult it is to understand this doctrine, it serves as a basis for a theory of the unity of soul and body. But Akan thinkers cannot strictly or unreservedly maintain such a theory, for it logically involves the impossibility of the doctrine of disembodied survival or life after death, which they tenaciously and firmly hold. The doctrine of the indivisible unity of soul and body is a doctrine that eliminates the notion of life after death, inasmuch as both soul and body are held to disintegrate together. The doctrine that the souls of the dead have some form of existence or life therefore cannot be maintained together with a doctrine of the indivisible unity of soul and body. The former doctrine implies an independent existence for the soul. I think their postulation of some kind of connection between the soul and blood is a response to the legitimate, and indeed fundamental, question as to how an entity (that is, the soul), supposed to be immaterial and separate, can "enter" the body. Though their response certainly bristles with difficulties and may be regarded as inadequate, like most theses on the soul, Akan thinkers had sufficient awareness to focus philosophical attention also on the intractable question regarding the beginnings of the connection of the soul to the body, of the immaterial to the material. Other philosophies attempt to demonstrate that man consists of soul and body, but they do not, to my knowledge, speculate on the manner of the soul's "entry" into the body.

In the Akan conception, the soul is held to be a spiritual entity (substance). It is not a bundle of qualities or perceptions, as it is held to be in some Western systems. The basis of this assertion is the Akan belief in disembodied survival. A bundle theory of substance implies the elimination of the notion of substance, for if a substance is held to be a bundle or collection of qualities or perceptions, when the qualities or perceptions are removed, nothing would be left. That is, there would then be no substance, that is, a substratum or an "owner" of

---

[27] This view was expressed also to Meyerowitz, *Sacred State*, p. 84.

those qualities.[28] Thus, if the soul is held to be a bundle of perceptions, as it is in the writings of David Hume, it would be impossible to talk of disembodied survival in the form of a soul or self since the bundle itself is an abstraction. One Akan maxim, expressed epigrammatically, is that "when a man dies he is not (really) dead" (*onipa wu a na onwui*). What is implied by this is that there is something in a human being that is eternal, indestructible, and that continues to exist in the world of spirits (*asamando*). An Akan motif expresses the following thought: "Could God die, I will die" (*Onyame bewu na m'awu*). In Akan metaphysics, . . . God is held to be eternal, immortal (*Ōdomankoma*). The above saying therefore means that since God will not die, a person, that is, his or her *'kra* (soul), conceived as an indwelling spark of God, will not die either. That is, the soul of man is immortal. The attributes of immortality make sense if, and only if, the soul is held to be a substance, an entity, and not a bundle of qualities or perceptions (experiences).

But where in a human being is this spiritual substance located? Descartes thought that the soul was in the pineal gland. The Akans also seem to hold that the soul is lodged in the head, although they do not specify exactly where. But "although it is in the head you cannot see it with your natural eyes," as they would put it, since it is immaterial. That the soul is "in the head (*ti*)" may be inferred from the following expressions: When they want to say that a person is lucky or fortunate they say: "His head is well (good)" (*ne ti ye*), or "His soul is well (good)" (*ne 'kra ye*). From such expressions one may infer some connection between the head and the soul. And although they cannot point to a specific part of the head as the "residence" of the soul, it may be conjectured that it is in the region of the brain which, as observed earlier, receives its energy from the *sunsum* (spirit), a part of the soul. That is, the soul acts on the brain in a specific locality, but it is itself not actually localized.

The Akan conception of a person, in my analysis, is dualistic, not tripartite, although the spiritual component of a person is highly complex. Such dualistic conception does not necessarily imply a belief in a causal relation or interaction between the two parts, the soul and body. For instance, some dualistic philosophers in the West maintain a doctrine of psychophysical parallelism, which completely denies interaction between soul and body. Other dualists advance a doctrine of epiphenomenalism, which, while not completely rejecting causal interaction, holds that the causality goes in one direction only, namely, from the body to the soul; such a doctrine, too, is thus not interactionist. Akan thinkers, however, are thoroughly interactionist on the relation between soul and body. They hold that not only does the body have a causal influence on the soul but also that the soul has a causal influence on the body (*honam*). What happens to the soul takes effect or reflects on the condition of the body. Thus, writing on Akan culture, Busia stated:

> They (that is, Akans) believed also that spiritual uncleanness was an element of ill-health and that the cleansing of the soul was necessary for health. When, for example, a patient was made to stand on a broom while being treated, it was to symbolize this cleansing. The broom sweeps filth away from the home and keeps it healthy; so the soul must be swept of filth to keep the body healthy.[29]

Similarly, what happens to the body reflects on the conditions of the soul. It is the actual bodily or physical behavior of a person that gives an idea of the condition of the soul. Thus, if the physical behavior of a man suggests that he is happy they would say, "His soul is happy" (*ne 'kra aniagye*); if unhappy or morose they would say, "His soul is sorrowful" (*ne 'kra di awerēhow*). When the soul is enfeebled or injured by evil spirits, ill health results; the poor conditions of the body affect the condition of the soul. The condition of the soul depends upon the condition of the body. The belief in psychophysical causal interaction is the whole basis of spiritual or psychical healing in Akan communities.

---

[28] See Kwame Gyekye, "An Examination of the Bundle Theory of Substance," *Philosophy and Phenomenological Research*, Vol. XXXIV, No. 1, September, 1973.

[29] Busia, *The Challenge of Africa*, p. 19.

There are certain diseases that are believed to be "spiritual diseases" (*sunsum yare*) and cannot be healed by the application of physical therapy. In such diseases attention must be paid to both physiological and spiritual aspects of the person. Unless the soul is healed, the body will not respond to physical treatment. The removal of a disease of the soul is the activity of the diviners or the traditional healers (*adunsifo*).

• • •

CONCLUSION

The Akan conception of the person, on my analysis, is both dualistic and interactionist. It seems to me that an interactionist psychophysical dualism is a realistic doctrine. Even apart from the prospects for disembodied survival that this doctrine holds out— prospects that profoundly affect the moral orientation of some people—it has had significant pragmatic consequences in Akan communities, as evidenced in the application of psychophysical therapies. There are countless testimonies of people who have been subjected to physical treatment for months or years in modern hospitals without being cured, but who have been healed by traditional healers applying both physical and psychical (spiritual) methods. In such cases the diseases are believed not to be purely physical, affecting only the body (*honam*). They are believed rather to have been inflicted on the *sunsum* through mystical or spiritual powers, and in time the body also gets affected. When Western-trained doctors pay attention only to the physical aspects of such diseases, they almost invariably fail to heal them. The fact that traditional healers, operating at both the physical and psychical levels, cope successfully with such diseases does seem to suggest a close relationship between the body and the soul.

From the point of view of the Akan metaphysics of the person and of the world in general, all this seems to imply that a human being is not just an assemblage of flesh and bone, that he or she is a complex being who cannot completely be explained by the same law of physics used to explain inanimate things, and that our world cannnot simply be reduced to physics.

QUESTION FOR DISCUSSION

1. Compare Gyekye's dualism with that of Descartes. Compare it with the dualism of the *Bhagavad-Gita*.

MATERIALIST CHALLENGES

India is viewed in the popular Western imagination as a land in which spirituality predominates over the practical side of life. Like most clichés, this is, perhaps, partially true. And yet modern India is one of the largest industrial nations in the world, while traditional India enjoyed a material culture far greater than that of Europe for most of its history. Moreover, although it is true that India's philosophies have, in the main, reflected a profound sense of spirituality, it is also true that India has always had its religious skeptics and materialist debunkers of the spiritual. The first selections below are taken from the oldest of these iconoclasts—the Cārvāka philosophers of the time of the Buddha, or rather, they are taken from their opponents' accounts of them, very few of their original works having survived the censorship of the orthodox over the centuries. "There is no heaven, no final liberation, nor any soul in another world," say the Cārvāka, according to these sources. "There is no evidence for any self distinct from the body." The ego dies with the body's death.

The same doctrine is expounded in England in the 1930s by the world-famous logician-philosopher Bertrand Russell, who debates these questions with Anglican bishops rather than Brahmin priests and saddhus. The ultimate argument, though bolstered with new forms of scientific evidence, remains the same in both cases. The data, the materialists claim, show that the relation of mind and body is such that we cannot expect mind or spirit to exist except where a living body sustains them.

ANCIENT INDIAN MATERIALISM

The Cārvāka School

The efforts of Cārvāka are indeed hard to be eradicated, for the majority of living beings hold by the current refrain—

> While life is yours, live joyously;
> None can escape Death's searching eye:
> When once this frame of ours they burn,
> How shall it e'er again return?

The mass of men, in accordance with the Śāstras of policy and enjoyment, considering wealth and desire the only ends of man and denying the existence of any object belonging to a future world, are found to follow only the doctrine of Cārvāka. Hence another name for that school is Lokāyata,—a name well accordant with the thing signified.*

In this school the four elements, earth, &c., are the original principles; from these alone, when transformed into the body, intelligence is produced, just as the inebriating power is developed from the mixing of certain ingredients; and when these are destroyed, intelligence at once perishes also. They quote the *śruti* [Vedic text] for this [*Bṛhadāraṇyaka Upaniṣad* II.iv.12]: "Springing forth from these elements, itself solid knowledge, it is destroyed when they are destroyed,—after death no intelligence remains." Therefore the soul is only the body distinguished by the attribute of intelligence, since there is no evidence for any self distinct from the body, as such cannot be proved, since this school holds that perception is the only source of knowledge and does not allow inference, &c.

The only end of man is enjoyment produced by sensual pleasures. Nor may you say that such cannot be called the end of man as they are always mixed with some kind of pain, because it is our wisdom to enjoy the pure pleasure as far as we can, and to avoid the pain which inevitably accompanies it; just as the man who desires fish takes the fish with

---

* "Loka" is Sanskrit for the material world (Eds.).

their scales and bones, and having taken as many as he wants, desists; or just as the man who desires rice, takes the rice, straw and all, and having taken as much as he wants, desists. It is not therefore for us, through a fear of pain, to reject the pleasure which our nature instinctively recognises as congenial. Men do not refrain from sowing rice, because forsooth there are wild animals to devour it; nor do they refuse to set the cooking-pots on the fire, because forsooth there are beggars to pester us for a share of the contents. If any one were so timid as to forsake a visible pleasure, he would indeed be foolish like a beast, as has been said by the poet—

The pleasure which arises to men from contact with sensible objects,
Is to be relinquished as accompanied by pain,—such is the reasoning of fools;
The berries of paddy, rich with the finest white grains,
What man, seeking his true interest, would fling away because covered with husk and dust?

If you object that, if there be no such thing as happiness in a future world, then how should men of experienced wisdom engage in the *Agnihotra*[1] and other sacrifices, which can only be performed with great expenditure of money and bodily fatigue, your objection cannot be accepted as any proof to the contrary, since the *Agnihotra,* &c., are only useful as means of livelihood, for the Veda is tainted by the three faults of untruth, self-contradiction, and tautology; then again the impostors who call themselves Vaidic [or Vedic] pandits are mutually destructive, as the authority of the *jñāna-kāṇḍa* (section on knowledge) is overthrown by those who maintain that of the *karma-kāṇḍa* (section on action), while those who maintain the authority of the *jñāna-kāṇḍa* reject that of the *karma-kāṇḍa*; and lastly, the three Vedas themselves are only the incoherent rhapsodies of knaves, and to this effect runs the popular saying—

The *Agnihotra,* the three Vedas, the ascetic's three staves, and smearing oneself with ashes,—

Bṛhaspati says these are but means of livelihood for those who have no manliness nor sense.

Hence it follows that there is no other hell than mundane pain produced by purely mundane causes, as thorns, &c.; the only Supreme is the earthly monarch whose existence is proved by all the world's eyesight; and the only liberation is the dissolution of the body. By holding the doctrine that the soul is identical with the body, such phrases as "I am thin," "I am black," &c., are at once intelligible, as the attributes of thinness, &c., and self-consciousness will reside in the same subject (the body); and the use of the phrase "my body" is metaphorical like "the head of Rāhu" [Rāhu being really *all head*].

All this has been thus summed up—
In this school there are four elements, earth, water, fire, and air;
And from these four elements alone is intelligence produced,—
Just like the intoxicating power from *kiṇva,* &c., mixed together;
Since in "I am fat," "I am lean," these attributes abide in the same subject,
And since fatness, &c., reside only in the body, it alone is the soul and no other,
And such phrases as "my body" are only significant metaphorically.

• • •

An opponent will say, if you thus do not allow *adṛṣṭa,*[2] the various phenomena of the world become destitute of any cause. But we cannot accept this objection as valid, since these phenomena can all be produced spontaneously from the inherent nature of things. Thus it has been said—

The fire is hot, the water cold, refreshing cool the breeze of morn;
By whom came this variety? from their own nature was it born

• • •

---

[1] Sacrificial offering to fire.

[2] The unseen force.

If beings in heaven are gratified by our offering the
    Śrāddha here,
Then why not give the food down below to those who
    are standing on the housetop?
While life remains let a man live happily, let him feed
    on ghee[1] even though he runs in debt;
When once the body becomes ashes, how can it ever re-
    turn again?
If he who departs from the body goes to another world,
How is it that he comes not back again, restless for love
    of his kindred?
Hence it is only as a means of livelihood that *brāhmins*
    have established here
All these ceremonies for the dead—there is no other
    fruit anywhere.
The three authors of the Vedas were buffoons, knaves,
    and demons.
All the well-known formulas of the pandits, *jarpharī,
    turpharī,* &c.[3]
And all the obscene rites for the queen commanded in
    the *Aśvamedha.*[4]
These were invented by buffoons, and so all the various
    kinds of presents to the priests,
While the eating of flesh was similarly commanded by
    night-prowling demons.

Hence in kindness to the mass of living beings
must we fly for refuge to the doctrine of Cārvāka.
Such is the pleasant consummation.

PRABODHA-CANDRODAYA OR THE RISE OF THE MOON OF INTELLECT

A Drama of Ancient India*

(A MATERIALIST and one of his pupils enter.)
    Materialist: My son, you know that Legislation
[the law of punishment by fear of which alone are
men influenced in their conduct] is the only Science, and that it comprises everything else. The

three Vedas are a cheat. Behold if Heaven be obtained through the officiating priest, sacrificial rites,
and the destruction of the substances employed,
why is not abundance of excellent fruit obtained
from the ashes of a tree which has been burnt up by
the fire of the forest. If the victims slain in sacrifices
ascend to heaven, why are not parents offered up in
sacrifice by their children? If funeral oblations
nourish the deceased, why is not the flame of an extinguished taper renovated by pouring on oil?
    Pupil: Venerable tutor, if to gratify the appetites
be the principal end of life, why do these men renounce sensual pleasures, and submit to pain arising from the severest mortifications?
    Materialist: These fools are deceived by the
lying Śāstras, and are fed with the allurements of
hope. But can begging, fasting, penance, exposure
to the burning heat of the sun, which emaciate the
body, be compared with the ravishing embraces of
women with large eyes, whose prominent breasts
are compressed with one's arms?
    Pupil: Do these pilgrims indeed torture them-
selves in order to remove the happiness which is
mingled with this miserable existence?
    Materialist: (*Smiling.*) You ignorant boy, such
are the fooleries of these unenlightened men. They
conceive that you ought to throw away the pleasures of life, because they are mixed with pain; but
what prudent man will throw away unpeeled rice
which incloses excellent grain because it is covered
with the husk?

 # PERSONS, DEATH, AND THE BODY

Bertrand Russell

Before we can profitably discuss whether we shall
continue to exist after death, it is well to be clear as
to the sense in which a man is the same person as he

---

[3] Clarified butter.
[4] A Vedic sacrifical ritual: the "horse sacrifice."
* This second selection on the Cārvāka school is taken from a
popular drama of ancient India. The school's doctrines are thus
seen to be a source of controversy that is not limited to the debates of scholars alone (Eds.).

was yesterday. Philosophers used to think that there were definite substances, the soul and the body, that each lasted on from day to day, that a soul, once created, continued to exist throughout all future time, whereas a body ceased temporarily from death till the resurrection of the body.

The part of this doctrine which concerns the present life is pretty certainly false. The matter of the body is continually changing by processes of nutriment and wastage. Even if it were not, atoms in physics are no longer supposed to have continuous existence; there is no sense in saying: this is the same atom as the one that existed a few minutes ago. The continuity of a human body is a matter of appearance and behavior, not of substance.

The same thing applies to the mind. We think and feel and act, but there is not, in addition to thoughts and feelings and actions, a bare entity, the mind or the soul, which does or suffers these occurrences. The mental continuity of a person is a continuity of habit and memory: there was yesterday one person whose feelings I can remember, and that person I regard as myself of yesterday; but, in fact, myself of yesterday was only certain mental occurrences which are now remembered and are regarded as part of the person who now recollects them. All that constitutes a person is a series of experiences connected by memory and by certain similarities of the sort we call habit.

If, therefore, we are to believe that a person survives death, we must believe that the memories and habits which constitute the person will continue to be exhibited in a new set of occurrences.

No one can prove that this will not happen. But it is easy to see that it is very unlikely. Our memories and habits are bound up with the structure of the brain, in much the same way in which a river is connected with the riverbed. The water in the river is always changing, but it keeps to the same course because previous rains have worn a channel. In like manner, previous events have worn a channel in the brain, and our thoughts flow along this channel. This is the cause of memory and mental habits. But the brain, as a structure, is dissolved at death, and memory therefore may be expected to be also dis-

solved. There is no more reason to think otherwise than to expect a river to persist in its old course after an earthquake has raised a mountain where a valley used to be.

All memory, and therefore (one may say) all minds, depend upon a property which is very noticeable in certain kinds of material structures but exists little if at all in other kinds. This is the property of forming habits as a result of frequent similar occurrences. For example: a bright light makes the pupils of the eyes contract; and if you repeatedly flash a light in a man's eyes and beat a gong at the same time, the gong alone will, in the end, cause his pupils to contract. This is a fact about the brain and nervous system—that is to say, about a certain material structure. It will be found that exactly similar facts explain our response to language and our use of it, our memories and the emotions they arouse, our moral or immoral habits of behavior, and indeed everything that constitutes our mental personality, except the part determined by heredity. The part determined by heredity is handed on to our posterity but cannot, in the individual, survive the disintegration of the body. Thus both the hereditary and the acquired parts of a personality are, so far as our experience goes, bound up with the characteristics of certain bodily structures. We all know that memory may be obliterated by an injury to the brain, that a virtuous person may be rendered vicious by encephalitis lethargica, and that a clever child can be turned into an idiot by lack of iodine. In view of such familiar facts, it seems scarcely probable that the mind survives the total destruction of brain structure which occurs at death.

It is not rational arguments but emotions that cause belief in a future life.

The most important of these emotions is fear of death, which is instinctive and biologically useful. If we genuinely and wholeheartedly believed in the future life, we should cease completely to fear death. The effects would be curious, and probably such as most of us would deplore. But our human and subhuman ancestors have fought and exterminated their enemies throughout many geological ages and have profited by courage; it is therefore an advantage to the victors in the struggle for life to be able, on occasion, to overcome the natural fear of death. Among animals and savages, instinctive pugnacity suffices for this purpose; but at a certain stage of development, as the Mohammedans first proved, belief in Paradise has considerable military value as reinforcing natural pugnacity. We should therefore admit that militarists are wise in encouraging the belief in immortality, always supposing that this belief does not become so profound as to produce indifference to the affairs of the world.

Another emotion which encourages the belief in survival is admiration of the excellence of man. As the Bishop of Birmingham says, "His mind is a far finer instrument than anything that had appeared earlier—he knows right and wrong. He can build Westminster Abbey. He can make an airplane. He can calculate the distance of the sun. . . . Shall, then, man at death perish utterly? Does that incomparable instrument, his mind, vanish when life ceases?"

The Bishop proceeds to argue that "the universe has been shaped and is governed by an intelligent purpose," and that it would have been unintelligent, having made man, to let him perish.

To this argument there are many answers. In the first place, it has been found, in the scientific investigation of nature, that the intrusion of moral or aesthetic values has always been an obstacle to discovery. It used to be thought that the heavenly bodies must move in circles because the circle is the most perfect curve, that species must be immutable because God would only create what was perfect and what therefore stood in no need of improvement, that it was useless to combat epidemics except by repentance because they were sent as a punishment for sin, and so on. It has been found, however, that, so far as we can discover, nature is indifferent to our values and can only be understood by ignoring our notions of good and bad. The Universe may have a purpose, but nothing that we know suggests that, if so, this purpose has any similarity to ours.

Nor is there in this anything surprising. Dr. Barnes tells us that man "knows right and wrong." But, in fact, as anthropology shows, men's views of right and wrong have varied to such an extent that

no single item has been permanent. We cannot say, therefore, that man knows right and wrong, but only that some men do. Which men? Nietzsche argued in favor of an ethic profoundly different from Christ's, and some powerful governments have accepted his teaching. If knowledge of right and wrong is to be an argument for immortality, we must first settle whether to believe Christ or Nietzsche, and then argue that Christians are immortal, but Hitler and Mussolini are not, or vice versa. The decision will obviously be made on the battlefield, not in the study. Those who have the best poison gas will have the ethic of the future and will therefore be the immortal ones.

Our feelings and beliefs on the subject of good and evil are, like everything else about us, natural facts, developed in the struggle for existence and not having any divine or supernatural origin. In one of Aesop's fables, a lion is shown pictures of huntsmen catching lions and remarks that, if he had painted them, they would have shown lions catching huntsmen. Man, says Dr. Barnes, is a fine fellow because he can make airplanes. A little while ago there was a popular song about the cleverness of flies in walking upside down on the ceiling, with the chorus: "Could Lloyd George do it? Could Mr. Baldwin do it? Could Ramsay Mac do it? Why, *no*." On this basis a very telling argument could be constructed by a theologically-minded fly, which no doubt the other flies would find most convincing.

Moreover, it is only when we think abstractly that we have such a high opinion of man. Of men in the concrete, most of us think the vast majority very bad. Civilized states spend more than half their revenue on killing each other's citizens. Consider the long history of the activities inspired by moral fervor: human sacrifices, persecutions of heretics, witch-hunts, pogroms leading up to wholesale extermination by poison gases, which one at least of Barnes's episcopal colleagues must be supposed to favor, since he holds pacifism to be un-Christian. Are these abominations, and the ethical doctrines by which they are prompted, really evidence of an intelligent Creator? And can we really wish that the men who practiced them should live forever? The world in which we live can be understood as a result of muddle and accident; but if it is the outcome of deliberate purpose, the purpose must have been that of a fiend. For my part, I find accident a less painful and more plausible hypothesis.

QUESTIONS FOR DISCUSSION

1. Russell says that, if our world is the outcome of deliberate purpose, it seems to him to be the purpose of a fiend rather than a good and loving God. Do you agree or disagree with this statement of Russell's? Why?

2. Russell believes that "all that constitutes a person is a series of experiences connected by memory and by certain similarities of the sort we call habit." Does this seem to you a correct analysis of what a person is? Why or why not?

THE SELF AS ACTIVITY

We end this chapter with yet another view of self. The twentieth-century Argentine philosopher Risieri Frondizi puts it succinctly: The self is constituted, not by a static, unchanging substance, but by its actions. It is our behavior that constitutes the self. In developing this view, he relies heavily upon psychology, invoking the psychological concept of Gestalt rather than "substance" to explain the unity of the self. Interestingly, Frondizi's essay is not, as one might expect, a translation from the Spanish. He spent much time lecturing in the United States as well as Argentina during his career and at times wrote in English as well as Spanish. Consequently, he was and is a presence in North American as well as in Latin American philosophy in this century.

THE DYNAMIC UNITY OF THE SELF

Risieri Frondizi

THE BEING AND THE DOING OF THE SELF

Experience shows us that the self does not depend upon any obscure or hidden substantial core but depends upon what it does, has done, proposes to do, or is able to do. The self is revealed in its action; it reveals itself and constitutes itself by acting. It is nothing before acting, and nothing remains of it if experiences cease completely. Its *esse* is equivalent to its *facere*. We are not given a ready-made self; we create our own self daily by what we do, what we experience. Our behavior—in which both our actual doing and our intentions should properly be included—is not an expression of our self but the very stuff which constitutes it.

What holds experiences together, what gives us personality, is not, therefore, a substantial bond but a functional one, a coordinated structure of activities. The self is not something already made but something that is always in the making. It is formed throughout the course of its life, just as any institution is formed—a family, a university, a nation.

There is no aboriginal nucleus of the self that exists prior to its actions; the self arises and takes on existence as it acts, as it undergoes experiences. The category of substance must be supplanted by that of function if we wish to interpret adequately the nature of the self. The concept of function connotes, in this case, the concepts of activity, process, and relation.

The functional link by no means includes only our past experiences. The self is memory, but it is not memory alone. Our personality depends upon what has happened to us, but it cannot be reduced to our personal history; the self is not the blind aggregate of our experiences. We get the push of the past, but we also get the pull of the future. There is, in the self, a note of novelty and creativity, a free will, an ability to control the eventual course of our experiences. Activity, therefore, contains an element of novelty; it cannot be grasped or comprehended by referring exclusively to its past. The self is not inert matter, deposited on the shore by the tide of experience, but creative will, plotting its own course for itself. It depends upon its past history but is able to mold its own history-to-be, to orient its life according to new courses. It is memory but memory projected toward the future, memory hurled ahead. The future conditions the nature of our self not only as it merges with the present but also while it is still more distantly future. What we plan to do, even if we never get to do it, gives sense to our activities. The future, however, is not a part of our self merely as a system of ideas and intentions; it also enters into the formation of the self through our emotions. In times of confusion and disaster the thought of the future of our country, our child, our own lives grieves us. Though it is true that this suffering is a present and not a future experience, its object is the future. It is like the pain caused by a splinter; the pain is not the splinter, but it could not exist without the presence of the splinter. Hope, despair, and many other experiences would be impossible if the future were not an element in our lives.

The self is a function already performed but also a function to be fulfilled, a capacity, a potentiality. Our being consists of what we have done but also of what we intend and are able to do. The past creates ability; the ability gives a sense of direction to the past. Even the capacity that was never realized, the potentiality that never had the chance of becoming actual, forms an integral part of our self.

The past and the future of the self are not, strictly speaking, separable parts; they form an indissoluble whole. The past acquires meaning in the light of the future; the future, in turn, depends upon the past. We cannot do whatever we want; our abilities depend upon our past experiences.

Some people have denied the dynamic character of the self or have relegated it to a position of secondary importance, thinking it to be incompatible with its unity. Unable to conceive of the unity of a changing being, they have considered that the process of alteration of the self only scratches its surface and that the self keeps an immutable central core. It is true that there is only one Ego for each experiential stream, but it is also true that the self is not immutable. We have seen that the self is constantly changing, that everything that happens to us enriches and modifies our self. But change does not mean substitution; rather, it means an alteration of the inner pattern. Thus, former experiences never quite disappear competely, though they can change their nature and meaning with the development of the self.

• • •

ANALYSIS AND ANALYTICISM

A study of the validity of the procedure utilized by the atomists reveals its weaknesses even more clearly than does an analysis of the results of the procedure itself.

The analysis of psychic complexes and their reduction to supposed primary elements has no empirical justification; it makes its appearance in atomism as a presupposition which, on the face of it, has the same philosophic value as the rationalist presupposition. We are aware of the difficulties which one has to face in an attempt to eliminate all presuppositions. It is nevertheless evident that atomism has made no serious effort to justify or examine critically the procedure which it employs. It has accepted and used the procedure with no thought for its philosophic basis or for the consequences which would result from its application.

As is well known, the method that is used conditions the nature of the object under observation. If, blinded by the prestige acquired by the scientific method, we commit the stupid blunder of the modern tourist who tries to examine under the microscope a city which he is visiting for the first time, we shall not succeed in seeing the houses, the people, the plants, and the flowers. It would imply an even greater blindness to maintain that in the city there are neither houses nor people nor flowers, without realizing that they have disappeared as a consequence of the instrument chosen. The naked eye, in such a case, is a better instrument than the microscope, which, though it shows us the detail, keeps us from seeing the whole.

The analytic method has often worked like a microscope. It has revealed details which no one had ever seen before, but it has impeded our view of the whole. Again, the naked eye and the free-ranging glances of the spirit are superior to the intellect provided with the perfected technique and instruments of analysis. We need only to glance within, if we hold no prejudicial theories, to see what is hidden from the philosophers using analytic methods and blinded by the postulates of their theory and by their technique of observation.

Why should we be surprised that the wholes are

not perceived if it has already been accepted in advance that analysis is the only form of apprehension? That which has been previously eliminated cannot be discovered, and it is impossible to reconstruct what should never have been destroyed.

The analytic philosophy which sprang from Hume's atomism is subject to an almost demoniac desire for destruction—destruction by reductions. When confronted by a whole, these philosophers make no effort to comprehend its nature and find the sense of the whole. They proceed immediately to chop the whole into as many parts as possible and to submit each part to the thoroughgoing test of analysis. It is like the little boy who wants to find out what makes his toy work and ends up defiantly facing a heap of loose nuts and bolts.

This destructive drive is based upon a metaphysical postulate from which another postulate, an epistemological one, is derived; these two postulates support what we might call "the fallacy of reduction." The metaphysical postulate may be stated thus: elements have a more actual reality than wholes. The epistemological consequence is obvious: the goal of philosophic knowledge is to come to grips with the basic elements which constitute reality.

From these two postulates a series of principles is derived and conditions the whole attitude of the analytic philosophers. There are two principles which particularly concern us in the study which we are making: a) that the "parts" or elements can be separated from the "whole" without undergoing any change; b) that these elements can be discovered by analysis and defined in such a way that leaves no room for doubt.

• • •

I am not proposing, of course, the abandonment of analysis as a philosophic method. It is not clear how analysis could be abandoned without falling into an attitude of contemplative mysticism, which would bring as its immediate consequence greater confusion and obscurity to the field of philosophy. What I am criticizing is *analyticism,* if we may so call it, which attempts to reduce to analysis every

philosophic task and actually analyzes away what is really important.

Analysis involves the disarticulation of a complex reality whose unity is destroyed when its component members are separated. It can be used in the realm of psychic life with a great deal of profit and very little danger, provided that one is constantly aware of its limitations and consequences and never loses sight of the fact that the elements which have been separated by analysis are members of a totality which must, of necessity, remain united. Analysis should therefore be used—always, of course, keeping the totality in mind—only in order to make clear the meaning of the whole and to comprehend its inner mechanism, not in order to eliminate the whole or reduce it to a heap of disjointed pieces. Hence analysis should be applied to a structure only after the structure has been taken in and recognized as a whole; reality should not be sacrificed to the method used.

• • •

The analytic attitude is moreover complemented by a mechanical conception of the psychic life which tries to "explain" everything by means of simple elements and the forces that move them. When the psychic life has been put together again in this way, it has lost its organic unity, its spontaneity, its very life—all that characterizes the human being. Hence the final result seems more like a robot than a man: the parts that make it up remain unalterable, and the forces that move it are completely mechanical. The process of reconstruction cannot give us what analysis has previously destroyed—the organic coherence of the inner life. Reconstruction is neither necessary nor possible, for this organic unity is a primary reality and not the conclusion of a system.

THE CONCEPT OF GESTALT

What is the self before its unity has been broken down by analysis? In what does its organic or structural unity consist?

Let us first make clear that this unity is not one that transcends the empirical world, the world of experiences. It is a unity derived from the very experiences themselves. There is nothing under or above the totality of experiences. If one overlooks the word "totality" or interprets it in an atomistic sense, this statement would be equivalent of subscribing to Hume's theory. But we should never interpret the totality or structure of experiences as a mere sum or aggregate of the same. The experiential totality has qualities which are not possessed by the members which constitute it. Consequently the characteristics of the total structure of the self cannot be deduced, necessarily from the characteristics of each of the experiences taken separately.

• • •

What is it that characterizes a Gestalt? Like any other fundamental concept, that of Gestalt presents a degree of complexity which does not allow one to enunciate in a few words all the richness of its content. Nevertheless, there are certain characteristics which seem to be fundamental. First, there is the one that has already been emphasized: a structural whole—a Gestalt—has qualities not possessed by any of the elements which form it. In this sense, a Gestalt or structure is set in contrast with a mere sum of elements. The physical and chemical qualities of a cubic yard of water are the same as those of each gallon that makes it up. The whole, in this case, is no more than the mere sum of its parts. In the case of a structure, on the other hand, this is not so, as we have seen in considering the character of a melody; it possesses qualities which cannot be found in any of the notes, for it can be transposed without being changed into another melody.

The above-mentioned characteristic does not mean, of course, that a Gestalt is completely independent of the members which constitute it. In the first place, there can be no structure without members. But the dependence of structure upon members does not stop here—the removal, addition, or fundamental alteration of a member modifies the whole structure, as can be seen in the case of an organism.* Any important alteration or suppression of a member alters the totality of an organism and may even cause its disappearance. This does not happen in the case of a sum. We can remove one, two, thirty, or forty gallons of water without causing the rest to undergo any important change in quality.

But not only does the structural whole suffer alteration when one of its members is taken away, the member that is taken away is also basically altered. A hand separated from the body is unable to feel or to seize an object—it ceases to be a hand—whereas the gallon of water separated from the rest retains practically all of its properties. This characteristic, taken along with the foregoing one, will suffice for the definition of a member of a structure. A member of a structure is that which cannot be removed without affecting the whole structure and losing its own nature when separated from the "whole." Conversely, we can characterize the "mere sum" as something made up of "parts" or "elements" that undergo no change when joined to other "parts" and which can be removed without producing any change either in itself or in what remains. The relationship between the parts is that of mere juxtaposition.

The difference between structure and mere sum does not stem solely from the fact that the parts of the latter are independent of the whole and that the members of the former are conditioned by the structure. There is also the fact that the parts may be homogeneous, whereas the members must offer diversity and even opposition of characteristics. One gallon of water is just as much water as any other gallon or measure. The same is true of one brick in a pile of bricks or of each grain of sand in the desert. On the contrary, in an organism each member has its own specific nature—the heart is the heart and cannot perform the functions of the liver or kidneys. There is not only diversity among the members but

---

* Lewin defines a Gestalt in his *Principles of Topological Psychology* (p. 208) as a "system whose parts are dynamically connected in such a way that a change of one part results in a change of all the other parts."

also opposition; and this opposition is subsumed into the unity which organizes them. The unification and organization of the members which make up a structure do not come about at the expense of the peculiar and distinctive qualities of each member. Organization is not the equivalent of homogenization, and unity does not contradict the multiplicity and diversity of the elements. This multiplicity and diversity must always be maintained as absolutely essential. Thus we find structure to be the result of a dialectic play of opposites, of a struggle between the members; it seems to hang by the thread which establishes a dynamic balance. But this unity is not of an abstract sort. A concept which organizes different members into a unity by grouping them in agreement with a common note does not constitute a structure. One essential aspect of the structure is lacking: its unity must be concrete. For that reason I use the term "structure" rather than "form" or "configuration" to translate the German word Gestalt, which, besides carrying the connotation of these two latter concepts, designates a unity that is *concrete*.

THE STRUCTURAL UNITY OF THE SELF

When we considered the applicability of the category of substance to the self, we noticed that none of the three classic characteristics of this concept—immutability, simplicity, and independence—belonged to the self. We obtained a similarly negative result from the consideration of the atomistic conception. In the first place, the supposed psychic atom is a poorly defined unit which, when one attempts to fix it with any precision, vanishes into thin air, becoming a mere arbitrary instant in an uninterrupted process. In the second place, the aggregation of atoms, which can have only a relationship of juxtaposition one to another, looks like a grotesque caricature of the real organic unity of the self. Let us now see if the category which we have called Gestalt or structure is any more successful.

It seems unquestionable that the psychic life is not chaotic, that each state or experience is connected to all the rest. This connection, however, is not of experience to experience, like the links of a chain, for if this were so there would be a fixed order of connections and in order to get to one link we should necessarily have to go by way of the preceding ones. But in the same way that Köhler showed that there is no constant relation between stimulus and response, it would be easy to show that in like manner there is no constant relation between one experience and another. No laboratory experiment is needed to prove this, for our daily experiences supply all the material we require—the sound and sight of the sea is exhilarating one day and depressing the next; the same piece of music arouses in us different reactions according to the situation in which we hear it; our arrival at the same port and in the same ship can start altogether different trains of reflection in us, depending on whether we have arrived to stay for the rest of our life or only for a short vacation; the memory of a disagreement with a friend, which irritated us so much when it happened, may now provoke only an indifferent smile. The relations of experiences to each other resemble the relations between stimuli and responses in the fact that they arise within a given context.

These undeniable data of the psychic life are founded on the fact that the self is not a sum of experiences or an aggregate of parts in juxtaposition but a structure—in the sense defined above; whatever happens to one of its elements affects the whole, and the whole in turn exerts an influence upon each element. It is because the whole reacts as a structural unity and not as a mechanism that a stimulus can provoke consequences in an altogether different field from the one in which it has arisen. Thus, a strictly intellectual problem can give rise to emotional torment, and a fact of an emotional sort can have far-reaching volitional consequences. The self is not departmentalized—like modern bureaucracy—but constitutes an organic unity with intimate, complex, and varied interrelations.

The self presents itself, then, as an organized whole, an integrated structure, and experiences are related to one another not through but within the whole. For that reason, when the structure is modified the nature of the experiences and of the relationships between them are also modified. The interdependence of the different experiential groups shows that the self is a structure which is organized and "makes sense" and that each member occupies its proper place within the structure.

This does not mean, of course, that the structure which constitutes the self cannot be analyzed and broken down, theoretically, into less complex structures. It does mean, however, that we are in fact dealing with a unity that is formed upon substructures and the intimate and complex interrelation of these substructures.*

And here we notice another characteristic of the concept of structure which is directly applicable to the self: the members of a structure are heterogeneous in contrast with the homogeneity of the parts of a nonstructural unity. Let us state, first of all, that the structure which constitutes the self, being a very complex structure, is made up not of "simple members" but of substructures; it is consequently to the heterogeneity of these substructures that we are referring. It must also be kept in mind that the substructures are not of an abstract nature, like concepts, and that we are not trying to reconstruct a reality by juxtaposing abstractions such as the so-called "faculties of the soul."

The complexity and heterogeneity of the structure are twofold: on the one hand there is the complexity which we may call transversal; on the other there is the horizontal or, better, the temporal complexity. In actuality the self embraces the combination of both complexes, which do not and cannot exist in separation.

If we make a cross section at a given moment in our life, we find that we have a slice of a process that is made up of bundles of three different kinds of experience: the intellectual, the emotive, and the volitive. This shows that not even in the briefest moment of our life is it possible to catch ourselves concentrated upon a single type of experience.

• • •

The atomists should not be blamed too much for their failure to perceive the structure that goes through time, its development and evolution. Their error in this case is due to their conception of time as an empty and indifferent form which may be filled by either one content or another, without making any difference. Psychological time, however, is not empty, and it is impossible to separate its content from its form. It cannot be disintegrated into the supposed instants which constitute it, for each psychological "moment" is a structure with unity of meaning. And, what is more, the "present" conceived of by the atomists is arbitrary. It aspires to be a fragment without extension. But for the present to make real sense it must contain the past and the future.

The gradual change of structure through time can be seen both by observing the development of the process itself and by comparing cross sections made at different points in the process. If one makes such a comparison, one will notice not only that the experiences vary but also that the type of structure does. At one moment the emotive is predominant and the intellectual and volitional are secondary; at another the intellectual is predominant, etc. The only thing that remains is the presence of a structure made up of three types of experiences.

This diversity and opposition among the elements which constitute the self should not lead us to forget the unity which characterizes every structure. The self is no exception. Its multiplicity does not exclude its unity or vice versa. And this is not the abstract unity of a concept which points to what is common; it is a concrete unity, of "flesh and blood" as Unamuno would say, for there is nothing more real and concrete than our self. Diversity underlies the structure but is in turn lost within it, for the elements uphold each other mutually in an intimate sort of interweaving in which it is impossible to distinguish warp from woof. This is not because the

---

* By substructure I mean any of the structural parts that constitute the total Gestalt that makes up the self.

three types of substructure have equivalent strength and no one of them dominates the other two—as in the theory of the so-called balance of power—but because they vary constantly. At a given moment one element stands forth as the figure and the others form the ground; after a while there is a change of roles. These changes are explained by the fact that the self is a dynamic structure and thus resembles a symphony rather than a painting.

We should perhaps stress the point that the changes undergone by the self are not due exclusively to a different distribution of the members, for the members themselves are of a dynamic nature. Moreover, the self is constituted not only of members but also of the *tensions* produced by the reciprocal play of influences. The breakdown of the equilibrium of tensions is what generally produces the most important changes.

It now appears obvious that the relations between the experiences are not fixed, for each experience as it is incorporated into the structure modifies its former state. This member in turn undergoes the influence of the whole, which is another characteristic of a Gestalt easy to find in the self. Thus, the perceptions which we have at this moment depend upon our former state. The new experience immediately acquires the coloration given it both by the basic structure of the self and by the particular situation in which it finds itself at that moment. If we are happy and in pleasant company, for example, the color of the spectacles we happen to be wearing has very little effect upon the emotive state of our spirit. This is not because visual perception ceases to have emotional tonality but because a greater affective tone—the happiness which results from a different cause—completely overshadows it. What is more, the stable nature of the self colors the transitory state. There are people who give the impression of seeing the world in the rosiest colors, whatever the tint of the spectacles they wear, and there are others who see clouds in the clearest sky.

This is the influence of the whole upon the member which is incorporated, but there is also an influence of the member upon the whole. We must not forget that a structure is not suspended in thin air but rests solely upon the members which constitute it. A symphonic orchestra is something more than the sum of the musicians that go to form it, but it cannot exist without the musicians. A self without the experiential structures that go to make it up would be the same as an orchestra without musicians, that is, a pure fantasy, the fantasy of a spiritual entity that would be unable to love, hate, decide, want, perceive, etc., and would pretend to be immutable substance. Such a concept would be immutable without doubt, but it would have the immutability of nothingness.

In the same way that the total suppression of the experiential structures would mean the suppression of the self, any change or alteration of a member has repercussions on the whole structure. By this I do not mean a man lacking in emotional life, for example, for it is obvious that he would not be a man but a mere caricature, or projection on a plane of two dimensions, of a three-dimensional reality. I am referring to the alteration of a structural subcomplex. Abulia, for example, is a disease of the will, but the changes which it provokes are not limited to the volitional—it has immediate repercussions in the emotive and intellectual spheres and consequently in the total structure. Its intellectual repercussions are easily seen, for the person suffering from abulia is unable to concentrate his attention, and thus his intellectual processes break down completely. And the emotional sphere is impaired too, for the sufferer is unable, by an act of the will, to get rid of the emotion which has taken control of him, so he lets himself be so possessed by this emotion that it changes his whole personality.

Of the characteristics of the structure that are applicable to the self we have only to consider now the first and most important, that is, the fact that the structure possesses qualities not possessed by the members that make it up. At this stage in our inquiry it seems a waste of time to insist that this is one of the characteristics of the self. Let us consider only the most obvious reasons. The self has a permanence—in the sense of constant presence—and a stability that the experiences and experiential groups do not have. Experiences are totally unstable; transiency is their characteristic. The self, on the other hand, remains stable in the face of the coming and going of experiences. If experiences do not have stability, even less can they have permanence, which is the fundamental characteristic of the self. And this is not all. The structure of the self is such that the members that make it up cannot exist in separation from it. There is no experience that does not belong to a particular self. The self depends, then, upon the experiences, but it is not equivalent to their sum. It is a structural quality.

• • •

PROBLEMS SOLVED BY THE STRUCTURAL CONCEPTION

A. Permanence and Mutability of the Self

At the beginning of this chapter we saw that both substantialism and atomism were unable to give an adequate picture of the self because they could not comprehend how its permanence and continuity could be compatible with the changes that it undergoes. Substantialism emphasized the permanence and atomism the mutability.

The structural conception that we are here proposing allows us to see that the two characteristics are not only compatible but also complementary. The historical survey of past thought on the subject, which occupied the first part of this book, showed us that substantialism could not understand the changing nature of the self because it held fast to an irreducible and immutable nucleus and that Hume's atomism, in its effort to destroy the doctrine of a substantial nucleus, confused it with the very real permanence and continuity of the self.

If we free ourselves of the limitations of both historical positions and observe reality just as it presents itself, we shall see that the permanence and continuity of the self are based upon its structural character, for it is a dynamic structure made up not only of the elements which we can isolate in a cross section of our life but also of the substructures that

form the complex longitudinal bundles that constitute the self. And change occurs each time a new element is taken in, which alters but does not destroy the structure.

In this way the constant alteration of the self insures its stability. It is undeniable that a new experience modifies, or can modify, the structure of the self. The loss of a child or a friend, a war, a religious experience, etc. can produce such an inner commotion that they may alter the total structure. From that time on we are not the same person as before. We act in a different way, we see life in a different perspective, and it may be that not only the future but also the past is colored by the new attitude. But it is just this experience causing us to change which gives endurance to the self. From now on we shall be the man who has lost his son or his friend or who had this or that religious experience. Other children that we may have or the new friends which we may take into our hearts may cover up but can never completely obliterate the existence of an experience that at one time shook us deeply and persists in the structure of our spirit despite all that may happen to us in the future.

What happens on a large scale in the case of experiences that are profoundly moving happens on a smaller scale in all the other experiences of our life. Each new experience alters the structure or substructure to which it is connected, and thus it is incorporated "definitively," so to speak. Whatever happens afterward may alter the meaning of the experience within the whole—increasing it or diminishing it—but it can never erase the experience completely.

An analogy of a physical sort, even though inadequate to characterize our psychic life, may perhaps make clear the meaning of what I am trying to put across. The self resembles, in this respect, a mixture of colors. If we add to the mixture a new color—for example, blue—the mixture will be altered to a degree that will depend upon the quantity and shade of blue added and upon the combination of colors that were there before. This quantity of blue which produces a change in the former mixture is incorporated definitively into the whole, and however many more colors we add we shall never be able completely to counteract its presence.

The nature of the whole and the influence of the element incorporated into it are controlled, in the case of the analogy, by certain stable physical laws in which quantity plays an important role. This is not the case with psychic structures, in which quantity gives way to equality. Psychic structures obey certain principles, carefully studied by the Gestalt psychologists in the case of visual perception, which also exist in all the other orders of life and in the constitution of the total structure of the self. These general principles governing the organization of our total personality are what the most psychologically acute educators use as the basis for their choice of one type of experience rather than another in their endeavor to devise a system of corrective education for an aberrant personality.

Every self has a center or axis around which its structure is organized. When the personality has already developed, this axis is what gives direction and organization to our life, not only in that new experiences do not succeed in dislodging it from its route but also in that it chooses the type of experience that it finds to be in tune with it. But it is not a nucleus immutable in itself or fixed in relation to the rest of the structure. In the first place it undergoes an evolution which we can consider normal. The axis that predominates changes at the different stages of our life. In our earliest childhood the predominant experiential substructure is that related to alimentation, later it is play, and so on through life.

What is more, the center undergoes sudden displacements caused by new experiences that shake and modify the total structure. This is the case with the soldier who, according to war records, after devoting his life to the acquisition or intensification of his capacity for destruction and after exercising this capacity for years at the cost of many lives, suddenly discovers "the truth," "finds himself," decides that "we are all brothers." The center of his personality is completely displaced. His technical capacity as a killer, in which he formerly took pride—and centered his whole personality—is now

a source of humiliation and shame. His personality must retrace its steps and choose another route.

These changes are due to many varied and complex reasons. Usually they have a long period of germination, as it were, in the world of the subconscious and burst forth full blown at a propitious moment. I recall the case of an American pilot who fought for several years in the Pacific; all of a sudden "the truth was revealed to him" while he was reading, more or less by chance, certain passages in the Bible. At other times the change comes about because of the intensification of the means of destruction; the explosion of the atomic bomb produced a psychological shock in many of those who had launched 200-pound bombs under the same flag. Most commonly it comes about because of the shock of contrast; the soldier, in the midst of hatred, destruction, and death, comes across people who are devoting their lives to healing, in a spirit of disinterested love, the physical and moral wounds that other men cause. These external situations usually act as the immediate cause for the eruption of subterranean currents; at other times they stir up for the first time currents that burst forth later on, if a propitious situation presents itself.

We should not be surprised that an apparently insignificant fact may be able to change the total structure of our personality after it has been stable for many years; in the psychological realm quantities are of no great importance. The principle, *causa aequat effectum,* is not valid in the interrelations of the different elements. Gestalt psychology has shown us how the constitution of the structure and its alteration are governed by principles that have nothing to do with the principle of causality in its simplistic interpretation as the equal of cause and effect.

• • •

B. Immanence and Transcendence of the Self

Another apparent paradox—similar to that of permanence and mutability—which is resolved by the structural conception is that of the immanence and transcendence of the self. For both atomism and substantialism, immanence and transcendence are incompatible. Either the self is equivalent to the totality of experiences—and in this sense is immanent to them—or it is something that transcends the experiences. Atomism holds the first position and substantialism the second.

According to the theory that I am proposing, the self is immanent and transcends experiences at the same time, though admittedly the terms have different meanings from those attributed to them both by atomism and by substantialism. The self is immanent because it is, indeed, equivalent to the totality of experiences; but this totality, in turn, should be interpreted not as the sum or aggregate of the experiences but as a structure that has properties that cannot be found in its parts. According to this interpretation of the concept of totality, the self transcends the experiences and becomes a structural quality, in the sense in which Ehrenfels used this expression. Nevertheless, this is not the transcendence defended by the substantialists when they affirm the existence of a being that supports states or experiences. Mine is a transcendence that not only does not exclude immanence but actually takes it for granted.

Let us look at the problem from another point of view. The relation beween the self and its experiences is so intimate that every experience reveals some aspect of the self; what is more, every experience forms part of the self. In this sense, the self seems to be represented in each one of the experiences, to be nothing but them. No experience, however, is able to reveal to us the self in its entirety. Not even the sum of all the experiences can do that. The self is able to transcend its autobiography; hence the possibility of a true repentance, a conversion, a new life. In the first instance the self seems to be immanent; in the second it is seen to be something that transcends its experiences.

The problem is clarified considerably if one turns his attention to those two propositions which Hume, and many others after him, considered to be incompatible: *a*) that the self is nothing apart from its experiences; *b*) that the self cannot be reduced to

its experiences. I, of course, affirm that both propositions are true. When Hume maintained that the self should be reduced to a bundle of perceptions because it could not exist without them, he let himself be misled by the substantialist prejudice in favor of the so-called independence of the self. But the self, though not independent of the perceptions, is not reducible to the mere sum of them.

The paradox of the immanence and transcendence of the self, just like the paradox which we examined before, has arisen as a consequence of the way in which substantialists stated the problem of the self, a statement that the atomists accepted without realizing its consequences. The problem, as stated, presupposes a metaphysics and a logic which our conception rejects. First, it conceives of real existence as substance, independent and immutable; and second, it interprets the principles of identity and of noncontradiction in a very rigid way. My concept, on the other hand, gives a very dynamic interpretation to both principles, to the point of seeing in contradiction much of the essence of the real. What is more, I believe that there is nothing independent and immutable. I can hardly believe, therefore, in the independence and immutability of the self, the stuff of which is relationship and the essence of which is creative process.

C. Unity and Multiplicity

A variant of the preceding paradoxes is that of unity and multiplicity. When atomism took over the analysis of the self, its unity was destroyed forever and the self was turned into a great mosaic of loose pieces. Each perception became a reality in itself, independent, separable, sharply delimited. With this conception of the elements it proved impossible to rewin the lost unity. Atomists maintained, therefore, the plurality of the self, even though they sighed from time to time for the unity that they themselves had destroyed. When atomists—and men like William James who criticized atomism without being able to free themselves from the source of its confusion—ask what unites the different parts constituting the self, one must simply answer that the self never ceased to constitute a unity. Atomism's difficulties in reaching the unity of the self are merely a consequence of the arbitrary way in which it was dismembered. First they build a wall; then they complain they cannot see beyond the wall.

Substantialism, on the other hand, takes as its point of departure the postulate of unity and relegates multiplicity to accidents. The self is only one, although many different things happen to it.

With the importance that these "happenings" have for us—the self is made up of what it does— the whole statement of the problem collapses; the self is one or multiple according to how one looks at it. It is one if one focuses on the whole; it is multiple if one focuses on the members that constitute it. The self is the unity of the multiplicity of its experiences.

The unity of the self is not like the pseudo unity of a concept that is arrived at by abstraction. Its unity is quite concrete and is arrived at by a process of integration. It is a unity that does not abolish but preserves the differences in the members that make it up. That the self has members does not mean that it can be divided, as one divides a generic concept into the different species that it contains. The self is indivisible, though this does not keep us from distinguishing the different members that constitute it. The self has no existence apart from its members, nor do the members, if separated from the totality of the self, have existence.

QUESTION FOR DISCUSSION

1. Is the self, as Frondizi argues, best viewed as an activity rather than a substance? Can its unity be constituted in the manner which he thinks it can?

Fatalism

Motse, *Anti-Fatalism*

Sarvepalli Radhakrishnan, *Karma and Freedom*

Radical Freedom

Fyodor Dostoevsky, *Notes from the Underground*

Jean-Paul Sartre, *Freedom and Action*

Human Beings Are Not Free

Okot p'Bitek, *Social Bonds*

B. F. Skinner, *Walden Two: Freedom and the Science of Human Behavior*

Can We Reconcile Freedom and Determinism?

Moritz Schlick, *Freedom and Responsibility*

Nancy Holmstrom, *Firming Up Soft Determinism*

Kitaro Nishida, *Freedom of the Will*

Patrick J. Sullivan, *The Fourth Dimension,* 1938, oil on canvas, 24 1/4″ x 30 1/4″. The Museum of Modern Art, New York. The Sidney and Harriet Janis Collection. Photograph © 1994 The Museum of Modern Art, New York.

CHAPTER 6

FATALISM, DETERMINISM, AND FREEDOM

What does it mean to be free? There is an obvious sociopolitical answer to this question. We are free insofar as we are permitted to do certain things or, conversely, insofar as there is nothing interfering with our acting as we wish. If we are enslaved or in prison, we are clearly not free. When government authorities tell us what we can read or say, what sexual acts we can and cannot perform, with whom we can associate, where we can travel, in short, when we are prevented from doing what we believe it is our right to do, we lack political freedom. On a smaller social scale, when someone physically threatens us, we experience ourselves as unfree. Some would extend this social and political concept to include nonphysical threats, e.g., when the boss threatens to fire us, and to situations where we lack the social and/or material resources to achieve our goals. In this last sense, we are not free if we cannot find employment (freedom to work), lack access to certain educational institutions (freedom to learn), or cannot obtain sufficient food or shelter (freedom from want). Where we draw the boundary lines has been a major source of political debate between liberals, conservatives, and radicals.

However, there is another issue of freedom, per- haps more subtle but, at least to those with a philosophical turn of mind, of equal importance. This is the issue of freedom versus determinism, which is the focus of Chapter 6. Consider the following hypothetical example: A woman lives in a society which grants what we believe are the appropriate political and human rights. She is gainfully employed in an agreeable situation. She has had a reasonable education and does not lack for material security. During her free time she goes to certain restaurants, supermarkets, and stores and consumes whatever she pleases. Is she free? If asked this question directly, she answers in the affirmative.

Before the reader, asked the same question, answers the same way, let us add one additional piece of information to our hypothetical scenario. She has been acting under the influence of a series of posthypnotic suggestions, but she has no memory of having been hypnotized. Is she still free?

The reader may protest at this point: "But I haven't been hypnotized. No one tells me what to buy, what career to pursue, who I may decide to marry, whether to join a political movement, etc." Let us think about our choices once again. Does modern advertising have anything to do with our choice of products? Does our socialization as males or females have anything to do with our choice of career, or who we marry, or our political orientation? How do we come to choose the things we do? Even if our choices cannot be traced to a straightforward suggestion by one or more persons, were there not some indirect suggestions? Were there not, at least, some factors in our personal history which motivated the choice?

Now, consider one of the key assumptions of modern science—the assumption of a universal cause and effect. If something occurs, we assume it was caused by something else. If psychology and the social sciences are to be truly scientific, must they not also assume that human action, emotions, and ideas are caused by certain factors in our past experience and perhaps partly by our genetic structure? This is the thesis of determinism. Then, if our actions and choices are themselves determined, how can we be free?

The selections in this chapter consider the philosophical problem of freedom from a number of points of view. In the first section, we consider a problem which precedes the scientific age but which still has many adherents—the problem of fatalism. Fatalism holds not merely that we are determined but that we are *predetermined* by certain universal cosmic forces—for example, the laws of Karma or the positions of the planets and stars as understood by astrology. The readings in this section by an ancient Chinese philosopher and a contemporary Indian one argue against the plausibility of fatalism in the forms that it has taken or presently takes in their respective cultures.

The readings in the chapter's second section argue for a radical concept of freedom, sometimes called "metaphysical freedom," or free will. Both the nineteenth-century Russian novelist Fyodor Dostoevsky and the contemporary French existentialist philosopher Jean-Paul Sartre insist that choice cannot be explained by reference to scientific, or causal, laws and that we have complete free will.

The readings in the third section of this chapter take the opposite position—that human beings are completely determined to think and act and choose as they do; that as individuals we are fettered by our social bonds (Okot p'Bitek); and that our behavior is the result of positive and negative reinforcement (B. F. Skinner).

Finally, in the fourth section of this chapter, we ask whether freedom is compatible with determinism. The first reading by Moritz Schlick argues yes, unequivocally; the second reading by Nancy Holmstrom argues yes, but only under certain conditions; and the final reading by Kitaro Nishida also argues yes, but for reasons that are significantly different than those advanced by Schlick and Holmstrom.

Readers of Section One might also want to look at the selection by Sarvepalli Radhakrishnan in Section Two of Chapter 3. Readers of Section Two of this chapter might want to consider also reading the selection by Sartre in Section One of Chapter 4. For those who want more about the logical positivist method which Schlick employs see the selection by Antony Flew in Section One of Chapter 3. Another selection by Kitaro Nishida can be found in Section Two of Chapter 3.

FATALISM

In the general introduction to this chapter we have already mentioned that fatalism refers to the belief that we are not only determined but predetermined by some universal cosmic force. In ancient China, for example, it was often said that "Heaven decreed" whether we were rich or poor, industrious or lazy, happy or unhappy, or whether our lives would be long or short. In India the idea of Karma, of a universal moral law, was often interpreted to mean that our present destiny was predetermined by our good or bad actions in former lives. In this section the ancient Chinese philosopher Motse (470–391 B.C.E.) and the contemporary Indian philosopher and statesman Sarvepalli Radhakrishnan respectively take issue with these interpretations.

Motse, who is said to have been originally a follower of Confucius, went on to found a rival school known as Moism. In this selection, he challenges what he takes to be a Confucian claim—it is unclear whether Confucius himself made this claim but it is thought that some of his followers did—that we are fated by Heaven to live or die as we do.

Motse's argument takes two forms. The first assumes the empiricist position that knowledge derives from sense experience. Since no one has ever seen or heard fate, on what basis can we believe that it exists? His second argument is a political one. The reason that people believe in fate is because wicked rulers have used this idea to cover over the ill consequences of their rule. He concludes that our destiny comes not from Heaven but is shaped by ourselves.

Sarvepalli Radhakrishnan is a major contemporary Indian philosopher and statesman—he was both vice president and president of India—who has attempted to reinterpret Hinduism in a way that reconciles some of its internal divisions and which makes it more accessible to Western philosophical thought. In the selection in this chapter he denies that the idea of Karma implies predestination.

Karma is understood as a moral counterpart to physical law. Just as there is cause and effect in the physical universe, so it exists in the moral universe. We reap morally as we have sown. If we do evil, we can expect evil to befall us; similarly, if we do good. Given the Hindu belief in reincarnation, it is often assumed that our destiny in this life is predestined by what we have done in our former lives.

Whereas Radhakrishnan would agree that the laws of Karma rule out free will in the sense of an undetermined action and that we always carry our whole past with us, he does not believe that our destiny is predetermined. He insists that the laws of Karma should be understood not as mechanical but as a spiritual principle and that, although our past is determined, our future is only conditioned. He compares the situation to a card game: "Cards in the game of life are given to us," but we can still choose how to play our hand. In short, we must confront the moral effects of our past actions, but we decide how to confront them, thus making it possible for us to change our destiny.

ANTI-FATALISM

Motse

Motse said: To make any statement or to publish any doctrine, there must first be established some standard of judgment. To discuss without a standard is like determining the directions of sunrise and sunset on a revolving potter's wheel. Even skilful artisans could not get accurate results in that way. Now that the truth and error (of a doctrine) in the world is hard to tell, there must be three tests. What are the three tests? They are the test of its basis, the test of its verifiability, and the test of its applicability. To test the basis of a doctrine we shall examine the will of Heaven and spirits and the deeds of the sage-kings.* To test its verifiability we shall go to the books of the early kings. As to its applicability it is to be tested by its use in the administration of justice and government. These then are the three tests of a doctrine.

Among the gentlemen of to-day some think there is fate, some think there is no fate. That I am able to judge whether there is fate or not is by the sense testimony of the multitude. If some have heard it and some have seen it I shall say there is fate. If none has heard it, if none has seen it, I shall say there is no fate. Why not then let us inquire into the sense testimony of the people? From antiquity to the present, since the beginning of man, has any seen such a thing as fate, or has heard the sound of fate? Of course, there is none. If the common people are considered stupid and their senses of hearing and sight unreliable, then why not inquire into the recorded statements of the feudal lords? But from antiquity to the present, since the beginning of man, has any of them heard the sound of fate or seen such a thing as fate? Of course, none of them has. Again,

---

* Traditional Chinese history assumed that there were ancient kings—*sage-kings*—who preceded the First Dynasty of the third millennium B.C.E. Motse, like Confucius and others, thought they were wise and good and could be invoked as the standard of right conduct and knowledge (Eds.).

why not let us inquire into the deeds of the sage-kings? The ancient kings promoted the filial sons and encouraged them to continue to serve their parents, and respected the virtuous and gentle and encouraged them to continue to do good. They published their orders to instruct (the people), and made reward and punishment fair to encourage (the good) and obstruct (the evil). In this way confusion could be reduced to order and danger could be converted to peace. If anyone doubts this, let us recall: In ancient times the confusion of Chieh was reduced to order by T'ang, and that of Chow by King Wu. Now, the times did not change and the people did not alter. Yet when the superior changed a regime the subordinates modified their conduct. Under T'ang and Wu it was orderly, but under Chieh and Chow it was disorderly. Hence peace and danger, order and disorder, all depend on the government of the superior. How can it be said everything is according to fate? So, assertions about there being fate are quite false.

The fatalists tell us: "This doctrine has not been invented by us in a late generation. Such a doctrine has appeared and been handed down since the Three Dynasties. Why do you, sir, now oppose it?" (In answer,) Motse asked: Was it from the sages and good men of the Three Dynasties or from the wicked and the vicious of the Three Dynasties that the fatalistic doctrine came? How can we find this out? In the beginning secretaries and ministers were careful in speech and intelligent in conduct. They could persuade their ruler above and instruct the people below. Thus they obtained reward from their ruler and applause from the people. And the fame of those secretaries and ministers has come down to the present day. The whole world remarks: "This is the result of endeavour." And it will never say: "I see fate there."

On the other hand, the wicked kings of the Three Dynasties did not control the lust of their ears and eyes and did not restrain the passions of their heart. When they went out they indulged in racing, hunting, and trapping. When they stayed indoors they revelled in wine and music. They did not attend to the government of the country and of the people, but they did much that was of no use. They oppressed the people, causing the subordinates not to love their superior. Hence the country became empty and without any future, and they themselves were in punishment and disaster. But they would not confess and say: "I am stupid and insolent and poor in administering the government." But they would say: "It is but my fate to perish." Even the miserable people of the Three Dynasties were like this. Within they could not well serve their parents, without they could not well serve their ruler. They disliked politeness and frugality but liked licence and ease. They indulged in drinking and eating and were lazy. The means of food and clothing became insufficient and they placed themselves in danger of hunger and cold. They would not confess: "I am stupid and insolent and was not diligent at work." But they would say: "It is but my fate to be poor." Such, then, also were the miserable people of the Three Dynasties.

Fatalism has been glossed over and taught the stupid people. This was of great concern to the sage-kings, and they put it down on the bamboos and silk and cut it in metals and and stone. Among the books of the early kings, "The Announcement of Chung Hui" says: "I have heard the man of Hsia issue orders, pretending them to be fate of Heaven. God was displeased and destroyed his forces." This shows how King Chieh of Hsia believed in fate and how both T'ang and Chung Hui thought it to be wrong. Among the books of early kings "The Great Declaration" says: "Chow became insolent and would not worship God, and pushed away the ancestors and spirits without offering them sacrifices. And he said: 'Fortune is with my people,' and neglected and betrayed his duty. Heaven thereupon deserted him and withdrew its protection." This shows how Chow believed in fate and how King Wu proclaimed it to be wrong with "The Great Declaration." Again, "The Three Dynasties and Hundred States" says: "Do not place too much faith in the fate in Heaven." So "The Three Dynasties and Hundred States" also says there is no fate. Also, "Shao Kung" in the same way discredits the belief in fate. It says: "Assuredly there is no fate in Heaven. Let us two not teach false doctrines. (One's destiny) does not come from Heaven, but is shaped by one's self." And it is said in the odes and books of Shang and Hsia: "Fate is born of the wicked kings."

So, then, if the gentlemen of the world desire to distinguish right and wrong, benefit and harm, fate of Heaven must be strenuously discredited. To hold there is fate is the great disaster of the world. And therefore Motse refuted it.

KARMA AND FREEDOM

Sarvepalli Radhakrishnan

. . . The doctrine of Karma is sometimes interpreted as implying a denial of human freedom, which is generally regarded as the basis of all ethical values. But when rightly viewed the law does not conflict with the reality of freedom. It is the principle of science which displaces belief in magic or the theory that we can manipulate the forces of the world at our pleasure. The course of nature is determined not by the passions and prejudices of personal spirits lurking behind it but by the operation of immutable laws. If the sun pursues his daily and the moon her nightly journey across the sky, if the silent procession of the seasons moves in light and shadow across the earth, it is because they are all guided in their courses by a power superior to them all. "Verily O Gārgī, at the command of that Imperishable, the sun and the moon stand apart, the earth and the sky stand apart . . . the moments, the hours, the days, the nights, the fortnights, the months, the seasons and the years stand apart. Verily O Gārgī, at the command of that Imperishable, some rivers flow from the snowy mountains to the east, others to the west in whatever direction each flows."[1] There is

---

[1] *Brh. Up.*, iii. 8. 9.

the march of necessity everywhere. The universe is lawful to the core.

The theory of Karma recognizes the rule of law not only in outward nature, but also in the world of mind and morals. *Rta* manifests itself equally in nature and in human society. We are every moment making our characters and shaping our destinies. "There is no loss of any activity which we commence nor is there any obstacle to its fulfilment. Even a little good that we may do will protect us against great odds."[2] What we have set our hearts on will not perish with this body. This fact inspires life with the present sense of eternity.

At a time when people were doing devil's work under divine sanction and consoling themselves by attributing everything to God's will, the principle of Karma insisted on the primacy of the ethical and identified God with the rule of law. All's law, yet all's God. Karma is not a mechanical principle but a spiritual necessity. It is the embodiment of the mind and will of God. God is its supervisor, *karmādhyakṣaḥ*.[3] Justice is an attribute of God. Character of God is represented by St. James as one "with whom can be no variation neither shadow that is cast by turning." Every act, every thought is weighed in the invisible but universal balance-scales of justice. The day of judgment is not in some remote future, but here and now, and none can escape it. Divine laws cannot be evaded. They are not so much imposed from without as wrought into our natures. Sin is not so much a defiance of God as a denial of soul, not so much a violation of law as a betrayal of self. We carry with us the whole of our past. It is an ineffaceable record which time cannot blur nor death erase.

There is room for repentance and consequent forgiveness on this scheme. The critic who urges that belief in Karma makes religious life, prayer and worship impossible has not a right understanding of it. In his opinion God has abdicated in favour of his law. To pray to God is as futile a superstition as to bid the storm give us strength, or the earthquake to forgive us our sins. Of course the Hindu does not look upon prayer as a sort of Aladdin's lamp to produce anything we want. God is not a magician stopping the sun in its course and staying the bullet in its march. But his truth and constancy, his mercy and justice find their embodiment in the implacable working of the moral law. Forgiveness is not a mitigation of God's justice but only an expression of it. We can insist with unflinching rigour on the inexorability of the moral law and yet believe in the forgiveness of sins. Spiritual growth and experience are governed by laws similar to those which rule the rest of the universe. If we sow to the flesh we shall of the flesh reap corruption. The punishment for a desecrated body is an enfeebled understanding and a darkened soul. If we deliberately fall into sin, shutting our eyes to moral and spiritual light, we may be sure that in God's world sin will find us out and our wilful blindness will land us in the ditch. A just God cannot refuse to any man that which he has earned. The past guilt cannot be wiped away by the atoning suffering of an outward substitute.[4] Guilt cannot be transferred. It must be atoned for through the sorrow entailed by self-conquest. God cannot be bought over and sin cannot be glossed over.

The principle of Karma reckons with the material or the context in which each individual is born. While it regards the past as determined, it allows that the future is only conditioned. The spiritual element in man allows him freedom within the limits of his nature. Man is not a mere mechanism of instincts. The spirit in him can triumph over the automatic forces that try to enslave him. The *Bhagavadgītā* asks us to raise the self by the self. We can use the material with which we are endowed to promote our ideals. The cards in the game of life are given to us. We do not select them. They are traced to our past Karma, but we can call as we please, lead what suit we will, and as we play, we gain or lose. And there is freedom.

---

[2] *Bhagavadgītā*, iii. 40.
[3] *Śvet. Up.*, vi. 11.

[4] Cp. munir manute mūrkho mucyate. The monk meditates and the fool is freed.

What the individual will be cannot be predicted beforehand, though there is no caprice. We can predict an individual's acts so far as they are governed by habit, that is, to the extent his actions are mechanical and not affected by choice. But choice is not caprice. Free will in the sense of an undetermined, unrelated, uncaused factor in human action is not admitted, but such a will defies all analysis. It has nothing to do with the general stream of cause and effect. It operates in an irregular and chaotic way. If human actions are determined by such a will, there is no meaning in punishment or training of character. The theory of Karma allows man the freedom to use the material in the light of his knowledge. Man controls the uniformities in nature, his own mind and society. There is thus scope for genuine rational freedom, while indeterminism and chance lead to a false fatalism.

The universe is not one in which every detail is decreed. We do not have a mere unfolding of a pre-arranged plan. There is no such thing as absolute prescience on the part of God, for we are all his fellow-workers. God is not somewhere above us and beyond us, he is also in us. The divine in us can, if utilized, bring about even sudden conversions. Evolution in the sense of epigenesis is not impossible. For the real is an active developing life and not a mechanical routine.

The law of Karma encourages the sinner that it is never too late to mend. It does not shut the gates of hope against despair and suffering, guilt and peril. It persuades us to adopt a charitable view towards the sinner, for men are more often weak than vicious. It is not true that the heart of man is desperately wicked and that he prefers evil to good, the easy descent to hell to the steep ascent to heaven.

Unfortunately, the theory of Karma became confused with fatality in India when man himself grew feeble and was disinclined to do his best. It was made into an excuse for inertia and timidity and was turned into a message of despair and not of hope. It said to the sinner, "Not only are you a wreck, but that is all you ever could have been. That was your preordained being from the beginning of time." But such a philosophy of despair is by no means the necessary outcome of the doctrine of Karma.

QUESTIONS FOR DISCUSSION

1. Consider one example of belief in fatalism in our society, belief in astrology. Would this form of fatalism be subject to Motse's political critique? What do you think is the psychological and/or social function of this belief? Do you believe in predestination in any form? Why or why not?
2. Evaluate Radhakrishnan's claim that according to the laws of Karma the past is determined but the future is only conditioned. Do you believe that our actions for good or evil can determine our destiny? Do you think that you can change your destiny?

RADICAL FREEDOM

It is not easy to categorize the Russian writer Fyodor Dostoevsky (1821–1881). Generally considered one of the greatest novelists of all times—his novels include *Crime and Punishment* and *The Brothers Karamazov*—his fiction has profound psychological, social, and philosophical merit. The main character in *Notes from the Underground,* from which this selection is taken, is an isolated, alienated, and self-avowedly spiteful and perverse individual who spends the first part of this work alternatively engaging in philosophical reflections and taunting a reader who, as far as he is concerned, does not exist. It is his philosophical musings which concern us in this section, but they cannot be entirely divorced from the character he creates.

The key claim made by this "underground" man is that what is most important to human beings is the assumption of a radical freedom—a freedom which challenges natural laws, reason, and even enlightened self-interest. Throughout history, he asserts, "men, *consciously,* that is, fully understanding their real interests, have left them in the background and have rushed headlong on another path." This is because human beings will not (and must not) allow themselves to become the object of scientific laws or mathematical predictions, for then they would be, in his words, mere "piano-keys" and "organ-stops." If human desires can be determined by the precision of a mathematical formula, they lose their quality as desires, as life can be predicted and plotted in advance. Human beings will do anything, he insists, to assert their freedom of will, even what is injurious and stupid "in order to have the right to desire for himself even what is stupid." This is why, in the last analysis, Dostoevsky believes that social reform is at best useless and more often pernicious. He decries the "Palace of Crystal," a phrase that refers to Russian proponents of utopian socialist ideas. Dostoevsky's specific target was the literary critic and novelist N. G. Chernyshevsky, whose novel *What Is to Be Done?* inspired Vladimir I.

Lenin to write a revolutionary treatise of the same name.

Dostoevsky's ideas can be appreciated as an overture to the more systematic view of human freedom proposed by the French existentialist philosopher and novelist Jean-Paul Sartre. For Sartre, as for Dostoevsky, freedom is absolute and entails an absolute responsibility. This aspect of Sartre's position is expressed forcefully in the selection in Chapter 4. The selection that we are now going to consider comes from his major work *Being and Nothingness,* and is an attempt to analyze the nature of choice and to demonstrate how it is possible for our choices to be absolutely free.

Sartre's position rests on his claim about how motives are formed. Our actions, he acknowledges, are always determined in the sense that they have motives. But it is human consciousness that freely creates these motives. Our choices are free, not in the sense that they are unconnected to our motives, but insofar as consciousness, which always operates "for-itself," has the power to withdraw from what *is,* the "in-itself," at any moment, to recognize that something is lacking in the present state of affairs, and, thus, to present this "negation" as a motive for action. Since according to this view, it is the absence of something rather than its presence which motivates us, no existing state of affairs can be said to cause my actions. This does not mean that my choices are arbitrary and that they have no relation to my character or to my past experience; each individual choice is part of an ensemble of choices, of an "organic totality of the projects which I am." And this ensemble, this totality, must, in turn, be referred to my original project of being who I am. And this original project is itself a choice that relates my consciousness to my body and both my consciousness and my body to the world and to other persons. It is the fundamental choice of my "being-in-the-world." As I am always free to make a new fundamental choice, I am ultimately free to reconstruct myself.

NOTES FROM THE UNDERGROUND[1]

Fyodor Dostoevsky

I am a sick man. . . . I am a spiteful man. I am an unattractive man. I believe my liver is diseased. However, I know nothing at all about my disease, and do not know for certain what ails me. I don't consult a doctor for it, and never have, though I have a respect for medicine and doctors. Besides, I am extremely superstitious, sufficiently so to respect medicine, anyway (I am well-educated enough not to be superstitious, but I am superstitious). No, I refuse to consult a doctor from spite. That you probably will not understand. Well, I understand it, though. Of course, I can't explain who it is precisely that I am mortifying in this case by my spite: I am perfectly well aware that I cannot "pay out" the doctors by not consulting them; I know better than any one that by all this I am only injuring myself and no one else. But still, if I don't consult a doctor it is from spite. My liver is bad, well—let it get worse!

I have been going on like that for a long time—twenty years. Now I am forty. I used to be in the government service, but am no longer. I was a spiteful official. I was rude and took pleasure in being so. I did not take bribes, you see, so I was bound to find a recompense in that, at least. (A poor jest, but I will not scratch it out. I wrote it thinking it would sound very witty; but now that I have seen myself that I only wanted to show off in a despicable way, I will not scratch it out on purpose!)

. . .

I was lying when I said just now that I was a spiteful official. I was lying from spite. I was simply amusing myself with the petitioners and with the officer, and in reality I never could become spiteful. I was conscious every moment in myself of many, very many elements absolutely opposite to that. I felt them positively swarming in me, these opposite elements. I knew that they had been swarming in me all my life and craving some outlet from me, but I would not let them, would not let them, purposely would not let them come out. They tormented me till I was ashamed: they drove me to convulsions and—sickened me, at last, how they sickened me! Now, are not you fancying, gentlemen, that I am expressing remorse for something now, that I am asking your forgiveness for something? I am sure you are fancying that. . . . However, I assure you I do not care if you are. . . .

It was not only that I could not become spiteful, I did not know how to become anything: neither spiteful nor kind, neither a rascal nor an honest man, neither a hero nor an insect. Now, I am living out my life in my corner, taunting myself with the spiteful and useless consolation that an intelligent man cannot become anything seriously, and it is only the fool who becomes anything. Yes, a man in the nineteenth century must and morally ought to be pre-eminently a characterless creature; a man of character, an active man, is pre-eminently a limited creature. That is my conviction of forty years. I am forty years old now, and you know forty years is a whole lifetime; you know it is extreme old age. To live longer than forty years is bad manners, is vulgar, immoral. Who does live beyond forty? Answer that, sincerely and honestly. I will tell you who do: fools and worthless fellows. I tell all old men that to their face, all these venerable old men, all these silver-haired and reverend seniors! I tell the whole world that to its face. I have a right to say so, for I shall go on living to sixty myself. To seventy! To eighty! . . . Stay, let me take breath. . . .

---

[1] The author of the diary and the diary itself are, of course, imaginary. Nevertheless it is clear that such persons as the writer of these notes not only may, but positively must, exist in our society, when we consider the circumstances in the midst of which our society is formed. I have tried to expose to the view of the public more distinctly than is commonly done one of the characters of the recent past. He is one of the representatives of a generation still living. In this fragment, entitled "Underground," this person introduces himself and his views, and, as it were, tries to explain the causes owing to which he has made his appearance and was bound to make his appearance in our midst. In the second fragment there are added the actual notes of this person concerning certain events in his life.—AUTHOR'S NOTE

You imagine no doubt, gentlemen, that I want to amuse you. You are mistaken in that, too. I am by no means such a mirthful person as you imagine, or as you may imagine; however, irritated by all this babble (and I feel that you are irritated) you think fit to ask me who am I—then my answer is, I am a collegiate assessor. I was in the service that I might have something to eat (and solely for that reason), and when last year a distant relation left me six thousand roubles in his will I immediately retired from the service and settled down in my corner. I used to live in this corner before, but now I have settled down in it. My room is a wretched, horrid one in the outskirts of the town. My servant is an old country-woman, ill-natured from stupidity, and, moreover, there is always a nasty smell about her. I am told that the Petersburg climate is bad for me, and that with my small means it is very expensive to live in Petersburg. I know all that better than all these sage and experienced counsellors and monitors. . . . But I am remaining in Petersburg; I am not going away from Petersburg! I am not going away because . . . ech! Why, it is absolutely no matter whether I am going away or not going away.

But what can a decent man speak of with most pleasure?

Answer: Of himself.

Well, so I will talk about myself.

I want now to tell you, gentlemen, whether you care to hear it or not, why I could not even become an insect. I tell you solemnly, that I have many times tried to become an insect. But I was not equal even to that. I swear, gentlemen, that to be too conscious is an illness—a real thorough-going illness. For man's everyday needs, it would have been quite enough to have the ordinary human consciousness, that is, half or a quarter of the amount which falls to the lot of a cultivated man of our unhappy nineteenth century, especially one who has the fatal ill-luck to inhabit Petersburg, the most theoretical and intentional town ˙on the whole terrestrial globe. (There are intentional and unintentional towns.) It would have been quite enough, for instance, to have the consciousness by which all so-called direct per-

sons and men of action live. I bet you think I am writing all this from affectation, to be witty at the expense of men of action; and what is more, that from ill-bred affectation, I am clanking a sword like my officer. But, gentlemen, whoever can pride himself on his diseases and even swagger over them?

Though, after all, every one does do that; people do pride themselves on their diseases, and I do, may be, more than any one. We will not dispute it; my contention was absurd. But yet I am firmly persuaded that a great deal of consciousness, every sort of consciousness, in fact, is a disease. I stick to that. Let us leave that, too, for a minute. Tell me this: why does it happen that at the very, yes, at the very moments when I am most capable of feeling every refinement of all that is "good and beautiful," as they used to say at one time, it would, as though of design, happen to me not only to feel but to do such ugly things, such that . . . Well, in short, actions that all, perhaps, commit; but which, as though purposely, occurred to me at the very time when I was most conscious that they ought not to be committed. The more conscious I was of goodness and of all that was "good and beautiful," the more deeply I sank into my mire and the more ready I was to sink in it altogether. But the chief point was that all this was, as it were, not accidental in me, but as though it were bound to be so. It was as though it were my most normal condition, and not in the least disease or depravity, so that at last all desire in me to struggle against this depravity passed. It ended by my almost believing (perhaps actually believing) that this was perhaps my normal condition. But at first, in the beginning, what agonies I endured in that struggle! I did not beleive it was the same with other people, and all my life I hid this fact about myself as a secret. I was ashamed (even now, perhaps, I am ashamed): I got to the point of feeling a sort of secret abnormal, despicable enjoyment in returning home to my corner on some disgusting Petersburg night, acutely conscious that that day I had committed a loathsome action again, that what was done could never be undone, and secretly, inwardly gnawing, gnawing at myself for it, tearing and consuming myself till at last the bitterness turned into a sort of shameful accursed sweetness, and at last—into positive real enjoyment! Yes, into enjoyment, into enjoyment! I insist upon that. I have spoken of this because I keep wanting to know for a fact whether other people feel such enjoyment. I will explain: the enjoyment was just from the too intense consciousness of one's own degradation; it was from feeling oneself that one had reached the last barrier, that it was horrible, but that it could not be otherwise; that there was no escape for you; that you never could become a different man; that even if time and faith were still left you to change into something different you would most likely not wish to change; or if you did wish to, even then you would do nothing; because perhaps in reality there was nothing for you to change into.

And the worst of it was, and the root of it all, that it was all in accord with the normal fundamental laws of overacute consciousness, and with the inertia that was the direct result of those laws, and that consequently one was not only unable to change but could do absolutely nothing. Thus it would follow, as the result of acute consciousness, that one is not to blame in being a scoundrel; as though that were any consolation to the scoundrel once he has come to realize that he actually is a scoundrel. But enough. . . . Ech, I have talked a lot of nonsense, but what have I explained? How is enjoyment in this to be explained? But I will explain it. I will get to the bottom of it! That is why I have taken up my pen. . . .

• • •

But these are all golden dreams. Oh, tell me, who was it first announced, who was it first proclaimed, that man only does nasty things because he does not know his own interests; and that if he were enlightened, if his eyes were opened to his real normal interests, man would at once cease to do nasty things, would at once become good and noble because, being enlightened and understanding his real advantage, he would see his own advantage in the good and nothing else, and we all know that not one man can, consciously, act against his own interests, consequently, so to say, through necessity, he would

begin doing good? Oh, the babe! Oh, the pure, innocent child! Why, in the first place, when in all these thousands of years has there been a time when man has acted only from his own interest? What is to be done with the millions of facts that bear witness that men, *consciously,* that is, fully understanding their real interests, have left them in the background and have rushed headlong on another path, to meet peril and danger, compelled to this course by nobody and by nothing, but, as it were, simply disliking the beaten track, and have obstinately, wilfully, struck out another difficult, absurd way, seeking it almost in the darkness. So, I suppose, this obstinacy and perversity were pleasanter to them than any advantage. . . . Advantage! What is advantage?

And will you take it upon yourself to define with perfect accuracy in what the advantage of man consists? And what if it so happens that a man's advantage, *sometimes,* not only may, but even must, consist in his desiring in certain cases what is harmful to himself and not advantageous. And if so, there can be such a case, the whole principle falls into dust. What do you think—are there such cases? You laugh; laugh away, gentlemen, but only answer me: have men's advantages been reckoned up with perfect certainty? Are there not some which not only have not been included but cannot possibly be included under any classification? You see, you gentlemen have, to the best of my knowledge, taken your whole register of human advantages from the averages of statistical figures and politico-economical formulas. Your advantages are prosperity, wealth, freedom, peace—and so on, and so on. So that the man who should, for instance, go openly and knowingly in opposition to all that list would, to your thinking, and indeed mine too, of course, be an obscurantist or an absolute madman: would not he? But, you know, this is what is surprising: why does it so happen that all these statisticians, sages and lovers of humanity, when they reckon up human advantages invariably leave out one? They don't even take it into their reckoning in the form in which it should be taken and the whole reckoning depends upon that. It would be no great matter, they would simply have to take it, this advantage, and add it to the list. But the trouble is, that this strange advantage does not fall under any classification and is not in place in any list. I have a friend for instance . . . Ech! gentlemen, but of course he is your friend, too; and indeed there is no one, no one, to whom he is not a friend!

When he prepares for any undertaking this gentleman immediately explains to you, elegantly and clearly, exactly how he must act in accordance with the laws of reason and truth. What is more, he will talk to you with excitement and passion of the true normal interests of man; with irony he will upbraid the short-sighted fools who do not understand their own interests, nor the true significance of virtue; and, within a quarter of an hour, without any sudden outside provocation, but simply through something inside him which is stronger than all his interests, he will go off on quite a different tack—that is, act in direct opposition to what he has just been saying about himself, in opposition to the laws of reason, in opposition to his own advantage—in fact, in opposition to everything. . . . I warn you that my friend is a compound personality, and therefore it is difficult to blame him as an individual. The fact is, gentlemen, it seems there must really exist something that is dearer to almost every man than his greatest advantages, or (not to be illogical) there is a most advantageous advantage (the very one omitted of which we spoke just now) which is more important and more advantageous than all other advantages, for the sake of which a man if necessary is ready to act in opposition to all laws; that is, in opposition to reason, honour, peace, prosperity—in fact, in opposition to all those excellent and useful things if only he can attain that fundamental, most advantageous advantage which is dearer to him than all. "Yes, but it's advantage all the same" you will retort. But excuse me, I'll make the point clear, and it is not a case of playing upon words. What matters is, that this advantage is remarkable from the very fact that it breaks down all our classifications, and continually shatters every system constructed by lovers of mankind for the benefit of mankind. In fact, it upsets everything. But before I mention this advantage

to you, I want to compromise myself personally, and therefore I boldly declare that all these fine systems—all these theories for explaining to mankind their real normal interests, in order that inevitably striving to pursue these interests they may at once become good and noble—are, in my opinion, so far, mere logical exercises! Yes, logical exercises. Why, to maintain this theory of the regeneration of mankind by means of the pursuit of his own advantage is to my mind almost the same thing as . . . as to affirm, for instance, following Buckle, that through civilization mankind becomes softer, and consequently less bloodthirsty, and less fitted for warfare.

Logically it does seem to follow from his arguments. But man has such a predilection for systems and abstract deductions that he is ready to distort the truth intentionally, he is ready to deny the evidence of his senses only to justify his logic. I take this example because it is the most glaring instance of it. Only look about you: blood is being spilt in streams, and in the merriest way, as though it were champagne. Take the whole of the nineteenth century in which Buckle lived. Take Napoleon—the Great and also the present one. Take North America—the eternal union. Take the farce of Schleswig-Holstein.* . . . And what is it that civilization softens in us? The only gain of civilization for mankind is the greater capacity for variety of sensations—and absolutely nothing more. And through the development of this many-sidedness man may come to finding enjoyment in bloodshed. In fact, this has already happened to him. Have you noticed that it is the most civilized gentlemen who have been the subtlest slaughterers, to whom the Attilas and Stenka Razins could not hold a candle, and if they are not so conspicuous as the Attilas and Stenka Razins it is simply because they are so often met with, are so ordinary and have become so familiar to us. In any case civilization has made mankind if

---

* The nineteenth-century controversy of the status of the territories of Schleswig and Holstein led to two German-Danish wars (Eds.).

not more bloodthirsty, at least more vilely, more loathsomely blood-thirsty. In old days he saw justice in bloodshed and with his conscience at peace exterminated those he thought proper. Now we do think bloodshed abominable and yet we engage in this abomination, and with more energy than ever. Which is worse? Decide that for yourselves.

They say that Cleopatra (excuse an instance from Roman history) was fond of sticking gold pins into her slave-girls' breasts and derived gratification from their screams and writhings. You will say that that was in the comparatively barbarous times; that these are barbarous times too, because also, comparatively speaking, pins are stuck in even now; that though man has now learned to see more clearly than in barbarous ages, he is still far from having learnt to act as reason and science would dictate. But yet you are fully convinced that he will be sure to learn when he gets rid of certain old bad habits, and when common sense and science have completely re-educated human nature and turned it in a normal direction. You are confident that then man will cease from *intentional* error and will, so to say, be compelled not to want to set his will against his normal interests. That is not all; then, you say, science itself will teach man (though to my mind it's a superfluous luxury) that he never has really had any caprice or will of his own, and that he himself is something of the nature of a piano-key or the stop of an organ, and that there are, besides, things called the laws of nature; so that everything he does is not done by his willing it, but is done of itself, by the laws of nature. Consequently we have only to discover these laws of nature, and man will no longer have to answer for his actions and life will become exceedingly easy for him. All human actions will then, of course, be tabulated according to these laws, mathematically, like tables of logarithms up to 108,000, and entered in an index; or, better still, there would be published certain edifying works of the nature of encyclopaedic lexicons, in which everything will be so clearly calculated and explained that there will be no more incidents or adventures in the world.

Then—this is all what you say—new economic relations will be established, all ready-made and worked out with mathematical exactitude, so that every possible question will vanish in the twinkling of an eye, simply because every possible answer to it will be provided. Then the "Palace of Crystal" will be built. Then . . . In fact, those will be halcyon days. Of course there is no guaranteeing (this is my comment) that it will not be, for instance, frightfully dull then (for what will one have to do when everything will be calculated and tabulated?), but on the other hand everything will be extraordinarily rational. Of course boredom may lead you to anything. It is boredom sets one sticking golden pins into people, but all that would not matter. What is bad (this is my comment again) is that I dare say people will be thankful for the gold pins then. Man is stupid, you know, phenomenally stupid; or rather he is not at all stupid, but he is so ungrateful that you could not find another like him in all creation. I, for instance, would not be in the least surprised if all of a sudden, apropos of nothing, in the midst of general prosperity a gentleman with an ignoble, or rather with reactionary and ironical, countenance were to arise and putting his arms akimbo, say to us all: "I say, gentlemen, hadn't we better kick over the whole show and scatter rationalism to the winds, simply to send these logarithms to the devil, and to enable us to live once more at our own sweet foolish will!" That again would not matter; but what is annoying is that he would be sure to find followers—such is the nature of man. And all that for the most foolish reason, which, one would think, was hardly worth mentioning: that is, that man everywhere and at all times, whoever he may be, has preferred to act as he chose and not in the least as his reason and advantage dictated. And one may choose what is contrary to one's own interests, and sometimes one *positively ought* (that is my idea). One's own free unfettered choice, one's own caprice—however wild it may be, one's own fancy worked up at times to frenzy—is that very "most advantageous advantage" which we have overlooked, which comes under no classification and against which all systems and theories are continually being shattered to atoms. And how do these wiseacres know that man wants a normal, a virtuous choice? What has made them conceive that man must want a rationally advantageous choice? What man wants is simply *independent* choice, whatever that independence may cost and wherever it may lead. And choice, of course, the devil only knows what choice. . . .

"Ha! ha! ha! But you know there is no such thing as choice in reality, say what you like," you will interpose with a chuckle. "Science has succeeded in so far analyzing man that we know already that choice and what is called freedom of will is nothing else than—"

Stay, gentlemen, I meant to begin with that myself. I confess, I was rather frightened. I was just going to say that the devil only knows what choice depends on, and that perhaps that was a very good thing, but I remembered the teaching of science . . . and pulled myself up. And here you have begun upon it. Indeed, if there really is some day discovered a formula for all our desires and caprices—that is, an explanation of what they depend upon, by what laws they arise, how they develop, what they are aiming at in one case and in another and so on, that is, a real mathematical formula—then, most likely, man will at once cease to feel desire, indeed, he will be certain to. For who would want to choose by rule? Besides, he will at once be transformed from a human being into an organ-stop or something of the sort; for what is a man without desires, without free will and without choice, if not a stop in an organ? What do you think? Let us reckon the chances—can such a thing happen or not?

"H'm!" you decide. "Our choice is usually mistaken from a false view of our advantage. We sometimes choose absolute nonsense because in our foolishness we see in that nonsense the easiest means for attaining a supposed advantage. But when all that is explained and worked out on paper (which is perfectly possible, for it is contemptible and senseless to suppose that some laws of nature man will never understand), then certainly so-called desires will no longer exist. For if a desire should

come into conflict with reason we shall then reason and not desire, because it will be impossible retaining our reason to be *senseless* in our desires, and in that way knowingly act against reason and desire to injure ourselves. And as all choice and reasoning can be really calculated—because there will some day be discovered the laws of our so-called free will—so, joking apart, there may one day be something like a table constructed of them, so that we really shall choose in accordance with it. If, for instance, some day they calculate and prove to me that I made a long nose at some one because I could not help making a long nose at him and that I had to do it in that particular way, what *freedom* is left me, especially if I am a learned man and have taken my degree somewhere? Then I should be able to calculate my whole life for thirty years beforehand. In short, if this could be arranged there would be nothing left for us to do; anyway, we should have to understand that. And, in fact, we ought unwearyingly to repeat to ourselves that at such and such a time and in such and such circumstances Nature does not ask our leave; that we have got to take her as she is and not fashion her to suit our fancy, and if we really aspire to formulas and tables of rules, and well, even . . . to the chemical retort, there's no help for it, we must accept the retort too, or else it will be accepted without our consent. . . ."

Yes, but here I come to a stop! Gentlemen, you must excuse me for being over-philosophical; it's the result of forty years underground! Allow me to indulge my fancy. You see, gentlemen, reason is an excellent thing, there's no disputing that, but reason is nothing but reason and satisfies only the rational side of man's nature, while will is a manifestation of the whole life, that is, of the whole human life including reason and all the impulses. And although our life, in this manifestation of it, is often worthless, yet it is life and not simply extracting square roots. Here I, for instance, quite naturally want to live, in order to satisfy all my capacities for life, and not simply my capacity for reasoning, that is, not simply one-twentieth of my capacity for life. What does reason know? Reason only knows what it has succeeded in learning (some things, perhaps, it will never learn; this is a poor comfort, but why not say so frankly?) and human nature acts as a whole, with everything that is in it, consciously or unconsciously, and, even if it goes wrong, it lives. I suspect, gentlemen, that you are looking at me with compassion; you tell me again that an enlightened and developed man, such, in short, as the future man will be, cannot consciously desire anything disadvantageous to himself, that that can be proved mathematically. I thoroughly agree, it can—by mathematics.

But I repeat for the hundredth time, there is one case, one only, when man may consciously, purposely, desire what is injurious to himself, what is stupid, very stupid—simply in order to have the right to desire for himself even what is very stupid and not to be bound by an obligation to desire only what is sensible. Of course, this very stupid thing, this caprice of ours, may be in reality, gentlemen, more advantageous for us than anything else on earth, especially in certain cases. And in particular it may be more advantageous than any advantage even when it does us obvious harm, and contradicts the soundest conclusions of our reason concerning our advantage—for in any circumstances it preserves for us what is more precious and most important—that is, our personality, our individuality. Some, you see, maintain that this really is the most precious thing for mankind; choice can, of course, if it chooses, be in agreement with reason; and especially if this be not abused but kept within bounds. It is profitable and sometimes even praiseworthy. But very often, and even most often, choice is utterly and stubbornly opposed to reason . . . and . . . and . . . do you know that that, too, is profitable, sometimes even praiseworthy? Gentlemen, let us suppose that man is not stupid. (Indeed one cannot refuse to suppose that, if only from the one consideration, that, if man is stupid, then who is wise?) But if he is not stupid, he is monstrously ungrateful! Phenomenally ungrateful. In fact, I believe that the best definition of man is the ungrateful biped. But that is not all, that is not his worst defect; his worst

defect is his perpetual moral obliquity, perpetual—from the days of the Flood to the Schleswig-Holstein period.

Moral obliquity and consequently lack of good sense; for it has long been accepted that lack of good sense is due to no other cause than moral obliquity. Put it to the test and cast your eyes upon the history of mankind. What will you see? Is it a grand spectacle? Grand, if you like. Take the Colossus of Rhodes,* for instance, that's worth something. With good reason Mr. Anaevsky testifies of it that some say that it is the work of man's hands, while others maintain that it has been created by Nature herself. Is it many-coloured? It may be it is many-coloured, too: if one takes the dress uniforms, military and civilian, of all peoples in all ages—that alone is worth something, and if you take the undress uniforms you will never get to the end of it; no historian would be equal to the job. Is it monotonous? It may be it's monotonous too: it's fighting and fighting; they are fighting now, they fought first and they fought last—you will admit that it is almost too monotonous. In short, one may say anything about the history of the world—anything that might enter the most disordered imagination.

The only thing one can't say is that it's rational. The very word sticks in one's throat. And, indeed, this is the odd thing that is continually happening: there are continually turning up in life moral and rational persons, sages and lovers of humanity, who make it their object to live all their lives as morally and rationally as possible, to be, so to speak, a light to their neighbours simply in order to show them that it is possible to live morally and rationally in this world. And yet we all know that those very people sooner or later have been false to themselves, playing some queer trick, often a most unseemly one. Now I ask you: what can be expected of man since he is a being endowed with such strange qual-

---

* The *Colossus of Rhodes* was a bronze statue over 100 feet high representing the ancient sun god Helios. It took twelve years to build (292–280 B.C.E.) and commemorated the raising of the siege in Rhodes 12 years earlier (Eds.).

ities? Shower upon him every earthly blessing, drown him in a sea of happiness, so that nothing but bubbles of bliss can be seen on the surface; give him economic prosperity, such that he should have nothing else to do but sleep, eat cakes and busy himself with the continuation of his species, and even then out of sheer ingratitude, sheer spite, man would play you some nasty trick. He would even risk his cakes and would deliberately desire the most fatal rubbish, the most uneconomical absurdity, simply to introduce into all this positive good sense his fatal fantastic element. It is just his fantastic dreams, his vulgar folly, that he will desire to retain, simply in order to prove to himself—as though that were so necessary—that men still are men and not the keys of a piano, which the laws of nature threaten to control so completely that soon one will be able to desire nothing but by the calendar. And that is not all: even if man really were nothing but a piano-key, even if this were proved to him by natural science and mathematics, even then he would not become reasonable, but would purposely do something perverse out of simple ingratitude, simply to gain his point. And if he does not find means he will contrive destruction and chaos, will contrive sufferings of all sorts, only to gain his point! He will launch a curse upon the world, and as only man can curse (it is his privilege, the primary distinction between him and other animals) it may be by his curse alone he will attain his object—that is, convince himself that he is a man and not a piano-key! If you say that all this, too, can be calculated and tabulated—chaos and darkness and curses, so that the mere possibility of calculating it all beforehand would stop it all, and reason would reassert itself—then man would purposely go mad in order to be rid of reason and gain his point! I believe in it, I answer for it, for the whole work of man really seems to consist in nothing but proving to himself every minute that he is a man and not a piano-key! It may be at the cost of his skin, it may be by cannibalism! And this being so, can one help being tempted to rejoice that it has not yet come off, and that desire still depends on something we don't know?

You will scream at me (that is, if you condescend

to do so) that no one is touching my free will, that all they are concerned with is that my will should of itself, of its own free will, coincide with my own normal interests, with the laws of nature and arithmetic.

Good heavens, gentlemen, what sort of free will is left when we come to tabulation and arithmetic, when it will all be a case of twice two makes four? Twice two makes four without my will. As if free will meant that!

FREEDOM AND ACTION

Jean-Paul Sartre

It is strange that philosophers have been able to argue endlessly about determinism and free-will, to cite examples in favor of one or the other thesis without ever attempting first to make explicit the structures contained in the very idea of *action*. The concept of an act contains, in fact, numerous subordinate notions which we shall have to organize and arrange in a hierarchy: to act is to modify the *shape* of the world; it is to arrange means in view of an end; it is to produce an organized instrumental complex such that by a series of concatenations and connections the modification effected on one of the links causes modifications throughout the whole series and finally produces an anticipated result. But this is not what is important for us here. We should observe first that an action is on principle *intentional*. The careless smoker who has through negligence caused the explosion of a powder magazine has not *acted*. On the other hand the worker who is charged with dynamiting a quarry and who obeys the given orders has acted when he has produced the expected explosion; he knew what he was doing or, if you prefer, he intentionally realized a conscious project.

This does not mean, of course, that one must foresee all the consequences of his act. The emperor

Constantine when he established himself at Byzantium, did not foresee that he would create a center of Greek culture and language, the apperance of which would ultimately provoke a schism in the Christian Church and which would contribute to weakening the Roman Empire. Yet he performed an act just in so far as he realized his project of creating a new residence for emperors in the Orient. Equating the result with the intention is here sufficient for us to be able to speak of action. But if this is the case, we establish that the action necessarily implies as its condition the recognition of a "desideratum"; that is, of an objective lack or again of a *négatité*.* *The intention* of providing a rival for Rome can come to Constantine only through the apprehension of an objective lack: Rome lacks a counterweight; to this still profoundly pagan city ought to be opposed a Christian city which at the moment is *missing.* Creating Constantinople is understood as an *act* only if first the conception of a new city has preceded the action itself or at least if this conception serves as an organizing theme for all later steps. But this conception can not be the pure representation of the city as *possible.* It apprehends the city in its essential characteristic, which is to be a *desirable* and not yet realized possible.

This means that from the moment of the first conception of the act, consciousness has been able to withdraw itself from the full world of which it is consciousness and to leave the level of being in order frankly to approach that of non-being. Conciousness in so far as it is considered exclusively in its being, is perpetually referred from being to being and can not find in being any motive for revealing non-being. The imperial system with Rome as its capital functions positively and in a certain real way which can be easily discovered. Will someone say that the taxes are collected badly, that Rome is not secure from invasions, that it does not have the geographical location which is suitable for the capital of a Mediterranean empire which is threatened by

barbarians, that its corrupt morals make the spread of the Christian religion difficult? How can anyone fail to see that all these considerations are *negative;* that is, that they aim at what is not, not at what is. To say that sixty per cent of the anticipated taxes have been collected can pass, if need be for a positive appreciation of the situation *such as it is.* To say that they are *badly* collected is to consider the situation across a situation which is posited as an absolute end but which precisely is *not.* To say that the corrupt morals at Rome hinder the spread of Christianity is not to consider this diffusion for what it is; that is, for a propagation at a rate which the reports of the clergy can enable us to determine. It is to posit the diffusion in itself as insufficient; that is, as suffering from a secret nothingness. But it appears as such only if it is surpassed toward a limiting-situation posited *a priori** as a value (for example, toward a certain rate of religious conversions, toward a certain mass morality). This limiting-situation can not be conceived in terms of the simple consideration of the real state of things; for the most beautiful girl in the world can offer only what she *has,* and in the same way the most miserable situation can by itself be designated only as it *is* without any reference to an ideal nothingness.

In so far as man is immersed in the historical situation, he does not even succeed in conceiving of the failures and lacks in a political organization or determined economy; this is not, as is stupidly said, because he "is accustomed to it," but because he apprehends it in its plenitude of being and because he can not even imagine that he can exist in it otherwise. For it is necessary here to reverse common opinion and on the basis of what it is not, to acknowledge the harshness of a situation or the sufferings which it imposes, both of which are motives for conceiving of another state of affairs in which things would be better for everybody. It is on the day that we can conceive of a different state of af-

---

* *Négatité* is Sartre's word for what is experienced as lacking or absent in the situation, e.g., that which is desired but does not exist.

* *a priori* is a Latin phrase meaning, literally, "from what comes before." In philosophy, it refers to something which precedes or is independent of sensory experience. Thus, what is *a priori* is true, valid, or exists by necessity (Eds.).

fairs that a new light falls on our troubles and our suffering and that we *decide* that these are unbearable. A worker in 1830 is capable of revolting if his salary is lowered, for he easily conceives of a situation in which his wretched standard of living would be not as low as the one which is about to be imposed on him. But he does not represent his sufferings to himself as unbearable; he adapts himself to them not through resignation but because he lacks the education and reflection necessary for him to conceive of a social state in which these sufferings would not exist. Consequently *he does not act.* Masters of Lyon following a riot, the workers at Croix-Rousse do not know what to do with their victory; they return home bewildered, and the regular army has no trouble in overcoming them. Their misfortunes do not appear to them "habitual" but rather *natural;* they *are,* that is all, and they constitute the worker's condition. They are not detached; they are not seen in the clear light of day, and consequently they are integrated by the worker with his being. He suffers without considering his suffering and without conferring value upon it. To suffer and to *be* are one and the same for him. His suffering is the pure affective tenor of his nonpositional consciousness, but he does not *contemplate* it. Therefore this suffering can not be in itself a *motive* for his acts. Quite the contrary, it is after he has formed the project of changing the situation that it will appear intolerable to him. This means that he will have had to give himself room, to withdraw in relation to it, and will have to have effected a double nihilation: on the one hand, he must posit an ideal state of affairs as a pure *present* nothingness; on the other hand, he must posit the actual situation as nothingness in relation to this state of affairs. He will have to conceive of a happiness attached to his class as a pure possible—that is, presently as a certain nothingness—and on the other hand, he will return to the present situation in order to illuminate it in the light of this nothingness and in order to nihilate it in turn by declaring: "I *am not* happy."

Two important consequences result. (1) No factual state whatever it may be (the political and economic structure of society, the psychological "state," *etc.*) is capable by itself of motivating any act whatsoever. For an act is a projection of the for-itself toward what is not, and what is can in no way determine by itself what is not. (2) No factual state can determine consciousness to apprehend it as a *négatité* or as a lack. Better yet no factual state can determine consciousness to define it and to circumscribe it since, as we have seen, Spinoza's statement, "Omnis determinatio est negatio," remains profoundly true. Now every action has for its express condition not only the discovery of a state of affairs as "lacking in——," *i.e.,* as a *négatité*—but also, and before all else, the constitution of the state of things under consideration into an isolated system. There is a factual state—satisfying or not—only by means of the nihilating power of the for-itself. But this power of nihilation can not be limited to realizing a simple *withdrawal* in relation to the world. In fact in so far as consciousness is "invested" by being, in so far as it simply suffers what is, it must be included in being. It is the organized form—worker-finding-his-suffering-natural—which must be surmounted and denied in order for it to be able to form the object of a revealing contemplation. This means evidently that it is by a pure wrenching away from himself and the world that the worker can posit his suffering as unbearable suffering and consequently cane *make of it the motive* for his revolutionary action. This implies for consciousness the permanent possibility of effecting a rupture with its own past, of wrenching itself away from its past so as to be able to consider it in the light of a non-being and so as to be able to confer on it the meaning which *it has* in terms of the project of a meaning which it *does not have.* Under no circumstances can the past in any way by itself produce *an act;* that is, the positing of an end which turns back upon itself so as to illuminate it. This is what Hegel caught sight of when he wrote that "the mind is the negative," although he seems not to have remembered this when he came to presenting his own theory of action and of freedom. In fact as soon as one attributes to consciousness this negative power with respect to the world and itself, as soon as the nihilation forms an integral part of the *positing* of an end, we must recognize that the indispensable and fundamental condition of all action is the freedom of the acting being.

Thus at the outset we can see what is lacking in those tedious discussions between determinists and the proponents of free will. The latter are concerned to find cases of decision for which there exists no prior cause, or deliberations concerning two opposed acts which are equally possible and possess causes (and motives) of exactly the same weight. To which the determinists may easily reply that there is no action without a cause and that the most insignificant gesture (raising the right hand rather than the left hand, *etc.*) refers to causes and motives which confer its meaning upon it. Indeed the case could not be otherwise since every action must be *intentional;* each action must, in fact, have an end, and the end in turn is referred to a cause. Such indeed is the unity of the three temporal ekstases*; the end or temporalization of my future implies a cause (or motive); that is, it points toward my past, and the present is the upsurge of the act. To speak of an act without a cause is to speak of an act which would lack the intentional structure of every act; and the proponents of free will by searching for it on the level of the act which is in the process of being performed can only end up by rendering the act absurd. But the determinists in turn are weighting the scale by stopping their investigation with the mere designation of the cause and motive. The essential question in fact lies beyond the complex organization "cause-intention-act-end"; indeed we ought to ask how a cause (or motive) can be constituted as such.

Now we have just seen that if there is no act without a cause, this is not in the sense that we can say that there is no phenomenon without a cause. In order to be a *cause,* the *cause* must be *experienced* as such. Of course this does not mean that it is to be thematically conceived and made explicit as in the case of deliberation. But at the very least it means that the for-itself* must confer on it its value as cause or motive. And, as we have seen, this constitution of the cause as such can not refer to another real and positive existence; that is, to a prior cause. For otherwise the very nature of the act as engaged intentionally in non-being would disappear. The motive is understood only by the end; that is, by the non-existent. It is therefore in itself a négatité. If I accept a niggardly salary it is doubtless because of fear; and fear is a motive. But it is *fear of dying from starvation;* that is, this fear has meaning only outside itself in an end ideally posited, which is the preservation of a life which I apprehend as "in danger." And this fear is understood in turn only in relation to the *value which I* implicitly give to this life; that is, it is referred to that hierarchal system of ideal objects which are values. Thus the motive makes itself understood as what it is by means of the ensemble of beings which "are not," by ideal existences, and by the future. Just as the future turns back upon the present and the past in order to elucidate them, so it is the ensemble of my projects which turns back in order to confer upon the *motive* its structure as a motive. It is only because I escape the in-itself† by nihilating myself toward my possibilities that this in-itself can take on value as cause or motive. Causes and motives have meaning only inside a projected ensemble which is precisely an ensemble of non-existents. And this ensemble is ultimately myself as transcendence; it is Me in so far as I have to be myself outside of myself.

If we recall the principle which we established earlier—namely that it is the apprehension of a revolution as possible which gives to the workman's suffering its value as a motive—we must thereby conclude that it is by fleeing a situation toward our

---

* *Temporal ekstases* are the temporal dimensions of existence—past, present, and future (Eds.).

* *For-itself* refers to the ability of consciousness to be for itself, to withdraw from and be always moving beyond the given, to be able to act on the given. Consciousness, then, is not a thing in the world but exists, according to Sartre, only for itself as consciousness (Eds.).

† *In-itself* is the given; what there is to be acted upon and transcended by consciousness, by the for-itself (Eds.).

possibility of changing it that we organize this situation into complexes of causes and motives. The nihilation by which we achieve a withdrawal in relation to the situation is the same as the ekstasis by which we project ourselves toward a modification of this situation. The result is that it is in fact impossible to find an act without a motive but that this does not mean that we must conclude that the motive causes the act; the motive is an integral part of the act. For as the resolute project toward a change is not distinct from the act, the motive, the act, and the end are all constituted in a single upsurge. Each of the these three structures claims the two others as its meaning. But the organized totality of the three is no longer explained by any particular structure, and its upsurge as the pure temporalizing nihilation of the in-itself is one with freedom. It is the act which decides its ends and its motives, and the act is the expression of freedom.

*   *   *

By the same token freedom appears as an unanalyzable totality; causes, motives, and ends, as well as the mode of apprehending causes, motives, and ends, are organized in a unity within the compass of this freedom and must be understood in terms of it. Does this mean that one must view freedom as a series of carpricious jerks comparable to the Epicurean clinamen? Am I free to wish anything whatsoever at any moment whatsoever? And must I at each instant when I wish to explain this or that project encounter the irrationality of a free and contingent choice? Inasmuch as it has seemed that the recognition of freedom had as its consequence these dangerous conceptions which are completely contradictory to experience, worthy thinkers have turned away from a belief in freedom. One could even state that determinism—if one were careful not to confuse it with fatalism—is "more human" than the theory of free will. In fact while determinism throws into relief the strict conditioning of our acts, it does at least give the *reason* for each of them. And if it is strictly limited to the psychic, if it gives up looking for a conditioning in the ensemble of the universe, it shows that the reason for our acts

is in ourselves: we act as we are, and our acts contribute to making us.

*   *   *

Thus we do not intend here to speak of anything arbitrary or capricious. An existent which as consciousness is necessarily separated from all others because they are in connection with it only to the extent that they are *for it,* an existent which decides its past in the form of a tradition in the light of its future instead of allowing it purely and simply to determine its present, an existent which makes known to itself what it is by means of *something other than it* (that is, by an end which it is not and which it projects from the other side of the world)— this is what we call a free existent. This does not mean that I am free to get up or to sit down, to enter or to go out, to flee or to face danger—if one means by freedom here a pure capricious, unlawful, gratuitous, and incomprehensible contingency. To be sure, each one of my acts, even the most trivial, is entirely free in the sense which we have just defined; but this does not mean that my act can be anything *whatsoever* or even that it is *unforeseeable.* Someone, nevertheless may object and ask how if my act can be understood *neither* in terms of the state of the world *nor* in terms of the ensemble of my past taken as an irremediable thing, it could possibly be anything but gratuitous. Let us look more closely.

Common opinion does not hold that to be free means only to choose oneself. A choice is said to be free if it is such that it could have been other than what it is. I start out on a hike with friends. At the end of several hours of walking my fatigue increases and finally becomes very painful. At first I resist and then suddenly I let myself go, I give up, I throw my knapsack down on the side of the road and let myself fall down beside it. Someone will reproach me for my act and will mean thereby that I was free—that is, not only was my act not determined by any thing or person, but also I could have succeeded in resisting my fatigue longer, I could have done as my companions did and reached the resting place before relaxing. I shall defend myself by saying that I was *too tired.* Who is right? Or rather is the debate not based on incorrect premises? There is no doubt that I could have done otherwise, but that is not the problem. It ought to be formulated rather like this: could I have done otherwise without perceptibly modifying the organic totality of the projects which I am; or is the fact of resisting my fatigue such that instead of remaining a purely local and accidental modification of my behavior, it could be effected only by means of a radical transformation of my being-in-the-world—a tranformation, moreover, which is *possible?* In other words: I could have done otherwise. Agreed, But *at what price?*

We are going to reply to this question by first presenting a *theoretical* description which will enable us to grasp the principle of our thesis. We shall see subsequently whether the concrete reality is not shown to be more complex and whether without contradicting the results of our theoretical inquiry, it will not lead us to enrich them and make them more flexible.

Let us note first that the fatigue by itself could not provoke my decision. As we saw with respect to physical pain, fatigue is only the way in which I exist my body.* It is not at first the object of a positional consciousness,† but it is the very facticity of my consciousness. If then I hike across the country, what is revealed to me is the surrounding world; this is the object of my consciousness, and this is what I transcend toward possibilities which are my own—those, for example, of arriving this evening at the place which I have set for myself in advance. Yet to the extent that I apprehend this countryside with my eyes which unfold distances, my legs which climb the hills and consequently cause new sights and new obstacles to appear and disappear,

with my back which carries the knapsack—to this extent I have a non-positional consciousness (of) this body which rules my relations with the world and which signifies my engagement in the world, in the form of fatigue. Objectively and in correlation with this non-thetic consciousness the roads are revealed as interminable, the slopes as *steeper,* the sun as more burning, *etc.* But I do not yet *think* of my fatigue; I apprehend it as the quasi-object of my reflection. Nevertheless there comes a moment when I do seek to consider my fatigue and to recover it. We really ought to provide an interpretation for this same intention; however, let us take it for what it is. It is not at all a contemplative apprehension of my fatigue; rather, as we saw with respect to pain, I *suffer* my fatigue. That is, a reflective consciousness is directed upon my fatigue in order to live it and to confer on it a value and a practical relation to myself. It is only on this plane that the fatigue will appear to me as bearable or intolerable. It will never be anything in itself, but it is the reflective For-itself which rising up suffers the fatigue as intolerable.

Here is posited the essential question: my companions are in good health—like me; they have had practically the same training as I so that although it is not possible to *compare* psychic events which occur in different subjectivities, I usually conclude—and witnesses after an objective consideration of our bodies-for-others conclude—that they are for all practical purposes "as fatigued as I am." How does it happen therefore that they suffer their fatigue differently? Someone will say that the difference stems from the fact that I am a "sissy" and that the others are not. But although this evaluation undeniably has a practical bearing on the case and although one could take this into account when there arose a question of deciding whether or not it would be a good idea to take me on another expedition, such an evaluation can not satisfy us here. We have seen that to be ambitious is to project conquering a throne or honors; it is not a *given* which would incite one to conquest; it is this conquest itself. Similarly to be a "sissy" can not be a factual given and is only a name given to the way in which I suffer my fatigue. If therefore I wish to understand

---

* Sartre is intentionally using the phrase *"exist my body"* to indicate that I do not exist *in* my body, for that would mean that I am separate from my body (Eds.).

† *Positional consciousness* is consciousness which is aware of itself, according to Sartre. If it is only conscious of any object (and not reflecting upon itself), it is nonpositional consciousness (Eds.).

under what conditions I can suffer a fatigue as unbearable, it will not help to address oneself to so-called factual givens, which are revealed as being only a choice; it is necessary to attempt to examine this choice itself and to see whether it is not explained within the perspective of a larger choice in which it would be integrated as a secondary structure. If I question one of my companions, he will explain to me that he is fatigued, of course, but that he *loves* his fatigue; he gives himself up to it as to a bath; it appears to him in some way as the privileged instrument for discovering the world which surrounds him, for adapting himself to the rocky roughness of the paths, for discovering the "mountainous" quality of the slopes. In the same way it is this light sunburn on the back of his neck and this slight ringing in his ears which will enable him to realize a direct contact with the sun. Finally the feeling of effort is for him that of fatigue overcome. But as his fatigue is nothing but the passion which he endures so that the dust of the highways, the burning of the sun, the roughness of the roads may exist to the fullest, his effort (*i.e.,* this sweet familiarity with a fatigue which he loves, to which he abandons himself and which nevertheless he himself directs) is given as a way of appropriating the mountain, of suffering it to the end and being victor over it. We shall see in the next chapter what is the meaning of the word *having* and to what extent *doing* is a method of *appropriating.* Thus my companion's fatigue is lived in a vaster project of a trusting abandon to nature, of a passion consented to in order that it may exist at full strength, and at the same time the project of sweet mastery and appropriation. It is only in and through this project that the fatigue will be able to be understood and that it will have meaning for him.

But this meaning and this vaster, more profound project are still by themselves *unselbständig.* They are not sufficient. For they precisely presuppose a particular relation of my companion to his body, on the one hand, and to things, on the other. It is easy to see, indeed, that there are as many ways of existing one's body as there are For-itselfs although naturally certain original structures are invariable and

in each For-itself constitute human-reality. We shall be concerned elsewhere with what is incorrectly called the relation of the individual to space and to the conditions of a universal truth. For the moment we can conceive in connection with thousands of meaningful events that there is, for example, a certain type of flight before facticity, a flight which consists precisely in abandoning oneself to this facticity; that is, in short, in trustingly reassuming it and loving it in order to try to recover it. This original project of recovery is therefore a certain choice which the For-itself makes of itself in the presence of the problem of being. Its project remains a nihilation, but this nihilation turns back upon the in-itself which it nihilates and expresses itself by a particular valorization of facticity. This is expressed especially by the thousands of behavior patterns called *abandon.* To abandon oneself to fatigue, to warmth, to hunger, to thirst, to let oneself fall back upon a chair or a bed with sensual pleasure, to relax, to attempt to let oneself be drunk in by one's own body, not now beneath the eyes of others as in masochism but in the original solitude of the For-itself—none of these types of behavior can ever be confined to itself. We perceive this clearly since in another person they irritate or attract. Their condition is an initial project of the recovery of the body; that is, an attempt at a solution of the problem of the absolute (of the In-itself-for-itself).*

This initial form can itself be limited to a profound acceptance of facticity; the project of "making oneself body" will mean then a happy abandon to a thousand little passing gluttonies, to a thousand little desires, a thousand little weaknesses. One may recall from Joyce's *Ulysses* Mr. Bloom satisfying his natural needs and inhaling with favor "the intimate odor rising from beneath him." But it is also possible (and this is the case with my companion)

---

* The *In-itself-for-itself* describes an impossible task, as the in-itself is the given and the for-itself is the movement of consciousness beyond the given. The phrase is ironic in that Sartre believes that human beings strive to become this impossibility. God is the only being who could be in-itself and for-itself simultaneously, completely within the world (immanent), yet beyond it (transcendent). And, for Sartre, there is no God (Eds.).

that by means of the body and by compliance to the body, the For-itself seeks to recover the totality of the non-conscious—that is, the whole universe as the ensemble of material *things*. In this case the desired synthesis of the in-itself with the for-itself will be the quasi pantheistic synthesis of the totality of the in-itself with the for-itself which recovers it. Here the body is the instrument of the synthesis; it loses itself in fatigue, for example, in order that this in-itself may exist to the fullest. And since it is the body which the for-itself exists as its own, this passion of the body coincides for the for-itself with the project of "making the in-itself exist." The ensemble of this attitude—which is that of one of my companions—can be expressed by the dim feeling of a kind of mission: he is going on this expedition because the mountain which he is going to climb and the forests which he is going to cross *exist;* his mission is to be the one by whom their meaning will be made manifest. Therefore he attempts to be the one who founds them in their very existence.

• • •

. . . It is evident following our analysis that the way in which my companion *suffers* his fatigue necessarily demands—if we are to understand it—that we undertake a regressive analysis which will lead us back to an initial project. Is this project we have outlined finally *selbständig?* Certainly—and it can be easily proved to be so. In fact by going further and further back we have reached the original relation which the for-itself chooses with its facticity and with the world. But this original relation is nothing other than the for-itself's being-in-the-world inasmuch as this being-in-the-world is a choice—that is, we have reached the original type of nihilation by which the for-itself has to be its own nothingness. No interpretation of this can be attempted, for it would implicitly suppose the being-in-the-world of the for-itself just as all the demonstrations attempted by Euclid's Postulate implicitly suppose the adoption of this postulate.

Therefore if I apply this same method to interpret the way in which I suffer my fatigue, I shall first apprehend in myself a distrust of my body—for example, a way of wishing not "to have anything to do with it," wanting not to take it into account, which is simply one of numerous possible modes in which I can *exist my body*. I shall easily discover an analogous distrust with respect to the in-itself and, for example, an original project for recovering the in-itself which I nihilate *through the intermediacy of others,* which project in turn refers me to one of the initial projects which we enumerated in our preceding discussion. Hence my fatigue instead of being suffered "flexibly" will be grasped "sternly" as an importunate phenomenon which I want to get rid of—and this simply because it incarnates my body and my brute contingency in the midst of the world at a time when my project is to preserve my body and my presence in the world by means of the looks of others. I am referred to myself as well as to my original project; that is, to my being-in-the-world in so far as this being is a choice.

QUESTIONS FOR DISCUSSION

1. Is Dostoevsky's underground man expressing any truths about the human condition (if so, what are they), or is he merely expressing his own very peculiar personality?

2. Analyze Sartre's example of the hiker who says that he is too tired to continue. How does Sartre interpret this situation as an example of freedom? What is your evaluation of Sartre's position?

3. Sartre believes that we are absolutely free in the sense that nothing but our free choices determine what we do and who we are. Do you agree or disagree? In arguing for your own position, use examples from your own life.

HUMAN BEINGS ARE NOT FREE

In the preceding section we saw how the radical freedom advocated by both Dostoevsky and Sartre puts human beings outside the natural laws of the universe and detaches the individual from his or her social conditions and past experience. A will that is absolutely free is a will that is not determined by anything outside itself. The authors represented in this section challenge that assumption and insist that who we are and what we do is determined by various factors outside ourselves. They insist, in effect, that human beings are not exceptions to the causal laws of the universe. This is the thesis of determinism.

We begin this section with a selection by Okot p'Bitek, who is a well-known East African poet and cultural critic. P'Bitek argues that the individual can never be separated from the society of which he or she is a part, because the very sense of who one is is always bound to a set of institutions and the roles that an individual occupies within those institutions. In sum, the "I" cannot stand alone, because it is itself constituted through the network of social relations within which it is embedded. Thus, "permanent bondage seems to be man's fate."

The next selection in this section is by the contemporary psychologist B. F. Skinner (1904–1990), perhaps the best-known representative of the behaviorist movement in the United States. Behaviorism as a systematic psychological theory was first developed in the United States by the early-twentieth-century psychologist John B. Watson, who insisted that if psychology was ever to become a rigorous experimental science, it must give up its introspective orientation. Psychology must no longer attempt to describe or analyze such intrinsically private states as feeling, thought, or desires and must focus instead on the relations between publically observable behavior and the environment. For Watson the key to this relation was the *conditioned reflex* which transferred a "response" from one "stimulus" to another. For example, as the famous Russian psychologist Ivan Petrovich Pavlov had demonstrated, a hungry dog presented with food and the ringing of a bell would eventually salivate when only the bell (the new stimulus) was rung.

B. F. Skinner, although agreeing with Watson's emphasis on the relation between observable behavior and the environment, argued that the conditioned reflex could account for only a small part of our human behavior. What shaped our behavior for the most part was what he called *operant conditioning*. This is a form of conditioning which utilizes positive and negative reinforcement; the former by rewarding certain behavior increases its frequency, the latter does the opposite. For example, if when a pigeon raises its head above a certain height it is given some food, the result will be that it will continue to do so more often; and for Skinner, positive reinforcement—which he prefers for reasons explained in the reading to negative reinforcement—can work as well with human beings as it does with pigeons.

The selection reprinted here is taken from Skinner's novel, *Walden Two,* which is a description of Skinner's vision of a utopian society run by behaviorist psychologists. The citizens of this society are conditioned by positive reinforcement to have desires and motives which make them behave as the psychologists in charge want them to behave. Skinner defends these practices through the voice of Frazier, the novel's protagonist and the creator of this psychological utopia. Frazier (Skinner) argues that, since human behavior is determined in any case, it ought to be determined by those who are well instructed in the behavioral sciences and who are concerned with the welfare of the individual and society. One of the interesting consequences of applying the technique of positive reinforcement is that the individual, although controlled, nonetheless feels free.

SOCIAL BONDS

Okot p'Bitek

. . . There is a false, and misleading assumption that on the one end, there is some notion called "philosophy" and on the other, some things and actions named "culture." Culture is philosophy as lived and celebrated in a society. Human beings do not behave like dry leaves, smoke or clouds which are blown here and there by winds. Men live in organisations called institutions; the family and clan, a chiefdom or kingdom or age-set system. He has a religion, an army, legal and other institutions. And all these institutions are formed by or built around the central issue of a people, what they believe, what life is all about, their social philosophy, their world view.

• • •

The bourgeois believe that liberty consists in absence of social organization; that liberty is a negative quality, a deprivation of existing obstacles to it; and not a positive quality, the reward of endeavour and wisdom. . . . Because of this basic fallacy this type of intellectual always *tries to cure positive social evils, such as wars, by negative individual actions, such as non-cooperation, passive resistance or conscientious objection.* This is because he cannot rid himself of the assumption that the individual is free. But we have shown that the individual is *never free.* He can only obtain freedom by *social cooperation.* He can only do what he wants by *using social forces.* But in order to use social relations he must understand them. He must become conscious of the laws of society, just as if he wants to lever up a stone, he must know the laws of levers.—*Christopher Caudwell*

The French philosopher Jean Jacques Rousseau (1712–1778) was quite wrong when he declared "Man is born free. . . ." Man is not born free. At birth he is firmly tied to his mother through the um-

bilical cord. He is physically cut free from her. But *this cutting free* is not merely a biological act. It is symbolic and most significant. Henceforth, he is an individual, who through upbringing is prepared to play his full role as a member of society.

Rousseau was not correct when he added, "and everywhere he is in chains." Man is not born free. He cannot be free. He is incapable of being free. For only by being in *chains* can he be and remain "human." What constitute these chains? Man has a bundle of *rights* and *privileges* that society owes him. In African belief, even death does not free him. If he had been an important member of society while he lived, his ghost continues to be revered and fed; and he in turn is expected to guide and protect the living. This is the essence of what is wrongly called "ancestor worship." Should he die a shameful death, his haunting ghost has to be laid. In some cases his ghost has to be "killed." "Till death do us part," the Christian vow made between man and woman at the wedding ritual, sounds hollow, in that at the death of the man, the woman does not walk out of the "home." She is *inherited* by one of the brothers of the dead man. Should the woman die her death does not extinguish the bonds between the man and his in-laws.

Man has always asked the most terrifying questions: What am I? What is the purpose of life? Why do people suffer? What is happiness? What is death? Is it the end? etc. etc. And, according to the "answers" provided by the "wise men," and have been accepted, society is then organised to achieve these ends. It is these fundamental ideas, the philosophy of life, which constitute the pillars, the foundations, on which the social institutions are erected.

Some have called these *myths* or *world-views;* others refer to them as ideologies (which, as in the case of socialism is even described as scientific): fanatics refer to them as *Truth,* as if these ideas are about verifiable or indisputable facts, or about the actual state of the matter. These fundamental ideas are concerned with *meaning.* The meaning of being alive in this world. And meaning is wider in scope than is truth. As John Dewey has put it ". . . truths are but one class of meanings, namely, those in which a claim to verifiability by their consequences is an intrinsic part of the meaning. Beyond this island of meanings, which in their own nature are true or false, lies the ocean of meanings to which truth or falsity are irrelevant.

Man cannot, and must not be free. "Son," "Mother," "Daughter," "Father," "Uncle," "Husband," "Grandfather," "Wife," "Clansman," "Mother-in-law," "Grandfather," "Chief," "Medicineman," and many other such terms, are the stamps of man's unfreedom. It is by such complex titles that a person is defined and identified. They order and determine human behaviour in society. The central question "Who am I?" cannot be answered in any meaningful way unless the relationship in question is known. Because "I" is not only one relationship, but numerous relationships: "I" has a clan, and a shrine, a country, a job. "I" may or may not be married, may or may not have children. Is "I" a chief? Then he has subjects or followers, etc. etc.

Permanent bondage seems to be man's fate. Because he cannot escape, he cannot be liberated, freed. The so-called "outcast" is not a free agent. Being "cast out" from society, for a while, does not sever the chains that bind him to society.

The act is a judgement, punishment and a lesson, not only for the victim, but for all members of the society. But the outcast, the refugee, the exile, soon joins another society and becomes a subscribed member of the group.

Even the hermit who pretends to withdraw to a solitary place for a life of religious seclusion, is not free. He peoples his cave, forest, mountain top, oasis, riverside, or whatever abode, with gods and spirits, devils and angels, etc.; and, as has been reported of one St. Francis of Asisi, these cowards (hermits), who exile themselves from human society, enter into communion with these non-existent, imaginary creations as well as with Nature: birds, flowers, animals, reptiles, trees, fruits, rocks and rivers etc.

WALDEN TWO: FREEDOM AND THE SCIENCE OF HUMAN BEHAVIOR

B. F. Skinner

"Mr. Castle," said Frazier very earnestly, "let me ask you a question. I warn you, it will be the most terrifying question of your life. *What would you do if you found yourself in possession of an effective science of behavior?* Suppose you suddenly found it possible to control the behavior of men as you wished. What would you do?"

"That's an assumption?"

"Take it as one if you like. *I* take it as a fact. And apparently you accept it as a fact, too. I can hardly be as despotic as you claim unless I hold the key to an extensive practical control."

"What would I do?" said Castle thoughtfully. "I think I would dump your science of behavior in the ocean."

"And deny men all the help you could otherwise give them?"

"And give them the freedom they would otherwise lose forever!"

"How could you give them freedom?"

"By refusing to control them!"

"But you would only be leaving the control in other hands."

"Whose?"

"The charlatan, the demagogue, the salesman, the ward heeler, the bully, the cheat, the educator, the priest—all who are now in possession of the techniques of behavioral engineering."

"A pretty good share of the control would remain in the hands of the individual himself."

"That's an assumption, too, and it's your only hope. It's your only possible chance to avoid the implications of a science of behavior. If man is free, then a technology of behavior is impossible. But I'm asking you to consider the other case."

"Then my answer is that your assumption is contrary to fact and any further consideration idle."

"And your accusations—?"

"—were in terms of intention, not of possible achievement."

Frazier sighed dramatically.

"It's a little late to be proving that a behavioral technology is well advanced. How can you deny it? Many of its methods and techniques are really as old as the hills. Look at their frightful misuse in the hands of the Nazis! And what about the techniques of the psychological clinic? What about education? Or religion? Or practical politics? Or advertising and salesmanship? Bring them all together and you have a sort of rule-of-thumb technology of vast power. No, Mr. Castle, the science is there for the asking. But its techniques and methods are in the wrong hands—they are used for personal aggrandizement in a competitive world or, in the case of the psychologist and educator, for futilely corrective purposes. My question is, have you the courage to take up and wield the science of behavior for the good of mankind? You answer that you would dump it in the ocean!"

"I'd want to take it out of the hands of the politicians and advertisers and salesmen, too."

"And the psychologists and educators? You see, Mr. Castle, you can't have that kind of cake. The fact is, we not only *can* control human behavior, we *must*. But who's to do it, and what's to be done?"

"So long as a trace of personal freedom survives, I'll stick to my position," said Castle, very much out of countenance.

"Isn't it time we talked about freedom?" I said. "We parted a day or so ago on an agreement to let the question of freedom ring. It's time to answer, don't you think?"

"My answer is simple enough," said Frazier. "I deny that freedom exists at all. I must deny it—or my program would be absurd. You can't have a science about a subject matter which hops capriciously about. Perhaps we can never *prove* that man isn't free; it's an assumption. But the increasing success of a science of behavior makes it more and more plausible."

"On the contrary, a simple personal experience makes it untenable," said Castle. "The experience of freedom. I *know* that I'm free."

"It must be quite consoling," said Frazier.

"And what's more—you do, too," said Castle hotly. "When you deny your own feedom for the sake of playing with a science of behavior, you're acting in plain bad faith. That's the only way I can explain it." He tried to recover himself and shrugged his shoulders. "At least you'll grant that you *feel* free."

"The 'feeling of freedom' should deceive no one," said Frazier. "Give me a concrete case."

"Well, right now," Castle said. He picked up a book of matches. "I'm free to hold or drop these matches."

"You will, of course, do one or the other," said Frazier. "Linguistically or logically there seem to be two possibilities, but I submit that there's only one in fact. The determining forces may be subtle but they are inexorable. I suggest that as an orderly person you will probably hold—ah! you drop them! Well, you see, that's all part of your behavior with respect to me. You couldn't resist the temptation to prove me wrong. It was all lawful. You had no choice. The deciding factor entered rather late, and naturally you couldn't foresee the result when you first held them up. There was no strong likelihood that you would act in either direction, and so you said you were free."

"That's entirely too glib," said Castle. "It's easy to argue lawfulness after the fact. But let's see you predict what I will do in advance. Then I'll agree there's law."

"I didn't say that behavior is always predictable, any more than the weather is always predictable. There are often too many factors to be taken into account. We can't measure them all accurately, and we couldn't perform the mathematical operations needed to make a prediction if we had the measurements. The legality is usually an assumption—but none the less important in judging the issue at hand."

"Take a case where there's no choice, then," said Castle. "Certainly a man in jail isn't free in the sense in which I am free now."

"Good! That's an excellent start. Let us classify the kinds of determiners of human behavior. One class, as you suggest, is physical restraint—handcuffs, iron bars, forcible coercion. These are ways in which we shape human behavior according to our wishes. They're crude, and they sacrifice the affection of the controllee, but they often work. Now, what other ways are there of limiting freedom?"

Frazier had adopted a professorial tone and Castle refused to answer.

"The threat of force would be one," I said.

"Right. And here again we shan't encourage any loyalty on the part of the controllee. He has perhaps a shade more of the feeling of freedom, since he can always 'choose to act and accept the consequences,' but he doesn't feel exactly free. He knows his behavior is being coerced. Now what else?"

I had to answer.

"Force or the threat of force—I see no other possibility," said Castle after a moment.

"Precisely," said Frazier.

"But certainly a large part of my behavior has no connection with force at all. There's my freedom!" said Castle.

"I wasn't agreeing that there was no other possibility—merely that *you* could see no other. Not being a good behaviorist—or a good Christian, for that matter—you have no feeling for a tremendous power of a different sort."

"What's that?"

"I shall have to be technical," said Frazier. "But only for a moment. It's what the science of behavior calls 'reinforcement theory.' The things that can happen to us fall into three classes. To some things we are indifferent. Other things we like—we want them to happen, and we take steps to make them happen again. Still other things we don't like—we don't want them to happen and we take steps to get rid of them or keep them from happening again.

"Now," Frazier continued earnestly, "if it's in our power to create any of the situations which a person likes or to remove any situation he doesn't like, we can control his behavior. When he behaves as we want him to behave, we simply create a situation he likes, or remove one he doesn't like. As a result, the probability that he will behave that way again goes up, which is what we want. Technically it's called 'positive reinforcement.'

"The old school made the amazing mistake of supposing that the reverse was true, that by removing a situation a person likes or setting up one he doesn't like—in other words by punishing him—it was possible to *reduce* the probability that he would behave in a given way again. That simply doesn't hold. It has been established beyond question. What is emerging at this critical stage in the evolution of society is a behavioral and cultural technology based on positive reinforcement alone. We are gradually discovering—at an untold cost in human suffering—that in the long run punishment doesn't reduce the probability that an act will occur. We have been so preoccupied with the contrary that we always take 'force' to mean punishment. We don't say we're using force when we send shiploads of food into a starving country, though we're displaying quite as much *power* as if we were sending troops and guns."

"I'm certainly not an advocate of force," said Castle. "But I can't agree that it's not effective."

"It's *temporarily* effective, that's the worst of it. That explains several thousand years of bloodshed. Even nature has been fooled. We 'instinctively' punish a person who doesn't behave as we like—we spank him if he's a child or strike him if he's a man. A nice distinction! The immediate effect of the blow teaches us to strike again. Retribution and revenge are the most natural things on earth. But in the long run the man we strike is no less likely to repeat his act."

"But he won't repeat it if we hit him hard enough," said Castle.

"He'll still *tend* to repeat it. He'll *want* to repeat it. We haven't really altered his potential behavior at all. That's the pity of it. If he doesn't repeat it in our presence, he will in the presence of someone else. Or it will be repeated in the disguise of a neurotic symptom. If we hit hard enough, we clear a little place for ourselves in the wilderness of civilization, but we make the rest of the wilderness still more terrible.

"Now, early forms of government are naturally based on punishment. It's the obvious technique when the physically strong control the weak. But we're in the throes of a great change to positive reinforcement—from a competitive society in which one man's reward is another man's punishment, to a cooperative society in which no one gains at the expense of anyone else.

"The change is slow and painful because the immediate, temporary effect of punishment overshadows the eventual advantage of positive reinforcement. We've all seen countless instances of the temporary effect of force, but clear evidence of the effect of not using force is rare. That's why I insist that Jesus, who was apparently the first to discover the power of refusing to punish, must have hit upon the principle by accident. He certainly had none of the experimental evidence which is available to us today, and I can't conceive that it was possible, no matter what the man's genius, to have discovered the principle from casual observation."

"A touch of revelation, perhaps?" said Castle.

"No, accident. Jesus discovered one principle because it had immediate consequences, and he got another thrown in for good measure."

I began to see the light.

"You mean the principle of 'love your enemies'?" I said.

"Exactly! To 'do good to those who despitefully use you' has two unrelated consequences. You gain the peace of mind we talked about the other day. Let the stronger man push you around—at least you avoid the torture of your own rage. *That's* the immediate consequence. What an astonishing discovery it must have been to find that in the long run you could *control the stronger man* in the same way!"

"It's generous of you to give so much credit to your early colleague," said Castle, "but why are we still in the throes of so much misery? Twenty centuries should have been enough for one piece of behavioral engineering."

"The conditions which made the principle difficult to discover made it difficult to teach. The history of the Christian Church doesn't reveal many cases of doing good to one's enemies. To inoffen-

sive heathens, perhaps, but not enemies. One must look outside the field of organized religion to find the principle in practice at all. Church governments are devotees of *power,* both temporal and bogus."

"But what has all this got to do with freedom?" I said hastily.

Frazier took time to reorganize his behavior. He looked steadily toward the window, against which the rain was beating heavily.

"Now that we *know* how positive reinforcement works and why negative doesn't," he said at last, "we can be more deliberate, and hence more successful, in our cultural design. We can achieve a sort of control under which the controlled, though they are following a code much more scrupulously than was ever the case under the old system, nevertheless *feel free.* They are doing what they want to do, not what they are forced to do. That's the source of the tremendous power of positive reinforcement—there's no restraint and no revolt. By a careful cultural design, we control not the final behavior, but the *inclination* to behave—the motives, the desires, the wishes.

"The curious thing is that in that case the *question of freedom never arises.* Mr. Castle was free to drop the matchbook in the sense that nothing was preventing him. If it had been securely bound to his hand he wouldn't have been free. Nor would he have been quite free if I'd covered him with a gun and threatened to shoot him if he let it fall. The question of freedom arises when there is restraint—either physical or psychological.

"But restraint is only one sort of control, and absence of restraint isn't freedom. It's not control that's lacking when one feels 'free,' but the objectionable control of force. Mr. Castle felt free to hold or drop the matches in the sense that he felt no restraint—no threat of punishment in taking either course of action. He neglected to examine his positive reasons for holding or letting go, in spite of the fact that these were more compelling in this instance than any threat of force.

"We have no vocabulary of freedom in dealing with what we want to do," Frazier went on. "The question never arises. When men strike for freedom, they strike against jails and the police, or the threat of them—against oppression. They never strike against forces which make them want to act the way they do. Yet, it seems to be understood that governments will operate only through force or the threat of force, and that all other principles of control will be left to education, religion, and commerce. If this continues to be the case, we may as well give up. A government can never create a free people with the techniques now allotted to it.

"The question is: Can men live in freedom and peace? And the answer is: Yes, if we can build a social structure which will satisfy the needs of everyone and in which everyone will want to observe the supporting code. But so far this has been achieved only in Walden Two. Your ruthless accusations to the contrary, Mr. Castle, this is the freest place on earth. And it is free precisely because we make no use of force or the threat of force. Every bit of our research, from the nursery through the psychological management of our adult membership, is directed toward that end—to exploit every alternative to forcible control. By skillful planning, by a wise choice of techniques we *increase* the feeling of freedom.

"It's not planning which infringes upon freedom, but planning which uses force. A sense of freedom was practically unknown in the planned society of Nazi Germany, because the planners made a fantastic use of force and the threat of force.

"No, Mr. Castle, when a science of behavior has once been achieved, there's no alternative to a planned society. We can't leave mankind to an accidental or biased control. But by using the principle of positive reinforcement—carefully avoiding force or the threat of force—we can preserve a personal sense of freedom."

Frazier threw himself back upon the bed and stared at the ceiling.

QUESTIONS FOR DISCUSSION

1. Consider some important decision that you have made in your life. How would Skinner explain this decision? How would Sartre (in the previous section) explain it? What is your own belief about your decision in regard to the question of free will versus determinism?

2. To what extent, if at all, do you believe that the individual is socially determined, that is, determined by social forces and social bonds? In your answer discuss Okot p'Bitek's position and the position of one other thinker in this chapter.

CAN WE RECONCILE FREEDOM AND DETERMINISM?

There are two kinds of determinism often labeled, respectively, "hard" and "soft" determinism. The difference between these two revolves around the problem of moral responsibility. We might recall that for Sartre—in Section Two of this chapter and in Chapter 4—since human beings are free, they must be responsible for their actions. Hard determinism would accept this implication, but insofar as it denies the antecedent, would draw a very different conclusion: since human beings are *not* free, they cannot be held morally responsible for their actions. This implication of determinism might be "hard" to accept, but the hard determinism insists that this is the way things are.

The soft determinist, in contrast, is a determinist who is uncomfortable with the above conclusion. Although equally deterministic, soft determinists want to hold human beings morally responsible for their actions. These determinists would also agree that unless human beings are free in a significant sense, they cannot be held responsible. The only possible solution to this dilemma is to claim that although human beings are determined, they are nonetheless free in a sense that is necessary for moral responsibility to exist. Thus, the soft determinist position is often called *compatibilism* or *reconciliationism,* because it takes freedom and moral responsibility to be compatible with determinism, because it claims to reconcile determinism with freedom.

The article by Moritz Schlick is one of the classic attempts to accomplish this task. Moritz Schlick was born in Berlin in 1882 and was shot to death in 1936 by a graduate student to whom he had denied the doctoral degree. Schlick was a founding member of the Vienna Circle, a small group of philosophers who came together in the early 1920s and formulated a philosophical position that has come to be known as "logical positivism." Logical positivism maintains that philosophy's chief task is to determine the conditions under which statements can be meaningful, in effect, to clarify the meaning

or to expose the lack of meaning of a variety of concepts. They claimed that many problems posed by traditional metaphysics turns out, on careful analysis, to be meaningless, hence, pseudoproblems.

In the selection that follows, Schlick analyzes the problem of free will as a pseudoproblem. The opposite of freedom is not determinism, he declares, but rather compulsion. As long as I can act upon my desires, as long as I am free from external compulsion, I have all the freedom I need to be considered morally responsible for my actions. Thus, the opposition "freedom versus determinism" is a pseudo-opposition.

Schlick maintains that psychological laws should not be understood as compelling our actions but simply as describing the desires on the basis of which we act. One possible problem with his analysis is that he does not inquire into the causes of these desires. Specifically, if human actions are motivated by desires, which are themselves determined by forces over which we have no control, then, even in the absence of external constraints, it is difficult to construe them as free actions. In other words, the problem of freedom, then, is not only, as Schlick would have it, the problem of external compulsion, but it is also the problem of internal psychological constraints and their causes. On this analysis, the program of soft determinism—to reconcile determinism and freedom—becomes problematic.

In the following article, Nancy Holmstrom, who teaches philosophy at Rutgers University, attempts to "firm up" soft determinism by having it take into account how our beliefs and desires are determined. She recognizes that at the heart of the question of freedom is not only being able to act upon our beliefs and desires but also having control over those beliefs and desires. In other words, soft determinism, in order to make good its compatibilist claim, must show how people can have control over the sources of the beliefs and desires that ultimately motivate them.

In the course of her analysis, Holmstrom indicates how a free action can be distinguished from an action performed as a result of brainwashing, subliminal advertising, and other forms of conditioning in which one's desires are acquired through coercion. The conclusion of her analysis ties the question of human freedom in the philosophical sense to social and political freedom, for only if people have control over the social conditions that shape their desires and beliefs can they be said to have control over their actions.

The last selection offers a very different attempt to reconcile freedom and determinism. Kitaro Nishida, a twentieth-century Japanese philosopher and Zen Buddhist, has attempted to give the Eastern mode of thinking a Western philosophical foundation, in effect, to synthesize the insights of East and West. His *Inquiry into the Good* from which this se-

lection is taken is heavily influenced by the phenomenological method.

Nishida criticizes both the notion of an absolute freedom and a mechanical determinism. He criticizes the former, because a will without a cause would be unintelligible and would, in any case, not be felt as free. He criticizes mechanical determinism, because consciousness is self-determined; it is not determined from without but is, nonetheless, determined by laws governing its own activity. Consciousness is free not because it acts without reason, not because it determines which ideas will initially arise, but because it can, through synthesizing and analyzing the ideas that do arise, come to know its own reason. Therefore, the more knowledge we have, the freer we become.

FREEDOM AND RESPONSIBILITY

Moritz Schlick

WHEN IS A MAN RESPONSIBLE?

1. The Pseudo-Problem of Freedom of the Will

With hesitation and reluctance I prepare to add this chapter to the discussion of ethical problems. For in it I must speak of a matter which, even at present, is thought to be a fundamental ethical question, but which got into ethics and has become a much discussed problem only because of a misunderstanding. This is the so-called problem of the freedom of the will. Moreover, this pseudo-problem has long since been settled by the efforts of certain sensible persons; and, above all, the state of affairs just described has been often disclosed—with exceptional clarity by Hume. Hence it is really one of the greatest scandals of philosophy that again and again so much paper and printer's ink is devoted to this mat-

ter, to say nothing of the expenditure of thought, which could have been applied to more important problems (assuming that it would have sufficed for these). Thus I should truly be ashamed to write a chapter on "freedom." In the chapter heading, the word "responsible" indicates what concerns ethics, and designates the point at which misunderstanding arises. Therefore the concept of responsibility constitutes our theme, and if in the process of its clarification I also must speak of the concept of freedom I shall, of course, say only what others have already said better; consoling myself with the thought that in this way alone can anything be done to put an end at last to that scandal.

• • •

The main task of ethics . . . is to explain moral behavior. To explain means to refer back to laws: every science, including psychology, is possible only in so far as there are such laws to which the events can be referred. Since the assumption that *all* events are subject to universal laws is called the principle of causality, one can also say, "Every science presupposes the principle of causality." Therefore every explanation of human behavior must also assume the validity of causal laws; in this case the existence of psychological laws.

• • •

All of our experience strengthens us in the belief that this presupposition is realized, at least to the extent required for all purposes of practical life in intercourse with nature and human beings, and also for the most precise demands of technique. Whether, indeed, the principle of causality holds universally, whether, that is, *determinism* is true, we do not know; no one knows. But we do know that it is impossible to settle the dispute between determinism and indeterminism by mere reflection and speculation, by the consideration of so many reasons for and so many reasons against (which collectively and individually are but pseudo-reasons). Such an attempt becomes especially ridiculous when one considers with what enormous expenditure of experimental and logical skill contemporary physics carefully approaches the question of whether causality can be maintained for the most minute intra-atomic events.

But the dispute concerning "freedom of the will" generally proceeds in such fashion that its advocates attempt to refute, and its opponents to prove, the validity of the causal principle, both using hackneyed arguments, and neither in the least abashed by the magnitude of the undertaking.

• • •

Fortunately, it is not necessary to lay claim to a final solution of the causal problem in order to say what is necessary in ethics concerning responsibility; there is required only an analysis of the concept, the careful determination of the meaning which is in fact joined to the words "responsibility" and "freedom" as these are actually used. If men had made clear to themselves the sense of those propositions, which we use in everyday life, that pseudo-argument which lies at the root of the pseudo-problem, and which recurs thousands of times within and outside of philosophical books, would never have arisen.

The argument runs as follows: "If determinism is true, if, that is, all events obey immutable laws, then my will too is always determined, by my innate character and my motives. Hence my decisions are necessary, not free. But if so, then I am not responsible for my acts, for I would be accountable for them only if I could do something about the way my decisions went; but I can do nothing about it, since they proceed with necessity from my character and the motives. And I have made neither, and have no power over them: the motives come from without, and my character is the necessary product of the innate tendencies and the external influences which have been effective during my lifetime. Thus determinism and moral responsibility are incompatible. Moral responsibility presupposes freedom, that is, exemption from causality."

This process of reasoning rests upon a whole series of confusions, just as the links of a chain hang together. We must show these confusions to be such, and thus destroy them.

2. Two Meanings of the Word "Law"

It all begins with an erroneous interpretation of the meaning of "law." In practice this is understood as a rule by which the state prescribes certain behavior to its citizens. These rules often contradict the natural desires of the citizens (for if they did not do so, there would be no reason for making them), and are in fact not followed by many of them; while others obey, but under *compulsion.* The state does in fact compel its citizens by imposing certain sanctions (punishments) which serve to bring their desires into harmony with the prescribed laws.

In natural science, on the other hand, the word "law" means something quite different. The natural law is not a *pre*scription as to how something should behave, but a formula, a *de*scription of how something does in fact behave. The two forms of "laws" have only this in common: both tend to be expressed in *formulae.* Otherwise they have absolutely nothing to do with one another, and it is very blameworthy that the same word has been used for two such different things; but even more so that philosophers have allowed themselves to be led into serious errors by this usage. Since natural laws are only descriptions of what happens, there can be in regard to them no talk of "compulsion." The laws of celestial mechanics do not prescribe to the planets how they have to move, as though the planets would actually like to move quite otherwise, and are only forced by these burdensome laws of Kepler to move in orderly paths; no, these laws do not in any way "compel" the planets, but express only what in fact planets actually do.

If we apply this to volition, we are enlightened at once, even before the other confusions are discovered. When we say that a man's will "obeys psychological laws," these are not civic laws, which compel him to make certain decisions, or dictate desires to him, which he would in fact prefer not to have. They are laws of nature, merely expressing which desires he *actually has* under given conditions; they describe the nature of the will in the same manner as the astronomical laws describe the nature of planets. "Compulsion" occurs where man is prevented from realizing his natural desires. How could the rule according to which these natural desires arise itself be considered as "compulsion"?

3. Compulsion and Necessity

But this is the second confusion to which the first leads almost inevitably: after conceiving the laws of nature, anthropomorphically, as order imposed *nolens volens* upon the events, one adds to them the concept of "necessity." This word, derived from "need," also comes to us from practice, and is used there in the sense of inescapable compulsion. To apply the word with this meaning to natural laws is of course senseless, for the presupposition of an opposing desire is lacking; and it is then confused with something altogether different, which is actually an attribute of natural laws. That is, universality. It is of the essence of natural laws to be universally valid, for only when we have found a rule which holds of events without exception do we *call* the rule a law of nature. Thus when we say "a natural law holds necessarily" this has but one legitimate

meaning: "It holds in *all* cases where it is applicable." It is again very deplorable that the word "necessary" has been applied to natural laws (or, what amounts to the same thing, with reference to causality), for it is quite superfluous, since the expression "universally valid" is available. Universal validity is something altogether different from "compulsion"; these concepts belong to spheres so remote from each other than once insight into the error has been gained one can no longer conceive the possibility of a confusion.

The confusion of two concepts always carries with it the confusion of their contradictory opposites. The opposite of the universal validity of a formula, of the existence of a law, is the nonexistence of a law, indeterminism, acausality; while the opposite of compulsion is what in practice everyone calls "freedom." Here emerges the nonsense, trailing through centuries, that freedom means "exemption from the causal principle," or "not subject to the laws of nature." Hence it is believed necessary to vindicate indeterminism in order to save human freedom.

4. Freedom and Indeterminism

This is quite mistaken. Ethics has, so to speak, no moral interest in the purely theoretical question of "determinism or indeterminism?," but only a theoretical interest, namely: in so far as it seeks the laws of conduct, and can find them only to the extent that causality holds. But that question of whether man is morally free (that is, has that freedom which, as we shall show, is the presupposition of moral responsibility) is altogether different from the problem of determinism. Hume was especially clear on this point. He indicated the inadmissible confusion of the concepts of "indeterminism" and "freedom"; but he retained, inappropriately, the word "freedom" for both, calling the one freedom of "the will," the other, genuine kind, "freedom of conduct." He showed that morality is interested only in the latter, and that such freedom, in general, is unquestionably to be attributed to mankind. And this is quite correct. Freedom means the opposite of compulsion; a man is *free* if he does not act under *compulsion,* and he is compelled or unfree when he is hindered from without in the realization of his natural desires. Hence he is unfree when he is locked up, or chained, or when someone forces him at the point of a gun to do what otherwise he would not do. This is quite clear, and everyone will admit that the everyday or legal notion of the lack of freedom is thus correctly interpreted, and that a man will be considered quite free and responsible if no such external compulsion is exerted upon him. There are certain cases which lie between these clearly described ones, as, say, when someone acts under the influence of alcohol or a narcotic. In such cases we consider the man to be more or less unfree, and hold him less accountable, because we rightly view the influence of the drug as "external," even though it is found within the body; it prevents him from making decisions in the manner peculiar to his nature. If he takes the narcotic of his own will, we make him completely responsible for *this* act and transfer a part of the responsibility to the consequences, making, as it were, an average or mean condemnation of the whole. In the case also of a person who is mentally ill we do not consider him free with respect to those acts in which the disease expresses itself, because we view the illness as a disturbing factor which hinders the normal functioning of his natural tendencies. We make not him but his disease responsible.

5. The Nature of Responsibility

But what does this really signify? What do we mean by this concept of responsibility which goes along with that of "freedom," and which plays such an important role in morality? It is easy to attain complete clarity in this matter; we need only carefully determine the manner in which the concept is used. What is the case in practice when we impute "responsibility" to a person? What is our aim in doing this? The judge has to discover who is responsible for a given act in order that he may *punish* him. We are inclined to be less concerned with the inquiry as to who deserves *reward* for an act, and we have no

special officials for this; but of course the principle would be the same. But let us stick to punishment in order to make the idea clear. What is punishment, actually? The view still often expressed, that it is a natural *retaliation* for past wrong, ought no longer to be defended in cultivated society; for the opinion that an increase in sorrow can be "made good again" by further sorrow is altogether barbarous. Certainly the origin of punishment may lie in an impulse of retaliation or vengeance; but what is such an impulse except the instinctive desire to destroy the *cause* of the deed to be avenged, by the destruction of or injury to the malefactor? Punishment is concerned only with the institution of causes, of *motives* of conduct, and this alone is its meaning. Punishment is an educative measure, and as such is a means to the formation of motives, which are in part to prevent the wrongdoer from repeating the act (reformation) and in part to prevent others from committing a similar act (intimidation). Analogously, in the case of reward we are concerned with an incentive.

Hence the question regarding responsibility is the question: Who, in a given case, is to be punished? Who is to be considered the true wrongdoer? This problem is not identical with that regarding the original instigator of the act; for the great-grandparents of the man, from whom he inherited his character, might in the end be the cause, or the statesmen who are responsible for his social milieu, and so forth. But the "doer" is the one *upon whom the motive must have acted* in order, with certainty, to have prevented the act (or called it forth, as the case may be). Consideration of remote causes is of no help here, for in the first place their actual contribution cannot be determined, and in the second place they are generally out of reach. Rather, we must find the person in whom the decisive junction of causes lies. The question of who is responsible is the question concerning the *correct point of application of the motive.* And the important thing is that in this its meaning is completely exhausted; behind it lurks no mysterious connection between transgression and requital, which is merely *indicated* by the described state of affairs. It is a matter only of knowing who is to be punished or rewarded, in order that punishment and reward function as such—be able to achieve their goal.

Thus, all the facts connected with the concepts of responsibility and imputation are at once made intelligible. We do not charge an insane person with responsibility, for the very reason that he offers no unified point for the application of a motive. It would be pointless to try to affect hm by means of promises or threats, when his confused soul fails to respond to such influence because its normal mechanism is out of order. We do not try to give him motives, but try to heal him (metaphorically, we make his sickness responsible, and try to remove its causes). When a man is forced by threats to commit certain acts we do not blame him, but the one who held the pistol at his breast. The reason is clear: the act would have been prevented had we been able to restrain the person who threatened him; and this person is the one whom we must influence in order to prevent similar acts in the future.

6. The Consciousness of Responsibility

But much more important than the question of when a man is said to be responsible is that of when he *himself* feels responsible. Our whole treatment would be untenable if it gave no explanation of this. It is, then, a welcome confirmation of the view here developed that the subjective feeling of responsibility coincides with the objective judgment. It is a fact of experience that, in general, the person blamed or condemned is conscious of the fact that he was "rightly" taken to account—of course, under the supposition that no error has been made, that the assumed state of affairs actually occurred. What is this consciousness of having been the true doer of the act, the actual instigator? Evidently not merely that it was he who took the steps required for its performance; but there must be added the awareness that he did it "independently," "of his own initiative," or however it be expressed. This feeling is simply the consciousness of *freedom,* which is merely the knowledge of having acted of one's *own* desires. And "one's own desires" are those which

have their origin in the regularity of one's character in the given situation, and are not imposed by an external power, as explained above. The absence of the external power expresses itself in the well-known feeling (usually considered characteristic of the consciousness of freedom) *that one could also have acted otherwise.* How this indubitable experience ever came to be an argument in favor of indeterminism is incomprehensible to me. It is of course obvious that I should have acted differently had I *willed* something else; but the feeling never says that I could also have willed something else, even though this is true, if, that is, other motives had been present. And it says even less than under *exactly the same* inner and outer conditions I could also have willed something else. How could such a feeling inform me of anything regarding the purely theoretical question of whether the principle of causality holds or not? Of course, after what has been said on the subject, I do not undertake to demonstrate the principle, but I do deny that from any such fact of consciousness the least follows regarding the principle's validity. This feeling is not the consciousness of the absence of a cause, but of something altogether different, namely, of *freedom,* which consists in the fact that I can act as I desire.

Thus the feeling of responsibility assumes that I acted freely, that my own desires impelled me; and if because of this feeling I willingly suffer blame for my behavior or reproach myself, and thereby admit that I might have acted otherwise, this means that other behavior was compatible with the laws of volition—of course, granted other motives. And I myself desire the existence of such motives and bear the pain (regret and sorrow) caused me by my behavior so that its repetition will be prevented. To blame oneself means just to apply motives of improvement to oneself, which is usually the task of the educator. But if, for example, one does something under the influence of torture, feelings of guilt and regret are absent, for one knows that according to the laws of volition no other behavior was possible—no matter what ideas, because of their feeling tones, might have functioned as motives. The important thing, always, is that the feeling of responsibility means the realization that one's self, one's own psychic processes constitute the point at which motives must be applied in order to govern the acts of one's body.

7. Causality as the Presupposition of Responsibility

We can speak of motives only in a causal context; thus it becomes clear how very much the concept of responsibility rests upon that of causation, that is, upon the regularity of volitional decisions. In fact if we should conceive of a decision as utterly without any cause (this would in all strictness be the indeterministic presupposition) then the act would be entirely a matter of *chance,* for chance is identical with the absence of a cause; there is no other opposite of causality. Could we under such conditions make the agent responsible? Certainly not. Imagine a man, always calm, peaceful and blameless, who suddenly falls upon and begins to beat a stranger. He is held and questioned regarding the motive of his action, to which he answers, in his opinion truthfully, as we assume: "There was no motive for my behavior. Try as I may I can discover no reason. My volition was without any cause—I desired to do so, and there is simply nothing else to be said about it." We should shake our heads and call him insane, because we have to believe that there was a cause, and lacking any other we must assume some mental disturbance as the only cause remaining; but certainly no one would hold him to be responsible. If decisions were causeless there would be no sense in trying to influence men; and we see at once that this is the reason why we could not bring such a man to account, but would always have only a shrug of the shoulders in answer to his behavior. One can easily determine that in practice we make an agent the more responsible the more motives we can find for his conduct. If a man guilty of an atrocity was an enemy of his victim, if previously he had shown violent tendencies, if some special circumstance angered him, then we impose severe punishment upon him; while the fewer the reasons to be found for an

offense the less do we condemn the agent, but make "unlucky chance," a momentary aberration, or something of the sort, responsible. We do not find the causes of misconduct in his character, and therefore we do not try to influence it for the better: this and only this is the significance of the fact that we do not put the responsibility upon him. And he too feels this to be so, and says, "I cannot understand how such a thing could have happened to me."

In general we know very well how to discover the causes of conduct in the characters of our fellow men; and how to use this knowledge in the prediction of their future behavior, often with as much certainty as that with which we know that a lion and a rabbit will behave quite differently in the same situation. From all this it is evident that in practice no one thinks of questioning the principle of causality, that, thus, the attitude of the practical man offers no excuse to the metaphysician for confusing freedom from compulsion with the absence of a cause. If one makes clear to himself that a causeless happening is identical with a chance happening, and that, consequently, an indetermined will would destroy all responsibility, then every desire will cease which might be father to an indeterministic thought. No one can prove determinism, but it is certain that we assume its validity in all of our practical life, and that in particular we can apply the concept of responsibility to human conduct only in so far as the causal principle holds of volitional processes.

For a final clarification I bring together again a list of those concepts which tend, in the traditional treatment of the "problem of freedom," to be confused. In the place of the concepts on the left are put, mistakenly, those on the right, and those in the vertical order form a chain, so that sometimes the previous confusion is the cause of that which follows:

Natural Law.	Law of State.
Determinism (Causality).	Compulsion.
(Universal Validity).	(Necessity).
Indeterminism (Chance).	Freedom.
(No Cause).	(No Compulsion).

FIRMING UP SOFT DETERMINISM

Nancy Holmstrom

I

An important position on the question of freedom and determinism holds that determinism and predictability *per se* constitute no threat to the freedom and responsibility of an agent. What matters, according to this view, called soft determinism, is the basis on which the prediction is made or the nature of the conditions such that given those conditions, the agent will do what he/she does.[1] When the agent does what he does because of his beliefs and desires[2] to do it, then what the agent does is "up to him"; the causal chain goes through the person or the self, as it were. In such cases the agent can be said to be the cause of the action. Such actions are free. On the other hand, when the causes of an action, or, more generally, of what a person does, are not his/her beliefs and desires to do that action,

then what happens is not "up to him" and the action is not free. However, it may not be compelled either. It is where the action is in contradiction to what the agent wants that the act can be said to be compelled. The agent is not responsible for the action because the action occurs in spite of him.

Among the objections that have been raised to this account of the distinction between free and unfree acts is that it provides an insufficient account of what it is for an agent to do an act freely. The problem is the source of the sources of one's allegedly free actions, i.e., the sources of one's beliefs and desires. Many philosophers have felt that if an agent's beliefs and desires are themselves determined, then actions proceeding from them must be as unfree as actions that are not caused by the agent's beliefs and desires. For example, Richard Taylor bids us to suppose that:

> while my behavior is entirely in accordance with my own volitions, and thus "free" in terms of the conception of freedom we are examining, my volitions themselves are caused. To make this graphic, we can suppose that an ingenious physiologist can induce in me any volition he pleases, simply by pushing various buttons on an instrument to which, let us suppose, I am attached by numerous wires. All the volitions I have in that situation, are, accordingly, precisely the ones he gives me . . . This is the description of a man who is acting in accordance with his inner volitions, a man whose body is unimpeded and unconstrained in its motions, these motions being the effects of those inner states. It is hardly the description of a free and responsible agent. It is the perfect description of a puppet.[3]

The same point can be made by examples of beliefs and desires acquired by brainwashing, hypnosis, subliminal advertising, etc. If a person acts because of beliefs and desires acquired in such ways, the action is clearly not free even though the action was done because of the agent's beliefs and desires. This

---

My thanks are due to all those whose comments on a closely related paper were invaluable help to me in writing this one and especially to Berent Enc, Haskell Fain, Bernard Gendron and Gary Young.

[1] Representative of contemporary approaches but somewhat different and less adequate in my opinion than the version I present are Moritz Schlick's "When Is a Man Responsible?" and R. E. Hobart's "Free Will as Involving Determinism and Inconceivable Without It" in *Free Will and Determinism* ed. by Bernard Berofsky (N. Y.: Harper and Row, 1966). Earlier versions are found in J. S. Mill, *An Examination of Sir William Hamilton's Philosophy* (London: Longman's Green and Co., Ltd., 1872) and David Hume's "Of Liberty and Necessity" in *An Inquiry Concerning Human Understanding* (Los Angeles: Henry Regnery Co., 1956).

[2] I intend "beliefs" and "desires" to cover all mental sources of action whatever exactly these are. I will not consider the question of the differences between these ostensible causes, (intentions, motives, wants, etc.), and their mutual relations, as this is a very involved issue and not crucial to my arguments. I use the word "desire" rather than "want" because there is one very weak sense of "want" in which I want to do everthing I do intentionally. When I do use "want" it should be understood in the stronger sense in which it is equivalent to "desire."

[3] Taylor, Richard, *Metaphysics* (Englewood Cliffs, N.J.: Prentice Hall, Inc., 1963), p. 45.

shows that it is not the case that an act is free just because it is caused by the beliefs and desires of the agent to do the act. The standard soft determinist position is inadequate as it stands.

One way of dealing with the objection might be to distinguish freedom of action and freedom of will and to maintain that the act was free but the will was not.[4] However, I think such examples show that these concepts cannot be so easily separated. Because the "will" is unfree in such cases, we would not call the act free. Taylor thinks his point applies much more generally than just to these sorts of examples and concludes that the standard conception of determinism cannot apply to a free act. He introduces, instead, a special notion of "agent causality."[5] I prefer to explore a response to the above objection that remains within the standard compatibilist framework.

I think that the objection I raised to soft determinism shows that soft determinists have too limited a notion of what is required for an agent to be the source of his/her actions. All that they require is that the agent do what he or she pleases. They ignore the question of whether the agent has control over the sources of the actions, his/her desires and beliefs. Taylor inferred that if the desires causing an action are themselves caused then the action is not free. This does not follow. Just because some causes of desires and beliefs, such as brainwashing, make actions resulting from them unfree, it does not follow that any cause of desires and beliefs has the same implications for the freedom of actions resulting from them.

Since the notion of having control is the heart of the notion of freedom for me,[6] let me stop to clarify the concept briefly. If I have control over x then x depends on what I do or do not do. I am an important part of the causal process producing x, such that if I did something different x would be different. Moreover, I must be conscious of x's dependence on me in order for x to be under my control. Whether some insect lives or not depends on whether or not I step on him as I walk down the street. But if I do not know he is there his life is not under my control. So for x to be under my control what I do or do not do must be an important part of the cause of x and I must know this. X therefore must depend on what I want or on my "will" in order for x to be under my control. Now since one can make more or less of a difference, be more or less important a part of the causal process, it therefore follows that one can have more or less control over something. The more control a person has the freer that person is. Clearly, then, a person is not simply free or unfree. Nor is every action simply free or unfree. Rather, there is a continuum between free and unfree with many or most acts lying somewhere in between. When I say that an act is free what I mean is that the act falls on the free side of the continuum. Or, since there is no line in the middle of a continuum, it might be clearer to say that a free act falls in the direction of the free end of the continuum. Acts are more or less free according to how close they are to the free end of the continuum.[7]

What I want to argue in this paper is that people can have differing amounts of control over what they desire and what they believe. People can be more or less important a part of the causal process leading to their having the desires and beliefs that they do. Our discussion thus far shows that only if

[4] Harry Frankfurt seems to do this although it is not entirely clear what he would say about this sort of example, in "Freedom of Will and the Concept of a Person," *Journal of Philosophy,* Vol. LXVIII, No. 1, January 14, 1971.

[5] Taylor, Richard, *Action and Purpose* (Englewood Cliffs, N.J.: Prentice Hall, Inc., 1966).

[6] If there are other conceptions of freedom in which control is not central then I am simply not interested in them and what I say may not apply to these other senses.

[7] It should be clear that I am using "free" and "unfree" (or "compelled") as contraries and not contradictories. Many acts we do every day, such as putting on our shoes, cannot sensibly be said to be either free or unfree. They belong in the middle of the continuum or—better perhaps—not on the continuum at all. Of other acts, it makes good sense to ask whether they are free or unfree; it is the answer that is complicated and which would place them somewhere in the middle of the continuum.

they have control over their beliefs and desires do they really have control over their actions. The key question, then is whether this idea of having control over one's beliefs and desires makes any sense and whether in fact we do have such control. Many people would probably say that while what we do is often up to us, what we believe and desire depends on factors completely beyond our control. Speaking generally, it depends on the way the world is; more specifically, it depends on our biological and psychological natures, the society in which we live, and our particular portion of it (i.e., our class, race, ethnic group, etc.). Others would object that it makes no sense to separate the person or self from his/her desires and beliefs, and hence makes no sense to talk of the person having control over his/her desires and beliefs. My major purpose in this paper will be to give substance to the idea that people can have control over the sources of their actions, that is, have control over their desires and beliefs.

If an agent can be said to be the source of his/her beliefs and desires, then it makes sense to say that the agent is a self-determining being. This is a concept that many have taken to be at the heart of freedom, whether they be determinists, indeterminists or hold to the idea of "agent causality."[8] If we can give substance to this notion of a person having control over his/her desires and beliefs, we will have given substance to the notion of a self-determining being.

II

Before turning directly to the central task, I wish to raise another sort of counterexample to soft determinism. Some acts that are done because of the agent's desires and beliefs to do them are nevertheless unfree, but for reasons other than the source of those desires and beliefs. However, we will see that these counterexamples do not challenge the fundamental thrust of soft determinism because the examples are all such that we have reason to say that the actions in the examples are not truly self-determined.

A heroin addict steals some money and uses it to buy heroin which he then takes. It might be said that all three acts (stealing, buying the drug and taking it) are done becuse of the addict's desire to achieve a certain state and the belief that these are ways of achieving it. If we imagine that this addict does not want to be an addict,[9] as is the case with most addicts, then these acts of his are crucially different from most acts done because of the agent's beliefs and desires. While the addict wants the heroin he also wants to not take the drug. Moreover, he wants a great number of things which he believes to be incompatible with taking the drug, e.g., health, self-respect, an ordinary life, etc. These contrary desires, values and beliefs are greater in number and also are part of an integrated whole. The desire to take the drug is not part of such an integrated whole, but nevertheless it outweighs all these contrary desires and beliefs. A kleptomaniac's desire to steal would probably be similar. Most actions done because of the agent's desires are not in conflict with a greater number of his/her integrated desires and beliefs. I think it is this factor which leads compatibilists to reject such cases as not really counterexamples to their analysis of a free act as one resulting from the wants of the agent. An act resulting from such a conflict does not seem to proceed from the self as a free act must; it occurs in spite of the person. Moritz Schlick says "We rightly consider the man to be more or less unfree, and hold him less responsible, because we rightly view the influence of the drug as "external" even though it is found within the body; it prevents him from making decisions in the manner peculiar to his nature."[10] This integrated set of desires, beliefs and values might be said to consti-

---

[8] "The principle of free will says 'I produce my volitions. Determinism says: My volitions are produced by me.' Determinism is free will expressed in the passive voice." R. E. Hobart, *op. cit.*, p. 71.

[9] If, on the other hand, we suppose that the addict does not mind being an addict, then none of the following holds.
[10] *Op. cit.*, p. 59.

tute the person's nature or self as it is at that time.[11] Acts proceeding from desires that are external to this and yet dominant would seem to be unfree. There are certain exceptions to this, however, which we will discover as we progress.

III

I wish at this point to introduce the notion of a second order volition as discussed by Harry Frankfurt in "Free Will and the Concept of a Person."[12] Someone has a volition of the second order when he wants to have a certain desire and, moreover, wants that desire to be his effective desire, i.e., his will, in Frankfurt's terminology. The addict in our example may simply suffer from a conflict between the desire to take the drug and a number of contradictory or incompatible desires. However, he may, further, want that the latter desires be his effective desires. If so, then the addict's desire to take the drug is in conflict not only with a greater number of integrated desires and beliefs, but with a second order volition as well. Yet it still determines the addict's actions. By being in conflict with the will he wants to have, it is in conflict with the want with which he has thereby identified himself. Hence, when this desire determines action, the action is in sharp contrast to most acts done because of the agent's beliefs and desires. Instead of being an act that depends on the agent, that is "up to him," it happens against his will. This provides further grounds for saying that the act does not proceed from the self. Quite aside

from the nature of the desire that is in conflict with the second order volition in our example, (i.e., the desire to take heroin), it would seem plausible to take as a sufficient condition for making an act unfree that it proceed from beliefs and desires that are in conflict with a second order volition. A necessary condition, then, of a free act is that it proceed from desires and beliefs that are consistent with second order volitions. This should be seen as a development of the compatibilist account of a free act as one caused by the self, specifically the agent's beliefs and desires.

IV

Consistency with an integrated set of beliefs and desires and with second order volitions is not sufficient for an act to be free. We saw at the outset that the source of the beliefs and desires causing an act is relevant to the freedom of that act. The sorts of examples which first showed us that the soft determinist position was unsatisfactory as thus far presented were examples of acts done because of beliefs and desires that seemed in some way to have been forced upon the agent. Whether the person acquired beliefs and desires (volitions or the reasons for doing what he/she does) by being hooked up to a machine someone else controls, or by being brainwashed or exposed to subliminal advertising, the following is true. The beliefs and desires were acquired by measures taken by others in order to induce them, which measures were taken either explicitly against the person's will (brainwashing), and/or without his/her knowledge (subliminal advertising). (Taylor's case could be either). Being ignorant of the measures taken to induce the beliefs and desires, the person is as much lacking in control over them as if they were taken explicitly against his/her will. In both cases the person, as an active determining being, is irrelevant to what happens. He/she has no control, and—more importantly— no possibility of control over the beliefs and desires he/she acquires. Actions done because of beliefs and desires acquired under such conditions are not free.

---

[11] It might be questioned whether the addict really does have such an integrated set at the time he/she is intent on procuring the heroin. (Alastair Hannay raised this question.) I think that when we ascribe wants or beliefs to a person we are talking of dispositions that a person has over some longish time period (the precise duration of which I could not say). So their having certain beliefs and desires is not contradicted by their behaving inconsistently with them on some occasion. If one prefers to say that they do not have these beliefs and desires when their behavior is inconsistent with them, then we could talk about the self as consisting of the integrated set of beliefs and desires that exist over some longish period of time, the precise duration of which it would be impossible to set.

[12] *Op. cit.*

Now is it really necessary that a person's beliefs and desires be caused by other people in order for it to be the case that they were forced upon him/her? Although it was true of our original examples, I do not think it is a necessary condition. While it may sound odd to say they were the result of force or coercion where no persons were the cause, it can certainly be said that the desires were not acquired freely, or even that they were acquired under coercive conditions. The issue about causation of beliefs and desires that is crucial to the freedom of acts resulting from them is whether the person enters into the causal process as an active determinant. If the person does not, then the beliefs and desires were not acquired freely, and acts resulting from them are not free because not self-determined. If, on the contrary, the beliefs and desires are opposed to the person's desires, first or second order, then acts resulting from them are unfree or compelled. All this can be true even though the causes of the beliefs and desires were not measures taken by others to induce them. Suppose that a person lives under conditions of economic scarcity, which entails that not everyone will get what he/she needs and wants. A consequence of a person getting enough for himself and his family is that others will not have enough. A person in these conditions might, partly as a survival mechanism, come to desire that others not have enough—and might act on this desire. If this occurred, it seems to me that such an act would be an unfree one, (although perhaps not at the very end of the continuum). If the person did not want to want that others not have enough, if in fact he/she wanted not to want this, then the desire would conflict with a second order volition. Acts resulting from such desires are unfree. However, in the absence of a conflicting or reinforcing second order volition, I would still wish to put the act on the unfree end of the continuum because the desires causing the act were produced under coercive conditions. The conditions were coercive because the person had no control over them, their existence was contrary to his/her desires, and his/her personality and character had little or no effect on their influence. Remove economic scarcity and the desire would be removed, (although perhaps not immediately). Similar examples could be given of beliefs and desires caused by particular social systems and particular institutions within a social system.

V

Let us examine in some greater detail the conditions I have given under which desires could be said to have been acquired unfreely or coercively. It might be thought that my conditions apply too widely and would make too many desires turn out to have been unfreely acquired. For example, suppose a person has a strong desire to hear Bach because her parents regularly played Bach records in order to induce that desire. Her desire was acquired because of her parents' efforts to induce the desire. Their efforts consisted of intensively exposing her to the object they wished her to desire. If my conditions apply to such cases then her going to a concert as an adult because she wants to hear Bach played would be unfree—and this is an unattractive conclusion. However, my conditions do not lead to this conclusion, because the conditions I set are not met in the example. The child was not unaware of the causes of her later desire, which is what my condition requires; in fact it was by being aware of the music that was regularly played that she came to desire to hear it. Conceivably, but improbably, she was unaware that hearing the music was the cause of her later desire or that her parents regularly played it in order to produce that desire in her. However, these are different conditions than the one I gave. In general, where the measures taken to induce a desire simply amount to exposing a person to the object of the hoped-for desire, this does not meet my conditions, because the person cannot be unaware of the causes of the desire, (although he/she may be unaware that they are the causes).[13]

---

[13] A desire acquired merely by exposure to the object or experience will not be a free desire if it meets other criteria for unfree desires. An example of such a desire might be the desire for heroin. The need for this qualification was pointed out to me by Gary Young.

I am inclined to think that my conditions as they stand thus far are in need of revision in the other direction, that is, to make them apply more widely. Suppose that what was done to induce the desire was not mere exposure to the object, but rather conditioning. If they had conditioned her, the parents would have accompanied the playing of the music with pleasurable stimuli and they would have negatively reinforced any expressions of negative feeling toward the music. If this had been done, the desire would be the result of more than the interrelation of the person and the object of the desire, as is the case when the desire for something comes into being because of exposure to it. A desire that is the result of conditioning is the result of pleasures and pains that accompany the object, but are external to the person, the object and the relation between them. When a person acquires desires and aversions for things because of pleasures and pains that are intrinsic to those things, such as the pleasures of eating good food, the pains of overeating, then those desires and aversions are freely acquired. Where the pleasures and pains are external, the *person* (i.e., his/her personality, reasoning, capacities, etc.), is bypassed in the process. This should make the process coercive. However, as my conditions stand they do not give this result. The person could be aware of the elements of the conditioning process, (the music, the accompanying pleasures and pains), though unaware of the connexions between them, the purposes behind them and their effect. She was aware of the measures taken and, therefore, if it were not explicitly against her will, the conditioning would not be coercive according to what I have said about coercion thus far. I take this to indicate that something more must be said.

In the hopes of working out how conditioning differs from mere exposure, let us go back to the example of the person who acquired a desire to hear the music of Bach because of repeated exposure to his music as a child. Whether the exposure was the deliberate work of others, as in our example, or not, acquisition of a desire through exposure differs from clearly coercive ways of acquiring desires. When people acquire a desire through being ac-

quainted with the object or experience, they have the possibility of coming to have that desire or not. Whether they do or not will depend on facts about them: their aptitudes, beliefs, personality, other desires, etc. Where this is the case they can be said to have control, or at least the possibility of control, over the desires they acquire. Where, on the other hand, the causes of their beliefs and desires would exist and would effectively operate regardless of the fact that their personality, character, other beliefs and desires are opposed to these causes, then they obviously have no chance of controlling what beliefs and desires they come to have.

We can distinguish, then, between cases where people can have control over their beliefs and desires and those where they cannot. Knowledge is necessary in order that a person have this possibility of control. In the account I gave of when a person could be said to have freely acquired his/her desires I only required that the person have knowledge of the causes, (and also that they not be against the person's will), in order that the causes not be coercive. Oftentimes, however, one needs to have more than simple knowledge of the causes. Conditioning is a case where the person being conditioned might know the causes, that is, might know the elements of the causal process, but might not know their interconnections or the purposes behind them. The person is acquainted with the causes but unaware that they are the causes of how and why they operate. If conditioning would operate regardless of whether a person knew the latter, then it is a causal process that the person cannot have any control over. Hence it is coercive.

Sometimes the efficacy of causal conditions depends on people's ignorance of them, that they are or may be causes, and how and why they operate. In such cases, people's ignorance of these facts would deprive them of whatever control knowledge might give them. People are less free to the extent that they operate on unconscious motives. Successful psychoanalysis can increase the patient's control and therefore freedom, by making conscious things that had hithertofore been unconscious. Sometimes just knowing the purposes behind potential causes, (e.g., that it is designed to convince you, scare you, buy you off, or get you to buy something), can make a difference to whether those purposes are realized. Without the knowledge, one's attitudes towards these purposes cannot come into play and one cannot exercise any control over them. If the efficacy of the causes depends on one's ignorance of such facts about the causes, then the causes are coercive. It is where knowledge about the causes would have made a difference that ignorance makes the causes coercive. Causes of beliefs and desires are coercive where they operate contrary to the person's other beliefs, desires, character and personality. This is so when the causes are explicitly against the person's will, or unknown to the person, or when they depend for their efficacy on the person's ignorance of certain facts about them. According to these conditions, conditioning would usually be coercive, which, I think, is as it should be.

Suppose one came to know that one was being conditioned and the knowledge made no difference to the efficacy of the causes. Is this a coercive way of acquiring desires? The answer depends on whether the conditioning process was against the person's will. If the causes operate against his/her will then they are coercive. On the other hand, suppose they are not operating against the person's will; in other words, suppose a person voluntarily chooses to be conditioned. A person might deliberately expose himself to conditions which will cause him to have (or not have) certain desires, e.g., not to smoke. Once he puts himself into the situation, the causes operate independent of his other beliefs and desires, personality, etc. His new effective desire not to smoke will be the result of conditioning, and we have said that conditioning is a form of coercion. However, I think that the circumstances of this kind of case make a significant difference. The person's self does enter into the causal process as an active determinant, whereas in most cases of conditioning this is not so. The person in our example who voluntarily has himself conditioned has a second order volition not to smoke, which is in conflict with his or her volition to smoke. If the second order volition were sufficiently strong to outweigh

the first order volition by itself, then the effective desire would be acquired in a completely free manner. However, it is not sufficiently strong to do this by itself. Causes that are independent of the person are necessary to change his desire. However, these other causes come into play only because of his second order volition. He had himself conditioned because he has a desire not to desire to smoke. So I think we can say that the cause of his new effective desire not to smoke is his second order volition. The new desire is not the result of coercion; it does spring from the self. However, it does not only spring from the self. It was not acquired in as free a manner as if the second order volition was sufficient by itself to cause it, but I would still put it towards the free end of the continuum.

What we have come up with is what we started with and that is, that to the extent that the causes of one's actions are themselves caused by things over which people have no control, (even with knowledge of them), to that extent one's actions are unfree. What I have tried to do is to make sense of the idea of having control over one's desires. In order to say that one has control over one's desires it is necessary that what we identify as the self determines what one desires and what desires one acts on. To put together the criteria elaborated thus far: in order for actions caused by desires to be free, these desires must first of all not have been coercively acquired. What this means has been explained. Knowledge was seen to be a key factor. Secondly, they must not be contrary to the person's second order volitions. This second condition implies that the person has second order volitions. We will not be able to say that these desires are the desires the person wants to have unless a) he/she has second order volitions and unless b) these volitions outweigh first order volitions in the case of a conflict. Thirdly, the desire must be in harmony with an integrated set of desires and beliefs—hence one's self at that given time. This third requirement must be qualified. A desire causing a free action may be inconsistent with this integrated set if the set does not meet one of the necessary conditions and the desire fulfills both the conditions. If the set was coercively acquired and the conflicting desire was not, or if the conflicting desire is supported by a second order volition and the set is not, then an action caused by the conflicting desire would be free. Any person missing second order volitions is missing an important kind of control over his/her actions, and hence an important dimension of freedom.[14] That is why an action that proceeds from a conflicting desire which is supported by a second order volition is freer than one that proceeded from the integrated set, where there are no effective second order volitions. This sort of situation could lead to a revision of the set—a restructuring of the self. However, lacking an integrated set which is responsible for his/her actions, the person is divided, and it is less possible for that person to be a self-determining being. Therefore, the person is most free when there is an integrated set which is in accordance with his/her second order volitions. Then we can say that this is a self-determining person.[15]

• • •

VII

As a prelude to concluding, I wish to consider the implications of my general and abstract analysis to the concrete question of just how free most people

are today. We shall see that although my view implies that people can be free, though determined, it is also an implication of my view that most people are quite unfree today. The answer to this question of how free people are is not one that applies to all people just in virtue of their being human, but rather depends on who the people are and where and when they are living. It turns out, then, on my view, that human freedom is closely tied to social and political freedom and is not a distinct metaphysical question. (In considering this part of the philosophical question we are invariably drawn into empirical issues, including political ones, so my own opinion on these matters will certainly intrude.)

Desires arise in us because of a whole complex set of conditions which affect one another. (Neither they nor their influence can actually be separated so the following remarks are unavoidably artificial.) These determining conditions include physical and psychological conditions, which to some extent we share with others, but which also differ from person to person. People today are capable of some but not much control over these conditions. Greater knowledge, aided by money, gives a person greater possibilities of control, but there are still very definite limits which no one today is capable of transcending. Greater knowledge will give greater possibilities of human control, but it is probable that there will always be limits that one cannot transcend. What is possible is for a person to exercise some control over the form of the desires these conditions tend to produce, and also over whether and how these desires are acted upon.

How much control a person can exercise over the social and political conditions causing his/her desires depends on the particular social system in which the person lives, and also the place that the person occupies in the system. Some changes are possible in the latter in most societies but usually quite little. In any case, it is only within the framework allowed by that system and it is not possible within the framework of *any* present society for *most* people to change their positions within that framework. As for the framework itself, one cannot change the time in which one lives, and since what

---

[14] What Frankfurt says is somewhat different. According to him, such a being would not be a person because having second order volitions is essential to being a person in his sense; a being without them is a wanton. We also differ in that I connect freedom of will and freedom of action whereas he separates them, and thirdly, in that I give a sense to the idea of controlling one's desires (freedom of will) independent of the idea of second order volitions.

[15] It may be worth pointing out that all of my criteria allow for the possibility that two people could perform the same act for the same reasons but one does it freely, the other unfreely. I do not see this as an objection of my account. (Paul Teller raised it as an objection.) All accounts of freedom allow the possibility of the same act (type) performed by one person being free and by another person being unfree. The act's (un)freedom depends on facts about its cause. Incompatibilists would say it depends on whether it's caused; compatibilists would say it depends on what the cause is. Since my account goes beyond the act, and its causes or lack thereof, to the causes of the causes of the act, it makes sense that the (un)freedom of the act would depend on facts about the causes of the causes.

social systems are possible depends on the time and place, there is a certain inevitable limitation. However, there are many fewer inevitable limitations on the degree of control one can exercise over social causes than over physical causes—in the future, but also in the present. Given the limitations of time and place, there is great potential today for people to collectively control the social conditions under which they live, and hence the beliefs and desires these conditions tend to produce, even if there are some conditions they still would not be able to control. However, with some notable exceptions, the ability to control the social conditions in which one lives is only potential today, not actual. This is partially because people do not realize they have this ability.[16] This lack of realization is strongly supported, of course, by the social system in which they live and by those who do control it. There is, again, the possibility of exercising some control over the form of the desires likely to be produced by these conditions, and also over whether and how these desires are acted upon. However, so long as one does not control the social causes of one's beliefs and desires, one does not have much chance of controlling the actual beliefs and desires one comes to have.

Leaving aside the nature of the influence, what is necessary in order to be able to exercise control over the influences acting upon one, is to be a certain kind of person, as well as to have knowledge and the cooperation of others. A person who is critical and discriminating and sees him/herself as actively shaping the world, history and also him/herself, is capable of doing just that—not alone, but in cooperation with others. There are, of course, varying conditions where people may be more or less aware and/or more or less able to be passive products. However, it seems that most people today are quite uncritical and undiscriminating and lack this self-conception. Many feel themselves to be more like passive products of history and their own particular environment—and their environment makes them feel that way. However, in the course of struggle against the oppressive aspects of their environment, they can come to realize their potential to bring the world under their conscious collective control. The realization of this is a first step towards changing the framework that keeps them without control. This capacity to change the world and consequently their own nature is unique to human beings. It gives them the potential of being free in their fullest sense that is possible in a deterministic world.[17]

FREEDOM OF THE WILL

Kitaro Nishida

I argued in the last chapter that in psychological terms the will is simply one phenomenon of consciousness but that in terms of its fundamental nature it is the base of reality. We now must consider whether the will is a free or determined activity, a question that has perplexed scholars since ancient times and that holds important implications for morality. Through this discussion we can clarify the philosophical character of the will.

---

[16] This is the phenomenon of fetishism that Marx discusses. "Such conditions are . . . independent of individuals and appear, although they are created by society, to be the same as natural conditions, i.e., uncontrollable by the individual." *The Grundrisse—Karl Marx,* edited by David McLellan (New York, Harper and Row, 1971), p. 72.

[17] This perspective is similar to that expressed by Marx in *Capital* where he says, "The freedom in this field [i.e., the realm of necessity] cannot consist of anything else but the fact that socialized man, the associated producers regulate their interchange with nature rationally, bring it under their human control, instead of being ruled by it as by some blind power; that they accomplish their task with the least expenditure of energy and under conditions most adequate to their human nature and most worthy of it. But it always remains a realm of necessity. Beyond it begins that development of human power, which is its own end, the true realm of freedom, which, however, can flourish only upon that realm of necessity as its basis." *Capital,* Vol. III, English translation, p. 820.

Judging from what people usually believe, we all consider the will to be free. Given our experience of our consciousness, within a certain sphere of action we are able to do something while also being able not to do it—that is, we believe we are free within that sphere. For this reason ideas of responsibility, irresponsibility, self-confidence, regret, praise, and blame arise in us. But let us now give careful thought to what is meant by "within a certain sphere."

We cannot freely control all things in the external world. Even our own bodies cannot be freely manipulated in any absolute sense. The voluntary movement of muscles seems to be free, but if we become ill we are no longer able to move our muscles freely. The only things we can freely manage are our own phenomena of consciousness. Even so, we have neither the freedom to create ideas anew nor the freedom to recall at any time something we once experienced. That which we regard as truly free is simply the activity of a union of ideas—that is, how we analyze ideas and how we synthesize them derives from the freedom of the self. And yet, an indisputable, a priori law functions in the analysis and synthesis of ideas, so we are not here able to do as we please either. Moreover, when a union of ideas stands alone or when a certain union is especially strong, we must fully obey it. We possess total freedom of choice only in the context of the a priori law of the establishment of ideas, and only when of two or more ways to unite ideas none has the strength to dominate.

Many of those who expound theories about the freedom of the will base their arguments on the facts of experience in the internal world. According to them, within that scope the selection of motives is in all respects a matter of our feedom and has no other reason than ourselves. They argue that decision is based on a type of mystical power—called the will—that is independent of both the various conditions in the external world and disposition, habit, and character in the internal world. In short, they posit a power that exists apart from the union of ideas while controlling it.

In contrast, those who expound deterministic theories of the will generally do so on the basis of observations of facts in the external world. According to them, the phenomena of the universe do not occur fortuitously; even extremely minute matters, when investigated in detail, necessarily possess a sufficient cause. This is the idea behind scholarly inquiry, and with the development of science it becomes increasingly certain. The causes and effects of natural phenomena formerly considered mysterious have since become clear, and we have advanced to the point where we can calculate them mathematically. At present, only our will is still regarded as having no cause. Even the will, however, cannot escape from the great, unchanging laws of nature. We continue to think that the will is free because the development of science is still in its infancy and because we cannot explain each of the causes of the will. It is true that in individual instances the action of the will appears to be irregular and devoid of any fixed cause, but if we look statistically at the actions of a large number of people, we discern that the actions are surprisingly orderly and that they have certain causes and effects. These observations strengthen our conviction that there are causes related to our will and bring us to the conclusion that our will, just like all other phenomena of nature, is ruled by a necessary, mechanical law of cause and effect and therefore is not some sort of mysterious power.

Which of these opposing theories is correct? As I stated before, those who uphold theories of free will in an extreme form tell us that we have a mysterious ability to choose motives freely without any cause or reason. But this assertion is totally mistaken, for there must be a sufficient reason for our choice of motives. Even if the reason does not appear clearly in consciousness, it must exist beneath consciousness. Moreover, if—as the proponents of free will contend—something decides things fortuitously without any reason, then at the time of decision we would not feel that the will is free; rather we would feel the decision to be a fortuitous event that has functioned from without, and our feeling of responsibility for the decision would be weak. Those who advance theories of free will set forth their arguments on the basis of experience in the internal world, but such internal experience actually proves the opposite—determinism.

Let us now offer a criticism of the determinist argument. These proponents claim that because natural phenomena are controlled by the law of mechanical necessity, phenomena of consciousness must be controlled by it as well. This stance is based on the assumption that phenomena of consciousness and natural phenomena (that is, material phenomena) are identical and controlled by the same law. But is this assumption correct? Whether phenomena of consciousness and material phenomena are controlled by the same law is an unsettled issue, and arguments marshalled on this assumption are extremely weak. Even if modern physiological psychology advances to the point where we can physically or chemically explain each of the functions of the brain at the base of consciousness, will we thereby be able to assert that phenomena of consciousness are controlled by a mechanical law of necessity? For example, the bronze that serves as the raw material of a statue perhaps cannot escape the domination of the laws of mechanical necessity, but can we not say that the meaning expressed by the statue exists apart from those laws? So-called spiritual meaning cannot be seen, heard, or counted; it transcends the laws of mechanical necessity.

In summary, the kind of will described by those who argue for the freedom of the will—a will that is totally without cause or reason—does not exist. Such a contingent will would not be felt to be free; rather, it would be felt to be oppressive. When we function for a certain reason, that is, from the internal character of the self, we feel ourselves to be free. And we feel most free when the cause of a motive emerges from the most profound internal character of the self. The reason behind the will, however, is now a mechanical cause as described by determinists. Our spirit contains a law governing its activity, and when spirit functions in accordance with its own law, it is truly free.

Freedom thus has two possible meanings: (1) being totally without cause, that is, fortuitous or contingent, and (2) having no external restrictions and therefore functioning of and by oneself. The latter indicates autonomous freedom, and this is the freedom of the will. At this point, the following problem arises. Assuming that freedom means to function according to one's character, we see that amongst the countless things around us nothing fails to function so. The flowing of water and the burning of fire are examples of this. Why then is only the will considered to be free and other things to be determined?

The occurrence of a phenomenon in the natural world is determined strictly by its circumstances. Only one, certain phenomenon—and no others—arises from a particular set of circumstances. All natural phenomena arise according to this sort of blind necessity. Phenomena of consciousness, however, do not simply arise, for they are phenomena of which we are conscious—that is, they arise and we know that they have arisen. Knowing something or being conscious of it includes other possibilities. To be conscious of taking something includes the possibility of not taking it. To put it more exactly, consciousness always possesses a universal character—consciousness always includes an idealistic element, otherwise it is not consciousness. That consciousness has such a character means that it harbors possibilities other than actual events. Being actual yet including ideals, being idealistic and yet not separating from actuality—this is the distinctive character of consciousness. Consciousness is in fact never controlled by other things, for it is always controlling them. Knowing this, even if our conduct occurs according to necessary laws we are not confined by the conduct. Moreover, actuality is simply one particular instance of the ideals that constitute the base of consciousness; that is, it is simply one process in which the ideals actualize themselves. Conduct therefore is not generated from without, but from within. And because we see actuality as simply one instance of the ideals, consciousness comes to include numerous other possibilities.

Consciousness is free not because it functions fortuitously beyond the laws of nature, but rather because it follows its own nature. It is free not because it functions for no reason, but because it knows well the reasons behind its functioning. As our knowledge advances, we become freer people. Even if we are controlled or oppressed by others, when we know this we extricate ourselves from the oppression. If we go even farther and realize the unavoidable reason for the situation, then the oppression turns into freedom—Socrates was freer than the Athenians who poisoned him. Pascal said that a person is as weak as a reed, but because he or she is a thinking reed, even if the whole world tries to destroy him, he is greater than that which kills him, for he himself knows that he will die.

As discussed earlier in the section on reality, the idealistic element—that is, the unifying activity—that constitutes the base of consciousness is not a product of nature; rather, it is because of this unity that nature comes to exist. This unity is the infinite power at the base of reality, and it cannot be limited quantitatively. It exists independently of the necessary laws of nature. Because our will is an expression of that power, it is free and goes beyond the control of such natural laws.

QUESTIONS FOR DISCUSSION

1. Discuss: freedom is a problem of both external physical constraints—consider Schlick's analysis of freedom as the absence of compulsion—and internal psychological constraints. What can we do to become more free in both senses?

2. Is freedom compatible with determinism? In your answer consider: (a) Schlick's analysis of freedom; and (b) the problem of conditioning and our ability to have control over the sources of our beliefs and desires.

3. Does Nancy Holmstrom's analysis of freedom really succeed in "firming up" soft determinism? In particular, does it succeed in drawing a clear distinction between conditioned acts which are unfree and those which are free?

4. Discuss Nishida's claim that consciousness is determined by laws governing its own activity. To what extent do you believe that consciousness is free from external determination? What is the role of knowledge and reason in human freedom?

Two Ragamuffins, "Didn't Live Nowhere," The Jacob A. Riis Collection, Museum of the City of New York.

CHAPTER 7

ETHICS

Of what does *ethics* consist? Is it the response in human volition and action to a moral law? Is it obedience to God? Or obedience to the rational? Both the Bhagavad-Gita and philosopher Immanuel Kant consider ethics to be based on duty, which is respect for a moral law. The Bhagavad-Gita sees that moral law ordained by God and written into human natures. Kant discerns the universal moral law through use of reason. Both assert that if all humanity followed this moral law, there would be harmony in society.

There are, however, critics of an ethics of duty. Mill's utilitarian theory insists that the right action is the one that would increase human happiness. Although we could say that it is one's "duty" to increase happiness for oneself and others, Kant's notion of duty specifically rules out concerns for happiness, so that "right" alone will prevail. Likewise, in the Bhagavad-Gita, the main character, Arjuna, is counselled to put aside all feelings of sadness and compassion so that he can do his duty.

It is just this abstract and "unfeeling" aspect of ethics of duty that Virginia Held criticizes in her analysis. The idea of a detached, rational analysis providing a guide for action belittles the positive role of emotion and care for others. It puts asunder all relationships of care between persons and replaces those relationships with respect for an abstract law. Such ethical systems are skewed, according to Held, because they come wholly from a male point of view and have neglected women's ethical experience.

Another theme, explored in the second section of this chapter, examines the issue of altruism or other-centered moral theories, in contrast to egoistic or self-centered theories. Throughout the centuries, moral theories and religious world views have described the moral life as opposed to the usual, amoral, and self-centered "survival instinct" acted upon naturally by so many humans. In our chapter, Riffat Hassan and Gunapala Dharmasiri show how concern for others is at the core of Islamic and Buddhist religions, respectively.

But not everyone agrees that one must give up one's egoistic concerns of survival and thriving, merely to fill the whims of others. Twentieth-century thinker Ayn Rand delivers a searing critique of altruistic moral theories and propounds what she considers a superior, egoistic basis for ethics.

It is obvious to even the beginner historian or an-

thropologist that different people have held different moral views at different times in history. Is this
because, as absolutists would claim, only some people were right and others were wrong? Or can the
same action be right in one context, wrong in another? Nowadays with sensitivity toward cultures
other than one's own emphasized, and the disasters
having ensued from cultural imperialism and forced
conversions better known (the destruction of Aztec
and Inca civilizations by Spanish conquistadors, the
burning of the Alexandrian library by overzealous
Christians, and so on), many are left wondering,
just where does tolerance and pluralism lead?
Should I apologize for my own views? Should I refrain from trying to convert others to my philosophy, for fear that I may damage their own valuable
belief system? Can I ever say that anyone else is
wrong? Can we ever use force to stop someone
from acting on their beliefs?

A religious figure named Maria was recently
popular in Russia and the Ukraine. She asserted that
the world would end on November 15, 1993. She
encouraged her followers to join her in Kiev for a
mass suicide on November 14. She and hundreds of
her followers were arrested. Being that we now
know that she was factually wrong, there remains
the issue, is it right to impose our value system on
her believers and insist that they cannot take their
lives, even if they want to? If we do insist, do we do
so by referring to an absolute standard of morality?
Or rather, can we argue that society as a whole creates standards by which individual members, or minority groups, are judged?

Wherever two cultures meet, and the newer one
tries to supplant the older, issues of how moral systems get their legitimacy and authority arise. Such
themes are often the central problematic of contemporary African novels, for in Africa longstanding
indigenous values and customs are challenged by
Christianity, Western secularism, and modernism.
Chinua Achebe's *Things Fall Apart* is a classic
when it comes to describing just how the intact and
self-coherent traditional lifestyle and belief system
of the Ibo in Nigeria were challenged and undermined, for better or worse, by the work of Christian
missionaries. Similar struggles can be seen in Nobel
prize author Wole Soyinka's account of his own upbringing in *Ake: Years of Childhood*. Such studies
bring to life the perennial moral dilemmas posed in
the third section by our two authors, Alejandro
Korn and Jeffrey Stout. Alejandro Korn argues that
indeed all moral judgments are subjective. There is
no universal standard and no criteria by which to
tell if a moral stance is the correct one. But Korn
thinks this subjectivity is fine. Others, of course,
would be dismayed. Jeffrey Stout argues that one
can admit that some actions are right in some circumstances and wrong in others, without therefore
becoming a complete relativist. Relativism has so
many senses; it would be best to be more specific
about what we mean by the term.

To explore further the issues of Buddhist reality,
and the Buddhist conception of the self, as background to Dharmasiri's article, see King Milindi,
Murti, and Izutsu in Chapter 5 and Hui Neng and
Thich Nhat Hanh in Chapter 1.

THE ETHICS OF DUTY AND CRITICS

Our first account of an ethics of duty is taken from India. The Bhagavad-Gita is a poem passed down through time by oral tradition. It found its way into the Hindu epic poem, the *Mahabharata,* which is the longest poem in the world. It is regarded as a sacred text, which encompasses Hindu wisdom of the centuries. The story line of the *Mahabharata* is a struggle between the forces of good and evil, and the story culminates with a war on a large battlefield. The "good" is represented by the Pandavas, and Arjuna is one of the sons of Pandu. The "evil" is represented by the Kuravas. The specific conflict that tears these related families apart has to do with rivalry caused by choosing an heir-apparent to the throne. Although many scholars argue that the storyline of the *Mahabharata* points to an actual historical event, the dialogue between Krishna and Arjuna is considered to be a spiritual masterpiece, set in the context of the larger storyline of the epic poem but possessing a spiritual insight that does not depend on its historical connection to the actual battle. It was included in the larger epic to ensure its preservation as a classic.

In this selection from Chapters 1 through 3 of the Bhagavad-Gita, we witness a dialogue between Arjuna, a young warrior, and Krishna, an avatar or incarnation of God, who advises him on the battleground. The story is used in the Hindu tradition to illustrate the proper attitude toward life and responsibility. In this particular battle, Arjuna does not want to fight, because he is moved by the sight of his friends, relatives, and teachers who are assembled to fight him on the battlefield. Yet, as a member of the warrior caste, it is his job to serve his community through selflessly fighting, and so it is not proper that he be moved to tears and put down his arms. This is explained to Arjuna by Krishna, who suggests that Arjuna should not be attached to the repercussions of his actions but should do his duty in a detached manner. Wars should not be fought for personal gain and power, but for a just cause. If one resists desire and the pleasures of the senses, the mind will not be clouded, and the soul will find peace.

Since Arjuna seems to be trying to enact a life of renunciation, as he has explained that he would rather be killed on the battlefield than fight, Krishna counsels against a life of renunciation and in favor of a life of duty, where one fulfills the tasks assigned and works happily with detachment: a spiritual practice called "Karma yoga." Based on this passage and others in the Hindu tradition, Hinduism has developed the concept of Karma yoga: it is aptly described as ethics of duty, in which not only must one do one's duty because God has ordained it, but also, because it is the way to true, spiritual happiness, in contrast to other pleasures which are passing and end in despair.

It should be noted that throughout the centuries there have been alternative interpretations of this passage that draw from it different conclusions about action. Although many might conclude that this passage attempts to reconcile young men to their position in military service, seeing it as a duty, Mohandas Gandhi held a somewhat unorthodox interpretation of the story. He insisted that the story did not describe a literal battlefield, and was not really about war. Rather, it was metaphorical, and represented the struggle between good and evil in the mind of each individual. In this way, one could regard the passage as not necessarily advocating violence—a position which is more consistent with Gandhi's devotion to the principle of *ahimsa* or nonviolence.

Although the practice of caste cannot be found in eighteenth-century Konigsberg, it is hard not to notice some similarities in disposition between the doctrines in the Bhagavad-Gita and Kant's concept of duty. Kant, like the Bhagavad-Gita, voices a fear of emotions that might sway one from the right course. However, the discernment of just what is one's duty he sees differently. The Bhagavad-Gita emphasizes God's ordination, presumably known through tradition; Kant emphasizes reason's ability to discern right action.

Kant begins his essay by emphasizing the central importance of the good will, meaning, the intention to do good. Regardless of its ability to enact what it desires, good will is valuable and praiseworthy for its own sake. Kant discerns that the goal of life is to do the good, in other words to do one's moral duty, which means to act in respect to the moral law. Kant asserts that an action has moral worth only if it is done from duty; to do what is right out of sympathy and compassion can no more give an action moral worth than a right action done for the motive of self-interest. Each of us can discern the proper course of action by making sure that the maxim of our action could become a universal law. This formula is known as Kant's "categorical imperative." As universality is the basic property of reason, it is pure reason itself, that is, reason free of emotions, from which our sense of duty is derived.

Kant's position is often contrasted to that of J. S. Mill. Mill argues that the goal of human life is happiness, and his "utilitarian" formulation of ethics argues that an action is the correct one if it results in the greatest happiness for the greatest number of people. Mill's position offers a challenge to Kant, in several ways. Firstly, Mill's position is hedonistic; he believes pleasure is the goal of human life. Of course, he makes distinctions, asserting that humans are capable of a pleasure more sophisticated than animal gratification. But that all humans seek pleasure as the highest end is a fact that Mill considers obvious. Second, Mill contends that intentions aren't important, as long as the consequences of an action increase happiness for the most number of people. This is what is referred to as the "consequentialist" aspect of his view, with this emphasis on consequences as justification for action being opposed to Kant's emphasis on intentions. As can be expected, a view entitled "utilitarianism" emphasizes the practical consequences which result from an action or policy. Although certainly in opposition to Kant's view, Mill himself thought there was an implicit consequentialism in Kant's intentional theory, in that the latter was implicitly appealing to the consequences of adopting the maxim of one's action as a universal law.

Needless to say, many philosophers have joined in this ethical debate between Kant and Mill, taking one side or the other or even criticizing both sides. For example, it could be argued that accepting Kant's "categorical imperative" is accepting too subjective a criterion, for it allows the callous to accept the possibility of harsh treatment, whereas the overly sensitive will rule out even minor inconveniences toward others. (For example, "it is acceptable to hurt others' feelings" may be a maxim accepted by some and not by others, as well as "it is acceptable to abandon people in need of help.") Criticisms of Mill's utilitarianism involve the unpredictability of the future, an aspect which especially wreaks havoc with an ethical view based wholly on the weighing of future consequences.

Our fourth author in this section, Virginia Held, has her own unique angle on the shortcomings of both Kant's and Mill's ethical theories. Her article not only puts forward her own view but attempts to represent some common threads of thought in the contemporary ethical theorizing of many women philosophers. Traditional ethical theories, she asserts, have been written from the male standpoint. Praise of reason and denigration of emotion, rather than being the obviously preferable moral position, is biased in favor of men's experience and relegates women to the status of inferiority. Male ethicists tend to abstract individuals from their family and their general social context, which obscures the true human situation, framing ethical obligations by means of a contextless, abstract, fictitious individual. Both Kant's and Mill's approaches to any moral dilemma are too abstracted from the concrete situation; such cool, calculated approaches to moral dilemmas denigrate the positive role of emotion, involvement, and the nuances of concrete situations. An alternative women's moral theory would entail appreciating the context of the dilemma. A fruitful resolution of a moral dilemma would show itself in the restoration of human relationships, not the upholding of a rule—such as the principle of utility or the categorical imperative. An "ethic of care" may be more important than the mere abstract and legalistic "ethic of justice."

RIGHT ACTION

Bhagavad-Gita

CHAPTER 1. THE HESITATION AND DESPONDENCY OF ARJUNA

The question

Dhrtarāṣṭra said:

1. In the field of righteousness, the field of the Kurus,[1] when my people and the sons of Pāndu had gathered together, eager for battle, what did they do, O Saṁjaya?[2]

Saṁjaya said:

2. Then, Duryodhana the prince, having seen the army of the Pāndavas drawn up in battle order, approached his teacher and spoke this word:

3. Behold, O Teacher, this mighty army of the sons of Pāndu organized by thy wise pupil, the son of Drupada.

4. Here are heroes, great bowmen equal in battle to Bhīma[3] and Arjuna[4]—Yuyudhāna, Virāṭa, and Drupada, a mighty warrior;

5. Dhrṣṭaketu, Cekitāna and the valiant King of Kāśi, also Purujit, Kuntibhoja and Śaibya, the foremost of men;

6. Yudhāmanyu, the strong and Uttamauja, the brave; and also the son of Subhadrā and sons of Draupadī, all of them great warriors.

7. Know also, O best of the twiceborn,[5] the leaders of my army, those who are most distinguished among us. I will name them now for thine information:

8. Thyself and Bhīṣma and Karṇa and Kṛpa, ever victorious in battle; Asvatthāman, Vikarṇa, and also the son of Somadatta;

9. And many other heroes who have risked their lives for my sake. They are armed with many kinds of weapons and are all well skilled in war.

10. Unlimited is this army of ours which is guarded by Bhīṣma, while that army of theirs, which is guarded by Bhīma, is limited.

11. Therefore do ye all support Bhīṣma, standing firm in all the fronts, in your respective ranks.

12. In order to cheer him up, the aged Kuru, his valiant grandsire, roared aloud like a lion and blew his conch.

13. Then conches and kettledrums, tabors and drums and horns suddenly blared forth and the noise was tumultuous.

14. When stationed in their great chariot yoked to white horses, Kṛṣṇa and Arjuna blew their celestial conches.

15. Kṛṣṇa blew his Pāñcajanya and Arjuna his Devadatta and Bhīma of terrific deeds blew his mighty conch, Paundra.

16. Prince Yudhiṣṭhira, the son of Kuntī, blew his Anantavijaya and Nakula and Sahadeva blew their Sughoṣa and Manipuṣpaka.

17. And the king of Kāśi, the Chief of archers, Śikhaṇḍin, the great warrior, Dhrṣṭadyumna and Virāṭa and the invincible Sātyaki;

18. Drupada and the sons of Draupadī, O Lord

---

[1] Kurukṣetra is the land of the Kurus, a leading clan of the period. It is a vast field near Hastināpura in the neighborhood of modern Delhi. When Dhrtarāṣṭra, the blind king of the Kurus, decided to give his throne to Yudhiṣṭhira, who is also known as Dharmarāja, the embodiment of virtue, in preference to his own eldest son, Duryodhana, the latter, by tricks and treachery, secured the throne for himself and attempted to destroy Yudhiṣṭhira and his four brothers. Kṛṣṇa, the head of the Yādava clan, sought to bring about a reconciliation between the cousins. When all attempts failed, a fratricidal war between the Kauravas and the Pāndavas became inevitable. Kṛṣṇa proposed that he and his vassals would join the two sides and left the choice to the parties. The vassals were selected by Duryodhana, and Kṛṣṇa himself joined the Pāndavas as the charioteer of Arjuna.

[2] Saṁjaya is the charioteer of the blind king, Dhrtarāṣṭra, who reports to him the events of the war. (Many of the other names used in the text are without philosophical significance and no attempt will be made to explain them.)

[3] Bhīma is Yudhiṣṭhira's Commander-in-Chief, though nominally Dhrṣṭadyumna holds that office.

[4] Arjuna is the friend of Kṛṣṇa and the great hero of the Pāndavas. Other names used for Arjuna are Bhārata (descended of Bhārata), Dhanaṁjaya (winner of wealth), Guḍākeśa (having the hair in a ball), Pārtha (son of Pṛthā), Paraṁtapa (oppressor of the enemy).

[5] One who is twice-born is one who is invested with the sacred thread, the symbol of initiation into the life of spirit, which is the aim of education.

of earth, and the strong-armed son of Subhadrā, on all sides blew their respective conches.

19. The tumultuous uproar resounding through earth and sky rent the hearts of Dhṛtarāṣṭra's sons.

20. Then Arjuna, whose banner bore the crest Hanumān, looked at the sons of Dhṛtarāṣṭra drawn up in battle order; and as the flight of missiles [almost] started, he took up his bow.

21. And, O Lord of earth, he spoke this word to Hṛṣīkeśa (Kṛṣṇa): Draw up my chariot, O Acyuta (Kṛṣṇa),[6] between the two armies.

22. So that I may observe these men standing, eager for battle, with whom I have to contend in this strife of war.

23. I wish to look at those who are assembled here, ready to fight and eager to achieve in battle what is dear to the evil-minded son of Dhṛtarāṣṭra.

24. Thus addressed by Guḍākeśa (Arjuna), Hṛṣīkeśa (Kṛṣṇa) drew up that best of chariots, O Bhārata (Dhṛtarāṣṭra), between the two armies.

25. In front of Bhīṣma, Droṇa, and all the chiefs he said: "Behold, O Pārtha (Arjuna), these Kurus assembled here."

26. There saw Arjuna standing fathers and grandfathers, teachers, uncles, brothers, sons and grandsons, as also companions;

27. And also fathers-in-law and friends in both the armies. When the son of Kuntī (Arjuna) saw all these kinsmen thus standing arrayed,

28. He was overcome with great compassion and uttered this in sadness:

The Distress of Arjuna

When I see my own people arrayed and eager for fight, O Kṛṣṇa,

29. My limbs quail, my mouth goes dry, my body shakes and my hair stands on end.

30. The bow Gāṇḍīva slips from my hand, and my skin too is burning all over. I am not able to stand steady. My mind is reeling.

31. And I see evil omens, O Keśava (Kṛṣṇa), nor do I foresee any good by slaying my own people in the fight.

32. I do not long for victory, O Kṛṣṇa, nor kingdom nor pleasures. Of what use is kingdom to us, O Kṛṣṇa, or enjoyment or even life?

33. Those for whose sake we desire kingdom, enjoyments and pleasures—they stand here in battle, renouncing their lives and riches:

34. Teachers, fathers, sons, and also grandfathers; uncles and fathers-in-law, grandsons and brothers-in-law, and other kinsmen.

35. These I would not consent to kill, though killed myself, O Madhusūdana (Kṛṣṇa), even for the kingdom of the three worlds; how much less for the sake of the earth?

36. What pleasure can be ours, O Kṛṣṇa, after we have slain the sons of Dhṛtarāṣṭra? Only sin will accrue to us if we kill these criminals.

37. So it is not right that we slay our kinsmen, the sons of Dhṛtarāṣṭra. Indeed, how can we be happy, O Mādhava (Kṛṣṇa), if we kill our own people?

38. Even if these whose minds are overpowered by greed see no wrong in the destruction of the family and no crime in treachery to friends;

39. Why should we not have the wisdom to turn away from this sin, O Janārdana (Kṛṣṇa), we who see the wrong in the destruction of the family?

40. In the ruin of a family, its ancient laws are destroyed: and when the laws perish, the whole family yields to lawlessness.

41. And when lawlessness prevails, O Vārṣṇeya (Kṛṣṇa), the women of the family become corrupted, and when women are corrupted, confusion of castes arises.

42. And to hell does this confusion bring the family itself as well as those who have destroyed it. For the spirits of their ancestors fall, deprived of their offerings of rice and water.

43. By the misdeeds of those who destroy a family and create confusion of *varṇas* [castes], the

---

[6] Acyuta (immovable) is another name for Kṛṣṇa. Other names used for Kṛṣṇa are Madhusūdana (slayer of the demon Madhu), Arisūdana (slayer of enemies), Govinda (herdsman or giver of enlightenment), Vāsudeva (son of Vasudeva), Yādava (descendent of Yadu), Keśava (having fine hair), Mādhava (the husband of Lakṣmī), Hṛṣīkeśa (lord of the senses, *hṛṣīka, īśā*) Janārdana (the liberator of men).

immemorial laws of the race and the family are destroyed.

44. And we have heard it said, O Janārdana (Kṛṣṇa), that the men of the families whose laws are destroyed needs must live in hell.

45. Alas, what a great sin have we resolved to commit in striving to slay our own people through our greed for the pleasures of the kingdom!

46. Far better would it be for me if the sons of Dhṛtarāṣṭra, with weapons in hand, should slay me in the battle, while I remain unresisting and unarmed.

47. Having spoken thus on the field of battle, Arjuna sank down on the seat of his chariot, casting away his bow and arrow, his spirit overwhelmed by sorrow.

In the Upaniṣad of the *Bhagavad-gītā,* the science of the Absolute, the scripture of *yoga,* and the dialogue between Śrīkṛṣṇa and Arjuna, this is the first chapter, entitled "The Depression of Arjuna."[7]

CHAPTER 2: SAMKHYA THEORY[8] AND YOGA PRACTICE

Kṛṣṇa's rebuke and exhortation to be brave

Saṁjaya said:

1. To him who was thus overcome by pity, whose eyes were filled with tears and troubled and who was much depressed in mind, Madhusūdana (Kṛṣṇa) spoke this word.

The Blessed Lord said:

2. Whence has come to thee this stain (this dejection) of spirit in this hour of crisis? It is unknown to men of noble mind [not cherished by the Āryans]; it does not lead to heaven; on earth it causes disgrace, O Arjuna.

3. Yield not to this unmanliness, O Pārtha (Arjuna), for it does not become thee. Cast off this petty faintheartedness and arise, O Oppressor of the foes (Arjuna).

Arjuna said:

4. How shall I strike Bhīṣma and Droṇa, who are worthy of worship, O Madhusūdana (Kṛṣṇa), with arrows in battle, O Slayer of foes (Kṛṣṇa)?

5. It is better to live in this world by begging than to slay these honoured teachers. Though they are mindful of their gains, they are my teachers, and by slaying them, I would enjoy in this world delights which are smeared with blood.

6. Nor do we know which for us is better, whether we conquer them or they conquer us. The sons of Dhṛtarāṣṭra, whom if we slew we should not care to live, are standing before us in battle array.

7. My very being is stricken with the weakness of sentimental pity. With my mind bewildered about my duty, I ask Thee. Tell me, for certain, which is better. I am Thy pupil; teach me, who am seeking refuge in Thee.

8. I do not see what will drive away this sorrow which dries up my senses even if I should attain rich and unrivalled kingdom on earth or even the sovereignty of the gods.

Saṁjaya said:

9. Having thus addressed Hṛṣīkeśa (Kṛṣṇa), the mighty Guḍākeśa (Arjuna) said to Govinda (Kṛṣṇa), "I will not fight," and became silent.

10. To him thus depressed in the midst of the two armies, O Bhārata (Dhṛtarāṣṭra), Hṛṣīkeśa (Kṛṣṇa), smiling as it were, spoke this word.

The distinction between self and body: we should not grieve for what is imperishable

The Blessed Lord said:

11. Thou grievest for those whom thou shouldst not grieve for, and yet thou speakest words about wisdom. Wise men do not grieve for the dead or for the living.

12. Never was there a time when I was not, nor

---

[7] This is the usual colophon, which is not a part of the text. There are slight variations in the titles of the chapters in the different versions, but they are not worth recording.

[8] The teacher explains in brief in verses 11–38 the wisdom of the Sāṁkhya philosophy. The Sāṁkhya does not refer to Kapila's system but to the teaching of the Upaniṣads.

Sāṁkhya and Yoga are not in the *Gītā* discordant systems. They have the same aim but differ in their methods.

thou, nor these lords of men, nor will there ever be a time hereafter when we shall cease to be.[9]

13. As the soul passes in this body through childhood, youth and age, even so is its taking on of another body. The sage is not perplexed by this.

14. Contacts with their objects, O son of Kuntī (Arjuna), give rise to cold and heat, pleasure and pain. They come and go and do not last forever; these learn to endure, O Bhārata (Arjuna).

15. The man who is not troubled by these, O Chief of men (Arjuna), who remains the same in pain and pleasure, who is wise, makes himself fit for eternal life.

16. Of the non-existent there is no coming to be; of the existent there is no ceasing to be. The conclusion about these two has been perceived by the seers of truth.

17. Know thou that that by which all this is pervaded is indestructible. Of this immutable being, no one can bring about the destruction.

18. It is said that these bodies of the eternal embodied soul, which is indestructible and incomprehensible, come to an end. Therefore fight, O Bhārata (Arjuna).

19. He who thinks that this slays and he who thinks that this is slain; both of them fail to perceive the truth; this one neither slays nor is slain.

20. He is never born, nor does he die at any time, nor having once come to be does he again cease to be. He is unborn, eternal, permanent, and primeval. He is not slain when the body is slain.

21. He who knows that it is indestructible and eternal, uncreated and unchanging—how can such a person slay any one, O Pārtha (Arjuna), or cause any one to slay?

22. Just as a person casts off worn-out garments and puts on others that are new, even so does the embodied soul cast off worn-out bodies and take on others that are new.

23. Weapons do not cleave this self; fire does not burn him; waters do not make him wet; nor does the wind make him dry.

24. He is uncleavable. He cannot be burnt. He

can be neither wetted nor dried. He is eternal, all-pervading, unchanging, and immovable. He is the same forever.

25. He is said to be unmanifest, unthinkable, and unchanging. Therefore, knowing him as such, thou shouldst not grieve.

We should not grieve over what is perishable

26. Even if thou thinkest that the self is perpetually born and perpetually dies, even then, O Mighty-armed (Arjuna), thou shouldst not grieve,

27. For to the one that is born death is certain, and certain is birth for the one that has died. Therefore, for what is unavoidable thou shouldst not grieve.

28. Beings are unmanifest in their beginnings, manifest in the middles, and unmanifest again in their ends, O Bhārata (Arjuna). What is there in this for lamentation?

29. One looks upon Him as a marvel; another likewise speaks of Him as a marvel; another hears of Him as a marvel; and even after hearing, no one whatsoever has known Him.

30. The dweller in the body of every one, O Bhārata (Arjuna), is eternal and can never be slain. Therefore, thou shouldst not grieve for any creature.

Appeal to a sense of duty

31. Further, having regard for thine own duty, thou shouldst not falter; there exists no greater good for a *kṣatriya* [warrior] than a war enjoined by duty.

32. Happy are the *kṣatriyas,* O Pārtha (Arjuna), for whom such a war comes of its own accord as an open door to heaven.

33. But if thou doest not this lawful battle, then thou wilt fail thy duty and glory and will incur sin.

34. Besides, men will ever recount thy ill-fame, and for one who has been honoured ill-fame is worse than death.

35. The greater warriors will think that thou hast abstained from battle through fear, and they by whom thou wast highly esteemed will make light of thee.

---

[9] While the Sāṁkhya system postulates a plurality of souls, the *Gītā* reconciles this with unity.

36. Many unseemly words will be uttered by thine enemies, slandering thy strength. Could anything be sadder than that?

37. Either slain thou shalt go to heaven; or victorious thou shalt enjoy the earth; therefore arise, O Son of Kuntī (Arjuna), resolve on battle.

38. Treating alike pleasure and pain, gain and loss, victory and defeat, then get ready for battle. Thus thou shalt not incur sin.

The insight of Yoga

39. This is the wisdom of the Sāṁkhya given to thee, O Pārtha (Arjuna). Listen now to the Yoga. If your intelligence accepts it, thou shalt cast away the bondage of works.

40. In this path, no effort is ever lost and no obstacle prevails; even a little of this righteousness (*dharma*) saves from great fear.

41. In this, O joy of the Kurus (Arjuna), the resolute understanding is single; but the thoughts of the irresolute are many-branched and endless.

No wisdom for the worldly-minded

42–43. The undiscerning, who rejoice in the letter of the Veda, who contend that there is nothing else, whose nature is desire, and who are intent on heaven, proclaim these flowery words that result in rebirth as the fruit of actions and lay down various specialized rites for the attainment of enjoyment and power.

44. The intelligence which is to be trained, of those who are devoted to enjoyment and power and whose minds are carried away by these words [of the Veda], is not well-established in the Self [or concentration].

45. The action of the threefold modes[10] is the subject matter of the Veda; but do thou become free, O Arjuna, from this threefold nature; be free from the dualities [the pairs of opposites]; be firmly fixed in purity, not caring for acquisition and preservation; and be possessed of the Self.

46. As is the use of a pond in a place flooded with water everywhere, so is that of all the Vedas for the *brāhmin* who understands.[11]

Work without concern for the results

47. To action alone hast thou a right and never at all to its fruit; let not the fruits of action be thy motive; neither let there be in thee any attachment to inaction.

48. Fixed in *yoga,* do thy work, O winner of wealth (Arjuna), abandoning attachment, with an even mind in success and failure, for evenness of mind is called *yoga.*

49. Far inferior indeed is mere action to the discipline of intelligence, O winner of wealth (Arjuna); seek refuge in intelligence. Pitiful are those who seek for the fruits of their action.

50. One who has yoked his intelligence [with the Divine] (or is established in his intelligence) casts away even here both good and evil. Therefore strive for *yoga*; *yoga* is skill in action.

51. The wise who have united their intelligence [with the Divine], renouncing the fruits which their action yields and freed from the bonds of birth, reach the sorrowless state.

52. When thine intelligence shall cross the whirl of delusion, then shalt thou become indifferent to what has been heard and what is yet to be heard.[12]

53. When thine intelligence, which is bewildered by the Vedic texts, shall stand unshaken and stable in spirit (*samādhi*), then shalt thou attain to insight (*yoga*).

The characteristics of the perfect sage

Arjuna said:
54. What is the description of the man who has this firmly founded wisdom, whose being is stead-

---

[10] The three modes (*guṇas*) are goodness (*sattva*), passion (*rajas*), and dullness or inertia (*tamas*). These are the primary constituents of nature and are the bases of all substances.

[11] That is, for those of illumined consciousness or spiritual insight ritual observances are of little value.
[12] Scriptures are unnecessary for the man who has attained insight.

fast in spirit, O Keśeva (Kṛṣṇa)? How does the man of settled intelligence speak; how does he sit; how does he walk?

The Blessed Lord said:

55. When a man puts away all the desires of his mind, O Pārtha (Arjuna), and when his spirit is content in itself, then is he called stable in intelligence.

56. He whose mind is untroubled in the midst of sorrows and is free from eager desire amid pleasures, he from whom passion, fear, and rage have passed away—he is called a sage of settled intelligence.

57. He who is without affection on any side, who does not rejoice or loathe as he obtains good or evil—his intelligence is firmly set [in wisdom].

58. He who draws away the senses from the objects of sense on every side as a tortoise draws in his limbs into the shell—his intelligence is firmly set [in wisdom].

59. The objects of sense turn away from the embodied soul who abstains from feeding on them, but the taste for them remains. Even the taste turns away when the Supreme is seen.

60. Even though a man may ever strive [for perfection] and be ever so discerning, O Son of Kuntī (Arjuna), his impetuous senses will carry off his mind by force.

61. Having brought all the senses under control, he should remain firm in *yoga,* intent on Me; for he, whose senses are under control, his intelligence is firmly set.

62. When a man dwells in his mind on the objects of sense, attachment to them is produced. From attachment springs desire, and from desire comes anger.

63. From anger arises bewilderment, from bewilderment loss of memory, and from loss of memory the destruction of intelligence; and from the destruction of intelligence he perishes.

64. But a man of disciplined mind, who moves among the objects of sense, with the senses under control and free from attachment and aversion—he attains purity of spirit.

65. And in that purity of spirit, there is produced for him an end of all sorrow; the intelligence of such a man of pure spirit is soon established [in the peace of the self].

66. For the uncontrolled, there is no intelligence; nor for the uncontrolled is there the power of concentration; and for him without concentration, there is no peace; and for the unpeaceful, how can there be happiness?

67. When the mind runs after the roving senses, it carries away the understanding, even as a wind carries away a ship on the waters.

68. Therefore, O Mighty-armed (Arjuna), he whose senses are all withdrawn from their objects—his intelligence is firmly set.

69. What is night for all beings is the time of waking for the disciplined soul; and what is the time of waking for all beings is night for the sage who sees (or the sage of vision).[13]

70. He unto whom all desires enter as waters into the sea, which, though ever being filled, is ever motionless, attains to peace, and not he who hugs his desires.

71. He who abandons all desires and acts free from longing, without any sense of mineness or egotism—he attains to peace.

72. This is the divine state, O Pārtha (Arjuna); having attained thereto, one is not again bewildered; fixed in that state at the end [at the hour of death] one can attain to the bliss of God.

This is the second chapter, entitled "The *Yoga* of Knowledge."

CHAPTER 3: KARMA-YOGA OR THE METHOD OF WORK

Why then work at all?

Arjuna said:

1. If thou deemest that the path of understanding is more excellent than the path of action, O Janārdana (Kṛṣṇa), why then dost thou urge me to do this savage deed, O Keśeva (Kṛṣṇa)?

---

[13] When all beings are attracted by the glitter of sense-objects, the sage is intent on understanding reality. He is wakeful to the nature of reality to which the unwise is asleep or indifferent.

2. With an apparently confused utterance thou seemest to bewilder my intelligence. Tell me, then, decisively the one thing by which I can attain to the highest good.

Life is work; unconcern for results is needful

The Blessed Lord said:

3. O blameless One, in this world a twofold way of life has been taught of yore by Me, the path of knowledge for men of contemplation and that of works for men of action.

4. Not by abstention from work does a man attain freedom from action; nor by mere renunciation does he attain to his perfection.

5. For no one can remain even for a moment without doing work; every one is made to act helplessly by the impulses born of nature.

6. He who restrains his organs of action but continues in his mind to brood over the objects of sense, whose nature is deluded, is said to be a hypocrite [a man of false conduct].

7. But he who controls the senses by the mind, O Arjuna, and without attachment engages the organs of action in the path of work, he is superior.

The importance of sacrifice

8. Do thou thine allotted work, for action is better than inaction; even the maintenance of thy physical life cannot be effected without action.

9. Save work done as and for a sacrifice[14] this world is in bondage to work. Therefore, O son of Kuntī (Arjuna), do thy work as a sacrifice, becoming free from all attachment.

10. In ancient days the Lord of creatures created men along with sacrifice, and said, "By this shall ye bring forth and this shall be unto you that which will yield the milk of your desires."

11. By this foster ye the gods and let the gods foster you; thus fostering each other you shall attain to the supreme good.

12. Fostered by sacrifice, the gods will give you enjoyments you desire. He who enjoys these gifts without giving to them in return is verily a thief.

13. The good people who eat what is left from the sacrifice are released from all sins, but those wicked people who prepare food for their own sake—verily they eat their sin.

14. From food creatures come into being; from rain is the birth of food; from sacrifice rain comes into being, and sacrifice is born of work.

15. Know the origin of *karma* [of the nature of sacrifices] to be in *Brahman* [the Veda], and the *Brahman* springs from the Imperishable. Therefore the *Brahman,* which comprehends all, ever centres round the sacrifice.

16. He who does not, in this world, turn the wheel thus set in motion, is evil in his nature, sensual in his delight, and he, O Pārtha (Arjuna), lives in vain.

Be satisfied in the Self

17. But the man whose delight is in the Self alone, who is content with the Self, who is satisfied with the Self—for him there exists no work that needs to be done.

18. Similarly, in this world he has no interest whatever to gain by the actions that he has done and none to be gained by the actions that he has not done. He does not depend on all these beings for any interest of his.

19. Therefore, without attachment, perform always the work that has to be done, for man attains to the highest by doing work without attachment.

Set an example to others

20. It was even by works that Janaka[15] and others attained to perfection. Thou shouldst do works

---

14 All work is to be done in a spirit of sacrifice, for the sake of the Divine.

15 Janaka was the king of Mithilā and the father of Sītā, the wife of Rāma. Janaka ruled, giving up his personal sense of being the worker.

also with a view to the maintenance of the world.[16]

21. Whatsoever a great man does, the same is done by others as well. Whatever standard he sets, the world follows.

22. There is not for me, O Pārtha (Arjuna), any work in the three worlds which has to be done or anything to be obtained which has not been obtained; yet I am engaged in work.

23. For, if ever I did not engage in work unwearied, O Pārtha (Arjuna), men would in every way follow my path.

24. If I should cease to work, these worlds would fall in ruin, and I should be the creator of disordered life and destroy these people.

25. As the unlearned act from attachment to their work, so should the learned also act, O Bhārata (Arjuna), but without any attachment, with the desire to maintain the world-order.

26. Let him not unsettle the minds of the ignorant who are attached to action. The enlightened man doing all works in a spirit of *yoga* should set others to act (as well).

The Self is no doer

27. While all kinds of work are done by the modes of nature (*guṇas*), he whose soul is bewildered by the self-sense thinks, "I am the doer."

28. But he who knows the true character of the distinction of the soul from the modes of nature and their works, O Mighty-armed (Arjuna), understanding that it is the modes which are acting on the modes themselves, does not get attached.

29. Those who are misled by the modes of nature get attached to the works produced by them. But let no one who knows the whole unsettle the minds of the ignorant who know only a part.

30. Resigning all thy works to Me, with thy con-

sciousness fixed in the Self, being free from desire and egoism, fight, delivered from thy fever.

31. Those men, too, who, full of faith and free from cavil, constantly follow this teaching of Mine are released from the bondage of works.

32. But those who slight My teaching and do not follow it, know them to be blind to all wisdom, lost and senseless.

Nature and duty

33. Even the man of knowledge acts in accordance with his own nature. Beings follow their nature. What can repression accomplish?

34. For every sense-attachment and [every] aversion are fixed in regard to the objects of that sense. Let no one come under their sway, for they are his two enemies.

35. Better is one's own law though imperfectly carried out than the law of another carried out perfectly. Better is death in the fulfilment of one's own law, for to follow another's law is perilous.

The enemy is desire and anger

Arjuna said:

36. But by what is a man impelled to commit sin, as if by force, even against his will, O Vārṣṇeya (Kṛṣṇa)?

The Blessed Lord said:

37. This is craving, this is wrath, born of the mode of passion, all devouring and most sinful. Know this to be the enemy here.

38. As fire is covered by smoke, as a mirror by dust, as an embryo is enveloped by the womb, so is this covered by that [passion].

39. Enveloped is wisdom, O Son of Kuntī (Arjuna), by this insatiable fire of desire, which is the constant foe of the wise.

40. The senses, the mind, and the intelligence are said to be its seat. Veiling wisdom by these, it deludes the embodied soul.

41. Therefore, O Best of Bhāratas (Arjuna), control thy senses from the beginning and slay this sinful destroyer of wisdom and discrimination.

---

[16] "The maintenance of the world" (*lokasaṁgraha*) stands for the unity of the world, the interconnectedness of society. If the world is not to sink into a condition of physical misery and moral degradation, if the common life is to be decent and dignified, religious ethics must control social action.

42. The senses, they say, are great; greater than the senses is the mind; greater than the mind is the intelligence; but greater than the intelligence is he [the self].

43. Thus knowing him who is beyond the intelligence, steadying the [lower] self by the Self, smite, O Mighty-armed (Arjuna), the enemy in the form of desire, so hard to get at.

This is the third chapter, entitled "The *Yoga* of Works."

MORAL DUTY

Immanuel Kant

It is impossible to conceive of anything anywhere in the world or even anywhere out of it that can without qualification be called good, except a Good Will. Reasoning, wit, judgment, or whatever the *talents* of the intellect may be called, or such qualities of *temperament* as courage, determination and constancy of purpose, are doubtless good and desirable in many respects. But they may also be extremely evil and harmful unless the will be good which is to make use of these natural gifts and whose particular quality we therefore designate as *character.* The same is true of the *gifts of fortune.* Power, riches, honor, even health, all comfort and contentment with one's condition which is called *happiness* frequently engender together with courage also an insolence, unless a good will is present which properly directs and thus fits to a general purpose their influence upon the mind and with it the entire principle of activity. Even an impartial sane witness can never take pleasure in the uninterrupted well-being of a person who shows no trace of a pure and good will. Consequently the good will seems to be the indispensable condition even of being worthy of happiness.

Certain qualities are even conducive to this good will itself and yet they have no intrinsic unquestioned value. Rather they still presuppose a good will which detracts from the esteem which we properly have for them and which makes it impossible to consider them absolutely good. Moderation in emotion and passion, self-control and sober consideration are not only in many respects good but they seem even to constitute a part of the *inner* worth of a person. And yet one can hardly call them unreservedly good (however much the ancients may have praised them). For without the principles of a good will they may become very evil indeed. The cold-bloodedness of a villain not only makes him far more dangerous, but also directly makes him seem more despicable to us than he would have seemed without it.

The good will is good not because of what it causes or accomplishes, not because of its usefulness in the attainment of some set purpose, but alone because of the willing, that is to say, of itself. Considered by itself, without any comparison, it is to be valued far more highly than all that might be accomplished through it in favor of some inclination or of the sum of all inclinations. Even though by some special disfavor of fortune or because of the meager provision of a stepmotherly nature this will were entirely lacking in ability to carry out its intentions; if with the greatest of efforts nothing were to be accomplished by it, and nothing were to remain except only the good will (not, to be sure, as a pious wish but as an exertion of every means in our power), it would still sparkle like a jewel by itself, like something that has its full value in itself. Its usefulness or fruitfulness can neither add nor detract from its worth. This would be, as it were, merely the setting to enable an easier handling of it in ordinary intercourse or to draw to it the attention of those who are not yet sufficiently expert in the knowledge of it, but not to recommend it to experts or to determine its worth.

There seems to be something so surprising in the idea of the absolute value of the mere will with no regard for its utility that, though even ordinary reason thoroughly agrees with it, we still must suspect that perhaps merely an extravagant fancy is at the basis of this assertion, and that we are interpreting wrongly the purpose of nature in making reason the ruler of our will. Therefore we will examine this idea from this point of view.

In the natural endowment of an organized being, that is, a being suitably adapted to life, we assume the principle that every organ to be found in it is best fitted and suited to it. If, therefore, in a being which possesses reason and a will the real purpose of nature were its *preservation* and its welfare, in a word, its *happiness,* then nature would have made a bad choice in selecting the reason of this being to carry out its intention. For all actions which such a being must perform to carry out this intention and the entire code of behavior could have been dictated far better and the purpose have been far better maintained by instinct than by reason. If the being was to be endowed also with reason, then the latter should have served only to make observations on the fortunate disposition of the nature of the being, to rejoice in it and be grateful for the beneficent cause of it; but it would not have wanted to entrust its desires to the weak and deceptive direction of reason and thus awkwardly to interfere with the intentions of nature. In a word, it would have prevented reason from breaking forth into *practical use* and assuming the impertinence to plan with its poor insight the structure of its happiness and the means of its attainment. Nature itself would have undertaken the selection not only of its purposes but also of the means of their attainment and with wise foresight would have entrusted both to instinct.

We do indeed find that the more a cultivated reason concerns itself with the meaning of happiness and the enjoyment of life, the farther away man gets from true satisfaction. Because of this there arises in many and even in those most tried in the use of reason, if only they are honest enough to admit it, a certain degree of *misology,* that is to say, a hatred of reason; because after viewing all the advantages which they derive, perhaps not merely from the discovery of the various arts of ordinary life but even from the sciences (which after all seem to them also a luxury of reason), they still find that they have burdened themselves with more

trouble than they have won of happiness. Finally they envy rather than despise the common run of men who are more nearly directed by the mere natural instincts and allow their reason to have little influence upon their conduct. In so far one must admit that the judgment of those, who belittle and even rate below zero the boastful glorification of the advantages which reason is supposed to give us in regard to the happiness and satisfaction of life, is in no sense peevish or lacking in gratitude to the kindness of providence. On the contrary, secretly there lies at the basis of this judgment the idea of another much worthier purpose of the existence of reason for which, rather than for the sake of happiness, it is really intended, and to which as a supreme condition the private intentions of man must for the most part yield.

However, reason is not sufficiently adapted to guide the will with certainty in respect to its objects and the satisfaction of all our needs which it in part even multiplies and for which purpose the inborn natural instincts would have served far better. Nevertheless reason has been allotted to us as a practical faculty, that is to say, a faculty which is meant to influence the *will.* Therefore, if we are to assume that nature in the distribution of its capacities has everywhere proceeded with expediency, the real destination of reason cannot be to serve as a means to other ends but to produce *a will good in itself,* for which reason is absolutely indispensable. Thus this will, though not the sole and entire good, must nevertheless be the highest good and a condition of every other, even of all desire for happiness. Therefore it is quite in accordance with the wisdom of nature when we realize that the cultivation of reason, demanded by the foremost and unconditional purpose, in various ways restricts, in this life at least, the attainment of the second and generally conditioned purpose, namely our happiness. Yes, it may even reduce its value to below nothing without injury to nature's purpose. For reason, which recognizes its highest office to be the establishing of a good will, in the attainment of this purpose is capable only of its own peculiar satisfaction which arises from the fulfilment of its purpose, even though it meets with many an obstruction raised by the inclinations.

Now, in order to develop the idea of a good will to be esteemed for no other reason than for itself, just as sound common sense already contains it and it therefore needs less to be taught than clarified, and which is foremost in the evaluation of all our actions and the condition of everything else, we will take the concept of *duty*. Duty includes the notion of a good will with certain subjective restrictions and hindrances. However, far from hiding and obscuring it, these rather serve to bring it out by contrast and make it shine forth all the brighter.

I shall pass over all those actions which are at once recognized as being contrary to duty however useful they may be in one or another respect. There can be no question whether or not they have arisen from duty since they plainly contradict the latter. I shall also omit those actions which really conform to duty but to which men have *no* immediate *inclination* because they are impelled to them by some other inclination. For in such actions it is easy to distinguish whether the dutiful action has been performed *out of duty* or for some selfish reason. It is much more difficult to observe the distinction where an action conforms to duty and the subject besides has an immediate inclination for it. For example, it is indeed a matter of duty that a merchant should not take advantage of an inexperienced customer and where business is flourishing no merchant will do so, but he will rather maintain a fixed common price for all. One is therefore served *honestly*. But that is not nearly reason enough to believe that the merchant has been acting out of duty or principles of honesty. It was his advantage to act so. It cannot be assumed in this case that he has besides a direct inclination for his customers which impels him out of love, as it were, to give none of them the advantage in price over the other. Consequently his action arose neither from duty nor from an immediate inclination, but merely out of some selfish purpose.

On the other hand, it is a duty to preserve one's life and besides everyone has an immediate inclination to do so. But the frequently anxious care which most men take of it has no intrinsic value and their maxim no moral content. They indeed preserve their life *dutifully,* but not *out of duty.* However, when adversities and hopeless grief have wholly destroyed the desire for living; when the unfortunate person, stout of soul and angered by his fate rather than dejected or despondent, nevertheless loves his life not because of inclination or fear, but as a matter of duty, then his maxim has a moral content.

It is a duty to help others wherever possible, and there is many a sympathetic soul that, without a trace of vanity or self-interest, takes delight in making others happy and is able to rejoice in the contentment of others, in so far as he has helped produce it. But I maintain that, however dutiful and amiable such an action may be, in this case it still has no moral value, but goes hand in hand with other inclinations as, for example, the inclination toward honor which, when it by chance coincides with what is in fact for the common good and in accordance with duty, and therefore honorable, deserves praise but not a high esteem. For the maxim lacks the moral content, namely, that such actions be done *from duty* and not from inclination. Let us assume, however, that the mind of such a philanthropist is beclouded by a private grief which destroys all his interest in the fate of others; that he still has the ability to alleviate the suffering of others, but that the strange need does not move him because he is sufficiently occupied with his own. If now, when there is no inclination to urge him to it, he nevertheless rouses himself from this deadly indifference and performs the act without any inclination, solely out of duty, then the action for the very first time has genuine moral value. Let us assume further still that nature has allotted very little power of sympathy to a certain person, he is cold by temperament and indifferent to the suffering of others, perhaps because he himself possesses the special gift of patience and the power of endurance in respect to his own suffering and presupposes or even demands the same in others. While such a person, who certainly is not its poorest product, has not been fashioned by nature into a philanthropist, will he not still find within himself a source which will afford him a far higher value than that of a friendly temperament can be? Assuredly! This is the very point at which that value of character begins to show which is moral and incomparably highest, namely, to do good, not from inclination, but from duty.

To safeguard one's happiness is a duty, at least indirectly; for discontent with one's condition amidst the press of worries and unsatisfied wants may easily become a great *temptation to the transgression of duties.* But, even without having regard for duty, all men already possess of themselves the strongest and deepest inclination to happiness, because in this very idea all inclinations unite. On the other hand, the prescription for happiness is often such that it greatly detracts from certain inclinations and thus makes it impossible for man to make a definite and certain concept of the satisfaction of all inclinations under the name of happiness. Therefore it is not hard to understand how a single inclination, because of what it promises and the time in which its gratification may be attained, is able to prove more powerful than such a fluctuating idea. For example, a gouty person may choose to enjoy what pleases his palate and suffer greatly because he calculates that, in this instance at least, he has not deprived himself of the enjoyment of the moment for the sake of the, perhaps groundless, expectation of the benefits that are said to lie in health. But also in this case, even though a general inclination to happiness did not determine his will and he did not consider health so necessary, at least for himself, there is still the law, here as in all other cases, namely the law to further his happiness not from inclination, but from duty. And that law alone will give his conduct its real moral worth.

That undoubtedly is the true interpretation of the Scriptures, where we are commanded to love our neighbor, even our enemy. For love from inclination cannot be commanded; but to do good out of duty, even though no inclination at all impels toward it, yes, even when a very natural and uncontrollable disinclination opposes it, is a *practical* and not a *pathological* love. Such a love lies in the will and not in some propensity of affection, in the prin-

ciples of action and not in tender sympathy. And such love alone can be commanded.

The second proposition is this: An action from duty does *not* have its moral worth *in the purpose* which is to be attained by it, but in the maxim according to which it has been formed. It therefore does not depend upon the actuality of the object of the action, but only on the *principle of volition* according to which the action has taken place, irrespective of all objects of desire. From what has been said above it is clear that, whatever the purpose of our actions, and whatever their effects as ends and drives of the will, these can afford the actions no absolute and moral value. In what then can this value be if it does not lie in the will or in relation to the expected effect? It can be nowhere except *in the principle of the will,* irrespective of the purposes that the action is to realize. For the will stands at the crossroads, as it were, between its *a priori* principle, which is formal, and its *a posteriori* drive, which is material. Since it must be determined by something, it follows that it must be determined by the formal principle of general volition, whenever an action is done from duty and consequently every material principle has been withdrawn from it.

The third proposition, a consequence of the two preceding, I would formulate thus: *Duty is the necessity of an action out of respect for the law.* For the object as the effect of my intended action I may indeed have an inclination, *but never respect,* for the very reason that it is merely an effect and not the activity of a will. Just so, I can have no respect for any inclination whatever, whether it be my own or another's. At most I may approve of my own and on occasion even have a fondness for another's, that is, consider it favorable to my interests. Only that can be an object of my respect, and hence a command, which has the relation of a basic principle to my will, but never that of an effect; which, instead of serving, rather outweighs my inclination or at least excludes it entirely from consideration in the making of a choice. Since then an action from duty must eliminate entirely the influence of the inclinations and thus every object of the will, there is nothing left to determine the will, except objectively the *law* and subjectively *pure respect* for this practical law, that is to say, the maxim[1] to be obey such a law, even at the expense of all my inclinations.

The moral worth of an action then does not lie in the effect which is expected of it, and consequently in no principle of an action which must borrow its motive from the expected effect. For all these effects (the comfort of one's condition or even the promotion of the happiness of others) could have been brought about by other causes and did not need the will of a rational being, in which alone, however, the highest and unconditioned good can be found. Therefore the supreme good which we call moral can consist only in *the conception of the law* in itself, *which indeed is possible only in a rational being,* in so far as this conception, and not the hoped-for effect, determines his will. This good, however, is already present in the person himself who acts in accordance with it, and it does not need to wait upon the effect to put in its appearance.[2]

---

[1] Maxim is the subjective principle of volition; the objective principle (that is, that which would also serve subjectively for all rational beings as a practical principle if reason had full power over the faculty of desire) is the practical law.

[2] I might be accused of taking refuge in some obscure feeling with the use of the word *respect,* instead of clarifying the question by means of a concept of reason. However, although respect is a feeling, still it is not a feeling which has been *received* through some influence, but one which a concept of reason has *produced of itself.* Consequently it is specifically distinct from all feelings of the former kind which can be traced to inclination or fear. What I recognize immediately as a law for me I acknowledge with respect, which merely means the consciousness of the submission of my will to a law, without the intervention of other influences upon my mind. The direct determination of the will by the law and the consciousness of it, we call *respect.* Therefore respect is considered to be the *effect* of the law upon the subject and not the *cause.* Respect is really the conception of a value which lessens my love of self. It is therefore something which is looked upon as an object neither of inclination nor of fear, though it has something analogous to both. The *object* of the respect, therefore, is solely the *law,* the law which we impose upon *ourselves* and yet consider necessary in itself. As a law we are subject to it without reference to our self-love, and thus it is analogous to fear; since we ourselves impose it upon ourselves it is certainly the result of our will, and thus it is analogous to inclination. All respect for a person is really nothing but a respect for the law (of righteousness, etc.,) of which the person is an example. Because we consider the expansion of our talents a duty we look upon a person of talents as a sort of an *example of the law* (to become like him by practice), and that constitutes our respect. All so-called moral *interest* consists purely and simply in the *respect* for the law.

But of what sort can this law possibly be, the conception of which, even without regard for the effect expected from it, must determine the will, in order that the latter may without qualification be called purely and simply good? Since I have deprived the will of every stimulus which it might receive from the results of a law, so there is nothing left to serve as principle for the will except the universal lawfulness of actions in general. That is to say, I am never to at otherwise than *so that I could at the same time will that my maxim should become a universal law.* Here the pure lawfulness in general, without the basis of any law whatever which is directed upon definite actions, is that which serves and must serve as principle for the will, unless duty everywhere is to be an empty delusion and a chimerical notion. Ordinary human reason in its practical judgment fully agrees with this and always has this suggested principle in view.

Take this question, for example. If I am sorely pressed, may I make a promise with the intention not to keep it? I readily distinguish between the two principal meanings of this question, whether it is clever or else a matter of duty to make a false promise. The first undoubtedly may quite often be the case. To be sure, I realize that it is not enough to want to extricate myself from a momentary embarrassment by means of this subterfuge, but that I ought to consider whether from this lie there might not arise later much greater difficulties than those from which I am at present freeing myself. Since the results of my assumed *cleverness* cannot easily be foreseen, I ought to consider whether the loss of confidence in me might not constitute a far greater harm than all the evil I am trying to avoid at present; whether I would not be acting *more prudently* if I proceeded according to a universal law and developed the habit of never making a promise except with the intention to keep it. However I soon realize that the basis of such a maxim is after all fear of the consequences of my action. Certainly it is a very different thing to be truthful from duty than because of fear of disadvantageous results. In the first case the very conception of the action in itself contains a law for me to follow, in the other case I must first look about to see what consequences might be connected with it for me. For if I deviate from the principle of duty then it is most certainly evil; if, however, I act against my maxim of cleverness I may at some time greatly profit by this faithlessness, even though it be safer for the present to adhere to it. However, in order to take the shortest and yet surest way toward an answer to this problem, whether or not a deceitful promise is in accordance with duty, I ask myself: Would I indeed be satisfied to have my maxim (to extricate myself from an embarrassing situation by a false promise) considered a universal law? Would I be able to say to myself: Everybody has the right to make a false promise if he finds himself in a difficulty from which he can escape in no other way? In that manner I soon realize that I may will the lie, but never a universal law to lie. For according to such a law there really would be no promise at all, because it would be vain to make a pretense of my will in respect to my future actions to those who have no faith in my pretensions or who, if they were rash enough to do so, would repay me in my own coin. Therefore my maxim would destroy itself as soon as it got to be a universal law.

Therefore I have need of no far-reaching perspicacity to know what to do in order that my volition may be morally good. Inexperienced in understanding the course of the world, incapable of being prepared for all that happens in it, I merely ask myself: Can you will that your maxim becomes a universal law? If not, then it is unsound; and indeed not because of a disadvantage arising from it for you or for others, but because it is not suited as a principle for a possible universal code of law. But reason forces upon me an immediate respect for this code, even though I do not yet *comprehend* upon what it is based (that is a matter for investigation by philosophers). But I at least understand this much: that it is an appreciation of that value which far outweighs all the worth of that which is esteemed by inclination; that the necessity of my action out of *pure* respect for the practical law is what constitutes duty and that, to duty, every other motive must yield because it is the condition of a will good *in itself,* than which there is no greater value.

UTILITARIANISM

John Stuart Mill

There are few circumstances among those which make up the present condition of human knowledge more unlike what might have been expected, or more significant of the backward state in which speculation on the most important subjects still lingers, than the little progress which has been made in the decision of the controversy respecting the criterion of right and wrong. From the dawn of philosophy, the question concerning the *summum bonum,* or, what is the same thing, concerning the foundation of morality, has been accounted the main problem in speculative thought, has occupied the most gifted intellects and divided them into sects and schools carrying on a vigorous warfare against one another. And after more than two thousand years the same discussions continue, philosophers are still ranged under the same contending banners, and neither thinkers nor mankind at large seem nearer to being unanimous on the subject than when the youth Socrates listened to the old Protagoras and asserted (if Plato's dialogue be grounded on a real conversation) the theory of utilitarianism against the popular morality of the so-called sophist.

• • •

To inquire how far the bad effects of this deficiency have been mitigated in practice, or to what extent the moral beliefs of mankind have been vitiated or made uncertain by the absence of any distinct recognition of an ultimate standard, would imply a complete survey and criticism of past and present ethical doctrine. It would, however, be easy to show that whatever steadiness or consistency these moral beliefs have attained has been mainly due to the tacit influence of a standard not recognized. Although the nonexistence of an acknowledged first principle has made ethics not so much a guide as a consecration of men's actual sentiments, still, as men's sentiments, both of favor and of aversion, are greatly influenced by what they suppose to be the effects of things upon their happiness, the principle of utility, or, as Bentham latterly called it, the greatest happiness principle, has had a large share in forming the moral doctrines even of those who most scornfully reject its authority. Nor is there any school of thought which refuses to admit that the influence of actions on happiness is a most material and even predominant consideration in many of the details of morals, however unwilling to acknowledge it as the fundamental principle of morality and the source of moral obligation. I might go much further and say that to all those *a priori* moralists who deem it necessary to argue at all, utilitarian arguments are indispensable. It is not my present purpose to criticize these thinkers; but I cannot help referring, for illustration, to a systematic treatise by one of the most illustrious of them, the *Metaphysics of Ethics* by Kant. This remarkable man, whose system of thought will long remain one of the landmarks in the history of philosophical speculation, does, in the treatise in question, lay down a universal first principle as the origin and ground of moral obligation; it is this: "So act that the rule on which thou actest would admit of being adopted as a law by all rational beings." But when he begins to deduce from this precept any of the actual duties of morality, he fails, almost grotesquely, to show that there would be any contradiction, any logical (not to say physical) impossibility, in the adoption by all rational beings of the most outrageously immoral rules of conduct. All he shows is that the *consequences* of their universal adoption would be such as no one would choose to incur.

On the present occasion, I shall, without further discussion of the other theories, attempt to contribute something toward the understanding and appreciation of the "utilitarian" or "happiness" theory, and toward such proof as it is susceptible of. It is evident that this cannot be proof in the ordinary and popular meaning of the term. Questions of ultimate ends are not amenable to direct proof. Whatever can be proved to be good must be so by being shown to be a means to something admitted to be good without proof. The medical art is proved to be good by its conducing to health; but how is it possible to prove that health is good? The art of music is good, for the reason, among others, that it produces pleasure; but what proof is it possible to give that pleasure is good? If, then, it is asserted that there is a comprehensive formula, including all things which are in themselves good, and that whatever else is good is not so as an end but as a means, the formula may be accepted or rejected, but is not a subject of what is commonly understood by proof. We are not, however, to infer that its acceptance or rejection must depend on blind impulse or arbitrary choice. There is a larger meaning of the word "proof," in which this question is as amenable to it as any other of the disputed questions of philosophy. The subject is within the cognizance of the rational faculty; and neither does that faculty deal with it solely in the way of intuition. Considerations may be presented capable of determining the intellect either to give or withhold its assent to the doctrine; and this is equivalent to proof.

We shall examine presently of what nature are these considerations; in what manner they apply to the case, and what rational grounds, therefore can be given for accepting or rejecting the utilitarian formula. But it is a preliminary condition of rational acceptance or rejection that the formula should be correctly understood. I believe that the very imperfect notion ordinarily formed of its meaning is the chief obstacle which impedes its reception, and that, could it be cleared even from only the grosser misconceptions, the question would be greatly simplified and a large proportion of its difficulties removed. Before, therefore, I attempt to enter into the philosophical grounds which can be given for assenting to the utilitarian standard, I shall offer some illustrations of the doctrine itself, with the view of showing more clearly what it is, distinguishing it from what it is not, and disposing of such of the practical objections to it as either originate in, or are closely connected with, mistaken interpretations of its meaning. Having thus prepared the ground, I shall afterwards endeavor to throw such light as I can call upon the question considered as one of philosophical theory.

• • •

A passing remark is all that needs be given to the ignorant blunder of supposing that those who stand up for utility as the test of right and wrong use the term in that restricted and merely colloquial sense in which utility is opposed to pleasure. An apology is due to the philosophical opponents of utilitarianism for even the momentary appearance of confounding them with anyone capable of so absurd a misconception; which is the more extraordinary, inasmuch as the contrary accusation, of referring everything to pleasure, and that, too, in its grossest form, is another of the common charges against utilitarianism: and, as has been pointedly remarked by an able writer, the same sort of persons, and often the very same persons, denounce the theory "as impracticably dry when the word 'utility' precedes the word 'pleasure,' and as too practicably voluptuous when the word 'pleasure' precedes the word 'utility.' " Those who know anything about the matter are aware that every writer, from Epicurus to Bentham, who maintained the theory of utility meant by it, not something to be contradistinguished from pleasure, but pleasure itself, together with exemption from pain; and instead of opposing the useful to the agreeable or the ornamental, have always declared that the useful means these, among other things. Yet the common herd, including the herd of writers, not only in newspapers and periodicals, but in books of weight and pretension, are perpetually falling into this shallow mistake. Having caught up the word "utilitarian," while knowing nothing whatever about it but its sound, they habitually express by it the rejection or the neglect of pleasure in some of its forms: of beauty, of ornament, or of amusement. Nor is the term thus ignorantly misapplied solely in disparagement, but occasionally in compliment, as though it implied superiority to frivolity and the mere pleasures of the moment. And this perverted use is the only one in which the word is popularly known, and the one from which the new generation are acquiring their sole notion of its meaning. Those who introduced the word, but who had for many years discontinued it as a distinctive appellation, may well feel themselves called upon to resume it if by doing so they can hope to contribute anything toward rescuing it from this utter degradation.

The creed which accepts as the foundation of morals "utility" or the "greatest happiness principle" holds that actions are right in proportion as they tend to promote happiness; wrong as they tend to produce the reverse of happiness. By happiness is intended pleasure and the absence of pain; by unhappiness, pain and the privation of pleasure. To give a clear view of the moral standard set up by the theory, much more requires to be said; in particular, what things it includes in the ideas of pain and pleasure, and to what extent this is left an open question. But these supplementary explanations do not affect the theory of life on which this theory of morality is grounded—namely, that pleasure and freedom from pain are the only things desirable as ends; and that all desirable things (which are as numerous in the utilitarian as in any other scheme) are desirable either for pleasure inherent in themselves or as means to the promotion of pleasure and the prevention of pain.

Now such a theory of life excites in many minds, and among them in some of the most estimable in feeling and purpose, inveterate dislike. To suppose that life has (as they express it) no higher end than pleasure—no better and nobler object of desire and pursuit—they designate as utterly mean and groveling, as a doctrine worthy only of swine, to whom the followers of Epicurus were, at a very early period, contemptuously likened; and modern holders of the doctrine are occasionally made the subject of equally polite comparisons by its German, French, and English assailants.

When thus attacked, the Epicureans have always answered that it is not they, but their accusers, who represent human nature in a degrading light, since the accusation supposes human beings to be capable of no pleasures except those of which swine are capable. If this supposition were true, the charge could not be gainsaid, but would then be no longer an imputation; for if the sources of pleasure were precisely the same to human beings and to swine, the rule of life which is good enough for the one would be good enough for the other. The comparison of the Epicurean life to that of beasts is felt as degrading, precisely because a beast's pleasures do not satisfy a human being's conceptions of happiness. Human beings have faculties more elevated than the animal appetites and, when once made conscious of them, do not regard anything as happiness which does not include their gratification. I do not, indeed, consider the Epicureans to have been by any means faultless in drawing out their scheme of consequences from the utilitarian principle. To do this in any sufficient manner, many Stoic, as well as Christian, elements require to be included. But there is no known Epicurean theory of life which does not assign to the pleasures of the intellect, of the feelings and imagination, and of the moral sentiments a much higher value as pleasures than to those of mere sensation. It must be admitted, however, that utilitarian writers in general have placed the superiority of mental over bodily pleasures chiefly in the greater permanency, safety, uncostliness, etc., of the former—that is, in their circumstantial advantages rather than in their intrinsic nature. And on all these points utilitarians have fully proved their case; but they might have taken the other and, as it may be called, higher ground with entire consistency. It is quite compatible with the principle of utility to recognize the fact that some kinds of pleasure are more desirable and more valuable than others. It would be absurd that, while in estimating all other things quality is considered as well as quantity, the estimation of pleasure should be supposed to depend on quantity alone.

If I am asked what I mean by difference of quality in pleasures, or what makes one pleasure more valuable than another, merely as a pleasure, except its being greater in amount, there is but one possible answer. Of two pleasures, if there be one to which all or almost all who have experience of both give a decided preference, irrespective of any feeling of moral obligation to prefer it, that is the more desirable pleasure. If one of the two is, by those who are competently acquainted with both, placed so far above the other that they prefer it, even though knowing it to be attended with a greater amount of discontent, and would not resign it for any quantity of the other pleasure which their nature is capable of, we are justified in ascribing to the preferred enjoyment a superiority in quality so far outweighing quantity as to render it, in comparison, of small account.

Now it is an unquestionable fact that those who are equally acquainted with and equally capable of appreciating and enjoying both do give a most marked preference to the manner of existence which employs their higher faculties. Few human creatures would consent to be changed into any of the lower animals for a promise of the fullest allowance of a beast's pleasures; no intelligent human being would consent to be a fool, no instructed person would be an ignoramus, no person of feeling and conscience would be selfish and base, even though they should be persuaded that the fool, the dunce, or the rascal is better satisfied with his lot than they are with theirs. They would not resign what they possess more than he for the most complete satisfaction of all the desires which they have in common with him. If they ever fancy they would, it is only in cases of unhappiness so extreme that to escape from it they would exchange their lot for almost any other, however undesirable in their own eyes. A being of higher faculties requires more to make him happy, is capable probably of more acute suffering, and certainly accessible to it at more points, than one of an inferior type; but in spite of these liabilities, he can never really wish to sink into what he feels to be a lower grade of existence. We may give what explanation we please of this unwillingness; we may attribute it to pride, a name which is given indiscriminately to some of the most and to some of the least estimable feelings of which mankind are capable; we may refer it to the love of liberty and personal independence, an appeal to which was with the Stoics one of the most effective means for the inculcation of it; to the love of power or to the love of excitement, both of which do really enter into and contribute to it; but its most appropriate appellation is a sense of dignity, which all human beings possess in one form or other, and in some, though by no means in exact, proportion to their higher faculties, and which is so essential a part of the happiness of those in whom it is strong that nothing which conflicts with it could be otherwise than momentarily an object of desire to them. Whoever supposes that this preference takes place at a sacrifice of happiness—that the superior being, in anything like equal circumstances, is not happier than the inferior—confounds the two very different ideas of happiness and content. It is indisputable that the being whose capacities of enjoyment are low has the greatest chance of having them fully satisfied; and a highly endowed being will always feel that any happiness which he can look for, as the world is constituted, is imperfect. But he can learn to bear its imperfections, if they are at all bearable; and they will not make him envy the being who is indeed unconscious of the imperfections, but only because he feels not at all the good which those imperfections qualify. It is better to be a human being dissatisfied than a pig satisfied; better to be Socrates dissatisfied than a fool satisfied. And if the fool, or the pig, are of a different opinion, it is because they only know their own side of the question. The other party to the comparison knows both sides.

It may be objected that many who are capable of the higher pleasures occasionally, under the influence of temptation, postpone them to the lower. But this is quite compatible with a full appreciation of the intrinsic superiority of the higher. Men often, from infirmity of character, make their election for the nearer good, though they know it to be the less valuable; and this no less when the choice is between two bodily pleasures than when it is between bodily and mental. They pursue sensual indulgences to the injury of health, though perfectly aware that health is the greater good. It may be further objected that many who begin with youthful enthusiasm for everything noble, as they advance in years, sink into indolence and selfishness. But I do not believe that those who undergo this very common change voluntarily choose the lower description of pleasures in preference to the higher. I believe that, before they devote themselves exclusively to the one, they have already become incapable of the other. Capacity for the nobler feelings is in most natures a very tender plant, easily killed, not only by hostile influences, but by mere want of sustenance; and in the majority of young persons it speedily dies away if the occupations to which their position in life has devoted them, and the society into which it has thrown them, are not favorable to keeping that higher capacity in exercise. Men lose their high aspirations as they lose their intellectual tastes, because they have not time or opportunity for indulging them; and they addict themselves to inferior pleasures, not because they deliberately prefer them, but because they are either the only ones to which they have access or the only ones which they are any longer capable of enjoying. It may be questioned whether anyone who has remained equally susceptible to both classes of pleasures ever knowingly and calmly preferred the lower, though many, in all ages, have broken down in an ineffectual attempt to combine both.

From this verdict of the only competent judges, I apprehend there can be no appeal. On a question which is the best worth having of two pleasures, or which of two modes of existence is the most grateful to the feelings, apart from its moral attributes and from its consequences, the judgment of those who are qualified by knowledge of both, or, if they differ, that of the majority among them, must be admitted as final. And there needs be the less hesitation to accept this judgment respecting the quality of pleasures, since there is no other tribunal to be referred to even on the question of quantity. What means are there of determining which is the acutest of two pains, or the intensest of two pleasurable sensations, except the general suffrage of those who are familiar with both? Neither pains nor pleasures are homogeneous, and pain is always heterogeneous with pleasure. What is there to decide whether a particular pleasure is worth purchasing at the cost of a particular pain, except the feelings and judgment of the experienced? When, therefore, those feeling and judgment declare the pleasures derived from the higher faculties to be preferable *in kind,* apart from the question of intensity, to those of which the animal nature, disjoined from the higher faculties, is susceptible, they are entitled on this subject to the same regard.

I have dwelt on this point as being a necessary part of a perfectly just conception of utility or happiness considered as the directive rule of human conduct. But it is by no means an indispensable condition to the acceptance of the utilitarian standard; for that standard is not the agent's own greatest happiness, but the greatest amount of happiness altogether; and if it may possibly be doubted whether a noble character is always the happier for its nobleness, there can be no doubt that it makes other people happier, and that the world in general is immensely a gainer by it. Utilitarianism, therefore, could only attain its end by the general cultivation of nobleness of character, even if each individual were only benefited by the nobleness of others, and his own, so far as happiness is concerned, were a sheer deduction from the benefit. But the bare enunciation of such an absurdity as this last renders refutation superfluous.

According to the greatest happiness principle, as above explained, the ultimate end, with reference to and for the sake of which all other things are desirable—whether we are considering our own good or that of other people—is an existence exempt as far as possible from pain, and as rich as possible in enjoyments, both in point of quantity and quality; the test of quality and the rule for measuring it against quantity being the preference felt by those who, in their opportunities of experience, to which must be added their habits of self-consciousness and self-observation, are best furnished with the means of comparison. This, being according to the utilitarian opinion the end of human action, is necessarily also the standard of morality, which may accordingly be defined "the rules and precepts for human conduct,"

by the observance of which an existence such as has been described might be, to the greatest extent possible, secured to all mankind; and not to them only, but, so far as the nature of things admits, to the whole sentient creation.

• • •

It has already been remarked that questions of ultimate ends do not admit of proof, in the ordinary acceptation of the term. To be incapable of proof by reasoning is common to all first principles, to the first premises of our knowledge, as well as to those of our conduct. But the former, being matters of fact, may be the subject of a direct appeal to the faculties which judge of fact—namely, our senses and our internal consciousness. Can an appeal be made to the same faculties on questions of practical ends? Or by what other faculty is cognizance taken of them?

Questions about ends are, in other words, questions what things are desirable. The utilitarian doctrine is that happiness is desirable, and the only thing desirable, as an end; all other things beings only desirable as means to that end. What ought to be required of this doctrine, what conditions is it requisite that the doctrine should fulfill—to make good its claim to be believed?

The only proof capable of being given that an object is visible is that people actually see it. The only proof that a sound is audible is that people hear it; and so of the other sources of our experience. In like manner, I apprehend, the sole evidence it is possible to produce that anything is desirable is that people do actually desire it. If the end which the utilitarian doctrine proposes to itself were not, in theory and in practice, acknowledged to be an end, nothing could ever convince any person that it was so. No reason can be given why the general happiness is desirable, except that each person, so far as he believes it to be attainable, desires his own happiness. This, however, being a fact, we have not only all the proof which the case admits of, but all which it is possible to require, that happiness is a good, that each person's happiness is a good to that person, and the general happiness, therefore, a good to the aggregate of all persons. Happiness has made out its title as *one* of the ends of conduct and, consequently, one of the criteria of morality.

FEMINIST TRANSFORMATION OF MORAL THEORY

Virginia Held

The history of philosophy, including the history of ethics, has been constructed from male points of view, and has been built on assumptions and concepts that are by no means gender-neutral.[1] Feminists characteristically begin with different concerns and give different emphases to the issues we consider than do non-feminist approaches. And, as Lorraine Code expresses it, "starting points and focal points shape the impact of theoretical discussion."[2] Within philosophy, feminists often start with, and focus on, quite different issues than those found in standard philosophy and ethics, however "standard" is understood. Far from providing mere additional insights which can be incorporated into traditional theory, feminist explorations often require radical transformations of existing fields of inquiry and theory. From a feminist point of view, moral theory along with almost all theory will have to be transformed to take adequate account of the experience of women.

• • •

Women have been seen as emotional rather than as rational beings, and thus as incapable of full moral personhood. Women's behavior has been interpreted as either "natural" and driven by instinct, and thus as irrelevant to morality and to the con-

struction of moral principles, or it has been interpreted as, at best, in need of instruction and supervision by males better able to know what morality requires and better able to live up to its demands.

The Hobbesian conception of reason is very different from the Platonic or Aristotelian conceptions before it, and from the conceptions of Rousseau or Kant or Hegel later; all have in common that they ignore and disparage the experience and reality of women. Consider Hobbes' account of man in the state of nature contracting with other men to establish society. These men hypothetically come into existence fully formed and independent of one another, and decide on entering or staying outside of civil society. As Christine Di Stefano writes, "What we find in Hobbes's account of human nature and political order is a vital concern with the survival of a self conceived in masculine terms . . . This masculine dimension of Hobbes's atomistic egoism is powerfully underscored in his state of nature, which is effectively built on the foundation of denied maternity."[3] In *The Citizen,* where Hobbes gave his first systematic exposition of the state of nature, he asks us to "consider men as if but even now sprung out of the earth, and suddenly, like mushrooms, come to full maturity, without all kind of engagement with each other."[4] As Di Stefano says, it is a most incredible and problematic feature of Hobbes's state of nature that the men in it "are not born of, much less nurtured by, women, or anyone else."[5] To abstract from the complex web of human reality an abstract man for rational perusal, Hobbes has, Di Stefano continues, "expunged human reproduction and early nurturance, two of the most basic and typically female-identified features of distinctively human life, from his account of basic human nature. Such a strategy ensures that he can present a

---

[1] See e.g. Cheshire Calhoun, "Justice, Care, Gender Bias," *The Journal of Philosophy* 85 (September, 1988): 451–63.
[2] Lorraine Code, "Second Persons," in *Science, Morality and Feminist Theory,* ed. Marsha Hanen and Kai Nielsen (Calgary: University of Calgary Press, 1987), p. 360.

[3] Christine Di Stefano, "Masculinity as Ideology in Political Theory: Hobbesian Man Considered," *Women's Studies International Forum* (Special Issue: *Hypatia*), Vol. 6, No. 6 (1983): 633–44, p. 637.
[4] Thomas Hobbes, *The Citizen: Philosophical Rudiments Concerning Government and Society,* ed. B. Gert (Garden City, New York: Doubleday, 1972 (1651)), p. 205.
[5] Di Stefano, op. cit., p. 638.
[6] Ibid.

thoroughly atomistic subject. . . ."[6] From the point of view of women's experience, such a subject or self is unbelievable and misleading, even as a theoretical construct. The Leviathan, Di Stefano writes, "is effectively comprised of a body politic of orphans who have reared themselves, whose desires are situated within and reflect nothing but independently generated movement. . . ."[7]

Rousseau, and Kant, and Hegel, paid homage to the emotional power, the aesthetic sensibility, and the familial concerns, respectively, of women. But since in their views morality must be based on rational principle, and women were incapable of full rationality, or a degree or kind of rationality comparable to that of men, women were deemed, in the view of these moralists, to be inherently wanting in morality. For Rousseau, women must be trained from childhood to submit to the will of men lest their sexual power lead both men and women to disaster. For Kant, women were thought incapable of achieving full moral personhood, and women lose all charm if they try to behave like men by engaging in rational pursuits. For Hegel, women's moral concern for their families could be admirable in its proper place, but is a threat to the more universal aims to which men, as members of the state, should aspire.[8]

These images, of the feminine as what must be overcome if knowledge and morality are to be achieved, of female experience as naturally irrelevant to morality, and of women as inherently deficient moral creatures, are built into the history of ethics.

• • •

Annette Baier recently speculated about why it is that moral philosophy has so seriously overlooked the trust between human beings that in her view is an utterly central aspect of moral life. She noted that "the great moral theorists in our tradition not only are all men, they are mostly men who had minimal adult dealings with (and so were then minimally influenced by) women."[9] They were for the most part "clerics, misogynists, and puritan bachelors," and thus it is not surprising that they focus their philosophical attention "so single-mindedly on cool, distanced relations between more or less free and equal adult strangers. . . ."[10]

• • •

And so we are groping to shape new moral theory. Understandably, we do not yet have fully worked out feminist moral theories to offer. But we can suggest some directions our project of developing such theories is taking. As Kathryn Morgan points out, there is not likely to be a "star" feminist moral theorist on the order of a Rawls or Nozick: "There will be no individual singled out for two reasons. One reason is that vital moral and theoretical conversations are taking place on a large dialectical scale as the feminist community struggles to develop a feminist ethic. The second reason is that this community of feminist theoreticians is calling into question the very model of the individualized autonomous self presupposed by a star-centered male-dominated tradition. . . . We experience it as a common labour, a common task."[11]

• • •

In the area of moral theory in the modern era, the priority accorded to reason has taken two major forms. A) On the one hand has been the Kantian, or Kantian-inspired search for very general, abstract, deontological, universal moral principles by which rational beings should be guided. Kant's Categorical Imperative is a foremost example: it suggests that all moral problems can be handled by applying

---

[7] Ibid., p. 639.
[8] For examples of relevant passages, see *Philosophy of Woman: Classical to Current Concepts,* ed. Mary Mahowald (Indianapolis: Hackett, 1978); and *Visions of Women,* ed. Linda Bell (Clifton, New Jersey: Humana, 1985). For discussion, see Susan Moller Okin, *Women in Western Political Thought* (Princeton, New Jersey: Princeton University Press, 1979); and Lorenne Clark and Lynda Lange, eds., *The Sexism of Social and Political Theory* (Toronto: University of Toronto Press, 1979).

[9] Annette Baier, "Trust and Anti-Trust," *Ethics* 96 (1986): 231–60, pp. 247–48.
[10] Ibid.
[11] Kathryn Morgan, "Women and Moral Madness," in *Science, Morality and Feminist Theory,* ed. Hanen and Nielsen, p. 223.

an impartial, pure, rational principle to particular cases. It requires that we try to see what the general features of the problem before us are, and that we apply an abstract principle, or rules derivable from it, to this problem. On this view, this procedure should be adequate for all moral decisions. We should thus be able to act as reason recommends, and resist yielding to emotional inclinations and desires in conflict with our rational wills.

B) On the other hand, the priority accorded to reason in the modern era has taken a Utilitarian form. The Utilitarian approach, reflected in rational choice theory, recognizes that persons have desires and interests, and suggests rules of rational choice for maximizing the satisfaction of these. While some philosophers in this tradition espouse egoism, especially of an intelligent and long-term kind, many do not. They begin, however, with assumptions that what are morally relevant are gains and losses of utility to theoretically isolatable individuals, and that the outcome at which morality should aim is the maximization of the utility of individuals. Rational calculation about such an outcome will, in this view, provide moral recommendations to guide all our choices. As with the Kantian approach, the Utilitarian approach relies on abstract general principles or rules to be applied to particular cases. And it holds that although emotion is, in fact, the source of our desires for certain objectives, the task of morality should be to instruct us on how to pursue those objectives most rationally. Emotional attitudes toward moral issues themselves interfere with rationality and should be disregarded. Among the questions Utilitarians can ask can be questions about which emotions to cultivate, and which desires to try to change, but these questions are to be handled in the terms of rational calculation, not of what our feelings suggest.

Although the conceptions of what the judgments of morality should be based on, and of how reason should guide moral decision, are different in Kantian and in Utilitarian approaches, both share a reliance on a highly abstract, universal principle as the appropriate source of moral guidance, and both share the view that moral problems are to be solved by the application of such an abstract principle to particular cases. Both share an admiration for the rules of reason to be appealed to in moral contexts, and both denigrate emotional responses to moral issues.

Many feminist philosophers have questioned whether the reliance on abstract rules, rather than the adoption of more context-respectful approaches, can possibly be adequate for dealing with moral problems, especially as women experience them.[12] Though Kantians may hold that complex rules can be elaborated for specific contexts, there is nevertheless an assumption in this approach that the more abstract the reasoning applied to a moral problem, the more satisfactory. And Utilitarians suppose that one highly abstract principle, The Principle of Utility, can be applied to every moral problem no matter what the context.

A genuinely universal or gender-neutral moral theory would be one which would take account of the experience and concerns of women as fully as it would take account of the experience and concerns of men. When we focus on the experience of women, however, we seem to be able to see a set of moral concerns becoming salient that differs from those of traditional or standard moral theory. Women's experience of moral problems seems to lead us to be especially concerned with actual relationships between embodied persons, and with what these relationships seem to require. Women are often inclined to attend to rather than to dismiss the particularities of the context in which a moral problem arises. And we often pay attention to feelings of empathy and caring to suggest what we ought to do rather than relying as fully as possible on abstract rules of reason.

Margaret Walker, for instance, contrasts feminist moral "understanding" with traditional moral "knowledge." She sees the components of the former as involving "attention, contextual and narra-

---

[12] For an approach to social and political as well as moral issues that attempts to be context-respectful, see Virginia Held, *Rights and Goods. Justifying Social Action* (Chicago: University of Chicago Press, 1989).

tive appreciation, and communications in the event of moral deliberation."[13] This alternative moral epistemology holds that "the adequacy of moral understanding decreases as its form approaches generality through abstraction."[14]

The work of psychologists such as Carol Gilligan and others has led to a clarification of what may be thought of as tendencies among women to approach moral issues differently. Rather than interpreting moral problems in terms of what could be handled by applying abstract rules of justice to particular cases, many of the women studied by Gilligan tended to be more concerned with preserving actual human relationships, and with expressing care for those for whom they felt responsible. Their moral reasoning was typically more embedded in a context of particular others than was the reasoning of a comparable group of men.[15] One should not equate tendencies women in fact display with feminist views, since the former may well be the result of the sexist, oppressive conditions in which women's lives have been lived. But many feminists see our own consciously considered experience as lending confirmation to the view that what has come to be called "an ethic of care" needs to be developed. Some think it should supercede "the ethic of justice" of traditional or standard moral theory. Others think it should be integrated with the ethic of justice and rules.

In any case, feminist philosophers are in the process of reevaluating the place of emotion in morality in at least two respects. First, many think morality requires the development of the moral emotions, in contrast to moral theories emphasizing the primacy of reason.

• • •

Secondly, emotion will be respected rather than dismissed by many feminist moral philosophers in the process of gaining moral understanding. The experience and practice out of which feminist moral theory can be expected to be developed will include embodied feeling as well as thought. In a recent overview of a vast amount of writing, Kathryn Morgan states that "feminist theorists begin ethical theorizing with embodied, gendered subjects who have particular histories, particular communities, particular allegiances, and particular visions of human flourishing. The starting point involves valorizing what has frequently been most mistrusted and despised in the western philosophical tradition. . . ."[16] Among the elements being reevaluated are feminine emotions. The "care" of the alternative feminist approach to morality appreciates rather than rejects emotion. The caring relationships important to feminist morality cannot be understood in terms of abstract rules or moral reasoning. And the "weighing" so often needed between the conflicting claims of some relationships and others cannot be settled by deduction or rational calculation. A feminist ethic will not just acknowledge emotion, as do Utilitarians, as giving us the objectives toward which moral rationality can direct us. It will embrace emotion as providing at least a partial basis for morality itself, and for moral understanding.

Annette Baier stresses the centrality of trust for an adequate morality.[17] Achieving and maintaining trusting, caring relationships is quite different from acting in accord with rational principles, or satisfying the individual desires of either self or other. Caring, empathy, feeling with others, being sensitive to each other's feelings, all may be better guides to what morality requires in actual contexts than may

---

[13] Margaret Urban Walker, "Moral Understandings: Alternative 'Epistemology' for a Feminist Ethics," *Hypatia* 4 (Summer, 1989): 15–28, p. 19.

[14] Ibid., p. 20. See also Iris Marion Young, "Impartiality and the Civil Public. Some Implications of Feminist Critiques of Moral and Political Theory," in Seyla Benhabib and Drucilla Cornell, *Feminism as Critique* (Minneapolis: University of Minnesota Press, 1987).

[15] See especially Carol Gilligan, *In a Different Voice. Psychological Theory and Women's Development* (Cambridge, Massachusetts: Harvard University Press, 1988); and Eva Feder Kittay and Diana T. Meyers eds., *Women and Moral Theory* (Totowa, New Jersey: Rowman and Allanheld, 1987).

[16] Kathryn Pauly Morgan, "Strangers in a Strange Land . . . ," p. 2.

[17] Annette Baier, "Trust and Anti-Trust."

abstract rules of reason, or rational calculation, or at least they may be necessary components of an adequate morality.

The fear that a feminist ethic will be a relativistic "situation ethic" is misplaced. Some feelings can be as widely shared as are rational beliefs, and feminists do not see their views as reducible to "just another attitude."[18] In her discussion of the differences between feminist medical ethics and non-feminist medical ethics, Susan Sherwin gives an example of how feminists reject the mere case by case approach that has come to predominate in non-feminist medical ethics. The latter also rejects the excessive reliance on abstract rules characteristic of standard ethics, and in this way resembles feminist ethics. But the very focus on cases in isolation from one another deprives this approach from attending to general features in the institutions and practices of medicine that, among other faults, systematically contribute to the oppression of women.[19] The difference of approach can be seen in the treatment of issues in the new reproductive technologies, where feminists consider how the new technologies may further decrease the control of women over reproduction.

This difference might be thought to be one of substance rather than of method, but Sherwin shows the implications for method also. With respect to reproductive technologies one can see especially clearly the deficiencies of the case by case approach: what needs to be considered is not only choice in the purely individualistic interpretation of the case by case approach, but control at a more general level and how it affects the structure of gender in society. Thus, a feminist perspective does not always counsel attention to specific case vs. appeal to general considerations, as some sort of methodological rule. But the general considerations are

often not the purely abstract ones of traditional and standard moral theory, they are the general features and judgments to be made about cases in actual (which means, so far, patriarchal) societies. A feminist evaluation of a moral problem should never omit the political elements involved; and it is likely to recognize that political issues cannot be dealt with adequately in purely abstract terms any more than can moral issues.

The liberal tradition in social and moral philosophy argues that in pluralistic society and even more clearly in a pluralistic world, we cannot agree on our visions of the good life, on what is the best kind of life for humans, but we can hope to agree on the minimal conditions for justice, for coexistence within a framework allowing us to pursue our visions of the good life.[20] Many feminists contend that the commitment to justice needed for agreement *in actual conditions* on even minimal requirements of justice is as likely to demand relational feelings as a rational recognition of abstract principles. Human beings can and do care, and are capable of caring far more than at present, about the sufferings of children quite distant from them, about the prospects for future generations, and about the well-being of the globe. The liberal tradition's mutually disinterested rational individualists would seem unlikely to care enough to take the actions needed to achieve moral decency at a global level, or environmental sanity for decades hence, as they would seem unable to represent caring relationships within the family and among friends.

•   •   •

The possibilities as well as the problems (and we are well aware of some of them) in a feminist reenvisioning of emotion and reason need to be further developed, but we can already see that the views of nonfeminist moral theory are unsatisfactory.

---

[18] See especially Kathryn Pauly Morgan, "Strangers in a Strange Land . . ."

[19] Susan Sherwin, "Feminist and Medical Ethics: Two Different Approaches to Contextual Ethics," *Hypatia* 4 (Summer, 1989): 57–72.

[20] See especially the work of John Rawls and Ronald Dworkin; see also Charles Larmore, *Patterns of Moral Complexity* (Cambridge: Cambridge University Press, 1987).

QUESTIONS FOR DISCUSSION

1. In what ways might it be fulfilling to, as the Bhagavad-Gita suggests, accept one's position in society, and do what one must do, in an attitude of detachment from results? What popular ideas in our society counsel against such an attitude? What is your own position on this debate, and why? Illustrate with an example or two from your own life.

2. Do you agree with Kant that practical love, which acts in response to duty, is more in line with morality than "pathological" love, based on feelings of affection which come and go? Or do you think that there is some moral value to a "feeling" like love? Would the contemporary crisis of marriage and divorce be abated if more people married due to practical love, rather than pathological? (Many contemporary societies still practice the tradition of arranged marriages, based on practical considerations. Do they know something we don't?)

3. Would you consider it moral to lie to bring happiness to many people? What would Kant say? What would a utilitarian say? Would you kill an innocent person to save the life of five others? These are some examples of moral dilemmas often posed to challenge utilitarian views. Explain why you would, or would not, do certain actions such as the above.

4. What is Held's criticism of both Kant and Mill? Is she right or wrong? Give your reasons for your judgment.

UNIVERSAL CONCERN FOR OTHERS: ALTRUISM VERSUS EGOISM

Our next author serves as a bridge from the preceding section, with its emphasis on duty, to our present section. Riffat Hassan shows how Islam connects an ethics of duty with an ethics of altruism.

Riffat Hassan is a contemporary Moslem thinker and a scholar of feminist theology. She was born in Lahore, Pakistan, and earned her Ph.D. from the University of Durham, England. Now at the University of Louisville, Hassan has been active over the years in Jewish-Christian-Moslem interreligious dialogue. In this reading, she describes the Islamic ethical view found in the Qur'an. Her goal is to distinguish the actual Islamic code of ethics from the prevalent stereotypes or distortions of Islamic belief held by many. Although her interpretations and emphases may not be in accordance with some or even many other followers of Islam, she backs up her claims with references to scripture.

Hassan begins by demonstrating that the central goal of Islam is being at peace with God or Allah, at peace with oneself, and at peace with other people. The follower of Islam must do what God approves; this is done by fulfilling one's duties toward both God and human beings. Verbal prayer is not enough; one must perform acts of kindness to those who are in need. For example, the tradition of *zakat* entails giving 2.5 percent of one's net worth yearly as a gift or investment for those who are in need. All humans have the right to life, to respect, and to justice. Likewise, all have a duty to act justly, which includes helping orphans, wayfarers, and beggars, as well as freeing those held in bondage.

Hassan holds firm to several points regarding women and morality that have been controversial in Islamic ethical theory and practice. She asserts that in court, the claims of two parties must be considered equally. In some Islamic countries, a woman's testimony is officially given half the weight of a man's testimony. Hassan also notes that the Qur'an

suggests similar punishments for men and women engaging in "unchastity," although the more common practice is to punish only the woman, or at least to punish her more severely than the man. In fact, she asserts that the Qur'an is concerned to free humans from the chains that bind them, including chains of racism and sexism. She further asserts that the Qur'an upholds religious freedom, and rules out political authoritarianism. She concludes by asserting that the only proper *jihad* or holy war for Moslems (followers of Islam) to engage in today would be the fight against ignorance and narrowness.

Gunapala Dharmasiri is concerned to argue for an ethics of altruism in the context of Buddhist ideas. He explains that Buddhist ethics' first challenge is to constitute an ethics without the concept of a substantial person who possesses a soul. For Buddhism, the person is a temporary arrangement of parts. However, there is still the notion that preceding events have a relationship to later events. And so, one still has a notion of causal responsibility, even without the permanent subject. Another metaphysical distinction influences Buddhist morality, in that Buddhism considers there to be two orders of "reality"—the conventional reality of our daily lives, and the higher, absolute reality in which there are no such things as persons and morality. However, the absolutely "realized" person will naturally act in such a way as to seem moral in the conventional sphere.

But, why should one devote oneself to the well-being of others if there "are" no others, in a substantive sense? Firstly, altruism arises from an acknowledgment of dependency. Since all of reality is interrelated, the extreme notions of altruism and egoism don't make sense; after all, one is part of a larger whole. A person who believes he or she is separate is in a state of illusion. Even the personality is a social construction, being shaped in interaction with others. One who mistreats nature or others sets off a causal chain of events that is bound to bounce back. One consequence of this view is a lifestyle of *ahimsa* or nonviolence, where one refrains from killing even the smallest of animals.

Our previous authors in this section have all been arguing in favor of individuals being able to control their own self-will and desires in order to respect and care for others. But is this the only possible ethical position? Is it wrong to care more for the self than for others? Arguing in defense of egoism is Ayn Rand, who was born in 1905 in St. Petersburg, Russia, but lived in the United States from 1926 onward. Rand is famous for her ethics of egoism, and she defends it against the ethics of altruism of the sort found in Buddhism, Christianity, and even Marxism. In her own life, Rand fled a Soviet government which often advocated the benefit of the society as a whole over individual rights, while condemning the capitalist ethic of getting ahead by exploiting others. To counter those notions, Rand developed her ethics of selfishness, which is unembarrassed by its egoistic claims. She first protects

egoism from stereotypes. Since egoism has to do with achieving one's own interests, the "brute's" grab at pleasure is not in the true self interest of the individual, and so can be ruled out. The evil of a robber's actions, for example, does not lie in his pursuing his interests, but rather in what the robber chooses as goal, and the way in which the goal is gained. In this way she distinguishes her position from the Nietzschean justification of any action which the strong may choose, in pursuit of his or her own interests. In fact, she has a theory of rights which must be upheld even by the egoist. (See Chapter 9 for Nietzsche's view.)

Rand considers altruism to be psychologically harmful. It implies that the desire to live is selfish and evil and suggests that any special love one might have for a family member, friend, or spouse is unwarranted or morally dangerous. She combats a view which she calls "moral cannibalism," which consists of the notion that any time one does something for oneself, someone else must be being hurt. In fact, the opposite may be the case.

ISLAMIC VIEW OF HUMAN RIGHTS

Riffat Hassan

It is profoundly ironic that stereotypes identify Islam with war and militancy, whereas the very term *islām* is derived from a root, one of whose basic meanings is "peace." Not only is the idea of peace of pivotal significance in the theological worldview of Islam, it also permeates the daily lives of Muslims. Each time two Muslims greet each other, they say *salam alaikum*, "peace be on you," and *alaikum assalum*, "peace be on you (too)." The regularity and fervor with which this greeting is exchanged shows that it is not a mechanical reiteration

of words that have little or no meaning but a religious ritual of great importance. The ideal of being at peace with oneself, one's fellow human beings, the world of nature, and God, is deeply cherished by Muslims in general. But if that is the case, why is there such manifest lack of peace, and so much talk of violence, in the present-day world of Islam? In order to answer this question it is necessary to understand what "peace" means according to the perspective of "normative" Islam.

Many, including some who are committed to the ideal of peacemaking, tend, unfortunately, to define peace negatively, as "absence of war" (just as some tend to define "health" as "absence of sickness"). But, in quranic terms, peace is much more than mere absence of war. It is a positive state of safety or security in which one is free from anxiety or fear.

It is this state that characterizes both *islām*,[1] self-surrender to God, and *īmān*,[2] true faith in God, and reference is made to it, directly or indirectly, on every page of the Qur'ān through the many derivatives of the roots "s-l-m" and "a-m-n" from which *islām* and *īmān* are derived, respectively. Peace is an integral part not only of the terms used for a believer, "muslim" (i.e., one who professes *islām*) and *mo'min* (i.e., one who possesses *īmān*), but also of God's names *As-Salām* and *Al-Mo'min* mentioned in the Qur'ān:

> He is Allāh, beside whom there is no God; the King, the Holy, the Author of Peace [As-Salām], the Granter of Security [Al-Mo'min], Guardian over all, the Mighty, the Supreme, the Possessor of greatness [Surah 59.23].[3]

As pointed out by G. A. Parwez, *As-Salām* is the Being who is the source of peace and concord and who assures peaceful existence to all beings. *Al-Mo'min* is the Being who shelters and protects all and bestows peace in every sphere of life.[4]

That God "invites" humanity to *dār as-salām* (i.e., the abode of peace) is stated by the Qur'ān (Surah 10.25), which also promises the reward of peace to those who live in accordance with God's will:

> God guides such as follow His pleasure into the ways of peace, and brings them out of darkness into light by His will, and guides them to the right path [Surah 5.16].[5]

• • •

In other words, peace on earth (which is a precondition of peace in heaven) is the result of living in accordance with God's will and pleasure. Here it is important to note that Islam conceives of God as

Rabb Al-'Alamīn: Creator and Sustainer of all the peoples and universes, whose purpose in creating (as stated in Surah 51.56) is that all creatures should engage in God's *'ibādat*. This term, which is commonly understood as "worship," in fact has a much broader meaning and refers to "doing what God approves."[6] In Islam "doing what God approves" is not conceived in terms of seeking salvation from the burden of original sin through belief in redemption or a redeemer (none of these ideas/concepts being present in the Qur'ān) or through renunciation of the world (monasticism not being required by God, according to the Qur'ān).[7] Rather, it is conceived in terms of the fulfillment of *Haquq Allāh* (rights of God) and *Haquq al-'ibād* (rights of God's servants—namely, human beings). The Qur'ān considers the two kinds of "rights" to be inseparable as indicated by the constant conjunction of *salāt* (signifying remembrance of, and devotion to, God) and *zakāt* (signifying the sharing of one's possessions with those in need). In fact, as Surah 107 shows, the Qur'ān is severe in its criticism of those who offer their prayers to God but are deficient in performing acts of kindness to those in need:

> Hast thou ever considered [the kind of person] who
> gives the lie to all moral law?
> Behold, it is this [kind of person] who thrusts the orphan
> away,
> and feels no urge to feed the needy.
> Woe, then, unto those praying ones whose hearts from
> their prayers are remote—
> those who want only to be seen and praised,
> and, withal, deny all assistance [to their fellows].[8]

In quranic terms, then, peace is obtained in any human society when human beings, conscious of their duty to God, fulfill their duty to other human beings. In fulfilling this duty they honor what I call the "human rights" of others. These rights are those that all human beings *ought* to possess because they are rooted so deeply in our humanness that their de-

---

[1] G. A. Parwez, *Lughat ul-Qur'ān* (Lahore, Idaru, Tulu'-e-Islam, 1960), vol. 2, p. 894.

[2] Ibid., vol. 1, p. 263.

[3] Muhammad Ali, *The Holy Qur'ān* (Chicago, Specialty Promotions, 1973).

[4] G. A. Parwez, *Islam: A Challenge to Religion* (Lahore, Idara Tulu'-e-Islam, 1968), p. 285.

[5] M. Ali, *Holy Qur'ān*.

[6] *Arabic-English Lexicon*, book 1, part 5, p. 1936.

[7] See Surah 57.27.

[8] Asad, *Message of the Qur'ān*.

nial or violation is tantamount to negation or degradation of that which makes us human. These rights came into existence when we did; they were created, as we were, by God in order that our human potential could be actualized. These rights not only provide us with an opportunity to develop all our inner resources, but they also hold before us a vision of what God would like us to be: what God wants us to strive for and live for and die for. Rights given by God are rights that ought to be exercised, because everything that God does is for "a just purpose" (Surah 15.85; 16.3; 44.39; 45.22; 46.3). Among these rights, there are some that have an important, perhaps even a crucial, bearing on whether or not a society can realize the ideal of peace; hence a brief account of them follows.

RIGHT TO LIFE

The sanctity and absolute value of human life is upheld by the Qur'ān, which states:

> And do not take any human being's life—which God has declared to be sacred—otherwise than in [the pursuit of] justice: this He has enjoined upon you so that you might use your reason [Surah 6.151].[9]

The Qur'ān also points out graphically in Surah 5.35 that in essence the life of each individual is comparable to the life of an entire community, and, therefore, should be treated with utmost care:

> We ordained
> For the Children of Israel
> That if any one slew
> A person—unless it be
> For murder or for spreading
> Mischief in the land—
> It would be as if
> He slew the whole people:
> And if anyone saved a life,
> It would be as if he saved
> The life of the whole people.[10]

RIGHT TO RESPECT

In Surah 17.70, the Qur'ān says: "Verily, we have honored every human being." Human beings are worthy of respect because they have been made "in the best of molds" (Surah 95.4), and possess the faculty of reason, which distinguishes them from all other creatures (Surah 2.30–34) and enables them to accept the "trust" of freedom of will, which no other creature is willing to accept (Surah 33.72). Human beings can acquire knowledge of good and evil, and strive to do the good and avoid the evil. Thus, they have the potential to be God's viceregents on earth. On account of the promise that is contained in being human, the humanness of all human beings is to be respected and regarded as an end in itself.

RIGHT TO JUSTICE

In the Qur'ān, tremendous emphasis is put on the duty to do justice:

> O ye who believe, be maintainers of justice, bearers of witness for Allah, even though it be against your own selves or [your] parents or near relatives—whether he be rich or poor, Allah has the better right over them both. So follow not low desires, lest you deviate. And if you distort or turn away from [truth], surely Allah is ever aware of what you do [Surah 4.135].[11]
>
> O ye who believe, be upright for Allah, bearers of witness with justice; and let not hatred of a people incite you not to act equitably. Be just; that is nearer to observance of duty. And keep your duty to Allah. Surely Allah is aware of what you do [Surah 5.8].[12]

In the context of justice, the Qur'ān uses two concepts: *adl* and *ihsan*. Both are enjoined (Surah 16.91) and both are related to the idea of balance, but they are not identical in meaning. A.A.A. Fyzee, a well-known scholar of Islamic laws, defined *adl* as "to be equal, neither more nor less," and stated: "in a court of justice the claims of the two

---

9 Ibid.
10 A. Y. Ali, *Holy Qur'ān.*

11 M. Ali, *Holy Qur'ān.*
12 Ibid.

parties must be considered evenly, without undue stress being laid upon one side or the other. Justice introduces balance in the form of scales that are evenly balanced."[13] Abu'l Kalam Azad, a noted Muslim scholar, described *adl* in similar terms: "What is justice but the avoiding of excess. There should be neither too much nor too little; hence the use of scales as the emblems of justice."[14] Lest anyone try to do too much or too little, the Qur'ān states that no human being can carry another's burden (Surah 53.38) or have anything without striving for it (ibid., 39).

It is important to note here that, according to the quranic perspective, justice is not to be interpreted as absolute equality of treatment, because human beings are not equal to far as their human potential or their human situation is concerned. Thus, though upholding the principle that the humanness of all human beings is to be respected, the Qur'ān maintains that the recognition of individual "merit" is also a fundamental human right. The Qur'ān teaches that merit is not determined by lineage, sex, wealth, success, or religion—but by righteousness. Righteousness consists not only of *īmān* (just belief) but also of *amal* (just action) as pointed out in the following passage:

> True piety does not consist in turning your faces towards the east or the west—but truly pious is he who believes in God, and the Last Day, and the angels, and revelation, and the prophets; and spends his substance—however much he himself may cherish it—upon the near of kin, and the orphans, and the needy, and the wayfarer, and the beggars, and for the freeing of human beings from bondage; and is constant in prayer, and renders the purifying dues; and [truly pious are] they who keep their promises whenever they promise, and are patient in misfortune and hardship and in time of peril: it is they who have proved themselves true, and it is they, they who are conscious of God.[15]

Surah 19.95 testifies to the higher merit of one who strives harder for the cause of God:

> Such of the believers as remain passive—other than the disabled—cannot be deemed equal to those who strive hard in God's cause with their possessions and their lives: God has exalted those who strive hard with their possessions and their lives far above those who remain passive. Although God has promised the ultimate good unto all [believers], yet has God exalted those who strive hard above those who remain passive by [promising them] a mighty reward—[many] degrees thereof—and forgiveness of sins, and His grace; for God is indeed much-forgiving, a dispenser of grace.[16]

Surah 49.13 affirms that "the most honored of you in the sight of God is the most righteous of you."

Just as it is in the spirit of *adl* that special merit be considered in the matter of rewards, so also special circumstances must be considered in the matter of punishments. In the case of punishment for crimes of "unchastity," for instance, the Qur'ān, being nonsexist, prescribes identical punishments for a man or a woman who is proved guilty (Surah 2.2), but it differentiates between different classes of women; for the same crime, a slave woman would receive half, and the Prophet's consort double, the punishment given to a "free" Muslim woman (Surah 4.25; 33.30). Making such a distinction shows compassion for the morally "disadvantaged," while upholding high moral standards for others, particularly those whose actions have a normative significance.

While constantly enjoining *adl,* the Qur'ān goes beyond this concept to *ihsan,* literally "restoring the balance by making up a loss or deficiency."[17] In order to understand this concept, it is necessary to understand the nature of the ideal community or society (*ummah*) envisaged by the Qur'ān. The word *ummah* comes from the term *umm* meaning "mother." The symbols of a mother and motherly

---

[13] A. A. A. Fyzee, *A Modern Approach to Islam* (Lahore, Universal Books, 1978), p. 17.
[14] Ibid.
[15] Asad, *Message of the Qur'ān.*

[16] Ibid.
[17] G. A. Parwez, *Tabweeb ul-Qur'ān* (Lahore, Idara Tulu'-e-Islam, 1977), vol. 1, p. 78.

love and compassion are also linked with the two attributes most characteristic of God, *Rahmān* and *Rahīm,* both of which are derived from the root r-h-m, meaning "womb." The ideal *ummah* cares about all its members as an ideal mother cares about all her children, knowing that all are not equal and that each has different needs. Although encouraging any one of her children to be parasitical would be injurious and unjust not only to her other children but also to the one who does not fulfill its human potential, she can, with justice, make up the deficiency of any child who, despite its best efforts, still cannot meet the requirements of life. *Ihsan* thus secures what even *adl* cannot; it shows the Qur'ān's sympathy for the downtrodden, oppressed, or weak classes of human beings (such as women, slaves, orphans, the poor, the infirm, minorities, etc.).

RIGHT TO FREEDOM

There is much in the Qur'ān that endorses J. J. Rousseau's famous statement: "Man is born free, and everywhere he is in chains." A large part of the Qur'ān's concern is to free human beings from the chains that bind them: traditionalism, authoritarianism (religious, political, economic), tribalism, racism, sexism, and slavery.

It is obvious that God alone is completely free and not subject to any constraints. The human condition necessitates that limits be set to what human beings may or may not do, so that liberty does not degenerate into license. Recognizing the human propensity toward dictatorship and despotism, the Qur'ān says with startling clarity and emphasis:

> It is not meet for a mortal that Allah should give him the Book and the judgment and the prophethood, then he should say to men: Be my servants besides Allah's; but [he would say]: Be worshippers of the Lord because you teach the Book and because you study [it] [Surah 3.78].[18]

The greatest guarantee of personal freedom for a Muslim lies in the quranic decree that no one other

than God can limit human freedom (Surah 42.21) and in the statement that "judgment is only Allah's" (Surah 12.40).

Although it is beyond the scope of this paper to cite quranic pronouncements relating to human freedom in the diverse realms of life, it is important to mention that the Qur'ān abolished slavery (Surah 47.4); that it established the principle of *shura* or government by mutual consultation (Surah 3.159)[19] in order to eliminate the possibility of political authoritarianism; and that it prohibited coercion in matters of religious belief as is clearly stated in Surah 2.256:

> Let there be no compulsion
> In religion: truth stands out
> Clear from error: whoever
> Rejects evil and believes
> In God hath grasped
> The most trustworthy
> Hand-hold, that never breaks.[20]

It is noteworthy that in the matter of religious freedom, the Qur'ān is "liberal" to an amazing degree. Not only does it state quite clearly that the mission of the Prophet (and Muslims) to non-Muslims consists only of a faithful transmission of the message of God and that the Prophet (and Muslims) ought not to feel responsible for the religious and moral choices made by other Muslims or by non-Muslims after they have received the message of God.[21] The Qur'ān also makes it clear that plurality of religions is part of God's plan for humanity:

---

[18] M. Ali, *Holy Qur'ān.*

[19] Of relevance here is the following passage: "The Qur'ān gives to responsible dissent the status of a fundamental right. In exercise of their powers, therefore, neither the legislature nor the executive can demand unquestioning obedience. . . . The Prophet, even though he was the recipient of Divine revelation, was required to consult the Muslims in public affairs. Allah addressing the Prophet says: '. . . consult with them upon the conduct of affairs. And . . . when thou art resolved, then put thy trust in Allah (Surah 3.159).' (K. Ishaque, "Islamic Law—Its Ideals and Principles," in *The Challenge of Islam,* A. Gauher, ed. [London, The Islamic Council of Europe, 1980], pp. 167–69).

[20] A. Y. Ali, *Holy Qur'ān.*

[21] See, e.g., Surah 6.107; 16.82; 42.48.

Those who believe [in the Qur'ān],
And those who follow the Jewish [scriptures],
And the Christians and the Sabians,
Any who believe in God
And the Last Day,
And work righteousness,
Shall have their reward
With their Lord,
Nor shall they grieve
[Surah 2.62].[22]

In other words, not only does the Qur'ān uphold the right of human beings in general to religious freedom, it also recognizes the religious equality of all those who have "iman" and act righteously.

• • •

In the context of the human right to religious freedom, it is necessary to mention that, according to traditional Islam, the punishment for apostasy is death. There is, however, nothing in the Qur'ān that suggests any punishment at all, let alone the punishment of death. There is absolutely no reason why the quranic imperative that there must be no compulsion in religion should not apply also to the Muslims who wish to renounce Islam. (I believe that the death penalty was not originally for apostasy but for apostasy accompanied by "acts of war" against Muslims. Later, however, this distinction was obliterated by Muslim jurists in order to compel "wavering" Muslims to remain within the fold of Islam.)

OTHER RIGHTS

Some other rights that may be mentioned in passing are: the right to be protected from defamation, sarcasm, offensive nicknames, and backbiting (Surah 49.11–12) as well as from being maligned on grounds of assumed guilt by scandal-mongers (Surah 24.16–19); the right to a secure place of residence (Surah 2.85); the right to a means of living (Surah 6.156; 11.6); the right to protection of one's

personal property or possessions (Surah 2.29); the right to protection of one's covenants/contracts (Surah 3.177; 5.1; 17.34); the right to move freely (Surah 67.15); the right to seek asylum if one is living under oppression (Surah 4.97–100); the right to social and judicial autonomy for minorities (Surah 5.42–48); the right to protection of one's holy places (Surah 9.17); and the right to protection of one's home life from undue intrusion (Surah 24.27–28, 58; 33.53; 49.12).

It is essential in the context of human rights in Islam to mention that there is more quranic legislation pertaining to the regulation of man-woman relationships than on any other subject. The Qur'ān is fully cognizant of the fact that women have been among the most exploited and oppressed groups in the world, and aims, in multifarious ways, to establish their equality with men in terms of their humanness and to secure justice for them in domestic and public matters. An idea of tremendous importance implicit in many teachings of the Qur'ān is that if human beings can learn to order their homes justly so that the rights of all within its jurisdiction are safeguarded, then they can also order their society and the world at large justly. In other words, the Qur'ān regards the home as a microcosm of the *ummah* and the world community, and emphasizes the importance of making it "the abode of peace" through just living.

Even a brief reflection on the "human rights"[23] mentioned above gives one a good idea of the quranic concept of "the good life." This good life, which is made up of many elements and is characterized by peace, is possible only with a just environment.

• • •

Without the elimination of the inequities, inequalities, and injustices that pervade the personal and

---

[22] Ibid. A. Y. Ali, *Holy Qur'ān.*

[23] For a more detailed discussion of human rights in Islam, see my article, "On Human Rights and the Qur'anic Perspective," in *Human Rights in Religious Traditions,* A. Swidler, ed. (New York, Pilgrim Press, 1982), pp. 51–65; also in *Journal of Ecumenical Studies,* 19/3 (Summer 1982) 51–65.

collective lives of human beings, it is not possible to talk of peace in Islamic terms. Such talk makes sense only in a society in which ignorance and oppression have been eliminated, in which the means of sustaining and developing human life and capabilities are accessible to all, in which there is freedom from fear, uncertainty, and anxiety—in short, in a society where justice prevails in every way.

• • •

It is obvious that the quranic ideal is not easy to achieve in a world such as the one in which we live, because it entails not simply the desire to abolish violence and war as means of conflict-resolution but the commitment to "doing what God approves." However, from the quranic perspective, the securing of peace either here and now or in the hereafter is not meant to be easy, as the Qur'ān states in Surah 3.141:

> Did you think that ye
> Would enter *al-jannah*
> [i.e., "the garden": the abode of peace]
> Without God testing
> Those of you who fought hard
> (in His cause) and
> Remained steadfast?[24]

Peace is dependent upon justice and justice is dependent upon *jihād fi sabil Allāh*: striving in the cause of God. It is most unfortunate that *jihād,* which is the means whereby God's vision of a peaceful world can come to be, has become identified in the minds of many non-Muslims and—what is much worse—in the minds of many present-day Muslims, with mere destruction. According to the Qur'ān, Muslims have the right to defend themselves against injustice and the duty to protect the weak from injustice.[25] But they are reminded, over and over, that the "limits set by God" (*hudud Allāh*) are not to be transgressed at any time, and that justice must be done even to an enemy."[26] Further-

more, any initiative toward peace taken by an enemy must be accepted and responded to in good faith and with good will.[27]

The thought with which I should like to conclude . . . is that, in my judgment, the greatest *jihād* for Muslims today lies in the making of war not upon real or assumed enemies of Islam but upon the ignorance and narrowness of heart, mind, and spirit that prevent Muslims from becoming *mo'minum*: those who have attained peace through right knowledge leading to right action. The duty to seek learning even in the midst of war is where the quranic emphasis lies, as pointed out in Surah 9.122:

> With all this, it is not desirable that all of the believers take the field [in time of war]. From within every group in their midst, some shall refrain from going forth to war, and shall devote themselves [instead] to acquiring a deeper knowledge of the faith, and [thus be able to] teach their home-coming brethren, so that these [too] might guard themselves against evil.[28]

BUGDHIST ETHICS

Gunapala Dharmasiri

There are some interesting issues that are specific to the Buddhist theory of ethics. These issues originate from the nature of the Buddhist theory of reality. A person does not have a self or a soul and is said to be made up of five factors. When these five factors come together, they constitute the person, just as a chariot is made up of the parts that constitute it. And, it is further said that these five factors are incessantly changing or are always in a state of flux. In this state of affairs, can one meaningfully speak of "a person"? If there is no person, there are problems for moral discourse, because ethical discourse

---

[24] A. Y. Ali, *Holy Qur'ān.*
[25] See, e.g., Surah 2.190–93, 217; 4.75–78; 22.39–40, 60; 57.25.
[26] See, e.g., Surah 5.8.

[27] See, e.g., Surah 8.61.
[28] Asad, *Message of the Qur'ān.*

presupposes the notions of "personal responsibility," "personal identity," "personal initiative" and "moral commitment."

One could imagine these problems easily solved if we were to accept the theory of a self. But for the Buddha, the idea of a self could not be made meaningful in any way. The only way to make the idea of self meaningful is to verify it, and if we look at ourselves objectively in order to verify it, all we see is the above five factors. And if we introspect and subjectively look for a self, all we see is an ever changing series of thoughts and sensations. Therefore, if the idea of self or soul is not meaningful, we will have to explain things with the help of existing facts.

Although Buddhism does not accept the idea of a person as an enduring entity, it accepts the existence of a person as a composite of factors. Two criteria are used in determining the identity of a person. A person is made up of two types of groups of events, physical and mental. As all these groups are ever changing, the preceding events disappear, giving birth to succeeding events. Thus the succeeding events inherit the characteristics of the preceding events. This results in a causal sequence of events. In Buddhism, it is through this "unbroken continuity or coherence of the series of events" (avicchinna santati sāmaggi—Buddhaghosa), that personal identity is traced. The person who lives at 9 a.m. this morning is a result of the person who lived at 7 a.m. this morning.

DOCTRINE OF KARMA

It is in this sense that the Buddhist doctrine of karma has to be interpreted. Though some assume that the doctrine of karma is a metaphysical doctrine, it is actually a psychological principle or a law based on the law of causation as applied to a series of mental events. If a person has a "bad" thought now, this will generate further "bad" thoughts, thus gradually leading to the formation of a karmic mental complex. This complex can generate various types of mental illnesses like anxiety and guilt, which gradually lead to further complications such as physical illnesses. The Buddha said that karma is

a principle that can be verified in this life itself by looking into the causal relationships between mental phenomena and between mental and physical phenomena. A "bad" thought leads to tension and anxiety, while a "good" thought leads to calmness and relaxation. Thus, the problem of personal identity and moral responsibility is solved in terms of causal connectedness.

Another problem that arises within Buddhist ethics is how to justify altruistic or "other-regarding" action. If real "persons" do not exist, how can we make the idea of moral commitment to others meaningful? A difficult problem that comes up in the Buddhist teaching of egolessness is "why should I do anything at all?"

Before we discuss acting or working for others, we must first be clear about what is meant by "work." Ordinarily, work is supposed to be physical. But Buddhism accepts two kinds of work: physical and spiritual. For example, a Brahmin farmer called Kasībhāradvāja accused the Buddha of leading an idle life, not doing any physical work or labor. The Buddha replied that he was also engaged in labor and that he was perhaps engaged in a task more important and arduous than what physical labor involves. Further, he said that if necessary, his work could also be easily described in the jargon of the physical labor of a farmer. The Buddha answers, "I also, O Brahmana, both plough and sow, and having ploughed and sown, I eat." Then the Brahmin retorts: "Thou professest to be a ploughman, and yet we do not see thy ploughing; asked about thy ploughing, tell us of it, that we may know thy ploughing." The Buddha answers, "Faith is the seed, penance the rain, understanding my yoke and plough, modesty the pole of the plough, mind the tie, thoughtfulness my ploughshare and goad. . . . Exertion is my beast of burden; carrying me to Nibbāna,[1] he goes without turning back to the place where, having gone, one does not grieve. So this ploughing is ploughed, it bears the fruit of immortality; having ploughed this ploughing, one is

---

[1] Sometimes spelled as "nirvana," this is the desireless state which is the goal of Buddhism [Eds.].

freed from all pain."[2] Therefore, the Buddhist approach to asceticism should be properly understood. The Buddha recommended forests and lonely places only as ideal sites for training in meditation, but never for living, and he always advised monks that they "should travel around for the benefit and happiness of the multitude of human beings" (*Caratha bhikkhave cārikaṃ bahu jana hitāya bahujana sukhāya*).

CONVENTIONAL REALITY AND ABSOLUTE REALITY

Buddhism also formulates another distinction we should be aware of, that beween two levels of reality: conventional reality and absolute reality. Persons and morality exist in the conventional realm, while in the realm of absolute reality both these ideas do not make much sense. Ordinary moral theory presupposes the sense of "a person." Ordinary moral theory is valid and meaningful for one who believes that he is "a person." Once one realizes that there is no person, then he goes beyond this type of morality. However, it should be clearly noted that by going beyond morality one does not get permission to contravene ordinary moral values. In other words, the absolute dimension has no power or privilege to abrogate ordinary moral values. The Buddha shows this distinction by saying that an ordinary person, when he is moral, is conditioned by morality (*sīlamayo*), but an enlightened person is moral by "nature" (*sīlavā*), because the nature of Nirvana is moral perfection, *i.e.*, when viewed from the conventional standpoint. Therefore, when we discuss morality we must be aware of the conventional level of reality which is presupposed in our analysis.

"OTHER REGARDING" ACTIONS

How does Buddhism recommend and justify "other-regarding" actions? It has several grounds for doing so. One reason stems from the theory of dependent origination (*paṭicca-samuppāda*), which emphasizes that everything originates dependent on everything else. Therefore, everything owes its existence to everything else. Actually, it is the *Anatta* doctrine that involves one in altruistic actions. The doctrine of interdependence rules out the possibility of a separate soul, because nothing can be independent in a world where everything is interrelated. I cannot think of myself as separate from the rest of the universe because, for example, if I take my body, it is dependent on food (which means that my body is dependent on plants, animals, water, oxygen, *etc.*). My mind also exists dependently because the existence of thoughts is dependent on sense data derived from the external world of objects and persons.

A Buddha's altruistic commitment to others and other objects originates from this dependency. Because my existence is dependent on the rest of the universe, I naturally owe a debt and an obligation to the rest of the universe. Therefore, my attitude to others and other objects should be one of respect and gratitude. Thus, Buddhism advocates a sense of awe and respect towards living beings and nature. Here, it is important to note that in Buddhism, the distinction between altruism and egoism breaks down as a meaningless distinction. The ideal moral attitude to other beings advocated by the Buddha is the "love a mother shows towards her one and only child" and the love relationship between mother and child cannot be characterized as egoistic or altruistic because it is a fluid mixture of both. Likewise, helping others is a way of helping oneself.

One has to understand that one is a part of a larger whole, and is not a separate person. That is why the ordinary unenlightened man is, in Buddhist terminology, called a "*Puthujjana*" (*puthu* = separate; *jana* = people), or a person who believes that he is separate. The relationship between the part and whole is organic. In the way the whole creates the part, the part also creates the whole. Therefore one should realize that one can play a creative (in a cosmic sense) part in the cosmic order of events. In a way, the whole determines the part. But, the Buddhist point is that the part can also play a role in determining the whole. This is, of course, an in-

---

[2] *Samyutta Nikāya.* (Polytechnic Society, London), pp. 13–14.

evitable implication of the principle of inter-relatedness.

• • •

What the doctrine of interdependence emphasizes is, from the fact that the rest of the universe is responsible for me, it follows that I too am responsible for the rest of the universe. In the *Sigālovāda Sutta,* the Buddha emphasizes that rights and duties imply each other. If the rights are not well reciprocated by the duties, a moral imbalance is bound to result. From the fact that nature treats us rightly, it follows that we should treat nature rightly. Buddhism strongly believes that morality is the best way to communicate with nature because morality is the nature of nature. If we mishandle or mistreat nature we are bound to get back our due.

LOVE THAT EMBRACES ALL BEINGS

It is from the above considerations that an attitude of deepest love towards other beings and nature, which the Buddha advocates is derived. It is important to note that Buddhism is much more than merely humanistic, because the Buddhist love embraces all types of beings. Whenever the Buddha talks about loving others, he always speaks of "all beings" (*sabbe sattā*). The same love that prompts a mother to care for her one and only son should prompt persons to do their best to help the rest of the community. This attitude fosters virtues like sharing and sympathy.

Another reason why we should do anything at all is grounded on sympathy. A central theme in Buddhist ethics is that "one should treat others in exactly the same way as one treats oneself" (*attānaṃ upamaṃ katvā*). In the *Anumāna Sutta,* the Buddha states that the basis of the "other-regarding" principle is an inference from oneself to another. The inference works in two ways. The first is thinking of oneself in terms of others. According to the Buddha, the sense of the value of oneself or of one's own personality is derived from others. Therefore, "personality" itself being a value concept, if one is to become a "person" in the proper sense, it must nec-

essarily be done in a social medium. For that reason, one should always be considerate of the value of others. Man's personality is largely a product and an item of the society around him. One becomes good or derives any value to one's personality only through the society, which is why one must consider and respect others. One does not become oneself without the help of others. Here, the so-called distinction between altruism and egoism breaks down. The Buddha states his inferential principle: "Therein, your reverences, self ought to be measured against self thus by a monk: 'That person who is of evil desires and who is in the thrall of evil desires, that person is displeasing and disagreeable to me; and similarly, if I were of evil desires and in the thrall of evil desires, I would be displeasing and disagreeable to other.' "[3] The dichotomy between egoism and altruism breaks down when he repeatedly emphasizes the necessity of "other-regarding" virtues for one's development as a person, not only on a social level, but even on the spiritual level where progress is impossible without cultivating "other-regarding" virtues.

• • •

In the *Karaṇīya Metta Suttahe* says that, in spreading love, one must think of all possible types of beings: "Whatever living beings there may be: feeble or strong, long (or tall), stout, or medium, short, small, or large, seen or unseen, those dwelling far or near, those who are born and those who are yet to be born: may all beings, without exception, be happy-minded."[4] We must respect all forms of life. What the Buddha believes is that whatever form it takes, life is life. As the Mahayanists say, all life forms are sacred because they all contain the seeds of Buddhahood or perfection. If one does not have this reverence towards life, one alienates oneself from life. Whether it is one's own or another's, life is treated as a commonly shared property. If one disrespects life that is manifested in

---

[3] *Majjhima Nikāya* (Polytechnic Society, London), I.97.
[4] *Sutta Nipāta* (Polytechnic Society, London), 146–147.

any form, one deteriorates morally and spiritually because one becomes alienated from the most basic and intrinsic value of the world. Here, it is important to note the significant fact that the Buddha prohibited monks from harming trees and plants because "they are creatures with one sense-faculty (*ekindriya*), (*i.e.* touch)" and therefore, "people are of the opinion that there is life in trees."[5] He also forbade monks to dig the earth because that would harm "tiny creatures living in earth"[6] (But he did not enjoin these rules for laymen because of the practical difficulties).

Although a complete practice of *Ahiṃsā* (non-injury) is even theoretically impossible because the process of living itself automatically involves a process of killing or injuring many beings, perfect *Ahiṃsā* is always regarded as the ideal that one should always try to live up to as far as possible. What truly matters is this genuine desire or motive to respect life. The Buddha says that the ultimate and intrinsic value of life will be self evident to any one who will care to look at one's own life. The Buddha's appeal to us is to realize that all other beings also think of themselves exactly in the same way one thinks about oneself. Therefore, in Buddhism, the sacredness of life is an ultimate ethical fact which is proved and made meaningful self-evidently, *i.e.,* through empathy.

---

[5] *Vinaya,* IV, 34.
[6] *Vinaya,* IV, 32–3.

THE VIRTUE OF SELFISHNESS*

Ayn Rand

In popular usage, the word "selfishness" is a synonym of evil; the image it conjures is of a murderous brute who tramples over piles of corpses to achieve his own ends, who cares for no living being and pursues nothing but the gratification of the mindless whims of any immediate moment.

Yet the exact meaning and dictionary definition of the word "selfishness" is: *concern with one's own interests.*

This concept does *not* include a moral evaluation; it does not tell us whether concern with one's own interests is good or evil; nor does it tell us what constitutes man's actual interests. It is the task of ethics to answer such questions.

The ethics of altruism has created the image of the brute, as its answer, in order to make men accept two inhuman tenets: (a) that any concern with one's own interests is evil, regardless of what these interests might be, and (b) that the brute's activities are *in fact* to one's own interest (which altruism enjoins man to renounce for the sake of his neighbors).

Altruism declares that any action taken for the benefit of others is good, and any action taken for one's own benefit is evil. Thus the *beneficiary* of an action is the only criterion of moral value—and so long as that beneficiary is anybody other than oneself, anything goes.

Hence the appalling immorality, the chronic injustice, the grotesque double standards, the insoluble conflicts and contradictions that have characterized human relationships and human societies throughout history, under all the variants of the altruist ethics.

Observe the indecency of what passes for moral judgments today. An industrialist who produces a fortune, and a gangster who robs a bank are regarded as equally immoral, since they both sought wealth for their own "selfish" benefit. A young man who gives up his career in order to support his parents and never rises beyond the rank of grocery clerk is regarded as morally superior to the young man who endures an excruciating struggle and achieves his personal ambition. A dictator is regarded as moral, since the unspeakable atrocities he committed were intended to benefit "the people," not himself.

Observe what this beneficiary-criterion of

---

*The Estate of Ayn Rand has requested the following: "The following are brief and potentially misleading excerpts from three different articles by Ayn Rand. An ellipsis sign indicates each omission of material from the original text."

morality does to a man's life. The first thing he learns is that morality is his enemy; he has nothing to gain from it, he can only lose; self-inflicted loss, self-inflicted pain and the gray, debilitating pall of an incomprehensible duty is all that he can expect. He may hope that others might occasionally sacrifice themselves for his benefit, as he grudgingly sacrifices himself for theirs, but he knows that the relationship will bring mutual resentment, not pleasure—and that, morally, their pursuit of values will be like an exchange of unwanted, unchosen Christmas presents, which neither is morally permitted to buy for himself. Apart from such times as he manages to perform some act of self-sacrifice, he possesses no moral significance: morality takes no cognizance of him and has nothing to say to him for guidance in the crucial issues of his life; it is only his own personal, private, "selfish" life and, as such, it is regarded either as evil or, at best, *amoral*.

Since nature does not provide man with an automatic form of survival, since he has to support his life by his own effort, the doctrine that concern with one's own interests is evil means that man's desire to live is evil—that man's life, as such, is evil. No doctrine could be more evil than that.

Yet that is the meaning of altruism, implicit in such examples as the equation of an industrialist with a robber. There is a fundamental moral difference between a man who sees his self-interest in production and a man who sees it in robbery. The evil of a robber does *not* lie in the fact that he pursues his own interests, but in *what* he regards as to his own interest; *not* in the fact that he pursues his values, but in *what* he chose to value; *not* in the fact that he wants to live, but in the fact that he wants to live on a subhuman level (see "The Objectivist Ethics").

If it is true that what I mean by "selfishness" is not what is meant conventionally, then *this* is one of the worst indictments of altruism: it means that altruism *permits no concept* of a self-respecting, self-supporting man—a man who supports his life by his own effort and neither sacrifices himself nor others. It means that altruism permits no view of men except as sacrificial animals and profiteers-on-sacri-

fice, as victims and parasites—that it permits no concept of a benevolent co-existence among men—that it permits no concept of *justice*.

If you wonder about the reasons behind the ugly mixture of cynicism and guilt in which most men spend their lives, these are the reasons: cynicism, because they neither practice nor accept the altruist morality—guilt, because they dare not reject it.

To rebel against so devastating an evil, one has to rebel against its basic premise. To redeem both man and morality, it is the concept of *"selfishness"* that one has to redeem.

The first step is to assert *man's right to a moral existence*—that is: to recognize his need of a moral code to guide the course and the fulfillment of his own life.

The Objectivist ethics holds that the actor must always be the beneficiary of his action and that man must act for his own *rational* self-interest. But his right to do so is derived from his nature as man and from the function of moral values in human life— and, therefore, is applicable *only* in the context of a rational, objectively demonstrated and validated code of moral principles which define and determine his actual self-interest. It is not a license "to do as he pleases" and it is not applicable to the altruists' image of a "selfish" brute nor to any man motivated by irrational emotions, feelings, urges, wishes or whims.

This is said as a warning against the kind of "Nietzschean egoists" who, in fact, are a product of the altruist morality and represent the other side of the altruist coin: the men who believe that any action, regardless of its nature, is good if it is intended for one's own benefit. Just as the satisfaction of the irrational desires of others is *not* a criterion of moral value, neither is the satisfaction of one's own irrational desires. Morality is not a contest of whims.

•   •   •

The *moral cannibalism* of all hedonist and altruist doctrines lies in the premise that the happiness of one man necessitates the injury of another.

Today, most people hold this premise as an absolute not to be questioned. And when one speaks of man's right to exist for his own sake, for his own rational self-interest, most people assume automatically that this means his right to sacrifice others. Such an assumption is a confession of their own belief that to injure, enslave, rob or murder others is in man's self-interest—which he must selflessly renounce. The idea that man's self-interest can be served only by a non-sacrificial relationship with others has never occurred to those humanitarian apostles of unselfishness, who proclaim their desire to achieve the brotherhood of men. And it will not occur to them, or to anyone, so long as the concept "rational" is omitted from the context of "values," "desires," "self-interest" and *ethics.*

The Objectivist ethics proudly advocates and upholds *rational selfishness*—which means: the values required for man's survival *qua* man—which means: the values required for *human* survival—not the values produced by the desires, the emotions, the "aspirations," the feelings, the whims or the needs of irrational brutes, who have never outgrown the primordial practice of human sacrifices, have never discovered an industrial society and can conceive of no self-interest but that of grabbing the loot of the moment.

The Objectivist ethics holds that *human* good does not require human sacrifices and cannot be achieved by the sacrifice of anyone to anyone. It holds that the *rational* interests of men do not clash—that there is no conflict of interests among men who do not desire the unearned, who do not make sacrifices nor accept them, who deal with one another as *traders,* giving value for value.

The principle of *trade* is the only rational ethical principle for all human relationships, personal and social, private and public, spiritual and material. It is the principle of *justice.*

A trader is a man who earns what he gets and does not give or take the undeserved. He does not treat men as masters or slaves, but as independent equals. He deals with men by means of a free, voluntary, unforced, uncoerced exchange—an exchange which benefits both parties by their own independent judgment. A trader does not expect to be paid for his defaults, only for his achievements. He does not switch to others the burden of his failures, and he does not mortgage his life into bondage to the failures of others.

In spiritual issues—(by "spiritual" I mean: "pertaining to man's consciousness")—the currency or medium of exchange is different, but the principle is the same. Love, friendship, respect, admiration are the emotional response of one man to the virtues of another, the spiritual *payment* given in exchange for the personal, selfish pleasure which one man derives from the virtues of another man's character. Only a brute or an altruist would claim that the appreciation of another person's virtues is an act of selflessness, that as far as one's own selfish interest and pleasure are concerned, it makes no difference whether one deals with a genius or a fool, whether one meets a hero or a thug, whether one marries an ideal woman or a slut. In spiritual issues, a trader is a man who does not seek to be loved for his weaknesses or flaws, only for his virtues, and who does not grant his love to the weaknesses or the flaws of others, only to their virtues.

To love is to value. Only a rationally selfish man, a man of *self-esteem,* is capable of love—because he is the only man capable of holding firm, consistent, uncompromising, unbetrayed values. The man who does not value himself, cannot value anything or anyone.

•   •   •

Love and friendship are profoundly personal, selfish values: love is an expression and assertion of self-esteem, a response to one's own values in the person of another. One gains a profoundly personal, selfish joy from the mere existence of the person one loves. It is one's own personal, selfish happiness that one seeks, earns and derives from love.

A "selfless," "disinterested" love is a contradiction in terms: it means that one is indifferent to that which one values.

Concern for the welfare of those one loves is a rational part of one's selfish interests. If a man who is passionately in love with his wife spends a fortune to cure her of a dangerous illness, it would be absurd to claim that he does it as a "sacrifice" for *her* sake, not his own, and that it makes no difference to *him,* personally and selfishly, whether she lives or dies.

Any action that a man undertakes for the benefit of those he loves is *not a sacrifice* if, in the hierarchy of his values, in the total context of the choices open to him, it achieves that which is of greatest *personal* (and rational) importance to *him.* In the above example, his wife's survival is of greater value to the husband than anything else that his money could buy, it is of greatest importance to his own happiness and, therefore, his action is *not* a sacrifice.

But suppose he let her die in order to spend his money on saving the lives of ten other women, none of whom meant anything to him—as the ethics of altruism would require. *That* would be a sacrifice. Here the difference between Objectivism and altruism can be seen most clearly: if sacrifice is the moral principle of action, then that husband *should* sacrifice his wife for the sake of ten other women. What distinguishes the wife from the ten others? Nothing but her value to the husband who has to make the choice—nothing but the fact that *his* happiness requires her survival.

The Objectivist ethics would tell him: your highest moral purpose is the achievement of your own happiness, your money is yours, use it to save your wife, *that* is your moral right and your rational, moral choice.

Consider the soul of the altruistic moralist who would be prepared to tell that husband the opposite. (And then ask yourself whether altruism is motivated by benevolence.)

The proper method of judging when or whether one should help another person is by reference to one's own rational self-interest and one's own hierarchy of values: the time, money or effort one gives or the risk one takes should be proportionate to the value of the person in relation to one's own happiness.

• • •

The virtue involved in helping those one loves is not "selflessness" or "sacrifice," but *integrity.* In-

tegrity is loyalty to one's convictions and values; it is the policy of acting in accordance with one's values, of expressing, upholding and translating them into practical reality. If a man professes to love a woman, yet his actions are indifferent, inimical or damaging to her, it is his lack of integrity that makes him immoral.

The same principle applies to relationships among friends. If one's friend is in trouble, one should act to help him by whatever nonsacrificial means are appropriate. For instance, if one's friend is starving, it is not a sacrifice, but an act of integrity to give him money for food rather than buy some insignificant gadget for oneself, because his welfare is important in the scale of one's personal values. If the gadget means more than the friend's suffering, one had no business pretending to be his friend.

The practical implementation of friendship, affection and love consists of incorporating the welfare (the *rational* welfare) of the person involved into one's own hierarchy of values, then acting accordingly.

But this is a reward which men have to earn by means of their virtues and which one cannot grant to mere acquaintances or strangers.

What, then, should one properly grant to strangers? The generalized respect and good will which one should grant to a human being in the name of the potential value he represents—until and unless he forfeits it.

A rational man does not forget that *life* is the source of all values and, as such, a common bond among living beings (as against inanimate matter), that other men are potentially able to achieve the same virtues as his own and thus be of enormous value to him. This does not mean that he regards human lives as interchangeable with his own. He recognizes the fact that his own life is the *source,* not only of all his values, but of *his capacity to value.* Therefore, the value he grants to others is only a consequence, an extension, a secondary projection of the primary value which is himself.

"The respect and good will that men of self-esteem feel toward other human beings is profoundly egoistic; they feel, in effect: 'Other men are of value because they are of the same species as myself.' In revering living entities, they are revering their *own* life. This is the psychological base of any emotion of sympathy and any feeling of 'species solidarity.' "[1]

• • •

It is only in emergency situations that one should volunteer to help strangers, if it is in one's power. For instance, a man who values human life and is caught in a shipwreck, should help to save his fellow passengers (though not at the expense of his own life). But this does not mean that after they all reach shore, he should devote his efforts to saving his fellow passengers from poverty, ignorance, neurosis or whatever other troubles they might have. Nor does it mean that he should spend his life sailing the seven seas in search of shipwreck victims to save.

Or to take an example that can occur in everyday life: suppose one hears that the man next door is ill and penniless. Illness and poverty are not metaphysical emergencies, they are part of the normal risks of existence; but since the man is temporarily helpless, one may bring him food and medicine, *if* one can afford it (as an act of good will, not of duty) or one may raise a fund among the neighbors to help him out. But this does not mean that one must support him from then on, nor that one must spend one's life looking for starving men to help.

In the normal conditions of existence, man has to choose his goals, project them in time, pursue them and achieve them by his own effort. He cannot do it if his goals are at the mercy of and must be sacrificed to any misfortune happening to others. He cannot live his life by the guidance of rules applicable only to conditions under which human survival is impossible.

The principle that one should help men in an emergency cannot be extended to regard all human suffering as an emergency and to turn the misfortune of some into a first mortgage on the lives of others.

• • •

[1] Nathaniel Branden, "Benevolence versus Altruism," *The Objectivist Newsletter,* July 1962.

The moral purpose of a man's life is the achievement of his own happiness. This does not mean that he is indifferent to all men, that human life is of no value to him and that he has no reason to help others in an emergency. But it *does* mean that he does not subordinate his life to the welfare of others, that he does not sacrifice himself to their needs, that the relief of their suffering is not his primary concern, that any help he gives is an *exception,* not a rule, an act of generosity, not of moral duty, that it is *marginal* and *incidental*—as disasters are marginal and incidental in the course of human existence—and that *values,* not disasters, are the goal, the first concern and the motive power of his life.

QUESTIONS FOR DISCUSSION

1. Islam has a tradition of *zakat,* where all believers are enjoined to give 2.5 percent of their net holding to those in need. But according to Rand, helping strangers in need is optional, and should only be done in emergencies. Who has the sounder view? Outline the arguments in favor of each view, and the value systems they imply, and then make your decision.

2. If Dharmasiri is right, and there is no "person," and personality is largely a product of social context, then who can we blame for evil deeds? Can there be an ethics without a potentially guilty subject? Why do what's right without the fear of punishment or the reward of an afterlife? Why wouldn't Buddhist egoless ethics end in the attitude, "why should I do anything at all?" How would a Buddhist defend him- or herself from the above challenges?

3. Certainly Rand's view is at odds with other views in this section. What would be some of our authors' criticisms of Rand's "selfishness" ethics? What would be Rand's criticisms of the others? Might there be some points of agreement between her view and the others?

SUBJECTIVISM AND THE PROBLEM OF RELATIVISM

Can there be universal moral claims? We'll look first at the views of Argentinean philosopher Alejandro Korn. Korn was born in San Vincente, district of Buenos Aires, in 1860. Korn had a large personal influence on many thinkers in Argentina, and due to his inspiration the positivism which had dominated Argentinean philosophy up to that point was overcome.

Korn argues that insofar as there is no God who can provide the standard for absolute, intrinsic claims of value for certain objects or concepts, valuation is always subjective. Valuation is always influenced by social context, and values change throughout time. Values proposed to be universal are never really upheld in practice. Korn instead insists that something is valuable only if humans value it. Each individual likes to keep her or his right of judging flexible at all times. And of course, there is no consensus among all people of all times as to what is valuable.

Korn insists that subjective valuations have not reduced human history to anarchy. During certain time frames, certain arguments, authorities, or interests hold sway over most people and introduce some temporary uniformity in values. Logical argumentation in itself is not sufficient to throw off the subjective aspect, for even logic is influenced by the times and the context. Those who claim that ideal values exist, especially philosophers, only deal with word play. This is because ideal values are just abstract ideas for unrealized ultimate aspirations. Ideal values can only become effective and efficacious when, through action, they are objec-

tivized in concrete form, destined to be a historical episode in the evolution of human culture. The historical process is the search for those values that are to triumph and prevail.

Contemporary philosopher and professor at Princeton University, Jeffrey Stout hopes to add some clarity to the questions of relativism and universal values. He draws a distinction between justification and truth. It may be that within the historical context of any given community, there is a way to justify ethical standards on a given issue. However, that does not mean that every society has the true position. Some may be wrong. Sometimes they may understandably be wrong, given the context, their lack of other information, and so on; however, sometimes holding a certain view may be due to willing disregard for legitimate counterclaims. By distinguishing between justification and truth, Stout argues that a society's upholding a certain moral claim could be, at one and the same time, justified and wrong. There are some ethical rules that would be wrong for all times and in all places; he uses slavery as an example. Holding this claim puts Stout in conflict with Korn and other subjectivist or relativist positions.

However, on many ethical topics Stout is willing to concede that the same action which would be moral in one situation would be immoral in another. Stout uses polygamy as an example of a relative moral claim. Stout concludes that sensitivity to error in cross-cultural moral judgments is important, but he does not rule out the possibility of making such judgments.

VALUES ARE SUBJECTIVE

Alejandro Korn

Valuation is a complex process in which all psychical activities participate in various proportions, as part of a whole, until they are synthesized in a volition. Psychological analysis can identify the confluence of the most elemental biological impulses, the most instinctive appetites, the most refined sensibility, the most prudent reflection, the most remote memories, the most headstrong faith, the most idealistic or mystical vision—all of which come together in the act of valuation, in the movement of will that approves or repudiates. The genesis of valuation is influenced by the historical moment in which we live, the collective atmosphere—cultural, ethnic, and associational—that envelops us, and the more or less social features of our character. In short, there is a slippery, personal dimension to valuation, which eludes all logical coercion. Although psychological analysis, armed with the intuition of a Dostoyevski, may penetrate to the murkiest depths of the human soul, there will always remain something, an undecipherable x. And this is to say nothing of those professional psychologists who are condemned to skim the surface.

If we judge another person's valuation to be naive or stupid, wise or brilliant, this is a valuation in its own right. Even valuations that are personally repugnant to us—that strike us as paradoxical, cynical, or extravagant—originate in a conscience that can declare them whenever it assumes the responsibility. They do not bind us, to be sure; they cannot even command our respect since we accept or reject them according to our own judgment. A universal conscience can deny the most pampered valuation, however attired in dogmatic authority. So many valuations, originally scorned and vilified, come to win general assent. Many others become silent, without echo, because they were isolated occurrences. We should realize not only that the valuations of our contemporaries disagree among themselves to infinity, but also that there is a continuing transformation of values throughout successive generations. How strange, indeed, if even in the course of our own brief existence we change our minds as we do!

We should not be led into error by the apparent existence of valuations that seem to be supported by indisputable evidence, as well as by our own assent. They would vanish as soon as one barely squeezed them. There is no need to choose a trivial example. Let us take the sixth of the Ten Commandments, but with its tacit qualifications: you shall not kill, if you are not a warrior, judge, or priest; you shall not kill, except for members of another tribe; you shall not kill but those who profess a different creed; you shall not kill, except in defense of your life, your honor, or your property; you shall not openly kill, although you may exploit the life of your neighbor; you shall not kill, as long as you have no motive for it. The author of this commandment was never concerned with living up to it; he must have been a very word-minded person. History is the history of human slaughter. Thinkers have justified it; poets have glorified it.

There is no need to multiply examples; they all lead to the same conclusion. Normative valuations may assume airs of universality, but that claim can be, and is, converted into a lie by historical reality. Effective valuation dwells in our inner authority; there is no judge outside the conscious will. We insist: it is impossible to point out a universal, permanent, or constant valuation that is esteemed by all people in all times. Conscience always reserves the right to choose or refuse the presumed obligation. I like it when someone else agrees with my evaluation; but I am not disposed to submit mine to an extraneous authority, whether that of the overwhelming majority of men or that of the highest magistrate. The decision is in the last resort that of the autonomous person. This is the common root of the infinite number of concrete valuations, and also the reason for their divergence.

Well, someone may say, these conclusions reflect historical and empirical reality, and in this sense they are beyond attack. And yet, valuations are not arbitrary: the will does not adopt them capriciously, nor can it ignore the existence of values independent of human whim—indeed, of human valuation. In other words, we do not create value, we are limited to discovering it, and the concept of it is independent of the psychological or historical process. Let us now examine this new problem.

Value, we have said, is the object of an affirmative valuation. It has to do with real or ideal objects. No one should attribute intrinsic value to real objects. Neither natural nor made objects have value if no one appreciates them, if they are unrelated to human interest. There are no values for science; there are only equally interesting or equally indifferent facts. When we attribute value to a thing, it is a shaky title; it is not the same for me as for another, nor the same today as yesterday. The Arab who was lost in the desert found what he took to be a sack of dates in the track of a caravan. He looked inside, and threw it away in disgust. They're only pearls, he said. The conditional value of real objects depends on our estimation of them. But let us leave the case of real objects: it is too simple.

We have examined the historical creations that pertain to the different order of valuations. The value of these creations depends on our evaluation. We can withhold it. The religious dogma, the work of art, the judicial formula, the practical advice, the philosophical truth—what other value should they have than what they receive from our assent? Has not the protest of the martyr or of the reforming genius always come under the scrutiny of the dominant valuation, armed perhaps with material power? When a secular value ceases to rule, first in one conscience and then in many, it ends by disappearing or by being replaced. Each person can bring this about, individually, within the jurisdiction of his own conscience, and he will do it if the dominant value strikes him as coercive. Historical, like material values, remain subject to our personal valuation.

Let us, then, get down to a discussion of the most important concepts: the great ideal values. Positivism manages to convert them into subjective postulates derived from the cosmic mechanism. The current metaphysical reaction classifies them as absolutes. In either case they are regarded as constant and immutable values, set apart from any act of will. They would continue to exist, whether or not any human mind conceived or esteemed them. Their own authority is enough to establish them; they cannot be denied: who would dare deny justice, beauty, truth?

It is commonsensical that such values do not exist. One does not find them in spatiotemporal reality. In what superreality or in what unreal limbo can one place them? They are the abstract name for still unrealized ultimate aspirations, and they put us in contact with the transcendent as we think about their fulfillment. They are pure ideas; they come to be but are not. Word on our lips, ideal concept in consciousness, they only become effective and efficacious when, through action, they are objectivized in concrete, relative, and deficient form, destined to be a historical episode in the evolution of human culture. These creations of will symbolize its ultimate aims. We cannot conceive of purposes as part of the mechanical process of nature as it is interpreted by science; only will proclaims them. Causal and teleological conceptions cannot be reconciled; they constitute a basic antinomy that is deepened, rather than avoided, by rational analysis. Let this be said for the naturalists.

Those axiological theories that make use of objective, unreal, and atemporal values represent a shamefaced metaphysics scarcely disguised by its mask of logic. We are by no means denying metaphysical need. Man keeps trying new roads to escape the greatest of his anxieties. Unfortunately, reason is no help. We deny the possibility of a logical and rational metaphysics and we require philosophies to set a neat boundary between empirical reality and metaphysical poetry. The "Great Demolisher" did his work to give the neo-rationalists a chance to hide amid the ruins of their miserable shacks. Any rational metaphysics is a sin against logic. We have no words—hardly even metaphors—to express the eternal—that is, the ineffable. There is no scholastic technique for finding the *coincidentia oppositorum* of irreducible antinomies. That can come only from the great creations of art and mystical vision, aesthetic and religious emotion.

The authors who are committed to discovering

absolute values, valid *a priori,* have already invented an *ad hoc* gnoseology. They will not discuss the historical and psychological consequences of valuations; they will maintain, however, that this process arises from values and does not create them. This assumes that our axiological knowledge transcends empirical reality and arrives at the notion of timeless values. In effect, they rely on a theory according to which spatiotemporal objects are only one kind of object within a multiplicity of objective orders. The unreal as well as the real can be an object. This is another effort to open the royal road to metaphysical truth.

It affirms, first, the autonomy of logical values, and then the autonomy of ethical values. They are objective and not subjective. They are born following a psychological gestation but, once the umbilical cord is cut, they have their own destiny. We know the offspring: the "substantial forms" of scholasticism, the old "rational entities," which prudent criticism, not daring to hypostasize, deprives of "being" and reduces to vague nonsense in a kingdom where they neither are, exist, nor act. If this paradox does not captivate us, it is, according to Rickert, because our mental habits are deficient.

We are dealing with wordplay, in which talented men waste their great erudition in byzantine discourse, a marvelous mixture of logical subtlety and essential intuitions (*Wesenschau*). They claim to have captured the unreal object, but they have only lost contact with reality. . . .

But now some terrified soul will break in: "In this case we are without fixed and binding values!" And indeed, we never had them; they do not exist. Is not the historical change of values an obvious fact, along with the incompatability of contemporary values? One finds different values at each geographical latitude, in each ethnic group, in each political alliance, and with each social interest. Within each group, however homogeneous it may seem, we find persons who resist the current valuation. There is always some dissent on the way to triumph or failure. Is it not amusing how the satisfied bourgeoisie try to turn their profit into a timeless value, or how the true believer hawks the promptings of his fanaticism like dogmas?

Philosophers are no better; indeed, they provide the most disconcerting spectacle. It is the very nature of philosophy, they say, to aspire to universality. Philosophical truth must be one. It is impossible to conceive it as circumscribed by geographical limits, or determined by the historical moment, or by the interests of a social level. Nevertheless, this is what happens. As in so many cases, the paradox is the real. We know of a Western philosophy and of another that is Eastern; of a Greek philosophy and of another that is modern, of an empirical position opposed to rationalism, skepticism to dogmatism, realism to idealism. All systems are logical, but their pied multiplicity simply shows how ineffective logical argumentation is. Each different philosophy is the expression of a different valuation. Thus it has to run the same risks as all valuations. Each philosophy is systematized as a legal brief for the will that inspires it. Sometimes, though, in periods of decadence, the professor's poor and empty pedantry reveals a lack of will, a lack of vital conviction.

People should not be so afraid of subjective valuation. Humanity has not fallen into anarchy just because valuations have always been subjective. Aristotle alerts us, with his usual sagacity, by his observation that man is a gregarious animal. An isolated individual is a rare event; as a member of a group, his personal impulses are toned down by the rule of the gregarious instinct. Without feeling himself restrained, he will recite the liturgical formula that he has been taught, he will revere the established legal norms, he will respect the hallowed commonplaces, and will dress according to the current fad. No one rebels against an oppression he does not feel. Satisfied souls do not change collective values.

If rebellious evaluation appears, it will take its chances. Only a closed mind would object to it; while if many experience the same coercion, the rebellious judgment will be generalized. But a subjective valuation will be extinguished without consequences if, after a short or long conflict, it comes to have no historical dignity. Expressions of the general will, to be effective, should at least express the will of a more or less large group.

How, then, are we to choose from among the available valuations those that ought to prevail? The historical process does this; those that triumph prevail. It is not always the most just valuation—namely, ours—that triumphs. So, to conciliate them, we have recourse to argumentation, to persuasion, to the coincidence of interests, or to authority—if we have it. And yet, let us not forget that valuations represent our reaction to physical or historical reality that is given to us, that common setting within which the individual and the collectivity act. . . .

THE PROBLEM OF RELATIVISM

Jeffrey Stout

Is moral relativism true? That depends on what we mean by relativism. Confusing the various senses of relativism is part of what fuels concerns over the significance of moral diversity. . . . I claim that which moral propositions you're justified in believing depends upon or is relative to where you find yourself in culture and history. All justification is relative in this way—scientific as well as moral. It doesn't follow, however, that the truth of a given proposition is relative. Furthermore, while justification is relative, it isn't relative to arbitrary, subjective choice on the part of an individual.

I maintain that the world isn't flat and that slavery is evil. We are now justified in believing both of these propositions, in holding them true. That is to say, we have good reason, given what else we're taking for granted at the current stage of inquiry and given the experience and wisdom we've accumulated so far, to believe that the world isn't flat and that slavery is evil. Anybody who wanted to deny these propositions in our context would have to bear the burden of proof.

It's clear, however, that people who lived thousands of years ago don't deserve epistemic blame for believing that the world is flat. There's a clear sense in which they were justified in so believing. Given the reasons and evidence available to them, it was rational to believe that the world is flat. Given the reasons and evidence that have since become available, and on which we draw in justifying our current beliefs about the shape of the earth, we would be unreasonable to doubt that the earth is in fact roundish.

We're now justified in believing slavery to be evil. Part of what justifies this belief is a failure, over the long haul of moral reasoning, to make clear what could conceivably justify treating people assigned to the role of slave in ways that we do not tolerate for other people. Some of the beliefs that used to underlie the practice of slavery—such as the belief that no society could survive without slavery and the belief that God had designated certain classes of people as slaves after the Flood—have not survived critical scrutiny. Let us suppose that most of these considerations were sufficiently evident to people even in the American South a hundred years ago that the proponents of slavery in that context weren't justified. Their reasons and arguments just weren't good enough, in the presence of reasons and counterarguments on the other side, for them to be justified in believing that slavery is morally legitimate. But we may imagine a time, or discover one through historical inquiry, when belief in slavery was justified, relative to available reasons and evidence.

Justification in morality, as in science, is relative—but relative to one's epistemic circumstance, including reasons and evidence available at the current stage of inquiry, not to the arbitrary choice of individuals. Just as an arbitrary change in scientific criteria wouldn't make it more reasonable for me to believe that the earth is flat, neither can an arbitrary change in moral principles make it more reasonable for me to believe that slavery is good. Being justified in believing something is a normative relation that exists among a given proposition, the person who accepts it, and a cognitive context. If I am justified in accepting a proposition, then the proposition, my context, and I are related in the required way. The relation is as objective as can be, not subject to worrisomely arbitrary subjective manipulation. What may make it seem subjective is that some of the facts about it are facts about the human subject involved. Facts about what my peers take for granted, about judgmental dispositions acquired by members of my society during successful training in the relevant practices, about the history of casuistical precedents in my tradition, about evidence available to me, and so on, all will be relevant features of the context, features open to objective inquiry.

This relativity does not carry over, at least in a case like the proposition that slavery is evil, to truth. What we're justified in believing about the evil of slavery varies according to the evidence and reasoning available to us in our place in culture and history. But the truth of the proposition that slavery is evil doesn't vary in the same way. It wasn't true several millennia ago that the earth was flat. When we say that it was true for people of the time that the earth was flat, we mean only that they believed it was true, not that the earth really was flat and only later became round. Similarly, slavery didn't become evil only when people discovered what was wrong with it. Perhaps it did become blameworthy then, but the discovery involved coming to know a truth about slavery—namely, that it was evil all along.

I hope this makes clear why some authors can sound relativistic for long stretches and then suddenly sound nonrelativistic about moral truth, especially when speaking as moralists. They need not be guilty of contradiction, for we can take them, charitably, to be able to see the difference between justification and truth. The facts of moral disagreement may well give us reason to insist upon the relativity of justification, since that insistence will help us explain forms of disagreement which might otherwise remain puzzling. But this insistence needn't render justification merely arbitrary or subjective, and it can swing free of concerns over moral truth.

Notice that a willingness to distinguish justification from truth allows us to be forthright in affirming the truth of our convictions without necessarily

blaming previous generations or distant cultures for believing differently. We can say that some of their practices were morally evil and that some of their related moral beliefs were false—for instance, beliefs about the treatment of slaves and women and witches—without implying that they were irrational, unreasonable, or blameworthy for behaving and believing as they did. Saying that slavery is evil is not the same thing as imputing blame for practicing it or supporting it or believing it morally unproblematical. We may disagree with our ancestors' moral judgments and thus hold their judgments to be false, explaining the difference by citing intervening historical developments that have significantly changed the epistemic situation. Reflection on such developments may make us want to excuse our ancestors for accepting false beliefs and hence for acting on them. If so, we shall say that they were justified but wrong.

• • •

When I affirmed that the proposition about the evil of slavery is true, always has been true, and would be true in any framework or context, I chose my example carefully. Given my purposes, it would only have clouded the issue to cite an ambiguous sentence, whose truth-value would depend on which of two or more plausible interpretations were assigned to it, such as: "It would be evil for us all to hang together." My interest here is in whether the truth-value of certain *interpreted* sentences is relative. The kind of relativity present in all instances of ambiguity is beside the point. By the same token, it would have been inappropriate to cite a sentence with what philosophers call indexical expressions, such as: "*I* am morally evil," "*This* is morally evil," or "The *current* investment policies of *our* university are morally evil." We are not concerned with sentences whose truth-value depends, for reasons that teach us nothing interesting about morality, on who spoke them, what demonstrative gestures accompanied them, when they were spoken, or the like. No one denies that the truth-value of sentences including indexical expressions is relative to features of context.

Nor does anyone deny that moral sentences often include an implicit indexical element. If I say, "Uttering falsehoods with the intent to deceive is evil," I may be leaving unstated a restriction of the form, "other things being equal" or "under circumstances of the sort being discussed," trusting that this will be clear from the context of the remark. A complete statement of my view would make any such specification of conditions explicit. Thus, the truth-value of a statement with an implicit reference to conditions of this sort will be relative to context; but this is not an issue in the debate over moral relativism. I am stipulating that propositions are fully interpreted, meaning by this that they have already been paired with paraphrases that resolve ambiguity, substitute nonindexical expressions for pronouns, demonstratives, and similar expressions, while making all implicit qualifications explicit.

The proposition in question, then, is that slavery, as defined in the previous chapter, is evil, period. No qualification of the form "under such-and-such conditions" or "other things being equal" is intended. My example needed to be a proposition nearly everyone likely to read this book would interpret fully and straightforwardly, accept without argument as true, and view as moral in content. The point I wanted to make wasn't about the relativity of uninterpreted sentences, the ethics of slavery, or the line between moral and nonmoral propositions. The example also needed to be a proposition whose truth does not seem, intuitively, to be relative in certain other ways. An unqualified proposition about the evil of slavery served my purposes well, for most of us are apt to condemn slavery as evil wherever and whenever we find it practiced, even in cases where those practicing it employ concepts quite different from ours, would fail to recognize our reasons for judging the practice evil, and don't know any better. If, however, you are reluctant to judge slavery *as such* evil, feel free to add the clause, "other things being equal." The addition will make the proposition weaker and thus perhaps easier to believe without further qualification, but the statement still serves my purposes by providing an example of a fully interpreted moral sentence whose truth is not relative.

Some propositions about the evil of some kinds of institution require more qualifications than does the one about slavery. Slavery, I want to say, is intrinsically evil in the sense that no variations in circumstances could make it good or morally indifferent. Polygamy seems to require different treatment. Many of us believe that while every society requires means for regulating sexual activity, and monogamy may be the best means for us, no single means is necessarily best for all societies. Polygamy may be evil under some conditions—for instance where a widely accepted institution of monogamy is in place and there are roughly equal numbers of heterosexual men and women—but not under others. We are not inclined to judge polygamy evil in a situation where most men have been killed at war and there is ample cultural precedent for taking more than one spouse, a condition that might obtain in a certain Bedouin tribe.

David Wong refers in this connection to *environmental relativity,* which he distinguishes from both the kind of relativity that denies that there is a "single true morality" and the kind of relativity involved in judgments with implicit qualifying clauses. He is right, I believe, in saying that environmental relativity does not threaten the notion that there is a truth of the matter about which practices are good or evil, morally speaking. It implies only that some practices which are in fact evil under particular social-historical conditions may not be so under others. There is a sense in which "Polygamy is evil" is true for us but not for the Bedouins just mentioned, a sense not captured by saying that we believe polygamy is evil and the Bedouins don't. But putting it in that way is apt to confuse the issue. It would be less misleading to say simply that in truth polygamy is not intrinsically evil, that whether a given instance of polygamy is evil depends on the social-historical conditions in which it is found.

This way of putting it makes clear, however, that environmental relativity differs only in scope from the kind brought out when implicit qualifications are made explicit in ordinary moral judgments. On my view, uttering falsehoods with the intent to deceive is evil, but only under certain conditions (namely, when one owes the truth as a debt of justice). The same holds for practicing polygamy—it, too, is evil only under certain conditions. The case of polygamy seems different only because the relevant conditions are always satisfied, as a matter of fact, in some societies but not in others. To discover that the truth-value of a given proposition is environmentally relative in Wong's sense is simply to discover that, in order to be true, the proposition needs a qualifying clause of the form "under conditions *C*," where *C* indicates a general type of social-historical setting instead of a type of moral circumstance one might find in any social-historical setting.

Given my beliefs about polygamy, I need to explain how others came to believe differently. Those within my own society who hold that polygamy is intrinsically evil pose one sort of problem. Bedouins who hold that polygamy is always acceptable, whatever conditions obtain, pose another. In each case, I may point to metaphysical beliefs I take to be mistaken, beliefs about what way of life God or Allah ordained for all humanity, beliefs whose presence helps account for what I take to be moral error concerning polygamy. Or I may point to ignorance of or insensitivity to social-historical conditions unlike one's own. In any event, however, I have differences to explain. Acknowledging environmental relativity is not a way of eliminating moral disagreement altogether. Environmental relatively remains a far cry from the idea that each society has its own moral truth, although it does help explain some of the differences that cause some people to embrace that idea.

Moreover, granting that there is a range of practices and institutions, among which one might be the best, objectively speaking, for a given society to adopt, depending on its social and historical circumstances, does not rule out holding that some practices are simply beyond the pale. Slavery, on my view, is such an institution. It is evil wherever and whenever it is found. Why do I not say, with equal conviction, that all slaveholders deserve blame? Because the truth-value of a judgment about blame is relative to the agent's circumstances in a way that the former judgment's truth-value is not.

In this respect, moral blame is like epistemic jus-

tification. People are epistemically justified in believing a proposition if, epistemically speaking, they are doing the best that could be done under the circumstances. They need not necessarily be believing truths, provided they are making proper use of available evidence and concepts, avoiding wishful thinking, and so forth. People are morally justified and hence morally blameless if, morally speaking, they are doing the best that could be done under the circumstances. They may be engaged in practices that we rightly judge to be evil and still be blameless, provided they could not have known the moral truth of the matter, have not been negligent, intend no injustice, and so forth. Before judging a given class of slaveholders blameworthy, we need to know, among other things, what they could have known about the intrinsic evil of slavery. Ignorance on that score, if the ignorance itself is morally blameless, will tend to excuse them for owning slaves.

This helps explain our reluctance to blame people in distant generations and cultures for engaging in practices and institutions we find evil. We cannot assume that their knowledge coincides with ours. Our knowledge about the evil of slavery may depend upon our use of concepts or styles of reasoning they lack; their judgment may have depended on no longer tenable empirical and metaphysical beliefs they had no compelling reason to question. This does not mean, of course, that we may never make judgments of blame across cultural boundaries. It means only that such judgments often require more subtlety, more sensitivity to context, than judgments about whether practices and institutions are evil. Certainly there are some people in every social group—and some actions of every member of every social group—that deserve our moral blame. Ceasing to apply the concept of blame across cultural boundaries is no way to avoid ethnocentrism. But figuring out who deserves blame and in what degree can be a complex matter, much complicated by differences in cultural setting.

In summary, I propose a metaphor. Propositions imputing moral blame and propositions describing people, practices, or institutions as evil fall at opposite ends of a spectrum of relativity. The truth-value of the former, like the truth-value of propositions about epistemic justification, is relative to certain features of the circumstances of the people referred to. The truth-value of the latter is not similarly relative. The closer you get to the former end of the spectrum, the more sensitivity to context a wise interpreter's moral judgments will need to show in judging members of other cultures. Even at that end of the spectrum, however, sound cross-cultural moral judgment remains possible—and often necessary—provided one is sensitive in the required ways and knows what one needs to know to judge well.

QUESTIONS FOR DISCUSSION

1. Given Korn's position, in what way could ethics be seen as a social enterprise? In what way is it a personal affair? What are the strengths or dangers of each (the social and the individual) approach?

2. If values are subjective, how will it be possible to arbitrate between diverse or opposing groups holding different values, when perhaps even the person chosen to arbitrate with a view to harmonizing the grieving parties will most likely as well be influenced by his or her own value system?

3. How can we be assured, if values are subjective, that the best view will prevail throughout history? Perhaps might makes right in too many cases of values. Can you think of some examples or counterexamples?

4. Stout argues that some ethical pronouncements can be considered universal and applicable to all people at all times. He gives the condemnation of slavery as an example. Can you think of others? Do your classmates agree with you, or can they argue that your example indeed depends on context?

Lewis Hine, "The Sky Boy," Avery Architectural and Fine Arts Library.

CHAPTER 8

THE MEANING OF LIFE AND DEATH

Does life have a meaning? What might the meaning of life be like? If it is seen as an ultimate reason for our existence, must that reason lie outside life? Or could it be found within life itself? Suppose life is found to have no meaning. Would that make it worthless? Would animal instinct and the force of habit then constitute our only reasons to live? Or, perhaps, are we—in asking this—approaching the problem in the wrong way? Might it not be that life's meaning is found within human satisfaction? In that case, the achievement of something like happiness would seem to be the meaning of life. But can it be any kind of happiness? And what is happiness anyway? These are among the questions debated in this chapter by thinkers from a great variety of cultures.

In the chapter's opening section, we are presented with two views that see human happiness as life's goal; the first—that of the great ancient Greek philosopher Aristotle—understands happiness in the context of Greek society; the second—that of a modern Shi'ite Moslem theologian—derives its norms from Islam's Holy Qur'an. A long historical dialogue, in fact, connects these thinkers' views over two millennia. The next two sections look at two different—but also historically related—viewpoints from Asia—Taoism and Buddhism. Next, the question of life's meaning is confronted more directly, where three very different modern Westerners—an analytic philosopher, an atheistic existentialist, and a psychologist—look at the question "What does life mean?"

Our fifth section explores how the confrontation with death sheds light on the meaning of life. What is the best attitude toward death? Should it be feared? Challenged? Accepted? Our first author, Miguel de Unamuno, a Spanish thinker of this century, describes the fear of death and longing for immortality that he and many others feel. Our second author, Canadian sociologist of religion Gregory Baum, suggests that the contemporary individual longing for immortality as Unamuno describes is a product of our individualistic culture. In earlier Christian accounts, individual survival of death was not central, and the focus was rather on the coming kingdom of God and the survival and well-being of the community. Baum suggests we could revive the communal sense, and face death from a different perspective. Our third author, Etty Hillesum, a Dutch Jew, shares her experience of confronting death at Auschwitz at the hands of the Nazis, and seeing her people's worldly existence destroyed. By clinging to spiritual values, she learns to accept her death without feeling destroyed as a person.

Readers of Section One might also want to look at the Ayatullah Murtaza Mutahari's essay in Chapter 2 and the selections on Islamic women in Chapter 4. Those interested in Aristotelian thought are re-

ferred to the first section of Chapter 5. Taoism is represented in the first two chapters. Buddhist thought appears in many chapters, but the reader is referred especially to Gunapala Dharmasiri's account of Buddhist ethics in Chapter 7. Jean-Paul Sartre's essay in Chapter 6 may shed some light on Albert Camus's existentialism.

HAPPINESS AND THE MEANING OF LIFE

Although Aristotle (384–322 B.C.) was the student of Plato—that other giant of Greek philosophy—his views on the ends of life were quite different from his teacher's. Whereas Plato has been the usual choice of mystics, teaching a philosophy whose aim is the transcendence of the physical world, Aristotle has appealed to the naturalistic tradition, having a view that sees life's goal as "functional": The supreme good is, for Aristotle, *eudaimonia,* which is usually translated from the Greek as "well being" or "happiness"—the term which the translator uses for it in our selection from Aristotle's *Nichomachean Ethics* that is presented below. Happiness is, in turn, understood by Aristotle as the exercise of our natural faculties in a manner which is virtuous. To act virtuously is to be happy and happiness is a mark that one is acting with virtue. Aristotle understands virtue as consisting of two varieties—intellectual and moral virtues. Virtue itself is seen by him as a skill appropriate to each of our natural human faculties. So, the skillful fulfillment of our human potential becomes the key to life. This view, of course, presupposes a particular understanding of human nature.

Although the belief systems of the Christian and Moslem Middle Ages had altered the view of human nature provided by Aristotle, the great philosophers of those civilizations salvaged enough of it to adapt Aristotle's thinking to both Catholic Christianity and Islam. Aristotle still holds a central place in the theology of Roman Catholicism, via St. Thomas Aquinas's interpretation of his work. Likewise, traditional Moslem theologians even today reflect a strong Aristotelian influence. It is, therefore, no accident that Allamah Sayyid Tabatabai's account of Islam's Holy Qur'an contains echoes of the *Nichomachean Ethics.* From his essay's very first paragraph, the Qur'an is exalted for its ability to provide a guide to happiness. It is this which makes it superior to other religions. In saying this, Tabatabai is probably thinking most particularly of Christianity and Judaism, whose Bibles are the Qur'an's scriptural competitors. For Islam reveres also the Jewish and Christian teachings, insisting only that its own holy book is the last and most perfect of God's revelations.

Allamah Sayyid Tabatabai is—like the Ayatollah Mutahari whose writings are represented in the book's second chapter—a present-day Shi'ite Moslem traditionalist. He is also Iranian. He represents, however, a different camp in Shi'ite thought from Mutahari and the Khomeini political regime. What Westerners term "Islamic fundamentalism" is a far more diverse movement than such journalistic classifications can encompass. Within traditional Islam, there still exists a rich intellectual tradition which finds its origins in the wisdom of the prophet Muhammad combined with the wisdom of the Greeks.

✴ THE RATIONAL LIFE

Aristotle

NICOMACHEAN ETHICS

Book I

Every art and every investigation, and likewise every practical pursuit or undertaking, seems to aim at some good: hence it has been well said that the Good is That at which all things aim. (It is true that a certain variety is to be observed among the ends at which the arts and sciences aim: in some cases the activity of practising the art is itself the end, whereas in others the end is some product over and above the mere exercise of the art; and in the arts whose ends are certain things beside the practice of the arts themselves, these products are essentially superior in value to the activities.) But as there are numerous pursuits and arts and sciences, it follows that their ends are correspondingly numerous: for instance, the end of the science of medicine is health, that of the art of shipbuilding a vessel, that of strategy victory, that of domestic economy wealth. Now in cases where several such pursuits are subordinate to some single faculty—as bridle-making and the other trades concerned with horses' harness are subordinate to horsemanship, and this and every other military pursuit to the science of strategy, and similarly other arts to different arts again—in all these cases, I say, the ends of the master arts are things more to be desired than all those of the arts subordinate to them; since the latter ends are only pursued for the sake of the former. (And it makes no difference whether the ends of the pursuits are the activities themselves or some other thing beside these, as in the case of the sciences mentioned.)

• • •

To resume, inasmuch as all studies and undertakings are directed to the attainment of some good, let us discuss what it is that we pronounce to be the aim of Politics, that is, what is the highest of all the goods that action can achieve. As far as the name goes, we may almost say that the great majority of mankind are agreed about this; for both the multitude and persons of refinement speak of it as Happiness, and conceive 'the good life' or 'doing well' to be the same thing as 'being happy' But what constitutes happiness is a matter of dispute; and the popular account of it is not the same as that given by the philosophers. Ordinary people identify it with some obvious and visible good, such as pleasure or wealth or honour—some say one thing and some another, indeed very often the same man says different things at different times: when he falls sick he thinks health is happiness, when he is poor, wealth. At other times, feeling conscious of their own ignorance, men admire those who propound something grand and above their heads; and it has been held by some thinkers that beside the many good things we have mentioned, there exists another Good, that is good in itself, and stands to all those goods as the cause of their being good.

Now perhaps it would be a somewhat fruitless task to review all the different opinions that are held. It will suffice to examine those that are most widely prevalent, or that seem to have some argument in their favour.

And we must not overlook the distinction between arguments that start from first principles and those that lead to first principles. It was a good practice of Plato to raise this question, and to enquire whether the right procedure was to start from or to lead up to the first principles, as in a race-course one may run from the judges to the far end of the track or reversely. Now no doubt it is proper to start from the known. But 'the known' has two meanings— 'what is known to us,' which is one thing, and 'what is knowable in itself,' which is another. Perhaps then for us at all events it is proper to start from what is known to us. This is why in order to be a competent student of the Right and Just, and in short of the topics of Politics in general, the pupil is bound to have been well trained in his habits. For the starting-point or first principle is the fact that a thing is so; if this be satisfactorily ascertained, there will be no need also to know the reason why it is so.

And the man of good moral training knows first principles already, or can easily acquire them. As for the person who neither knows nor can learn, let him hear the words of Hesiod:

> Best is the man who can himself advise;
> He too is good who hearkens to the wise;
> But who, himself being witless, will not heed
> Another's wisdom, is worthless indeed.

But let us continue from the point where we digressed. To judge from men's lives, the more or less reasoned conceptions of the Good or Happiness that seem to prevail among them are the following. On the one hand the generality of men and the most vulgar identify the Good with pleasure, and accordingly are content with the Life of Enjoyment—for there are three specially prominent Lives, the one just mentioned, the Life of Politics, and thirdly, the Life of Contemplation. The generality of mankind then show themselves to be utterly slavish, by preferring what is only a life for cattle; but they get a hearing for their view as reasonable because many persons of high position share the feelings of Sardanapallus.

Men of refinement, on the other hand, and men of action think that the Good is honour—for this may be said to be the end of the Life of Politics. But honour after all seems too superficial to be the Good for which we are seeking; since it appears to depend on those who confer it more than on him upon whom it is conferred, whereas we instinctively feel that the Good must be something proper to its possessor and not easy to be taken away from him. Moreover men's motive in pursuing honour seems to be to assure themselves of their own merit; at least they seek to be honoured by men of judgement and by people who know them, that is, they desire to be honoured on the ground of virtue. It is clear therefore that in the opinion at all events of men of action, virtue is a greater good than honour; and one might perhaps accordingly suppose that virtue rather than honour is the end of the Political Life. But even virtue proves on examination to be too incomplete to be the End; since it appears possible to possess it while you are asleep, or without

putting it into practice throughout the whole of your life; and also for the virtuous man to suffer the greatest misery and misfortune—though no one would pronounce a man living a life of misery to be happy, unless for the sake of maintaining a paradox. But we need not pursue this subject, since it has been sufficiently treated in the ordinary discussions.

The third type of life is the Life of Contemplation, which we shall consider in the sequel.

• • •

We may now return to the Good which is the object of our search, and try to find out what exactly it can be. For good appears to be one thing in one pursuit or art and another in another: it is different in medicine from what it is in strategy, and so on with the rest of the arts. What definition of the Good then will hold true in all the arts? Perhaps we may define it as that for the sake of which everything else is done. This applies to something different in each different art—to health in the case of medicine, to victory in that of strategy, to a house in architecture, and to something else in each of the other arts; but in every pursuit or undertaking it describes the end of that pursuit or undertaking, since in all of them it is for the sake of the end that everything else is done. Hence if there be something which is the end of all the things done by human action, this will be the practicable Good—or if there be several such ends, the sum of these will be the Good. Thus by changing its ground the argument has reached the same result as before. We must attempt however to render this still more precise.

Now there do appear to be several ends at which our actions aim; but as we choose some of them—for instance wealth, or flutes, and instruments generally—as a means to something else, it is clear that not all of them are final ends; whereas the Supreme Good seems to be something final. Consequently if there be some one thing which alone is a final end, this thing—or if there be several final ends, the one among them which is the most final—will be the Good which we are seeking. In speaking of degrees of finality, we mean that a thing pursued as an end in itself is more final than one pursued as a means to something else, and that a thing never chosen as a means to anything else is more final than things chosen both as ends in themselves and as means to that thing; and accordingly a thing chosen always as an end and never as a means we call absolutely final. Now happiness above all else appears to be absolutely final in this sense, since we always choose it for its own sake and never as a means to something else; whereas honour, pleasure, intelligence, and excellence in its various forms, we choose indeed for their own sakes (since we should be glad to have each of them although no extraneous advantage resulted from it), but we also choose them for the sake of happiness, in the belief that they will be a means to our securing it. But no one chooses happiness for the sake of honour, pleasure, etc., nor as a means to anything whatever other than itself.

The same conclusion also appears to follow from a consideration of the self-sufficiency of happiness—for it is felt that the final good must be a thing sufficient in itself. The term self-sufficient, however, we employ with reference not to oneself alone, living a life of isolation, but also to one's parents and children and wife, and one's friends and fellow citizens in general, since man is by nature a social being. On the other hand a limit has to be assumed in these relationships; for if the list be extended to one's ancestors and descendants and to the friends of one's friends, it will go on *ad infinitum*. But this is a point that must be considered later on; we take a self-sufficient thing to mean a thing which merely standing by itself alone renders life desirable and lacking in nothing, and such a thing we deem happiness to be. Moreover, we think happiness the most desirable of all good things without being itself reckoned as one among the rest; for if it were so reckoned, it is clear that we should consider it more desirable when even the smallest of other good things were combined with it, since this addition would result in a larger total of good, and of two goods the greater is always the more desirable.

Happiness, therefore, being found to be something final and self-sufficient, is the End at which all actions aim.

To say however that the Supreme Good is happiness will probably appear a truism; we still require a more explicit account of what constitutes happiness. Perhaps then we may arrive at this by ascertaining what is man's function. For the goodness or efficiency of a flute-player or sculptor or craftsman of any sort, and in general of anybody who has some function or business to perform, is thought to reside in that function; and similarly it may be held that the good of man resides in the function of man, if he has a function.

Are we then to suppose that, while the carpenter and the shoemaker have definite functions or businesses belonging to them, man as such has none, and is not designed by nature to fulfil any function? Must we not rather assume that, just as the eye, the hand, the foot and each of the various members of the body manifestly has a certain function of its own, so a human being also has a certain function over and above all the functions of his particular members? What then precisely can this function be? The mere act of living appears to be shared even by plants, whereas we are looking for the function peculiar to man; we must therefore set aside the vital activity of nutrition and growth. Next in the scale will come some form of sentient life; but this too appears to be shared by horses, oxen, and animals generally. There remains therefore what may be called the practical life of the rational part of man. (This part has two divisions, one rational as obedient to principle, the other as possessing principle and exercising intelligence). Rational life again has two meanings; let us assume that we are here concerned with the active exercise of the rational faculty, since this seems to be the more proper sense of the term. If then the function of man is the active exercise of the soul's faculties in conformity with rational principle, or at all events not in dissociation from rational principle, and if we acknowledge the function of an individual and of a good individual of the same class (for instance, a harper and a good harper, and so generally with all classes) to be generically the same, the qualification of the latter's superiority in excellence being added to the function in his case (I mean that if the function of a harper is to play the harp, that of a good harper is to play the harp well): if this is so, and if we declare that the function of man is a certain form of life, and define that form of life as the exercise of the soul's faculties and activities in association with rational principle, and say that the function of a good man is to perform these activities well and rightly, and if a function is well performed when it is performed in accordance with its own proper excellence—from these premises it follows that the Good of man is the active exercise of his soul's faculties in conformity with excellence or virtue, or if there be several human excellences or virtues, in conformity with the best and most perfect among them. Moreover this activity must occupy a complete lifetime; for one swallow does not make spring, nor does one fine day; and similarly one day or a brief period of happiness does not make a man supremely blessed and happy.

• • •

Book II

Virtue being, as we have seen, of two kinds, intellectual and moral, intellectual virtue is for the most part both produced and increased by instruction, and therefore requires experience and time; whereas moral or ethical virtue is the product of habit (*ethos*), and has indeed derived its name, with a slight variation of form, from that word. And therefore it is clear that none of the moral virtues is engendered in us by nature, for no natural property can be altered by habit. For instance, it is the nature of a stone to move downwards, and it cannot be trained to move upwards, even though you should try to train it to do so by throwing it up into the air ten thousand times; nor can fire be trained to move downwards, nor can anything else that naturally behaves in one way be trained into a habit of behaving in another way. The virtues therefore are engendered in us neither by nature nor yet in violation of nature; nature gives us the capacity to receive them, and this capacity is brought to maturity by habit.

Moreover, the faculties given us by nature are bestowed on us first in a potential form; we exhibit their actual exercise afterwards. This is clearly so with our senses: we did not acquire the faculty of sight or hearing by repeatedly seeing or repeatedly listening, but the other way about—because we had the senses we began to use them, we did not get them by using them. The virtues on the other hand we acquire by first having actually practised them, just as we do the arts. We learn an art or craft by doing the things that we shall have to do when we have learnt it: for instance, men become builders by building houses, harpers by playing on the harp. Similarly we become just by doing just acts, temperate by doing temperate acts, brave by doing brave acts. This truth is attested by the experience of states: lawgivers make the citizens good by training them in habits of right action—this is the aim of all legislation, and if it fails to do this it is a failure; this is what distinguishes a good form of constitution from a bad one. Again, the actions from or through which any virtue is produced are the same as those through which it also is destroyed—just as is the case with skill in the arts, for both the good harpers and the bad ones are produced by harping, and similarly with builders and all the other craftsmen: as you will become a good builder from building well, so you will become a bad one from building badly. Were this not so, there would be no need for teachers of the arts, but everybody would be born a good or bad craftsman as the case might be. The same then is true of the virtues. It is by taking part in transactions with our fellow-men that some of us become just and others unjust; by acting in dangerous situations and forming a habit of fear or of confidence we become courageous or cowardly. And the same holds good of our dispositions with regard to the appetites, and anger; some men become temperate and gentle, other profligate and irascible, by actually comporting themselves in one way or the other in relation to those passions. In a word, our moral dispositions are formed as a result of the corresponding activities. Hence it is incumbent on us to control the character of our activities, since on the quality of these depends the quality of our dispositions. It is therefore not of small moment whether we are trained from childhood in one set of habits or another; on the contrary it is of very great, or rather of supreme, importance.

As then our present study, unlike the other branches of philosophy, has a practical aim (for we are not investigating the nature of virtue for the sake of knowing what it is, but in order that we may become good, without which result our investigation would be of no use), we have consequently to carry our enquiry into the region of conduct, and to ask how we are to act rightly; since our actions, as we have said, determine the quality of our dispositions.

Now the formula 'to act in conformity with right principle' is common ground, and may be assumed as the basis of our discussion. (We shall speak about this formula later, and consider both the definition of right principle and its relation to the other virtues.)

But let it be granted to begin with that the whole theory of conduct is bound to be an outline only and not an exact system, in accordance with the rule we laid down at the beginning, that philosophical theories must only be required to correspond to their subject matter; and matters of conduct and expediency have nothing fixed or invariable about them, any more than have matters of health. And if this is true of the general theory of ethics, still less is exact precision possible in dealing with particular cases of conduct; for these come under no science or professional tradition, but the agents themselves have to consider what is suited to the circumstances on each occasion, just as is the case with the art of medicine or of navigation. But although the discussion now proceeding is thus necessarily inexact, we must do our best to help it out.

First of all then we have to observe, that moral qualities are so constituted as to be destroyed by excess and by deficiency—as we see is the case with bodily strength and health (for one is forced to explain what is invisible by means of visible illustrations). Strength is destroyed both by excessive and by deficient exercises, and similarly health is destroyed both by too much and by too little food and drink; while they are produced, increased and preserved by suitable quantities. The same therefore is true of Temperance, Courage, and the other virtues. The man who runs away from everything in fear and never endures anything becomes a coward; the

man who fears nothing whatsoever but encounters everything becomes rash. Similarly he that indulges in every pleasure and refrains from none turns out a profligate, and he that shuns all pleasure, as boorish persons do, becomes what may be called insensible. Thus Temperance and Courage are destroyed by excess and deficiency, and preserved by the observance of the mean.

But not only are the virtues both generated and fostered on the one hand, and destroyed on the other, from and by the same actions, but they will also find their full exercise in the same actions. This is clearly the case with the other more visible qualities, such as bodily strength: for strength is produced by taking much food and undergoing much exertion, while also it is the strong man who will be able to eat most food and endure most exertion. The same holds good with the virtues. We become temperate by abstaining from pleasures, and at the same time we are best able to abstain from pleasures when we have become temperate. And so with Courage: we become brave by training ourselves to despise and endure terrors, and we shall be best able to endure terrors when we have become brave.

An index of our dispositions is afforded by the pleasure or pain that accompanies our actions. A man is temperate if he abstains from bodily pleasures and finds this abstinence itself enjoyable, profligate if he feels it irksome; he is brave if he faces danger with pleasure or at all events without pain, cowardly if he does so with pain.

In fact pleasures and pains are the things with which moral virtue is concerned.

For (1) pleasure causes us to do base actions and pain causes us to abstain from doing noble actions. Hence the importance, as Plato points out, of having been definitely trained from childhood to like and dislike the proper things; this is what good education means.

(2) Again, if the virtues have to do with actions and feelings, and every feeling and every action is attended with pleasure or pain, this too shows that virtue has to do with pleasure and pain.

(3) Another indication is the fact that pain is the medium of punishment; for punishment is a sort of

medicine, and it is the nature of medicine to work by means of opposites.

(4) Again, as we said before, every formed disposition of the soul realizes its full nature in relation to and in dealing with that class of objects by which it is its nature to be corrupted or improved. But men are corrupted through pleasures and pains, that is, either by pursuing and avoiding the wrong pleasures and pains, or by pursuing and avoiding them at the wrong time, or in the wrong manner, or in one of the other wrong ways under which errors of conduct can be logically classified. This is why some thinkers define the virtues as states of impassivity or tranquillity, though they make a mistake in using these terms absolutely, without adding 'in the right (or wrong) manner' and 'at the right (or wrong) time' and the other qualifications.

We assume therefore that moral virtue is the quality of acting in the best way in relation to pleasures and pains, and that vice is the opposite.

But the following considerations also will give us further light on the same point.

(5) There are three things that are the motives of choice and three that are the motives of avoidance; namely, the noble, the expedient, and the pleasant, and their opposites, the base, the harmful, and the painful. Now in respect of all these the good man is likely to go right and the bad to go wrong, but especially in respect of pleasure; for pleasure is common to man with the lower animals, and also it is a concomitant of all the objects of choice, since both the noble and the expedient appear to us pleasant.

(6) Again, the susceptibility to pleasure has grown up with all of us from the cradle. Hence this feeling is hard to eradicate, being engrained in the fabric of our lives.

(7) Again, pleasure and pain are also the standards by which we all, in a greater or less degree, regulate our actions. On this account therefore pleasure and pain are necessarily our main concern, since to feel pleasure and pain rightly or wrongly has a great effect on conduct.

(8) And again, it is harder to fight against pleasure than against anger (hard as that is, as Heracleitus says); but virtue, like art, is constantly dealing with what is harder, since the harder the task the better is success. For this reason also therefore pleasure and pain are necessarily the main concern both of virtue and of political science, since he who comports himself towards them rightly will be good, and he who does so wrongly, bad.

We may then take it as established that virtue has to do with pleasures and pains, that the actions which produce it are those which increase it, and also, if differently performed, destroy it, and that the actions from which it was produced are also those in which it is exercised.

A difficulty may however be raised as to what we mean by saying that in order to become just men must do just actions, and in order to become temperate they must do temperate actions. For if they do just and temperate actions, they are just and temperate already, just as, if they spell correctly or play in tune, they are scholars or musicians.

But perhaps this is not the case even with the arts. It is possible to spell a word correctly by chance, or because some one else prompts you; hence you will be a scholar only if you spell correctly in the scholar's way, that is, in virtue of the scholarly knowledge which you yourself possess.

Moreover the case of the arts is not really analogous to that of the virtues. Works of art have their merit in themselves, so that it is enough if they are produced having a certain quality of their own; but acts done in conformity with the virtues are not done justly or temperately if they themselves are of a certain sort, but only if the agent also is in a certain state of mind when he does them: first he must act with knowledge; secondly he must deliberately choose the act, and choose it for its own sake; and thirdly the act must spring from a fixed and permanent disposition of character. For the possession of an art, none of these conditions is included, except the mere qualification of knowledge; but for the possession of the virtues, knowledge is of little or no avail, whereas the other conditions, so far from being of little moment, are all-important, inasmuch as virtue results from the repeated performance of just and temperate actions. Thus although actions are entitled just and temperate when they are such acts as just and temperate men would do, the agent is just and temperate not when he does these acts merely, but when he does them in the way in which just and temperate men do them. It is correct therefore to say that a man becomes just by doing just actions and temperate by doing temperate actions; and no one can have the remotest chance of becoming good without doing them. But the mass of mankind, instead of doing virtuous acts, have recourse to discussing virtue, and fancy that they are pursuing philosophy and that this will make them good men. In so doing they act like invalids who listen carefully to what the doctor says, but entirely neglect to carry out his prescriptions. That sort of philosophy will no more lead to a healthy state of soul than will the mode of treatment produce health of body.

• • •

Book X, vi

Having now discussed the various kinds of Virtue, of Friendship and of Pleasure, it remains for us to treat in outline of Happiness, inasmuch as we count this to be the End of human life. But it will shorten the discussion if we recapitulate what has been said already.

Now we stated that happiness is not a certain disposition of character; since if it were it might be possessed by a man who passed the whole of his life asleep, living the life of a vegetable, or by one who was plunged in the deepest misfortune. If then we reject this as unsatisfactory, and feel bound to class happiness rather as some form of activity, as has been said in the earlier part of this treatise, and if activities are of two kinds, some merely necessary means and desirable only for the sake of something else, others desirable in themselves, it is clear that happiness is to be classed among activities desirable in themselves, and not among those desirable as a means to something else; since happiness lacks nothing, and is self-sufficient.

But those activities are desirable in themselves which do not aim at any result beyond the mere exercise of the activity. Now this is felt to be the nature of actions in conformity with virtue; for to do noble and virtuous deeds is a thing desirable for its own sake.

But agreeable amusements also are desirable for their own sake; we do not pursue them as a means to something else, for as a matter of fact they are more often harmful than beneficial, causing men to neglect their health and their estates. Yet persons whom the world counts happy usually have recourse to such pastimes; and this is why adepts in such pastimes stand in high favour with princes, because they make themselves agreeable in supplying what their patrons desire, and what they want is amusement. So it is supposed that amusements are a component part of happiness, because princes and potentates devote their leisure to them.

But (i) perhaps princes and potentates are not good evidence. Virtue and intelligence, which are the sources of man's higher activities, do not depend on the possession of power; and if these persons, having no taste for pure and liberal pleasure, have recourse to the pleasures of the body, we must not on that account suppose that bodily pleasures are the more desirable. Children imagine that the things they themselves value are actually the best; it is not surprising therefore that, as children and grown men have different standards of value, so also should the worthless and the virtuous. Therefore, as has repeatedly been said, those things are actually valuable and pleasant which appear so to the good man; but each man thinks that activity most desirable which suits his particular disposition, and therefore the good man thinks virtuous activity most desirable. It follows therefore that happiness is not to be found in amusements.

(ii) Indeed it would be strange that amusement should be our End—that we should toil and moil all our life long in order that we may amuse ourselves. For virtually every object we adopt is pursued as a means to something else, excepting happiness, which is an end in itself; to make amusement the object of our serious pursuits and our work seems foolish and childish to excess: Anacharsis's motto, Play in order that you may work, is felt to be the right rule. For amusement is a form of rest; but we need rest because we are not able to go on working without a break, and therefore it is not an end, since we take it as a means to further activity.

(iii) And the life that conforms with virtue is thought to be a happy life; but virtuous life involves serious purpose, and does not consist in amusement.

(iv) Also we pronounce serious things to be superior to things that are funny and amusing; and the nobler a faculty or a person is, the more serious, we think, are their activities; therefore, the activity of the nobler faculty or person is itself superior, and therefore more productive of happiness.

(v) Also anybody can enjoy the pleasures of the body, a slave no less than the noblest of mankind; but no one allows a slave any measure of happiness, any more than a life of his own. Therefore happiness does not consist in pastimes and amusements, but in activities in accordance with virtue, as has been said already.

But if happiness consists in activity in accordance with virtue, it is reasonable that it should be activity in accordance with the highest virtue; and this will be the virtue of the best part of us. Whether then this be the intellect, or whatever else it be that is thought to rule and lead us by nature, and to have cognizance of what is noble and divine, either as being itself also actually divine, or as being relatively the divinest part of us, it is the activity of this part of us in accordance with the virtue proper to it that will constitute perfect happiness; and it has been stated already that this activity is the activity of contemplation.

And that happiness consists in contemplation may be accepted as agreeing both with the results already reached and with the truth. For contemplation is at once the highest form of activity (since the intellect is the highest thing in us, and the objects with which the intellect deals are the highest things that can be known), and also it is the most continuous, for we can reflect more continuously than we can carry on any form of action. And again we suppose that happiness must contain an element of pleasure; now activity in accordance with wisdom is admittedly the most pleasant of the activities in accordance with virtue: at all events it is held that philosophy or the pursuit of wisdom contains pleasures of marvellous purity and permanence, and it is reasonable to suppose that the enjoyment of knowledge is a still pleasanter occupation than the pursuit of it. Also the activity of contemplation will be found to possess in the highest degree the quality that is termed self-sufficiency; for while it is true that the wise man equally with the just man and the rest requires the necessaries of life, yet, these being adequately supplied, whereas the just man needs other persons towards whom or with whose aid he may act justly, and so likewise do the temperate man and the brave man and the others, the wise man on the contrary can also contemplate by himself, and the more so the wiser he is; no doubt he will study better with the aid of fellow-workers, but still he is the most self-sufficient of men. Also the activity of contemplation may be held to be the only activity that is loved for its own sake: it produces no result beyond the actual act of contemplation, whereas from practical pursuits we look to secure some advantage, greater or smaller, beyond the action itself. Also happiness is thought to involve leisure; for we do business in order that we may have leisure, and carry on war in order that we may have peace. Now the practical virtues are exercised in politics or in warfare; but the pursuits of politics and war seem to be unleisured—those of war indeed entirely so, for no one desires to be at war for the sake of being at war, nor deliberately takes steps to cause a war: a man would be thought an utterly blood-thirsty character if he declared war on a friendly state for the sake of causing battles and massacres. But the activity of the politician also is unleisured, and aims at securing something beyond the mere participation in politics—positions of authority and honour, or, if the happiness of the politician himself and of his fellow-citizens, this happiness conceived as something distinct from political activity (indeed we are clearly investigating it as so distinct). If then among practical pursuits displaying the virtues, politics and war stand out pre-eminent in nobility and grandeur, and yet they are unleisured, and directed to some further end, not chosen for their own sakes: whereas the activity of the intellect is felt to excel in serious worth, consisting as it does in contemplation, and to aim at no end beyond itself, and also to contain a pleasure peculiar to itself, and therefore augmenting its activity: and if accordingly the attributes of this activity are found to be self-sufficiency, leisuredness, such freedom from fatigue as is possible for man, and all the other attributes of blessedness: it follows that it is the activity of the intellect that constitutes complete human happiness—provided it be granted a complete span of life, for nothing that belongs to happiness can be incomplete.

Such a life as this however will be higher than the human level: not in virtue of his humanity will a man achieve it, but in virtue of something within him that is divine; and by as much as this something is superior to his composite nature, by so much is its activity superior to the exercise of the other forms of virtue. If then the intellect is something divine in comparison with man, so is the life of the intellect divine in comparison with human life. Nor ought we to obey those who enjoin that a man should have man's thoughts and a mortal the thoughts of mortality, but we ought so far as possible to achieve immortality, and do all that man may to live in accordance with the highest thing in him; for though this be small in bulk, in power and value it far surpasses all the rest.

It may even be held that this is the true self of each, inasmuch as it is the dominant and better part; and therefore it would be a strange thing if a man should choose to live not his own life but the life of some other than himself.

Moreover what was said before will apply here also: that which is best and most pleasant for each creature is that which is proper to the nature of each; accordingly the life of the intellect is the best and the pleasantest life for man, inasmuch as the intellect more than anything else is man; therefore this life will be the happiest.

The life of moral virtue, on the other hand, is happy only in a secondary degree. For the moral activities are purely human: Justice, I mean, Courage and the other virtues we display in our intercourse with our fellows, when we observe what is due to each in contracts and services and in our various actions, and in our emotions also; and all of these things seem to be purely human affairs. And some moral actions are thought to be the outcome of the physical constitution, and moral virtue is thought to have a close affinity in many respects with the passions. Moreover, Prudence is intimately connected with Moral Virtue, and this with Prudence, inasmuch as the first principles which Prudence employs are determined by the Moral Virtues, and the right standard for the Moral Virtues is determined by Prudence. But these being also connected with the passions are related to our composite nature; now the virtues of our composite nature are purely human; so therefore also is the life that manifests these virtues, and the happiness that belongs to it. Whereas the happiness that belongs to the intellect is separate: so much may be said about it here, for a full discussion of the matter is beyond the scope of our present purpose. And such happiness would appear to need but little external equipment, or less than the happiness based on moral virtue. Both, it may be granted, require the mere necessaries of life, and that in an equal degree (though the politician does as a matter of fact take more trouble about bodily requirements and so forth than the philosopher); for in this respect there may be little difference between them. But for the purpose of their special activities their requirements will differ widely. The liberal man will need wealth in order to do liberal actions, and so indeed will the just man in order to discharge his obligations (since mere intentions are invisible, and even the unjust pretend to wish to act justly); and the brave man will need strength if he is to perform any action displaying his virtue; and the temperate man opportunity for indulgence: otherwise how can he, or the possessor of any other virtue, show that he is virtuous? It is disputed also whether purpose or performance is the more important factor in virtue, as it is alleged to depend on both; now the perfection of virtue will clearly consist in both; but the performance of virtuous actions requires much outward equipment, and the more so the greater and more noble the actions are. But the student, so far as the pursuit of his activity is concerned, needs no external apparatus: on the contrary, worldly goods may almost be said to be a hinderance to contemplation; though it is true that, being a man and living in the society of others, he chooses to engage in virtuous action, and so will need external goods to carry on his life as a human being.

The following considerations also will show that perfect happiness is some form of contemplative activity. The gods, as we conceive them, enjoy supreme felicity and happiness. But what sort of actions can we attribute to them? Just actions? but will it not seem ridiculous to think of them as making contracts, restoring deposits and the like? Then brave actions—enduring terrors and running risks for the nobility of so doing? Or liberal actions? but to whom will they give? Besides, it would be absurd to suppose that they actually have a coinage or currency of some sort! And temperate actions—what will these mean in their case? surely it would be derogatory to praise them for not having evil desires! If we go through the list we shall find that all forms of virtuous conduct seem trifling and unworthy of the gods. Yet nevertheless they have always been conceived as, at all events, living, and therefore living actively, for we cannot suppose they are always asleep like Endymion. But for a living being, if we eliminate action, and *a fortiori* creative action, what remains save contemplation? It follows that the activity of God, which is transcendent in blessedness, is the activity of contemplation; and therefore among human activities that which is most akin to the divine activity of contemplation will be the greatest source of happiness.

A further confirmation is that the lower animals cannot partake of happiness, because they are completely devoid of the contemplative activity. The whole of the life of the gods is blessed, and that of man is so in so far as it contains some likeness to the divine activity; but none of the other animals possess happiness, because they are entirely incapable of contemplation. Happiness therefore is co-extensive in its range with contemplation: the more a class of beings possesses the faculty of contemplation, the more it enjoys happiness, not as an accidental concomitant of contemplation but as inherent in it, since contemplation is valuable in itself. It follows that happiness is some form of contemplation.

But the philosopher being a man will also need external well-being, since man's nature is not self-sufficient for the activity of contemplation, but he must also have bodily health and a supply of food and other requirements. Yet if supreme blessedness is not possible without external goods, it must not be supposed that happiness will demand many or great possessions; for self-sufficiency does not depend on excessive abundance, nor does moral conduct, and it is possible to perform noble deeds even without being ruler of land and sea: one can do virtuous acts with quite moderate resources. This may be clearly observed in experience: private citizens do not seem to be less but more given to doing virtuous actions than princes and potentates. It is sufficient then if moderate resources are forthcoming; for a life of virtuous activity will be essentially a happy life.

Solon also doubtless gave a good description of happiness, when he said that in his opinion those men were happy who, being moderately equipped with external goods, had performed noble exploits and had lived temperately; for it is possible for a man of but moderate possessions to do what is right. Anaxagoras again does not seem to have conceived the happy man as rich or powerful, since he says that he would not be surprised if he were to appear a strange sort of person in the eyes of the many; for most men judge by externals, which are all that they can perceive. So our theories seem to be in agreement with the opinions of the wise.

Such arguments then carry some degree of conviction; but it is by the practical experience of life and conduct that the truth is really tested, since it is there that the final decision lies. We must therefore examine the conclusions we have advanced by bringing them to the test of the facts of life. If they are in harmony with the facts, we may accept them; if found to disagree, we must deem them mere theories.

And it seems likely that the man who pursues intellectual activity, and who cultivates his intellect and keeps that in the best condition, is also the man most beloved of the gods. For if, as is generally believed, the gods exercise some superintendence over human affairs, then it will be reasonable to suppose that they take pleasure in that part of man which is best and most akin to themselves, namely the intellect, and that they recompense with their favours those men who esteem and honour this most, because these care for the things dear to themselves, and act rightly and nobly. Now it is clear that all these attributes belong most of all to the wise man. He therefore is most beloved by the gods; and if so, he is naturally most happy. Here is another proof that the wise man is the happiest.

ISLAM IS THE ROAD TO HAPPINESS

Tabatabai

The religion of Islam is superior to any other in that it guarantees happiness in man's life. For Muslims, Islam is a belief system with moral and practical laws that have their source in the Qur'an.

God, may He be exalted, says, *"Indeed this Qur'an guides to the path which is clearer and straighter than any other"* [XVII:9]. He also says, *"We have revealed to you the book which clarifies every matter"* [XVI:89].

These references exemplify the numerous Qur'anic verses *(āyāt)* which mention the principles of religious belief, moral virtues and a general legal system governing all aspects of human behavior.

A consideration of the following topics will enable one to understand that the Qur'an provides a comprehensive programme of activity for man's life.

Man has no other aim in life but the pursuit of happiness and pleasure, which manifests itself in much the same way as love of ease or wealth. Although some individuals seem to reject this happiness, for example, by ending their lives in suicide, or by turning away from a life of leisure, they too, in their own way, confirm this principle of happiness; for, in seeking an end to their life or of material pleasure, they are still asserting their own personal choice of what happiness means to them. Human actions, therefore, are directed largely by the prospects of happiness and prosperity offered by a certain idea, whether that idea be true or false.

Man's activity in life is guided by a specific plan or programme. This fact is self-evident, even though it is sometimes concealed by its very apparentness. Man acts according to his will and desires; he also weighs the necessity of a task before undertaking it.

In this he is promoted by an inherent scientific law, which is to say that he performs a task for "himself" in fulfilling needs which he perceives are necessary. There is, therefore, a direct link between the objective of a task and its execution.

Any action undertaken by man, whether it be eating, sleeping or walking, occupies its own specific place and demands its own particular efforts. Yet an action is implemented according to an inherent law, the general concept of which is stored in man's perception and is recalled by motions associated with that action. This notion holds true whether or not one is obliged to undertake the action or whether or not the circumstances are favourable.

Every man, in respect of his own actions, is as the state in relation to its individual citizens, whose activity is controlled by specific laws, customs and behaviour. Just as the active forces in a state are obliged to adapt their actions according to certain laws, so is the social activity of a community composed of the actions of each individual. If this were not the case, the different components of society would fall apart and be destroyed in anarchy in the shortest time imaginable.

If a society is religious, its government will reflect that religion; if it is secular, it will be regulated by a corresponding code of law. If a society is uncivilized and barbaric, a code of behaviour imposed by a tyrant will appear; otherwise, the conflict of various belief-systems within such a society will produce lawlessness.

Thus man, as an individual element of society, has no option but to possess and pursue a goal. He is guided in the pursuit of his goal by the path which corresponds to it and by the rules which must necessarily accompany his programme of activity. The Qur'an affirms this idea when it says that *"every man has a goal to which he is turning, so compete with each other in good action"* [II:148]. In the usage of the Qur'an, the word *dīn* is basically applied to a way, a pattern of living, and neither the believer nor the non-believer is without a path, be it prophetic or man-made.

God, may He be exalted, describes the enemies of the divine *dīn* (religion) as those *"who prevent others from the path of God and would have it crooked"* [VII:45].

This verse shows that the term *Sabāil Allāh*—the path of God—used in the verse refers to the *dīn* of *fitrah*—the inherent pattern of life intended by God for man). It also indicates that even those who do not believe in God implement His *dīn*, albeit in a deviated form; this deviation, which becomes their *dīn*, is also encompassed in God's programme.

The best and firmest path in life for man is the one which is dictated by his innate being and not by the sentiments of any individual or society. A close examination of any part of creation reveals that, from its very inception, it is guided by an innate purpose towards fulfilling its nature along the most appropriate and shortest path; every aspect of each part of creation is equipped to do so, acting as a blueprint for defining the nature of its existence. Indeed all of creation, be it animate or inanimate, is made up in this manner.

As an example, we may say that a green-tipped shoot, emerging from a single grain in the earth, is "aware" of its future existence as a plant which will yield an ear of wheat. By means of its inherent characteristics, the shoot acquires various mineral elements for its growth from the soil and changes, day by day, in form and strength until it becomes a fully-matured grain-bearing plant—and so comes to the end of its natural cycle.

Similarly, if we investigate the life-cycle of the walnut tree, we observe that it too is "aware," from the very beginning, of its own specific purpose in life, namely, to grow into a big walnut tree. It reaches this goal by developing according to its own distinct inherent characteristics; it does not, for example, follow the path of the wheat-plant in fulfilling its goal just as the wheat-plant does not follow the life pattern of the walnut tree.

Since every created object which makes up the visible world is subject to this same general law, there is no reason to doubt that man, as a species of creation, is not. Indeed his physical capabilities are the best proof of this rule; like the rest of creation, they allow him to realize his purpose, and ultimate happiness, in life.

Thus, we observe that man, in fact, guides himself to happiness and well-being merely by applying the fundamental laws inherent in his own nature.

This law is confirmed by God in the Qur'an, through His Prophet Moses, when he says, *"Our Lord is He who gave everything its nature, then guided it"* [XX:50]. It is further explained in LXXXVII:2–3 as *"He who created and fashioned in balanced proportion and He who measures and guides."*

As to the creation and the nature of man, the Qur'an says,

> By the soul and Him who fashioned it and then inspired it with wrong action and fear of God; he is truly successful who causes it to grow and purifies it and he is a failure who corrupts and destroys it.
> [XCI:7–10].

God enjoins upon man the duty to *"strive toward a sincere application of the dīn,"* (that is, the *fitrah* of God, or the natural code of behaviour upon which He has created mankind), since *"there is no changing (the laws of) the creation of God"* [XXX:30].

He also says that *"In truth, the only* deen *recognized by God is Islam"* [III:19]. Here, Islam means submission, the method of submission to these very laws. The Qur'an further warns that *"the actions of the man who chooses a dīn other than Islam will not be accepted"* [III:85].

The gist of the above verses, and other references on the same subject, is that God has guided every creature—be it man, beast or vegetable—to a state of well-being and self-fulfilment appropriate to its individual make-up.

Thus the appropriate path for man lies in the adoption of personal and social laws particular to his own *fiṭrah* (or innate nature), and in avoiding people who have become "denaturalized" by following their own notions or passions. It is clearly underlined that *fiṭrah*, far from denying man's feelings and passions, accords each its proper due and allows man's conflicting spiritual and material needs to be fulfilled in a harmonious fashion.

Thus, we may conclude that the intellect *'aql* should rule man in matters pertaining to individual or personal decisions, rather than his feelings. Similarly, truth and justice should govern society and not the whim of a tyrant or even the will of a majority, if that be contrary to a society's true benefit.

From this we may conclude that only God is empowered to make laws, since the only law useful to man are those which are made according to his inherent nature.

It also follows that man's needs, arising from his outward circumstance and his inner reality, are fulfilled only by obeying God's instructions (or laws). These needs may arise through events beyond man's control or as a result of the natural demands of his body.

Both are encompassed in the plan of life that God has designated for man. For, as the Qur'an says, the *"decision rests with God only,"* [XII: 40, 67] which is to say that there is no governance (of man or society, of the inner or the outer) except that of God.

Without a specific creational plan, based on the innate disposition for man, life would be fruitless and without meaning. We may understand this only through belief in God and a knowledge of his Unity, as explained in the Qur'an.

From here we may proceed to an understanding of the Day of Judgement, when man is rewarded or punished according to his deeds. Thereafter, we may arrive at a knowledge of the prophets and of prophetic teachings, since man cannot be judged without being first instructed in the matter of obedience and disobedience. These three fundamental teachings are considered to be the roots of the Islamic way of life.

To these we may add the fundamentals of good character and morals which a true believer must possess, and which are a necessary extension of the three basic beliefs mentioned above. The laws governing daily activity not only guarantee man's happiness and moral character but, more importantly, increase his understanding of these beliefs and of the fundamentals of Islam.

QUESTION FOR DISCUSSION

1. Compare Aristotle's account of happiness with that presented by Tabatabai. In what ways is Tabatabai influenced by Aristotle? Where does he differ from Aristotle's approach?

TAOIST VIEWS

Taoism is a mysticism. It does not believe that life's meaning can be expressed in words. The Chinese classic *Tao Te Ching* (attributed to the sixth-century B.C. sage Lao Tzu) from which our first selection is taken, appears to state this when it says:

> The ancient Masters were profound and subtle
> Their wisdom was unfathomable
> There is no way to describe it;
> all we can describe is their appearance

So we are to understand wisdom through observing the actions and styles of the wise. Will this show us what life's meaning is? Do those who have wisdom necessarily know what life means? How will we ever know the answer to this, if wisdom cannot be described? But then, how can there be a question about life's meaning, if the meaning of life is also beyond words?

Chuang Tzu, our second author, the fourth-century B.C. Chinese sage, goes directly to the actions expressive of wisdom in the story of Prince Wen Hui's cook who used Tao to cut up oxen; Ch'ui, the draftsman who draws perfect circles freehand; Chi Hsing Tzu, the patient trainer of fighting cocks; and himself, Chuang Tzu, when he turned down the offer to become Prime Minister. The same spirit as that exemplified in these tales is also to be found in the dialogue and essays of the contemporary American logician-philosopher Raymond Smullyan, who plays in his work with the Taoist paradoxes of action and inaction.

 LIVING IN THE TAO

Lao Tzu

8

The highest form of goodness is like water.
Water knows how to benefit all things without striving with them.
It stays in places loathed by all men.
Therefore, it comes near the Tao.

In choosing your dwelling, know how to keep to the ground.
In cultivating your mind, know how to dive in the hidden deeps.
In dealing with others, know how to be gentle and kind.
In speaking, know how to keep your words.
In governing, know how to maintain order.
In transacting business, know how to be efficient.
In making a move, know how to choose the right moment.

If you do not strive with others,
You will be free from blame.

9

As for holding to fullness,
Far better were it to stop in time!

Keep on beating and sharpening a sword,
And the edge cannot be preserved for long.

Fill your house with gold and jade,
And it can no longer be guarded.

Set store by your riches and honour,
And you will only reap a crop of calamities.

Here is the Way of Heaven:
When you have done your work, retire!

• • •

12

The five colours blind the eye.
The five tones deafen the ear.
The five flavours cloy the palate.
Racing and hunting madden the mind.
Rare goods tempt men to do wrong.

Therefore, the Sage takes care of the belly, not the eye.
He prefers what is within to what is without.

13

"Welcome disgrace as a pleasant surprise.
Prize calamities as your own body."

Why should we "welcome disgrace as a pleasant surprise"?
Because a lowly state is a boon:
Getting it is a pleasant surprise,
And so is losing it!
That is why we should "welcome disgrace as a pleasant surprise."

Why should we "prize calamities as our own body"?
Because our body is the very source of our calamities.
If we have no body, what calamities can we have?

Hence, only he who is willing to give his body for the sake of the world is fit to be entrusted with the world.
Only he who can do it with love is worthy of being the steward of the world.

• • •

15

The ancient adepts of the Tao were subtle and flexible, profound and comprehensive.
Their minds were too deep to be fathomed.

Because they are unfathomable,
One can only describe them vaguely by their appearance.

Hesitant like one wading a stream in winter;
Timid like one afraid of his neighbours on all sides;
Cautious and courteous like a guest;
Yielding like ice on the point of melting;
Simple like an uncarved block;
Hollow like a cave;
Confused like a muddy pool;
And yet who else could quietly and gradually evolve from the muddy to the clear?
Who else could slowly but steadily move from the inert to the living?

He who keeps the Tao does not want to be full.
But precisely because he is never full,
He can always remain like a hidden sprout,
And does not rush to early ripening.

16

Attain to utmost Emptiness.
Cling single-heartedly to interior peace.

While all things are stirring together,
I only contemplate the Return.
For flourishing as they do,
Each of them will return to its root.
To return to the root is to find peace.
To find peace is to fulfill one's destiny.
To fulfill one's destiny is to be constant.
To know the Constant is called Insight.

If one does not know the Constant,
One runs blindly into disasters.
If one knows the Constant,
One can understand and embrace all.
If one understands and embraces all,
One is capable of doing justice.
To be just is to be kingly;
To be kingly is to be heavenly;
To be heavenly is to be one with the Tao;
To be one with the Tao is to abide forever.
Such a one will be safe and whole
Even after the dissolution of his body.

• • •

22

Bend and you will be whole.
Curl and you will be straight.
Keep empty and you will be filled.
Grow old and you will be renewed.

Have little and you will gain.
Have much and you will be confused.

Therefore, the Sage embraces the One,
And becomes a Pattern to all under Heaven.
He does not make a show of himself,
Hence he shines;
Does not justify himself,
Hence he becomes known;
Does not boast of his ability,
Hence he gets his credit;
Does not brandish his success,
Hence he endures;
Does not compete with anyone,
Hence no one can compete with him.
Indeed, the ancient saying: "Bend and you will remain whole" is no idle word.
Nay, if you have really attained wholeness, everything will flock to you.

• • •

24

One on tip-toe cannot stand.
One astride cannot walk.
One who displays himself does not shine.
One who justifies himself has no glory.
One who boasts of his own ability has no merit.
One who parades his own success will not endure.
In Tao these things are called "unwanted food and extra-
neous growths,"
Which are loathed by all things.
Hence, a man of Tao does not set his heart upon them.

• • •

38

High Virtue is non-virtuous;
Therefore it has Virtue.
Low Virtue never frees itself from virtuousness;
Therefore it has no Virtue.

High Virtue makes no fuss and has no private ends to
serve:
Low Virtue not only fusses but has private ends to serve.

High humanity fusses but has no private ends to serve:
High morality not only fusses but has private ends to
serve.
High ceremony fusses but finds no response;
Then it tries to enforce itself with rolled-up sleeves.

Failing Tao, man resorts to Virtue.
Failing Virtue, man resorts to humanity.
Failing humanity, man resorts to morality.
Failing morality, man resorts to ceremony.
Now, ceremony is the merest husk of faith and loyalty;
It is the beginning of all confusion and disorder.

As to foreknowledge, it is only the flower of Tao,
And the beginning of folly.

Therefore, the full-grown man sets his heart upon the
substance rather than the husk;
Upon the fruit rather than the flower.
Truly, he prefers what is within to what is without.

• • •

43

The softest of all things
Overrides the hardest of all things.

Only Nothing can enter into no-space.
Hence I know the advantages of Non-Ado.

Few things under heaven are as instructive as the
lessons of Silence,
Or as beneficial as the fruits of Non-Ado.

44

As for your name and your body, which is the dearer?
As for your body and your wealth, which is the more to
be prized?
As for gain and loss, which is the more painful?

Thus, an excessive love for anything will cost you dear
in the end.
The storing up of too much goods will entail a heavy
loss.

To know when you have enough is to be immune from
disgrace.
To know when to stop is to be preserved from perils.
Only thus can you endure long.

45

The greatest perfection seems imperfect,
And yet its use is inexhaustible.
The greatest fullness seems empty,
And yet its use is endless.

The greatest straightness looks like crookedness.
The greatest skill appears clumsy.
The greatest eloquence sounds like stammering.

Restlessness overcomes cold,
But calm overcomes heat.

The peaceful and serene
Is the Norm of the World.

• • •

63

Do the Non-Ado.
Strive for the effortless.
Savour the savourless.
Exalt the low.
Multiply the few.
Requite injury with kindness.

Nip troubles in the bud.
Sow the great in the small.

Difficult things of the world
Can only be tackled when they are easy.
Big things of the world
Can only be achieved by attending to their small begin-
nings.
Thus, the Sage never has to grapple with big things,
Yet he alone is capable of achieving them!

He who promises lightly must be lacking in faith.
He who thinks everything easy will end by finding
everything difficult.
Therefore, the Sage, who regards everything as difficult,
Meets with no difficulties in the end.

. . .

68

A good soldier is never aggressive;
A good fighter is never angry.
The best way of conquering an enemy
Is to win him over by not antagonizing him.
The best way of employing a man
Is to serve under him.
This is called the virtue of non-striving!
This is called using the abilities of men!
This is called being wedded to Heaven as of old!

. . .

74

When the people are no longer afraid of death,
Why scare them with the spectre of death?

If you could make the people always afraid of death,
And they still persisted in breaking the law,
Then you might with reason arrest and execute them,
And who would dare to break the law?

Is not the Great Executor always there to kill?
To do the killing for the Great Executor
Is to chop wood for a master carpenter,
And you would be lucky indeed if you did not hurt your
own hand!

. . .

76

When a man is living, he is soft and supple.
When he is dead, he becomes hard and rigid.

When a plant is living, it is soft and tender.
When it is dead, it becomes withered and dry.

Hence, the hard and rigid belongs to the company of the
dead:
The soft and supple belongs to the company of the living.

Therefore, a mighty army tends to fall by its own
weight,
Just as dry wood is ready for the axe.

The mighty and great will be laid low;
The humble and weak will be exalted.

. . .

81

Sincere words are not sweet,
Sweet words are not sincere.
Good men are not argumentative,
The argumentative are not good.
The wise are not erudite,
The erudite are not wise.

The Sage does not take to hoarding.
The more he lives for others, the fuller is his life.
The more he gives, the more he abounds.

The Way of Heaven is to benefit, not to harm.
The Way of the Sage is to do his duty, not to strive with
anyone.

LOST IN THE TAO

Chuang Tzu

CUTTING UP AN OX

Prince Wen Hui's cook
Was cutting up an ox.
Out went a hand,
Down went a shoulder,
He planted a foot,
He pressed with a knee,
The ox fell apart
With a whisper,

The bright cleaver murmured
Like a gentle wind.
Rhythm! Timing!
Like a sacred dance,
Like "The Mulberry Grove,"
Like ancient harmonies!

"Good work!" the Prince exclaimed,
"Your method is faultless!"
"Method?" said the cook
Laying aside his cleaver,
"What I follow is Tao
Beyond all methods!

"When I first began
To cut up oxen
I would see before me
The whole ox
All in one mass.

"After three years
I no longer saw this mass.
I saw the distinctions.

"But now, I see nothing
With the eye. My whole being
Apprehends.
My senses are idle. The spirit
Free to work without plan
Follows its own instinct
Guided by natural line,
By the secret opening, the hidden space,
My cleaver finds its own way.
I cut through no joint, chop no bone.

"A good cook needs a new chopper
Once a year—he cuts.
A poor cook needs a new one
Every month—he hacks!

"I have used this same cleaver
Nineteen years.
It has cut up
A thousand oxen.
Its edge is as keen
As if newly sharpened.

"There are spaces in the joints;
The blade is thin and keen;
When this thinness
Finds that space
There is all the room you need!
It goes like a breeze!

Hence I have this cleaver nineteen years
As if newly sharpened!

"True, there are sometimes
Tough joints. I feel them coming,
I slow down, I watch closely,
Hold back, barely move the blade,
And whump! the part falls away
Landing like a clod of earth.

"Then I withdraw the blade,
I stand still
And let the joy of the work
Sink in.
I clean the blade
And put it away."

Prince Wan Hui said,
"This is it! My cook has shown me
How I ought to live
My own life!"

• • •

MAN IS BORN IN TAO

Fishes are born in water
Man is born in Tao.
If fishes, born in water,
Seek the deep shadow
Of pond and pool,
All their needs
Are satisfied.
If man, born in Tao,
Sinks into the deep shadow
Of non-action
To forget aggression and concern,
He lacks nothing
His life is secure.

Moral: "All the fish needs
Is to get lost in water.
All man needs is to get lost
In Tao."

• • •

CRACKING THE SAFE

For security against robbers who snatch purses, rifle
    luggage, and crack safes,
One must fasten all property with ropes, lock it up with
    locks, bolt it with bolts.

This (for property owners) is elementary good sense.
But when a strong thief comes along he picks up the
    whole lot,
Puts it on his back, and goes on his way with only one
    fear:
That ropes, locks, and bolts may give way.
Thus what the world calls good business is only a way
To gather up the loot, pack it, make it secure
In one convenient load for the more enterprising thieves.
Who is there, among those called smart,
Who does not spend his time amassing loot
For a bigger robber than himself?

• • •

In the land of Khi, from village to village,
You could hear cocks crowing, dogs barking.
Fishermen cast their nets,
Ploughmen ploughed the wide fields,
Everything was neatly marked out
By boundary lines. For five hundred square miles
There were temples for ancestors, altars
For field-gods and corn-spirits.
Every canton, country, and district
Was run according to the laws and statutes—
Until one morning the Attorney General, Tien Khang
    Tzu,
Did away with the King and took over the whole state.
Was he content to steal the land? No,
He also took over the laws and statutes at the same time,
And all the lawyers with them, not to mention the po-
    lice.
They all formed part of the same package.

Of course, people called Khang Tzu a robber,
But they left him alone
To live as happy as the Patriarchs.
No small state would say a word against him,
No larger state would make a move in his direction,
So for twelve generations the state of Khi
Belonged to his family. No one interfered
With his inalienable rights.

• • •

The invention
Of weights and measures
Makes robbery easier.
Signing contracts, settings seals,
Makes robbery more sure.
Teaching love and duty

Provides a fitting language
With which to prove that robbery
Is really for the general good.
A poor man must swing
For stealing a belt buckle
But if a rich man steals a whole state
He is acclaimed
As statesman of the year.

Hence if you want to hear the very best speeches
On love, duty, justice, etc.,
Listen to statesmen.

But when the creek dries up
Nothing grows in the valley.
When the mound is levelled
The hollow next to it is filled.
And when the statesmen and lawyers
And preachers of duty disappear
There are no more robberies either
And the world is at peace.

Moral: the more you pile up ethical principles
And duties and obligations
To bring everyone in line
The more you gather loot
For a thief like Khang.
By ethical argument
And moral principle
The greatest crimes are eventually shown
To have been necessary, and, in fact,
A signal benefit
To mankind.

• • •

ACTION AND NON-ACTION

The non-action of the wise man is not inaction.
It is not studied. It is not shaken by anything.
The sage is quiet because he is not moved,
Not because he *wills* to be quiet.
Still water is like glass.
You can look in it and see the bristles on your chin.
It is a perfect level;
A carpenter could use it.
If water is so clear, so level,
How much more the spirit of man?
The heart of the wise man is tranquil.
It is the mirror of heaven and earth

The glass of everything.
Emptiness, stillness, tranquillity, tastelessness,
Silence, non-action: this is the level of heaven and earth.
This is perfect Tao. Wise men find here
Their resting place.
Resting, they are empty.

From emptiness comes the unconditioned.
From this, the conditioned, the individual things.
So from the sage's emptiness, stillness arises:
From stillness, action. From action, attainment.
From their stillness comes their non-action, which is
   also action
And is, therefore, their attainment.
For stillness is joy. Joy is free from care
Fruitful in long years.

Joy does all things without concern:
For emptiness, stillness, tranquillity, tastelessness,
Silence, and non-action
Are the root of all things.

      •   •   •

THE MAN OF TAO

The man in whom Tao
Acts without impediment
Harms no other being
By his actions
Yet he does not know himself
To be "kind," to be "gentle."

The man in whom Tao
Acts without impediment
Does not bother with his own interests
And does not despise
Others who do.
He does not struggle to make money
And does not make a virtue of poverty.
He goes his way
Without relying on others
And does not pride himself
On walking alone.
While he does not follow the crowd
He won't complain of those who do.
Rank and reward
Make no appeal to him;
Disgrace and shame
Do not deter him.
He is not always looking

For right and wrong
Always deciding "Yes" or "No."
The ancients said, therefore:

"The man of Tao
Remains unknown
Perfect virtue
Produces nothing
'No-Self'
Is 'True-Self.'
And the greatest man
Is Nobody."

THE TURTLE

Chuang Tzu with his bamboo pole
Was fishing in Pu river.

The Prince of Chu
Sent two vice-chancellors
With a formal document:
"We hereby appoint you
Prime Minister."

Chuang Tzu held his bamboo pole.
Still watching Pu river,
He said:
"I am told there is a sacred tortoise,
Offered and canonized
Three thousand years ago,
Venerated by the prince,
Wrapped in silk,
In a precious shrine
On an altar
In the Temple.

"What do you think:
Is it better to give up one's life
And leave a sacred shell
As an object of cult
In a cloud of incense
Three thousand years,

Or better to live
As a plain turtle
Dragging its tail in the mud?"

"For the turtle," said the Vice-Chancellor,
"Better to live
And drag its tail in the mud!"

"Go home!" said Chuang Tzu.
"Leave me here
To drag my tail in the mud!"

      •   •   •

PERFECT JOY

Is there to be found on earth a fullness of joy, or is there no such thing? Is there some way to make life fully worth living, or is this impossible? If there is such a way, how do you go about finding it? What should you try to do? What should you seek to avoid? What should be the goal in which your activity comes to rest? What should you accept? What should you refuse to accept? What should you love? What should you hate?

What the world values is money, reputation, long life, achievement. What it counts as joy is health and comfort of body, good food, fine clothes, beautiful things to look at, pleasant music to listen to.

What it condemns is lack of money, a low social rank, a reputation of being no good, and an early death.

What it considers misfortune is bodily discomfort and labor, no chance to get your fill of good food, not having good clothes to wear, having no way to amuse or delight the eye, no pleasant music to listen to. If people find that they are deprived of these things, they go into a panic or fall into despair. They are so concerned for their life that their anxiety makes life unbearable, even when they have the things they think they want. Their very concern for enjoyment makes them unhappy.

The rich make life intolerable, driving themselves in order to get more and more money which they cannot really use. In so doing they are alienated from themselves, and exhaust themselves in their own service as though they were slaves of others.

The ambitious run day and night in pursuit of honors, constantly in anguish about the success of their plans, dreading the miscalculation that may wreck everything. Thus they are alienated from themselves, exhausting their real life in service of the shadow created by their insatiable hope.

The birth of a man is the birth of his sorrow. The longer he lives, the more stupid he becomes, because his anxiety to avoid unavoidable death becomes more and more acute. What bitterness! He lives for what is always out of reach! His thirst for survival in the future makes him incapable of living in the present.

• • •

I cannot tell if what the world considers "happiness" is happiness or not. All I know is that when I consider the way they go about attaining it, I see them carried away headlong, grim and obsessed, in the general onrush of the human herd, unable to stop themselves or to change their direction. All the while they claim to be just on the point of attaining happiness.

For my part, I cannot accept their standards, whether of happiness or unhappiness. I ask myself if after all their concept of happiness has any meaning whatever.

My opinion is that you never find happiness until you stop looking for it. My greatest happiness consists precisely in doing nothing whatever that is calculated to obtain happiness: and this, in the minds of most people, is the worst possible course.

I will hold to the saying that: "Perfect joy is to be without joy. Perfect praise is to be without praise."

If you ask "what ought to be done" and "what ought not to be done" on earth in order to produce happiness, I answer that these questions do not have an answer. There is no way of determining such things.

Yet at the same time, if I cease striving for happiness, the "right" and the "wrong" at once become apparent all by themselves.

Contentment and well-being at once become possible the moment you cease to act with them in view, and if you practice non-doing (*wu wei*), you will have both happiness and well-being.

Here is how I sum it up:

Heaven does nothing: its non-doing is its serenity.
Earth does nothing: it non-doing is its rest.

From the union of these two non-doings
All actions proceed,
All things are made.
How vast, how invisible
This coming-to-be!
All things come from nowhere!

How vast, how invisible—
No way to explain it!
All beings in their perfection
Are born of non-doing.
Hence it is said:
"Heaven and earth do nothing
Yet there is nothing they do not do."

Where is the man who can attain
To this non-doing?

• • •

THE FIGHTING COCK

Chi Hsing Tzu was a trainer of fighting cocks
For King Hsuan.
He was training a fine bird.
The King kept asking if the bird were
Ready for combat.
"Not yet," said the trainer.
"He is full of fire.
He is ready to pick a fight
With every other bird. He is vain and confident
Of his own strength."
After ten days, he answered again:
"Not yet. He flares up
When he hears another bird crow."
After ten more days:
"Not yet. He still gets
The angry look
And ruffles his feathers."
Again ten days:
The trainer said, "Now he is nearly ready.
When another bird crows, his eye
Does not even flicker.
He stands immobile
Like a cock of wood.
He is a mature fighter.
Other birds
Will take one look at him
And run."

• • •

WHEN THE SHOE FITS

Ch'ui the draftsman
Could draw more perfect circles freehand
Than with a compass.

His fingers brought forth
Spontaneous forms from nowhere. His mind
Was meanwhile free and without concern
With what he was doing.

No application was needed
His mind was perfectly simple
And knew no obstacle.

So, when the shoe fits
The foot is forgotten,
When the belt fits
The belly is forgotten,
When the heart is right
"For" and "against" are forgotten.

No drives, no compulsions,
No needs, no attractions:
Then your affairs
Are under control.
You are a free man.

Easy is right. Begin right
And you are easy.
Continue easy and you are right.
The right way to go easy
Is to forget the right way
And forget that the going is easy.

• • •

MEANS AND ENDS

The gatekeeper in the capital city of Sung became
such an expert mourner after his father's death, and
so emaciated himself with fasts and austerities, that
he was promoted to high rank in order that he might
serve as a model of ritual observance.

As a result of this, his imitators so deprived
themselves that half of them died. The others were
not promoted.

The purpose of a fish trap is to catch fish, and
when the fish are caught, the trap is forgotten.

The purpose of a rabbit snare is to catch rabbits.
When the rabbits are caught, the snare is forgotten.

The purpose of words is to convey ideas. When
the ideas are grasped, the words are forgotten.

Where can I find a man who has forgotten
words? He is the one I would like to talk to.

FLIGHT FROM THE SHADOW

There was a man who was so disturbed by the sight of his own shadow and so displeased with his own footsteps that he determined to get rid of both. The method he hit upon was to run away from them.

So he got up and ran. But every time he put his foot down there was another step, while his shadow kept up with him without the slightest difficulty.

He attributed his failure to the fact that he was not running fast enough. So he ran faster and faster, without stopping, until he finally dropped dead.

He failed to realize that if he merely stepped into the shade, his shadow would vanish, and if he sat down and stayed still, there would be no more footsteps.

WHICHEVER THE WAY

Raymond M. Smullyan

1. MY SYSTEM OF ETHICS

Whichever the way the wind blows,
Whichever the way the world goes,
Is perfectly all right with me!
(Anonymous Taoist)

2. WHICHEVER THE WAY

Moralist: I have just read your poem:

Whichever the way the wind blows,
Whichever the way the world goes,
Is good enough for me!

Taoist: You misquoted it. The last line is "Is perfectly all right with me." But I like your version at least as well as mine—in a way, even better.

Moralist: At any rate, I regard the poem as childish, irresponsible, illogical and morally reprehensible.

Taoist: That's perfectly all right with me!

Moralist: No, seriously, I cannot go along with the quietistic philosophy in your poem.

Taoist: I don't think of it as quietistic.

Moralist: Of course it is! Superficially your poem bears a resemblance to the Zen poem:

Sitting quietly doing nothing,
Spring comes, and the grass grows by itself.[1]

Taoist: I love that poem; I think it is my favorite.

Moralist: You would love it! Actually, I myself have nothing against that poem. There is nothing wrong with sitting quietly while the grass is growing because growing grass is something of value. But it is a very different thing to sit quietly while the world is going up in flames!

Taoist: I never advocated sitting quietly while the world goes up in flames. I never advocated sitting quietly at all. In fact, my poem does not advocate anything.

Moralist: You say the way things are going is good enough for you. Well, it may be good enough for you, but it sure is not good enough for me! With all the misery and injustice in the world, you might be content to sit quietly doing nothing, letting the wind blow where it listeth, but *I* intend to go out in the world and do something about it, whether you like it or not!

Taoist: Whether *I* like it or not! Whether *I* like it? I just told you:

Whichever the way the wind blows,
Whichever the way the world goes,
Is good enough for me!

So if you wish to go out and make changes in the world, your doing so is good enough for me.

Moralist: Sure it's good enough for you if *I* go to the trouble of making changes in the world, but it evidently is not good enough for you if you have to go to the trouble of making the changes.

Taoist: Why not? If I go out in the world and make changes, that is also good enough for me.

Moralist: But if things are already good enough for you, why would you want to make any changes?

---

[1] See Alan Watts, *The Way of Zen* (Vintage Books, 1957), p. 134.

Taoist: Why not?

Moralist: Oh come now, don't be silly! Either things are good enough for you or they are not. You can't have it both ways. If things are good enough for you, then there is no need for you to make changes; if not, then there is. I judge whether things really are good enough for you on the basis of how you act.

Taoist: I don't see it that way. I lead a very active life, as a matter of fact; I am always busy with some project or other. But I still say that whatever happens is good enough for me. Suppose some of my projects fail. Then I keep trying further until I succeed. Some of my projects I may not succeed in accomplishing in my lifetime. And this very fact is good enough for me.

Moralist: Suppose you were a doctor and were working hard to save a patient's life. Would you honestly say to yourself, "I am trying my best to save the patient's life, but if he dies, it is perfectly all right with me?

Taoist: Of course not! I would think it highly inappropriate to express this sentiment at such a time.

Moralist: Ah, I've caught you! You are being inconsistent! On the one hand you say that *all* the things which happen are good enough for you, and yet you admit of a particular happening that it is not good enough for you. So plainly you are inconsistent!

Taoist: Oh, for God's sake, come off it! You the great logician have caught *me* in an inconsistency! I affirm a universal statement and yet I deny an instance! Tut, tut, isn't that just terrible!

Moralist: Well, what do you have to say for yourself?

Taoist: What do I have to say for myself? Mainly that you are a first-class dope! That is the main thing I have to say.

Now look, will it make you any happier if I change the poem as follows? Suppose some very unpleasant event occurs—call it event E—then I can change the poem thus:

> Whichever the way the wind blows,
> Whichever the way the world goes,
> Is perfectly all right with me
> Except for event E.

Moralist: That is still no good. This means that you have to change the poem every time you come across a different unpleasant event.

Taoist: Not at all! I can simply use the symbol "E" once and for all as a variable ranging over all unpleasant events.

Moralist: I think you are being facetious!

Taoist: Of course I am! My facetiousness is obviously only an annoyance reaction to your pedantry.

Moralist: But honestly now, why should you regard it as pedantic that I object to a simple inconsistency? How can you seriously maintain that everything that happens is all right with you and yet admit that certain things which happen are not all right with you.

Taoist: I never maintained that everything that happens is all right with me. I never said that taking each thing that happens, that very thing is all right with me. I said "whichever the way the world goes" is all right with me. I was thinking of the direction of the world as a whole as one *unit*. The fact that I like the world as a whole does not mean that I like each part in isolation from the rest.

Moralist: It has suddenly occurred to me that maybe I have misjudged you. Perhaps all you are trying to say is that you accept the will of God. Maybe you are trying to say, "Let thy will, not mine, be done."

Taoist: If it makes you happy to think of it in these theological terms, by all means do so. I would not put it in those words, but perhaps they are not too far from what I have in mind. Your first suggestion, that I accept the will of God, comes closer than "Let thy will, not mine, be done."

Moralist: What is the difference between the two?

Taoist: To me they are, at least psychologically, very different. I recall in my bachelor days I spent one summer in Chicago in which I resided in a theological seminary. I had many conversations with the resident minister. One day he asked me whether I would not attend the evening services for the house. Although I did not feel quite right about it, I accepted as a matter of courtesy. And so I went, and at one point we were to fold our hands and pray to

God, "Let thy will, not mine, be done." I vividly re-call at this point that I felt hypocritical—indeed as if I actually were lying. Could I in all sincerity re-ally wish that God would do his will rather than mine? Suppose, for example, that Christianity were true, and that God would will that I be damned and suffer eternal punishment. Could I really *sanction* God doing this to me? Or to anyone else, for that matter? Even Satan himself? Besides, if the Christ-ian God really exists, it would seem rather ludicrous for a weak defenceless creature like myself to have to give his approval of God carrying out his own will. Obviously God will do what he wills, whether I like it or not. I'm sure this sentiment has often been expressed before, but I cannot help expressing it again. Anyhow, for these reasons, the phrase "Let thy will, not mine, be done" has never sounded right in my ears. Your first idea of "accepting the will of God" is different. Accepting something is not the same as desiring it. And that is why I say that your first suggestion comes closer to my meaning than your second although it still is not quite what I mean.

Moralist: Well, if this is not what your poem means, then I am still puzzled as to what it really means.

Taoist: Why do you work so hard trying to find its *meaning?* Can't you just accept if for what it is, and simply say "It's a good poem" or "It's a rotten poem"?

Moralist: No, no, there must be a meaning in it. You say you are not advocating quietism, surely you are not advocating activism. I guess you are just advocating accepting the world as it is.

Taoist: No, I am not *advocating* anything.

Moralist: Surely your idea must somehow affect your attitude towards the world, and have some ef-fect on your behavior.

Taoist: Attitude, yes; behavior, no.

Moralist: Have you always had this attitude?

Taoist: Definitely not.

Moralist: Well, since you had it, would you say that you have become more or less active than for-merly?

Taoist: Neither. My external actions have under-gone no appreciable change.

Moralist: But you must have *some* ethical mes-sage in your poem. Why did you choose such a pompous title as "My system of Ethics"? According to the last few things you have said, you seem to have no system at all.

Taoist (laughing): I deliberately chose such a pompous title as a jest at moralists, who tend to take themselves so seriously! I was delighted at the very pomposity of the title "My System of Ethics" lead-ing the reader to expect that I was going to come out with some ponderous analysis of what is the ulti-mate nature of the "Good," and how people should conduct their lives. And then all that comes out is this silly little poem. And yet, in a way, I honestly believe that this poem does contain—mainly, per-haps, on an unconscious level—a very serious mes-sage.

Moralist: But you cannot tell me what the mes-sage is?

Taoist: I have the same difficulty I would have in trying to explain why a joke is funny.

Moralist: Well, now, you say that the message does not so much concern people's actions.

Taoist: That's right.

Moralist: It just concerns change in attitudes.

Taoist: Right.

Moralist: Can you give me any inkling as to what attitude you have in mind? Do you have any idea of what attitudes you hope your message might engender?

Taoist: I think so. I think it would tend to make one's actions no less directed or efficient than be-fore—indeed, hopefully even more so—but it would tend to make the actions performed with less fear and anxiety.

Moralist: Oh, then you *do* have a significant message. In which case I think you owe it to your-self and others to express it more precisely and clearly.

Taoist: The clearest way *I* can express it is by saying

Whichever the way the wind blows,
Whichever the way the world goes,
It's all the same to me!

EPILOGUE

Several days after I completed this chapter, there was a storm during the night and the wind blew out many of the screens from the porch. Next morning I was standing there looking at the desolation, and my wife came down and said: "Well Raymond, are you still satisfied with whichever the way the wind blows?"

QUESTIONS FOR DISCUSSION

1. Discuss the *Tao Te Ching*'s claim that true wisdom seems foolish.

2. Evaluate Chuang Tzu's claim that the longer we live the stupider we become because our anxiety over death becomes more and more acute.

3. Evaluate Smullyan's dialogue between the Taoist and the Moralist. With whom do you agree more and why? Or do you disagree with both? What is your own position on "whichever the way the wind blows"?

A BUDDHIST VIEW

In a sense, the Buddhist answer to the question of life's meaning is that it has none. Life, as most of us know it, is an error, a confused dream produced by delusion and hatred and greed. This would seem to be a deeply pessimistic view of life, if the Buddhists left the matter there. But they do not. For they claim also to know the way to wake up from the nightmare. In another sense then, the Buddhist answers the question of life's meaning by seeing its potential as an educational process. Life is a meaningless cycle of birth and death for those who do not know and follow the eight-fold path to awakening. For those who do, life is a process of learning. As to any deeper meaning that life might have, Buddha was consciously silent. To ask questions about how this world was ultimately created is to be, on his view, like a man with an arrow wound who will not let the surgeon operate until he knows who has shot him.

The selection is taken from a modern Buddhist teacher. Chögyam Trungpa was a Tibetan lama, who fled his country after the Chinese invasion of Tibet, settling first in Scotland and later in the United States. He was founder of Naropa Institute in Boulder, Colorado, a center for the advanced study of religion.

THE MYTH OF FREEDOM

Chögyam Trungpa

As we grow older, in one way or another we begin to ask, "What is the meaning of life?" We might say, "What isn't the meaning of life? Everything is life." But that is too cute, too clever, and the question still remains. We could say that the meaning of life is to exist. Again, exist for what? What are we trying to achieve by leading our lives? Some people say that the meaning of life is to put our effort and energy toward higher goals: commuting between the earth and moon or becoming enlightened, becoming a great professor, great scientist, great mystic, to improve the world, clean up the earth's pollution. Maybe that is the meaning of life—that we are supposed to work hard and achieve something. We should discover wisdom and share it with others. Or we should create a better political order, reinforcing democracy so that all men are equal and everyone has a right to do whatever he wants within the limits of mutual responsibility. Perhaps we should raise the level of our civilization to the highest point so that our world becomes a fantastic place, a seat of wisdom, of enlightenment, of learning and the highest technological developments. There should be plenty to eat, pleasant houses, amiable company. We should become sophisticated, rich and happy, without quarrels, war or poverty, with tremendously powerful intellects that know all the answers, the scientific explanations of how the jellyfish began and how the cosmos operates.

I am not mocking this mentality, not at all, but have we considered the significance of death? The counterpart of life is death. Have we considered that? The very message of death is painful. If you were to ask your fifteen-year-old child to write his will, people would regard that as being completely absurd. No one would do that. We refuse to acknowledge death, but our highest ideals, our speculations on the meaning of life, the highest forms of civilization—all are impractical if we do not consider the process of birth, suffering and death.

From moment to moment, birth, suffering and

death take place. Birth is opening into a new situation. Immediately after birth, there is the sense of refreshment, freshness, like watching the sun rise in the early morning. The birds begin to wake up and sing their songs, the air is fresh, we begin to see the hazy silhouettes of the trees and mountains. As the sun rises, the world becomes clearer and more defined. We watch the sun become redder and redder, finally turning into white light, bright sunshine. One would prefer to hold on to the dawn and sunrise, to keep the sun from rising completely, to hold on to the glowing promise. We would prefer to do this, but we cannot. No one has ever achieved it. We struggle to maintain the new situation, but finally we cannot hold on to anything and we are dead. When we die, there is a gap between the death and the next birth; but still that gap is filled with all kinds of subconscious gossip, questions as to what we should do, and we latch on to a new situation and are born again. We repeat this process again and again and again.

From this point of view, when you give birth to a child, if you really want to cling to life, you should not cut the umbilical cord as he is born. But you must. Birth is an expression of the separateness between mother and child. Either you are going to witness your child's death or the child is going to witness your death. Perhaps this is a very grim way of looking at life, but still it is true. Every move we make is an expression of birth, suffering and death.

There are three categories of suffering or pain in the Buddhist tradition: all-pervading pain, the pain of alternation and the pain of pain. All-pervading pain is the general pain of dissatisfaction, separation and loneliness. We are alone, we are lonely people, we cannot regenerate our umbilical cord, we cannot say of our birth that "it was a rehearsal." It has already happened. So pain is inevitable as long as there is the presence of discontinuity and insecurity.

All-pervading pain is general frustration resulting from aggression. Whether you are polite or blunt, a seemingly happy or unhappy person, is irrelevant. As long as we try to hold on to our existence, we become a bundle of tense muscles protecting ourselves. This creates discomfort. We tend to feel that our existence is slightly inconvenient. Even if we are self-contained and have plenty of money, food, shelter, companionship, still there is this little thing in our being which is in the way. Something is protruding from which we constantly have to shield and hide ourselves. We have to be watchful in case we goof up, but we are uncertain as to what we are going to goof up. There is a sort of universal understanding that there is something we must keep secret, something we should not goof up, something unnameable. It is not logical, but there is still some sort of threat.

So fundamentally, no matter how happy we may be, we are still careful and angry. We do not really want to be exposed, we do not really want to encounter this thing, whatever it is. Of course we could attempt to rationalize this feeling saying, "I didn't get enough sleep last night so I feel funny today and don't want to do difficult work—I might goof up." But such self-justifications are not valid. The concern over goofing up involves being angry as well as hiding. We are angry at the unnameable private parts that we do not want exposed. "If only I could get rid of this thing, then I would be relieved, I would feel free."

This fundamental pain takes innumerable forms —the pain of losing a friend, the pain of having to attack an enemy, the pain of making money, the pain of wanting credentials, the pain of washing dishes, the pain of duty, the pain of feeling that someone is watching over your shoulder, the pain of thinking that we haven't been efficient or successful, the pain of relationships of all kinds.

In addition to all-pervading pain, there is the pain of alternation, which is realizing that you are carrying a burden. Sometimes you begin to feel that the burden has disappeared because you feel free, that you do not have to keep up with yourself anymore. But the sense of alternation between pain and its absence, between sanity and insanity, again and again, is itself painful. Shouldering the burden again is very painful.

And then there is the pain of pain, which is the third type. You are already insecure, feeling uncertain about your territory. On top of that you worry about your condition and develop an ulcer. While rushing to the doctor to treat the ulcer you stub your toe. Resisting pain only increases its intensity. The three types of pain quickly follow one another in life, they pervade life. First you feel fundamental pain, and then the pain of alternation, from pain to its absence and back again; and then you have the pain of pain, the pain of all those life situations you do not want.

You decide to take a vacation in Paris, planning to have a good time, but something goes wrong. Your longtime French friend had an accident. He is in the hospital and his family is very upset, unable to provide you with the hospitality you had expected. Instead you have to stay in a hotel, which you cannot afford, as your money is running out. You decide to change your money on the black market and you get swindled. And your supposed friend, who had an accident and is in the hospital, suddenly starts to dislike you, begins to regard you as a nuisance. You want to return home, but you can't. All flights are cancelled because of bad weather. You are really desperate. Every hour, every second is important to you. You are pacing up and down in the airport and your visa is running out. You have to get out of the country soon. And explaining to the officials is very difficult because you do not speak French.

. . . Such situations occur all the time. We are speeding, trying to get rid of our pain, and we find more pain by doing so. Pain is very real. We cannot pretend that we are all happy and secure. Pain is our constant companion. It goes on and on—all-pervading pain, the pain of alternation and the pain of pain. If we are seeking eternity or happiness or security, then the experience of life is one of pain, *duhkha*, suffering.

. . . The effort to secure our happiness, to maintain ourselves in relation to something else, is the process of ego. But this effort is futile because there are continual gaps in our seemingly solid world, continual cycles of death and rebirth, constant change. The sense of continuity and solidity of self is an illusion. There is really no such thing as ego, soul or *atman*. It is a succession of confusions that create ego. The process which is ego actually consists of a flicker of confusion, a flicker of aggression, a flicker of grasping—all of which exist only in the moment. Since we cannot hold on to the present moment, we cannot hold on to me and mine and make them solid things.

The experience of oneself relating to other things is actually a momentary discrimination, a fleeting thought. If we generate these fleeting thoughts fast enough, we can create the illusion of continuity and solidity. It is like watching a movie, the individual film frames are played so quickly that they generate the illusion of continual movement. So we build up an idea, a preconception, that self and other are solid and continuous. And once we have this idea, we manipulate our thoughts to confirm it, and are afraid of any contrary evidence. It is this fear of exposure, this denial of impermanence that imprisons us. It is only by acknowledging impermanence that there is the chance to die and the space to be reborn and the possibility of appreciating life as a creative process.

There are two stages to understanding egolessness. In the first stage we perceive that ego does not exist as a solid entity, that it is impermanent, constantly changing, that it was our concepts that made it seem solid. So we conclude that ego does not exist. But we still have formulated a subtle concept of egolessness. There is still a watcher of the egolessness, a watcher to identify with it and maintain his existence. The second stage is seeing through this subtle concept and dropping the watcher. So true egolessness is the absence of the concept of egolessness. In the first stage there is a sense of someone perceiving egolessness. In the second, even the perceiver does not exist. In the first, we perceive that there is no fixed entity because everything is relative to something else. In the second stage there is the understanding that the notion of relativity needs a watcher to perceive it, to confirm it, which introduces another relative notion, the watcher and the watched.

To say that egolessness does exist because things are constantly changing is quite feeble, since we still hold on to change as something solid. Egolessness is not simply the idea that, since there is discontinuity, therefore there is nothing to hang on to. True egolessness involves the non-existence of the discontinuity as well. We cannot hang on to the idea of discontinuity either. In fact, discontinuity really does not operate. Our perception of discontinuity is the product of insecurity; it is concept. So too is any idea about the oneness behind or within phenomena.

The idea of egolessness has often been used to obscure the reality of birth, suffering and death. The problem is that, once we have a notion of egolessness and a notion of pain, birth and death, then we can easily entertain or justify ourselves by saying that pain does not exist because there is no ego to experience it, that birth and death do not exist because there is no one to witness them. This is just cheap escapism. The philosophy of *shunyata* has often been distorted by the presentation of the idea that: "There is no one to suffer, so who cares? If you suffer, it must be your illusion." This is pure opinion, speculation. We can read about it, we can think about it, but when we actually suffer, can we remain indifferent? Of course not; suffering is stronger than our petty opinions. A true understanding of egolessness cuts through opinion. The absence of a notion of egolessness allows us to fully experience pain, birth and death because then there are no philosophical paddings.

The whole idea is that we must drop all reference points, all concepts of what is or what should be. Then it is possible to experience the uniqueness and vividness of phenomena directly. There is tremendous room to experience things, to allow experience to occur and pass away. Movement happens within vast space. Whatever happens, pleasure and pain, birth and death and so forth, are not interfered with but are experienced in their fullest flavor. Whether they are sweet or sour, they are experienced completely, without philosophical overlays or emotional attitudes to make things seem lovable or presentable.

We are never trapped in life, because there are constant opportunities for creativity, challenges for improvisation. Ironically, by seeing clearly and acknowledging our egolessness, we may discover that suffering contains bliss, impermanence contains continuity or eternity and egolessness contains the earth quality of solid being. But this transcendental bliss, continuity and beingness is not based on fantasies, ideas or fears.

• • •

. . . In order to cut through the ambition of ego, we must understand how we set up me and my territory, how we use our projections as credentials to prove our existence. The source of the effort to confirm our solidity is an uncertainty as to whether or not we exist. Driven by this uncertainty, we seek to prove our own existence by finding a reference point outside ourselves, something with which to have a relationship, something solid to feel separate from. But the whole enterprise is questionable if we really look back and back and back. Perhaps we have perpetrated a gigantic hoax?

The hoax is the sense of the solidity of I and other. This dualistic fixation comes from nothingness. In the beginning there is open space, zero, self-contained, without relationship. But in order to confirm zeroness, we must create one to prove that zero exists. But even that is not enough; we might get stuck with just one and zero. So we begin to advance, venture out and out. We create two to confirm one's existence, and then we go out again and confirm two by three, three by four and so on. We set up a background, a foundation from which we can go on and on to infinity. This is what is called *samsara*, the continuous vicious cycle of confirmation of existence. One confirmation needs another confirmation needs another. . . .

The attempt to confirm our solidity is very painful. Constantly we find ourselves suddenly slipping off the edge of a floor which had appeared to extend endlessly. Then we must attempt to save ourselves from death by immediately building an extension to the floor in order to make it appear endless again. We think we are safe on our seemingly solid floor, but then we slip off again and have to build another extension. We do not realize that the whole process is unnecessary, that we do not need a floor to stand on, that we have been building all these floors on the ground level. There was never any danger of falling or need for support. In fact, our occupation of extending the floor to secure our ground is a big joke, the biggest joke of all, a cosmic joke. But we may not find it funny: it may sound like a serious double cross.

To understand more precisely the process of confirming the solidity of I and other, that is, the development of ego, it is helpful to be familiar with the five *skandhas*, a set of Buddhist concepts which describe ego as a five-step process.

The first step or skandha, the birth of ego, is called "form" or basic ignorance. We ignore the open, fluid, intelligent quality of space. When a gap or space occurs in our experience of mind, when there is a sudden glimpse of awareness, openness, absence of self, then a suspicion arises: "Suppose I find that there is no solid me? That possibility scares me. I don't want to go into that." That abstract paranoia, the discomfort that something may be wrong, is the source of karmic chain reactions. It is the fear of ultimate confusion and despair. The fear of the absence of self, of the egoless state, is a constant threat to us. "Suppose it is true, what then? I am afraid to look." We want to maintain some solidity but the only material available with which to work is space, the absence of ego, so we try to solidify or freeze that experience of space. Ignorance in this case is not stupidity, but it is a kind of stubbornness. Suddenly we are bewildered by the discovery of selflessness and do not want to accept it; we want to hold on to something.

Then the next step is the attempt to find a way of occupying ourselves, diverting our attention from our aloneness. The karmic chain reaction begins. Karma is dependent upon the relativity of this and that—my existence and my projections—and karma is continually reborn as we continually try to busy ourselves. In other words, there is a fear of not being confirmed by our projections. One must constantly try to prove that one does exist by feeling one's projections as a solid thing. Feeling the solidity of something seemingly outside you reassures you that you are a solid entity as well. This is the second skandha, "feeling."

In the third stage, ego develops three strategies or impulses with which to relate to its projections: in-

difference, passion and aggression. These impulses are guided by perception. Perception, in this case, is the self-conscious feeling that you must officially report back to central headquarters what is happening in any given moment. Then you can manipulate each situation by organizing another strategy.

In the strategy of indifference, we numb any sensitive areas that we want to avoid, that we think might hurt us. We put on a suit of armor. The second strategy is passion—trying to grasp things and eat them up. It is a magnetizing process. Usually we do not grasp if we feel rich enough. But whenever there is a feeling of poverty, hunger, impotence, then we reach out, we extend our tentacles and attempt to hold onto something. Aggression, the third strategy, is also based upon the experience of poverty, the feeling that you cannot survive and therefore must ward off anything that threatens your property or food. Moreover, the more aware you are of the possibilities of being threatened, the more desperate your reaction becomes. You try to run faster and faster in order to find a way of feeding or defending yourself. This speeding about is a form of aggression. Aggression, passion, indifference are part of the third skandha, "perception/impulse."

Ignorance, feeling, impulse and perception—all are instinctive processes. We operate a radar system which senses our territory. Yet we cannot establish ego properly without intellect, without the ability to conceptualize and name. By now we have an enormously rich collection of things going on inside us. Since we have so many things happening, we begin to categorize them, putting them into certain pigeon-holes, naming them. We make it official, so to speak. So "intellect" or "concept" is the next stage of ego, the fourth skandha, but even this is not quite enough. We need a very active and efficient mechanism to keep the instinctive and intellectual processes of ego coordinated. That is the last development of ego, the fifth skandha, "consciousness."

Consciousness consists of emotions and irregular thought patterns, all of which taken together form the different fantasy worlds with which we occupy ourselves. These fantasy worlds are referred to in the scriptures as the "six realms." The emotions are the highlights of ego, the generals of ego's army; subconscious thought, daydreams and other thoughts connect one highlight to another. So thoughts form ego's army and are constantly in motion, constantly busy. Our thoughts are neurotic in the sense that they are irregular, changing direction all the time and overlapping one another. We continually jump from one thought to the next, from spiritual thoughts to sexual fantasies to money matters to domestic thoughts and so on. The whole development of the five skandhas—ignorance/form, feeling, impulse/perception, concept and consciousness—is an attempt on our part to shield ourselves from the truth of our insubstantiality.

The practice of meditation is to see the transparency of this shield. But we cannot immediately start dealing with the basic ignorance itself; that would be like trying to push a wall down all at once. If we want to take this wall down, we must take it down brick by brick; we start with immediately available material, a stepping stone. So the practice of meditation starts with the emotions and thoughts, particularly with the thought process.

• • •

Meditation practice is not a matter of trying to produce a hypnotic state of mind or create a sense of restfulness. Trying to achieve a restful state of mind reflects a mentality of poverty. Seeking a restful state of mind, one is on guard against restlessness. There is a constant sense of paranoia and limitation. We feel a need to be on guard against the sudden fits of passion or aggression which might take us over, make us lose control. This guarding process limits the scope of the mind by not accepting whatever comes.

Instead, meditation should reflect a mentality of richness in the sense of using everything that occurs in the state of mind. Thus, if we provide enough room for restlessness so that it might function within the space, then the energy ceases to be restless because it can trust itself fundamentally. Meditation is giving a huge, luscious meadow to a restless cow. The cow might be restless for a while in its huge meadow, but at some stage, because there is so much space, the restlessness becomes irrelevant. So the cow eats and eats and eats and relaxes and falls asleep.

Acknowledging restlessness, identifying with it, requires mindfulness, whereas providing a luscious meadow, a big space for the restless cow requires awareness. So mindfulness and awareness always complement each other. Mindfulness is the process of relating with individual situations directly, precisely, definitely. You communicate or connect with problematic situations or irritating situations in a simple way. There is ignorance, there is restlessness, there is passion, there is aggression. They need not be praised or condemned. They are just regarded as fits. They are conditioned situations, but they could be seen accurately and precisely by the unconditioned mindfulness. Mindfulness is like a microscope; it is neither an offensive nor a defensive weapon in relation to the germs we observe through it. The function of the microscope is just to clearly present what is there. Mindfulness need not refer to the past or the future; it is fully in the now.

• • •

In the Tibetan tradition the watcher is called *dzinba* (*'dzin pa*), which means "fixation" or "holding." If we give up the watcher, then we have nothing left for which to survive, nothing left for which to continue. We give up hope of holding on to something. That is a very big step toward true asceticism. You have to give up the questioner and the answer—that is, discursive mind, the checking mechanism that tells you whether you are doing well or not doing well. "I am this, I am that." "Am I doing all right, am I meditating correctly, am I studying well, am I getting somewhere?" If we give all this up, then how do we know if we are advancing in spiritual practice? Quite possibly there is no such thing as spiritual practice except stepping out of self-deception, stopping our struggle to get hold of spiritual states. Just give that up. Other than that there is no spirituality. It is a very desolate situation. It is like living among snowcapped peaks with clouds wrapped around them and the sun and moon starkly shining over them. Below, tall alpine trees are swayed by strong, howling winds and beneath them is a thundering waterfall. From our point of view, we may appreciate this desolation if we are an occasional tourist who photographs it or a mountain climber trying to climb to the mountain top. But we do not really want to live in those desolate places. It's no fun. It is terrifying, terrible.

But it is possible to make friends with the desolation and appreciate its beauty. Great sages like Milarepa relate to the desolation as their bride. They marry themselves to desolation, to the fundamental psychological aloneness. They do not need physical or psychological entertainment. Aloneness be-comes their companion, their spiritual consort, part of their being. Wherever they go they are alone, whatever they do they are alone. Whether they re-late socially with friends or meditate alone or per-form ceremonies together or meditate together, aloneness is there all the time. That aloneness is freedom, fundamental freedom.

QUESTION FOR DISCUSSION

1. Discuss Trungpa's claim that a huge "cosmic joke" lies at the bottom of human existence.

DOES LIFE HAVE A MEANING?: CONTEMPORARY WESTERN VIEWS

Some questions are so general in their scope that some philosophers have suggested that—though they have the grammatical form of real questions—they actually have no meaning. The question "Why is there something instead of nothing?" is often cited as such a question. It makes sense as a question, if an answer like "Because God created the world" is accepted as a possible answer; but, if the inquirer says "No, I'm including God in the 'something.' . . . I'm asking the question about *everything*!" knowing what sort of answer could make sense becomes difficult. If meaningful questions should be—in theory at least—answerable, then this question is highly suspect. The closely related question "What is the meaning of it all?" or "What is the meaning of life?" is often also subjected to this scrutiny. Thus, the first order of business in setting out to discover life's meaning appears to be to discover whether the search for it can even be undertaken. In our first selection, the contemporary British analytic philosopher John Wisdom argues that it seems as if it can, though he warns that we cannot expect a simple answer to the question of the form "The meaning of life is. . . ."

Starting from the point of view of the "absurd" that life is essentially meaningless, the French existentialist Albert Camus (1913–1960) asks if it can nonetheless be worth living. Using the image of the torments of Sisyphus from mythology, he argues that it can be. Life is in fact all the better for having no meaning outside itself. Despite the eternally futile tasks the gods have given him, "one must imagine Sisyphus happy." The psychotherapist Carl Rogers approaches the question quite differently, attempting to discover in the psychotherapeutic process what it is that constitutes a meaningful life.

THE MEANINGS OF THE QUESTIONS OF LIFE

John Wisdom

When one asks "What is the meaning of life?" one begins to wonder whether this large, hazy and bewildering question itself has any meaning. Some people indeed have said boldly that the question has no meaning. I believe this is a mistake. But it is a mistake which is not without excuse. And I hope that by examining the excuse we may begin to remedy the mistake, and so come to see that whether or not life has a meaning it is not senseless to enquire whether it has or not. First, then, what has led some people to think that the whole enquiry is senseless?

There is an old story which runs something like this: A child asked an old man "What holds up the world? What holds up all things?" The old man answered "A giant." The child asked "And what holds up the giant? You must tell me what holds up the giant." The old man answered "An elephant." The child said, "And what holds up the elephant?" The old man answered "A tortoise." The child said "You still have not told me what holds up all things. For what holds up the tortoise." The old man answered "Run away and don't ask me so many questions."

From this story we can see how it may happen that a question which looks very like sensible meaningful questions may turn out to be a senseless, meaningless one. Again and again when we ask "What supports this?" it is possible to give a sensible answer. For instance what supports the top-most card in a house of cards? The cards beneath it which are in their turn supported by the cards beneath them. What supports all the cards? The table. What supports the table? The floor and the earth. But the question "What supports all things, absolutely all things?" is different. It is absurd, it is senseless, like the question "What is bigger than the largest thing in the world?" And it is easy to see why the question "What supports all things?" is absurd. Whenever we ask, "What supports thing A or these things A, B, C," then we can answer this question only by mentioning some thing other than the thing A or things A, B, C about which we are asked "What supports it or them." We must if we are to answer the question mention something D other than those things which form the subject of our question, and we must say that this thing is what supports them. If we mean by the phrase "all things" absolutely all things which exist then obviously there is nothing outside that about which we are now asked "What supports all this?" Consequently any answer to the question will be self-contradictory just as any answer to the question "What is bigger than the biggest of all things" must be self-contradictory. Such questions are absurd, or, if you like, silly and senseless.

In a like way again and again when we ask "What is the meaning of this?" we answer in terms of something other than this. For instance imagine that there has been a quarrel in the street. One man is hitting another man on the jaw. A policeman hurries up. "Now then" he says, "what is the meaning of all this?" He wants to know what led up to the quarrel, what caused it. It is no good saying to the policeman "It's a quarrel." He knows there is a quarrel. What he wants to know is what went before the quarrel, what led up to it. To answer him we must mention something other than the quarrel itself. Again suppose a man is driving a motor car and sees in front of him a road sign, perhaps a red flag, perhaps a skull and cross bones. "What does this mean?" he asks and when he asks this he wants to know what the sign points to. To answer we must mention something other than the sign itself, such as a dangerous corner in the road. Imagine a doctor sees an extraordinary rash on the face of his patient. He is astonished and murmurs to himself "What is the meaning of this?" He wants to know what

caused the strange symptoms, or what they will lead to, or both. In any case in order to answer his question he must find something which went before or comes after and lies outside that about which he asks "What does this mean?" This need to look before or after in order to answer a question of the sort "What is the meaning of this?" is so common, so characteristic, a feature of such questions that it is natural to think that when it is impossible to answer such a question in this way then the question has no sense. Now what happens when we ask "What is the meaning of life?"

Perhaps someone here replies, the meaning, the significance of this present life, this life on earth, lies in a life hereafter, a life in heaven. All right. But imagine that some persistent enquirer asks, "But what I am asking is what is the meaning of all life, life here and life beyond, life now and life hereafter? What is the meaning of all things in earth and heaven?" Are we to say that this question is absurd because there cannot be anything beyond all things while at the same time any answer to "What is the meaning of all things?" must point to some thing beyond all things?

Imagine that we come into a theatre after a play has started and are obliged to leave before it ends. We may then be puzzled by the part of the play that we are able to see. We may ask "What does it mean?" In this case we want to know what went before and what came after in order to understand the part we saw. But sometimes even when we have seen and heard a play from the beginning to the end we are still puzzled and still ask what does the whole thing mean. In this case we are not asking what came before or what came after, we are not asking about anything outside the play itself. We are, if you like asking a very different sort of question from that we usually put with the words "What does this mean?" But we are still asking a real question, we are still asking a question which has sense and is not absurd. For our words express a wish to grasp the character, the significance of the whole play. They are a confession that we have not yet done this and they are a request for help in doing it. Is the play a tragedy, a comedy or a tale told by an idiot? The pattern of it is so complex, so bewildering, our grasp of it still so inadequate, that we don't know what to say, still less whether to call it good or bad. But this question is not senseless.

In the same way when we ask "what is the meaning of all things?" we are not asking a senseless question. In this case, of course, we have not witnessed the whole play, we have only an idea in outline of what went before and what will come after that small part of history which we witness. But with the words "What is the meaning of it all?" we are trying to find the order in the drama of Time. The question may be beyond us. A child may be able to understand, to grasp a simple play and be unable to understand and grasp a play more complex and more subtle. We do not say on this account that when he asks of the larger more complex play "What does it mean?" then his question is senseless, nor even that it is senseless for him. He has asked and even answered such a question in simpler cases, he knows the sort of effort, the sort of movement of the mind which such a question calls for, and we do not say that a question is meaningless to him merely because he is not yet able to carry out quite successfully the movement of that sort which is needed in order to answer a complex question of that sort. We do not say that a question in mathematics which is at present rather beyond us is meaningless to us. We know the type of procedure it calls for and may make efforts which bring us nearer and nearer to an answer. We are able to find the meaning which lies not outside but within very complex but still limited wholes whether these are dramas of art or of real life. When we ask "What is the meaning of all things?" we are bewildered and have not that grasp of the order of things the desire for which we express when we ask that question. But this does not render the question senseless nor make it impossible for us to move towards an answer.

We must however remember that what one calls answering such a question is not giving an answer. I mean we cannot answer such a question in the form: "The meaning is this."

Such an idea about what form answering a question must take may lead to a new despair in which we feel we cannot do anything in the way of answering such a question as "What is the meaning in it all?" merely because we are not able to sum up our results in a phrase or formula.

When we ask what is the meaning of this play or this picture we cannot express the understanding which this question may lead to in the form of a list of just those things in the play or the picture which give it its meaning. No. The meaning eludes such a list. This does not mean that words quite fail us. They may yet help us provided that we do not expect of them more than they can do.

A person who is asked what he finds so hateful or so lovable in another may with words help himself and us in grasping what it is that so moves him. But he will only mislead us and himself if he pretends that his words are a complete account of all that there is in the matter.

It is the same when we ask what is it in all things that makes it all so good, so bad, so grand, so contemptible. We must not anticipate that the answer can be given in a word or in a neat list. But this does not mean that we can do nothing towards answering these questions nor even that words will not help us. Indeed surely the historians, the scientists, the prophets, the dramatists and the poets have said much which may help any man who asks himself: Is the drama of time meaningless as a tale told by an idiot? Or is it not meaningless? And if it is not meaningless is it a comedy or a tragedy, a triumph or a disaster, or is it a mixture in which sweet and bitter are for ever mixed?

THE ABSURD AND THE MYTH OF SISYPHUS

Albert Camus

There is but one truly serious philosophical problem, and that is suicide. Judging whether life is or is not worth living amounts to answering the fundamental question of philosophy. All the rest—whether or not the world has three dimensions, whether the mind has nine or twelve categories—comes afterwards. These are games; one must first answer. And if it is true, as Nietzsche claims, that a philosopher, to deserve our respect, must preach by example, you can appreciate the importance of that reply, for it will precede the definitive act. These are facts the heart can feel; yet they call for careful study before they become clear to the intellect.

If I ask myself how to judge that this question is more urgent than that, I reply that one judges by the actions it entails. I have never seen anyone die for the ontological argument. Galileo, who held a scientific truth of great importance, abjured it with the greatest ease as soon as it endangered his life. In a certain sense, he did right.[1] That truth was not worth the stake. Whether the earth or the sun revolves around the other is a matter of profound indifference. To tell the truth, it is a futile question. On the other hand, I see many people die because they judge that life is not worth living. I see others paradoxically getting killed for the ideas or illusions that give them a reason for living (what is called a reason for living is also an excellent reason for dying). I therefore conclude that the meaning of life is the most urgent of questions.

• • •

I don't know whether this world has a meaning that transcends it. But I know that I do not know that meaning and that it is impossible for me just now to know it. What can a meaning outside my condition mean to me? I can understand only in human terms. What I touch, what resists me—that is what I understand. And these two certainties—my appetite for the absolute and for unity and the impossibility of reducing this world to a rational and reasonable principle—I also know that I cannot reconcile them. What other truth can I admit without lying, without bringing in a hope I lack and which means nothing within the limits of my condition?

---

[1] From the point of view of the relative value of truth. On the other hand, from the point of view of virile behavior, this scholar's fragility may well make us smile.

If I were a tree among trees, a cat among animals, this life would have a meaning, or rather this problem would not arise, for I should belong to this world. I should *be* this world to which I am now opposed by my whole consciousness and my whole insistence upon familiarity. This ridiculous reason is what sets me in opposition to all creation. I cannot cross it out with a stroke of the pen. What I believe to be true I must therefore preserve. What seems to me so obvious, even against me, I must support. And what constitutes the basis of that conflict, of that break between the world and my mind, but the awareness of it? If therefore I want to preserve it, I can through a constant awareness, ever revived, ever alert. This is what, for the moment, I must remember. At this moment the absurd, so obvious and yet so hard to win, returns to a man's life and finds its home there. At this moment, too, the mind can leave the arid, dried-up path of lucid effort. That path now emerges in daily life. It encounters the world of the anonymous impersonal pronoun "one," but henceforth man enters in with his revolt and his lucidity. He has forgotten how to hope. This hell of the present is his Kingdom at last. All problems recover their sharp edge. Abstract evidence retreats before the poetry of forms and colors. Spiritual conflicts become embodied and return to the abject and magnificent shelter of man's heart. None of them is settled. But all are transfigured. Is one going to die, escape by the leap, rebuild a mansion of ideas and forms to one's own scale? Is one, on the contrary, going to take up the heart-rending and marvelous wager of the absurd? Let's make a final effort in this regard and draw all our conclusions. The body, affection, creation, action, human nobility will then resume their places in this mad world. At last man will again find there the wine of the absurd and the bread of indifference on which he feeds his greatness.

• • •

Now I can broach the notion of suicide. It has already been felt what solution might be given. At this point the problem is reversed. It was previously a question of finding out whether or not life had to have a meaning to be lived. It now becomes clear, on the contrary, that it will be lived all the better if it has no meaning. Living an experience, a particular fate, is accepting it fully.

• • •

The gods had condemned Sisyphus to ceaselessly rolling a rock to the top of a mountain, whence the stone would fall back of its own weight. They had thought with some reason that there is no more dreadful punishment than futile and hopeless labor.

If one believes Homer, Sisyphus was the wisest and most prudent of mortals. According to another tradition, however, he was disposed to practice the profession of highwayman. I see no contradiction in this. Opinions differ as to the reasons why he became the futile laborer of the underworld. To begin with, he is accused of a certain levity in regard to the gods. He stole their secrets. Ægina, the daughter of Æsopus, was carried off by Jupiter. The father was shocked by that disappearance and complained to Sisyphus. He, who knew of the abduction, offered to tell about it on condition that Æsopus would give water to the citadel of Corinth. To the celestial thunderbolts he preferred the benediction of water. He was punished for this in the underworld. Homer tells us also that Sisyphus had put Death in chains. Pluto could not endure the sight of his deserted, silent empire. He dispatched the god of war, who liberated Death from the hands of her conqueror.

It is said also that Sisyphus, being near to death, rashly wanted to test his wife's love. He ordered her to cast his unburied body into the middle of the public square. Sisyphus woke up in the underworld. And there, annoyed by an obedience so contrary to human love, he obtained from Pluto permission to return to earth in order to chastise his wife. But when he had seen again the face of this world, enjoyed water and sun, warm stones and the sea, he no longer wanted to go back to the infernal darkness. Recalls, signs of anger, warnings were of no avail. Many years more he lived facing the curve of the gulf, the sparkling sea, and the smiles of earth. A decree of the gods was necessary. Mercury came and seized the impudent man by the col-

lar and, snatching him from his joys, led him forcibly back to the underworld, where his rock was ready for him.

You have already grasped that Sisyphus is the absurd hero. He *is*, as much through his passions as though his torture. His scorn of the gods, his hatred of death, and his passion for life won him that unspeakable penalty in which the whole being is exerted toward accomplishing nothing. This is the price that must be paid for the passions of this earth. Nothing is told us about Sisyphus in the underworld. Myths are made for the imagination to breathe life into them. As for this myth, one sees merely the whole effort of a body straining to raise the huge stone, to roll it and push it up a slope a hundred times over; one sees the face screwed up, the cheek tight against the stone, the shoulder bracing the clay-covered mass, the foot wedging it, the fresh start with arms outstretched, the wholly human security of two earth-clotted hands. At the very end of his long effort measured by skyless space and time without depth, the purpose is achieved. Then Sisyphus watches the stone rush down in a few moments toward that lower world whence he will have to push it up again toward the summit. He goes back down to the plain.

It is during that return, that pause, that Sisyphus interests me. A face that toils so close to stones is already stone itself! I see that man going back down with a heavy yet measured step toward the torment of which he will never know the end. That hour like a breathing-space which returns as surely as his suffering, that is the hour of consciousness. At each of those moments when he leaves the heights and gradually sinks toward the lairs of the gods, he is superior to his fate. He is stronger than his rock.

If this myth is tragic, that is because its hero is conscious. Where would his torture be, indeed, if at every step the hope of succeeding upheld him? The workman of today works every day in his life at the same tasks, and this fate is no less absurd. But it is tragic only at the rare moments when it becomes conscious. Sisyphus, proletarian of the gods, powerless and rebellious, knows the whole extent of his wretched condition: it is what he thinks of during his descent. The lucidity that was to constitute his torture at the same time crowns his victory. There is no fate that cannot be surmounted by scorn.

• • •

If the descent is thus sometimes performed in sorrow, it can also take place in joy. This word is not too much. Again I fancy Sisyphus returning toward his rock, and the sorrow was in the beginning. When the images of earth cling too tightly to memory, when the call of happiness becomes too insistent, it happens that melancholy rises in man's heart: this is the rock's victory, this is the rock itself. The boundless grief is too heavy to bear. These are our nights of Gethsemane.* But crushing truths perish from being acknowledged. Thus, Œdipus at the outset obeys fate without knowing it. But from the moment he knows, his tragedy begins. Yet at the same moment, blind and desperate, he realizes that the only bond linking him to the world is the cool hand of a girl. Then a tremendous remark rings out: "Despite so many ordeals, my advanced age and the nobility of my soul make me conclude that all is well." Sophocles' Œdipus, like Dostoevsky's Kirilov, thus gives the recipe for the absurd victory. Ancient wisdom confirms modern heroism.

One does not discover the absurd without being tempted to write a manual of happiness. "What! by such narrow ways—?" There is but one world, however. Happiness and the absurd are two sons of the same earth. They are inseparable. It would be a mistake to say that happiness necessarily springs from the absurd discovery. It happens as well that the feeling of the absurd springs from happiness. "I conclude that all is well," says Œdipus, and that remark is sacred. It echoes in the wild and limited universe of man. It teaches that all is not, has not been, exhausted. It drives out of this world a god who had come into it with dissatisfaction and a preference for futile sufferings. It makes of fate a human matter, which must be settled among men.

All Sisyphus' silent joy is contained therein. His fate belongs to him. His rock is his thing. Likewise, the absurd man, when he contemplates his torment, silences all the idols. In the universe suddenly restored to its silence, the myriad wondering little voices of the earth rise up. Unconscious, secret calls, invitations from all the faces, they are the necessary reverse and price of victory. There is no sun without shadow, and it is essential to know the night. The absurd man says yes and his effort will henceforth be unceasing. If there is a personal fate, there is no higher destiny, or at least there is but one which he concludes is inevitable and despicable. For the rest, he knows himself to be the master of his days. At that subtle moment when man glances backward over his life, Sisyphus returning toward his rock, in that slight pivoting he contemplates that series of unrelated actions which becomes his fate, created by him, combined under his memory's eye and soon sealed by his death. Thus, convinced of the wholly human origin of all that is human, a blind man eager to see who knows that the night has no end, he is still on the go. The rock is still rolling.

I leave Sisyphus at the foot of the mountain! One always finds one's burden again. But Sisyphus teaches the higher fidelity that negates the gods and raises rocks. He too concludes that all is well. This universe henceforth without a master seems to him neither sterile nor futile. Each atom of that stone, each mineral flake of that night-filled mountain, in itself forms a world. The struggle itself toward the heights is enough to fill a man's heart. One must imagine Sisyphus happy.

TO BE THE SELF WHICH ONE TRULY IS

Carl Rogers

The Questions

"What is my goal in life?" "What am I striving for?" "What is my purpose?" These are questions which every individual asks himself at one time or another, sometimes calmly and meditatively, some-

---

* *Gethsemane* is the garden where Jesus prayed the night of his arrest and before he was crucified.

times in agonizing uncertainty or despair. They are old, old questions which have been asked and answered in every century of history. Yet they are also questions which every individual must ask and answer for himself, in his own way. They are questions which I, as a counselor, hear expressed in many differing ways as men and women in personal distress try to learn, or understand, or choose, the directions which their lives are taking.

In one sense there is nothing new which can be said about these questions. Indeed the opening phrase in the title I have chosen for this paper is taken from the writings of a man who wrestled with these questions more than a century ago. Simply to express another personal opinion about this whole issue of goals and purposes would seem presumptuous. But as I have worked for many years with troubled and maladjusted individuals I believe that I can discern a pattern, a trend, a commonality, an orderliness, in the tentative answers to these questions which they have found for themselves. And so I would like to share with you my perception of what human beings appear to be striving for, when they are free to choose.

Some Answers

Before trying to take you into this world of my own experience with my clients, I would like to remind you that the questions I have mentioned are not pseudo-questions, nor have men in the past or at the present time agreed on the answers. When men in the past have asked themselves the purpose of life, some have answered, in the words of the catechism, that "the chief end of man is to glorify God." Others have thought of life's purpose as being the preparation of oneself for immortality. Others have settled on a much more earthy goal—to enjoy and release and satisfy every sensual desire. Still others—and this applies to many today—regard the purpose of life as being to achieve—to gain material possessions, status, knowledge, power. Some have made it their goal to give themselves completely and devotedly to a cause outside of themselves such as Christianity, or Communism. A Hitler has seen his goal as that of becoming the

leader of a master race which would exercise power over all. In sharp contrast, many an Oriental has striven to eliminate all personal desires, to exercise the utmost of control over himself. I mention these widely ranging choices to indicate some of the very different aims men have lived for, to suggest that there are indeed many goals possible.

In a recent important study Charles Morris investigated objectively the pathways of life which were preferred by students in six different countries—India, China, Japan, the United States, Canada, and Norway (5). As one might expect, he found decided differences in goals between these national groups. He also endeavored, through a factor analysis of his data, to determine the underlying dimensions of value which seemed to operate in the thousands of specific individual preferences. Without going into the details of his analysis, we might look at the five dimensions which emerged, and which, combined in various positive and negative ways, appeared to be responsible for the individual choices.

The first such value dimension involves a preference for a responsible, moral, self-restrained participation in life, appreciating and conserving what man has attained.

The second places stress upon delight in vigorous action for the overcoming of obstacles. It involves a confident initiation of change, either in resolving personal and social problems, or in overcoming obstacles in the natural world.

The third dimension stresses the value of a self-sufficient inner life with a rich and heightened self-awareness. Control over persons and things is rejected in favor of a deep and sympathetic insight into self and others.

The fourth underlying dimension values a receptivity to persons and to nature. Inspiration is seen as coming from a source outside the self, and the person lives and develops in devoted responsiveness to this source.

The fifth and final dimension stresses sensuous enjoyment, self-enjoyment. The simple pleasures of life, an abandonment to the moment, a relaxed openness to life, are valued.

This is a significant study, one of the first to measure objectively the answers given in different cultures to the question, what is the purpose of my life? It has added to our knowledge of the answers given. It has also helped to define some of the basic dimensions in terms of which the choice is made. As Morris says, speaking of these dimensions, "it is as if persons in various cultures have in common five major tones in the musical scales on which they compose different melodies." (5, p. 185)

Another View

I find myself, however, vaguely dissatisfied with this study. None of the "Ways to Live" which Morris put before the students as possible choices, and none of the factor dimensions, seems to contain satisfactorily the goal of life which emerges in my experience with my clients. As I watch person after person struggle in his therapy hours to find a way of life for himself, there seems to be a general pattern emerging, which is not quite captured by any of Morris' descriptions.

The best way I can state this aim of life, as I see it coming to light in my relationship with my clients, is to use the words of Søren Kierkegaard— "to be that self which one truly is." (3, p. 29) I am quite aware that this may sound so simple as to be absurd. To be what one is seems like a statement of obvious fact rather than a goal. What does it mean? What does it imply? I want to devote the remainder of my remarks to those issues. I will simply say at the outset that it seems to mean and imply some strange things. Out of my experience with my clients, and out of my own self-searching, I find myself arriving at views which would have been very foreign to me ten or fifteen years ago. So I trust you will look at these views with critical scepticism, and accept them only in so far as they ring true in your own experience.

DIRECTIONS TAKEN BY CLIENTS

Let me see if I can draw out and clarify some of the trends and tendencies which I see as I work with clients. In my relationship with these individuals my aim has been to provide a climate which con-

tains as much of safety, of warmth, of empathic understanding, as I can genuinely find in myself to give. I have not found it satisfying or helpful to intervene in the client's experience with diagnostic or interpretative explanations, nor with suggestions and guidance. Hence the trends which I see appear to me to come from the client himself, rather than emanating from me.

Away from Façades

I observe first that characteristically the client shows a tendency to move away, hesitantly and fearfully, from a self that he is *not*. In other words even though there may be no recognition of what he might be moving toward, he is moving away from something. And of course in so doing he is beginning to define, however negatively, what he *is*.

At first this may be expressed simply as a fear of exposing what he is. Thus one eighteen-year-old boy says, in an early interview: "I know I'm not so hot, and I'm afraid they'll find it out. That's why I do these things. . . . They're going to find out some day that I'm not so hot. I'm just trying to put that day off as long as possible. . . . If you know me as I know myself—. (*Pause*) I'm not going to tell you the person I really think I am. There's only one place I won't cooperate and that's it. . . . It wouldn't help your opinion of me to know what I think of myself."

It will be clear that the very expression of this fear is a part of becoming what he is. Instead of simply *being* a façade, as if it were himself, he is coming closer to being *himself*, namely a frightened person hiding behind a façade because he regards himself as too awful to be seen.

Away from "Oughts"

Another tendency of this sort seems evident in the client's moving away from the compelling image of what he "ought to be." Some individuals have absorbed so deeply from their parents the concept "I ought to be good," or "I have to be good," that it is only with the greatest of inward struggle that they find themselves moving away from this goal. Thus one young woman, describing her unsatisfactory relationship with her father, tells first how much she wanted his love. "I think in all this feeling I've had about my father, that *really* I *did* very much want a good relationship with him. . . . I wanted so much to have him care for me, and yet didn't seem to get what I really wanted." She always felt she had to meet all of his demands and expectations and it was "just too much. Because once I meet one there's another and another and another, and I never really meet them. It's sort of an endless demand." She feels she has been like her mother, submissive and compliant, trying continually to meet his demands. "And really *not* wanting to be that kind of person. I find it's not a good way to be, but yet I think I've had a sort of belief that that's the way you *have* to be if you intend to be thought a lot of and loved. And yet who would *want* to love somebody who was that sort of wishy washy person?" The counselor responded, "Who really would love a door mat?" She went on, "At least I wouldn't want to be loved by the kind of person who'd love a door mat!"

Thus, though these words convey nothing of the self she might be moving toward, the weariness and disdain in both her voice and her statement make it clear that she is moving away from a self which *has* to be good, which *has* to be submissive.

Curiously enough a number of individuals find that they have felt compelled to regard themselves as bad, and it is this concept of themselves that they find they are moving away from. One young man shows very clearly such a movement. He says: "I don't know how I got this impression that being ashamed of myself was such an *appropriate* way to feel. . . . Being ashamed of me was the way I just *had* to be. . . . There was a world where being ashamed of myself was the best way to feel. . . . If you are something which is disapproved of very much, then I guess the only way you can have any kind of self-respect is to be ashamed of that part of you which isn't approved of. . . .

"But now I'm adamantly refusing to do things from the old viewpoint. . . . It's as if I'm convinced that someone said, 'The way you will *have* to be is to be *ashamed* of yourself—so *be* that way!' And I accepted it for a long, long time, saying 'OK, that's

me!' And now I'm standing up against that somebody, saying, 'I don't care *what* you say. I'm *not* going to feel ashamed of myself!' " Obviously he is abandoning the concept of himself as shameful and bad.

Away from Meeting Expectations

Other clients find themselves moving away from what the culture expects them to be. In our current industrial culture, for example, as Whyte has forcefully pointed out in his recent book (7), there are enormous pressures to become the characteristics which are expected of the "organization man." Thus one should be fully a member of the group, should subordinate his individuality to fit into the group needs, should become "the well-rounded man who can handle well-rounded men."

In a newly completed study of student values in this country Jacob summarizes his findings by saying, "The main overall effect of higher education upon student values is to bring about general acceptance of a body of standards and attitudes characteristic of collegebred men and women in the American community. . . . The impact of the college experience is . . . to *socialize* the individual, to refine, polish, or 'shape up' his values so that he can fit comfortably into the ranks of American college alumni." (1, p. 6)

Over against these pressures for conformity, I find that when clients are free to be any way they wish, they tend to resent and to question the tendency of the organization, the college or the culture to mould them to any given form. One of my clients says with considerable heat: "I've been so long trying to live according to what was meaningful to other people, and what made no sense at *all* to me, really. I somehow felt so much *more* than that, at some level." So he, like others, tends to move away from being what is expected.

Away from Pleasing Others

I find that many individuals have formed themselves by trying to please others, but again, when they are free, they move away from being this person. So one professional man, looking back at some of the process he has been through, writes, toward the end of therapy: "I finally felt that I simply *had* to begin doing what *I wanted* to do, not what I thought I *should* do, and regardless of what other people feel I *should* do. This is a complete reversal of my whole life. I've always felt I *had* to do things because they were expected of me, or more important, to make people like me. The hell with it! I think from now on I'm going to just be me—rich or poor, good or bad, rational or irrational, logical or illogical, famous or infamous. So thanks for your part in helping me to rediscover Shakespeare's— 'To thine own *self* be true.' "

So one may say that in a somewhat negative way, clients define their goal, their purpose, by discovering, in the freedom and safety of an understanding relationship, some of the directions they do *not* wish to move. They prefer not to hide themselves and their feelings from themselves, or even from some significant others. They do not wish to be what they "ought" to be, whether that imperative is set by parents, or by the culture, whether it is defined positively or negatively. They do not wish to mould themselves and their behavior into a form which would be merely pleasing to others. They do not, in other words, choose to be anything which is artificial, anything which is imposed, anything which is defined from without. They realize that they do not value such purposes or goals, even though they may have lived by them all their lives up to this point.

Toward Self-Direction

But what is involved positively in the experience of these clients? I shall try to describe a number of the facets I see in the directions in which they move.

First of all, the client moves toward being autonomous. By this I mean that gradually he chooses the goals toward which *he* wants to move. He becomes responsible for himself. He decides what activities and ways of behaving have meaning for him, and what do not. I think this tendency toward self-direction is amply illustrated in the examples I have given.

I would not want to give the impression that my clients move blithely or confidently in this direction. No indeed. Freedom to be oneself is a frighteningly responsible freedom, and an individual moves toward it cautiously, fearfully, and with almost no confidence at first.

Nor would I want to give the impression that he always makes sound choices. To be responsibly self-directing means that one chooses—and then learns from the consequences. So clients find this a sobering but exciting kind of experience. As one client says—"I feel frightened, and vulnerable, and cut loose from support, but I also feel a sort of surging up or force or strength in me." This is a common kind of reaction as the client takes over the self-direction of his own life and behavior.

Toward Being Process

The second observation is difficult to make, because we do not have good words for it. Clients seem to move toward more openly being a process, a fluidity, a changing. They are not disturbed to find that they are not the same from day to day, that they do not always hold the same feelings toward a given experience or person, that they are not always consistent. They are in flux, and seem more content to continue in this flowing current. The striving for conclusions and end states seems to diminish.

One client says, "Things are sure changing, boy, when I can't even predict my own behavior in here anymore. It was something I was able to do before. Now I don't know what I'll say next. Man, it's quite a feeling. . . . I'm just surprised I even said these things. . . . I see something new every time. It's an adventure, that's what it is—into the unknown. . . . I'm beginning to enjoy this now, I'm joyful about it, even about all these old negative things." He is beginning to appreciate himself as a fluid process, at first in the therapy hour, but later he will find this true in his life. I cannot help but be reminded of Kierkegaard's description of the individual who really exists. "An existing individual is constantly in process of becoming, . . . and translates all his thinking into terms of process. It is with (him) . . . as it is with a writer and his style; for he only has a style who never has anything finished, but 'moves the waters of the language' every time he begins, so that the most common expression comes into being for him with the freshness of a new birth." (2, p. 79) I find this catches excellently the direction in which clients move, toward being a process of potentialities being born, rather than being or becoming some fixed goal.

Toward Being Complexity

It also involves being a complexity of process. Perhaps an illustration will help here. One of our counselors, who has himself been much helped by psychotherapy, recently came to me to discuss his relationship with a very difficult and disturbed client. It interested me that he did not wish to discuss the client, except in the briefest terms. Mostly he wanted to be sure that he was clearly aware of the complexity of his own feelings in the relationship—his warm feelings toward the client, his occasional frustration and annoyance, his sympathetic regard for the client's welfare, a degree of fear that the client might become psychotic, his concern as to what others would think if the case did not turn out well. I realized that his overall attitude was that if he could *be*, quite openly and transparently, all of his complex and changing and sometimes contradictory feelings in the relationship, all would go well. If, however, he was only part of his feelings, and partly façade or defense, he was sure the relationship would not be good. I find that this desire to be *all* of oneself in each moment—all the richness and complexity, with nothing hidden from oneself, and nothing feared in oneself—this is a common desire in those who have seemed to show much movement in therapy. I do not need to say that this is a difficult, and in its absolute sense an impossible goal. Yet one of the most evident trends in clients is to move toward becoming all of the complexity of one's changing self in each significant moment.

Toward Openness to Experience

"To be that self which one truly is" involves still other components. One which has perhaps been im-

plied already is that the individual moves toward living in an open, friendly, close relationship to his own experience. This does not occur easily. Often as the client senses some new facet of himself, he initially rejects it. Only as he experiences such a hitherto denied aspect of himself in an acceptant climate can he tentatively accept it as a part of himself. As one client says with some shock after experiencing the dependent, small boy aspect of himself, "That's an emotion I've never felt clearly—one that I've never been!" He cannot tolerate the experience of his childish feelings. But gradually he comes to accept and embrace them as a part of himself, to live close to them land in them when they occur.

Another young man, with a very serious stuttering problem, lets himself be open to some of his buried feelings toward the end of his therapy. He says, "Boy, it was a terrible fight. I never realized it. I guess it was too painful to reach that height. I mean I'm just beginning to feel it now. Oh, the *terrible* pain. . . . It was *terrible* to talk. I mean I wanted to talk and then I didn't want to. . . . I'm feeling—I think I know—it's just plain strain—terrible strain—*stress*, that's the word, just so much *stress* I've been feeling. I'm just beginning to *feel* it now after all these years of it. . . . it's terrible. I can hardly get my breath now too, I'm just all choked up inside, all *tight* inside. . . I just feel like I'm *crushed*. (*He begins to cry.*) I never realized that, I never knew that." (6) Here he is opening himself to internal feelings which are clearly not new to him, but which up to this time, he has never been able fully to experience. Now that he can permit himself to experience them, he will find them less terrible, and he will be able to live closer to his own experiencing.

Gradually clients learn that experiencing is a friendly resource, not a frightening enemy. Thus I think of one client who, toward the close of therapy, when puzzled about an issue, would put his head in his hands and say, "Now what *is* it I'm feeling? I want to get next to it. I want to learn what it is." Then he would wait, quietly and patiently, until he could discern the exact flavor of the feelings occurring in him. Often I sense that the client is trying to listen to himself, is trying to hear the messages and meanings which are being communicated by his own physiological reactions. No longer is he so fearful of what he may find. He comes to realize that his own inner reactions and experiences, the messages of his senses and his viscera, are friendly. He comes to want to be close to his inner sources of information rather than closing them off.

Maslow, in his study of what he calls self-actualizing people, has noted this same characteristic. Speaking of these people, he says, "Their ease of penetration to reality, their closer approach to an animal-like or child-like acceptance and spontaneity imply a superior awareness of their own impulses, their own desires, opinions, and subjective reactions in general." (4, p. 210)

This greater openness to what goes on within is associated with a similar openness to experiences of external reality. Maslow might be speaking of clients I have known when he says, "self-actualized people have a wonderful capacity to appreciate again and again, freshly and naively, the basic goods of life with awe, pleasure, wonder, and even ecstasy, however stale these experiences may be for other people." (4, p. 214)

Toward Acceptance of Others

Closely related to this openness to inner and outer experience in general is an openness to and an acceptance of other individuals. As a client moves toward being able to accept his own experience, he also moves toward the acceptance of the experience of others. He values and appreciates both his own experience and that of others for what it *is*. To quote Maslow again regarding his self-actualizing individuals: "One does not complain about water because it is wet, nor about rocks because they are hard. . . . As the child looks out upon the world with wide, uncritical and innocent eyes, simply noting and observing what is the case, without either arguing the matter or demanding that it be otherwise, so does the self-actualizing person look upon human nature both in himself and in others." (4, p. 207) This acceptant attitude toward that which exists, I find developing in clients in therapy.

Toward Trust of Self

Still another way of describing this pattern which I see in each client is to say that increasingly he trusts and values the process which is himself. Watching my clients, I have come to a much better understanding of creative people. El Greco, for example, must have realized as he looked at some of his early work, that "good artists do not paint like that." But somehow he trusted his own experiencing of life, the process of himself, sufficiently that he could go on expressing his own unique perceptions. It was as though he could say, "Good artists do not paint like this, but *I* paint like this." Or to move to another field, Ernest Hemingway was surely aware that "good writers do not write like this." But fortunately he moved toward being Hemingway, being himself, rather than toward some one else's conception of a good writer. Einstein seems to have been unusually oblivious to the fact that good physicists did not think his kind of thoughts. Rather than drawing back because of his inadequate academic preparation in physics, he simply moved toward being Einstein, toward thinking his own thoughts, toward being as truly and deeply himself as he could. This is not a phenomenon which occurs only in the artist or the genius. Time and again in my clients, I have seen simple people become significant and creative in their own spheres, as they have developed more trust of the processes going on within themselves, and have dared to feel their own feelings, live by values which they discover within, and express themselves in their own unique ways.

The General Direction

Let me see if I can state more concisely what is involved in this pattern of movement which I see in clients, the elements of which I have been trying to describe. It seems to mean that the individual moves toward *being*, knowingly and acceptingly, the process which he inwardly and actually *is*. He moves away from being what he is not, from being a façade. He is not trying to be more than he is, with the attendant feelings of insecurity or bombastic defensiveness. He is not trying to be less than he is, with the attendant feelings of guilt or self-deprecation. He is increasingly listening to the deepest recesses of his physiological and emotional being, and finds himself increasingly willing to be, with greater accuracy and depth, that self which he most truly is. One client, as he begins to sense the direction he is taking, asks himself wonderingly and with incredulity in one interview, "You mean if I'd really be what I feel like being, that that would be all right?" His own further experience, and that of many another client, tends toward an affirmative answer. To be what he truly is, this is the path of life which he appears to value most highly, when he is free to move in any direction. It is not simply an intellectual value choice, but seems to be the best description of the groping, tentative, uncertain behaviors by which he moves exploringly toward what he wants to be.

REFERENCES

1. Jacob, P. E. *Changing Values in College*. New Haven: Hazen Foundation, 1956.
2. Kierkegaard, S. *Concluding Unscientific Postscript*. Princeton University Press, 1941.
3. Kierkegaard, S. *The Sickness Unto Death*. Princeton University Press, 1941.
4. Maslow, A. H. *Motivation and Personality*. Harper and Bros., 1954.
5. Morris, C. W. *Varieties of Human Value*. University of Chicago Press, 1956.
6. Seeman, Julius. *The Case of Jim*. Nashville, Tennessee: Educational Testing Bureau, 1957.
7. Whyte, W. H., Jr. *The Organization Man*. Simon & Schuster, 1956.

QUESTIONS FOR DISCUSSION

1. Although he begins by asking a question about the question "What is the meaning of life?" rather than simply asking for life's meaning, by the end of his essay, John Wisdom seems to have made some progress in dealing with both questions. Compare his viewpoint with that of Albert Camus. Compare it with Carl Rogers'. (*Suggestion:* You might do this by inventing an imaginary conversation between them all in which they discuss the question of life's meaning.)

2. Carl Rogers cites a study which claims that in America "the impact of the college experience is . . . to socialize the individual, to . . . 'shape up' his values so that he can fit into the ranks" of educated Americans. From your own experience of college education, do you feel that this is true? If you are reading this book in the context of taking a college course, is it true of the course? Is it true of this book? What is Carl Rogers's reaction to the study cited? Do you feel his reaction is justified? Why or why not?

FACING DEATH

Plato quotes Socrates as saying, as he waited in prison for his execution, that a philosopher's whole life's goal is to prepare for death. Martin Heidegger, a German existentialist philosopher of this century, suggested that it wasn't possible to lead an authentic life until one took stock of one's human finitude, for only the sense of dread that this produces can lift us out of scurrying self-forgetfulness.

Miguel de Unamuno is not at all happy with the prospect of death and is certainly expressing the dread to which Heidegger referred. He claims to speak for others as well when he describes his ardent desire to live forever. Unamuno was born in the Basque region of Spain in 1864. The passion and drama of Unamuno's life is reflected in his works. Because of his outspoken political criticisms over the years, he was at various times deported, placed under house arrest, and dismissed from his rectorship at the University of Salamanca. His struggles parallel those of Don Quixote, a hero in one of Unamuno's books, infamous for taking on even the most impossible of battles, caring not for whether he is ridiculed. One could say that that describes the same vigor and dedication with which Unamuno takes on his enemy, death.

Unamuno is determined to resist death, if not physically, at least in his mind. He first describes how ardently humanity longs for immortality. Since this intense desire exists, either it can be filled (as faith claims), or it can be thwarted (as reason suggests). But for our internal desire to be so thwarted would make life tragic. In fact, some come to the conclusion that if we can't live forever, then what's the use of living for this short while—and they decide to commit suicide. Unamuno insists that one must look death in the eye, and not turn away. Only this experience of confronting death, and the ensuing anguish, can make life real, can make every moment important. Unamuno's final advice is to follow the heart, the heart that wants immortality, and with Pascal to choose to believe.

Our next author, Gregory Baum of McGill University in Montreal, Canada, is familiar with the view that Unamuno describes, but sees it in its social context. The desire of the individual to live forever is a product of our times, with its emphasis on the individual ego. In earlier times, the community was more important; the early Christian church had a much different understanding of life after death than its contemporary position.

Gregory Baum's course of studies is a fascinating one. Born a Jew in Berlin, Baum fled in 1939 at age 16, taking refuge first in England, and then Canada, which became his permanent home. He converted to Christianity in 1946 and became well-known as a theologian. Later pursuing studies in sociology at the New School for Social Research, he combined the two fields and began to produce works such as *Religion and Alienation*, of which our passage is an excerpt.

Baum argues that death, like any other aspect of life, must be understood in its social context, for society gives the act meaning and to a large extent shapes the individual's reaction to death. In contrast to views of heaven meant to placate the suffering, toiling masses, the Bible accounts speak of a coming kingdom of God to happen in this world in the near future. Baum suggests that attitudes toward death are socially grounded, and, depending on the society's imagination of the future, death will be either feared or accepted. Death is only a dreaded enemy for those who love the self, an attitude encouraged by our contemporary individualistic society. However, if Christians are able to have as their longing a just society for others, focus can be taken off the self, and death loses its fearfulness.

Our final author in this first section, Etty Hillesum, is perhaps an example of what Baum describes as fearlessness in the face of death born of caring for others. Hillesum was a Dutch Jew, born in 1914 in Middleburg, Netherlands. The selections are excerpts from her diary and letters, entitled *An Interrupted Life*, that was published after her death at Auschwitz concentration camp in 1943. Her diary, which begins in 1941, gives a detailed description of the slowly dawning realization, experienced by so many Jews in Nazi-occupied countries, that they are methodically being exterminated as a people. What is first experienced as restriction and discrimination finally results in annihilation.

Holland had capitulated to the Nazis in May 1940, and the Germans were working at isolating the Jews, throwing them out of jobs, forcing them to wear the star of David, and finally deporting them to work camps.

Hillesum's diaries and letters give a close account not only of her own states of mind but also of those of the people around her. Not a philosopher by profession, Hillesum's reflections yet show evidence of a philosophy formed and lived in the crucible of trying times.

Because Hillesum saw physical death as inevitable, she sought not to flee it but to accept it. Since she was convinced of the spirituality of the self, she interpreted death as no loss, as long as one could face it with calm happiness and in selfless service. Hillesum preferred this attitude of quiet bravery to attempts at saving oneself, which she saw as selling one's integrity, snatching at a few brief moments of worldly life while losing the spiritual significance of the moment, and exhibiting a lack of solidarity with the suffering of others.

Though some have criticized such attitudes toward the holocaust, Hillesum's account remains insightful and moving as an account of one young woman's coming to terms with the finitude of her own life and the moral collapse of the society around her.

The selections contained here begin with entries during March 1942. By that summer, she had a job with the Jewish Council. Working in these offices briefly, Hillesum decided by August that what she really wanted to do was to accompany Jews sent to Westerbork work camp and minister to their needs within the camp. Westerbork was a temporary community, uprooted weekly by transport trains which were packed with prisoners bound for Auschwitz. Eventually her whole family, and even Hillesum herself, were packed onto the Poland-bound trains. The last correspondence of Hillesum's was a postcard thrown off from the moving train on which she was sent to her death in Auschwitz in Autumn 1943. In the postcard, she asserted that she and others left the camp singing; these brave last words attest to her consistency in her attitude even to her end.

THE TRAGIC VIEW OF LIFE

Miguel de Unamuno

Let us pause to consider this immortal yearning for immortality—even though the gnostics or intellectuals may be able to say that what follows is not philosophy but rhetoric. Moreover, the divine Plato, when he discussed the immortality of the soul in his *Phædo,* said that it was proper to clothe it in legend. . . .

First of all let us recall once again—and it will not be for the last time—that saying of Spinoza that every being endeavours to persist in itself, and that this endeavour is its actual essence, and implies indefinite time, and that the soul, in fine, sometimes with a clear and distinct idea, sometimes confusedly, tends to persist in its being with indefinite duration, and is aware of its persistency [*Ethic*, Part III., Props. VI.-X.].

It is impossible for us, in effect, to conceive of ourselves as not existing, and no effort is capable of enabling consciousness to realize absolute unconsciousness, its own annihilation. Try, reader, to imagine to yourself, when you are wide awake, the condition of your soul when you are in a deep sleep; try to fill your consciousness with the representation of no-consciousness, and you will see the impossibility of it. The effort to comprehend it causes the most tormenting dizziness. We cannot conceive ourselves as not existing.

The visible universe, the universe that is created by the instinct of self-preservation, becomes all too narrow for me. It is like a cramped cell, against the bars of which my soul beats its wings in vain. Its lack of air stifles me. More, more, and always more! I want to be myself, and yet without ceasing to be myself to be others as well, to merge myself into the totality of things visible and invisible, to extend myself into the illimitable of space and to prolong myself into the infinite of time. Not to be all and for ever is as if not to be—at least, let me be my whole self, and be so for ever and ever. And to be the whole of myself is to be everybody else. Either all or nothing!

All or nothing! And what other meaning can the Shakespearean "To be or not to be" have, or that passage in *Coriolanus* where it is said of Marcius "He wants nothing of a god but eternity"? Eternity, eternity!—that is the supreme desire! The thirst of eternity is what is called love among men, and whosoever loves another wishes to eternalize himself in him. Nothing is real that is not eternal.

From the poets of all ages and from the depths of their souls this tremendous vision of the flowing away of life like water has wrung bitter cries—from Pindar's "dream of a shadow," . . . to Calderón's "life is a dream" and Shakespeare's "we are such stuff as dreams are made on," this last a yet more tragic sentence than Calderón's, for whereas the Castilian only declares that our life is a dream, but not that we ourselves are the dreamers of it, the Englishman makes us ourselves a dream, a dream that dreams.

The vanity of the passing world and love are the two fundamental and heart-penetrating notes of true poetry. And they are two notes of which neither can be sounded without causing the other to vibrate. The feeling of the vanity of the passing world kindles love in us, the only thing that triumphs over the vain and transitory, the only thing that fills life again and eternalizes it. In appearance at any rate, for in reality . . . And love, above all when it struggles against destiny, overwhelms us with the feeling of the vanity of this world of appearances and gives us a glimpse of another world, in which destiny is overcome and liberty is law.

Everything passes! Such is the refrain of those who have drunk, lips to the spring, of the fountain of life, of those who have tasted of the fruit of the tree of the knowledge of good and evil.

To be, to be for ever, to be without ending! thirst of being, thirst of being more! hunger of God! thirst of love eternalizing and eternal! to be for ever! to be God!

"Ye shall be as gods!" we are told in Genesis that the serpent said to the first pair of lovers (Gen. iii. 5). "If in this life only we have hope in Christ, we are of all men most miserable," wrote the Apostle (I Cor. xv. 19); and all religion has sprung historically from the cult of the dead—that is to say, from the cult of immortality.

The tragic Portuguese Jew of Amsterdam* wrote that the free man thinks of nothing less than of death; but this free man is a dead man, free from the impulse of life, for want of love, the slave of his liberty. This thought that I must die and the enigma of what will come after death is the very palpitation of my consciousness. When I contemplate the green serenity of the fields or look into the depths of clear eyes through which shines a fellow-soul, my consciousness dilates, I feel the diastole of the soul and am bathed in the flood of the life that flows about me, and I believe in my future; but instantly the voice of mystery whispers to me, "Thou shalt cease to be!" the angel of Death touches me with his wing, and the systole of the soul floods the depths of my spirit with the blood of divinity.

Like Pascal, I do not understand those who assert that they care not a farthing for these things, and this indifference "in a matter that touches themselves, their eternity, their all, exasperates me rather than moves me to compassion, astonishes and shocks me," and he who feels thus "is for me," as for Pascal, whose are the words just quoted, "a monster."

---

* Here Unamuno once again refers to philosopher Benedict Spinoza, born in Amsterdam in 1632 [Ed.].

It has been said a thousand times and in a thousand books that ancestor-worship is for the most part the source of primitive religions, and it may be strictly said that what most distinguishes man from the other animals is that, in one form or another, he guards his dead and does not give them over to the neglect of teeming mother earth; he is an animal that guards its dead. And from what does he thus guard them? From what does he so futilely protect them? The wretched consciousness shrinks from its own annihilation, and, just as an animal spirit, newly severed from the womb of the world, finds itself confronted with the world and knows itself distinct from it, so consciousness must needs desire to possess another life than that of the world itself. And so the earth would run the risk of becoming a vast cemetery before the dead themselves should die again.

When mud huts or straw shelters, incapable of resisting the inclemency of the weather, sufficed for the living, tumuli were raised for the dead, and stone was used for sepulchres before it was used for houses. It is the strong-builded houses of the dead that have withstood the ages, not the houses of the living; not the temporary lodgings but the permanent habitations.

This cult, not of death but of immortality, originates and preserves religions. In the midst of the delirium of destruction, Robespierre induced the Convention to declare the existence of the Supreme Being and "the consolatory principle of the immortality of the soul," the Incorruptible being dismayed at the idea of having himself one day to turn to corruption.

A disease? Perhaps; but he who pays no heed to his disease is heedless of his health, and man is an animal essentially and substantially diseased. A disease? Perhaps it may be, like life itself to which it is thrall, and perhaps the only health possible may be death; but this disease is the fount of all vigorous health. From the depth of this anguish, from the abyss of the feeling of our mortality, we emerge into the light of another heaven, as from the depth of Hell Dante emerged to behold the stars once again . . . .

Although this meditation upon mortality may soon induce in us a sense of anguish, it fortifies us in the end. Retire, reader, into yourself and imagine a slow dissolution of yourself—the light dimming about you—all things becoming dumb and soundless, enveloping you in silence—the objects that you handle crumbling away between your hands—the ground slipping from under your feet—your very memory vanishing as if in a swoon—everything melting away from you into nothingness and you yourself also melting away—the very consciousness of nothingness, merely as the phantom harbourage of a shadow, not even remaining to you.

I have heard it related of a poor harvester who died in a hospital bed, that when the priest went to anoint his hands with the oil of extreme unction, he refused to open his right hand, which clutched a few dirty coins, not considering that very soon neither his hand nor he himself would be his own any more. And so we close and clench, not our hand, but our heart, seeking to clutch the world in it.

A friend confessed to me that, foreseeing while in the full vigour of physical health the near approach of a violent death, he proposed to concentrate his life and spend the few days which he calculated still remained to him in writing a book. Vanity of vanities!

If at the death of the body which sustains me, and which I call mine to distinguish it from the self that is I, my consciousness returns to the absolute unconsciousness from which it sprang, and if a like fate befalls all my brothers in humanity, then is our toil-worn human race nothing but a fatidical procession of phantoms, going from nothingness to nothingness, and humanitarianism the most inhuman thing known.

And the remedy is not that suggested in the quatrain that runs—

> *Cada vez que considero*
> *que me tengo de morir,*
> *tiendo la capa en el suelo*
> *y no me harto de dormir.*[1]

---

[1] Each time that I consider that it is my lot to die, I spread my cloak upon the ground and am never surfeited with sleeping.

No! The remedy is to consider our mortal destiny without flinching, to fasten our gaze upon the gaze of the Sphinx, for it is thus that the malevolence of its spell is discharmed.

If we all die utterly, wherefore does everything exist? Wherefore? It is the Wherefore of the Sphinx; it is the Wherefore that corrodes the marrow of the soul; it is the begetter of that anguish which gives us the love of hope.

Among the poetic laments of the unhappy Cowper there are some lines written under the oppression of delirium, in which, believing himself to be the mark of the Divine vengeance, he exclaims—

Hell might afford my miseries a shelter.

This is the Puritan sentiment, the preoccupation with sin and predestination. . . . And I must confess, painful though the confession be, that in the days of the simple faith of my childhood, descriptions of the tortures of hell, however terrible, never made me tremble, for I always felt that nothingness was much more terrifying. He who suffers lives, and he who lives suffering, even though over the portal of his abode is written "Abandon all hope!" loves and hopes. It is better to live in pain than to cease to be in peace. The truth is that I could not believe in this atrocity of Hell, of an eternity of punishment, nor did I see any more real hell than nothingness and the prospect of it. And I continue in the belief that if we all believed in our salvation from nothingness we should all be better.

What is this *joie de vivre** that they talk about nowadays? Our hunger for God, our thirst of immortality, of survival, will always stifle in us this pitiful enjoyment of the life that passes and abides not. It is the frenzied love of life, the love that would have life to be unending, that most often urges us to long for death. "If it is true that I am to die utterly," we say to ourselves, "then once I am annihilated the world has ended so far as I am concerned—it is finished. Why, then, should it not end forthwith, so that no new consciousnesses, doomed to suffer the tor-

menting illusion of a transient and apparential existence, may come into being? If, the illusion of living being shattered, living for the mere sake of living or for the sake of others who are likewise doomed to die, does not satisfy the soul, what is the good of living? Our best remedy is death." And thus it is that we chant the praises of the never-ending rest because of our dread of it, and speak of liberating death.

Leopardi, the poet of sorrow, of annihilation, having lost the ultimate illusion, that of believing in his immortality . . . perceived how close is the kinship between love and death, and how "when love is born deep down in the heart, simultaneously a languid and weary desire to die is felt in the breast." The greater part of those who seek death at their own hand are moved thereto by love; it is the supreme longing for life, for more life, the longing to prolong and perpetuate life, that urges them to death, once they are persuaded of the vanity of this longing.

The problem is tragic and eternal, and the more we seek to escape from it, the more it thrusts itself upon us. Four-and-twenty centuries ago, in his dialogue on the immortality of the soul, the serene Plato—but was he serene?—spoke of the uncertainty of our dream of being immortal and of the *risk* that the dream might be vain, and from his own soul there escaped this profound cry—Glorious is the risk! . . . glorious is the risk that we are able to run of our souls never dying—a sentence that was the germ of Pascal's famous argument of the wager.

Faced with this risk, I am presented with arguments designed to eliminate it, arguments demonstrating the absurdity of the belief in the immortality of the soul; but these arguments fail to make any impression upon me, for they are reasons and nothing more than reasons, and it is not with reasons that the heart is appeased. I do not want to die—no; I neither want to die nor do I want to want to die; I want to live for ever and ever and ever. I want this "I" to live—this poor "I" that I am and that I feel myself to be here and now, and therefore the problem of the duration of my soul, of my own soul, tortures me.

_____

* Joy of living [Eds.].

I am the centre of my universe, the centre of the universe, and in my supreme anguish I cry. . . . What is a man profited if he shall gain the whole world and lose his own soul? (Matt. xvi. 26). Egoism, you say? There is nothing more universal than the individual, for what is the property of each is the property of all. Each man is worth more than the whole of humanity, nor will it do to sacrifice each to all save in so far as all sacrifice themselves to each. That which we call egoism is the principle of psychic gravity, the necessary postulate. "Love thy neighbour as thyself," we are told, the presupposition being that each man loves himself; and it is not said "Love thyself." And, nevertheless, we do not know how to love ourselves.

Put aside the persistence of your own self and ponder what they tell you. Sacrifice yourself to your children! And sacrifice yourself to them because they are yours, part and prolongation of yourself, and they in their turn will sacrifice themselves to their children, and these children to theirs, and so it will go on without end, a sterile sacrifice by which nobody profits. I came into the world to create my self, and what is to become of all our selves? Live for the True, the Good, the Beautiful! We shall see presently the supreme vanity and the supreme insincerity of this hypocritical attitude.

"That art thou!" they tell me with the Upanishads.* And I answer: Yes, I am that, if that is I and all is mine, and mine the totality of things. As mine I love the All, and I love my neighbour because he lives in me and is part of my consciousness, because he is like me, because he is mine.

Oh, to prolong this blissful moment, to sleep, to eternalize oneself in it! Here and now, in this discreet and diffused light, in this lake of quietude, the storm of the heart appeased and stilled the echoes of the world! Insatiable desire now sleeps and does not even dream; use and wont, blessed use and wont, are the rule of my eternity; my disillusions have

died with my memories, and with my hopes my fears.

And they come seeking to deceive us with a deceit of deceits, telling us that nothing is lost, that everything is transformed, shifts and changes, that not the least particle of matter is annihilated, not the least impulse of energy is lost, and there are some who pretend to console us with this! Futile consolation! It is not my matter or my energy that is the cause of my disquiet, for they are not mine if I myself am not mine—that is, if I am not eternal. No, my longing is not to be submerged in the vast All, in an infinite and eternal Matter or Energy, or in God; not to be possessed by God, but to possess Him, to become myself God, yet without ceasing to be I myself, I who am now speaking to you. Tricks of monism avail us nothing; we crave the substance and not the shadow of immortality.

Materialism, you say? Materialism? Without doubt; but either our spirit is likewise some kind of matter or it is nothing. I dread the idea of having to tear myself away from my flesh; I dread still more the idea of having to tear myself away from everything sensible and material, from all substance. Yes, perhaps this merits the name of materialism; and if I grapple myself to God with all my powers and all my senses, it is that He may carry me in His arms beyond death, looking into these eyes of mine with the light of His heaven when the light of earth is dimming in them for ever. Self-illusion? Talk not to me of illusion—let me live!

They also call this pride—"stinking pride" Leopardi called it—and they ask us who are we, vile earthworms, to pretend to immortality; in virtue of what? wherefore? by what right? "In virtue of what?" you ask; and I reply, In virtue of what do we now live? "Wherefore?"—and wherefore do we now exist? "By what right?"—and by what right are we? To exist is just as gratuitous as to go on existing for ever. Do not let us talk of merit or of right or of the wherefore of our longing, which is an end in itself, or we shall lose our reason in a vortex of absurdities. I do not claim any right or merit; it is only a necessity; I need it in order to live.

And you, who are you? you ask me; and I reply

---

* The Upanishads are part of the Vedas, or Hindu scriptures, where metaphysical topics are directly addressed. See Chapter 1 of this book for the selection of the Upanishads to which Unamuno is referring [Eds.].

with Obermann, "For the universe, nothing; for myself, everything!" Pride? Is it pride to want to be immortal? Unhappy men that we are! 'Tis a tragic fate, without a doubt, to have to base the affirmation of immortality upon the insecure and slippery foundation of the desire for immortality; but to condemn this desire on the ground that we believe it to have been proved to be unattainable, without undertaking the proof, is merely supine. I am dreaming . . .? Let me dream, if this dream is my life. Do not awaken me from it. I believe in the immortal origin of this yearning for immortality, which is the very substance of my soul. But do I really believe in it . . .? And wherefore do you want to be immortal? you ask me, wherefore? Frankly, I do not understand the question, for it is to ask the reason of the reason, the end of the end, the principle of the principle.

 # SOCIAL CONCEPTIONS OF DEATH

Gregory Baum

The great critics of religion have looked upon the Christian teaching on the kingdom of God and the expectation of eternal life as principal causes of human alienation. Otherworldliness, according to these critics, leads to the contempt of this world. The hope for an eternal life of happiness makes people shrug their shoulders in regard to their earthly existence and prevents them from becoming concerned enough about their situation to change the conditions of social life. The doctrine of eternal life trivializes history. A religion that promises heaven consoles people in their misery, makes them patient and meek, and protects the existing social and political orders. Otherworldly religion, according to this analysis, is inevitably ideological.

Since critical theology intends to make the church assume theological responsibility for the un-

intended, social consequences of its religion and free the proclamation of the gospel from the alienating trends associated with it, contemporary theologians regard the Christian teaching on the last things as a topic of special challenge. Is it possible to understand Christ's preaching of the kingdom as utopian rather than ideological religion? The great critics of religion have measured Christian teaching in the light of the common understanding held by the church over the last centuries, with its almost exclusive concentration on individual destiny. The message of the kingdom has been reduced, in the church's preaching and in the minds of the faithful, to an assurance of personal survival after death and entry into the happiness of heaven. Hell was preached as a possibility for the unrepentant sinner, and in the Catholic Church purgatory was presented as the realm where the faithful departed of good will undergo the painful transformation that enables them to enter into eternal bliss. What we find in this common understanding is an almost complete privatization of the gospel promises. The first task of critical theology then, here as in connection with other doctrines, is the deprivatization of the church's teaching.

. . . According to the New Testament the center of Christ's preaching was the kingdom of God. Jesus was the servant and instrument of God's reign in the lives of men, promised to Israel in the ancient days, inaugurated in his person, and about to be made manifest in all its power. This kingdom was no "otherworldy reality"; it was God's reign, promised from the beginning, anticipated in the covenanted people and the sacramental church, and finally coming upon history as judgment and new creation. This kingdom was not conceived as a realm parallel to history; it was not a heavenly dominion above the realms of the earth; the kingdom was, rather, the divine reign that emerged in history as the longing of the cosmos and the fulfillment of the people's hopes. The kingdom was preached as the new age. It will destroy the sin in the hearts of men and the injustices present in their institutions, it will rectify the inequalities in the world and give people access to the sources of life. It was this kingdom that was to have no end. The promises made in the New Testament, then, affect individual people as well as society, the heart as well as the world, the body as well as the soul, present history as well as the world to come. The Christian promises are offered globally; they are not sorted out in detail. We admit, of course, that the New Testament language regarding the kingdom is dualistic, but this refers not to a dualism between mind and body, or between person and society, but to the contrast between the old age and the new. Christ ushered in a new age. The New Testament records the different ways in which the early Christians understood God's promises, from the eager expectation of the final judgment and the end of the world, to the patient confidence that the kingdom present in Christ and his church would be a source of a gradual humanization in history.

In the patristic age the message of eternal life remained focused on the community. It is true that the eschatological tension of the early church was lost very soon, but if we are to believe Henri de Lubac's famous study, *Catholicism*,[1] in the age of the fathers the thrust of the church's teaching, including the doctrine of eternal life, focused on the redemption and destiny of the whole community. Lubac developed the thesis of his book in the thirties, after prolonged conversation with Marxist thought; he tried to demonstrate that the individualism implicit in modern Christianity was due to the privatization of religion which had distorted, against the genius of Catholicism, the collectivist understanding of sin, grace and glory proclaimed and celebrated by the church of the fathers. The church as God's people was the bearer of the divine promises, and it was this people that was to live eternally. The church was the sign and symbol of the whole human race, the one human family, whose destiny was disclosed and made visible in the fellowship of the faithful. The doctrine of eternal life revealed first and foremost the divine end and purpose of history. It di-

rected people's imagination toward the last days of God's ultimate victory of evil and the creation of a new heaven and a new earth. The question of personal survival after death was not in the foreground. The liturgy of Christian burial confined itself to the simple words of *requies, lux* and *pax*. Dominant in the Christian imagination and the church's liturgy was the hope for the final accomplishment, the completion of history, and the resurrection of the entire people.

For the first thousand years the Christian people looked forward to the resurrection of the last day as the complete fulfillment of the divine promises and showed comparatively little interest in the state of the soul after the death of the body. This changed gradually. When the theologians in the 14th century, responding to the religion of the faithful, taught that after death the soul encounters the living God, undergoes the particular judgment, and if approved is admitted to eternal bliss in the *visio beatifica*,* Pope John XXII, relying on the more ancient tradition, condemned this new trend. "The soul separated from the body," he taught, "does not enjoy the vision of God which is its total reward and will not enjoy it prior to the resurrection."[2] Pope John XXII was the last witness of the ancient church's collectivist imagination, which saw salvation primarily as the entry of the entire people into grace and glory. However individualistic culture had superseded the Pope. He himself changed his mind; and the next pontiff, Pope Benedict XII, revoked the position of his predecessor, solemnly proposed the new teaching, and confirmed the shift of the church's religious longing from the crowning of history in the new creation to the soul's eternal happiness after death. Until recently, this has been the common stance of modern Christianity.

In the modern period the church's teaching of eternal life was understood almost exclusively in

---

[1] Henri de Lubac, *Catholicism*, trans. L. C. Sheppard, Burns & Oates, London, 1962, especially pp. 49–62.

* Literally, "beatific vision": a state of bliss in which the human soul beholds God's presence [Eds.].
[2] *Enchiridion Symbolorum*, edit. Denzinger-Schönmetzer, Herder, Freiburg, 1963, p. 295.

terms of the fate that awaited the individual after his or her death. The eschatological framework of the gospel was largely abandoned. Christians no longer experienced themselves as a people on pilgrimage, as a people with an historical destiny; instead they regarded the society to which they belonged, and the church within it, as abiding elements of the divine plan and reduced the great Christian adventure to the personal journey from birth to death. Church and society were the unchanging stage on which people worked out their personal salvation. The Church's liturgy, on the whole, retained the historical vision and recalled that God had acted in Christ on behalf of all mankind and brought history to the new and final age, but the individualistic culture did not allow this ancient teaching to affect the people's piety. Death became the end of the journey and salvation the pledge of one's own personal happiness beyond the grave.

This privatizing trend in religion corresponds to the growing individualism in secular culture, which has reached its high point in modern, *Gesellschaft*-type society. Here the individual is wholly severed from the social matrix. At the same time, acting as impersonal agents in a rationalized society, people feel that they have lost the sense of self. The triumph and agony of individualism have made people focus on personal death as the great enemy which threatens the meaning of their lives in the present. Modern secularity imitates the church's concentration on death. For Heidegger, the fear of death marks a person's entire life and produces a metaphysical anguish that reveals man's authentic nature. This concentration on personal death has even found entry into sociological reflection. Alfred Schutz integrates Heidegger's view of death into his phenomenology of the social world, and Peter Berger assigns personal death a primary role in his sociology of religion and the construction of reality.[3] The fear of death overshadows the whole of a person's life; it convicts her efforts of building the

world and her quest for happiness of finitude and imbues them with a peculiar anxiety. This anguish, this fear of death, the horror of chaos is, according to Berger's sociology, the generating force that makes people seek a safe and stable world, and create sacred symbols that legitimate the present order and promise future security. Religion is created as the answer to personal death and its anxiety-producing power. What we have here, it seems to me, is a psychology rather than a sociology of religion.

While it may not be surprising that such a privatizing perspective takes hold of philosophers in the modern age, it is curious to see this perspective applied in sociology. For why should a social thinker hold that death is the universal fact that has meaning apart from the social context in which it occurs? Is the reaction of people to their mortality a transcendent phenomenon, independent of their cultural world, and hence a solid ground, beyond the changing social circumstances, on which to construct a sociology of religion? The old-fashioned literature glorifying the self-sacrifice of soldiers on the battlefield is a good illustration that the attitude toward one's own death depends on social environment. Max Weber may have been only half-serious when he suggested that death has become such an absurd event only in modern, competitive, achievement-oriented society because there people daily sacrifice happiness for the sake of work, and when they finally encounter death, they feel that after having postponed happiness all their lives, they are now cheated of their reward and their entire life is being mocked and invalidated. Weber may have thought that in other cultures people were willing to live more wholeheartedly in the present with its joys and pains, and when death awaited them as the long sleep at the end of their lives, they may not have been that frightened by it. Even the attitude toward death is socially grounded. To regard the anxiety over one's mortality as a primary principle of human behavior, I conclude, corresponds not to the nature of reality but to the privatizing trend of the social world.

The attitude toward death depends on the imagination of the future, mediated throughout society by

---

[3] Peter Berger, *The Sacred Canopy*, pp. 23–28; *The Social Construction of Reality*, pp. 27, 101–102.

cultural or religious movements. In tribal society, the imagination of people projected the ongoing existence of the tribe and hence they found it easy to speak of life beyond the grave. They felt themselves embedded in a living reality that would perdure in the future. In the ages of nationalism and its accompanying conflicts and wars, to give another example, people's imagination of the future circled around the emergence and flowering of the nation, and when confronted with death in this struggle, they did not fear for themselves but dreamt of their nation's future. Nationalist poetry is full of accounts of such sacrificial deaths. In modern society, people's imagination of the future tends to be caught in their own personal lives. They dream of what life will be like for them in ten years, in twenty years, in thirty years. In the consumers' society of today our imagination is taught to concentrate on the rising standard of living and the ever greater personal well-being. Death, in such a context, seems utterly frightful. But already if a person is profoundly attached to her children and their families, then her imagination will circle around their future and her own personal death will not appear as the great enemy. Herbert Marcuse, the great atheistic social philosopher, has made one of the most profound remarks about death, one that one might expect to find in the great literatures of religion. "Men can die without anxiety," Marcuse wrote, "if they know that what they love is protected from misery and oblivion."[4] If the object of a person's love is protected from harm and assured of well-being, then the nothingness of her own tomorrow, threatened in death, is not a great source of anguish. But if we love ourselves, and our future imagination circles around our own well-being—this is almost inevitable in *Gesellschaft*-type society—then what we love is wholly unprotected, and death becomes the dreaded enemy. How does Marcuse's important remark apply to the Christian faith? If we yearn for the kingdom of God, if we long for God's victory over

evil and all the enemies of life and believe that in Christ this victory is assured, then what we love is protected and it should not be so difficult to die.

The Christian teaching of eternal life, we conclude, rather than making the believers focus on their own death and worry about what happens to them after they die, liberates them for a greater love and makes them yearn for the reconciliation and deliverance of all peoples. The Christian message of resurrection, understood in this deprivatizing perspective, far from making Christians concentrate on their own heaven, frees them from anxiety about their own existence and directs their hope to the new creation. The doctrine of God's approaching kingdom, the central Christian symbol, summons people to forget themselves, to serve the kingdom of God coming into the lives of men and women, and to rejoice with the Christian community, gathered at worship, that in Christ God's final victory has been assured. God will have the last word. Evil will not be allowed to stand. The entry into personal salvation and future life is not prepared by concentrating on one's own life but by trusting and loving God's coming reign. The dialect of personal-and-social, which we observed when speaking of sin and grace, must also be observed when interpreting the Christian doctrine of eternal life.

This deprivatizing trend is operative in contemporary spirituality. Perhaps one of the first signs of this reorientation was given by a remarkable woman who in many ways was a conventional saint, Thérèse of Lisieux.* In her oft-quoted statement, "I want to spend my heaven doing good on earth," she subtly criticized the individualism of traditional Catholic spirituality. She thought that she would not be able to rest with God as long as people were still suffering and the promised kingdom had not been established. This was then a startling innovation. In contemporary spiritual writers, such

---

[4] Herbert Marcuse, *Eros and Civilization*, Vintage Books, New York, 1962, p. 216.

---

* Author of the religious classic, *Story of a Soul,* Thérèse of Lisieux was born in 1873 in Alencon, France. She joined the Carmelite Monastery at age 15 and died an early and painful death in 1897. Devotion to Thérèse, and claims of her ongoing help and influence, continue to this day [Eds.].

as Thomas Merton, Daniel Berrigan, Ernesto Cardinale, and James Douglas, the passage to a more collective understanding of divine salvation has been completed. While these authors attach much importance to personal life and one's personal union with God as the ground for a life that will never die, they understand this personal life as participation in the human community and a share in the salvation which is meant for all. Here each person is damaged by the misery inflicted on others. In this new spirituality there is no communion with God unless mediated by Jesus, that is, by a total solidarity with humanity, especially the underprivileged and dispossessed. Here entry into eternal life is again understood, following the New Testament, as repentance and identification with God's coming reign. Anguish about one's death and concern about one's personal heaven are not the entry into the Christian life. Nor is the question of personal survival after death the best way to approach the Christian teaching on eternal life.

The common theological approach to death and dying has also been privatized from another point of view. Usually, in sermons and books on pastoral theology, we speak of death as if people normally die peacefully in their beds. Death is here looked upon as the startling end of a person's life in a settled context of friendly faces. Yet by thinking of death in this way, we forget that vast numbers of people die very differently as victims of society. A glance at a statistics of people killed by wars, acts of genocide, unrelieved famines, and other forms of collective violence reminds us that a peaceful death in bed is by no means the normal way for people to die in the 20th century. A certain, highly private theology of dying, it seems to me, disguises from consciousness the cruel world to which we belong. We tend to think that the terms which make sense to us in our protected context apply to people everywhere. But death in bed, after a life well spent, is for many people the object of great hope. To focus on this kind of death as if it were the great enemy overlooks the political realities of the 20th century. Asking the reader's permission for a very personal remark, I recall that my own mother, hiding in Berlin

from Nazi persecution of the Jews and deportation to the death camps, became overwhelmed with exhaustion, fell gravely ill, and still died in bed surrounded by friendly faces, not by enemies. This was a grace. A Christian theology of death ought to take the political dimension seriously. To die in bed, after a long, affirmative life, is not so bad, and we can't really wish anything better for ourselves. At the same time, we do not want an imagination of the future that circles around our own personal fate. The Christian message of the coming kingdom promises deliverance from evil on a universal scale including all the peoples of the earth, and thanks to this message we want to think of our personal lives as situated in this holy, dread and universal drama.

FACING DEATH

Etty Hillesum

The branches of the tree outside my window have been lopped off.

The night before the stars had still hung like glistening fruit in the heavy branches, and now they climbed, unsure of themselves, up the bare, ravaged trunk. Oh, yes, the stars: for a few nights, some of them, lost, deserted, grazed over the wide, forsaken, heavenly plain.

For a moment, when the branches were being cut, I became sentimental. And for that moment I was deeply sad. Then I suddenly knew: I should love the new landscape, too, love it in my own way. Now the two trees rise up outside my window like imposing, emaciated ascetes, thrusting into the bright sky like two daggers.

And on Thursday evening the war raged once again outside my window and I lay there watching it all from my bed. Bernard was playing a Bach record next door. It had sounded so powerful and glowing, but then, suddenly, there were planes, ack-ack fire, shooting, bombs—much noisier than they have been for a long time. It seemed to go on right beside the house. And it suddenly came to me again: there must be so many houses all over the world which are collapsing each day under just such bombs as these.

And Bach went gallantly on, now faint and small. And I lay there in my bed in a very strange mood. Filaments of light along the menacing bare trunk outside my window. A constant pounding. And I thought to myself: any minute now a piece of shrapnel could come through that window. It's quite possible. And it's equally possible that there would be a lot of pain. And yet I felt so deeply peaceful and grateful, there in my bed, and meekly resigned to all the disasters and pains that might be in store for me.

• • •

SATURDAY MORNING, 7:30. [. . .] The bare trunks which climb past my window now shelter under a cover of young green leaves. A springy fleece along their naked, tough, ascetic limbs.

I went to bed early last night and from my bed I stared out through the large open window. And it was once more as if life with all its mysteries was close to me, as if I could touch it. I had the feeling that I was resting against the naked breast of life, and could feel her gentle and regular heartbeat. I felt safe and protected. And I thought: how strange. It is wartime. There are concentration camps. I can say of so many of the houses I pass: here the son has been thrown into prison, there the father has been taken hostage, and an 18-year-old boy in that house over there has been sentenced to death. And these streets and houses are all so close to my own. I know how very nervous people are, I know about the mounting human suffering. I know the persecution and oppression and despotism and the impotent fury and the terrible sadism. I know it all.

And yet—at unguarded moments, when left to myself, I suddenly lie against the naked breast of life and her arms round me are so gentle and so protective and my own heartbeat is difficult to describe: so slow and so regular and so soft, almost muffled, but so constant, as if it would never stop.

That is also my attitude to life and I believe that neither war nor any other senseless human atrocity will ever be able to change it.

• • •

Many accuse me of indifference and passivity when I refuse to go into hiding; they say that I have given up. They say everyone who can must try to stay out of their clutches, it's our bounden duty to try. But that argument is specious. For while everyone tries to save himself, vast numbers are nevertheless disappearing. And the funny thing is I don't feel I'm in their clutches anyway, whether I stay or am sent away. I find all that talk so cliché-ridden and naive and can't go along with it any more. I don't feel in anybody's clutches; I feel safe in God's arms, to put it rhetorically, and no matter whether I am sitting at this beloved old desk now, or in a bare room in the Jewish district or perhaps in a labour camp under SS guards in a month's time—I shall always feel safe in God's arms. They may well succeed in breaking me physically, but no more than that. I may face cruelty and deprivation the likes of which I cannot imagine in even my wildest fantasies. Yet all this is as nothing to the immeasurable expanse of my faith in God and my inner receptiveness.

I shall always be able to stand on my own two feet even when they are planted on the hardest soil of the harshest reality. And my acceptance is not indifference or helplessness. I feel deep moral indignation at a regime that treats human beings in such a way. But events have become too overwhelming and too demonic to be stemmed with personal resentment and bitterness. These responses strike me as being utterly childish and unequal to the fateful course of events.

People often get worked up when I say it doesn't really matter whether I go or somebody else does, the main thing is that so many thousands *have* to go. It is not as if I want to fall into the arms of destruction with a resigned smile—far from it. I am only bowing to the inevitable and even as I do so I am sustained by the certain knowledge that ultimately they cannot rob us of anything that matters. But I don't think I would feel happy if I were exempted from what so many others have to suffer. They keep telling me that someone like me has a duty to go into hiding, because I have so many things to do in life, so much to give. But I know that whatever I may have to give to others, I can give it no matter where I am, here in the circle of my friends or over there, in a concentration camp. And it is sheer arrogance to think oneself too good to share the fate of the masses.

And if God Himself should feel that I still have a great deal to do, well then, I shall do it after I have suffered what all the others have to suffer. And whether or not I am a valuable human being will only become clear from my behaviour in more arduous circumstances. And if I should not survive, how I die will show me who I really am. Of course that doesn't mean I will turn down a medical exemption if they give me one on account of my inflamed kidneys and bladder. And I have been recommended for some sort of soft job with the Jewish Council. They had permission to hire 180 people last week, and the desperate are thronging there in droves, as shipwrecked people might cling for dear life to a piece of driftwood. But that is as far as I am prepared to go and, beyond that, I am not willing to pull any strings. In any case, the Jewish Council seems to have become a hotbed of intrigue, and resentment against this strange agency is growing by the hour. And sooner or later it will be their turn to go, anyway.

But, of course, by then the English may have landed. At least that's what those people say who have not yet abandoned all political hope. I believe that we must rid ourselves of all expectations of help from the outside world, that we must stop guessing about the duration of the war and so on. And now I am going to set the table.

• • •

14 JULY, TUESDAY EVENING. Everyone must follow the way of life that suits him best. I simply cannot make active preparations to save myself, it seems so pointless to me and would make me nervous and unhappy. My letter of application to the Jewish Council on Jaap's urgent advice has upset my cheerful yet deadly serious equilibrium. As if I had done something underhand. Like crowding on to a small piece of wood adrift on an endless ocean after a shipwreck and then saving oneself by pushing others into the water and watching them drown. It is all so ugly. And I don't think much of this particular crowd, either. I would much rather join those who prefer to float on their backs for a while, drifting on the ocean with their eyes turned towards heaven and who then go down with a prayer. I cannot help myself. My battles are fought out inside, with my own demons; it is not in my nature to tilt against the savage, cold-blooded fanatics who clamour for our destruction. I am not afraid of them either, I don't know why; I am so calm it is sometimes as if I were standing on the parapets of the palace of history looking down over far-distant lands. This bit of history we are experiencing right now is something I know I can stand up to. I know what is happening and yet my head is clear. But sometimes I feel as if a layer of ashes were being sprinkled over my heart, as if my face were withering and decaying before my very eyes, and as if everything were falling apart in front of me and my heart were letting everything go. But these are brief moments; then everything falls back into place, my head is clear again and I can once more bear and stand up to this piece of history which is ours. For once you have begun to walk with God, you need only keep on walking with Him and all of life becomes one long stroll—such a marvellous feeling.

We go too far in fearing for our unhappy bodies, while our forgotten spirit shrivels up in some corner.

• • •

10 July 1943

Maria, hallo,

Ten thousand have passed through this place, the clothed and the naked, the old and the young, the sick and the healthy—and I am left to live and work and stay cheerful. It will be my parents' turn to leave soon, if by some miracle not this week then certainly one of the next. And I must learn to accept this as well. Mischa insists on going along with them and it seems to me that he probably should; if he has to watch his parents leave this place it will totally unhinge him. I shan't go, I just can't. It is easier to pray for someone from a distance than to see him suffer by your side. It is not fear of Poland that keeps me from going along with my parents, but fear of seeing them suffer. And that, too, is cowardice.

This is something people refuse to admit to themselves: at a given point you can no longer *do,* but can only *be* and accept. And although that is something I learned a long time ago, I also know that one can only accept for oneself and not for others. And that is what is so desperately difficult for me here. Mother and Mischa still want to "do," to turn the whole world upside down, but I know we can't do anything about it. I have never been able to "do" anything; I can only let things take their course and if need be suffer. This is where my strength lies and it is great strength indeed. But for myself, not for others.

Mother and Father have definitely been turned down for Barneveld; we heard the news yesterday. They were also told to be ready to leave here on next Tuesday's transport. Mischa wanted to rush straight to the commandant and call him a murderer. We'll have to watch him carefully. Outwardly, Father appears very calm, but he would have gone to pieces in a matter of days in these vast barracks if I hadn't been able to have him taken into the hospital.

• • •

24 August 1943

There was a moment when I felt in all seriousness that, after this night, it would be a sin ever to laugh again. But then I reminded myself that some of those who had gone away had been laughing, even if only a handful of them this time . . . There will be some who will laugh now and then in Poland, too, though not many from this transport, I think.

When I think of the faces of that squad of armed, green-uniformed guards—my God, those faces! I looked at them, each in turn, from behind the safety of a window, and I have never been so frightened of anything in my life as I was of those faces. I sank to my knees with the words that preside over human life: And God made man after His likeness. That passage spent a difficult morning with me.

I have told you often enough that no words and images are adequate to describe nights like these. But still I must try to convey something of it to you. One always has the feeling here of being the ears and eyes of a piece of Jewish history, but there is also the need sometimes to be a still, small voice. We must keep one another in touch with everything that happens in the various outposts of this world, each one contributing his own little piece of stone to the great mosaic that will take shape once the war is over.

After a night in the hospital barracks, I took an early morning walk past the punishment barracks, and prisoners were being moved out. The deportees, mainly men, stood with their packs behind the barbed wire. So many of them looked tough and ready for anything. An old acquaintance—I didn't recognise him straightaway, a shaven head often changes people completely—called out to me with a smile, "If they don't manage to do me in, I'll be back."

But the babies, those tiny piercing screams of the babies, dragged from their cots in the middle of the night . . . I have to put it all down quickly, in a muddle because if I leave it until later I probably won't be able to go on believing that it really happened. It is like a vision, and drifts further and further away. The babies were easily the worst.

And then there was that paralysed young girl, who didn't want to take her dinner plate along and found it so hard to die. Or the terrified young boy: he had thought he was safe, that was his mistake, and when he realised he was going to have to go anyway, he panicked and ran off. His fellow Jews had to hunt him down—if they didn't find him, scores of others would be put on the transport in his place. He was caught soon enough, hiding in a tent, but "notwithstanding" . . . "notwithstanding," all those others had to go on transport anyway, as a deterrent, they said. And so, many good friends were dragged away by that boy. Fifty victims for one moment of insanity. Or rather: he didn't drag them away—our commandant did, someone of whom it is sometimes said that he is a gentleman. Even so, will the boy be able to live with himself, once it dawns on him exactly what he's been the cause of? And how will all the other Jews on board the train react to him? That boy is going to have a very hard time. The episode might have been overlooked, perhaps, if there hadn't been so much unnerving activity over our heads that night. The commandant must have been affected by that too. "*Donnerwetter,* some flying tonight!" I heard a guard say as he looked up at the stars.

People still harbour such childish hopes that the transport won't get through. Many of us were able from here to watch the bombardment of a nearby town, probably Emden. So why shouldn't it be possible for the railway line to be hit too, and for the train to be stopped from leaving? It's never been known to happen yet, but people keep hoping it will with each new transport and with never-flagging hope . . .

The evening before that night, I walked through the camp. People were grouped together between the barracks, under a grey, cloudy sky. "Look, that's just how people behave after a disaster, standing about on street corners discussing what's happened," my companion said to me. "But that's what makes it so impossible to understand," I burst out. "This time, it's *before* the disaster!"

Whenever misfortune strikes, people have a natural instinct to lend a helping hand and to save what can be saved. Tonight I shall be "helping" to dress babies and to calm mothers and that is all I can hope to do. I could almost curse myself for that. For we all know that we are yielding up our sick and defenceless brothers and sisters to hunger, heat, cold, exposure and destruction, and yet we dress them and escort them to the bare cattle trucks—and if they can't walk we carry them on stretchers. What

is going on, what mysteries are these, in what sort of fatal mechanism have we become enmeshed? The answer cannot simply be that we are all cowards. We're not that bad. We stand before a much deeper question . . .

In the afternoon I did a round of the hospital barracks one more time, going from bed to bed. Which beds would be empty the next day? The transport lists are never published until the very last moment, but some of us know well in advance that our names will be down. A young girl called me. She was sitting bolt upright in her bed, eyes wide open. This girl has thin wrists and a peaky little face. She is partly paralysed, and has just been learning to walk again, between two nurses, one step at a time. "Have you heard? I have to go." We look at each other for a long moment. It is as if her face has disappeared, she is all eyes. Then she says in a level, grey little voice, "Such a pity, isn't it? That everything you have learned in life goes for nothing." And, "How hard it is to die." Suddenly the unnatural rigidity of her expression gives way and she sobs, "Oh, and the worst of it all is having to leave Holland!" and, "Oh, why wasn't I allowed to die before . . ." Later, during the night, I saw her again, for the last time.

There was a little woman in the wash-house, a basket of dripping clothes on her arm. She grabbed hold of me. She looked deranged. A flood of words poured over me, "That isn't right, how can that be right, I've got to go and I won't even be able to get my washing dry by tomorrow. And my child is sick, he's feverish, can't you fix things so that I don't have to go? And I don't have enough things for the child, the rompers they sent me are too small, I need the bigger size, oh, it's enough to drive you mad. And you're not even allowed to take a blanket along, we're going to freeze to death, you didn't think of that, did you? There's a cousin of mine here, he came here the same time I did, but he doesn't have to go, he's got the right papers. Couldn't you help me to get some, too? Just say I don't have to go, do you think they'll leave the children with their mothers, that's right, you come back again tonight, you'll help me then, won't you, what do you think, would my cousin's papers . . . ?"

If I were to say that I was in hell that night, what would I really be telling you? I caught myself saying it aloud in the night, aloud to myself and quite soberly, "So that's what hell is like." You really can't tell who is going and who isn't this time. Almost everyone is up, the sick help each other to get dressed. There are some who have no clothes at all, whose luggage has been lost or hasn't arrived yet. Ladies from the "Welfare" walk about doling out clothes, which may fit or not, it doesn't matter so long as you've covered yourself with something. Some old women look a ridiculous sight.

We are being hunted to death right through Europe . . .

I wander in a daze through other barracks. I walk past scenes that loom up before my eyes in crystal-clear detail, and at the same time seem like blurred age-old visions. I see a dying old man being carried away, reciting the Sh'ma[1] to himself . . .

* * *

Slowly but surely six o'clock in the morning has arrived. The train is due to depart at eleven, and they are starting to load it with people and luggage. Paths to the train have been staked out by men of the *Ordedienst,* the Camp Service Corps. Anyone not involved with the transport has to keep to barracks. I slip into one just across from the siding. "There's always been a splendid view from here . . ." I hear a cynical voice say. The camp has been cut in two halves since yesterday by the train: a depressing series of bare, unpainted goods wagons in the front, and a proper carriage for the guards at the back. Some of the wagons have paper mattresses on the floor. These are for the sick. There is more and more movement now along the asphalt path beside the train. . . .

Suddenly there are a lot of green-uniformed men swarming over the asphalt. I can't imagine where they have sprung from. Knapsacks and guns over their shoulders. I study their faces. I try to look at them without prejudice. . . .

My God, are the doors really being shut now? Yes, they are. Shut on the herded, densely packed, mass of people inside. Through small openings at the top we can see heads and hands, hands that will wave to us later when the train leaves. The commandant takes a bicycle and rides once again along the entire length of the train. Then he makes a brief gesture, like royalty in an operetta. A little orderly comes flying up and deferentially relieves him of the bicycle. The train gives a piercing whistle, and 1,020 Jews leave Holland.

This time the quota was really quite small, all considered: a mere thousand Jews, the extra twenty being reserves, for it is always possible, indeed quite certain this time, that a few will die or be crushed to death on the way. So many sick people and not a single nurse . . .

The tide of helpers gradually recedes; people go back to their sleeping quarters. So many exhausted, pale and suffering faces. One more piece of our camp has been amputated. Next week yet another piece will follow. This is what has been happening now for over a year, week in, week out. We are left with just a few thousand. A hundred thousand Dutch members of our race are toiling away under an unknown sky or lie rotting in some unknown soil. We know nothing of their fate. It is only a short while, perhaps, before we find out, each one of us in his own time, for we are all marked down to share that fate, of that I have not a moment's doubt. But I must go now and lie down and sleep for a little while. I am a bit tired and dizzy. Then later I have to go to the laundry to track down the face cloth that got lost. But first I must sleep. As for the future, I am firmly resolved to return to you after my wanderings. In the meantime, my love once again, you dear people.

---

[1] "Hear, O Israel: the Lord our God, the Lord is one." This is a line of the prayer said when death is approaching.

QUESTIONS FOR DISCUSSION

1. Do you agree with Unamuno that the heart wants immortality, but reason counsels against it? Or can you think of examples where the heart may not want immortality and reason may dictate it, or at least show it to be plausible?

2. The Unamuno selection suggests adoption of an attitude of resistance to death and clinging to life (whether in this life or a projected next life). Hillesum, however, thinks that fighting death is unproductive. When, or in what way, do you think, is it appropriate to cultivate acceptance of death? When might it be better to "fight" death?

3. Baum suggests a theological interpretation of the Christian position on life after death that is quite different than the layperson's understanding. Is Baum's view convincing? Or do you find giving up the standard contemporary Christian view of individual survival after death difficult?

The Just Ruler
Confucius, *Ruler as Moral Model*
Plato, *The Philosopher King*
Hannah Arendt, *Against Conceiving Politics as the Ruler and the Ruled*
Vaclav Havel, *Trust in Leaders*

Domination and the Struggle against Domination
Friedrich Nietzsche, *Master and Slave Morality*
Karl Marx and Friedrich Engels, *The Communist Manifesto*

Frantz Fanon, *Violence and Self-Definition*
Sandra Lee Bartky, *The Psychological Oppression of Women*
Paulo Freire, *Oppression and Liberation*
Malcolm X, *By Any Means Necessary*
Mohandas K. Gandhi, *Non-violent Resistance*

Birmingham, Alabama, May 1963. (Charles Moore/Black Star)

CHAPTER 9

SOCIAL JUSTICE

Philosophy is essentially a theoretical discipline, but theories are related to practice. In social and political philosophy, philosophers turn their thoughts to the question of human social formations and forms of government: What is the ideal government? What is the individual's relationship to government? What is required in our relationship to one another? Justice is a central ethical notion on the societal level. What constitutes exploitation or discrimination?

In matters of politics, philosophers throughout history have been more than armchair speculators. Some have helped to legitimate the governments in which they lived; often, philosophers have questioned that legitimation and helped to topple governments. Our chapter includes prestigious thinkers who have also been community leaders and activists. Several had to flee for their lives from governmental persecution; some were shot down or executed for their views.

The chapter centers on two themes. In the first part, the concept of the ruler is explored. The first two readings, from Confucius and Plato, put forward similar sentiments: that a ruler should be of exemplary moral virtue. What virtue consists of and how that virtue shows itself are explained a bit dif-

ferently by the two authors. However, common in its absence is a critique of hierarchical government in general. Confucius takes for granted that the people need a ruler and that the good ruler is of course what all people hope for; whereas Plato takes the more cynical position. For Plato, the people would not necessarily want or choose the moral ruler, even though they should. That is what is wrong with democracy, according to Plato; the people would be better off, on this account, having their just ruler (the philosopher-king) chosen for them by competent judges.

This supposition of the benefits of hierarchy and rulership is called into question by our contemporary authors, Hannah Arendt and Vaclav Havel. Arendt emphasizes that leaders are dependent on the support of their followers; yet the history of political philosophy has obscured this fact by its overemphasis on rulership. By making a split between those who command and those who obey, the majority of the people are reduced to subjects of government. Such a setup leads, over time, to the kind of society Havel describes. Havel critiques the "post-totalitarian society," different than traditional dictatorships in that most people have become used to the idea that they are just cogs in the societal machine and are willing to play out their limited role, following the dictates given them, in exchange for survival and security. The only possible challenge to such a system would be an "existential revolution," where people would regain a sense of moral responsibility and choose new leaders who exhibit attributes of honesty and dedication to the good of all. On this note we come full circle, with a reassertion of the need for moral leadership, but in a totally different structural context.

In the second section, we look at the results when rulership goes astray, and people are oppressed by unjust political or economic systems. Just what is morally wrong with relationships of domination and submission? Nietzsche argues that nothing is wrong; others assert that the dominated have a right to reassert and fight for their dignity and freedom. But just how that fight will be waged—through violence and threat of violence, nonviolent activism, or education—differs from author to author. Marx and Engels focus on a revolutionary challenge to the political and economic sys-

tems of capitalism. Fanon, Bartky, and Freire explore the psychological dimensions of domination. Fanon studies the emasculation of the colonized under not only the degrading system of slavery, but even by paternalistic-humanitarian treatment by colonizers. He advocates violent revolution to restore a sense of agency and human worth to the colonized. Bartky draws parallels between what Fanon describes as the psychology of the oppressed and women's acceptance of domination through subtle psychological controls. Freire insists that education will help oppressed peoples recognize their situation as one of oppression, and this insight will lead to developing their plan for liberation (which might indeed be violent). Malcolm X sees the need to challenge and eradicate racist practices in the United States; violent threats may be needed to startle a complacent and entrenched system. Gandhi, on the contrary, thinks that love can reform the system of foreign oppression in colonial India; he uses the same rationale as well to combat the caste discrimination that exists in his society.

THE JUST RULER

This section focuses on issues of moral rulership and contrasts ancient views with contemporary perspectives. All four authors in this section have good reasons from their own life circumstances and experiences to be gravely concerned with the issue of moral leadership. Therefore, we will discuss each author in the context of her or his life experience.

Confucius (a name which is a latinized version of "Kong Fuzi" or "Master Kong") was born around 551 B.C. in the province of Lu in China. He was upset at the state of government in China, which was then dominated by warring princes motivated by greed. He wanted to use his influence to reform the government through persuasion, not force. He began a school to educate young men in ceremony and virtues, so that they might enter politics and influence it for the good by exercising loyalty to principles, not people. Confucius himself sought political office, but no one would appoint him, so he went traveling from state to state in the region, advising local rulers, until his final retirement to his home in Lu.

The text from the Confucian tradition is in the form of an interview with a local ruler, Duke Ai. In this short passage, Confucius sums up his views on political philosophy. *Li* guides proper relationships between ruler and ruled, leaders and juniors, and so on. Ceremony and ritual sacrifice are all-important as expressions of respect.

The sovereign is a role model. Confucius's word for the ruler was *chuntse* which means ruler, sovereign, prince, but also "superior man," explicitly meaning superior in the moral sense. Confucius's humanism is evident in this piece, as he avoids the need to depend on revelation to know the will of God. Since God manifests through nature, living according to nature and according to God are the same.

Plato (born around 428 B.C.), the famous student of Socrates who wrote many dialogues based on Socrates' teaching, had good reason to be con-

cerned about politics. After all, the democratic government of his city-state, Athens, had voted to put Socrates to death. The charges against Socrates, corruption of the youth and impiety, probably had to do with his encouraging the youth to question their government. His influence on a couple of young men who had been part of the temporary "Thirty Tyrants" takeover of Athens' democratic government, and his friendship with Alcibiades, an infamous traitor, led to Socrates' "guilt by association." Although Socrates saw his practice of philosophy as a positive exercise of inquiry and judgment, Athenian elders seemingly preferred to have a more docile body of citizens who would not be so apt to raise criticisms and question authority. Plato's negative appraisal of democracy was certainly influenced by watching his teacher sentenced to death by a popular vote of the people, and the knowledgeable navigator in the upcoming parable in the Plato reading is surely modeled on Socrates.

Socrates is the principal speaker in Plato's *Republic* and Plato's mouthpiece in the work. Socrates dialogues with Glaucon. According to Socrates, philosophers should be set up as guardians and rulers of the city, because they know how to conceptualize universals (such as justice) as standards to judge the ever-changing happenings of the city. However, when Glaucon complains that philosophers are often considered useless, Socrates explains why philosophers seem to be useless to the people by recounting the parable of the ship crew's neglect of the navigator. The people are like the captain, strong but uneducated and shortsighted. Those who wish to rule in a democracy court the people, but don't have the required knowledge. The philosopher, the only one who can do the job, is the neglected navigator. His neglect is due in part to people's ignorance as to their need for guidance according to eternal principles.

Hannah Arendt, born of German Jewish descent in Koenigsberg, Prussia (present-day Russia), in

1906, often said that her interest in politics stemmed from her early frustration at being shut out of the public realm. Studying in Germany during the 1930s, she was disturbed at the rise of the Nazi Party and began working underground to gather evidence against the Party. Caught and imprisoned, she talked her way out of a German jail and fled the country, only to later find herself interned in a camp at Gurs in France. Escaping again, she eventually made her way to the United States. In the United States, she became well-known first through her analyses of totalitarianism and later for her works on political philosophy that encompassed wider issues.

Rather than describe the moral ruler, as Confucius and Plato do, Arendt is skeptical that the structure of rulership is a positive development in politics. Arendt notes that because human actions are boundless and unpredictable, people turn to rulers for security; in turn, the rulers try to take away the impulse or ability to act from the people. Society then becomes divided between, on the one hand, those who know but do not act; and on the other hand, those who act but do not know. In this way, government parallels the master-slave relationship. Implicit in her work here, and manifest in other of her writings, is the idea that for each person in society to be fulfilled, she or he must experience action in its fullest sense, and be both an originator and a participant in an idea's fruition.

The Czech playwright and essayist Vaclav Havel was a leading dissident throughout the years of Soviet domination. After the August 1968 invasion of Czechoslovakia by Soviet forces, Havel authored and was chief signatory of "Charta 77," a document calling for respect for human rights in his country. Imprisoned for four years after the publication of his essay, "The Power of the Powerless," written in 1978 (included here), Havel began to see that his critique of modern society referred not only to communist governments but to modern "consumer societies" around the globe. His call for an "existential revolution" finally had its chance when in November 1989, during what has been called the "velvet revolution," Czechoslovakia was free to follow its own course apart from Soviet dictates. Havel was voted president of the new republic but resigned in 1992 when Czechoslovakia was dissolved and split into two separate countries. In 1993, he was voted president of the Czech republic.

Havel posits a moral criterion for future leaders but only after a thorough critique of the structure of his own society (in this essay, communist-ruled Czechoslovakia) as one that encourages obedience to a vast and complex structure of government, which he refers to as the "post-totalitarian system." Havel describes a society where individuals' actions are constrained and shaped to continually prop up a system that denies life, creativity, and moral responsibility. In such a society, people easily become demoralized in that they see their only responsibility as being their own survival in the system. In this context, those who try to exercise responsibility for their actions are seen as crazy. Dissidents do not want to fix the system, so that people will become better; rather, dissidents want to challenge individuals to become more human, to stop living the lie and accept responsibility for their actions. A new society, what Havel projects as a coming "existential revolution," would have to be built on the "rehabilitation of values" such as trust, responsibility, and solidarity. The less formal structure the better; leaders who crop up in this future, alternative government, will derive their authority from the people's confidence in their virtue.

RULER AS MORAL MODEL

Confucius

Duke Ai asked Confucius, "What is this great *li*? Why is it that you talk about *li* as though it were such an important thing?"

Confucius replied, "Your humble servant is really not worthy to understand *li*."

"But you do constantly speak about it," said Duke Ai.

Confucius: "What I have learned is this, that of all the things that the people live by, *li* is the greatest. Without *li*, we do not know how to conduct a proper worship of the spirits of the universe; or how to establish the proper status of the king and the ministers, the ruler and the ruled, and the elders and the juniors; or how to establish the moral relationships between the sexes, between parents and children and between brothers; or how to distinguish the different degrees of relationships in the family. That is why a gentleman holds *li* in such high regard, and proceeds to teach its principles to the people and regulate the forms of their social life. When these are established, then he institutes different insignia and ceremonial robes as symbols of authority to perpetuate the institutions. When everything is in order, then he proceeds to fix the periods of burial and mourning, provide the sacrificial vessels and the proper offerings, and beautify the ancestral temples. Every year sacrifices are made in their proper seasons, in order to bring about social order in the clans and tribes. Then he retires to his private dwelling where he lives in simple contentment, dressed simply and housed simply, without carved carriages and without carved vessels, sharing the same food and the same joys with the people. That was how the ancient princes lived in accordance with *li*."

Duke Ai: "Why don't the princes of today do the same?"

Confucius: "The princes of today are greedy in their search after material goods. They indulge themselves in pleasure and neglect their duties and carry themselves with a proud air. They take all they can from the people and invade the territory of good rulers against the will of the people, and they go out to get what they want without regard for what is right. This is the way of the modern rulers, while that was the way of the ancient rulers whom I just spoke of. The rulers of today do not follow *li*."

Confucius was sitting in the company of Duke Ai, and the Duke asked: "What, in your opinion, is the highest principle of human civilization?" Confucius looked very grave and replied: "It is the good fortune of the people that Your Highness has asked this question. I must do my best to answer it. The highest principle of human civilization is government."

The Duke: "May I ask what is the art of government?"

Confucius: "The art of government simply consists in making things right, or putting things in their right places. When the ruler himself is "right," then the people naturally follow him in his right course. The people merely follow what the ruler does, for what the ruler himself does not do, wherewithal shall the people know how and what to follow?"

The Duke: "Tell me more in detail about this art of government."

Confucius: "The husband and wife should have different duties. The parents and children should be affectionate toward each other. The king and his subjects should have rigid discipline. When these three things are right, then everything follows."

The Duke: "Can you enlighten me a little more on the method to carry out these three things, unworthy as I am?"

Confucius: "The ancient rulers regarded loving the people as the chief principle of their government, and *li* as the chief principle by which they ruled the people they loved. In the cultivation of *li*, the sense of respect is the most important, and as the ultimate symbol of this respect, the ceremony of royal marriage is the most important. The ceremony of royal marriage is the ultimate symbol of respect, and as it is the ultimate symbol of respect, the king goes with his crown to welcome the princess from her own home personally because he regards the bride as so close in relationship to him. He goes personally because the relationship is regarded as personal. Therefore the sovereign cultivates the sense of respect and personal relationship. To neglect to show respect is to disregard the personal relationship. Without love, there will be no *personal* relationship, and without respect, there will be no *right* relationship. So love and respect are the foundation of government."

Duke Ai: "I want to say something. Isn't it making the royal marriage a little too serious by requiring a king to wear his crown and welcome the princess from her own home?"

Confucius looked very grave and replied: "Why do you say so? A royal marriage means the union of two ruling houses for the purpose of carrying on the royal lineage and producing offspring to preside over the worship of Heaven and Earth, of the ancestral spirits, and of the gods of land and grains."

Duke Ali: "Excuse me for pressing the question, for if I do not persist, I shall not be able to hear your opinions on this point. I want to ask you something, but do not know how to put it. Will you please proceed further?"

Confucius: "You see, if Heaven and Earth (representing *yin* and *yang*) do not come together, there is no life in this world. A royal marriage is for the purpose of perpetuating the ruling house for thousands of generations. How can one take it too seriously?"

Confucius then said: "In the art of government, *li* comes first. It is the means by which we establish the forms of worship, enabling the ruler to appear before the spirits of Heaven and Earth at sacrifices on the one hand; and on the other, it is the means by which we establish the forms of intercourse at the court and a sense of piety or respect between the ruler and the ruled. It revives or resuscitates the social and political life from a condition of disgraceful confusion. Therefore *li* is the foundation of government."

Confucius then went on to say: "The ancient great kings always showed respect or proper consideration to their wives and children in accordance with a proper principle. How can one be disrespectful (or show disregard) toward one's wife since she is the center of the home? And how can one be disrespectful toward (or be lacking in regard for) one's children, since the children perpetuate the family? A gentleman is always respectful or always shows regard for everything. First of all he is respectful, or shows a pious regard toward himself. How dare he be disrespectful or have no pious regard for himself since the self is a branch of the family line? Not to show regard for one's self is to injure the family, and to injure the family is to injure the root, and when the root is injured, the branches die off. These three things, the relationship toward one's wife, toward one's children and toward one's self, are a symbol of the human relationships among the people. By showing respect for his own self, he teaches the people respect for their selves; by showing regard for his own children, he teaches the people regard for their children; and by showing regard for his own wife, he teaches the people regard for their wives. When a sovereign carries out these three things, his example will be imitated by the entire country. This is the principle of King T'ai (grandfather of King Wen). Thus harmonious relationships will prevail in the country."

Duke Ai: "May I ask what is meant by showing respect for one's self?"

Confucius: "When the sovereign makes a mistake in his speech, the people quote him, and when a sovereign makes a mistake in his conduct, the people imitate him. When a sovereign makes no mistakes in his speech or his conduct, then the people learn respect for him without any laws or regulations. In this way the sovereign shows respect for himself, and by showing respect for himself, he glorifies his ancestors."

Duke Ai: "May I ask what you mean by 'glorifying one's ancestors'?"

Confucius: "When a man becomes famous, we call him 'a prince' or 'a princely man,' and the people gladly follow him and honor him, saying that he is 'a prince's son' (or 'son of a gentleman'). Thus his own father is called a 'prince' through him and his name is glorified."

Confucius went on to say: "The ancient rulers considered loving the people as the first thing in their government. Without loving the people, the ruler cannot realize his true self, and without realizing or taking possession of his true self, he cannot establish peace in his land; without peace in his land, he cannot enjoy life in conformity with God's law; and being unable to enjoy life in conformity with God's law, he cannot live a full life."

Duke Ai: "May I ask what you mean by 'living a full life'?"

Confucius: "Just follow the natural law of things."

Duke Ai: "May I ask why the gentleman lays such stress on the laws of God?"

Confucius: "The gentleman lays such stress upon God's law, because it is eternal. For instance, you see the sun and the moon eternally following one another in their courses—that is God's law. Life in this universe never stops and continues forever—that is God's law. Things are created or produced without any effort or interference—that is God's law. When the things are created or produced, the universe is illuminated—that is God's law."

Duke Ai: "I'm stupid and confused. Will you make it clearer and simplify it so that I can remember?"

A change came over Confucius' countenance. He rose from his seat and said: "A great man simply follows the natural law of things. A good son simply follows the natural law of things. Therefore, a great man feels he is serving God when he serves his parents, and feels he is serving his parents when he serves God. Therefore, a good son lives a full life."

Duke Ai: "I am extremely fortunate to have heard these words from you, and I crave your pardon if I fail to live up to them hereafter."

Confucius: "The pleasure is mine."

THE PHILOSOPHER KING

Plato

I said*—"since philosophers alone are able to lay hold of the ever same and unchangeable, and those who cannot do so, but keep wandering amid the changeable and manifold are not philosophers,—which ought to be leaders of a city?"

"I hardly know what to say, without saying too much," he said.

"Whichever of the two," said I, "appear able to guard the laws and habits of cities, set them up as guardians."

"Quite right," he said.

"Here is another question," said I: "Ought a guardian to be blind or sharp-sighted when he watches anything? Is that clear?"

"Of course it is clear," he said.

"Well then, are those any better than blind men who are in truth deprived of knowledge of what truly each thing is?—who have no bright-shining pattern in the soul; who cannot fix their eyes on the truest, like painters, always referring to it and beholding it most exactly, and only thus lay down ordinances here as regards what is beautiful and just and good, if that is necessary, and preserve and keep safe those already laid down?"

"No indeed," he said, "they are not much better than the blind."

"Then shall we choose to establish these as guardians, or those who do know everything that really is, and in experience are not inferior to the others, and in any portion of virtue, too, are not behind them?"

"Really it would be extraordinary," said he, "to choose others, provided that the philosophers were not otherwise inferior, when they would be superior

---

*The main speaker is Socrates. He is speaking with Glaucon, and occasionally with Glaucon's brother Adeimantos [Eds.].

in this very knowledge—perhaps the greatest of superiorities."

"Then let us say now, in what way the same persons will be able to have both qualifications."

"By all means."

"Then we should first learn their nature, as we said when we began this talk. And I believe that if we can satisfy ourselves as to that, we shall agree both that the same persons are able to have both, and that these and no others ought to be leaders of cities."

"How?"

"One thing in the nature of philosophers let us take as agreed, that they always are in love with learning, that is, whatever makes clear to them anything of that being[1] which is eternal, and does not merely wander about between the limits of birth and death."

"Let that be taken as agreed."

"Further," said I, "they never leave hold of this being, if they can help it, the whole or a part, neither a greater part nor smaller, neither a more honourable part nor less honourable. We have shown that already in discussing lovers of honour and the amorous."

"You are right," he answered.

"Next, consider if there be necessity to have something else, in the nature of those who are to be such as we described."

"What?"

"Truthfulness—never to admit willingly a falsehood, to hate it and to love the truth."

"That is likely," said he.

"Not only likely, my friend," said I; "it is absolute necessity that one who is in love with anything by his nature should be fond of all that is akin to his beloved and at home in his beloved."

"But further, if the desires in anyone weigh strongly towards some one thing, we know, I suppose, that they are weaker for other things, like a flow of water drawn away to one place by a channel."

"Certainly."

"Well, when the desires in anyone flow towards learning and every such object, their concern would surely be with the pleasure of the soul within itself, and they would leave alone bodily pleasures, if one were a true lover of wisdom, not a sham."

"That is utterly necessary."

"Again, such a one would be temperate, and in no wise a money-lover, for to seek earnestly those things for which wealth with its great expenditure is earnestly sought belongs to anyone but him."

"That is so."

"There is something more which you must ask if you mean to distinguish the philosopher's nature from the sham."

"What is that?"

"Has it a touch of meanness? Don't overlook that; for littleness is the most opposite, I take it, to a soul which is always yearning to reach after what is whole and complete, both human and divine."

"Very true," said he.

"Then if a mind has magnificence, and a view over all time and all being, do you believe such a one thinks human life a great thing?"

"Impossible," said he.

"Then he will consider death to be no terror?"

"Not in the least," said he.

"Then a cowardly and mean nature could have no part in true philosophy, as it seems."

"I think not."

"Very well; one well-ordered and not covetous, not mean or cowardly, no impostor, could never become a hard bargainer or unjust?"

"It is not possible."

• • •

"Then can you find a fault anywhere in such a pursuit, which a man would never be able to practise competently unless he were by nature good at remembering and learning, endowed with magnificence and grace, friendly and akin to truth, justice, courage, temperance?" "Not Fault-finding himself* personified," said he, "could find any fault in that."

---

[1] "Being," of course, is not a person, but abstract, all that really is, as distinct from what seems to be, or what changes.

*Momos, the god of blame [Eds.].

"Very well," I said, "when such men are perfected by education and ripe age, you would commit the city to them alone, wouldn't you?"

And Adeimantos answered, "What you say, Socrates, no one could contradict. But you should know what happens to those who hear you each time you speak in this way. They feel their own inexperience in question and answer, and they think they are led astray a little in each question, so that at the end of an argument the many littles make a muckle; they stumble badly and find themselves contradicting what they said at first. It is like a game of checkers, when bad players in the end are held in check by the good players and can't make a move: so they also find themselves in check and can't make a speech in this other game with words for counters; and they feel indeed that they have not grasped the truth any better by this game. I speak with an eye to the present case. As things are, one might say that in each question he could not contradict you in argument; but they say what they see in fact is that of those who apply themselves to philosophy and spend a long time in the study, not those who only touch it as a part of education and drop it while still young, most become regular cranks, not to say quite worthless, and those who are considered the finest are made useless to their cities by the very pursuit which you praise."

I listened to this and said, "Then do you think that those who say this are saying untruths?"

"I don't know," said he, "but I would gladly hear your opinion."

"You would hear then," said I, "that they appear to me to be speaking the truth."

"Then how can it be right," said he, "to say that cities will have no end to their miseries until philosophers rule in them, when we admit that philosophers are useless to them?"

"You ask a question," said I, "which must be answered in a parable."

"And you never use parables, of course!" he said.

"Oh, all right!" I said. "You make fun of me after dumping me into an argument so hard to prove! Listen to my parable then, and see more than ever how greedy I am of parables. The fact is, that what happens to the finest philosophers in their relation to cities is hard; there is no single thing in the world like it, but one must compile a parable from all sorts of things to defend them, like a painter painting a goat-stag* and other such mixtures. Imagine a ship or a fleet of ships in the following state. The captain† is above all on board in stature and strength, but rather deaf and likewise rather short-sighted, and he knows navigation no better than he sees and hears. The crew are quarrelling about pilotage; everyone thinks he ought to be pilot, although he knows nothing of the art, and cannot tell us who taught him or where he learnt it. Besides, they all declared that it cannot be taught, and they are ready to tear in pieces anyone who says it can; they all keep crowding round the solitary captain, begging and praying and doing anything and everything to get him to hand over the helm to them. Sometimes one party fails but another succeeds better; then one party kills the other, or throws them overboard, and the good, honest captain they bind hand and foot by some opiate or intoxicant or some other means and take command of the ship. They use up all the stores, drinking and feasting, and make such a voyage as you might expect with such men. Besides, they have their votes of thanks: one has a testimonial as Good Navigator, another is a Born Pilot and Master Mariner. These are for any who are good hands at backing them up when they try to persuade or compel the captain to let them rule; for those who will not they have a vote of censure, Good-For-Nothing, and the true pilot is nowhere—they won't listen to him. They fail to understand that he must devote his attention to year and seasons, sky and stars and winds, and all that belongs to his art, if he is really to be anything like a ruler of the ship; but that as for gaining control of the helm, with the approval of some people and the disapproval of others, neither art not practice of this can be comprehended at the same time as the art of navigation.

---

*One of the Greek mythical creatures; cf. the centaur, part man ad part horse. [Eds.].
†The people in a democracy [Eds.].

With such a state of things on board the ships, don't you believe the true-born pilot would be dubbed stargazer, bibble-babbler, good-for-nothing, by those afloat in ships so provided?"

"That he would," said Adeimantos.

"I don't suppose," I said, "you want us to examine the parable bit by bit, and so to see how this is exactly what happens between the true philosopher and the city; I think you understand what I mean."

"Certainly," he said.

"Well, then, if anyone is surprised that philosophers are not honoured in a city, first teach him this parable, and try to persuade him that it would be much more surprising if they were."

"That I will," said he.

"And tell him he is quite right in saying that the finest philosophers are useless to the multitude; but tell him it is *their* fault for not using them, no fault of these fine men. For it is not natural that a pilot should beg the sailors to be ruled by him; nor that the wise should wait at the rich man's door.[2] No, the author of that neat saying told a lie, but the truth is that the sick man must wait at the doctor's door, whether he is rich or poor; and anyone who needs to be ruled should wait at the door of one who is able to rule him, not that the ruler should petition the subjects to be ruled, if there is truly any help in him. But you will make no mistake in likening the present political rulers to the sailors I described just now, and those whom they call good-for-nothing and stargazing babblers to the true pilots."

"Quite right," said he.

AGAINST CONCEIVING POLITICS AS THE RULER AND THE RULED

Hannah Arendt

History is full of examples of the impotence of the strong and superior man who does not know how to

enlist the help, the co-acting of his fellow men. His failure is frequently blamed upon the fatal inferiority of the many and the resentment every outstanding person inspires in those who are mediocre. Yet true as such observations are bound to be, they do not touch the heart of the matter.

In order to illustrate what is at stake here we may remember that Greek and Latin, unlike the modern languages, contain two altogether different and yet interrelated words with which to designate the verb "to act." To the two Greek verbs *archein* ("to begin," "to lead," finally "to rule") and *prattein* ("to pass through," "to achieve," "to finish") correspond the two Latin verbs *agere* ("to set into motion," "to lead") and *gerere* (whose original meaning is "to bear"). Here it seems as though each action were divided into two parts, the beginning made by a single person and the achievement in which many join by "bearing" and "finishing" the enterprise, by seeing it through. Not only are the words interrelated in a similar manner, the history of their usage is very similar too. In both cases the word that originally designated only the second part of action, its achievement—*prattein* and *gerere*—became the accepted word for action in general, whereas the words designating the beginning of action became specialized in meaning, at least in political language. *Archein* came to mean chiefly "to rule" and "to lead" when it was specifically used, and *agere* came to mean "to lead" rather than "to set into motion."

Thus the role of the beginner and leader, who was a *primus inter pares* (in the case of Homer, a king among kings), changed into that of a ruler; the original interdependence of action, the dependence of the beginner and leader upon others for help and the dependence of his followers upon him for an occasion to act themselves, split into two altogether different functions: the function of giving commands, which became the prerogative of the ruler, and the function of executing them, which became the duty of his subjects. This ruler is alone, isolated against others by his force, just as the beginner was isolated through his initiative at the start, before he had found others to join him. Yet the strength of the beginner and leader shows itself only in his initiative and the risk he takes, not in the actual achievement. In the case of the successful ruler, he may claim for himself what actually is the achievement of many—something that Agamemnon, who was a king but no ruler, would never have been permitted. Through this claim, the ruler monopolizes, so to speak, the strength of those without whose help he would never be able to achieve anything. Thus, the delusion of extraordinary strength arises and with it the fallacy of the strong man who is powerful because he is alone.

Because the actor always moves among and in relation to other acting beings, he is never merely a "doer" but always and at the same time a sufferer. To do and to suffer are like opposite sides of the same coin, and the story that an act starts is composed of its consequent deeds and sufferings. These consequences are boundless, because action, though it may proceed from nowhere, so to speak, acts into a medium where every reaction becomes a chain reaction and where every process is the cause of new processes. Since action acts upon beings who are capable of their own actions, reaction, apart from being a response, is always a new action that strikes out on its own and affects others. Thus action and reaction among men never move in a closed circle and can never be reliably confined to two partners. This boundlessness is characteristic not of political action alone, in the narrower sense of the word, as though the boundlessness of human interrelatedness were only the result of the boundless multitude of people involved, which could be escaped by resigning oneself to action within a limited, graspable framework of circumstances; the smallest act in the most limited circumstances bears the seed of the same boundlessness, because one deed, and sometimes one word, suffices to change every constellation.

· · ·

Escape from the frailty of human affairs into the solidity of quiet and order has in fact so much to recommend it that the greater part of political philosophy since Plato could easily be interpreted as various attempts to find theoretical foundations and practical ways for an escape from politics altogether. The hallmark of all such escapes is the concept of rule, that is, the notion that men can lawfully and politically live together only when some are entitled to command and the others forced to obey. The commonplace notion already to be found in Plato and Aristotle that every political community consists of those who rule and those who are ruled (on which assumption in turn are based the current definitions of forms of government—rule by one or monarchy, rule by few or oligarchy, rule by many or democracy) rests on a suspicion of action rather than on a contempt for men, and arose from the earnest desire to find a substitute for action rather than from any irresponsible or tyrannical will to power.

Theoretically, the most brief and most fundamental version of the escape from action into rule occurs in the *Statesman,* where Plato opens a gulf between the two modes of action, *archein* and *prattein* ("beginning" and "achieving"), which according to Greek understanding were interconnected. The problem, as Plato saw it, was to make sure that the beginner would remain the complete master of what he had begun, not needing the help of others to carry it through. In the realm of action, this isolated mastership can be achieved only if the others are no longer needed to join the enterprise of their own accord, with their own motives and aims, but are used to execute orders, and if, on the other hand, the beginner who took the initiative does not permit himself to get involved in the action itself. To begin (*archein*) and to act (*prattein*) thus can become two altogether different activities, and the beginner has become a ruler (an *archōn* in the twofold sense of the word) who "does not have to act at all (*prattein*), but rules (*archein*) over those who are capable of execution." Under these circumstances, the essence of politics is "to know how to begin and to rule in the gravest matters with regard to timeliness and untimeliness"; action as such is entirely eliminated and has become the mere "execution of orders."[3] Plato was the first to introduce the division between those who know and do not act and those

_____

[3] *Statesman* 305.

who act and do not know, instead of the old articulation of action into beginning and achieving, so that knowing what to do and doing it became two altogether different performances.

. . . According to Greek understanding, the relationship between ruling and being ruled, between command and obedience, was by definition identical with the relationship between master and slaves and therefore precluded all possibility of action. Plato's contention, therefore, that the rules of behavior in public matters should be derived from the master-slave relationship in a well-ordered household actually meant that action should not play any part in human affairs.

It is obvious that Plato's scheme offers much greater chances for a permanent order in human affairs than the tyrant's efforts to eliminate everybody but himself from the public realm. Although each citizen would retain some part in the handling of public affairs, they would indeed "act" like one man without even the possibility of internal dissension, let alone factional strife: through rule, "the many become one in every respect" except bodily appearance.[4] Historically, the concept of rule, though originating in the household and family realm, has played its most decisive part in the organization of public matters and is for us invariably connected with politics. This should not make us overlook the fact that for Plato it was a much more general category. He saw in it the chief device for ordering and judging human affairs in every respect. This is not only evident from his insistence that the city-state must be considered to be "man writ large" and from his construction of a psychological order which actually follows the public order of his utopian city, but is even more manifest in the grandiose consistency with which he introduced the principle of domination into the intercourse of man with himself. The supreme criterion of fitness for ruling others is, in Plato and in the aristocratic tradition of the West, the capacity to rule one's self. Just as the philosopher-king commands the city, the soul commands the body and reason commands the passions. In Plato himself, the legitimacy of this tyranny in everything pertaining to man, his conduct toward himself no less than his conduct toward others, is still firmly rooted in the equivocal significance of the word *archein*, which means both beginning and ruling; it is decisive for Plato, as he says expressly at the end of the *Laws*, that only the beginning (*archē*) is entitled to rule (*archein*). In the tradition of Platonic thought, this original, linguistically predetermined identity of ruling and beginning had the consequence that all beginning was understood as the legitimation for rulership, until, finally, the element of beginning disappeared altogether from the concept of rulership. With it the most elementary and authentic understanding of human freedom disappeared from political philosophy.

The Platonic separation of knowing and doing has remained at the root of all theories of domination which are not mere justifications of an irreducible and irresponsible will to power. By sheer force of conceptualization and philosophical clarification, the Platonic identification of knowledge with command and rulership and of action with obedience and execution overruled all earlier experiences and articulations in the political realm and became authoritative for the whole tradition of political thought.

TRUST IN LEADERS

Vaclav Havel

The smaller a dictatorship and the less stratified by modernization the society under it, the more directly the will of the dictator can be exercised. In other words, the dictator can employ more or less naked discipline, avoiding the complex processes of relating to the world and of self-justification which ideology involves. But the more complex the mechanisms of power become, the larger and more

---

[4] *Republic* 443E.

stratified the society they embrace, and the longer they have operated historically, the more individuals must be connected to them from outside, and the greater the importance attached to the ideological excuse. It acts as a kind of bridge between the regime and the people, across which the regime approaches the people and the people approach the regime. This explains why ideology plays such an important role in the post-totalitarian system: that complex machinery of units, hierarchies, transmission belts, and indirect instruments of manipulation which ensure in countless ways the integrity of the regime, leaving nothing to chance, would be quite simply unthinkable without ideology acting as its all-embracing excuse and as the excuse for each of its parts. . . .

Between the aims of the post-totalitarian system and the aims of life there is a yawning abyss: while life, in its essence, moves toward plurality, diversity, independent self-constitution, and self-organization, in short, toward the fulfillment of its own freedom, the post-totalitarian system demands conformity, uniformity, and discipline. While life ever strives to create new and improbable structures, the post-totalitarian system contrives to force life into its most probable states. The aims of the system reveal its most essential characteristic to be introversion, a movement toward being ever more completely and unreservedly itself, which means that the radius of its influence is continually widening as well. This system serves people only to the extent necessary to ensure that people will serve it. Anything beyond this, that is to say, anything which leads people to overstep their predetermined roles is regarded by the system as an attack upon itself. And in this respect it is correct: every instance of such transgression is a genuine denial of the system. It can be said, therefore, that the inner aim of the post-totalitarian system is not mere preservation of power in the hands of a ruling clique, as appears to be the case at first sight. Rather, the social phenomenon of self-preservation is subordinated to something higher, to a kind of blind automatism which drives the system. No matter what position individuals hold in the hierarchy of power, they are not

considered by the system to be worth anything in themselves, but only as things intended to fuel and serve this automatism. For this reason, an individual's desire for power is admissible only in so far as its direction coincides with the direction of the automatism of the system.

Ideology, in creating a bridge of excuses between the system and the individual, spans the abyss between the aims of the system and the aims of life. It pretends that the requirements of the system derive from the requirements of life. It is a world of appearances trying to pass for reality.

The post-totalitarian system touches people at every step, but it does so with its ideological gloves on. This is why life in the system is so thoroughly permeated with hypocrisy and lies: government by bureaucracy is called popular government; the working class is enslaved in the name of the working class; the complete degradation of the individual is presented as his ultimate liberation; depriving people of information is called making it available; the use of power to manipulate is called the public control of power, and the arbitrary abuse of power is called observing the legal code; the repression of culture is called its development; the expansion of imperial influence is presented as support for the oppressed; the lack of free expression becomes the highest form of freedom; farcical elections become the highest form of democracy; banning independent thought becomes the most scientific of world views; military occupation becomes fraternal assistance. Because the regime is captive to its own lies, it must falsify everything. It falsifies the past. It falsifies the present, and it falsifies the future. It falsifies statistics. It pretends not to possess an omnipotent and unprincipled police apparatus. It pretends to respect human rights. It pretends to persecute no one. It pretends to fear nothing. It pretends to pretend nothing.

Individuals need not believe all these mystifications, but they must behave as though they did, or they must at least tolerate them in silence, or get along well with those who work with them. For this reason, however, they must live within a lie. They need not accept the lie. It is enough for them to have accepted their life with it and in it. For by this very fact, individuals confirm the system, fulfill the system, make the system, *are* the system.

· · ·

I see a renewed focus of politics on real people as something far more profound than merely returning to the everyday mechanisms of Western (or, if you like, bourgeois) democracy. In 1968, I felt that our problem could be solved by forming an opposition party that would compete publicly for power with the Communist Party. I have long since come to realize, however, that it is just not that simple and that no opposition party in and of itself, just as no new electoral laws in and of themselves, could make society proof against some new form of violence. No "dry" organizational measures in themselves can provide that guarantee, and we would be hard-pressed to find in them that God who alone can save us.

I may . . . be asked the question: What then is to be done?

My skepticism toward alternative political models and the ability of systemic reforms or changes to redeem us does not, of course, mean that I am skeptical of political thought altogether. Nor does my emphasis on the importance of focusing concern on real human beings disqualify me from considering the possible structural consequences flowing from it. On the contrary, if A was said, then B should be said as well. Nevertheless, I will offer only a few very general remarks.

Above all, any existential revolution should provide hope of a moral reconstitution of society, which means a radical renewal of the relationship of human beings to what I have called the "human order," which no political order can replace. A new experience of being, a renewed rootedness in the universe, a newly grasped sense of higher responsibility, a newfound inner relationship to other people and to the human community—these factors clearly indicate the direction in which we must go.

And the political consequences? Most probably they could be reflected in the constitution of structures that will derive from this new spirit, from

human factors rather than from a particular formalization of political relationships and guarantees. In other words, the issue is the rehabilitation of values like trust, openness, responsibility, solidarity, love. I believe in structures that are not aimed at the technical aspect of the execution of power, but at the significance of that execution in structures held together more by a commonly shared feeling of the importance of certain communities than by commonly shared expansionist ambitions directed outward. There can and must be structures that are open, dynamic, and small; beyond a certain point, human ties like personal trust and personal responsibility cannot work. There must be structures that in principle place no limits on the genesis of different structures. Any accumulation of power whatsoever (one of the characteristics of automatism) should be profoundly alien to it. They would be structures not in the sense of organizations or institutions, but like a community. Their authority certainly cannot be based on long-empty traditions, like the tradition of mass political parties, but rather on how, in concrete terms, they enter into a given situation. Rather than a strategic agglomeration of formalized organizations, it is better to have organizations springing up ad hoc, infused with enthusiasm for a particular purpose and disappearing when that purpose has been achieved. The leaders' authority ought to derive from their personalities and be personally tested in their particular surroundings, and not from their position in any *nomenklatura*. They should enjoy great personal confidence and even great lawmaking powers based on that confidence.

QUESTIONS FOR DISCUSSION

1. Find in the newspapers an account of a contemporary politician. How would Confucius regard this politician, and why? How would Plato regard her or him? Would you agree or disagree with their critique? Why or why not?

2. Havel suggested later in his career that this cri-

tique of government structures, and ensuing demoralization, applies to all consumer societies. Can you find evidence or examples from your daily life that illustrate Havel's points? What does "living a lie" mean in the U.S. context?

3. Is the idea of a moral, responsible citizenry in a democracy an impossible ideal? Or must the people depend on a ruling elite that is able to uphold moral standards that the general public could not practice? Give reasons for your answer.

DOMINATION AND THE STRUGGLE AGAINST DOMINATION

This section focuses on the ever-recurrent political problem that stems from abuses of rulership. What constitutes unjust rulership, or domination? Dictionary accounts define *domination* as an "exercise of power in ruling" but add that the term also refers to "arbitrary or insolent sway." Not all thinkers agree on where to draw the line, in specific instances as well as in theory, between legitimate authority and use of power and brutal or disrespectful abuse of power.

Our first author, Friedrich Nietzsche, argues that there is nothing wrong with using others and that relationships of inequality are natural. The authors following him all argue that some sort of struggle against systems of domination is necessary to restore human dignity at some level. Some authors define domination in practical terms; others are primarily interested in its psychological effects on individuals. An examination of our authors' ideas in the context of their lives will prove illuminating, as the personal experiences of each contributed greatly to the views he or she held.

Friedrich Nietzsche was born in 1844 in Rocken, Prussia. Noticed early in his career for his brilliance, he was appointed an associate professor at the University of Basel at the age of 24. Nietzsche in his brief career wrote many controversial philosophical works and was an important participant in the intellectual climate of the time in Germany.

In the selection presented below, Nietzsche advocates the moral philosophy of the "master" or superior man, who loves life and does not apologize for surviving and thriving by whatever means necessary. After all, all of life is exploitation, as everyone can tell by pondering their own "exploitation" of animals and plants to enrich themselves in the daily act of eating. Those who don't get others to do for them as the master does are too weak to assert their wills and are general failures at life, deserving any mistreatment they receive. "Slave" moralities, such as that of Christianity, condemn those who ex-

ploit as evil, while claiming themselves and their attributes of humility and helpfulness to be "good." Nietzsche, however, is suspicious of their true motives; their condemnation of the master is based on resentment. To console themselves with feelings of their own moral superiority, they castigate the master and wish upon him eternal hellfire. The master would be better off seeing through this veneer of false slave morality and relying on his own moral code. Certainly during the times that Nietzsche was writing, something similar to "master morality" was being practiced on a grand scale by the imperializing nations of Europe, and so of course his ideas were not produced without a context.

For Nietzsche, morality is not what it appears to be; morality appeals to timeless standards of right and wrong, but it always serves a purpose, or, should we say, certain interests. In this way his critique of morality is similar to that of Marx and Engels. According to Marx and Engels, what counts as virtue and what counts as criminal activity is always decided by the ruling class of any given era and framed in such a way as to legitimate the ruling class's own actions while appealing to universal impartiality.

Karl Marx (1818–1883) was born in Trier in the Rhineland of Germany of a Jewish family. He received a doctorate in philosophy from the University of Jena. He was involved in journalism which criticized the government's policies and soon found himself exiled, first in France and then in England. His partnership with German-born Friedrich Engels (1820–1895) solidified in England, where Engels worked in his father's textile industry and helped to support Marx in his studies.

In *The Communist Manifesto,* Marx and Engels describe, first, how societies through the ages, from ancient to feudal to modern times, have always been set up to legitimate exploitation. Although capitalism has served its purpose in society, by furthering the means of production, its usefulness has passed. In the near future, they predict, the time will be ripe for the workers to become self-aware and gather their forces together, to oust the capitalists from their position of privilege and give the factories to their rightful owners: the workers themselves.

Frantz Fanon carries this same theme out of the inter-European context and into the context of the fight against European imperialism. Born in 1925 of African ancestry, and a native of Martinique, a Caribbean island colonized by the French, Fanon had witnessed the nonviolent transfer of power in 1946, when France granted Martinique the right to self-government. He then went to France, became a psychiatrist, and was assigned to a hospital in Algeria during that country's fight for independence from France. There, he saw firsthand the devastating psychological effects for both colonizer and colonized that result from domination. Yet he saw in the violent fight for survival of the native Algerians a healthy and necessary struggle for psychological as well as political self-determination.

In the passage included here, Fanon applies German philosopher Hegel's account of the master-slave dialectic to the Martinican situation. Since Martinique had been given its independence without a fight, Fanon feels humiliation instead of relief, for it is in the struggle against the master for liberation that one gains self-definition. We all need to be recognized by others; whether one gains recognition as a "gift" or because one fought to deserve it makes all the difference. By risking one's life in struggle, one wins one's freedom.

Sandra Lee Bartky, contemporary feminist philosopher and professor, uses Fanon's psychological study of the colonized in the context of colonial rule to understand the internalized oppression experienced by women in societies where men are in power. Psychological oppression, she explains, has as its goal the obfuscation of the real source and nature of subjugation, so that women turn interiorly to find the source of their suffering within their own psyches, in a list of their own faults and failings, rather than in the male monopoly of power. The constant desire to please men distracts women from

self-fulfillment and inner peace, and diffuses any possible concerted action to change the status of women in society.

For Paulo Freire, liberation from oppression happens first through education. Freire, born in Recife, Brazil, in 1921, became well-known as a teacher of literacy among the poor of Brazil. Freire showed his students how to use words as a tool to express their demands and challenge the political and economic system in which they lived. While professor at the University of Recife in the early 1960s, Freire implemented his educational program throughout northeastern Brazil. However, when a military coup occurred in 1964, Freire was jailed, and later exiled, to return to Brazil 20 years later.

In this excerpt from Freire's *Pedagogy of the Oppressed*, the influence of existentialism on his work is evident. He describes becoming human as a project or vocation, to be accomplished in history; to be fully human people must struggle against the distortion of human life found in unjust social systems. Although the oppressed will most likely have to use violence to win their freedom, there is a love implicit in this uprising that is not present in the oppressor's use of violence. Destroying the oppressive system sets free the oppressors from their own negative roles, so that they can embrace a fuller humanity for themselves.

Malcolm X, later known as El Hajj Malik El Shabazz, describes his struggle for respect and self-recognition for all African Americans, in their attempt to combat U.S. racism. Malcolm X was born Malcolm Little in Michigan. His father was killed by Ku Klux Klan members when he was still a child, and his mother struggled with poverty in the years that followed. Years later, in prison, he studied Islam, prompted by correspondence with the founder of the black-based Nation of Islam, Elijah Muhammad. An eloquent and fiery spokesman on his release from prison, Malcolm X became a preacher for the Nation of Islam, and was well-known to Americans for not mincing words about the situation of race relations in the United States. Heralded by some as a truth-teller and derided by others as a hate-monger, it is important to scrutinize his works to accurately understand his message.

The speech excerpted here was delivered on December 3, 1964 during a debate at Britain's Oxford University, in which he and others on his debate team defended the proposition, "Extremism in defense of liberty is no vice, moderation in the pursuit of justice is no virtue." Many in the audience were loudly enthusiastic in their applause of Malcolm; however, in the vote recorded after the debate, Malcolm's position received 137 votes, compared to 228 votes against. In this excerpt from the speech, Malcolm explains what he means by his now famous saying, "By any means necessary."

Malcolm argues that since racism is such a terrible blight upon society, extreme measures are justified in eradicating unjust racist structures. Certainly he argues, as he summed up elsewhere, the ballot would be better than the bullet; but if we look more closely at the so-called democratic system of government in the United States, we see that racist structures make reform impossible. In this context Malcolm insists that fear born from threats of violence may be the only thing that will be able to shake the system.

Our final author, Mohandas K. Gandhi, argues that colonial India should only attempt to win its freedom from British rule by nonviolent means. Gandhi was born in 1869 in Porbandar, India, an area highly influenced by Jainism with its emphasis on the practice of "ahimsa" or nonviolence. Gandhi would change the emphasis of this traditional spiritual virtue from "refraining to act" to acting in a context of resistance, while using nonviolent means. He termed his actions "satyagraha," meaning "soul-force" or "truth-force," and was determined to reinforce through his actions this new method of seeking social change and justice.

As the selections in our chapter mention, there was much concern in India in the years preceding independence, as to whether Gandhi's nonviolent methods would work. There had been a massacre at Jalianwala Bagh, located in Amritsar, in April, 1919. General Dyer of the British forces decided to order his troops to open fire on a peaceful assembly of protestors, because they disobeyed the order against holding public meetings. Over three hundred people were killed and over one thousand were wounded. Although Gandhi mourned for those who were killed, he said that he felt worse when he heard reports of Indians who had used violence against the British; so set was he to show that India could use the method of nonviolence to win freedom.

Gandhi was a Hindu (and Hindus make up about 80 percent of the population of India, while Muslims account for about 15 percent), and yet his movement was vigorously in favor of Hindu-Muslim unity. The Khalifat Committee mentioned in the following passages was created to show united support in India for the Caliph, or religious leader in Islam, who was in a troubled position after the defeat of Turkey in World War I. Both Hindus and Muslims braved arrests and beatings in many satyagraha campaigns. The Great Salt Satyagraha was one of the most famous and widespread of the nonviolent campaigns, and its success resulted in the Round Table talks in London between British government officials, Gandhi, and other members of the Indian National Congress in 1931, as a prelude to independence.

MASTER AND SLAVE MORALITY

Friedrich Nietzsche

Refraining mutually from injury, violence, and exploitation and placing one's will on a par with that of someone else—this may become, in a certain rough sense, good manners among individuals if the appropriate conditions are present (namely, if these men are actually similar in strength and value standards and belong together in *one* body). But as soon as this principle is extended, and possibly even accepted as the *fundamental principle of society*, it immediately proves to be what it really is—a will to the *denial* of life, a principle of disintegration and decay.

Here we must beware of superficiality and get to the bottom of the matter, resisting all sentimental weakness: life itself is *essentially* appropriation, injury, overpowering of what is alien and weaker; suppression, hardness, imposition of one's own forms, incorporation and at least, at its mildest, exploitation—but why should one always use those words in which a slanderous intent has been imprinted for ages?

Even the body within which individuals treat each other as equals, as suggested before—and this happens in every healthy aristocracy—if it is a living and not a dying body, has to do to other bodies what the individuals within it refrain from doing to each other: it will have to be an incarnate will to power, it will strive to grow, spread, seize, become predominant—not from any morality or immorality but because it is *living* and because life simply *is* will to power. But there is no point on which the ordinary consciousness of Europeans resists instruction as on this: everywhere people are now raving, even under scientific disguises, about coming conditions of society in which "the exploitative aspect" will be removed—which sounds to me as if they promised to invent a way of life that would dispense with all organic functions. "Exploitation" does not belong to a corrupt or imperfect and primitive society: it belongs to the *essence* of what lives, as a basic organic function; it is a consequence of the will to power, which is after all the will of life.

If this should be an innovation as a theory—as a reality it is the *primordial fact* of all history: people ought to be honest with themselves at least that far.

Wandering through the many subtler and coarser moralities which have so far been prevalent on earth, or still are prevalent, I found that certain features recurred regularly together and were closely associated—until I finally discovered two basic types and one basic difference.

There are *master morality* and *slave morality*—I add immediately that in all the higher and more mixed cultures there also appear attempts at mediation between these two moralities, and yet more often the interpenetration and mutual misunderstanding of both, and at times they occur directly alongside each other—even in the same human being, within a *single* soul. The moral discrimination of values has originated either among a ruling group whose consciousness of its difference from the ruled group was accompanied by delight—or among the ruled, the slaves and dependents of every degree.

In the first case, when the ruling group determines what is "good," the exalted, proud states of the soul are experienced as conferring distinction and determining the order of rank. The noble human being separates from himself those in whom the opposite of such exalted, proud states finds expression: he despises them. It should be noted immediately that in this first type of morality the opposition of "good" and "*bad*" means approximately the same as "noble" and "contemptible." (The opposition of "good" and "*evil*" has a different origin.) One feels contempt for the cowardly, the anxious, the petty, those intent on narrow utility; also for the suspicious with their unfree glances, those who humble themselves, the doglike people who allow themselves to be maltreated, the begging flatterers, above all the liars: it is part of the fundamental faith of all aristocrats that the common people lie. "We truthful ones"—thus the nobility of ancient Greece referred to itself.

It is obvious that moral designations were everywhere first applied to *human beings* and only later, derivatively, to actions. Therefore it is a gross mistake when historians of morality start from such questions as: why was the compassionate act praised? The noble type of man experiences *itself* as determining values; it does not need approval; it judges, "what is harmful to me is harmful in itself"; it knows itself to be that which first accords honor to things; it is *value-creating*. Everything it knows as part of itself it honors: such a morality is self-glorification. In the foreground there is the feeling of fullness, of power that seeks to overflow, the happiness of high tension, the consciousness of wealth that would give and bestow: the noble human being, too, helps the unfortunate, but not, or almost not, from pity, but prompted more by an urge begotten by excess of power. The noble human being honors himself as one who is powerful, also as one who has power over himself, who knows how to speak and be silent, who delights in being severe and hard with himself and respects all severity and hardness. "A hard heart Wotan put into my breast," says an old Scandinavian saga: a fitting poetic expression, seeing that it comes from the soul of a proud Viking. Such a type of man is actually proud of the fact that he is *not* made for pity, and the hero of the saga therefore adds as a warning: "If the heart is not hard in youth it will never harden." Noble and courageous human beings who think that way are furthest removed from that morality which finds the distinction of morality precisely in pity, or in acting for others, or in *désintéressement;* faith in oneself, pride in oneself, a fundamental hostility and irony against "selflessness" belong just as definitely to noble morality as does a slight disdain and caution regarding compassionate feelings and a "warm heart."

It is the powerful who *understand* how to honor; this is their art, their realm of invention. The profound reverence for age and tradition—all law rests on this double reverence—the faith and prejudice in favor of ancestors and disfavor of those yet to come are typical of the morality of the powerful; and when the men of "modern ideas," conversely, believe almost instinctively in "progress" and "the future" and more and more lack respect for age, this in itself would sufficiently betray the ignoble origin of these "ideas."

A morality of the ruling group, however, is most alien and embarrassing to the present taste in the severity of its principle that one has duties only to one's peers; that against beings of lower rank, against everything alien, one may behave as one pleases or "as the heart desires," and in any case "beyond good and evil"—here pity and like feelings may find their place. The capacity for, and the duty of, long gratitude and long revenge—both only among one's peers—refinement in repaying, the sophisticated concept of friendship, a certain necessity for having enemies (as it were, as drainage ditches for the affects of envy, quarrelsomeness, exuberance—at bottom, in order to be capable of being good *friends*): all these are typical characteristics of noble morality which, as suggested, is not the morality of "modern ideas" and therefore is hard to empathize with today, also hard to dig up and uncover.

It is different with the second type of morality, *slave morality*. Suppose the violated, oppressed, suffering, unfree, who are uncertain of themselves and weary, moralize: what will their moral valuations have in common? Probably, a pessimistic suspicion about the whole condition of man will find expression, perhaps a condemnation of man along with his condition. The slave's eye is not favorable to the virtues of the powerful: he is skeptical and suspicious, *subtly* suspicious, of all the "good" that is honored there—he would like to persuade himself that even their happiness is not genuine. Conversely, those qualities are brought out and flooded with light which serve to ease existence for those who suffer: here pity, the complaisant and obliging hand, the warm heart, patience, industry, humility, and friendliness are honored—for here these are the most useful qualities and almost the only means for enduring the pressure of existence. Slave morality is essentially a morality of utility.

Here is the place for the origin of that famous opposition of "good" and "evil": into evil one's feelings project power and dangerousness, a certain terribleness, subtlety, and strength that does not permit contempt to develop. According to slave morality, those who are "evil" thus inspire fear; according to master morality it is precisely those who are "good" that inspire, and wish to inspire, fear, while the "bad" are felt to be contemptible.

The opposition reaches its climax when, as a logical consequence of slave morality, a touch of disdain is associated also with the "good" of this morality—this may be slight and benevolent—because the good human being has to be *undangerous* in the slaves' way of thinking: he is good-natured, easy to deceive, a little stupid perhaps, *un bonhomme!** Wherever slave morality becomes preponderant, language tends to bring the words "good" and "stupid" closer together.

One last fundamental difference: the longing for *freedom*, the instinct for happiness and the subtleties of the feeling of freedom belong just as necessarily to slave morality and morals as artful and enthusiastic reverence and devotion are the regular symptom of an aristocratic way of thinking and evaluating.

This makes plain why love *as passion*—which is our European specialty—simply must be of noble origin: as is well known, its invention must be credited to the Provençal knight-poets, those magnificent and inventive human beings of the *"gai saber"*† to whom Europe owes so many things and almost owes itself.—

---

*A good person [Eds.].
†Translates as "gay science." Refers to the art of the troubadours [Eds.].

THE COMMUNIST MANIFESTO

Karl Marx and Friedrich Engels

The history of all hitherto existing society[1] is the history of class struggles.

Freeman and slave, patrician and plebeian, lord and serf, guild-master[2] and journeyman, in a word, oppressor and oppressed, stood in constant opposition to one another, carried on an uninterrupted, now hidden, now open fight, a fight that each time ended, either in a revolutionary reconstitution of society at large, or in the common ruin of the contending classes.

In the earlier epochs of history, we find almost everywhere a complicated arrangement of society into various orders, a manifold gradation of social rank. In ancient Rome we have patricians, knights, plebeians, slaves; in the Middle Ages, feudal lords, vassals, guild-masters, journeymen, apprentices, serfs; in almost all of these classes, again, subordinate gradations.

The modern bourgeois society that has sprouted from the ruins of feudal society, has not done away with class antagonisms. It has but established new classes, new conditions of oppression, new forms of struggle in place of the old ones.

---

[1] That is, all *written* history. In 1837, the pre-history of society, the social organization existing previous to recorded history, was all but unknown. Since then Haxthausen [August von, 1792–1866] discovered common ownership of land in Russia, Maurer [Georg Ludwig von] proved it to be the social foundation from which all Teutonic races started in history, and, by and by, village communities were found to be, or to have been, the primitive form of society everywhere from India to Ireland. The inner organization of this primitive communistic society was laid bare, in its typical form, by Morgan's [Lewis H., 1818–1881] crowning discovery of the true nature of the *gens* and its relation to the *tribe*. With the dissolution of these primeval communities, society begins to be differentiated into separate and finally antagonistic classes. I have attempted to retrace this process of dissolution in *The Origin of the Family, Private Property and the State*.
[2] Guild-master, that is a full member of a guild, a master within, not a head of a guild.

Our epoch, the epoch of the bourgeoisie, possesses, however, this distinctive feature: It has simplified the class antagonisms. Society as a whole is more and more splitting up into two great hostile camps, into two great classes directly facing each other—bourgeoisie and proletariat.[3]

From the serfs of the Middle Ages sprang the chartered burghers[4] of the earliest towns. From these burgesses the first elements of the bourgeoisie were developed.

The discovery of America, the rounding of the Cape, opened up fresh ground for the rising bourgeoisie. The East Indian and Chinese markets, the colonization of America, trade with the colonies, the increase in the means of exchange and in commodities generally, gave to commerce, to navigation, to industry, an impulse never before known, and thereby, to the revolutionary element in the tottering feudal society, a rapid development.

The feudal system of industry in which industrial production was monopolized by closed guilds,[5] now no longer sufficed for the growing wants of the new markets. The manufacturing system took its place. The guild-masters were pushed aside by the manufacturing middle class; division of labor between the different corporate guilds vanished in the face of division of labor in each single workshop.

Meantime the markets kept ever growing, the demand ever rising. Even manufacture no longer sufficed. Thereupon, steam and machinery revolutionized industrial production. The place of manufacture was taken by the giant, modern industry, the place of the industrial middle class, by industrial millionaires—the leaders of whole industrial armies, the modern bourgeois.

Modern industry has established the world market, for which the discovery of America paved the way. This market has given an immense development to commerce, to navigation, to communication by land. This development has, in its turn, reacted on the extension of industry; and in proportion as industry, commerce, navigation, railways extended, in the same proportion the bourgeoisie developed, increased its capital, and pushed into the background every class handed down from the Middle Ages.

We see, therefore, how the modern bourgeoisie is itself the product of a long course of development, of a series of revolutions in the modes of production and of exchange.

Each step in the development of the bourgeoisie was accompanied by a corresponding political advance of that class. An oppressed class under the sway of the feudal nobility, it became an armed and self-governing association in the medieval commune[6] here independent urban republic (as in Italy and Germany), there taxable "third estate" of the monarchy (as in France); afterwards, in the period of manufacture proper, serving either the semi-feudal or the absolute monarchy as a counterpoise against the nobility, and, in fact, cornerstone of the great monarchies in general—the bourgeoisie has at last, since the establishment of modern industry and of the world market, conquered for itself, in the modern representative state, exclusive political sway. The executive of the modern state is but a committee for managing the common affairs of the whole bourgeoisie.

The bourgeoisie has played a most revolutionary role in history.

---

[3] By bourgeoisie is meant the class of modern capitalists, owners of the means of social production and employers of wage-labor; by proletariat, the class of modern wage-laborers who, having no means of production of their own, are reduced to selling their labor power in order to live.

[4] Chartered burghers were freemen who had been admitted to the privileges of a chartered borough thus possessing full political rights.—*Ed.*

[5] Craft guilds, made up of exclusive and privileged groups of artisans were, during the feudal period, granted monopoly rights to markets by municipal authorities. The guilds imposed minute regulations on their members controlling such matters as working hours, wages, prices, tools, and the hiring of workers.—*Ed.*

---

[6] "Commune" was the name taken in France by the nascent towns even before they had conquered from their feudal lords and masters local self-government and political rights as the "Third Estate." Generally speaking, for the economic development of the bourgeoisie, England is here taken as the typical country, for its political development, France.

The bourgeoisie, wherever it has got the upper hand, has put an end to all feudal, patriarchal, idyllic relations. It has pitilessly torn asunder the motley feudal ties that bound man to his "natural superiors," and has left no other bond between man and man than naked self-interest, than callous "cash payment." It has drowned the most heavenly ecstasies of religious fervor, of chivalrous enthusiasm, of philistine sentimentalism, in the icy water of egotistical calculation. It has resolved personal worth into exchange value, and in place of the numberless indefeasible chartered freedoms, has set up that single, unconscionable freedom—Free Trade. In one word, for exploitation, veiled by religious and political illusions, it has substituted naked, shameless, direct, brutal exploitation.

The bourgeoisie has stripped of its halo every occupation hitherto honored and looked up to with reverent awe. It has converted the physician, the lawyer, the priest, the poet, the man of science, into its paid wage-laborers.

The bourgeoisie has torn away from the family its sentimental veil, and has reduced the family relation to a mere money relation.

The bourgeoisie has disclosed how it came to pass that the brutal display of vigor in the Middle Ages, which reactionaries so much admire, found its fitting complement in the most slothful indolence. It has been the first to show what man's activity can bring about. It has accomplished wonders far surpassing Egyptian pyramids, Rome aqueducts, and Gothic cathedrals; it has conducted expeditions that put in the shade all former migrations of nations and crusades.

The bourgeoisie cannot exist without constantly revolutionizing the instruments of production, and thereby the relations of production, and with them the whole relations of society. Conservation of the old modes of production in unaltered form, was, on the contrary, the first condition of existence for all earlier industrial classes. Constant revolutionizing of production, uninterrupted disturbance of all social conditions, everlasting uncertainty and agitation distinguish the bourgeois epoch from all earlier ones. All fixed, fast-frozen relations, with their train

of ancient and venerable prejudices and opinions, are swept away, all new-formed ones become antiquated before they can ossify. All that is solid melts into air, all that is holy is profaned, and man is at last compelled to face with sober senses his real conditions of life and his relations with his kind.

The need of a constantly expanding market for its products chases the bourgeoisie over the whole surface of the globe. It must nestle everywhere, settle everywhere, establish connections everywhere.

The bourgeoisie has through its exploitation of the world market given a cosmopolitan character to production and consumption in every country. To the great chagrin of reactionaries, it has drawn from under the feet of industry the national ground on which it stood. All old-established national industries have been destroyed or are daily being destroyed. They are dislodged by new industries, whose introduction becomes a life and death question for all civilized nations, by industries that no longer work up indigenous raw material, but raw material drawn from the remotest zones; industries whose products are consumed, not only at home, but in every quarter of the globe. In place of the old wants, satisfied by the production of the country, we find new wants, requiring for their satisfaction the products of distant lands and climes. In place of the old local and national seclusion and self-sufficiency, we have intercourse in every direction, universal inter-dependence of nations. And as in material, so also in intellectual production. The intellectual creations of individual nations become common property. National one-sidedness and narrow-mindedness become more and more impossible, and from the numerous national and local literatures there arises a world literature.

The bourgeoisie, by the rapid improvement of all instruments of production, by the immensely facilitated means of communication, draws all nations, even the most barbarian, into civilization. The cheap prices of its commodities are the heavy artillery with which it batters down all Chinese walls, with which it forces the barbarians' intensely obstinate hatred of foreigners to capitulate. It compels all nations, on pain of extinction, to adopt the bourgeois mode of production; it compels them to introduce what it calls civilization into their midst, i.e., to become bourgeois themselves. In a word, it creates a world after its own image.

The bourgeoisie has subjected the country to the rule of the towns. It has created enormous cities, has greatly increased the urban population as compared with the rural, and has thus rescued a considerable part of the population from the idiocy of rural life. Just as it has made the country dependent on the towns, so it has made barbarian and semi-barbarian countries dependent on the civilized ones, nations of peasants on nations of bourgeois, the East on the West.

More and more the bourgeoisie keeps doing away with the scattered state of the population, of the means of production, and of property. It has agglomerated population, centralized means of production, and has concentrated property in a few hands. The necessary consequence of this was political centralization. Independent, or but loosely connected provinces, with separate interests, laws, governments, and systems of taxation, became lumped together into one nation, with one government, one code of laws, one national class interest, one frontier, and one customs tariff.

The bourgeoisie, during its rule of scarce one hundred years, has created more massive and more colossal productive forces than have all preceding generations together. Subjection of nature's forces to man, machinery, application of chemistry to industry and agriculture, steam-navigation, railways, electric telegraphs, clearing of whole continents for cultivation, canalisation of rivers, whole populations conjured out of the ground—what earlier century had even a presentiment that such productive forces slumbered in the lap of social labour?

We see then that the means of production and of exchange, which served as the foundation for the growth of the bourgeoisie, were generated in feudal society. At a certain stage in the development of these means of production and of exchange, the conditions under which feudal society produced and exchanged, the feudal organisation of agriculture and manufacturing industry, in a word, the feu-

dal relations of property became no longer compatible with the already developed productive forces; they became so many fetters. They had to be burst asunder; they were burst asunder.

Into their place stepped free competition, accompanied by a social and political constitution adapted to it, and by the economic and political sway of the bourgeois class.

A similar movement is going on before our own eyes. Modern bourgeois society with its relations of production, of exchange and of property, a society that has conjured up such gigantic means of production and of exchange, is like the sorcerer who is no longer able to control the powers of the nether world whom he has called up by his spells. For many a decade past the history of industry and commerce is but the history of the revolt of modern productive forces against modern conditions of production, against the property relations that are the conditions for the existence of the bourgeoisie and of its rule. It is enough to mention the commercial crises that by their periodical return put the existence of the entire bourgeois society on trial, each time more threateningly. In these crises a great part not only of the existing products, but also of the previously created productive forces, are periodically destroyed. In these crises there breaks out an epidemic that, in all earlier epochs, would have seemed an absurdity—the epidemic of over-production. Society suddenly finds itself put back into a state of momentary barbarism; it appears as if a famine, a universal war of devastation had cut off the supply of every means of subsistence; industry and commerce seem to be destroyed. And why? Because there is too much civilization, too much means of subsistence, too much industry, too much commerce. The productive forces at the disposal of society no longer tend to further the development of the conditions of bourgeois property; on the contrary, they have become too powerful for these conditions, by which they are fettered, and no sooner do they overcome these fetters than they bring disorder into the whole of bourgeois society, endanger the existence of bourgeois property. The conditions of bourgeois society are too narrow to comprise the wealth created by them. And how does the bourgeoisie get over these crises? On the one hand, by enforced destruction of a mass of productive forces; on the other, by the conquest of new markets, and by the more thorough exploitation of the old ones. That is to say, by paving the way for more extensive and more destructive crises, and by diminishing the means whereby crises are prevented.

The weapons with which the bourgeoisie felled feudelism to the ground are now turned against the bourgeoisie itself.

But not only has the bourgeoisie forged the weapons that bring death to itself; it has also called into existence the men who are to wield those weapons—the modern working class—the proletarians.

In proportion as the bourgeoisie, i.e., capital, is developed, in the same proportion is the proletariat, the modern working class, developed—a class of laborers, who live only so long as they find work, and who find work only so long as their labor increases capital. These laborers, who must sell themselves piecemeal, are a commodity, like every other article of commerce, and are consequently exposed to all the vicissitudes of competition, to all the fluctuations of the market.

Owing to the extensive use of machinery and to division of labor, the work of the proletarians has lost all individual character, and consequently, all charm for the workman. He becomes an appendage of the machine, and it is only the most simple, most monotonous, and most easily acquired knack, that is required of him. Hence, the cost of production of a workman is restricted, almost entirely, to the means of subsistence that he requires for his maintenance, and for the propagation of his race. But the price of a commodity, and therefore also of labor, is equal to its cost of production. In proportion, therefore, as the repulsiveness of the work increases, the wage decreases. Nay more, in proportion as the use of machinery and division of labor increases, in the same proportion the burden of toil also increases, whether by prolongation of the working hours, by increase of the work exacted in a given time, or by increased speed of the machinery, etc.

Modern industry has converted the little workshop of the patriarchal master into the great factory of the industrial capitalist. Masses of laborers, crowded into the factory, are organized like soldiers. As privates of the industrial army they are placed under the command of a perfect hierarchy of officers and sergeants. Not only are they slaves of the bourgeois class, and of the bourgeois state; they are daily and hourly enslaved by the machine, by the over-looker, and, above all, by the individual bourgeois manufacturer himself. The more openly this despotism proclaims gain to be its end and aim, the more petty, the more hateful and the more embittering it is.

The less the skill and exertion of strength implied in manual labor, in other words, the more modern industry develops, the more is the labor of men superseded by that of women. Differences of age and sex have no longer any distinctive social validity for the working class. All are instruments of labor, more or less expensive to use, according to their age and sex.

No sooner has the laborer received his wages in cash, for the moment escaping exploitation by the manufacturer, than he is set upon by the other portions of the bourgeoisie, the landlord, the shopkeeper, the pawnbroker, etc.

The lower strata of the middle class—the small tradespeople, shopkeepers, and retired tradesmen generally, the handicraftsmen and peasants—all these sink gradually into the proletariat, partly because their diminutive capital does not suffice for the scale on which modern industry is carried on, and is swamped in the competition with the large capitalists, partly because their specialized skill is rendered worthless by new methods of production. Thus the proletariat is recruited from all classes of the population.

The proletariat goes through various stages of development. With its birth begins its struggle with the bourgeoisie. At first the contest is carried on by individual laborers, then by the work people of a factory, then by the operatives of one trade, in one locality, against the individual bourgeois who directly exploits them. They direct their attacks not against the bourgeois conditions of production, but against the instruments of production themselves; they destroy imported wares that compete with their labor, they smash machinery to pieces, they set factories ablaze, they seek to restore by force the vanished status of the workman of the Middle Ages.

At this stage the laborers still form an incoherent mass scattered over the whole country, and broken up by their mutual competition. If anywhere they unite to form more compact bodies, this is not yet the consequence of their own active union, but of the union of the bourgeoisie, which class, in order to attain its own political ends, is compelled to set the whole proletariat in motion, and is moreover still able to do so for a time. At this stage, therefore, the proletarians do not fight their enemies, but the enemies of their enemies, the remnants of absolute monarchy, the landowners, the nonindustrial bourgeois, the petty bourgeoisie. Thus the whole historical movement is concentrated in the hands of the bourgeoisie; every victory so obtained is a victory for the bourgeoisie.

But with the development of industry the proletariat not only increases in number; it becomes concentrated in greater masses, its strength grows, and it feels that strength more. The various interests and conditions of life within the ranks of the proletariat are more and more equalized, in proportion as machinery obliterates all distinctions of labor and nearly everywhere reduces wages to the same low level. The growing competition among the bourgeois, and the resulting commercial crises, make the wages of the workers ever more fluctuating. The unceasing improvement of machinery, ever more rapidly developing, makes their livelihood more and more precarious; the collisions between individual workmen and individual bourgeois take more and more the character of collisions between two classes. Thereupon the workers begin to form combinations (trade unions) against the bourgeoisie; they club together in order to keep up the rate of wages; they found permanent associations in order to make provision beforehand for these occasional revolts. Here and there the contest breaks out into riots.

Now and then the workers are victorious, but only for a time. The real fruit of their battles lies, not in the immediate result, but in the ever expanding union of the workers. This union is furthered by the improved means of communication which are created by modern industry, and which place the workers of different localities in contact with one another. It was just this contact that was needed to centralize the numerous local struggles, all of the same character, into one national struggle between classes. But every class struggle is a political struggle. And that union, to attain which the burghers of the Middle Ages, with their miserable highways, required centuries, the modern proletarians, thanks to railways, achieve in a few years.

This organization of the proletarians into a class, and consequently into a political party, is continually being upset again by the competition between the workers themselves. But it ever rises up again, stronger, firmer, mightier. It compels legislative recognition of particular interests of the workers, by taking advantage of the divisions among the bourgeoisie itself. Thus the ten-hour bill[7] in England was carried.

Altogether, collisions between the classes of the old society further the course of development of the proletariat in many ways. The bourgeoisie finds itself involved in a constant battle. At first with the aristocracy; later on, with those portions of the bourgeoisie itself whose interests have become antagonistic to the progress of industry; at all times with the bourgeoisie of foreign countries. In all these battles it sees itself compelled to appeal to the proletariat, to ask for its help, and thus, to drag it into the political arena. The bourgoisie itself, therefore, supplies the proletariat with its own elements of political and general education, in other words, it furnishes the proletariat with weapons for fighting the bourgeoisie.

Further, as we have already seen, entire sections of the ruling classes are, by the advance of industry, precipitated into the proletariat, or are at least threatened in their conditions of existence. These

---

[7] The 10-Hour Bill, for which the English workers had been fighting for 30 years, was made a law in 1847.—*Ed.*

also supply the proletariat with fresh elements of enlightenment and progress.

Finally, in times when the class struggle nears the decisive hour, the process of dissolution going on within the ruling class, in fact within the whole range of old society, assumes such a violent, glaring character, that a small section of the ruling class cuts itself adrift, and joins the revolutionary class, the class that holds the future in its hands. Just as, therefore, at an earlier period, a section of the nobility went over to the bourgeoisie, so now a portion of the bourgeoisie goes over to the proletariat, and in particular, a portion of the bourgeois ideologists, who have raised themselves to the level of comprehending theoretically the historical movement as a whole.

Of all the classes that stand face to face with the bourgeoisie today, the proletariat alone is a really revolutionary class. The other classes decay and finally disappear in the face of modern industry; the proletariat is its special and essential product.

The lower middle class, the small manufacturer, the shopkeeper, the artisan, the peasant, all these fight against the bourgeoisie, to save from extinction their existence as fractions of the middle class. They are therefore not revolutionary, but conservative. Nay more, they are reactionary, for they try to roll back the wheel of history. If by chance they are revolutionary, they are so only in view of their impending transfer into the proletariat; they thus defend not their present, but their future interests; they desert their own standpoint to adopt that of the proletariat.

The "dangerous class," the social scum (*Lumpenproletariat*), that passively rotting mass thrown off by the lowest layers of old society, may, here and there, be swept into the movement by a proletarian revolution; its conditions of life, however, prepare it far more for the part of a bribed tool of reactionary intrigue.

The social conditions of the old society no longer exist for the proletariat. The proletarian is without property; his relation to his wife and children has no longer anything in common with bourgeois family relations; modern industrial labor, modern subjection to capital, the same in England as in France, in America as in Germany, has stripped him of every trace of national character. Law, morality, religion, are to him so many bourgeois prejudices, behind which lurk in ambush just as many bourgeois interests.

All the preceding classes that got the upper hand, sought to fortify their already acquired status by subjecting society at large to their conditions of appropriation. The proletarians cannot become masters of the productive forces of society, except by abolishing their own previous mode of appropriation, and thereby also every other previous mode of appropriation. They have nothing of their own to secure and to fortify; their mission is to destroy all previous securities for, and insurances of, individual property.

All previous historical movements were movements of minorities, or in the interest of minorities. The proletarian movement is the self-conscious, independent movement of the immense majority, in the interest of the immense majority. The proletariat, the lowest stratum of our present society, cannot stir, cannot raise itself up, without the whole superincumbent strata of official society being sprung into the air.

Though not in substance, yet in form, the struggle of the proletariat with the bourgeoisie is at first a national struggle. The proletariat of each country must, of course, first of all settle matters with its own bourgeoisie.

In depicting the most general phases of the development of the proletariat, we traced the more or less veiled civil war, raging within existing society, up to the point where that war breaks out into open revolution, and where the violent overthrow of the bourgeoisie lays the foundation for the sway of the proletariat.

Hitherto, every form of society has been based, as we have already seen, on the antagonism of oppressing and oppressed classes. But in order to oppress a class, certain conditions must be assured to it under which it can, at least, continue its slavish existence. The serf, in the period of serfdom, raised himself to membership in the commune, just as the petty bourgeois, under the yoke of feudal absolutism, managed to develop into a bourgeois. The modern laborer, on the contrary, instead of rising with the progress of industry, sinks deeper and deeper below the conditions of existence of his own class. He becomes a pauper, and pauperism develops more rapidly than population and wealth. And here it becomes evident, that the bourgeoisie is unfit any longer to be the ruling class in society, and to impose its conditions of existence upon society as an overriding law. It is unfit to rule because it is incompetent to assure an existence to its slave within his slavery, because it cannot help letting him sink into such a state, that it has to feed him, instead of being fed by him. Society can no longer live under this bourgeoisie, in other words, its existence is no longer compatible with society.

The essential condition for the existence and sway of the bourgeois class, is the formation and augmentation of capital; the condition for capital is wage-labor. Wage-labor rests exclusively on competition between the laborers. The advance of industry, whose involuntary promoter is the bourgeoisie, replaces the isolation of the laborers, due to competition, by their revolutionary combination, due to association. The development of modern industry, therefore, cuts from under its feet the very foundation on which the bourgeoisie produces and appropriates products. What the bourgeoisie therefore produces, above all, are its own grave-diggers. Its fall and the victory of the proletariat are equally inevitable.

VIOLENCE AND SELF-DEFINITION

Frantz Fanon

Self-consciousness exists in itself *and* for itself, *in that and by the fact that it exists for another self-consciousness; that is to say, it is only by being acknowledged or recognized.*
—Hegel, The Phenomenology of Mind

Man is human only to the extent to which he tries to impose his existence on another man in order to be recognized by him. As long as he has not been effectively recognized by the other, that other will remain the theme of his actions. It is on that other being, on recognition by that other being, that his own human worth and reality depend. It is that other being in whom the meaning of his life is condensed.

There is not an open conflict between white and black. One day the White Master, *without conflict,* recognized the Negro slave.

But the former slave wants to *make himself recognized.*

• • •

In its immediacy, consciousness of self is simple being-for-itself. In order to win the certainty of oneself, the incorporation of the concept of recognition is essential. Similarly, the other is waiting for recognition by us, in order to burgeon into the universal consciousness of self. Each consciousness of self is in quest of absoluteness. It wants to be recognized as a primal value without reference to life, as a transformation of subjective certainty (*Gewissheit*) into objective truth (*Wahrheit*).

When it encounters resistance from the other, self-consciousness undergoes the experience of *desire*—the first milestone on the road that leads to the dignity of the spirit. Self-consciousness accepts the risk of its life, and consequently it threatens the other in his physical being. "It is solely by risking life that freedom is obtained; only thus is it tried and proved that the essential nature of self-consciousness is not *bare existence*, is not the merely immediate form in which it at first makes its appearance, is not its mere absorption in the expanse of life."[1]

Thus human reality in-itself-for-itself can be achieved only through conflict and through the risk that conflict implies. This risk means that I go beyond life toward a supreme good that is the transformation of subjective certainty of my own worth into a universally valid objective truth.

[1] G. W. F. Hegel, *The Phenomenology of Mind*, trans. by J. B. Baillie, 2nd rev. ed. (London, Allen & Unwin, 1949), p. 233.

As soon as I *desire* I am asking to be considered. I am not merely here-and-now, sealed into thingness. I am for somewhere else and for something else. I demand that notice be taken of my negating activity insofar as I pursue something other than life; insofar as I do battle for the creation of a human world—that is, of a world of reciprocal recognitions.

He who is reluctant to recognize me opposes me. In a savage struggle I am willing to accept convulsions of death, invincible dissolution, but also the possibility of the impossible.

The other, however, can recognize me without struggle: "The individual, who has not staked his life, may, no doubt, be recognized as a *person*, but he has not attained the truth of this recognition as an independent self-consciousness."[2]

Historically, the Negro steeped in the inessentiality of servitude was set free by his master. He did not fight for his freedom.

Out of slavery the Negro burst into the lists where his masters stood. Like those servants who are allowed once every year to dance in the drawing room, the Negro is looking for a prop. The Negro has not become a master. When there are no longer slaves, there are no longer masters.

The Negro is a slave who has been allowed to assume the attitude of a master.

The white man is a master who has allowed his slaves to eat at his table.

One day a good white master who had influence said to his friends, "Let's be nice to the niggers. . . ."

The other masters argued, for after all it was not an easy thing, but then they decided to promote the machine-animal-men to the supreme rank of *men*.

Slavery shall no longer exist on French soil.

The upheaval reached the Negroes from without. The black man was acted upon. Values that had not been created by his actions, values that had not been born of the systolic tide of his blood, danced in a hued whirl round him. The upheaval did not make a difference in the Negro. He went from one way of

life to another, but not from one life to another. Just as when one tells a much improved patient that in a few days he will be discharged from the hospital, he thereupon suffers a relapse, so the announcement of the liberation of the black slaves produced psychoses and sudden deaths.

It is not an announcement that one hears twice in a lifetime. The black man contented himself with thanking the white man, and the most forceful proof of the fact is the impressive number of statues erected all over France and the colonies to show white France stroking the kinky hair of this nice Negro whose chains had just been broken.

"Say thank you to the nice man," the mother tells her little boy . . . but we know that often the little boy is dying to scream some other, more resounding expression. . . .

The white man, in the capacity of master,[3] said to the Negro, "From now on you are free."

But the Negro knows nothing of the cost of freedom, for he has not fought for it. From time to time he has fought for Liberty and Justice, but these were always white liberty and white justice; that is, values secreted by his masters. The former slave, who can find in his memory no trace of the struggle for liberty or of that anguish of liberty of which Kierkegaard speaks, sits unmoved before the young white man singing and dancing on the tightrope of existence.

When it does happen that the Negro looks fiercely at the white man, the white man tells him: "Brother, there is no difference between us." And yet the Negro *knows* that there is a difference. He *wants* it. He wants the white man to turn on him and

---

[2]Ibid.

[3] I hope I have shown that here the master differs basically from the master described by Hegel. For Hegel there is reciprocity; here the master laughs at the consciousness of the slave. What he wants from the slave is not recognition but work.

In the same way, the slave here is in no way identifiable with the slave who loses himself in the object and finds in his work the source of his liberation.

The Negro wants to be like the master.

Therefore he is less independent than the Hegelian slave.

In Hegel the slave turns away from the master and turns toward the object.

Here the slave turns toward the master and abandons the object.

shout: "Damn nigger." Then he would have that unique chance—to "show them. . . ."

But most often there is nothing—nothing but indifference, or a paternalistic curiosity.

The former slave needs a challenge to his humanity, he wants a conflict, a riot. But it is too late: The French Negro is doomed to bite himself and just to bite. I say "the French Negro," for the American Negro is cast in a different play. In the United States, the Negro battles and is battled. There are laws that, little by little, are invalidated under the Constitution. There are other laws that forbid certain forms of discrimination. And we can be sure that nothing is going to be given free.

There is war, there are defeats, truces, victories.

"The twelve million black voices" howled against the curtain of the sky. Torn from end to end, marked with the gashes of teeth biting into the belly of interdiction, the curtain fell like a burst balloon.

On the field of battle, its four corners marked by the scores of Negroes hanged by their testicles, a monument is slowly being built that promises to be majestic.

And, at the top of this monument, I can already see a white man and a black man *hand in hand*.

For the French Negro the situation is unbearable. Unable ever to be sure whether the white man considers him consciousness in-itself-for-itself, he must forever absorb himself in uncovering resistance, opposition, challenge.

This is what emerges from some of the passages of the book that Mounier has devoted to Africa.[4] The young Negroes whom he knew there sought to maintain their alterity. Alterity of rupture, of conflict, of battle.

The self takes its place by opposing itself, Fichte said. Yes and no.

I said in my introduction that man is a *yes*. I will never stop reiterating that.

Yes to life. Yes to love. *Yes* to generosity.

But man is also a *no. No* to scorn of man. *No* to degradation of man. *No* to exploitation of man. *No* to the butchery of what is most human in man: freedom.

Man's behavior is not only reactional. And there is always resentment in a *reaction.* Nietzsche had already pointed that out in *The Will to Power.*

To educate man to be *actional*, preserving in all his relations his respect for the basic values that constitute a human world, is the prime task of him who, having taken thought, prepares to act.

THE PSYCHOLOGICAL OPPRESSION OF WOMEN

Sandra Lee Bartky

In *Black Skin, White Masks*, Frantz Fanon offers an anguished and eloquent description of the psychological effects of colonialism on the colonized, a "clinical study" of what he calls the "psychic alienation of the black man." "Those who recognize themselves in it," he says, "will have made a step forward."[1] Fanon's black American readers saw at once that he had captured the corrosive effects not only of classic colonial oppression but of domestic racism too, and that his study fitted well the picture of black America as an internal colony. Without wanting in any way to diminish the oppressive and stifling realities of black experience that Fanon reveals, let me say that I, a white woman, recognize myself in this book too, not only in my "shameful livery of white incomprehension,"[2] but as myself the victim of a "psychic alienation" similar to the one Fanon has described. In this paper I shall try to explore that moment of recognition, to reveal the ways in which the psychological effects of sexist

---

[4] Emmanuel Mounier, *L'éveil de l'Afrique noire* (Paris, Éditions du Seuil, 1948).

[1] Frantz Fanon, *Black Skins, White Masks* (New York: Grove Press, 1967), p. 12.
[2] Ibid.

oppression resemble those of racism and colonialism.

To oppress, says Webster, is "to lie heavy on, to weigh down, to exercise harsh dominion over." When we describe a people as oppressed, what we have in mind most often is an oppression that is economic and political in character. But recent liberation movements, the black liberation movement and the women's movement in particular, have brought to light forms of oppression that are not immediately economic or political. It is possible to be oppressed in ways that need involve neither physical deprivation, legal inequality, nor economic exploitation;[3] one can be oppressed psychologically—the "psychic alienation" of which Fanon speaks. To be psychologically oppressed is to be weighed down in your mind; it is to have a harsh dominion exercised over your self-esteem. The psychologically oppressed become their own oppressors; they come to exercise harsh dominion over their own self-esteem. Differently put, psychological oppression can be regarded as the "internalization of intimations of inferiority."[4]

Like economic oppression, psychological oppression is institutionalized and systematic; it serves to make the work of domination easier by breaking the spirit of the dominated and by rendering them incapable of understanding the nature of those agencies responsible for their subjugation. This allows those who benefit from the established order of things to maintain their ascendancy with more appearance of legitimacy and with less recourse to overt acts of violence than they might otherwise require. Now, poverty and powerlessness can destroy a person's self-esteem, and the fact that one occupies an inferior position in society is all too often racked up to one's being an inferior sort of

person. Clearly, then, economic and political oppression are themselves psychologically oppressive. But there are unique modes of psychological oppression that can be distinguished from the usual forms of economic and political domination. Fanon offers a series of what are essentially phenomenological descriptions of psychic alienation.[5] In spite of considerable overlapping, the experiences of oppression he describes fall into three categories: stereotyping, cultural domination, and sexual objectification. These, I shall contend, are some of the ways in which the terrible messages of inferiority can be delivered even to those who may enjoy certain material benefits; they are special modes of psychic alienation. In what follows, I shall examine some of the ways in which American women—white women and women of color—are stereotyped, culturally dominated, and sexually objectified. In the course of the discussion, I shall argue that our ordinary concept of oppression needs to be altered and expanded, for it is too restricted to encompass what an analysis of psychological oppression reveals about the nature of oppression in general. Finally, I shall be concerned throughout to show how both fragmentation and mystification are present in each mode of psychological oppression, although in varying degrees: fragmentation, the splitting of the whole person into parts of a person which, in stereotyping, may take the form of a war between a "true" and "false" self—or, in sexual objectification, the form of an often coerced and degrading identification of a person with her body; mystification, the systematic obscuring of both the

---

[3] For an excellent comparison of the concepts of exploitation and oppression, see Judith Farr Tormey, "Exploitation, Oppression and Self-Sacrifice," in *Women and Philosophy,* ed. Carol C. Gould and Marx W. Wartofsky (New York: G. P. Putnam's Sons, 1976), pp. 206–221.

[4] Joyce Mitchell Cook, paper delivered at Philosophy and the Black Liberation Struggle Conference, University of Illinois, Chicago Circle, November 19–20, 1970.

[5] Fanon's phenomenology of oppression, however, is almost entirely a phenomenology of the oppression of colonized *men*. He seems unaware of the ways in which the oppression of women by their men in the societies he examines is itself similar to the colonization of natives by Europeans. Sometimes, as in *A Dying Colonialism* (New York: Grove Press, 1968), he goes so far as to defend the clinging to oppressive practices, such as the sequestration of women in Moslem countries, as an authentic resistance by indigenous people to Western cultural intrusion. For a penetrating critique of Fanon's attitude toward women, see Barbara Burris, "Fourth World Manifesto," in *Radical Feminism*, ed. A. Koedt, E. Levine, and A. Rapone (New York: Quadrangle, 1973), pp. 322–357.

reality and agencies of psychological oppression so that its intended effect, the depreciated self, is lived out as destiny, guilt, or neurosis.

The stereotypes that sustain sexism are similar in many ways to those that sustain racism. Like white women, black and brown persons of both sexes have been regarded as childlike, happiest when they are occupying their "place"; more intuitive than rational, more spontaneous than deliberate, closer to nature, and less capable of substantial cultural accomplishment. Black men and women of all races have been victims of sexual stereotyping: the black man and the black woman, like the "Latin spitfire," are lustful and hotblooded; they are thought to lack the capacities for instinctual control that distinguish people from animals. What is seen as an excess in persons of color appears as a deficiency in the white woman; comparatively frigid, she has been, nonetheless, defined by her sexuality as well, here her reproductive role or function. In regard to capability and competence, black women have, again, an excess of what in white women is a deficiency. White women have been seen as incapable and incompetent: no matter, for these are traits of the truly feminine woman. Black women, on the other hand, have been seen as overly capable, hence, as unfeminine bitches who threaten, through their very competence, to castrate their men.

Stereotyping is morally reprehensible as well as psychologically oppressive on two counts, at least. First, it can hardly be expected that those who hold a set of stereotyped beliefs about the sort of person I am will understand my needs or even respect my rights. Second, suppose that I, the object of some stereotype, believe in it myself—for why should I not believe what everyone else believes? I may then find it difficult to achieve what existentialists call an authentic choice of self, or what some psychologists have regarded as a state of self-actualization. Moral philosophers have quite correctly placed a high value, sometimes the highest value, on the development of autonomy and moral agency. Clearly, the economic and political domination of women— our concrete powerlessness—is what threatens our autonomy most. But stereotyping, in its own way,

threatens our self-determination too. Even when economic and political obstacles on the path to autonomy are removed, a depreciated alter ego still blocks the way. It is hard enough for me to determine what sort of person I am or ought to try to become without being shadowed by an alternate self, a truncated and inferior self that I have, in some sense, been doomed to be all the time. For many, the prefabricated self triumphs over a more authentic self which, with work and encouragement, might sometimes have emerged. For the talented few, retreat into the *imago* is raised to the status of art or comedy. Muhammad Ali has made himself what he could scarcely escape being made into—a personification of Primitive Man; while Zsa Zsa Gabor is not so much a woman as the parody of a woman.

Female stereotypes threaten the autonomy of women not only by virtue of their existence but also by virtue of their content. In the conventional portrait, women deny their femininity when they undertake action that is too self-regarding or independent. As we have seen, black women are condemned (often by black men) for supposedly having done this already; white women stand under an injunction not to follow their example. Many women in many places lacked (and many still lack) the elementary right to choose our own mates; but for some women even in our society today, this is virtually the only major decision we are thought capable of making without putting our womanly nature in danger; what follows ever after is or ought to be a properly feminine submission to the decisions of men. We cannot be autonomous, as men are thought to be autonomous, without in some sense ceasing to be women. When one considers how interwoven are traditional female stereotypes with traditional female roles—and these, in turn, with the ways in which we are socialized—all this is seen in an even more sinister light: White women, at least, are psychologically conditioned not to pursue the kind of autonomous development that is held by the culture to be a constitutive feature of masculinity.

The truncated self I am to be is not something manufactured out there by an anonymous Other which I encounter only in the pages of *Playboy* or the *Ladies' Home Journal;* it is inside of me, a part of myself. I may become infatuated with my feminine persona and waste my powers in the more or less hopeless pursuit of a *Vogue* figure, the look of an *Essence* model, or a home that "expresses my personality." Or I may find the parts of myself fragmented and the fragments at war with one another. Women are only now learning to identify and struggle against the forces that have laid these psychic burdens upon us. More often than not, we live out this struggle, which is really a struggle against oppression, in a mystified way: What we are enduring we believe to be entirely intrapsychic in character, the result of immaturity, maladjustment, or even neurosis.

Tyler, the great classical anthropologist, defined culture as all the items in the general life of a people. To claim that women are victims of cultural domination is to claim that all the items in the general life of our people—our language, our institutions, our art and literature, our popular culture— are sexist; that all, to a greater or lesser degree, manifest male supremacy. There is some exaggeration in this claim, but not much. Unlike the black colonial whom Fanon describes with such pathos, women *qua* women are not now in possession of an alternate culture, a "native" culture which, even if regarded by everyone, including ourselves, as decidedly inferior to the dominant culture, we could at least recognize as our own. However degraded or distorted an image of ourselves we see reflected in the patriarchal culture, the culture of our men is still our culture. Certainly in some respects, the condition of women is like the condition of a colonized people. But we are not a colonized people; we have never been more than half a people.

This lack of cultural autonomy has several important consequences for an understanding of the condition of women. A culture has a global character; hence, the limits of my culture are the limits of my world. The subordination of women, then, because it is so pervasive a feature of my culture, will (if uncontested) appear to be natural—and because it is natural, unalterable. Unlike a colonized people, women have no memory of a "time before"; a time

before the masters came, a time before we were subjugated and ruled. Further, since one function of cultural identity is to allow me to distinguish those who are like me from those who are not, I may feel more kinship with those who share my culture, even though they oppress me, than with the women of another culture, whose whole experience of life may well be closer to my own than to any man's.

Our true situation in regard to male supremacist culture is one of domination and exclusion. But this manifests itself in an extremely deceptive way; mystification once more holds sway. Our relative absence from the "higher" culture is taken as proof that we are unable to participate in it ("Why are there no great women artists?"). Theories of the female nature must then be brought forward to try to account for this.[6] The splitting or fragmenting of women's consciousness which takes place in the cultural sphere is also apparent. While remaining myself, I must at the same time transform myself into that abstract and "universal" subject for whom cultural artifacts are made and whose values and experience they express. This subject is not universal at all, however, but *male*. Thus, I must approve the taming of the shrew, laugh at the mother-in-law or the dumb blonde, and somehow identify with all those heroes of fiction from Faust to the personae of Norman Mailer and Henry Miller, whose *Bildungsgeschichten* involve the sexual exploitation of women. Women of color have, of course, a special problem: The dominant cultural subject is not only male, but *white*, so their culture alienation is doubled; they are expected to assimilate cultural motifs that are not only masculinist but racist.

Women of all races and ethnicities, like Fanon's "black man," are subject not only to stereotyping and cultural depreciation but to sexual objectification as well. Even though much has been written

---

[6] The best-known modern theory of this type is, of course, Freud's. He maintains that the relative absence of women from the higher culture is the consequence of a lesser ability to sublimate libidinal drives. See "Femininity" in *New Introductory Lectures in Psychoanalysis* (New York: W. W. Norton, 1933).

about sexual objectification in the literature of the women's movement, the notion itself is complex, obscure, and much in need of philosophical clarification. I offer the following preliminary characterization of sexual objectification: A person is sexually objectified when her sexual parts or sexual functions are separated out from the rest of her personality and reduced to the status of mere instruments or else regarded as if they were capable of representing her. On this definition, then, the prostitute would be a victim of sexual objectification, as would the *Playboy* bunny, the female breeder, and the bathing beauty.

To say that the sexual part of a person is regarded as if it could represent her is to imply that it cannot, that the part and the whole are incommensurable. But surely there are times, in the sexual embrace perhaps, when a woman might want to be regarded as nothing but a sexually intoxicating body and when attention paid to some other aspect of her person—say, to her mathematical ability—would be absurdly out of place. If sexual relations involve some sexual objectification, then it becomes necessary to distinguish situations in which sexual objectification is oppressive from the sorts of situations in which it is not. The identification of a person with her sexuality becomes oppressive, one might venture, when such an identification becomes habitually extended into every area of her experience. To be routinely perceived by others in a sexual light on occasions when such a perception is inappropriate is to have one's very being subjected to that compulsive sexualization that has been the traditional lot of both white women and black men and women of color generally. "For the majority of white men," says Fanon, "the Negro is the incarnation of a genital potency beyond all moralities and prohibitions."[7] Later in *Black Skin, White Masks*, he writes that "the Negro is the genital."[8]

• • •

Subject to the evaluating eye of the male connoisseur, women learn to evaluate themselves first and best. Our identities can no more be kept separate from the appearance of our bodies than they can be kept separate from the shadow-selves of the female stereotype. "Much of a young woman's identity is already defined in her kind of attractiveness and in the selectivity of her search for the man (or men) by whom she wishes to be sought."[9] There is something obsessional in the preoccupation of many women with their bodies, although the magnitude of the obsession will vary somewhat with the presence or absence in a woman's life of other sources of self-esteem and with her capacity to gain a living independent of her looks. Surrounded on all sides by images of perfect female beauty—for, in modern advertising, the needs of capitalism and the traditional values of patriarchy are happily married—of course we fall short. The narcissism encouraged by our identification with the body is shattered by these images. Whose nose is not the wrong shape, whose hips are not too wide or too narrow? Anyone who believes that such concerns are too trivial to weigh very heavily with most women has failed to grasp the realities of the feminine condition.

• • •

The foregoing examination of three modes of psychological oppression, so it appears, points up the need for an alteration in our ordinary concept of oppression. Oppression, I believe, is ordinarily conceived in too limited a fashion. This has placed undue restrictions both on our understanding of what oppression itself is and on the categories of persons we might want to classify as oppressed. Consider, for example, the following paradigmatic case of oppression:

> And the Egyptians made the children of Israel to serve with rigor; and they made their lives bitter

---

[7] Fanon, *Black Skin, White Masks*, p. 177. Eldridge Cleaver sounds a similar theme in *Soul on Ice* (New York: Dell, 1968). The archetypal white man in American society, for Cleaver, is the "Omnipotent Administrator," the archetypal black man the "Super-Masculine Menial."
[8] P. 180.

[9] Erik Erikson, "Inner and Outer Space: Reflections on Womanhood," *Daedalus,* Vol. 93, 1961, pp. 582–606.

with hard bondage, in mortar and in brick, and in all manner of service in the field; all their service wherein they made them serve, was with rigor.[10]

Here the Egyptians, one group of persons, exercise harsh dominion over the Israelites, another group of persons. It is not suggested that the Israelites, however great their sufferings, have lost their integrity and wholeness *qua* persons. But psychological oppression is dehumanizing and depersonalizing; it attacks the person in her personhood. I mean by this that the nature of psychological oppression is such that the oppressor and oppressed alike come to doubt that the oppressed have the capacity to do the sorts of things that only persons can do, to be what persons, in the fullest sense of the term, can be. The possession of autonomy, for example, is widely thought to distinguish persons from nonpersons; but some female stereotypes, as we have seen, threaten the autonomy of women. Oppressed people might or might not be in a position to exercise their autonomy, but the psychologically oppressed may come to believe that they lack the capacity to be autonomous whatever their position.

Similarly, the creation of culture is a distinctly human function, perhaps the most human function. In its cultural life, a group is able to affirm its values and to grasp its identity in acts of self-reflection. Frequently, oppressed persons, cut off from the cultural apparatus, are denied the exercise of this function entirely. To the extent that we are able to catch sight of ourselves in the dominant culture at all, the images we see are distorted or demeaning. Finally, sexual objectification leads to the identification of those who undergo it with what is both human and not quite human—the body. Thus, psychological oppression is just what Fanon said it was—"psychic alienation"—the estrangement or separating of a person from some of the essential attributes of personhood.

Mystification surrounds these processes of human estrangement. The special modes of psychological oppression can be regarded as some of the many ways in which messages of inferiority are delivered to those who are to occupy an inferior position in society. But it is important to remember that messages of this sort are neither sent nor received in an unambiguous way. We are taught that white women and (among others) black men and women are deficient in those capacities that distinguish persons from nonpersons, but at the same time we are assured that we are persons after all. *Of course* women are persons; *of course* blacks are human beings. Who but the lunatic fringe would deny it? The Antillean Negro, Fanon is fond of repeating, is a *Frenchman*. The official ideology announces with conviction that "all men are created equal"; and in spite of the suspect way in which this otherwise noble assertion is phrased, we women learn that they mean to include us after all.

It is itself psychologically oppressive both to believe and at the same time not to believe that one is inferior—in other words, to believe a contradiction. Lacking an analysis of the larger system of social relations which produced it, one can only make sense of this contradiction in two ways. First, while accepting in some quite formal sense the proposition that "all men are created equal," I can believe, inconsistently, what my oppressors have always believed: that some types of persons are less equal than others. I may then live out my membership in my sex or race in *shame;* I am "only a woman" or "just a nigger." Or, somewhat more consistently, I may reject entirely the belief that my disadvantage is generic; but having still to account for it somehow, I may locate the cause squarely within myself, a bad destiny of an entirely private sort—a character flaw, an "inferiority complex," or a neurosis.

Many oppressed persons come to regard themselves as uniquely unable to satisfy normal criteria of psychological health or moral adequacy. To believe that my inferiority is a function of the kind of person I am may make me ashamed of being one of *this* kind. On the other hand, a lack I share with many others just because of an accident of birth would be unfortunate indeed, but at least I would not have to regard myself as having failed uniquely to measure up to standards that people like myself are expected to meet. It should be pointed out, however, that both of these "resolutions"—the ascrip-

---

[10] Exod. 1:13–14.

tion of one's inferiority to idiosyncratic or else to generic causes—produces a "poor self-image," a bloodless term of the behavioral sciences that refers to a very wide variety of possible ways to suffer.[11]

To take one's oppression to be an inherent flaw of birth, or of psychology, is to have what Marxists have characterized as "false consciousness." Systematically deceived as we are about the nature and origin of our unhappiness, our struggles are directed inward toward the self, or toward other similar selves in whom we may see our deficiencies mirrored, not outward upon those social forces responsible for our predicament. Like the psychologically disturbed, the psychologically oppressed often lack a viable identity. Frequently we are unable to make sense of our own impulses or feelings, not only because our drama of fragmentation gets played out on an inner psychic stage, but because we are forced to find our way about in a world which presents itself to us in a masked and deceptive fashion. Regarded as persons, yet depersonalized, we are treated by our society the way the parents of some schizophrenics are said by R. D. Laing to treat their children—professing love at the very moment they shrink from their children's touch.

In sum, then, to be psychologically oppressed is to be caught in the double bind of a society which both affirms my human status and at the same time bars me from the exercise of many of those typically human functions that bestow this status. To be denied an autonomous choice of self, forbidden cultural expression, and condemned to the immanence of mere bodily being is to be cut off from the sorts of activities that define what it is to be human. A person whose being has been subjected to these cleavages may be described as "alienated." Alien-

ation in any form causes a rupture within the human person, an estrangement from self, a "splintering of human nature into a number of misbegotten parts."[12] Any adequate theory of the nature and varieties of human alienation, then, must encompass psychological oppression—or, to use Fanon's term once more, "psychic alienation."

---

[12] Bertell Ollman, *Alienation: Marx's Conception of Man in Capitalist Society* (London and New York: Cambridge University Press, 1971), p. 135.

OPPRESSION AND LIBERATION

Paulo Freire

Dehumanization, which marks not only those whose humanity has been stolen, but also (though in a different way) those who have stolen it, is a *distortion* of the vocation of becoming more fully human. This distortion occurs within history; but it is not an historical vocation. Indeed, to admit of dehumanization as an historical vocation would lead either to cynicism or total despair. The struggle for humanization, for the emancipation of labor, for the overcoming of alienation, for the affirmation of men as persons would be meaningless. This struggle is possible only because dehumanization, although a concrete historical fact, is *not* a given destiny but the result of an unjust order that engenders violence in the oppressors, which in turn dehumanizes the oppressed.

Because it is a distortion of being more fully human, sooner or later being less human leads the oppressed to struggle against those who made them so. In order for this struggle to have meaning, the oppressed must not, in seeking to regain their humanity (which is a way to create it), become in turn oppressors, but rather restorers of the humanity of both.

This, then, is the great humanistic and historical task of the oppressed: to liberate themselves and

---

[11] The available clinical literature on the psychological effects of social inferiority supports this claim. See William H. Grier and Price M. Cobbs, *Black Rage* (New York: Grosset & Dunlap, 1969); Pauline Bart, "Depression in Middle-Aged Women," in *Women in Sexist Society,* ed. Vivian Gornick and Barbara Moran (New York: New American Library, 1971), pp. 163–186; also Phyllis Chesler, *Women and Madness* (New York: Doubleday, 1972).

their oppressors as well. The oppressors, who oppress, exploit, and rape by virtue of their power, cannot find in this power the strength to liberate either the oppressed or themselves. Only power that springs from the weakness of the oppressed will be sufficiently strong to free both. Any attempt to "soften" the power of the oppressor in deference to the weakness of the oppressed almost always manifests itself in the form of false generosity; indeed, the attempt never goes beyond this. In order to have the continued opportunity to express their "generosity," the oppressors must perpetuate injustice as well. An unjust social order is the permanent fount of this "generosity," which is nourished by death, despair, and poverty. That is why the dispensers of false generosity become desperate at the slightest threat to its source.

True generosity consists precisely in fighting to destroy the causes which nourish false charity. False charity constrains the fearful and subdued, the "rejects of life," to extend their trembling hands. True generosity lies in striving so that these hands—whether of individuals or entire peoples—need be extended less and less in supplication, so that more and more they become human hands which work and, working, transform the world.

This lesson and this apprenticeship must come, however, from the oppressed themselves and from those who are truly solidary with them. As individuals or as peoples, by fighting for the restoration of their humanity they will be attempting the restoration of true generosity. Who are better prepared than the oppressed to understand the terrible significance of an oppressive society? Who suffer the effects of oppression more than the oppressed? Who can better understand the necessity of liberation? They will not gain this liberation by chance but through the praxis* of their quest for it, through their recognition of the necessity to fight for it. And this fight, because of the purpose given it by the oppressed, will actually constitute an act of love opposing the lovelessness which lies at the heart of the oppres-

sors' violence, lovelessness even when clothed in false generosity.

But almost always, during the initial stage of the struggle, the oppressed, instead of striving for liberation, tend themselves to become oppressors, or "sub-oppressors." The very structure of their thought has been conditioned by the contradictions of the concrete, existential situation by which they were shaped. Their ideal is to be men; but for them, to be men is to be oppressors. This is their model of humanity. This phenomenon derives from the fact that the oppressed, at a certain moment of their existential experience, adopt an attitude of "adhesion" to the oppressor. Under these circumstances they cannot "consider" him sufficiently clearly to objectivize him—to discover him "outside" themselves. This does not necessarily mean that the oppressed are unaware that they are downtrodden. But their perception of themselves as oppressed is impaired by their submersion in the reality of oppression. At this level, their perception of themselves as opposites of the oppressor does not yet signify engagement in a struggle to overcome the contradiction[1]; the one pole aspires not to liberation, but to identification with its opposite pole.

In this situation the oppressed do not see the "new man" as the man to be born from the resolution of this contradiction, as oppression gives way to liberation. For them, the new man is themselves become oppressors. Their vision of the new man is individualistic; because of their identification with the oppressor, they have no consciousness of themselves as persons or as members of an oppressed class. It is not to become free men that they want agrarian reform, but in order to acquire land and thus become landowners—or, more precisely, bosses over other workers. It is a rare peasant who, once "promoted" to overseer, does not become more of a tyrant towards his former comrades than the owner himself. This is because the context of

---

* Action based on theory [Eds.].

---

[1] As used throughout this book, the term "contradiction" denotes the dialectical conflict between opposing social forces.—Translator's note.

the peasant's situation, that is, oppression, remains unchanged. In this example, the overseer, in order to make sure of his job, must be as tough as the owner—and more so. Thus is illustrated our previous assertion that during the initial stage of their struggle the oppressed find in the oppressor their model of "manhood."

Even revolution, which transforms a concrete situation of oppression by establishing the process of liberation, must confront this phenomenon. Many of the oppressed who directly or indirectly participate in revolution intend—conditioned by the myths of the old order—to make it their private revolution. The shadow of their former oppressor is still cast over them.

The "fear of freedom" which afflicts the oppressed,[2] a fear which may equally well lead them to desire the role of oppressor or bind them to the role of oppressed, should be examined. One of the basic elements of the relationship between oppressor and oppressed is *prescription*. Every prescription represents the imposition of one man's choice upon another, transforming the consciousness of the man prescribed to into one that conforms with the prescriber's consciousness. Thus, the behavior of the oppressed is a prescribed behavior, following as it does the guidelines of the oppressor.

The oppressed, having internalized the image of the oppressed and adopted his guidelines, are fearful of freedom. Freedom would require them to eject this image and replace it with autonomy and responsibility. Freedom is acquired by conquest, not by gift. It must be pursued constantly and responsibly. Freedom is not an ideal located outside of man; nor is it an idea which becomes myth. It is rather the indispensable condition for the quest for human completion.

To surmount the situation of oppression, men must first critically recognize its causes, so that

through transforming action they can create a new situation, one which makes possible the pursuit of a fuller humanity. But the struggle to be more fully human has already begun in the authentic struggle to transform the situation. Although the situation of oppression is a dehumanized and dehumanizing totality affecting both the oppressors and those whom they oppress, it is the latter who must, from their stifled humanity, wage for both the struggle for a fuller humanity; the oppressor, who is himself dehumanized because he dehumanizes others, is unable to lead this struggle.

However, the oppressed, who have adapted to the structure of domination in which they are immersed, and have become resigned to it, are inhibited from waging the struggle for freedom so long as they feel incapable of running the risks it requires. Moreover, their struggle for freedom threatens not only the oppressor, but also their own oppressed comrades who are fearful of still greater repression. When they discover within themselves the yearning to be free, they perceive that this yearning can be transformed into reality only when the same yearning is aroused in their comrades. But while dominated by the fear of freedom they refuse to appeal to others, or to listen to the appeals of others, or even to the appeals of their own conscience. They prefer gregariousness to authentic comradeship; they prefer the security of conformity with their state of unfreedom to the creative communion produced by freedom and even the very pursuit of freedom.

The oppressed suffer from the duality which has established itself in their innermost being. They discover that without freedom they cannot exist authentically. Yet, although they desire authentic existence, they fear it. They are at one and the same time themselves and the oppressor whose consciousness they have internalized. The conflict lies in the choice between being wholly themselves or being divided; between ejecting the oppressor within or not ejecting him; between human solidarity or alienation; between following prescriptions or having choices; between being spectators or actors; between acting or having the illusion of acting

---

[2] This fear of freedom is also to be found in the oppressors, though, obviously, in a different form. The oppressed are afraid to embrace freedom; the oppressors are afraid of losing the "freedom" to oppress.

through the action of the oppressors; between speaking out or being silent, castrated in their power to create and re-create, in their power to transform the world. This is the tragic dilemma of the oppressed which their education must take into account.

This book will present some aspects of what the writer has termed the pedagogy of the oppressed, a pedagogy which must be forged *with,* not *for,* the oppressed (whether individuals or peoples) in the incessant struggle to regain their humanity. This pedagogy makes oppression and its causes objects of reflection by the oppressed, and from that reflection will come their necessary engagement in the struggle for their liberation. And in the struggle this pedagogy will be made and remade.

The central problem is this: How can the oppressed, as divided, unauthentic beings, participate in developing the pedagogy of their liberation? Only as they discover themselves to be "hosts" of the oppressor can they contribute to the midwifery of their liberating pedagogy. As long as they live in the duality in which *to be* is *to be like,* and *to be like* is *to be like the oppressor,* this contribution is impossible. The pedagogy of the oppressed is an instrument for their critical discovery that both they and their oppressors are manifestations of dehumanization. . . .

The pedagogy of the oppressed, as a humanist and libertarian pedagogy, has two distinct stages. In the first, the oppressed unveil the world of oppression and through the praxis commit themselves to its transformation. In the second stage, in which the reality of oppression has already been transformed, this pedagogy ceases to belong to the oppressed and becomes a pedagogy of all men in the process of permanent liberation. In both stages, it is always through action in depth that the culture of domination is culturally confronted.[3] In the first stage this confrontation occurs through the change in the way the oppressed perceive the world of oppression; in the second stage, through the expulsion of the myths created and developed in the old order, which like specters haunt the new structure emerging from the revolutionary transformation.

The pedagogy of the first stage must deal with the problem of the oppressed consciousness and the oppressor consciousness, the problem of men who oppress and men who suffer oppression. It must take into account their behavior, their view of the world, and their ethics. A particular problem is the duality of the oppressed: they are contradictory, divided beings, shaped by and existing in a concrete situation of oppression and violence.

Any situation in which "A" objectively exploits "B" or hinders his pursuit of self-affirmation as a responsible person is one of oppression. Such a situation in itself constitutes violence, even when sweetened by false generosity, because it interferes with man's ontological and historical vocation to be more fully human. With the establishment of a relationship of oppression, violence has *already* begun. Never in history has violence been initiated by the oppressed. How could they be the initiators, if they themselves are the result of violence? How could they be the sponsors of something whose objective inauguration called forth their existence as oppressed? There would be no oppressed had there been no prior situation of violence to establish their subjugation.

Violence is initiated by those who oppress, who exploit, who fail to recognize others as persons—not by those who are oppressed, exploited, and unrecognized. It is not the unloved who initiate disaffection, but those who cannot love because they love only themselves. It is not the helpless, subject to terror, who initiate terror, but the violent, who with their power create the concrete situation which begets the "rejects of life." It is not the tyrannized who initiate despotism, but the tyrants. It is not the despised who initiate hatred, but those who despise. It is not those whose humanity is denied them who negate man, but those who denied that humanity (thus negating their own as well). Force is used not by those who have become weak under the prepon-

---

[3] This appears to be the fundamental aspect of Mao's Cultural Revolution [Eds.].

derance of the strong, but by the strong who have emasculated them.

For the oppressors, however, it is always the oppressed (whom they obviously never call "the oppressed" but—depending on whether they are fellow countrymen or not—"those people" or "the blind and envious masses" or "savages" or "natives" or "subversives") who are disaffected, who are "violent," "barbaric," "wicked," or "ferocious" when they react to the violence of the oppressors.

Yet it is—paradoxical though it may seem—precisely in the response of the oppressed to the violence of their oppressors that a gesture of love may be found. Consciously or unconsciously, the act of rebellion by the oppressed (an act which is always, or nearly always, as violent as the initial violence of the oppressors) can initiate love. Whereas the violence of the oppressors prevents the oppressed from being fully human, the response of the latter to this violence is grounded in the desire to pursue the right to be human. As the oppressors dehumanize others and violate their rights, they themselves also become dehumanized. As the oppressed, fighting to be human, take away the oppressors' power to dominate and suppress, they restore to the oppressors the humanity they has lost in the exercise of oppression.

It is only the oppressed who, by freeing themselves, can free their oppressors. The latter, as an oppressive class, can free neither others nor themselves. It is therefore essential that the oppressed wage the struggle to resolve the contradiction in which they are caught; and the contradiction will be resolved by the appearance of the new man: neither oppressor nor oppressed, but man in the process of liberation. If the goal of the oppressed is to become fully human, they will not achieve their goal by merely reversing the terms of the contradiction, by simply changing poles.

This may seem simplistic; it is not. Resolution of the oppressor-oppressed contradiction indeed implies the disappearance of the oppressors as a dominant class. However, the restraints imposed by the former oppressed on their oppressors, so that the latter cannot reassume their former position, do not

constitute *oppression*. An act is oppressive only when it prevents men from being more fully human. Accordingly, these necessary restraints do not *in themselves* signify that yesterday's oppressed have become today's oppressors. Acts which prevent the restoration of the oppressive regime cannot be compared with those which create and maintain it, cannot be compared with those by which a few men deny the majority their right to be human.

However, the moment the new regime hardens into a dominating "bureaucracy"[4] the humanist dimension of the struggle is lost and it is no longer possible to speak of liberation. Hence our insistence that the authentic solution of the oppressor-oppressed contradiction does not lie in a mere reversal of position, in moving from one pole to the other. Nor does it lie in the replacement of the former oppressors with new ones who continue to subjugate the oppressed—all in the name of their liberation.

But even when the contradiction is resolved authentically by a new situation established by the liberated laborers, the former oppressors do not feel liberated. On the contrary, they genuinely consider themselves to be oppressed. Conditioned by the experience of oppressing others, any situation other than their former seems to them like oppression. Formerly, they could eat, dress, wear shoes, be educated, travel, and hear Beethoven; while millions did not eat, had no clothes or shoes, neither studied nor traveled, much less listened to Beethoven. Any restriction on this way of life, in the name of the rights of the community, appears to the former oppressors as a profound violation of their individual rights—although they had no respect for the millions who suffered and died of hunger, pain, sorrow, and despair. For the oppressors, "human beings" refers only to themselves; other people are "things." For the oppressors, there exists only one right: their

---

4 This rigidity should not be identified with the restraints that must be imposed on the former oppressors so they cannot restore the oppressive order. Rather, it refers to the revolution which becomes stagnant and turns against the people, using the old repressive, bureaucratic State apparatus (which should have been drastically suppressed, as Marx so often emphasized).

right to live in peace, over against the right, not always even recognized, but simply conceded, of the oppressed to survival. And they make this concession only because the existence of the oppressed is necessary to their own existence.

This behavior, this way of understanding the world and men (which necessarily makes the oppressors resist the installation of a new regime) is explained by their experience as a dominant class. Once a situation of violence and oppression has been established, it engenders an entire way of life and behavior for those caught up in it—oppressors and oppressed alike. Both are submerged in this situation, and both bear the marks of oppression. Analysis of existential situations of oppression reveals that their inception lay in an act of violence—initiated by those with power. This violence, as a process, is perpetuated from generation to generation of oppressors, who become its heirs and are shaped in its climate. This climate creates in the oppressor a strongly possessive consciousness—possessive of the world and of men. Apart from direct, concrete, material possession of the world and of men, the oppressor consciousness could not understand itself—could not even exist. Fromm said of this consciousness that, without such possession, "it would lose contact with the world." The oppressor consciousness tends to transform everything surrounding it into an object of its domination. The earth, property, production, the creations of men, men themselves, time—everything is reduced to the status of objects at its disposal.

In their unrestrained eagerness to possess, the oppressors develop the conviction that it is possible for them to transform everything into objects of their purchasing power; hence their strictly materialistic concept of existence. Money is the measure of all things, and profit the primary goal. For the oppressors, what is worthwhile is to have more—always more—even at the cost of the oppressed having less or having nothing. For them, *to be is to have* and to be the class of the "haves."

As beneficiaries of a situation of oppression, the oppressors cannot perceive that if *having* is a condition of *being,* it is a necessary condition for all

men. This is why their generosity is false. Humanity is a "thing," and they possess it as an exclusive right, as inherited property. To the oppressor consciousness, the humanization of the "others," of the people, appears not as the pursuit of full humanity, but as subversion.

The oppressors do not perceive their monopoly on *having more* as a privilege which dehumanizes others and themselves. They cannot see that, in the egoistic pursuit of *having* as a possessing class, they suffocate in their own possessions and no longer *are;* they merely *have.* For them, *having more* is an inalienable right, a right they acquired through their own "effort," with their "courage to take risks." If others do not have more, it is because they are incompetent and lazy, and worst of all is their unjustifiable ingratitude towards the "generous gestures" of the dominant class. Precisely because they are "ungrateful" and "envious," the oppressed are regarded as potential enemies who must be watched.

It could not be otherwise. If the humanization of the oppressed signifies subversion, so also does their freedom; hence the necessity for constant control. And the more the oppressors control the oppressed, the more they change them into apparently inanimate "things." This tendency of the oppressor consciousness to "in-animate" everything and everyone it encounters, in its eagerness to possess, unquestionably corresponds with a tendency to sadism.

> The pleasure in complete domination over another person (or other animate creature) is the very essence of the sadistic drive. Another way of formulating the same thought is to say that the aim of sadism is to transform a man into a thing, something animate into something inanimate, since by complete and absolute control the living loses one essential quality of life—freedom.[5]

Sadistic love is a perverted love—a love of death, not of life. One of the characteristics of the oppressor consciousness and its necrophilic view of the world is thus sadism. As the oppressor conscious-

---

[5] Eric Fromm, *The Heart of Man* (New York, 1985), p. 32.

ness, in order to dominate, tries to deter the drive to search, the restlessness, and the creative power which characterize life, it kills life. More and more, the oppressors are using science and technology as unquestionably powerful instruments for their purpose: the maintenance of the oppressive order through manipulation and repression. The oppressed, as objects, as "things," have no purposes except those their oppressors prescribe for them.

Given the preceding context, another issue of indubitable importance arises: the fact that certain members of the oppressor class join the oppressed in their struggle for liberation, thus moving from one pole of the contradiction to the other. Theirs is a fundamental role, and has been so throughout the history of this struggle. It happens, however, that as they cease to be exploiters or indifferent spectators or simply the heirs of exploitation and move to the side of the exploited, they almost always bring with them the marks of their origin: their prejudices and their deformations, which include a lack of confidence in the people's ability to think, to want, and to know. Accordingly, these adherents to the people's cause constantly run the risk of falling into a type of generosity as malefic as that of the oppressors. The generosity of the oppressors is nourished by an unjust order, which must be maintained in order to justify that generosity. Our converts, on the other hand, truly desire to transform the unjust order; but because of their background they believe that they must be the executors of the transformation. They talk about the people, but they do not trust them; and trusting the people is the indispensable precondition for revolutionary change. A real humanist can be identified more by his trust in the people, which engages him in their struggle, than by a thousand actions in their favor without that trust.

Those who authentically commit themselves to the people must re-examine themselves constantly. This conversion is so radical as not to allow of ambiguous behavior. To affirm this commitment but to consider oneself the proprietor of revolutionary wisdom—which must then be given to (or imposed on) the people—is to retain the old ways. The man who proclaims devotion to the cause of liberation

yet is unable to enter into *communion* with the people, whom he continues to regard as totally ignorant, is grievously self-deceived. The convert who approaches the people but feels alarm at each step they take, each doubt they express, and each suggestion they offer, and attempts to impose his "status," remains nostalgic towards his origins.

Conversion to the people requires a profound rebirth. Those who undergo it must take on a new form of existence; they can no longer remain as they were. Only through comradeship with the oppressed can the converts understand their characteristic ways of living and behaving, which in diverse moments reflect the structure of domination. One of these characteristics is the previously mentioned existential duality of the oppressed, who are at the same time themselves and the oppressor whose image they have internalized. Accordingly, until they concretely "discover" their oppressor and in turn their own consciousness, they nearly always express fatalistic attitudes toward their situation. . . .

It is only when the oppressed find the oppressor out and become involved in the organized struggle for their liberation that they begin to believe in themselves. This discovery cannot be purely intellectual but must involve action; nor can it be limited to mere activism, but must include serious reflection: only then will it be a praxis.

Critical and liberating dialogue, which presupposes action, must be carried on with the oppressed at whatever the stage of their struggle for liberation.[6] The content of that dialogue can and should vary in accordance with historical conditions and the level at which the oppressed perceive reality. But to substitute monologue, slogans, and communiqués for dialogue is to attempt to liberate the oppressed with the instruments of domestication. Attempting to liberate the oppressed without their reflective participation in the act of liberation is to treat them as objects which must be saved from a burning building; it is to lead them into the populist pitfall and transform them into masses which can be manipulated.

---

[6] Not in the open, of course; that would only provoke the fury of the oppressor and lead to still greater repression.

At all stages of their liberation, the oppressed must see themselves as men engaged in the ontological and historical vocation of becoming more fully human. Reflection and action become imperative when one does not erroneously attempt to dichotomize the content of humanity from its historical forms.

The insistence that the oppressed engage in reflection on their concrete situation is not a call to armchair revolution. On the contrary, reflection—true reflection—leads to action. On the other hand, when the situation calls for action, that action will constitute an authentic praxis only if its consequences become the object of critical reflection. In this sense, the praxis is the new *raison d'être* of the oppressed; and the revolution, which inaugurates the historical moment of this *raison d'être,* is not viable apart from their concomitant conscious involvement. Otherwise, action is pure activism.

To achieve this praxis, however, it is necessary to trust in the oppressed and in their ability to reason. Whoever lacks this trust will fail to initiate (or will abandon) dialogue, reflection, and communication, and will fall into using slogans, communiqués, monologues, and instructions. Superficial conversions to the cause of liberation carry this danger.

Political action on the side of the oppressed must be pedagogical action in the authentic sense of the word, and, therefore, action *with* the oppressed. Those who work for liberation must not take advantage of the emotional dependence of the oppressed—dependence that is the fruit of the concrete situation of domination which surrounds them and which engendered their unauthentic view of the world. Using their dependence to create still greater dependence is an oppressor tactic.

Libertarian action must recognize this dependence as a weak point and must attempt through reflection and action to transform it into independence. However, not even the best-intentioned leadership can bestow independence as a gift. The liberation of the oppressed is a liberation of men, not things. Accordingly, while no one liberates himself by his own efforts alone, neither is he liberated by others. Liberation, a human phenomenon, cannot be achieved by semihumans. Any attempt to treat men as semihumans only dehumanizes them. When men are already dehumanized, due to the oppression they suffer, the process of their liberation must not employ the methods of dehumanization.

The correct method for a revolutionary leadership to employ in the task of liberation is, therefore, *not* "libertarian propaganda." Nor can the leadership merely "implant" in the oppressed a belief in freedom, thus thinking to win their trust. The correct method lies in dialogue. The conviction of the oppressed that they must fight for their liberation is not a gift bestowed by the revolutionary leadership, but the result of their own *conscientização.**

The revolutionary leaders must realize that their own conviction of the necessity for struggle (an indispensable dimension of revolutionary wisdom) was not given to them by anyone else—if it is authentic. This conviction cannot be packaged and sold; it is reached, rather, by means of a totality of reflection and action. Only the leaders' own involvement in reality, within an historical situation, led them to criticize this situation and to wish to change it.

Likewise, the oppressed (who do not commit themselves to the struggle unless they are convinced, and who, if they do not make such a commitment, withhold the indispensable conditions for this struggle) must reach this conviction as Subjects, not as objects. They also must intervene critically in the situation which surrounds them and whose mark they bear; propaganda cannot achieve this. While the conviction of the necessity for struggle (without which the struggle is unfeasible) is indispensable to the revolutionary leadership (indeed, it was this conviction which constituted that leadership), it is also necessary for the oppressed. It is necessary, that is, unless one tends to carry out the transformation *for* the oppressed rather than *with* them. It is my belief that only the latter form of transformation is valid.

---

* Conscientization: a process whereby one learns to perceive political, social, and economic conditions, leading to taking action against the source of oppression. [Eds.].

BY ANY MEANS NECESSARY

Malcolm X

You make my point, [*Laughter*] that as long as a white man does it, it's all right. A Black man is supposed to have no feelings. [*Applause*] So when a Black man strikes back, he's an extremist. He's supposed to sit passively and have no feelings, be nonviolent, and love his enemy. No matter what kind of attack, be it verbal or otherwise, he's supposed to take it. But if he stands up and in any way tries to defend himself, [*Malcolm laughs*] then he's an extremist. [*Laughter and applause*]

No. I think that the speaker who preceded me is getting exactly what he asked for. [*Laughter*] My reason for believing in extremism—intelligently directed extremism, extremism in defense of liberty, extremism in quest of justice—is because I firmly believe in my heart that the day that the Black man takes an uncompromising step and realizes that he's within his rights, when his own freedom is being jeopardized, to use any means necessary to bring about his freedom or put a halt to that injustice, I don't think he'll be by himself.

I live in America, where there are only 22 million Blacks against probably 160 million whites. One of the reasons that I'm in no way reluctant or hesitant to do whatever is necessary to see that Black people do something to protect themselves [is that] I honestly believe that the day that they do, many whites will have more respect for them. And there will be more whites on their side than are now on their side with this little wishy-washy "love-thy-enemy" approach that they've been using up to now.

And if I'm wrong, then you are racialists. [*Malcolm laughs; laughter and applause from the audience*]

As I said earlier, in my conclusion, I'm a Muslim. I believe in the religion of Islam. I believe in Allah, I believe in Muhammad, I believe in all of the prophets. I believe in fasting, prayer, charity, and that which is incumbent upon a Muslim to ful-

fill in order to be a Muslim. In April I was fortunate to make the hajj to Mecca, and went back again in September to try and carry out my religious functions and requirements.

But at the same time that I believe in that religion, I have to point out I'm also an American Negro, and I live in a society whose social system is based upon the castration of the Black man, whose political system is based on castration of the Black man, and whose economy is based upon the castration of the Black man. A society which, in 1964, has more subtle, deceptive, deceitful methods to make the rest of the world think that it's cleaning up its house, while at the same time the same things are happening to us in 1964 that happened in 1954, 1924, and in 1984.

They came up with what they call a civil rights bill in 1964, supposedly to solve our problem, and after the bill was signed, three civil rights workers were murdered in cold blood. And the FBI head, [J. Edgar] Hoover, admits that they know who did it. They've known ever since it happened, and they've done nothing about it. Civil rights bill down the drain. No matter how many bills pass, Black people in that country where I'm from—still, our lives are not worth two cents. And the government has shown its inability, or its unwillingness, to do whatever is necessary to protect life and property where the Black American is concerned.

So my contention is that whenever a people come to the conclusion that the government which they have supported proves itself unwilling or proves itself unable to protect our lives and protect our property because we have the wrong color skin, we are not human beings unless we ourselves band together and do whatever, however, whenever is necessary to see that our lives and our property is protected. And I doubt that any person in here would refuse to do the same thing, were he in the same position. Or I should say, were he in the same condition. [*Applause*]

Just one step farther to see, am I justified in this stand? And I say, I'm speaking as a Black man from America, which is a racist society. No matter how much you hear it talk about democracy, it's as racist as South Africa or as racist as Portugal, or as racist as any other racialist society on this earth. The only difference between it and South Africa: South Africa preaches separation and practices separation; America preaches integration and practices segregation. This is the only difference. They don't practice what they preach, whereas South Africa preaches and practices the same thing. I have more respect for a man who lets me know where he stands, even if he's wrong, than one who comes up like an angel and is nothing but a devil. [*Applause*]

The system of government that America has consists of committees. There are sixteen senatorial committees that govern the country and twenty congressional committees. Ten of the sixteen senatorial committees are in the hands of southern racialists, senators who are racialists. Thirteen of the twenty—well this was before the last election, I think it's even more so now. Ten of the sixteen committees, senatorial committees, are in the hands of senators who are southern racialists. Thirteen of the twenty congressional committees were in the hands of southern congressmen who are racialists. Which means out of the thirty-six committees that govern the foreign and domestic direction of that government, twenty-three are in the hands of southern racialists—men who in no way believe in the equality of man, and men who would do anything within their power to see that the Black man never gets to the same seat or to the same level that they are on.

The reason that these men from that area have that type of power is because America has a seniority system. And these who have that seniority have been there longer than anyone else because the Black people in the areas where they live can't vote. And it is only because the Black man is deprived of his vote that puts these men in positions of power, that gives them such influence in the government beyond their actual intellectual or political ability, or even beyond the number of people from the areas that they represent.

So we can see in that country that no matter what the federal government professes to be doing, the power of the federal government lies in these committees. And any time any kind of legislation is pro-

posed to benefit the Black man or give the Black man his just due, we find it is locked up in these committees right here. And when they let something through the committee, usually it is so chopped up and fixed up that by the time it becomes law, it's a law that can't be enforced.

Another example is the Supreme Court desegregation decision that was handed down in 1954. This is a law, and they have not been able to implement this law in New York City, or in Boston, or in Cleveland, or Chicago, or the northern cities. And my contention is that any time you have a country, supposedly a democracy, supposedly the land of the free and the home of the brave, and it can't enforce laws—even in the northernmost, cosmopolitan, and progressive part of it—that will benefit a Black man, if those laws can't be enforced or that law can't be enforced, how much heart do you think we will get when they pass some civil rights legislation which only involves more laws? If they can't enforce this law, they will never enforce those laws.

So my contention is that we are faced with a racialistic society, a society in which they are deceitful, deceptive, and the only way we can bring about a change is to talk the kind of language—speak the language that they understand. The racialists never understand a peaceful language. The racialist never understands the nonviolent language. The racialist we have, he's spoken his language to us for four hundred years.

We have been the victim of his brutality. We are the ones who face his dogs that tear the flesh from our limbs, only because we want to enforce the Supreme Court decision. We are the ones who have our skulls crushed, not by the Ku Klux Klan but by policemen, only because we want to enforce what they call the Supreme Court decision. We are the ones upon whom water hoses are turned, with pressure so hard that it rips the clothes from our backs—not men, but the clothes from the backs of women and children. You've seen it yourselves. Only because we want to enforce what they call the law.

Well, any time you live in a society supposedly based upon law, and it doesn't enforce its own law because the color of a man's skin happens to be wrong, then I say those people are justified to resort to any means necessary to bring about justice where the government can't give them justice. [*Prolonged applause*]

I don't believe in any form of unjustified extremism. But I believe that when a man is exercising extremism, a human being is exercising extremism in defense of liberty for human beings, it's no vice. And when one is moderate in the pursuit of justice for human beings, I say he's a sinner.

And I might add, in my conclusion—In fact, America is one of the best examples, when you read its history, about extremism. Old Patrick Henry said, "Liberty or death!" That's extreme, very extreme. [*Laughter and applause*]

I read once, passingly, about a man named Shakespeare. I only read about him passingly, but I remember one thing he wrote that kind of moved me. He put it in the mouth of Hamlet, I think it was, who said, "To be or not to be"—he was in doubt about something. [*Laughter*] "Whether it was nobler in the mind of man to suffer the slings and arrows of outrageous fortune"—moderation—"or take up arms against a sea of troubles and by opposing end them."

And I go for that. If you take up arms, you'll end it. But if you sit around and wait for the one who's in power to make up his mind that he should end it, you'll be waiting a long time.

And in my opinion the young generation of whites, Blacks, browns, whatever else there is—you've living at a time of extremism, a time of revolution, a time when there's got to be a change. People in power have misused it, and now there has to be a change and a better world has to be built, and the only way it's going to be built is with extreme methods. And I for one will join in with anyone, I don't care what color you are, as long as you want to change this miserable condition that exists on this earth.

Thank you. [*Applause*]

NON-VIOLENT RESISTANCE

Mohandas. K. Gandhi

MEANS AND ENDS

Reader: Why should we not obtain our goal, which is good, by any means whatsoever, even by using violence? Shall I think of the means when I have to deal with a thief in the house? My duty is to drive him out anyhow. You seem to admit that we have received nothing, and that we shall receive nothing by petitioning. Why, then, may we not do so by using brute force? And, to retain what we may receive we shall keep up the fear by using the same force to the extent that it may be necessary. You will not find fault with a continuance of force to prevent a child from thrusting its foot into fire? Somehow or other we have to gain our end.

Gandhi: Your reasoning is plausible. It has deluded many. I have used similar arguments before now. But I think I know better now, and I shall endeavour to undeceive you. Let us first take the argument that we are justified in gaining our end by using brute force because the English gained theirs by using similar means. It is perfectly true that they used brute force and that it is possible for us to do likewise, but by using similar means we can get only the same thing that they got. You will admit that we do not want that. Your belief that there is no connection between the means and the end is a great mistake. Through that mistake even men who have been considered religious have committed grievous crimes. Your reasoning is the same as saying that we can get a rose through planting a noxious weed. If I want to cross the ocean, I can do so only by means of a vessel; if I were to use a cart for that purpose, both the cart and I would soon find the bottom. "As is the God, so is the votary", is a maxim worth considering. Its meaning has been distorted and men have gone astray. The means may be likened to a seed, the end to a tree; and there is just the same inviolable connection between the means and the end as there is between the seed and the tree.

I am not likely to obtain the result flowing from the worship of God by laying myself prostrate before Satan. If, therefore, any one were to say: "I want to worship God; it does not matter that I do so by means of Satan," it would be set down as ignorant folly. We reap exactly as we sow. The English in 1833 obtained greater voting power by violence. Did they by using brute force better appreciate their duty? They wanted the right of voting, which they obtained by using physical force. But real rights are a result of performance of duty; these rights they have not obtained. We, therefore, have before us in England the force of everybody wanting and insisting on his rights, nobody thinking of his duty. And, where everybody wants rights, who shall give them to whom? I do not wish to imply that they do no duties. They don't perform the duties corresponding to those rights; and as they do not perform that particular duty, namely, acquire fitness, their rights have proved a burden to them. In other words, what they have obtained is an exact result of the means they adopted. They used the means corresponding to the end. If I want to deprive you of your watch, I shall certainly have to fight for it; if I want to buy your watch, I shall have to pay for it; and if I want a gift, I shall have to plead for it; and, according to the means I employ, the watch is stolen property, my own property, or a donation. Thus we see three different results from three different means. Will you still say that means do not matter?

Now we shall take the example given by you of the thief to be driven out. I do not agree with you that the thief may be driven out by any means. If it is my father who has come to steal I shall use one kind of means. If it is an acquaintance I shall use another; and in the case of a perfect stranger I shall use a third. If it is a white man, you will perhaps say you will use means different from those you will adopt with an Indian thief. If it is a weakling, the means will be different from those to be adopted for dealing with an equal in physical strength; and if the thief is armed from top to toe, I shall simply remain quiet. Thus we have a variety of means between the father and the armed man. Again, I fancy that I should pretend to be sleeping whether the thief was my father or that strong armed man. The reason for this is that my father would also be armed and I should succumb to the strength possessed by either and allow my things to be stolen. The strength of my father would make me weep with pity; the strength of the armed man would rouse in me anger and we should become enemies. Such is the curious situation. From these examples we may not be able to agree as to the means to be adopted in each case. I myself seem clearly to see what should be done in all these cases, but the remedy may frighten you. I therefore hesitate to place it before you. For the time being I will leave you to guess it, and if you cannot, it is clear you will have to adopt different means in each case. You will also have seen that any means will not avail to drive away the thief. You will have to adopt means to fit each case. Hence it follows that your duty is not to drive away the thief by any means you like.

Let us proceed a little further. That well-armed man has stolen your property; you have harboured the thought of his act; you are filled with anger; you argue that you want to punish that rogue, not for your own sake, but for the good of your neighbours; you have collected a number of armed men, you want to take his house by assault; he is duly informed of it, he runs away; he too is incensed. He collects his brother robbers, and sends you a defiant message that he will commit robbery in broad daylight. You are strong, you do not fear him, you are prepared to receive him. Meanwhile, the robber pesters your neighbours. They complain before you. You reply that you are doing all for their sake, you do not mind that your own goods have been stolen. Your neighbours reply that the robber never pestered them before, and that he commenced his depredations only after you declared hostilities against him. You are between Scylla and Charybdis. You are full of pity for the poor men. What they say is true. What are you to do? You will be disgraced if you now leave the robber alone. You, therefore, tell the poor men: "Never mind. Come, my wealth is yours, I will give you arms, I will teach you how to use them; you should belabour the rogue; don't you leave him alone." And so the battle grows; the robbers increase in numbers; your neighbours have deliberately put themselves to inconvenience. Thus the result of wanting to take revenge upon the robber is that you have disturbed your own peace; you are in perpetual fear of being robbed and assaulted; your courage has given place to cowardice. If you will patiently examine the argument, you will see that I have not overdrawn the picture. This is one of the means. Now let us examine the other. You set this armed robber down as an ignorant brother; you intend to reason with him at a suitable opportunity; you argue that he is, after all, a fellow man; you do not know what prompted him to steal. You, therefore, decide that, when you can, you will destroy the man's motive for stealing. Whilst you are thus reasoning with yourself, the man comes again to steal. Instead of being angry with him you take pity on him. You think that this stealing habit must be a disease with him. Henceforth, you, therefore, keep your doors and windows open, you change your sleeping-place, and you keep your things in a manner most accessible to him. The robber comes again and is confused as all this is new to him; nevertheless, he takes away your things. But his mind is agitated. He inquires about you in the village, he comes to learn about your broad and loving heart, he repents, he begs your pardon, returns you your things, and leaves off the stealing habit. He becomes your servant, and you will find for him honourable employment. This is the second method. Thus, you see, different means have brought about totally different results. I do not wish to deduce from this that robbers will act in the above manner or that all will have the same pity and love like you, but I only wish to show that fair means alone can produce fair results, and that, at least in the majority of cases, if not indeed in all, the force of love and pity is infinitely greater than the force of arms. There is harm in the exercise of brute force, never in that of pity.

Now we will take the question of petitioning. It is a fact beyond dispute that a petition, without the backing of force, is useless. However, the late Justice Ranade used to say that petitions served a useful purpose because they were a means of educating people. They give the latter an idea of their condition and warn the rulers. From this point of view, they are not altogether useless. A petition of an equal is a sign of courtesy; a petition from a slave is a symbol of his slavery. A petition backed by force is a petition from an equal and, when he transmits his demand in the form of a petition, it testifies to his nobility. Two kinds of force can back petitions. "We shall hurt you if you do not give this," is one kind of force; it is the force of arms, whose evil results we have already examined. The second kind of force can thus be stated: "If you do not concede our demand, we shall be no longer your petitioners. You can govern us only so long as we remain the governed; we shall no longer have any dealings with you." The force implied in this may be described as love-force, soul-force, or, more popularly but less accurately, passive resistance.[1] This force is indestructible. He who uses it perfectly understands his position. We have an ancient proverb which literally means: "One negative cures thirty-six diseases." The force of arms is powerless when matched against the force of love or the soul.

Now we shall take your last illustration, that of the child thrusting its foot into fire. It will not avail you. What do you really do to the child? Supposing that it can exert so much physical force that it renders you powerless and rushes into fire, then you cannot prevent it. There are only two remedies open to you—either you must kill it in order to prevent it from perishing in the flames, or you must give your own life because you do not wish to see it perish before your very eyes. You will not kill it. If your heart is not quite full of pity, it is possible that you will not surrender yourself by preceding the child and going into the fire yourself. You, therefore, helplessly allow it to go to the flames. Thus, at any rate, you are not using physical force. I hope you will not consider that it is still physical force, though of a low order, when you would forcibly prevent the child from rushing toward the fire if you could. That

---

[1] Finding the word misleading Gandhiji later called the same force Satyagraha or non-violent resistance.—Ed.

force is of a different order and we have to understand what it is.

Remember that, in thus preventing the child, you are minding entirely its own interest, you are exercising authority for its sole benefit. Your example does not apply to the English. In using brute force against the English you consult entirely your own, that is the national, interest. There is no question here either of pity or of love. If you say that the actions of the English, being evil, represent fire, and that they proceed to their actions through ignorance, and that therefore they occupy the position of a child and that you want to protect such a child, then you will have to overtake every evil action of that kind by whomsoever committed and, as in the case of the evil child, you will have to sacrifice yourself. If you are capable of such immeasurable pity, I wish you well in its exercise.

(*Hind Swaraj or Indian Home Rule,* chap. xvi)

• • •

THE LAW OF SUFFERING

No country has ever risen without being purified through the fire of suffering. Mother suffers so that her child may live. The condition of wheat growing is that the seed grain should perish. Life comes out of Death. Will India rise out of her slavery without fulfilling this eternal law of purification through suffering?

If my advisers are right, evidently India will realize her destiny without travail. For their chief concern is that the events of April, 1919, should not be repeated. They fear non-co-operation because it would involve the sufferings of many. If Hampdon had argued thus he would not have withheld payment of ship-money, nor would Wat Tayler have raised the standard of revolt. English and French histories are replete with instances of men continuing their pursuit of the right irrespective of the amount of suffering involved. The actors did not stop to think whether ignorant people would not have involuntarily to suffer. Why should we expect to write our history differently? It is possible for us,

if we would, to learn from the mistakes of our predecessors to do better, but it is impossible to do away with the law of suffering which is the one indispensable condition of our being. The way to do better is to avoid, if we can, violence from our side and thus quicken the rate of progress and to introduce greater purity in the methods of suffering. We can, if we will, refrain, in our impatience, from bending the wrong-doer to our will by physical force as Sinn Feiners are doing today, or from coercing our neighbours to follow our methods as was done last year by some of us in bringing about *hartal.* Progress is to be measured by the amount of suffering undergone by the sufferer. The purer the suffering, the greater is the progress. Hence did the sacrifice of Jesus suffice to free a sorrowing world. In his onward march he did not count the cost of suffering entailed upon his neighbours whether it was undergone by them voluntarily or otherwise. Thus did the sufferings of a Harishchandra suffice to re-establish the kingdom of truth. He must have known that his subjects would suffer involuntarily by his abdication. He did not mind because he could not do otherwise than follow truth.

I have already stated that I do not deplore the massacre of Jalianwala Bagh so much as I deplore the murders of Englishmen and destruction of property by ourselves. The frightfulness at Amritsar drew away public attention from the greater though slower frightfulness at Lahore where attempt was made to emasculate the inhabitants by slow processes. But before we rise higher we shall have to undergo such processes many more times till they teach us to take up suffering voluntarily and to find joy in it. I am convinced that the Lahorians never deserved the cruel insults that they were subjected to; they never hurt a single Englishman; they never destroyed any property. But a wilful ruler was determined to crush the spirit of a people just trying to throw off his chafing yoke. And if I am told that all this was due to my preaching Satyagraha, my answer is that I would preach Satyagraha all the more forcibly for that so long as I have breath left in me, and tell the people that next time they would answer O'Dwyer's insolence not by opening shops by reason of threats of forcible sales but by allowing the tyrant to do his worst and let him sell their all but their unconquerable souls. Sages of old mortified the flesh so that the spirit within might be set free, so that their trained bodies might be proof against any injury that might be inflicted on them by tyrants seeking to impose their will on them. And if India wishes to revive her ancient wisdom and to avoid the errors of Europe, if India wishes to see the Kingdom of God established on earth instead of that of Satan which has enveloped Europe, then I would urge her sons and daughters not to be deceived by fine phrases, the terrible subtleties that hedge us in, the fears of suffering that India may have to undergo, but to see what is happening today in Europe and from it understand that we must go through suffering even as Europe has gone through, but not the process of making others suffer. Germany wanted to dominate Europe and the Allies wanted to do likewise by crushing Germany. Europe is no better for Germany's fall. The Allies have proved themselves to be just as deceitful, cruel, greedy and selfish as Germany was or would have been. Germany would have avoided the sanctimonious humbug that one sees associated with the many dealings of the Allies.

The miscalculation that I deplored last year was not in connection with the sufferings imposed upon the people, but about the mistakes made by them and violence done by them owing to their not having sufficiently understood the message of Satyagraha. What then is the meaning of non-co-operation in terms of the law of suffering? We must voluntarily put up with the losses and inconveniences that arise from having to withdraw our support from a Government that is ruling against our will. Possession of power and riches is a crime under an unjust Government, poverty in that case is a virtue, says Thoreau. It may be that in the transition state we may make mistakes; there may be avoidable suffering. These things are preferable to national emasculation.

We must refuse to wait for the wrong to be righted till the wrong-doer has been roused to a sense of his iniquity. We must not, for fear of ourselves or others having to suffer, remain participators in it. But we must combat the wrong by ceasing to assist the wrong-doer directly or indirectly.

If a father does an injustice it is the duty of his children to leave the parental roof. If the headmaster of a school conducts his institution on an immoral basis, the pupils must leave the school. If the chairman of a corporation is corrupt the members thereof must wash their hands clean of his corruption by withdrawing from it; even so if a Government does a grave injustice the subjects must withdraw co-operation wholly or partially, sufficiently to wean the ruler from his wickedness. In each case conceived by me there is an element of suffering whether mental or physical. Without such suffering it is not possible to attain freedom.

(*Young India,* 16-6-'20)

HOW TO WORK NON-CO-OPERATION

Perhaps the best way of answering the fears and criticism as to non-co-operation is to elaborate more fully the scheme of non-co-operation. The critics seem to imagine that the organizers propose to give effect to the whole scheme at once. The fact however is that the organizer have fixed definite, progressive four stages. The first is the giving up of titles and resignation of honorary posts. If there is no response or if the response received is not effective, recourse will be had to the second stage. The second stage involves much previous arrangement. Certainly not a single servant will be called out unless he is either capable of supporting himself and his dependents or the Khilafat Committee is able to bear the burden. All the classes of servants will not be called out at once and never will any pressure be put upon a single servant to withdraw himself from Government service. Nor will a single private employee be touched, for the simple reason that the movement is not anti-English. It is not even anti-Government. Co-operation is to be withdrawn because the people must not be party to a wrong—a broken pledge—a violation of deep religious sentiment. Naturally, the movement will receive a check, is there is any undue influence brought to bear upon any Government servant, or if any violence is used or countenanced by any member of the Khilafat Committee. The second stage must be entirely successful, if the response is at all on an adequate scale. For no Government—much less the Indian Government—can subsist if the people cease to serve it. The withdrawal therefore of the police and the military—the third stage—is a distant goal. The organizers however wanted to be fair, open and above suspicion. They did not want to keep back from Government or the public a single step they had in contemplation even as a remote contingency. The fourth, i.e. suspension of taxes, is still more remote. The organizers recognize that suspension of general taxation is fraught with the greatest danger. It is likely to bring a sensitive class in conflict with the police. They are therefore not likely to embark upon it, unless they can do so with the assurance that there will be no violence offered by the people.

I admit, as I have already done, that non-co-operation is not unattended with risk, but the risk of supineness in the face of a grave issue is infinitely greater than the danger of violence ensuing from organizing non-co-operation. To do nothing is to invite violence for a certainty.

It is easy enough to pass resolutions or write articles condemning non-co-operation. But it is no easy task to restrain the fury of a people incensed by a deep sense of wrong. I urge those who talk or work against non-co-operation to descend from their chairs and go down to the people, learn their feelings and write, if they have the heart, against non-co-operation. They will find, as I have found, that the only way to avoid violence is to enable them to give such expression to their feelings as to compel redress. I have found nothing save non-co-operation. It is logical and harmless. It is the inherent right of a subject to refuse to assist a government that will not listen to him.

Non-co-operation as a voluntary movement can only succeed, if the feeling is genuine and strong enough to make people suffer to the utmost. If the religious sentiment of the Mohammedans is deeply hurt and if the Hindus entertain neighbourly regard towards their Muslim brethren, they both will count no cost too great for achieving the end. Non-co-operation will not only be an effective remedy but will also be an effective test of the sincerity of the Muslim claim and the Hindu profession of friendship.

(*Young India*, 5-5-'20)

• • •

MY FAITH IN NON-VIOLENCE

[From a talk after the evening prayer on board the ship at Suez on the way to London for the Round Table Conference.]

I have found that life persists in the midst of destruction and, therefore, there must be a higher law than that of destruction. Only under that law would a well-ordered society be intelligible and life worth living. And if that is the law of life, we have to work it out in daily life. Wherever there are jars, wherever you are confronted with an opponent, conquer him with love. In a crude manner I have worked it out in my life. That does not mean that all my difficulties are solved. I have found, however, that this law of love has answered as the law of destruction has never done. In India we have had an ocular demonstration of the operation of this law on the widest scale possible. I do not claim therefore that non-violence has necessarily penetrated the three hundred millions, but I do claim that it has penetrated deeper than any other message, and in an incredibly short time. We have not been all uniformly non-violent; and with the vast majority, non-violence has been a matter of policy. Even so, I want you to find out if the country has not made phenomenal progress under the protecting power of non-violence.

It takes a fairly strenuous course of training to attain to a mental state of non-violence. In daily life it has to be a course of discipline though one may not like it, like for instance, the life of a soldier. But I agree that, unless there is a hearty co-operation of the mind, the mere outward observance will be simply a mask, harmful both to the man himself and to others. The perfect state is reached only when mind and body and speech are in proper co-ordination.

But it is always a case of intense mental struggle. It is not that I am incapable of anger, for instance, but I succeed on almost all occasions to keep my feelings under control. Whatever may be the result, there is always in me a conscious struggle for following the law of non-violence deliberately and ceaselessly. Such a struggle leaves one stronger for it. Non-violence is a weapon of the strong. With the weak it might easily be hypocrisy. Fear and love are contradictory terms. Love is reckless in giving away, oblivious as to what it gets in return. Love wrestles with the world as with the self and ultimately gains a mastery over all other feelings. My daily experience, as of those who are working with me, is that every problem lends itself to solution if we are determined to make the law of truth and non-violence the law of life. For truth and non-violence are, to me, faces of the same coin.

The law of love will work, just as the law of gravitation wi¹l work, whether we accept it or not. Just as a scientist will work wonders out of various applications of the law of nature, even so a man who applies the law of love with scientific precision can work greater wonders. For the force of non-violence is infinitely more wonderful and subtle than the material forces of nature, like, for instance, electricity. The men who discovered for us the law of love were greater scientists than any of our modern scientists. Only our explorations have not gone far enough and so it is not possible for every one to see all its working. Such, at any rate, is the hallucination, if it is one, under which I am labouring. The more I work at this law the more I feel the delight in life, the delight in the scheme of this universe. It gives me a peace and a meaning of the mysteries of nature that I have no power to describe.

(*The Nation's Voice,* part II, pp. 109–10)

THE FUTURE

A friend writing from America propounds the following two questions:

"1. Granted that Saytagraha is capable of winning India's independence, what are the chances of its being accepted as a principle of State policy in a free India? In other words, would a strong and independent India rely on Satyagraha as a method of self-preservation, or would it lapse back to seeking refuge in the age-old institution of war, however defensive its character? To restate the question on the basis of a purely theoretic problem: In Satyagraha likely to be accepted only in an up-hill battle, when the phenomenon of martyrdom is fully effective, or is it also to be the instrument of a sovereign authority which has neither the need nor the scope of behaving on the principle of martyrdom?

"2. Suppose a free India adopts Saytagraha as an instrument of State policy how would she defend herself against probable aggression by another sovereign State? To restate the question on the basis of a purely theoretic problem: What would be the Satyagrahic action-patterns to meet the invading army at the frontier? What kind of resistance can be offered the opponent before a common area of action, such as the one now existing in India between the Indian nationalists and the British Government, is established? Or should the Satyagrahis withhold their action until after the opponent has taken over the country?"

The questions are admittedly theoretical. They are also premature for the reason that I have not mastered the whole technique of non-violence. The experiment is still in the making. It is not even in its advanced stage. The nature of the experiment requires one to be satisfied with one step at a time. The distant scene is not for him to see. Therefore, my answers can only be speculative.

In truth, as I have said before, now we are not having unadulterated non-violence even in our struggle to win independence.

As to the first question, I fear that the chances of non-violence being accepted as a principle of State policy are very slight, so far as I can see at present. If India does not accept non-violence as her policy after winning independence, the second question becomes superfluous.

But I may state my own individual view of the potency of non-violence. I believe that a State can be administered on a non-violent basis if the vast majority of the people are non-violent. So far as I know, India is the only country which has a possibility of being such a State. I am conducting my experiment in that faith. Supposing, therefore, that India attained independence through pure non-violence, India could retain it too by the same means. A non-violent man or society does not anticipate or provide for attacks from without. On the contrary, such a person or society firmly believes that nobody is going to disturb them. If the worst happens, there are two ways open to non-violence. To yield possession but non-co-operate with the aggressor. Thus, supposing that a modern edition of Nero descended upon India, the representatives of the State will let him in but tell him that he will get no assistance from the people. They will prefer death to submission. The second way would be non-violent resistance by the people who have been trained in the non-violent way. They would offer themselves unarmed as fodder for the aggressor's cannon. The underlying belief in either case is that even a Nero is not devoid of a heart. The unexpected spectacle of endless rows upon rows of men and women simply dying rather than surrender to the will of an aggressor must ultimately melt him and his soldiery. Practically speaking there will be probably no greater loss in men than if forcible resistance was offered; there will be no expenditure in armaments and fortifications. The non-violent training received by the people will add inconceivably to their moral height. Such men and women will have shown personal bravery of a type far superior to that shown in armed warfare. In each case the bravery consists in dying, not in killing. Lastly, there is no such thing as defeat in non-violent resistance. That such a thing has not happened before is no answer to my speculation. I have drawn no impossible picture. History is replete with instances of individual non-violence of the type I have mentioned. There is no warrant for saying or thinking that a group of men and women cannot by sufficient training act non-violently as a group or nation. Indeed the sum total of the experience of mankind is

that men somehow or other live on. From which fact I infer that it is the law of love that rules mankind. Had violence, i.e. hate, ruled us, we should have become extinct long ago. And yet the tragedy of it is that the so-called civilized men and nations conduct themselves as if the basis of society was violence. It gives me ineffable joy to make experiments proving that love is the supreme and only law of life. Much evidence to the contrary cannot shake my faith. Even the mixed non-violence of India has supported it. But if it is not enough to convince an unbeliever, it is enough to incline a friendly critic to view it with favour.

(*Harijan*, 13-4-'40)

QUESTIONS FOR DISCUSSION

1. Do you think, in your experience, that there is any truth to Nietzsche's critique of Christianity as a slave morality? Is pity a vice, rather than a virtue—in all or some circumstances? Explain.

2. Fanon, Bartky, and Freire describe the important process of getting the oppressor or colonizer out of one's own head: of evaluating oneself by independent criteria, and learning to love oneself, rather than see only how one does not measure up to another person's standard. In what ways in your own life have you had to go through the same process?

3. Familiarize yourself with some of the struggles of contemporary workers around the world. What would Marx and Engels have to say to them? How is the situation of workers in the United States different from, or similar to, the portrayal of proletarians which Marx and Engels give?

4. Several of our authors (Marx, Fanon, and Freire) advocate violence to combat a situation of injustice. Gandhi, however advocates nonviolence. Who do you think has the more effective method? Who do you think has the best moral position (or are both positions moral)?

PERMISSIONS ACKNOWLEDGMENTS

Chapter 1

Plato, "The Parable of the Cave." "The Republic" from *The Great Dialogues of Plato* by Plato. Translated by W. H. D. Rouse. Translation copyright © 1956, renewed 1984 by J. C. G. Rouse. Used by permission of Dutton Signet, a division of Penguin Books USA Inc.

Plato, "The Symposium." "The Symposium" from *The Great Dialogues of Plato* by Plato. Translated by W. H. D. Rouse. Translation copyright © 1956, renewed 1984 by J. C. G. Rouse. Used by permission of Dutton Signet, a division of Penguin Books USA Inc.

Black Elk, "A Lakota Vision." Reprinted from *Black Elk Speaks,* pp. 85–87, by John G. Neihardt, by permission of the University of Nebraska Press. Copyright 1932, 1959, 1972, by John G. Neihardt. Copyright © 1961 by the John G. Neihardt Trust.

The Upanishads, "Thou Art That." From F. Frederick Max Müller, trans., *The Upanishads,* vol. 1 of *The Sacred Books of the East* (New York: Dover, 1962), pp. 101–105. Facsimile reprint of 1879 edition published by Clarendon Press, Oxford, England.

Sankara, "A Commentary on the Upanishads." From George Thibaut, trans., *The Vedanta Sutras of Badarayana with the Commentary by Sankara, Part I* (New York: Dover, 1961), pp. 185–187, 312–313, 321–323. Facsimile reprint of 1890 edition of vol. 34 of *The Sacred Books of the East* published by Clarendon Press, Oxford, England.

George Berkeley, "Subjective Idealism." From George Berkeley, "Three Dialogues between Hylas and Philonous . . . ," in *The Empiricists* (Garden City, N.Y.: Doubleday, Dolphin Books, 1970), pp. 217–237, 252–256.

Arthur Schopenhauer, "The World as Will and Idea." From Arthur Schopenhauer, *The World as Will and Idea,* trans. R. B. Haldane and J. Kemp (London: Kegan Paul, Trench and Trubner, 1896), pp. 452–461.

Hui Neng, "Sutra of Hui Neng." From *The Diamond Sutra and the Sutra of Hui Neng,* pp. 11–24, translated by Wong Mou-Lam. Reprinted by arrangement with Shambhala Publications, Inc., 300 Massachusetts Avenue, Boston, MA 02115.

Thich Nhat Hanh, "Zen Keys." From *Zen Keys* by Thich Nhat Hanh, pp. 103–105. Copyright © 1974 by Doubleday, a division of Bantam Doubleday Dell Publishing Group, Inc. Used by permission of Doubleday, a division of Bantam Doubleday Dell Publishing Group, Inc.

Lao Tzu, "The Way and Its Power." From Lao Tzu, *Tao Teh Ching,* trans. John C. H. Wu: 1, 4, 5, 11, 25, 32, 34, 35, 37, 51, 77. © 1961 by St. John's University Press, New York; published in 1989 by Shambhala Publications. Reprinted by arrangement with Shambhala Publications, Inc., 300 Massachusetts Avenue, Boston, MA 02115.

Wang Fu-Chih, "Neo-Confucian Materialism." From Wang Fu-Chih, in *A Sourcebook in Chinese Philosophy,* translated and compiled by Wing-Tsit Chan, pp. 694–698. Copyright © 1963 and renewed by Princeton University Press. Reprinted by permission of Princeton University Press.

Friedrich Engels, "Materialism and the Scientific World View." Reprinted by permission from Friedrich Engels, *Dialectics of Nature,* trans. and ed. Clemens Dutt (New York: International Publishers, 1949), pp. 13–25.

Chapter 2

Bertrand Russell, "Problem of Induction." Reprinted by permission of Oxford University Press from Bertrand Russell, *The Problems of Philosophy* (Oxford, England: Oxford University Press, 1912), ch. 6, pp. 60–69.

The Cārvāka School, "Scepticism." From Sarvepalli Radhakrishnan and Charles Moore, eds., *A Sourcebook in Indian Philosophy,* pp. 236–238. Copyright © 1957, renewed 1985, by Princeton University Press. Reprinted by permission of Princeton University Press.

Charles Sanders Peirce, "The Fixation of Belief." Reprinted by permission of the publishers from *Collected Papers of Charles Sanders Peirce,* Vol. V, *Pragmatism and Pragmaticism,* edited by Charles Hartshorne and Paul Weiss, Cambridge, Mass.: The Belknap Press of Harvard University Press, Copyright © 1934, 1935 by the President and Fellows of Harvard College.

Albert Einstein, "Creativity and Science." From *Ideas and Opinions,* pp. 270–274, by Albert Einstein. Copyright © 1954, 1982 by Crown Publishers, Inc. Reprinted by permission of Crown Publishers, Inc.

Paul K. Feyerabend, "Against Method." Reprinted by permission from Paul K. Feyerabend, "Against Method: Outline of an Anarchistic Theory of Knowledge," in Michael Radner and Stephen Winokur, eds., *Analyses of Theories and Methods of Physics and Psychology,* vol. 4 in Minnesota Studies in the Philosophy of Science, pp. 17–26. Copyright 1970 by the University of Minnesota. Published by the University of Minnesota Press.

Chinua Achebe, "The Truth of Fiction." From *Hopes and Impediments* by Chinua Achebe, pp. 138–153. Copyright © 1988 by Chinua Acheba. Used by permission of Doubleday, a division of Bantam Doubleday Dell Publishing Group, Inc., and Harold Ober Associates Incorporated.

Mao Tse-tung, "On Practice." From *Mao Tse-tung: An Anthology of His Writings,* ed. Anne Fremantle (New York: Mentor, New American Library, 1971), pp. 201–213.

Mao Tse-tung, "Where Do Correct Ideas Come From?" From *Mao Tse-tung: An Anthology of His Writings,* ed. Anne Fremantle (New York: Mentor, New American Library, 1971), pp. 303–304.

Ayatullah Murtaza Mutahhari, "Limits of Science." Reprinted by permission of the publisher from Ayatullah Murtaza Mutahhari, *Fundamentals of Islamic Thought: God, Man, and the Universe* (Berkeley, Calif.: Mizan Press, 1985), pp. 68–75.

Chuang Tzu, "Knowledge and Relativity." First part from Wang Fu-Chih, in *A Sourcebook in Chinese Philosophy,* translated and compiled by Wing-Tsit Chan, pp. 182–190. Copyright © 1963 and renewed by Princeton University Press. Reprinted by permission of Princeton University Press. Second part from Thomas Merton, *The Way of Chuang-Tzu.* Copyright © 1965 by The Abbey of Gethsemani. Reprinted by permission of New Directions Publishing Corp.

Jorge Luis Borges, "Averroës' Search." From *A Personal Anthology* by Jorge Luis Borges, translated by Anthony Kerrigan. Copyright © 1967 by Grove Press, Inc. Used by permission of Grove/Atlantic, Inc.

Daisetz T. Suzuki, "Zen Knowledge." From Daisetz T. Suzuki, "The Meaning of Satori," in *Philosophical Explorations,* ed. Peter A. French (Morristown, N.J.: General Learning Press, 1975), pp. 633–639. Originally from Daisetz T. Suzuki, "The Meaning of Satori," *The Middle Way,* The Journal of the Buddhist Society, 1969, London.

Milton Munitz, "Boundless Existence." From Milton Munitz, *The Question of Reality,* pp. 192–207. Copyright © 1990 by Princeton University Press. Reprinted by permission of Princeton University Press.

Chapter 3

A. C. Ewing, "Proofs of God's Existence." Reprinted with permission of Routledge & Kegan Paul from A. C. Ewing, *The Fundamental Questions of Philosophy,* © 1962, pp. 237–247.

Antony Flew, "Theology and Falsification." Reprinted with the permission of Macmillan Publishing Company and SCM Press from *New Essays in Philosophical Theology* by Antony Flew and Alasdair MacIntyre. Copyright 1955, renewed 1983 by Antony Flew and Alasdair MacIntrye.

Sigmund Freud, "A Philosophy of Life." Reprinted from *New Introductory Lectures on Psycho-analysis,* by Sigmund Freud, translated by James Strachey, with the permission of W. W. Norton & Company, Inc., and Random House UK Limited. Copyright © 1965, 1964 by James Strachey.

Sarvepalli Radhakrishnan, "Personal Experience of God." Reprinted by permission of HarperCollins Ltd. from Sarvepalli Radhakrishnan, *An Idealist View of Life* (London: Unwin Hyman, 1988), pp. 70–81.

Black Elk, "The Sacred Pipe." Reprinted by permission from *The Sacred Pipe: Black Elk's Account of the Seven Rites of the Oglala Sioux* by Joseph Epes Brown. Copyright © 1953 by the University of Oklahoma Press.

Kitaro Nishida, "The Essence of Religion." Reprinted by permission from Kitaro Nishida, *An Inquiry into the Good,* trans. Masao Abe and Christopher Ives (New Haven, Conn.: Yale University Press, 1990), pp. 153–157, 79–83.

Buddhadasa, "No Religion." Source: Reprinted from Buddhadasa, *No Religion!* trans. Bhikkhu Punno (Bangkok, Thailand: Sublime Life Mission, 1967), pp. 1–7.

Karl Marx and Friedrich Engels, "Critique of Religion." Reprinted from Karl Marx and Friedrich Engels, *On Religion* (New York: Schocken Books, 1964), pp. 41–42, 135–136, 147–149, 316–317, 82–84.

Leonardo Boff and Clodovis Boff, "Liberation Theology." Reprinted by permission from Leonardo Boff and Clodovis Boff, *Introducing Liberation Theology* (Maryknoll, N.Y.: Orbis, 1987), pp. 1–10, 28–35, 49–58.

Carol P. Christ, "Why Women Need the Goddess." Reprinted by permission of the author from Carol P. Christ, "Why Women Need the Goddess," in Carol P. Christ and Judith Plaskow, eds., *Womanspirit Rising: A Feminist Reader in Religion* (New York: HarperCollins, 1992), pp. 273–287. Carol P. Christ is an internationally known feminist thealogian. Her book *Laughter of Aphrodite: Reflections on a Journey to the Goddess* (Harper & Row) discusses issues raised in this essay in greater detail.

Chapter 4

Mencius, "Human Nature Is Good." From Wang Fu-Chih, in *A Sourcebook in Chinese Philosophy,* translated and compiled by Wing-Tsit Chan, pp. 51–59, 65–66. Copyright © 1963 and renewed by Princeton University Press. Reprinted by permission of Princeton University Press.

Hsün Tzu, "Human Nature is Evil." From Hsün Tzu, "Man's Nature is Evil," in *Basic Writings of Mo Tzu, Hsün Tzu, and Han Fei Tzu,* trans. Burton Watson (New York: Columbia University Press, 1967), pp. 157–165. © Columbia University Press, New York. Reprinted with permission of the publisher.

Ch'eng Hao, "Human Nature Is Good But Can Become Evil." From Wang Fu-Chih, in *A Sourcebook in Chinese Philosophy,* translated and compiled by Wing-Tsit Chan, pp. 527–528. Copyright © 1963 and renewed by Princeton University Press. Reprinted by permission of Princeton University Press.

Han Yü, "Three Grades of Human Nature." From Wang Fu-Chih, in *A Sourcebook in Chinese Philosophy,* translated and compiled by Wing-Tsit Chan, pp. 451–453. Copyright © 1963 and renewed by Princeton University Press. Reprinted by permission of Princeton University Press.

Bithika Mukerji, "A Hindu View." Reprinted with permission from Mukerji Bithika, *The Hindu Tradition* (Rockport, Mass.: Element Books, 1991).

Thomas Hobbes, "Human Nature as Competitive." Reprinted from Thomas Hobbes, *Leviathan,* ed. Michael Oakeshott (New York: Collier Books, Macmillan Publishing, 1962), pp. 98–102.

Pëtr Kropotkin, "Mutual Aid." From Pëtr Kropotkin, *Mutual Aid,* Extending Horizons Books, 1976, Porter Sargent Publishers, Inc., 11 Beacon Street, Boston, MA 02108.

John Dewey, "Changing Human Nature." Excerpts from *Human Nature and Conduct: An Introduction to Social Psychology* by John Dewey, copyright 1922 by Holt, Rinehart & Winston, Inc., and renewed 1950 by John Dewey, reprinted by permission of the publisher.

Jean-Paul Sartre, "There Is No Human Nature." From *Existentialism and Human Emotions,* pp. 9–33, 51, by Jean-Paul Sartre, © 1949 by Wisdom Library. Published by arrangement with Carol Publishing Group. A Citadel Press Book.

Shin'ichi Hisamatsu, "A Zen View." "A Zen View" is a section from Shin'ichi Hisamatsu, "Zen: Its Meaning for Modern Civilization," translated by Richard DeMartino and Gishin Tokiwa, in *Eastern Buddhist,* new series 1, 1 (1965). Reprinted by permission.

Abuhamid Muhammad Al-Ghazali, "The Proper Role for Women." From Abuhamid Muhammad Al-Ghazali, "Describing Women and Their Good and Bad Points," in his *Ghazali's Book of Counsel for Kings,* trans. F. R. C. Bagley (University of Durham Publications, 1964), pp. 158–173. Reprinted by permission of Oxford University Press.

Fatima Mernissi, "Beyond the Veil." Source: Reprinted by permission from Fatima Mernissi, *Beyond the Veil: Male-Female Dynamics in Modern Muslim Society,* rev. ed. (Bloomington: Indiana University Press, 1987), pp. 18–20, 27–33, 41–45.

Simone de Beauvoir, "The Second Sex." From *The Second Sex* by Simone De Beauvoir. Copyright © 1952 and renewed 1980 by Alfred A. Knopf, Inc. Reprinted by permission of Alfred A. Knopf, Inc., a subsidiary of Random House, Inc.

Ann Ferguson, "Androgyny as an Ideal for Human Development." Reprinted by permission from Ann Ferguson, "Androgyny as an Ideal for Human Development," in *Feminism and Philosophy,* ed. Mary Vetterling-Braggin (Lanham, Md.: Littlefield, Adams, 1977), pp. 45–69.

Richard D. Mohr, "Is Homosexuality Unnatural?" Reprinted by permission of the author from Richard D. Mohr, "Gay Basics: Some Questions, Facts, and Values," in *The Right Thing to Do: Basic Readings in Moral Philosphy,* ed. James Rachels (New York: Random House, 1989), pp. 147–148, 155–160, 162–163.

Chapter 5

Plato, "The Phaedo." "The Phaedo" from *The Great Dialogues of Plato* by Plato. Translated by W. H. D. Rouse. Translation copyright © 1956, renewed 1984 by J. C. G. Rouse. Used by permission of Dutton Signet, a division of Penguin Books USA Inc.

Aristotle, "On the Soul." Reprinted by permission of the publishers and the Loeb Classical Library from Aristotle, *Aristotle on the Soul, Parva Naturalia, On Breath,* translated by W. S. Hett, Cambridge, Mass.: Harvard University Press, 1957, pp. 67–73.

René Descartes, "Meditations." Copyright © 1952. From *New Studies in the Philosophy of Descartes* by Norman Kemp Smith. Reprinted with permission of St. Martin's Press, Inc.

David Hume, "Personal Identity." Reprinted from David Hume, *A Treatise on Human Nature* (Cleveland: World Publishing, 1962), pp. 300–305.

Edmund Husserl, "Transcendental Subjectivity." From Edmund Husserl, *The Paris Lectures,* trans. Peter Koestenbaum (The Hague, The Netherlands: Martinus-Nijoff, 1964), pp. 3–15. Reprinted by permission of Kluwer Academic Publishers.

Bhagavad-Gita, "Samkhya Dualism." Reprinted from Sarvepalli Radhakrishnan and Charles Moore, eds., *A Sourcebook in Indian Philosophy,* pp. 145–147. Copyright © 1957, renewed 1985, by Princeton University Press. Reprinted by permission of Princeton University Press.

The Upanishads, "The True Self." From F. Frederick Max Müller, trans., *The Upanishads,* vol. 1 of *The Sacred Books of the East,* (New York: Dover, 1962), pp. 125–127, 48. Facsimile reprint of 1879 edition published by Clarendon Press, Oxford, England.

Questions of King Milinda, "No Self." From *The Questions of King Milinda,* in vol. 35 of *The Sacred Books of the East,* trans. T. W. Rhys Davids (New York: Dover, 1963), pp. 40–45, 86–89. Facsimile reprint of 1874 edition published by Clarendon Press, Oxford, England.

T. R. V. Murti, "The Middle Way." From T. R. V. Murti, *The Central Philosophy of Buddhism* (London: George Allen & Unwin), pp. 10–11, 201–207. Reprinted by permission of HarperCollins Ltd.

Toshiko Izutsu, "Ego-less Consciousness: A Zen View." From *Toward a Philosophy of Zen Buddhism,* pp. 65–77, 82–83, by Toshihiko Izutsu. © 1977 by the Imperial Iranian Academy of Philosophy. Reprinted by arrangement with Shambhala Publications, Inc., 300 Massachusetts Avenue, Boston, MA 02115.

Derek Parfit, "Divided Minds and the 'Bundle' Theory of Self." Reprinted by permission of Blackwell Publishers from Derek Parfit, "Divided Minds and the Nature of Persons," in *Mindwaves: Thoughts on Intelligence, Identity, and Consciousness,* ed. Colin Blakemore and Susan Greenfield (Oxford, England: Basil Blackwell, 1987), pp. 19–26.

Kwame Gyekye, "Interactionist Dualism." Reprinted from Kwame Gyekye, *An Essay on African Philosophical Thought: The Akan Conceptual Scheme.* Copyright © 1987 Cambridge University Press. Reprinted with the permission of Cambridge University Press.

The Cārvāka School, "Ancient Indian Materialism." First part from Madhava Acarya, *Sarvadarsanas-Samgraha,* trans. E. B. Cowell and A. E. Gough (London: Kegan Paul, Trench & Trubner, 1904). Second part from Krsna Misra, *Prabodhacandrodaya,* trans. J. Taylor (Bombay, 1811).

Bertrand Russell, "Persons, Death, and the Body." Reprinted by permission of Routledge, ITPS, from Bertrand Russell, "Do We Survive Death?" in *Why I Am Not a Christian,* ed. Paul Edwards (New York: Simon & Schuster, 1957).

Risieri Frondizi, "Dynamic Unity of the Self." From Risieri Frondizi, *The Nature of the Self: A Functional Interpretation* (Carbondale and Edwardsville: Southern Illinois University Press, 1971), pp. 145–147, 158–163, 170–177, 180–184, 188–193, 197–201.

Chapter 6

Motse, "Anti-Fatalism." From Motse, "Anti-Fatalism," in *The Ethical and Political Works of Motse,* trans. Yi-Pao Mei (Westport, Conn.: Hyperion Press, 1973), pp. 189–193.

Sarvepalli Radhakrishnan, "Karma and Freedom." From Sarvepalli Radhakrishnan, *The Hindu View of Life* (New York: Macmillan, 1969), pp. 52–55. Reprinted by permission of HarperCollins Ltd.

Fyodor Dostoyevsky, "Notes from the Underground." Reprinted with the permission of Macmillan Publishing Company from *White Nights and Other Stories,* pp. 25–51, by Fyodor Dostoevsky, translated from the Russian by Constance Garnett. New York: Macmillan Publishing Company, 1923.

Jean-Paul Sartre, "Freedom and Action." From *Being and Nothingness* by Jean-Paul Sartre, translated by Hazel E. Barnes. Copyright 1956 by Philosophical Library. Published by arrangement with Carol Publishing Group.

Okot p'Bitek, "Social Bondage." From Okot p'Bitek, "On Culture, Man, and Freedom," in *Philosophy and Cultures,* ed. H. Odera Oruka and D. A. Masolo (Nairobi: Bookwise Limited, 1983), pp. 106, 108–110. Reprinted by permission of the Philosophical Association of Kenya.

B. F. Skinner, "Walden Two: Freedom and the Science of Human Behavior." Reprinted with the permission of Macmillan College Publishing Company from *Walden Two* by B. F. Skinner, pp. 240–248. Copyright © 1948, 1976 by B. F. Skinner.

Moritz Schlick, "Freedom and Responsibility." Reprinted by permission from Moritz Schlick, "When Is a Man Responsible?" in his *Problems of Ethics,* trans. David Rynin (Dover, 1939), pp. 143–158.

Nancy Holmstrom, "Firming Up Soft Determinism." Reprinted by permission of Blackwell Publications from *The Personalist,* vol. 58, no. 1 (January 1977).

Kitarō Nishida, "Freedom of the Will." Reprinted by permission from Kitarō Nishida, *An Inquiry into the Good,* trans. Masao Abe and Christopher Ives (New Haven, Conn.: Yale University Press, 1990), pp. 95–99.

Chapter 7

Bhagavad-Gita, "Right Action." From Sarvepalli Radhakrishnan and Charles Moore, eds., *A Sourcebook in Indian Philosophy,* pp. 102–116. Copyright © 1957, renewed 1985, by Princeton University Press. Reprinted by permission of Princeton University Press.

Immanuel Kant, "Moral Duty." From Immanuel Kant, *The Fundamental Principles of the Metaphysics of Ethics,* trans. Otto Manthey-Zorn (New York: Appleton-Century-Crofts, 1938), pp. 8–19.

John Stuart Mill, "Utilitarianism." From John Stuart Mill, *Utilitarianism,* ed. Oscar Priest (Library of Liberal Arts, Bobbs-Merrill, 1957), pp. 3–16, 44–45.

Virginia Held, "Feminist Transformations of Moral Theory." Reprinted by permission from Virginia Held, "Feminist Transformations of Moral Theory," *Philosophy and Phenomenological Research,* vol. 50, Supplement (Fall 1990): 321–334.

Riffat Hassan, "Islamic View of Human Rights." Reprinted by permission from Riffat Hassan, "Peace Education: A Muslim Perspective," in *Education for Peace*, ed. Haim Gordon and Leonard Grob (Maryknoll, N.Y.: Orbis Books, 1987), pp. 96–106.

Gunapala Dharmasiri, "Buddhist Ethics." Reprinted by permission from Gunapala Dharmasiri, "Motivation in Buddhist Ethics," in *Fundamentals of Buddhist Ethics* (Antioch, Calif.: Golden Leaves, 1989), pp. 12–21.

Ayn Rand, "The Virtue of Selfishness." Reprinted by permission of the Ayn Rand Estate from Ayn Rand, *The Virtue of Selfishness* (New York: Signet/Penguin, 1964), pp. vii–xi, 34–35, 51–56. Originally in *The Objectivist Newsletter*, February 1963.

Alejandro Korn, "Values Are Subjective." From Alejandro Korn, "Axiología," in *Obras* (La Plata: Universidad Nacional de La Plata, 1938), 1: 129–144. Excerpted in *Latin American Philosophy in the Twentieth Century*, ed. Jorge J. E. Garcia and trans. Francis Myers (Buffalo, N.Y.: Prometheus Books, 1980), pp. 167–171.

Jeffrey Stout, "The Problem of Relativism." From *Ethics after Babel* by Jeffrey Stout. Copyright © 1988 by Jeffrey Stout. Reprinted by permission of Beacon Press.

Chapter 8

Aristotle, "The Rational Life." Reprinted by permission of the publishers and the Loeb Classical Library from *Aristotle in Twenty-Three Volumes, xix: The Nichomachean Ethics*, translated by H. Rackham (Cambridge, Mass.: Harvard University Press, 1968), pp. 3–5, 11–17, 25–33, 71–87, 607–629.

Tabatabai, "Islam Is the Road to Happiness." From Allāmah Sayyid M. H. Tabatabai, *The Qur'an in Islam: Its Impact and Influence on the Life of Muslims* (London: Zahra Publications, Routledge & Kegan Paul, 1987), pp. 17–21.

Lao Tzu, "Living in the Tao." From Lao Tzu, *Tao Teh Ching*, trans. John C. H. Wu: 8, 9, 12, 13, 15, 16, 22, 24, 38, 43–45, 63, 68, 74, 76, 81. © 1961 by St. John's University Press, New York; published in 1989 by Shambhala Publications. Reprinted by arrangement with Shambhala Publications, Inc., 300 Massachusetts Avenue, Boston, MA 02115.

Chuang Tzu, "Lost in the Tao." From Thomas Merton, *The Way of Chuang-Tzu*. Copyright © 1965 by The Abbey of Gethsemani. Reprinted by permission of New Directions Publishing Corp.

Raymond M. Smullyan, "Whichever the Way." Chapter 19 from *The Tao Is Silent* by Raymond Smullyan. Copyright © 1977 by Raymond M. Smullyan. Reprinted by permission of HarperCollins Publishers, Inc.

Chögyam Trungpa, "The Myth of Freedom." From *The Myth of Freedom and the Way of Meditation* by Chögyam Trungpa. © 1976 by Chögyam Trungpa. Reprinted by arrangement with Shambhala Publications, Inc., 300 Massachusetts Avenue, Boston, MA 02115.

John Wisdom, "The Meanings of the Questions of Life." Reprinted by permission of Blackwell Publishers from John Wisdom, "The Meanings of the Questions of Life," in his *Paradox and Discovery* (Berkeley: University of California Press, 1970), pp. 38–42.

Albert Camus, "The Absurd and the Myth of Sisyphus." From *The Myth of Sisyphus and Other Essays* by Albert Camus. Copyright © 1955 by Alfred A. Knopf, Inc. Reprinted by permission of Alfred A. Knopf, Inc., a subsidiary of Random House, Inc.

Carl Rogers, "To Be the Self Which One Truly Is." From Carl R. Rogers, *On Becoming a Person*, pp. 164–176. Copyright © 1961 by Houghton Mifflin Company. Used with permission.

Miguel de Unamuno, "The Tragic View of Life." Reprinted by permission from Miguel de Unamuno, "The Hunger of Immortality," in his *The Tragic Sense of Life*, trans. J. Crawford Fitch (New York: Dover, 1954), pp. 38–48.

Gregory Baum, "Social Conceptions of Death." Reprinted from *Religion and Alienation: A Theological Reading of Sociology* by Gregory Baum. © 1975 by the Missionary Society of St. Paul the Apostle in the State of New York. Used by permission of Paulist Press.

Etty Hillesum, "Facing Death." From *An Interrupted Life* by Etty Hillesum. English translation copyright © 1983 by Jonathan Cape Ltd. Reprinted by permission of Pantheon Books, a division of Random House, Inc.

Chapter 9

Confucius, "Ruler as Moral Model." From *Wisdom of China and India*, pp. 196–203, by Lin Yutang. Copyright

INDEX OF AUTHORS
AND TITLES